The British
BOXING
Board of Control
YEARBOOK
2003

Edited and compiled by
Barry J. Hugman

Queen Anne Press

First published in 2002

© Barry J. Hugman

Barry J. Hugman has asserted his right under
the Copyright, Designs and Patent Act, 1988
to be identified as the author of this work

First published in Great Britain in 2002 by
Queen Anne Press
a division of Lennard Associates
Mackerye End, Harpenden
Hertfordshire, AL5 5DR

A CIP catalogue record for this book
is available from the British Library

ISBN 1 85291 649 4

Typeset and designed by Typecast (Artwork and Design)
8 Mudford Road, Yeovil, Somerset, BA21 4AA

Printed and bound in Great Britain by
Butler & Tanner, London and Frome

Front cover: Lennox Lewis defaets Mike Tyson in Memphis (Al Bello/ Getty Images)
Back cover: Ricky Hatton beats Jason Rowland
to retain his WBU Light Welterweight title in Manchester (Les Clark)

Contents

ST. ANDREW'S SPORTING CLUB

EXCLUSIVE GENTLEMEN'S CLUB
AND
THE HOME OF SCOTTISH BOXING

2002/2003 Fixture List

Monday 23rd September 2002

Monday 21st October 2002

Monday 18th November 2002

Saturday 7th December 2002
(Ladies Night Dinner/Dance)

Monday 20th January 2003
(Burns Night)

Monday 17th February 2003

Monday 17th March 2003

Monday 14th April 2003

Saturday 10th May 2003
(Summer Ball)

Monday 2nd June 2003

TEAM 2002

FLYWEIGHT
JASON BOOTH
British & Commonwealth Champion
DALE ROBINSON
Central Area Champion

BANTAMWEIGHT
NICKY BOOTH
British & Commonwealth Champion
JAMIL HUSSAIN

FEATHERWEIGHT
ALSTON BUCHANAN
ANDREW FERRANS

SUPER-FEATHERWEIGHT
ALEX MOON
Former Commonwealth Champion
CRAIG DOCHERTY
GWYN WALE

LIGHTWEIGHT
JAMES ARMAH
Commonwealth Champion
TONY McPAKE
GARY REID

LIGHT-WELTERWEIGHT
PABLO SARMIENTO
I.B.O. World Champion
GARY RYDER
JOHN MARSHALL

WELTERWEIGHT
JAWAID KHALIQ
I.B.O. World Champion
JAMES HARE
Commonwealth Champion
DEREK ROCHE
Former British Champion
DAVID KEIR
RITCHIE MURRAY
SCOTT MILLAR

LIGHT-MIDDLEWEIGHT
JOE TOWNSLEY
Former I.B.O. Continental Champion
JAMIE MOORE
CIARAN DUFFY
ANDY GIBSON

MIDDLEWEIGHT
WAYNE PINDER
MARK NILSEN
BIAGIO FALCONE

SUPER-MIDDLEWEIGHT
DEAN COCKBURN
LEE MOLLOY

CRUISERWEIGHT
MARK HOBSON
BILLY McCLUNG
TONY MORAN

HEAVYWEIGHT
DAVID McKENNA

ADMINISTRATIVE OFFICES: HOLIDAY INN, BOTHWELL STREET, GLASGOW G2 7EN, SCOTLAND
Telephone: +44 141 248 5461 and +44 141 275 4265
Fax: +44 141 248 5922 Email: gilmourjnr@aol.com
DIRECTOR: TOMMY GILMOUR Jnr

Acknowledgements

In going from strength to strength, it is once again my pleasure to thank all of those who have helped to establish the *Yearbook*, now in its 19th year, as an essential annual for the sport, and one that in its own way is just as important to the boxing public as receiving *Boxing News* every week.

As in previous years, I am indebted to the BBBoC's General Secretary, Simon Block, for his continued support and help in placing information at my disposal and being of assistance when required. His assistant, Robert Smith, who is also the Southern Area Secretary and a former pro fighter of note, was again extremely helpful, as was Dai Corp, the Welsh and Western Area Secretary, who now works out of the Board's Cardiff office.

Once again, I would like to thank Bernard Hart, the Managing Director of Lonsdale Sports Equipment Ltd, for his efforts on behalf of the *Yearbook*, especially in organising the annual British Boxing Board of Control Awards Luncheon where the book will be launched. He was ably supported in this exercise by Kymberly and Chas Taylor and Peter Chapman. At the same time, I would like to thank Jonathan Ticehurst, the Managing Director of the Sports Division of Windsor Insurance Brokers Ltd, for his continued support and sponsorship of the *Yearbook*.

Ron Olver has been with the *Yearbook* from day one and, as ever, remains a tower of strength with his help and support. Once again, despite it being a difficult year and suffering continued ill-health, Ron has produced the Directory of Ex-Boxers' Associations. A former Assistant Editor of both *Boxing News* and *Boxing World*, he is also well known as the British correspondent of the *Ring*; the author of *The Professionals*; for producing the boxing section within *Encyclopedia Britannica*; his work on *Boxing*, Foyles' library service; and as the former co-editor of the *Boxing News Annual*. His honorary work which includes being the Chairman of the BBBoC Charity Grants' Committee; the Vice-President of many ex-boxers' associations; the Public Relations Officer of the London Ex-Boxers' Association; membership of the Commonwealth Boxing Council as New Zealand's representative; and the International Hall of Fame – has, in recent years, seen him honoured by the Boxing Writers' Club, the BBBoC, and the Commonwealth Boxing Council. He has recently been further honoured by the Boxing Writers' Club, who have made him an Honorary Life Member. It was due to Ron's promptings that the ex-boxers' associations came into being as we now know them, and he will always be remembered by the *Boxing News*' readership as the man responsible for the 'Old Timers' page, now in its 35th year.

Members of the *Yearbook* 'team' who wrote articles for this year's edition and who have recently been published, or are in the process of publishing their own books are: John Jarrett (*Dynamite Gloves*); Bob Lonkhurst (*East End Idol, the biography of Terry Spinks*); Ralph Oates (*The Heavyweight Boxing Quizbook*), Tony Gee (*Up To Scratch*) and Melanie Lloyd (*Sweet Fighting Man*). This is Mel's first venture into the world of book publishing and I am sure that the readership of this book will enjoy dipping into the pages of *Sweet Fighting Man*.

Another lady boxing writer, Tracey Pollard, who as a local freelance journalist covers boxing for the Manchester-based *Reporter* and *Chronicle* Newspaper Group, has written about Brian London, the former heavyweight champion, while we welcome on board Wynford Jones, the Class 'A' referee. Wynford, who also came to my rescue when travelling to the Board's offices on a regular basis in order to collate vital data required for this publication, has produced an article titled: A Century of Welsh Boxing Greats. Other members of the *Yearbook* team are Bob Yalen, who covers boxing with ABC across the world and looks after the World Title Bouts' section; Harold Alderman, an unsung hero who has spent over 40 years researching the early days of boxing through to modern times; Chris Kempson, our man in the world of amateur boxing; Eric Armit, who is a leading authority on current boxers' records throughout the world, and who is responsible for the 'World Scene' column within *Boxing News*; and Derek O'Dell, a long-time friend, who produced the Obituaries section of the book following a heart attack and prior to going back into hospital to have a kidney removed. They are a tough breed, these boxing writers!

Regarding photographs, as in previous years the great majority were produced by Les Clark (he also writes the Boxing Quiz with a Few Below the Belt within these pages), who has possibly the largest library of both action and poses from British rings. If anyone requires a copy of a photo that has appeared in the *Yearbook* credited to Les, or requires a list, he can be reached at 352 Trelawney Avenue, Langley, Bucks SL3 7TS. Other photos were supplied by my good friends, Derek Rowe and Harry Goodwin, and Paul Speak and Chris Bevan.

Also, additional help came from Neil Blackburn (who yet again provided information to make the Obituaries section as complete as possible); Mrs Enza Jacoponi, the Secretary of the European Boxing Union (EBU Championship data covering the past 12 months); Simon Block (Commonwealth and British Championship data); Patrick Myler (Irish amateur boxing information); Ray Allen (Welsh amateur boxing information); Sid Turp, Peter Foley and Dave Cockell (ABA Championship information); and Dai Corp, John Jarrett, Brian McAllister, Ken Morton, Les Potts, and Robert Smith (Area title data). Although the research on world title bouts since gloves continues to wind down, I would again like to praise the efforts of men such as Tracy Callis, Luckett Davis and John Hogg, who are always available to help track down old fighters' records. At the same time, I would like to pay my respects to Fred Snelling and Bob Soderman, both 'grand old men of boxing', who both passed away during the last year. They will be sorely missed.

Finally, my thanks go to Jean Bastin, who continued to produce a high standard of typesetting and design, and my wife, Jennifer, who looks after the proof reading.

TARA BOXING PROMOTIONS & MANAGEMENT

Doughty's Gym, Princess Road, Shaw, Oldham OL2 7AZ
Tel/Fax: 01706-845753 (Office)   Tel: 01706-846762 (Gym)

Jack Doughty with left to right: Ady Lewis, Bobby Vanzie and Charles Shepherd

Trainer/Manager: JACK DOUGHTY
Trainers: Eamonn Vickers, Ray Ashton, Chris Fuller, Andy Jessiman, Maurice Core
Matchmaker: Richard Poxon M.C: Michael Pass

BOXERS

Shinny Bayaar - Flyweight
•Ady Lewis - Former British & Commonwealth Fly & Bantamweight Champion
Choi Tseveenpurev - British Masters Featherweight Champion
•Charles Shepherd - Former British, Commonwealth & IBO World
Super-Featherweight Champion
•Bobby Vanzie - British Lightweight Champion
Shaun Horsfall - Welterweight
Gary Hadwin - Welterweight
Wayne Shepherd - Light-Middleweight
Gary Dixon - Middleweight
Darren Stubbs - Super-Middleweight

•Co-managed

Introduction

by Barry J. Hugman

Welcome to the latest edition of the *British Boxing Yearbook*. Fast approaching the 20-year mark, the *Yearbook* picked up where the old *Boxing News'* Annuals left off and the two give a complete record of British boxing since the last World War. The format hasn't changed dramatically, as myself and the team continue to monitor and update the current goings on, while also continuing to research the past and pass on our findings.

Starting with the modern era, once again we have decided to stay with the way we produce Current British Based-Boxers: Complete Records. The decision to have one alphabet, instead of separating champions, being taken on the grounds that because there are so many champions these days – British, Commonwealth, European, IBF, WBA, WBC, WBO, and more recently WBU, IBO, WBF, etc, etc, and a whole host of Inter-Continental and International titles – it would cause confusion rather than what was really intended. If you wish to quickly locate whether or not a boxer fought during the past season (1 July 2001 to 30 June 2002) then the Boxers' Record Index at the back of the *Yearbook* is the place to look.

Regarding records, if a fighter is counted out standing up we have continued to show it as a stoppage rather than that of a kayo, as in fights where the referee dispenses with the count. Thus fights are recorded as count outs (the count being tolled with the fighter still on the canvas), retirements (where a fighter is retired on his stool) and referee stopped contest. Of course, other types of decisions would take in draws, no contests, and no decisions. In these days of health and safety fears, more and more boxers are being counted out either standing up or when initially floored, especially when a referee feels that the man on the receiving end is unable to defend himself adequately or requires immediate medical attention. One of the reasons that we have yet to discriminate between cut-eye stoppages and other types of endings, is because a fighter who is stopped because of cuts is often on his way to a defeat in the first place. Thus, if you want to get a true reflection on the fight it is probably better to consult the trade paper, *Boxing News*, rather than rely on a referee's decision to tell you all you want to know; the recorded result merely being a guide.

Continuing the trend, there are always new articles to match the old favourites. Regular features such as Home and Away with British Boxers (John Jarrett), World Title Bouts During the Season (Bob Yalen), A-Z of Current World Champions (Eric Armit), Highlights from the Amateur Season (Chris Kempson), Directory of Ex-Boxers' Associations (Ron Olver), Obituaries (Derek O'Dell) and two regular quizzes (Ralph Oates and Les Clark), etc, being supported this year with interesting articles such as 'Smiling' Sammy McCarthy; The Pride of East London (Bob Lonkhurst), John H.Stracey: Against All The Odds (Ralph Oates), The Quiet Man in the Corner (Melanie Lloyd), A Century of Welsh Boxing Greats (Wynford Jones), Brian London: The Man Who Followed in his Father's Footsteps (Tracey Pollard) and A Brief Introduction to Prize-Fighting in Popular Street Literature (Tony Gee).

Elsewhere, hopefully, you will find all you want to know about British (Area), Commonwealth, European and world title bouts that took place in 2001-2002, along with the amateur championships that were held in England, Scotland, Wales and Ireland.

Historically, what was started several years ago under the heading of Early Gloved Boxing, was extended to 138lbs in last year's edition. Much of this work was due to Harold Alderman painstakingly piecing together results for the pre-Lonsdale Belt and named weight-division period. There are still many who believe as gospel much of what was reported down the ages by 'respected' men such as Nat Fleischer, the owner of *The Ring* Magazine and the *Ring Record Book*, and then copied by numerous historians who failed to grasp what the sport was really like before the First World War. This year, we have compiled a list of all major fights from the beginning of gloves for all weights below 112lbs, the current flyweight limit, thus highlighting the rise and fall of the little known paperweight (light bantams) class.

Basically, boxing prior to the period in question was a shambles, following bare fists with an assortment of driving gloves, knuckle gloves, and two-ounce gloves, etc, until it arrived at what we recognise today. There were no Commissions, newspapermen becoming all powerful by naming their own champions at all kinds of weights, and in much of America the sport was illegal, no-decision contests rescuing it from being abolished. If you thought today was dire, then boxing prior to that period was almost impossible in all divisions bar the heavyweights. Because travel was difficult and news travelled slowly, fighters were able to move from town to town proclaiming themselves to be the best and 'ringers' constantly prevailed. With today's research being aided by access to early newspapers, and the use of computers, it is becoming clear that men like Fleischer 'took' the best fighters of the day and then 'fitted' them into the named weight divisions we now know so well. If that is still as clear as mud, then turn to the pages in question.

Finally, I would like to thank you all for your continued support of the *British Boxing Yearbook* and, at the same time, place on record my gratitude to Windsor's Jonathan Ticehurst, for his continued support of the *Yearbook* during these difficult times for the BBBoC.

Abbreviations and Definitions used in the record sections of the Yearbook:
PTS (Points), CO (Count Out), RSC (Referee Stopped Contest), RTD (Retired), DIS (Disqualification), NC (No Contest), ND (No Decision).

British Boxing Board of Control Ltd: Structure

(Members of the World Boxing Council, World Boxing Association, International Boxing Federation, World Boxing Organisation, Commonwealth Boxing Council and European Boxing Union)

PRESIDENT	Leonard E. Read, QPM
CHAIRMAN	Lord Brooks of Tremorfa, DL
VICE CHAIRMAN	His Honour Alan Simpson, MA, Oxon
GENERAL SECRETARY	Simon Block
ADMINISTRATIVE STEWARDS	Dennis Lockton Lincoln Crawford, OBE Charles Giles John Handelaar Nicky Piper Billy Walker Rt. Hon. Lord Pendry
HONORARY STEWARDS*	Dr Oswald Ross Mary Peters, DBE Frank Butler, OBE Bill Sheeran Sir Henry Cooper, OBE, KSG Capt. Robert Graham, BEM
STEWARDS OF APPEAL*	Robin Simpson, QC Peter Richards FRCS John Mathew, QC Nicholas Valios, QC William Tudor John Geoffrey Finn His Honour Brian Capstick, QC Colin Ross-Munroe, QC Prof. Andrew Lees Timothy Longdale, QC Robert Kidby
HEAD OFFICE	The Old Library Trinity Street Cardiff CF10 1BH Tel: 02920 367000 Fax: 02920 367019 E-mail: sblock@bbbofc.com Website: www.bbbofc.com

* Not directors of the company

AREA COUNCILS - AREA SECRETARIES

AREA NO 1 (SCOTLAND)
Brian McAllister
11 Woodside Crescent, Glasgow G3 7UL
Telephone 0141 3320392

AREA NO 2 (NORTHERN IRELAND)
John Campbell
8 Mount Eden Park, Belfast, Northern Ireland BT9 6RA
Telephone 02890 683310

AREA NO 3 (WALES)
Dai Corp
13 Hill Crest, Brynna, Llanharan, Pontyclun,
Mid Glamorgan CF7 9SN
Telephone 01443 226465

AREA NO 4 (NORTHERN)
(Northumberland, Cumbria, Durham, Cleveland, Tyne and Wear, North Yorkshire [north of a line drawn from Whitby to Northallerton to Richmond, including these towns].)
John Jarrett
5 Beechwood Avenue, Gosforth, Newcastle upon Tyne NE3 5DH
Telephone 0191 285 6556

AREA NO 5 (CENTRAL)
(North Yorkshire [with the exception of the part included in the Northern Area - see above], Lancashire, West and South Yorkshire, Greater Manchester, Merseyside and Cheshire, Isle of Man, North Humberside.)
Richard Jones
1 Churchfields, Croft, Warrington, Cheshire WA3 7JR
Telephone 01925 765167

AREA NO 6 (SOUTHERN)
(Bedfordshire, Berkshire, Buckinghamshire, Cambridgeshire, Channel Islands, Isle of Wight, Essex, Hampshire, Kent, Hertfordshire, Greater London, Norfolk, Suffolk, Oxfordshire, East and West Sussex.)
Robert W. Smith
The Old Library, Trinity Street, Cardiff CF10 1BH
Telephone 02920 367000

AREA NO 7 (WESTERN)
(Cornwall, Devon, Somerset, Dorset, Wiltshire, Avon, Gloucestershire.)
Dai Corp
13 Hill Crest, Brynna, Llanharan, Pontyclun,
Mid Glamorgan CF7 9SN
Telephone 01443 226465

AREA NO 8 (MIDLANDS)
(Derbyshire, Nottinghamshire, Lincolnshire, Salop, Staffordshire, Herefordshire and Worcestershire, Warwickshire, West Midlands, Leicestershire, South Humberside, Northamptonshire.)
Alec Kirby
105 Upper Meadow Road, Quinton, Birmingham B32
Telephone 0121 421 1194

Foreword

by Simon Block *(General Secretary, British Boxing Board of Control)*

In my Foreword to last year's *Yearbook* I commented on the defeats of Lennox Lewis and Naseem Hamed and expressed the view that both were capable of making it back to the top. In the case of Naseem Hamed, we still await confirmation of his enthusiasm to become champion again after his come back win against Manuel Calvo of Spain. Although a lot of critics were disappointed, Calvo was a lot tougher than many had appreciated beforehand. In the case of Lennox Lewis, however, he more than lived up to expectations when brutally disposing of his former conqueror, Hasim Rahman, to recapture the title in November of 2001, before going on to confirm his superiority in the heavyweight division by defeating the fading, but still dangerous Mike Tyson in June 2002 to secure his place as a 'great', not just in boxing but right across the sporting spectrum. Lewis aside, Johnny Nelson and Joe Calzaghe have maintained their positions as Britain's most successful champions, while Richard Hatton is without question British boxing's top 'box office' attraction.

Are we to see Scotland re-establish itself as a fight country? Scott Harrison has already established himself as one of Britain's better champions and a genuine world title contender. Alex Arthur looks to be one of the best Scottish prospects for years and his eagerly awaited British super-featherweight title challenge against fellow Scot and prospect, Willie Limond, may turn out to be the finest domestic pairing since Ken Buchanan defeated Jim Watt for the British lightweight championship 30 years ago. That was the contest which topped the bill of the inaugural St Andrew's Sporting Club in Glasgow. The club, which will be celebrating its anniversary during the year, has maintained its position as Scotland's premier dinner/boxing club, but since the demise of the National Sporting Club, the Midlands Sporting Club and Wolverhampton Sporting Club, etc, it can now rightly claim to be Britain's premier sporting club.

I continue to remain optimistic about British boxing and its future. We still produce exciting talent within these islands and revenue from Sky and BBC television, and the occasional backing of HBO and Showtime in the USA, make the sport viable at the top level, while the popularity of Sunday afternoon boxing is helping to keep some of the smaller promoters going. The campaign for the abolition of the sport undertaken by the British Medical Association in 1984 was ill-conceived, did not appear to have the backing of the majority of its own members and has now utterly failed. My only reservation continues to be the proliferation of titles with the resultant loss of prestige of British, Commonwealth, European and even World Championships, with the best boxers in the same weight division often avoiding each other. Anticipation is essential for the survival of any major sport and what fills major boxing venues are genuine matches, where both boxers are known to the ticket-buying public. There is no doubt that a full venue and great matches make for great television.

In November of 2001 the Board resolved the question of the damages claim by the former boxer, Michael Watson, after his successful legal action, and we came out of Adminstration. However, this involved paying over a substantial percentage of the value of Jack Petersen House, the Board's Headquarters, and the question of alternative accommodation was an option that had to be considered. Following a very generous offer made to us by Cardiff Council, the Board took the bold step of relocating out of London to Cardiff. This was something of a controversial move and a number of Licenceholders expressed their reservations. In fact, the transition has been much smoother than might have been anticipated and we are working from our offices in a beautiful old building, The Old Library, in the centre of Cardiff. Our new staff here have capably filled the positions occupied by the excellent staff that we had in London. Frank Warren and his staff are to be commended for their excellent fundraising event they ran for Michael at the Grosvenor House Hotel on 8 July 2002, which was attended by just about every big name in British boxing, including Lennox Lewis, and which raised a considerable sum to help him achieve a quality of life, despite his on-going disability, over and above those monies that he receives as a result of the Board's settlement. The Stewards of the Board were delighted to support the fundraising event.

It is not possible to sit in my chair for too long without controversy finding its way into my tray. We have certainly had that over the last couple of years in respect of the boxer, Wayne McCullough, who was refused an Alien Permit to box in Belfast in October 2000 following a query concerning his MRI brain scan. This case served to highlight the difficulties that face the Stewards, even with the benefit of eminent medical advice in reaching an appropriate decision in the case of professional boxers. Most medical matters are fairly straight forward and it is easy, even for the non-medical person, to determine that in any particular case a person may or may not be fit to box. However, there are a percentage of cases where the evidence is not so clear, but we still have an obligation both morally and legally to act in the best interests of the boxer. Faced with conflicting evidence, the Board will always err on the side of safety, but following advice received from the Chairman of our Panel of Appeal Stewards, Robin Simpson QC (the Appeal Stewards are independent from the rest of the Board and only meet to hear appeals by Licenceholders against decisions of the Board or Area Councils), in an unrelated matter, it became necessary for the Stewards of the Board to review the procedures for determining brain scan queries. In each and every case the Board now receives independent advice from Consultants in Neuroradiology, Neurosurgery and Neurology and it became possible to review the case of Mr McCullough when he subsequently applied for a full Licence here. Unfortunately, this led to the resignation of our Acting Chief Medical Officer, Dr George O'Neil, who had been such a valuable servant of the Board over many years, which caused even further controversy. However, when a meeting of our Area Chief Medical Officers was called quickly afterwards each Medical Officer in attendance came to the conclusion separately and without discussion, having had an opportunity to review all the available reports, that the Board had made the correct decision.

The Board itself will be undergoing some restructuring during the 2002-2003 season to ensure that it continues to meet the highest standards required in licensing and regulating this still great sport of ours. This will not only be in a form that is acceptable to our Licenceholders, but also to Parliament, where we have had a number of meetings with the All-Party Parliamentary Boxing Group chaired by Jimmy Wray MP, and to the general public at large in order to maintain our position as one of the world's leading boxing regulatory authorities.

We look forward in the coming season to maintain our dialogue with the ABA of England and Amateur Boxing Scotland and we hope that these discussions can be extended to include Northern Ireland and Wales in the future. Our congratulations go to the domestic teams for their successes in the 2002 Commonwealth Games in Manchester, particularly to England and Wales, whose teams did exceptionallly well. Although some of their stars will come over to professional boxing not all will and I would dearly love to see the re-establishment of amateur boxing of Great Britain and Northern Ireland to the position of its former eminence. I also believe that both we and the amateurs can co-exist to mutual benefit and that the stronger the amateur game the stronger will be the professional one.

The *Yearbook* contains just about everything you need to know about boxing over the last season. Having seen the work that Barry Hugman and his team have to put in to produce this every year, I congratulate them all on another excellent job, which I am sure you will enjoy as much as I will.

British Boxing Board of Control Awards

The Awards, inaugurated in 1984 in the form of statuettes of boxers, and designed by Morton T. Colver, are supplied by Len Fowler Trophies of Holborn. Len was an early post-war light-heavyweight favourite. As in 2001, the Awards Ceremony, which has reverted back to a luncheon format, is due to be held this coming Autumn in London and will again be hosted by the Lonsdale International Sporting Club's Bernard Hart, the Managing Director of Lonsdale Sports Equipment Ltd, and sponsor of the Awards.

British Boxer of the Year: The outstanding British Boxer at any weight. 1984: Barrry McGuigan. 1985: Barry McGuigan. 1986: Dennis Andries. 1987: Lloyd Honeyghan. 1988: Lloyd Honeyghan. 1989: Dennis Andries. 1990: Dennis Andries. 1991: Dave McAuley. 1992: Colin McMillan. 1993: Lennox Lewis. 1994: Steve Robinson. 1995: Nigel Benn. 1996: Prince Naseem Hamed. 1997: Robin Reid. 1998: Carl Thompson. 1999: Billy Schwer. 2000: Glenn Catley. 2001: Joe Calzaghe.

British Contest of the Year: Although a fight that took place in Europe won the 1984 Award, since that date, the Award, presented to both participants, has applied to the best all-action contest featuring a British boxer in a British ring. 1984: Jimmy Cable v Said Skouma. 1985: Barry McGuigan v Eusebio Pedroza. 1986: Mark Kaylor v Errol Christie. 1987: Dave McAuley v Fidel Bassa. 1988: Tom Collins v Mark Kaylor. 1989: Michael Watson v Nigel Benn. 1990: Orlando Canizales v Billy Hardy. 1991: Chris Eubank v Nigel Benn. 1992: Dennis Andries v Jeff Harding. 1993: Andy Till v Wally Swift Jnr. 1994: Steve Robinson v Paul Hodkinson. 1995: Steve Collins v Chris Eubank. 1996: P. J. Gallagher v Charles Shepherd. 1997: Spencer Oliver v Patrick Mullings. 1998: Carl Thompson v Chris Eubank. 1999: Shea Neary v Naas Scheepers. 2000: Simon Ramoni v Patrick Mullings. 2001: Colin Dunne v Billy Schwer.

Overseas Boxer of the Year: For the best performance by an overseas boxer in a British ring. 1984: Buster Drayton. 1985: Don Curry. 1986: Azumah Nelson. 1987: Maurice Blocker. 1988: Fidel Bassa. 1989: Brian Mitchell. 1990: Mike McCallum. 1991: Donovan Boucher. 1992: Jeff Harding. 1993: Crisanto Espana. 1994: Juan Molina. 1995: Mike McCallum. 1996: Jacob Matlala. 1997: Ronald Wright. 1998: Tim Austin. 1999: Vitali Klitschko. 2000: Keith Holmes. 2001: Harry Simon.

Special Award: Covers a wide spectrum, and is an appreciation for services to boxing. 1984: Doctor Adrian Whiteson. 1985: Harry Gibbs. 1986: Ray Clarke. 1987: Hon. Colin Moynihan. 1988: Tom Powell. 1990: Frank Bruno. 1991: Muhammad Ali. 1992: Doctor Oswald Ross. 1983: Phil Martin. 1994: Ron Olver. 1995: Gary Davidson. 1996: Reg Gutteridge and Harry Carpenter. 1997: Miguel Matthews and Pete Buckley. 1998: Mickey Duff and Tommy Miller. 1999: Jim Evans and Jack Lindsey. 2000: Henry Cooper. 2001: John Morris and Leonard 'Nipper' Read.

Sportsmanship Award: This Award recognises boxers who set a fine example, both in-and-out of the ring. 1986: Frank Bruno. 1987: Terry Marsh. 1988: Pat Cowdell. 1989: Horace Notice. 1990: Rocky Kelly. 1991: Wally Swift Jnr. 1992: Duke McKenzie. 1993: Nicky Piper. 1994: Francis Ampofo. 1995: Paul Wesley. 1996: Frank Bruno. 1997: Lennox Lewis. 1998: Johnny Williams. 1999: Brian Coleman. 2000: Michael Ayers and Wayne Rigby. 2001: Billy Schwer.

Joe Calzaghe (right) receives the 2001 'British Boxer of the Year' award from Sir Henry Cooper, Britain's first Knight of the ring
Les Clark

Insure You Keep your Guard Up

Insurance Brokers and Insurance Consultants to the:

British Boxing Board of Control, British Olympic Association,
International Cricket Council, Professional Footballers' Association,
Many Premier League and Football League Clubs
The Scottish Football Association, The Scottish Football League,
The Scottish Premier League, The Football Association of Wales,
The Football Association of Ireland, The Football League of Ireland,
The Irish Football Association, The Football Trust,
Event Organisers, Event Sponsors,
Individual Sportsmen and Sportswomen, Sports Agents

Windsor is one of the world's largest Specialist Sports, Leisure and
Entertainment Brokers, servicing National Sports Associations, Leagues,
Clubs and Players throughout the UK, Europe and North America.

While Personal Accident forms the major part of our Sports-related business,
the Group can also offer many other types of insurance cover at highly
competitive rates, including the following:-

- Stadium Risks
- Commercial Fire
- High Risk Liability
- Professional Indemnity
- Marine and Aviation

For Sponsors and Organisers, we offer a wide experience of Contingency risks such as:

- Event Cancellation/Abandonment
- Prize Indemnity
- Death and Disgrace
- Bonus Protection

**Do not leave yourselves exposed to the elements of chance
inherent in the sporting life.**

ASK WINDSOR TO HELP YOU

Windsor Insurance Brokers Limited
2 America Square
London EC3N 2LU

TEL: 020 7133 1200   FAX: 020 7133 1500

Boxing and the Need for Insurance

by Jonathan Ticehurst (Managing Director, Sports Division of Windsor Insurance Brokers Ltd)

To all of us in the insurance industry, our clients are of paramount importance. But, in our case, not only are they important, they are also in the public eye – because our speciality is professional sports and, in particular, boxing.

Boxing is, of course, a national sport, enjoyed at amateur level through schools and clubs by thousands of people and watched at top professional level by millions worldwide through the eyes of television.

How many of us see claims, or potential claims, occurring on television, or read about them in the papers before we get to the office? Millions have seen both promising, mature and lucrative careers ended in a matter of seconds as we have watched late night title fights and supporting bouts from our sitting room chairs.

Many people might wonder how such a direct contact sport can possibly qualify for Accident and Injury insurance cover. The answer lies in the definition of 'injury' and the definition of 'disablement'. For many years, the British Boxing Board of Control has provided and paid for a Personal Accident Policy for every one of its licensed boxers. This includes overseas boxers who have acquired a temporary licence for the purposes of fighting in this country in specific bouts. Traditionally, that policy provided cover for death, blindness, deafness and loss of limbs or parts of limbs whilst the licensed boxer was in the ring or climbing into or out of the ring.

Windsor have been managing the insurance affairs of the world of professional football and cricket for 20 years or more. During this time, various policies have paid out millions of pounds against claims by the national associations, the leagues, the clubs and counties, in respect of players who have gone out of the game early through injury. Some names you will only remember, others you may well have seen or, in early days, even played with, like Ian Storey-Moore, Steve Coppell, Gary Bailey, Alan Brazil, John O'Neill, Norman Whiteside, Gary Stevens, Siggi Jonsson, Mick McCarthy, Paul Elliott, John Fashanu, 'Syd' Lawrence, Paul Downton, Nigel Felton, Rodney Ontong and many others.

It was, perhaps, no surprise, therefore, that the Board should turn to Windsor in the course of its review of the insurance cover which has been available historically for boxers. The London insurance market is nothing if not imaginative and when brokers who are experts in their field put their heads together with underwriters who have made it their business to specialise in a particular class of insurance worldwide, then almost anything is possible at an affordable premium. The result was that the Board has now been able to include within their policy the all-important additional cover of Permanent & Total Disablement.

Experience has taught us that where an association, a federation, or affinity body takes out insurance for the benefit of its membership, then any individual member who needs additional or more wide-ranging cover for his own particular needs, should be able to buy his or her own cover as an extension to the group cover. That is what happens in football, cricket and many other sports. The Board's policy provides basic benefits for its licensed members and, although the benefits could not be, and, as is generally known, was never intended to be, regarded as a 'retirement fund', the policy is a very important starting point.

The Professional Boxers' Association recognised the hard work and imagination that the Board put into their new policy and were quick to endorse its value to all their members. Perhaps, more importantly, the PBA then worked closely with Windsor in designing tailor-made additional insurance cover which could be purchased, through their association, by members individually.

It is an ideal arrangement. The British Boxing Board of Control, through their own funds, are providing a general benefit for all their licensed boxers which can act as a platform for individual members to buy top-up cover, at their own expense, to suit their own particular requirements and financial obligations. The insurance wraps itself around the actual business of boxing and those in it and responds directly to the risks associated with it. It may be marginally more expensive than 'off the shelf' Accident & Injury policies, but then "off the shelf" policies will not respond to the peculiarities and the particular risks associated with a sport having such pugnacious characteristics.

Between them, the Board and the PBA have taken a giant leap forward for the benefit of all professional boxers. We, at Windsor, are happy that another high profile professional sport has the protection from the insurance market that it needs and deserves.

EVANS-WATERMAN PROMOTIONS

Licensed to the British Boxing Board of Control

Members of the Professional Boxing Promoters' Association

**88 WINDSOR ROAD
BRAY, MAIDENHEAD
BERKS SL6 2DJ**

Tel: 01628 623640   Fax: 01628 684633   Mobile: 07768 954643

e-mail: jimbox@tinyworld.co.uk

HEAVYWEIGHTS

Jacklord Jacobs	–	6-8-10 Rounds
Mike Holden	–	6-8-10 Rounds
Roman Greenberg	–	4-6 Rounds
Hovik Keuchkerian	–	4-6-8 Rounds

CRUISERWEIGHT

Graham Nolan	–	4 Rounds

LIGHT-HEAVYWEIGHTS

James Hearn	–	Debut
Shpetim Hoti	–	4 Rounds

MIDDLEWEIGHTS

Alan Gilbert	–	6-8-10 Rounds
Kevin Phelan	–	Debut
Mo	–	4 Rounds
Matthew Barr	–	4-6-8 Rounds

WELTERWEIGHTS

Sammy Smith	–	6-8 Rounds
Adrian Chase	–	6-8 Rounds

LIGHT-WELTERWEIGHTS

Jon Honney	–	4-6 Rounds
Nathan Ward	–	Debut
Iain Eldridge	–	6-8 Rounds
Robert Taylor	–	Debut

LIGHTWEIGHT

Chris McDonagh	–	4-6 Rounds

FEATHERWEIGHT

Mickey Bowden	–	6-8 Rounds

BANTAMWEIGHT

Jamie Yelland	–	6-8-10 Rounds

FLYWEIGHT

Darren Taylor	–	6-8 Rounds

JIM EVANS STABLE OF TRAINERS:-

Johnny Bloomfield
Derek Andrews
Mark Haines
Darren Whitman
Paul Rees

WEST LONDON'S FASTEST RISING STABLE

'Smiling' Sammy McCarthy: The Pride of East London

by Bob Lonkhurst

'The Nicest Man in Boxing' is the phrase which for years has been used to describe former British featherweight champion, Sammy McCarthy. I find it moving that despite some serious setbacks in his life, this genuinely nice man is still held in great esteem.

An extremely polite, quiet and well-mannered man, he remains as popular today as he was back in the 1950s when he packed London boxing arenas, particularly in the East End. Warmth radiates from Sammy, and he still has that familiar smile which earned him the affectionate title of 'Smiling Sammy' when he was a young amateur boxer with the Stepney and St George's club.

I have been fortunate to witness many instances of McCarthy's popularity. It was, however, never more apparent to me than one sunny spring morning a couple of years ago as we strolled along Commercial Road in the East End. What should have been a 15-minute trip was nearer to an hour as people of all ages stopped to pass the time of day. Each time Sammy's response was the same – a warm handshake, polite conversation and the familiar McCarthy smile.

Born at Stepney on Guy Fawkes day 1931, Sammy was the sixth child of a family of 10 – six girls and four boys. "As far as I can say, I am half Irish and half Jewish," he told me. "Both my grandmothers were Jewish, and my grandfathers were from the Emerald Isle."

Following the outbreak of the second world war, Sammy, along with many other youngsters from the East End, was evacuated to Egham in Surrey. He remained there for five years, and only when he returned home to Stepney did he become involved in boxing. His elder brother, Freddie, a good amateur who won a Junior ABA championship in 1938, persuaded him to join Stepney and St George's Amateur Boxing Club to learn to look after himself. His grandfather had also been a notable performer in his day.

Under the guidance of former professional, Johnny Mann, Sammy developed well. He had an abundance of natural talent, and desperately wanted to follow in Freddie's footsteps. After his first amateur contest in early 1946, he always believed he would win a title.

It was not long coming, and in 1947 he won the North-East London Divisional Junior title at seven stone. In February the following year, at Seymour Hall, he won a London Youth Class 'B' championship at seven stone seven. That success moved him into the Junior ABA Championship semi-finals at Wembley nine days later. In a close and thrilling contest, he was outpointed by the eventual champion, R. T. Parker (Roadmender BC, Northampton).

Although he was a good junior, Sammy really came to notice at Camberwell Baths in January 1949. In his first senior contest he boxed brilliantly to outpoint Norman Watts (Fitzroy Lodge). The packed audience watched in amazement at the youngster's skill and maturity against a proven competitor. Watts had won the North-West London Divisional bantam title the previous year, and was being tipped to win an ABA title.

Three weeks later Sammy proved his victory was no fluke when, before another packed house at Mile End Baths, he beat Watts again with a masterful display over four rounds. *Boxing News* described it as one of the finest bouts seen in London that season.

From that moment, Sammy's following grew rapidly, and he became unpaid boxing's 'Golden Boy'. The 'Sammy McCarthy Fan Club' was formed and, whenever he boxed, at least a dozen coach loads of fans would leave the Hope & Anchor pub at Watney Street to support him. Throughout the East End, bill-boards were posted advertising: 'McCARTHY FIGHTS TONIGHT - FARE 2/6d.'

Throughout his amateur career, Sammy worked for his father who had a green-grocery business. Every morning he was up at 5.30am and caught a bus to Spitafields Market. There he loaded a barrow full of vegetables and pulled it the two miles back to Watney Street. After helping his father lay out his own barrow, he pulled the empty one back to the market, returned home again, and then accompanied his father through the streets of Stepney on the regular round.

"I didn't need to do roadwork," recalled Sammy. "I was on the go all the time, and it was hard work."

Four evenings a week, he trained in the boxing gyms – Monday and Friday at the Stepney Institute Club, Smithy Street, and on Tuesday and Thursday at Stepney & St George's, Cable Street. His trainer, Johnny Mann, had great respect for him and in an interview once remarked: "Sammy is a very efficient pupil who always makes a point to enquire whether there have been any faults in his boxing, and is always ready to go back into the ring to rectify them."

As an amateur, it was always obvious that Sammy boxed for fun. Whenever Mann issued final instructions before a contest, he just smiled. At the bell, he skipped to the centre of the ring with a smile of mischievous anticipation etched across his face. Throughout the duration of his fights, the smile remained, even after the most vicious exchanges.

After beating Norman Watts, Sammy became something of an idol, and a crowd invariably packed into his dressing room following each contest. Despite all the attention, he remained the same gentle, unassuming lad. He always had a smiling greeting for every visitor, and a polite acknowledgement at the slightest compliment.

At first, he found all the attention quite daunting, but once he got used to it, he loved having his followers behind him. Consequently, he rarely boxed outside London.

Despite his tremendous ability, injury prevented McCarthy from pursuing ABA titles in 1949 and 1950. In 1951, when fit and determined, he was narrowly outpointed by the experienced Ron Hinson (West Ham) in the North-

East London Divisional Championships at York Hall, Bethnal Green. They had met twice before in 1950, winning one apiece. Following his latest success, Ron progressed to become the ABA lightweight champion.

Although he failed to win a major amateur title, Sammy was extremely successful in the unpaid ranks, and one of the finest boxers never to win an ABA Championship. From about 90 contests, he lost only seven, and boxed for England on four occasions. In 1949 he outpointed A. Bertieaux of Belgium at Wembley, and the following year beat J. Cummins (Ireland) and J. Steiner (Austria), but was outpointed by F. Dyma of Austria. One of his team mates for the two matches in Austria was Ron Hinson, with whom he formed a close friendship. Today he remains good friends with Ron's brothers Dennis and Tommy.

From a young age Sammy was a fine advertisement for boxing. An example of his sporting nature occurred one night at Poplar Baths during a 'needle fight'. When the fans loudly booed an indiscretion by his opponent, Sammy leaned over the ropes and shouted: "No, don't do that. It's alright."

McCarthy was just 19 when he turned professional with Jack King, although before anything was agreed Jack asked trainer, Snowy Buckingham, to look him over. When Sammy arrived at Jack Solomons' Windmill Street gym, Snowy couldn't believe he was a fighter. "He looked so smart and acted like a gentleman," the trainer recalled years later. When Sammy opened his training bag, Buckingham got another shock. "I've never seen a bag more neatly, cleanly and carefully packed," he remarked.

The East End lad made a superb start to his professional career, knocking out Hector Macrow in 57 seconds of the first round at Earls Court on 30 April 1951. A vicious left hook to the liver ended the contest, and as they left the ring Jack King asked Buckingham what he thought of Sammy. "How the hell do I know," snapped the trainer. "I never saw anything."

Top of the bill that night was a British Empire featherweight championship contest between Ronnie Clayton and Roy Ankrah (Gold Coast), both of whom would become opponents of Sammy as his career developed.

During the next five weeks, three more quick victories followed. Roy Groome was knocked out in three rounds, Jackie Leonard went in three before a capacity crowd at Mile End, and Peter Morrison was also stopped in the third.

After beating Jackie Horseman (points) and Teddy Odus (rsf 2), Sammy faced a real test in Freddie Hicks of Bermondsey. There were occasions during the fight when it looked as though he had been over-matched and, although the referee called it a draw, many people considered Sammy to be extremely fortunate.

McCarthy has a good recollection of that fight. "Freddie was a real handful," he told me. "Perhaps the referee was rather kind to me that night. I wouldn't have complained if I lost."

Sammy's popularity was incredible and increased with every contest. It was not just confined to the East End, and

in February 1952 readers of *Boxing News* voted him as the 'Best British-Born Boxer in 1951'.

During 1952, Sammy was gradually stepped up in class and successfully dealt with every opponent put in front of him. Fourteen more consecutive victories followed, seven opponents failing to last the distance. After beating Jackie Lucraft in three rounds, he considerably enhanced his reputation by forcing Hugh Mackie of British Guiana to retire after six rounds before a capacity crowd at Manor Place Baths in January. His display showed him to be one of the finest prospects in the country.

Boxing at fortnightly intervals, Sammy outpointed Jim McCann (Belfast) over eight rounds in a thrilling contest at Seymour Hall, and went on to beat Laurie McShane (ret 6) and Pat Kelly (rsc 4). Manor Place Baths was packed to capacity on 21 April when he won six of the eight rounds to clearly outpoint Central Area Champion, Denny Dawson, of Sheffield.

Recognising McCarthy's potential, promoter Jack Solomons put up a purse of £1,000, to be split £600 to £400, for him to meet Freddie King of Walworth. Both were making rapid progress in the featherweight division so the contest was a natural.

The fight took place at Harringay on 20 May 1952 and King gave Sammy a terrific battle for five rounds. The east Londoner then punished him badly, forcing referee, Austin O'Connor, to call a halt in the seventh.

Another wonderful exhibition of box-fighting earned McCarthy victory over Jackie Turpin (Leamington), who was stopped in four rounds at the White City. That success elevated him to number three in *Boxing News'* featherweight ratings for July.

Although just a shy 20-year-old barrow-boy, Sammy had aroused fight frenzy in the East End just like Teddy Baldock, Ted 'Kid' Lewis and Jack 'Kid' Berg years earlier. He hit harder than in his amateur days, and his exciting style ensured that whenever he boxed the venue was sold out. People loved Sammy because not only was he a wonderful entertainer, but a genuinely nice young man with a mischievous smile.

On 27 July 1952, Mile End Arena was packed for what Sammy always describes as the hardest fight of his career. His opponent, Johnny Molloy from St Helens, had been a professional for nine years. He had faced Ray Famecheon of France and most of the top men in Britain, including Ronnie Clayton, whom he beat in 1948, but lost to in a title fight the following year.

Molloy took everything Sammy threw at him, and by round five looked well in command. In the sixth, McCarthy bled badly from the nose and was cut over the left eye. He was in serious trouble, but dug deep and hit back viciously only to play into Molloy's hands. Heavy rights put him down for a count of 'nine', the first time he had been on the floor as a pro. When he rose, he was driven across the ring before going down again for 'eight'.

Sammy never lacked courage and, with wonderful fighting instinct, he fought back and boxed coolly to avoid further trouble. His tremendous attacking skills then turned the fight around, and he frustrated Molloy's efforts and took a very close decision. The fight was in fact so hard that Sammy could remember nothing about it when he was back in his dressing room. At one stage he turned to his brother Freddie and said, "I'm sorry I lost." He couldn't believe it when told he had won.

Even now Sammy has only one recollection of the fight, that being at a stage when he was hanging over the ropes being battered by Molloy. Freddie recalls the fight well, and describes how Sammy fought on instinct alone.

Points victories over Charlie Smithers (Leeds) and former Scottish champion, George Stewart, followed before Sammy faced his first overseas opponent, Jan Maas, featherweight champion of Holland. Heavy punches, particularly to the body, put the Dutchman down for five counts before the fight was stopped in round three.

By this stage, Sammy was the leading contender for Ronnie Clayton's British title, and promoters were clamouring for his services. Four weeks later, Freddie Mills matched him with former Scottish champion, Jim Kenny. It was the Londoner's biggest test to date because three months earlier Kenny had beaten Clayton in a non-title fight and had gone the distance with him for the title in 1950.

Boxing as well as at any time in his career, Sammy scored a brilliant victory, taking the last four rounds in great style. It was his first fight over ten rounds, and his fans snapped up over £1,000 worth of tickets more than two weeks in advance.

As Clayton was now the only British boxer left for McCarthy to face, Jack Solomons matched them over ten rounds at catchweights. They met at Harringay on 10 December 1952 on a show in aid of the National Playing Fields Association in the presence of HRH, The Duke of Edinburgh.

Although Clayton did most of the attacking, Sammy boxed brilliantly on the retreat. He had a scare in the fifth when, bleeding badly from the nose, he was floored for a count of 'eight'. Sticking to his boxing, however, he recovered well to win the last two rounds and take a close, but conclusive decision.

As Sammy was putting on his dressing gown and preparing to leave the ring, a voice suddenly said, "Stay where you are son, the Duke wants to see you." McCarthy and Clayton were then escorted to the ringside and introduced to the Duke. "That was a good fight," he told them. "I enjoyed every second of it." Both thanked him and were about to walk away when he added, "You two boys will have to box again, and I'll see if I can get a night off to come and see it."

Readers of *Boxing News* again recognised Sammy's achievements, and voted him 'The Fighter Who Did Most For British Boxing in 1952'. He was a clear winner over his nearest rival, Randolph Turpin, and at a luncheon at the Albany Club in London, Board of Control President, J. Onslow Fane, presented him with the *Boxing News* silver belt. Sammy also received a Certificate of Merit for his victory over Clayton.

Progress continued in 1953 with a series of victories over continental opposition. Eugene Servais of Belgium was stopped in three, former Italian bantamweight champion, Amleto Falcinelli, outpointed over ten, Louis Cabo, featherweight champion of Belgium, retired after eight rounds, and Jacques Lengendre of France was outpointed over ten. All were workmanlike performances as the east-London lad patiently awaited a shot at the British title.

For periods, Sammy trained at the Crown & Anchor gym, Preston Park, Brighton, with Albert Finch, Lew Lazar, Ansell Adams, Ron Pudney and Yolande Pompey. He also trained at Solomons gym at Windmill Street, where

McCarthy (left) on his way to victory against Scotland's Jim Kenny

Pompey gave him tremendous help before one of his fights. Wanting to show his appreciation, he asked Snowy Buckingham what he could give the Trinidad boxer as a present. "Go and ask him," said Snowy, "he's in the shower."

Sammy was fully clothed and without thinking walked straight into the shower room and got absolutely soaked. Undaunted, he told Pompey what was on his mind. "I don't help you because I want something," said the man from Trinidad, "but if you insist, I would like a quarter of boiled sweets." McCarthy revealed the story in the *Empire News* during 1955 because he believed it was important for people to know there is both friendship and humour in boxing.

In September 1953, Sammy received the news he had been patiently waiting for. The Board of Control finally ordered Ronnie Clayton to defend the British featherweight title against him. Jack Solomons wanted to stage the fight before Christmas, but the Board extended Clayton's period of grace to allow him to fulfil an engagement in South Africa.

Outside boxing, McCarthy, together with other London boxers, Jack Hobbs, Lew Lazar, Joe Lucy, George Walker and Tommy Barnham, accompanied a party of 250 East End children on a three hour riverboat trip on the Thames. Organised by the Albany Club Fair Play Fund, refreshments and musical entertainment were arranged and invitations extended to members of the press.

Anxious to keep active before his title fight, Sammy beat Gene Caffrey (rsc 7) and Ken Lawrence (disq 6), but then met with his first professional defeat. His opponent was Hogan Bassey who, since arriving in England less than two years earlier, had a record of 19 victories from 26 fights. Nobody in London knew much about the Nigerian because he had only boxed in the capital twice, winning one and losing the other. He was therefore not expected to pose Sammy any particular problems.

The fight, full of brilliant boxing by both men, was one for the connoisseurs, and everything rested on the final round. Bassey won it narrowly on aggression and took the decision much to the dismay of the London fans. Sammy, however, had no complaints because he learned a great deal from the fight.

Often when a boxer loses a long unbeaten record, further defeats follow. Sammy was no exception, and four weeks after losing to Bassey, he was outpointed by the brilliant Frenchman, Ray Famecheon. They were originally matched for Ray's European title, but when he lost it to Jean Sneyers, Solomons re-scheduled the fight for ten rounds.

Although McCarthy never gave up trying, the Frenchman was too clever and experienced. A veteran of 90 contests since 1944, including nine for the European featherweight title, he had lost just seven, one of which was on points to Willie Pep for the world title.

After the fight, Famecheon went to Sammy's dressing room, and before a captivated audience, proceeded to give the youngster useful hints of defence, demonstrating bobbing, weaving and swaying techniques. He said Sammy was too nice, and offered to take him to France for sparring. "Sammy will soon be a champion," insisted Ray. "He is a great fighter and boxer, and I hold it a great compliment to be able in some small way to help him."

Sammy was due to meet Ronnie Clayton at Harringay on 16 February 1954, but when the champion withdrew, Solomons matched him with Jean Sneyers of Belgium over 15 rounds for the European title. It proved to be a massive step-up in class, and although every round was close and bitterly contested, McCarthy was out-boxed and out-fought. Only amazing courage and fighting spirit kept him on his feet until the final bell. Yet he never gave up trying and stirred his fans with a rousing effort in the last two rounds. It was not enough and, with typical sportsmanship, Sammy was the first to congratulate the Belgian.

It was no disgrace to lose to a man of Sneyer's quality. Since 1948, he had lost just five of his 54 professional contests and had held the European fly and bantamweight titles before taking the featherweight title from Ray Famecheon.

After two months rest, McCarthy was back to his best and in April outpointed Teddy Peckham over eight rounds before a packed house at Manor Place Baths. Peckham, a veteran of more than 120 fights, provided Sammy with an ideal warm-up for his re-scheduled British title fight.

Whilst training to meet Clayton, Sammy received a telephone call from a man saying he had read that Ronnie had a boxer dog. "I am a McCarthy fan and breed boxers," he said. "I don't see any reason why Clayton should have something you don't have. So will you accept one as a present?"

Expecting to be given a puppy, Sammy accepted, but when the dog was brought to the gym, he found it was fully grown and needed a great deal of handling. Being too polite to refuse the dog, Sammy took it to his parents house at 705 Commercial Road. They called him Ricky, and he stayed with the family for several years until one night he escaped through the back gate and was never seen again. The family tell many amusing stories about the dog, one being how one night he smashed down his father's chicken house.

The fight with Clayton finally went ahead at the White City on 1 June 1954. When they met in the centre of the ring for the referee's final instructions, Clayton said, "Evening Sammy, let's have a nice fight." With his usual courtesy, Sammy replied, "Yes, of course Mr Clayton."

Having finally got his chance, Sammy made no mistake. He boxed brilliantly and the contest became very one-sided. His left jab repeatedly found the champion's head, and Clayton retired at the end of round eight suffering from loss of vision.

Three weeks after becoming champion, Sammy was taken to Pinewood Studios where Norman Wisdom was making the film *One Good Turn*. Norman was a former Army flyweight champion, and the film featured a scene at a boxing booth. He was delighted to meet Sammy, who quickly became the centre of attention and spent a lot of time signing autographs and posing for photos.

McCarthy insisted on being a fighting champion, and in

August stopped Enrico Macale of Italy at Clapton Greyhound Stadium. a crowd of 4,000 braving drizzle and gusting winds to see him produce a dazzling display.

Victories over Joe Woussem of Belgium (points) and Pierre Richard of France (rsc 6) followed. For the Richard fight, Sammy trained behind closed doors at Tommy Farr's old gym at the Crown & Anchor, Preston Park. No press interviews were given and even promoter, Harry Levene, was refused admission. Sammy was having weight problems, but didn't want anyone to know.

Jack Solomons then attempted to launch McCarthy into world class by matching him with Baby Ortiz, rated eighth in the rankings, but twice the Mexican champion pulled out. Solomons then tried to bring in Roy Ankrah, but Sammy wanted more money to fight him. He was even prepared to fake injury and pull out if Solomons failed to meet his demands. The situation became so desperate that Teddy Waltham, then General Secretary of the Board of Control, even visited Sammy at his home and tried to persuade him to go through with the fight. It was highly unethical, and Waltham remarked, "When you write your memoirs you can say that I humbled myself."

After a great deal of negotiation, the fight went ahead, with both men putting up side stakes of £500. Sammy gave a wonderful display and won most of the ten rounds. Knowing he could only win by a knock-out, Ankrah went for broke in the final round, but Sammy punched him to a stand-still.

The victory, however, was not without its complications, because McCarthy sustained serious damage to his right hand. He knew it required specialist treatment, but whenever his father or brother tried to persuade him, Sammy always said 'tomorrow', which never came. Failure to get proper treatment would have disastrous consequences.

Meanwhile, Irish promoter, Bob Gardner, offered Sammy £3,000 to defend his British title against the Empire champion, Billy 'Spider' Kelly, in Belfast. At first Jack King ignored the offer because Solomons promised to out-bid Gardner and stage the fight in London. Unfortunately, he made no bid so the fight went ahead at King's Hall, Belfast, on 22 January 1955.

Almost from that moment, things started to go wrong for Sammy. Whilst training at Brighton there was a recurrence of the damage to his right hand. He made no mention of it to Jack King or Snowy Buckingham because he knew they would call the fight off.

Adverse weather conditions then seriously affected his trip to Belfast. All planes were grounded due to thick fog, so he spent 19 hours getting there by train and boat. Instead of spending the night before the fight in a hotel bed, he made the long train journey from Euston to Heysham, where at 2am he boarded a night ferry. The next eight hours were spent at sea.

Kelly gave a fine exhibition of boxing and took a wide points decision, and it was Sammy's poorest performance since he drew with Freddie Hicks in 1951. Only in the final round did he slug it out in a desperate attempt to hang on to his title.

Typically, Sammy made no excuse for his defeat. It would have been easy to have put forward any of a number of reasons, particularly as his hand went in round four. In fact he was so honest that he said if the fight had been staged on the very same night in the East End, he would still have been beaten. What he failed to disclose was that weight problems had seriously weakened him.

The situation seriously affected Sammy's attitude, and his zest for boxing suddenly left him. As he climbed from the ring at Belfast he turned to his trainer and said, "Mr Snowy, if I don't fight again, I don't care." It wasn't reaction to losing the title, but how he felt.

In an article in the *Empire News* some months later, McCarthy admitted that by losing the title a strange feeling of relief came over him. It was as if a burden had been lifted from his shoulders. "I woke up one day to find myself a champion," he said, "but somehow from that moment I was never able to relax."

Although it was a strange comment, anyone who knew Sammy accepted that it was a true expression of his feelings. His muddled thinking persisted for two weeks after the fight. He alternated between feeling sorry for himself because he had lost the title and pleased because he no longer had to worry about it. Even to this day, he agrees that he felt tremendous pressure.

Sammy was out of the ring for five months, during which time he got his damaged right hand treated by a specialist. Suddenly, he wanted to be a champion again, so he got back into training. He found new confidence, and when he returned to the ring the familiar smile was replaced by an expression of grim determination. He stopped Teddy Peckham in three rounds, and a string of victories followed. Jesus Rubio (rsc 7), Andre Younsi (ko 3), Juan Alvarez (rsc 6), Willie Swobada (ko 3) and Lucien Meraint (pts).

On 29 November 1955, Sammy faced old foe, Jean Sneyers, over ten rounds at Streatham Ice Rink. It was a brilliant fight – fast and clever throughout, and thoroughly entertaining. Again the Belgian got the decision, but this time it was very close. Knowing he was behind, McCarthy made tremendous efforts in rounds eight and nine, but could not get on top. In the final session, they stood toe-to-toe and punched non-stop until the bell. There were resounding cheers for both men at the end.

Moving up to lightweight, Sammy faced British champion, Frank Johnson, over ten rounds at the Royal Albert Hall on 24 January 1956. More confident at the higher weight, he gave the champion a real beating by winning every round. It was McCarthy at his very best, and Johnson showed great courage to last the distance.

Just when it seemed that Sammy was headed for another title, everything came apart. In April, in a fight which attracted tremendous betting, he was narrowly outpointed by the young up-and-coming Dave Charnley. It was a wonderful fight, and although he was on the floor for long counts in the second and third rounds, Sammy attacked for all he was worth. His biggest obstacle, however, was that he was facing a southpaw for the first time in his career.

Charnley was still not 21, and not eligible to fight for the title. Sammy was therefore matched with the champion, Joe Lucy of Mile End, over 15 rounds at Wembley on 26 June 1956. Although it was an all East End affair, it was a tame fight. Sammy was down for 'seven' in the opening round, and fell a long way behind. When referee, Ike Powell, went to his corner at the end of the 12th round to enquire how he felt, Sammy replied with typical courtesy, "I am alright thank you Mr Powell."

In the next round, however, the referee considered he was too far behind to have a realistic chance of winning, so he stopped the fight. Although he was in no physical difficulty, Sammy was deprived of his extremely credible record of never having been stopped.

Still believing he had plenty to offer, Sammy beat Johnny Mann on points twice over ten rounds and stopped former French champion, Jacques Dumesnil, in four rounds before the end of the year.

McCarthy's last fight was on 22 January 1957 at the Royal Albert Hall when he was outpointed by Guy Gracia. The good Frenchman who had beaten Charnley and Lucy, put Sammy on the floor three times. Once again, the Londoner sustained damage to his right hand and sensibly realised he was past his best.

Two months later, the BBC honoured Sammy with a *This Is Your Life* programme. Unbeknown to him members of his family had attended two rehersals. Freddie convinced Sammy that a story was being written about his life, and the writer wanted to interview him the following evening. His first reaction was that he didn't want to go because it would mean he would miss seeing *Gun Law* on television.

The next evening, a cab called for Sammy and his family, and he recalls that it drove around for ages before stopping at the rear of a building. He was left alone in the cab for 20 minutes before being escorted into the building to be confronted by Eamonn Andrews holding the familiar red book. "Sammy McCarthy," he said: "This is your life."

Among the guests were former opponents, Hector Macrow, Jean Sneyers and Ronnie Clayton. Although in a state of shock, Sammy waited for an appropriate moment and then announced his retirement from the ring. It was a fitting end to the career of one of Britain's most popular champions.

Another celebrity guest was Terry Spinks who, as a young schoolboy, idolised Sammy and often sat on his doorstep at Commercial Road waiting for him to come home. Three months earlier, the 19-year-old Canning Town lad had won the Olympic flyweight championship at Melbourne. He told Sammy he was about to turn professional and wanted him to become his manager. The former featherweight champion was delighted, and immediately agreed.

McCarthy took out a manager's license and, apart from Spinks, also handled Canning Town boxers, Terry Gill, Terry Brown and Brian Bissmire, amongst others. Spinks was by far the most successful, winning the British featherweight title, while Gill was Southern Area welterweight champion.

All of Sammy's boxers trained at the Thomas A' Beckett gym in the Old Kent Road. Whilst they were dedicated to their work, he was constantly on his guard. "They all needed careful watching," he recalled with a smile. "They were young lads who liked the beer, so I had to make sure they trained properly."

Although he has remained in touch with boxing throughout his life, Sammy has retained special affection for Spinks, his life-long friend. "We have stuck together through many highs and lows," he remarked, "but we are as close today as when Terry was boxing. He is my dearest friend."

Indeed, when Spinks was extremely ill during the early 1990s, Sammy was a frequent visitor to both the hospital and clinic over a 21-month period. He gave incredible support to Terry's family, and still does. When Spinks was awarded the MBE in 2002, Sammy was one of the three guests who accompanied him to Buckingham Palace.

Both are now honorary Vice-Presidents of the London ex-Boxers' Association. They represent the Association at many events, attend funerals and visit sick members and friends in hospital. They are also tireless workers for charity. Together with their close mate, Ron Cooper, a former Navy, Imperial Services and ABA champion, they spend days recalling the good old days, and are affectionately known as *Last of the Summer Wine*.

More than 45 years since he retired from boxing, Sammy McCarthy is still loved and respected by all who know him. He is one of the nicest men ever to have climbed into the ring, and there can be few modern day fighters with the following he had.

He has frequently expressed his thanks to everyone who made it possible for an ordinary East End lad to become a household name. Of his parents he said; "I fully realise that but for their indulgence which made it possible for me to train when I might have been earning much needed money for the family, I could never have made the grade."

When he retired from the ring in 1957, Sammy had the credible record of 44 wins, one draw and eight defeats, Joe Lucy being the only man to beat him inside the distance. His success and popularity were recognised when his effigy in wax was exhibited at Madam Tussauds during the 1950s.

Sammy McCarthy sets a wonderful example to the sport of boxing. Many of us are privileged to know him.

John H. Stracey: Against All Odds

by Ralph Oates

It was quite clear from the off that John H. Stracey had the ability to become a welterweight champion in the professional ranks. The big question was, at which level would John eventually reign. The British and Commonwealth titles looked a good bet, possibly even the European crown appeared to be within his reach. The world championship, well that may have been a little too much to have hoped for. After all there were a number of very talented fighters in the 147 lb division. In fact, it wouldn't be an under-statement to say that there were some exceptional men plying their trade at that poundage. Over the years the welterweight division had produced many fine fighters at the weight, a number of them could even be called great. Sugar Ray Robinson, Kid Gavilan, Carmen Basilio, Emile Griffith and Curtis Cokes, were just a few of the class names who had previously ruled over the division with distinction.

Stracey, who was born on 22 September 1950, had a very impressive amateur pedigree, which included winning the ABA light-welterweight crown in 1969. Prior to that achievement, John, at the very tender age of 18, represented Great Britain at the 1968 Olympic Games which took place in Mexico. Stracey may have failed to bring back a medal, but he gave a good account of himself against good opposition. Being at the Games also gave him valuable experience which would stand him in good stead for the future. At the same Games, Chris Finnegan won gold at middleweight to give British amateur boxing a massive boost.

On 17 September 1969, John made his foray into the professional ranks, knocking out Santos Martins in two rounds. Stracey was just days away from his 19th birthday and, at this stage, it looked as if the boxing world was well and truly his oyster. John had joined the fashionable stable of East-End manager, Terry Lawless, who appeared to have the magical knack of turning out champions. Fortunate to be young with time on his side, John would be able to serve his fistic apprenticeship by mixing it with an assortment of opponents with various style. Stracey's second contest took place on 2 October and once again he wasted very little time, knocking out Ron Clifford in two rounds, to confirm he had impressive punching power to go with his boxing skills. He had a further two winning bouts before the year came to a close, once again stopping both his opponents, before opening his account early in 1970, stopping Tommy Carson in round seven on 20 January. Carson proved to be a stubborn opponent who did not wilt easily, giving John an interesting night's work. Stracey returned quickly to the ring on 10 February, stopping Tei Dovie in three rounds to push his undefeated record to six, all inside the scheduled distance. However, a cloud of despondency had descended over the Lawless camp that night, since on the same bill

John's stable mate, the highly-rated Ralph Charles, the holder of the British and Commonwealth welterweight titles, had lost a ten-round points decision to Raul Soriano. This was a set back for Charles, for this was a contest many had expected him to win, but Soriano had proven to be a very tricky opponent and Ralph now had to fight his way back if he was to get a shot at the world crown. This too was a lesson for Stracey, for he had seen at first hand how easy it was to have both your dreams and ambitions dashed in just one night and, indeed, one fight.

During the course of 1970, John had a further six winning bouts with just one opponent, David Pesenti, taking him the full distance of eight rounds. In this contest, which took place on 12 May, Pesenti proved to be a very artful opponent who knew how to use the ring and was also able to absorb a punch. The contest was a valuable one for the London-born fighter, since while it is great to be able to

John poses with the Lonsdale Belt and European title-winning belt

put an opponent away early, it is also a necessity to be able to cope should the man in the opposite corner be able to last the respective course.

1971 looked like being another good year for advancement and all was going along well until he and his opponent, Frankie Lewis, stepped into the ring on 5 October. It was obvious from the sound of the bell to start round one that this was one ring-wise boxer, yet John took the fight to his man, throwing solid punches to both head and body, but when the contest eventually came to a close the referee decided that both men had shared the points, the result being a draw after eight rounds. This was an obvious disappointment, but it was one which John just had to put behind him in order to move on. This was the strategy the Lawless camp quickly employed on the 27th of the same month when Stracey was back in action, stopping Dave Wyatt in three rounds. Then, on 16 November, another victory followed when Guy Vercoutter was stopped in seven rounds. The year had been a good one, for John had continued to make progress and was fast climbing the ladder to the top of the domestic tree.

He started 1972 well, with a four-round knockout over Yvon Mariolle, being too clever and too powerful for his game opponent. The next contest, on 15 February, was really a test for Stracey since the man in the other corner was Bernie Terrell. Terrell was an experienced fighter, who, in his previous outing on 7 December 1971, had challenged for the British and Commonwealth welterweight titles, being stopped in round eight by Ralph Charles. Another point of obvious interest was that Terrell had also outpointed Frankie Lewis over eight rounds on 19 October 1971. Against Stracey, Bernie would be having his 28th contest with a record of 23 wins, one draw and three defeats. The question was had John taken that one step too far too soon. The answer was a emphatic no. John did not give Terrell a chance to settle and was all over his man, punching hard and fast to bring about the referee's intervention in round two.

Next up on John's fistic agenda was Des Rea, a man who had made boxing history on 27 February 1968 by becoming the first holder of the British junior-welterweight championship (later to be called the British light-welterweight title). Rea achieved this honour by outpointing Vic Andreetti over 15 hard rounds. It may have been true to say that, at this stage, Des's career was on a downward spiral, yet he had met many quality names like Jose Napoles, Bruno Arcari, Brian Curvis, Johnny Cooke, Jorgen Hansen and Chuck Henderson. Rea's record very much resembled a travel catalogue, with him having fought in Italy, America, Australia (twice), France, Denmark and South Africa. 'Have Gloves Will Travel' should have been stamped on his passport. During his career the man from Belfast had also won the Northern Ireland and All-Ireland crowns in putting together a record of 24 wins, 19 losses and two draws. It was clear that Des would fight anybody at anytime, anywhere, and

the growing reputation of Stracey held no fears for him. Rea was coming into the ring with two previous winning bouts behind him and was confident that on the night of 3 March he would make it a hat-trick. John, however, had other ideas, making light of Rea's vast ring experience to stop him in round two. Stracey delighted his fans with a hard-hitting display, which once again gave notice that he was a little special.

The next man selected was the ever reliable Ricky Porter, on 4 April. Ricky was another fighter who could extend the very best on his night, but once again he found, like many before him, that he had no answer to this fast-punching opponent in front of him, but at least gained a modicum of satisfaction by lasting the full course of eight rounds. Just when it looked as if all was warm and sunny a man by the name of Marshall Butler came along 21 days later to bring a cold front to Stracey's career, by out-pointing him over eight close rounds in an interesting match. Both fighters gave the fans a good-night's boxing. Some pundits were of the opinion that John did just enough to get the nod, while others agreed with the verdict. In a strange way the result did not harm the progress of the London-born fighter, since it was one of those bouts where both winner and loser emerged with credit.

It soon became obvious that John's confidence was not dented in any way by the result and he was quickly back in action in May and June, winning both his bouts inside the distance. On 10 October, John took part in his most important contest so far – a final eliminator for the British welterweight crown. Ralph Charles, John's stablemate, had relinquished the title and very clearly the Lawless camp wanted to reclaim the crown. On the night in question, the man facing John was Les Pearson, a good, honest fighter, who gave his very all when ever in action, but John made short work of his man, stopping him in round two. Stracey now looked an excellent bet to be the next holder of the British welterweight championship. Yet life can play some very strange tricks.

The contest for the vacant championship took place on the 31 October and John, fresh from the Pearson win, was the firm favourite to collect the title. Bobby Arthur, the man in the opposite corner, like John, was full of ambition and was one of those fighters who should not be written off without a thought. Arthur had paid his dues, having fought former British lightweight champion, Maurice Cullen, Angel Garcia, Jorgen Hansen, Jose Duran and also twice defeated the once highly-touted Jackie Turpin, putting together in the process a record of 29 bouts, with 22 victories and seven defeats. Bobby had also put together a winning sequence of six wins prior to facing Stracey. Before the bell rang out to start the much anticipated contest, the atmosphere was pure electric, with the fans chanting John's name and expecting to see their man blow away Arthur to gain the championship. At the start of the contest, John went straight in, attacking his opponent with classy combinations, while Arthur, to his credit, attempted to contain his man and counter when he could. The battle continued with John boxing well to have the upper hand until round seven when he caught Arthur with a punch to the body, sending him to the canvas. It looked as if the fight was over and it was, with Stracey being disqualified for hitting on the break. This was a shock. John had looked home and dry and about to bring the title back to the East End, but it was not to be. Stracey was disappointed, but knew deep down that under the circumstances a return bout would be made in the not too distant future. For now, Bobby Arthur was the British welterweight champion, but John, in the eyes of many, was the uncrowned king.

Before the year was out he got back in the win column, stopping David Melendez in round seven on 5 December. Stracey was quickly back into fistic action on 15 January 1973, knocking out Otho Tyson in three rounds. Then, on 14 February, Stracey had his first professional fight abroad, meeting Danny McAloon in America. McAloon was one of those fighters who did not win that often, but was one hard, rugged individual who did not look for the easy way out. He always came to fight and that he did on the night he crossed gloves in Las Vegas with the British fighter. Proving that he was growing in ring maturity, John had an answer for everything McAloon attempted, running out a good points winner over the respective ten rounds. It was the first time that Stracey had travelled the full distance of ten rounds and the fact that he did so without any problems was an excellent sign for the future. On the same bill, fellow Britons, Joe Bugner and John Conteh, also fought. Bugner lost a 12-round points decision to Muhammad Ali, while Conteh stopped his opponent, Terry Daniels, in six rounds.

In the following months, John scored two more victories, then, on 5 June, his return with Bobby Arthur took place. Since defeating Stracey, Arthur had not fought at all, while in the same period of time John had boxed five times. The outlook did not look good for Arthur, as he had more than his hands full when he first contested this title against Stracey. Now, the Londoner was that more experienced and ring sharp, while the defending champion had to shake off ring rust. John was once again the clear favourite to take the championship and so it was. In truth, Arthur gave a good account of himself in the first three rounds, jabbing well, but in round four John brought proceedings to a close, knocking out the champion with a good right hand. The fans gave Stracey a tremendous cheer and at last their man was a champion. John was now wearing the crown which in bygone years had been worn by men like Matt Wells, Ted 'Kid' Lewis, Ernie Roderick, Eddie Thomas, Brian Curvis and many other eminent exponents of the noble art.

Everything in the garden of John H. Stracey looked very rosy at that time and British boxing had a welterweight who clearly had a great deal more in store to offer. Exciting times ahead looked certain as John next stepped between the ropes on 10 September, stopping Jose Melendez in three rounds. This was promptly followed by a further two victories in the months of October and November. Then, on 11 December, disaster struck when Stracey suffered a three-round cut eye loss to 'Top Cat' Jackson. This was one cat that was lucky to get the cream, since John had looked to be on his way to yet another win. The defeat was only a slight set-back, yet a defeat is a defeat and the Lawless camp knew that they would have to work fast and hard to ensure that John maintained his world ranking. On 26 March 1974, John once again put on the gloves for further ring action, stopping the highly regarded Jack Tillman in round four, which was followed by a further winning bout on 23 April when he knocked out Vernon Mason, also in round four.

On 27 May, Stracey took a major step into the big time when challenging Roger Menetrey for the European title. This was no easy task. It was, in fact, a fight which John could quite easily lose, the odds in fact being against him. The British fighter had to travel to France to meet the Frenchman and was thus going into the lion's den to meet a very dangerous and experienced man, a lion who still had very sharp teeth. Roger, an exceptional European champion, would be making his sixth defence against the Londoner. The Stracey camp knew Menetrey quite well, since he had taken the continental crown from Ralph Charles by a seven-round knockout on 4 June 1971 and then defended the title successfully against quality fighters like Sylvan Bertini, Robert Gallois, Jorgen Hansen and former world light-welterweight champion, Sandro Lopopolo. The French fighter even went the full 15 rounds on 23 June 1973 against Jose Napoles, when challenging for the world title. A betting man, when considering the form and experience of both men, would have put his money on the Frenchman, who appeared to have everything in his favour. Yet, on the night at the Roland Garros Stadium in Paris, John took the champion apart, boxing superbly and scoring with classy jabs to the head of Menetrey, who was not able to come to grips with his opponent. John looked every inch a class act, moving around the ring and not giving the champion a chance to connect with his blows. The referee stopped the bout in round eight in Stracey's favour and John had not only gained revenge for Ralph Charles, but had brought the championship back to Britain. In fact, the night was a great one for British boxing, since, on the same bill, Kevin Finnegan had also obtained a magnificent win when outpointing another world-ranked Frenchman, Jean Claude-Bouttier, over 15 rounds to capture the European middleweight championship. Like Stracey, Finnegan appeared to have the odds against him, but like his fellow countryman he more than rose to the occasion.

John H. Stracey was now a name to be taken seriously by the other contenders in the division. The champion, Jose Napoles, loomed large in the sights of the British fighter, despite him not being a highly ranked contender. However, John had to keep the momentum going – keep active and keep winning to secure a world title shot. On 1 October 1974, Stracey pulled off another solid win, stopping Tony Garcia in three rounds before taking a good testing match, against ranked opponent, Ernie (Red) Lopez, on the 29th of the same month. A win here by Stracey would further enhance his fistic reputation, since Lopez was a highly respected fighter, a man who could mix it with the very best and would not come to Britain to roll over. The American knew that a win here over Stracey would push him back up the ratings and hence into other big-money bouts. The incentive for Lopez was therefore quite massive. The same of course could be said for Stracey. When the bell rang to send the two gladiators into battle, Stracey's face was a picture of concentration, while Lopez, a man who had already challenged twice for the world title against Jose Napoles, found out that he would not be able to use the young British boxer as a stepping stone to get back into the championship picture. John boxed to perfection, outclassing the American in every department, but Lopez was a brave man, full of both dignity and pride, who was clearly not going to give up without a fight. Yet flesh and bone can only take so much and the contest was duly stopped in Stracey's favour in round seven, much to the delight of the many fans who cheered his every move.

Soon after, John suffered a set-back when he went down with appendicitis. However, after a successful operation, he made a ring return on 29 April 1975, making the first defence of his European title against Max Hebeison of Switzerland. In truth, Hebeison did not stand a chance and Stracey had too much of everything for him to cope with, the bout being stopped in round six. John looked good once again in victory and showed no ill effects from his operation. A further two wins followed, before John was given the opportunity to challenge for the world welterweight championship against the man who was regarded as a modern day great, Jose Napoles.

Napoles, who was born in Cuba on 13 April 1940, had made Mexico his home and was treated like a king. He had made his professional debut on 2 August 1958, in Havana, knocking out Julio Rojas in round one. In the years which followed, Napoles fought his way to the top, boxing an assortment of fighters, until his moment came on 18 April 1969 when, in his 59th contest, he stopped the defending titleholder, Curtis Cokes, in round 13 to capture the welterweight championship of the world. On 29 June 1969, Napoles proved that his victory had been no fluke when he repeated his win over Cokes, this time forcing him to retire in round ten. A few months later, on 17 October, Jose made a second defence of his crown, outpointing another fighter whose name was ranked among the greats, Emile Griffith. A three-time holder of the world welterweight championship and twice holder of the middleweight title, Griffith gave it his best shot but was clearly beaten by Jose on points over 15 rounds. After defeating Ernie (Red) Lopez by a stoppage in round 15 on 14 February 1970, Jose later took part in two winning non-title bouts, but in a shock

result on 3 December he lost his welterweight title when stopped in round four by Billy Backus. This was a fight he was expected to win without too many problems. The defeat came due to an eye injury but, nevertheless, Napoles was now a former champion. Backus, a nephew of former world welterweight and middleweight champion, Carmen Basilio, enjoyed his moment of glory. However, matters were soon put right on 4 June 1971, when Napoles, having secured a return with Backus for the crown, regained the title with a stoppage victory in round eight. Napoles went on to defeat Hedgemon Lewis (twice), Ralph Charles, Adolph Pruitt, Ernie (Red) Lopez (a second time), Roger Menetrey, Clyde Gray, Horacio Saldano and Armano Muniz (twice). There was no doubt that Napoles faced the very top men in his division and turned back their respective challenges, but on 9 February 1974, Jose overreached himself when challenging Carlos Monzon for the world middleweight title. The Argentinian was just too big and strong for him and he retired in round six. In truth, the mighty Monzon was never troubled by the welterweight king. Regardless of that, Jose was still the main man in the 147 lb division.

Stracey was most certainly up against it and his task was made even worse when it was confirmed that he would have to venture to Mexico City to take his chance. Everything would be against Stracey. Not only was the British fighter meeting a man who would be difficult enough to defeat, even in his own backyard, but to meet Napoles in his adopted country and get acclimatised to the high altitude of Mexico as well as overcoming the educated fists of the champion was a tall order. John had fought in Mexico as an amateur, when representing Great Britain at the Olympic Games, so he knew what to expect with regards to the altitude, thus the experience would not give him any nasty shocks. Also, the Lawless camp had seen Napoles close up in 1972 when he came to Britain in defence of his welterweight crown and duly knocked out their then charge, Ralph Charles, in seven rounds. Yet there was no doubt that Stracey had the odds stacked against him, big time. Although he had faced a number of good fighters to get his crack at the championship, Napoles was something else, and a man who could box like a master with a devastating punch which could take an opponent out anytime it struck home. However, John was full of confidence and felt he had the talent and the desire to tear the crown off Napoles' head even in Mexico. While many fight experts admired Stracey's confidence and attitude going into the contest they feared that Napoles would have too much of everything for him and that he would do well just to last the distance, let alone win the championship. The heart wanted a British win, but the head said Napoles.

On the night of 6 December 1975 at the Plaza De Toros, the situation did not look too bright for the British prospect when he was sent to the canvas for a count in the opening round and it looked as if the confident champion would be having an early night. However, Stracey was not going to make life that easy for Napoles as he had come to win the crown and, with the heart of a lion, he fought back to force the referee, Octavio Meyran, to stop the contest in his favour in the sixth round. It was a glorious victory which shook many boxing pundits to their boots. It wasn't that they doubted John's ability in any way, it was that Napoles was such an outstanding champion, a man who had met and dispatched so many excellent welterweights in his reign at the top. Stracey was now on top of the world, the first British fighter to hold the world welterweight crown since Ted 'Kid' Lewis lost the championship to Jack Britton on 17 March 1919 by a ninth-round knockout. Stracey was the talk of the boxing world and a man who looked ready to reign for many years.

Although John was regarded as the *real* world champion, Napoles had already relinquished the WBA version of the title to concentrate on the WBC crown. Puerto Rican, Angel Espada, had taken the vacant version of the WBA title on 28 June, following a 15-round points victory over Clyde Gray of Canada, and had made a first successful defence on 11 October with another 15-round points decision over Johnny Gant of America. A match up for the undisputed championship between Stracey and Espada looked like an excellent contest along the line. In the meantime, both men had to take care of immediate business with their respective title defences and look good in doing so, to ensure their meeting would be a box-office winner when made.

The first defence for the British fighter came on 20 March 1976 at Wembley against the classy American, Hedgemon Lewis. Hedgemon had twice challenged Napoles for the world title without success, being outpointed over 15 rounds on 14 December 1971, and then being stopped on 3 August 1974 in nine rounds. However, Lewis did gain a measure of recognition as world champion when he outpointed former world welterweight king, Billy Backus, over 15 rounds for the vacant New York version of the championship on 16 June 1972 and repeated the victory in his first defence on 8 December with another 15-round points victory over Backus. That aside, any claims Lewis may have had on the welterweight championship quickly disappeared when he met Napoles for the second time in 1974. Some critics were of the opinion that Lewis was a little past his best, but it was clear by his attitude that he had not come to take in the sights of London; he wanted Stracey's crown and knew that this would be his last chance. On the night, Lewis did not disappoint. From the first round, the American challenger took the fight to the British world champion, with classy jabs and hooks appearing to catch Stracey with ultimate ease. At the end of the first round the situation looked far from good for Stracey. Lewis was really fired up and there was a danger that he just might overwhelm the British fighter, but the contest had only just started and Stracey had only just begun to show his wares. From the second round onwards, the champion came forward, attacking his challenger with a constant stream of punches to both head

In one of boxing's great upsets, John (left) demolished the legendary Jose Napoles

and body with relentless aggression. Lewis would fight back, attempting to put the champion on the backfoot with an array of punches, but John would have none of it, keeping the pressure on the challenger and hooking beautifully to the body. With only experience and courage keeping Lewis going, he was determined to stay in the contest with the slight hope that he just might be able to find the punch to turn the fight around. However, the fans were on their feet in round ten when the referee, Harry Gibbs, stepped in to save the stricken American from further punishment after Stracey had let loose with a whirlwind of punches. Lewis was defeated, but he went out with his pride intact, knowing that he had given all he had but had lost to a better fighter, a true champion. This had been a magnificent performance from Stracey.

The name of John H. Stracey was now well and truly one to contend with and he was the man to beat in the division. At that moment in time, it appeared that the British fighter had the tools to defeat anyone in the division and the next challenger selected was Mexican-American, Carlos Palomino, a fighter who had a good record but in all truth did not look too serious a threat. After taking care of Napoles and Lewis, Stracey looked a class above this man. True, Carlos had held Lewis to a draw over ten rounds in Los Angeles on 22 November 1975, but apart from that result the challenger appeared to be quite a good fighter, although not really an outstanding one. Yet, on the night of 22 June 1976 at the Empire Pool Wembley, the world of boxing was in for a shock. With Palomino proving to be something a little special, Stracey could not get to grips with his man and it was apparent from the early rounds that the defending champion had a fight on his hands. John lacked nothing in the courage department and took his licks while still advancing. However, in round 12, much to the dismay of the fans the referee, Sid Nathan, moved in to stop the contest. Stracey had lost his world title.

The result was hard to believe. How could the man who took the championship off a great like Jose Napoles in Mexico lose the title to a man who looked lucky to be given a chance in the first place. Yet Palomino performed in a way which suggested that he was so much better than his record indicated and that he was a man who would prove a worthy champion (Palomino went on to defend the championship successfully seven times before losing it to Wilfred Benitez on 14 January 1979, via a 15-round points decision). John was of course disappointed, but a champion in victory is also a champion in defeat, and he accepted that on the night the better man won. John was a very popular figure with the fight fans and many felt that this defeat was down to an off night, a bad day at the office no less.

Stracey did not fight again that year and took a well-earned rest before a battle plan was put together. While John H. had been contesting world titles, another domestic fighter was making headlines. His name was Dave 'Boy' Green, a hard-punching rugged battler from Chatteris, nicknamed the 'Fen Tiger', who was undefeated in 23 fights, winning 18 inside the distance, along with the British and European light-welterweight titles. Green was no soft option and the match was set for 29 March 1977, being made a final eliminator for the WBC world welterweight championships. Green was full of determination and confidence and there was no doubt in his mind that he would defeat the former world champion and push on to challenge Palomino. The fight was a box office magnet; it was the fight everyone wanted to see. The view on who the victor would be was somewhat mixed amongst the fans. Some felt Green's chance had come a little too soon and that Stracey would know too much for him, while others wondered if the Palomino defeat had taken something out of Stracey. It was in every sense of the word a fascinating contest.

At the start of the bell, Green came out of his corner looking for Stracey, every jab, every hook thrown with mean intention. Dave took no prisoners but Stracey, in his 50th contest, managed to evade much of the leather thrown in his direction. At that particular moment in time, Green was not showing anything that Stracey had seen before. John was able to counter and show his opponent that this was not a one-way street and that he too had come to fight and win. Each round was hard fought and no one was giving an inch. After all the victor was going for the world title. The prize was thus a massive one, with the loser having to tread a long and hard road back. Round after round the two men threw punches in a breathtaking way in a fight which was really living up to all expectations. During the course of the epic encounter the heads of the two boxers would bump on various occasions when they came in for close quarter work. This was one hard, bitter battle with both men pushing each other to the very limit of their endurance. On the night the fans had the privilege of watching one of the fights to remember, one in which it was a shame there had to be a loser, such was the effort both men put into this bout. The end came finally in round ten when Harry Gibbs stepped in to stop the fight in favour of Green. John had lost, but what a magnificent contest it had been with both fighters emerging with credit from the encounter. Green duly went on in his next fight to challenge Carlos Palomino for the world title on 14 June, losing by a knockout in round 11 after giving the champion a very hard night. There were, in fact, moments when it looked as if Green would defeat Palomino and return the championship to domestic shores. However, in the years that followed, Green went on to capture the European welterweight title and even had a second crack at the world title against the great 'Sugar' Ray Leonard on 31 March 1980, this time failing when knocked out in round four.

For John H. it was a different story and he stayed out of the ring for over a year before returning to action on 23 May 1978 to stop the Frenchman, Georges Warusfel, in round nine. Considering the length of time that Stracey had been out of the ring, he gave a good performance against a solid fighter and it looked as if the former world champion still had much to offer to the sport. However, this proved to be John's last professional contest at the age of just 28 and he had the satisfaction of bowing out of the game with a win on his record. John's departure from the sport was a big loss, for he was a fighter who always gave of his best and brought credit to British boxing with his bulldog spirit and never-say-die attitude. Having won the British, European and world welterweight titles, and having taken part in 51 bouts, winning 45, drawing one and losing just five against a number of good fighters. John can look back in pride on a truly magnificent career, which his fight record more than confirms.

However, the Stracey story does not end there. After his retirement from the ring, John later turned his attention to the entertainment world and proved to be a exceptionally good singer. He is also one of the few fighters to have a pub named after him (The John H. Stracey in Briston, Norfolk). Recently I spoke to John on behalf of the *Yearbook* and asked his views on various aspects of the sport and about his new life in the entertainment business.

(Ralph Oates) How old were you when you first started boxing?
(John H. Stracey) 11 years and six months.
(RO) What made you take up the sport of boxing?
(JS) Because I was always fighting at school, or where we lived on the Council Estate, so my dad took me to Repton in 1962.
(RO) Have any other members of your family ever boxed?
(JS) No they haven't. I am the first and so far only one.
(RO) Who was your most difficult opponent in the amateur ranks?
(JS) Alan Smith, who boxed for West Ham ABC, defeated me on three occasions. A great boxer, Alan's a referee now.
(RO) How many amateur bouts did you have?
(JS) About 130 and I lost just 15.
(RO) Which amateur clubs did you box for?
(JS) Repton (1962-1964), St George's (1964-1966), Robert Browning (1966-1967) and Repton (1967-1969).
(RO) Who was your most difficult opponent in the professional ranks?
(JS) Carlos Palomino, because I lost my world title to him.
(RO) Who is your favourite old-time fighter?
(JS) 'Sugar' Ray Robinson, because he had everything. I actually met him when I boxed in Vegas on the Ali-Bugner bill in 1973. My ultimate British favourite is Ken Buchanan, whom I am proud to be able to call a friend.
(RO) Who is your favourite modern-day fighter?
(JS) I think Steve Collins, who held the WBO middle and super-middleweight titles, because he was so strong. Steve would never give up, his mental attitude was just about perfect. I feel Steve would have defeated Roy Jones had the match been made.
(RO) What changes would you like to see in boxing?
(JS) Amateur boxers not wearing headguards, which really

offer little if any protection at all. During the course of the bout, the fighters often have to stop to adjust the respective guard. I also feel the boxer can become too self reliant on the headguard and this can prove to be counter-productive at a later stage of his career.
(RO) Which is your favourite weight division?
(JS) Welterweight – because many of the all-time greats have boxed in this division. 'Sugar' Ray Robinson, 'Sugar' Ray Leonard and Roberto Duran, etc.
(RO) What changes would you like to see in boxing and how do you feel about the many world boxing organisations in the sport these days?
(JS) We all agree that there are too many world titles now. It would be really great to go back to the undisputed days. Then you would see the best in each division meeting to contest the respective titles. These days it's difficult to know who the champion is and let's face it how can you have a world title bout taking place at a small venue. A world championship fight should be a big event, taking place at major sites. When John Conteh won the world light-heavyweight crown he did it at Wembley, Lloyd Honeyghan won the world welterweight title in Atlantic City, Alan Minter won the world middleweight championship in Las Vegas and I won my crown in Mexico. These were all capital events. A world title should not be commonplace and should be held in high esteem and be contested by the best the said division has to offer at that time at a top venue.
(RO) How do you feel boxers of today compare with fighters of the past?
(JS) Well, in some ways lucky. They can have half the

John (right) pictured with his good friend Ken Buchanan, the former world lightweight champion

fights we had and get to the top much quicker. However, overall, many of them are just as good as we were.

(RO) How do you feel about title fights being held over the duration of 12 rounds rather than 15?

(JS) I still feel the true test of a champion is 15 rounds. How many fighters have lost in the 13th, 14th or 15th round in the history of the sport; quite a few.

(RO) Many boxers do not like fighting southpaws. How did you feel about meeting them?

(JS) I didn't mind to be honest. You just have to fathom them out quickly, or they can build up an early lead.

(RO) I noticed that you didn't contest the Commonwealth title during your professional career.

(JS) No I didn't. However, I fully believe I could have won the title, but my battle plan took me along another road.

(RO) You did not win a Lonsdale Belt outright. Were you sorry about that?

(JS) Yes I was very sorry. I would have loved to have won that belt. In my opinion any fighter who has held a British title and then goes on to win a *major* world championship, should be awarded the belt automatically. After all, the fighter in question has won the world title not only for himself but for British boxing. John Conteh was another, like myself, who won the highest honours but did not win the Lonsdale Belt outright. When I was British champion, there was no outstanding challenger for my title and after I won and lost the world title it was very difficult to get up for a domestic title fight. I feel this situation should be looked at.

(RO) Did you at any time ever consider making a come-back to boxing?

(JS) Once or twice, but in all truth I knew I was right to retire when I did. I did not have the desire anymore, so I know I was right not to fight again.

(RO) How do you feel about boxers who fight on well into middle age?

(JS) This I don't agree with. They should be told to pack it in by the people who look after them. It's easy to spot someone going on too long.

(RO) What made you retire from boxing when you did?

(JS) I had won everything by the time I was 25 and at the age of 27 I retired. I knew I was right to do so.

(RO) What advice would you give to a young boxer just starting out?

(JS) To be happy with whoever you sign with, but to make all the decisions about your career. Be content and remember at the end of the day you are the one who is getting hit.

(RO) Apart from boxing what is your favourite sport?

(JS) Cricket. I am an Essex supporter.

(RO) Do you have a hobby?

(JS) Yes – I play golf. I also go swimming quite a lot and am an avid Spurs' supporter.

(RO) How long have you been married?

(JS) Eight years to my lovely wife, Kathy Jane.

(RO) Do you have any children?

(JS) Yes I have a 23-year-old daughter, Laura, who is a singer, and a son, Daniel, who is 14.

(RO) Have you ever considered being a boxing manager, promoter or trainer?

(JS) No not really. As soon as I retired I went straight into business that had nothing to do with boxing. However, I do hold a BBBoC M.C. license, the only boxer to date to do so.

(RO) How do you feel about women boxing?

(JS) Well I don't particularly like it, but freedom of choice and to do what you like is paramount in life. So I don't object to it. However, it is a pity they can't swap shirts at the end of the contest.

(RO) What made you go into the entertainment business?

(JS) I started singing before I started boxing at the age of eight. I won a Pontins holiday competition and went to Toynbee Hall voice training. However, as soon as I discovered boxing I dropped the singing. Now it's nice to go back into something I originally wanted to do.

(RO) Who is your favourite singer?

(JS) I have two, Roy Orbison and Matt Munro.

(RO) What are your ambitions for the future?

(JS) To keep working until I drop. I just love entertaining and after-dinner speaking. I really enjoy keeping busy. It gives me a real buzz.

There is no doubt that John H. Stracey played a vital role in his career to boost British boxing, giving the fans many exciting moments along the way. It is good to see that today, John is still full of fight with his ambitions in the entertainment world. I feel sure that all boxing fans wish John and his family all the very best for the future.

The Quiet Man in the Corner

by Melanie Lloyd

Switch to your television to watch a bit of boxing on a Saturday evening and the chances are you will see a familiar face in one of the corners. Pop into London to catch a small hall show without the luxury of TV coverage, and he's there again. Mention his name to anybody involved in boxing and they'll tell you, "He's been around for years." Because, over the decades this character has been in the corner for literally thousands of fights. He has worked alongside Angelo Dundee and Archie Moore, has washed out the gum shields of George Foreman, Lennox Lewis and Mike Tyson, has shaken the hand of Sugar Ray Robinson and Joe Louis and, quite frankly, boxing is his life. He even named his house, 'The Noble Art'. His name is Lenny Lee.

When I asked Lenny if I could interview him for this article he was kind enough to invite me to his exquisite home in Barnet. I stepped out of the tube station and there was Lenny, waiting to collect me, with a wide friendly grin that remained in evidence for the entire day. We arrived at the house and Lenny's wife, Iris, was waiting on the doorstep with a welcoming smile and a roast lamb Sunday dinner in the oven. Their daughter, Karen, was also present and she greeted me with a hug and a kiss and a sunny disposition. Then we all sat and enjoyed a summer Sunday afternoon in the conservatory, overlooking the swimming pool in the garden, if you don't mind!

Lenny and Iris are the original childhood sweethearts. "We got married when Iris was 17 and I was 21. We've been married for 44 years. We used to live in the same block of flats. That's how we met. I was a friend of her brother. I would go and knock for her brother and there she would be. She was five and I was ten. I remember it like it was yesterday. So we virtually grew up together." Iris told me, "Let's put it this way, we've been a couple since I was 14-years old. That was when he went in the Air Force. He did his National Service and I used to write to him. When he came out we got married." Lenny and Iris have two daughters, Karen and Debbie and a son, Perry. They also have three grandchildren.

'The Noble Art' is a far cry from the bleak surroundings of Lenny's childhood years. "I was born one of six children, in a very tough part of Islington called Hornsey Rise and if you didn't know how to fight you was in trouble. I used to get into a lot of fights because going back then, I couldn't stand people being bullied at school so I would sort of champion their cause if you know what I mean. No one ever bullied me because I was nearly six foot tall at the age of 14.

"It was hard really because my mum could only afford to serve up one good meal and my dad had to have that because he was the one going out to work, bringing the money into the house. The rest of us used to have bread and dripping most of the time. As kids see, because we was so poor there was nowhere to go, because we never had any money. Sometimes we would just sit in the gutter and talk about boxing. And people like Bruce Woodcock were around at the time. He was the British hero. Everybody knew Bruce Woodcock. And Freddie Mills, of course. They were fighters that stick in your mind for ever. I mean, I've got a film somewhere of Bruce Woodcock boxing Lee Savold at White City and there was thousands upon thousands of people. And people right at the back, who would pay to watch it, just to say they were there. I mean, they were what I call magic fighters. They kind of brought something out of you. They were the good old days."

Despite his early fascination with boxing, Lenny does not come from a traditional boxing family. "Not really, no. Except my uncle. He won every single Army

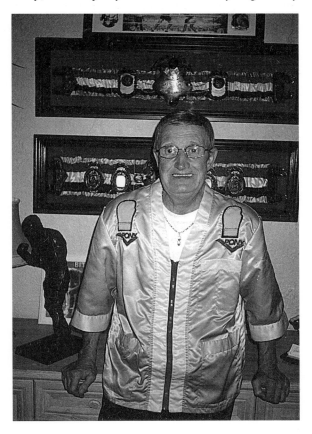

title you could win. That's going back into the '30s, so he slightly inspired me. But I must be honest, I was really inspired by Joe Louis. Joe Louis was my idol. My absolute idol. And then along came Sugar Ray Robinson.

"One day the gym master (at school) said I should take up boxing. Because in those days they used to put the rope square in the hall and encourage kids to put the gloves on and have a little fisticuffs. So I went in for the Schoolboy Championships and I didn't do bad, because I was only a novice and didn't really know much. Then, after the Schoolboys, I joined Blythe Amateur Boxing Club and we had a really good trainer there called George Digby. He taught me how to box. I started off as a southpaw and he switched me round to box orthodox, because basically I was an orthodox boxer. As a schoolboy, I used to get caught quite a lot, especially with straight rights coming at me. George said to me, "As a southpaw you'll always get caught with straight rights and left hooks." I started off in the amateurs very light, probably round about featherweight. I was a six foot featherweight. I was so skinny that when I turned sideways they couldn't hit me. That's probably why I was successful as an amateur boxer really. I picked up some sort of youth title when I was about 17, I'm not sure what it was now."

"Then I got called up for my National Service and went in the RAF, going on to win the Command Championship at light-welterweight in 1954. I was very lucky in the RAF because, basically, there weren't too many boxers about who were light-welters. I went in for the Britannia Shield. That was something really big because it was all the American Air Force and I think the French, German and British Air Forces combined to win this Britannia Shield and I was actually beaten by the chap who won it so that wasn't too bad."

"I sparred once with Brian London, and he knocked me out. He sent me to hospital. He was called Brian Harper then. I think he was a Corporal actually. Anyway, they wanted someone to spar with him and they couldn't find a heavyweight and with me being six foot tall, I think I was a bit taller than him actually. Anyway, in those days he was an absolute bully. Mind you, these days, he's a really lovely fella' and I wouldn't say anything bad about him. It was unfortunate what happened really. We had an American trainer from the United States Air Force and he said to us, just move around really and I happened to catch him."

"Then I got badly hurt in a fight when boxing against one of the Royal Marines. When I was born my belly button used to stick out, so obviously I wasn't tied up properly. But it never really worried me when I was boxing because my stomach was as strong as an ox; I was really tough round there. But this time I took a punch and it severed the navel cord, causing haemorrhaging. I was still in the RAF at the time, which

was towards the end of my service. I ended up in RAF Halton Hospital for a couple of months. It was quite serious because since I've spoken to surgeons, they have said they would have had to cut me a little bit, but in those days they cut me from hip to hip. They more or less cut me in half. I can vaguely remember lying on the stretcher, still in my boxing boots, looking in a mirror and seeing my stomach all swollen, because I was bleeding internally into my stomach, and they were drawing off this blood with a great big syringe. Then they sedated me. I was in hospital for a long time because they put clips in my stomach and I got an infection, so they had to open me up again. After that they said I would never box again. Although I never boxed for the RAF again, when I came out I got a job with this firm and there was a guy there who was one of the people that ran the Enterprise Club at Tottenham. I'd been out of training for about 18 months but he knew I'd done a bit of boxing and he asked me if I would like to come to the club and box for them. So I went down there and started training again and I had one bout at the Municipal Hall in Tottenham, which is no longer there. I got beaten on points by this kid who was quite good and I decided to call it a day. I did actually sign a pro contract. When I was in the Air Force they put a picture of me in the paper and we had a guy come up to the camp one day and he asked me if I wanted to turn pro when I left the RAF. I said, 'Yeah, sure.' But I never followed it through because I'd been boxing then for 11 or 12 years, which was a long time. I'd started going out and being with my mates and I'd had enough, that's the strength of it. And I honestly didn't think that I'd make a good pro so I decided to hang up the gloves." Lenny had 52 fights as an amateur, winning 42.

"In my day you would go out there and you would box and score points and you'd come back to the corner and the trainer would say, 'You done that comfortably.' So therefore, that's how you won the decision. I didn't have many stoppages in my career. I was a purist. That's why I've got a straight nose now. People say, 'You never boxed in your life.' And I say, 'I *did*.' Because I haven't got any scars or anything. I used to tuck up tight, and I used my straight left. Because if you keep pumping away with that... But of course things change and styles change. Now they come out in the first round with the straight intention of knocking their opponent out in the first round. I've watched the amateurs on television and I can't believe the speed of the blows. It's like a fight, as opposed to seeing superior boxing. Mind you, that's just my opinion."

Lenny believes that amateur boxers should be allowed to train with professionals in this country. "I don't see why not. Because you see, whereas you might get boys who have come through the amateurs and have won the amateur titles, when they get in the ring they don't make good pros. They can't make that transition.

Whereas basically, if they were allowed to train with pros and spar with pros, and I don't mean hard sparring, they would learn a lot more and they'd know what their ability is when they *do* turn pro. But I mean, who am I to say?"

Years after Lenny unlaced his last glove, he suddenly found his interest in boxing re-born. "I had a friend who was a bit of a tearaway, because there were a lot of tearaways at Hornsey Rise. He had a friend in boxing; his name was Dave Stone. I didn't know at that time but I had actually boxed on the same bill as Dave Stone as an amateur. I wasn't interested but he persuaded me, 'Come on. Come with me.' So I went with him, it was at Shoreditch Town Hall and I saw this Dave Stone fight and I'll tell you what, it brought back all the enthusiasm. So I decided that I'd try and be an amateur trainer and coach somebody. I wanted to coach a heavyweight and I saw this guy, who was about 15 at the time, whose name was Jumbo. His real name was Carl Figaro, but they called him Jumbo because he was about 20 stone and six foot four, and he was only 15. I actually met him on the street. I approached him and asked him if he wanted to become a boxer and he readily agreed. So I took him to Haverstock Hill, to the famous gym where George Francis used to train John Conteh and Bunny Sterling. I took him up there and taught him how to box. And as an amateur he didn't do bad, not great, but not bad. Then after that I started as an amateur trainer at Cheshunt ABC and did my trainers course. I must have been in my early 30s by then."

At this point Lenny got to his feet and showed me his training methods adopted at Cheshunt. His approach to teaching is uncomplicated and effective, and one aspect that I particularly liked was the way he taught a boy to keep his right hand up. He would tell them to imagine they had a beard, and to hold on to it. "It gives them something to hold on to, psychologically." I tried it myself when I got home, and it works! "I was at Cheshunt for about ten years. I used to stand in the shadows of the other trainers I suppose, but that didn't bother me. You can get a kid come in as a junior and work with him and think, 'Oh great!' and you get home at night and you've got this buzz, because you've *made* something. A kid's come off the street who doesn't know his left from his right and you teach him to become near enough a decent boxer. And then he goes to a disco and he meets a girl and it all goes out the window! Because he don't want to come training and wants to go and meet his girlfriend instead. That's the difference between the amateurs and the pros. When you get a good decent pro, he'll work for it. He knows if he wants to get to the top he's got to make sacrifices."

I asked Lenny how he made the transition from amateur to professional boxing. "One day me luck changed. I'd known Ernie Fossey for many, many years. Ernie has been an exceptional friend to me and I doubt I would have got as far as I have in boxing if it hadn't been for him. Anyway, one day Ernie persuaded me to go for my pro licence (second's). I said, 'You sure?' He said. 'Yeah. You can come and work with me then at the Twentieth Century Sporting Club,' because he was the matchmaker there. So I applied to the Boxing Board of Control and fortunately, because of my little bit of pedigree, I got my second's licence. The first fight I cornered for was a British title fight between Chris Christian and Herol Graham in Sheffield. Unfortunately, Chris got beat, but Herol Graham was an exceptional fighter. No one could beat him. He was virtually unbeatable."

"In the meantime, I was still frequenting the gyms, and one day I met up with this manager called Billy Wynter. He had about six boxers and said to me that he wanted me and Brian Lawrence and himself to work as a team. And I really enjoyed that time. I didn't have a full trainer's licence then but when you were in the gym you'd still go on the pads and give them their ground work and things like that. And, eventually, I put in for a trainer's licence and got that, no problem. And I used to

James Cook, the former British and European super-middleweight champion   Les Clark

work with Billy, training James Cook and Chris Christian."

"I had some fantastic times with Billy. I remember when James Cook was fighting Tony Burke, I think it was up in Manchester (October 1995, Solihull). Anyway, we left London in James' car. I met them up at the M1 at about 10 o'clock in the morning. There was five of us all together because we had another guy on the bill. We hadn't gone far when we had a blow-out on the back tyre. Anyway, we pulled over on to the hard shoulder and James found out that he never had a spare! We were all standing there deliberating over what we were going to do, and it was really windy and cold. Anyway, James took the wheel off and took it up the motorway – and remember he's fighting that night, defending his Southern Area title against Burke – to a garage and managed to get it repaired. We couldn't believe it. He's come running down the motorway with this tyre in his arms. Anyway, eventually we got on our way and we broke down again! This time the car overheated. So we pulled up on the hard shoulder again but it was in a contra flow, where no one should stop. Well, suddenly, the police pulled up behind us didn't they? So I ran down towards the police and said, 'Excuse me. This is James Cook in the car.' I didn't tell them the Southern Area, I said, 'He's fighting for the British title tonight.' So the police said, 'Oh well, come on and follow us.' And they took us off the contra flow and we got the water in the radiator and eventually we got there. But, of course, we missed the weigh-in and everything and, unfortunately, James got knocked out (Burke stopped Cook in two) so that was that. But he's a nice fella' James, a good friend and a good trainer today." For the record, James Cook went on to become British and European super-middleweight champion.

"But we had loads and loads of good times with Billy and it was a shame when he eventually packed it in and decided to call it a day. It was great working with them because I never, ever felt inferior. Not that I felt superior mind you, far from it, but with Billy Wynter and James Cook it was great. I was at ease with them. Chris Christian had retired then. Chris won the Southern Area title and I think it would have been at light-middleweight. He was a good fighter. However, he came to the gym one Sunday morning to spar, but said he had a terrible headache. So I took him down the hospital and he had a detached retina. I went to see him a few days later at his home and he really thanked me for taking him, because who knows what might of happened. Anyway, obviously he never fought again and I don't know where he is today."

For many years Lenny has worked as House Second for Frank Warren. "It started when Ernie Fossey was telling me about this young chap who was beginning in the boxing game called Frank Warren, who had big things to do. I didn't work with Frank at first because I think he had his brother working with him and when he stopped I just filled in the gap. So Ernie got me the job with Frank and I've had it ever since. I've been working for Frank for a good 20 years now. It's been great because it's given me the opportunity to be in the corner with great fighters like Barry McGuigan. I mean, you couldn't even get near Barry McGuigan to get his autograph and suddenly I'm in the corner washing his gumshield out. And Mike Tyson. I was in his corner both times he came over here to fight. He was alright. I had a conversation with him just briefly, when he came over here the first time. The second time he wouldn't talk to anybody, but I mean you couldn't get near him anyway. But the first time I went up to his room to ask him to autograph one of my golden gloves. When they opened the door he was playing on this Gameboy machine in the hotel room. I said to this big guy, I'm the corner man, and will he sign my glove?' So he took the glove into the room and I said (to Tyson), 'Hello.' And he looked up and said, 'Oh, hi.'" I put it to Lenny that it was a shame when the controversy happened after the Savarese fight because it detracted from the fact that it was such a brilliant knockdown. It was the Tyson of old; underneath the right cross and left hook to the temple. I was pleased when Lenny agreed. "Oh yes! It was brilliant! Really. The biggest problem was, of course, the rain. It was raining like hell. Luckily, the ring was covered so we weren't getting wet, but all the crowd had disappeared. They had all gone back to try and get some shelter. There were those who had umbrellas but no, it was sheet rain. You couldn't really see anything. I never actually did anything in the corner in that fight anyway because it only lasted a round, but I was there. It's something to tell the grandchildren if they're interested."

"I was in Lennox Lewis' corner at the Albert Hall, back in the early days. I was in Razor Ruddock's corner when he got knocked out. Then I was in Oliver McCall's corner when he stopped Lewis with that sneak right-hand punch, bosh! Which I thought Tyson was going to do (against Lewis). I thought Tyson was going to do the same thing." I got the feeling that Lenny, like myself, had been a long-term Tyson fan, back to the good old days when he took the boxing world by storm. Yet at the same time, I personally feel that if Tyson had beat Lewis, sadly, it would have bad thing for boxing. Because there has been too much water under the bridge and many people would have turned their backs on boxing, because Tyson has upset too many people. Lenny agreed. "Yes, Tyson was a great fighter but there comes a point when you've got to draw a line."

The first time two women had a licensed professional boxing match in this country, Lenny was in the corner. "I did the very first womens' fight in this country. It was Jane Couch and a German girl. That was at Caesar's Night Club in Streatham. And I worked in the corner with the German girl." I asked Lenny how he felt that first time, working in the corner with a female boxer. "Oh, very apprehensive. Totally apprehensive. Because you know, when you've worked in the corner with hundreds and hundreds of male boxers, when they get hurt it's *sad*, I mean you *feel* for them. I must admit, you really feel for them but not as much as you would for a woman. I mean, you'd really want to jump in and help her. But I've never really seen what I would call serious injuries. I've certainly never seen a cut eye. I've never seen one cut yet, and you rarely see them with a bleeding nose, because they punch very fast, but not hard enough to *hurt* each other. So really, what can you say? I've got no problem there." I asked Lenny how he feels about women boxing generally, which made him chuckle. "Well, I've got no problem with it at all really, to be honest. I mean, if they want to do it, what can you say? I mean, Cathy Brown you know, *lovely* little girl. She's a *lovely* little person. But I'd feel bad if they started really getting hurt."

Lenny has always been happy with his status as House Second, never seeking the deeper involvement of training or management., "I was running a business, I was a plumbing engineer (hence the beautiful home) and I never really had the time to become a professional

One of Lenny's idols, Sugar Ray Robinson (left), is pictured losing his world middleweight title to Britain's Randy Turpin in July 1951

trainer because that was a day job. So I was always happy to do the house seconding because that was an evening job. Also, there's not really a lot of money in training and some of the small promoters can lose thousands. I don't think I could stomach that because I've never been a gambling man. I've never gambled in me life. But being a second, I'm involved in boxing, I get a free ringside seat and I've worked with the top fighters. I've met Floyd Patterson. He wasn't in the corner but he was there with Angelo Dundee. So there we are in the corner, Razor Ruddock, Angelo Dundee, and me! And when George Foreman boxed, I was in the corner with Archie Moore! Archie was great. He didn't really talk a lot, a lot of them don't, but we had a chat. The fact that I was actually there with these guys; it's been marvellous."

I asked Lenny if he ever gets frustrated as a second, to stand there and watch with no verbal input. "Sometimes, but I never say anything. Because I would be so embarrassed if the trainer turned around to me and said: 'Shut up and mind your own business.' I feel that if that trainer is training that kid and *he* can't teach him, then who am *I*, you know? But yes, it does get frustrating sometimes. Mainly, with Frank Warren, I nearly always work with the house fighters who are in retrospect the better fighters. Unless it's a closely contested championship fight, or an upset happens, which is very rare, but it does happen. Most top trainers that I work in the corner with are people like Jimmy Tibbs or Billy Graham, or someone like that. They know exactly what's got to be done."

It would be impossible to count the number of corners Lenny Lee has worked in. "Oh, it's got to be thousands. I mean, literally thousands. Because I've worked for every promoter, certainly in the London area for the last 20 years, and that's including small shows that people never hear of, apart from the television shows. These days I must go out at least four times a month."

Over the years Lenny has met hundreds of his heroes, usually in boxing gyms or during his trips around the world to watch his favourites in action. "I've met Sugar Ray Robinson and I've got a lovely photo of him. And I've met Joe Louis." I asked Lenny how he found the 'Brown Bomber', his childhood idol. "Oh he was a lovely, lovely man. And of course, he was like a God to me; I couldn't believe it. I was in Caesar's Palace, having gone out there to watch the Ali versus Bugner fight and in comes Joe Louis. But they roped him off because of the fans. So there was a kind of roped square and he was in there with a couple of security guards. So I went up to one of them and said. 'Joe Louis is like a God to me. Could I possibly shake his hand?' They said 'No' at first, but after a while they said 'Okay, go on.' And they let me in. Anyway, luckily I had one of my golden gloves, and Louis signed it and he shook my hand. I could not *believe* it, I was shaking. And then I'm sitting there at the ringside and who come to sit down just near me was Sugar Ray Robinson. I couldn't believe it. So I got up and said: 'I'm one of your biggest fans.' And he said, 'Thank you very much' and he autographed my glove as well." Lenny has a pair of golden gloves that are signed just by world champions. "I bought them in 1971 when I went to see the Ali versus Frazier fight. And they were selling these golden gloves around the ring. They are real Everlast boxing gloves. I bought two sets and used to always take one of these gloves around with me. I've had them signed by Archie Moore, Floyd Patterson, George Foreman, Joe Frazier, Muhammad Ali, Sugar Ray Robinson, Willie Pep, Carmen Basilio, the list is endless.

"If I sat down and thought about it I could relate boxing stories all day. Lots of things have happened in my life as far as boxing goes and I think I've been very lucky. Possibly luckier than a lot of blokes who have probably put a lot more into it than I have. I'm proud to be involved in boxing because it's a wonderful sport. But I don't think I'm very important really, in fact I'm not very important at all."

Brian London: The Man Who Followed in his Father's Footsteps

by Tracey Pollard

Steve Foster (Jnr) is unlikely to do it, Ross Minter can only hope to do it, and only Billy 'Spider' Kelly and Brian London have managed it. Many boxers follow their fathers into the sport hoping to emulate their success, but only Billy 'Spider' Kelly and Brian London have ever managed to capture the very same titles held by their fathers. At bantamweight, Steve Foster is unlikely to fight for the light-middleweight title and welterweight, Ross Minter, would have to move up to middleweight to fight for Alan's British title. Billy 'Spider' Kelly won the British feather-weight title held by his dad in 1938. And when he won the British and Empire heavyweight titles in 1958, Brian London became the first British heavyweight to hold the same title as his father, Jack London, who was the British and Empire heavyweight champion in 1944.

Like his father, Brian had started boxing in the RAF and had toppled a giant to become champion. Both were to lose their titles on the first defence and they even managed to fight the same opponent, but, unlike his father, Brian hated boxing and saw it purely as a way to make a living.

He could have ended up as a journeyman, but his natural talent and determination made him a champion. With the right management he could have been a world-beater. As it was, his rather colourful career saw him face six European champions, four British champions and four world champions and a veritable who's who of heavyweights. He fought barefoot in the rain on one occasion and is remembered for the fight that came after the fight. He was always entertaining and certainly never dull.

Brian had never liked boxing and it was his brother, Jack, who was expected to follow in his father's footsteps. When Jack London (Snr), was knocked out by Bruce Woodcock, Brian swore he would never take up boxing, while his brother vowed to one day bring back the heavyweight title. But once he joined the RAF the decision was made for him. "Because I was Jack London's son I was expected to fight. They thought I'd be a good fighter, but I couldn't fight at all, I was just a big, strong guy." He can't have been too bad because Brian Harper, as he was then, was soon cutting a swathe through the amateur ranks,

Brian, flanked by Jack Bates and his dad, acknowledges the cheers of the crowd

winning the RAF and Imperial Services championships and the ABA heavyweight title. In August 1954 he won the Empire Games gold medal in Vancouver. It was the first time the son of a professional heavyweight champion had taken the amateur title at the same weight.

As British and Empire amateur champion, Brian was offered good money to turn professional. Like his father, he changed his name to London and was paid £65 to knock out Dennis Lockton (now a BBBoC steward) in his pro debut. That was £64, eight shillings and sixpence more than his father received for his first contest. The 'Blackpool Bomber' won his first 12 contests, usually in under three rounds, and was beginning to attract attention. The press dubbed him the 'British Marciano', but Brian knew that these were fighters that he was supposed to be able to knock out. It was during this time that he disposed of Prosper Beck before the end of the first round. It must have seemed like déjà vu for poor Prosper. In 1949, in his British debut contest, he had taken a pounding from Brian's dad before the referee stopped the fight in the fifth. It must have disheartened him because in the six intervening years he had only had four more fights, or perhaps he was saving himself for the Harper family!

Any dreams of being the second Marciano were shattered when Brian suffered his first defeat at the hands of the man who would become his nemesis, Henry Cooper. Brian had already seen off Henry's brother, Jim, when the second 'Bellingham Twin' finished him in the first round. An overconfident Brian walked straight onto a left hook and staggered under a barrage of punches, before the referee stopped the fight.

Of his dad, Brian says: "My dad was one hell of a fantastic feller, he was the nicest feller in the world." Of his trainer, Jack Bates, he says: "He was my best friend. He was a fantastic man, the nicest, quietest, best trainer in the world." The two had met in the RAF and would see Brian through his tumultuous career. The legendary Bates had trained champions, Jackie Brown, Jock McAvoy, Johnny King and Johnny Cusick. He would die a year to the day after his old friend Jack London had passed away.

Brian soon recovered from his loss to Cooper and scored nine victories, including wins over the two Tongans, George Naufahu and Kitione Lave, and Peter Bates, before facing Joe Erskine for the British and Empire titles. The champion, Erskine, had successfully defended his title between 1956 and 1958 when he met London at the White

Jack London (left) shakes hands with the American, Aaron Wilson, prior to his final contest on 29 November 1949

City Stadium. Despite confident boxing from Erskine in the first five rounds, Brian was never in any danger. Cheered on by his dad and his brother, Brian overwhelmed Erskine with his superior power and his heavy chopping rights finished him in the eighth. Brian would go on to fight some of the top boxers in history, but he is full of praise for Erskine. "Joe Erskine was the best boxer ever, very, very clever. Better than all the pro's I've ever fought. The only thing he couldn't do, he couldn't punch so you weren't worried." The 'Blackpool Bomber' had made boxing history by winning the same British and Empire titles as his dad, the 'West Hartlepool Giant' who had wrested his title from Freddie Mills back in '44.

Brian's next fight that year was a return with Willie Pastrano. He had stunned the boxing world with his performance in February, when he had given Pastrano a close fight, only narrowly dropping the verdict which many people thought he deserved. If there was controversy over that first verdict then it was Pastrano's turn to feel cheated when the referee stopped the fight at the end of the fifth because of a cut over his eye. Brian had dominated the opening rounds, but Pastrano was reduced to tears by the stoppage.

Like his father, Brian would lose his title in his first defence. Bruce Woodcock had taken Jack's crown, Brian would see his old foe, Henry Cooper, take his title. Cooper looked in danger of being stopped by cuts in the seventh but, after 15 gory rounds, and with both fighters covered in blood, Cooper was a clear points winner.

When Cooper turned down a fight with world champion, Floyd Patterson, in Indianapolis, Brian stepped in. The BBBoC objected and imposed a £1,000 fine, but Brian defied them and made his first trip to America. He says of Patterson: "He was one hulluva fighter, very, very fast." He was also the first fighter to knock Brian out, although it took 11 rounds to do it. The Board, though, were not impressed and fined Brian a further £1,000 on his return. Brian had won 22 of his 28 fights, his losses being to the likes of Cooper (2), Heinz Neuhaus, Patterson, Pastrano and Nino Valdes.

In April 1960 he knocked out Pete Rademacher in the seventh at Wembley. Rademacher had the distinction of fighting for a world title in his first professional bout. He was a boxer who, it was said, started at the top and worked his way down. Following that, in 1961, came the famous 'Porthcawl Brawl'. Pitting the fiery London against the equally fiery Dick Richardson, who had been disqualified for butting Cleveland Williams in their fight, was bound to produce fireworks, and it did. According to Brian, it was a needle match because he had knocked out Richardson as an amateur. At stake was Richardson's European title. London was well ahead when a clash of heads split his eye. "I always said it was the best left hand, right hand, head. The referee said: 'It's finished'. I said: 'You dare not stop this fight', so the referee said: 'I'll give you one more round'. So when I went out my aim was to knock Richardson out. The bell went and the referee stopped the fight! If I'd won it I would've been the European champion. I was fuming. All of a sudden this guy came over to console me from Richardson's corner, only I thought he was coming to have a go so I blew my top, belted him, and that's how the fight started. Everybody jumped in. You've never seen anything like it in your life!" In the film of the fight, Jack Bates can be seen laughing and trying to hold two of the brawlers apart. According to *Boxing Illustrated*, at one time six men lay stretched out on the canvas. Order was restored when an entire precinct-full of bobbies piled into the ring.

Brian faced more than his fair share of Americans; more, he says, than any other British heavyweight. The names are impressive and, prior to the Richardson fight,

World title challenge number one and defeat at the hands of Floyd Patterson

Brian seen listening intently to Jack Bates

Brian had already met Howie Turner, Pastrano (2), Patterson, Valdez and Rademacher. He would eventually go on to fight Billy Hunter, Eddie Machen, Young Jack Johnson, Howard King, Von Clay, Tom McNeely, Don Warner, Billy Nielsen, Chip Johnson, Roger Rischer, Thad Spencer, Amos Johnson, Muhammad Ali, Jerry Quarry (2), James J. Woody, Zora Folley, Roberto Davilla, Henry Clark and Jim Fletcher. There were 26 fights, all told, and Brian won 15 of them with one draw. Brian says: "Machen was probably the best fighter I ever fought; he really tanned me". Regarding him not going further in the game, he puts a lot of it down to living in Blackpool, rather than in London, and not having the right people behind him, including managers who would advise him and would have provided him with the sparring partners he never had. "They would get me a fight and they never bothered what his record was or who he was. My best sparring partner was my brother, Jack. When I fought Patterson, they got me this 22-stone American when Patterson was around 13 stone."

Brian was always happy to fight at home and noticably he didn't do too well when he fought abroad. He couldn't have been more pleased when he had to fight Howard King in Blackpool in 1962, but he hadn't allowed for the British weather. When he woke up the sun was shining for this outdoor contest, but they climbed into the ring in torrential rain. Referee, Wally Thom, in raincoat and rainhat, swept huge pools of rain over the side of the ring with a broom as the fighters removed their socks and boxing boots. King, who had once forced Archie Moore to a draw, seemed almost relieved when a right from London finished it in the sixth.

Then, it was another trip abroad again, in 1963, to fight former world champion, Ingemar Johansson. Johansson had won the European title from Dick Richardson in 1962

and the fight with London was supposed to be a walkover. But Brian fought an unexpectedly clever fight and, although he was known for his bludgeoning right, it was his left hook that troubled Johansson throughout. Johansson was probably edging the fight when, with four seconds to go, Brian landed a vicious left to his jaw. After a count of four the final bell rang, but referee, Andy Smythe, said: "If the bell hadn't rung I would've stopped it. Ingemar was in no position to defend himself."

Brian next had wins over Warner, Nielson, Chip Johnson, Giorgio Masteghin, Billy Walker, Rischer and Amos Johnson, and losses to Cooper, Spencer and Johnny Prescott, before he fought Muhammad Ali for the world title at Earls Court. What does he think of the man who knocked him out in three rounds? "He was a nice feller really. All that talking he was doing was just for publicity. Cassius Clay was a big guy, six foot four inches, and like lightning, bam-bam-bam!"

In the late '60s, Brian continued to fight class fighters but, as the losses began to outnumber the wins, he decided he'd made enough money from boxing. After a second loss to Jerry Quarry, at 35, he went out against Joe Bugner when the referee stopped the fight in the fifth. Addressing the crowd through the ring microphone, he said: "Thanks for putting up with me for 15 years."

Having made his money, Brian opened the first nightclub in Blackpool, the '007 Club'. Today, at 68, he continues to run at five o'clock every morning before working out on the bags at the home he shares with Beryl ("I'd have been world champion if I'd been with her all along," says Brian). And did he go on hating boxing? "Well, I did get to like it," he admits. "Let's face it, it's a hell of a way to make a living."

World title challenge number two and another defeat, this time his conquerer being the incomparable Muhammad Ali

Brian as he looks today   Paul Speak

A Century of Welsh Boxing Greats

by Wynford Jones

Looking back to the early years of the 20th century, Wales was blessed with an abundance of boxing talent.

Beginning with the featherweight division there was 'Peerless' Jim Driscoll from Cardiff. Jim became British featherweight champion at the National Sporting Club and won the NSC Challenge Belt put up by Lord Lonsdale. Regarded as a highly accomplished boxer, he went on to America to face Abe Attell, the world champion. He gave Attell a boxing lesson and, as with the case in No-Decision contests, there was usually an agreement in force to go along with the decision of the journalists present. With those present favouring Driscoll, Attell reneged on his earlier agreement so Jim was deprived of universal acclaim.

He is remembered for his charitable work and, in particular, for his efforts on behalf of Nazareth House in Cardiff. When Driscoll made his final appearance at the NSC, where he had become a huge favourite over the years, he was already suffering from tuberculosis, the disease which was to kill him barely five years later. However, he still managed to put up an amazing performance against the Frenchman, Charles Ledoux, until he was finally forced to succumb to his younger and stronger opponent in the 16th round.

Freddie Welsh, from Pontypridd, won the British lightweight title by beating Johnny Summers at the NSC. He boxed many times in America but became world champion by beating Willie Ritchie at Olympia, and finally lost his title to the legendary Benny Leonard.

Before Jimmy Wilde gained recognition as flyweight champion of the world, Wales had already had one holder in this division in the form of Percy Jones of Porth, who gained recognition by defeating Bill Ladbury and confirmed his status by beating Eugene Criqui.

As the century ran its course and various lists were compiled, Jimmy Wilde still retained his position among the all-time greats. He became world champion by defeating Young Zulu Kid in London in 1916 and had been virtually inactive for two years when he lost his crown to Pancho Villa in 1923.

Another figure of importance was Tom Thomas from Penygraig. He won the British middleweight title, but his achievements were curtailed by ill health which led to his untimely death at the age of 32. Barely a month earlier it had seemed probable that agreement might be reached for him to face Billy Papke for the world title.

Gipsy Daniels, the British light-heavyweight champion, went to Germany and knocked out Max Schmeling in a round, though he subsequently lost the return on points. At this moment in time, Schmeling is the oldest surviving heavyweight champion of the world.

Frank Moody should also be given credit for his campaign in America. During his time there he met several champions, including Jack Delaney, but he also boxed Tiger Flowers and Harry Greb, two of the toughest men ever to lace on boxing gloves.

At welterweight, Johnny Basham won the British title in 1914, finally losing it in 1920 to Ted Kid Lewis, one of British boxing's genuine greats. In all, they met four times with Lewis clearly the master.

During the 1940s, Gwyn Williams, Eddie Thomas and Cliff Curvis revived Welsh interest in the division, with Thomas and Curvis winning major championships. Cliff's connection with the very same British title continued into the 1960s when his younger brother, Brian, reigned supreme as British and Empire champion from 1960 to 1966. Brian went on to challenge Emile Griffith for the world title, but was painfully beaten on points over 15 rounds. Griffith confirmed his greatness when he went on to win a second world title at middleweight.

The contribution of Eddie Thomas to the sport was immense. As a boxer he won the British Empire and European welterweight titles, but the part he played as one of our leading managers went even further. As the manager of Gorseinon welterweight, Colin Jones, his protege captured those very same titles in the '80s and, after emulating the achievements of Thomas, went on to challenge for two versions of the world title. He drew with Milton McCrory in Reno in a contest for the WBC title and was adjudged to have lost their return. Colin later fought Don Curry for the WBA version of the crown, but was badly beaten. He sustained a horizontal gash on the bridge of his nose, which made it impossible for him to continue.

Before this, Eddie had enjoyed great success in the '60s and '70s in taking Howard Winstone to British, European and world featherweight titles. He then took Ken Buchanan to the British lightweight title and the Scot brought off a richly deserved victory when beating Ismael Laguna in San Juan, Puerto Rico to win the world lightweight title. Another of Eddie's protegees, namely Eddie Avoth of Cardiff, won the British and Commonwealth light-heavyweight titles, while Carl Gizzi, another member of the stable, was taken to a British title challenge against Jack Bodell at heavyweight.

In the heavyweight division the list of champions is impressive. Jack Petersen enjoyed enormous popularity and drew huge crowds for his wins over the immaculate Len Harvey and the Irish glamour boy, Jack Doyle, not to mention the temperamental Jock McAvoy. His career was unfortunately curtailed by eye injuries and three defeats at the hands of the powerful German, Walter Neusel.

Tommy Farr eventually enjoyed similar popularity after beating the likes of Neusel and Max Baer and he will be forever remembered for his 15-round challenge against Joe Louis, the Brown Bomber, one of the greatest heavyweight champions of all time.

Johnny Williams won the British title during the '50s as did Joe Erskine, who once outboxed one of the most skilful boxers ever, namely Willie Pastrano, who later went on to win the world title at light-heavyweight.

Newport's Dick Richardson brought off an unexpected

victory in Germany, defeating Hans Kalbfell and winning the European heavyweight title in the process. He finally lost his crown to Ingemar Johannson, the Swede who had beaten Floyd Patterson to become world champion.

During the '40s, Ronnie James was a major figure in the lightweight division, defeating Eric Boon to become British champion. In 1946, he lost against Ike Williams, one of the division's all time greats, in a contest for the world title at Ninian Park, Cardiff.

In the '50s, flyweight Dai Dower from Abercynon, was sensational, beating the likes of Eric Marsden and Jake Tuli in winning British and Empire titles respectively. He became European champion by beating Nazzareno Giannelli in London, but by the time he challenged Pascual Perez in Buenos Aires for the world title he was experiencing serious weight problems and was knocked out in the first round.

In the late '70s, Merthyr's Johnny Owen won British, Commonwealth and European bantamweight honours and had earned his place as challenger for Lupe Pintor's world title. After doing well during the early rounds disaster struck in the 12th when he was knocked out. He subsequently underwent brain surgery and sadly lost his battle for life several weeks later. Away from the ring, Johnny was almost anonymous, but the ring was his kingdom and that was where he was best able to express himself. He was a delight to watch and I shall always remember the character he showed in beating Paul Ferreri of Australia on his way to the Commonwealth title.

During the '90s, boxing in Wales enjoyed something of a revival, with Joe Calzaghe winning the WBO super-

middleweight title, Robbie Regan the WBO bantamweight title and Steve Robinson the WBO featherweight title. Steve enjoyed a successful reign, beating boxers of stature in former champions Duke McKenzie and Paul Hodkinson. His reign ended when Naseem Hamed occupied the opposite corner, but to his eternal credit Steve had come back to rule as European champion as the century ended.

Amidst all this activity, Barry Jones of Cardiff was given an opportunity to challenge for the WBO super-featherweight title against Wilson Palacio. Barry came home with the title, but his reign was shortlived because of differences of opinion on his brain scan, a problem which was to keep him out of the ring for some time and which resulted in his championship being taken away.

For a very short period, Calzaghe, Regan and Jones were reigning WBO champions at the same time and a picture of them holding the WBO belt was taken. I was reminded of the picture taken early in the century of Driscoll, Welsh and Tom Thomas wearing their Lonsdale Belts. There seemed to be a certain symmetry to it all, a sense that the wheel had turned full circle. And now we are in the 21st century, we can but hope that Celtic fists will continue to play such an important part as the history of the 'Noble Art' unfolds.

Steve Robinson, the former WBO featherweight champion
Les Clark

Tommy Farr, the man who took Joe Louis to the wire

A Brief Introduction to Prize-Fighting in Popular Street Literature

by Tony Gee

Prize-fighting appears to have been one of the more favoured subjects for topical street literature (in particular the broadside, in both its prose and ballad forms). It is scarcely surprising that this should be so, for until the advent of cheap books and newspapers such items could be said to have constituted the major part of the reading matter of the labouring classes (who had always made up the hardcore of the Fancy). Indeed, Sheila O'Connell, Assistant Keeper of the Department of Prints and Drawings, British Museum, has likened low-priced prints, including broadsides, to today's tabloid newspapers, "which are their equivalent to a great extent in both function and subject matter". A broadside is usually considered to be a sheet of paper printed on just one side (as opposed to a broadsheet printed on both), with a content consisting of prose, verse, picture, or any combination thereof. Relatively few fistic broadsides (especially prose examples) have remained intact, particularly in relation to the number produced, since again like today's newspapers they were ephemeral items usually discarded after reading. Most of those that have survived are from the last great outpouring of street literature which occurred in the 19th century.

Maurice Rickards, an expert on ephemera, in his recent encyclopedia on the subject, wrote that with regard to pugilistic prose broadsides, accounts were unreliable. He even mentioned it was said that on one occasion a detailed report was printed of a contest which had never occurred. Rickards' comments were in connection with broadsides produced by the entrepreneurial James Catnach and other publishers from Seven Dials (the centre for the printing of such literature in 19th century London). Certainly Catnach, as stated by Leslie Shepard in *The History of Street Literature*, was noted for "fictitious narratives printed up when real news was scarce". The writer of this article, however, has not, at least thus far, located an example of a broadside describing a prize-fight between known pugilists that obviously never took place. Even so there is little doubt that, whilst they can be useful as a source of information, enough evidence exists to show that the accuracy of these accounts should not always be relied upon.

That this is true, and not just with regard to broadsides published in London, can be illustrated by quoting the example of an item in the Glasgow University Library's Department of Special Collections. It is a broadside printed by John Muir of Glasgow detailing the first contest between Irishman Simon Byrne and the prodigiously strong Highlander, Alexander (Sandy) M'Kay (both of whom were later to lose their lives because of pugilistic participation, M'Kay as a result of the return encounter with Byrne and the latter after a desperate affair with James 'Deaf' Burke). The match in question, as reported in both Scottish and sporting newspapers, ended in success for Byrne, albeit somewhat controversially. The broadside, though, stated that "after a slashing battle the victory was declared in favour of the Scotchman". Interestingly, following Byrne's 47th round win in their second confrontation, *The Scotsman* wrote that one of the "numberless printed nuisances" being sold on the streets of Edinburgh proclaimed a triumph for M'Kay. The *Glasgow Chronicle*, moreover, describing the excitement in Paisley, told of a "bulletin extraordinary" (and, indeed, a second edition) naming M'Kay the victor which "found a ready market with the credulous multitude". After Byrne's trial at Buckingham for the Highlander's manslaughter, *The Scotsman* related that an Edinburgh street publication telling of the defendant having been sentenced to be hanged had completely outsold one revealing the truth that he had, in fact, been acquitted.

Moving on to broadside ballads, it is likewise prudent to regard the accuracy of their content with some suspicion. Nevertheless such song sheets with a fistic theme should not be totally dismissed by boxing historians as being of mere entertainment value only, for topical broadside ballads were, as Shepard asserted in his book on Catnach's great rival John Pitts, a "kind of musical journalism". Again like prose broadsides generally, ballads were often illustrated by crude woodcuts. Indeed, John Ashton maintained in the introduction to his 1888 publication *Modern Street Ballads* that these were usually "served out with charming impartiality, and without the slightest regard to the subject of the ballad". This actually does not appear to have been so true with examples appertaining to pugilism as it does perhaps with those covering other subjects, both topical and traditional. However, if any illustrations happened to bear a likeness to the combatants featured, this seems on the whole to have been purely coincidental. It was apparently quite common, moreover, for exactly the same picture to be included on different fistic items. For instance, amongst examples located of the use of identical woodcuts are two broadside ballads telling of the celebrated Tom Sayers' contests against Bob Brettle and John C. Heenan, to be found in a collection in the Language and Literature Department, Central Library, Manchester. These are embellished with the same crude print of a couple of prize-fighters squaring up to one another, despite the fact that there was a considerable disparity in the height and weight of the popular Birmingham favourite Brettle and Sayers' American challenger. Incidentally, it was not unusual for more than one ballad to be printed on a single sheet and both of these broadsides are good examples of that practice. Generally speaking the literary quality of the broadside ballads was also inferior, but as Ashton remarked "we must ever bear in mind the class for whom they were produced, who listened to them, and – practical proof of interest – bought them".

It is perhaps surprising to note that the subject matter of fistic broadside ballads was not always confined to major contests between pugilists with nationwide reputations. This is evident from some examples held by the Norfolk Heritage Centre, Norwich. One such item, for instance, detailed a contest between two provincial bruisers named Dan and Gale (a butcher), which was not included in the sport's 'official' record book *Fistiana; or, The Oracle of the Ring*. No date was given in the verses for the encounter but it was obviously the same bout, between "Dan a stone-mason, and Gale a butcher", which received a brief mention in the *Norfolk Chronicle and Norwich Gazette* of 8 July 1820. The newspaper stated that Gale was victorious after 120 rounds of "hard milling" lasting one hour 22 minutes; the ballad described a similarly competitive battle in which

> An hour and twenty minutes they fought with
>   courage bold,
> The claret did so briskly flow, and every blow it
>   told;
> They fought above a hundred rounds till faint
>   from loss of blood,
> And though they scarce got strength to stand yet
>   still their hearts were good.

Also at the Norfolk Heritage Centre are both broadside ballads and broadsides containing a combination of prose and verse relating to Jem Mace. (Often considered the father of the modern scientific school of pugilism, Mace was born at Beeston-next-Mileham in Norfolk and for at least part of his career was billed out of Norwich.) Included amongst these items are some which demonstrate how derogatory certain broadsides could be and cover two questionable episodes in Mace's pre-championship days. The first incident, which resulted in the future legend gaining an early reputation for cowardice, was, as reported in the authoritative sporting newspaper *Bell's Life in London and Sporting Chronicle*, a bizarre bolting on catching sight of an intended opponent Mike Madden, Mace having previously refused to fight him because of an objection to the appointed referee. Mace's reluctance to face his proposed antagonist, so several of the broadside ballads purported, was because of a fear that he would suffer the same tragic fate as had befallen the unfortunate Jack Jones after a second encounter with Madden. Titles such as 'A New Song, Called the Norfolk Duffer; or, Jack Jones' Ghost!!' and 'A Mid-night Visit!! or, Jones' Ghost appearance to Duffer Mace!' left little doubt of the less than flattering content to follow. Ironically, the ballad with the least disparaging title was the most insulting, containing crude verses such as

> But what we none of us can like,
>   Is that there twice should be no fighting,
> But soon as ever he saw Mike,
>   He should run off and take to sh——g

The manner of Mace's subsequent loss to Bob Brettle further increased the Fancy's poor opinion of him. His brief performance ended in the second round when he received a right hand blow and, as the *News of the World* reported, "the 'white plumed warrior' went to grass, remaining deaf to the call of time". *Bell's Life in London* was convinced that Mace could have continued the fight had he so desired, and described what seemed to have been his determined efforts to resist assistance from his seconds. Included amongst the mixed prose and verse broadsides at the Norfolk Heritage Centre appertaining to this event is a tongue-in-cheek reward poster for a missing "White-liver'd Cur" who "Answers to the name of 'JEM', and smells like damaged 'MASE'".

Broadsides, like the prize-ring itself, did not disappear overnight. However it seems, as Shepard pointed out, that the advent of "cheap, well-edited, illustrated newspapers in place of the old single-sheets found a ready-made public". This viewpoint, that broadsides do appear to die out in the second half of the 19th century as illustrated newspapers became more common, is certainly one to which Sheila O'Connell subscribes. It looks, therefore, as if the period of the gradual demise of the broadside roughly coincided with that of the prize-ring. Moreover, it can be said that by the time pugilism had been completely transformed into boxing as we know it today, these entertaining examples of street literature, along with the traditional bareknuckle sport, had been consigned to history. Although its quality and accuracy may often have left much to be desired, there is little reason to doubt Shepard's assertion that the part street literature played in the spread of literacy cannot be underestimated.

Home and Away with British Boxers During 2001-2002

by John Jarrett

JULY

The WBO cruiserweight champion, Johnny Nelson, may not be everyone's cup of tea but more and more he is becoming an acquired taste, as he keeps doing what he does best...winning! In front of his local fans, the Sheffield stylist clocked up a unanimous decision over former WBC champion, Marcelo Dominguez, to retain his title for the eighth time and, at 34, was looking for a big one. The man from Buenos Aires made a strong start, but Nelson boxed well and was on top coming down the stretch to take his pro log to 40-12-1.

Manchester fans of Richard Hatton were hanging off the wall at the local Velodrome when their favourite came home to retain his WBU light-welterweight championship against former titleholder, Jason Rowland, knocking his man out in the fourth round for his 24th straight win, 19 inside. Frank Warren was delighted with the 22-year old, an ace in the hand of Britain's top promoter, and promised Richard would be back in the Manchester ring soon. Hatton is ruthless when he has his man going. By the fourth round, Rowland was rocked, then dropped with a searing left to the body and one to the head. He made it back to his feet but another left hook ripped into his body and by the time he got off the canvas it was all over.

At Wembley Conference Centre big Danny Williams retained his British and Commonwealth heavyweight titles and, in the process, avenged his only professional defeat when he blasted the former champion, Julius Francis, to the canvas in round four with a superb left uppercut. The punch caught Francis on the right eye and he was in agony as Mickey Vann counted him out. The Brixton man tends to loaf at times when he should be working, but when he did put his mind to it he was the better man. Just turned 28, Danny took his record to 24-1 and at 17½ stones is big enough to do it all.

When a fighter comes into the ring with "Rose Funerals" as one of his sponsors, it does not augur well for his chances, and so it proved for the South African, Soon Botes, when he tried to relieve Robin Reid of his WBF super-middleweight title at Liverpool's Olympia. Although holding a second-division belt, Reid is a former WBC champion and looks the part. Taking his log to 29-3-1 (22 early), the Runcorn man had too much power and cut Botes down to size in the fourth round. A big right hand dropped the South African and when he got up was taken to the ropes where another guided missile blew him off his feet again. He beat the count but the third man had seen enough. Maybe Botes should look for another sponsor.

Billy Schwer reached the end of the road, as they all do, at the Wembley Conference Centre where the awkward Argentinian, Pablo Sarmiento, wore him down for a stoppage halfway through the 11th round to take Billy's IBO light-welterweight title and convince the Luton man it was time to call it a career. It was quite a career at that.

Billy was British, Commonwealth and European light-weight champion, but couldn't win a world title until moving up a division to take the lightly regarded IBO title. He was beaten in legitimate lightweight world title shots by Rafael Ruelas (IBF), Steve Johnston (WBC) and by Colin Dunne in a cracker for the WBU championship, three of the six defeats in a 45-bout career. Good luck, champ!

It was no happy return for Bristol's Glenn Catley when he went back to Montreal to fight Eric Lucas for the vacant WBC super-middleweight title. When they met in the same ring 18 months previously, Catley had hammered the Canadian to a 12th round defeat in a final eliminator for this title. This time Lucas made no mistake and a terrific right to the jaw in the seventh round sent the Bristol boy down in a heap to be counted out.

Another Bristol entry on the world scene was out of luck when Adrian Stone tangled with WBC welterweight champion, Sugar Shane Mosley, in Las Vegas. The man they were calling America's latest superstar ended matters in round three with a chilling knockout. Three sizzling rights to the head followed by a left hook-right cross left the Bristolian flat out on the canvas and the referee didn't even bother counting. Stone had performed well up to that point but there was only going to be one winner, Mosley finishing the job in style for his 38th straight win, 34 inside.

There was some success for Brits fighting abroad. In Brakpan, South Africa, the British and Commonwealth super-middleweight champion, David Starie, forced Argentine's Bruno Godoy to quit in round three, claiming a problem with his right leg after being decked. And in Amsterdam, former British welterweight champion Derek Roche took his record to 25-2 when he outpunched Zoltan Szili of Hungary in four rounds, the towel coming in after the Leeds' man dropped Zoltan for the second time. On the same card, the Oldham lightweight, Gary Hibbert, had an easy ride when stopping Belgium's Gaetan Trovato inside three minutes. Meanwhile, the Blackpool heavyweight, Matthew Ellis, was in Houston, USA to rack up a lop-sided decision over Ronnie Smith in a six rounder.

Manchester's Anthony Farnell had won all of his 26 fights and maybe he was starting to think he only had to turn up to clock another victory as his fans raised the roof. He was brought rudely down to earth in just two minutes and three seconds of the first round by Takaloo at a packed Velodrome. The Margate man calmly took his man to school and a searing right uppercut drove home the lesson as Farnell crashed. He managed to beat the count but was still shaky and, with Takaloo throwing punches and nothing coming back, the referee stopped it.

Yet another Manchester favourite in Michael Gomez had a shock on the Velodrome card when tangling with former conqueror Laszlo Bognar. The Hungarian southpaw had taken Michael's WBO Inter-Continental super-featherweight title with a ninth-round stoppage five months previously and looked headed for a repeat performance when he floored Gomez in the first round and again in round two. Yet Michael got off the deck to force the champion back and drop him at the bell. The third round lasted only a minute as Gomez decked his man again and it was stopped. Revenge is sweet!

It was a bad night for young Nicky Booth as the British and Commonwealth bantamweight champion reached for the stars and fell on his face. Going against Colombian southpaw, Jose Sanjuanelo, for the vacant IBO belt at Wembley, the Nottingham lad was beaten all ends up, floored twice, before being stopped in the ninth round.

The Harrow southpaw, Patrick Mullings, came through a thriller to avenge a previous defeat by Michael Alldis for the British super-bantamweight title, scraping a one-point win after 12 gruelling rounds at Wembley Conference Centre. A point deduction for a low blow in the final round cost Alldis his title.

Bradford light-welterweight, Junior Witter, chasing a fight with Ricky Hatton, kept his tools sharp with a fifth-round knockout over Hartlepool's former lightweight contender, Alan Temple…At York Hall, IBO flyweight champion Damaen Kelly showed he could punch as well as box when upending South Africa's Sipho Mantyi twice with body shots for a fourth-round stoppage…Russian heavyweight Alexei Osokin was in playful mood at Liverpool, but no-nonsense Herbie Hide, back after two years, blasted his man to the deck three times for a third-round stoppage to take his record to 32-2 with 31 inside.

AUGUST

Just two small hall shows kept the flag flying in Britain this holiday month, at Dewsbury and Warrington. Making his first hometown appearance at Dewsbury Town Hall, super-featherweight Steve Conway drew a packed house for his eight-twos with the tough Welsh light-welterweight, Keith Jones, and sent his fans home happy with a well-earned decision, taking his record to 23-4. Jones has a lousy record on paper, just seven wins in 66 fights and three draws, but he is better than that as he again proved with Conway, fighting the local man all the way to the final bell. Conway, just 23, has set his sights on Michael Gomez, a man he beat as an amateur.

The White brothers from Cardiff came unstuck against Ingle fighters, with southpaw Jason getting off the floor in round one to lose a decision to unbeaten Leeds' favourite Jesse James Daniel, and David lost a gruelling battle to Darlington's unbeaten Oscar Hall. In an upset, local lightweight Mally MacIver crashed in the first round to Mark Bowen and Simeon Cover outpointed Rob Stevenson after losing his debut.

Shades of the prize ring days! In a tent behind a pub on a Sunday afternoon, the Birkenhead cruiserweight, Peter Merrall, got his debut off on a winning note against Adam Cale, taking the six-rounds decision. Lee Holmes made it a Mersey double with a points win over Neil Read, but Accrington's Colin McCash crashed to first round defeat at the fists of Neil Bonner. The poor attendance was down to the fact that 200-ticket seller Tony Burns, the Preston light-middleweight, pulled out with a reported stomach upset.

Richard Hatton (left) successfully defended his WBU light-welter title for the first time when knocking out Jason Rowland inside four rounds in July 2001

Les Clark

From Southampton came news that the 78-year-old veteran fight man, Jack Bishop, was planning to promote in the town again, at the Guild Hall, mainly to give work to his fighters, Colin Kenna (heavyweight) and Joe Brame (light-heavyweight).

Promoters Stephen Vaughan and Lee Maloney had to cancel their show at Everton Park Sports Centre when two of their best ticket sellers in the local light-welterweight, Jason Vlasman, and Liverpool southpaw light-middle-weight, Carl Wall, were forced to pull out with injuries. Vaughan said he hoped to run in four weeks time.

A long way from home but still a winner, Coventry middleweight, Steven Bendall, was in Hammanskraal, South Africa, for an eight-rounder with Filipino, Bert Bado. It was a bad-do for Bert as Bendall made full use of a ten-pound pull in the weights to force a stoppage at 1.48 of round one. The Filipino was cut between the eyes and outclassed as the Midlander chalked up his 12th straight win.

There was a win for the Irish heavyweight, Kevin McBride, on Lou Di Bella's show in Little Rock, Arkansas, with Kevin taking a unanimous ten rounds decision over Willie Phillips. McBride took his log to 24-3 in a so-so fight. Across country in Connecticut, at the Uncasville Pavilion, Belfast's 35-year-old John Lowey, banned from British rings because of a brain scan irregularity, and having only his fourth fight in almost four years, blew a 12-rounds decision to Emanuel Lucero, a Mexican based in the Bronx, New York City, for the WBC Continental Americas super-bantamweight title. Lowey sleepwalked through ten rounds and when he tried to throw some leather it was far too late and too little.

On a lighter note, big Joe Bugner was back in London to make a comeback, but not as a fighter. The Hungarian-born former world heavyweight title challenger, now living in Australia, was in town to make a gangster spoof entitled *Juice Express*, along with son Joe. At 51, big Joe was still talking a good fight.

SEPTEMBER

Olympic super-heavyweight champion Audley Harrison was not the big noise at the Telewest Arena in Newcastle. The big noise was Herbie Hide hitting the floor four times inside two rounds, courtesy of the blazing fists of Zambia's Joseph Chingangu, who was expected to be a stepping stone for the former two-time WBO heavyweight champion to challenge Danny Williams for the British and Commonwealth titles later in the year. The bout ended with Hide flat on his face, his future behind him.

Harrison didn't set the crowd alight as he was taken the six rounds distance by willing Derek McCafferty, even if he was a good winner of his second professional outing. The big fellow didn't appear in top condition as he was blowing for the last three rounds and at the final bell it was underdog McCafferty who earned the cheers.

Stephen Smith was a good fighter looking for a good fight. He didn't get one from South Africa's Melikhaya August, who was beaten all ends up before Smith knocked him out in the fourth. Smith's IBC light-welterweight title was supposedly on the line.

Hartlepool's Ian Cooper, Northern Area super-middle-weight champion, dropped down to middleweight to contest the vacant British Masters title against Jason Collins and came out with the decision after ten hard rounds. Darlington's unbeaten Oscar Hall picked up the vacant Northern Area welterweight title when Dean Nicholas was ruled out in the ninth for using his head and elbow.

Manchester favourite, Richard Hatton, was not tested at the MEN Arena with his hometown fans cheering him on as he retained his WBU light-welterweight title against the American, John Bailey, the referee stopping it in the fifth after the unfortunate visitor had been decked four times. It was Richard's 25th consecutive victory, but he will need to meet tougher opposition than Bailey was able to provide.

That other Manchester favourite, Anthony Farnell, was looking to get back on the winning trail after the disastrous one-round loss to Takaloo last time out. Farnell had won 26 straight before coming a cropper, so he jumped gyms from Brian Hughes to Billy Graham and shaped up to the Wigan southpaw, Lee Blundell, for the vacant WBO Inter-Continental light-middleweight bauble. Anthony got the win he wanted in round two when a left hook to the jaw lifted Blundell off his feet and when he got up the referee stopped it, despite his protests.

Scott Harrison, honoured by the Boxing Writers' Club as 'Young Boxer of the Year', outboxed and outpunched Gary Thornhill to keep his British and Commonwealth featherweight belts with a fifth-round stoppage of the former champion and was looking for a European title shot…Former amateur star, Alex Arthur, took only 2.42 of round one to dismantle Russia's Dimitri Gorodetsky, the Edinburgh prospect chalking up his sixth straight win.

Former heavyweight contender, Dave Garside, is doing well with his Sunday afternoon shows at Seaton Carew just down the coast from Hartlepool and a packed Mayfair Suite saw local former amateur star, Michael Hunter, win the vacant Northern Area super-bantamweight title with an eighth-round stoppage of Sunderland's John Barnes. Hunter was just too strong for John who failed to go the distance for the first time in 26 fights. Michael took his unbeaten log to 8-0 and looked promising.

Commonwealth light-heavyweight champion, Tony Oakey, tuned up for a British title shot at Neil Simpson with a fourth-round stoppage of Ukrainian, Konstantin Ochrej, at the Elephant & Castle in Southwark…WBU lightweight champion Colin Dunne had looked on his way to bigger things when beating Billy Schwer in a cracker, but almost a year later he was having only his second non-title bout, stopping Russia's Sergey Starkov in round three with a cut eye at York Hall.

Clinton Woods finally got his WBC final eliminator with Yawe Davis and came through with a fine decision victory over the Italian-based Ugandan veteran in front of his hometown fans at Sheffield. Woods thus cleared the way for a crack at superstar Roy Jones for the world light-heavyweight title. He should also have picked up the European championship held by Davis, but for some cockeyed reason the EBU refused to sanction the fight, afterwards asking for purse bids to be submitted for a

Woods-Davis European title bout. You figure it out, and when you do, tell Clinton Woods!

In an official eliminator for the British heavyweight title, former champion Mike Holden was outworked over ten rounds by Brixton's Keith Long on the Sheffield bill.

Nottingham fans saw their IBO welterweight champion, Jawaid Khaliq, retain his championship with a stunning fifth-round knockout over the Polish challenger, Jacek Bielski. It was a so-so fight up to the dramatic finish, but the local star struck like a cobra with a dynamic left-right to the jaw and it was all over for Bielski...Defending his WBF light-middleweight title for the fifth time, the unbeaten West Hammer, Steve Roberts, had to make do with Andrzej Butowicz, a Polish southpaw substitute, who had taken enough after seven rounds and retired on his stool.

Bouncing back from his IBO title defeat, local Nicky Booth retained his British and Commonwealth bantamweight titles in a thriller with Jim Betts in the Nottingham ring, the Scunthorpe man being stopped in the seventh round as the 21-year-old champion turned on the pressure. In a clash of former British and Commonwealth champions, Ady Lewis outpunched Tommy Waite in a six rounds thriller.

That pocket battleship of a battler, Baby Jake Matlala, at 39, still had too much of everything for Mickey Cantwell at the Elephant & Castle and retained his WBU light-flyweight title with a fifth-round stoppage of the gutsy Londoner. The South African said one more and he hangs them up for good!

A scene from the British heavyweight title eliminator between Mike Holden and Keith Long (right), won by the latter   Les Clark

OCTOBER

It was a good payday for Joe Calzaghe, plus television exposure, so he accepted a bout on the Mike Tyson versus Brian Nielsen card in Copenhagen. Why not, that's his business. Professional fighter. Good one, too. Still unbeaten in 31 fights and WBO super-middleweight champion with eight defences logged up, the handsome Welsh southpaw was looking for bigger and better fights.

So they gave him Will McIntyre, a substitute for Antwun Echols, with only two defeats in his 31 fights but strictly a club fighter from Louisiana.

What happened? Well, Calzaghe won it without raising a sweat, the American referee, Rudy Battle, stopping it in round four. Calzaghe stopped it in the third. He knew McIntyre was finished, had nothing left, and Joe appealed to the referee to save his abject opponent from unecessary punishment. But Mr Battle gave Will an eight count and the bell ended the round. Reluctantly Calzaghe hit his man a few times in the fourth and when Will fell to his hands and knees, then bravely pulled himself up, the referee waved it off. Another win for Joe, but that's all.

Richard Hatton was back in action again at the MEN Arena in Manchester, defending his WBU light-welter-weight title against the American veteran, Fred Pendleton, 12 rounds or less. With young Mr Hatton it is usually less. In 25 professional fights, he had finished work early in all but five of them. Although 38, Pendleton had been in with the best in the business and was a former IBF lightweight champion. It didn't make any difference. At 2.40 of the second round, Freddie was wondering what hit him. What hit him was one of Hatton's Saturday night specials, a sizzling left hook into the body that left the American rolling on the canvas in agony. "If you can do that to me," Freddie told Hatton afterwards, "you can do it to anyone."

Michael Gomez was another two-round winner on the Manchester card, retaining his British super-featherweight title with a second-round stoppage of Craig Docherty. The Glasgow boy was unbeaten in 14 (1 draw) but it was too much too soon. Trying to trade in close with Gomez he ran a poor second and was being outpunched when it was stopped...Nobody was working overtime this night as Junior Witter got his job done inside two rounds, claiming the vacant WBU Inter-Continental light-welterweight title after dismantling South Africa's Colin Mayisela. Junior had too much of everything and the South African had no answer to his speed and flashy combinations. When Colin was knocked down in the second, the referee took one look at him and waved it off...Anthony Farnell had to work for his money to retain his WBO Inter-Continental light-middleweight title against a tough Russian named Pavel Melnikov. There were only ten seconds remaining in the last round when Farnell's final assault brought the referee's intervention. It was close but Anthony left nothing to chance in getting his man out of there. But it had been a hard day's night!

On the big Manchester show Belfast hard man, Eamonn Magee, was looking to impress with a view to meeting Hatton, but was taken the distance by the lanky South African, Matthews Zulu, as he retained his Commonwealth light-welterweight title. In taking his pro log to 22-2, Magee didn't look a threat to Richard Hatton.

Nobbins were once commonplace in British boxing halls, a rare occurence these days. Well, the punters dug into their pockets at the end of ten thrilling rounds at the Elephant & Castle Leisure Centre in Southwark as Hussain Osman outlasted Gary Logan to take his Southern Area middleweight title. Osman made Gary fight his fight in the early rounds and Logan went with him instead of boxing his man. It made for a helluva fight, but it was Osman's fight and he survived cuts over both eyes to punch his way to victory, the crowd as exhausted as the fighters at the finish.

The Audley Harrison roadshow moved into Glasgow for the big fellow's third outing in the money ranks against a poorly conditioned Pole named Piotr Jurczyk. It was all over halfway through the second round as a terrific right to the body left Piotr turning away, doubled over in pain. He touched down and was still in pain when getting to his feet, prompting the referee to call a halt. It was better stuff from the former Olympic champ, if hardly main event stuff. He seemed happy anyway…The usual supporting cast was on hand with Robin Reid defending his WBF super-middle-weight title against the Argentinian challenger, Jorge Sclarandi, who looked as though he would have preferred to have been somewhere else, like Argentine for instance. It wasn't much of a fight, ending in the third when a clash of heads sent Sclarandi down claiming a nose injury. He was counted out and everybody was happy except Sclarandi.

At Portsmouth, the local favourite, Tony Oakey, thrilled a capacity crowd as he retained his Commonwealth light-heavyweight title in a nip-and-tuck battle with Chris Davies. The Welshman was the better boxer, but his clever work was negated by Oakey's all-out aggression and with his crowd behind him the champion kept the punches coming to catch the eye of Dave Parris, the referee… Commonwealth light-middleweight champion, Richard Williams, got himself a good workout at the expense of Viktor Fesetchko, the Ukrainian being stopped in the sixth and last round after taking a hard right from Williams that knocked him into the ropes and out of the fight.

At Barnsley, the British lightweight champion, Bobby Vanzie, was in no mood to hang about, which was bad news for his challenger, Anthony Maynard, who was on his way to the showers after just 70 seconds of round one. That amazing veteran, Affif Djelti, wrecked another British hope when the Commonwealth super-featherweight champion, Alex Moon, was devastated with a superb left hook in the sixth, the 42-year-old Frenchman retaining his IBO championship. Next!

NOVEMBER

It was almost ringtime at the Mandalay Bay Hotel in Las Vegas and there was world heavyweight champion, Hasim Rahman, hammering on the door of Lennox Lewis' dressing room, demanding to see the former champion's hands being wrapped! Rahman would see those big hands soon enough, out there in the ring, and he didn't like what he saw. He saw those big hands encased in red leather gloves coming at him like guided missiles for three-and-a-half rounds, and then he couldn't see them anymore. He couldn't see much of anything! He had been sent crashing on his back in that fourth round and when he tried to get up he fell down again and when he did get up he was no longer heavyweight champion of the world.

Lennox Lewis was back in the driving seat, back on top of the boxing world and over the upset of that South African nightmare last April when Rahman poleaxed him with a big right hand consigned to history. This night in Las Vegas, Lewis was a winner. Big Time! In taking back his WBC/IBF/IBO titles, Lennox didn't put a glove wrong as Rahman unravelled in the ring before him. It was Lewis at his best and even the Americans were beginning to think he wasn't such a bad fighter after all. And as Lewis came out of the ring, the talk was already of his next fight…Mike Tyson!

In a supporting fight on the bill, the former Lewis conqueror (and victim), Oliver McCall, clashed with another Lewis victim in big Henry Akinwande, now fighting out of Florida. Henry, a former WBO champion, outboxed McCall, who had taken the WBC title from Lewis in a shocker not unlike the Rahman defeat, in the early rounds with McCall coming on strong over the last half of the fight and sealing victory with a devastating right to the chin in round ten to knock Akinwande out cold! Although he suffered only his second defeat in 43 fights, 36-year-old Henry looked finished.

It was so nearly a great British double on the Vegas card as Howard Eastman ended the final round of his challenge to WBA middleweight champion, William Joppy, with two smashing rights to the head to send the American touching down for an eight count. The bell ended the fight and when the decision was announced Howard Eastman knew that he had left it too late. On a majority decision Joppy was the winner and still champion. Eastman had won 32 straight fights in taking British, Commonwealth, and European titles on his way to the big one, and now he had blown it. In many rounds he had looked the better fighter, but he didn't do enough to convince the judges. He'll know what to do next time. There should be a next time, now that Howard is with Don King.

This game is all about moving up and moving down. At the Bellahouston Leisure Centre in Glasgow, the local favourite, Scott Harrison, was moving up and Cardiff's Steve Robinson was moving down. At 32, his best days behind him, former WBO featherweight champion, Robinson, was going for Harrison's British and Common-wealth titles, but he had lost his last four big fights. He would lose this one to the improving Scot who took his pro log to 15-1-1, scoring his seventh inside win when referee Richie Davies stopped it in round three. It was fight number 50 for the Cardiff man but his 16th defeat. Moving down…

On the Glasgow show, Wayne Alexander scored an away win, the Croydon British light-middleweight champion destroying the dream of Motherwell challenger Joe Townsley, who was decked twice in the first round and once in round two for the finish. Joe made it to his feet but it was waved off just 29 seconds into the round. Wayne had tripped and gone down in the opener and was angry when it was called a knockdown. He took it out on the Scot to rack up his 14th early win in 17 bouts against one defeat.

Britain's busiest boxing venue has to be York Hall in Bethnal Green. Three shows in six days this month left local fans punch-drunk. On Friday night, the Northampton light-welterweight, Alan Bosworth, earned a crack at the

British title when he beat Daniel James on a cut eye stoppage in the seventh round of a fight that could have gone either way. If you saved your money for the Saturday night show to see Johnny Nelson defend his WBO cruiserweight title against Napoleon Tagoe you would have been disappointed, as the Ghanaian was ruled out at the weigh-in on medical grounds. But Nelson still topped the bill, in a re-arranged contest for the vacant WBU heavyweight title against Russian Alex Vasiliev. Nelson won a lop-sided decision but it was another of his disappointing displays that left you thinking he could have done better. Then it was Wednesday and Stephen Smith was topping the bill, defending his IBC light-welterweight title against the Argentine veteran, Victor Hugo Paz, and coming out with an easy decision win, Paz not winning a round as Smith took his record to 30-1.

Another veteran who looked at the end of the road was Carl Thompson. Defending his IBO cruiserweight title against the American southpaw, Ezra Sellers, at Wythenshawe Forum, Thompson floored his challenger twice and was decked himself four times. He only got up three times and it was all over at 1.36 of the fourth round. At 37, it was time for Carl to think about his future. Outside the ring.

A new British welterweight champion was crowned in Glasgow as the Belfast puncher, Neil Sinclair, climbed off the floor to flatten Harry Dhami in round five. Former British lightweight champion, Wayne Rigby, had to dig deep to beat Antonio Ramirez of the Dominican Republic to take the vacant WBF light-welter title in a gruelling scrap at Wythenshawe. Rigby's former conqueror, Michael Ayers, took a beating from IBO light-welter champ, Pablo Sarmiento, at Wembley. Ayers was there at the finish of the fight, but at 36 it looked like the finish of Michael's career.

Michael Ayers (left), in what was possibly his last contest, lost to Pablo Sarmiento in an IBO light-welterweight title challenge   Les Clark

DECEMBER

Manchester's Richard Hatton earned himself a few bob for Christmas with an easy defence of his WBU light-welterweight title before a packed Wembley Conference Centre, Australia's Justin Rowsell lasting only three minutes, 36 seconds. Even having Aussie legend, Jeff

Fenech, in his corner didn't help Justin. He should have stayed in his corner and sent Fenech out to face Hatton's guns. Richard's fans had followed him to London and he didn't let them down, almost finishing matters in the opening round.

The Australian didn't have the power to bother Hatton and the champion crowded him to the ropes, setting up a fierce attack, ending in a vicious left hook that sent Rowsell almost out of the ring. The bell rang before Hatton could finish him, but Richard wasted no time in round two and with Justin not firing back it was stopped, giving Hatton his 27th straight win. The Manchester boy did what he had to do against an opponent who was unable to provide opposition!

The undercard featured two eliminators for the British lightweight title, with Steve Murray stopping Jason Hall inside four rounds and Graham Earl beating Mark Winter on points. Harlow's Murray looked favourite to get his second crack at the champion, Bobby Vanzie, who stopped him in seven for his only defeat in 20 bouts. Steve had too much power for Hall and when Jason sustained a damaged right eye in the fourth it was called off.

Former British light-welter champion, Winter, made it a close run thing, but Luton's Earl was just too sharp for him and boxed his way to a decision over the Northern Irishman. Graham had already won the Southern Area title, now he was after the British bauble.

WBF super-middleweight champion, Robin Reid, had a fight on his hands at the Coventry Skydome. Fighters from the Argentine are usually tough guys and Julio Cesar Vasquez didn't let the side down. Although 35, Vasquez had 14 title bouts in two reigns as WBA light-middleweight champion and only three defeats in a 66-fight career with 42 stoppages of one sort or another. But, while his best days were at 11 stone, he was fighting Reid at 12 stone and it made the difference. Reid is a good looking fighter and he looked good against the veteran, taking a unanimous decision over the South American, who was still throwing leather at the final bell.

Another Argentinian veteran in 36-year-old Ramon Britez held the IBO super-middleweight title, but not for long. Eight months after knocking out Adrian Dodson to become champ, Britez was demolished in just 1.56 of the opening round by Brian Magee in Liverpool. The all-southpaw contest ended with Britez counted out on the third knockdown as Magee jumped for joy at his 14th straight win, 12 inside schedule.

Former Commonwealth welterweight champion and WBC title challenger, Shannan Taylor, came to the York Hall to fight Commonwealth light-middleweight champion, Richard Williams, for the vacant IBO title. But it was not a good month for Australian entries and Taylor was no match for the classy Williams once the Londoner opened up in round four to force a stoppage. On the same bill, WBU bantamweight champion, Johnny Armour, won a fight without bleeding all over the place when outpointing Ian Turner in eight good rounds, the Welshman surviving a fourth-round knockdown.

A couple of British heavyweights won their fights

overseas which was nice. Michael Sprott boxed well to take an eight-round decision over the American journeyman, Jermell Lamar Barnes, in Rotterdam, while British and Commonwealth champion, Danny Williams, won his first fight for Don King, taking out Shawn Robinson in round two at Mashantucket, Connecticut.

And still they try. At 37, Crawford Ashley could look back on a 14-year pro career that saw him crowned British, Commonwealth, and European light-heavyweight champion and have two cracks at a world title. At Goresbrook Leisure Centre in Dagenham, the Leeds' puncher went up against the WBU cruiserweight champion, Sebastiaan Rothmann. He may as well have gone up against a brick wall! As the eighth round was ending, the South African smashed a right to Ashley's jaw and it was all over. Hopefully, Crawford's career will also be over.

The career of the Ukrainian, Viktor Fesetchko, received a boost when he was matched with Darren Dorrington at Bristol for the WBF European middleweight title. Nine times Victor had fought here and nine times he had lost. But the title tag, however dubious, inspired the Ukrainian and he outfought the local favourite to finally become a champion.

They crowned a new British Masters featherweight champion at Shaw when Choi Tseveenpurev, a Mongolian fighting out of Oldham (who is ineligible for a British title), beat Kevin Gerowski (well at least he was born in Leicester) on a debatable stoppage in the fifth…The British Masters light-middleweight title was on the line in Birmingham, as Jimmy Vincent retained in a hard ten rounder with former champion, Ojay Abrahams.

The Birmingham heavyweight, Pele Reid, showed Audley Harrison, sitting at ringside, how to do it when he stopped Kettering's Derek McCafferty inside three rounds after decking him in the opening round. Derek was never off his feet in losing a six rounder to the former Olympic champion three months earlier. British and Commonwealth super-middleweight champion, David Starie, knocked out Paul Wesley in 2.59 of round one at Dagenham and would be looking for a world title shot in the New Year. I hope Santa got his letter...

JANUARY

When Wayne Alexander hits them, they usually go! In winning 17 pro fights, only three opponents have managed to survive his hammering fists and hear the final bell. He did it again at the old York Hall in Bethnal Green, demolishing Italy's Paolo Pizzamiglio in three rounds to add the vacant European light-middleweight title to his British championship. Wayne stunned his man in the opener with a left hook but Paolo boxed well enough to edge the second. Round three was a different story as Alexander sent a crashing right to the jaw and the Italian hit the deck. He managed to beat the count but couldn't beat Wayne, who was belting him along the ropes when the referee waved it off, just as the towel came in from Paolo's corner. Alexander became the first Briton to win the title since Chris Pyatt in 1986.

Colin Dunne hung on to his WBU lightweight title in Dagenham with a split decision over the South African challenger, Martin Jacobs, but he has seen better nights, in fact there were many who thought he lost it. Among them was Martin's trainer, former world champ, Brian Mitchell, who voiced his displeasure angily at the verdict. It looked like an early win for Mitchell's man when Jacobs floored Dunne in the first round, but the Holloway-based Liverpool lad fought his way back and it was nip and tuck with Colin finishing like a train to clinch victory. "Can't a fighter have a bad night anymore," Dunne asked of his critics, who thought Jacobs had won.

In a support, Hussain Osman outfought Matthew Barney who was pulled out by his corner in the ninth round of a hard-fought struggle for the vacant IBO super-middleweight title as well as Barney's Southern Area belt…Hartlepool's former double ABA champion, Michael Hunter, was looking for a British title chance after his second-round kayo of Stevie Quinn, that took his record to 10-0.

Belfast's Wayne McCullough was refused a licence by the British Boxing Board who decreed that a small cyst near his brain was life threatening. But the Las Vegas-based 'Pocket Rocket' got himself a fight in his adopted hometown after claiming he had been cleared by no less than 14 American doctors. So Wayne was back in the ring against a clubfighter, Alvin Brown, who was decked twice in the second round for the knockout. Of course the fight didn't prove anything, but the former WBC bantam-weight champ, at 31, was happy to be back and take his record to 24-3.

The cut eye bogie hit Damaen Kelly again, in the very first round of his fight with the South African southpaw, Simphewe Xabendlini, at the Coventry Skydome, and the brilliant Belfast flyweight reacted immediately he felt the blood. The former British, Commonwealth, European and IBO champion, cut his taller rival down with a body shot followed by a left to the jaw and it was all over at 2.51. Kelly was looking for another world title shot.

Defending his WBU welterweight title at the York Hall, South Africa's Jan Bergman kept knocking Derek Roche down, but Derek kept getting up and maybe Jan got tired of hitting him because the Leeds' Irishman was still there at the final bell, beaten but still enjoying himself. Six times the former British champion was knocked down and six times he got up to fight back, but it was Bergman by unanimous decision.

Maybe Pele Reid should have done a bit of homework on British heavyweight champions. He would have learned that one of our most unlikely champions was an ungainly southpaw named Jack Bodell, who came out of Swadlincote in Derbyshire. Luke Simpkin is another awkward fellow from Swadlincote, with 14 defeats in 20 fights, and he didn't figure to give Reid much trouble in their four rounder in Streatham. But he did just that, and the Brummie had to be happy with a draw as Simpkin fought out of his skin. Maybe Luke just got tired of losing.

It seems like just about everybody in the British light-middleweight division has a title of some sort or other. The West Ham southpaw, Steve Roberts, carries the WBF flag when he goes into battle these days and at the Barnsley Metrodome he turned back an American attack from Troy Lowry, sometimes called 'TNT', although on this occasion Troy failed to detonate. Roberts had the blasting powder in his shots and halfway through the fourth round the referee had seen enough, sending Mr Lowry off to the showers on the first leg of his journey back to Minnesota. Steve remained undefeated after 28 fights. Next!

The European Boxing Union diluted their own championships when they introduced ten-round European Union titles, for whatever reason. In fact, by the time you read this, even I should have a belt of some sort to keep my pants up! James Hare is a good fighter and he was still undefeated in 21 fights (1 draw) after taking a decision over the French-African, Monney Seka, on the Barnsley show to win the inaugural welterweight championship... Hartlepool's Ian Cooper had won the Northern Area super-middleweight title as well as the British Masters middleweight championship in putting eight straight wins in the book. But he didn't win this one, being docked a point for holding against Ojay Abrahams, who took the six rounds decision much to Cooper's disgust.

In Berlin, southpaw London heavyweight, Wayne Llewellyn, had an easy ride as he knocked out the German veteran, Andreas Sidon, in the first round. Another London heavyweight in John McDermott learned little in extending his unbeaten run to 10-0 at the expence of Tony Booth who was dropped twice for a first-round stoppage at York Hall. A former British light-heavyweight title challenger, Booth was giving two stones to big John (17st 5lbs) in a contest that was strictly no contest.

FEBRUARY

British and Commonwealth heavyweight champion, Danny Williams, retained his titles at the York Hall when Michael Sprott's trainer Jimmy Tibbs pulled him out after just 26 seconds of round seven. Sprott had taken the fight on a week's notice when original challenger Keith Long withdrew with a stomach bug, and he was carrying extra weight although claiming he was in condition. Michael gave it a try but the champion was just too big, too heavy, and, when he wanted to be, too good. That's the trouble with Danny. After the fight, trainer Jim McDonnell even said his charge was bored, found it hard to "get up for domestic fights."

However, now that Don King is promoting him, Williams would do well to 'get up' for whomever he fights from now on. One problem, despite McDonnell claiming otherwise, could be Danny's weight. He came into the ring against Sprott weighing his heaviest ever, 18st 5lbs, which is a lot of Danny to carry around at any sort of pace. This may explain why he fought in spurts, easing off when his foot should have been to the floor. A heavy right decked Sprott in the fourth, but Danny was in no hurry and Michael lived to fight another few rounds. The champion made his effort in the seventh and with Sprott in trouble on the ropes, Tibbs had seen enough. In taking his record to 26-1, with 15 early, Williams said he could do better. Then why the hell didn't he? If Sprott wasn't a worthy

challenger, get him out of there! No wonder the fans booed. They didn't pay to see what McDonnell likened to 'a walk in the park!' They paid to see a fight. They didn't get one.

Actually, the York Hall fans did see a fight, a bloody good one! They saw Bradley Pryce stop Chesterfield's Gavin Down in nine rounds to win the vacant IBF Inter-Continental light-welterweight title. This one was a walk on the wild side! By the end, Pryce was bleeding from the nose and his left eye, which required four stitches. Down bled from the nose and an eye that took eight stitches at the finish. There was a nasty discoloured bump on his right cheek. Yes, these guys had a FIGHT! Going in, Pryce was unbeaten in 13 starts while Gavin was 22-1. Something had to give. In round six it was Pryce who almost didn't make it. A left uppercut followed by a right-handed barrage left Bradley shell-shocked at the bell. He came back firing and in the ninth it was Gavin who was in big trouble when the referee called it off. It mightn't be much of a title, but Pryce was a champion.

Richard Hatton is a champion, wearing the WBU light-welterweight belt, and he is after better things. He is well on the way going off his ninth-round stoppage of the tough Russian, Mikhail Krivolapov, which gave the Manchester favourite his 28th straight victory (23 inside) and sent the 12,000 capacity crowd at the MEN Arena into raptures. Richard's three main qualities as a fighter are pressure, pressure, and pressure. His left hook isn't bad either. In 36 fights, the Russian had never been stopped inside the distance. Until he met Richard Hatton, that is.

On the Manchester bill, Belfast's Eamonn Magee kept his name in the frame as a future Hatton opponent with a sixth-round stoppage of Jonathan Thaxton to retain his Commonwealth light-welter title for the fifth time. In this all-southpaw battle, Magee showed he can box as well as bang as he took his pro log to 23-2 (18 inside) and said he wanted Hatton ASAP! Over to you Mr Warren.

Another visitor who had never been stopped was Australia's Kevin Kelly. Big punching Gary Lockett soon sorted that out, a right and a left hook sending Kelly crashing for the count in round four. With his victory, Gary took the vacant WBO Inter-Continental light-middleweight title as he maintained his unbeaten pro record, now 16 wins with 13 inside.

A big punch is a fighter's 'Get out of jail' card. Nottingham's IBO welterweight champion, Jawaid Khaliq, saved his title when a long right to the jaw sent the Russian challenger, Maxim Nesterenko, crashing in the 12th round. The former European champion beat the count but he was still shaken, if not stirred, and the referee called it off. Khaliq had seen better nights but not many better rights than the one that put the issue beyond doubt 45 seconds into that final round.

The battling Booth brothers, Nicky and Jason, won their fights to keep their local fans happy. British and Commonwealth bantamweight champion, Nicky, retained his titles and made the Lonsdale Belt his own when he stopped the Fulham challenger, Stephen Oates, in the seventh round of a thriller. Oates fought his heart out, climbing off the canvas twice in the fifth before Booth got to him in the seventh. Stephen beat the count but it was waved off. Brother Jason's British and Commonwealth flyweight titles were not on the line against the Welsh southpaw, Jason Thomas, who gave the champion a good workout over six rounds.

At an age when most boxers are thinking retirement, 39 in this case, Nigel Senior won the British Masters lightweight title when the champion, Brian Gentry, was ruled out with a cut over his left eye in round eight at Slough. The Nottingham veteran had been fighting pro since 1985 with an eight-year gap (1991-99) and deserved his '15 minutes of fame.'

Former champions Richie Woodhall and Ali Forbes finally hung the gloves up forever. Former WBC super-middleweight and European and Commonwealth middleweight titleholder, Woodhall, had suffered recurring back trouble so, at 33, has moved to the safe side of the ropes, working with BBC television. Ali was British super-middle champ in 1995 but, at 40, figured it was time to walk away from the sport after 13 years as a pro.

Michael Sprott (left), challenging Danny Williams for the British and Commonwealth heavyweight titles, is seen on the ropes immediately prior to being retired in the seventh round
Les Clark

MARCH

Bristol's Glenn Catley did everything right in his challenge to Germany's Danilo Haeussler for his European super-middleweight championship in Frankfurt/Oder. He lost a majority decision. Maybe if he had done a little bit more, he would have won. After the fight Glenn ruefully admitted, "I could have done more...I thought I was comfortably ahead." Not a good assumption to make fighting a German in Germany for his championship! Even, it seems, with neutral officials. Even when your opponent comes out of the ring looking like he'd lost an argument with a runaway truck. Haeussler's face was a mass of bruises, nose swollen, eyes almost hammered shut from the belts he received from Catley's fists. But the belt Danilo received from the EBU official at the end of 12 gruelling rounds, made it all worth while. The winner and still champion!

Another British fighter to return home empty-handed from a trip abroad was the West Ham cruiserweight, Garry Delaney, beaten on a unanimous decision when challenging Sebastiaan Rothmann for his WBU title in Brakpan, South African. Garry was understandably not in the best frame of mind for an important fight as his brother's baby son had died of cot death a week before the fight. Rothmann looked too good for Delaney in any event, and may well have ended matters early had he not injured his right hand in the fourth round. On the same show, David Starie retained his Commonwealth super-middleweight title with an easy first-round blowout of the Australian champion, Marc Bargero, while Coventry's Steven Bendall retained his WBU Inter-Continental middleweight title in an all-southpaw battle with Ahmet Dottouev, the Russian veteran being pulled out by his corner after four rounds in which he had been floored twice and suffered a cut over his right eye.

Going into the ring at Crawley Leisure Centre, the local favourite, Michael Alldis, hoped it would come out right this time and he would once again be British super-bantam-weight champion, with the Lonsdale Belt his for keeps. He had been in this situation before, against Patrick Mullings, but lost the title and the belt on a final round point deduction. Mullings subsequently failed a drugs test, was stripped of the title, and now Alldis was boxing the Commonwealth champion, Brian Carr, for both titles and the Lonsdale Belt. Well, Michael did it this time, prevailing in a sometimes bad-tempered contest to come out with the decision and all the marbles. At 33 he still had a few shots left in his locker.

Northampton's Alan Bosworth was not so fortunate in his British title challenge, going in with Junior Witter for the vacant light-welterweight championship. Against the brilliant Bradford switch-hitter, Bosworth needed more than the noisy support of his hometown fans as Witter decked him and forced the third man's intervention in the third round. Junior is growing up!

The proliferation of sanctioning bodies in boxing today with titles almost being given away with so many box-tops, has resulted in more fighters contesting championships of one sort or another when they are either not ready, or not worthy, or never will be. Many so-called contenders for Commonwealth titles just don't measure up. One such fighter was Australia's Tony Wehbee. He had the misfortune to be thrust into a fight with Scott Harrison, the British and Commonwealth featherweight champion who is a very good fighter. Wehbee found that out as Harrison dismantled him inside three rounds at Glasgow to retain his Commonwealth title. In support, the Edinburgh super-featherweight, Alex Arthur, picked up what could be the first of several titles when he stopped Polish veteran, Dariusz Snarski, in the tenth to win the IBF Inter-Continental championship. Alex won his tenth straight fight, eight inside. Watch this space!

The sanctioning bodies were out in force at York Hall with three title bouts labelled WBO, WBC, and WBU. Tony Oakey's fans had followed him from Portsmouth to see him contest the vacant (they usually are!) WBU light-heavyweight title against Konstantin Shvets from the Ukraine. In winning a unanimous decision over his awkward opponent, Oakey forfeited his Commonwealth title, but could now claim to be a world champion! Yeah, and I'm marrying Julia Roberts at Christmas.

The WBO Inter-Continental lightweight title was vacant so they tossed it into the pot for Steve Murray while he marked time for another crack at Bobby Vanzie's British title. Steve had a fight on his hands before stopping Russia's Viktor Baranov in five rounds and looked good doing it, decking his man twice before it was called off. In challenging another Russian in Dennis Bakhtov for his WBC International heavy-weight crown, Blackpool's Matthew Ellis was hoping to notch the double over a man he had beaten over four rounds a year-and-a-half ago. But Ellis failed to make an impression this time around and it was Baranov's fight in the fifth round as the referee intervened with the Englishman in trouble from some big punches.

When TV pays the bill the show must go on, no matter what. And that means a title fight, of course. Wayne Rigby was due to defend his WBF light-welterweight belt against Spain's Miguel Angel Pena at the Wythenshawe Forum. When Pena pulled out, they wheeled in Sedat Puskullu who was claiming the French lightweight title. The French-Turk lasted 2.17 of round one and Board officials had a hard think before letting him have his full purse.

We lost a good fighter when Billy Schwer decided to hang up his gloves after an exemplary pro career taking in 45 fights with only six defeats. The Luton boxer won British, Commonwealth and European titles at lightweight, lost three world title shots before copping the IBO light-welter belt. He was a class act.

An action shot from the Michael Alldis (right) v Brian Carr contest, which involved the British and Commonwealth super-bantamweight titles　　　　　Les Clark

APRIL

Joe Calzaghe seems to have put his injury troubles behind him and is surging forward, seeking his place in the boxing pantheon as a true champion. With a capacity crowd at Cardiff's International Arena cheering him on, as well as Showtime viewers in the United States, the WBO super-middleweight titleholder came through a tough one with America's Charles 'The Hatchet' Brewer to cop a unanimous decision and retain his title for the tenth time. In keeping his unbeaten record, 33-0 (27) the Welsh favourite

survived some tough moments against the Philadelphia veteran, a former IBF champion at the weight. In round seven, the American set his feet and teed off on Calzaghe, ripping solid punches to head and body, and Joe felt them. But he stood up to them and won the next round and at the final bell he had won the fight, "one of my hardest," he later admitted.

On the Cardiff show it was third time lucky for the Russian visitor, Yuri Tsarenko, beaten in previous UK fights by Ryan Rhodes and Ossie Duran, as he hammered Gary Lockett loose from his unbeaten record to take a split decision and the Welsh boy's WBO Inter-Continental light-middleweight title. Gary had won 16 straight, his terrific punching accounting for 13 inside-the-distance victories, and this was his first fight before his own countrymen and the Showtime audience in USA. But it all went horribly wrong and at the final bell Lockett's face was a mess, both eyes swollen and discoloured, his nose broken and a cheekbone fractured. The kid they were calling 'The Rocket' had fizzled out and fallen to earth!

At Liverpool, another Australian Commonwealth title challenger was found wanting as Alex Moon clinically dismantled Mick O'Malley in eight rounds to keep his title, the towel coming in as the referee was waving it off.

It was another one of those Johnny Nelson fights, or rather contests, as the Sheffield enigma retained his WBO cruiserweight title in Copenhagen with an eighth-round knockout of Ezra Sellers. The American, who had beaten Carl Thompson for the IBO title which he forfeited when taking this fight, went down from a right hand punch that landed on his right eye, leaving him in obvious pain. Sellers wasn't winning the fight so much as Nelson was losing it. Johnny still has this tendency to box way below his capabilities. The man is big, fast, can box and can punch. When he puts it all together he can be a world-beater. Trouble is he doesn't believe it.

On the Copenhagen bill, Liverpool's WBU flyweight champion, Peter Culshaw, got back in the ring after ten months with an easy second-round stoppage of Estonia's Sergei Tasimov. Peter's title was not on the line as he took his pro log to 21-1-1.

If you thought Audley Harrison was big at 6'5½" and 18st 4lbs, wait till you see the other guy! American Julius Long stood 7'2" in his socks and bounced the scales at a solid 20st. In the second round Julius bounced off the canvas at the Wembley Conference Centre and when he got up it was all over. As he lunged in with a right that missed, Harrison countered with a left that didn't and the Olympic champion had his fourth straight win, three inside the distance.

Stephen Smith is part of the 'Harrison Road Show' and he performed adequately enough to retain his IBC light-welterweight title for the third time against a rugged Mexican, Ray Martinez, with a unanimous decision, even after being docked two points for low blows in the fifth and sixth rounds…Dean Francis made a winning comeback after three-and-a-half years out due to a dislocated shoulder and a short term as a guest of Her Majesty. The former European super-middleweight champion had no trouble taking a lop-sided decision over South Africa's Mondili Mbonambi, although Dean was still not happy with the shoulder afterwards.

Unbeaten Coventry southpaw, Steven Bendall, made his hometown debut at the Skydome (he actually lives in Bournemouth) with a tenth-round stoppage of the rugged Ukrainian, Viktor Fesetchko, to claim the vacant IBO Inter-Continental middleweight title, just another trinket for his collection. Steven already has the WBU Inter-Continental belt for what it is worth.

At the Huddersfield Sports Centre, James Hare racked up a sixth-round stoppage win over Julian Holland to take the Australian's Commonwealth welterweight title. It was a fine performance from Hare, a resident of nearby Roberttown, as he took his record to 21-0-1. After boxing his way into the lead, Hare threw a hard right to the chin in the sixth round and Holland fell on his face. He managed to beat the count but was being hammered when the referee called it off.

As one champion arrives, so another departs. The 33-year-old Welsh veteran, Steve Robinson, his glory days as WBO featherweight champion long behind him, blew an eight-rounds decision to Dewsbury southpaw, Steve Conway, and called it quits. "I really didn't want it to end this way," he said afterwards, "but that's the way it goes."

Opportunity knocked for Liverpool super-middleweight Tony Dodson when the IBO champion, Brian Magee, refused to take a fight with America's Brian Barbosa at Everton Park Sports Centre. Magee was off the show and Dodson was given the chance of fighting the American. He jumped at it and made good by dumping Barbosa on the canvas in the seventh round and taking a well-earned decision.

Putney southpaw Allan Gray finally got it right as he took the vacant Southern Area middleweight title after a terrific nobbins fight with a former rival, Alan Gilbert, at the Elephant & Castle in Southwark, giving veteran manager Dennie Mancini his 18th Southern Area champion.

Joe Calzaghe (right) wades into Charles Brewer in defence of his WBO super-middleweight crown   Les Clark

MAY

Naseem Hamed was twice stripped bare for his comeback fight with Spain's Manuel Calvo at the London Arena. He had to remove his shorts to make the featherweight limit at the official weigh-in, much to his annoyance, yelling at the Board's inspector, "This is against my religion." And he was stripped bare of his once prodigious talents the next night in the ring, much to the annoyance of the fans who had paid good money to see something they didn't get – Hamed back to something like the fighter he was before Marco Antonio Barrera gave him a boxing lesson in Las Vegas 13 months previously.

After that showing, Naz had to do something special to prove he still could. But on what was on display against Calvo, a hand-picked opponent who himself had been inactive for 12 months, Hamed looked a poor copy of himself. After the fight he claimed to have damaged his left hand in the second round, yet there was little evidence of the injury during the contest. From the seventh round, people began walking out of the arena and at the end there were shouts of "What a load of rubbish!" That says it all, but Naseem Hamed wasn't listening. He hasn't been listening since Barrerra took him to school, and now it may be too late.

Hamed's contest was something of an anti-climax coming after the war between Michael Brodie and the Argentine tough guy, Pastor Maurin, for the vacant WBF featherweight title, won by Brodie on a unanimous decision. Michael came out of the ring looking like the loser, his right eye swollen and bleeding and his nose damaged, and he had to climb off the deck in the tenth round to finish a winner. Brodie had floored Maurin in the sixth, but the Latin fought back and both men well earned the standing ovation they were given at the final bell.

Colin Dunne roared back to silence those critics who said he was worn out when beating Martin Jacobs in January, forcing Manchester's Wayne Rigby to retire on his stool after ten one-sided rounds on the London Arena show. In retaining his WBU lightweight championship, Dunne was the master throughout, even though Dave Parris gave two counts against him when one looked a trip and one a slip. Rigby, the WBF light-welterweight champion, was floored in round six, having tripped over a superb left hook from the champion. Wayne survived for another four rounds before calling it a day. Dunne took his record to 37-1 and that defeat was more than five years ago. At 31, he looked far from being worn out.

Coventry's Neil Simpson gave up his British light-heavyweight title to fight Tony Oakey for the WBU championship, but after dropping a unanimous decision to the hometown favourite in Portsmouth, Neil would be looking for his old title again. It was a gruelling fight with the shorter Oakey (5'8" to Neil's 6'2") battling hard to keep his title and his unbeaten record, now 16-0. That done, Tony packed his case and headed off for a well-earned holiday in Jamaica.

Return fights rarely live up to the first time around. But there are exceptions, and Johnny Armour v Francis Ampofo for the Chatham southpaw's WBU bantamweight title at Dagenham's Goresbrook Leisure Centre was almost a carbon copy of their first encounter in December 2000. Armour won that one and he won this one according to the

WBU rules after two of the officials voted a draw, the other going for Armour. Most ringsiders had Francis winning this time as he appeared the harder puncher of the two, continually taking the fight to the champion, and he didn't lose it for two of the judges who scored it even. But Karl Rogers marked Armour a lop-sided 116-112 winner which threw the verdict once again at the champion and Ampofo, at 34, won't have too many fights like this left in him.

Michael Alldis didn't have much to beat in South Africa's Vuyanu Phulo when defending his Commonwealth super-bantamweight title on the Dagenham bill, ending matters in the eighth round with a knockout of an opponent who, to be fair, was a substitute on a week's notice. The champion moved to 24-8, 14 inside.

The big fellow was back in action again, second time in a month, for fight number five at the Custom House in London. This time, Audley Harrison took on Mark Krence, the unbeaten Chesterfield man coming in for Dominic Negus, down with a viral infection. Harrison had previously used Krence as a sparmate and Mark gave him six rounds this time before losing the decision. The former Olympic champion still left questions to be answered as his stamina was again found wanting and Krence never looked like being knocked out...Former British, Commonwealth, European and IBO flyweight champion, Damaen Kelly, collected another title when he outscored Celso Dangud to pick up the vacant WBF championship on the Harrison show.

Takaloo's progress continued with a tenth-round stoppage win over Gary Logan, who is seen taking a count   Les Clark

Plenty of action at the York Hall when Takaloo put his WBU light-middleweight title on the line for Gary Logan. It was Gary's boxing skills against the Margate man's relentless aggression and the latter prevailed in round ten when the referee called it off. The champion did not get off lightly, coming out with cuts over both eyes that took eight stitches to close. In a support, IBF Inter-Continental lightweight champion, Steve Murray, kept his tools sharp when he knocked out Russia's Rosalin Nasibulin in the fifth round of a non-title bout.

Former British and Commonwealth heavyweight champion, Julius Francis, figured to ease back into contention after losing his titles to Danny Williams, but caught a tartar in unfashionable Luke Simpkin who fought his way to a draw over six rounds at Millwall. This fellow Simpkin will bear some watching after fighting a draw with Pele Reid, and now Francis. One of these days...

JUNE

Mike Tyson had talked the talk but when the time came he couldn't walk the walk. In the ring at the Pyramid Arena in Memphis, the former champion shaped up to Lennox Lewis like David against Goliath, only David had forgotten his slingshot. He tried just throwing the stone with his right hand, but when it bounced off Lewis, Mike knew he was never going to beat Lennox, even with the help of a friendly referee. Defending his world heavyweight championship (forget the alphabet boys, this was the only title that mattered), Lennox Lewis was just too big, too powerful, too good and too everything for what was left of Mike Tyson. By the eighth round the lamb was ready for the slaughter and it took just one big crushing right hand to the jaw to end it. Mike never looked like beating the count and they all had to admit that Lennox Lewis was 'The Man'! The Heavyweight Champion of the World! What now for Lewis? Tyson was to be the defining fight of his career. There was nothing left for him to prove and, just three months off his 37th birthday, the wise thing to do would be to retire with all the (and his) marbles. I hope he does.

The British and Commonwealth super-middleweight champion, David Starie, made it a double for the home team when he blew away Ron Martinez in just 88 seconds of a mismatch. Martinez was decked three times in what was a paid holiday jaunt for the champion, now 30-2.

The moment of truth arrived for Richard Hatton in the very first round of his WBU light-welterweight title defence against arch rival, Eamonn Magee, at the MEN Arena in Manchester. Richard had thrown two of his favourite left hooks to the body when the Belfast man, his back to the ropes, threw a counter right hook to the side of Hatton's head and sent him down on his backside.

As his legion of fans held their collective breath, Richard got to his feet halfway through Mickey Vann's mandatory count and got right back into the fight. Magee did it again in the second round, although Richard didn't fall this time. But he had learned that this fellow from Belfast was dangerous and he set out to win the fight. He did, taking a unanimous decision by keeping the pressure on the former Commonwealth champion, who was content to counterpunch. It had been tough, but Hatton had his 29th straight victory and would be a better fighter for it.

Upset of the night was the shock defeat of Michael Gomez by unheralded Kevin Lear in what was hastily arranged as a fight for the vacant WBU super-featherweight title. On paper it was a fight too far for the kid from West Ham, undefeated in 12 fights but all six-rounders, going against the former undefeated British champion. But it was Lear who looked like a champion and he was when Gomez retired on his stool after eight rounds, eyes cut and swollen and nose bleeeding heavily. A star is born!

Manchester's other favourite son, Anthony Farnell, came out a loser after a bruising, bad-tempered fight with Ruben Groenewald, who was floored twice and finished with both eyes cut, the right one almost shuttered tight. But when the slips were collected the South African was the winner and new WBU middleweight champion. It had been close but Farnell carelessly lost three vital points for low punches and it cost him the decision and the title as his record fell to 29-2. British lightweight champion, Bobby Vanzie, was anything but impressive taking a decision over Russia's Viktor Baranov.

It was not third time lucky for Jason Booth as Nottingham's British and Commonwealth flyweight champion made his third assault on the European title in Le Havre against former unbeaten French champion, Mimoun Chent. Jason had lost in previous efforts against David Guerault and Russia's Alex Mahmutov and he lost this one when the fight was stopped in the eighth round with the Frenchman cut over both eyes. Belgian referee Bob Logist ruled that the injuries had been caused accidentally so the fight went to the scorecards. And on the scorecards, Monsieur Chent was ahead. Winner and new champion…

Glasgow's Scott Harrison was to have fought Julio Pablo Chacon for the WBO featherweight title at Renfrew, but when the Argentinian withdrew through injury, the British and Commonwealth champion was matched with Victor Santiago for something called the 'interim' title. Harrison took his frustration out on the Puerto Rican, who was well beaten when stopped in round six. Scott moved to 17-1-1 and is ready for better things.

Some nights you hammer away for ten, 12 rounds and there's blood everywhere and next day you wake up aching in places you didn't know you had places. And some nights you just walk out there and you see the opening and bang! It's all over. It was for the former British welterweight champion, Derek Roche, as he tried to get his title back. But Neil Sinclair didn't want to give it up and a sizzling left to the stomach dropped Roche for the count after just two minutes two seconds.

A couple of guys who just love getting in there for a punch-up are Paul Bonson and Wayne Shepherd. At Leeds, the 43-year-old Carlisle veteran, Shepherd, finally got a chance at something good when meeting Lee Murtagh for the vacant British Masters middleweight title. Wayne gave it a shot and finished strong but the local was a good winner. And at Southwark, Bonson came out a winner for a change when taking a four rounds decision over the Leicester southpaw, Scott Lansdowne. Featherstone cruiser-weight, Bonson, had lost 47 of his 68 fights (6 draws) going in and won for only the 15th time in his seven-year career. Well done, lad!

Facts and Figures, 2001-2002

There were 612 (643 in 2000-2001) British-based boxers who were active between 1 July 2001 and 30 June 2002, spread over 185 (191 in 2000-2001) promotions held in Britain, not including the Republic of Ireland, during the same period. The above figure comprised 501 boxers already holding licenses or having been re-licensed, and 111 (149 in 2000-2001) new professionals. These figures include eight licensed women boxers – Cathy Brown, Clair Cooper, Jane Couch, Adele Dean, Audrey Guthrie, Michelle Sutcliffe, Jan Wild and Juliette Winter. Also included are two foreign-born boxers, Varuzhan Davtyan and Ossie Duran, who began their careers elsewhere but are now domiciled in Britain.

Unbeaten During Season (Minimum Qualification: 6 Contests)
7: Alex Arthur, David Barnes. 6: Oscar Hall, Richard Hatton, Colin Lynes, Matthew Macklin.

Longest Unbeaten Sequence (Minimum Qualification: 10 Contests)
33: Joe Calzaghe. 29: Richard Hatton, Lester Jacobs, Steve Roberts. 23: James Hare (1 draw). 22: Oscar Hall (1 draw), Noel Wilders. 19: Colin Lynes. 18: Thomas McDonagh (2 draws), Tony Mulholland (1 draw). 17: Nicky Cook, Johnny Nelson, Wayne Pinder (1 draw). 16: Steven Bendall, Colin Dunne, Michael Jones, Willie Limond, Brian Magee, Tony Oakey, Bradley Pryce. 15: Graham Earl, Scott Harrison (1 draw), Michael Jennings, Gavin Rees. 14: Mehrdud Takaloo, David Walker (1 draw), Richard Williams (1 draw). 13: Jawaid Khaliq, Kevin Lear, Clinton Woods. 12: Jason Cook, Paul Halpin (1 draw), Matthew Hatton, Michael Hunter (1 draw), Elvis Michailenko (1 draw). 11: Alex Arthur, Barry Hughes, Brett James (2 draws), John McDermott, Lee Meager (1 draw), Leo O'Reilly, Danny Williams. 10: David Burke, Lawrence Murphy (1 draw).

Most Wins During Season (Minimum Qualification: 6 Contests)
7: Alex Arthur, David Barnes, Erik Teymour. 6: Tony Dodson, Oscar Hall, Richard Hatton, Mark Krence, Colin Lynes, Matthew Macklin.

Most Contests During Season (Minimum Qualification: 10 Contests)
16: Paul Bonson, Pete Buckley. 15: Harry Butler. 13: Richard Inquieti. 12: Darren Ashton, Adam Cale, Keith Jones, Arv Mittoo, Nigel Senior, Leigh Wicks. 11: Tony Booth, David Kirk, Daniel Thorpe, Joel Viney. 10: Woody Greenaway.

Most Contests During Career (Minimum Qualification: 50 Contests)

184: Pete Buckley. 136: Brian Coleman. 113: Tony Booth. 79: Nigel Senior. 78: Karl Taylor. 77: Keith Jones. 75: Anthony Hanna. 71: Paul Bonson, Arv Mittoo. 68: Paul Wesley, Leigh Wicks. 66: Mark Ransey. 65: Michael Pinnock. 62: Darren Ashton, Harry Butler. 61: Ojay Abrahams, Wayne Shepherd. 59: Howard Clarke. 58: Gary Flear, Gary Williams. 55: David Kirk, Johnny Nelson, Ram Singh. 51: Steve Robinson, Rob Stevenson. 50: Dave Hinds.

Stop Press: Results for July/August 2002

Grosvenor House, Mayfair, London – 8 July (Promoter: Sports Network)

Junior Witter w rsc 2 Laatekwei Hammond (Commonwealth L. Welterweight Title). Keith Long w rsc 4 Alexei Varakin. Gavin Rees w rsc 5 Ernie Smith. Steve Foster w rsc 1 Ian Turner. Martin Power w pts 4 Darren Cleary.

The Conference Centre, Wembley – 10 July (Promoter: Harding)

Audley Harrison w pts 6 Dominic Negus. Robin Reid w pts 12 Francisco Mora (WBF S. Middleweight Title). Glenn Catley w pts 8 Vage Kocharyan. Mark Potter w rsc 6 Derek McCafferty. Nicky Cook w pts 8 Andrei Devyataykin. Michael Sprott w pts 6 Garing Lane. Scott Dann w pts 4 Mike Phillips.

The Guildhall, Southampton – 12 July (Promoter: Bishop)

Colin Kenna w rsc 3 Gary Williams. Chill John w pts 4 Daniel Thorpe. Tony Montana w pts 4 Chris McDonagh. Danny Quillian w pts 6 Mo Qais Ariya.

The Skydrome, Coventry – 13 July (Promoter: Capitol Promotions)

Dean Pithie w pts 12 Alex Moon (Commonwealth S. Featherweight Title). Steven Bendall w rsc 5 Phillip Bystrikov. Mark Smallwood w rsc 3 Ganny Dovidovas. Craig Docherty w pts 6 Dariusz Snarski. Darren McInulty drew 6 Pedro Thompson. Tony Conroy w rsc 3 Woody Greenaway. Gary Greenwood w rsc 5 Gary Reid. Andy Hadler w pts 4 Martin Scotland. Tony McPake w rsc 3 Dave Hinds.

The Light Bar, Wolverhampton – 13 July (Promoter: Bradley)

Steve Saville w rsc 2 Wayne Wheeler. Conroy McIntosh w pts 4 Darren Covill. Danny Norton w pts 4 Liam Lathbury. Dean Hickman w rsc 1 Dai Bando. Paul Bonson w pts 6 Jason Brewster.

York Hall, Bethnal Green, London – 20 July (Promoter: Sports Network)

Hussain Osman w pts 12 Gary Logan (WBO Inter-Continental Middleweight Title). Matthew Hatton w rtd 2 Karl Taylor. Steve Foster w co 1 Paddy Folan. Matt Legg w rsc 2 Dave Clarke. Jeff Thomas w pts 4 Pete Buckley.

The Willows, Salford – 21 July (Promoter: VIP Promotions)

Wayne Pinder w co 2 Darren Covill. Eddie Nevins w pts 4 Carl Allen. Lee Whitehead w pts 6 Eamonn Glennon. John Marshall w rsc 1 Daniel Thorpe.

Boston, Mass, USA – 26 July

Kevin McBride w rsc 3 Reynaldo Minus.

Harvey Hadden Leisure Centre, Nottingham – 27 July (Promoters: Matchroom/Prince Promotions)

Andrei Pestriaev w pts 12 Steve Roberts (WBF L. Middleweight Title). Jawaid Khaliq w pts 12 Jose Rosa (IBO Welterweight Title). Nicky Booth w co 5 Moses Kinyua (Commonwealth Bantamweight Title). Jim Betts w rsc 3 Colin Moffett. Mihaly Kotai w rsc 1 Howard Clarke. Albert Sosnowski w pts 4 Paul Bonson. Craig Spacie w pts 4 Jason Nesbitt. Jason McKay w rsc 3 Simon Andrews. John Mackay w pts 4 Chris Hooper.

Norbreck Castle Hotel, Blackpool – 3 August (Promoters: Garside/Veitch)

Lee Blundell w rsc 6 Alan Gilbert (WBF Inter-Continental Middleweight Title). Jane Couch w pts 6 Borislava Goranova. Peter Jackson w pts 4 Jimmy Steel. Eamonn Glennon w pts 6 Lee Whitehead. Jeff Thomas w dis 2 Gareth Wiltshaw. Isaac Ward w rsc 1 Neil Read.

Storm Centre, Derby – 3 August (Promoters: Evans-Waterman Promotions/Ingle)

Damon Hague w co 5 andrew Facey (Final Elim. WBF Middleweight Title). Mark Krence w pts 4 Tony Booth. Lee Swaby w rsc 4 Greg Scott-Briggs. Gifford Shillingford w rsc 4 Petr Horacek. Simeon Cover w rsc 2 Mike Duffield. Dean Walker w pts 6 Richard Inquieti.

San Mango D'Aquino, Italy – 3 August

Jason Cook w rsc 3 Sandro Casamonica (European Lightweight Title).

The Castle, Cardiff – 17 August (Promoter: Sports Network)

Joe Calzaghe w pts 12 Miguel Jimenez (WBO S. Middleweight Title). Daniel Santos w pts 12 Mehrdud Takaloo (WBO L. Middleweight Title). Joan Guzman w co 3 Fabio Oliva (WBO S. Bantamweight Title). Neil Sinclair w rsc 4 Dmitri Kashkan. Ted Bami w rsc 6 Bradley Pryce. Alex Arthur w co 1 Pvel Potipko. Gavin Rees w rtd 1 Sergei Andreychikov. Enzo Maccarinelli w rtd 2 Tony Booth. Jeff Lacy w co 1 Jason Collins. Valery Odin w pts 6 Nathan King. Wayne Elcock w pts 4 Ojay Abrahams. Henry Castle w rsc 1 Joel Viney.

York Hall, Bethnal Green, London – 23 August (Promoter: Burns)

David Walker w rsc 2 Robert B urton. Brett James w pts 6 Brian Coleman. Mark Potter w pts 6 Luke Simpson. Carl Froch w rsc 1 Darren Covill. Matthew Thirwall w rsc 3 Harry Butler. Billy Corcoran w pts 4 Jason Nesbitt. Ben Hudson drew 4 Pete Buckley.

Diary of British Boxing Tournaments, 2001-2002

Tournaments are listed by date, town, venue and promoter, and cover the period 1 July 2001 – 30 June 2002

Code: SC = Sporting Club

Date	Town	Venue	Promoters
04.01.01	Bloomsbury	Royal National Hotel	Casey
07.07.01	Manchester	The Velodrome	Sports Network
14.07.01	Wembley	Conference Centre	Matchroom/Prince Promotions
14.07.01	Liverpool	Olympia	Harding
21.07.01	Sheffield	Ponds Forge International Sports Centre	Sports Network
26.07.01	Blackpool	Paradise Rooms	Veitch
27.07.01	Sheffield	Don Valley Stadium	Hobson/Panix Promotions
28.07.01	Wembley	Conference Centre	Sports Network
31.07.01	Bethnal Green	York Hall	Panix Promotions
18.08.01	Dewsbury	Town Hall	Ingle
26.08.01	Warrington	The Bank Quay	Showsport International
07.09.01	Bethnal Green	York Hall	Harding
07.09.01	West Bromwich	Gala Baths	Bradley
07.09.01	Glasgow	Thistle Hotel	Morrison
09.09.01	Southwark	Elephant & Castle Leisure Centre	Maloney
09.09.01	Hartlepool	Seaton Carew Mayfair Suite	Garside
13.09.01	Sheffield	Grosvenor House Hotel	Rhodes
13.09.01	Sheffield	Ponds Forge International Sports Centre	Panix Promotions
15.09.01	Swansea	The Leisure Centre	Boyce
15.09.01	Manchester	MEN Arena	Sports Networks
15.09.01	Nottingham	Harvey Hadden Leisure Centre	Matchroom/Prince Promotions
15.09.01	Derby	Storm Arena	Ingle
17.09.01	Glasgow	Holiday Inn	St Andrew's SC
20.09.01	Blackfriars	Mermaid Theatre	Jacobs
22.09.01	Bethnal Green	York Hall	Sports Network
22.09.01	Newcastle	Telewest Arena	Harding
22.09.01	Canning Town	Marquee, Victoria Dock Road,	Peacock Promotions
23.09.01	Shaw	Tara Leisure Centre	Tara Promotions
24.09.01	Cleethorpes	Winter Gardens	Dalton
25.09.01	Liverpool	Everton Park Sports Centre	Matchroom/Prince Promotions
28.09.01	Millwall	Britannia Hotel	Peacock Promotions
29.09.01	Southwark	Elephant & Castle Leisure Centre	Lion Promotions/Golden Fists Promotions
30.09.01	Bristol	Whitchurch Leisure Centre	Sanigar
04.10.01	Finsbury	Porter Tun Rooms	Pyle/World Sports Organisation
04.10.01	Sunderland	Marriott Hotel	Conroy
06.10.01	Manchester	Wythenshawe Forum	Matchroom/Prince Promotions
07.10.01	Wolverhampton	The Light Bar	Bradley
08.10.01	Barnsley	The Metrodome	Matchroom/Prince Promotions
08.10.01	Birmingham	Burlington Hotel	Cowdell
09.10.01	Cardiff	Ice Rink	Sports Network
10.10.01	Stoke	Moat House Hotel	Brogan
15.10.01	Southampton	The Guildhall	Bishop
15.10.01	Bradford	Hilton Hotel	Yorkshire Executive SC
20.10.01	Portsmouth	Mountbatten Centre	Matchroom/Prince Promotions
20.10.01	Glasgow	Kelvin Hall	Harding/GSC Promotions
21.10.01	Pentre Halkyn	Springfield Hotel	Williams
22.10.01	Glasgow	Holiday Inn	St Andrew's SC
27.10.01	Manchester	MEN Arena	Sports Network
28.10.01	Southwark	Elephant & Castle Leisure Centre	Maloney
31.10.01	Birmingham	Burlington Hotel	Cowdell
01.11.01	Hull	City Hall	Pollard

03.11.01	Glasgow	Bellahouston Leisure Centre	Matchroom/Prince Promotions
10.11.01	Wembley	Conference Centre	Matchroom/Prince Promotions
13.11.01	Leeds	Marquee, Elland Road	Spratt
16.11.01	Preston	The Guildhall	Williams
16.11.01	West Bromwich	Gala Baths	Bradley
17.11.01	Dewsbury	Town Hall	Ingle
17.11.01	Glasgow	Bellahouston Leisure Centre	Sports Network
17.11.01	Coventry	Leofric Hotel	Capitol Promotions
19.11.01	Glasgow	Holiday Inn	St Andrew's SC
22.11.01	Mayfair	Marriott Hotel	Jacobs
22.11.01	Paddington	Hilton Metropole Hotel	Evans-Waterman Promotions
23.11.01	Bethnal Green	York Hall	Panix Promotions/Peacock Promotions
24.11.01	Bethnal Green	York Hall	Sports Network
24.11.01	Wakefield	Light Waves Leisure Centre	Prince Promotions
26.11.01	Manchester	Wythenshawe Forum	Matchroom/Prince Promotions
28.11.01	Bethnal Green	York Hall	Harding
29.11.01	Hartlepool	Seaton Carew Mayfair Suite	Garside
30.11.01	Hull	The University	Hull & District SC
01.12.01	Bethnal Green	York Hall	Matchroom/Prince Promotions
03.12.01	Leeds	Queen's Hotel	Walker
06.12.01	Stoke	Moat House Hotel	Brogan
06.12.01	Sunderland	Marriott Hotel	Conroy
08.12.01	Dagenham	Goresbrook Leisure Centre	Lion Promotions/Golden Fists Promotions
08.12.01	Chesterfield	Queen's Park Leisure Centre	Ingle
08.12.01	Millwall	Britannia Hotel	Peacock Promotions
09.12.01	Shaw	Tara Leisure Centre	Tara Promotions
09.12.01	Blackpool	Paradise Rooms	Veitch
10.12.01	Liverpool	Everton Park Sports Centre	Matchroom/Prince Promotions
10.12.01	Nottingham	Post House Hotel	Gill/Brogan
10.12.01	Bradford	Hilton Hotel	Yorkshire Executive SC
10.12.01	Birmingham	Burlington Hotel	Cowdell
12.12.01	Clydach	Manor Park Country House	Boyce
13.12.01	Leicester Square	Equinox Nightclub	Pyle/World Sports Organisation
15.12.01	Sheffield	Don Valley Stadium	Panix Promotions/Hobson
15.12.01	Wembley	Conference Centre	Sports Network
15.12.01	Chigwell	Prince Regent Hotel	Burns
16.12.01	Southwark	Elephant & Castle Leisure Centre	Maloney
16.12.01	Bristol	Whitchurch Leisure Centre	Sanigar
16.12.01	Glasgow	Thistle Hotel	Morrison
17.12.01	Cleethorpes	Winter Gardens	Dalton
19.12.01	Coventry	The Skydrome	Harding
23.12.01	Salford	The Willows	VIP Promotions
18.01.02	Coventry	The Skydrome	Harding
19.01.02	Bethnal Green	York Hall	Sports Network
21.01.02	Glasgow	Holiday Inn	St Andrew's SC
26.01.02	Bethnal Green	York Hall	Lion Promotions/Golden Fists Promotions
26.01.02	Dagenham	Goresbrook Leisure Centre	Matchroom/Prince Promotions
27.01.02	Streatham	Caesar's Nightclub	Pyle
28.01.02	Barnsley	The Metrodome	Matchroom/Prince Promotions
31.01.02	Piccadilly	Café Royal	Lion Promotions/Golden Fists Promotions
07.02.02	Stoke	Moat House Hotel	Brogan
08.02.02	Preston	The Guildhall	Williams
09.02.02	Manchester	MEN Arena	Sports Network
09.02.02	Coventry	Sports Connexion	Capitol Promotions
10.02.02	Southwark	Elephant & Castle Leisure Centre	Maloney
11.02.02	Southampton	The Guildhall	Bishop
11.02.02	Shrewsbury	Albrighton Hall Hotel	Cowdell

12.02.02	Bethnal Green	York Hall	Maloney
17.02.02	Salford	The Willows	VIP Promotions
17.02.02	Wolverhampton	The Light Bar	Bradley
18.02.02	Glasgow	Holiday Inn	St Andrew's SC
21.02.02	Sunderland	Marriott Hotel	Conroy
23.02.02	Nottingham	Harvey Hadden Leisure Centre	Matchroom/Prince Promotions
25.02.02	Slough	Montem Leisure Centre	Evans-Waterman Promotions
01.03.02	Irvine	Volunteer Rooms	St Andrew's SC
02.03.02	Bethnal Green	York Hall	Sports Network
02.03.02	Wakefield	Light Waves Leisure Centre	Prince Promotions
03.03.02	Shaw	Tara Leisure Centre	Tara Promotions
04.03.02	Bradford	Hilton Hotel	Yorkshire Executive SC
04.03.02	Birmingham	Burlington Hotel	Cowdell
08.03.02	Ellesmere Port	Epic Leisure Centre	Williams
09.03.02	Manchester	Wythenshawe Forum	Matchroom/Prince Promotions
11.03.02	Glasgow	Kelvin Hall	Sports Network
13.03.02	Mayfair	Marriott Hotel	Pyle/World Sports Organisation
15.03.02	Spennymoor	The Leisure Centre	Callighan
15.03.02	Glasgow	Thistle Hotel	Morrison
15.03.02	Millwall	Britannia Hotel	Peacock Promotions
16.03.02	Northampton	Derngate Centre	Sanigar
16.03.02	Bethnal Green	York Hall	Panix Promotions
18.03.02	Crawley	The Leisure Centre	Matchroom/Prince Promotions
18.03.02	Glasgow	Holiday Inn	St Andrew's SC
19.03.02	Slough	Montem Leisure Centre	Evans-Waterman Promotions
22.03.02	Coventry	Leofric Hotel	Capitol Promotions
23.03.02	Southwark	Elephant & Castle Leisure Centre	Matchroom/Prince Promotions
24.03.02	Streatham	Caesar's Nightclub	Honeyghan
25.03.02	Sunderland	Stadium of Light Function Rooms	Conroy
27.03.02	Mayfair	Marriott Hotel	Jacobs
08.04.02	Southampton	The Guildhall	Bishop
13.04.02	Norwich	Sports Village	Ingle
13.04.02	Liverpool	Everton Park Sports Centre	Matchroom/Prince Promotions
13.04.02	Wolverhampton	The Light Bar	Bradley
15.04.02	Shrewsbury	Albrighton Hall Hotel	Cowdell
17.04.02	Stoke	Moat House Hotel	Brogan
19.04.02	Darlington	Dolphin Leisure Centre	Walker
20.04.02	Cardiff	International Arena	Sports Network
20.04.02	Wembley	Conference Centre	Harding
20.04.02	Derby	Pennine Hotel	Ingle
22.04.02	Glasgow	Holiday Inn	St Andrew's SC
25.04.02	Hull	Willerby Manor Hotel	Pollard
26.04.02	Coventry	The Skydrome	Capitol Promotions
26.04.02	Glasgow	Thistle Hotel	Morrison
27.04.02	Huddersfield	The Leisure Centre	Matchroom/Prince Promotions
28.04.02	Southwark	Elephant & Castle Leisure Centre	Maloney
29.04.02	Bradford	Hilton Hotel	Yorkshire Executive SC
04.05.02	Bethnal Green	York Hall	Sports Network
05.05.02	Hartlepool	Seaton Carew Mayfair Suite	Garside
09.05.02	Sunderland	Marriott Hotel	Conroy
09.05.02	Leicester Square	Equinox Nightclub	Pyle/World Sports Organisation
10.05.02	Bethnal Green	York Hall	Sanigar
10.05.02	Millwall	Britannia Hotel	Peacock Promotions
10.05.02	Preston	Leyland Leisure Centre	Williams
11.05.02	Dagenham	Goresbrook Leisure Centre	Matchroom/Prince Promotions
11.05.02	Newark	Grove Leisure Centre	Gill
11.05.02	Chesterfield	Queen's Park Leisure Centre	Ingle

13.05.02	Birmingham	Burlington Hotel	Cowdell
18.05.02	Millwall	London Arena	Matchroom/Prince Promotions
21.05.02	Custom House	Excel Exhibition Centre	Harding
25.05.02	Portsmouth	Mountbatten Centre	Sports Network
28.05.02	Leeds	Marquee, Elland Road	Spratt
28.05.02	Liverpool	Everton Park Sports Centre	Matchroom/Prince Promotions
31.05.02	Hull	The University	Hull & District SC
01.06.02	Manchester	MEN Arena	Sports Network
02.06.02	Shaw	Tara Leisure Centre	Tara Promotions
03.06.02	Glasgow	Holiday Inn	St Andrew's SC
08.06.02	Renfrew	Braehead Arena	Sports Network
13.06.02	Leicester Square	Equinox Nightclub	Pyle/World Sports Organisation
15.06.02	Tottenham	The Green Leisure Centre	World Sports Organisation
15.06.02	Norwich	Sports Village	Ingle
15.06.02	Leeds	Town Hall	Matchroom/Prince Promotions
21.06.02	Leeds	Queen's Hotel	Walker
23.06.02	Southwark	Elephant & Castle Leisure Centre	Maloney
24.06.02	Bradford	Hilton Hotel	Yorkshire Executive SC
25.06.02	Rugby	Benn Hall	Capitol Promotions
29.06.02	Brentwood	International Centre	Matchroom/Prince Promotions

Active British-Based Boxers: Career Records

Shows the complete record for all British-based boxers who have been active between 1 July 2001 and 30 June 2002. Names in brackets are real names, where they differ from ring names, and the first place name given is the boxer's domicile. Boxers are either shown as being self-managed or with a named manager, the information being supplied by the BBBoC shortly before going to press. Also included are foreign-born fighters who made their pro debuts in Britain, along with others like Varuzhan Davtyan (Armenia) and Ossie Duran (Ghana) who, although starting their careers elsewhere, now hold BBBoC licenses.

Ojay Abrahams

Watford. *Born* Lambeth, 17 December, 1964
Middleweight. Former British Masters
L. Middleweight Champion. Ht. 5'8½"
Manager Self

21.09.91	Gordon Webster W RSC 3 Tottenham
26.10.91	Mick Reid W RSC 5 Brentwood
26.11.91	John Corcoran W PTS 6 Bethnal Green
21.01.92	Dave Andrews DREW 6 Norwich
31.03.92	Marty Duke W RSC 2 Norwich
19.05.92	Michael Smyth L PTS 6 Cardiff
16.06.92	Ricky Mabbett W PTS 6 Dagenham
13.10.92	Vince Rose L RSC 3 Mayfair
30.01.93	Vince Rose DREW 6 Brentwood
19.05.93	Ricky Mabbett L RSC 4 Leicester
18.09.93	Ricky Mabbett L PTS 6 Leicester
09.12.93	Nick Appiah W PTS 6 Watford
24.01.94	Errol McDonald W RSC 2 Glasgow
09.02.94	Vince Rose W PTS 6 Brentwood
23.05.94	Spencer McCracken L PTS 6 Walsall
11.06.94	Darren Dyer W RSC 1 Bethnal Green
29.09.94	Gary Logan L PTS 10 Bethnal Green *(Southern Area Welterweight Title Challenge)*
13.12.94	Geoff McCreesh L PTS 6 Potters Bar
11.02.95	Gary Murray L PTS 8 Hamanskraal, South Africa
17.07.95	Andreas Panayi L PTS 8 Mayfair
02.10.95	Larbi Mohammed L RTD 5 Mayfair
08.12.95	Jason Beard W CO 2 Bethnal Green
09.04.96	Kevin Thompson W RSC 3 Stevenage
07.05.96	Harry Dhami L RSC 5 Mayfair *(Vacant Southern Area Welterweight Title)*
12.11.96	Spencer McCracken L PTS 8 Dudley
22.04.97	Paul King W RSC 4 Bethnal Green
29.05.97	Paul Ryan L RSC 3 Mayfair
30.06.97	Ahmet Dottuev L RSC 4 Bethnal Green
08.11.97	Anthony McFadden L PTS 8 Southwark
24.03.98	Leigh Wicks W PTS 6 Bethnal Green
28.04.98	Jim Webb W RSC 2 Belfast
10.09.98	Delroy Leslie L PTS 10 Acton *(Vacant Southern Area L. Middleweight Title)*
19.12.98	Michael Jones L PTS 6 Liverpool
23.01.99	Wayne Alexander L DIS 1 Cheshunt *(Vacant Southern Area L. Middleweight Title)*
01.05.99	Wayne Alexander L RSC 3 Crystal Palace
26.06.99	Geoff McCreesh L PTS 8 Millwall
05.10.99	Hussain Osman L PTS 4 Bloomsbury
23.10.99	Paul Samuels L PTS 8 Telford
18.01.00	Howard Eastman L RSC 2 Mansfield
23.03.00	Pedro Thompson DREW 6 Bloomsbury
08.04.00	Anthony Farnell L PTS 8 Bethnal Green
16.05.00	Ryan Rhodes L PTS 6 Warrington
23.05.00	Alexandru Andrei L PTS 6 Paris, France
04.07.00	Lester Jacobs L PTS 4 Tooting
21.09.00	Harry Butler W PTS 6 Bloomsbury
07.10.00	Kofi Jantuah L RTD 3 Doncaster
25.11.00	Donovan Smillie W RSC 2 Manchester
16.12.00	Marlon Hayes L RTD 6 Sheffield
15.01.01	Gordon Behan DREW 6 Manchester
24.02.01	Ruben Groenewald L PTS 6 Bethnal Green
22.04.01	Harry Butler W PTS 6 Streatham
17.05.01	Lee Murtagh W RSC 2 Leeds *(Vacant British Masters L. Middleweight Title)*
21.06.01	Charden Ansoula L PTS 4 Earls Court
28.07.01	Gary Logan L RSC 4 Wembley
10.12.01	Jimmy Vincent L PTS 10 Birmingham *(British Masters L. Middleweight Title Challenge)*
28.01.02	Ian Cooper W PTS 6 Barnsley
16.03.02	John Humphrey L PTS 10 Bethnal Green *(Vacant Southern Area L. Middleweight Title)*
13.04.02	Mihaly Kotai L PTS 6 Liverpool
20.04.02	Freeman Barr L PTS 8 Cardiff
10.05.02	Carl Froch L RSC 1 Bethnal Green
15.06.02	Sam Soliman L PTS 4 Tottenham

Career: 61 contests, won 19, drew 4, lost 38.

Andy Abrol　　　　　Les Clark

Andy Abrol

Blackpool. *Born* Middlesbrough, 19
October, 1973
Welterweight. Ht. 5'10"
Manager L. Veitch

08.03.01	Chris Steele W RSC 6 Blackpool
18.03.01	Paddy Martin W RSC 3 Shaw
26.07.01	Ernie Smith W PTS 6 Blackpool

Career: 3 contests, won 3.

Babatunde Ajayi

Peckham. *Born* London, 10 July, 1974
Welterweight. Ht. 5'7¾"
Manager Self

18.02.01	Brian Gifford W RSC 1 Southwark
01.04.01	Arv Mittoo W PTS 6 Southwark
03.06.01	Ernie Smith W PTS 4 Southwark
09.09.01	James Paisley W PTS 4 Southwark
28.10.01	Karl Taylor W PTS 4 Southwark

Career: 5 contests, won 5.

Babatunde Ajayi　　　　　Les Clark

Henry Akinwande

Dulwich. *Born* London, 12 October, 1965
WBC FeCarBox Heavyweight Champion.
Former Undefeated WBO, European &
Commonwealth Heavyweight Champion.
Ht. 6'7"
Manager Self

04.10.89	Carlton Headley W CO 1 Kensington
08.11.89	Dennis Bailey W RSC 2 Wembley
06.12.89	Paul Neilson W RSC 1 Wembley
10.01.90	John Fairbairn W RSC 1 Kensington
14.03.90	Warren Thompson W PTS 6 Kensington
09.05.90	Mike Robinson W CO 1 Wembley
10.10.90	Tracy Thomas W PTS 6 Kensington
12.12.90	Francois Yrius W RSC 1 Kensington
06.03.91	J. B. Williamson W RSC 2 Wembley
06.06.91	Ramon Voorn W PTS 8 Barking
28.06.91	Marshall Tillman W PTS 8 Nice, France
09.10.91	Gypsy John Fury W CO 3 Manchester *(Elim. British Heavyweight Title)*
06.12.91	Tim Bullock W CO 3 Dussledorf, Germany
28.02.92	Young Joe Louis W RSC 3 Issy les Moulineaux, France
26.03.92	Tucker Richards W RSC 2 Telford
10.04.92	Lumbala Tshimba W PTS 8 Carquefou, France
05.06.92	Kimmuel Odum W DIS 6 Marseille, France
18.07.92	Steve Garber W RTD 2 Manchester
19.12.92	Axel Schulz DREW 12 Berlin, Germany *(Vacant European Heavyweight Title)*
18.03.93	Jimmy Thunder W PTS 12 Lewisham *(Vacant Commonwealth Heavyweight Title)*
01.05.93	Axel Schulz W PTS 12 Berlin, Germany *(Vacant European Heavyweight Title)*
06.11.93	Frankie Swindell W PTS 10 Sun City, South Africa
01.12.93	Biagio Chianese W RSC 4 Kensington *(European Heavyweight Title Defence)*
05.04.94	Johnny Nelson W PTS 10 Bethnal Green
23.07.94	Mario Schiesser W CO 7 Berlin, Germany *(European Heavyweight Title Defence)*
08.04.95	Calvin Jones W CO 2 Las Vegas, USA
22.07.95	Stanley Wright W RSC 2 Millwall
16.12.95	Tony Tucker W PTS 10 Philadelphia, USA
27.01.96	Brian Sergeant W RSC 1 Phoenix, USA
23.03.96	Gerard Jones W DIS 7 Miami, USA
29.06.96	Jeremy Williams W CO 3 Indio, USA *(Vacant WBO Heavyweight Title)*
09.11.96	Alexander Zolkin W RSC 10 Las Vegas, USA *(WBO Heavyweight Title Defence)*
11.01.97	Scott Welch W PTS 12 Nashville, USA *(WBO Heavyweight Title Defence)*
12.07.97	Lennox Lewis L DIS 5 Lake Tahoe, USA *(WBC Heavyweight Title Challenge)*
13.12.97	Orlin Norris W PTS 12 Pompano Beach, USA *(Final Elim. WBA Heavyweight Title)*
06.03.99	Reynaldo Minus W RSC 2 St Paul, USA
15.05.99	Najeed Shaheed W RSC 9 Miami, USA
22.02.00	Chris Serengo W RSC 1 Capetown, South Africa
25.05.00	Russull Chasteen W CO 5 Tunica, USA
08.12.00	Ken Craven W CO 1 Tallahassee, USA *(Vacant WBC FeCarBox Heavyweight Title)*
17.03.01	Peter McNeeley W CO 2 Tallahassee, Florida, USA
16.06.01	Maurice Harris W CO 1 Cincinnati, USA
17.11.01	Oliver McCall L CO 10 Las Vegas, Nevada, USA
08.03.02	Curt Paige W RSC 1 Kissimmee, Florida, USA

Career: 44 contests, won 41, drew 1, lost 2.

Mark Alexander　　　　　　　Les Clark

Mark Alexander

Finsbury Park. *Born* Hackney, 18 November, 1975
S. Bantamweight. Ht. 5'9½"
Manager A. Gee

10.04.01	Steve Hanley W PTS 4 Wembley
31.07.01	Damien Dunnion W PTS 4 Bethnal Green
19.12.01	Dazzo Williams L PTS 6 Coventry

Career: 3 contests, won 2, lost 1.

Wayne Alexander

Croydon. *Born* Tooting, 17 July, 1973
British & European L. Middleweight Champion. Former Undefeated Southern Area L. Middleweight Champion. Ht. 5'8¾"
Manager F. Warren

10.11.95	Andrew Jervis W RTD 3 Derby

Wayne Alexander　　　　　　　Les Clark

13.02.96	Paul Murray W PTS 4 Bethnal Green	
11.05.96	Jim Webb W RSC 2 Bethnal Green	
13.07.96	John Janes W RSC 3 Bethnal Green	
05.06.97	Prince Kasi Kaihau W CO 4 Bristol	
29.11.97	John Janes W RSC 1 Norwich	
21.03.98	Darren Covill W RSC 2 Bethnal Green	
09.05.98	Pedro Carragher W CO 2 Sheffield	
14.07.98	Lindon Scarlett W RSC 5 Reading	
05.12.98	Jimmy Vincent W RSC 3 Bristol	
23.01.99	Ojay Abrahams W DIS 1 Cheshunt	

*(Vacant Southern Area
L. Middleweight Title)*

01.05.99	Ojay Abrahams W RSC 3 Crystal Palace
07.08.99	George Richards W RSC 2 Dagenham
19.02.00	Paul Samuels W RSC 3 Dagenham

(Vacant British L. Middleweight Title)

12.08.00	Paul Denton W RSC 1 Wembley
10.02.01	Harry Simon L RSC 5 Widnes

(WBO L. Middleweight Title Challenge)

28.07.01	Viktor Fesetchko W PTS 8 Wembley
17.11.01	Joe Townsley W RSC 2 Glasgow

(British L. Middleweight Title Defence)

19.01.02	Paolo Pizzamiglio W RSC 3 Bethnal Green

(Vacant European L. Middleweight Title)

Career: 19 contests, won 18, lost 1.

Michael Alldis

Crawley. *Born* London, 25 May, 1968
British & Commonwealth S. Bantamweight
Champion. Former Undefeated British
Masters S. Bantamweight Champion. Ht. 5'6"
Manager B. Hearn

15.09.92	Ceri Farrell W RSC 3 Crystal Palace
10.11.92	Kid McAuley W PTS 6 Dagenham
12.12.92	Kid McAuley W CO 1 Muswell Hill
16.02.93	Ceri Farrell W CO 1 Tooting
29.06.93	Ady Benton L DIS 3 Mayfair
28.09.93	Alan Ley W PTS 6 Bethnal Green
06.11.93	Pete Buckley W PTS 8 Bethnal Green
09.04.94	Fernando Lugo W CO 1 Bethnal Green
11.06.94	Conn McMullen W PTS 8 Bethnal Green
20.12.94	Pete Buckley W PTS 6 Bethnal Green
17.02.95	Miguel Matthews W PTS 8 Crawley
25.03.95	Chip O'Neill W RSC 2 Chester
13.06.95	Laureano Ramirez L PTS 12 Basildon

*(Vacant WBO Inter-Continental
S. Bantamweight Title)*

25.11.95	Conn McMullen W CO 4 Dagenham
13.01.96	Garry Burrell W RSC 7 Halifax
14.02.96	Billy Hardy L PTS 12 Sunderland

(Commonwealth Featherweight Title Challenge)

04.04.97	Ervine Blake W RSC 3 Brighton
28.04.97	Paul Ingle L RTD 11 Hull

(British Featherweight Title Challenge)

06.01.98	Luigi Mancini L RSC 4 Brighton
03.10.98	Jason Thomas W PTS 6 Crawley
15.12.98	Simon Ramoni L RSC 2 Durban, South Africa

(IBO S. Bantamweight Title Challenge)

27.04.99	Garry Burrell W RSC 1 Bethnal Green
29.06.99	David Jeffrey W CO 1 Bethnal Green

(British Masters S. Bantamweight Final)

06.11.99	Patrick Mullings W PTS 12 Bethnal Green

(Vacant British S. Bantamweight Title)

24.01.00	Shaun Anderson W PTS 12 Glasgow

(British S. Bantamweight Title Defence)

16.06.00	Bagdad Touama W RSC 4 Bloomsbury
04.11.00	Drew Docherty W RSC 6 Bethnal Green

(British S. Bantamweight Title Defence)

23.01.01	Salem Bouita W RSC 6 Crawley
14.07.01	Patrick Mullings L PTS 12 Wembley

(British S.Bantamweight Title Defence)

20.10.01	Mahyar Monshipour L RTD 4 Portsmouth
18.03.02	Brian Carr W PTS 12 Crawley

*(Vacant British S. Bantamweight Title.
Commonwealth S. Bantamweight Title
Challenge)*

11.05.02	Vuyani Phulo W CO 8 Dagenham

*(Commonwealth S. Bantamweight Title
Defence)*

Career: 32 contests, won 24, lost 8.

Carl Allen

Wolverhampton. *Born* Wolverhampton, 20
November, 1969
S. Featherweight. Midlands Area S.
Bantamweight Champion. Ht. 5'7¼"
Manager Self

26.11.95	Gary Jenkinson W PTS 6 Birmingham
29.11.95	Jason Squire L PTS 6 Solihull
17.01.96	Andrew Robinson L PTS 6 Solihull
13.02.96	Ervine Blake W RSC 5 Wolverhampton
21.02.96	Ady Benton L PTS 6 Batley
29.02.96	Chris Jickells W PTS 6 Scunthorpe
27.03.96	Jason Squire DREW 6 Whitwick
26.04.96	Paul Griffin L RSC 3 Cardiff
30.05.96	Roger Brotherhood W RSC 5 Lincoln
26.09.96	Matthew Harris W PTS 10 Walsall

*(Midlands Area S. Bantamweight Title
Challenge)*

07.10.96	Emmanuel Clottey L RTD 3 Lewisham
21.11.96	Miguel Matthews W PTS 8 Solihull
30.11.96	Floyd Havard L RTD 3 Tylorstown
29.01.97	Pete Buckley W PTS 8 Stoke
11.02.97	David Morris DREW 8 Wolverhampton
28.02.97	Ian McLeod L RTD 3 Kilmarnock
21.05.97	David Burke L PTS 4 Liverpool
30.06.97	Duke McKenzie L PTS 8 Bethnal Green
12.09.97	Brian Carr L PTS 8 Glasgow
04.10.97	Sergei Devakov L PTS 6 Muswell Hill
03.12.97	Chris Lyons W PTS 8 Stoke
21.05.98	Roy Rutherford L PTS 6 Solihull
09.06.98	Scott Harrison L RSC 6 Hull
30.11.98	Gary Hibbert L PTS 4 Manchester
09.12.98	Chris Jickells W RSC 3 Stoke
04.02.99	Mat Zegan L PTS 4 Lewisham
17.03.99	Craig Spacie W PTS 8 Stoke
08.05.99	Phillip Ndou L RSC 2 Bethnal Green
14.06.99	Pete Buckley W PTS 6 Birmingham
22.06.99	David Lowry L PTS 4 Ipswich
11.10.99	Lee Williamson L PTS 6 Birmingham
19.10.99	Tontcho Tontchev L CO 2 Bethnal Green
20.12.99	Nicky Cook L CO 3 Bethnal Green
08.02.00	Lee Williamson W PTS 8 Wolverhampton
29.02.00	Bradley Pryce L PTS 4 Widnes
28.03.00	Lee Williamson W PTS 8 Wolverhampton
16.05.00	Bradley Pryce L RSC 3 Warrington
24.06.00	Michael Gomez L CO 2 Glasgow
10.10.00	Steve Hanley W PTS 8 Brierley Hill
05.02.01	Lee Meager DREW 6 Hull
12.03.01	Pete Buckley W PTS 6 Birmingham
27.03.01	Pete Buckley W PTS 8 Brierley Hill
15.09.01	Esham Pickering L PTS 6 Derby
17.11.01	Steve Conway L PTS 8 Dewsbury
08.12.01	Esham Pickering L PTS 8 Chesterfield
07.02.02	Mark Bowen L PTS 6 Stoke
20.04.02	Esham Pickering L PTS 6 Derby

Career: 47 contests, won 16, drew 3, lost 28.

Peter Allen

Birkenhead. *Born* Birkenhead, 13 August,
1978
Lightweight. Ht. 5'5"
Manager T. Miller

30.04.98	Sean Grant L PTS 6 Pentre Halkyn
21.06.98	Garry Burrell W PTS 6 Liverpool
20.09.98	Simon Chambers L PTS 6 Sheffield
16.11.98	Stevie Kane W PTS 6 Glasgow
07.12.98	Simon Chambers L PTS 6 Bradford
28.02.99	Amjid Mahmood L PTS 6 Shaw
12.03.99	Marc Callaghan L PTS 4 Bethnal Green
15.09.99	Steve Brook L PTS 6 Harrogate
07.10.99	Nicky Wilders L PTS 6 Sunderland
18.10.99	Mark Hudson L PTS 6 Bradford
15.11.99	Craig Docherty L RSC 1 Glasgow
09.12.01	Jeff Thomas L PTS 6 Blackpool
01.03.02	Andrew Ferrans L PTS 8 Irvine
15.03.02	Ricky Burns L PTS 6 Glasgow
17.04.02	Andrew Smith W PTS 6 Stoke
24.06.02	Tasawar Khan L PTS 6 Bradford

Career: 16 contests, won 3, lost 13.

Adnan Amar

Nottingham. *Born* Nottingham, 17
February, 1983
Lightweight. Ht. 5'9"
Manager M. Shinfield

11.06.01	Steve Hanley W PTS 4 Nottingham
13.11.01	Duncan Armstrong W PTS 6 Leeds

Career: 2 contests, won 2.

Francis Ampofo

Bethnal Green. *Born* Ghana, 5 June, 1967
Bantamweight. Former IBO Inter-
Continental Bantamweight Champion.
Former Undefeated British Flyweight
Champion. Former Commonwealth
Flyweight Champion. Ht. 5'1½"
Manager D. Powell

30.01.90	Neil Parry W PTS 6 Bethnal Green
06.03.90	Robbie Regan L PTS 6 Bethnal Green
29.05.90	Eric George W RSC 3 Bethnal Green
12.09.90	Eric George W CO 2 Bethnal Green
26.03.91	Ricky Beard W RSC 8 Bethnal Green
22.06.91	Neil Johnston W RSC 2 Earls Court
03.09.91	Robbie Regan W RSC 11 Cardiff

(British Flyweight Title Challenge)

17.12.91	Robbie Regan L PTS 12 Cardiff

(British Flyweight Title Defence)

25.02.92	Ricky Beard W PTS 8 Crystal Palace
16.06.92	Shaun Norman RSC 4 Dagenham
22.12.92	James Drummond W PTS 12 Mayfair

(Vacant British Flyweight Title)

17.02.93	Alberto Cantu W RSC 5 Bethnal Green
29.06.93	Albert Musankabala W RSC 3 Mayfair

(Vacant Commonwealth Flyweight Title)

11.06.94	Jacob Matlala L RTD 9 Bethnal Green

(WBO Flyweight Title Challenge)

20.09.94	James Drummond W RSC 3 Musselburgh

(British Flyweight Title Defence)

20.12.94	Daren Fifield W RSC 2 Bethnal Green

(British Flyweight Title Defence. Commonwealth Flyweight Title Challenge)

06.03.95	Danny Ward L CO 12 Mayfair

(Commonwealth Flyweight Title Defence)

27.11.96	Rowan Williams W PTS 6 Bethnal Green
08.04.97	Vince Feeney L PTS 10 Bethnal Green

(Vacant Southern Area Bantamweight Title)

19.09.97	Gary Hickman W RSC 2 Southend
25.10.97	Paul Lloyd L PTS 12 Queensferry

(Commonwealth Bantamweight Title Challenge. Vacant British Bantamweight Title)

08.09.98	Graham McGrath W RTD 3 Bethnal Green
25.01.99	Shaun Anderson W RSC 9 Glasgow

(Vacant IBO Inter-Continental Bantamweight Title)

30.10.99	Noel Wilders L PTS 12 Peterlee

(Vacant British Bantamweight Title)

01.04.00	Ady Lewis L PTS 12 Bethnal Green

(Vacant British & Commonwealth Bantamweight Titles)

09.12.00	John Armour L PTS 12 Southwark

(Vacant WBU Bantamweight Title)

11.05.02	John Armour L PTS 12 Dagenham

(WBU Bantamweight Title Challenge)

Career: 27 contests, won 17, lost 10.

Simon Andrews

Plymouth. *Born* Birmingham, 24 April, 1970
S. Middleweight. Ht. 5'9½"
Manager Self

19.09.95	J. P. Matthews L RSC 3 Plymouth
13.11.95	Carl Winstone L PTS 6 Barnstaple
03.12.95	Jason Hart L PTS 6 Southwark
12.02.96	Neville Smith L RSC 3 Heathrow
04.04.96	Jetty Williams W PTS 6 Plymouth
10.05.96	Graham Townsend L RSC 5 Wembley
18.10.96	Gareth Thomas W RSC 5 Barnstaple
07.11.96	Gary Reyniers DREW 6 Battersea
10.12.96	Gareth Thomas W RSC 4 Plymouth
15.02.97	Neville Smith L PTS 4 Tooting
19.04.97	Peter Vosper L PTS 10 Plymouth

(Vacant Western Area L. Heavyweight Title)

12.07.97	Markus Beyer L RSC 5 Earls Court
02.12.97	Gary Reyniers L PTS 6 Windsor
24.02.98	Alex Mason L PTS 6 Edgbaston
24.03.98	Gordon Behan L RSC 6 Wolverhampton
24.09.98	Alex Mason L PTS 8 Edgbaston
17.03.99	Matthew Barney L RTD 6 Kensington
03.10.99	Damon Hague L PTS 6 Chesterfield
20.11.99	Damon Hague L RSC 4 Grantham
27.02.00	Matt Mowatt L PTS 6 Plymouth
29.03.00	Gareth Hogg L RSC 5 Piccadilly
02.06.00	Steven Bendall L RSC 5 Ashford
25.02.01	Joe Brame L RSC 5 Streatham
12.05.01	Freddie Yemofio W PTS 4 Plymouth
30.09.01	Darren Dorrington L RSC 4 Bristol

(Western Area S. Middleweight Title Challenge)

12.12.01	Mark Phillips L PTS 6 Clydach
16.03.02	Mike Thompson L PTS 4 Northampton
13.04.02	Peter Jackson L PTS 4 Wolverhampton

Career: 28 contests, won 4, drew 1, lost 23.

John Armour

Chatham. *Born* Chatham, 26 October, 1968
WBU Bantamweight Champion. Former Undefeated European & Commonwealth Bantamweight Champion. Ht. 5'4¾"
Manager Self

24.09.90	Lupe Castro W PTS 6 Lewisham
31.10.90	Juan Camero W RSC 4 Crystal Palace
21.01.91	Elijro Mejia W RSC 1 Crystal Palace
30.09.91	Pat Maher W CO 1 Kensington
29.10.91	Pete Buckley W PTS 6 Kensington
14.12.91	Gary Hickman W RSC 6 Bexleyheath
25.03.92	Miguel Matthews W PTS 6 Dagenham
30.04.92	Ndabe Dube W RSC 12 Kensington

(Vacant Commonwealth Bantamweight Title)

17.10.92	Mauricio Bernal W PTS 8 Wembley
03.12.92	Albert Musankabala W RSC 5 Lewisham

(Commonwealth Bantamweight Title Defence)

28.01.93	Ricky Romero W CO 1 Southwark
10.02.93	Morgan Mpande W PTS 12 Lewisham

(Commonwealth Bantamweight Title Defence)

09.06.93	Boualem Belkif W PTS 10 Lewisham
01.12.93	Karl Morling W CO 3 Kensington
14.01.94	Rufus Adebayo W RSC 7 Bethnal Green

(Commonwealth Bantamweight Title Defence)

23.09.94	Shaun Anderson W RSC 11 Bethnal Green

(Commonwealth Bantamweight Title Defence)

14.02.95	Tsitsi Sokutu W RSC 7 Bethnal Green

(Commonwealth Bantamweight Title Defence)

19.04.95	Antonio Picardi W RSC 8 Bethnal Green

(Vacant European Bantamweight Title)

19.05.95	Matthew Harris W RSC 3 Southwark
29.11.95	Redha Abbas W CO 5 Bethnal Green

(European Bantamweight Title Defence)

17.12.96	Lyndon Kershaw W RSC 8 Bethnal Green
29.01.97	Petrica Paraschiv W PTS 12 Bethnal Green

(Vacant Interim WBC International Bantamweight Title)

20.05.97	Anatoly Kvitko W RSC 8 Gillingham
28.11.97	Ervine Blake W PTS 10 Bethnal Green
12.12.98	Carlos Navarro L RSC 4 Southwark

(WBU S. Bantamweight Title Challenge)

19.06.99	Mohamed Ouzid W RSC 5 Dublin
25.07.00	Alexander Tiranov W PTS 8 Southwark
09.12.00	Francis Ampofo W PTS 12 Southwark

(Vacant WBU Bantamweight Title)

01.12.01	Ian Turner W PTS 8 Bethnal Green
11.05.02	Francis Ampofo W PTS 12 Dagenham

(WBU Bantamweight Title Defence)

Career: 30 contests, won 29, lost 1.

Duncan Armstrong

South Shields. *Born* South Shields, 29 November, 1977
Lightweight. Ht. 5'10"
Manager T. Callighan

26.11.99	Chris Hall L PTS 6 Wakefield
02.03.00	Joel Viney L PTS 6 Blackpool
28.03.00	Dave Travers W PTS 6 Wolverhampton
06.06.00	Andrew Ferrans L PTS 6 Motherwell
23.07.00	James Rooney L RSC 3 Hartlepool
20.11.00	Andrew Ferrans L PTS 6 Glasgow
05.12.00	Dave Cotterill L PTS 6 Nottingham
26.02.01	Inderpaul Sandhu L PTS 4 Nottingham
19.03.01	Pete Buckley W PTS 6 Glasgow
09.04.01	Leo Turner L PTS 6 Bradford
27.07.01	Chris Hall L PTS 4 Sheffield
13.11.01	Adnan Amar L PTS 6 Leeds

Career: 12 contest, won 2, lost 10.

(Shaun) Lee Armstrong

Huddersfield. *Born* Hartlepool, 18 October, 1972
Welterweight. Former Undefeated Central Area S. Featherweight Champion. Ht. 5'8"
Manager Self

26.04.96	Daryl McKenzie W RSC 4 Glasgow
10.05.96	Charlie Rumbol W PTS 6 Wembley
23.05.96	Ian Richardson W PTS 6 Queensferry
04.10.96	Michael Gibbons L RSC 3 Wakefield
18.11.96	Garry Burrell W PTS 6 Glasgow
20.02.97	Carl Greaves W RSC 4 Mansfield
10.04.97	Chris Lyons W PTS 6 Sheffield
28.04.97	Hugh Collins W RTD 5 Glasgow
26.06.97	Garry Burrell W PTS 6 Sheffield
06.10.97	Roger Sampson L PTS 6 Bradford
13.11.97	Graeme Williams W PTS 6 Bradford
30.11.97	Gary Jenkinson W PTS 6 Shaw
06.02.98	Nigel Leake W PTS 6 Wakefield
05.04.98	John T. Kelly W PTS 4 Shaw
21.05.98	Pete Buckley W PTS 6 Bradford
14.06.98	Pete Buckley W PTS 6 Shaw
23.10.98	Nigel Leake W RSC 3 Wakefield

(Vacant Central Area S. Featherweight Title)

11.12.98	Ian McLeod L RSC 8 Prestwick

(IBO Inter-Continental S. Featherweight Title Challenge)

21.02.99	Bobby Lyndon W RSC 5 Bradford
03.04.99	John T. Kelly L PTS 6 Carlisle
25.04.99	Chris Lyons W PTS 8 Leeds
02.10.99	Jamie McKeever DREW 6 Cardiff
14.11.99	Keith Jones W PTS 6 Bradford
11.12.99	Jason Dee L RSC 4 Merthyr
21.02.00	Gary Flear W PTS 8 Glasgow
27.03.00	Sebastian Hart L CO 4 Barnsley
24.09.00	Dave Travers W PTS 6 Shaw
23.10.00	Craig Docherty DREW 8 Glasgow
10.12.01	Arv Mittoo W PTS 6 Bradford
27.04.02	Keith Jones W PTS 6 Huddersfield
09.05.02	Richard Inquieti L RSC 5 Sunderland

Career: 31 contests, won 22, drew 2, lost 7.

Alex Arthur

Edinburgh. *Born* Edinburgh, 26 June, 1978
IBF & WBO Inter-Continental S. Featherweight Champion. Ht. 5'9"
Manager F. Warren/F. Maloney

25.11.00 Richmond Asante W RSC 1 Manchester
10.02.01 Eddie Nevins W RSC 1 Widnes
26.03.01 Woody Greenaway W RTD 2 Wembley
28.04.01 Dafydd Carlin W PTS 4 Cardiff
21.07.01 Rakhim Mingaleev W PTS 4 Sheffield
15.09.01 Dimitri Gorodetsky W RSC 1 Manchester
27.10.01 Alexei Slyautchin W RSC 1 Manchester
17.11.01 Laszlo Bognar W RSC 3 Glasgow
19.01.02 Vladimir Borov W RSC 2 Bethnal Green
11.03.02 Dariusz Snarski W RSC 10 Glasgow
(Vacant IBF Inter-Continental S.Featherweight Title)
08.06.02 Nikolai Eremeev W RTD 5 Renfrew
(Vacant WBO Inter-Continental S.Featherweight Title)

Career: 11 contests, won 11.

Alex Arthur   Les Clark

Richmond Asante

East Ham. *Born* Ghana, 7 July, 1976
Featherweight. Ht. 5'5½"
Manager Self

25.11.00 Alex Arthur L RSC 1 Manchester
18.02.01 Gareth Wiltshaw W PTS 4 Southwark
01.04.01 Stevie Quinn L PTS 4 Southwark
03.06.01 Steve Gethin W PTS 4 Southwark
09.09.01 Mickey Coveney L PTS 4 Southwark
26.01.02 Marc Callaghan L PTS 4 Dagenham
27.04.02 Jesse James Daniel W PTS 6 Huddersfield

Career: 7 contests, won 3, lost 4.

Richmond Asante   Les Clark

(Gary) Crawford Ashley (Crawford)

Leeds. *Born* Leeds, 20 May, 1964
Cruiserweight. Former British, Commonwealth & European L. Heavyweight Champion. Former Undefeated Central Area L. Heavyweight Champion. Ht. 6'3"
Manager Self

26.03.87 Steve Ward W RSC 2 Merton
29.04.87 Lee Woolis W RSC 3 Stoke
14.09.87 Glazz Campbell L PTS 8 Bloomsbury
07.10.87 Joe Frater W RSC 4 Burnley
28.10.87 Ray Thomas W RSC 1 Stoke
03.12.87 Jonjo Greene W RSC 7 Leeds
04.05.88 Johnny Nelson L PTS 8 Solihull
15.11.88 Richard Bustin W CO 3 Norwich
22.11.88 Cordwell Hylton W CO 3 Basildon
24.01.89 John Foreman W RSC 4 Kings Heath
08.02.89 Lavell Stanley W CO 1 Kensington
28.03.89 Blaine Logsdon L RSC 2 Glasgow
10.05.89 Serg Fame W RTD 7 Solihull
31.10.89 Carl Thompson W RSC 6 Manchester
(Vacant Central Area L. Heavyweight Title)
24.01.90 Brian Schumacher W RSC 3 Preston
(Central Area L. Heavyweight Title Defence)
25.04.90 Dwain Muniz W RSC 1 Brighton
26.11.90 John Williams W RSC 1 Mayfair
12.02.91 Melvin Ricks W CO 1 Belfast
01.03.91 Graciano Rocchigiani L PTS 12 Dusseldorf, Germany
(Vacant European L. Heavyweight Title)
25.07.91 Roy Skeldon W RSC 7 Dudley
(Vacant British L. Heavyweight Title)
30.01.92 Jim Peters W RSC 1 Southampton
(British L. Heavyweight Title Defence)
25.04.92 Glazz Campbell W RSC 8 Belfast

(British L. Heavyweight Title Defence)
23.09.92 Yawe Davis DREW 12 Campione d'Italia, Italy
(Vacant European L. Heavyweight Title)
23.04.93 Michael Nunn L RSC 6 Memphis, USA
(WBA S. Middleweight Title Challenge)
29.01.94 Dennis Andries L RTD 4 Cardiff
19.11.94 Nicky Piper W PTS 12 Cardiff
(Vacant British L. Heavyweight Title)
25.02.95 Hunter Clay W RTD 3 Millwall
01.04.95 Virgil Hill L PTS 12 Stateline, USA
(WBA L. Heavyweight Title Challenge)
01.07.95 Lenzie Morgan W PTS 8 Kensington
24.11.95 Jesus Castaneda W RSC 3 Manchester
10.02.96 Frank Minton W RSC 1 Cottbus, Germany
02.03.96 Ray Kane W CO 2 Newcastle
11.12.96 Tony Booth W RSC 1 Southwark
11.01.97 Peter Kamarenko W RSC 1 Bethnal Green
01.03.97 Roberto Dominguez W CO 3 Liverpool
(Vacant European L. Heavyweight Title)
31.05.97 Pascal Warusfel W PTS 12 Paris, France
(European L. Heavyweight Title Defence)
04.10.97 Ole Klemetsen L RSC 2 Muswell Hill
(European L. Heavyweight Title Defence)
14.03.98 Monty Wright W RSC 2 Bethnal Green
British L. Heavyweight Title Defence)
09.06.98 Tony Booth W RSC 6 Hull
(British L. Heavyweight Title Defence. Vacant Commonwealth L. Heavyweight Title)
26.09.98 Jo Siluvangi W PTS 12 York
(Vacant European L. Heavyweight Title)
13.03.99 Clinton Woods L RSC 8 Manchester
(British, Commonwealth & European L. Heavyweight Title Defences)
05.02.01 Shane Woollas W RSC 4 Hull
24.03.01 Lee Swaby W PTS 8 Sheffield
08.12.01 Sebastiaan Rothmann L RSC 8 Dagenham
(WBU Cruiserweight Title Challenge)

Career: 44 contests, won 33, drew 1, lost 10.

Darren Ashton

Stoke. *Born* Stoke, 26 February, 1969
Cruiserweight. Midlands Area L. Heavyweight Champion. Former Undefeated Midlands Area S. Middleweight Champion. Ht. 6'1"
Manager Self

13.10.93 Tony Colclough W RSC 1 Stoke
08.12.93 Nigel Rafferty W PTS 6 Stoke
23.03.94 L. A. Williams W PTS 6 Stoke
23.05.94 Nigel Rafferty W PTS 6 Walsall
30.11.94 Carlos Christie L PTS 6 Solihull
04.03.95 John Wilson NC 3 Livingston
06.05.95 Dale Nixon W RSC 4 Shepton Mallet
13.05.95 Stefan Wright W PTS 6 Glasgow
11.10.95 Neil Simpson L RSC 3 Solihull
17.11.95 Mark Baker L RSC 1 Bethnal Green
12.01.96 Frederic Alvarez L PTS 6 Copenhagen, Denmark

27.05.96 Harri Hakulinen L PTS 4 Helsinki, Finland
09.07.96 Chris Johnson L RSC 1 Bethnal Green
08.02.97 Paul Bowen L PTS 4 Millwall
04.04.97 Mark Snipe W RSC 2 Brighton
26.06.97 Clinton Woods L PTS 6 Sheffield
02.09.97 Adrian Strachan W PTS 4 Southwark
15.09.97 Darren Dorrington W DIS 2 Bristol
21.11.97 Stuart Fleet W RSC 4 Hull
(Vacant Midlands Area S. Middleweight Title)
07.02.98 Sven Hamer L RSC 6 Cheshunt
27.03.98 Toks Owoh L RSC 2 Telford
16.05.98 Ali Forbes L PTS 6 Chigwell
23.05.98 Howard Eastman L RSC 4 Bethnal Green
23.09.98 Bobby Banghar L RSC 2 Bloomsbury
13.11.98 Graham Townsend L DIS 6 Brighton
30.11.98 Mervyn Penniston-John L PTS 4 Manchester
19.12.98 Ole Klemetsen L RSC 2 Liverpool
11.02.99 Alex Mason W PTS 10 Dudley
(Vacant Midlands Area L. Heavyweight Title)
13.03.99 Glenn Williams L PTS 4 Manchester
17.05.99 Tony Booth L PTS 6 Cleethorpes
04.06.99 Lee Osie Manuel L RSC 5 Vigo, Spain
(Transcontinental L. Heavyweight Title Challenge)
31.07.99 Darren Corbett L RSC 2 Carlisle
09.10.99 Glenn Williams L PTS 6 Manchester
28.10.99 Warren Stowe W PTS 6 Burnley
04.12.99 Mike Gormley L PTS 4 Manchester
21.02.00 Tony Oakey L PTS 4 Southwark
04.03.00 Neil Linford L PTS 6 Peterborough
20.03.00 Brian Magee L RTD 5 Mansfield
29.05.00 Roy Finlay L PTS 4 Manchester
21.10.00 Tony Oakey L PTS 4 Wembley
31.10.00 Konstantin Schvets L RSC 1 Hammersmith
30.11.00 Neil Linford L PTS 4 Peterborough
08.12.00 Delroy Leslie L RTD 3 Crystal Palace
27.01.01 Peter Haymer L PTS 4 Bethnal Green
17.02.01 Faisal Mohammed L RSC 1 Bethnal Green
28.03.01 Michael Pinnock DREW 6 Piccadilly
20.04.01 Tony Griffiths W PTS 4 Millwall
28.04.01 Enzo Maccarinelli L CO 1 Cardiff
27.05.01 Lee Whitehead W RSC 2 Manchester
15.06.01 Garry Delaney L RTD 4 Millwall
(Vacant British Masters Cruiserweight Title)
13.09.01 Mark Brookes L PTS 4 Sheffield
20.09.01 Tony Strong W PTS 4 Blackfriars
09.10.01 Nathan King L PTS 6 Cardiff
27.10.01 Steven Spartacus L PTS 4 Manchester
19.11.01 Billy McClung L PTS 6 Glasgow
19.01.02 Steven Spartacus L PTS 4 Bethnal Green
10.02.02 Blue Stevens L PTS 4 Southwark
02.03.02 Pinky Burton L PTS 6 Wakefield
18.03.02 Paul Bowen L PTS 6 Crawley
20.04.02 Andrew Facey L PTS 6 Derby
28.04.02 Scott Baker L RSC 6 Southwark
13.06.02 John Killian L PTS 4 Leicester Square
Career: 62 contests, won 15, drew 1, lost 45, no contest 1.

Dean Ashton

Stoke. *Born* Stoke, 26 November, 1967
S. Middleweight. Ht. 5'9"
Manager Self

13.10.93 Phil Ball W PTS 6 Stoke
08.12.93 Mark Hale W RSC 1 Stoke
23.03.94 Shaun McCrory DREW 6 Stoke
23.05.94 Mark Smallwood L RTD 3 Walsall
28.03.98 Andy Wright L RSC 2 Crystal Palace
16.05.98 Earl Ling DREW 6 Chigwell
02.07.98 Earl Ling W RSC 2 Ipswich
17.09.98 Peter Mitchell L PTS 6 Brighton
25.10.98 Mike Whittaker L PTS 6 Shaw
13.11.98 Jimmy Millen W RSC 3 Brighton
30.11.98 Mike Gormley L PTS 4 Manchester
14.12.98 Damon Hague L PTS 6 Cleethorpes
19.01.99 Adrian Houldey W PTS 8 Ipswich
22.02.99 John Docherty L PTS 6 Glasgow
13.03.99 Brian Magee L RSC 2 Manchester
22.04.99 Alex Mason L PTS 10 Dudley
(Vacant Midlands Area S. Middleweight Title)
26.06.99 Frode Steinsvik L RSC 2 Millwall
19.09.99 Lee Blundell L RSC 4 Shaw
28.10.99 Mike Whittaker L PTS 6 Burnley
14.11.99 Danny Thornton L PTS 4 Bradford
01.12.99 Ian Cooper L PTS 4 Yarm
14.12.99 Peter Federenko L PTS 4 Coventry
22.01.00 Gordon Behan L RSC 2 Birmingham
20.03.00 Ivan Botton L RSC 2 Mansfield
11.05.00 Ian Toby L PTS 6 Sunderland
22.05.00 Edwin Cleary DREW 4 Coventry
29.05.00 Darren Rhodes L RSC 3 Manchester
25.07.00 Butch Lesley L PTS 6 Southwark
08.09.00 Richard Williams L RSC 1 Hammersmith
12.11.00 Alan Page L RSC 2 Manchester
23.02.01 Tony Griffiths L PTS 8 Barking
28.03.01 Wayne Asker L PTS 6 Piccadilly
20.04.01 Elvis Michailenko L RSC 4 Millwall
27.05.01 Wayne Pinder L PTS 6 Manchester
16.06.01 Damon Hague W DIS 1 Derby
14.07.01 Erik Teymour L RSC 2 Liverpool
15.09.01 Damon Hague L RTD 2 Derby
(Vacant Midlands Area S.Middleweight Title)
22.11.01 John Killian L PTS 4 Mayfair
03.12.01 Andy Vickers L PTS 6 Leeds
16.12.01 George Robshaw L RTD 2 Southwark
Career: 40 contests, won 6, drew 3, lost 31.

Wayne Asker

Bury St Edmunds. *Born* Bury St Edmunds, 20 November, 1975
Middleweight. Ht. 5'9"
Manager Self

02.07.98 Dennis Griffin W PTS 4 Ipswich
03.10.98 Delroy Mellis W PTS 6 Crawley
19.01.99 David Baptiste W PTS 6 Ipswich
09.05.99 Hussan Osman L PTS 4 Bracknell
22.06.99 David Baptiste L PTS 4 Ipswich
28.03.01 Dean Ashton W PTS 6 Piccadilly
08.12.01 Leigh Wicks W PTS 4 Dagenham
10.02.02 Ruben Groenewald L PTS 10 Southwark
(Vacant British Masters S.Middleweight Title)
15.06.02 Donovan Smillie DREW 6 Norwich
Career: 9 contests, won 5, drew 1, lost 3.

Michael Ayers

Tooting. *Born* London, 26 January, 1965
Former Undefeated British, IBO, WBC

International & Southern Area Lightweight Champion. Ht. 5'8"
Manager B. Hearn

16.05.89 Young Joe Rafiu W RSC 5 Wandsworth
27.06.89 Greg Egbuniwe W CO 1 Kensington
15.11.89 Mille Markovic W RSC 2 Lewisham
05.12.89 Darren Mount W RSC 2 Catford
26.04.90 Nick Hall W CO 3 Wandsworth
04.06.91 Stuart Rimmer W CO 1 Bethnal Green
22.06.91 Wayne Weekes W RSC 6 Earls Court
(Vacant Southern Area Lightweight Title)
21.09.91 Peter Till W RSC 5 Tottenham
(Elim. British Lightweight Title)
28.01.92 Jorge Pompey W PTS 8 Hamburg, Germany
19.02.92 Rudy Valentino W RSC 7 Muswell Hill
(Southern Area Lightweight Title Defence. Elim. British Lightweight Title)
27.06.92 Sugar Gibiliru W RSC 6 Quinta do Lago, Portugal
13.10.92 Scott Brouwer W RSC 4 Mayfair
(Vacant WBC International Lightweight Title)
20.02.93 Danny Myburgh W RSC 5 Earls Court
(WBC International Lightweight Title Defence)
16.04.93 Giovanni Parisi L PTS 12 Rome, Italy
(WBO Lightweight Title Challenge)
24.05.94 Karl Taylor DREW 8 Sunderland
30.09.94 John O. Johnson W RSC 3 Bethnal Green
07.11.94 Bamana Dibateza W PTS 6 Bethnal Green
17.02.95 Paul Burke W RSC 6 Crawley
(Vacant British Lightweight Title)
31.03.95 Karl Taylor W RSC 8 Crystal Palace
(British Lightweight Title Defence)
23.05.95 Charles Shepherd W RSC 3 Potters Bar
(British Lightweight Title Defence)
30.09.95 Dave Anderson W RTD 7 Basildon
(British Lightweight Title Defence)
27.09.96 Tony Swift W RSC 5 Stevenage
20.11.96 Colin Dunne W RSC 9 Wembley
(British Lightweight Title Defence)
21.03.98 Alan Temple W RSC 2 Bethnal Green
30.05.98 Anthony Maynard L PTS 8 Bristol
06.11.98 Steve Tuckett W RSC 5 Mayfair
03.12.98 Roger Sampson L PTS 6 Mayfair
12.01.99 Jean Gomis W RTD 5 Bethnal Green
12.03.99 Luis Flores W RSC 4 Bethnal Green
(Vacant IBO Lightweight Title)
25.05.99 Mkhuseli Kondile W CO 3 Mayfair
(IBO Lightweight Title Defence)
02.10.99 Pablo Sarmiento W RSC 6 Cardiff
(IBO Lightweight Title Defence)
20.12.99 Tony Miller W RSC 10 Bethnal Green
(IBO Lightweight Title Defence)
01.07.00 Wayne Rigby W RSC 10 Manchester
(IBO Lightweight Title Defence)
19.08.00 Mehdi Labdouni W CO 1 Brentwood
(IBO Lightweight Title Defence)
03.03.01 Wayne Rigby W PTS 12 Wembley
(IBO Lightweight Title Defence)
10.11.01 Pablo Sarmiento L PTS 12 Wembley
(IBO L.Welterweight Title Challenge)
Career: 36 contests, won 31, drew 1, lost 4.

Chris P. Bacon

Manchester. *Born* Australia, 8 October, 1969
Cruiserweight. Former Undefeated WBF European S. Cruiserweight Champion.
Ht. 6'0"
Manager Self

21.12.97	Tim Brown W PTS 6 Salford
23.02.98	Tim Brown W PTS 6 Salford
08.05.98	Lee Swaby W RSC 3 Manchester
30.05.98	Phill Day W RSC 4 Bristol
17.07.98	Lee Swaby W PTS 6 Mere
18.09.98	Kevin Mitchell W RSC 1 Manchester
16.10.98	Luke Simpkin W PTS 6 Salford
16.11.98	Paul Bonson W PTS 8 Glasgow
25.02.99	Israel Ajose W PTS 10 Kentish Town
	(Vacant WBF European
	S. Cruiserweight Title)
19.06.99	Kelly Oliver L PTS 8 Dublin
09.10.99	Chris Woollas W PTS 4 Manchester
03.02.01	Collice Mutizwa W RSC 1 Manchester
14.07.01	Garry Delaney L RSC 10 Liverpool
	(British Masters Cruiserweight Title
	Challenge)

Career: 13 contests, won 11, lost 2.

Martyn Bailey   Les Clark

Martyn Bailey

Wrexham. *Born* Wrexham, 16 January, 1976
L. Middleweight. Ht. 5'8"
Manager R. Jones

07.10.99	John Marsden W PTS 6 Sunderland
27.11.99	Lee Molloy L RSC 2 Liverpool
18.02.00	Donovan Davey W PTS 6 Pentre Halkyn
06.03.00	Richard Inquieti L RSC 5 Bradford
05.05.00	Richard Inquieti W PTS 6 Pentre Halkyn
22.09.00	David Smales W RSC 3 Wrexham
28.11.00	Paul Martin W PTS 6 Brierley Hill
04.02.01	Pedro Thompson W PTS 6 Queensferry
08.04.01	Peter Dunn W PTS 6 Wrexham
10.06.01	Robert Burton DREW 6 Ellesmere Port
08.10.01	Reagan Denton L PTS 4 Barnsley
21.10.01	Wayne Shepherd W PTS 6 Pentre Halkyn
16.11.01	Robert Burton DREW 4 Preston
08.03.02	Danny Moir W PTS 6 Ellesmere Port
29.04.02	Paul Lomax DREW 6 Bradford

Career: 15 contests, won 9, drew 3, lost 3.

Scott Baker

Walthamstow. *Born* Londonderry, 29 August, 1977
Cruiserweight. Ht. 6'2"
Manager R. Davies

22.06.99	Adam Cale W PTS 4 Ipswich
13.09.99	Georgie Stevens L PTS 4 Bethnal Green
01.10.99	Jason Brewster W RTD 5 Cleethorpes
16.06.00	Adam Cale W PTS 4 Bloomsbury
08.09.00	Mark Dawson L RSC 3 Hammersmith
03.02.01	Slick Miller L RSC 4 Brighton
16.12.01	Jimmy Steel W PTS 4 Southwark
28.04.02	Darren Ashton W RSC 6 Southwark

Career: 8 contests, won 5, lost 3.

Ted Bami (Minsende)

Brixton. *Born* Zaire, 2 March, 1978
L. Welterweight. Ht. 5'7"
Manager Self

26.09.98	Des Sowden W RSC 1 Southwark
11.02.99	Gary Reid W RSC 2 Dudley
10.03.00	David Kehoe W PTS 4 Bethnal Green
08.09.00	Jacek Bielski L RSC 4 Hammersmith
29.03.01	Keith Jones W PTS 4 Hammersmith
05.05.01	Francis Barrett W PTS 6 Edmonton
31.07.01	Lance Crosby W PTS 6 Bethnal Green
19.03.02	Michael Smyth W CO 4 Slough
23.06.02	Keith Jones W RSC 4 Southwark

Career: 9 contests, won 8, lost 1.

David Baptiste

Balham. *Born* Luton, 5 March, 1966
Welterweight. Ht. 5'7"
Manager Self

20.09.96	Robbie Dunn W CO 2 Tooting
08.11.97	Darren Covill L PTS 4 Southwark
04.03.98	Scott Garrett L PTS 6 Bloomsbury
02.07.98	Mark Weller L PTS 4 Ipswich
08.08.98	Darren Christie L PTS 4 Scarborough
12.10.98	Ray Newby L RSC 6 Nottingham
30.11.98	Neil Linford L PTS 4 Peterborough
12.12.98	Shane Thomas W RSC 2 Chester
19.12.98	Paolo Roberto L RSC 6 Liverpool
19.01.99	Wayne Asker L PTS 6 Ipswich
26.02.99	Joel Ani W RSC 5 Longford
13.03.99	Brian Knudsen L RSC 4 Manchester
29.04.99	Sergei Dzindziruk L RTD 2 Bethnal Green
22.06.99	Wayne Asker W PTS 4 Ipswich
21.07.99	Lester Jacobs L RSC 2 Bloomsbury
15.09.99	James Lowther W RSC 3 Harrogate
26.11.99	Adrian Chase L RSC 2 Bayswater
	(Vacant British Masters Welterweight
	Title)

29.02.00	Jamie Moore L RSC 3 Manchester
07.04.00	Jason Williams L PTS 6 Bristol
06.05.00	Zoltan Sarossy L PTS 8 Neuss, Germany
29.05.00	Thomas McDonagh L PTS 6 Manchester
16.09.00	Kevin McCarthy W RSC 6 Bethnal Green
04.11.00	Gary Lockett L PTS 4 Bethnal Green
11.11.00	Jim Rock L PTS 4 Belfast
30.11.00	Lester Jacobs L RSC 3 Bloomsbury
02.02.01	Paul Dyer L PTS 10 Portsmouth
	(Vacant Southern Area Welterweight
	Title)
23.02.01	Chris Nembhard L PTS 8 Barking
17.03.01	Thomas McDonagh L PTS 4 Manchester
26.03.01	Clive Johnson L PTS 6 Peterborough
04.05.02	David Barnes L CO 3 Bethnal Green

Career: 30 contests, won 6, lost 24.

David Barnes (Smith)

Manchester. *Born* Manchester, 16 January, 1981
Welterweight. Ht. 5'8½"
Manager F. Warren

07.07.01	Trevor Smith W RSC 2 Manchester
15.09.01	Karl Taylor W PTS 4 Manchester
27.10.01	Mark Sawyers W RSC 2 Manchester
15.12.01	James Paisley W RTD 2 Wembley
09.02.02	David Kirk W RTD 1 Manchester
04.05.02	David Baptiste W CO 3 Bethnal Green
01.06.02	Dimitri Protkunas W RSC 1 Manchester

Career: 7 contests, won 7.

David Barnes   Les Clark

John Barnes

Sunderland. *Born* Sunderland, 7 July, 1975
S. Bantamweight. Ht. 5'6½"
Manager T. Conroy

02.10.97	Nicky Wilders W PTS 6 Sunderland
04.12.97	Sean Grant W PTS 6 Sunderland
26.01.98	Alston Buchanan L PTS 6 Glasgow
07.05.98	Kevin Gerowski W PTS 6 Sunderland

06.05.99	Simon Chambers W PTS 6 Sunderland	
12.07.99	Mark Payne L PTS 4 Coventry	
20.09.99	Craig Docherty L PTS 6 Glasgow	
30.10.99	Paul Quarmby W PTS 4 Peterlee	
27.11.99	Nicky Cook L PTS 6 Liverpool	
07.02.00	Jezz D'Agostino W PTS 4 Peterborough	
24.02.00	Sebastian Hart L PTS 6 Sunderland	
04.03.00	Jezz D'Agostino W PTS 4 Peterborough	
20.03.00	Andrew Ferrans DREW 6 Glasgow	
01.04.00	Marc Callaghan L PTS 4 Bethnal Green	
11.05.00	Nigel Senior W PTS 6 Sunderland	
01.07.00	Jason Booth L PTS 6 Manchester	
25.09.00	Dale Robinson L PTS 4 Barnsley	
05.10.00	Steve Brook W PTS 6 Sunderland	
23.10.00	Shaun Anderson W PTS 6 Glasgow	
31.10.00	Jamie Yelland L PTS 6 Hammersmith	
20.11.00	Barry Hawthorne L PTS 6 Glasgow	
19.03.01	Shaun Anderson W PTS 6 Glasgow	
07.04.01	Jamie Yelland L PTS 4 Wembley	
30.04.01	Chris Emanuele W PTS 4 Glasgow	
12.05.01	Frankie DeMilo L PTS 10 Plymouth *(British Masters S. Bantamweight Title Challenge)*	
09.09.01	Michael Hunter L RSC 8 Hartlepool *(Vacant Northern Area S.Bantamweight Title)*	

Career: 26 contests, won 12, drew 1, lost 13.

Chris Barnett

Manchester. *Born* Coventry, 15 July, 1973
Lightweight. Former Undefeated IBO
International L. Welterweight Champion.
Ht. 5.5½"
Manager Self

18.02.95	Wayne Jones W RSC 5 Shepton Mallet
24.11.95	Brian Coleman W PTS 6 Manchester
09.04.96	Charlie Paine W RSC 2 Salford
25.10.96	John Smith W PTS 6 Mere
22.12.96	Wayne Shepherd W PTS 6 Salford
18.01.97	Kid McAuley W RTD 3 Manchester
24.02.97	Jay Mahoney L PTS 6 Manchester
20.03.97	Mike Watson W RSC 2 Salford
08.05.98	David Kirk W PTS 6 Manchester
17.07.98	Ivan Walker W RSC 1 Mere
17.10.98	Trevor Smith W RSC 4 Manchester
10.07.99	Karim Bouali DREW 6 Southwark
09.10.99	Mick Mulcahy W RSC 2 Manchester
27.11.99	Glenn McClarnon W PTS 12 Liverpool *(Vacant IBO International L. Welterweight Title)*
29.02.00	Victor Barinov L PTS 8 Manchester
19.08.00	Newton Villareal L RSC 3 Brentwood *(IBO L.Welterweight Title Challenge)*
06.10.01	Jason Dee W DIS 5 Manchester
26.11.01	Viktor Baranov L PTS 6 Manchester
28.05.02	James Armah L PTS 8 Liverpool

Career: 19 contests, won 13, drew 1, lost 5.

Matthew Barney

Southampton. *Born* Fareham, 25 June, 1974
IBO Inter-Continental & Southern Area S.
Middleweight Champion. Former
Undefeated British Masters S.
Middleweight Champion. Ht. 5'10¾"
Manager Self

04.06.98	Adam Cale W PTS 6 Barking

23.07.98	Adam Cale W PTS 6 Barking
02.10.98	Dennis Doyley W PTS 4 Cheshunt
22.10.98	Kevin Burton W PTS 6 Barking
07.12.98	Freddie Yemofio W PTS 4 Acton
17.03.99	Simon Andrews W RTD 4 Kensington
09.05.99	Gareth Hogg W PTS 4 Bracknell
20.05.99	Bobby Banghar W RSC 5 Kensington *(British Masters S. Middleweight Final)*
05.06.99	Paul Bowen DREW 10 Cardiff *(Southern Area S. Middleweight Title Challenge)*
20.08.99	Adam Cale W PTS 4 Bloomsbury
05.10.99	Delroy Leslie L PTS 10 Bloomsbury *(Vacant Southern Area Middleweight Title)*
15.04.00	Mark Dawson W PTS 6 Bethnal Green
06.05.00	Jason Hart W PTS 10 Southwark *(Vacant Southern Area S. Middleweight Title)*
30.09.00	Neil Linford L PTS 10 Peterborough *(Elim. British S. Middleweight Title)*
02.02.01	Darren Covill W PTS 6 Portsmouth
16.03.01	Matt Mowatt W RSC 1 Portsmouth *(British Masters S. Middleweight Title Defence)*
14.07.01	Robert Milewics W PTS 8 Wembley
20.10.01	Jon Penn W RSC 4 Portsmouth
26.01.02	Hussain Osman L RTD 9 Dagenham *(Vacant IBO Inter-Continental S.Middleweight Title. Southern Area S.Middleweight Title Defence)*
08.04.02	Hussain Osman W PTS 12 Southampton *(IBO Inter-Continental & Southern Area S. Middleweight Title Challenges)*

Career: 20 contests, won 16, drew 1, lost 3.

Matthew Barr

Walton. *Born* Kingston, 22 May, 1977
L. Middleweight. Ht. 5'11"
Manager Self

02.12.97	Keith Palmer L RSC 3 Windsor
23.02.98	Martin Cavey W RSC 1 Windsor
14.05.98	Gerard Lawrence L RSC 1 Acton
29.10.98	Sonny Thind W RSC 2 Bayswater
20.05.99	Paul Knights L RSC 1 Barking
31.10.99	Allan Gray W PTS 4 Raynes Park
25.02.00	John Humphrey W RSC 1 Newmarket
06.05.00	Ernie Smith W PTS 4 Southwark
22.10.00	Ernie Smith W PTS 4 Streatham
23.11.00	Harry Butler W PTS 4 Bayswater
23.11.01	John Humphrey L RSC 2 Bethnal Green

Career: 11 contests, won 7, lost 4.

Francis Barrett

Wembley. *Born* Galway, 7 February, 1977
L. Welterweight. Ht. 5'7"
Manager F. Warren

12.08.00	Mohamed Helel W PTS 4 Wembley
23.09.00	Trevor Smith W RSC 1 Bethnal Green
21.10.00	Keith Jones W PTS 4 Wembley
24.02.01	David White W PTS 4 Bethnal Green
10.03.01	Karl Taylor W RSC 3 Bethnal Green
26.03.01	Tony Montana W PTS 4 Wembley
05.05.01	Ted Bami L PTS 6 Edmonton
22.09.01	Gary Reid W PTS 4 Bethnal Green
19.01.02	Dafydd Carlin W PTS 4 Bethnal Green
25.05.02	David Kirk W PTS 6 Portsmouth

Career: 10 contests, won 9, lost 1.

Kevin Barrett

Hackney. *Born* Hackney, 15 October, 1973
Heavyweight. Ht. 5'9"
Manager B. Lawrence

27.01.01	Mark McManus W RSC 1 Bethnal Green
10.04.01	Brian Gascoigne W RSC 1 Wembley
13.09.01	Lee Swaby L PTS 4 Sheffield
15.12.01	Enzo Maccarinelli L RSC 2 Wembley
09.05.02	Terry Dixon DREW 4 Leicester Square

Career: 5 contests, won 2, drew 1, lost 2.

Kevin Barrett   Les Clark

Ryan Barrett

Thamesmead. *Born* London, 27 December, 1982
Lightweight. Ht. 5'10"
Manager D. Powell

13.06.02	Gareth Wiltshaw W PTS 4 Leicester Square

Career: 1 contest, won 1.

(Shinebayer) Shinny Bayaar (Sukhbaatar)

Carlisle. *Born* Mongolia, 27 August, 1977
Flyweight. Ht. 5'0"
Manager J. Doughty

10.10.01	Damien Dunnion L PTS 8 Stoke
09.12.01	Delroy Spencer W PTS 4 Shaw

Career: 2 contests, won 1, lost 1.

Jimmy Beech

Walsall. *Born* Walsall, 19 January, 1979
S. Featherweight. Ht. 5'7"
Manager Self

23.06.99	Ike Halls W RTD 2 West Bromwich
03.09.99	Tom Wood W PTS 6 West Bromwich
07.04.00	Willie Limond L RSC 2 Glasgow
28.01.01	Lenny Hodgkins W PTS 6 Wolverhampton

16.11.01 Pete Buckley W PTS 6 West Bromwich
23.11.01 Henry Castle L PTS 4 Bethnal Green
07.02.02 Dave Cotterill W PTS 6 Stoke
25.02.02 Mickey Bowden W PTS 4 Slough
09.03.02 Tony Mulholland L PTS 6 Manchester
05.05.02 James Rooney W RSC 5 Hartlepool
25.05.02 Henry Castle L PTS 4 Portsmouth
Career: 11 contests, won 7, lost 4.

Jimmy Beech   Les Clark

Steven Bendall

Coventry. *Born* Coventry, 1 December, 1973
IBO Inter-Continental Middleweight Champion. Former Undefeated WBU Inter-Continental Middleweight Champion. Ht. 6'0"
Manager Self

15.05.97 Dennis Doyley W RSC 2 Reading
13.09.97 Gary Reyniers W PTS 4 Millwall
27.02.99 Israel Khumalo W PTS 4 Oldham
02.07.99 Darren Covill W RTD 3 Bristol
24.09.99 Sean Pritchard W PTS 6 Merthyr
03.12.99 Ian Toby W PTS 6 Peterborough
07.04.00 Des Sowden W RSC 3 Bristol
02.06.00 Simon Andrews W RSC 5 Ashford
08.09.00 Jason Barker W PTS 6 Bristol
03.11.00 Eddie Haley W RSC 1 Ebbw Vale
01.12.00 Peter Mitchell W PTS 8 Peterborough
22.08.01 Bert Bado W RSC 1 Hammanskraal, South Africa
29.09.01 Alan Gilbert W RTD 3 Southwark
08.12.01 Jason Collins W PTS 12 Dagenham
(Vacant WBU Inter-Continental Middleweight Title)
02.03.02 Ahmet Dottouev W RTD 4 Brakpan, South Africa
(WBU Inter-Continental Middleweight Title Defence)
26.04.02 Viktor Fesetchko W RSC 10 Coventry
(Vacant IBO Inter-Continental Middleweight Title)
Career: 16 contests, won 16.

Kevin Bennett

Hartlepool. *Born* Birmingham, 15 August, 1975
L. Welterweight. Ht. 5'7"
Manager M. Marsden

01.12.99 Karim Bouali W PTS 4 Yarm
28.03.00 Les Frost W RSC 2 Hartlepool
25.06.00 Steve Hanley W PTS 6 Wakefield
23.07.00 Gary Reid W RSC 4 Hartlepool
28.10.00 Gary Harrison W RTD 2 Coventry
27.11.00 Keith Jones W PTS 4 Birmingham
23.01.01 Tommy Peacock W RSC 5 Crawley
03.03.01 Iain Eldridge W PTS 6 Wembley
08.05.01 Keith Jones W PTS 6 Barnsley
04.06.01 Gary Ryder L RSC 6 Hartlepool
20.10.01 Paul Denton W PTS 4 Portsmouth
03.11.01 Mark Ramsey W PTS 6 Glasgow
26.01.02 Glenn McClarnon L PTS 8 Dagenham
18.05.02 Colin Lynes L RSC 4 Millwall
Career: 14 contests, won 11, lost 3.

Jim Betts

Scunthorpe. *Born* Tickhill, 6 October, 1977
Former Undefeated British Masters Flyweight Champion. Ht. 5'6½"
Manager M. Marsden

26.03.98 Des Gargano W PTS 6 Scunthorpe
13.05.98 David Jeffrey W RSC 3 Scunthorpe
05.06.98 Chris Price W PTS 6 Hull
11.09.98 Marty Chestnut W PTS 6 Newark
16.10.98 Marty Chestnut W PTS 6 Salford
28.11.98 Ola Dali W PTS 4 Sheffield
17.05.99 Dave Travers W RTD 4 Cleethorpes
17.07.99 Ross Cassidy W RSC 1 Doncaster
27.09.99 Graham McGrath W PTS 6 Cleethorpes
19.02.00 Chris Price W PTS 6 Newark
19.06.00 Chris Price W PTS 4 Burton
30.08.00 David Coldwell W RSC 2 Scunthorpe
(Vacant British Masters Flyweight Title. Elim. British Flyweight Title)
26.02.01 Chris Emanuele L PTS 6 Nottingham
08.05.01 Sean Grant W RSC 3 Barnsley
11.06.01 Daniel Ring W PTS 6 Nottingham
15.09.01 Nicky Booth L RSC 7 Nottingham
(British & Commonwealth Bantamweight Title Challenges)
18.03.02 Ian Turner W RTD 4 Crawley
18.05.02 Gareth Payne W PTS 6 Millwall
Career: 18 contests, won 16, lost 2.

Lee Blundell

Wigan. *Born* Wigan, 11 August, 1971
WBF Inter-Continental Middleweight Champion. Former Undefeated Central Area L. Middleweight Champion. Ht. 6'2"
Manager L. Veitch

25.04.94 Robert Harper W RSC 2 Bury
20.05.94 Freddie Yemofio W RSC 6 Acton
08.09.94 Gordon Blair DREW 6 Glasgow
07.12.94 Kesem Clayton W RTD 2 Stoke
18.02.95 Glenn Catley L RSC 6 Shepton Mallet
11.12.95 Martin Jolley W PTS 6 Morecambe
16.03.97 Martin Jolley W PTS 6 Shaw
08.05.97 Paul Jones L RSC 4 Mansfield
19.09.99 Dean Ashton W RSC 4 Shaw
28.10.99 Jason Collins DREW 6 Burnley
06.12.99 Danny Thornton W PTS 6 Bradford
05.03.00 Ian Toby W RTD 3 Shaw
21.05.00 Phil Epton W RSC 2 Shaw

30.11.00 Danny Thornton W RSC 8 Blackpool
(Vacant Central Area L. Middleweight Title)
08.03.01 Paul Wesley W RSC 3 Blackpool
03.04.01 Spencer Fearon W PTS 6 Bethnal Green
26.07.01 Harry Butler W RSC 4 Blackpool
15.09.01 Anthony Farnell L RSC 2 Manchester
(Vacant WBO Inter-Continental L. Middleweight Title)
09.12.01 Neil Bonner W RSC 3 Blackpool
16.03.02 Ryan Rhodes L RSC 3 Bethnal Green
(Vacant WBF Inter-Continental Middleweight Title)
Career: 20 contests, won 15, drew 2, lost 3.

Lee Blundell   Les Clark

Neil Bonner

Abergele. *Born* Enfield, 13 October, 1975
Middleweight. Ht. 5'9"
Manager Self

22.09.00 Drea Dread W RSC 4 Wrexham
03.11.00 James Lee L PTS 4 Ebbw Vale
04.02.01 Richard Inquieti W PTS 6 Queensferry
26.08.01 Colin McCash W RSC 1 Warrington
09.09.01 Peter Jackson L PTS 6 Hartlepool
21.10.01 Matt Scriven NC 1 Glasgow
09.12.01 Lee Blundell L RSC 3 Blackpool
08.03.02 Paul Buchanan L PTS 6 Ellesmere Port
19.04.02 Lee Murtagh L PTS 6 Darlington
11.05.02 Darrell Grafton L PTS 6 Chesterfield
08.06.02 Joe Townsley L PTS 6 Renfrew
Career: 11 contests, won 3, lost 7, no contest 1.

Paul Bonson

Featherstone. *Born* Castleford, 18 October, 1971
Cruiserweight. Former Central Area L. Heavyweight Champion. Ht. 5'10"
Manager M. Marsden

04.10.96 Michael Pinnock W PTS 6 Wakefield
14.11.96 Michael Pinnock DREW 6 Sheffield

22.12.96	Pele Lawrence DREW 6 Salford
20.04.97	Shamus Casey W PTS 6 Leeds
26.06.97	Andy Manning L PTS 6 Sheffield
19.09.97	Mike Gormley W PTS 6 Salford
03.10.97	Rudi Marcussen L PTS 4 Copenhagen, Denmark
03.12.97	Alex Mason DREW 6 Stoke
14.12.97	Willie Quinn L RSC 4 Glasgow
15.01.98	Alex Mason L PTS 6 Solihull
13.02.98	Peter Mason L PTS 4 Seaham
23.02.98	Martin McDonough W PTS 6 Windsor
07.03.98	Michael Bowen L PTS 6 Reading
14.03.98	Alain Simon L PTS 6 Pont St Maxence, France
08.04.98	Tim Brown DREW 4 Liverpool
21.05.98	Mark Hobson L PTS 6 Bradford
21.06.98	Kenny Rainford L PTS 6 Liverpool
01.09.98	Roberto Dominguez L PTS 8 Vigo, Spain
23.10.98	Rob Galloway W PTS 6 Wakefield
16.11.98	Chris P. Bacon L PTS 8 Glasgow
11.12.98	Robert Zlotkowski L PTS 4 Prestwick
20.12.98	Glenn Williams L PTS 6 Salford
24.04.99	Kenny Gayle DREW 6 Peterborough
29.05.99	Dave Johnson L PTS 6 South Shields
19.06.99	Sebastiaan Rothmann L PTS 8 Dublin
12.07.99	Jim Twite L PTS 4 Coventry
07.08.99	Kid Dongo L PTS 8 Arona, Tenerife
11.09.99	Mark Hobson L PTS 4 Sheffield
02.10.99	Enzo Maccarinelli L PTS 4 Cardiff
16.10.99	Robert Zlotkowski L PTS 6 Bethnal Green
27.10.99	Peter McCormack W PTS 6 Birmingham
04.12.99	Glenn Williams W PTS 4 Manchester
11.12.99	Chris Davies L PTS 4 Merthyr
05.02.00	Paul Maskell L PTS 4 Bethnal Green
11.03.00	Tony Dodson L PTS 4 Kensington
26.03.00	Wayne Buck L PTS 8 Nottingham
29.04.00	Cathal O'Grady L PTS 4 Wembley
13.05.00	Mark Hobson L PTS 4 Barnsley
25.06.00	Andy Manning W PTS 10 Wakefield
	(Vacant Central L. Heavyweight Title)
08.09.00	Robert Milewicz L PTS 4 Hammersmith
21.10.00	Jon Penn L PTS 6 Sheffield
12.11.00	Glenn Williams L PTS 10 Manchester
	(Central Area L.Heavyweight Title Defence)
24.11.00	Alex Mason L PTS 6 Darlington
09.12.00	Mark Baker L PTS 6 Solihull
23.01.01	Calvin Stonestreet W PTS 4 Crawley
03.02.01	Tony Dodson L PTS 4 Manchester
18.02.01	Butch Lesley L PTS 6 Southwark
13.03.01	Konstantin Schvets L PTS 6 Plymouth
07.04.01	Rob Hayes-Scott L PTS 4 Wembley
26.04.01	Mike White L PTS 6 Gateshead
17.05.01	Clint Johnson W PTS 6 Leeds
24.05.01	Sven Hamer L PTS 4 Kensington
04.06.01	Joe Gillon DREW 6 Glasgow
11.06.01	Darren Chubbs L PTS 4 Nottingham
21.06.01	Michael Pinnock W PTS 6 Sheffield
27.07.01	Clinton Woods L PTS 6 Sheffield
09.09.01	Eamonn Glennon W PTS 6 Hartlepool
28.09.01	Elvis Michailenko L PTS 6 Millwall
13.11.01	Tony Moran W PTS 6 Leeds
23.11.01	Elvis Michailenko L PTS 6 Bethnal Green
06.12.01	Shaun Bowes W RSC 5 Sunderland
16.12.01	Tommy Eastwood L PTS 4 Southwark
26.01.02	Dominic Negus L PTS 4 Bethnal Green
10.02.02	Butch Lesley L PTS 4 Southwark
25.02.02	Roman Greenberg L PTS 6 Slough

15.03.02	Michael Thompson L PTS 6 Spennymoor
22.03.02	Mark Smallwood L PTS 6 Coventry
19.04.02	Michael Thompson L PTS 6 Darlington
11.05.02	Mark Brookes L PTS 4 Chesterfield
15.06.02	Peter Haymer L PTS 4 Tottenham
23.06.02	Scott Lansdowne W PTS 4 Southwark

Career: 71 contests, won 15, drew 6, lost 50.

Jason Booth

Nottingham. *Born* Nottingham, 7 November, 1977
British & Commonwealth Flyweight Champion. Ht. 5'4"
Manager Self

13.06.96	Darren Noble W RSC 3 Sheffield
24.10.96	Marty Chestnut W PTS 6 Lincoln
27.11.96	Jason Thomas W PTS 4 Swansea
18.01.97	David Coldwell W PTS 4 Swadlincote
07.03.97	Pete Buckley W PTS 6 Northampton
20.03.97	Danny Lawson W RSC 3 Newark
10.05.97	Anthony Hanna W PTS 6 Nottingham
19.05.97	Chris Lyons W PTS 6 Cleethorpes
31.10.97	Mark Reynolds W PTS 6 Ilkeston
31.01.98	Anthony Hanna W PTS 6 Edmonton
20.03.98	Louis Veitch W CO 2 Ilkeston
	(Elim. British Flyweight Title)
09.06.98	Dimitar Alipiev W RSC 2 Hull
17.10.98	Graham McGrath W RSC 4 Manchester
07.12.98	Louis Veitch W RSC 5 Cleethorpes
08.05.99	David Guerault L PTS 12 Grande Synthe, France
	(European Flyweight Title Challenge)
12.07.99	Mark Reynolds W RSC 3 Coventry
16.10.99	Keith Knox W RSC 10 Belfast
	(British & Commonwealth Flyweight Title Challenges)
22.01.00	Abie Mnisi W PTS 12 Birmingham
	(Commonwealth Flyweight Title Defence)
01.07.00	John Barnes W PTS 6 Manchester
13.11.00	Ian Napa W PTS 12 Bethnal Green
	(British & Commonwealth Flyweight Title Defences)
26.02.01	Nokuthula Tshabangu W CO 2 Nottingham
	(Commonwealth Flyweight Title Defence)
30.06.01	Alexander Mahmutov L PTS 12 Madrid, Spain
	(European Flyweight Title Challenge)
23.02.02	Jason Thomas W PTS 6 Nottingham
01.06.02	Mimoun Chent L TD 8 Le Havre, France
	(Vacant European Flyweight Title)

Career: 24 contests, won 21, lost 3.

Nicky Booth

Nottingham. *Born* Nottingham, 21 January, 1980
British & Commonwealth Bantamweight Champion. Ht. 5'5"
Manager M. Shinfield

26.02.98	Shane Mallon W RSC 4 Hull
15.05.98	Marty Chestnut W PTS 6 Nottingham
14.07.98	Ian Napa L PTS 6 Reading
11.09.98	Anthony Hanna DREW 6 Cleethorpes
25.11.98	Anthony Hanna L PTS 6 Clydach
30.04.99	Delroy Spencer W PTS 6 Scunthorpe

06.06.99	Delroy Spencer W PTS 4 Nottingham
20.09.99	Russell Laing W PTS 8 Glasgow
03.12.99	David Jeffrey W PTS 4 Peterborough
03.03.00	Shaun Anderson W PTS 6 Irvine
22.05.00	Gareth Payne W PTS 4 Coventry
24.09.00	Gary Ford W PTS 6 Shaw
09.10.00	Tommy Waite W PTS 12 Liverpool
	(British & Commonwealth Bantamweight Title Challenges)
26.02.01	Ady Lewis W RSC 7 Nottingham
	(British & Commonwealth Bantamweight Title Defences)
11.06.01	Kevin Gerowski W RSC 4 Nottingham
14.07.01	Jose Sanjuanelo L RSC 9 Wembley
	(Vacant IBO Bantamweight Title)
15.09.01	Jim Betts W RSC 7 Nottingham
	(British & Commonwealth Bantamweight Title Defences)
23.02.02	Stephen Oates W RSC 7 Nottingham
	(British & Commonwealth Bantamweight Title Defences)

Career: 18 contests, won 14, drew 1, lost 3.

Tony Booth

Hull. *Born* Hull, 30 January, 1970
Heavyweight. Former Undefeated British Masters L. Heavyweight Champion. Former Undefeated British Central Area Cruiserweight Champion. Ht. 5'11¼"
Manager M. Dalton

08.03.90	Paul Lynch L PTS 6 Watford
11.04.90	Mick Duncan W PTS 6 Dewsbury
26.04.90	Colin Manners W PTS 6 Halifax
16.05.90	Tommy Warde W PTS 6 Hull
05.06.90	Gary Dyson W PTS 6 Liverpool
05.09.90	Shaun McCrory L PTS 6 Hull
08.10.90	Bullit Andrews W RSC 3 Cleethorpes
23.01.91	Darron Griffiths DREW 6 Stoke
06.02.91	Shaun McCrory L PTS 6 Liverpool
06.03.91	Billy Brough L PTS 6 Glasgow
18.03.91	Billy Brough L PTS 6 Glasgow
28.03.91	Neville Brown L PTS 6 Alfreton
17.05.91	Glenn Campbell L RSC 2 Bury
	(Central Area S. Middleweight Title Challenge)
25.07.91	Paul Murray W PTS 6 Dudley
01.08.91	Nick Manners DREW 8 Dewsbury
11.09.91	Jim Peters L PTS 8 Hammersmith
28.10.91	Eddie Smulders L RSC 6 Arnhem, Holland
09.12.91	Steve Lewsam L PTS 8 Cleethorpes
30.01.92	Serg Fame W PTS 6 Southampton
12.02.92	Tenko Ernie W RSC 4 Wembley
05.03.92	John Beckles W RSC 6 Battersea
26.03.92	Dave Owens W PTS 6 Hull
08.04.92	Michael Gale L PTS 8 Leeds
13.05.92	Phil Soundy W PTS 6 Kensington
02.06.92	Eddie Smulders L RSC 1 Rotterdam, Holland
18.07.92	Maurice Core L PTS 6 Manchester
07.09.92	James Cook L PTS 8 Bethnal Green
30.10.92	Roy Richie DREW 6 Istrees, France
18.11.92	Tony Wilson DREW 8 Solihull
25.12.92	Francis Wanyama L PTS 6 Izegem, Belgium
09.02.93	Tony Wilson W PTS 8 Wolverhampton
01.05.93	Ralf Rocchigiani DREW 8 Berlin, Germany
03.06.93	Victor Cordoba L PTS 8 Marseille, France
23.06.93	Tony Behan W PTS 6 Gorleston
01.07.93	Michael Gale L PTS 8 York

17.09.93 Ole Klemetsen L PTS 8 Copenhagen, Denmark
07.10.93 Denzil Browne DREW 8 York
02.11.93 James Cook L PTS 8 Southwark
12.11.93 Carlos Christie W PTS 6 Hull
28.01.94 Francis Wanyama L RSC 2 Waregem, Belgium
(Vacant Commonwealth Cruiserweight Title)
26.03.94 Torsten May L PTS 6 Dortmund, Germany
21.07.94 Mark Prince L RSC 3 Battersea
24.09.94 Johnny Held L PTS 8 Rotterdam, Holland
07.10.94 Dirk Wallyn L PTS 6 Waregem, Belgium
27.10.94 Dean Francis L CO 1 Bayswater
23.01.95 Jan Lefeber L PTS 8 Rotterdam, Holland
07.03.95 John Foreman L PTS 6 Edgbaston
27.04.95 Art Stacey W PTS 10 Hull
(Vacant Central Area Cruiserweight Title)
04.06.95 Montell Griffin L RSC 2 Bethnal Green
06.07.95 Nigel Rafferty W RSC 7 Hull
22.07.95 Mark Prince L RSC 2 Millwall
06.09.95 Leif Keiski L PTS 8 Helsinki, Finland
25.09.95 Neil Simpson W PTS 8 Cleethorpes
06.10.95 Don Diego Poeder L RSC 2 Waregem, Belgium
11.11.95 Bruce Scott L RSC 3 Halifax
16.12.95 John Marceta L RSC 2 Cardiff
20.01.96 Johnny Nelson L RSC 2 Mansfield
15.03.96 Slick Miller W PTS 6 Hull
27.03.96 Neil Simpson L PTS 6 Whitwick
17.05.96 Mark Richardson W RSC 2 Hull
13.07.96 Bruce Scott L PTS 8 Bethnal Green
03.09.96 Paul Douglas L PTS 4 Belfast
14.09.96 Kelly Oliver L RSC 2 Sheffield
06.11.96 Martin Jolley W PTS 4 Hull
22.11.96 Slick Miller W RSC 5 Hull
11.12.96 Crawford Ashley L RSC 1 Southwark
18.01.97 Kelly Oliver L RSC 4 Swadlincote
27.02.97 Kevin Morton L PTS 6 Hull
25.03.97 Nigel Rafferty DREW 8 Wolverhampton
04.04.97 John Wilson L PTS 6 Glasgow
16.04.97 Robert Norton L RSC 4 Bethnal Green
15.05.97 Phill Day W PTS 4 Reading
11.09.97 Steve Bristow L PTS 4 Widnes
22.09.97 Martin Langtry L PTS 6 Cleethorpes
04.10.97 Bruce Scott W PTS 8 Muswell Hill
28.11.97 Martin Jolley W PTS 6 Hull
15.12.97 Nigel Rafferty W PTS 6 Cleethorpes
06.03.98 Peter Mason W RSC 3 Hull
09.06.98 Crawford Ashley L RSC 4 Hull
(British L. Heavyweight Title Challenge. Vacant Commonwealth L. Heavyweight Title)
18.07.98 Omar Sheika W PTS 8 Sheffield
26.09.98 Toks Owoh L PTS 6 Norwich
29.10.98 Nigel Rafferty W PTS 8 Bayswater
14.12.98 Sven Hamer L PTS 6 Cleethorpes
05.01.99 Ali Saidi W RSC 4 Epernay, France
17.05.99 Darren Ashton W PTS 6 Cleethorpes
12.07.99 Neil Simpson L PTS 10 Coventry
(Elim. British L. Heavyweight Title)
27.09.99 Adam Cale W PTS 8 Cleethorpes
16.10.99 Cathal O'Grady L CO 4 Belfast
18.01.00 Michael Sprott L PTS 6 Mansfield
12.02.00 Thomas Hansvoll L PTS 6 Sheffield
29.02.00 John Keeton L RSC 2 Widnes
09.04.00 Greg Scott-Briggs W PTS 10 Alfreton

(Vacant British Masters L. Heavyweight Title)
15.05.00 Michael Pinnock W PTS 6 Cleethorpes
19.06.00 Toks Owoh L RSC 3 Burton
08.09.00 Dominic Negus W PTS 6 Bristol
30.09.00 Robert Norton L RSC 3 Peterborough
31.10.00 Firat Aslan L RSC 2 Hammersmith
11.12.00 Mark Krence L PTS 6 Sheffield
05.02.01 Denzil Browne L RSC 5 Hull
(Vacant Central Area Cruiserweight Title)
01.04.01 Kenny Gayle DREW 4 Southwark
10.04.01 Mark Baker L PTS 4 Wembley
16.06.01 Butch Lesley L RSC 3 Dagenham
09.09.01 Tommy Eastwood L PTS 4 Southwark
22.09.01 Peter Haymer L PTS 4 Bethnal Green
15.10.01 Colin Kenna L PTS 6 Southampton
01.11.01 Terry Morrill W RSC 7 Hull
24.11.01 Matt Legg L PTS 4 Bethnal Green
16.12.01 Blue Stevens L PTS 4 Southwark
19.01.02 John McDermott L RSC 1 Bethnal Green
20.04.02 Enzo Maccarinelli L PTS 4 Cardiff
28.04.02 Scott Lansdowne W RSC 4 Southwark
10.05.02 Paul Buttery L PTS 4 Preston
23.06.02 Neil Linford L RSC 5 Southwark
Career: 113 contests, won 38, drew 8, lost 67.

Alan Bosworth

Northampton. *Born* Northampton, 31 December, 1967
L. Welterweight. Ht. 5'7"
Manager N. Christian

17.10.95 Simon Hamblett W RSC 2 Wolverhampton
29.10.95 Shaun Gledhill W PTS 6 Shaw
16.11.95 Brian Coleman W PTS 6 Evesham
23.11.95 David Thompson W RSC 4 Tynemouth
13.01.96 Jason Blanche W PTS 6 Halifax
31.01.96 Arv Mittoo W PTS 6 Stoke
16.02.96 John Docherty W PTS 6 Irvine
24.03.96 Scott Walker DREW 6 Shaw
16.05.96 Yifru Retta W PTS 6 Dunstable
07.03.97 Wayne Rigby L RSC 5 Northampton
09.09.97 Colin Dunne L RSC 4 Bethnal Green
31.10.98 Alan Temple L PTS 6 Basingstoke
26.02.99 Des Sowden W PTS 6 Longford
13.03.99 Paul Burke L PTS 6 Manchester
24.04.99 Jan Bergman L RSC 6 Munich, Germany
02.07.99 Keith Jones W PTS 6 Bristol
24.09.99 Woody Greenaway L PTS 6 Merthyr
03.12.99 Darren Underwood W CO 5 Peterborough
20.01.00 Brian Coleman W PTS 6 Piccadilly
24.03.00 Allan Vester L PTS 12 Aarhus, Denmark
(IBF Inter-Continental L. Welterweight Title Challenge)
28.04.00 George Scott L PTS 8 Copenhagen, Denmark
02.06.00 Mohamed Helel W PTS 6 Ashford
25.07.00 Shea Neary L PTS 10 Southwark
01.12.00 David Kirk DREW 8 Peterborough
13.03.01 Eamonn Magee L RSC 5 Plymouth
23.06.01 Keith Jones W PTS 6 Peterborough
23.11.01 Daniel James W RSC 7 Bethnal Green
(Elim. British L. Welterweight Title)
16.03.02 Junior Witter L RSC 3 Northampton
(Vacant British L. Welterweight Title)
Career: 28 contests, won 15, drew 2, lost 11.

Ivan Botton

Newark. *Born* Nottingham, 8 October, 1979
Cruiserweight. Ht. 6'1¼"
Manager D. Smith

20.03.00 Dean Ashton W RSC 2 Mansfield
11.05.00 Matthew Pepper W RSC 4 Newark
29.01.01 Michael Pinnock L PTS 4 Peterborough
02.06.01 Adam Cale W PTS 4 Wakefield
20.04.02 Adam Cale DREW 4 Wembley
11.05.02 Dave Clarke W PTS 6 Newark
Career: 6 contests, won 4, drew 1, lost 1.

Mickey Bowden

Forest Hill. *Born* Lewisham, 30 June, 1975
Featherweight. Ht. 5'8"
Manager Self

25.02.99 Kevin Gerowski W PTS 4 Kentish Town
09.05.99 Graham McGrath W RSC 4 Bracknell
07.08.99 Brendan Bryce W PTS 4 Dagenham
26.05.01 Anthony Hanna W PTS 4 Bethnal Green
25.02.02 Jimmy Beech L PTS 4 Slough
25.04.02 Nelson Valez L PTS 4 Las Vegas, Nevada, USA
Career: 6 contests, won 4, lost 2.

Mark Bowen

Bilston. *Born* Wolverhampton, 11 September, 1974
Lightweight. Ht. 5'7"
Manager P. Bowen

08.03.01 Woody Greenaway DREW 6 Stoke
18.08.01 Mally McIver W RSC 1 Dewsbury
07.02.02 Carl Allen W PTS 6 Stoke
17.04.02 Craig Spacie W PTS 8 Stoke
Career: 4 contests, won 3, drew 1.

Paul Bowen

West Ham. *Born* Barking, 14 May, 1973
L. Heavyweight. Former Undefeated Southern Area S. Middleweight Champion. Ht. 6'0"
Manager Self

13.02.96 Lee Bird W RSC 2 Bethnal Green
13.04.96 Pat Durkin W RSC 3 Wythenshawe
13.07.96 Mark Dawson W RSC 3 Bethnal Green
08.02.97 Darren Ashton W PTS 4 Millwall
29.11.97 Ian Toby W RSC 4 Norwich
17.01.98 Mark Dawson W PTS 4 Bristol
16.05.98 Eddie Knight W RSC 3 Bethnal Green
10.10.98 Enzo Giordano W RSC 10 Bethnal Green
(Vacant Southern Area S. Middleweight Title)
27.02.99 Phil Epton W RSC 2 Oldham
05.06.99 Matthew Barney DREW 10 Cardiff
(Southern Area S. Middleweight Title Defence)
25.07.00 Andy Manning W PTS 4 Southwark
18.11.00 Paul Wesley W PTS 4 Dagenham
03.04.01 Ruben Groenewald L PTS 6 Bethnal Green
18.03.02 Darren Ashton W PTS 6 Crawley
Career: 14 contests, won 12, drew 1, lost 1.

Shaun Bowes

Esh Winning. *Born* Durham, 4 October, 1973
Heavyweight. Ht. 5'10"
Manager G. McCrory

26.04.01 Tony Moran W PTS 6 Gateshead
06.12.01 Paul Bonson L RSC 5 Sunderland
15.03.02 Dave Clarke W PTS 6 Spennymoor
Career: 3 contests, won 2, lost 1.

Christian Brady

Birmingham. *Born* Birmingham, 23 July,
1970
Midlands Area Welterweight Champion.
Ht. 5'8"
Manager Self

02.12.96 Shaun Gledhill W RTD 3 Birmingham
03.03.97 Vic Broomhead W PTS 6 Birmingham
09.06.97 Tony Smith W RSC 4 Birmingham
06.10.97 David Kirk W PTS 6 Birmingham
08.12.97 Craig Kelley W PTS 8 Birmingham
02.03.98 Craig Kelley W RTD 5 Birmingham
08.06.98 Dean Bramhald W PTS 6 Birmingham
12.10.98 Brian Coleman W PTS 6 Birmingham
26.10.98 Darren McInulty W PTS 6 Manchester
26.11.98 Dewi Roberts W RSC 7 Edgbaston
13.03.00 Harry Butler W PTS 6 Birmingham
15.05.00 Delroy Mellis L RSC 6 Birmingham
21.05.01 Matt Scriven W RSC 5 Birmingham
*(Vacant Midlands Area Welterweight
Title)*
08.10.01 Michael Smyth L RSC 3 Birmingham
Career: 14 contests, won 12, lost 2.

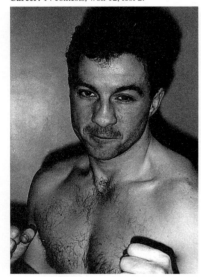

Christian Brady   Les Clark

Joe Brame

London. *Born* Portsmouth, 2 October, 1975
Cruiserweight. Ht. 5'8¼"
Manager J. Bishop

25.02.01 Simon Andrews W RSC 5 Streatham
15.10.01 Oneal Murray L RSC 2 Southampton
08.04.02 Brodie Pearmaine L RSC 1
Southampton
Career: 3 contests, won 1, lost 2.

Joe Brame   Les Clark

Jason Brewster

Coseley. *Born* Wolverhampton, 6 February,
1971
Heavyweight. Ht. 6'1"
Manager Self

23.06.99 Mark Williams DREW 6 West
Bromwich
03.09.99 Adam Cale W PTS 6 West Bromwich
01.10.99 Scott Baker L RTD 5 Cleethorpes
18.02.00 Nigel Rafferty L PTS 6 West
Bromwich
11.05.00 Tony Dowling L RSC 2 Newark
09.06.00 Paul Richardson L PTS 6 Blackpool
10.09.00 Adam Cale W PTS 4 Walsall
06.11.00 Nigel Rafferty W PTS 8
Wolverhampton
13.11.00 Mark McManus L RTD 2 Bethnal
Green
01.04.01 Paul Richardson L RSC 4
Wolverhampton
20.05.01 Kevin Burton W PTS 6
Wolverhampton
07.09.01 Slick Miller W PTS 6 West Bromwich
24.09.01 Lee Nicholson W PTS 6 Cleethorpes
15.12.01 Butch Lesley L RSC 1 Chigwell
17.02.02 Lee Nicholson W PTS 6
Wolverhampton
Career: 15 contests, won 7, drew 1, lost 7.

Michael Brodie

Manchester. *Born* Manchester, 10 May,
1974
WBF Featherweight Champion. Former
Undefeated British, European &
Commonwealth S. Bantamweight
Champion. Ht. 5'6"
Manager J. Trickett

03.10.94 Graham McGrath W RSC 5
Manchester
20.10.94 Chip O'Neill W CO 3 Middleton
28.11.94 Muhammad Shaffique W CO 2
Manchester
13.12.94 Pete Buckley W PTS 6 Potters Bar
16.02.95 G. G. Goddard W PTS 6 Bury
03.04.95 Garry Burrell W RSC 4 Manchester
05.05.95 G. G. Goddard W PTS 6 Swansea
17.05.95 Ian Reid W RSC 3 Ipswich
10.06.95 Chris Clarkson W PTS 6 Manchester
14.11.95 Niel Leggett W CO 1 Bury
25.11.95 Karl Morling W RSC 1 Dagenham
18.12.95 Marty Chestnut W RTD 3 Mayfair
26.02.96 Bamana Dibateza W PTS 6 Manchester
13.04.96 John Sillo W CO 1 Liverpool
07.05.96 Elvis Parsley W RSC 1 Mayfair
06.07.96 Colin Innes W RSC 2 Manchester
19.09.96 Ervine Blake W RSC 4 Manchester
09.11.96 Miguel Matthews W PTS 6 Manchester
22.03.97 Neil Swain W RSC 10 Wythenshawe
(Vacant British S. Bantamweight Title)
30.08.97 Pete Buckley W PTS 8 Cheshunt
01.11.97 Wilson Docherty W CO 4 Glasgow
*(British S. Bantamweight Title Defence.
Vacant Commonwealth
S. Bantamweight Title)*
31.01.98 Brian Carr W RSC 10 Edmonton
*(British & Commonwealth
S. Bantamweight Title Defences)*
23.05.98 Simon Ramoni W PTS 12 Bethnal
Green
*(Commonwealth S. Bantamweight Title
Defence)*
17.10.98 Sergei Devakov W PTS 12 Manchester
*(European S. Bantamweight Title
Challenge)*
13.03.99 Salim Medjkoune W RSC 9
Manchester
*(European S. Bantamweight Title
Defence)*
31.07.99 Serge Poilblan W RSC 12 Carlisle
*(European S. Bantamweight Title
Defence)*
01.10.99 Drew Docherty W RSC 6 Bethnal
Green
*(European S. Bantamweight Title
Defence)*

Michael Brodie   Les Clark

26.02.00 Salim Medjkoune W RSC 9 Carlisle
(European S. Bantamweight Title Defence)
01.07.00 Mustapha Hame W CO 4 Manchester
(European S.Bantamweight Title Defence)
09.09.00 Willie Jorrin L PTS 12 Manchester
(Vacant WBC S.Bantamweight Title)
03.02.01 Sergio Aguila W RSC 4 Manchester
06.10.01 Frederic Bonifai W RSC 5 Manchester
26.11.01 Sean Fletcher W CO 2 Manchester
18.05.02 Pastor Maurin W PTS 12 Millwall
(Vacant WBF Featherweight Title)
Career: 34 contests, won 33, lost 1.

Mark Brookes

Swinton. *Born* Doncaster, 1 December, 1979
L. Heavyweight. Ht. 6'0"
Manager D. Hobson

21.10.00 Rob Galloway W RSC 5 Sheffield
11.12.00 Jimmy Steel W PTS 6 Sheffield
24.03.01 Matthew Pepper W RSC 1 Sheffield
18.06.01 Clint Johnson W PTS 6 Bradford
27.07.01 Michael Pinnock W PTS 4 Sheffield
13.09.01 Darren Ashton W PTS 4 Sheffield
22.09.01 Valery Odin L PTS 4 Canning Town
15.12.01 Clint Johnson W PTS 4 Sheffield
11.05.02 Paul Bonson W PTS 4 Chesterfield
Career: 9 contests, won 8, lost 1.

Mark Brookes   Les Clark

Cathy Brown

Peckham. *Born* Leeds, 28 July, 1970
WBF European Flyweight Champion. Ht. 5'2"
Manager Self

31.10.99 Veerle Braspenningsx W PTS 5 Raynes Park
05.02.00 Veerle Braspenningsx W RSC 6 Sint-Truiden, Belgium
01.07.00 Jan Wild W PTS 6 Southwark
(Vacant WBF European Flyweight Title)

31.10.00 Viktoria Vargal W RSC 3 Hammersmith
28.02.01 Marietta Ivanova W PTS 4 Kensington
26.04.01 Oksana Vasilieva L PTS 4 Kensington
16.06.01 Romona Gughie W RSC 3 Wembley
22.11.01 Audrey Guthrie W PTS 6 Mayfair
(WBF European Flyweight Title Defence)
13.12.01 Ilina Boneva W RSC 5 Leicester Square
13.03.02 Svetla Taskova W PTS 4 Mayfair
13.06.02 Alina Shaternikova L PTS 10 Leicester Square
(Vacant WBF Womens Flyweight Title)
Career: 11 contests, won 9, lost 2.

(Taiwo) Ty Browne

Portsmouth. *Born* London, 28 June, 1977
Middleweight. Ht. 5'8¾"
Manager R. Davies

03.02.01 Chris Duggan W RSC 1 Brighton
05.05.01 Leigh Wicks W PTS 6 Brighton
20.10.01 Harry Butler W PTS 4 Portsmouth
11.02.02 Conroy McIntosh DREW 4 Southampton
08.04.02 Kreshnik Qato L PTS 4 Southampton
21.05.02 Conroy McIntosh DREW 4 Custom House
08.06.02 Tom Cannon L PTS 4 Renfrew
Career: 7 contests, won 3, drew 2, lost 2.

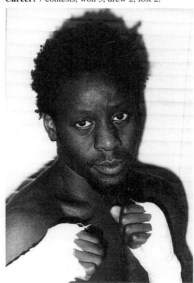

Ty Browne   Les Clark

Darren Bruce

Grays. *Born* Orsett, 1 December, 1972
Former Undefeated IBO Inter-Continental Welterweight Champion. Ht. 5'11"
Manager B. Hearn

28.11.97 Noel Henry W RSC 1 Bethnal Green
27.01.98 Darren McInulty W PTS 4 Bethnal Green
11.03.98 Kevin Lang W RSC 6 Bethnal Green
02.05.98 Harry Butler W RSC 6 Kensington
05.06.98 Leigh Wicks W PTS 6 Southend

08.09.98 Darren McInulty W CO 1 Bethnal Green
31.10.98 Shaun O'Neill W RSC 1 Southend
06.11.98 Delroy Mellis W RTD 3 Mayfair
11.12.98 John Green W RSC 1 Cheshunt
26.02.99 George Richards W PTS 6 Coventry
27.04.99 Dennis Berry W RSC 3 Bethnal Green
29.06.99 Frederic Noto L PTS 10 Bethnal Green
16.10.99 Charlie Kane W RTD 5 Bethnal Green
(Vacant IBO Inter-Continental Welterweight Title)
05.02.00 Michael Smyth W CO 5 Bethnal Green
(IBO Inter-Continental Welterweight Title Defence)
11.03.00 Mark Ramsey DREW 6 Kensington
02.12.00 Willy Wise L PTS 12 Bethnal Green
(Vacant IBO Welterweight Title)
14.07.01 Mark Ramsey L PTS 6 Wembley
29.06.02 Peter Dunn W PTS 6 Brentwood
Career: 18 contests, won 14, drew 1, lost 3.

Alston Buchanan

Glasgow. *Born* Glasgow, 25 December, 1972
Featherweight. Ht. 5'5"
Manager T. Gilmour

26.04.96 Amjid Mahmood W RTD 1 Glasgow
24.05.96 Marty Chestnut W PTS 6 Glasgow
20.09.96 Gary Hickman W PTS 6 Glasgow
29.11.96 Pete Buckley W PTS 8 Glasgow
12.02.97 Benny Jones L CO 5 Glasgow
02.06.97 Jason Whitaker W RSC 6 Glasgow
26.01.98 John Barnes W PTS 6 Glasgow
23.02.98 Nicky Wilders W RSC 2 Glasgow
27.04.98 Pete Buckley W PTS 8 Glasgow
21.09.98 Kevin Sheil W PTS 8 Glasgow
26.02.99 Nicky Wilders W CO 1 Irvine
22.03.99 Kevin Gerowski W PTS 6 Glasgow
07.06.99 Anthony Hanna L RSC 3 Glasgow
03.06.02 Tasawar Khan L RSC 3 Glasgow
Career: 14 contests, won 11, lost 3.

Andrew Buchanan

West Denton. *Born* Newcastle, 24 March, 1980
Middleweight. Ht. 6'0"
Manager T. Conroy

01.12.00 Paul Johnson W PTS 4 Peterborough
28.03.01 Wayne Shepherd W RSC 2 Piccadilly
26.04.01 Steve Timms W RSC 4 Gateshead
18.03.02 Jason Collins L PTS 4 Crawley
Career: 4 contests, won 3, lost 1.

Paul Buchanan

West Denton. *Born* Newcastle, 23 October, 1981
S. Middleweight. Ht. 5'10"
Manager T. Conroy

31.01.01 Gary Jones W RTD 1 Piccadilly
26.04.01 Lee Woodruff W PTS 6 Gateshead
08.03.02 Neil Bonner W PTS 6 Ellesmere Port
25.03.02 Dean Cockburn W PTS 6 Sunderland
Career: 4 contests, won 4.

Pete Buckley

Birmingham. *Born* Birmingham, 9 March, 1969
Lightweight. Former Undefeated Midlands

Area S. Featherweight Champion. Former
Midlands Area S. Bantamweight
Champion. Ht. 5'8"
Manager Self

04.10.89	Alan Baldwin DREW 6 Stafford
10.10.89	Ronnie Stephenson L PTS 6 Wolverhampton
30.10.89	Robert Braddock W PTS 6 Birmingham
14.11.89	Neil Leitch W PTS 6 Evesham
22.11.89	Peter Judson W PTS 6 Stafford
11.12.89	Stevie Woods W PTS 6 Bradford
21.12.89	Wayne Taylor W PTS 6 Kings Heath
10.01.90	John O'Meara W PTS 6 Kensington
19.02.90	Ian McGirr L PTS 6 Birmingham
27.02.90	Miguel Matthews DREW 6 Evesham
14.03.90	Ronnie Stephenson DREW 6 Stoke
04.04.90	Ronnie Stephenson L PTS 8 Stafford
23.04.90	Ronnie Stephenson W PTS 6 Birmingham
30.04.90	Chris Clarkson L PTS 8 Mayfair
17.05.90	Johnny Bredahl L PTS 6 Aars, Denmark
04.06.90	Ronnie Stephenson W PTS 8 Birmingham
28.06.90	Robert Braddock W RSC 5 Birmingham
01.10.90	Miguel Matthews W PTS 8 Cleethorpes
09.10.90	Miguel Matthews L PTS 8 Wolverhampton
17.10.90	Tony Smith W PTS 6 Stoke
29.10.90	Miguel Matthews W PTS 8 Birmingham
21.11.90	Drew Docherty L PTS 8 Solihull
10.12.90	Neil Leitch W PTS 8 Birmingham
10.01.91	Duke McKenzie L RSC 5 Wandsworth
18.02.91	Jamie McBride L PTS 8 Glasgow
04.03.91	Brian Robb W RSC 7 Birmingham
26.03.91	Neil Leitch DREW 8 Wolverhampton
01.05.91	Mark Geraghty W PTS 8 Solihull
05.06.91	Brian Robb W PTS 10 Wolverhampton *(Vacant Midlands Area S. Featherweight Title)*
09.09.91	Mike Deveney L PTS 8 Glasgow
24.09.91	Mark Bates W RTD 5 Basildon
29.10.91	John Armour L PTS 6 Kensington
14.11.91	Mike Deveney L PTS 6 Edinburgh
28.11.91	Craig Dermody L PTS 6 Liverpool
19.12.91	Craig Dermody L PTS 6 Oldham
18.01.92	Alan McKay DREW 8 Kensington
20.02.92	Brian Robb W RSC 10 Oakengates *(Midlands Area S. Featherweight Title Defence)*
27.04.92	Drew Docherty L PTS 8 Glasgow
15.05.92	Ruben Condori L PTS 10 Augsburg, Germany
29.05.92	Donnie Hood L PTS 8 Glasgow
07.09.92	Duke McKenzie L RTD 3 Bethnal Green
12.11.92	Prince Naseem Hamed L PTS 6 Liverpool
19.02.93	Harald Geier L PTS 12 Vienna, Austria *(Vacant WBA Penta-Continental S. Bantamweight Title)*
26.04.93	Bradley Stone L PTS 8 Lewisham
18.06.93	Eamonn McAuley L PTS 6 Belfast
01.07.93	Tony Silkstone L PTS 8 York
06.10.93	Jonjo Irwin L PTS 8 Solihull
25.10.93	Drew Docherty L PTS 8 Glasgow
06.11.93	Michael Alldis L PTS 8 Bethnal Green
30.11.93	Barry Jones L PTS 4 Cardiff
19.12.93	Shaun Anderson L PTS 6 Glasgow
22.01.94	Barry Jones L PTS 6 Cardiff
29.01.94	Prince Naseem Hamed L RSC 4 Cardiff
10.03.94	Tony Falcone L PTS 4 Bristol
29.03.94	Conn McMullen W PTS 6 Bethnal Green
05.04.94	Mark Bowers L PTS 6 Bethnal Green
13.04.94	James Murray L PTS 6 Glasgow
06.05.94	Paul Lloyd L RTD 4 Liverpool
03.08.94	Greg Upton L PTS 6 Bristol
26.09.94	John Sillo L PTS 6 Liverpool
05.10.94	Matthew Harris L PTS 6 Wolverhampton
07.11.94	Marlon Ward L PTS 4 Piccadilly
23.11.94	Justin Murphy L PTS 4 Piccadilly
29.11.94	Neil Swain L PTS 6 Cardiff
13.12.94	Michael Brodie L PTS 6 Potters Bar
20.12.94	Michael Alldis L PTS 6 Bethnal Green
10.02.95	Matthew Harris L RSC 6 Birmingham *(Midlands Area S. Bantamweight Title Challenge)*
23.02.95	Paul Ingle L PTS 8 Southwark
20.04.95	John Sillo L PTS 6 Liverpool
27.04.95	Paul Ingle L PTS 8 Bethnal Green
09.05.95	Ady Lewis L PTS 4 Basildon
23.05.95	Spencer Oliver L PTS 4 Potters Bar
01.07.95	Dean Pithie L PTS 4 Kensington
21.09.95	Patrick Mullings L PTS 6 Battersea
29.09.95	Marlon Ward L PTS 4 Bethnal Green
25.10.95	Matthew Harris L PTS 10 Telford *(Midlands Area S. Bantamweight Title Defence)*
08.11.95	Vince Feeney L PTS 8 Bethnal Green
28.11.95	Barry Jones L PTS 6 Cardiff
15.12.95	Patrick Mullings L PTS 4 Bethnal Green
05.02.96	Patrick Mullings L PTS 8 Bexleyheath
09.03.96	Paul Griffin L PTS 4 Millstreet
21.03.96	Colin McMillan L RSC 3 Southwark
14.05.96	Venkatesan Deverajan L PTS 4 Dagenham
29.06.96	Matt Brown W RSC 1 Erith
03.09.96	Vince Feeney L PTS 4 Bethnal Green
28.09.96	Fabrice Benichou L PTS 8 Barking
09.10.96	Gary Marston DREW 8 Stoke
06.11.96	Neil Swain L PTS 4 Tylorstown
29.11.96	Alston Buchanan L PTS 8 Glasgow
22.12.96	Brian Carr L PTS 6 Glasgow
11.01.97	Scott Harrison L PTS 4 Bethnal Green
29.01.97	Carl Allen L PTS 8 Stoke
12.02.97	Ronnie McPhee L PTS 6 Glasgow
25.02.97	Dean Pithie L PTS 4 Sheffield
07.03.97	Jason Booth L PTS 6 Northampton
20.03.97	Thomas Bradley W PTS 6 Newark
08.04.97	Sergei Devakov L PTS 6 Bethnal Green
25.04.97	Matthew Harris L PTS 6 Cleethorpes
08.05.97	Gregorio Medina L RTD 2 Mansfield
13.06.97	Mike Deveney L PTS 6 Paisley
19.07.97	Richard Evatt L PTS 4 Wembley
30.08.97	Michael Brodie L PTS 8 Cheshunt
06.10.97	Brendan Bryce W PTS 6 Piccadilly
20.10.97	Kelton McKenzie L PTS 6 Leicester
20.11.97	Ervine Blake L PTS 8 Solihull
06.12.97	Danny Adams L PTS 4 Wembley
13.12.97	Gary Thornhill L PTS 6 Sheffield
31.01.98	Scott Harrison L PTS 4 Edmonton
05.03.98	Steve Conway L PTS 6 Leeds
18.03.98	Ervine Blake L PTS 8 Stoke
26.03.98	Graham McGrath W RTD 4 Solihull
11.04.98	Salim Medjkoune L PTS 6 Southwark
18.04.98	Tony Mulholland L PTS 4 Manchester
27.04.98	Alston Buchanan L PTS 8 Glasgow
11.05.98	Jason Squire W RTD 2 Leicester
21.05.98	Lee Armstrong L PTS 6 Bradford
06.06.98	Tony Mulholland L PTS 6 Liverpool
14.06.98	Lee Armstrong L PTS 6 Shaw
21.07.98	David Burke L PTS 6 Widnes
05.09.98	Michael Gomez L PTS 6 Telford
17.09.98	Brian Carr L PTS 6 Glasgow
03.10.98	Justin Murphy L PTS 6 Crawley
05.12.98	Lehlohonolo Ledwaba L PTS 8 Bristol
19.12.98	Acelino Freitas L RTD 3 Liverpool
09.02.99	Chris Jickells L PTS 6 Wolverhampton
16.02.99	Franny Hogg L PTS 6 Leeds
26.02.99	Richard Evatt L RSC 5 Coventry
17.04.99	Martin O'Malley L RSC 3 Dublin
29.05.99	Richie Wenton L PTS 6 Halifax
14.06.99	Carl Allen L PTS 6 Birmingham
26.06.99	Paul Halpin L PTS 4 Millwall
15.07.99	Salim Medjkoune L PTS 6 Peterborough
07.08.99	Steve Murray L PTS 6 Dagenham
12.09.99	Kevin Gerowski L PTS 6 Nottingham
20.09.99	Mat Zegan L PTS 6 Peterborough
02.10.99	Jason Cook L PTS 4 Cardiff
09.10.99	Brian Carr L PTS 6 Manchester
19.10.99	Gary Steadman L PTS 6 Bethnal Green
27.10.99	Miguel Matthews W PTS 8 Birmingham
20.11.99	Carl Greaves L PTS 10 Grantham *(British Masters S. Featherweight Title Challenge)*
11.12.99	Gary Thornhill L PTS 6 Liverpool
29.01.00	Bradley Pryce L PTS 4 Manchester
19.02.00	Gavin Rees L PTS 4 Dagenham
29.02.00	Tony Mulholland L PTS 4 Widnes
20.03.00	Carl Greaves L PTS 4 Mansfield
27.03.00	James Rooney L PTS 4 Barnsley
08.04.00	Delroy Pryce L PTS 4 Bethnal Green
17.04.00	Franny Hogg L PTS 8 Glasgow
11.05.00	Craig Spacie L PTS 4 Newark
25.05.00	Jimmy Phelan DREW 6 Hull
19.06.00	Delroy Pryce L PTS 4 Burton
01.07.00	Richard Evatt L PTS 4 Manchester
16.09.00	Lee Meager L PTS 4 Bethnal Green
23.09.00	Gavin Rees L PTS 4 Bethnal Green
02.10.00	Brian Carr L PTS 4 Glasgow
14.10.00	Gareth Jordan L PTS 4 Wembley
13.11.00	Kevin Lear L PTS 6 Bethnal Green
24.11.00	Lee Williamson L PTS 6 Hull
09.12.00	Leo O'Reilly L PTS 4 Southwark
15.01.01	Eddie Nevins L PTS 4 Manchester
23.01.01	David Burke L PTS 4 Crawley
31.01.01	Tony Montana L PTS 6 Piccadilly
19.02.01	Kevin England W PTS 6 Glasgow
12.03.01	Carl Allen L PTS 6 Birmingham
19.03.01	Duncan Armstrong L PTS 6 Glasgow
27.03.01	Carl Allen L PTS 8 Brierley Hill
05.05.01	Danny Hunt L PTS 4 Edmonton
09.06.01	Gary Thornhill L PTS 4 Bethnal Green
21.07.01	Scott Miller L PTS 4 Sheffield
28.07.01	Kevin Lear L PTS 4 Wembley
25.09.01	Ricky Eccleston L PTS 4 Liverpool
07.10.01	Nigel Senior L PTS 6 Wolverhampton
31.10.01	Woody Greenaway L PTS 6 Birmingham
16.11.01	Jimmy Beech L PTS 6 West Bromwich
01.12.01	Chill John L PTS 4 Bethnal Green
09.12.01	Nigel Senior W PTS 6 Shaw
26.01.02	Scott Lawton L PTS 4 Bethnal Green
09.02.02	Sam Gorman L PTS 6 Coventry
23.02.02	Alex Moon L PTS 4 Nottingham
04.03.02	Leo Turner L PTS 6 Bradford
11.03.02	Martin Watson L PTS 4 Glasgow
26.04.02	Scott Lawton L PTS 4 Coventry
10.05.02	Lee Meager L PTS 6 Bethnal Green
08.06.02	Bradley Pryce L RSC 1 Renfrew

Career: 184 contests, won 28, drew 7, lost 149.

David Burke

Liverpool. *Born* Liverpool, 3 February, 1975
Lightweight. Ht. 5'9"
Manager J. Hyland

01.03.97	Ervine Blake W PTS 4 Liverpool
21.05.97	Carl Allen W PTS 4 Liverpool
26.09.97	Rudy Valentino W PTS 4 Liverpool
12.03.98	Bamana Dibateza W PTS 6 Liverpool
08.04.98	John O. Johnson W RSC 1 Liverpool
23.05.98	Mike Deveney W PTS 6 Bethnal Green
21.07.98	Pete Buckley W PTS 6 Widnes
24.10.98	Gary Flear W PTS 6 Liverpool
12.12.98	Justin Murphy W RSC 4 Southwark
05.03.99	Alan Temple W PTS 8 Liverpool
15.05.99	Marian Leonardu L RSC 3 Blackpool
19.06.99	Chris Williams W RTD 1 Dublin
13.12.99	Chris Jickells W PTS 6 Glasgow
09.03.00	Woody Greenaway W RSC 2 Liverpool
23.01.01	Pete Buckley W PTS 4 Crawley
03.02.01	Keith Jones W PTS 4 Manchester
03.03.01	Marco Fattore W RSC 1 Wembley
24.04.01	Jason Dee W RSC 1 Liverpool
26.05.01	Matthew Zulu W PTS 6 Bethnal Green
25.09.01	Richard Howard W PTS 6 Liverpool
09.03.02	Anthony Maynard W PTS 6 Manchester

Career: 21 contests, won 20, lost 1.

Matthew Burke

Stratford. *Born* London, 7 October, 1980
Lightweight. Ht. 5'11¼"
Manager B. Hearn

29.06.02	Joel Viney W PTS 4 Brentwood

Career: 1 contest, won 1.

Ricky Burns

Coatbridge. *Born* Bellshill, 13 April, 1983
L. Welterweight. Ht. 5'10"
Manager R. Bannan

20.10.01	Woody Greenaway W PTS 4 Glasgow
15.03.02	Peter Allen W PTS 6 Glasgow
08.06.02	Gary Harrison W RSC 1 Renfrew

Career: 3 contests, won 3.

Pinky Burton

Sheffield. *Born* Perth, 13 December, 1979
L. Heavyweight. Ht. 5'11½"
Manager F. Warren

28.04.01	Nathan King L PTS 4 Cardiff
28.01.02	Rob Galloway W RSC 4 Barnsley
02.03.02	Darren Ashton W PTS 6 Wakefield

Career: 3 contests, won 2, lost 1.

Robert Burton

Barnsley. *Born* Barnsley, 1 April, 1971
Central Area Welterweight Champion.
Ht. 5'9"
Manager T. Schofield

05.02.01	Gavin Pearson W RSC 3 Bradford
23.02.01	Scott Millar W CO 5 Irvine
20.03.01	Peter Dunn W PTS 6 Leeds
08.05.01	Arv Mittoo W PTS 4 Barnsley
10.06.01	Martyn Bailey DREW 6 Ellesmere Port
08.10.01	Gavin Pearson W RSC 2 Barnsley
16.11.01	Martyn Bailey DREW 4 Preston
24.11.01	Peter Dunn L PTS 6 Wakefield
28.01.02	Peter Dunn W RSC 8 Barnsley
	(Vacant Central Area Welterweight Title)

Career: 9 contests, won 6, drew 2, lost 1.

Robert Burton   Les Clark

Harry Butler

Worcester. *Born* Wisbech, 12 August, 1977
S. Middleweight. Ht. 5'8"
Manager Self

19.07.97	Mehrdud Takaloo L RSC 1 Wembley
30.08.97	Patrick Pasi L PTS 4 Cheshunt
26.09.97	Darren Williams L PTS 6 Port Talbot
21.10.97	John Green L PTS 6 Yarm
15.11.97	Michael Jones L PTS 4 Bristol
02.12.97	Ross McCord W RSC 3 Swansea
13.12.97	Hercules Kyvelos L PTS 4 Sheffield
06.01.98	Alan Gilbert L PTS 4 Brighton
13.02.98	Gareth Hogg L RSC 3 Weston super Mare
14.03.98	Sonny Thind L PTS 4 Bethnal Green
03.04.98	Jon Foster L PTS 6 Ebbw Vale
18.04.98	Anthony Farnell L PTS 6 Manchester
02.05.98	Darren Bruce L RSC 6 Kensington
04.06.98	Adrian Houldey L PTS 6 Dudley
14.06.98	Gerard Lawrence L PTS 6 Golders Green
08.08.98	Sonny Pollard W RSC 4 Scarborough
05.09.98	Jawaid Khaliq L PTS 4 Telford
26.09.98	James Lowther L RSC 6 York
21.11.98	Brian Knudsen L RSC 4 Southwark
18.02.99	Clive Johnson L PTS 6 Barking
05.03.99	Paul Burns L RSC 5 Liverpool
23.04.99	Jason Williams L RSC 7 Clydach
26.06.99	Lawrence Murphy L RSC 1 Glasgow
19.09.99	Mick Mulcahy L PTS 6 Shaw
14.10.99	Lester Jacobs L PTS 6 Bloomsbury
06.11.99	Junior Witter L PTS 6 Widnes
06.12.99	Malcolm Melvin L PTS 8 Birmingham
20.12.99	Richard Williams L RSC 1 Bethnal Green
26.02.00	Jason Cook L PTS 6 Swansea
13.03.00	Christian Brady L PTS 6 Birmingham
20.03.00	Jamie Moore L RSC 2 Mansfield
15.05.00	Ernie Smith W PTS 6 Birmingham
26.05.00	Barry Connell L PTS 4 Glasgow
21.09.00	Ojay Abrahams L PTS 6 Bloomsbury
07.10.00	Michael Alexander L PTS 6 Doncaster
26.10.00	Matthew Ashmole W PTS 6 Clydach
23.11.00	Matthew Barr L PTS 4 Bayswater
30.11.00	Shpetim Hoti W PTS 4 Bloomsbury
11.12.00	Jimmy Vincent L PTS 6 Birmingham
28.01.01	Peter Jackson L PTS 6 Wolverhampton
10.02.01	Thomas McDonagh L PTS 6 Widnes
24.02.01	Spencer Fearon L PTS 4 Bethnal Green
09.03.01	John Humphrey L RSC 1 Millwall
22.04.01	Ojay Abrahams L PTS 6 Streatham
05.05.01	Liam Lathbury L PTS 6 Brighton
19.05.01	Delroy Leslie L PTS 6 Wembley
21.06.01	Shpetim Hoti W PTS 4 Earls Court
04.07.01	Darren Covill W RSC 4 Bloomsbury
26.07.01	Lee Blundell L RSC 4 Blackpool
20.09.01	Ruben Groenewald L PTS 4 Blackfriars
08.10.01	Roddy Doran L PTS 6 Birmingham
20.10.01	Ty Browne L PTS 4 Portsmouth
31.10.01	Roddy Doran DREW 6 Birmingham
16.11.01	Mark Richards L PTS 6 West Bromwich
23.11.01	Erik Teymour L RSC 2 Bethnal Green
26.01.02	Jamie Moore L RSC 3 Dagenham
04.03.02	Malcolm Melvin L PTS 8 Birmingham
15.03.02	Tom Cannon L PTS 6 Glasgow
24.04.02	Jim Rock L PTS 6 Dublin
11.05.02	Jason McKay L PTS 4 Dagenham
01.06.02	Mickey Quinn L PTS 4 Manchester
15.06.02	Darren Rhodes L PTS 4 Leeds

Career: 62 contests, won 7, drew 1, lost 54.

Paul Buttery

Preston. *Born* Preston, 12 May, 1977
Heavyweight. Ht. 6'2½"
Manager B. Devine

03.02.01	Luke Simpkin L RSC 1 Manchester
24.04.01	Dave Faulkner W CO 1 Liverpool
16.11.01	Eamonn Glennon W RSC 1 Preston
10.05.02	Tony Booth W PTS 4 Preston

Career: 4 contests, won 3, lost 1.

Lee Byrne

Manchester. *Born* Manchester, 23 July, 1981
Welterweight. Ht. 5'7"
Manager J. Trickett

09.09.00	Ram Singh W RSC 2 Manchester
14.07.01	Arv Mittoo W PTS 4 Wembley
06.10.01	Peter Dunn W RSC 4 Manchester
26.11.01	Young Muttley L RSC 1 Manchester

Career: 4 contests, won 3, lost 1.

Tony Byrne

Preston. *Born* Preston, 17 November, 1978
L. Middleweight. Ht. 5'7"
Manager Self

10.06.01	Paul Lomax W PTS 6 Ellesmere Port
16.11.01	Gary Jones W PTS 6 Preston
09.12.01	Paul Lomax W PTS 6 Blackpool
08.02.02	Jamie Logan W RTD 3 Preston
08.03.02	Andrei Ivanov W PTS 6 Ellesmere Port
10.05.02	Scott Millar W RSC 2 Preston

Career: 6 contests, won 6.

Adam Cale

Worcester. *Born* Worcester, 11 April, 1972
Cruiserweight. Ht. 6'2"
Manager Self

04.06.98	Matthew Barney L PTS 6 Barking
23.07.98	Matthew Barney L PTS 6 Barking
07.10.98	Kevin Burton W PTS 6 Stoke
31.10.98	Faisal Mohammed L RSC 2 Basingstoke
09.02.99	Kevin Burton W PTS 8 Wolverhampton
26.02.99	Neil Simpson L RSC 3 Coventry
27.05.99	Carl Smallwood L PTS 6 Edgbaston
06.06.99	Wayne Buck L PTS 6 Nottingham
22.06.99	Scott Baker L PTS 4 Ipswich
20.08.99	Matthew Barney L PTS 4 Bloomsbury
03.09.99	Jason Brewster L PTS 6 West Bromwich
20.09.99	Kenny Gayle L PTS 4 Peterborough
27.09.99	Tony Booth L PTS 6 Cleethorpes
11.10.99	Stevie Pettit L PTS 6 Birmingham
20.10.99	Stevie Pettit L PTS 6 Stoke
08.12.99	Nigel Rafferty L PTS 6 Stoke
12.02.00	Tony Dowling L PTS 4 Sheffield
26.02.00	Chris Davies L RSC 4 Swansea
18.05.00	Elvis Michailenko L PTS 4 Bethnal Green
16.06.00	Scott Baker L PTS 4 Bloomsbury
10.09.00	Jason Brewster L PTS 4 Walsall
21.10.00	Scott Lansdowne L RSC 5 Sheffield
25.11.00	Peter Haymer L RSC 1 Manchester
22.04.01	Radcliffe Green L CO 5 Streatham
02.06.01	Ivan Botton L PTS 4 Wakefield
26.07.01	Eamonn Glennon L PTS 6 Blackpool
26.08.01	Peter Merrall L PTS 6 Warrington
09.09.01	Rob Hayes-Scott L RSC 1 Southwark
01.11.01	Mark Ellwood L PTS 6 Hull
16.11.01	Gary Thompson L PTS 6 Preston
22.11.01	Tony Strong L CO 1 Mayfair
27.01.02	Oneal Murray L PTS 6 Streatham
12.02.02	Tommy Eastwood L PTS 4 Bethnal Green
08.03.02	Spencer Wilding L PTS 6 Ellesmere Port
19.03.02	Blue Stevens L RSC 4 Slough
20.04.02	Ivan Botton DREW 4 Wembley
02.06.02	Darren Stubbs L RSC 6 Shaw

Career: 37 contests, won 2, drew 1, lost 34.

Marc Callaghan

Barking. *Born* Barking, 13 November, 1977
S. Bantamweight. Ht. 5'6"
Manager B. Hearn

08.09.98	Kevin Sheil W PTS 4 Bethnal Green
31.10.98	Nicky Wilders W RSC 1 Southend
12.01.99	Nicky Wilders W RTD 2 Bethnal Green
12.03.99	Peter Allen W PTS 4 Bethnal Green
25.05.99	Simon Chambers L RSC 1 Mayfair
16.10.99	Nigel Leake W PTS 4 Bethnal Green
20.12.99	Marc Smith W PTS 4 Bethnal Green
05.02.00	Steve Brook W RSC 2 Bethnal Green
01.04.00	John Barnes W PTS 4 Bethnal Green
19.08.00	Anthony Hanna W PTS 4 Brentwood
09.10.00	Jamie McKeever L PTS 6 Liverpool
04.11.00	Nigel Senior W RSC 4 Bethnal Green
03.03.01	Anthony Hanna W PTS 6 Wembley
26.05.01	Roy Rutherford L RSC 3 Bethnal Green
01.12.01	Nigel Senior L CO 1 Bethnal Green
26.01.02	Richmond Asante W PTS 4 Dagenham
18.03.02	Michael Hunter DREW 6 Crawley
11.05.02	Andrew Ferrans W PTS 6 Dagenham

Career: 18 contests, won 13, drew 1, lost 4.

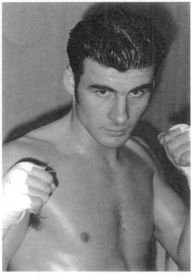

Joe Calzaghe   Les Clark

Joe Calzaghe

Newbridge. *Born* Hammersmith, 23 March, 1972
WBO S. Middleweight Champion. Former Undefeated British S. Middleweight Champion. Ht. 5'11"
Manager F. Warren

01.10.93	Paul Hanlon W RSC 1 Cardiff
10.11.93	Stinger Mason W RSC 1 Watford
16.12.93	Spencer Alton W RSC 2 Newport
22.01.94	Martin Rosamond W RSC 1 Cardiff
01.03.94	Darren Littlewood W RSC 1 Dudley
04.06.94	Karl Barwise W RSC 1 Cardiff
01.10.94	Mark Dawson W RSC 1 Cardiff
30.11.94	Trevor Ambrose W RSC 2 Wolverhampton
14.02.95	Frank Minton W CO 1 Bethnal Green
22.02.95	Bobbi Joe Edwards W PTS 8 Telford
19.05.95	Robert Curry W RSC 1 Southwark
08.07.95	Tyrone Jackson W RSC 4 York
30.09.95	Nick Manners W RSC 4 Basildon
28.10.95	Stephen Wilson W RSC 8 Kensington
	(Vacant British S. Middleweight Title)
13.02.96	Guy Stanford W RSC 1 Cardiff
13.03.96	Anthony Brooks W RSC 2 Wembley
20.04.96	Mark Delaney W RSC 5 Brentwood
	(British S. Middleweight Title Defence)
04.05.96	Warren Stowe W RTD 2 Dagenham
15.05.96	Pat Lawlor W RSC 2 Cardiff
21.01.97	Carlos Christie W CO 2 Bristol
22.03.97	Tyler Hughes W CO 1 Wythenshawe
05.06.97	Luciano Torres W RSC 3 Bristol
11.10.97	Chris Eubank W PTS 12 Sheffield
	(Vacant WBO S. Middleweight Title)

24.01.98	Branco Sobot W RSC 3 Cardiff
	(WBO S. Middleweight Title Defence)
25.04.98	Juan Carlos Gimenez W RTD 9 Cardiff
	(WBO S. Middleweight Title Defence)
13.02.99	Robin Reid W PTS 12 Newcastle
	(WBO S. Middleweight Title Defence)
05.06.99	Rick Thornberry W PTS 12 Cardiff
	(WBO S. Middleweight Title Defence)
29.01.00	David Starie W PTS 12 Manchester
	(WBO S. Middleweight Title Defence)
12.08.00	Omar Sheika W RSC 5 Wembley
	(WBO S.Middleweight Title Defence)
16.12.00	Richie Woodhall W RSC 10 Sheffield
	(WBO S. Middleweight Title Defence)
28.04.01	Mario Veit W RSC 1 Cardiff
	(WBO S. Middleweight Title Defence)
13.10.01	Will McIntyre W RSC 4 Copenhagen, Denmark
	(WBO S. Middleweight Title Defence)
20.04.02	Charles Brewer W PTS 12 Cardiff
	(WBO S. Middleweight Title Defence)

Career: 33 contests, won 33.

Alan Campbell

Kirkham. *Born* Greenock, 5 April, 1974
L. Middleweight. Ht. 5'11"
Manager L. Veitch

08.03.01	Richard Inquieti W PTS 6 Blackpool
26.07.01	Brian Gifford W PTS 6 Blackpool

Career: 2 contests, won 2.

Alan Campbell   Les Clark

Tom Cannon

Coatbridge. *Born* Bellshill, 18 March, 1980
Middleweight. Ht. 5'11½"
Manager R. Bannon

15.06.01	Valery Odin L PTS 4 Millwall
20.10.01	Andrew Lowe L PTS 4 Glasgow
26.01.02	Arthur Chekmuroz DREW 4 Bethnal Green
15.03.02	Harry Butler W PTS 6 Glasgow
08.06.02	Ty Browne W PTS 4 Renfrew

Career: 5 contests, won 2, drew 1, lost 2.

Mickey Cantwell

Eltham. *Born* London, 23 November, 1964
Former Undefeated British Flyweight
Champion. Former Undefeated Southern
Area Flyweight Champion. Ht. 5'2½"
Manager Self

21.01.91	Eduardo Vallejo W RSC 4 Crystal Palace	
26.03.91	Mario Alberto Cruz W PTS 6 Bethnal Green	
30.09.91	Ricky Beard W PTS 8 Kensington	
23.10.91	Carlos Manrigues W RSC 5 Bethnal Green	
14.12.91	Shaun Norman W PTS 8 Bexleyheath	
16.05.92	Louis Veitch W PTS 6 Muswell Hill	
10.02.93	Louis Veitch DREW 8 Lewisham	
14.04.93	Daren Fifield W PTS 10 Kensington	
	(Vacant Southern Area Flyweight Title)	
15.09.93	Pablo Tiznado L PTS 12 Bethnal Green	
	(Vacant WBC International L. Flyweight Title)	
03.11.93	Anthony Hanna W PTS 8 Bristol	
27.04.94	Luigi Camputaro L PTS 12 Bethnal Green	
	(European Flyweight Title Challenge)	
15.06.94	Lyndon Kershaw L PTS 8 Southwark	
27.04.95	Anthony Hanna W PTS 6 Bethnal Green	
02.07.95	Anthony Hanna W PTS 6 Dublin	
21.03.96	Keith Knox W PTS 12 Southwark	
	(Vacant British Flyweight Title)	
29.06.96	Krasimir Tcholakov W PTS 6 Erith	
08.02.97	Jacob Matlala L PTS 12 Millwall	
	(WBO L. Flyweight Title Challenge)	
03.05.97	David Coldwell W PTS 8 Manchester	
19.12.97	Eric Jamili L RSC 8 Millwall	
	(Vacant WBO M. Flyweight Title)	
01.05.99	David Coldwell W PTS 6 Crystal Palace	
02.06.00	Zolani Petelo L RSC 8 Ashford	
	(IBF M. Flyweight Title Challenge)	
29.09.01	Jake Matlala L RSC 5 Southwark	
	(WBU L.Flyweight Title Challenge)	

Career: 22 contests, won 14, drew 1, lost 7.

Richie Caparelli (Cas)

Blackburn. *Born* Canada, 24 July, 1968
L. Welterweight. Ht. 5'6½"
Manager T. Miller

06.12.01	Nicky Leech L PTS 6 Stoke
16.12.01	Martin Watson L PTS 6 Glasgow
17.02.02	Gary Reid L PTS 6 Salford
15.03.02	Tony McPake L RSC 3 Glasgow
17.04.02	Robbie Sivyer L RSC 6 Stoke

Career: 5 contests, lost 5.

(Barry) Baz Carey

Coventry. *Born* Coventry, 11 March, 1971
S. Featherweight. Ht. 5'4½"
Manager J. Griffin

19.12.01	J.J. Moore L PTS 4 Coventry
18.01.02	J.J. Moore DREW 4 Coventry
25.02.02	Chris McDonagh L PTS 6 Slough
19.03.02	Ilias Miah W PTS 6 Slough

Career: 4 contests, won 1, drew 1, lost 2.

Baz Carey   Les Clark

Dafydd Carlin

Belfast. *Born* Brecon, 2 August, 1978
L. Welterweight. Ht. 5'6"
Manager A. Wilton

01.04.01	Paddy Folan W PTS 4 Southwark
28.04.01	Alex Arthur L PTS 4 Cardiff
03.06.01	Dave Hinds W PTS 4 Southwark
22.09.01	Danny Hunt L PTS 4 Bethnal Green
15.12.01	Matthew Hatton L PTS 6 Wembley
19.01.02	Francis Barrett L PTS 4 Bethnal Green
12.02.02	Scott Miller L PTS 4 Bethnal Green
20.04.02	Bradley Pryce L RSC 8 Cardiff

Career: 8 contests, won 2, lost 6.

Dafydd Carlin   Les Clark

Brian Carr

Moodiesburn. *Born* Glasgow, 20 June, 1969
Former Commonwealth S. Bantamweight
Champion. Scottish Featherweight
Champion. Ht. 5'6"
Manager A. Morrison

18.12.94	Fred Reeve W CO 2 Glasgow	
21.01.95	Shaun Anderson W PTS 6 Glasgow	
04.03.95	G. G. Goddard W PTS 8 Livingston	
13.05.95	Paul Wynn W RTD 2 Glasgow	
08.06.95	Abdul Manna W PTS 6 Glasgow	
13.10.95	Muhammad Shaffique W PTS 6 Glasgow	
17.12.95	Abdul Mannon W PTS 8 Glasgow	
16.03.96	Chip O'Neill W PTS 4 Glasgow	
26.04.96	Mike Deveney W PTS 10 Glasgow	
	(Vacant Scottish Featherweight Title)	
20.09.96	Fred Reeve W RSC 3 Glasgow	
06.11.96	Mike Deveney W PTS 10 Glasgow	
	(Scottish Featherweight Title Defence)	
22.12.96	Pete Buckley W PTS 6 Glasgow	
04.04.97	Lyndon Kershaw W PTS 10 Glasgow	
	(Elim. British S. Bantamweight Title)	
05.07.97	Kevin Sheil W RSC 5 Glasgow	
12.09.97	Carl Allen W PTS 8 Glasgow	
01.11.97	Steve Conway W PTS 6 Glasgow	
31.01.98	Michael Brodie L RSC 10 Edmonton	
	(British & Commonwealth S. Bantamweight Title Challenges)	
17.09.98	Pete Buckley W PTS 6 Glasgow	
06.02.99	Patrick Mullings L PTS 12 Halifax	
	(Vacant British S. Bantamweight Title)	
27.02.99	Fondil Madani W CO 3 Bethnal Green	
09.04.99	Keith Jones W PTS 8 Glasgow	
26.06.99	Cassius Baloyi L RTD 9 Glasgow	
	(WBU Featherweight Title Challenge)	
09.10.99	Pete Buckley W PTS 6 Manchester	
12.11.99	Harry Woods W PTS 6 Glasgow	
11.12.99	Lee Williamson DREW 6 Liverpool	
18.03.00	Nedal Hussein L PTS 12 Glasgow	
	(Vacant Commonwealth S. Bantamweight Title)	
26.05.00	Ian Turner W PTS 6 Glasgow	
24.06.00	Dave Hinds W PTS 4 Glasgow	
02.10.00	Pete Buckley W PTS 4 Glasgow	
03.11.01	Mishek Kondwani W PTS 12 Glasgow	
	(Vacant Commonwealth S.Bantamweight Title)	
18.03.02	Michael Alldis L PTS 12 Crawley	
	(Vacant British S. Bantamweight Title. Commonwealth S. Bantamweight Title Defence)	

Career: 31 contests, won 25, drew 1, lost 5.

Henry Castle

Salisbury. *Born* Southampton, 7 February, 1979
Featherweight. Ht. 5'6¾"
Manager K. Sanders

29.01.01	Jason Nesbitt W CO 6 Peterborough
26.03.01	Eddie Nevins W RSC 2 Peterborough
23.11.01	Jimmy Beech W PTS 4 Bethnal Green
11.03.02	David Lowry W RSC 1 Glasgow
20.04.02	Jason Nesbitt W PTS 4 Cardiff
25.05.02	Jimmy Beech W PTS 4 Portsmouth

Career: 6 contests, won 6.

Glenn Catley

Bristol. *Born* Sodbury, 15 March, 1972
Former WBC S. Middleweight Champion.
Former Undefeated IBF & WBO Inter-
Continental S. Middleweight Champion.
Former Undefeated British Middleweight
Champion. Former WBC International
Middleweight Champion. Ht. 5'8"
Manager C. Sanigar/F. Warren

27.05.93	Rick North W PTS 4 Bristol
26.06.93	Chris Vassiliou W CO 2 Keynsham
31.08.93	Marty Duke W RSC 2 Croydon
13.09.93	Barry Thorogood W PTS 4 Bristol
03.11.93	Marty Duke W RSC 1 Bristol
13.12.93	Shamus Casey W PTS 4 Bristol
10.03.94	Mark Cichocki W PTS 6 Bristol
23.03.94	Carlo Colarusso L RSC 5 Cardiff
25.05.94	Chris Davies W RSC 1 Bristol
02.07.94	Martin Jolley W RSC 1 Keynsham
22.11.94	Kirkland Laing W RSC 5 Bristol
18.02.95	Lee Blundell W RSC 6 Shepton Mallet
06.05.95	Mark Dawson W RSC 5 Shepton Mallet
28.07.95	Kevin Adamson W CO 1 Bristol
02.09.95	Quinn Paynter W RSC 1 Wembley
30.09.95	John Duckworth W RSC 3 Cardiff
28.10.95	Carlos Christie W PTS 8 Bristol
10.11.95	Carlos Christie W CO 3 Bristol
16.12.95	Peter Vosper W RSC 2 Cardiff
26.04.96	Lee Crocker W RSC 2 Cardiff
19.10.96	Paul Wesley W RSC 7 Bristol
21.01.97	George Bocco W RTD 4 Bristol *(Vacant WBC International Middleweight Title)*
05.06.97	Andras Galfi L RSC 7 Bristol *(WBC International Middleweight Title Defence)*
17.01.98	Neville Brown W RTD 8 Bristol *(British Middleweight Title Challenge)*
05.09.98	Richie Woodhall L PTS 12 Telford *(WBC S. Middleweight Title Challenge)*
24.10.98	Andras Galfi W PTS 12 Bristol *(Vacant WBO Inter-Continental S. Middleweight Title)*
05.12.98	Andrew Flute W RSC 5 Bristol *(Vacant IBF Inter-Continental S. Middleweight Title)*
10.12.99	Eric Lucas W RSC 12 Montreal, Canada *(Final Elim. WBC S. Middleweight Title)*
06.05.00	Markus Beyer W RSC 12 Frankfurt, Germany *(WBC S. Middleweight Title Challenge)*
01.09.00	Dingaan Thobela L CO 12 Brakpan, South Africa *(WBC S.Middleweight Title Defence)*
10.07.01	Eric Lucas L RSC 7 Montreal, Canada *(Vacant WBC S.Middleweight Title)*
09.03.02	Danilo Haeussler L PTS 12 Frankfurt, Germany *(European S. Middleweight Title Challenge)*

Career: 32 contests, won 26, lost 6.

Mark Chesters

Preston. *Born* Cape Town, South Africa, 15 February, 1973
S. Middleweight. Ht. 5'10³/₄"
Manager L. Veitch

17.09.01	Dean Cockburn L RSC 4 Glasgow
22.10.01	Biagio Falcone L RSC 2 Glasgow
09.12.01	Gary Firby L PTS 6 Blackpool
17.12.01	Donovan Smillie L PTS 6 Cleethorpes
21.01.02	Gary Firby L RSC 1 Glasgow

Career: 5 contests, lost 5.

Stephen Chinnock

Rugeley. *Born* Lichfield, 4 December, 1975
Midlands Area Featherweight Champion.
Ht. 5'10"
Manager Self

10.09.00	Neil Read W RSC 5 Walsall
06.11.00	Jason Nesbitt W PTS 6 Wolverhampton
27.11.00	Jason White W PTS 4 Birmingham
20.05.01	Gareth Wiltshaw W PTS 6 Wolverhampton
07.10.01	Kevin Gerowski W PTS 10 Wolverhampton *(Vacant Midlands Area Featherweight Title)*
18.01.02	John Mackay W PTS 4 Coventry
13.04.02	Neil Read W CO 3 Wolverhampton *(Midlands Area Featherweight Title Defence)*

Career: 7 contests, won 7.

Stephen Chinnock   Les Clark

Anthony Christopher

Aberystwyth. *Born* Aberystwyth, 18 August, 1981
Welterweight. Ht. 5'8¹/₄"
Manager D. Davies

23.09.01	Arv Mittoo DREW 6 Shaw

Career: 1 contest, drew 1.

Darren Chubbs   Les Clark

Darren Chubbs

Southport. *Born* Southport, 4 October, 1968
Heavyweight. Ht. 6'3"
Manager B. Devine

09.10.00	Geoff Hunter W RSC 3 Liverpool
08.12.00	Eamonn Glennon W PTS 4 Crystal Palace
24.04.01	Luke Simpkin W PTS 4 Liverpool
11.06.01	Paul Bonson W PTS 4 Nottingham
25.09.01	Mark Krence L PTS 4 Liverpool

Career: 5 contests, won 4, lost 1.

Dave Clarke

Blackpool. *Born* Dover, 20 June, 1976
Cruiserweight. Ht. 6'1"
Manager L. Veitch

22.11.01	Roman Greenberg L RSC 5 Paddington
11.02.02	Colin Kenna L RSC 4 Southampton
15.03.02	Shaun Bowes L PTS 6 Spennymoor
24.03.02	Tommy Eastwood L PTS 6 Streatham
11.05.02	Ivan Botton L PTS 6 Newark
03.06.02	Tony Moran L PTS 6 Glasgow
25.06.02	Carl Wright L PTS 6 Rugby

Career: 7 contests, lost 7.

Dave Clarke   Les Clark

Howard Clarke

Warley. *Born* London, 23 September, 1967
L. Middleweight. Ht. 5'10"
Manager Self

15.10.91	Chris Mylan W PTS 4 Dudley
09.12.91	Claude Rossi W RSC 3 Brierley Hill
04.02.92	Julian Eavis W PTS 4 Alfreton
03.03.92	Dave Andrews W RSC 3 Cradley Heath
21.05.92	Richard O'Brien W CO 1 Cradley Heath
29.09.92	Paul King W PTS 6 Stoke
27.10.92	Gordon Blair L RSC 4 Cradley Heath
16.03.93	Paul King W PTS 6 Edgbaston
07.06.93	Dean Bramhald W RTD 2 Walsall
29.06.93	Paul King W PTS 6 Edgbaston

06.10.93	Julian Eavis L PTS 8 Solihull
30.11.93	Julian Eavis W PTS 8 Wolverhampton
08.02.94	Nigel Bradley W RTD 6 Wolverhampton
18.04.94	Andy Peach W PTS 6 Walsall
28.06.94	Dennis Berry L RSC 3 Edgbaston
12.10.94	Julian Eavis W PTS 8 Stoke
25.10.94	Andy Peach W RSC 3 Edgbaston
02.11.94	Julian Eavis W PTS 8 Birmingham
29.11.94	Julian Eavis W PTS 6 Cannock
07.12.94	Peter Reid W PTS 8 Stoke
25.01.95	Dennis Berry L PTS 8 Stoke
08.03.95	Andrew Jervis W PTS 6 Solihull
11.05.95	David Bain W RSC 1 Dudley
20.09.95	Michael Smyth DREW 6 Ystrad
02.10.95	Nigel Wenton L PTS 6 Mayfair
02.12.96	Martin Smith L PTS 8 Birmingham
29.01.97	Gary Beardsley W PTS 6 Stoke
11.02.97	Prince Kasi Kaihau L RSC 4 Wolverhampton
19.03.97	Mark Cichocki W PTS 6 Stoke
15.04.97	Prince Kasi Kaihau W PTS 6 Edgbaston
30.04.97	Allan Gray W PTS 8 Acton
22.05.97	Michael Alexander W RSC 3 Solihull
21.06.97	Paul Samuels L PTS 8 Cardiff
09.09.97	Harry Dhami L PTS 8 Bethnal Green
05.11.97	Andras Galfi W PTS 8 Tenerife
27.01.98	Mack Razor L PTS 8 Hammanskraal, South Africa
23.03.98	Lindon Scarlett DREW 6 Crystal Palace
18.07.98	Jason Papillion W PTS 8 Sheffield
13.03.99	Fernando Vargas L RSC 4 New York City, USA *(IBF L. Middleweight Title Challenge)*
05.11.99	Michael Rask L PTS 12 Aalberg, Denmark *(WBA Inter-Continental L. Middleweight Title Challenge)*
29.05.00	Anthony Farnell L PTS 12 Manchester *(WBO Inter-Continental L. Middleweight Title Challenge)*
12.08.00	Mehrdud Takaloo L PTS 12 Wembley *(Vacant IBF Inter-Continental L.Middleweight Title)*
04.11.00	Richard Williams L CO 4 Bethnal Green
16.12.00	Ryan Rhodes L PTS 6 Sheffield
03.02.01	Michael Jones L PTS 4 Manchester
26.02.01	Jawaid Khaliq L PTS 6 Nottingham
07.04.01	Gary Lockett L RSC 2 Wembley
06.05.01	Ian Cooper L PTS 6 Hartlepool
04.06.01	James Docherty L PTS 6 Hartlepool
14.07.01	Gary Lockett L CO 1 Wembley
15.09.01	Thomas McDonagh L PTS 6 Manchester
10.11.01	Ossie Duran L PTS 6 Wembley
26.11.01	Wayne Pinder L PTS 6 Manchester
16.12.01	Erik Teymour L PTS 6 Southwark
27.01.02	Paul Samuels L PTS 6 Streatham
03.03.02	Lee Murtagh NC 2 Shaw
20.04.01	Wayne Elcock L PTS 4 Cardiff
25.05.02	Ross Minter W RSC 2 Portsmouth
08.06.02	Alexander Vetoux L RSC 4 Renfrew

Career: 59 contests, won 27, drew 2, lost 29, no contest, 1.

Darren Cleary

Salford. *Born* Salford, 28 February, 1980
Flyweight. Ht. 5'5"
Manager S. Foster/S. Wood

27.05.01	Marty Kayes W PTS 4 Manchester
07.07.01	Marty Kayes W PTS 4 Manchester
18.03.02	Jamil Hussain DREW 4 Crawley
27.04.02	Jamil Hussain DREW 4 Huddersfield
11.05.02	Jimbo Rooney W PTS 4 Dagenham

Career: 5 contests, won 3, drew 2.

Andrew Close

Hartlepool. *Born* Hartlepool, 20 September, 1981
Welterweight. Ht. 5'11½"
Manager M. Marsden

09.09.01	Mark Halstead DREW 6 Hartlepool
04.10.01	Mark Halstead W PTS 6 Sunderland
29.11.01	Emmanuel Marcos W PTS 6 Hartlepool
18.03.02	Lee Minter L PTS 4 Crawley

Career: 4 contests, won 2, drew 1, lost 1.

Dean Cockburn

Doncaster. *Born* Doncaster, 28 March, 1979
L. Heavyweight. Ht. 5'9½"
Manager T. Gilmour/G. Rhodes

17.09.01	Mark Chesters W RSC 4 Glasgow
17.11.01	Paul Wesley W PTS 4 Glasgow
25.03.02	Paul Buchanan L PTS 6 Sunderland
21.06.02	Darren Stubbs W RSC 1 Leeds

Career: 4 contests, won 3, lost 1.

Dean Cockburn Les Clark

Brian Coleman

Birmingham. *Born* Birmingham, 27 July, 1969
Welterweight. Ht. 5'11"
Manager Self

21.11.91	Jamie Morris DREW 6 Stafford
11.12.91	Craig Hartwell DREW 6 Leicester
22.01.92	John O. Johnson L PTS 6 Stoke
20.02.92	Davy Robb L PTS 6 Oakengates
31.03.92	Blue Butterworth L PTS 6 Stockport
17.05.92	Korso Aleain L RSC 5 Harringay

17.09.92	Nicky Bardle L RSC 4 Watford
21.10.92	Jason Barker W PTS 6 Stoke
10.12.92	A. M. Milton DREW 4 Bethnal Green
31.03.93	A. M. Milton L PTS 4 Bethnal Green
26.04.93	Jason Beard L PTS 6 Lewisham
06.05.93	Mark Allen W PTS 6 Walsall
18.05.93	Sean Metherell DREW 6 Kettering
27.05.93	Blue Butterworth L PTS 6 Burnley
23.06.93	Jonathan Thaxton L PTS 6 Gorleston
11.08.93	Steve Howden L RSC 4 Mansfield
13.09.93	Mick Hoban L PTS 6 Middleton
01.12.93	A. M. Milton L PTS 4 Bethnal Green
08.12.93	Chris Pollock W PTS 6 Stoke
16.12.93	Mark Newton L PTS 6 Newport
11.01.94	Paul Knights L RSC 4 Bethnal Green
08.02.94	Andy Peach W PTS 6 Wolverhampton
18.02.94	Cam Raeside L PTS 6 Leicester
08.03.94	Chris Pollock L PTS 6 Edgbaston
29.03.94	P. J. Gallagher L PTS 6 Bethnal Green
14.04.94	Cham Joof L CO 3 Battersea
02.06.94	Scott Walker L CO 1 Middleton
12.09.94	Shabba Edwards L PTS 6 Mayfair
19.09.94	Mark Breslin L CO 1 Glasgow
09.11.94	Kenny Scott L PTS 6 Stafford
23.11.94	Billy McDougall W PTS 4 Piccadilly
29.11.94	Warren Stephens W PTS 6 Wolverhampton
09.12.94	Danny Stevens L RTD 2 Bethnal Green
24.01.95	Wayne Jones L PTS 6 Piccadilly
07.02.95	Alan Temple L PTS 6 Ipswich
23.02.95	Darren Covill L PTS 4 Southwark
16.03.95	Paul Knights L RSC 2 Basildon
02.07.95	Tommy Lawler L PTS 4 Dublin
08.09.95	George Naylor L PTS 6 Liverpool
27.09.95	Allan Gray L PTS 6 Bethnal Green
20.10.95	Mikael Nilsson L PTS 4 Ipswich
02.11.95	Marco Fattore W PTS 6 Mayfair
16.11.95	Alan Bosworth L PTS 6 Evesham
24.11.95	Chris Barnett L PTS 6 Manchester
02.12.95	Neil Sinclair L RTD 1 Belfast
20.01.96	James Hare L PTS 6 Mansfield
29.01.96	Dave Fallon L PTS 6 Piccadilly
13.02.96	Martin Holgate L PTS 4 Bethnal Green
21.02.96	Marco Fattore W PTS 6 Piccadilly
13.03.96	Paul Samuels L PTS 6 Wembley
03.04.96	Ian Honeywood L PTS 6 Bethnal Green
20.04.96	Ray Robinson L PTS 6 Brentwood
24.05.96	Scott Dixon L PTS 8 Glasgow
08.06.96	Mark Winters L PTS 4 Newcastle
06.07.96	Nick Boyd L PTS 4 Manchester
16.08.96	Charlie Paine W PTS 6 Liverpool
27.08.96	Dave Brazil L PTS 6 Windsor
19.09.96	Ricky Sackfield W RSC 3 Manchester
27.09.96	Nicky Bardle L PTS 4 Stevenage
08.10.96	Marcus McCrae W PTS 6 Battersea
09.11.96	Mark Haslam L PTS 6 Manchester
27.11.96	Bernard Paul L PTS 6 Bethnal Green
09.12.96	Wayne Windle L PTS 6 Chesterfield
18.01.97	Paul Burke L PTS 6 Manchester
19.02.97	Anthony Campbell L PTS 6 Acton
25.03.97	Craig Stanley DREW 4 Lewisham
03.04.97	Kevin McCarthy L PTS 6 Wembley
22.04.97	Georgie Smith L PTS 6 Bethnal Green
19.05.97	John O.Johnson DREW 6 Cleethorpes
02.06.97	Steve McLevy W RSC 5 Glasgow
02.08.97	Junior Witter L PTS 4 Barnsley
13.09.97	Jason Rowland L PTS 8 Millwall
04.10.97	Everald Williams L PTS 4 Muswell Hill
24.10.97	Anthony Maynard L CO 1 Birmingham
27.01.98	Kevin McCarthy L PTS 6 Streatham
23.02.98	Kevin McKillan L PTS 6 Salford

79

05.03.98 Junior Witter L PTS 6 Leeds
24.03.98 Jon Harrison DREW 6 Wolverhampton
03.04.98 Peter Nightingale L PTS 6 West Bromwich
23.04.98 Marc Smith W PTS 6 Edgbaston
06.05.98 Stuart Rimmer L PTS 6 Blackpool
18.05.98 Steve Conway L PTS 6 Cleethorpes
26.05.98 Rimvidas Billius L PTS 4 Mayfair
06.06.98 Jamie McKeever L PTS 4 Liverpool
18.06.98 Shaun Stokes L PTS 6 Sheffield
12.09.98 Graham Earl L PTS 4 Bethnal Green
03.10.98 Peter Nightingale L PTS 6 West Bromwich
12.10.98 Christian Brady L PTS 6 Birmingham
22.10.98 Colin Lynes L RSC 2 Barking
25.11.98 Arv Mittoo W PTS 6 Clydach
07.12.98 Gavin Down L PTS 6 Manchester
21.01.99 Dennis Griffin W PTS 6 Piccadilly
06.02.99 Tontcho Tontchev L PTS 6 Halifax
26.02.99 Peter Nightingale L PTS 6 West Bromwich
08.03.99 Sammy Smith W PTS 8 Birmingham
25.03.99 Ernie Smith W PTS 6 Edgbaston
03.04.99 Richard Hatton L CO 2 Kensington
27.05.99 Ernie Smith L PTS 6 Edgbaston
04.06.99 Steve Conway L PTS 6 Hull
26.06.99 Steve Murray L PTS 6 Millwall
07.08.99 Jonathan Thaxton L PTS 6 Dagenham
13.09.99 Bobby Vanzie L PTS 6 Bethnal Green
27.09.99 Steve Conway L PTS 6 Leeds
24.10.99 Peter Nightingale L PTS 10 Wolverhampton
(Midlands Area Welterweight Title Challenge)
06.11.99 Jacek Bielski L PTS 4 Bethnal Green
22.11.99 Sonny Thind W RSC 5 Piccadilly
30.11.99 Ernie Smith W PTS 8 Wolverhampton
11.12.99 Oscar Hall L PTS 6 Liverpool
20.01.00 Alan Bosworth L PTS 6 Piccadilly
12.02.00 Shaun Stokes W PTS 4 Sheffield
24.02.00 Ernie Smith W PTS 6 Edgbaston
09.03.00 Paul Burns L PTS 6 Liverpool
25.03.00 Michael Jennings L PTS 6 Liverpool
16.05.00 Michael Jennings L PTS 6 Warrington
25.05.00 Lee Molyneux L PTS 6 Peterborough
19.06.00 Gavin Down L PTS 4 Burton
19.08.00 Glenn McClarnon L PTS 6 Brentwood
25.09.00 Derek Roche L PTS 6 Barnsley
14.10.00 Colin Lynes L PTS 6 Wembley
31.10.00 Ivan Kirpa L RSC 3 Hammersmith
02.12.00 John Tiftik L PTS 4 Chigwell
11.12.00 Lee Bird W CO 4 Cleethorpes
23.01.01 Paul Knights L PTS 6 Crawley
03.02.01 Darren Spencer L PTS 6 Manchester
10.02.01 Carl Wall L RSC 1 Widnes
17.03.01 Bradley Pryce L PTS 4 Manchester
26.03.01 Ross Minter L PTS 4 Wembley
28.04.01 Ismail Khalil L PTS 4 Cardiff
08.05.01 Gavin Wake L PTS 4 Barnsley
21.05.01 Ernie Smith L PTS 6 Birmingham
09.06.01 Matthew Hatton L RTD 2 Bethnal Green
08.12.01 Gavin Down L RSC 1 Chesterfield
23.02.02 Young Muttley L PTS 4 Nottingham
22.03.02 Sam Gorman L PTS 6 Coventry
26.04.02 Andy Egan L PTS 6 Coventry
08.06.02 Ronnie Nailen L PTS 4 Renfrew
Career: 136 contests, won 22, drew 7, lost 107.

Jason Collins
Walsall. *Born* Walsall, 5 December, 1972
Middleweight. Ht. 5'9"
Manager Self

18.02.99 Biagio Falcone L PTS 6 Glasgow
17.03.99 Stuart Harper W RSC 2 Stoke
06.06.99 Jon Foster DREW 6 Nottingham
15.08.99 Matt Galer W PTS 6 Derby
28.10.99 Lee Blundell DREW 6 Burnley
20.11.99 Dennis Berry L PTS 6 Grantham
14.12.99 Jorge Araujo L PTS 6 Telde, Gran Canaria, Spain
15.01.00 Martin Jolley W RTD 1 Doncaster
18.02.00 Oscar Hall DREW 6 West Bromwich
27.02.00 Jawaid Khaliq L PTS 6 Leeds
05.03.00 Wayne Shepherd W PTS 6 Shaw
21.03.00 Sharden Ansoula W PTS 6 Telde, Gran Canaria
21.05.00 Neville Brown L RSC 2 Derby
08.07.00 Darren Rhodes DREW 4 Widnes
04.09.00 Darren Rhodes W PTS 4 Manchester
01.10.00 Juergen Braehmer L CO 1 Hamburg, Germany
13.11.00 Mehrdud Takaloo L RSC 2 Bethnal Green
16.12.00 Louis Swales DREW 4 Sheffield
27.01.01 Spencer Fearon W PTS 4 Bethnal Green
26.03.01 P.J. Maxwell W PTS 4 Wembley
20.04.01 Jim Rock L PTS 6 Dublin
08.06.01 Leigh Wicks W PTS 4 Hull
21.06.01 Lester Jacobs L CO 9 Earls Court
(WBF Middleweight Title Challenge)
07.09.01 Delroy Mellis W DIS 5 Bethnal Green
22.09.01 Ian Cooper L PTS 10 Newcastle
(Vacant British Masters Middleweight Title)
27.10.01 Ryan Rhodes L PTS 4 Manchester
17.11.01 Gerard Murphy L PTS 4 Glasgow
08.12.01 Steven Bendall L PTS 12 Dagenham
(Vacant WBU Inter-Continental Middleweight Title)
12.02.02 Delroy Leslie L RSC 1 Bethnal Green
18.03.02 Andrew Buchanan W PTS 4 Crawley
01.06.02 Wayne Elcock L RSC 2 Manchester
Career: 31 contests, won 11, drew 5, lost 15.

Tony Conroy
Coventry. *Born* Coventry, 18 December, 1977
Welterweight. Ht. 5'9"
Manager Self

22.10.99 Mark Halstead W PTS 4 Coventry
24.02.00 Dave Gibson W PTS 4 Edgbaston
22.05.00 Dave Hinds W PTS 4 Coventry
28.10.00 Chris Hall W RSC 1 Coventry
02.01.01 Woody Greenaway W PTS 4 Coventry
25.06.02 Robin Thomas W RSC 1 Rugby
Career: 6 contests, won 6.

Steve Conway
Dewsbury. *Born* Hartlepool, 6 October, 1977
S. Featherweight. Ht. 5'8"
Manager M. Marsden

21.02.96 Robert Grubb W PTS 6 Batley
24.04.96 Ervine Blake W PTS 6 Solihull
20.05.96 Chris Lyons W PTS 6 Cleethorpes
30.05.96 Ram Singh W PTS 6 Lincoln
03.02.97 Jason Squire W PTS 6 Leicester
11.04.97 Marc Smith W PTS 4 Barnsley
22.09.97 Arv Mittoo W PTS 6 Cleethorpes
09.10.97 Arv Mittoo W PTS 6 Leeds
01.11.97 Brian Carr L PTS 6 Glasgow
14.11.97 Brendan Bryce W PTS 6 Mere
04.12.97 Kid McAuley W RSC 5 Doncaster

15.12.97 Nicky Wilders W PTS 6 Cleethorpes
05.03.98 Pete Buckley W PTS 6 Leeds
25.04.98 Dean Phillips W PTS 6 Cardiff
09.05.98 Gary Flear W PTS 4 Sheffield
18.05.98 Brian Coleman W PTS 6 Cleethorpes
05.09.98 Benny Jones W PTS 4 Telford
19.12.98 Gary Thornhill L RSC 9 Liverpool
(WBO Inter-Continental S. Featherweight Title Challenge)
04.06.99 Brian Coleman W PTS 6 Hull
27.09.99 Brian Coleman W PTS 6 Leeds
27.02.00 Chris Price W RTD 3 Leeds
21.03.00 Pedro Miranda L RSC 3 Telde, Gran Canaria
15.07.00 Arv Mittoo W PTS 6 Norwich
20.10.00 Junior Witter L RTD 4 Belfast
25.02.01 Ram Singh W RSC 2 Derby
02.06.01 Jimmy Phelan W PTS 4 Wakefield
18.08.01 Keith Jones W PTS 8 Dewsbury
17.11.01 Carl Allen W PTS 8 Dewsbury
27.04.02 Steve Robinson W PTS 8 Huddersfield
Career: 29 contests, won 25, lost 4.

Jason Cook
Maesteg. *Born* Maesteg, 27 February, 1975
Lightweight. Welsh L. Welterweight Champion. Ht. 5'9"
Manager B. Hearn

11.10.96 Brian Robb W RSC 2 Mayfair
27.11.96 Andrew Reed W RSC 3 Bethnal Green
27.05.97 Marc Smith W PTS 4 Mayfair
31.10.97 Marc Smith W PTS 4 Mayfair
24.01.98 David Kirk W RSC 3 Cardiff
26.05.98 Trevor Smith L RSC 1 Mayfair
23.02.99 Darren Woodley W RSC 4 Cardiff
28.05.99 Dave Hinds W RSC 1 Liverpool
02.10.99 Pete Buckley W PTS 4 Cardiff
11.12.99 Woody Greenaway W RSC 1 Merthyr
(Vacant Welsh L. Welterweight Title)
26.02.00 Harry Butler W PTS 6 Swansea
17.04.00 Andrei Sinepupov W RTD 3 Birmingham
12.05.00 Keith Jones W PTS 10 Swansea
(Welsh L. Welterweight Title Defence)
09.10.00 Assen Vasilev W PTS 6 Liverpool
17.02.01 Dariusz Snarski W PTS 8 Kolbrzeg, Poland
18.03.02 Nono Junior W RSC 1 Crawley
11.05.02 Andrei Devyataykin W PTS 6 Dagenham
29.06.02 Viktor Baranov W PTS 6 Brentwood
Career: 18 contests, won 17, lost 1.

Nicky Cook
Dagenham. *Born* Stepney, 13 September, 1979
WBF Inter-Continental S. Featherweight Champion. Ht. 5'6½"
Manager J. Harding

11.12.98 Sean Grant W CO 1 Cheshunt
26.02.99 Graham McGrath W CO 2 Coventry
27.04.99 Vasil Paskelev W CO 1 Bethnal Green
25.05.99 Wilson Acuna W PTS 4 Mayfair
12.07.99 Igor Sakhatarov W PTS 4 Coventry
20.08.99 Vlado Varhegyi W PTS 4 Bloomsbury
27.11.99 John Barnes W PTS 6 Liverpool
20.12.99 Carl Allen W CO 3 Bethnal Green
10.03.00 Chris Jickells W RSC 1 Bethnal Green
27.05.00 Anthony Hanna W PTS 6 Mayfair
16.06.00 Salem Bouaita W PTS 6 Bloomsbury

04.11.00	Vladimir Borov W RSC 1 Bethnal Green
08.12.00	Rakhim Mingaleev W PTS 8 Crystal Palace
19.05.01	Foudil Madani W RSC 1 Wembley
28.11.01	Woody Greenaway W RSC 3 Bethnal Green
19.12.01	Marcelo Ackermann W RSC 3 Coventry
	(Vacant WBF Inter-Continental S.Featherweight Title)
20.04.02	Jackie Gunguluza W RTD 4 Wembley
	(WBF Inter-Continental S.Featherweight Title Defence)

Career: 17 contests, won 17.

Claire Cooper

Thornbury. *Born* Bristol, 10 December, 1978
Bantamweight. Ht. 5'5"
Manager T. Woodward

20.09.01	Juliet Winter W RSC 4 Blackfriars

Career: 1 contest, won 1.

Ian Cooper

Hartlepool. *Born* Hartlepool, 3 May, 1974
Former Undefeated British Masters Middleweight Champion. Northern Area S. Middleweight Champion. Ht. 5'11"
Manager D. Garside

01.12.99	Dean Ashton W PTS 4 Yarm
09.06.00	Richie Jenkins W PTS 6 Blackpool
23.07.00	Martin Jolley W PTS 6 Hartlepool
01.10.00	Ian Toby W RSC 4 Hartlepool
11.02.01	Mike White W RSC 9 Hartlepool
	(Vacant Northern Area S.Middleweight Title)
06.05.01	Howard Clarke W PTS 6 Hartlepool
22.09.01	Jason Collins W PTS 10 Newcastle
	(Vacant British Masters Middleweight Title)
01.12.01	Jim Rock W PTS 6 Bethnal Green
28.01.02	Ojay Abrahams L PTS 6 Barnsley

Career: 9 contests, won 8, lost 1.

Ian Cooper   Les Clark

Darren Corbett

Belfast. *Born* Belfast, 8 July, 1972
Former Undefeated IBO Inter-Continental L. Heavyweight Champion. Former Commonwealth, IBO Inter-Continental & All-Ireland Cruiserweight Champion. Ht. 5'11"
Manager Self

10.12.94	David Jules W RSC 1 Manchester
13.12.94	Carl Gaffney W RSC 1 Potters Bar
21.02.95	Steve Garber W PTS 6 Sunderland
18.03.95	Gary Williams DREW 6 Millstreet
14.04.95	Dennis Bailey W RSC 2 Belfast
27.05.95	R. F. McKenzie L PTS 6 Belfast
26.08.95	Nigel Rafferty W PTS 6 Belfast
07.10.95	Nigel Rafferty W PTS 6 Belfast
02.12.95	Bobbi Joe Edwards W PTS 6 Belfast
07.05.96	Cliff Elden W RSC 1 Mayfair
28.05.96	Darren Fearn W RSC 1 Belfast
03.09.96	Chris Woollas W RSC 7 Belfast
05.11.96	Ray Kane W RSC 5 Belfast
	(Vacant All-Ireland Cruiserweight Title)
17.12.96	Chris Woollas W RSC 1 Doncaster
28.01.97	Nigel Rafferty W PTS 10 Belfast
	(All-Ireland Cruiserweight Title Defence)
29.04.97	Noel Magee W CO 2 Belfast
	(All-Ireland Cruiserweight Title Defence)
02.06.97	Chris Okoh W RSC 3 Belfast
	(Commonwealth Cruiserweight Title Challenge)
17.10.97	Hector Sanjuro W PTS 6 Ledyard, USA
20.12.97	Robert Norton W PTS 12 Belfast
	(Commonwealth Cruiserweight Title Defence)
21.02.98	Dirk Wallyn W PTS 10 Belfast
28.04.98	Konstantin Ochrej W RSC 4 Belfast
	(Vacant IBO Inter-Continental Cruiserweight Title)
26.05.98	Roberto Dominguez W CO 1 Mayfair
	(IBO Inter-Continental Cruiserweight Title Defence)
28.11.98	Bruce Scott L RSC 10 Belfast
	(Commonwealth Cruiserweight Title Defence. Vacant British Cruiserweight Title)
10.04.99	Stephane Allouane L RSC 9 Manchester
	(Vacant IBO Inter-Continental Cruiserweight Title)
31.07.99	Darren Ashton W RSC 2 Carlisle
14.12.99	Neil Simpson W PTS 12 Coventry
	(Vacant IBO Inter-Continental L. Heavyweight Title)
25.03.00	Lennox Lewis W RSC 2 Liverpool
	(IBO Inter-Continental L. Heavyweight Title Defence)
16.06.01	Tyler Hughes W RSC 1 New York City, USA
16.11.01	Radcliffe Green W PTS 8 Dublin

Career: 29 contests, won 25, drew 1, lost 3.

Dave Cotterill

Hemsworth. *Born* Pontefract, 25 April, 1977
S. Featherweight. Ht. 5'8"
Manager S. Butler

26.10.00	Leo Turner L PTS 6 Stoke
04.11.00	Scott Spencer L PTS 4 Bethnal Green
30.11.00	Joel Viney W RSC 1 Blackpool
05.12.00	Duncan Armstrong W PTS 6 Nottingham
23.02.01	Andrew Ferrans W RSC 2 Irvine
30.04.01	Andrew Ferrans L RSC 1 Glasgow
18.06.01	Nigel Senior W PTS 6 Bradford
08.10.01	James Rooney L RSC 4 Barnsley
24.11.01	Dave Curran W PTS 6 Wakefield
07.02.02	Jimmy Beech L PTS 6 Stoke
08.03.02	Lee Holmes L PTS 6 Ellesmere Port
22.03.02	Gary Greenwood L PTS 6 Coventry
31.05.02	Lance Crosby L RSC 1 Hull

Career: 13 contests, won 5, lost 8.

Jane Couch   Harry Goodwin

Jane Couch

Fleetwood. *Born* Fleetwood, 12 August, 1968
Former Undefeated WBF Lightweight Champion. Former Undefeated WIBF & WBF Welterweight Champion. Ht. 5'7"
Manager Tex Woodward

30.10.94	Kalpna Shah W RSC 2 Wigan
29.01.95	Fosteres Joseph W PTS 6 Fleetwood
18.04.95	Jane Johnson W RSC 4 Fleetwood
01.07.95	Julia Shirley W PTS 6 Fleetwood
24.05.96	Sandra Geiger W PTS 10 Copenhagen, Denmark
	(WIBF Welterweight Title Challenge)
01.03.97	Andrea Deshong W RSC 7 New Orleans, USA
	(WIBF Welterweight Title Defence)
24.08.97	Leah Mellinger W PTS 10 Connecticut, USA
	(WIBF Welterweight Title Defence)
24.10.97	Dora Webber L PTS 6 Mississippi, USA
10.01.98	Dora Webber L PTS 10 Atlantic City, USA
25.11.98	Simone Lukic W RSC 2 Streatham
20.02.99	Marisch Sjauw W PTS 10 Thornaby
	(WIBF Welterweight Title Defence. Vacant WBF Welterweight Title)

01.04.99	Heike Noller W PTS 8 Birmingham	
31.10.99	Sharon Anyos W PTS 10 Raynes Park	
	(Vacant WBF Lightweight Title)	
09.03.00	Michelle Straus W RSC 3 Bethnal Green	
01.07.00	Galina Gumliska W RSC 6 Southwark	
	(WBF Lightweight Title Defence)	
19.08.00	Liz Mueller L PTS 6 Mashantucket, Connecticut, USA	
16.06.01	Viktoria Oleynikov W PTS 4 Wembley	
31.07.01	Shakurah Witherspoon W PTS 4 Montego Bay, Jamaica	
16.12.01	Tzanka Karova W RSC 3 Bristol	
21.06.02	Sumya Anani L RSC 4 Waco, Texas, USA	
	(Vacant WIBA L. Welterweight Title)	

Career: 20 contests, won 16, lost 4.

Mickey Coveney

West Ham. *Born* London, 26 November, 1981
Featherweight. Ht. 5'4"
Manager F. Maloney

12.06.00	Stevie Quinn W PTS 4 Belfast
30.11.00	Gareth Wiltshaw W PTS 4 Peterborough
24.02.01	Dazzo Williams L CO 1 Bethnal Green
03.06.01	Gareth Wiltshaw W PTS 4 Southwark
09.09.01	Richmond Asante W PTS 4 Southwark
28.11.01	Steve Gethin W PTS 4 Bethnal Green
24.03.02	Anthony Hanna W PTS 4 Streatham

Career: 7 contests, won 6, lost 1.

Mickey Coveney   Les Clark

Simeon Cover

Worksop. *Born* Clapton, 12 March, 1978
S. Middleweight. Ht. 5'11"
Manager D. Ingle

28.03.01	Danny Smith L PTS 6 Piccadilly
18.08.01	Rob Stevenson W PTS 6 Dewsbury
24.09.01	Colin McCash L PTS 6 Cleethorpes
01.11.01	Rob Stevenson L PTS 6 Hull
16.11.01	Jon O'Brien L PTS 6 Dublin
24.11.01	Darren Rhodes L RSC 5 Wakefield
31.01.02	Shpetim Hoti W PTS 6 Piccadilly
13.04.02	Earl Ling L CO 4 Norwich
13.05.02	Roddy Doran DREW 8 Birmingham
02.06.02	Gary Dixon W PTS 6 Shaw

Career: 10 contests, won 3, drew 1, lost 6.

Darren Covill

Welling. *Born* Welling, 11 April, 1970
Middleweight. Ht. 5'8"
Manager Self

23.02.95	Brian Coleman W PTS 4 Southwark
19.05.95	Allan Gray L PTS 6 Southwark
04.06.95	Dick Hanns-Kat W RSC 3 Bethnal Green
14.09.95	Gavin Barker W CO 1 Battersea
21.09.95	Shaun Stokes L PTS 6 Sheffield
22.11.95	Jason Barker L PTS 4 Sheffield
05.02.96	Jason Barker W RSC 1 Bexleyheath
21.03.96	Paul Miles L PTS 4 Southwark
11.07.97	Leigh Wicks W RSC 2 Brighton
26.09.97	Jason Williams L PTS 6 Port Talbot
08.10.97	Steve Roberts L PTS 6 Poplar
08.11.97	David Baptiste W PTS 4 Southwark
06.12.97	Ali Khattab L PTS 4 Wembley
31.01.98	Paolo Roberto L PTS 6 Edmonton
13.02.98	John Docherty W RSC 1 Barrhead
21.03.98	Wayne Alexander L RSC 2 Bethnal Green
04.06.98	Darren McInulty DREW 6 Barking
10.09.98	Cornelius Carr L RTD 2 Acton
25.11.98	Leigh Wicks L PTS 4 Streatham
16.01.99	Anthony McFadden L RSC 2 Bethnal Green
18.02.99	Adrian Stone L RSC 2 Barking
24.03.99	Lester Jacobs L RSC 2 Bayswater
02.07.99	Steven Bendall L RTD 3 Bristol
27.02.00	Gareth Hogg L RSC 3 Plymouth
02.02.01	Matthew Barney L PTS 6 Portsmouth
24.03.01	Allan Foster L RTD 3 Sheffield
12.05.01	Hughie Doherty L PTS 4 Plymouth
04.07.01	Harry Butler L RSC 4 Bloomsbury
20.09.01	Lester Jacobs L CO 2 Blackfriars
22.11.01	Dean Powell L PTS 4 Mayfair
08.12.01	Tomas da Silva L PTS 4 Millwall
15.12.01	Reagan Denton L PTS 4 Sheffield
27.03.02	John Tiftik W RSC 2 Mayfair
25.04.02	Brendan Rollinson L PTS 4 Hull
21.05.02	Elroy Edwards L PTS 4 Custom House

Career: 35 contests, won 8, drew 1, lost 26.

Lance Crosby

Hull. *Born* Hull, 15 June, 1974
Lightweight. Ht. 5'8½"
Manager D. Smith

20.03.00	Delroy Mellis W PTS 4 Mansfield
25.05.00	Trevor Smith W PTS 6 Hull
16.11.00	Arv Mittoo W RSC 3 Hull
05.02.01	David White DREW 4 Hull
02.06.01	Woody Greenaway W PTS 6 Wakefield
31.07.01	Ted Bami L PTS 6 Bethnal Green
01.11.01	Ernie Smith W PTS 6 Hull

16.03.02	Leo O'Reilly L PTS 8 Bethnal Green
31.05.02	Dave Cotterill W RSC 1 Hull

Career: 9 contests, won 6, drew 1, lost 2.

Peter Culshaw

Liverpool. *Born* Liverpool, 15 May, 1973
WBU Flyweight Champion. Former
Undefeated WBU International S.
Flyweight Champion. Former
Commonwealth Flyweight Champion.
Former Undefeated Central Area Flyweight
Champion. Ht. 5'6"
Manager Self

02.07.93	Graham McGrath W PTS 6 Liverpool
28.09.93	Vince Feeney W PTS 6 Liverpool
11.12.93	Nick Tooley W RSC 1 Liverpool
25.02.94	Des Gargano W PTS 6 Chester
06.05.94	Neil Swain W PTS 6 Liverpool
26.09.94	Daryl McKenzie W PTS 6 Liverpool
20.04.95	Rowan Williams W CO 6 Liverpool
29.09.95	Maxim Pougatchev DREW 8 Liverpool
05.03.96	Louis Veitch W RSC 3 Barrow
	(Central Area Flyweight Title Challenge)
13.04.96	Lyndon Kershaw W RSC 3 Liverpool
25.06.96	Danny Ward W RSC 3 Stevenage
	(Commonwealth Flyweight Title Challenge)
27.09.96	James Wanene W RSC 7 Stevenage
	(Commonwealth Flyweight Title Defence)
02.08.97	Jason Thomas W PTS 8 Barnsley
11.09.97	Ady Lewis L RSC 8 Widnes
	(Commonwealth Flyweight Title Defence. British Flyweight Title Challenge)
12.03.98	Foudil Madani W RSC 4 Liverpool
	(Vacant WBU International S. Flyweight Title)
24.10.98	Mzukisi Marali W RSC 7 Liverpool
	(Vacant WBU Flyweight Title)
05.03.99	Zolile Mbityi W PTS 12 Liverpool
	(WBU Flyweight Title Defence)
15.05.99	Adrian Ochoa W RSC 9 Blackpool
	(WBU Flyweight Title Defence)
09.03.00	Oscar Andrade W PTS 12 Liverpool
	(WBU Flyweight Title Defence)
24.05.00	Jake Matlala W PTS 12 Carnival City, South Africa
	(WBU Flyweight Title Defence)
11.11.00	Dimitar Alipiev W CO 1 Belfast
	(WBU Flyweight Title Defence)
09.06.01	Ian Napa W RSC 8 Bethnal Green
	(WBU Flyweight Title Defence)
06.04.02	Sergei Tasimov W RSC 2 Copenhagen, Denmark

Career: 23 contests, won 21, drew 1, lost 1.

Dave Curran

Doncaster. *Born* Tipperary, 15 January, 1977
L. Welterweight. Ht. 5'7¾"
Manager T. Petersen/G. Rhodes

24.11.01	Dave Cotterill L PTS 6 Wakefield
29.04.02	Mark Hudson W RSC 1 Bradford
28.05.02	Martin Hardcastle L RSC 3 Leeds

Career: 3 contests, won 1, lost 2.

(Daniel) Jesse James Daniel (James)

Leeds. *Born* Leeds, 21 July, 1975
S. Featherweight. Ht. 5'9"
Manager Self

17.05.99	Dave Hinds W PTS 6 Cleethorpes
15.08.99	Graham McGrath W PTS 6 Derby
27.09.99	Marc Smith W PTS 6 Cleethorpes
13.12.99	Sean Grant W RSC 5 Cleethorpes
27.02.00	Les Frost W PTS 6 Leeds
15.05.00	Chris Jickells W PTS 6 Cleethorpes
29.05.00	Gary Flear W PTS 4 Manchester
04.09.00	Steve Hanley W PTS 4 Manchester
07.10.00	Arv Mittoo W PTS 4 Doncaster
19.11.00	Chris Price W PTS 4 Chesterfield
18.08.01	Jason White W PTS 6 Dewsbury
17.11.01	Sean Grant W RSC 1 Dewsbury
02.03.02	Gareth Wiltshaw W RSC 3 Wakefield
27.04.02	Richmond Asante L PTS 6 Huddersfield
15.06.02	Jason Nesbitt W PTS 4 Leeds

Career: 15 contests, won 14, lost 1.

Scott Dann   Les Clark

Scott Dann

Plymouth. *Born* Plymouth, 23 July, 1974
Former Undefeated IBO Inter-Continental
Middleweight Champion. Ht. 5'10¹/₂"
Manager C. Sanigar/F. Warren

15.11.97	Jon Rees W RSC 1 Bristol
25.04.98	Israel Khumalo W RSC 3 Cardiff
30.05.98	Michael Alexander W PTS 4 Bristol
14.07.98	Richard Glaysher W RSC 1 Reading
24.10.98	James Donoghue W PTS 6 Bristol
27.02.00	James Donoghue W RSC 1 Plymouth
07.04.00	Martin Jolley W RSC 2 Bristol
08.09.00	Sean Pritchard W RSC 5 Bristol
06.10.00	Peter Mitchell W RSC 3 Maidstone
03.11.00	Anthony Ivory W PTS 8 Ebbw Vale

13.03.01	Jason Hart W RSC 2 Plymouth
12.05.01	Elvis Adonesi W CO 7 Plymouth
	(Vacant IBO Inter-Continental Middleweight Title)
13.09.01	Jon Penn L RSC 5 Sheffield
10.05.02	Mark Phillips W PTS 6 Bethnal Green

Career: 14 contests, won 13, lost 1.

Shaune Danskin

Peterborough. *Born* Spalding, 28
December, 1975
L. Welterweight. Ht. 5'5"
Manager M. Goodall

08.12.95	Gary Jenkinson L PTS 6 Leeds
19.02.96	Paul Hamilton L CO 2 Glasgow
04.10.96	Nicky Wilders L PTS 6 Wakefield
24.05.01	Martin Watson L RSC 3 Glasgow
15.10.01	Paul Philpott L RSC 5 Southampton
17.11.01	Sam Gorman L RSC 3 Coventry

Career: 6 contests, lost 6.

Shaune Danskin   Les Clark

Tomas da Silva

London. *Born* Sao Luiz Maranhao, Brazil,
19 May, 1976
L. Middleweight. Ht. 5'11"
Manager A. Bowers

22.09.01	Conroy McIntosh W PTS 4 Canning Town
03.11.01	Ryan Kerr L PTS 4 Glasgow
16.11.01	Tommy Tolan W RSC 6 Dublin
08.12.01	Darren Covill W PTS 4 Millwall
16.12.01	Duje Postenjak L PTS 6 Glasgow
09.02.02	Thomas McDonagh DREW 4 Manchester
18.02.02	Biagio Falcone W RSC 3 Glasgow
19.04.02	Mark Graversen L PTS 6 Aarhus, Denmark

Career: 8 contests, won 4, drew 1, lost 3.

James Davenport

Manchester. *Born* Salford, 8 January, 1977
Middleweight. Ht. 5'9"
Manager S. Wood/T. Gilmour

| 23.12.01 | William Webster W RSC 5 Salford |

17.02.02	Chris Steele W PTS 6 Salford
09.03.02	Martin Scotland W RSC 1 Manchester
28.05.02	Paul Lomax L CO 3 Liverpool

Career: 4 contests, won 3, lost 1.

Chris Davies

Blaenclydach. *Born* Pontypridd, 24 August,
1974
L. Heavyweight. Ht. 5'9"
Manager D. Gardiner

27.04.94	Craig Joseph L PTS 6 Solihull
25.05.94	Glenn Catley L RSC 1 Bristol
29.05.96	Mark Hickey W RSC 1 Ebbw Vale
19.07.96	Michael Pinnock W PTS 6 Ystrad
31.08.96	James Branch L PTS 4 Dublin
02.10.96	Neil Simpson L PTS 4 Cardiff
02.10.99	Carl Nicholson W CO 1 Cardiff
22.10.99	Jim Twite W CO 1 Coventry
30.10.99	Ganny Dovidavas W PTS 4 Southwark
11.12.99	Paul Bonson W PTS 4 Merthyr
26.02.00	Adam Cale W RSC 4 Swansea
18.03.00	Neville Brown W RSC 2 Glasgow
11.04.00	Lee Manuel Ossie L PTS 10 Vigo, Spain
12.06.00	Cathal O'Grady W RSC 1 Belfast
29.01.01	Peter Oboh L RSC 8 Peterborough
	(Elim. Commonwealth L. Heavyweight Title)
07.09.01	Mark Williams W RSC 4 Bethnal Green
20.10.01	Tony Oakey L PTS 12 Portsmouth
	(Commonwealth L. Heavyweight Title Challenge)

Career: 17 contests, won 10, lost 7.

Chris Davies   Les Clark

Gary Davis

St Helens. *Born* Liverpool, 17 October,
1982
S. Bantamweight. Ht. 5'6"
Manager F. Maloney/F. Warren

| 01.06.02 | Steve Gethin L RSC 2 Manchester |

Career: 1 contest, lost 1.

Varuzhan Davtyan

Birmingham. *Born* Armenia, 11 August, 1972
L. Heavyweight. Ht. 5'8½"
Manager D. Bradley

Previous record unknown
09.03.02   Tony Dodson W PTS 6 Manchester
09.05.02   Rasmus Ojemaye W RSC 3 Leicester Square
29.06.02   Elvis Michailenko L PTS 6 Brentwood
Career: 3 contests, won 2, lost 1.

Adele Dean

Wigan. *Born* Wigan, 22 June, 1981
Featherweight. Ht. 5'7"
Manager L. Veitch

10.05.02   Audrey Guthrie W RSC 1 Preston
Career: 1 contest, won 1.

Rocky Dean

Thetford. *Born* Bury St Edmonds, 17 June, 1978
Bantamweight. Ht. 5'5"
Manager Self

14.10.99   Lennie Hodgkins W PTS 6 Bloomsbury
30.10.99   Lennie Hodgkins W PTS 6 Southwark
18.05.00   Danny Lawson W RSC 1 Bethnal Green
29.09.00   Anthony Hanna W PTS 4 Bethnal Green
10.11.00   Chris Jickells L RSC 1 Mayfair
19.04.02   Peter Svendsen W PTS 6 Aarhus, Denmark
Career: 6 contests, won 5, lost 1.

Rocky Dean   Les Clark

Jason Dee (Davies)

Pontardawe. *Born* Londonderry, 18 August, 1972
Lightweight. Ht. 5'7"
Manager Self

11.10.96   Danny Thomas W RSC 3 Mayfair
28.04.97   David Jay W RSC 3 Enfield
08.10.97   Andrew Reed W RSC 1 Poplar
18.11.97   Dewi Roberts W PTS 4 Mansfield
27.01.98   Mark McGowan L RSC 1 Piccadilly
06.11.98   Gary Jenkinson W RSC 2 Mayfair
23.02.99   Woody Greenaway W CO 6 Cardiff
31.07.99   Stefy Bull W RSC 4 Carlisle
02.10.99   Keith Jones W RSC 5 Cardiff
11.12.99   Lee Armstrong W RSC 4 Merthyr
24.04.01   David Burke L RSC 1 Liverpool
06.10.01   Chris Barnett L DIS 5 Manchester
26.01.02   Patrick Gallagher L DIS 6 Dagenham
Career: 13 contests, won 9, lost 4.

Jason Dee   Les Clark

Garry Delaney

West Ham. *Born* Newham, 12 August, 1970
British Masters & Southern Area Cruiserweight Champion. Former Commonwealth, WBO Inter-Continental & Southern Area L. Heavyweight Champion. Ht. 6'3"
Manager A. Bowers

02.10.91   Gus Mendes W RSC 1 Barking
23.10.91   Joe Frater W RSC 1 Bethnal Green
13.11.91   John Kaighin W PTS 6 Bethnal Green
11.12.91   Randy B. Powell W RSC 1 Basildon
11.02.92   Simon Harris DREW 8 Barking
12.05.92   John Williams W PTS 6 Crystal Palace
16.06.92   Nigel Rafferty W CO 5 Dagenham
15.09.92   Gil Lewis W CO 2 Crystal Palace
06.10.92   Simon McDougall W PTS 8 Antwerp, Belgium
10.11.92   John Oxenham W CO 5 Dagenham
12.12.92   Simon McDougall W PTS 8 Muswell Hill
30.01.93   Simon Collins W PTS 8 Brentwood
28.09.93   Glazz Campbell W CO 6 Bethnal Green
     (Southern Area L. Heavyweight Title Challenge)
06.11.93   John Kaighin W CO 1 Bethnal Green

21.12.93   Ray Albert W RSC 3 Mayfair
     (Vacant WBO Inter-Continental L. Heavyweight Title)
11.01.94   Jim Murray W RSC 7 Bethnal Green
     (WBO Inter-Continental L. Heavyweight Title Defence)
09.04.94   Simon Harris W CO 6 Bethnal Green
     (WBO Inter-Continental & Southern Area L. Heavyweight Title Defences)
09.07.94   Sergio Merani W PTS 12 Earls Court
     (WBO Inter-Continental L. Heavyweight Title)
30.09.94   Arigoma Chiponda W CO 2 Bethnal Green
     (Vacant Commonwealth L. Heavyweight Title)
18.03.95   Ernest Mateen W RTD 7 Millstreet
     (Vacant WBO Inter-Continental L. Heavyweight Title)
09.05.95   Noel Magee L RTD 7 Basildon
     (Commonwealth L. Heavyweight Title Defence)
06.02.96   Francis Wanyama W PTS 6 Basildon
09.04.96   Joey Paladino W RSC 1 Stevenage
07.02.97   John Kiser W PTS 6 Las Vegas, USA
04.03.97   Peter Oboh W DIS 8 Southwark
27.09.97   Julius Francis L RSC 6 Belfast
     (Vacant British Heavyweight Title. Commonwealth Heavyweight Title Challenge)
05.06.98   Darron Griffiths W PTS 6 Southend
23.01.99   John Keeton L PTS 12 Cheshunt
     (Vacant WBO Inter-Continental Cruiserweight Title)
01.05.99   Tim Brown W PTS 8 Crystal Palace
04.09.99   Lee Swaby W PTS 8 Bethnal Green
29.04.00   Jesper Kristiansen L RTD 10 Varde, Denmark
     (Vacant WBO Inter-Continental Cruiserweight Title)
06.10.00   Dominic Negus W PTS 10 Maidstone
     (Southern Area Cruiserweight Title Challenge)
10.03.01   Bruce Scott L RTD 3 Bethnal Green
     (British Cruiserweight Title Challenge. Vacant Commonwealth Cruiserweight Title)
15.06.01   Darren Ashton W RTD 4 Millwall
     (Vacant British Masters Cruiserweight Title)
14.07.01   Chris P. Bacon W RSC 10 Liverpool
     (British Masters Cruiserweight Title Defence)
20.10.01   Tony Dowling W RSC 6 Glasgow
02.03.02   Sebastiaan Rothmann L PTS 12 Brakpan, South Africa
     (WBU Cruiserweight Title Challenge)
Career: 37 contests, won 30, drew 1, lost 6.

(Mtabingwa) Frankie DeMilo

Bristol. *Born* Rwanda, 6 April, 1974
British Masters & Western Area S. Bantamweight Champion. Ht. 5'7½"
Manager C. Sanigar

26.02.99   Danny Lawson W PTS 6 Longford
17.03.99   Daniel Ring W RSC 2 Kensington
02.07.99   Graham McGrath W PTS 4 Bristol
24.09.99   Jason Thomas L RSC 2 Merthyr
22.11.99   Anthony Hanna W PTS 6 Piccadilly
03.12.99   Ian Turner W PTS 6 Peterborough
20.01.00   David Jeffrey W RSC 8 Piccadilly
     (Vacant Western Area S. Bantamweight Title)

29.03.00 Jason Thomas W RSC 8 Piccadilly
*(Vacant British Masters
S. Bantamweight Title)*
02.06.00 Kevin Gerowski W RSC 7 Ashford
*(British Masters S.Bantamweight Title
Defence)*
08.09.00 Harry Woods W RTD 6 Bristol
*(British Masters S.Bantamweight Title
Defence)*
03.11.00 Ian Turner W PTS 10 Ebbw Vale
*(British Masters S.Bantamweight Title
Defence)*
12.05.01 John Barnes W PTS 10 Plymouth
*(British Masters S. Bantamweight Title
Defence)*
30.09.01 Sean Green W PTS 6 Bristol
16.12.01 Rakhim Mingaleev W PTS 6 Bristol
08.02.02 Francisco Tejedor W PTS 6
Copenhagen, Denmark
14.06.02 Jadgar Abdulla L PTS 4 Copenhagen,
Denmark

Career: 16 contests, won 14, lost 2.

Frankie DeMilo   Les Clark

Paul Denton (Ramsey)

Birmingham. *Born* Birmingham, 12 April,
1970
Welterweight. Ht. 5'10"
Manager Self

18.03.93 Mark O'Callaghan W RSC 4 Lewisham
29.04.93 Dave Maj DREW 6 Mayfair
11.08.93 Billy McDougall W PTS 6 Mansfield
01.10.93 Ferid Bennecer W CO 3 Waregem,
Belgium
01.12.93 Brian Hickey W CO 1 Kensington
28.01.94 Youssef Bakhouche L PTS 6 Waregem,
Belgium
07.05.94 Viktor Fesechko L PTS 6
Dnepropetrousk, Ukraine
23.09.94 Roy Rowland W RSC 5 Bethnal Green
03.01.95 Patrick Charpentier L RSC 4 Epernay,
France
25.02.95 Paul Ryan L RSC 4 Millwall
25.11.95 Michael Carruth L PTS 8 Dublin

03.02.96 George Naylor W RSC 3 Liverpool
26.04.96 Ross Hale W RSC 4 Cardiff
15.11.96 Frank Olsen L RSC 4 Nestved,
Denmark
14.03.97 Mark Winters L PTS 8 Reading
13.06.97 Alan McDowall DREW 6 Paisley
21.03.98 Naas Scheepers L PTS 8
Hammanskraal, South Africa
19.09.98 Neil Sinclair L RSC 1 Dublin
19.12.98 Richard Hatton L RSC 6 Liverpool
16.02.99 Steve Tuckett L PTS 6 Leeds
27.02.99 Michael Carruth L RSC 5 Bethnal
Green
27.05.00 Jacek Bielski L PTS 6 Mayfair
19.06.00 Oscar Hall L PTS 4 Burton
08.07.00 Michael Jennings L PTS 6 Widnes
12.08.00 Wayne Alexander L RSC 1 Wembley
02.10.00 Kevin McIntyre L PTS 6 Glasgow
18.11.00 Pavel Melnikov L PTS 4 Dagenham
01.12.00 Paul Dyer L PTS 4 Peterborough
11.12.00 Michael Jennings L PTS 4 Widnes
17.02.01 David Walker L PTS 4 Bethnal Green
26.02.01 James Hare L PTS 4 Nottingham
07.04.01 Brett James L PTS 4 Wembley
24.04.01 Paul Burns L PTS 4 Liverpool
08.05.01 Derek Roche L PTS 6 Barnsley
27.05.01 Jamie Moore L RSC 3 Manchester
07.07.01 Thomas McDonagh L PTS 6
Manchester
20.10.01 Kevin Bennett L PTS 4 Portsmouth
26.11.01 James Hare L RTD 4 Manchester
09.02.02 Matthew Hatton L PTS 6 Manchester
02.03.02 Ross Minter L PTS 6 Bethnal Green
10.05.02 Leo O'Reilly L PTS 6 Bethnal Green

Career: 41 contests, won 7, drew 2, lost 32.

Reagan Denton

Sheffield. *Born* Sheffield, 26 June, 1978
L. Middleweight. Ht. 5'11"
Manager Self

15.05.99 Pedro Thompson W PTS 4 Sheffield
15.11.99 Colin Vidler W PTS 4 Bethnal Green
25.09.00 William Webster W PTS 4 Barnsley
08.10.01 Martyn Bailey W PTS 4 Barnsley
15.12.01 Darren Covill W PTS 4 Sheffield

Career: 5 contests, won 5.

Norman Dhalie

Birmingham. *Born* Birmingham, 24 March,
1971
L. Welterweight. Ht. 5'7"
Manager Self

06.04.92 Karl Morling L PTS 6 Northampton
27.04.92 Wilson Docherty L RSC 2 Glasgow
02.07.92 John White L RSC 6 Middleton
29.09.92 Gary Marston DREW 6 Stoke
07.10.92 Jacob Smith W PTS 6 Sunderland
03.12.92 Bradley Stone L CO 4 Lewisham
26.01.93 Neil Smith L PTS 4 Leicester
13.02.93 John White L CO 2 Manchester
20.04.93 Bobby Guynan L PTS 6 Brentwood
29.04.93 Kevin Toomey L PTS 6 Hull
23.05.93 Mike Anthony Brown W PTS 4
Brockley
09.06.93 Joey Moffat L RTD 4 Liverpool
30.09.93 Simon Frailing W PTS 6 Hayes
06.10.93 Kevin McKillan L RSC 1 Solihull
06.12.93 Colin Innes W PTS 6 Bradford
16.12.93 Peter Till L PTS 8 Walsall
19.01.94 John Naylor L RSC 3 Stoke
21.02.94 Hugh Collins L RTD 4 Glasgow

14.04.94 Mike Anthony Brown L PTS 6
Battersea
28.04.94 John Stovin DREW 6 Hull
06.05.94 Sugar Gibiliru L RTD 5 Liverpool
02.09.94 Dave Fallon L DIS 4 Spitalfields
28.09.94 Tanveer Ahmed L CO 5 Glasgow
24.11.94 Tony Foster L RTD 7 Hull
17.02.95 Paul Knights L RTD 5 Crawley
16.06.95 George Naylor L PTS 6 Liverpool
25.10.95 Joe Donohoe W PTS 6 Stoke
20.12.95 J. T. Williams L CO 2 Usk
16.03.96 Robbie Sivyer L CO 4 Barnstaple
15.10.96 Wayne Windle W PTS 6
Wolverhampton
02.12.96 Andrew Robinson W PTS 6
Birmingham
06.10.97 Vic Broomhead W PTS 6 Birmingham
14.10.97 Chris Pegg W RSC 5 Wolverhampton
11.11.97 Vic Broomhead W PTS 6 Edgbaston
02.03.98 Wayne Windle W PTS 6 Birmingham
23.04.98 Thomas Bradley L CO 5 Edgbaston
27.05.99 Carl Tilley W RSC 1 Edgbaston
04.03.02 Nicky Leech L PTS 6 Birmingham

Career: 38 contests, won 12, drew 2, lost 24.

(Hardip) Harry Dhami

Gravesend. *Born* Gravesend, 17 April, 1972
Former British Welterweight Champion.
Former Undefeated Southern Area
Welterweight Champion. Ht. 5'10"
Manager T. Toole

29.10.92 Johnny Pinnock W PTS 6 Hayes
20.05.94 Nick Appiah W RSC 4 Acton
27.05.94 Chris Vassiliou W RSC 5 Ashford
11.10.94 Steve McNess DREW 6 Bethnal Green
09.11.94 Clay O'Shea L PTS 6 Millwall
30.11.94 Robert Wright L PTS 8
Wolverhampton
17.11.95 John Bosco L PTS 6 Bethnal Green
08.12.95 Nicky Thurbin L PTS 8 Bethnal Green
25.04.96 Chris Pollock W PTS 6 Mayfair
07.05.96 Ojay Abrahams W RSC 5 Mayfair
*(Vacant Southern Area Welterweight
Title)*
20.11.96 Andy Peach W RTD 3 Wembley
14.03.97 Paul Dyer W PTS 10 Reading
*(Southern Area Welterweight Title
Defence)*
20.05.97 Paul Miles W RTD 2 Gillingham
*(Southern Area Welterweight Title
Defence)*
09.09.97 Howard Clarke W PTS 8 Bethnal
Green
26.09.98 Allan Gray W PTS 10 Southwark
*(Southern Area Welterweight Title
Defence)*
12.12.98 Kevin McCarthy W PTS 10 Southwark
*(Southern Area Welterweight Title
Defence)*
15.05.99 Paul Burns W PTS 8 Blackpool
12.12.99 Lee Bird W PTS 6 Chigwell
27.03.00 Derek Roche W PTS 12 Barnsley
(British Welterweight Title Challenge)
14.10.00 Malcolm Melvin W PTS 12 Wembley
(British Welterweight Title Defence)
27.11.00 Spencer McCracken W PTS 12
Birmingham
(British Welterweight Title Defence)
19.11.01 Neil Sinclair L RSC 5 Glasgow
(British Welterweight Title Defence)

Career: 22 contests, won 16, drew 1, lost 5.

Haroon Din

Sheffield. *Born* Middlesbrough, 21 May, 1978
S. Featherweight. Ht. 5'8"
Manager D. Ingle

21.09.98	Les Frost L PTS 6 Cleethorpes	
14.12.98	Les Frost L RSC 1 Cleethorpes	
02.05.99	Amjid Mahmood W PTS 6 Shaw	
20.05.00	Dave Travers W PTS 6 Leicester	
24.06.00	Willie Limond L PTS 4 Glasgow	
30.08.00	Leon Dobbs W CO 1 Scunthorpe	
19.11.00	Carl Greaves L RSC 4 Chesterfield	
24.09.01	Nigel Senior W PTS 6 Cleethorpes	
17.12.01	Nigel Senior W PTS 6 Cleethorpes	
31.01.02	Ilias Miah W RSC 3 Piccadilly	
20.04.02	Gareth Wiltshaw W PTS 6 Derby	

Career: 11 contests, won 7, lost 4.

Gary Dixon

Carlisle. *Born* Carlisle, 2 November, 1974
S. Middleweight. Ht. 5'10½"
Manager J. Doughty

18.03.01	Jamie Logan W PTS 6 Shaw	
10.05.01	Paul Owen L RSC 3 Sunderland	
26.07.01	Michael Thompson W PTS 6 Blackpool	
23.09.01	Mark Sawyers DREW 6 Shaw	
09.12.01	Danny Wray W RSC 4 Shaw	
03.03.02	William Webster W PTS 6 Shaw	
02.06.02	Simeon Cover L PTS 6 Shaw	

Career: 7 contests, won 4, drew 1, lost 2.

Gary Dixon   Les Clark

Scott Dixon

Hamilton. *Born* Hamilton, 28 September, 1976
WBO Inter-Continental L. Middleweight Champion. Former Undefeated Commonwealth Welterweight Champion. Former Undefeated WBB & Scottish Welterweight Champion. Ht. 5'9"
Manager A. Bowers

13.10.95	Andrew Smith W PTS 4 Glasgow	

17.12.95	Martin Evans W RSC 4 Glasgow	
12.02.96	Colin Innes W PTS 6 Glasgow	
16.03.96	Ian Richardson W PTS 4 Glasgow	
26.04.96	Andy Green W RSC 5 Glasgow	
24.05.96	Brian Coleman W PTS 8 Glasgow	
20.09.96	Alan Temple W PTS 4 Glasgow	
06.11.96	Rocky Ferrari DREW 6 Glasgow	
22.12.96	Marc Smith W PTS 6 Glasgow	
04.04.97	Jimmy Phelan W PTS 6 Glasgow	
16.05.97	Dean Bramhald W PTS 6 Glasgow	
13.06.97	Chris Price W PTS 6 Paisley	
05.07.97	Mark McGowan W PTS 4 Glasgow	
12.09.97	Gerard Murphy W PTS 8 Glasgow	
01.11.97	Nigel Bradley W PTS 4 Glasgow	
12.11.97	John Green DREW 8 Glasgow	
14.12.97	Tony Walton W PTS 6 Glasgow	
27.02.98	Chris Saunders W PTS 10 Glasgow *(Elim. British Welterweight Title)*	
19.09.98	Michael Carruth L PTS 12 Dublin *(Vacant WAA Welterweight Title)*	
13.11.98	Lee Molyneux W PTS 4 Brighton	
26.02.99	Edwin Murillo W CO 6 Bethnal Green *(WBB Welterweight Title Challenge)*	
07.06.99	Mark Ramsey W PTS 8 Glasgow	
22.10.99	Derek Roche L PTS 12 Coventry *(British Welterweight Title Challenge)*	
05.02.00	Sean Sullivan W PTS 12 Bethnal Green *(Vacant Commonwealth Welterweight Title)*	
06.06.00	Charlie Kane W RSC 6 Motherwell *(Commonwealth Welterweight Title Defence. Vacant Scottish Welterweight Title)*	
24.06.00	Leith Wicks W PTS 4 Glasgow	
19.08.00	Steve Roberts L RSC 9 Brentwood *(Vacant WBF L. Middleweight Title)*	
25.11.00	Anthony Farnell L RSC 7 Manchester *(WBO Inter-Continental L. Middleweight Title Challenge)*	
20.03.01	Wayne Shepherd W PTS 6 Glasgow	
27.04.01	Anders Styve L PTS 4 Aalborg, Denmark	
18.05.01	Ruben Varon W RSC 5 Guadalajara, Spain	
07.07.01	Jamie Moore W CO 5 Manchester *(Vacant WBO Inter-Continental L.Middleweight Title)*	
22.09.01	Mehrdud Takaloo L CO 1 Bethnal Green *(WBU L.Middleweight Title Challenge)*	
15.03.02	Michael Rask L PTS 8 Vilborg, Denmark	

Career: 34 contests, won 25, drew 2, lost 7.

Terry Dixon

West Ham. *Born* London, 29 July, 1966
Cruiserweight. Ht. 5'11"
Manager J. Oyebola

21.09.89	Dave Mowbray W RSC 1 Southampton	
30.11.89	Brendan Dempsey W RSC 8 Barking	
08.03.90	Cordwell Hylton W PTS 8 Watford	
06.04.90	Prince Rodney W RSC 7 Stevenage	
23.10.90	Dennis Bailey W PTS 6 Leicester	
07.03.91	Carl Thompson L PTS 8 Basildon	
22.04.91	Everton Blake L RSC 8 Mayfair	
25.03.92	Mark Bowen W RTD 1 Kensington	
27.04.92	Ian Bulloch W RSC 4 Mayfair	
17.10.92	Darren McKenna L RSC 3 Wembley	
04.10.93	Steve Yorath W RSC 4 Mayfair	
03.08.94	Chemek Saleta L PTS 8 Bristol	
09.05.02	Kevin Barrett DREW 4 Leicester Square	

Career: 13 contests, won 8, drew 1, lost 4.

Craig Docherty

Glasgow. *Born* Glasgow, 27 September, 1979
S. Featherweight. Ht. 5'7"
Manager T. Gilmour

16.11.98	Kevin Gerowski W PTS 6 Glasgow	
22.02.99	Des Gargano W PTS 6 Glasgow	
19.04.99	Paul Quarmby W RSC 4 Glasgow	
07.06.99	Simon Chambers W PTS 6 Glasgow	
20.09.99	John Barnes W PTS 6 Glasgow	
15.11.99	Peter Allen W RSC 1 Glasgow	
24.01.00	Lee Williamson W PTS 6 Glasgow	
19.02.00	Steve Hanley W PTS 6 Prestwick	
05.06.00	Sebastian Hart W RSC 1 Glasgow	
23.10.00	Lee Armstrong DREW 8 Glasgow	
22.01.01	Nigel Senior W RSC 4 Glasgow	
20.03.01	Jamie McKeever W RSC 3 Glasgow	
11.06.01	Rakhim Mingaleev W PTS 8 Nottingham	
27.10.01	Michael Gomez L RSC 2 Manchester *(British S.Featherweight Title Challenge)*	
18.03.02	Joel Viney W CO 1 Glasgow	

Career: 15 contests, won 13, drew 1, lost 1.

Tony Dodson

Liverpool. *Born* Liverpool, 2 July, 1980
Central Area S. Middleweight Champion. Ht. 6'0½"
Manager B. Devine

31.07.99	Michael McDermott W RTD 1 Carlisle	
02.10.99	Sean Pritchard W RSC 3 Cardiff	
22.01.00	Mark Dawson W PTS 4 Birmingham	
11.03.00	Paul Bonson W PTS 4 Kensington	
19.08.00	Jimmy Steel W RSC 3 Brentwood	
09.09.00	Danny Southam W RSC 2 Manchester	
09.10.00	Elvis Michailenko DREW 6 Liverpool	
03.02.01	Paul Bonson W PTS 4 Manchester	
25.09.01	Paul Wesley W PTS 6 Liverpool	
13.10.01	Roman Divisek W CO 1 Budapest, Hungary	
10.11.01	Valery Odin W RSC 4 Wembley	
10.12.01	Jon Penn W RSC 2 Liverpool *(Vacant Central Area S.Middleweight Title)*	
23.02.02	Jason Hart W RSC 2 Nottingham	
09.03.02	Varuzhan Davtyan L PTS 6 Manchester	
13.04.02	Brian Barbosa W PTS 8 Liverpool	

Career: 15 contests, won 13, drew 1, lost 1.

Francie Doherty

Wellingborough. *Born* Cardiff, 12 October, 1977
Middleweight. Ht. 5'6"
Manager K. Sanders

29.01.01	Freddie Yemofio W RSC 4 Peterborough	
24.03.01	Lee Bird W RSC 3 Sheffield	
23.06.01	Conroy McIntosh W PTS 4 Peterborough	
13.09.01	John Tiftik W PTS 4 Sheffield	

Career: 4 contests, won 4.

Roddy Doran

Shrewsbury. *Born* Shrewsbury, 15 March, 1972
Middleweight. Ht. 5'11"
Manager P. Cowdell/R. Gray

08.10.01 Harry Butler W PTS 6 Birmingham
31.10.01 Harry Butler DREW 6 Birmingham
11.02.02 Freddie Yemofio W PTS 8 Shrewsbury
15.04.02 William Webster W PTS 8 Shrewsbury
13.05.02 Simeon Cover DREW 8 Birmingham
Career: 5 contests, won 3, drew 2.

Darren Dorrington

Bristol. *Born* Bristol, 24 July, 1968
Middleweight. Western Area
S. Middleweight Champion. Ht. 5'11"
Manager C. Sanigar

13.09.93 Justin Smart DREW 4 Bristol
03.11.93 Russell Washer W PTS 4 Bristol
20.01.94 Shamus Casey W PTS 6 Battersea
29.01.94 Barry Thorogood DREW 6 Cardiff
10.03.94 Ray Price W RSC 6 Bristol
25.05.94 Steve Thomas W PTS 4 Bristol
02.07.94 Paul Murray W RSC 3 Keynsham
03.08.94 Gary Pemberton W CO 4 Bristol
07.10.94 Peter Vosper W RSC 6 Taunton
        (Vacant Western Area S. Middleweight Title)
27.10.94 Russell Washer W PTS 8 Bayswater
22.11.94 Robert Allen L RSC 5 Bristol
21.03.95 Lee Crocker L PTS 6 Swansea
19.10.96 Peter Vosper W RSC 3 Bristol
09.12.96 Ernie Loveridge W PTS 6 Bristol
21.01.97 Peter Mitchell W RSC 5 Bristol
24.03.96 Peter Mitchell W RSC 7 Bristol
05.06.97 Paul Carr W PTS 6 Bristol
15.09.97 Darren Ashton L DIS 2 Bristol
11.10.97 Jason Matthews L RSC 7 Sheffield
        (WBO Inter-Continental Middleweight Title Challenge)
17.01.98 Rob Stevenson W RSC 3 Bristol
30.03.98 Bruno Girard L PTS 8 Tenerife
30.05.98 Jason Hart W RTD 2 Bristol
14.07.98 Adrian Riley W RTD 2 Reading
24.10.98 Jimmy Vincent DREW 6 Bristol
02.07.99 Elvis Adonesi L RTD 11 Bristol
        (Vacant WBU Inter-Continental L. Middleweight Title)
07.04.00 Elvis Adonesi L PTS 12 Bristol
        (Vacant WBU Inter-Continental Middleweight Title)
30.09.01 Simon Andrews W RSC 4 Bristol
        (Western Area S.Middleweight Title Defence)
16.12.01 16/12/01 Viktor Fesetchko L PTS 10 Bristol
        (Vacant WBF European Middleweight Title)
Career: 28 contests, won 17, drew 3, lost 8.

(Genadijus) Ganny Dovidovas

Beckton. *Born* Lithuania, 29 October, 1974
S. Middleweight. Ht. 6'1"
Manager C. Smith

26.02.99 Jimmy Steel W PTS 6 Bethnal Green
30.09.99 Peter Mason W RSC 3 Kensington
14.10.99 Anthony Wright W PTS 6 Bloomsbury
30.10.99 Chris Davies L PTS 4 Southwark
26.11.99 Reece McAllister W RSC 1 Bayswater
25.02.00 Jason Barker DREW 4 Newmarket
09.03.00 Ossie Duran W PTS 4 Bethnal Green
20.05.00 Paul Jones L PTS 6 Rotherham
03.11.00 Juan Francisco Galvez L PTS 8 Erandio, Spain
31.05.02 Marian Diaconu L CO 3 Bucharest, Romania
Career: 10 contests, won 5, drew 1, lost 4.

Tony Dowling

Lincoln. *Born* Lincoln, 5 January, 1976
Cruiserweight. Ht. 6'2"
Manager J. Ashton

22.03.96 Slick Miller W RSC 4 Mansfield
30.05.96 Nigel Rafferty W PTS 6 Lincoln
29.07.96 Albert Call L RSC 4 Skegness
12.02.00 Adam Cale W PTS 4 Sheffield
20.03.00 Danny Southam W PTS 4 Mansfield
11.05.00 Jason Brewster W RSC 2 Newark
08.07.00 Slick Williams W PTS 4 Widnes
09.09.00 Lee Swaby L RSC 9 Newark
        (Vacant British Masters Cruiserweight Title)
20.04.01 Cathal O'Grady L RSC 1 Dublin
15.09.01 Michael Pinnock W PTS 6 Derby
20.10.01 Garry Delaney L RSC 6 Glasgow
11.05.02 Gary Thompson W RSC 3 Newark
Career: 12 contests, won 8, lost 4.

Gavin Down

Chesterfield. *Born* Chesterfield, 2 February, 1977
British Masters & Midlands Area
L. Welterweight Champion. Ht. 5'9"
Manager J. Ingle

21.09.98 Peter Lennon W RSC 1 Cleethorpes
27.11.98 Trevor Tacy L PTS 6 Nottingham
07.12.98 Brian Coleman W PTS 6 Manchester
26.02.99 Brian Gifford W PTS 6 West Bromwich
27.03.99 Lee Molyneux W PTS 4 Derby
15.05.99 Les Frost W RSC 1 Sheffield
27.06.99 Lee Molyneux W PTS 6 Alfreton
03.10.99 Ernie Smith W RSC 1 Chesterfield
28.11.99 Dave Gibson W PTS 6 Chesterfield
09.04.00 Sammy Smith W PTS 6 Alfreton
21.05.00 Arv Mittoo W PTS 6 Derby
19.06.00 Brian Coleman W PTS 4 Burton
13.08.00 Lee Bird W PTS 6 Nottingham
30.08.00 Ram Singh W PTS 6 Scunthorpe
04.11.00 Sebastian Hart W RSC 4 Derby
19.11.00 David Kirk W PTS 10 Chesterfield
        (Vacant British Masters L. Welterweight Title)
11.12.00 Dave Gibson W RSC 5 Cleethorpes
25.02.01 Jay Mahoney W RSC 1 Derby
01.04.01 Steve Saville W RSC 3 Alfreton
        (Vacant Midlands Area L. Welterweight Title)
16.06.01 Arv Mittoo W PTS 6 Derby
21.07.01 Tommy Peacock W RSC 1 Sheffield
15.09.01 Lee Williamson W PTS 6 Derby
08.12.01 Brian Coleman W RSC 1 Chesterfield
12.02.02 Bradley Pryce L RSC 9 Bethnal Green
        (Vacant IBF Inter-Continental L.Welterweight Title)
11.05.02 Woody Greenaway W RSC 3 Chesterfield
Career: 25 contests, won 23, lost 2.

(Andre) Drea Dread (Francis)

Nottingham. *Born* Nottingham, 4 November, 1969
Welterweight. Ht. 5'11"
Manager J. Gill

22.09.00 Neil Bonner L RSC 4 Wrexham
06.12.01 Stuart Rimmer L PTS 6 Stoke
Career: 2 contests, lost 2.

Mike Duffield

Cleethorpes. *Born* Cleethorpes, 9 April, 1969
Middleweight. Ht. 6'2½"
Manager Self

22.09.97 Ian Toby L PTS 6 Cleethorpes
21.10.97 Ian Toby W PTS 6 Yarm
14.11.97 Mike Gormley L RSC 2 Mere
15.12.97 Jon Penn L RSC 2 Cleethorpes
16.03.98 Matt Galer L PTS 6 Nottingham
28.04.98 Gary Reyniers DREW 6 Brentford
18.05.98 Carlton Williams W PTS 6 Cleethorpes
17.07.98 Mike White W PTS 6 Mere
21.09.98 Phil Ball W RSC 2 Cleethorpes
26.11.98 Gordon Behan L RSC 3 Edgbaston
        (Vacant Midlands Area Middleweight Title)
18.02.99 Lawrence Murphy L RSC 2 Glasgow
29.05.99 Eddie Haley L RSC 6 South Shields
28.11.99 Martin Jolley W PTS 6 Chesterfield
18.01.00 Gary Beardsley L RTD 2 Mansfield
15.05.00 William Webster L PTS 6 Birmingham
15.07.00 Earl Ling L PTS 6 Norwich
30.08.00 Matthew Pepper W RSC 4 Scunthorpe
04.11.00 Damon Hague L RSC 3 Derby
        (Vacant WBF European S. Middleweight Title)
20.04.02 Donovan Smillie W PTS 4 Derby
31.05.02 Jamie Wilson W PTS 6 Hull
Career: 20 contests, won 8, drew 1, lost 11.

Ciaran Duffy

Glasgow. *Born* Donegal, 11 September, 1980
L. Middleweight. Ht. 5'11"
Manager T. Gilmour

03.11.01 Wayne Shepherd W PTS 6 Glasgow
03.12.01 Pedro Thompson W PTS 6 Leeds
22.04.02 Richard Inquieti W PTS 6 Glasgow
Career: 3 contests, won 3.

Chris Duggan   Les Clark

Chris Duggan

Coatbridge. *Born* Glasgow, 26 May, 1981
Welterweight. Ht. 5'10½"
Manager P. Cowdell

03.02.01 Ty Browne L RSC 1 Brighton

27.07.01 Dean Walker L RSC 4 Sheffield
10.12.01 Carl Walton W PTS 6 Birmingham
15.04.02 Arv Mittoo W PTS 6 Shrewsbury
13.05.02 Lee Williamson L RSC 3 Birmingham
Career: 5 contests, won 2, lost 3.

Peter Dunn

Pontefract. *Born* Doncaster, 15 February, 1975
Welterweight. Ht. 5'8"
Manager Self

08.12.97 Leigh Daniels W PTS 6 Bradford
15.05.98 Peter Lennon W PTS 6 Nottingham
18.09.98 Jan Cree L RSC 5 Belfast
23.10.98 Bobby Lyndon W PTS 6 Wakefield
03.12.98 Craig Smith L RSC 3 Sunderland
17.03.99 Des Sowden W PTS 6 Kensington
15.05.99 Ray Wood DREW 4 Blackpool
29.05.99 Dean Nicholas L PTS 6 South Shields
01.10.99 Jon Honney L PTS 4 Bethnal Green
18.10.99 Jan Cree W PTS 6 Glasgow
26.11.99 Gavin Pearson DREW 6 Wakefield
18.02.00 John T. Kelly L PTS 6 Pentre Halkyn
11.03.00 Iain Eldridge L RSC 2 Kensington
18.09.00 Joe Miller L PTS 6 Glasgow
26.10.00 Ram Singh W PTS 6 Stoke
27.11.00 Young Muttley L RSC 3 Birmingham
22.02.01 Darren Spencer W PTS 6 Sunderland
03.03.01 Glenn McClarnon L PTS 4 Wembley
20.03.01 Robert Burton L PTS 6 Leeds
08.04.01 Martyn Bailey L PTS 6 Wrexham
17.05.01 Gavin Pearson L PTS 6 Leeds
25.09.01 Darren Spencer L PTS 4 Liverpool
06.10.01 Lee Byrne L RSC 4 Manchester
13.11.01 Richard Inquieti DREW 6 Leeds
24.11.01 Robert Burton W PTS 6 Wakefield
28.01.02 Robert Burton L RSC 8 Barnsley
(Vacant Central Area Welterweight Title)
23.03.02 Colin Lynes L PTS 4 Southwark
19.04.02 Oscar Hall L PTS 6 Darlington
28.05.02 Matt Scriven L PTS 8 Leeds
29.06.02 Darren Bruce L PTS 6 Brentwood
Career: 30 contests, won 8, drew 3, lost 19.

Colin Dunne

Holloway. *Born* Liverpool, 19 September, 1970
WBU & WBF Lightweight Champion. Former Undefeated Southern Area Lightweight Champion. Ht. 5'6"
Manager T. Toole

07.12.93 Mark O'Callaghan W RSC 1 Bethnal Green
14.01.94 Wayne Jones W RSC 3 Bethnal Green
04.03.94 Malcolm Thomas W CO 1 Bethnal Green
26.04.94 Steve Burton W CO 2 Bethnal Green
17.05.94 Phil Found W PTS 6 Kettering
23.09.94 Steve Howden W CO 1 Bethnal Green
11.10.94 Jimmy Phelan W PTS 6 Bethnal Green
09.11.94 Mark O'Callaghan W RSC 2 Millwall
09.12.94 David Thompson W RSC 3 Bethnal Green
20.01.95 Chris Aston W RSC 4 Bethnal Green
03.03.95 Marco Fattore W RSC 3 Bethnal Green
19.04.95 Rudy Valentino W PTS 6 Bethnal Green
12.05.95 Chris Aston W RSC 4 Bethnal Green

27.09.95 Steve Howden W RSC 4 Bethnal Green
28.10.95 Chris Clarkson W RSC 4 Kensington
08.12.95 Jonathan Thaxton W RSC 5 Bethnal Green
(Vacant Southern Area Lightweight Title)
05.03.96 Rudy Valentino W RSC 4 Bethnal Green
03.04.96 Kino Rodriguez W RSC 2 Bethnal Green
10.05.96 Lajos Nagy W RSC 5 Wembley
03.07.96 Marian Stoica W PTS 8 Wembley
24.10.96 Bamana Dibateza W PTS 8 Wembley
20.11.96 Michael Ayers L RSC 9 Wembley
(British Lightweight Title Challenge)
24.04.97 Lewis Reynolds W CO 4 Mayfair
(Southern Area Lightweight Title Defence)
30.06.97 Demir Nanev W RSC 8 Bethnal Green
09.09.97 Alan Bosworth W RSC 8 Bethnal Green
28.11.97 Zoltan Kalocsai W PTS 12 Bethnal Green
(Vacant WBU Lightweight Title)
23.05.98 Emmanuel Clottey W PTS 12 Bethnal Green
(WBU Lightweight Title Defence)
21.07.98 Affif Djelti W PTS 12 Widnes
(WBU Lightweight Title Defence)
12.12.98 Sedat Puskullu W RSC 3 Southwark
27.02.99 Phillip Holiday W PTS 12 Bethnal Green
(WBU Lightweight Title Defence)
13.07.00 Leonti Voronchuk W CO 4 Bethnal Green
25.07.00 Rakhim Mingaleev W RTD 5 Southwark
14.10.00 Billy Schwer W PTS 12 Wembley
(WBU Lightweight Title Defence)
16.06.01 Barrie Kelley W CO 3 Dagenham
07.09.01 Sergei Starkov W RSC 3 Bethnal Green
10.11.01 Alan Temple W RSC 7 Wembley
26.01.02 Martin Jacobs W PTS 12 Dagenham
(WBU Lightweight Title Defence)
18.05.02 Wayne Rigby W RTD 10 Millwall
(WBU Lightweight Title Defence. Vacant WBF Lightweight Title)
Career: 38 contests, won 37, lost 1.

Damien Dunnion

Newport. *Born* Manchester, 9 January, 1977
S. Bantamweight. Ht. 5'6"
Manager T. Borg

31.07.01 Mark Alexander L PTS 4 Bethnal Green
10.10.01 Shinny Bayaar W PTS 8 Stoke
Career: 2 contests, won 1, lost 1.

(Osumanu) Ossie Duran (Yahaya)

London. *Born* Accra, Ghana, 23 April, 1977
WBF European Welterweight Champion. Former Undefeated Ghanaian Lightweight Champion. Ht. 5'10"
Manager Self

28.08.96 Dick Dotse W RSC 4 Togo
20.09.96 Victor Abbey W RSC 2 Ivory Coast

30.11.96 David Allotey W PTS 8 Accra, Ghana
28.12.96 Neuziwere Apolo W RSC 1 Accra, Ghana
05.03.97 Ike Obi L PTS 10 Nigeria
26.04.97 Abas de Souza W RSC 6 Benin
28.06.97 Tony Danso DREW 12 Accra, Ghana
(Ghanaian Lightweight Title Challenge)
06.09.97 Iron Cutter W RSC 2 Accra, Ghana
04.10.97 Tony Danso W PTS 12 Accra, Ghana
(Ghanaian Lightweight Title Challenge)
06.06.98 David Tetteh L PTS 12 Accra, Ghana
(Commonwealth Lightweight Title Challenge)
09.03.00 Ganny Dovidovas L PTS 4 Bethnal Green
19.04.00 Vincent Nobela W PTS 6 Kensington
28.09.00 Mark Ramsey W RSC 2 Kensington
31.10.00 Yuri Tsarenko W PTS 4 Hammersmith
28.02.01 David Kirk W PTS 8 Kensington
(Vacant WBF European Welterweight Title)
26.04.01 Geoff McCreesh W PTS 6 Kensington
10.11.01 Howard Clarke W PTS 6 Wembley
13.12.01 Delroy Mellis W PTS 10 Leicester Square
(WBF European Welterweight Title Defence)
Career: 18 contests, won 14, drew 1, lost 3.

Paul Dyer

Portsmouth. *Born* Portsmouth, 11 July, 1970
Former Southern Area Welterweight Champion. Ht. 5'11½"
Manager C. Sanigar

24.09.91 Mick Reid W PTS 6 Basildon
19.11.91 Dave Andrews W PTS 6 Norwich
23.02.93 Kevin Mabbutt L PTS 6 Kettering
17.06.94 Dewi Roberts W PTS 6 Plymouth
27.10.94 George Wilson W PTS 4 Bayswater
25.01.95 John Janes W PTS 6 Cardiff
08.03.95 Anthony Huw Williams W PTS 6 Cardiff
06.05.95 Wahid Fats W PTS 4 Shepton Mallet
15.09.95 Mark Ramsey W PTS 6 Mansfield
16.12.95 Dennis Gardner W RSC 1 Cardiff
26.01.96 Danny Quacoe W PTS 6 Brighton
30.11.96 Mark Winters L PTS 6 Tylorstown
09.12.96 Paul Miles W PTS 6 Bristol
08.02.97 Michael Carruth L PTS 4 Millwall
14.03.97 Harry Dhami L PTS 10 Reading
(Southern Area Welterweight Title Challenge)
24.03.99 Steve Brumant W PTS 4 Bayswater
16.10.99 Neil Sinclair L RSC 8 Belfast
16.05.00 Neil Sinclair L RSC 6 Warrington
01.12.00 Paul Denton W PTS 4 Peterborough
02.02.01 David Baptiste W PTS 10 Portsmouth
(Vacant Southern Area Welterweight Title)
16.03.01 Peter Nightingale W PTS 6 Portsmouth
01.12.01 Paul Knights L PTS 10 Bethnal Green
(Southern Area Welterweight Title Defence)
16.03.02 David Walker L RSC 6 Bethnal Green
(Vacant Southern Area Welterweight Title)
Career: 23 contests, won 15, lost 8.

Graham Earl

Luton. *Born* Luton, 26 August, 1978
Southern Area Lightweight Champion.
Ht. 5'5¾"
Manager F. Maloney

02.09.97	Mark O'Callaghan W RSC 2 Southwark
06.12.97	Mark McGowan W PTS 4 Wembley
11.04.98	Danny Lutaaya W RSC 2 Southwark
23.05.98	David Kirk W PTS 4 Bethnal Green
12.09.98	Brian Coleman W PTS 4 Bethnal Green
10.12.98	Marc Smith W RSC 1 Barking
16.01.99	Lee Williamson W RSC 4 Bethnal Green
08.05.99	Benny Jones W PTS 6 Bethnal Green
15.07.99	Simon Chambers W CO 6 Peterborough
04.03.00	Ivo Golakov W RSC 1 Peterborough
29.04.00	Marco Fattore W PTS 6 Wembley
21.10.00	Lee Williamson W RSC 3 Wembley
10.03.01	Brian Gentry W RSC 8 Bethnal Green
	(Vacant Southern Area Lightweight Title)
22.09.01	Liam Maltby W CO 1 Bethnal Green
	(Southern Area Lightweight Title Defence)
15.12.01	Mark Winters W PTS 10 Wembley
	(Elim. British Lightweight Title)

Career: 15 contests, won 15.

Howard Eastman

Battersea. *Born* New Amsterdam, Guyana,
8 December, 1970
British & Commonwealth Middleweight
Champion. Former Undefeated European,
IBO Inter-Continental & WBA Inter-
Continental Middleweight Champion.
Former Undefeated Southern Area
Middleweight Champion. Ht. 5'11"
Manager Self

06.03.94	John Rice W RSC 1 Southwark
14.03.94	Andy Peach W PTS 6 Mayfair
22.03.94	Steve Phillips W RSC 5 Bethnal Green
17.10.94	Barry Thorogood W RSC 6 Mayfair
06.03.95	Marty Duke W RSC 1 Mayfair
20.04.95	Stuart Dunn W RSC 2 Mayfair
23.06.95	Peter Vosper W RSC 1 Bethnal Green
16.10.95	Carlo Colarusso W RSC 1 Mayfair
29.11.95	Brendan Ryan W RSC 2 Bethnal Green
31.01.96	Paul Wesley W RSC 1 Birmingham
13.03.96	Steve Goodwin W RSC 5 Wembley
29.04.96	John Duckworth W RSC 5 Mayfair
11.12.96	Sven Hamer W RSC 10 Southwark
	(Vacant Southern Area Middleweight Title)
18.02.97	John Duckworth W CO 7 Cheshunt
25.03.97	Rachid Serdjane W RSC 7 Lewisham
14.02.98	Vitali Kopitko W PTS 8 Southwark
28.03.98	Terry Morrill W RTD 4 Hull
23.05.98	Darren Ashton W RSC 4 Bethnal Green
30.11.98	Steve Foster W RSC 7 Manchester
	(Vacant British Middleweight Title)
04.02.99	Jason Barker W RSC 6 Lewisham
06.03.99	Jon Penn W RSC 3 Southwark
	(Vacant IBO Inter-Continental S. Middleweight Title)
22.05.99	Roman Babaev W RSC 6 Belfast

	(WBA Inter-Continental Middleweight Title Challenge)
10.07.99	Teimouraz Kikelidze W RSC 6 Southwark
	(WBA Inter-Continental Middleweight Title Defence)
13.09.99	Derek Wormald W RSC 3 Bethnal Green
	(British Middleweight Title Defence)
13.11.99	Mike Algoet W RSC 8 Hull
	(WBA Inter-Continental Middleweight Title Defence)
18.01.00	Ojay Abrahams W RSC 2 Mansfield
04.03.00	Viktor Fessetchko W RTD 4 Peterborough
29.04.00	Anthony Ivory W RTD 6 Wembley
25.07.00	Ahmet Dottouev W RTD 5 Southwark
	(WBA Inter-Continental Middleweight Title Defence)
16.09.00	Sam Soliman W PTS 12 Bethnal Green
	(Commonwealth Middleweight Title Challenge)
05.02.01	Mark Baker W RTD 5 Hull
10.04.01	Robert McCracken W RSC 10 Wembley
	(British & Commonwealth Middleweight Title Defences. Vacant European Middleweight Title)
17.11.01	William Joppy L PTS 12 Las Vegas, Nevada, USA
	(Vacant WBA Interim Middleweight Title)

Career: 33 contests, won 32, lost 1.

Tommy Eastwood

Epsom. *Born* Epsom, 16 May, 1979
Cruiserweight. Ht. 5'11½"
Manager F. Maloney

09.09.01	Tony Booth W PTS 4 Southwark
16.12.01	Paul Bonson W PTS 4 Southwark
12.02.02	Adam Cale W PTS 4 Bethnal Green
24.03.02	Dave Clarke W PTS 6 Streatham
23.06.02	Brodie Pearmaine W PTS 4 Southwark

Career: 5 contests, won 5.

Ricky Eccleston

Liverpool. *Born* Liverpool, 22 September,
1981
Lightweight. Ht. 5'8½"
Manager B. Hearn

01.07.00	Dave Hinds W PTS 4 Manchester
09.09.00	Billy Smith W PTS 4 Manchester
09.10.00	Nigel Senior W PTS 4 Liverpool
27.11.00	Dave Hinds W PTS 4 Birmingham
03.02.01	Steve Hanley W PTS 4 Manchester
24.04.01	Gary Flear W PTS 4 Liverpool
25.09.01	Pete Buckley W PTS 4 Liverpool
27.10.01	Gary Flear W PTS 4 Manchester
28.05.02	David Kehoe W RSC 4 Liverpool

Career: 9 contests, won 9.

Howard Eastman   Les Clark

Chris Edwards

Stoke. *Born* Stoke, 6 May, 1976
Flyweight. Ht. 5'3"
Manager Self

03.04.98	Chris Thomas W RSC 2 Ebbw Vale
21.09.98	Russell Laing L PTS 6 Glasgow
26.02.99	Delroy Spencer L PTS 6 West Bromwich
17.04.99	Stevie Quinn L RSC 4 Dublin
19.10.99	Lee Georgiou L RSC 2 Bethnal Green
03.12.99	Daniel Ring L PTS 4 Peterborough
15.05.00	Paddy Folan L PTS 6 Bradford
07.10.00	Andy Roberts W PTS 4 Doncaster
27.11.00	Levi Pattison W PTS 4 Birmingham
16.03.01	Jamie Evans L PTS 6 Portsmouth
03.06.01	Darren Taylor DREW 6 Hanley
08.10.01	Levi Pattison L PTS 4 Barnsley
06.12.01	Neil Read W PTS 8 Stoke

Career: 13 contests, won 4, drew 1, lost 8.

Elroy Edwards

Brixton. *Born* Jamaica, 12 October, 1971
L. Middleweight. Ht. 5'9½"
Manager A. Gee

21.05.02	Darren Covill W PTS 4 Custom House

Career: 1 contest, won 1.

Greg Edwards

Hereford. *Born* Hereford, 26 June, 1978
S. Featherweight. Ht. 5'7"
Manager D. Gardiner

28.01.02	Chris Hooper L RSC 2 Barnsley
27.03.02	Jason Nesbitt L RSC 5 Mayfair

Career: 2 contests, lost 2.

Greg Edwards   Les Clark

Andy Egan

Coventry. *Born* Coventry, 16 September, 1977
Welterweight. Ht. 5'8¾"
Manager J. Griffin/J. Harding

02.01.01	Gareth Jones L PTS 4 Coventry

19.12.01	Brian Gifford W RSC 1 Coventry
18.01.02	Marcus Portman L PTS 4 Coventry
09.02.02	Tony Smith W PTS 4 Coventry
26.04.02	Brian Coleman W PTS 6 Coventry

Career: 5 contests, won 3, lost 2.

Andy Egan   Les Clark

Wayne Elcock

Birmingham. *Born* Birmingham, 12 February, 1974
Middleweight. Ht. 5'9½"
Manager F. Maloney

02.12.99	William Webster W PTS 6 Peterborough
04.03.00	Sonny Pollard W RSC 3 Peterborough
07.07.01	Darren Rhodes W PTS 4 Manchester
09.10.01	Valery Odin W PTS 4 Cardiff
02.03.02	Charles Shodiya W RSC 1 Bethnal Green
20.04.02	Howard Clarke W PTS 4 Cardiff
01.06.02	Jason Collins W RSC 2 Manchester

Career: 7 contests, won 7.

Iain Eldridge

Watford. *Born* Watford, 26 February, 1975
L. Welterweight. Ht. 5'8"
Manager Self

18.11.99	Des Sowden W RSC 4 Mayfair
21.02.00	Lee Sharp L PTS 6 Glasgow
11.03.00	Peter Dunn W RSC 2 Kensington
22.07.00	Ross McCord W RSC 2 Watford
19.08.00	Karl Taylor W PTS 4 Brentwood
03.03.01	Kevin Bennett L PTS 6 Wembley
23.11.01	Costas Katsantonis L RSC 1 Bethnal Green
	(Vacant Southern Area L.Welterweight Title)

Career: 7 contests, won 4, lost 3.

Matthew Ellis

Blackpool. *Born* Oldham, 12 April, 1974
Heavyweight. Ht. 5'11¾"
Manager Self

03.02.96	Laurent Rouze W CO 1 Liverpool
01.04.96	Ladislav Husarik W RTD 4 Den Bosch, Holland

06.09.96	Darren Fearn W RSC 6 Liverpool
26.10.96	Daniel Beun W RSC 1 Liverpool
01.03.97	Yuri Yelistratov L RSC 5 Liverpool
20.07.97	Ricardo Phillips W PTS 4 Indio, USA
26.09.97	Albert Call DREW 6 Liverpool
12.03.98	Yuri Yelistratov W RSC 1 Liverpool
21.07.98	Chris Woollas W RSC 5 Widnes
24.10.98	Peter Hrivnak W RSC 1 Liverpool
12.12.98	Harry Senior W PTS 8 Southwark
27.02.99	Michael Murray W PTS 8 Bethnal Green
15.05.99	Biko Botowamungu W PTS 8 Blackpool
27.05.00	Alex Vasiliev W CO 4 Southwark
16.09.00	Dimitri Bakhtov W PTS 4 Bethnal Green
18.11.00	Chris Woollas W PTS 4 Dagenham
17.02.01	Alexei Osokin W PTS 8 Bethnal Green
12.07.01	Ronnie Smith W PTS 6 Houston, Texas, USA
22.09.01	Colin Abelson W CO 1 Bethnal Green
02.03.02	Dennis Bakhtov L RSC 5 Bethnal Green
	(WBC International Heavyweight Title Challenge)

Career: 20 contests, won 17, drew 1, lost 2.

Mark Ellwood

Hull. *Born* Hull, 13 June, 1963
S. Middleweight. Ht. 5'9½"
Manager S. Pollard

01.11.01	Adam Cale W PTS 6 Hull
25.04.02	Mark Phillips W PTS 6 Hull

Career: 2 contests, won 2.

(Christoforo) Chris Emanuele

Nuneaton. *Born* Nuneaton, 26 November, 1973
Former British Masters Bantamweight Champion. Ht. 5'5¾"
Manager Self

08.12.97	Marty Chestnut W PTS 6 Leicester
17.01.98	Stephen Oates L RSC 4 Bristol
18.05.98	Anthony Hanna L RSC 3 Cleethorpes
11.09.98	Dave Travers L RSC 2 Newark
27.11.98	Terry Gaskin W PTS 6 Nottingham
21.02.99	Paddy Folan DREW 6 Bradford
17.05.99	Daniel Ring DREW 6 Cleethorpes
17.07.99	Andy Roberts W PTS 4 Doncaster
26.11.99	Paddy Folan W RSC 5 Wakefield
11.03.00	Jamie Yelland L PTS 4 Kensington
17.04.00	Tommy Waite L PTS 6 Bradford
20.05.00	Sean Grant W RSC 5 Rotherham
06.06.00	Shaun Anderson L PTS 6 Motherwell
08.07.00	Tiger Singh W RSC 1 Rotherham
13.07.00	Lee Georgiou W CO 1 Bethnal Green
01.10.00	Michael Hunter L PTS 6 Hartlepool
28.10.00	Gareth Payne L CO 1 Coventry
26.02.01	Jim Betts W PTS 6 Nottingham
17.03.01	Stephen Oates L PTS 8 Manchester
30.04.01	John Barnes L PTS 4 Glasgow
15.06.01	John Mackay W RSC 4 Millwall
21.07.01	Noel Wilders L PTS 6 Sheffield
15.09.01	Colin Moffett W RSC 4 Nottingham
17.11.01	Jason Thomas W RSC 1 Coventry
09.02.02	Sean Green W RSC 6 Coventry
	(Vacant British Masters Bantamweight Title)
22.03.02	Choi Tseveenpurev L PTS 4 Coventry
26.04.02	Gareth Payne L RSC 3 Coventry
	(British Masters Bantamweight Title Defence)

Career: 27 contests, won 12, drew 2, lost 13.

Andrew Facey

Sheffield. *Born* Wolverhampton, 20 May, 1972
Central Area Middleweight Champion.
Ht. 6'0"
Manager J. Ingle

06.12.99	Peter McCormack W CO 2 Birmingham	
09.06.00	Matthew Pepper W RSC 1 Hull	
04.11.00	Earl Ling W PTS 6 Derby	
11.12.00	Gary Jones W PTS 6 Cleethorpes	
10.02.01	Louis Swales W RSC 3 Widnes	
17.03.01	Darren Rhodes L PTS 4 Manchester	
24.03.01	Matthew Tait W PTS 4 Chigwell	
16.06.01	Earl Ling DREW 6 Derby	
09.12.01	Michael Pinnock W PTS 6 Shaw	
02.03.02	Darren Rhodes W RSC 6 Wakefield *(Vacant Central Area Middleweight Title)*	
20.04.02	Darren Ashton W PTS 6 Derby	
13.04.02	Leigh Wicks W PTS 6 Norwich	

Career: 12 contests, won 10, drew 1, lost 1.

Andrew Facey   Les Clark

Biagio Falcone

Falkirk. *Born* Edinburgh, 1 February, 1973
Middleweight. Ht. 5'9"
Manager T. Gilmour

24.04.98	Mark Owens W PTS 6 Glasgow
17.09.98	Mark Owens W PTS 6 Glasgow
18.02.99	Jason Collins W PTS 6 Glasgow
09.04.99	Ian Toby W RSC 3 Glasgow
26.06.99	Ian Toby W PTS 4 Glasgow
04.10.99	Pedro Carragher W PTS 6 Glasgow
12.11.99	William Webster W PTS 6 Glasgow
13.12.99	William Webster W RSC 1 Glasgow

24.02.00	Mike Watson W RSC 2 Glasgow
18.03.00	Ernie Smith W PTS 4 Glasgow
08.04.00	Mehrdud Takaloo L RTD 4 Bethnal Green
26.05.00	Ernie Smith W PTS 4 Glasgow
02.10.00	Jason Barker L PTS 10 Glasgow *(Vacant Scottish S.Middleweight Title)*
30.04.01	Ian Toby W RSC 2 Glasgow
22.10.01	Mark Chesters W RSC 2 Glasgow
18.02.02	Tomas da Silva L RSC 3 Glasgow

Career: 16 contests, won 13, lost 3.

Anthony Farnell

Manchester. *Born* Manchester, 1 July, 1978
Middleweight. Former Undefeated WBO
Inter-Continental L. Middleweight
Champion. Ht. 5'10"
Manager F. Warren

03.05.97	Lee Molyneux W PTS 4 Manchester
02.08.97	Martin Renaghan W RSC 3 Barnsley
20.09.97	Dominique van der Steene W CO 1 Aachen, Germany
13.12.97	Paul Scott W RSC 3 Sheffield
24.01.98	Steve Brumant W PTS 4 Cardiff
21.03.98	Hughie Davey W PTS 6 Bethnal Green
18.04.98	Harry Butler W PTS 6 Manchester
09.05.98	David Thompson W CO 1 Sheffield
18.07.98	Lee Molyneux W CO 3 Sheffield
05.09.98	Darren Williams W RTD 4 Telford
31.10.98	Mark Richardson W PTS 6 Atlantic City, USA
28.11.98	George Richards W RSC 7 Sheffield
19.12.98	Koba Kulu W RTD 5 Liverpool
27.02.99	Koba Kulu W RSC 1 Oldham
01.05.99	Alan Gilbert W RSC 8 Crystal Palace
29.05.99	John Long W RSC 6 Halifax *(Vacant WBO Inter-Continental L. Middleweight Title)*
07.08.99	Israel Ponce W RSC 3 Atlantic City, USA
09.10.99	Javier Santibanez W CO 1 Manchester *(WBO Inter-Continental L. Middleweight Title Defence)*
27.11.99	Marino Monteyne W CO 6 Lubeck, Germany
29.01.00	Ian Toby W RSC 3 Manchester
08.04.00	Ojay Abrahams W PTS 8 Bethnal Green
29.05.00	Howard Clarke W PTS 12 Manchester *(WBO Inter-Continental L. Middleweight Title Defence)*
04.09.00	Juan Carlos Sanchez W PTS 12 Manchester *(WBO Inter-Continental L. Middleweight Title Defence)*
25.11.00	Scott Dixon W RSC 7 Manchester *(WBO Inter-Continental L. Middleweight Title Defence)*
15.01.01	Sergio Acuna W PTS 12 Manchester *(WBO Inter-Continental L. Middleweight Title Defence)*
17.03.01	Shakir Ashanti W RSC 2 Manchester *(WBO Inter-Continental L. Middleweight Title Defence)*
07.07.01	Mehrdud Takaloo L RSC 1 Manchester *(Vacant WBU L.Middleweight Title)*
15.09.01	Lee Blundell W RSC 2 Manchester *(Vacant WBO Inter-Continental L.Middleweight Title)*
27.10.01	Pavel Melnikov W RSC 12 Manchester *(WBO Inter-Continental L. Middleweight Title Defence)*

09.02.02	Matt Galer W RSC 3 Manchester
01.06.02	Ruben Groenewald L PTS 12 Manchester *(Vacant WBU Middleweight Title)*

Career: 31 contests, won 29, lost 2.

Anthony Farnell   Paul Speak

Andrew Ferrans   Les Clark

Andrew Ferrans

New Cumnock. *Born* Irvine, 4 February, 1981
S. Featherweight. Ht. 5'9"
Manager T. Gilmour

19.02.00	Chris Lyons W PTS 6 Prestwick
03.03.00	Gary Groves W RSC 1 Irvine
20.03.00	John Barnes DREW 6 Glasgow
06.06.00	Duncan Armstrong W PTS 6 Motherwell
18.09.00	Steve Brook W PTS 6 Glasgow
20.11.00	Duncan Armstrong W PTS 6 Glasgow
23.02.01	Dave Cotterill L RSC 2 Irvine
30.04.01	Dave Cotterill W RSC 1 Glasgow
04.06.01	Jason Nesbitt W RSC 2 Glasgow
17.09.01	Gary Flear W PTS 8 Glasgow
10.12.01	Jamie McKeever L PTS 6 Liverpool
21.01.02	Joel Viney W PTS 8 Glasgow
01.03.02	Peter Allen W PTS 8 Irvine
13.04.02	Tony Mulholland L PTS 4 Liverpool
11.05.02	Marc Callaghan L PTS 6 Dagenham

Career: 15 contests, won 10, drew 1, lost 4.

Gary Firby

Gateshead. *Born* Gateshead, 5 October, 1979
Middleweight. Ht. 5'10"
Manager T. Conroy

09.12.01	Mark Chesters W PTS 6 Blackpool
21.01.02	Mark Chesters W RSC 1 Glasgow
21.02.02	Craig Lynch L RSC 3 Sunderland
09.05.02	Ian Thomas DREW 6 Sunderland

Career: 4 contests, won 2, drew 1, lost 1.

Gary Flear

Birmingham. *Born* Birmingham, 28 May, 1965
L. Welterweight. Former Undefeated British Masters Lightweight Champion. Ht. 5'8"
Manager Self

20.09.84	Wayne Trigg W PTS 4 Dudley
10.10.84	Neville Fivey W PTS 6 Stoke
29.10.84	Muhammad Lovelock L PTS 6 Birmingham
07.11.84	Ray Newby W PTS 6 Evesham
19.11.84	Henry Arnold W RSC 5 Leicester
27.11.84	Andy Williams DREW 6 Wolverhampton
10.12.84	Nicky Day W PTS 6 Birmingham
04.02.85	Tyrell Wilson W CO 2 Birmingham
12.02.85	Peter Bowen W PTS 6 Wolverhampton
20.02.85	George Jones W PTS 8 Stafford
04.03.85	Teddy Anderson W RSC 5 Birmingham
20.03.85	Tommy Frankham W PTS 6 Solihull
22.04.85	George Jones W PTS 8 Birmingham
08.05.85	Michael Marsden W RTD 5 Solihull
20.05.85	Edward Lloyd W PTS 8 Nottingham
23.09.85	Peter Bradley L PTS 6 Mayfair
02.10.85	Paul Cook W PTS 8 Solihull
15.10.85	Dave Henderson W PTS 8 Wolverhampton
06.11.85	George Jones W PTS 8 Evesham
20.11.85	George Kerr W PTS 8 Solihull
09.12.85	Gerry Beard W PTS 8 Birmingham
22.01.86	Andy Mayers W PTS 8 Solihull
11.02.86	Lenny Gloster W PTS 8 Wolverhampton
27.02.86	Errol McDonald L RSC 5 Bethnal Green
21.04.86	Dean Barclay L RSC 1 Birmingham
28.05.86	Billy Edwards W PTS 8 Lewisham
03.10.91	Chris Saunders W PTS 6 Burton
06.10.97	Chris Lyons W PTS 6 Piccadilly

27.10.97	Isaac Sebaduka W PTS 6 Nottingham
20.11.97	Elvis Parsley L PTS 6 Solihull
27.03.98	Anthony Maynard L RSC 9 Telford
	(Vacant Midlands Area Lightweight Title)
09.05.98	Steve Conway L PTS 4 Sheffield
01.06.98	Bobby Vanzie L PTS 6 Manchester
24.10.98	David Burke L PTS 6 Liverpool
12.01.99	David Kehoe W PTS 4 Bethnal Green
06.03.99	Stephen Smith L RTD 7 Southwark
	(Vacant IBO Inter-Continental Lightweight Title)
12.10.99	Steve Saville L RSC 6 Wolverhampton
11.12.99	Tony Mulholland L PTS 4 Liverpool
21.02.00	Lee Armstrong L PTS 8 Glasgow
18.03.00	Barry Hughes L RSC 4 Glasgow
29.05.00	Jesse James Daniel L PTS 4 Manchester
12.06.00	David Lowry L PTS 4 Belfast
01.07.00	Jamie McKeever W PTS 4 Manchester
15.07.00	Bradley Pryce L RSC 1 Millwall
08.09.00	Brian Gentry W RSC 6 Hammersmith
	(Vacant British Masters Lightweight Title)
11.11.00	David Lowry W PTS 4 Belfast
18.11.00	David Walker L PTS 4 Dagenham
02.12.00	James Rooney L PTS 4 Bethnal Green
01.04.01	Jason Hall L PTS 8 Southwark
24.04.01	Ricky Eccleston L PTS 4 Liverpool
17.09.01	Andrew Ferrans L PTS 8 Glasgow
09.10.01	Gareth Jordan L PTS 4 Cardiff
27.10.01	Ricky Eccleston L PTS 4 Manchester
24.11.01	Kevin Lear L PTS 4 Bethnal Green
10.12.01	Tony Mulholland L PTS 4 Liverpool
02.03.02	Danny Hunt L PTS 4 Bethnal Green
13.03.02	Ajose Olusegun L PTS 4 Mayfair
20.04.02	Gavin Rees L RTD 4 Cardiff

Career: 58 contests, won 28, drew 1, lost 29.

(Patrick) Paddy Folan (Powders)

Huddersfield. *Born* Birmingham, 25 June, 1972
Featherweight. Ht. 5'7"
Manager Self

25.10.98	Waj Khan W PTS 6 Shaw
26.11.98	Daniel Ring DREW 6 Bradford
07.12.98	Kevin Gerowski L PTS 6 Bradford
21.02.99	Chris Emanuele DREW 6 Bradford
19.04.99	Gary Groves L CO 1 Bradford
19.09.99	Gary Ford L PTS 6 Shaw
14.11.99	Shane Mallon W PTS 6 Bradford
26.11.99	Chris Emanuele L RSC 5 Wakefield
05.03.00	Gary Ford L PTS 6 Shaw
15.05.00	Chris Edwards W PTS 6 Bradford
25.06.00	Levi Pattison L PTS 6 Wakefield
30.11.00	Neil Read W PTS 6 Blackpool
07.12.00	John-Paul Ryan L PTS 6 Stoke
11.02.01	Michael Hunter L RSC 6 Hartlepool
20.03.01	Sean Grant DREW 6 Leeds
01.04.01	Dafydd Carlin L PTS 4 Southwark
09.04.01	Sean Grant L PTS 6 Bradford
10.06.01	Lee Holmes L PTS 6 Ellesmere Port
31.07.01	Jamie Yelland L RSC 5 Bethnal Green
22.10.01	Sean Grant L PTS 6 Glasgow
19.11.01	Gary Groves W PTS 6 Glasgow
09.12.01	Joel Viney L PTS 6 Blackpool
21.02.02	Gypsy Boy Mario W PTS 6 Sunderland
02.03.02	Sean Hughes L PTS 6 Wakefield
28.05.02	John Paul Ryan L PTS 6 Leeds
24.06.02	Gary Groves W RSC 2 Bradford

Career: 26 contests, won 7, drew 3, lost 16.

Ali Forbes

Sydenham. *Born* London, 7 March, 1961
L. Heavyweight. Former British S. Middleweight Champion. Former Undefeated Southern Area S. Middleweight Champion. Ht. 5'9"
Manager Self

16.02.89	David Haycock W RSC 4 Battersea
22.06.90	Andy Marlow W RTD 4 Gillingham
26.09.90	Peter Vosper W PTS 6 Mayfair
06.02.91	Adrian Wright W PTS 6 Battersea
03.04.91	Karl Barwise W RTD 4 Bethnal Green
16.05.91	Quinn Paynter DREW 6 Battersea
01.06.91	Paul McCarthy W CO 2 Bethnal Green
11.03.92	Ian Strudwick L PTS 10 Solihull
	(Southern Area S. Middleweight Title Challenge)
29.10.92	Nick Manners W RSC 3 Leeds
28.11.93	Carlos Christie W CO 4 Southwark
06.03.94	Richard Bustin W PTS 10 Southwark
	(Vacant Southern Area S. Middleweight Title)
29.09.94	Darron Griffiths W PTS 12 Bethnal Green
	(Final Elim. British S. Middleweight Title)
23.01.95	Fidel Castro W PTS 12 Bethnal Green
	(Vacant British S. Middleweight Title)
27.04.95	Sammy Storey L PTS 12 Bethnal Green
	(British S. Middleweight Title Defence)
16.05.98	Darren Ashton W PTS 6 Chigwell
21.11.98	David Starie L CO 11 Southwark
	(Commonwealth S. Middleweight Title Challenge. Vacant British S. Middleweight Title)
18.12.99	Mark Delaney L PTS 8 Southwark
09.03.00	Mark Baker L PTS 12 Bethnal Green
	(Vacant WBF L. Heavyweight Title)
09.06.00	Kid Dongo L RTD 10 Santa Cruz, Tenerife, Spain
	(WBA International L. Heavyweight Title Challenge)
14.10.00	Thomas Ulrich L PTS 8 Cologne, Germany
24.03.01	Clinton Woods L RTD 10 Sheffield
	(Vacant WBC Inter-Continental L. Heavyweight Title)
21.06.01	Mark Williams W PTS 4 Earls Court
08.12.01	Jason Hart W RSC 3 Millwall
26.01.02	Neil Linford L PTS 6 Bethnal Green
12.02.02	Andrew Lowe L PTS 4 Bethnal Green

Career: 25 contests, won 14, drew 1, lost 10.

Maurice Forbes

Brixton. *Born* Jamaica, 24 June, 1968
L. Middleweight. Ht. 5'10½"
Manager Self

23.05.93	Michael Dick W RSC 1 Brockley
25.06.93	Kenny Scott W RSC 2 Battersea
14.08.93	Phil Found W PTS 4 Hammersmith
14.04.94	Dave Maj W RTD 2 Battersea
22.05.94	Trevor Meikle W RTD 3 Crystal Palace
21.07.94	Michael Smyth L RSC 3 Battersea
27.11.94	Marty Duke W PTS 6 Southwark
31.03.95	Steve McGovern W PTS 6 Crystal Palace
02.06.95	Gordon Blair W RSC 4 Bethnal Green
03.05.97	Chris Pyatt L PTS 8 Manchester
27.02.98	Danny Quacoe W RSC 5 Brighton
04.10.01	Charden Ansoula L PTS 4 Finsbury

Career: 12 contests, won 9, lost 3.

Allan Foster

Northampton. *Born* Kilmarnock, 8
November, 1973
S. Middleweight. Ht. 5'11"
Manager C. Sanigar

03.12.99	Steve Timms W RSC 4 Peterborough
05.03.00	Richie Jenkins W PTS 6 Peterborough
02.06.00	Leigh Wicks W PTS 4 Ashford
06.10.00	Paul Johnson W PTS 4 Maidstone
01.12.00	Michael Pinnock W PTS 4 Peterborough
17.02.01	Tommy Matthews W PTS 4 Bethnal Green
24.03.01	Darren Covill W RTD 3 Sheffield
31.07.01	Mark Snipe W PTS 6 Bethnal Green
16.03.02	Alan Jones DREW 6 Northampton

Career: 9 contests, won 8, drew 1.

Steve Foster

Salford. *Born* Salford, 16 September, 1980
Featherweight. Ht. 5'6"
Manager S. Foster/S. Wood/F. Maloney

15.09.01	Andy Greenaway W PTS 4 Manchester
27.10.01	Gareth Wiltshaw W PTS 4 Manchester
02.03.02	Andy Greenaway W RSC 1 Bethnal Green
04.05.02	Gareth Wiltshaw W PTS 4 Bethnal Green

Career: 4 contests, won 4.

Steve Foster   Les Clark

Dean Francis

Basingstoke. *Born* Basingstoke, 23 January, 1974
S. Middleweight. Former Undefeated

British, European & WBO Inter-Continental S. Middleweight Champion.
Ht. 5'10½"
Manager C. Sanigar

28.05.94	Darren Littlewood W PTS 4 Queensway
17.06.94	Martin Jolley W PTS 6 Plymouth
21.07.94	Horace Fleary W RSC 4 Tooting
02.09.94	Steve Osborne W RTD 4 Spitalfields
27.10.94	Tony Booth W CO 1 Bayswater
22.11.94	Darron Griffiths W RTD 1 Bristol
30.03.95	Paul Murray W RSC 2 Bethnal Green
25.05.95	Hunter Clay W RSC 8 Reading
16.06.95	Paul Murray W RTD 3 Southwark
20.10.95	Zafarou Ballogou L RSC 10 Ipswich *(WBC International S. Middleweight Title Challenge)*
16.12.95	Kid Milo W RSC 3 Cardiff
13.02.96	Mike Bonislawski W RSC 2 Bethnal Green
26.04.96	Neil Simpson W RSC 3 Cardiff
08.06.96	John Marceta W RSC 8 Newcastle
14.09.96	Larry Kenny W RSC 2 Sheffield
19.10.96	Rolando Torres W RSC 4 Bristol *(Vacant WBO Inter-Continental S. Middleweight Title)*
14.03.97	Cornelius Carr W RSC 7 Reading *(WBO Inter-Continental S. Middleweight Title Defence)*
15.05.97	Kit Munro W RSC 2 Reading *(WBO Inter-Continental S. Middleweight Title Defence)*
19.07.97	David Starie W RSC 6 Wembley *(British S. Middleweight Title Challenge)*
19.12.97	Frederic Seillier W RSC 9 Millwall *(Vacant European S. Middleweight Title)*
07.03.98	Mark Baker W RSC 12 Reading *(British & WBO Inter-Continental S. Middleweight Title Defences)*
22.08.98	Xolani Ngemntu W CO 2 Hammanskraal, South Africa *(WBO Inter-Continental S. Middleweight Title Defence)*
31.10.98	Undra White L RTD 4 Basingstoke *(Vacant IBO Inter-Continental S. Middleweight Title)*
20.04.02	Mondili Mbonambi W PTS 8 Wembley

Career: 24 contests, won 22, lost 2.

Julius Francis

Woolwich. *Born* Peckham, 8 December, 1964
Former Undefeated Commonwealth Heavyweight Champion. Former British Heavyweight Champion. Former Undefeated Southern Area Heavyweight Champion. Ht. 6'2"
Manager Self

23.05.93	Graham Arnold W RSC 5 Brockley
23.06.93	Joey Paladino W CO 4 Edmonton
24.07.93	Andre Tisdale W PTS 4 Atlantic City, USA
28.08.93	Don Sargent W RSC 2 Bismark, USA
01.12.93	John Keeton W PTS 4 Bethnal Green
27.04.94	Manny Burgo W PTS 4 Bethnal Green
25.05.94	John Ruiz L CO 4 Bristol
12.11.94	Conroy Nelson W RSC 4 Dublin

23.11.94	Gary Charlton W RSC 1 Piccadilly
23.02.05	Damien Caesar W RSC 8 Southwark *(Vacant Southern Area Heavyweight Title)*
27.04.95	Keith Fletcher W PTS 10 Bethnal Green *(Southern Area Heavyweight Title Defence)*
25.05.95	Steve Garber W PTS 8 Reading
01.07.95	Scott Welch L RSC 10 Kensington *(Southern Area Heavyweight Title Defence. Final Elim. British Heavyweight Title)*
24.10.95	Neil Kirkwood W RSC 7 Southwark
30.11.95	Nikolai Kulpin L PTS 10 Saratov, Russia
05.02.96	Michael Murray L PTS 10 Bexleyheath *(Elim. British Heavyweight Title)*
09.04.96	Damien Caesar W CO 1 Stevenage *(Vacant Southern Area Heavyweight Title)*
07.05.96	Darren Fearn W PTS 8 Mayfair
09.07.96	Mike Holden W PTS 10 Bethnal Green
28.09.96	James Oyebola W RSC 5 Barking *(Southern Area Heavyweight Title Defence)*
15.02.97	Zeljko Mavrovic L RSC 8 Vienna, Austria *(European Heavyweight Title Challenge)*
30.06.97	Joseph Chingangu W PTS 12 Bethnal Green *(Vacant Commonwealth Heavyweight Title)*
27.09.97	Garry Delaney W RSC 6 Belfast *(Commonwealth Heavyweight Title Defence. Vacant British Heavyweight Title)*
28.02.98	Axel Schulz L PTS 12 Dortmund, Germany
18.04.98	Vitali Klitschko L RSC 2 Aachen, Germany
30.01.99	Pele Reid W RSC 3 Bethnal Green *(British & Commonwealth Heavyweight Title Defences)*
03.04.99	Danny Williams W PTS 12 Kensington *(British & Commonwealth Heavyweight Title Defences)*
26.06.99	Scott Welch W PTS 12 Millwall *(British & Commonwealth Heavyweight Title Defences)*
29.01.00	Mike Tyson L RSC 2 Manchester
13.03.00	Mike Holden L PTS 12 Bethnal Green *(British Heavyweight Title Defence)*
03.04.01	Mike Holden W PTS 12 Bethnal Green *(Final Elim. British Heavyweight Title)*
28.07.01	Danny Williams L CO 4 Wembley *(British & Commonwealth Heavyweight Title Challenges)*
10.05.02	Luke Simpkin DREW 6 Millwall

Career: 33 contests, won 22, drew 1, lost 10.

Carl Froch

Nottingham. *Born* Nottingham, 2 July, 1977
S. Middleweight. Ht. 6'4"
Manager R. McCracken

16.03.02	Michael Pinnock W RSC 4 Bethnal Green
10.05.02	Ojay Abrahams W RSC 1 Bethnal Green

Career: 2 contests, won 2.

Matt Galer

Burton. *Born* Burton, 15 December, 1973
Middleweight. Ht. 5'8"
Manager J. Ashton

30.09.97	Martin Cavey W CO 1 Edgbaston
18.11.97	Chris Pollock W PTS 6 Mansfield
16.03.98	Mike Duffield W PTS 6 Nottingham
14.05.98	Freddie Yemofio W RSC 4 Acton
14.10.98	Carlton Williams L PTS 6 Stoke
25.03.99	Gordon Behan L RSC 9 Edgbaston
	(Midlands Area Middleweight Title Challenge)
15.08.99	Jason Collins L PTS 6 Derby
13.11.01	Danny Thornton W RSC 4 Leeds
09.02.02	Anthony Farnell L RSC 3 Manchester

Career: 9 contests, won 5, lost 4.

Patrick Gallagher

Islington. *Born* Manchester, 23 July, 1971
Lightweight. Ht. 5'7½"
Manager Self

22.12.92	Karl Taylor W RSC 3 Mayfair
20.02.93	Joe Fannin W RTD 1 Earls Court
21.12.93	Karl Taylor W PTS 6 Mayfair
11.01.94	Mark Antony W RSC 3 Bethnal Green
15.03.94	Karl Taylor W PTS 6 Mayfair
07.11.94	Rudy Valentino W PTS 6 Bethnal Green
27.05.95	Paul Burke L PTS 8 Belfast
27.01.98	Elvis Parsley W CO 3 Bethnal Green
11.03.98	David Kirk W PTS 6 Bethnal Green
28.04.98	Ian McLeod L RSC 7 Belfast
	(Vacant IBO Inter-Continental S. Featherweight Title)
27.04.99	Demir Nanev W RSC 3 Bethnal Green
28.04.01	Gareth Jordan W PTS 4 Cardiff
26.01.02	Jason Dee W DIS 6 Dagenham

Career: 13 contests, won 11, lost 2.

Rob Galloway

Barnsley. *Born* Barnsley, 30 May, 1974
Cruiserweight. Ht. 5'11"
Manager Self

17.02.98	Clint Johnson L PTS 6 Leeds
15.05.98	Johnny Hooks L PTS 6 Nottingham
20.09.98	Clint Johnson L PTS 6 Sheffield
23.10.98	Paul Bonson L PTS 6 Wakefield
03.12.98	Tony Rowbotham L PTS 6 Hull
20.12.98	Mike White L PTS 6 Salford
01.02.99	Shamus Casey L PTS 6 Bradford
26.02.99	Joe Gillon L PTS 6 Irvine
05.03.99	Brian Kilbride L PTS 4 Liverpool
19.04.99	Joe Gillon L PTS 6 Glasgow
29.05.99	Darren Kirby L PTS 6 South Shields
14.06.99	Lee Simpkin DREW 6 Bradford
12.09.99	Lee Simpkin L RSC 4 Nottingham
30.10.99	Andy Vickers L PTS 6 Peterlee
26.11.99	Kent Davis W PTS 6 Hull
06.12.99	Eamonn Glennon L PTS 6 Bradford
20.12.99	Paul Maskell L RSC 1 Bethnal Green
02.03.00	Eamonn Glennon L PTS 6 Blackpool
14.04.00	Kent Davis L PTS 6 Manchester
09.06.00	Kent Davis L CO 3 Hull

21.10.00	Mark Brookes L RSC 5 Sheffield
10.12.01	Gary Thompson L PTS 6 Bradford
28.01.02	Pinky Burton L RSC 4 Barnsley

Career: 23 contests, won 1, drew 1, lost 21.

(Terrace) Terry Gaskin

Doncaster. *Born* Doncaster, 20 October, 1974
Former Central Area Flyweight Champion.
Ht. 5'4"
Manager Self

28.03.94	Keith Knox L PTS 6 Musselburgh
09.05.94	Tiger Singh L RSC 2 Bradford
26.09.94	Ian Baillie W RSC 3 Bradford
29.10.94	Neil Parry L PTS 6 Cannock
28.11.94	Tiger Singh L PTS 6 Manchester
08.12.94	Ian Baillie W RTD 3 Hull
11.03.95	Neil Parry DREW 6 Barnsley
22.03.95	Neil Parry L PTS 8 Stoke
19.05.95	Shaun Hall L RSC 3 Leeds
21.09.95	Darren Noble DREW 6 Sheffield
20.10.95	Steve Williams L PTS 6 Mansfield
12.05.97	Paul Squire DREW 6 Leicester
20.10.97	Tiny Pope W CO 3 Leicester
04.12.97	Chris Thomas W PTS 6 Doncaster
13.12.97	Zoltan Lunka L CO 2 Hamburg, Germany
27.11.98	Chris Emanuele L PTS 6 Nottingham
18.03.99	Andy Roberts W RSC 8 Doncaster
17.07.99	David Coldwell L CO 5 Doncaster
	(Central Area Flyweight Title Challenge)
15.01.00	Andy Roberts W RSC 8 Doncaster
	(Vacant Central Area Flyweight Title)
08.05.01	Dale Robinson L RTD 3 Barnsley
	(Central Area Flyweight Title Defence)
18.02.02	Jimbo Rooney L RSC 3 Glasgow

Career: 21 contests, won 6, drew 3, lost 12.

Brian Gentry

Morden. *Born* Balham, 2 January, 1975
Lightweight. Ht. 5'6"
Manager B. Baker

29.11.95	Des Gargano W PTS 4 Southwark
20.09.96	Stevie Bolt W RSC 3 Tooting
07.11.96	Wayne Jones L PTS 6 Battersea
15.02.97	David Jeffrey W PTS 6 Tooting
02.12.97	Wee Barry W PTS 6 Windsor
03.10.98	Benny Jones W PTS 6 Crawley
25.11.98	Des Sowden W RSC 6 Streatham
24.03.99	Wayne Jones W PTS 6 Bayswater
21.07.99	Arv Mittoo W RSC 4 Bloomsbury
31.10.99	Dennis Griffin W PTS 4 Raynes Park
06.05.00	Dean Murdoch W RSC 3 Southwark
08.09.00	Gary Flear L RSC 6 Hammersmith
	(Vacant British Masters Lightweight Title)
10.03.01	Graham Earl L RSC 8 Bethnal Green
	(Vacant Southern Area Lightweight Title)
22.04.01	Keith Jones W PTS 8 Streatham
25.02.02	Nigel Senior L RSC 8 Slough
	(British Masters Lightweight Title Defence)

Career: 15 contests, won 11, lost 4.

Lee Georgiou

Romford. *Born* Rush Green, 25 April, 1977
Flyweight. Ht. 5'2½"
Manager F. Maloney

19.10.99	Chris Edwards W RSC 2 Bethnal Green
29.11.99	Delroy Spencer W PTS 4 Wembley
15.04.00	Delroy Spencer W PTS 4 Bethnal Green
13.07.00	Chris Emanuele L CO 1 Bethnal Green
26.01.02	Marty Kayes W PTS 6 Bethnal Green
13.06.02	Sunkanbi Ogunbiyi L CO 1 Leicester Square

Career: 6 contests, won 4, lost 2.

Kevin Gerowski   Les Clark

Kevin Gerowski

Nottingham. *Born* Leicester, 6 February, 1971
Bantamweight. Ht. 5'4½"
Manager J. Gill

07.05.98	John Barnes L PTS 6 Sunderland
12.10.98	Brendan Bryce W PTS 6 Nottingham
16.11.98	Craig Docherty L PTS 6 Glasgow
28.11.98	Barry Waite L PTS 4 Belfast
07.12.98	Paddy Folan W PTS 6 Bradford
22.01.99	Ady Benton W PTS 4 Carlisle
25.02.99	Mickey Bowden L PTS 4 Kentish Town
22.03.99	Alston Buchanan L PTS 6 Glasgow
03.04.99	Shaun Anderson L PTS 4 Carlisle
17.04.99	Willie Valentine L PTS 6 Dublin
06.06.99	Waj Khan W PTS 6 Nottingham
12.09.99	Pete Buckley W PTS 6 Nottingham
01.10.99	Salim Medjkoune L PTS 6 Bethnal Green
18.10.99	Shaun Anderson L PTS 6 Glasgow
27.11.99	Tommy Waite W PTS 6 Liverpool
13.12.99	Sean Green W PTS 6 Cleethorpes
19.02.00	Esham Pickering L PTS 10 Newark
	(Vacant British Masters Bantamweight Title. Elim. British Bantamweight Title)
02.06.00	Frankie DeMilo L RSC 7 Ashford
	(British Masters S. Bantamweight Title Challenge)
26.10.00	Leon Dobbs W CO 1 Stoke
05.12.00	Jason Thomas W PTS 8 Nottingham
11.06.01	Nicky Booth L RSC 4 Nottingham

07.10.01 Stephen Chinnock L PTS 10
Wolverhampton
*(Vacant Midlands Area Featherweight
Title)*
10.11.01 Stephen Oates L PTS 6 Wembley
09.12.01 Choi Tseveenpurev L RSC 5 Shaw
*(Vacant British Masters Featherweight
Title)*

Career: 24 contests, won 9, lost 15.

Steve Gethin

Walsall. *Born* Walsall, 30 July, 1978
Featherweight. Ht. 5'9"
Manager Self

03.09.99 Ike Halls W RSC 3 West Bromwich
24.10.99 Ricky Bishop W RSC 4
Wolverhampton
22.01.00 Sebastian Hart L PTS 4 Birmingham
10.09.00 Nigel Senior DREW 6 Walsall
03.06.01 Richmond Asante L PTS 4 Southwark
28.11.01 Mickey Coveney L PTS 4 Bethnal
Green
09.12.01 Gary Groves W PTS 6 Shaw
17.02.02 Gary Groves W PTS 6 Wolverhampton
01.06.02 Gary Davis W RSC 2 Manchester
Career: 9 contests, won 5, drew 1, lost 3.

Alex Gething

Abergavenny. *Born* Gelligaer, 10 May,
1977
L. Heavyweight. Ht. 6'1"
Manager D. Gardiner

24.03.02 Calvin Stonestreet DREW 4 Streatham
Career: 1 contest, drew 1.

Brian Gifford

Hull. *Born* Hull, 27 January, 1972
Welterweight. Ht. 5'6"
Manager M. Toomey

26.02.99 Gavin Down L PTS 6 West Bromwich
05.03.99 Ray Wood L CO 2 Liverpool
22.04.99 Lee Williamson L PTS 6 Dudley
17.05.99 Dave Gibson W PTS 6 Cleethorpes
29.05.99 Oscar Hall L RSC 1 Halifax
27.09.99 Karim Bouali L RSC 3 Cleethorpes
18.02.01 Babatunde Ajayi L RSC 1 Southwark
10.05.01 Gary Greenwood L PTS 6 Sunderland
08.06.01 Ram Singh L PTS 6 Hull
23.06.01 Ram Singh DREW 4 Peterborough
26.07.01 Alan Campbell L PTS 6 Blackpool
07.09.01 Daniel Thorpe DREW 4 Bethnal Green
30.11.01 Tony Montana L PTS 6 Hull
19.12.01 Andy Egan L RSC 1 Coventry
09.02.02 Jason Rushton L RSC 1 Manchester
Career: 15 contests, won 1, drew 2, lost 12.

Alan Gilbert

Crawley. *Born* Bromley, 17 November, 1970
Middleweight. Ht. 5'11"
Manager Self

02.12.97 Martin Cavey W RSC 1 Windsor
06.01.98 Harry Butler W PTS 4 Brighton
23.02.98 Jon Harrison W PTS 6 Windsor
21.04.98 Paul Henry L PTS 4 Edmonton
08.08.98 Lee Murtagh L PTS 4 Scarborough
03.10.98 C. J. Jackson W RSC 3 Crawley
25.02.99 Justin Simmons W RSC 5 Kentish Town
01.05.99 Anthony Farnell L RSC 8 Crystal Palace

07.08.99 Wayne Shepherd DREW 8 Dagenham
*(Vacant British Masters
L. Middleweight Title)*
11.03.00 Michael Jones L RTD 3 Kensington
12.06.00 Jim Rock L PTS 6 Belfast
22.07.00 Delroy Mellis L RSC 3 Watford
*(Vacant Southern Area L.Middleweight
Title)*
23.01.01 Delroy Mellis L RSC 3 Crawley
*(Southern Area L. Middleweight Title
Challenge)*
29.09.01 Steven Bendall L RTD 3 Southwark
10.02.02 Allan Gray DREW 4 Southwark
28.04.02 Allan Gray L PTS 10 Southwark
*(Vacant Southern Area Middleweight
Title)*
Career: 16 contests, won 5, drew 2, lost 9.

Joe Gillon

Motherwell. *Born* Motherwell, 24 April,
1977
L. Heavyweight. Ht. 6'3"
Manager T. Gilmour

26.02.99 Rob Galloway W PTS 6 Irvine
19.04.99 Rob Galloway W PTS 6 Glasgow
23.10.00 Clint Johnson W CO 4 Glasgow
20.03.01 Michael Pinnock W PTS 6 Glasgow
04.06.01 Paul Bonson DREW 6 Glasgow
03.11.01 Clint Johnson L CO 3 Glasgow
Career: 6 contests, won 4, drew 1, lost 1.

Mark Gladwell

Southampton. *Born* Portsmouth, 26 August,
1977
Heavyweight. Ht. 6'2"
Manager J. Bishop

11.02.02 Brodie Pearmaine L RSC 3
Southampton
Career: 1 contest, lost 1.

Mark Gladwell   Les Clark

Eamonn Glennon

Blackpool. *Born* Blackpool, 12 February,
1970
Heavyweight. Ht. 5'10"
Manager L. Veitch

06.12.99 Rob Galloway W PTS 6 Bradford
02.03.00 Rob Galloway W PTS 6 Blackpool
09.06.00 Mark Dawson L PTS 6 Blackpool
25.09.00 Dave Faulkner W PTS 4 Barnsley
08.12.00 Darren Chubbs L PTS 4 Crystal Palace
27.01.01 John McDermott L RSC 1 Bethnal
Green
10.03.01 Danny Percival L PTS 4 Bethnal Green
22.04.01 Colin Kenna L PTS 4 Streatham
30.04.01 Lee Swaby L PTS 6 Glasgow
26.07.01 Adam Cale W PTS 6 Blackpool
09.09.01 Paul Bonson L PTS 6 Hartlepool
29.09.01 Dominic Negus L PTS 6 Southwark
09.10.01 Enzo Macarinelli L RSC 1 Cardiff
16.11.01 Paul Buttery L RSC 1 Preston
15.12.01 Mark Krence L RSC 2 Sheffield
10.05.02 Tony Moran L RTD 1 Preston
24.06.02 Lee Mountford W PTS 6 Bradford
Career: 17 contests, won 5, lost 12.

Michael Gomez (Armstrong)

Manchester. *Born* Dublin, 21 June, 1977
Former Undefeated WBO Inter-Continental
& British S. Featherweight Champion.
Former WBO Inter-Continental S.
Featherweight Champion. Former
Undefeated Central Area & IBF Inter-
Continental Featherweight Champion.
Ht. 5'5"
Manager F. Warren

10.06.95 Danny Ruegg W PTS 6 Manchester
15.09.95 Greg Upton L PTS 4 Mansfield
24.11.95 Danny Ruegg L PTS 4 Manchester
19.09.96 Martin Evans W RSC 1 Manchester
09.11.96 David Morris W PTS 4 Manchester
22.03.97 John Farrell W RSC 2 Wythenshawe
03.05.97 Chris Williams L PTS 4 Manchester
11.09.97 Wayne Jones W RSC 2 Widnes
18.04.98 Benny Jones W PTS 4 Manchester
16.05.98 Craig Spacie W RSC 3 Bethnal Green
05.09.98 Pete Buckley W PTS 6 Telford
14.11.98 David Jeffrey W RSC 1 Cheshunt
19.12.98 Kevin Sheil W RSC 4 Liverpool
13.02.99 Dave Hinds W PTS 6 Newcastle
27.02.99 Chris Jickells W RSC 5 Oldham
*(Vacant Central Area Featherweight
Title)*
29.05.99 Nigel Leake W RSC 2 Halifax
*(Vacant IBF Inter-Continental
Featherweight Title)*
07.08.99 William Alverzo W PTS 6 Atlantic
City, USA
04.09.99 Gary Thornhill W RSC 2 Bethnal
Green
(Vacant British S. Featherweight Title)
06.11.99 Jose Juan Manjarrez W PTS 12
Widnes
*(WBO Inter-Continental
S. Featherweight Title Defence)*
11.12.99 Oscar Galindo W RSC 11 Liverpool
*(WBO Inter-Continental
S. Featherweight Title Defence)*
29.01.00 Chris Jickells W RSC 4 Manchester
29.02.00 Dean Pithie W PTS 12 Widnes
*(British S. Featherweight Title
Defence)*

24.06.00 Carl Allen W CO 2 Glasgow
08.07.00 Carl Greaves W CO 2 Widnes
          (British S. Featherweight Title
          Defence)
19.10.00 Awel Abdulai W PTS 8 Harrisburg,
          USA
11.12.00 Ian McLeod W PTS 12 Widnes
          (British S.Featherweight Title
          Defence)
10.02.01 Laszlo Bognar L RSC 9 Widnes
          (WBO Inter-Continental
          S. Featherweight Title Defence)
07.07.01 Laszlo Bognar W RSC 3 Manchester
          (WBO Inter-Continental
          S. Featherweight Title Challenge)
27.10.01 Craig Docherty W RSC 2 Manchester
          (British S.Featherweight Title Defence)
01.06.02 Kevin Lear L RTD 8 Manchester
          (Vacant WBU S. Featherweight Title)

Career: 30 contests, won 25, lost 5.

Jason Gonzalez

Birmingham. *Born* Birmingham, 5 January,
1970
Lightweight. Ht. 5'6"
Manager N. Nobbs

22.11.01 Chris McDonagh L PTS 6 Paddington
10.12.01 Daniel Thorpe L RSC 2 Birmingham
09.02.02 Gary Greenwood L PTS 6 Coventry
28.04.02 Albi Hunt L PTS 6 Southwark
15.06.02 Jackson Williams L PTS 6 Norwich
23.06.02 James Paisley L PTS 6 Southwark

Career: 6 contests, lost 6.

Sam Gorman

Alfreton. *Born* Nuneaton, 19 October, 1981
Welterweight. Ht. 5'9"
Manager J. Weaver

17.11.01 Shaune Danskin W RSC 3 Coventry
09.02.02 Pete Buckley W PTS 6 Coventry
22.03.02 Brian Coleman W PTS 6 Coventry
25.06.02 Pedro Thompson W PTS 6 Rugby

Career: 4 contests, won 4.

Jimmy Gould

Coseley. *Born* Wolverhampton, 8 July,
1977
L. Welterweight. Ht. 5'10"
Manager Self

23.06.99 Benny Jones W PTS 6 West
          Bromwich
03.09.99 Dave Travers W PTS 6 West
          Bromwich
06.11.00 Jon Honney W PTS 6 Wolverhampton
28.01.01 David White W PTS 6
          Wolverhampton
20.05.01 Keith Jones W PTS 6 Wolverhampton
07.09.01 Woody Greenaway W PTS 6 West
          Bromwich
07.10.01 Steve Hanley W PTS 6 Wolverhampton
13.04.02 Keith Jones W PTS 8 Wolverhampton
25.05.02 Raymond Narh L RSC 3 Portsmouth

Career: 9 contests, won 8, lost 1.

Darrell Grafton

Chesterfield. *Born* Chesterfield, 14 July,
1974
Welterweight. Ht. 5'10"
Manager M. Shinfield

11.06.01 Chris Steele W RSC 1 Nottingham
15.09.01 Ram Singh W DIS 5 Nottingham
22.10.01 Emmanuel Marcos W RSC 2 Glasgow
10.12.01 Prince Kasi Kaihau W RSC 5
          Nottingham
23.02.02 Jon Honney W RTD 1 Nottingham
11.05.02 Neil Bonner W PTS 6 Chesterfield

Career: 6 contests, won 6.

Darrell Grafton   Les Clark

Sean Grant

Newton Aycliffe. *Born* Bishop Auckland,
18 January, 1971
Featherweight. Ht. 5'6"
Manager T. Callighan

04.12.97 John Barnes L PTS 6 Sunderland
03.02.98 Graham McGrath W PTS 6 Yarm
30.04.98 Peter Allen W PTS 6 Pentre Halkyn
18.07.98 Noel Wilders L RSC 4 Sheffield
19.09.98 Willie Valentine L PTS 4 Dublin
11.12.98 Nicky Cook L CO 1 Cheshunt
29.05.99 Gary Groves W PTS 6 South Shields
29.06.99 Barry Waite L RSC 3 Bethnal Green
16.10.99 David Lowry L RSC 1 Belfast
13.12.99 Jesse James Daniel L RSC 5
          Cleethorpes
22.01.00 Gareth Payne L RSC 1 Birmingham
20.05.00 Chris Emanuele L RSC 5 Rotherham
23.07.00 Michael Hunter L PTS 6 Hartlepool
20.10.00 Stevie Quinn L RSC 2 Belfast
20.03.01 Paddy Folan DREW 6 Leeds
09.04.01 Paddy Folan W PTS 6 Bradford
08.05.01 Jim Betts L RSC 3 Barnsley
09.06.01 Martin Power L PTS 4 Bethnal Green
22.10.01 Paddy Folan W PTS 6 Glasgow
17.11.01 Jesse James Daniel L RSC 1 Dewsbury
08.02.02 Lee Holmes L CO 5 Preston
15.06.02 Noel Wilders L RSC 3 Leeds

Career: 22 contests, won 5, drew 1, lost 16.

Allan Gray

Putney. *Born* Roehampton, 4 August, 1971
Southern Area Middleweight Champion.
Ht. 5'9"
Manager D. Mancini

19.05.95 Darren Covill W PTS 6 Southwark
23.06.95 Wayne Jones W PTS 6 Bethnal Green
27.09.95 Brian Coleman W PTS 6 Bethnal Green
28.10.95 John O. Johnson W PTS 6 Kensington
29.11.95 Justin Simmons L PTS 6 Bethnal
          Green
08.12.95 Mike Watson W PTS 8 Bethnal Green
15.03.96 Mike Watson DREW 6 Dunstable
29.04.96 Mike Watson W PTS 6 Mayfair
03.07.96 Jon Harrison W PTS 6 Wembley
24.10.96 Costas Katsantonis W PTS 6 Mayfair
29.01.97 Gary Hiscox W PTS 6 Bethnal Green
19.02.97 Costas Katsantonis W PTS 6 Acton
30.04.97 Howard Clarke L PTS 8 Acton
27.01.98 Peter Nightingale W PTS 6 Streatham
26.09.98 Harry Dhami L PTS 10 Southwark
          (Southern Area Welterweight Title
          Challenge)
16.02.99 Lee Bird W PTS 6 Brentford
31.10.99 Matthew Barr L PTS 4 Raynes Park
15.04.00 Jim Rock L PTS 10 Bethnal Green
          (Vacant All-Ireland L. Middleweight
          Title)
22.10.00 Delroy Mellis L RSC 6 Streatham
          (Southern Area L.Middleweight Title
          Challenge)
28.10.01 Leigh Wicks W PTS 4 Southwark
16.12.01 Leigh Wicks W PTS 4 Southwark
10.02.02 Alan Gilbert DREW 4 Southwark
28.04.02 Alan Gilbert W PTS 10 Southwark
          (Vacant Southern Area Middleweight
          Title)

Career: 23 contests, won 15, drew 2, lost 6.

Carl Greaves

Newark. *Born* Nottingham, 12 June, 1976
Former Undefeated British Masters &
Midlands Area S. Featherweight Champion.
Ht. 5'7"
Manager J. Ashton

22.03.96 Paul Hamilton W PTS 6 Mansfield
30.05.96 Kevin Sheil W PTS 6 Lincoln
02.10.96 Robert Grubb W PTS 8 Stoke
01.11.96 Benny Jones W PTS 6 Mansfield
26.11.96 Danny Ruegg W RTD 4 Sheffield
04.12.96 Des Gargano W PTS 6 Stoke
20.02.97 Lee Armstrong L RSC 4 Mansfield
10.04.97 Kevin Sheil W PTS 6 Sheffield
08.05.97 Benny Jones L RSC 4 Mansfield
10.07.97 Stefy Bull L PTS 6 Doncaster
18.08.97 Graham McGrath W PTS 6
          Nottingham
06.10.97 Ervine Blake L PTS 10 Birmingham
          (Vacant Midlands Area
          S. Featherweight Title)
30.10.97 Graham McGrath W PTS 6 Newark
18.11.97 Garry Burrell W CO 4 Mansfield
07.05.98 John T. Kelly W PTS 6 Sunderland
14.10.98 Andrew Robinson W PTS 6 Stoke
02.12.98 Graham McGrath W PTS 6 Stoke
18.03.99 Ernie Smith W PTS 6 Doncaster
27.06.99 Chris Jickells W PTS 10 Alfreton
          (British Masters S. Featherweight
          Final)
20.11.99 Pete Buckley W PTS 10 Grantham
          (British Masters S. Featherweight Title
          Defence)
18.01.00 Keith Jones W PTS 6 Mansfield
19.02.00 Marc Smith W PTS 6 Newark
20.03.00 Pete Buckley W PTS 4 Mansfield
11.05.00 Marco Fattore W PTS 8 Newark

08.07.00 Michael Gomez L CO 2 Widnes
(British S. Featherweight Title Challenge)
09.09.00 Dave Hinds W PTS 6 Newark
19.11.00 Haroon Din W RSC 4 Chesterfield
24.03.01 Nigel Senior W CO 6 Newark
(Vacant Midlands Area S. Featherweight Title)
16.06.01 Dave Hinds W PTS 6 Derby
11.05.02 Wayne Wheeler W RSC 1 Newark
Career: 30 contests, won 25, lost 5.

(Roger) Radcliffe Green

Balham. *Born* Jamaica, 24 November, 1973
L. Heavyweight. Ht. 5'9½"
Manager I. Akay

26.03.01 Peter Haymer L PTS 4 Wembley
22.04.01 Adam Cale W CO 5 Streatham
03.06.01 Rob Hayes-Scott W RSC 4 Southwark
21.07.01 John Keeton L PTS 4 Sheffield
28.10.01 Michael Pinnock W PTS 4 Southwark
16.11.01 Darren Corbett L PTS 8 Dublin
10.02.02 Valery Odin L PTS 6 Southwark
20.04.02 Nathan King L PTS 5 Cardiff
04.05.02 Andrew Lowe L PTS 4 Bethnal Green
Career: 9 contests, won 3, lost 6.

Radcliffe Green   Les Clark

Sean Green

Rotherham. *Born* Doncaster, 2 November, 1977
Bantamweight. Ht. 5'6"
Manager J. Rushton

17.12.96 Willie Smith W PTS 6 Doncaster
17.02.97 Jason Whitaker W PTS 6 Bradford
24.02.97 Neil Armstrong L PTS 6 Glasgow
08.05.97 Ross Cassidy DREW 6 Mansfield
27.09.97 Tommy Waite W RSC 3 Belfast
24.10.97 Graham McGrath DREW 6 Birmingham
04.12.97 Jason Thomas DREW 4 Doncaster
21.01.98 Graham McGrath W PTS 6 Stoke
19.03.98 Steve Williams L PTS 6 Doncaster

06.05.98 Louis Veitch W PTS 6 Blackpool
10.10.98 Ian Napa L PTS 6 Bethnal Green
09.12.98 Graham McGrath W PTS 6 Stoke
21.05.99 Chris Jickells W PTS 6 Glasgow
01.06.99 Samir Laala L RSC 3 Levallois, France
27.10.99 Graham McGrath W PTS 6 Birmingham
30.11.99 Phil Lashley W PTS 6 Wolverhampton
13.12.99 Kevin Gerowski L PTS 6 Cleethorpes
15.01.00 Levi Pattison W PTS 4 Doncaster
07.10.00 Hussein Hussein L RSC 1 Doncaster
02.12.00 Danny Costello L PTS 4 Chigwell
16.06.01 Danny Costello W RSC 3 Dagenham
30.09.01 Frankie DeMilo L PTS 6 Bristol
09.02.02 Chris Emanuele L RSC 6 Coventry
(Vacant British Masters Bantamweight Title)
Career: 23 contests, won 11, drew 3, lost 9.

Andy Greenaway

Gelligaer. *Born* Caerphilly, 13 January, 1974
S. Bantamweight. Ht. 5'1"
Manager D. Gardiner

12.12.00 Danny Lawson W PTS 6 Clydach
18.03.01 Gary Ford L RSC 1 Shaw
05.05.01 Gwyn Evans DREW 6 Brighton
27.05.01 Anthony Hughes L PTS 4 Manchester
28.07.01 Martin Power L RSC 3 Wembley
15.09.01 Steve Foster L PTS 4 Manchester
08.10.01 Jamil Hussain L RSC 3 Barnsley

24.11.01 Levi Pattison L PTS 6 Wakefield
02.03.02 Steve Foster L RSC 1 Bethnal Green
Career: 9 contests, won 1, drew 1, lost 7.

(Paul) Woody Greenaway

Gelligaer. *Born* Gelligaer, 5 February, 1972
Lightweight. Ht. 5'7"
Manager Self

23.07.98 Terry Butwell W PTS 6 Barking
17.09.98 Pat Larner L RSC 3 Brighton
13.11.98 Daniel James L PTS 4 Brighton
24.11.98 Ernie Smith W PTS 6 Wolverhampton
07.12.98 Barry Hughes L PTS 4 Acton
14.12.98 Steve Saville W PTS 6 Birmingham
23.02.99 Jason Dee L CO 6 Cardiff
03.04.99 Steve Murray L CO 2 Kensington
26.06.99 Nwajcvenki Sambo L PTS 6 Glasgow
15.07.99 Koba Gogoladze L RSC 2 Peterborough
24.09.99 Alan Bosworth W PTS 6 Merthyr
22.10.99 Roy Rutherford L PTS 4 Coventry
06.11.99 Jason Hall L RSC 5 Bethnal Green
11.12.99 Jason Cook L RSC 1 Mayfair
(Vacant Welsh L. Welterweight Title)
26.02.00 Ross McCord W PTS 4 Swansea
09.03.00 David Burke L RSC 2 Liverpool
19.04.00 Nono Junior L PTS 4 Kensington
12.05.00 Dave Tatton L PTS 4 Swansea
30.05.00 Manzo Smith L PTS 4 Kensington
09.09.00 Gary Hibbert L RSC 2 Manchester
26.10.00 Barrie Kelley L PTS 6 Clydach

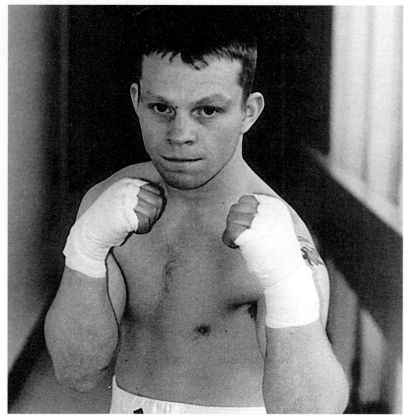

Andy Greenaway   Les Clark

06.11.00	Steve Saville L CO 5 Wolverhampton
12.12.00	Ross McCord W PTS 6 Clydach
02.01.01	Tony Conroy L PTS 4 Coventry
05.02.01	Leo O'Reilly L CO 1 Hull
08.03.01	Mark Bowen DREW 6 Stoke
16.03.01	Jon Honney L PTS 6 Portsmouth
26.03.01	Alex Arthur L RTD 2 Wembley
27.04.01	Dave Stewart L PTS 6 Glasgow
05.05.01	Chill John L PTS 6 Brighton
19.05.01	Mark Hawthorne L PTS 4 Wembley
02.06.01	Lance Crosby L PTS 6 Wakefield
11.06.01	Anthony Maynard L PTS 4 Nottingham
21.06.01	Ajose Olusegun L RSC 1 Earls Court
31.07.01	Costas Katsantonis L RSC 4 Bethnal Green
07.09.01	Jimmy Gould L PTS 6 West Bromwich
15.09.01	Andy McLean L RSC 3 Manchester
20.10.01	Ricky Burns L PTS 4 Glasgow
31.10.01	Pete Buckley W PTS 6 Birmingham
17.11.01	Dean Pithie L PTS 6 Coventry
28.11.01	Nicky Cook L RSC 3 Bethnal Green
19.01.02	Nigel Wright L CO 2 Bethnal Green
15.03.02	Barry Hughes L PTS 8 Glasgow
11.05.02	Gavin Down L RSC 3 Chesterfield

Career: 44 contest, won 8, drew 1, lost 35.

Roman Greenberg

Maidenhead. *Born* Russia, 18 May, 1982
Heavyweight. Ht. 6'2½"
Manager J. Evans

22.11.01	Dave Clarke W RSC 5 Paddington
25.02.02	Paul Bonson W PTS 6 Slough
25.04.02	Jakarta Nakyru W RSC 4 Las Vegas, Nevada, USA

Career: 3 contests, won 3.

Roman Greenberg　　　　Les Clark

Gary Greenwood

Hinckley. *Born* Leicester, 9 December, 1974
Lightweight. Ht. 5'8"
Manager J. Weaver

09.03.00	Ray Wood W PTS 4 Liverpool
03.12.00	Tony Montana DREW 6 Shaw
13.02.01	Dave Travers W PTS 6 Brierley Hill
10.05.01	Brian Gifford W PTS 6 Sunderland
23.06.01	Jay Mahoney L PTS 4 Peterborough
17.11.01	Nigel Senior W PTS 6 Coventry
09.02.02	Jason Gonzalez W PTS 6 Coventry
22.03.02	Dave Cotterill W PTS 6 Coventry
02.06.02	Mally McIver W RSC 1 Shaw

Career: 9 contests, won 7, drew 1, lost 1.

Gary Greenwood　　　　Les Clark

Kenny Griffith

Carmarthen. *Born* Bangor, 23 June, 1978
S. Middleweight. Ht. 5'11½"
Manager R. Jones

21.10.01	Alan Jones L RSC 4 Pentre Halkyn

Career: 1 contest, lost 1.

Kenny Griffith　　　　Les Clark

Gary Groves

Walsall. *Born* Walsall, 17 November, 1969
Featherweight. Ht. 5'6"
Manager Self

21.02.99	Mark Hudson L RSC 3 Bradford
19.04.99	Paddy Folan W CO 1 Bradford
27.04.99	Gary Steadman L RSC 2 Bethnal Green
29.05.99	Sean Grant L PTS 6 South Shields
08.02.00	Neil Read L PTS 6 Wolverhampton
03.03.00	Andrew Ferrans L RSC 1 Irvine
24.11.00	Michael Hunter L RSC 2 Darlington
19.11.01	Paddy Folan L PTS 6 Glasgow
09.12.01	Steve Gethin L PTS 6 Shaw
17.02.02	Steve Gethin L PTS 6 Wolverhampton
24.06.02	Paddy Folan L RSC 2 Bradford

Career: 11 contests, won 1, lost 10.

Audrey Guthrie

Newcastle. *Born* Newcastle, 19 April, 1964
Bantamweight. Ht. 5'0"
Manager Self

01.12.99	Jan Wild L PTS 4 Yarm
01.04.01	Sara Hall L RSC 2 Alfreton
22.11.01	Cathy Brown L PTS 6 Mayfair
	(WBF European Flyweight Title Challenge)
10.05.02	Adele Dean L RSC 1 Preston

Career: 4 contests, lost 4.

Danny Gwilym

Bristol. *Born* Bristol, 15 January, 1975
Welterweight. Ht. 5'7"
Manager T. Woodward

16.12.01	Wayne Wheeler L RSC 2 Bristol
11.02.02	James Lee L PTS 6 Southampton

Career: 2 contests, lost 2.

Danny Gwilym　　　　Les Clark

Gary Hadwin
Oldham. *Born* Carlisle, 10 February, 1969
Welterweight. Ht. 5'9"
Manager J. Doughty

02.06.02 Andrei Ivanov L PTS 6 Shaw
Career: 1 contest, lost 1.

Damon Hague (Wheatley)
Derby. *Born* Derby, 29 October, 1970
WBF European & Midlands Area
S. Middleweight Champion. Ht. 6'0"
Manager D. Ingle

27.11.98 Jimmy Steel DREW 6 Nottingham
14.12.98 Dean Ashton W PTS 6 Cleethorpes
26.02.99 Adrian Houldey W RSC 5 West Bromwich
27.03.99 Mark Owens W RSC 2 Derby
15.05.99 Michael Pinnock W PTS 4 Sheffield
27.06.99 Mark Owens W RSC 5 Alfreton
15.08.99 Ian Toby W PTS 6 Derby
03.10.99 Simon Andrews W PTS 6 Chesterfield
20.11.99 Simon Andrews W RSC 4 Grantham
15.01.00 Matthew Pepper W CO 1 Doncaster
09.04.00 Matthew Pepper W RSC 3 Alfreton
21.05.00 Martin Jolley W PTS 6 Derby
19.06.00 William Webster W PTS 4 Burton
13.08.00 Martin Jolley W RTD 1 Nottingham
04.11.00 Mike Duffield W RSC 3 Derby
(Vacant WBF European S. Middleweight Title)
25.02.01 Rob Stevenson W PTS 8 Derby
16.06.01 Dean Ashton L DIS 1 Derby
21.07.01 Leigh Wicks W PTS 4 Sheffield
15.09.01 Dean Ashton W RTD 2 Derby
(Vacant Midlands Area S.Middleweight Title)
08.12.01 Rob Stevenson W RSC 7 Chesterfield
20.04.02 Jimmy Steel W PTS 6 Derby
Career: 21 contests, won 19, drew 1, lost 1.

Brendan Halford
Rugby. *Born* Folkestone, 30 July, 1973
L. Middleweight. Ht. 5'8¹/₂"
Manager J. Weaver

09.02.02 Wayne Shepherd W PTS 6 Coventry
Career: 1 contest, won 1.

Chris Hall
Sheffield. *Born* Sheffield, 25 September, 1980
L. Welterweight. Ht. 5'7"
Manager Self

11.09.99 Ricky Bishop W PTS 4 Sheffield
26.11.99 Duncan Armstrong W PTS 6 Wakefield
18.03.00 Kevin McIntyre L RSC 3 Glasgow
20.05.00 Craig Goodman W PTS 6 Rotherham
28.10.00 Tony Conroy L RSC 1 Coventry
27.07.01 Duncan Armstrong W PTS 4 Sheffield
Career: 6 contests, won 4, lost 2.

Jason Hall
Hanwell. *Born* Perivale, 19 November, 1975
Lightweight. Ht. 5'8¹/₂"
Manager F. Maloney

19.04.97 Johannes Musa W RSC 3 Las Vegas, USA
06.06.97 Raul Basulto L RSC 10 Las Vegas, USA
30.07.97 Mark Chang w pts 4 Las Vegas, USA
27.06.98 Andrew Poulos W PTS 4 Vancouver, Canada
29.06.99 Brendan Ahearne W PTS 6 Bethnal Green
20.08.99 Keith Jones W PTS 6 Bloomsbury
05.10.99 John Paul Temple W PTS 6 Bloomsbury
06.11.99 Woody Greenaway W RSC 5 Bethnal Green
10.03.00 Arv Mittoo L RSC 3 Bethnal Green
18.02.01 Marco Fattore W PTS 6 Southwark
01.04.01 Gary Flear W PTS 8 Southwark
28.04.01 Bradley Pryce L PTS 12 Cardiff
(Vacant WBO Inter-Continental Lightweight Title)
15.12.01 Steve Murray L RSC 4 Wembley
(Elim. British Lightweight Title)
Career: 13 contests, won 9, lost 4.

(Michael) Oscar Hall
Darlington. *Born* Darlington, 8 November, 1974
Northern Area Welterweight Champion. Ht. 5'9"
Manager D. Ingle

09.05.98 Trevor Smith W PTS 4 Sheffield
27.02.99 Lee Molyneux W PTS 4 Oldham
15.05.99 Chris Price W PTS 4 Sheffield
29.05.99 Brian Gifford W RSC 1 Halifax
04.06.99 Arv Mittoo W PTS 6 Hull
27.09.99 Dave Gibson W PTS 6 Leeds
11.12.99 Brian Coleman W PTS 6 Liverpool
18.02.00 Jason Collins DREW 6 West Bromwich
02.03.00 Ernie Smith W PTS 6 Birkenhead
09.06.00 Dave Gibson W PTS 6 Hull
19.06.00 Paul Denton W PTS 4 Burton
13.08.00 Lee Molyneux W PTS 6 Nottingham
04.11.00 Ram Singh W PTS 6 Derby
24.11.00 Dean Nicholas W PTS 6 Darlington
11.12.00 Ram Singh W CO 4 Cleethorpes
16.06.01 David Kirk W PTS 6 Derby
18.08.01 David White W PTS 6 Dewsbury
22.09.01 Dean Nicholas W DIS 9 Newcastle
(Vacant Northern Area Welterweight Title)
17.11.01 Paul Lomax W PTS 4 Dewsbury
15.03.02 Stuart Rimmer W RSC 4 Spennymoor
19.04.02 Peter Dunn W PTS 4 Darlington
10.05.02 Arv Mittoo W PTS 4 Bethnal Green
Career: 22 contests, won 21, drew 1.

Paul Halpin
Brighton. *Born* Brighton, 4 August, 1974
S. Featherweight. Former Undefeated Southern Area Featherweight Champion. Ht. 5'5"
Manager F. Warren

04.04.97 Graham McGrath W PTS 6 Brighton
20.05.97 David Jeffrey W PTS 6 Gillingham
11.07.97 Wayne Jones W RSC 5 Brighton
08.10.97 Greg Upton DREW 4 Poplar
27.02.98 Taffy Evans W RSC 3 Brighton
16.05.98 Chris Lyons W PTS 6 Chigwell
26.02.99 Justin Murphy W RSC 2 Bethnal Green
(Vacant Southern Area Featherweight Title)

26.06.99 Pete Buckley W PTS 4 Millwall
15.11.99 Chris Jickells W PTS 6 Bethnal Green
19.06.00 Chris Jickells W RSC 4 Burton
12.08.00 Eddie Nevins W PTS 6 Wembley
02.03.02 Gary Reid W RSC 3 Bethnal Green
Career: 12 contests, won 11, drew 1.

Mark Halstead
Halifax. *Born* Halifax, 14 July, 1974
L. Welterweight. Ht. 5'7"
Manager Self

30.03.98 Leigh Daniels DREW 6 Bradford
14.06.98 Terry Butwell L PTS 6 Golders Green
12.10.98 Mark Harrison DREW 6 Bradford
25.11.98 Malcolm Thomas L PTS 6 Clydach
07.12.98 Gavin McGill L PTS 6 Nottingham
01.02.99 Les Frost DREW 6 Bradford
21.05.99 Ram Singh DREW 6 Glasgow
04.06.99 Chris Price DREW 6 Hull
01.10.99 Dale Lowe L PTS 6 Cleethorpes
22.10.99 Tony Conroy L PTS 4 Coventry
26.11.99 Kevin Abdy W PTS 6 Wakefield
11.12.99 Dariusz Snarski L PTS 6 Merthyr
08.03.01 Elias Boswell W RSC 5 Blackpool
09.09.01 Andrew Close DREW 6 Hartlepool
04.10.01 Andrew Close L PTS 6 Sunderland
20.10.01 Chill John L PTS 4 Portsmouth
Career: 16 contests, won 2, drew 6, lost 8.

Terry Ham
Manchester. *Born* Manchester, 21 March, 1977
Welterweight. Ht. 5'10"
Manager M. Goodall

16.11.01 Arv Mittoo W PTS 6 Preston
Career: 1 contest, won 1.

Prince Naseem Hamed
Sheffield. *Born* Sheffield, 12 February, 1974
IBO Featherweight Champion. Former Undefeated WBO, IBF & WBC Featherweight Champion. Former Undefeated WBC International S. Bantamweight Champion. Former Undefeated European Bantamweight Champion. Ht. 5'3"
Manager Self

14.04.92 Ricky Beard W CO 2 Mansfield
25.04.92 Shaun Norman W RSC 2 Manchester
23.05.92 Andrew Bloomer W RSC 2 Birmingham
14.07.92 Miguel Matthews W RSC 3 Mayfair
07.10.92 Des Gargano W RSC 4 Sunderland
12.11.92 Pete Buckley W PTS 6 Liverpool
24.02.93 Alan Ley W CO 2 Wembley
26.05.93 Kevin Jenkins W RSC 3 Mansfield
24.09.93 Chris Clarkson W CO 2 Dublin
29.01.94 Pete Buckley W RSC 4 Cardiff
09.04.94 John Miceli W CO 1 Mansfield
11.05.94 Vincenzo Belcastro W PTS 12 Sheffield
(European Bantamweight Title Challenge)
17.08.94 Antonio Picardi W RSC 3 Sheffield
(European Bantamweight Title Defence)
12.10.94 Freddy Cruz W RSC 6 Sheffield
(Vacant WBC International S. Bantamweight Title)

19.11.94 Laureano Ramirez W RTD 3 Cardiff
(WBC International S. Bantamweight Title Defence)
21.01.95 Armando Castro W RSC 4 Glasgow
(WBC International S. Bantamweight Title Defence)
04.03.95 Sergio Liendo W RSC 2 Livingston
(WBC International S. Bantamweight Title Defence)
06.05.95 Enrique Angeles W CO 2 Shepton Mallet
(WBC International S. Bantamweight Title Defence)
01.07.95 Juan Polo Perez W CO 2 Kensington
(WBC International S. Bantamweight Title Defence)

30.09.95 Steve Robinson W RSC 8 Cardiff
(WBO Featherweight Title Challenge)
16.03.96 Said Lawal W RSC 1 Glasgow
(WBO Featherweight Title Defence)
08.06.96 Daniel Alicea W RSC 2 Newcastle
(WBO Featherweight Title Defence)
31.08.96 Manuel Medina W RSC 11 Dublin
(WBO Featherweight Title Defence)
09.11.96 Remigio Molina W RSC 2 Manchester
(WBO Featherweight Title Defence)
08.02.97 Tom Johnson W RSC 8 Millwall
(WBO Featherweight Title Defence. IBF Featherweight Title Challenge)
03.05.97 Billy Hardy W RSC 1 Manchester
(WBO & IBF Featherweight Title Defences)

19.07.97 Juan Cabrera W RSC 2 Wembley
(WBO Featherweight Title Defence)
11.10.97 Jose Badillo W RSC 7 Sheffield
(WBO Featherweight Title Defence)
19.12.97 Kevin Kelley W CO 4 New York City, USA
(WBO Featherweight Title Defence)
18.04.98 Wilfredo Vasquez W RSC 7 Manchester
(WBO Featherweight Title Defence)
31.10.98 Wayne McCullough W PTS 12 Atlantic City, USA
(WBO Featherweight Title Defence)
10.04.99 Paul Ingle W RSC 11 Manchester
(WBO Featherweight Title Defence)
22.10.99 Cesar Soto W PTS 12 Detroit, USA
(WBO Featherweight Title Defence. WBC Featherweight Title Challenge)
11.03.00 Vuyani Bungu W CO 4 Kensington
(WBO Featherweight Title Defence)
19.08.00 Augie Sanchez W RSC 4 Mashantucket, Connecticut, USA
(WBO Featherweight Title Defence)
07.04.01 Marco Antonio Barrera L PTS 12 Las Vegas, USA
(Vacant IBO Featherweight Title)
18.05.02 Manuel Calvo W PTS 12 Millwall
(Vacant IBO Featherweight Title)

Career: 37 contests, won 36, lost 1.

Gary Hamilton

Belfast. *Born* Belfast, 27 May, 1980
L. Welterweight. Ht. 5'8¹/₂"
Manager Self

20.10.00 Gyula Szabo W PTS 4 Belfast
10.12.00 Patrick Dominguez L RSC 3 Elgin, Illinois, USA
21.01.02 John Marshall L PTS 4 Glasgow
18.02.02 Tony McPake L PTS 4 Glasgow
24.04.02 Robert Murray L PTS 6 Dublin
Career: 5 contests, won 1, lost 4.

Steve Hanley

Redditch. *Born* Bromsgrove, 30 April, 1970
Lightweight. Ht. 5'8"
Manager Self

15.11.99 Kevin Lear L RSC 1 Bethnal Green
13.12.99 Willie Limond L PTS 6 Glasgow
08.02.00 Barrie Kelley L PTS 6 Wolverhampton
19.02.00 Craig Docherty L PTS 6 Prestwick
05.03.00 Mark Hargreaves W RTD 4 Shaw
25.03.00 Tony Mulholland L PTS 6 Liverpool
13.04.00 Danny Hunt L PTS 4 Holborn
25.05.00 Liam Maltby L PTS 4 Peterborough
06.06.00 Barrie Kelley W RSC 5 Brierley Hill
25.06.00 Kevin Bennett L PTS 6 Wakefield
15.07.00 Jan Jansen L RSC 1 Millwall
04.09.00 Jesse James Daniel L PTS 4 Manchester
25.09.00 Franny Hogg L PTS 6 Barnsley
10.10.00 Carl Allen L PTS 8 Brierley Hill
13.11.00 Gavin Rees L RSC 1 Bethnal Green
03.02.01 Ricky Eccleston L PTS 4 Manchester
10.02.01 Scott Miller L RSC 3 Widnes
17.03.01 Andy McLean L PTS 4 Manchester
24.03.01 Mally McIver L PTS 4 Sheffield
03.04.01 Kevin Lear L PTS 6 Bethnal Green
10.04.01 Mark Alexander L PTS 4 Wembley
04.06.01 James Rooney L PTS 4 Hartlepool
11.06.01 Adnan Amar L PTS 4 Nottingham
04.07.01 Chill John L PTS 4 Bloomsbury

Prince Naseem Hamed   Les Clark

31.07.01 Lee Meager L PTS 6 Bethnal Green
09.09.01 David Lowry L PTS 6 Southwark
23.09.01 Choi Tseveenpurev L PTS 6 Shaw
07.10.01 Jimmy Gould L PTS 6 Wolverhampton
Career: 28 contests, won 2, lost 26.

Anthony Hanna

Birmingham. *Born* Birmingham, 22
September, 1974
S. Bantamweight. Midlands Area Flyweight
Champion. Ht. 5'6"
Manager Self

19.11.92 Nick Tooley L PTS 6 Evesham
10.12.92 Daren Fifield L RSC 6 Bethnal Green
11.05.93 Tiger Singh W PTS 6 Norwich
24.05.93 Lyndon Kershaw L PTS 6 Bradford
16.09.93 Chris Lyons W PTS 6 Southwark
06.10.93 Tiger Singh W PTS 6 Solihull
03.11.93 Mickey Cantwell L PTS 8 Bristol
25.01.94 Marty Chestnut W PTS 4 Picadilly
10.02.94 Allan Mooney W RTD 1 Glasgow
13.04.94 Allan Mooney L PTS 6 Glasgow
22.04.94 Jesper Jensen L PTS 6 Aalborg,
Denmark
03.08.94 Paul Ingle L PTS 6 Bristol
01.10.94 Mark Hughes L PTS 4 Cardiff
30.11.94 Shaun Norman W PTS 10 Solihull
(Vacant Midlands Area Flyweight Title)
24.02.95 Darren Greaves W RSC 5 Weston
super Mare
06.03.95 Mark Hughes L PTS 6 Mayfair
27.04.95 Mickey Cantwell L PTS 6 Bethnal
Green
05.05.95 Mark Cokely W RSC 4 Swansea
04.06.95 Mark Reynolds L PTS 10 Bethnal
Green
(Elim. British Flyweight Title)
02.07.95 Mickey Cantwell L PTS 6 Dublin
02.11.95 Shaun Norman DREW 10 Mayfair
*(Midlands Area Flyweight Title
Defence)*
31.01.96 Marty Chestnut DREW 6 Stoke
20.03.96 Harry Woods L PTS 6 Cardiff
22.04.96 Neil Parry W PTS 6 Manchester
14.05.96 Dharmendra Singh Yadav L PTS 4
Dagenham
08.10.96 Marty Chestnut W PTS 6 Battersea
11.12.96 Mark Reynolds DREW 8 Southwark
28.01.97 Colin Moffett L PTS 4 Belfast
28.02.97 Paul Weir L PTS 8 Kilmarnock
14.03.97 Jesper Jensen L PTS 6 Odense, Denmark
30.04.97 Clinton Beeby DREW 6 Acton
10.05.97 Jason Booth L PTS 6 Nottingham
02.06.97 Keith Knox L PTS 6 Glasgow
14.10.97 Louis Veitch L PTS 6 Kilmarnock
27.10.97 Russell Laing W PTS 4 Musselburgh
13.11.97 Noel Wilders L PTS 6 Bradford
24.11.97 Shaun Anderson L PTS 8 Glasgow
20.12.97 Damaen Kelly L PTS 4 Belfast
31.01.98 Jason Booth L PTS 6 Edmonton
23.02.98 David Coldwell W PTS 6 Salford
19.03.98 Andy Roberts L PTS 6 Doncaster
18.05.98 Chris Emanuele W RSC 3 Cleethorpes
11.09.98 Nicky Booth DREW 6 Cleethorpes
18.09.98 Colin Moffett DREW 4 Belfast
29.10.98 Nick Tooley W RTD 6 Bayswater
25.11.98 Nicky Booth W PTS 6 Clydach
21.01.99 Ola Dali W PTS 6 Piccadilly
13.03.99 Damaen Kelly L PTS 12 Manchester
*(Vacant British Flyweight Title.
Commonwealth Flyweight Title
Challenge)*

24.04.99 Noel Wilders L PTS 6 Peterborough
07.06.99 Alston Buchanan W RSC 3 Glasgow
29.06.99 Tommy Waite L PTS 4 Bethnal Green
16.10.99 Stevie Quinn W PTS 4 Belfast
22.11.99 Frankie DeMilo L PTS 6 Piccadilly
04.12.99 Ady Lewis L PTS 6 Manchester
19.02.00 Ian Napa L PTS 6 Dagenham
13.03.00 Mzukisi Sikali L PTS 6 Bethnal Green
27.05.00 Nicky Cook L PTS 6 Mayfair
25.07.00 David Lowry L PTS 4 Southwark
19.08.00 Marc Callaghan L PTS 4 Brentwood
29.09.00 Rocky Dean L PTS 4 Bethnal Green
07.10.00 Oleg Kiryukhin L PTS 6 Doncaster
14.10.00 Danny Costello DREW 4 Wembley
31.10.00 Dmitri Kirilov L PTS 6 Hammersmith
10.02.01 Tony Mulholland L PTS 4 Widnes
19.02.01 Alex Moon L PTS 6 Glasgow
03.03.01 Marc Callaghan L PTS 6 Wembley
24.04.01 Silence Mabuza L PTS 6 Liverpool
06.05.01 Michael Hunter L PTS 4 Hartlepool
26.05.01 Mickey Bowden L PTS 4 Bethnal Green
04.06.01 Michael Hunter L PTS 4 Hartlepool
01.11.01 Nigel Senior L PTS 6 Hull

24.11.01 Martin Power L PTS 4 Bethnal Green
08.12.01 Faprakob Rakkiatgym L PTS 8
Dagenham
24.03.02 Mickey Coveney L PTS 4 Streatham
23.06.02 Johannes Maisa L PTS 4 Southwark
Career: 75 contests, won 18, drew 7, lost 50.

Martin Hardcastle

Leeds. *Born* Pontefract, 27 August, 1976
L. Welterweight. Ht. 5'6"
Manager M. Marsden

02.03.02 Mick McPhilbin W RSC 4 Wakefield
28.05.02 Dave Curran W RSC 3 Leeds
Career: 2 contests, won 2.

James Hare

Robertown. *Born* Dewsbury, 16 July, 1976
Commonwealth Welterweight Champion.
Former Undefeated European Union
Welterweight Champion. Ht. 5'6"
Manager T. Gilmour/C. Aston

James Hare   Les Clark

20.01.96	Brian Coleman W PTS 6 Mansfield
25.06.96	Mike Watson W PTS 4 Mansfield
13.07.96	Dennis Griffin W RSC 4 Bethnal Green
14.09.96	Paul Salmon W RSC 4 Sheffield
14.12.96	Jon Harrison W PTS 4 Sheffield
25.02.97	Kid McAuley W PTS 4 Sheffield
12.04.97	Andy Peach W RSC 1 Sheffield
13.12.97	Costas Katsantonis W RSC 3 Sheffield
09.05.98	Peter Nightingale W PTS 4 Sheffield
18.07.98	Karl Taylor W PTS 4 Sheffield
28.11.98	Peter Nightingale W PTS 6 Sheffield
15.05.99	Lee Williamson W RSC 2 Sheffield
23.10.99	Mark Winters DREW 6 Telford
23.10.00	Dean Nicholas W RSC 1 Glasgow
23.01.01	Mark Ramsey W PTS 6 Crawley
26.02.01	Paul Denton W PTS 4 Nottingham
08.05.01	Jessy Moreaux W RSC 3 Barnsley
26.05.01	John Humphrey W RSC 7 Bethnal Green
	(Elim. British Welterweight Title)
08.10.01	John Ameline W PTS 8 Barnsley
26.11.01	Paul Denton W RTD 4 Manchester
28.01.02	Monney Seka W PTS 10 Barnsley
	(Vacant European Union Welterweight Title)
27.04.02	Julian Holland W RSC 6 Huddersfield
	(Commonwealth Welterweight Title Challenge)
15.06.02	Abdel Mehidi W PTS 8 Leeds

Career: 23 contests, won 22, drew 1.

Audley Harrison

Edmonton. *Born* Park Royal, 26 October, 1971
Heavyweight. Ht. 6'4³/₄"
Manager C. McMillan

19.05.01	Michael Middleton W RSC 1 Wembley
22.09.01	Derek McCafferty W PTS 6 Newcastle
20.10.01	Piotr Jurczyk W RSC 2 Glasgow
20.04.02	Julius Long W CO 2 Wembley
21.05.02	Mark Krence W PTS 6 Custom House

Career: 5 contests, won 5.

Audley Harrison   Les Clark

Gary Harrison

Swadlincote. *Born* Burton, 26 May, 1969
L. Welterweight. Ht. 5'8"
Manager R. Davies

20.05.99	Chris Lyons W PTS 6 Barking
29.04.00	Mike Yikealo L PTS 4 Wembley
13.07.00	Costas Katsantonis L PTS 4 Bethnal Green
28.10.00	Kevin Bennett L RTD 2 Coventry
03.02.01	Casey Brooke W PTS 6 Brighton
05.05.01	Jason McElligott W PTS 6 Brighton
15.09.01	Michael Jennings L PTS 6 Manchester
23.11.01	Manzo Smith W PTS 4 Bethnal Green
10.05.02	Costas Katsantonis L PTS 10 Millwall
	(Southern Area L.Welterweight Title Challenge)
08.06.02	Ricky Burns L RSC 1 Renfrew

Career: 10 contests, won 4, lost 6.

Jon Harrison

Plymouth. *Born* Scunthorpe, 18 March, 1977
L. Middleweight. Ht. 5'11¹/₂"
Manager N. Christian

13.01.96	Mark Haslam L PTS 6 Manchester
13.02.96	Paul Samuels L CO 1 Cardiff
16.05.96	Dave Fallon W RSC 4 Dunstable
03.07.96	Allan Gray L PTS 6 Wembley
01.10.96	Cam Raeside L PTS 6 Birmingham
07.11.96	Nicky Bardle L PTS 6 Battersea
14.12.96	James Hare L PTS 4 Sheffield
19.04.97	Jason Williams W PTS 6 Plymouth
11.07.97	Pat Larner L PTS 6 Brighton
07.10.97	Paul Salmon L PTS 6 Plymouth
23.02.98	Alan Gilbert L PTS 6 Windsor
24.03.98	Brian Coleman DREW 6 Wolverhampton
14.07.98	Jason Williams L RTD 2 Reading
12.05.01	Ernie Smith W PTS 4 Plymouth
15.09.01	Darren Williams L PTS 6 Swansea

Career: 15 contests, won 3, drew 1, lost 11.

Scott Harrison

Cambuslang. *Born* Bellshill, 19 August, 1977
British, Commonwealth & WBO Interim
Featherweight Champion. Former
Undefeated IBO Inter-Continental
Featherweight Champion. Ht. 5'7"
Manager F. Maloney

07.10.96	Eddie Sica W RSC 2 Lewisham
11.01.97	Pete Buckley W PTS 4 Bethnal Green
25.03.97	David Morris W PTS 4 Lewisham
04.10.97	Miguel Matthews L RSC 4 Muswell Hill
16.12.97	Stephane Fernandez DREW 6 Grand Synthe, France
31.01.98	Pete Buckley W PTS 4 Edmonton
09.06.98	Carl Allen W RSC 6 Hull
17.10.98	Rakhim Mingaleev W PTS 8 Manchester
06.03.99	John Matthews W RSC 4 Southwark
10.07.99	Smith Odoom W PTS 12 Southwark
	(IBO Inter-Continental Featherweight Title Challenge)
24.01.00	Patrick Mullings W PTS 12 Glasgow
	(Commonwealth Featherweight Title Challenge)
29.04.00	Tracy Harris Patterson W PTS 10 New York City, USA
15.07.00	Tom Johnson W PTS 12 Millwall
	(IBO Inter-Continental Featherweight Title Defence)

11.11.00	Eric Odumasi W RSC 12 Belfast
	(Commonwealth Featherweight Title Defence)
24.03.01	Richie Wenton W RSC 4 Sheffield
	(Vacant British Featherweight Title. Commonwealth Featherweight Title Defence)
15.09.01	Gary Thornhill W RSC 5 Manchester
	(British & Commonwealth Featherweight Title Defences)
17.11.01	Steve Robinson W RSC 3 Glasgow
	(British & Commonwealth Featherweight Title Defences)
11.03.02	Tony Wehbee W RSC 3 Glasgow
	(Commonwealth Featherweight Title Defence)
08.06.02	Victor Santiago W RSC 6 Renfrew
	(Vacant WBO Interim Featherweight Title)

Career: 19 contests, won 17, drew 1, lost 1.

Scott Harrison   Les Clark

Jason Hart

Bromley. *Born* Beckenham, 23 January, 1970
L. Heavyweight. Ht. 5'9¹/₂"
Manager Self

02.06.94	Paul Matthews L RSC 3 Tooting
28.07.94	Julian Eavis W PTS 6 Tooting
30.09.94	Freddie Yemofio W PTS 6 Bethnal Green
31.03.95	Andy Ewen W PTS 6 Crystal Palace
20.09.95	Steve Roberts L RSC 5 Potters Bar
03.12.95	Simon Andrews W PTS 6 Southwark
30.01.96	Ernie Loveridge W PTS 6 Barking
05.03.96	Martin Jolley W PTS 6 Bethnal Green
03.04.96	Michael Pinnock W PTS 6 Bethnal Green
24.10.96	Graham Townsend L RSC 5 Mayfair
	(Vacant Southern Area S. Middleweight Title)
13.04.97	Sven Ottke L RSC 2 Cologne, Germany
20.05.97	Johnny Hooks W PTS 6 Gillingham

28.03.98	Rob Stevenson W PTS 6 Crystal Palace
30.05.98	Darren Dorrington L RTD 2 Bristol
26.09.98	Jimmy Hawk DREW 6 Southwark
25.11.98	Lester Jacobs L RSC 6 Streatham
	(Vacant WBF European Middleweight
	Title)
05.11.99	Evans Ashira L RTD 3 Aalberg,
	Denmark
06.05.00	Matthew Barney L PTS 10 Southwark
	(Vacant Southern Area S. Middleweight
	Title)
25.07.00	Michael Bowen L RSC 1 Southwark
13.03.01	Scott Dann L RSC 2 Plymouth
08.12.01	Ali Forbes L RSC 3 Millwall
23.02.02	Tony Dodson L RSC 2 Nottingham

Career: 22 contests, won 9, drew 1, lost 12.

Sebastian Hart

Wisbech. *Born* Burnley, 10 May, 1980
S. Featherweight. Ht. 5'4"
Manager B. Lee

26.11.99	Gary Wilson W PTS 6 Wakefield
08.12.99	Phil Lashley W RSC 3 Stoke
22.01.00	Steve Gethin W PTS 4 Birmingham
24.02.00	John Barnes W PTS 6 Sunderland
05.03.00	Chris Lyons W PTS 6 Peterborough
27.03.00	Lee Armstrong W CO 4 Barnsley
13.05.00	James Rooney L PTS 6 Barnsley
05.06.00	Craig Docherty L RSC 1 Glasgow
04.11.00	Gavin Down L RSC 4 Derby
25.09.01	Jamie McKeever L PTS 4 Liverpool

Career: 10 contests, won 6, lost 4.

Matthew Hatton

Manchester. *Born* Stockport, 15 May, 1981
L. Welterweight. Ht. 5'8¹/₂"
Manager F. Warren

23.09.00	David White W PTS 4 Bethnal Green
25.11.00	David White W PTS 4 Manchester
11.12.00	Danny Connelly W PTS 4 Widnes
15.01.01	Keith Jones W PTS 4 Manchester
10.02.01	Karl Taylor W PTS 4 Widnes
17.03.01	Assen Vassilev W RSC 5 Manchester
09.06.01	Brian Coleman W RTD 2 Bethnal Green
21.07.01	Ram Singh W RSC 2 Sheffield
15.09.01	Marcus Portman W RSC 3 Manchester
15.12.01	Dafydd Carlin W PTS 6 Wembley
09.02.02	Paul Denton W PTS 6 Manchester
04.05.02	Karl Taylor W RSC 3 Bethnal Green

Career: 12 contests, won 12.

Richard Hatton

Manchester. *Born* Stockport, 6 October, 1978
WBU L. Welterweight Champion. Former
Undefeated British, WBO Inter-Continental
& Central Area L. Welterweight Champion.
Ht. 5'7¹/₂"
Manager Self

11.09.97	Kid McAuley W RTD 1 Widnes
19.12.97	Robert Alvarez W PTS 4 New York
	City, USA
17.01.98	David Thompson W RSC 1 Bristol
27.03.98	Paul Salmon W RSC 1 Telford
18.04.98	Karl Taylor W RSC 1 Manchester
30.05.98	Mark Ramsey W PTS 6 Bristol
18.07.98	Anthony Campbell W PTS 6 Sheffield
19.09.98	Pascal Montulet W CO 2 Oberhausen,
	Germany
31.10.98	Kevin Carter W RSC 1 Atlantic City,
	USA
19.12.98	Paul Denton W RSC 6 Liverpool

27.02.99	Tommy Peacock W RSC 2 Oldham
	(Vacant Central Area L. Welterweight
	Title)
03.04.99	Brian Coleman W CO 2 Kensington
29.05.99	Dillon Carew W RSC 5 Halifax
	(Vacant WBO Inter-Continental
	L. Welterweight Title)
17.07.99	Mark Ramsey W PTS 6 Doncaster
09.10.99	Bernard Paul W RTD 4 Manchester
	(WBO Inter-Continental
	L. Welterweight Title Defence)
11.12.99	Mark Winters W RSC 4 Liverpool
	(WBO Inter-Continental
	L. Welterweight Title Defence)
29.01.00	Leoncio Garces W RSC 3 Manchester
25.03.00	Pedro Teran W RSC 4 Liverpool
	(WBO Inter-Continental
	L. Welterweight Title Defence)
16.05.00	Ambioris Figuero W RSC 4 Warrington
	(WBO Inter-Continental
	L. Welterweight Title Defence)
10.06.00	Gilbert Quiros W CO 2 Detroit, USA
	(WBO Inter-Continental
	L. Welterweight Title Defence)

23.09.00	Giuseppe Lauri W RSC 5 Bethnal Green
	(WBO Inter-Continental
	L. Welterweight Title Defence. WBA
	Inter-Continental L. Welterweight Title
	Challenge)
21.10.00	Jonathan Thaxton W PTS 12 Wembley
	(Vacant British L.Welterweight Title)
26.03.01	Tony Pep W CO 4 Wembley
	(Vacant WBU L. Welterweight Title)
07.07.01	Jason Rowland W CO 4 Manchester
	(WBU L.Welterweight Title Defence)
15.09.01	John Bailey W RSC 5 Manchester
	(WBU L.Welterweight Title Defence)
27.10.01	Fred Pendleton W CO 2 Manchester
	(WBU L.Welterweight Title Defence)
15.12.01	Justin Rowsell W RSC 2 Wembley
	(WBU L.Welterweight Title Defence)
09.02.02	Mikhail Krivolapov W RSC 9
	Manchester
	(WBU L. Welterweight Title Defence)
01.06.02	Eamonn Magee W PTS 12 Manchester
	(WBU L. Welterweight Title Defence)

Career: 29 contests, won 29.

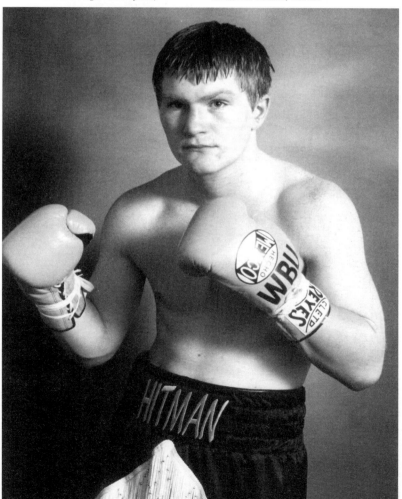

Richard Hatton   Paul Speak

103

Barry Hawthorne

Port Glasgow. *Born* Greenock, 21 July, 1978
Featherweight. Ht. 5'9"
Manager T. Gilmour

18.10.99	Paul Quarmby W PTS 6 Glasgow
15.11.99	Jason Edwards W PTS 6 Glasgow
24.01.00	Steve Brook DREW 4 Glasgow
19.02.00	Stevie Quinn L RSC 5 Prestwick
06.06.00	Nigel Senior W PTS 6 Motherwell
18.09.00	Nigel Leake W RSC 4 Glasgow
20.11.00	John Barnes W PTS 6 Glasgow
04.06.01	Joel Viney W PTS 8 Glasgow
13.04.02	Jamie McKeever L PTS 6 Liverpool

Career: 9 contests, won 6, drew 1, lost 2.

Mark Hawthorne

Lowestoft. *Born* Great Yarmouth, 20
March, 1973
Lightweight. Ht. 5'7¾"
Manager J. Harding

10.03.00	Dean Murdoch W RSC 1 Bethnal Green
17.04.00	David Kehoe W PTS 4 Birmingham
19.05.01	Woody Greenaway W PTS 4 Wembley
07.09.01	Tony Montana W CO 3 Bethnal Green

Career: 4 contests, won 4.

Rob Hayes-Scott

Kennington. *Born* Lambeth, 4 January, 1976
Cruiserweight. Ht. 6'0"
Manager T. Follett

18.02.01	Kevin Burton W RSC 1 Southwark
07.04.01	Paul Bonson W PTS 4 Wembley
03.06.01	Radcliffe Green L RSC 4 Southwark
09.09.01	Adam Cale W RSC 1 Southwark

Career: 4 contests, won 3, lost 1.

Peter Haymer

Enfield. *Born* London, 10 July, 1978
Cruiserweight. Ht. 6'1¼"
Manager F. Maloney

25.11.00	Adam Cale W RSC 1 Manchester
27.01.01	Darren Ashton W PTS 4 Bethnal Green
10.03.01	Daniel Ivanov W CO 2 Bethnal Green
26.03.01	Radcliffe Green W PTS 4 Wembley
05.05.01	Terry Morrill W PTS 4 Edmonton
22.09.01	Tony Booth W PTS 4 Bethnal Green
24.11.01	Nathan King L PTS 4 Bethnal Green
12.02.02	Nathan King L PTS 4 Bethnal Green
09.05.02	Mark Snipe W PTS 4 Leicester Square
15.06.02	Paul Bonson W PTS 4 Tottenham

Career: 10 contests, won 8, lost 2.

Gary Hibbert

Oldham. *Born* Oldham, 5 February, 1975
Central Area Lightweight Champion.
Ht. 5'8½"
Manager B. Hearn

02.06.96	John T. Kelly W PTS 6 Shaw
13.10.96	Sean Morrison W RSC 2 Shaw
16.03.97	David Kirk W PTS 6 Shaw
08.06.97	Bamana Dibateza W PTS 4 Shaw
18.09.98	Jimmy Phelan W PTS 6 Manchester
17.10.98	Dennis Griffin W RSC 4 Manchester
30.11.98	Carl Allen W PTS 4 Manchester
13.03.99	Mark Haslam W PTS 10 Manchester
	(Vacant Central Area Lightweight Title)

01.07.00	Marco Fattore W PTS 4 Manchester
09.09.00	Woody Greenaway W RSC 2 Manchester
03.02.01	Franck Benoni L PTS 6 Manchester
04.06.01	Alan Temple L PTS 6 Hartlepool
07.07.01	Gaeten Trovato W RSC 1 Amsterdam, Holland
06.10.01	Yannick Paget W RSC 2 Manchester
26.11.01	Rosalin Nasibulin W RSC 3 Manchester
09.03.02	Alan Temple W RSC 1 Manchester
23.03.02	Andrei Devyataykin L RSC 4 Southwark

Career: 17 contests, won 14, lost 3.

Dean Hickmam

West Bromwich. *Born* West Bromwich, 24
November, 1979
L. Welterweight. Ht. 5'7"
Manager D. Bradley

17.02.02	Wayne Wheeler DREW 6 Wolverhampton
13.04.02	Wayne Wheeler W PTS 6 Wolverhampton

Career: 2 contests, won 1, drew 1.

Herbie Hide

Norwich. *Born* Nigeria, 27 August, 1971
Former WBO Heavyweight Champion.
Former Undefeated British, WBC
International & Penta-Continental
Heavyweight Champion. Ht. 6'1½"
Manager Self

24.10.89	L. A. Williams W CO 2 Bethnal Green
05.11.89	Gary McCrory W RTD 1 Kensington
19.12.89	Steve Osborne W RSC 8 Bethnal Green
27.06.90	Alek Penarski W RSC 3 Kensington
05.09.90	Steve Lewsam W RSC 4 Brighton
26.09.90	Jonjo Greene W RSC 1 Manchester
17.10.90	Gus Mendes W RSC 2 Bethnal Green
18.11.90	Steve Lewsam W RSC 1 Birmingham
29.01.91	Lennie Howard W RSC 1 Wisbech
09.04.91	David Jules W RSC 1 Mayfair
14.05.91	John Westgarth W RTD 4 Dudley
03.07.91	Tucker Richards W RSC 3 Brentwood
15.10.91	Eddie Gonzalez W CO 2 Hamburg, Germany
29.10.91	Chris Jacobs W RSC 1 Cardiff
21.01.92	Conroy Nelson W RSC 2 Norwich
	(Vacant WBC International Heavyweight Title)
03.03.92	Percell Davis W CO 1 Amsterdam, Holland
08.09.92	Jean Chanet W RSC 7 Norwich
06.10.92	Craig Peterson W RSC 7 Antwerp, Belgium
	(WBC International Heavyweight Title Defence)
12.12.92	James Pritchard W RSC 2 Muswell Hill
30.01.93	Juan Antonio Diaz W RSC 3 Brentwood
	(Vacant Penta-Continental Heavyweight Title)
27.02.93	Michael Murray W RSC 5 Dagenham
	(Vacant British Heavyweight Title)
11.05.93	Jerry Halstead W RSC 4 Norwich
	(Penta-Continental Heavyweight Title Defence)
18.09.93	Everett Martin W PTS 10 Leicester
06.11.93	Mike Dixon W RSC 9 Bethnal Green
	(Penta-Continental Heavyweight Title Defence)

04.12.93	Jeff Lampkin W RSC 2 Sun City, South Africa
	(WBC International Heavyweight Title Defence)
19.03.94	Michael Bentt W CO 7 Millwall
	(WBO Heavyweight Title Challenge)
11.03.95	Riddick Bowe L CO 6 Las Vegas, USA
	(WBO Heavyweight Title Defence)
06.07.96	Michael Murray W RSC 6 Manchester
09.11.96	Frankie Swindell W CO 1 Manchester
28.06.97	Tony Tucker W RSC 2 Norwich
	(Vacant WBO Heavyweight Title)
18.04.98	Damon Reed W RSC 1 Manchester
	(WBO Heavyweight Title Defence)
26.09.98	Willi Fischer W RSC 2 Norwich
	(WBO Heavyweight Title Defence)
26.06.99	Vitali Klitschko L CO 2 Millwall
	(WBO Heavyweight Title Defence)
14.07.01	Alexei Osokin W RSC 3 Liverpool
22.09.01	Joseph Chingangu L RSC 2 Newcastle

Career: 35 contests, won 32, lost 3.

Dave Hinds

Birmingham. *Born* Leicester, 5 January, 1971
Lightweight. Ht. 5'5"
Manager Self

19.09.95	Martin Evans W RSC 5 Plymouth
08.11.95	Wayne Pardoe L CO 4 Walsall
04.04.96	Paul Salmon L RTD 5 Plymouth
06.10.97	Eddie Sica L RSC 1 Piccadilly
25.11.97	Graham McGrath W PTS 6 Wolverhampton
06.12.97	Adam Spelling W RSC 1 Wembley
27.01.98	Malcolm Thomas L PTS 6 Piccadilly
06.03.98	Jon Dodsworth W RSC 1 Hull
12.03.98	Jamie McKeever L PTS 4 Liverpool
20.03.98	John O'Johnson L PTS 6 Ilkeston
23.04.98	Roy Rutherford L RSC 5 Edgbaston
26.05.98	David Kehoe L RSC 5 Mayfair
07.10.98	Steve Saville L PTS 6 Stoke
26.10.98	Eddie Nevins L PTS 6 Manchester
26.11.98	Steve Saville L PTS 6 Edgbaston
07.12.98	Danny Bell L PTS 6 Nottingham
13.02.99	Michael Gomez L PTS 6 Newcastle
23.04.99	Mark Ramsey L PTS 6 Clydach
17.05.99	Jesse James Daniel L PTS 6 Cleethorpes
28.05.99	Jason Cook L RSC 1 Liverpool
17.07.99	Bradley Pryce L PTS 4 Doncaster
03.09.99	Young Muttley L RSC 4 West Bromwich
13.11.99	Humberto Soto L PTS 6 Hull
11.12.99	Gavin Rees L RSC 2 Liverpool
07.02.00	Liam Maltby L PTS 4 Peterborough
13.03.00	Danny Hunt L PTS 4 Bethnal Green
23.03.00	Marco Fattore L PTS 6 Bloomsbury
13.05.00	Alan Kershaw L PTS 4 Barnsley
22.05.00	Tony Conroy L PTS 4 Coventry
09.06.00	Elias Boswell W RSC 5 Blackpool
24.06.00	Brian Carr L PTS 4 Glasgow
01.07.00	Ricky Eccleston L PTS 4 Manchester
25.07.00	Kevin Lear L PTS 6 Southwark
09.09.00	Carl Greaves L PTS 6 Newark
16.09.00	Leo O'Reilly L RSC 2 Bethnal Green
27.11.00	Ricky Eccleston L PTS 4 Birmingham
04.12.00	Gavin Pearson L PTS 6 Bradford
11.12.00	Miguel Matthews W PTS 6 Birmingham
11.02.01	James Rooney L PTS 6 Hartlepool
26.03.01	Kevin Lear L CO 1 Wembley
03.06.01	Dafydd Carlin L PTS 4 Southwark
16.06.01	Carl Greaves L PTS 6 Derby
29.09.01	Scott Lawton L RSC 2 Southwark
15.12.01	Danny Hunt L PTS 4 Wembley
26.01.02	Chris McDonagh L PTS 4 Bethnal Green

03.03.02 Mally McIver L PTS 6 Shaw
11.03.02 Willie Limond L PTS 6 Glasgow
11.05.02 Craig Spacie L PTS 6 Chesterfield
15.06.02 Dave Stewart L PTS 6 Tottenham
23.06.02 Peter McDonagh L PTS 6 Southwark
Career: 50 contests, won 6, lost 44.

Mark Hobson

Huddersfield. *Born* Workington, 7 May, 1976
Cruiserweight. Ht. 6'5"
Manager C. Aston/T. Gilmour

09.06.97 Michael Pinnock W PTS 6 Bradford
06.10.97 P. R. Mason W PTS 6 Bradford
13.11.97 P. R. Mason W PTS 6 Bradford
27.02.98 Colin Brown DREW 6 Irvine
21.05.98 Paul Bonson W PTS 6 Bradford
15.06.98 Martin Jolley W RSC 3 Bradford
25.10.98 Mark Snipe W RSC 3 Shaw
26.11.98 Danny Southam W RSC 5 Bradford
19.04.99 Mark Levy L PTS 8 Bradford
11.09.99 Paul Bonson W PTS 4 Sheffield
06.12.99 Brian Gascoigne W RSC 3 Bradford
11.03.00 Nikolai Ermenkov W RSC 3 Kensington
27.03.00 Luke Simpkin W PTS 4 Barnsley
13.05.00 Paul Bonson W PTS 4 Barnsley
25.09.00 Mark Dawson W CO 1 Barnsley
26.02.01 Billy Bessey W PTS 6 Nottingham
24.04.01 Sebastiaan Rothmann L RTD 9 Liverpool
(WBU Cruiserweight Title Challenge)
08.10.01 Firat Arslan L RSC 7 Barnsley
10.12.01 Luke Simpkin W RTD 3 Liverpool
23.02.02 Valery Semishkur W PTS 6 Nottingham
27.04.02 Lee Swaby W PTS 10 Huddersfield
(Final Elim. British Cruiserweight Title)
Career: 21 contests, won 17, drew 1, lost 3.

Gareth Hogg

Torquay. *Born* Newton Abbott, 21 October, 1977
L. Heavyweight. Ht. 6'2"
Manager C. Sanigar

13.02.98 Harry Butler W RSC 3 Weston super Mare
09.05.99 Matthew Barney L PTS 4 Bracknell
07.08.99 Clive Johnson W PTS 4 Dagenham
27.02.00 Darren Covill W RSC 3 Plymouth
29.03.00 Simon Andrews W RSC 5 Piccadilly
12.05.01 Oddy Papantoniou W RSC 2 Plymouth
10.07.01 Kevin Rainey W RSC 1 Montreal, Canada
23.06.02 Mark Phillips W PTS 4 Southwark
Career: 8 contests, won 7, lost 1.

Mike Holden

Manchester. *Born* Ashton under Lyme, 13 March, 1968
Former Undefeated British Heavyweight Champion. Ht. 6'4"
Manager Self

04.10.94 Gary Williams W RSC 4 Mayfair
20.12.94 Pat Passley L RTD 3 Bethnal Green
07.10.95 R. F. McKenzie W RSC 2 Belfast
14.11.95 Michael Murray L PTS 6 Bury
09.07.96 Julius Francis L PTS 10 Bethnal Green
28.09.96 Mikael Lindblad W PTS 6 Barking
26.06.97 Israel Ajose W RSC 1 Salford

02.09.97 Mika Kihlstrom W RSC 1 Southwark
12.12.98 Nigel Rafferty W RTD 2 Chester
08.05.99 Harry Senior L PTS 8 Bethnal Green
15.07.99 Derek McCafferty W RSC 1 Peterborough
13.03.00 Julius Francis W PTS 12 Bethnal Green
(British Heavyweight Title Challenge)
03.04.01 Julius Francis L PTS 10 Bethnal Green
(Final Elim. British Heavyweight Title)
13.09.01 Keith Long L PTS 10 Sheffield
(Elim.British Heavyweight Title)
15.03.02 Luke Simpkin W PTS 6 Millwall
Career: 15 contests, won 9, lost 6.

Martin Holgate

Walthamstow. *Born* Waltham Forest, 24 November, 1968
L. Welterweight. Ht. 5'6½"
Manager Self

02.06.95 Adam Baldwin W PTS 6 Bethnal Green
22.07.95 Mike Watson W PTS 6 Millwall
02.09.95 Trevor Smith W RSC 2 Wembley
21.10.95 John O. Johnson W PTS 4 Bethnal Green
09.12.95 Andrew Reed W RSC 1 Bethnal Green
13.02.96 Brian Coleman W PTS 4 Bethnal Green
13.07.96 John Smith W PTS 4 Bethnal Green
27.03.97 Danny Stevens W RSC 3 Norwich
29.05.97 Gary Hiscox W PTS 4 Mayfair
13.09.97 Jawaid Khaliq L RSC 6 Millwall
12.05.98 Steve Tuckett L PTS 6 Leeds
13.12.01 Liam Maltby W RSC 4 Leicester Square
09.05.02 Keith Jones W PTS 6 Leicester Square
Career: 13 contests, won 11, lost 2.

Lee Holmes

Ellesmere Port. *Born* Chester, 18 April, 1975
S. Bantamweight. Ht. 5'6"
Manager M. Goodall

10.06.01 Paddy Folan W PTS 6 Ellesmere Port
26.08.01 Neil Read W PTS 6 Warrington
08.02.02 Sean Grant W CO 5 Preston
08.03.02 Dave Cotterill W PTS 6 Ellesmere Port
Career: 4 contests, won 4.

Jon Honney

Basingstoke. *Born* Basingstoke, 6 August, 1975
L. Welterweight. Ht. 5'7"
Manager Self

01.10.99 Peter Dunn W PTS 4 Bethnal Green
18.12.99 Marco Fattore W PTS 4 Southwark
21.02.00 Costas Katsantonis L RSC 1 Southwark
13.07.00 Mickey Yikealo L PTS 4 Bethnal Green
29.09.00 Manzo Smith L PTS 4 Bethnal Green
06.11.00 Jimmy Gould L PTS 6 Wolverhampton
16.03.01 Woody Greenaway W PTS 6 Portsmouth
07.09.01 Young Muttley L RSC 1 West Bromwich
20.10.01 Martin Watson L RSC 3 Glasgow
23.02.02 Darrell Grafton L RTD 1 Nottingham
Career: 10 contests, won 3, lost 7.

Chris Hooper

Scarborough. *Born* Barking, 28 September, 1977
Featherweight. Ht. 5'9"
Manager S. Pollard

01.11.01 Jason Nesbitt W RSC 6 Hull
28.01.02 Greg Edwards W RSC 2 Barnsley
Career: 2 contests, won 2.

Petr Horacek

Maidenhead. *Born* Czechoslovakia, 11 January, 1974
Heavyweight. Ht. 6'4"
Manager J. Evans

29.01.00 Gary Williams W PTS 4 Manchester
08.09.00 Chris Woollas W PTS 4 Hammersmith
23.11.00 Neil Kirkwood W RSC 2 Bayswater
10.04.01 Shane Woollas DREW 4 Wembley
13.09.01 Mal Rice L RSC 1 Sheffield
22.11.01 Slick Miller W PTS 4 Paddington
09.02.02 Vladislav Druso W PTS 6 Prague, Czechoslovakia
15.02.02 Ervin Slonka W PTS 4 Brno, Czechoslovakia
Career: 8 contests, won 6, drew 1, lost 1.

Petr Horacek   Les Clark

Shaun Horsfall

Colne. *Born* Burnley, 15 November, 1975
L. Middleweight. Ht. 5'7"
Manager J. Doughty

19.09.99 Danny Bance W PTS 6 Shaw
28.10.99 Lee Molyneux W PTS 6 Burnley
05.03.00 Dave Gibson W PTS 6 Shaw
21.05.00 Tony Smith W RSC 4 Shaw
24.09.00 Ernie Smith W PTS 6 Shaw
03.12.00 Ernie Smith W PTS 6 Shaw
03.03.02 Dean Walker L PTS 6 Shaw
Career: 7 contests, won 6, lost 1.

Neil Hosking

Reading. *Born* Plymouth, 6 December, 1972
Heavyweight. Ht. 6'4"
Manager J. Evans

31.07.01 Slick Miller W RSC 2 Bethnal Green
Career: 1 contest, won 1.

Shpetim Hoti

New Cross. *Born* Montenegro, 29 November, 1974
L. Heavyweight. Ht. 5'11½"
Manager A. Gee

21.09.00 Elvis Michailenko L PTS 4 Bloomsbury
30.11.00 Harry Butler L PTS 4 Bloomsbury
21.06.01 Harry Butler L PTS 4 Earls Court
31.01.02 Simeon Cover L PTS 6 Piccadilly
Career: 4 contests, lost 4.

Mark Hudson

Bradford. *Born* Bradford, 18 April, 1975
S. Featherweight. Ht. 5'7"
Manager J. Celebanski

21.02.99 Gary Groves W RSC 3 Bradford
18.10.99 Peter Allen W PTS 6 Bradford
29.04.02 Dave Curran L RSC 1 Bradford
Career: 3 contests, won 2, lost 1.

Anthony Hughes

Manchester. *Born* Salford, 8 May, 1981
Bantamweight. Ht. 5'6"
Manager S. Foster/S. Wood

27.05.01 Andrew Greenaway W PTS 4 Manchester
07.07.01 Daniel Ring W RSC 1 Manchester
Career: 2 contests, won 2.

Barry Hughes

Glasgow. *Born* Glasgow, 18 November, 1978
Lightweight. Ht. 5'8"
Manager Self

07.12.98 Woody Greenaway L PTS 6 Acton
18.02.99 Leon Dobbs W RSC 1 Glasgow
09.04.99 Gareth Dooley W PTS 6 Glasgow
26.06.99 Des Sowden W CO 1 Glasgow
04.10.99 Tony Smith W RSC 5 Glasgow
12.11.99 Brendan Ahearne W RSC 5 Glasgow
13.12.99 Jason Vlasman W RSC 2 Glasgow
24.02.00 Nono Junior W RSC 1 Glasgow
18.03.00 Gary Flear W RSC 4 Glasgow
07.04.00 Billy Smith W PTS 6 Glasgow
12.08.00 Dave Travers W PTS 4 Wembley
15.03.02 Woody Greenaway W PTS 8 Glasgow
Career: 12 contests, won 11, lost 1.

Sean Hughes

Pontefract. *Born* Pontefract, 5 June, 1982
S. Bantamweight. Ht. 5'9"
Manager M. Marsden

02.03.02 Paddy Folan W PTS 6 Wakefield
25.06.02 John Paul Ryan W PTS 6 Rugby
Career: 2 contests, won 2.

John Humphrey

Newmarket. *Born* Kings Lynn, 24 July, 1980
Southern Area L. Middleweight Champion. Former Undefeated British Masters Welterweight Champion. Ht. 6'2"
Manager A. Bowers

20.05.99 Arv Mittoo W PTS 6 Barking
13.09.99 Les Frost W CO 1 Bethnal Green
05.10.99 David Kehoe W PTS 4 Bloomsbury
06.11.99 Emmanuel Marcos W PTS 4 Bethnal Green
25.02.00 Matthew Barr L RSC 1 Newmarket
18.05.00 Lee Molyneux W PTS 6 Bethnal Green
29.09.00 Chris Henry W RSC 4 Bethnal Green
15.02.01 Kevin McIntyre W RSC 4 Glasgow
09.03.01 Harry Butler W RSC 1 Millwall
20.04.01 Mark Ramsey W PTS 10 Millwall
(Vacant British Masters Welterweight Title)
26.05.01 James Hare L RSC 7 Bethnal Green
(Elim. British Welterweight Title)
28.09.01 Clive Johnson W PTS 6 Millwall
23.11.01 Matthew Barr W RSC 2 Bethnal Green
16.03.02 Ojay Abrahams W PTS 10 Bethnal Green
(Vacant Southern Area L.Middleweight Title)
Career: 14 contests, won 12, lost 2.

John Humphrey   Les Clark

Albi Hunt

Ealing. *Born* Hammersmith, 20 April, 1974
L. Welterweight. Ht. 5'9"
Manager E. Maloney

28.04.02 Jason Gonzalez W PTS 6 Southwark
Career: 1 contest, won 1.

Danny Hunt

Southend. *Born* Rochford, 1 May, 1981
Lightweight. Ht. 5'7"
Manager F. Maloney

29.11.99 Chris Lyons W PTS 4 Wembley
13.03.00 Dave Hinds W PTS 4 Bethnal Green
13.04.00 Steve Hanley W PTS 4 Holborn

13.07.00 Dave Travers W PTS 4 Bethnal Green
27.01.01 Lee Williamson L RSC 2 Bethnal Green
03.04.01 Lee Williamson W PTS 4 Bethnal Green
05.05.01 Pete Buckley W PTS 4 Edmonton
22.09.01 Dafydd Carlin W PTS 4 Bethnal Green
15.12.01 Dave Hinds W PTS 4 Wembley
02.03.02 Gary Flear W PTS 4 Bethnal Green
04.05.02 Jason Nesbitt W PTS 4 Bethnal Green
Career: 11 contests, won 10, lost 1.

Michael Hunter

Hartlepool. *Born* Hartlepool, 5 May, 1978
Northern Area S. Bantamweight Champion. Ht. 5'7½"
Manager D. Garside

23.07.00 Sean Grant W PTS 6 Hartlepool
01.10.00 Chris Emanuele W PTS 6 Hartlepool
24.11.00 Gary Groves W RSC 2 Darlington
09.12.00 Chris Jickells W PTS 4 Southwark
11.02.01 Paddy Folan W RSC 6 Hartlepool
06.05.01 Anthony Hanna W PTS 4 Hartlepool
04.06.01 Anthony Hanna W PTS 4 Hartlepool
09.09.01 John Barnes W RSC 8 Hartlepool
(Vacant Northern Area S.Bantamweight Title)
29.11.01 Joel Viney W PTS 6 Hartlepool
26.01.02 Stevie Quinn W CO 2 Dagenham
18.03.02 Marc Callaghan DREW 6 Crawley
18.05.02 Mark Payne W PTS 8 Millwall
Career: 12 contests, won 11, drew 1.

Jamil Hussain

Bradford. *Born* Pakistan, 15 September, 1979
Bantamweight. Ht. 5'7"
Manager C. Aston/T. Gilmour

08.10.01 Andy Greenaway W RSC 3 Barnsley
28.01.02 Neil Read W CO 2 Barnsley
18.03.02 Darren Cleary DREW 4 Crawley
27.04.02 Darren Cleary DREW 4 Huddersfield
Career: 4 contests, won 2, drew 2.

Jamil Hussain   Les Clark

Richard Inquieti　　　　　Les Clark

Richard Inquieti

Nottingham. *Born* Langley Mill, 19
October, 1968
Welterweight. Ht. 6'3¹/₄"
Manager Self

30.09.96	Peter Varnavas L CO 2 Manchester
20.02.97	Paul Johnson W PTS 6 Mansfield
12.03.97	Tony Smith W RSC 2 Stoke
19.03.97	Andy Peach L RSC 1 Stoke
18.08.97	Jawaid Khaliq L RSC 5 Nottingham
18.09.97	Danny Bell L RSC 1 Alfreton
11.11.97	Trevor Smith L RSC 3 Edgbaston
08.12.97	Danny Bell L RSC 1 Nottingham
07.10.98	Sean O'Sullivan W PTS 6 Stoke
29.10.98	Dean Nicholas L RSC 1 Newcastle
02.12.98	Martyn Thomas L RSC 3 Stoke
25.03.99	Shane Junior L CO 2 Edgbaston
06.03.00	Martyn Bailey W RSC 5 Bradford
28.03.00	David Smales W PTS 6 Hartlepool
05.05.00	Martyn Bailey L PTS 6 Pentre Halkyn
20.11.00	Darren Spencer L RSC 1 Glasgow
04.02.01	Neil Bonner L PTS 6 Queensferry
23.02.01	Dean Nicholas L PTS 6 Irvine
08.03.01	Alan Campbell L PTS 6 Blackpool
01.04.01	Stuart Elwell L PTS 6 Wolverhampton
09.04.01	Gavin Wake L PTS 6 Bradford
20.04.01	Darren Williams L PTS 6 Dublin
03.06.01	Nicky Leech L PTS 6 Hanley
15.09.01	Andrei Ivanov DREW 6 Nottingham
23.09.01	Wayne Shepherd L PTS 6 Shaw
04.10.01	Danny Moir L PTS 6 Sunderland
15.10.01	Danny Parkinson L RSC 1 Bradford
13.11.01	Peter Dunn DREW 6 Leeds
24.11.01	Gavin Wake L PTS 6 Wakefield
06.12.01	John Jackson W RSC 3 Sunderland
08.02.02	Mark Paxford L PTS 6 Preston
18.03.02	Gavin Pearson L PTS 6 Glasgow
22.04.02	Ciaran Duffy L PTS 6 Glasgow
29.04.02	Gavin Pearson L PTS 6 Bradford

09.05.02	Lee Armstrong W RSC 5 Sunderland
03.06.02	Gary Porter L PTS 6 Glasgow

Career: 36 contests, won 7, drew 2, lost 27.

Andrei Ivanov

Nottingham. *Born* Rostov, Russia, 15 April,
1980
Nottingham. Ht. 6'0"
Manager J. Gill

15.09.01	Richard Inquieti DREW 6 Nottingham
10.10.01	Paddy Martin W RSC 2 Stoke
16.11.01	Peter Jackson L PTS 6 West Bromwich
12.12.01	Wayne Shepherd L PTS 6 Nottingham
17.12.01	Tony Montana DREW 6 Cleethorpes
07.02.02	Chris Steele W PTS 6 Stoke
08.03.02	Tony Byrne L PTS 6 Ellesmere Port
15.03.02	Paul Lomax L PTS 6 Spennymoor
02.06.02	Greg Hadwin W PTS 6 Shaw

Career: 9 contests, won 3, drew 2, lost 4.

John Jackson

Gateshead. *Born* Birkenhead, 5 June, 1980
L. Welterweight. Ht. 5'9"
Manager T. Conroy

06.12.01	Richard Inquieti L RSC 3 Sunderland
25.03.02	Scott Millar L RSC 4 Sunderland

Career: 2 contests, lost 2.

Peter Jackson

Halesowen. *Born* Wordsley, 27 January,
1976
S. Middleweight. Ht. 5'11"
Manager D. Bradley

28.01.01	Harry Butler W PTS 6 Wolverhampton
01.04.01	Jamie Logan W PTS 6 Wolverhampton
20.05.01	Jamie Logan W PTS 6 Wolverhampton
09.09.01	Neil Bonner W PTS 6 Hartlepool
16.11.01	Andrei Ivanov W PTS 6 West Bromwich
17.02.02	Alan Jones L PTS 6 Wolverhampton
13.04.02	Simon Andrews W PTS 4 Wolverhampton

Career: 7 contests, won 6, lost 1.

Jacklord Jacobs

Kingston. *Born* Nigeria, 1 January, 1970
British Masters Heavyweight Champion.
Ht. 6'1"
Manager J. Evans

Jacklord Jacobs　　　　　Les Clark

03.03.94	Cordwell Hylton W RSC 3 Ebbw Vale
30.07.94	Cordwell Hylton W RSC 4 Bethnal Green
01.11.94	Bobby Anderson DREW 4 Las Vegas, USA
14.11.95	John Pierre W PTS 6 Yarm
05.02.96	Tim Redman DREW 6 Bexleyheath
22.04.96	Chris Woollas DREW 4 Crystal Palace
27.08.96	Andrew Benson L CO 2 Windsor
22.01.00	Pele Reid W RSC 2 Birmingham
23.11.00	Gordon Minors W RSC 4 Bayswater
	(Vacant British Masters Heavyweight Title)
15.03.02	Rene Lillebuen L CO 4 Vilborg, Denmark
25.04.02	Omran Awaldi L RTD 2 Las Vegas, Nevada, USA

Career: 11 contests, won 5, drew 3, lost 3.

Lester Jacobs

Peckham. *Born* London, 29 January, 1962
WBF Middleweight Champion. Former
Undefeated WBF European Middleweight
Champion. Ht. 5'7"
Manager Self

01.03.89	Peter Vosper W PTS 6 Bethnal Green
29.03.89	Reuben Thurley W RSC 4 Bethnal Green
30.01.90	David Brown W PTS 6 Battersea
12.09.90	Peter Gorny W RSC 2 Battersea
18.10.90	Alan Pennington W RSC 2 Wandsworth
20.03.91	Karl Barwise W PTS 6 Battersea
16.05.91	Paul McCarthy W PTS 6 Battersea
11.09.91	John Kaighin W RSC 2 Hammersmith
05.03.92	John Kaighin W RSC 1 Battersea
17.05.92	Marvin O'Brien W PTS 6 Harringay
16.11.94	Stinger Mason W PTS 6 Bloomsbury
23.02.95	Paul Murray W RSC 2 Southwark
08.03.95	Mark Dawson W PTS 6 Bloomsbury
22.07.95	Mark Dawson W PTS 4 Millwall
02.09.95	Butch Lesley W PTS 4 Wembley
27.11.97	Leigh Wicks W PTS 6 Bloomsbury
04.03.98	Mike Whittaker W RSC 3 Bloomsbury
23.09.98	Paul Wesley W CO 4 Bloomsbury
25.11.98	Jason Hart W RSC 6 Streatham
	(Vacant WBF European Middleweight Title)
24.03.99	Darren Covill W RSC 2 Bayswater
21.07.99	David Baptiste W RSC 2 Bloomsbury
14.10.99	Harry Butler W PTS 6 Bloomsbury
23.03.00	Paul Wesley W PTS 6 Bloomsbury
04.07.00	Ojay Abrahams W PTS 4 Tooting
08.09.00	Delroy Leslie W RSC 8 Hammersmith
	(WBF Middleweight Title Challenge)
30.11.00	David Baptiste W RSC 3 Bloomsbury
29.03.01	Leigh Wicks W PTS 6 Hammersmith
21.06.01	Jason Collins W CO 9 Earls Court
	(WBF Middleweight Title Defence)
20.09.01	Darren Covill W CO 2 Blackfriars

Career: 29 contests, won 29.

Brett James (Eleftheriou)

St Pancras. *Born* London, 3 November, 1975
Welterweight. Ht. 5'8"
Manager D. Powell

20.01.00	Colin Vidler W PTS 6 Piccadilly
21.02.00	Julian Kacanolli W PTS 4 Southwark
04.07.00	Colin Vidler W PTS 4 Tooting
04.11.00	Matt Scriven W RTD 1 Bethnal Green

20.01.01	Jay Mahoney W PTS 4 Bethnal Green
07.04.01	Paul Denton W PTS 4 Wembley
16.06.01	Karl Taylor DREW 4 Wembley
14.07.01	Lee Williamson W PTS 6 Wembley
29.09.01	Ernie Smith W PTS 6 Southwark
12.02.02	Karl Taylor DREW 4 Bethnal Green
23.06.02	Lee Williamson W PTS 6 Southwark

Career: 11 contests, won 9, drew 2.

Brett James   Les Clark

Daniel James

Newmarket. *Born* Lincoln, 15 December, 1975
Former Undefeated Southern Area L.
Welterweight Champion. Ht. 5'9"
Manager A. Bowers

24.10.96	Shaba Edwards W PTS 6 Wembley
20.11.96	Costas Katsantonis W PTS 6 Wembley
11.02.97	Vince Burns W CO 2 Bethnal Green
03.04.97	Mark Allen W RSC 4 Wembley
09.09.97	Peter Nightingale W PTS 6 Bethnal Green
11.11.97	Marco Fattore W RSC 3 Bethnal Green
13.11.98	Woody Greenaway W PTS 4 Brighton
26.02.99	Tony Swift W PTS 6 Bethnal Green
20.05.99	Delroy Mellis W PTS 4 Barking
16.10.99	Steve Tuckett W RSC 1 Bethnal Green
25.02.00	John Paul Temple W PTS 10 Newmarket
	(Vacant Southern Area L. Welterweight Title)
06.10.00	Stephen Carr L RTD 5 Maidstone
28.09.01	Keith Jones W PTS 6 Millwall
23.11.01	Alan Bosworth L RSC 7 Bethnal Green
	(Elim. British L.Welterweight Title)

Career: 14 contests, won 12, lost 2.

Michael Jennings

Chorley. *Born* Preston, 9 September, 1977
Welterweight. Ht. 5'9¹/₂"
Manager F. Warren

15.05.99	Tony Smith W RSC 1 Blackpool
11.12.99	Lee Molyneux W PTS 4 Liverpool
29.02.00	Lee Molyneux W PTS 6 Widnes

25.03.00	Brian Coleman W PTS 6 Liverpool
16.05.00	Brian Coleman W PTS 6 Warrington
29.05.00	William Webster W PTS 6 Manchester
08.07.00	Paul Denton W PTS 6 Widnes
04.09.00	Mark Ramsey W PTS 6 Manchester
25.11.00	Ernie Smith W PTS 4 Manchester
11.12.00	Paul Denton W PTS 4 Widnes
10.02.01	Mark Haslam W RSC 2 Widnes
07.07.01	David Kirk W PTS 6 Manchester
15.09.01	Gary Harrison W PTS 6 Manchester
09.02.02	James Paisley W RSC 3 Manchester
01.06.02	Lee Williamson W PTS 4 Manchester

Career: 15 contests, won 15.

(Garnet) Chill John

Brighton. *Born* St Vincent, 11 August, 1977
Lightweight. Ht. 5'7"
Manager R. Davies

22.10.00	Paul Philpott W PTS 6 Streatham
03.02.01	Dave Travers W PTS 4 Brighton
25.02.01	Scott Hocking W RSC 4 Streatham
05.05.01	Woody Greenaway W PTS 6 Brighton
04.07.01	Steve Hanley W PTS 4 Bloomsbury
20.10.01	Mark Halstead W PTS 4 Portsmouth
01.12.01	Pete Buckley W PTS 4 Bethnal Green
13.04.02	Jonathan Thaxton L RSC 2 Norwich

Career: 8 contests, won 7, lost 1.

Chill John   Les Clark

Clint Johnson

Leeds. *Born* Leeds, 13 April, 1974
Cruiserweight. Ht. 6'2"
Manager T. O'Neill

11.11.97	Jon Penn W RSC 2 Leeds
04.12.97	John O'Byrne L PTS 6 Sunderland
17.02.98	Rob Galloway W PTS 6 Leeds
20.09.98	Rob Galloway W PTS 6 Sheffield
29.10.98	Mike White L PTS 6 Newcastle
06.11.98	Gerard Zdiarski W PTS 4 Mayfair
07.12.98	Carl Nicholson W PTS 6 Bradford
16.02.99	Danny Southam L RSC 5 Leeds
15.09.99	Steve Loftus W PTS 6 Harrogate
28.03.00	Martin Jolley W PTS 6 Hartlepool

17.04.00 Alex Mason L PTS 6 Birmingham
20.05.00 Jason Barker L RSC 1 Rotherham
23.10.00 Joe Gillon L CO 4 Glasgow
17.05.01 Paul Bonson L PTS 6 Leeds
18.06.01 Mark Brookes L PTS 6 Bradford
13.09.01 Darren Littlewood W PTS 6 Sheffield
03.11.01 Joe Gillon W CO 3 Glasgow
03.12.01 Jimmy Steel DREW 6 Leeds
15.12.01 Mark Brookes L PTS 4 Sheffield
18.02.02 Billy McClung L PTS 6 Glasgow
01.03.02 Billy McClung L PTS 6 Irvine
16.03.02 Clinton Woods L RSC 3 Bethnal Green

Career: 22 contests, won 9, drew 1, lost 12.

Clive Johnson

Basingstoke. *Born* Botswana, 18 October, 1977
L. Middleweight. Ht. 5'10"
Manager C. Sanigar

18.02.99 Harry Butler W PTS 6 Barking
20.05.99 Joe Skeldon W PTS 6 Barking
07.08.99 Gareth Hogg L PTS 4 Dagenham
09.10.99 Jamie Moore L RSC 3 Manchester
07.04.00 Kevin Lang W RSC 1 Bristol
08.09.00 Chris Henry L PTS 4 Bristol
06.10.00 Colin Vidler L PTS 6 Maidstone
26.03.01 David Baptiste W PTS 6 Peterborough
28.09.01 John Humphrey L PTS 6 Millwall
09.02.02 Darren McInulty L PTS 8 Coventry

Career: 10 contests, won 4, lost 6.

Alan Jones

Aberystwyth. *Born* Aberystwyth, 6 October, 1976
S. Middleweight. Ht. 6'1"
Manager D. Davies

15.09.01 Martyn Woodward W CO 3 Swansea
21.10.01 Kenny Griffith W RSC 4 Pentre Halkyn
17.02.02 Peter Jackson W PTS 6 Wolverhampton
16.03.02 Allan Foster DREW 6 Northampton

Career: 4 contests, won 3, drew 1.

Franny Jones

Darlington. *Born* Burnley, 7 February, 1981
L. Middleweight. Ht. 5'9½"
Manager M. Marsden

05.05.02 Surinder Sekhon W PTS 6 Hartlepool

Career: 1 contest, won 1.

Gary Jones

Birmingham. *Born* Birmingham, 26 October, 1976
Middleweight. Ht. 6'1"
Manager Self

15.07.00 Danny Smith L RSC 1 Norwich
16.09.00 Liam Lathbury L RSC 5 Bethnal Green
11.12.00 Andrew Facey L PTS 6 Cleethorpes
31.01.01 Paul Buchanan L RTD 1 Piccadilly
16.11.01 Tony Byrne L PTS 6 Preston
06.12.01 Danny Moir L PTS 6 Sunderland

Career: 6 contests, lost 6.

Keith Jones

Cefn Hengoed. *Born* Bradwell, 4 December, 1968
L. Welterweight. Former Undefeated

British Masters Lightweight Champion. Ht. 5'5¾"
Manager Self

17.05.94 Abdul Mannon L PTS 6 Kettering
13.06.94 G. G. Goddard L PTS 6 Liverpool
21.07.94 G. G. Goddard L RSC 1 Battersea
12.09.94 Marco Fattore L PTS 6 Mayfair
29.09.94 Marlon Ward L PTS 4 Bethnal Green
21.10.94 James Murray L CO 3 Glasgow
27.11.94 Daniel Lutaaya L CO 1 Southwark
03.09.96 Benny May W RSC 2 Bethnal Green
18.09.96 Kevin Sheil W PTS 4 Tylorstown
04.10.96 Andy Ross DREW 6 Pentre Halkyn
18.10.96 Wayne Jones DREW 6 Barnstaple
06.11.96 Robert Grubb W PTS 4 Tylorstown
22.11.96 Tony Mulholland L PTS 4 Liverpool
03.12.96 Alex Moon L RTD 5 Liverpool
21.01.97 Greg Upton DREW 6 Bristol
26.02.97 Greg Upton L PTS 4 Cardiff
07.03.97 Dean Murdoch L PTS 6 Weston super Mare
20.03.97 Kevin Sheil DREW 8 Solihull
04.04.97 Tony Mulholland L PTS 4 Liverpool
22.05.97 Darrell Easton L PTS 4 Southwark
02.10.98 Dean Pithie L PTS 8 Cheshunt
10.10.98 Steve Murray L RSC 4 Bethnal Green
21.11.98 Mat Zegan L PTS 4 Southwark
30.11.98 Eddie Nevins L PTS 4 Manchester
14.12.98 Roy Rutherford L PTS 6 Birmingham
12.01.99 Richard Evatt L CO 3 Bethnal Green
23.02.99 Simon Chambers DREW 4 Cardiff
12.03.99 Maurycy Gojko L PTS 6 Bethnal Green
09.04.99 Brian Carr L PTS 8 Glasgow
23.04.99 Dewi Roberts W PTS 6 Clydach
01.05.99 Steve Murray L RSC 6 Crystal Palace
04.06.99 Luis Navarro L RSC 5 Malaga, Spain
02.07.99 Alan Bosworth L PTS 6 Bristol
15.07.99 Tomas Jansson L PTS 4 Peterborough
20.08.99 Jason Hall L PTS 6 Bloomsbury
02.10.99 Jason Dee L RSC 5 Cardiff
06.11.99 Isaac Sebaduka L PTS 4 Bethnal Green
14.11.99 Lee Armstrong L PTS 6 Bradford
04.12.99 Franny Hogg L PTS 4 Manchester
14.12.99 Roy Rutherford L PTS 4 Coventry
18.01.00 Carl Greaves L PTS 6 Mansfield
29.01.00 Steve Murray L PTS 4 Manchester
27.02.00 Mark McGowan W RSC 7 Plymouth
          (British Masters Lightweight Title Challenge)
25.03.00 Alex Moon L PTS 6 Liverpool
12.05.00 Jason Cook L PTS 10 Swansea
          (Welsh L. Welterweight Title Challenge)
01.07.00 Matty Leonard W RSC 4 Southwark
25.07.00 Koba Gogoladze L PTS 4 Southwark
19.08.00 Richard Evatt L PTS 6 Brentwood
16.09.00 David Walker L PTS 4 Bethnal Green
21.10.00 Francis Barrett L PTS 4 Wembley
16.11.00 Jimmy Phelan DREW 6 Hull
27.11.00 Kevin Bennett L PTS 4 Birmingham
11.12.00 Steve Saville L PTS 8 Birmingham
02.01.01 Mark Payne L PTS 6 Coventry
15.01.01 Matthew Hatton L PTS 4 Manchester
03.02.01 David Burke L PTS 4 Manchester
10.02.01 Nigel Wright L PTS 4 Widnes
23.02.01 Darren Melville L PTS 4 Barking
29.03.01 Ted Bami L PTS 4 Hammersmith
10.04.01 Dean Pithie L PTS 4 Wembley
22.04.01 Brian Gentry L PTS 8 Streatham
08.05.01 Kevin Bennett L PTS 6 Barnsley
20.05.01 Jimmy Gould L PTS 6 Wolverhampton
02.06.01 Mally McIver L PTS 6 Wakefield

23.06.01 Alan Bosworth L PTS 6 Peterborough
14.07.01 Wayne Rigby L CO 3 Wembley
18.08.01 Steve Conway L PTS 8 Dewsbury
28.09.01 Daniel James L PTS 6 Millwall
20.10.01 Ronnie Nailen L PTS 4 Glasgow
10.11.01 Colin Lynes L PTS 6 Wembley
17.11.01 Willie Limond L PTS 4 Glasgow
24.11.01 Steve Murray L RSC 4 Bethnal Green
13.04.02 Jimmy Gould L PTS 8 Wolverhampton
27.04.02 Lee Armstrong L PTS 6 Huddersfield
09.05.02 Martin Holgate L PTS 6 Leicester Square
13.06.02 Ajose Olusegun L PTS 6 Leicester Square
23.06.02 Ted Bami L RSC 4 Southwark

Career: 77 contests, won 7, drew 6, lost 64.

Michael Jones

Liverpool. *Born* Liverpool, 14 November, 1974
Commonwealth L. Middleweight Champion. Ht. 6'0¼"
Manager J. Trickett

15.11.97 Harry Butler W PTS 4 Bristol
17.01.98 Martin Cavey W CO 1 Bristol
07.03.98 Darren McInulty W PTS 4 Reading
25.04.98 Koba Kulu W RSC 3 Cardiff
06.06.98 G. L. Booth W RSC 2 Liverpool
10.10.98 Mehrdud Takaloo W PTS 6 Bethnal Green
19.12.98 Ojay Abrahams W PTS 6 Liverpool
26.06.99 Paul King W PTS 6 Glasgow
11.03.00 Alan Gilbert W RTD 3 Kensington
02.06.00 Mohammed Boualleg W PTS 8 Ashford
03.02.01 Howard Clarke W PTS 4 Manchester
24.04.01 Judicael Bedel W PTS 6 Liverpool
06.10.01 Delroy Mellis W PTS 8 Manchester
10.12.01 Piotr Bartnicki W RSC 4 Liverpool
13.04.02 Mark Richards W RSC 1 Liverpool
28.05.02 Joshua Onyango W RSC 6 Liverpool
          (Commonwealth L. Middleweight Title Challenge)

Career: 16 contests, won 16.

Paul Jones

Sheffield. *Born* Sheffield, 19 November, 1966
Middleweight. Former Undefeated WBC International S. Middleweight Champion. Former Commonwealth Middleweight Champion. Former Undefeated WBO, WBO Inter-Continental & Central Area L. Middleweight Champion. Ht. 6'0"
Manager Self

08.12.86 Paul Gillings W PTS 6 Liverpool
28.10.87 Pat Durkin W PTS 4 Sheffield
10.11.87 David Binns L PTS 6 Batley
11.01.88 Humphrey Harrison L PTS 8 Manchester
27.09.88 George Sponagle DREW 8 Halifax, Canada
07.12.88 Jimmy Thornton W PTS 6 Stoke
23.01.89 Donovan Boucher L DIS 6 Toronto, Canada
13.03.89 Dale Moreland W PTS 6 Toronto, Canada
30.03.89 Benoit Boudreau W PTS 10 Moncton, Canada
19.04.89 Tony Collier W CO 3 Toronto, Canada

109

06.06.89	George Sponagle L PTS 8 Halifax, Canada
06.09.89	Kid Ford W PTS 6 Mississouga, Canada
13.11.89	Ian Midwood-Tate W RSC 4 Manchester
08.12.89	Antoine Tarver L PTS 4 Doncaster
06.03.90	Antonio Fernandez W PTS 8 Stoke
22.03.90	Darren Pilling W RTD 7 Gateshead
26.04.90	Newton Barnett W PTS 8 Mayfair
20.05.90	Jim Beckett W CO 1 Sheffield
22.05.90	Wayne Ellis L PTS 6 St Albans
14.11.90	Jason Rowe W PTS 10 Sheffield *(Central Area L. Middleweight Title Challenge)*
12.03.91	Tony Velinor W PTS 8 Mansfield
16.08.91	Hugo Marinangelli L CO 2 Marbella, Spain

01.10.91	Simon Eubank W CO 6 Sheffield
14.04.92	Paul Lynch W RSC 3 Mansfield
19.05.92	Trevor Ambrose W PTS 6 Cardiff
02.06.92	Patrick Vungbo W PTS 10 Rotterdam, Holland
19.09.92	Ernie Loveridge W PTS 6 Glasgow
24.11.92	Paul Wesley L RSC 2 Doncaster
17.01.95	Julian Eavis W RSC 4 Worcester
06.03.95	Peter Waudby W PTS 6 Mayfair
14.04.95	Damien Denny W CO 1 Belfast *(Vacant WBO Inter-Continental L. Middleweight Title)*
26.08.95	Danny Juma W PTS 12 Belfast *(WBO Inter-Continental L. Middleweight Title Defence)*
02.10.95	Eric Spalding W RSC 2 Mayfair *(WBO Inter-Continental L. Middleweight Title Defence)*

22.11.95	Verno Phillips W PTS 12 Sheffield *(WBO L. Middleweight Title Challenge)*
14.12.96	Ryan Rhodes L RSC 8 Sheffield *(Vacant British L. Middleweight Title)*
08.05.97	Lee Blundell W RSC 4 Mansfield
31.10.97	Johnson Tshuma L PTS 12 Mayfair *(Vacant Commonwealth Middleweight Title)*
24.03.98	Johnson Tshuma W PTS 12 Bethnal Green *(Commonwealth Middleweight Title Challenge)*
27.02.99	Jason Matthews L DIS 7 Oldham *(Commonwealth Middleweight Title Defence)*
20.05.00	Ganny Dovidovas W PTS 6 Rotherham
08.07.00	Jason Barker W RSC 5 Rotherham
09.10.00	Olivier Beard W RSC 1 Liverpool *(Vacant WBC International S.Middleweight Title)*
03.03.01	Adrian Dodson L CO 3 Wembley *(Vacant IBO S.Middleweight Title)*
10.05.02	Kreshnik Qato W PTS 6 Millwall

Career: 44 contests, won 31, drew 1, lost 12.

Gareth Jordan

Monmouth. *Born* Usk, 19 December, 1971
S. Featherweight. Ht. 5'6¾"
Manager Self

02.11.92	Con Cronin W RSC 2 Wolverhampton
04.12.92	Jason White W RSC 2 Telford
16.03.93	Lee Fox W RSC 3 Wolverhampton
26.05.93	Mark O'Callaghan W RSC 3 Mansfield
27.10.93	Dave Madden W RSC 5 West Bromwich
16.12.93	Phil Found W PTS 6 Newport
04.06.94	T. J. Smith W RSC 1 Cardiff
01.10.94	Wayne Jones W RSC 2 Cardiff
30.11.94	Kevin McKenzie W PTS 6 Wolverhampton
04.02.95	Mark O'Callaghan W RSC 2 Cardiff
21.04.95	Peter Till W PTS 6 Dudley
07.07.95	Kelton McKenzie W PTS 4 Cardiff
25.10.95	Mervyn Bennett L PTS 10 Cardiff *(Welsh Lightweight Title Challenge)*
13.02.96	Bamana Dibateza W PTS 8 Cardiff
16.05.96	Billy Schwer L RSC 3 Dunstable
03.04.97	Anthony Campbell W PTS 6 Wembley
07.07.00	Billy Smith W PTS 6 Chigwell
14.10.00	Pete Buckley W PTS 4 Wembley
28.04.01	Patrick Gallagher L PTS 4 Cardiff
09.10.01	Gary Flear W PTS 4 Cardiff
28.05.02	Gary Reid DREW 6 Liverpool

Career: 21 contests, won 17, drew 1, lost 3.

(Fation) Nono Junior (Kacanolli)

Hayes. *Born* Kosovo, 20 October, 1977
Lightweight. Ht. 5'7"
Manager D. Currivan

18.11.99	Darren Woodley W RSC 1 Mayfair
19.12.99	Gary Reid W PTS 6 Salford
24.02.00	Barry Hughes L RSC 1 Glasgow
19.04.00	Woody Greenaway W PTS 4 Kensington
30.05.00	Phil Lashley W CO 2 Kensington
24.06.00	Steve Murray L RSC 4 Glasgow
10.03.01	Ivan Kirpa L RSC 1 Bethnal Green
04.10.01	Isaac Sebaduka W RSC 4 Finsbury
18.03.02	Jason Cook L RSC 1 Crawley

Career: 9 contests, won 5, lost 4.

Michael Jones   Les Clark

Prince Kasi Kaihau

Doncaster. *Born* Doncaster, 3 October, 1967
Welterweight. Ht. 5'11"
Manager J. Rushton

12.10.93	Prince Louis W PTS 6 Wolverhampton
24.11.93	Steve Levene W PTS 6 Solihull
13.12.93	Rob Stevenson W RSC 5 Doncaster
07.03.94	Steve Levene W RSC 3 Doncaster
10.05.94	Billy McDougall W RTD 4 Doncaster
12.09.94	Rick North W PTS 6 Doncaster
12.10.94	Andy Peach W PTS 6 Stoke
30.11.94	Billy McDougall W PTS 6 Solihull
12.12.94	Andy Peach W PTS 6 Doncaster
28.03.95	David Bain L PTS 6 Wolverhampton
05.05.95	Andy Peach W PTS 6 Doncaster
02.11.95	Robbie Bell L PTS 6 Houghton le Spring
26.01.96	Ozzy Orrock W RSC 5 Doncaster
29.03.96	Chris Pollock L RSC 2 Doncaster
10.05.96	Jon Stocks L PTS 6 Liverpool
28.05.96	Neil Sinclair L RSC 2 Belfast
26.09.96	Joe Townsley L PTS 8 Glasgow
07.10.96	Carl Winstone W RSC 5 Birmingham
24.10.96	George Richards L PTS 6 Birmingham
09.12.96	Stuart Dunn W RSC 2 Leicester
16.01.97	George Richards L PTS 8 Solihull
11.02.97	Howard Clarke W RSC 4 Wolverhampton
27.02.97	Terry Morrill L PTS 6 Hull
15.04.97	Howard Clarke L PTS 6 Edgbaston
25.04.97	Brian Dunn W RSC 1 Cleethorpes
05.06.97	Wayne Alexander L CO 4 Bristol
08.10.97	Alex Mason DREW 6 Stoke
20.10.97	Carlton Williams DREW 6 Leicester
21.11.97	Peter Waudby DREW 6 Hull
06.12.97	Ahmet Oner L PTS 4 Offenbach, Germany
13.12.97	Harry Simon L RSC 4 Sheffield
24.01.98	Paul Samuels L CO 3 Cardiff
27.03.98	Spencer McCracken L PTS 8 Telford
08.04.98	Paul Burns W RSC 2 Liverpool
30.05.98	Jason Williams L CO 2 Bristol
18.09.98	Jim Webb L RSC 4 Belfast
14.11.98	Spencer Fearon L CO 5 Cheshunt
21.05.99	Gerard Murphy L PTS 6 Glasgow
04.10.99	Brian Dunn W RSC 2 Glasgow
23.10.99	Mehrdud Takaloo L RSC 3 Telford
08.12.99	Martin Jolley L PTS 8 Stoke
12.11.00	Jamie Moore L RSC 2 Manchester
17.12.00	Gerard Murphy L PTS 6 Glasgow
27.10.01	P.J. Maxwell L CO 4 Manchester
10.12.01	Darrell Grafton L RSC 5 Nottingham

Career: 45 contests, won 17, drew 3, lost 25.

Costas Katsantonis

St Pancras. *Born* London, 16 October, 1970
Southern Area L. Welterweight Champion.
Ht. 5'8"
Manager Self

09.07.96	Gilbert Eastman L RSC 1 Bethnal Green
28.09.96	Jason Campbell W PTS 6 Barking
24.10.96	Allan Gray L PTS 6 Mayfair
20.11.96	Daniel James L PTS 6 Wembley
19.02.97	Allan Gray L PTS 6 Acton
30.04.97	Kevin McCarthy W RSC 6 Acton
13.12.97	James Hare L RSC 3 Sheffield
21.02.98	Martin Renaghan L PTS 4 Belfast
21.02.00	Jon Honney W RSC 1 Southwark
13.07.00	Gary Harrison W PTS 4 Bethnal Green
18.11.00	Peter Richardson L PTS 4 Dagenham
17.02.01	Trevor Smith W RSC 3 Bethnal Green
10.04.01	Karl Taylor W PTS 4 Wembley
31.07.01	Woody Greenaway W RSC 4 Bethnal Green
23.11.01	Iain Eldridge W RSC 1 Bethnal Green *(Vacant Southern Area L.Welterweight Title)*
10.05.02	Gary Harrison W PTS 10 Millwall *(Southern Area L. Welterweight Title Defence)*

Career: 16 contests, won 9, lost 7.

Costas Katsantonis Les Clark

Marty Kayes Les Clark

Marty Kayes

Downpatrick. *Born* Ashton under Lyne, 16
December, 1975
Flyweight. Ht. 5'5 1/2"
Manager N. Nobbs

27.05.01	Darren Cleary L PTS 4 Manchester
07.07.01	Darren Cleary L PTS 4 Manchester
15.10.01	Darren Taylor L PTS 4 Southampton
26.01.02	Lee Georgiou L PTS 6 Bethnal Green
13.03.02	Sunkanmi Ogunbiyi L PTS 4 Mayfair

Career: 5 contests, lost 5.

John Keeton Les Clark

John Keeton

Sheffield. *Born* Sheffield, 19 May, 1972
WBF Cruiserweight Champion. Former
Undefeated WBO Inter-Continental
Cruiserweight Champion. Ht. 6'0"
Manager D. Ingle

11.08.93	Tony Colclough W RSC 1 Mansfield
15.09.93	Val Golding L PTS 6 Ashford
27.10.93	Darren McKenna W RSC 3 Stoke
01.12.93	Julius Francis L PTS 4 Bethnal Green
19.01.94	Dennis Bailey W RTD 2 Stoke
17.02.94	Dermot Gascoyne L RSC 1 Dagenham
09.04.94	Eddie Knight W RTD 5 Mansfield
11.05.94	John Rice W RSC 5 Sheffield
02.06.94	Devon Rhooms W RSC 2 Tooting
06.09.94	Mark Walker W RSC 5 Stoke
24.09.94	Dirk Wallyn L CO 3 Middlekerke, Belgium
26.10.94	Lee Archer W PTS 6 Stoke
09.12.94	Bruce Scott L CO 2 Bethnal Green
11.02.95	Rudiger May L PTS 6 Frankfurt, Germany
06.03.95	Simon McDougall W RSC 5 Mayfair
07.07.95	Nicky Piper L RTD 2 Cardiff
15.09.95	Steve Osborne W RSC 4 Mansfield
27.10.95	Nicky Wadman W RSC 1 Brighton
03.11.95	Monty Wright W RSC 4 Dudley
11.11.95	Denzil Browne W RSC 4 Halifax
30.01.96	Cesar Kazadi W RSC 3 Lille, France
11.05.96	Terry Dunstan L RSC 1 Bethnal Green *(British Cruiserweight Title Challenge)*

111

14.09.96	John Pierre W PTS 4 Sheffield
14.12.96	Nigel Rafferty W RTD 3 Sheffield
12.04.97	Nigel Rafferty W RSC 6 Sheffield
11.10.97	Kelly Oliver L RSC 8 Sheffield
	(Vacant WBO Inter-Continental Cruiserweight Title)
16.05.98	Jacob Mofokeng L RTD 4 Hammanskraal, South Africa
18.07.98	Kelly Oliver W RSC 2 Sheffield
23.01.99	Garry Delaney W PTS 12 Cheshunt
	(Vacant WBO Inter-Continental Cruiserweight Title)
15.05.99	William Barima W RTD 3 Sheffield
29.02.00	Tony Booth W RSC 2 Widnes
16.12.00	Bruce Scott L CO 6 Sheffield
	(Vacant British Cruiserweight Title)
21.07.01	Radcliffe Green W PTS 4 Sheffield
19.03.02	Butch Lesley W PTS 12 Slough
	(Vacant WBF Cruiserweight Title)

Career: 34 contests, won 23, lost 11.

David Kehoe

Northampton. *Born* Northampton, 24 December, 1972
Lightweight. Ht. 5'10½"
Manager Self

06.02.96	Simon Frailing W CO 1 Basildon
20.04.96	Paul Salmon W PTS 6 Brentwood
12.11.96	Peter Nightingale L PTS 6 Dudley
28.04.97	Craig Kelley L DIS 3 Enfield
18.11.97	Peter Nightingale DREW 4 Mansfield
27.01.98	Paul Miles L PTS 4 Bethnal Green
11.03.98	Trevor Tacy W RTD 1 Bethnal Green
28.03.98	David Thompson W PTS 6 Crystal Palace
26.05.98	Dave Hinds W RSC 5 Mayfair
08.09.98	Marc Smith W PTS 6 Bethnal Green
12.01.99	Gary Flear L PTS 4 Bethnal Green
25.01.99	Roger Sampson L PTS 4 Glasgow
12.03.99	Jamie McKeever L RSC 2 Bethnal Green
02.07.99	Mark McGowan L RSC 3 Bristol
	(Vacant British Masters Lightweight Title)
13.09.99	Stephen Smith L DIS 2 Bethnal Green
05.10.99	John Humphrey L PTS 4 Bloomsbury
24.10.99	Young Muttley L RTD 1 Wolverhampton
02.12.99	Liam Maltby L PTS 4 Peterborough
19.02.00	Dariusz Snarski DREW 6 Prestwick
10.03.00	Ted Bami L PTS 4 Bethnal Green
17.04.00	Mark Hawthorne L PTS 4 Birmingham
25.07.00	P.J.Gallagher L PTS 6 Southwark
08.09.00	Dariusz Snarski W PTS 4 Hammersmith
27.11.00	Anthony Maynard L RSC 5 Birmingham
16.03.02	Wayne Wheeler DREW 6 Northampton
28.05.02	Ricky Eccleston L RSC 4 Liverpool

Career: 26 contests, won 7, drew 3, lost 16.

David Keir

Liverpool. *Born* Liverpool, 23 September, 1977
Welterweight. Ht. 5'9½"
Manager T. Gilmour

10.12.01	Lee Williamson DREW 4 Liverpool
11.02.02	Sammy Smith L PTS 6 Southampton
13.04.02	Lee Williamson W PTS 4 Liverpool
03.06.02	Paul McIlwaine W CO 2 Glasgow

Career: 4 contests, won 2, drew 1, lost 1.

David Keir   Les Clark

Damaen Kelly

Belfast. *Born* Belfast, 3 April, 1973
WBF Flyweight Champion. Former Undefeated IBO Flyweight Champion. Former Undefeated European Flyweight Champion. Former Undefeated WBC International S. Flyweight Champion. Former British & Commonwealth Flyweight Champion. Ht. 5'5"
Manager Self

27.09.97	Chris Thomas W RSC 1 Belfast
22.11.97	Bojidar Ivanov W CO 1 Manchester
20.12.97	Anthony Hanna W PTS 4 Belfast
14.02.98	Hristo Lessov W RSC 2 Southwark
14.03.98	Mark Reynolds W RSC 4 Bethnal Green
02.05.98	Krasimir Tcholakov W RSC 3 Kensington
26.09.98	Mike Thomas W PTS 6 Uncasville, USA
12.12.98	Alfonso Zvenyika W PTS 12 Chester
	(Commonwealth Flyweight Title Challenge)
13.03.99	Anthony Hanna W PTS 12 Manchester
	(Vacant British Flyweight Title. Commonwealth Flyweight Title Defence)
22.05.99	Keith Knox L RTD 6 Belfast
	(British & Commonwealth Flyweight Title Defences)
16.10.99	Igor Gerasimov W RSC 4 Belfast
	(Vacant WBC International S. Flyweight Title)
12.02.00	Alexander Mahmutov W PTS 12 Sheffield
	(European Flyweight Title Challenge)
12.06.00	Jose Antonio Lopez Bueno W PTS 12 Belfast
	(European Flyweight Title Defence)
30.09.00	Zolile Mbitye W PTS 12 Peterborough
	(IBO Flyweight Title Challenge)
17.02.01	Paulino Villabos W PTS 12 Bethnal Green
	(IBO Flyweight Title Defence)
31.07.01	Sipho Mantyi W RSC 4 Bethnal Green

18.01.02	Simphewe Xabendini W RSC 1 Coventry
21.05.02	Celso Dangud W PTS 12 Custom House
	(Vacant WBF Flyweight Title)

Career: 18 contests, won 17, lost 1.

Colin Kenna

Dublin. *Born* Dublin, 28 July, 1976
Heavyweight. Ht. 6'1"
Manager J. Bishop

25.02.01	Slick Miller W RSC 3 Streatham
22.04.01	Eamonn Glennon W PTS 4 Streatham
15.10.01	Tony Booth W PTS 6 Southampton
11.02.02	Dave Clarke W RSC 4 Southampton
08.04.02	James Gilbert W RSC 1 Southampton

Career: 5 contests, won 5.

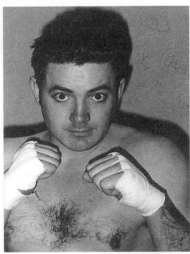

Colin Kenna   Les Clark

Ryan Kerr

Stirling. *Born* Falkirk, 19 March, 1982
L. Middleweight. Ht. 5'9"
Manager T. Conroy

17.09.01	Pedro Thompson W RSC 1 Glasgow
04.10.01	Colin McCash W PTS 6 Sunderland
03.11.01	Tomas da Silva W PTS 4 Glasgow
21.02.02	Wayne Shepherd W PTS 6 Sunderland

Career: 4 contests, won 4.

Jawaid Khaliq (Akhtar)

Nottingham. *Born* Reading, 30 July, 1970
IBO Welterweight Champion. Former Undefeated Commonwealth & Midlands Area Welterweight Champion. Former Undefeated Midlands Area & WBF European L. Middleweight Champion. Ht. 5'10½"
Manager T. Gilmour/C. Aston

18.08.97	Richard Inquieti W RSC 5 Nottingham
13.09.97	Martin Holgate W RSC 6 Millwall
13.12.97	Mark Ramsey DREW 4 Sheffield
07.02.98	Mehrdud Takaloo W RSC 4 Cheshunt
07.03.98	Koba Kulu W PTS 4 Reading
05.09.98	Harry Butler W PTS 4 Telford

03.12.98	Frederic Klose L PTS 8 Epernay, France	
27.09.99	Lee Murtagh W RSC 5 Leeds	
	(Vacant WBF European L. Middleweight Title)	
14.12.99	Dirk Kaltenbach W CO 2 Telde, Gran Canaria	
15.01.00	Lee Bird W RSC 4 Doncaster	
27.02.00	Jason Collins W PTS 6 Leeds	
21.05.00	Dennis Berry W RSC 6 Derby	
	(Vacant Midlands Area L. Middleweight Title)	
13.08.00	Ernie Smith W RSC 4 Nottingham	
	(Vacant Midlands Area Welterweight Title)	
28.10.00	Trevor Smith W RSC 1 Coventry	
27.11.00	Sean Sullivan W PTS 12 Birmingham	
	(Vacant Commonwealth Welterweight Title)	

26.02.01	Howard Clarke W PTS 6 Nottingham
11.06.01	Willy Wise W PTS 12 Nottingham
	(IBO Welterweight Title Challenge)
15.09.01	Jacek Bielski W CO 5 Nottingham
	(IBO Welterweight Title Defence)
03.11.01	Luther Smith W RSC 3 Glasgow
23.02.02	Maxim Nesterenko W RSC 12 Nottingham
	(IBO Welterweight Title Defence)

Career: 20 contests, won 18, drew 1, lost 1.

Tasawar Khan

Bradford. *Born* Bradford, 10 June, 1980
S. Featherweight. Ht. 5'5"
Manager C. Ashton

10.06.01	Jason Edwards L PTS 6 Ellesmere Port
15.10.01	Joel Viney W PTS 6 Bradford
11.05.02	Steve Williams L PTS 6 Newark

Jawaid Khaliq   Les Clark

03.06.02	Alston Buchanan W RSC 3 Glasgow
24.06.02	Peter Allen W PTS 6 Bradford

Career: 5 contests, won 3, lost 2.

John Killian

Finchley. *Born* South Africa, 24 August, 1976
L. Heavyweight. Ht. 6'0"
Manager J. Oyebola

16.06.01	Calvin Stonestreet W PTS 4 Wembley
22.11.01	Dean Ashton W PTS 4 Mayfair
13.06.02	Darren Ashton W PTS 4 Leicester Square

Career: 3 contests, won 3.

Nathan King

Mountain Ash. *Born* Aberdare, 19 March, 1981
L. Heavyweight. Ht. 6'3"
Manager F. Warren/E. Calzaghe

27.01.01	Tony Oakey L PTS 6 Bethnal Green
28.04.01	Pinky Burton W PTS 4 Cardiff
09.06.01	Michael Pinnock W PTS 4 Bethnal Green
09.10.01	Darren Ashton W PTS 6 Cardiff
24.11.01	Peter Haymer W PTS 4 Bethnal Green
12.02.02	Peter Haymer W PTS 4 Bethnal Green
20.04.02	Radcliffe Green W PTS 6 Cardiff

Career: 7 contests, won 6, lost 1.

David Kirk

Sutton in Ashfield. *Born* Mansfield, 5 October, 1974
L. Welterweight. Former Undefeated WBF European Welterweight Champion. Ht. 5'8"
Manager J. Ashton

01.11.96	Arv Mittoo W PTS 6 Mansfield
04.12.96	Stuart Rimmer W PTS 6 Stoke
20.02.97	Chris Price W PTS 6 Mansfield
16.03.97	Gary Hibbert L PTS 6 Shaw
25.03.97	Miguel Matthews W PTS 6 Wolverhampton
28.04.97	Mark Breslin L PTS 8 Glasgow
06.10.97	Christian Brady L PTS 6 Birmingham
30.10.97	Trevor Tacy L PTS 6 Newark
08.12.97	Nick Hall L PTS 6 Nottingham
12.01.98	Juha Temonen DREW 6 Helsinki, Finland
24.01.98	Jason Cook L RSC 3 Cardiff
24.02.98	Roy Rutherford L PTS 6 Edgbaston
11.03.98	Patrick Gallagher L PTS 6 Bethnal Green
27.04.98	Tommy Peacock L PTS 6 Manchester
08.05.98	Chris Barnett L PTS 6 Manchester
23.05.98	Graham Earl L PTS 4 Bethnal Green
04.06.98	Mark Richards L PTS 6 Dudley
21.09.98	Steve McLevy L PTS 8 Glasgow
12.10.98	Malcolm Melvin L PTS 10 Birmingham
	(Midlands Area L. Welterweight Title Challenge)
31.10.98	Bernard Paul L PTS 6 Southend
28.11.98	Glenn McClarnon L PTS 4 Belfast
11.12.98	Charlie Kane L PTS 8 Prestwick
20.02.99	Dennis Berry L PTS 10 Thornaby
	(Vacant Continental European Welterweight Title)
09.05.99	Sammy Smith L PTS 6 Bracknell
20.05.99	Steve Brumant W PTS 4 Kensington
05.06.99	Neil Sinclair L PTS 8 Cardiff
11.09.99	Glenn McClarnon L PTS 6 Sheffield

20.10.99 Dave Gibson W PTS 6 Stoke
18.11.99 Adrian Chase W PTS 10 Mayfair
(Vacant WBF European Welterweight Title)
26.11.99 Gerard Murphy L RTD 3 Hull
25.03.00 Jacek Bielski L PTS 6 Liverpool
29.04.00 Eamonn Magee L RSC 8 Wembley
13.08.00 Ram Singh W PTS 6 Nottingham
09.09.00 Mally McIver L PTS 6 Newark
23.09.00 Steve Murray L PTS 4 Bethnal Green
09.10.00 Steve Saville W PTS 8 Birmingham
19.11.00 Gavin Down L PTS 10 Chesterfield
(Vacant British Masters L.Welterweight Title)
01.12.00 Alan Bosworth DREW 8 Peterborough
04.02.01 Mark Winters L PTS 6 Queensferry
28.02.01 Ossie Duran L PTS 8 Kensington
(Vacant WBF European Welterweight Title)
10.03.01 Junior Witter L RSC 2 Bethnal Green
10.04.01 Colin Lynes L PTS 6 Wembley
20.04.01 Mark Winters L PTS 6 Dublin
16.06.01 Oscar Hall L PTS 6 Derby
07.07.01 Michael Jennings L PTS 6 Manchester
28.07.01 Jonathan Thaxton L PTS 4 Wembley
13.09.01 David Walker DREW 8 Sheffield
17.11.01 Kevin McIntyre L PTS 4 Glasgow
24.11.01 Ivan Kirpa L PTS 4 Bethnal Green
08.12.01 Chris Saunders L CO 2 Chesterfield
26.01.02 Colin Lynes L PTS 6 Dagenham
09.02.02 David Barnes L RTD 1 Manchester
11.03.02 Matthew Macklin L PTS 4 Glasgow
25.05.02 Francis Barrett L PTS 6 Portsmouth
08.06.02 Kevin McIntyre L RTD 4 Renfrew
Career: 55 contests, won 9, drew 3, lost 43.

Adrian Kirkbride

Carlisle. *Born* Penrith, 11 February, 1971
L. Middleweight. Ht. 5'10"
Manager P. McCausland

22.01.99 Shaun O'Neill W PTS 6 Carlisle
03.04.99 Lee Molloy L PTS 4 Carlisle
19.02.00 Piotr Bartnicki L RSC 1 Prestwick
06.06.00 Scott Millar L RSC 2 Motherwell
20.10.00 Balazs Szabo W PTS 6 Belfast
01.04.01 Gary Logan L RSC 1 Southwark
24.04.02 Darren Williams L RSC 2 Dublin
Career: 7 contests, won 2, lost 5.

Neil Kirkwood

Barnsley. *Born* Barnsley, 30 November, 1969
Central Area Heavyweight Champion.
Ht. 6'4"
Manager Self

17.03.94 Gary Williams W RSC 1 Lincoln
16.05.94 Joey Paladino W RSC 2 Cleethorpes
26.08.94 Shane Woollas W RSC 6 Barnsley
11.03.95 Carl Gaffney W RSC 2 Barnsley
(Vacant Central Area Heavyweight Title)
24.10.95 Julius Francis L RSC 7 Southwark
08.10.96 Nikolai Valouev L RSC 2 Battersea
11.04.97 Johnny Davison W RSC 3 Barnsley
23.10.98 Lennox Williams W RSC 2 Wakefield
27.05.00 Albert Sosnowski L RSC 1 Mayfair
21.10.00 Mark Krence L PTS 6 Sheffield
23.11.00 Petr Horacek L RSC 2 Bayswater
16.03.02 Mark Krence L RSC 4 Bethnal Green
28.04.02 Mark Potter L RSC 1 Southwark
Career: 13 contests, won 6, lost 7.

Eddie Knight

Ashford. *Born* Ashford, 4 October, 1966
Cruiserweight. Former Southern Area L.
Heavyweight Champion. Ht. 5'11"
Manager Self

05.10.92 Shaun McCrory L PTS 6 Bristol
29.10.92 Adrian Wright L PTS 6 Bayswater
25.11.92 Julian Johnson L RSC 2 Mayfair
15.09.93 Terry Duffus W PTS 6 Ashford
09.04.94 John Keeton L RTD 5 Mansfield
27.05.94 Lee Sara W CO 2 Ashford
09.07.94 Mark Delaney L CO 4 Earls Court
17.09.94 Mark Hale W PTS 6 Crawley
13.12.94 Tim Robinson W RTD 2 Potters Bar
09.05.95 Mark Delaney L RSC 2 Basildon
30.01.96 Graham Townsend W PTS 4 Barking
04.03.96 Marko Salminen W RSC 2 Helsinki, Finland
17.12.96 Monty Wright L RSC 5 Bethnal Green
(Vacant Southern Area L. Heavyweight Title)
20.05.97 Martin Jolley W PTS 6 Gillingham
09.09.97 Graham Townsend W RSC 6 Bethnal Green
16.05.98 Paul Bowen L RSC 3 Bethnal Green
16.01.99 Monty Wright W RSC 2 Bethnal Green
(Southern Area L. Heavyweight Title Challenge)
02.06.00 Martin Jolley W RSC 5 Ashford
14.10.00 Butch Lesley L RSC 6 Wembley
(Southern Area L.Heavyweight Title Defence)
08.12.01 Dominic Negus L CO 2 Dagenham
(Vacant WBU Inter-Continental S.Cruiserweight Title)
Career: 20 contests, won 10, lost 10.

Paul Knights

Redhill. *Born* Redhill, 5 February, 1971
Former Undefeated Southern Area
Welterweight Champion. Ht. 5'10"
Manager B. Hearn

26.11.91 Steve Hearn W RSC 4 Bethnal Green
19.02.92 Seth Jones W RSC 5 Muswell Hill
16.06.92 Seth Jones W PTS 6 Dagenham
10.11.92 Alex Moffatt W CO 3 Dagenham
30.01.93 Dave Lovell W PTS 6 Brentwood
20.04.93 Mark Allen W PTS 6 Brentwood
26.06.93 Phil Found W PTS 4 Earls Court
28.09.93 Pat Delargy W RSC 3 Bethnal Green
11.01.94 Brian Coleman W RSC 4 Bethnal Green
09.02.94 Mark Allen W RSC 2 Brentwood
19.03.94 Alan Peacock W PTS 6 Millwall
11.06.94 John O. Johnson L PTS 6 Bethnal Green
17.09.94 Dewi Roberts W PTS 6 Crawley
17.02.95 Norman Dhalie W RTD 5 Crawley
16.03.95 Brian Coleman W RSC 2 Basildon
09.05.95 Alan Peacock W PTS 6 Basildon
28.10.95 Tony Swift W PTS 6 Kensington
23.01.96 Karl Taylor DREW 6 Bethnal Green
08.03.97 Dave Brazil L RSC 2 Brentwood
22.04.97 Peter Nightingale W PTS 6 Bethnal Green
11.07.97 Paul Miles W PTS 6 Brighton
27.01.98 Adrian Chase L RSC 1 Bethnal Green
20.05.99 Matthew Barr W RSC 1 Barking
29.06.99 Dean Nicholas W RSC 2 Bethnal Green
01.04.00 Delroy Mellis L RSC 3 Bethnal Green
23.01.01 Brian Coleman W PTS 6 Crawley
01.12.01 Paul Dyer W PTS 10 Bethnal Green
(Southern Area Welterweight Title Challenge)
Career: 27 contests, won 22, drew 1, lost 4.

Paul Knights   Les Clark

Mark Krence

Chesterfield. *Born* Chesterfield, 24 August, 1976
Heavyweight. Ht. 6'5"
Manager D. Hobson

09.04.00 Slick Miller W PTS 6 Alfreton
21.10.00 Neil Kirkwood W PTS 6 Sheffield
11.12.00 Tony Booth W PTS 6 Sheffield
20.01.01 Nigel Rafferty W PTS 4 Bethnal Green
24.03.01 Mark Williams W PTS 4 Sheffield
27.07.01 Shane Woollas W PTS 4 Sheffield
13.09.01 Luke Simpkin W PTS 4 Sheffield
25.09.01 Darren Chubbs W PTS 4 Liverpool
15.12.01 Eamonn Glennon W RSC 2 Sheffield
16.03.02 Neil Kirkwood W RSC 4 Bethnal Green
11.05.02 Gary Williams W PTS 6 Chesterfield
21.05.02 Audley Harrison L PTS 6 Custom House
Career: 12 contests, won 11, lost 1.

Mark Krence   Les Clark

Kenroy Lambert

Luton. *Born* Grenada, WI, 14 March, 1972
Middleweight. Ht. 5'9"
Manager T. Toole

17.02.02 Mark Nilsen L PTS 6 Salford
27.03.02 Freddie Yemofio W PTS 6 Mayfair

Career: 2 contests, won 1, lost 1.

Kenroy Lambert　　　　　Les Clark

Scott Lansdowne

Leicester. *Born* Leicester, 11 August, 1972
Cruiserweight. WBF European S.
Cruiserweight Champion. Ht. 5'10"
Manager D. Hobson

15.12.98 Gary Williams W PTS 6 Sheffield
11.09.99 Luke Simpkin W PTS 4 Sheffield
09.12.99 Geoff Hunter W PTS 6 Sheffield
20.05.00 Gary Williams W RSC 1 Leicester
　　　　　(Vacant WBF European
　　　　　S. Cruiserweight Title)
21.10.00 Adam Cale W RSC 5 Sheffield
29.01.01 Nigel Rafferty W PTS 4 Peterborough
28.04.02 Tony Booth L RSC 4 Southwark
23.06.02 Paul Bonson L PTS 4 Southwark

Career: 8 contests, won 6, lost 2.

Liam Lathbury

Chippenham. *Born* Bath, 10 February, 1981
Middleweight. Ht. 5'10"
Manager C. Sanigar

16.09.00 Gary Jones W RSC 5 Bethnal Green
09.12.00 Freddie Yemofio W PTS 4 Southwark
03.02.01 Rob Stevenson W PTS 6 Brighton
05.05.01 Harry Butler W PTS 6 Brighton
30.09.01 Leigh Wicks W PTS 4 Bristol

Career: 5 contests, won 5.

Scott Lawton

Stoke. *Born* Stoke, 23 September, 1976
Lightweight. Ht. 5'10"
Manager P. Dykes

29.09.01 Dave Hinds W RSC 2 Southwark
08.12.01 Ilias Miah W PTS 4 Dagenham
26.01.02 Pete Buckley W PTS 4 Bethnal Green
26.04.02 Pete Buckley W PTS 4 Coventry

Career: 4 contests, won 4.

Scott Lawton　　　　　Les Clark

Kevin Lear

West Ham. *Born* Whitechapel, 3 May, 1977
WBU S. Featherweight Champion.
Ht. 5'7¼"
Manager F. Maloney

13.09.99 Demir Nanev W RSC 4 Bethnal Green
15.11.99 Steve Hanley W RSC 1 Bethnal Green
19.02.00 Lee Williamson W PTS 4 Dagenham
13.03.00 Marco Fattore W PTS 4 Bethnal Green
13.04.00 Rakhim Mingaleev W PTS 4 Holborn
25.07.00 Dave Hinds W PTS 6 Southwark
13.11.00 Pete Buckley W PTS 6 Bethnal Green
10.03.01 Joel Viney W RSC 2 Bethnal Green
26.03.01 Dave Hinds W CO 1 Wembley
03.04.01 Steve Hanley W PTS 6 Bethnal Green
28.07.01 Pete Buckley W PTS 4 Wembley
24.11.01 Gary Flear W PTS 4 Bethnal Green
01.06.02 Michael Gomez W RTD 8 Manchester
　　　　　(Vacant WBU S. Featherweight Title)

Career: 13 contests, won 13.

James Lee (Birchall)

Portsmouth. *Born* Portsmouth, 29
December, 1974
L. Middleweight. Ht. 5'11"
Manager N. Christian

03.11.00 Neil Bonner W PTS 4 Ebbw Vale
11.12.00 Dean Walker W PTS 6 Sheffield
02.02.01 Robert Weston L PTS 6 Portsmouth
16.03.01 Jed Tytler W RSC 3 Portsmouth
15.10.01 Mark Sawyers L PTS 6 Southampton

12.12.01 Darren Williams L PTS 4 Clydach
11.02.02 Danny Gwilym W PTS 6 Southampton
08.04.02 Richie Murray L PTS 6 Southampton

Career: 8 contests, won 4, lost 4.

Nicky Leech

Nottingham. *Born* Nottingham, 6 June,
1981
Welterweight. Ht. 5'10"
Manager Self

03.06.01 Richard Inquieti W PTS 6 Hanley
06.12.01 Richie Caparelli W PTS 6 Stoke
04.03.02 Norman Dhalie W PTS 6 Birmingham
13.04.02 Tony Montana W PTS 6
　　　　　Wolverhampton
11.05.03 Chris Steele W PTS 6 Newark

Career: 5 contests, won 5.

Matt Legg

Milton Keynes. *Born* Northampton, 17
April, 1976
Heavyweight. Ht. 6'2"
Manager F. Maloney

28.07.01 Mal Rice W PTS 4 Wembley
24.11.01 Tony Booth W PTS 4 Bethnal Green

Career: 2 contests, won 2.

Matt Legg　　　　　Les Clark

(Herbert) Butch Lesley

Islington. *Born* Chelmsford, 21 April, 1973
Cruiserweight. Former Southern Area L.
Heavyweight Champion. Ht. 6'2½"
Manager A. Simms

02.09.95 Lester Jacobs L PTS 4 Wembley
16.10.95 David Larkin L RSC 4 Mayfair
23.01.96 Michael Pinnock W PTS 4 Bethnal
　　　　　Green
09.04.96 Jerry Mortimer W RSC 3 Stevenage
25.06.96 Graham Townsend L PTS 6 Stevenage
05.11.96 Sammy Storey L DIS 3 Belfast
08.03.97 Mark Delaney L PTS 6 Brentwood
11.11.97 Martin Jolley W PTS 6 Bethnal Green

10.01.98	Martin Jolley W PTS 4 Bethnal Green
30.03.98	Waldemar Barta W PTS 6 Tenerife
27.02.99	Dennis Doyley W RSC 5 Bethnal Green
12.12.99	Rob Stevenson W PTS 6 Chigwell
25.07.00	Dean Ashton W PTS 6 Southwark
14.10.00	Eddie Knight W RSC 6 Wembley
	(Southern Area L.Heavyweight Title Challenge)
02.12.00	Jason Barker W RSC 1 Chigwell
18.02.01	Paul Bonson W PTS 6 Southwark
26.03.01	Tony Oakey L PTS 10 Wembley
	(Southern Area L. Heavyweight Title Defence)
16.06.01	Tony Booth W RSC 3 Dagenham
29.09.01	Andrei Kiarsten L PTS 12 Southwark
	(Vacant WBU Inter-Continental L.Heavyweight Title)
15.12.01	Jason Brewster W RSC 1 Chigwell
10.02.02	Paul Bonson W PTS 4 Southwark
19.03.02	John Keeton L PTS 12 Slough
	(Vacant WBF Cruiserweight Title)

Career: 22 contests, won 14, lost 8.

Delroy Leslie

Carshalton. *Born* Jamaica, 22 February, 1970
Middleweight. Former WBF Middleweight Champion. Former Undefeated Southern Area Middleweight Champion. Former Undefeated Southern Area L. Middleweight Champion. Ht. 5'11½"
Manager Self

29.04.93	Phil Found W PTS 6 Mayfair
14.06.93	Jason Barker W RTD 3 Bayswater
16.09.93	Jamie Davidson W PTS 6 Southwark
06.03.95	Shaun Cogan W RSC 1 Mayfair
20.04.95	Clayton Hollingsworth W PTS 6 Mayfair
23.06.95	Jonathan Thaxton L PTS 6 Bethnal Green
03.12.95	Adrian Chase W RSC 4 Southwark
02.04.96	Richie Edwards L RSC 3 Southwark
17.06.97	Ben Lockhart W CO 1 Nashville, USA
24.06.97	Julius Brown W CO 2 Nashville, USA
01.07.97	Booker T. Mulline W RSC 3 Nashville, USA
08.07.97	Dexter Phillips W RSC 3 Nashville, USA
24.07.97	Cassius Caldwell W CO 2 Cayce, USA
29.07.97	Mario Hereford W RSC 2 Nashville, USA
05.08.97	Charles Brown W RSC 1 Nashville, USA
12.08.97	William Lee W RSC 1 Nashville, USA
30.09.97	Don Greene W PTS 4 Nashville, USA
07.10.97	Reggie Strickland W PTS 4 Nashville, USA
14.10.97	Reggie Strickland W PTS 6 Nashville, USA
21.10.97	Tim Green W RSC 1 Nashville, USA
04.11.97	Jason Stewart W CO 1 Nashville, USA
25.11.97	Mario Hereford W RSC 3 Nashville, USA
14.05.98	Matthew Tait L PTS 6 Acton
10.09.98	Ojay Abrahams W PTS 10 Acton
	(Vacant Southern Area L. Middleweight Title)
20.08.99	Ensley Bingham L RSC 9 Bloomsbury
	(British L. Middleweight Title Challenge)

05.10.99	Matthew Barney W PTS 10 Bloomsbury
	(Vacant Southern Area Middleweight Title)
10.03.00	Ruben Groenewald W PTS 12 Bethnal Green
	(Interim WBF Middleweight Title)
08.09.00	Lester Jacobs L RSC 8 Hammersmith
	(WBF Middleweight Title Defence)
08.12.00	Darren Ashton W RTD 3 Crystal Palace
19.05.01	Harry Butler W PTS 6 Wembley
09.09.01	Viktor Fesetchko W PTS 6 Southwark
12.02.02	Jason Collins W RSC 1 Bethnal Green

Career: 32 contests, won 27, lost 5.

Delroy Leslie　　　　　　Les Clark

Ady Lewis

Bury. *Born* Bury, 31 May, 1975
Bantamweight. Former British & Commonwealth Bantamweight Champion. Former Undefeated Commonwealth, British & Central Area Flyweight Champion. Ht. 4'10½"
Manager J. Doughty/T. Gilmour

25.04.94	Darren Greaves W RSC 1 Bury
02.06.94	Dave Campbell W RSC 1 Middleton
22.09.94	Neil Parry W RSC 3 Bury
21.11.94	Daryl McKenzie W RSC 4 Glasgow
17.01.95	Yusuf Vorajee W RSC 2 Worcester
16.02.95	Chip O'Neill W RSC 1 Bury
06.03.95	Mark Cokely W RSC 5 Mayfair
09.05.95	Pete Buckley W PTS 4 Basildon
25.06.96	Graham McGrath W RSC 1 Stevenage
13.10.96	Gary Hickman W RSC 3 Shaw
01.12.96	Louis Veitch W PTS 10 Shaw
	(Vacant Central Area Flyweight Title)
27.01.97	Keith Knox W PTS 12 Glasgow
	(Vacant British Flyweight Title)
27.05.97	Mark Reynolds W PTS 12 Mayfair
	(British Flyweight Title Defence)

11.09.97	Peter Culshaw W RSC 8 Widnes
	(British Flyweight Title Defence. Commonwealth Flyweight Title Challenge)
22.11.97	David Guerault L RSC 4 Manchester
	(European Flyweight Title Challenge)
08.04.98	Nicky Wilders W RSC 3 Liverpool
25.10.98	Ian Turner DREW 8 Shaw
22.01.99	Louis Veitch W RSC 2 Carlisle
22.06.99	Noel Wilders L RSC 6 Ipswich
	(Final Elim. British Bantamweight Title)
04.12.99	Anthony Hanna W PTS 6 Manchester
01.04.00	Francis Ampofo W PTS 12 Bethnal Green
	(Vacant British & Commonwealth Bantamweight Titles)
09.09.00	Tommy Waite L RSC 4 Manchester
	(British & Commonwealth Bantamweight Title Defences)
26.02.01	Nicky Booth L RSC 7 Nottingham
	(British & Commonwealth Bantamweight Title Challenges)
15.09.01	Tommy Waite W PTS 6 Nottingham
06.10.01	Jose Sanjuelo L RSC 2 Manchester
	(IBO Bantamweight Title Challenge)

Career: 25 contests, won 19, drew 1, lost 5.

Ady Lewis　　　　　　Les Clark

Lennox Lewis

Hadley Wood. *Born* London, 2 September, 1965
WBC, IBF & IBO Heavyweight Champion. Former Undefeated WBA, British, European & Commonwealth Heavyweight Champion. Ht. 6'4¾"
Manager Self

27.06.89	Al Malcolm W CO 2 Kensington
21.07.89	Bruce Johnson W RSC 2 Atlantic City, USA
25.09.89	Andrew Gerrard W RSC 4 Crystal Palace

10.10.89 Steve Garber W CO 1 Hull
05.11.89 Melvin Epps W DIS 2 Kensington
18.12.89 Greg Gorrell W RSC 5 Kitchener, Canada
31.01.90 Noel Quarless W RSC 2 Bethnal Green
22.03.90 Calvin Jones W CO 1 Gateshead
14.04.90 Mike Simwelu W CO 1 Kensington
09.05.90 Jorge Dascola W CO 1 Kensington
20.05.90 Dan Murphy W RSC 6 Sheffield
27.06.90 Ossie Ocasio W PTS 8 Kensington
11.07.90 Mike Acey W RSC 2 Mississuaga, Canada
31.10.90 Jean Chanet W RSC 6 Crystal Palace
(European Heavyweight Title Challenge)
06.03.91 Gary Mason W RSC 7 Wembley
(British Heavyweight Title Challenge. European Heavyweight Title Defence)
12.07.91 Mike Weaver W CO 6 Lake Tahoe, USA
30.09.91 Glenn McCrory W CO 2 Kensington
(British & European Heavyweight Title Defence)
21.11.91 Tyrell Biggs W RSC 3 Atlanta, USA
01.02.92 Levi Billups W PTS 10 Las Vegas, USA
30.04.92 Derek Williams W RSC 3 Kensington
(British & European Heavyweight Title Defence. Commonwealth Heavyweight Title Challenge)
11.08.92 Mike Dixon W RSC 4 Atlantic City, USA
31.10.92 Razor Ruddock W RSC 2 Earls Court
(Final Elim. WBC Heavyweight Title & Commonwealth Heavyweight Title Defence)
08.05.93 Tony Tucker W PTS 12 Las Vegas, USA
(WBC Heavyweight Title Defence)
01.10.93 Frank Bruno W RSC 7 Cardiff
(WBC Heavyweight Title Defence)
06.05.94 Phil Jackson W RSC 8 Atlantic City
(WBC Heavyweight Title Defence)
24.09.94 Oliver McCall L RSC 2 Wembley
(WBC Heavyweight Title Defence)
13.05.95 Lionel Butler W RSC 5 Sacramento, USA
(Elim. WBC Heavyweight Title)
02.07.95 Justin Fortune W RSC 4 Dublin
07.10.95 Tommy Morrison W RSC 6 Atlantic City, USA
10.05.96 Ray Mercer W PTS 10 New York City, USA
07.02.97 Oliver McCall W RSC 5 Las Vegas, USA
(Vacant WBC Heavyweight Title)
12.07.97 Henry Akinwande W DIS 5 Lake Tahoe, USA
(WBC Heavyweight Title Defence)
04.10.97 Andrew Golota W RSC 1 Atlantic City, USA
(WBC Heavyweight Title Defence)
28.03.98 Shannon Briggs W RSC 5 Atlantic City, USA
(WBC Heavyweight Title Defence)
26.09.98 Zeljko Mavrovic W PTS 12 Uncasville, USA
(WBC Heavyweight Title Defence)
13.03.99 Evander Holyfield DREW 12 New York City, USA
(WBC Heavyweight Title Defence. WBA & IBF Heavyweight Title Challenges)

13.11.99 Evander Holyfield W PTS 12 Las Vegas, USA
(WBC Heavyweight Title Defence. WBA & IBF Heavyweight Title Challenges)
29.04.00 Michael Grant W CO 2 New York City, USA
(WBC & IBF Heavyweight Title Defences)
15.07.00 Frans Botha W RSC 2 Millwall
(WBC, IBF & IBO Heavyweight Title Defences)
11.11.00 David Tua W PTS 12 Las Vegas, USA
(WBC, IBF & IBO Heavyweight Title Defences)
22.04.01 Hasim Rahman L CO 5 Brakpan, South Africa

(WBC, WBA & IBO Heavyweight Title Defences)
17.11.01 Hasim Rahman W CO 4 Las Vegas, Nevada, USA
(WBC, IBF & IBO Heavyweight Title Challenges)
08.06.02 Mike Tyson W CO 8 Memphis, Tennessee, USA
(WBC, IBF & IBO Heavyweight Title Defences)

Career: 43 contests, won 40, drew 1, lost 2.

Willie Limond

Glasgow. *Born* Glasgow, 2 February, 1979
S. Featherweight. Ht. 5'7"
Manager A. Morrison/F. Warren

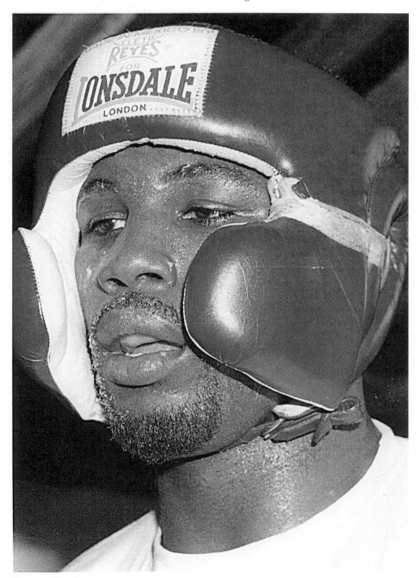

Lennox Lewis

Les Clark

117

12.11.99	Lennie Hodgkins W RTD 1 Glasgow
13.12.99	Steve Hanley W PTS 6 Glasgow
24.02.00	Nigel Senior W RSC 6 Glasgow
18.03.00	Phil Lashley W RSC 1 Glasgow
07.04.00	Jimmy Beech W RSC 2 Glasgow
26.05.00	Billy Smith W PTS 4 Glasgow
24.06.00	Haroon Din W PTS 4 Glasgow
10.11.00	Danny Connelly W PTS 6 Glasgow
17.12.00	Billy Smith W PTS 6 Glasgow
15.02.01	Marcus Portman W PTS 6 Glasgow
03.04.01	Trevor Smith W PTS 4 Bethnal Green
27.04.01	Choi Tseveenpurev W PTS 6 Glasgow
07.09.01	Gary Reid W PTS 8 Glasgow
03.11.01	Rakhim Mingaleev W PTS 6 Glasgow
17.11.01	Keith Jones W PTS 4 Glasgow
11.03.02	Dave Hinds W PTS 6 Glasgow

Career: 16 contests, won 16.

Willie Limond   Les Clark

Neil Linford

Leicester. *Born* Leicester, 29 September, 1977
L. Heavyweight. Ht. 5'10¾"
Manager K. Sanders

30.10.98	Israel Khumalo W RSC 2 Peterborough
30.11.98	David Baptiste W PTS 4 Peterborough
15.12.98	Johannes Ngiba W CO 2 Durban, South Africa
16.01.99	Dean Powell W RSC 1 Bethnal Green
22.02.99	Leigh Wicks W PTS 4 Peterborough
24.04.99	Adrian Houldey W RSC 2 Peterborough
17.05.99	Jason Barker L RSC 3 Peterborough
15.07.99	Hussain Osman L RSC 5 Peterborough
07.02.00	Mark Dawson W PTS 4 Peterborough
04.03.00	Darren Ashton W PTS 6 Peterborough
25.05.00	Michael Pinnock W PTS 4 Peterborough
30.09.00	Matthew Barney W PTS 10 Peterborough
	(Elim. British S. Middleweight Title)
30.11.00	Darren Ashton W PTS 4 Peterborough
29.01.01	Brian Magee L PTS 12 Peterborough

	(Vacant IBO Inter-Continental S. Middleweight Title)
23.06.01	Jon Penn W RSC 3 Peterborough
29.09.01	David Starie L RSC 6 Southwark
	(British & Commonwealth S.Middleweight Title Challenges)
26.01.02	Ali Forbes W PTS 6 Bethnal Green
23.06.02	Tony Booth W RSC 5 Southwark

Career: 18 contests, won 14, lost 4.

Earl Ling

Norwich. *Born* Kings Lynn, 9 March, 1972
L. Heavyweight. Ht. 5'10"
Manager Self

08.09.92	Eddie Collins W PTS 6 Norwich
11.05.93	Mark Hale L RSC 2 Norwich
12.12.94	Clinton Woods L RSC 5 Cleethorpes
04.12.95	Jeff Finlayson L PTS 6 Manchester
26.02.96	Peter Waudby L PTS 6 Hull
19.03.96	James Lowther L RSC 4 Leeds
16.05.98	Dean Ashton DREW 6 Chigwell
02.07.98	Dean Ashton L RSC 2 Ipswich
17.09.98	Jimmy Steel DREW 6 Brighton
19.01.99	Israel Khumalo L RSC 1 Ipswich
15.07.00	Mike Duffield W PTS 6 Norwich
04.11.00	Andrew Facey L PTS 6 Derby
16.06.01	Andrew Facey DREW 6 Derby
04.07.01	Calvin Stonestreet L PTS 4 Bloomsbury
13.04.02	Simeon Cover W CO 4 Norwich
25.04.02	Lee Whitehead W PTS 6 Hull

Career: 16 contests, won 4, drew 3, lost 9.

Darren Littlewood

Sheffield. *Born* Sheffield, 6 November, 1974
S. Middleweight. Ht. 6'0"
Manager Self

24.11.93	Mark Smallwood L PTS 8 Solihull
02.12.93	Martin Jolley W PTS 6 Evesham
01.03.94	Joe Calzaghe L RSC 1 Dudley
28.05.94	Dean Francis L PTS 4 Queensway
17.08.94	Chris Woollas L RSC 4 Sheffield
26.10.94	John Duckworth W PTS 6 Stoke
24.11.94	Tim Robinson W PTS 6 Hull
12.12.94	Martin Jolley W PTS 6 Cleethorpes
23.01.95	Roland Ericsson W RSC 4 Bethnal Green
11.11.95	Jetty Williams L PTS 6 Halifax
06.07.96	Paschal Collins W PTS 4 Manchester
17.09.96	Roberto Dominguez L RSC 5 Porrino, Spain
10.04.97	Clinton Woods L RSC 6 Sheffield
	(Central Area S. Middleweight Title Challenge)
03.10.98	Andrew Flute L PTS 6 West Bromwich
13.11.98	Willie Quinn L RSC 3 Glasgow
28.02.99	Mike Whittaker L PTS 6 Shaw
13.09.01	Clint Johnson L PTS 6 Sheffield
15.03.02	Erik Teymour L RSC 1 Millwall

Career: 18 contests, won 6, lost 12.

Wayne Llewelyn

Beckenham. *Born* Greenwich, 20 April, 1970
Heavyweight. Ht. 6'3½"
Manager Self

18.01.92	Chris Coughlan W RSC 3 Kensington

30.03.92	Steve Stewart W RSC 4 Eltham
23.04.92	Gary Charlton W RSC 6 Eltham
10.12.92	Gary McCrory W RSC 2 Glasgow
23.05.93	Cordwell Hylton W PTS 6 Brockley
01.12.93	Manny Burgo W PTS 6 Bethnal Green
14.04.94	Vance Idiens W RSC 1 Battersea
22.05.94	Cordwell Hylton W CO 2 Crystal Palace
03.05.95	Mitch Rose W PTS 4 New York City, USA
07.07.95	Vance Idiens W RSC 1 Cardiff
11.08.95	Carlos Monroe W RSC 3 Louisiana, USA
26.04.96	Steve Garber W CO 1 Cardiff
08.06.96	Dermot Gascoyne W RSC 4 Newcastle
22.03.97	Mike Sedillo W CO 2 Wythenshawe
20.09.97	Michael Murray W RTD 4 Aachen, Germany
21.03.98	Everton Davis W PTS 8 Bethnal Green
06.06.98	Pele Reid L CO 1 Liverpool
	(Elim. British Heavyweight Title)
18.02.99	Derek Williams W RSC 3 Bossier City, USA
03.06.99	Frankie Swindell L CO 2 Mount Pleasant, USA
21.08.99	Terry Veners W RSC 3 Coachella, USA
28.11.99	Terry Veners W CO 2 Monterey, USA
10.03.00	William Barima W CO 1 Bethnal Green
19.03.00	Augustin Corpus L PTS 8 Tunica, USA
14.10.00	Michael Sprott W RSC 3 Wembley
08.12.00	Alex Vasiliev L RSC 1 Crystal Palace
01.04.01	Luke Simpkin W PTS 6 Southwark
19.01.02	Andreas Simon W CO 1 Berlin, Germany
22.03.02	Ladislav Husarik W PTS 6 Berlin, Germany

Career: 28 contests, won 24, lost 4.

Gary Lockett

Cwmbran. *Born* Pontypool, 25 November, 1976
Former WBO Inter-Continental L. Middleweight Champion. Ht. 5'10"
Manager B. Hearn/B. Devine

06.09.96	Ernie Loveridge W PTS 4 Liverpool
26.10.96	Charlie Paine W RSC 4 Liverpool
24.10.98	Lee Bird W RSC 2 Liverpool
27.02.99	Carl Smith W RSC 2 Bethnal Green
15.05.99	Mike Whittaker W RSC 2 Blackpool
19.06.99	Kid Halls W CO 1 Dublin
09.03.00	Kevin Thompson W CO 2 Liverpool
04.11.00	David Baptiste W PTS 4 Bethnal Green
23.01.01	Abdul Mehdi W RSC 2 Crawley
03.03.01	Hussain Osman W CO 2 Wembley
07.04.01	Howard Clarke W RSC 2 Wembley
08.05.01	Mike Algoet W PTS 6 Barnsley
14.07.01	Howard Clarke W CO 1 Wembley
25.09.01	Denny Dalton W RSC 1 Liverpool
24.11.01	Chris Nembhard W RSC 2 Bethnal Green
09.02.02	Kevin Kelly W CO 4 Manchester
	(Vacant WBO Inter-Continental L.Middleweight Title)
20.04.02	Youri Tsarenko L PTS 12 Cardiff
	(WBO Inter-Continental L.Middleweight Title Defence)

Career: 17 contests, won 16, lost 1.

Gary Logan

Croydon. *Born* Lambeth, 10 October, 1968
L. Middleweight. Former Southern Area
Middleweight Champion. Former
Undefeated Southern Area Welterweight
Champion. Ht. 5'8¾"
Manager Self

05.10.88	Peppy Muire W RTD 3 Wembley
02.11.88	Tony Gibbs W PTS 6 Southwark
07.12.88	Pat Dunne W PTS 6 Piccadilly
12.01.89	Mike Russell W CO 1 Southwark
20.02.89	Dave Griffiths W RSC 5 Mayfair
29.03.89	Ronnie Campbell W PTS 6 Wembley
10.05.89	Tony Britland W CO 1 Kensington
07.06.89	Davey Hughes W CO 1 Wembley
24.08.89	Mike English W CO 2 Tampa, USA
04.10.89	Simon Eubank W PTS 6 Kensington
12.10.89	Jimmy Thornton W PTS 6 Southwark
08.11.89	Chris Blake L PTS 8 Wembley
10.01.90	Julian Eavis W PTS 8 Kensington
03.03.90	Anthony Joe Travis W CO 5 Wembley
09.05.90	Joseph Alexander W PTS 8 Wembley
13.09.90	Manuel Rojas W PTS 8 Watford
16.01.91	Julian Eavis W RSC 5 Kensington
18.02.91	Gordon Blair W CO 1 Mayfair
25.04.91	Trevor Ambrose W PTS 8 Mayfair
17.10.91	Des Robinson W PTS 8 Southwark
15.10.92	Mick Duncan W PTS 8 Lewisham
17.12.92	Roy Rowland W RSC 4 Wembley
	(Vacant Southern Area Welterweight Title)
23.05.93	Glyn Rhodes W CO 3 Brockley
25.06.93	Gordon Blair W RSC 6 Battersea
14.08.93	Paul King W CO 2 Hammersmith
28.11.93	Paul King W CO 4 Southwark
11.12.93	Horace Fleary W PTS 8 Dusseldorf, Germany
09.02.94	Graham Cheney L RSC 10 Bethnal Green
	(WBC International Welterweight Title Challenge)
29.09.94	Ojay Abrahams W PTS 10 Bethnal Green
	(Southern Area Welterweight Title Defence)
25.10.94	Nick Hall DREW 8 Southwark
02.06.95	Del Bryan L RSC 11 Bethnal Green
	(British Welterweight Title Challenge)
21.03.96	Paul Wesley W PTS 6 Southwark
13.04.96	Ensley Bingham L RSC 6 Wythenshawe
	(British L. Middleweight Title Challenge)
01.04.01	Adrian Kirkbride W RSC 1 Southwark
03.06.01	Spencer Fearon W RSC 2 Southwark
	(Vacant Southern Area Middleweight Title)
28.07.01	Ojay Abrahams W RSC 4 Wembley
28.10.01	Hussain Osman L PTS 10 Southwark
	(Southern Area Middleweight Title Defence)
04.05.02	Mehrdud Takaloo L RSC 10 Bethnal Green
	(WBU L.Middleweight Title Challenge)

Career: 38 contests, won 31, drew 1, lost 6.

Jamie Logan

Nottingham. *Born* Lincoln, 9 April, 1975
L. Middleweight. Ht. 6'1"
Manager J. Gill

07.12.00	David Smales L PTS 6 Stoke

18.03.01	Gary Dixon L PTS 6 Shaw
01.04.01	Peter Jackson L PTS 6 Wolverhampton
20.05.01	Peter Jackson L PTS 6 Wolverhampton
03.06.01	Paul Martin L PTS 6 Hanley
10.10.01	Tony Smith W PTS 6 Stoke
08.02.02	Tony Byrne L RTD 3 Preston

Career: 7 contests, won 1, lost 6.

Paul Lomax

Sunderland. *Born* Sunderland, 11 May,
1974
S. Middleweight. Ht. 6'0½"
Manager T. Callighan

23.07.00	Reece McAllister L PTS 6 Hartlepool
10.06.01	Tony Byrne L PTS 6 Ellesmere Port
17.11.01	Oscar Hall L PTS 4 Dewsbury
09.12.01	Tony Byrne L PTS 6 Blackpool
15.03.02	Andrei Ivanov W PTS 6 Spennymoor
29.04.02	Martyn Bailey DREW 6 Bradford
28.05.02	James Davenport W CO 3 Liverpool

Career: 7 contests, won 2, drew 1, lost 4.

Keith Long

Brixton. *Born* Greenwich, 30 July, 1968
Heavyweight. Ht. 5'11½"
Manager D. Williams/F. Warren

15.02.97	Steve Cranston W PTS 4 Tooting
04.02.99	Gordon Minors W PTS 6 Lewisham
24.04.99	Derek McCafferty L PTS 4 Peterborough
07.08.99	Israel Ajose DREW 6 Dagenham
29.11.99	Mark Potter W PTS 8 Wembley
13.04.00	Harry Senior W PTS 10 Holborn
18.11.00	Luke Simpkin W RSC 3 Dagenham
13.09.01	Mike Holden W PTS 10 Sheffield
	(Elim.British Heavyweight Title)

Career: 8 contests, won 6, drew 1, lost 1.

Andrew Lowe   Les Clark

Andrew Lowe

Hackney. *Born* Hackney, 23 June, 1974
L. Heavyweight. Ht. 5'10"
Manager T. Sims

19.05.01	Rob Stevenson W PTS 4 Wembley

16.06.01	William Webster W RSC 2 Dagenham
20.10.01	Tom Cannon W PTS 4 Glasgow
24.11.01	Paul Wesley W PTS 4 Bethnal Green
15.12.01	Mark Snipe W PTS 4 Chigwell
12.02.02	Ali Forbes W PTS 4 Bethnal Green
04.05.02	Radcliffe Green W PTS 4 Bethnal Green

Career: 7 contests, won 7.

David Lowry

Belfast. *Born* Belfast, 1 March, 1975
S. Featherweight. Ht. 5'7"
Manager F. Maloney

13.03.99	Chris Lyons W PTS 4 Manchester
22.05.99	Wee Barry W RTD 1 Belfast
22.06.99	Carl Allen W PTS 4 Ipswich
16.10.99	Sean Grant W RSC 1 Belfast
10.12.99	Assen Vassilev L PTS 4 Nicosia, Cyprus
12.06.00	Gary Flear W PTS 4 Belfast
25.07.00	Anthony Hanna W PTS 4 Southwark
11.11.00	Gary Flear L PTS 4 Belfast
09.09.01	Steve Hanley W PTS 6 Southwark
11.03.02	Henry Castle L RSC 1 Glasgow

Career: 10 contests, won 7, lost 3.

Craig Lynch

Edinburgh. *Born* Edinburgh, 22 July, 1974
Welterweight. Ht. 6'1"
Manager A. Bowers

13.05.95	James Clamp DREW 6 Glasgow
08.06.95	Gary Silvester W PTS 3 Glasgow
15.09.95	Adam Baldwin W PTS 6 Glasgow
25.11.95	Jim Rock L PTS 4 Dublin
02.03.96	Hughie Davey L PTS 4 Newcastle
08.06.96	Hughie Davey L PTS 4 Newcastle
24.10.96	Pat Wright L PTS 6 Wembley
21.02.02	Gary Firby W RSC 3 Sunderland
26.04.02	Kevin McIntyre L PTS 10 Glasgow
	(Vacant Scottish Welterweight Title)

Career: 9 contests, won 3, drew 1, lost 5.

Colin Lynes

Hornchurch. *Born* Whitechapel, 26
November, 1977
L. Welterweight. Ht. 5'7½"
Manager Self

04.05.98	Les Frost W CO 1 Barking
23.07.98	Ram Singh W CO 1 Barking
22.10.98	Brian Coleman W RSC 2 Barking
31.10.98	Marc Smith W PTS 4 Basingstoke
10.12.98	Trevor Smith W RSC 1 Barking
25.02.99	Dennis Griffin W PTS 6 Kentish Town
20.05.99	Mark Haslam W PTS 4 Barking
18.05.00	Jason Vlasman W RSC 2 Bethnal Green
16.09.00	Karl Taylor W PTS 6 Bethnal Green
14.10.00	Brian Coleman W PTS 6 Wembley
09.12.00	Jimmy Phelan W PTS 6 Southwark
17.02.01	Mark Ramsey W PTS 6 Bethnal Green
10.04.01	David Kirk W PTS 6 Wembley
10.11.01	Keith Jones W PTS 6 Wembley
01.12.01	Leonti Voronchuk W PTS 6 Bethnal Green
26.01.02	David Kirk W PTS 6 Dagenham
23.03.02	Peter Dunn W PTS 4 Southwark
18.05.02	Kevin Bennett W RSC 4 Millwall
29.06.02	Ian Smith W RSC 7 Brentwood

Career: 19 contests, won 19.

(Gary) Reece McAllister

Newton Aycliffe. *Born* Bishop Auckland,
30 March, 1970
S. Middleweight. Ht. 6'0¹/₂"
Manager T. Callighan

26.11.99	Ganny Dovidovas L RSC 1 Bayswater	
26.02.00	Mike White L PTS 4 Carlisle	
25.03.00	Albert Rybacki L RSC 2 Liverpool	
23.07.00	Paul Lomax W PTS 6 Hartlepool	
10.10.00	Craig Clayton W RSC 4 Brierley Hill	
24.11.00	Paul Owen W PTS 6 Darlington	
17.05.01	Andy Vickers W RSC 1 Leeds	
21.06.01	Paul Owen DREW 6 Sheffield	
13.09.01	Paul Owen L RSC 1 Sheffield	

Career: 9 contests, won 4, drew 1, lost 4.

Kevin McBride

Clones. *Born* Monaghan, 10 May, 1973
All-Ireland Heavyweight Champion.
Ht. 6'5"
Manager Self

17.12.92	Gary Charlton DREW 6 Barking	
13.02.93	Gary Williams W PTS 4 Manchester	
15.09.93	Joey Paladino W CO 2 Bethnal Green	
13.10.93	Chris Coughlan W PTS 4 Bethnal Green	
01.12.93	John Harewood W RSC 3 Bethnal Green	
06.05.94	Edgar Turpin W RSC 1 Atlantic City, USA	
04.06.94	Roger Bryant W CO 1 Reno, USA	
17.06.94	Stanley Wright W PTS 6 Atlantic City, USA	
26.08.94	James Truesdale W RSC 3 Upper Marlboro, USA	
24.09.94	Graham Arnold W RSC 2 Wembley	
12.11.94	Dean Storey W RSC 3 Dublin	
10.12.94	John Lamphrey W RSC 1 Portland, USA	
07.02.95	Carl Gaffney W RSC 1 Ipswich	
03.03.95	Carl McGrew W RSC 5 Boston, USA	
22.04.95	Jimmy Harrison W RSC 1 Boston, USA	
13.05.95	Atelea Kalhea W CO 1 Sacramento, USA	
02.07.95	Steve Garber W RSC 7 Dublin	
06.11.96	Shane Woollas W RSC 2 Hull	
03.12.96	R.F. McKenzie W RSC 6 Liverpool	
21.01.97	Tui Toia W RSC 2 Kansas City, USA	
07.02.97	Louis Monaco L RSC 5 Las Vegas, USA	
28.04.97	Stoyan Stoyanov W RSC 1 Hull	
02.06.97	Paul Douglas W RSC 5 Belfast	
	(Vacant All-Ireland Heavyweight Title)	
30.08.97	Axel Schulz L RSC 9 Berlin, Germany	
22.11.97	Yuri Yelistratov W RSC 1 Manchester	
11.04.98	Michael Murray L RSC 3 Southwark	
26.06.99	Domingo Monroe W CO 1 Boston, USA	
11.08.01	Willie Phillips W PTS 10 Little Rock, Arkansas, USA	
01.11.01	Rodney McSwain W PTS 10 Little Rock, Arkansas, USA	

Derek McCafferty

Kettering. *Born* Aberdeen, 10 November, 1968
Heavyweight. Ht. 6'3¹/₂"
Manager K. Sanders

22.02.99	Gary Williams W CO 1 Peterborough	
24.04.99	Keith Long W PTS 4 Peterborough	
15.07.99	Mike Holden L RSC 1 Peterborough	
13.09.99	Mark Potter L PTS 6 Bethnal Green	
18.12.99	Georgi Kandelaki L PTS 8 Southwark	
22.09.01	Audley Harrison L PTS 6 Newcastle	
13.12.01	Pele Reid L RSC 3 Leicester Square	
26.01.02	Mark Potter L PTS 6 Bethnal Green	
25.05.02	Georgie Kandelaki L RTD 5 Portsmouth	

Career: 9 contests, won 2, lost 7.

Enzo Maccarinelli

Swansea. *Born* Swansea, 20 August, 1980
Cruiserweight. Ht. 6'4"
Manager F. Warren

02.10.99	Paul Bonson W PTS 4 Cardiff	
11.12.99	Mark Williams W RSC 1 Merthyr	
26.02.00	Nigel Rafferty W RSC 3 Swansea	
12.05.00	Lee Swaby L CO 3 Swansea	
11.12.00	Chris Woollas W PTS 4 Widnes	
28.04.01	Darren Ashton W CO 1 Cardiff	
09.10.01	Eamonn Glennon W RSC 2 Cardiff	
15.12.01	Kevin Barrett W RSC 2 Wembley	
12.02.02	James Gilbert W RSC 2 Bethnal Green	
20.04.02	Tony Booth W PTS 4 Cardiff	

Career: 10 contests, won 9, lost 1.

Colin McCash

Accrington. *Born* Dundee, 29 October, 1977
L. Middleweight. Ht. 5'11"
Manager B. Myers

22.09.00	Mark Paxford DREW 6 Wrexham	
21.10.00	Dean Walker DREW 6 Sheffield	
05.12.00	Chris Steele W RSC 4 Nottingham	
26.08.01	Neil Bonner L RSC 1 Warrington	
24.09.01	Simeon Cover W PTS 6 Cleethorpes	
04.10.01	Ryan Kerr L PTS 6 Sunderland	
08.02.02	Danny Moir L RSC 3 Preston	

Career: 7 contests, won 2, drew 2, lost 3.

Glenn McClarnon

Lurgan. *Born* Carrickfergus, 1 July, 1974
L. Welterweight. Ht. 5'9"
Manager Self

20.12.97	Marc Smith W PTS 4 Belfast	
21.02.98	Andrew Reed W CO 1 Belfast	
28.04.98	Brian Robb W RSC 2 Belfast	
18.09.98	Mark Ramsey W PTS 4 Belfast	
28.11.98	David Kirk W PTS 4 Belfast	
12.01.99	Ram Singh W RSC 1 Bethnal Green	
25.01.99	Dean Nicholas W CO 1 Glasgow	
12.03.99	Mark Ramsey W PTS 6 Bethnal Green	
25.05.99	Steve Tuckett W PTS 6 Mayfair	
11.09.99	David Kirk W PTS 6 Sheffield	
27.11.99	Chris Barnett L PTS 12 Liverpool	

18.01.02	Davarryl Williamson L RSC 5 Las Vegas, Nevada, USA	
27.05.02	Gary Winmon W RSC 2 Revere, Mass, USA	

Career: 31 contests, won 26, drew 1, lost 4.

	(Vacant IBO International L. Welterweight Title)	
01.04.00	Bernard Paul W RTD 5 Bethnal Green	
19.08.00	Brian Coleman W PTS 6 Brentwood	
13.10.00	Allan Vester L PTS 12 Aarhus, Denmark	
	(IBF Inter-Continental L.Welterweight Title Challenge)	
02.12.00	John Ameline L PTS 4 Bethnal Green	
03.03.01	Peter Dunn W PTS 4 Wembley	
28.04.01	Jacek Bielski L PTS 12 Wroclaw, Poland	
	(Vacant IBO Inter-Continental Welterweight Title)	
25.09.01	Gary Ryder L PTS 8 Liverpool	
10.11.01	Rosalin Nasibulin W PTS 6 Wembley	
26.01.02	Kevin Bennett W PTS 8 Dagenham	

Career: 20 contests, won 15, lost 5.

Billy McClung

Kilmarnock. *Born* Irvine, 13 March, 1982
L. Heavyweight. Ht. 6'3"
Manager T. Gilmour

19.11.01	Darren Ashton W PTS 6 Glasgow	
18.02.02	Clint Johnson W PTS 6 Glasgow	
01.03.02	Clint Johnson W PTS 6 Irvine	
18.03.02	Shane White L RTD 4 Glasgow	

Career: 4 contests, won 3, lost 1.

Ross McCord

Swansea. *Born* Swansea, 31 August, 1977
L. Welterweight. Ht. 5'10"
Manager Self

02.12.97	Harry Butler L RSC 3 Swansea	
23.05.98	Sony Thind W RSC 1 Bethnal Green	
25.11.98	Pedro Thompson W RSC 2 Clydach	
07.12.98	Sammy Smith L RSC 5 Acton	
20.02.99	Scott Garrett L RSC 2 Thornaby	
23.04.99	Darren Underwood W RSC 1 Clydach	
31.10.99	Arv Mittoo W PTS 6 Raynes Park	
26.02.00	Woody Greenaway L PTS 4 Swansea	
09.03.00	Karim Bouali L RSC 1 Bethnal Green	
22.07.00	Iain Eldridge L RSC 2 Watford	
12.12.00	Woody Greenaway L PTS 6 Clydach	
15.09.01	Tony Smith W PTS 6 Swansea	
12.12.01	Marcus Portman DREW 4 Clydach	
24.04.02	Paul McIlwaine W PTS 4 Dublin	

Career: 14 contests, won 6, drew 1, lost 7.

John McDermott

Horndon. *Born* Basildon, 26 February, 1980
Heavyweight. Ht. 6'3"
Manager J. Branch

23.09.00	Slick Miller W RSC 1 Bethnal Green	
21.10.00	Gary Williams W PTS 4 Wembley	
13.11.00	Geoff Hunter W RSC 1 Bethnal Green	
27.01.01	Eamonn Glennon W RSC 1 Bethnal Green	
24.02.01	Alexei Osokin W PTS 4 Bethnal Green	
26.03.01	Mal Rice W RSC 2 Wembley	
09.06.01	Luke Simpkin W PTS 6 Bethnal Green	
22.09.01	Gary Williams W RSC 4 Bethnal Green	
24.11.01	Gordon Minors W RSC 3 Bethnal Green	
19.01.02	Tony Booth W RSC 1 Bethnal Green	
04.05.02	Martin Roothman W RSC 1 Bethnal Green	

Career: 11 contests, won 11.

John McDermott   Les Clark

Chris McDonagh

Maidenhead. *Born* Ascot, 9 July, 1978
L. Welterweight. Ht. 5'10"
Manager J. Evans

22.11.01	Jason Gonzalez W PTS 6 Paddington
26.01.02	Dave Hinds W PTS 4 Bethnal Green
25.02.02	Baz Carey W PTS 6 Slough
19.03.02	Ray Wood W PTS 4 Slough
25.04.02	Vatche Wartanian L PTS 4 Las Vegas, Nevada, USA
21.05.02	Daniel Thorpe W PTS 6 Custom House

Career: 6 contests, won 5, lost 1.

Chris McDonagh   Les Clark

Peter McDonagh

Bermondsey. *Born* Galway, 21 December, 1977
L. Welterweight. Ht. 5'9"
Manager E. Maloney

28.04.02	Arv Mittoo W PTS 6 Southwark
23.06.02	Dave Hinds W PTS 6 Southwark

Career: 2 contests, won 2.

Thomas McDonagh

Manchester. *Born* Manchester, 8 December, 1980
L. Middleweight. Ht. 6'0"
Manager F. Warren

09.10.99	Lee Molyneux W PTS 4 Manchester
06.11.99	Lee Molyneux W PTS 4 Widnes
11.12.99	Arv Mittoo W RSC 2 Liverpool
29.01.00	Emmanuel Marcos W PTS 4 Manchester
29.02.00	William Webster W RTD 2 Widnes
25.03.00	Lee Molyneux W PTS 6 Liverpool
16.05.00	Richie Murray W PTS 4 Warrington
29.05.00	David Baptiste W PTS 6 Manchester
04.09.00	Colin Vidler W PTS 6 Manchester
11.12.00	Richie Murray W PTS 6 Widnes
15.01.01	Kid Halls W RSC 4 Manchester
10.02.01	Harry Butler W PTS 6 Widnes
17.03.01	David Baptiste W PTS 4 Manchester
07.07.01	Paul Denton W PTS 6 Manchester
15.09.01	Howard Clarke W PTS 6 Manchester
27.10.01	Mark Richards DREW 4 Manchester
09.02.02	Tomas da Silva DREW 4 Manchester
01.06.02	Delroy Mellis W PTS 4 Manchester

Career: 18 contests, won 16, drew 2.

Paul McIlwaine

Bangor, NI. *Born* Belfast, 18 June, 1980
Welterweight. Ht. 5'5"
Manager P. McCausland

16.11.01	Robert Murray L RSC 6 Dublin
21.01.02	Tony McPake L RTD 1 Glasgow
11.03.02	Gary Young L CO 2 Glasgow
24.04.02	Ross McCord L PTS 4 Dublin
03.06.02	David Keir L CO 2 Glasgow

Career: 5 contests, lost 5.

Conroy McIntosh

Wolverhampton. *Born* Wolverhampton, 5 December, 1973
Middleweight. Ht. 5'7"
Manager T. Marshall

31.01.01	Ross Murray W CO 1 Piccadilly
23.06.01	Francie Doherty L PTS 4 Peterborough
22.09.01	Tomas da Silva L PTS 4 Canning Town
11.02.02	Ty Browne DREW 4 Southampton
03.03.02	Wayne Shepherd DREW 6 Shaw
21.05.02	Ty Browne DREW 4 Custom House

Career: 6 contests, won 1, drew 3, lost 2.

Kevin McIntyre

Paisley. *Born* Paisley, 5 May, 1978
Scottish Welterweight Champion.
Ht. 5'10½"
Manager N. Sweeney/A. Morrison

13.11.98	Ray Wood W RSC 4 Glasgow
18.02.99	Gareth Dooley W RSC 3 Glasgow
21.05.99	Mohamed Helel W PTS 6 Glasgow
26.06.99	Karim Bouali L RTD 1 Glasgow
18.03.00	Chris Hall W RSC 3 Glasgow
07.04.00	Dave Travers W RSC 4 Glasgow
26.05.00	Tommy Peacock W RSC 5 Glasgow
24.06.00	Lee Williamson W PTS 4 Glasgow
02.10.00	Paul Denton W PTS 6 Glasgow
10.11.00	Mark Ramsey W RSC 4 Glasgow
17.12.00	Ernie Smith W PTS 6 Glasgow
15.02.01	John Humphrey L RSC 4 Glasgow
27.04.01	Michael Smyth W PTS 6 Glasgow
17.11.01	David Kirk W PTS 4 Glasgow
16.12.01	Manzo Smith W PTS 6 Glasgow
11.03.02	Karl Taylor W PTS 4 Glasgow
26.04.02	Craig Lynch W PTS 10 Glasgow
	(Vacant Scottish Welterweight Title)
08.06.02	David Kirk W RTD 5 Renfrew

Career: 18 contests, won 16, lost 2.

Darren McInulty

Bedworth. *Born* Coventry, 10 November, 1970
L. Middleweight. Ht. 5'11"
Manager Self

20.05.91	Derek Binstead DREW 6 Leicester
01.10.91	Dean Carr W PTS 6 Bedworth
11.11.91	Rick North W PTS 6 Stratford upon Avon
20.01.92	Chris Mulcahy W PTS 6 Coventry
04.02.92	Richard O'Brien L PTS 4 Alfreton
11.03.92	Eddie King W RSC 1 Stoke
25.03.92	Robert Riley L PTS 6 Hinckley
28.04.92	Dean Bramhald W PTS 6 Wolverhampton
11.05.92	Dean Bramhald W PTS 6 Coventry
10.09.92	Hughie Davey L PTS 6 Sunderland
23.11.92	Mark Antony W PTS 6 Coventry
02.12.92	Dean Hiscox DREW 6 Bardon
27.02.93	Andreas Panayi L PTS 6 Ellesmere Port
24.03.93	Barry Thorogood L PTS 6 Cardiff
26.04.93	Ricky Mabbett L CO 3 Cleethorpes
17.06.93	Mark Antony L CO 2 Bedworth
25.11.97	Andy Peach W PTS 6 Wolverhampton
15.01.98	Ray Newby L PTS 6 Solihull
27.01.98	Darren Bruce L PTS 4 Bethnal Green
23.02.98	Derek Roche L PTS 6 Glasgow
07.03.98	Michael Jones L PTS 4 Reading
24.03.98	Nick Hall L PTS 6 Wolverhampton
23.04.98	Kevin Lang W PTS 6 Edgbaston
02.05.98	Georgie Smith L CO 2 Kensington
04.06.98	Darren Covill DREW 6 Barking
08.09.98	Darren Bruce L CO 1 Bethnal Green
26.10.98	Christian Brady L PTS 6 Manchester
30.01.99	Mehrdud Takaloo L RSC 5 Bethnal Green
17.11.01	Robbie Sivyer W RSC 1 Coventry
09.02.02	Clive Johnson W PTS 8 Coventry
26.04.02	Jimmy Vincent L CO 6 Coventry
	(British Masters L. Middleweight Title Challenge)

Career: 31 contests, won 11, drew 3, lost 17.

(Malcolm) Mally McIver

Dewsbury. *Born* Dewsbury, 29 January, 1974
Lightweight. Ht. 5'9"
Manager Self

12.02.00	Arv Mittoo W PTS 4 Sheffield
27.05.00	Paul Philpott W PTS 4 Southwark
09.09.00	David Kirk W PTS 6 Newark
05.02.01	Alan Kershaw W PTS 4 Hull

24.03.01 Steve Hanley W PTS 4 Sheffield
02.06.01 Keith Jones W PTS 6 Wakefield
18.08.01 Mark Bowen L RSC 1 Dewsbury
17.11.01 Daniel Thorpe W PTS 6 Dewsbury
03.03.02 Dave Hinds W PTS 6 Shaw
02.06.02 Gary Greenwood L RSC 1 Shaw
Career: 10 contests, won 8, lost 2.

Jason McKay

County Down. *Born* Craigavon, NI, 11 October, 1977
S. Middleweight. Ht. 6'1"
Manager B. Hearn

18.02.02 Jimmy Steel W PTS 4 Glasgow
11.05.02 Harry Butler W PTS 4 Dagenham
Career: 2 contests, won 2.

John Mackay (Mukaya)

Canning Town. *Born* Uganda, 20 October, 1981
S. Bantamweight. Ht. 5'6"
Manager T. Bowers

15.06.01 Chris Emanuele L RSC 4 Millwall
22.09.01 Jason Nesbitt W PTS 4 Canning Town
16.11.01 Willie Valentine W RSC 4 Dublin
28.11.01 Jamie Yelland W RSC 6 Bethnal Green
18.01.02 Stephen Chinnock L PTS 4 Coventry
20.04.02 Dazzo Williams W PTS 6 Wembley
02.06.02 Choi Tseveenpurev L RSC 5 Shaw
Career: 7 contests, won 4, lost 3.

John Mackay   Les Clark

Jamie McKeever

Birkenhead. *Born* Birkenhead, 7 July, 1979
Featherweight. Ht. 5'6½"
Manager B. Hearn

12.03.98 Dave Hinds W PTS 4 Liverpool
08.04.98 Kid McAuley W RTD 1 Liverpool
06.06.98 Brian Coleman W PTS 4 Liverpool
21.07.98 Stuart Rimmer W PTS 4 Widnes
31.10.98 John T. Kelly L PTS 6 Southend
22.01.99 Garry Burrell W RSC 2 Carlisle

12.03.99 David Kehoe W RSC 2 Bethnal Green
28.05.99 Arv Mittoo W PTS 6 Liverpool
02.10.99 Lee Armstrong DREW 6 Cardiff
27.11.99 Nigel Leake W RSC 2 Liverpool
01.07.00 Gary Flear L PTS 4 Manchester
09.10.00 Marc Callaghan W PTS 6 Liverpool
20.03.01 Craig Docherty L RSC 3 Glasgow
25.09.01 Sebastian Hart W PTS 4 Liverpool
10.12.01 Andrew Ferrans W PTS 6 Liverpool
09.03.02 James Rooney W PTS 6 Manchester
13.04.02 Barry Hawthorne W PTS 6 Liverpool
Career: 17 contests, won 13, drew 1, lost 3.

Dave McKenna

Port Glasgow. *Born* Greenock, 8 January, 1975
Heavyweight. Ht. 6'3"
Manager T. Gilmour

18.03.02 Leighton Morgan L DIS 3 Glasgow
Career: 1 contest, lost 1.

Matthew Macklin

Birmingham. *Born* Birmingham, 14 May, 1982
Welterweight. Ht. 5'10"
Manager F. Maloney/F. Warren

17.11.01 Ram Singh W RSC 1 Glasgow
15.12.01 Christian Hodorogea W CO 1 Wembley
09.02.02 Dimitri Protkunas W RTD 3 Manchester
11.03.02 David Kirk W PTS 4 Glasgow
20.04.02 Illia Spassov W CO 3 Cardiff
01.06.02 Guy Alton W RSC 3 Manchester
Career: 6 contests, won 6.

Matthew Macklin   Les Clark

Andy McLean

Newcastle. *Born* Durham, 13 January, 1976
Lightweight. Ht. 5'8"
Manager T. Callighan

17.03.01 Steve Hanley W PTS 4 Manchester

15.09.01 Woody Greenaway W RSC 3 Manchester
15.03.02 Leo Turner W RSC 4 Spennymoor
05.05.02 Joel Viney W PTS 6 Hartlepool
Career: 4 contests, won 4.

Tony McPake

Salsburgh. *Born* Bellshill, 3 December, 1979
Lightweight. Ht. 5'10"
Manager T. Gilmour

21.01.02 Paul McIlwaine W RTD 1 Glasgow
18.02.02 Gary Hamilton W PTS 4 Glasgow
15.03.02 Richie Caparelli W RSC 3 Glasgow
22.04.02 Leo Turner W RTD 4 Glasgow
28.05.02 Joel Viney W RSC 1 Liverpool
Career: 5 contests, won 5.

Mick McPhilbin

Bulwell. *Born* Nottingham, 31 March, 1980
Lightweight. Ht. 5'5"
Manager M. Shinfield

10.12.01 John Spence W RSC 6 Nottingham
02.03.02 Martin Hardcastle L RSC 4 Wakefield
Career: 2 contests, won 1, lost 1.

Brian Magee

Belfast. *Born* Lisburn, 9 June, 1975
IBO S. Middleweight Champion. Former Undefeated IBO Inter-Continental S. Middleweight Champion. Ht. 6'0"
Manager Self

13.03.99 Dean Ashton W RSC 2 Manchester
22.05.99 Richard Glaysher W RSC 1 Belfast
22.06.99 Chris Howarth W RSC 1 Ipswich
13.09.99 Dennis Doyley W RSC 3 Bethnal Green
16.10.99 Michael Pinnock W RSC 3 Belfast
12.02.00 Terry Morrill W RTD 4 Sheffield
21.02.00 Rob Stevenson W RSC 5 Southwark
20.03.00 Darren Ashton W RTD 5 Mansfield
15.04.00 Pedro Carragher W CO 2 Bethnal Green
12.06.00 Jason Barker W PTS 8 Belfast
11.11.00 Teimouraz Kikelidze W RSC 4 Belfast
29.01.01 Neil Linford W PTS 12 Peterborough
    (Vacant IBO Inter-Continental S. Middleweight Title)
31.07.01 Chris Nembhard W RSC 6 Bethnal Green
10.12.01 Ramon Britez W CO 1 Liverpool
    (IBO S. Middleweight Title Challenge)
18.03.02 Vage Kocharyan W PTS 8 Crawley
15.06.02 Mpush Makambi W RSC 7 Leeds
    (IBO S. Middleweight Title Defence)
Career: 16 contests, won 16.

Eamonn Magee

Belfast. *Born* Belfast, 13 July, 1971
Former Undefeated Commonwealth L. Welterweight Champion. Ht. 5'9"
Manager Self

25.11.95 Pete Roberts W CO 4 Dublin
09.03.96 Steve McGovern W PTS 4 Millstreet
28.05.96 John Stovin W RSC 2 Belfast
03.09.96 Kevin McKillan W RTD 4 Belfast
05.11.96 Shaun Stokes W RSC 2 Belfast

28.01.97	Karl Taylor W PTS 6 Belfast	
03.03.97	Troy Townsend W RSC 1 Austin, USA	
28.03.97	Teddy Reid L PTS 6 Boston, USA	
29.04.97	Peter Nightingale W RTD 2 Belfast	
02.06.97	Kevin McKillan W RSC 3 Belfast	
	(Elim. All-Ireland L. Welterweight Title)	
14.02.98	Dennis Griffin W RSC 2 Southwark	
26.09.98	Allan Hall W RSC 7 York	
30.11.98	Paul Burke L PTS 12 Manchester	
	(Vacant Commonwealth L. Welterweight Title)	
22.05.99	Alan Temple W CO 3 Belfast	
10.07.99	Karl Taylor W RTD 3 Southwark	
13.09.99	Paul Burke W RSC 6 Bethnal Green	
	(Commonwealth L. Welterweight Title Challenge)	
16.10.99	Radoslav Gaidev W RSC 1 Belfast	
04.03.00	Joseph Miyumo W RSC 1 Peterborough	
	(Commonwealth L. Welterweight Title Defence)	
29.04.00	David Kirk W RSC 8 Wembley	
16.09.00	Pavel Melnikov W PTS 8 Bethnal Green	
11.11.00	Shea Neary W PTS 12 Belfast	
	(Commonwealth L. Welterweight Title Defence)	
13.03.01	Alan Bosworth W RSC 5 Plymouth	
12.05.01	Harrison Methula W RSC 7 Plymouth	
	(Commonwealth L. Welterweight Title Defence)	
27.10.01	Matthews Zulu W PTS 12 Manchester	
	(Commonwealth L.Welterweight Title Defence)	
09.02.02	Jonathan Thaxton W RSC 6 Manchester	
	(Commonwealth L. Welterweight Title Defence)	
01.06.02	Richard Hatton L PTS 12 Manchester	
	(WBU L. Welterweight Title Challenge)	

Career: 26 contests, won 23, lost 3.

Liam Maltby

Yaxley. *Born* Peterborough, 17 May, 1979
Lightweight. Ht. 5'9¼"
Manager K. Sanders

30.10.98	Dave Travers W PTS 4 Peterborough	
30.11.98	Benny Jones L RSC 1 Peterborough	
22.02.99	Ernie Smith L PTS 4 Peterborough	
20.09.99	Dave Travers W PTS 4 Peterborough	
02.12.99	David Kehoe W PTS 4 Peterborough	
07.02.00	Dave Hinds W PTS 4 Peterborough	
04.03.00	Lee Williamson W PTS 6 Peterborough	
25.05.00	Steve Hanley W PTS 4 Peterborough	
30.09.00	Marco Fattore W PTS 6 Peterborough	
30.11.00	Alan Kershaw W PTS 6 Peterborough	
29.01.01	Trevor Smith W PTS 6 Peterborough	
26.03.01	Lee Williamson W PTS 6 Peterborough	
23.06.01	Jimmy Phelan W RTD 3 Peterborough	
22.09.01	Graham Earl L CO 1 Bethnal Green	
	(Southern Area Lightweight Title Challenge)	
13.12.01	Martin Holgate L RSC 4 Leicester Square	

Career: 15 contests, won 11, lost 4.

Emmanuel Marcos

Haringey. *Born* Luanda, 13 July, 1976
Welterweight. Ht. 5'4"
Manager Self

06.11.99	John Humphrey L PTS 4 Bethnal Green	
29.01.00	Thomas McDonagh L PTS 4 Manchester	
21.10.00	Isam Khalil L RSC 1 Wembley	
22.10.01	Darrell Grafton L RSC 2 Glasgow	
29.11.01	Andrew Close L PTS 6 Hartlepool	

Career: 5 contests, lost 5.

(Ahmed) Gypsy Boy Mario (Mahmud)

Middlesbrough. *Born* Yugoslavia, 5 June, 1969
Featherweight. Ht. 5'3"
Manager M. Marsden

21.02.02	Paddy Folan L PTS 6 Sunderland	

Career: 1 contest, lost 1.

John Marshall

Glossop. *Born* Australia, 28 May, 1975
L. Welterweight. Ht. 5'6"
Manager S. Wood/T. Gilmour

07.09.01	Dave Stewart L PTS 6 Glasgow	
23.12.01	Arv Mittoo W RSC 1 Salford	
21.01.02	Gary Hamilton W PTS 4 Glasgow	
17.02.02	Joel Viney W RSC 6 Salford	
31.05.02	Tony Montana W PTS 6 Hull	

Career: 5 contests, won 4, lost 1.

(Patrick) Paddy Martin

Nuneaton. *Born* Birmingham, 6 April, 1974
Welterweight. Ht. 6'0"
Manager J. Griffin

20.05.00	Martin Scotland L RSC 5 Leicester	
09.10.00	Simon Sherrington L RSC 5 Birmingham	
03.12.00	Mark Paxford L RSC 3 Shaw	
18.03.01	Andy Abrol L RSC 3 Shaw	
10.10.01	Andrei Ivanov L RSC 2 Stoke	

Career: 5 contests, lost 5.

Paul Martin   Les Clark

Paul Martin

Birmingham. *Born* Meriden, 24 April, 1973
Middleweight. Ht. 5'8"
Manager R. Gray/P. Cowdell

28.11.00	Martyn Bailey L PTS 6 Brierley Hill	
03.06.01	Jamie Logan W PTS 6 Hanley	
26.07.01	Lee Woodruff L RSC 1 Blackpool	

Career: 3 contests, won 1, lost 2.

(Patrick) P.J. Maxwell (Drinkwater)

Manchester. *Born* USA, 20 March, 1979
Middleweight. Ht. 5'8"
Manager F. Warren

17.03.98	Danny Thornton W PTS 6 Sheffield	
12.08.00	Matthew Ashmole W RSC 3 Wembley	
26.03.01	Jason Collins L PTS 4 Wembley	
27.10.01	Prince Kasi Kaihau W CO 4 Manchester	
09.02.02	Leigh Wicks W PTS 4 Manchester	

Career: 5 contests, won 4, lost 1.

Anthony Maynard

Birmingham. *Born* Birmingham, 12 January, 1972
Midlands Area Lightweight Champion. Ht. 5'8"
Manager Self

17.10.94	Malcolm Thomas W PTS 6 Birmingham	
02.11.94	Dean Phillips W PTS 6 Birmingham	
25.01.95	Neil Smith L PTS 6 Stoke	
07.02.95	Anthony Campbell W PTS 8 Wolverhampton	
08.03.95	Scott Walker W PTS 6 Solihull	
28.03.95	Kid McAuley W PTS 8 Wolverhampton	
11.05.95	Gary Hiscox W RSC 4 Dudley	
06.06.95	Richard Swallow L RSC 2 Leicester	
02.10.95	Jay Mahoney W PTS 8 Birmingham	
26.10.95	Ray Newby W PTS 8 Birmingham	
17.01.96	Tom Welsh W RSC 8 Solihull	
06.03.96	G. G. Goddard W RSC 3 Solihull	
20.03.97	Richard Swallow W PTS 6 Solihull	
24.10.97	Brian Coleman W CO 1 Birmingham	
27.03.98	Gary Flear W RSC 9 Telford	
	(Vacant Midlands Area Lightweight Title)	
30.05.98	Michael Ayers W PTS 8 Bristol	
21.11.98	Stephen Smith L PTS 10 Southwark	
27.11.00	David Kehoe W RSC 5 Birmingham	
07.04.01	Alfred Kotey L RTD 6 Wembley	
	(Vacant WBF Inter-Continental Lightweight Title)	
11.06.01	Woody Greenaway W PTS 4 Nottingham	
08.10.01	Bobby Vanzie L RSC 1 Barnsley	
	(British Lightweight Title Challenge)	
09.03.02	David Burke L PTS 6 Manchester	

Career: 22 contests, won 16, lost 6.

Lee Meager

Salford. *Born* Salford, 18 January, 1978
Lightweight. Ht. 5'8"
Manager Self

16.09.00	Pete Buckley W PTS 4 Bethnal Green	
14.10.00	Chris Jickells W PTS 4 Wembley	
18.11.00	Billy Smith W RSC 1 Dagenham	
09.12.00	Jason Nesbitt W RSC 2 Southwark	
05.02.01	Carl Allen DREW 6 Hull	

13.03.01	Lennie Hodgkins W RSC 3 Plymouth
12.05.01	Jason White W PTS 4 Plymouth
31.07.01	Steve Hanley W PTS 6 Bethnal Green
13.09.01	Arv Mittoo W PTS 6 Sheffield
16.03.02	Jason Nesbitt W PTS 6 Bethnal Green
10.05.02	Pete Buckley W PTS 6 Bethnal Green

Career: 11 contests, won 10, drew 1.

Delroy Mellis

Brixton. *Born* Jamaica, 7 January, 1971
Former Undefeated Southern Area L.
Middleweight Champion. Ht. 5'8"
Manager Self

27.02.98	Pat Larner L PTS 4 Brighton
16.04.98	Sonny Thind L RTD 5 Mayfair
09.06.98	Darren Christie L PTS 4 Hull
10.09.98	Paul Miles W RSC 3 Acton
03.10.98	Wayne Asker L PTS 6 Crawley
06.11.98	Darren Bruce L RTD 3 Mayfair
21.01.99	Darren Christie L PTS 6 Piccadilly
04.02.99	Sergei Dzindziruk L RSC 3 Lewisham
24.03.99	Martyn Thomas W RSC 3 Bayswater
20.05.99	Daniel James L PTS 4 Barking
02.07.99	Jason Williams L PTS 6 Bristol
30.09.99	Steve Brumant L PTS 6 Kensington
16.10.99	Jacek Bielski L PTS 4 Bethnal Green
18.11.99	Dennis Griffin W RSC 5 Mayfair
29.11.99	George Scott L PTS 6 Wembley
20.03.00	Lance Crosby L PTS 4 Mansfield
01.04.00	Paul Knights W RSC 3 Bethnal Green
15.05.00	Christian Brady W RSC 6 Birmingham
01.07.00	Cham Joof DREW 6 Southwark
22.07.00	Alan Gilbert W RSC 3 Watford
	(Vacant Southern Area L.Middleweight Title)
22.10.00	Allan Gray W RSC 6 Streatham
	(Southern Area L.Middleweight Title Defence)
23.01.01	Alan Gilbert W RSC 3 Crawley
	(Southern Area L. Middleweight Title Defence)
20.04.01	Chris Nembhard W RSC 8 Millwall
	(Southern Area L. Middleweight Title Defence)
07.09.01	Jason Collins L DIS 5 Bethnal Green
06.10.01	Michael Jones L PTS 8 Manchester
13.12.01	Ossie Duran L PTS 10 Leicester Square
	(WBF European Welterweight Title Challenge)
01.06.02	Thomas McDonagh L PTS 4 Manchester
15.06.02	Chardan Ansoula L RTD 4 Tottenham

Career: 28 contests, won 9, drew 1, lost 18.

Darren Melville

Canning Town. *Born* Tobago, 13
September, 1975
L. Welterweight. Ht. 5'8"
Manager T. Bowers

29.09.00	Lee Williamson W RSC 4 Bethnal Green
10.11.00	Jason McElligott W RSC 2 Mayfair
23.02.01	Keith Jones W PTS 4 Barking
09.03.01	Billy Smith W PTS 4 Millwall
29.03.01	Jaz Malik W RSC 1 Hammersmith
20.04.01	Marcus Portman W RSC 3 Millwall
15.06.01	Isaac Sebaduka W PTS 6 Millwall
22.09.01	Steve Murray L PTS 8 Bethnal Green
08.12.01	Christian Hodoragea W PTS 4 Millwall
15.03.02	Mark Ramsey W PTS 6 Millwall
19.04.02	Jan Jensen DREW 6 Aarhus, Denmark

Career: 11 contests, won 9, drew 1, lost 1.

Malcolm Melvin

Birmingham. *Born* Birmingham, 5
February, 1967
Welterweight. Former Undefeated All-
Ireland & Midlands Area L. Welterweight
Champion. Ht. 5'7"
Manager Self

28.11.85	Steve Foster DREW 6 Ilkeston
04.12.85	Simon Collins L PTS 6 Stoke
24.03.86	Rocky McGran L PTS 6 Mayfair
10.04.86	Lincoln Pennant W PTS 6 Leicester
21.04.86	Malcolm Davies W PTS 6 Birmingham
07.05.86	Julian Monville W PTS 6 Solihull
19.01.88	Antonio Fernandez L RSC 4 Kings Heath
07.03.88	John Ellis L PTS 6 Piccadilly
03.12.89	Dave Jenkins W PTS 6 Birmingham
05.02.90	Trevor Meikle W PTS 6 Brierley Hill
22.02.90	Chris Saunders L PTS 4 Hull
19.03.90	Barry North W PTS 6 Brierley Hill
30.04.90	Andy Kent W RSC 5 Brierley Hill
04.06.90	Brendan Ryan L RSC 7 Edgbaston
03.09.90	Dave Jenkins W PTS 8 Dudley
13.11.90	Brendan Ryan W PTS 10 Edgbaston
	(Vacant Midlands Area L. Welterweight Title)
18.03.91	Carl Brasier W PTS 6 Piccadilly
17.06.91	Dean Bramhald W PTS 6 Edgbaston
21.05.92	Mark Kelly W PTS 8 Cradley Heath
05.10.92	Ross Hale L PTS 10 Bristol
	(Elim. British L. Welterweight Title)
17.11.92	Tusikoleta Nkalankete DREW 8 Paris, France
16.03.93	Shaun Cogan W PTS 10 Edgbaston
	(Vacant All-Ireland L. Welterweight Title & Midlands Area L. Welterweight Title Defence)
29.06.93	Mark Kelly W PTS 6 Edgbaston
24.11.93	Alan Peacock W PTS 8 Solihull
08.03.94	Julian Eavis W PTS 6 Edgbaston
28.06.94	John Smith W PTS 6 Edgbaston
18.02.95	Ross Hale L PTS 12 Shepton Mallet
	(British & Commonwealth L. Welterweight Title Challenges)
21.05.96	Karl Taylor W PTS 10 Edgbaston
	(Midlands Area L. Welterweight Title Defence)
03.06.96	Jamie Morris W RSC 2 Birmingham
09.06.97	Jimmy Phelan W RSC 2 Birmingham
30.09.97	Wayne Windle W PTS 6 Edgbaston
24.02.98	Ray Newby W PTS 6 Edgbaston
12.10.98	David Kirk W PTS 10 Birmingham
	(Midlands Area L. Welterweight Title Defence)
13.02.99	Junior Witter L RSC 2 Newcastle
	(Vacant WBF L. Welterweight Title)
06.12.99	Harry Butler W PTS 8 Birmingham
13.03.00	Peter Nightingale W PTS 6 Birmingham
14.10.00	Harry Dhami L PTS 12 Wembley
	(British Welterweight Title Challenge)
04.03.02	Harry Butler W PTS 8 Birmingham

Career: 38 contests, won 26, drew 2, lost 10.

Peter Merrall

Wirral. *Born* Bebington, 25 October, 1973
Cruiserweight. Ht. 5'11¼"
Manager M. Goodall

26.08.01	Adam Cale W PTS 6 Warrington
21.10.01	Michael Pinnock DREW 6 Pentre Halkyn

Career: 2 contests, won 1, drew 1.

Ilias Miah

Hanwell. *Born* Bangladesh, 12 November,
1980
Lightweight. Ht. 5'7"
Manager D. Currivan

08.12.01	Scott Lawton L PTS 4 Dagenham
31.01.02	Haroon Din L RSC 3 Piccadilly
19.03.02	Baz Carey L PTS 6 Slough

Career: 3 contests, lost 3.

Ilias Miah   Les Clark

(Elviss) Elvis Michailenko

Canning Town. *Born* Jormala, Latvia, 13
September, 1976
WBF European L. Heavyweight Champion.
Ht. 5'11½"
Manager A. Bowers

18.05.00	Adam Cale W PTS 4 Bethnal Green
21.09.00	Shpetim Hoti W PTS 4 Bloomsbury
09.10.00	Tony Dodson DREW 6 Liverpool
02.11.00	Freddie Yemofio W PTS 6 Kensington
28.02.01	Tommy Matthews W PTS 4 Kensington
09.03.01	Tommy Matthews W PTS 4 Millwall
20.04.01	Dean Ashton W RSC 4 Millwall
16.06.01	Sven Hamer W RSC 6 Wembley
	(Vacant WBF European L. Heavyweight Title)
28.09.01	Paul Bonson W PTS 6 Millwall
23.11.01	Paul Bonson W PTS 6 Bethnal Green
15.03.02	Hastings Rasani W RSC 5 Millwall
29.06.02	Varuzhan Davtyan W PTS 6 Brentwood

Career: 12 contests, won 11, drew 1.

Scott Millar

Ayr. *Born* Irvine, 30 November, 1976
Welterweight. Ht. 6'0"
Manager T. Gilmour

21.02.00	William Webster W PTS 6 Glasgow
03.03.00	David Smales DREW 6 Irvine

06.06.00	Adrian Kirkbride W RSC 2 Motherwell	
23.02.01	Robert Burton L CO 5 Irvine	
19.11.01	Sam Mottram W PTS 6 Glasgow	
01.03.02	David Smales L PTS 6 Irvine	
25.03.02	John Jackson W RSC 4 Sunderland	
22.04.02	Chris Steele W PTS 6 Glasgow	
10.05.02	Tony Byrne L RSC 2 Preston	

Career: 9 contests, won 5, drew 1, lost 3.

Scott Miller

Hull. *Born* Hull, 27 July, 1979
L. Welterweight. Ht. 5'5"
Manager F. Maloney

16.12.00	Jason White W PTS 4 Sheffield
10.02.01	Steve Hanley W RSC 3 Widnes
21.07.01	Pete Buckley W PTS 4 Sheffield
12.02.02	Dafydd Carlin W PTS 4 Bethnal Green
08.06.02	Martin Watson L RSC 2 Renfrew

Career: 5 contests, won 4, lost 1.

Scott Miller   Les Clark

(Alvin) Slick Miller

Doncaster. *Born* Doncaster, 12 May, 1968
Heavyweight. Ht. 6'2"
Manager J. Rushton

28.04.94	Declan Faherty L RSC 2 Hull
06.10.94	Kent Davis L PTS 6 Hull
17.11.94	Graham Wassell L RSC 1 Sheffield
29.09.95	Mark Richardson L PTS 6 Hartlepool
13.01.96	Geoff Hunter DREW 6 Halifax
13.02.96	Danny Williams L RSC 1 Bethnal Green
15.03.96	Tony Booth L PTS 6 Hull
22.03.96	Tony Dowling L RSC 4 Mansfield
26.09.96	Steve Pettit L PTS 6 Walsall
22.11.96	Tony Booth L RSC 5 Hull
17.03.97	Michael Sprott L CO 1 Mayfair
25.04.97	Pele Lawrence L PTS 6 Mere
16.05.97	Edwin Cleary DREW 6 Hull

20.10.97	Neil Simpson L RTD 1 Leicester
16.04.98	Kevin Mitchell L RSC 2 Mayfair
08.06.98	Stevie Pettit W CO 1 Birmingham
30.11.98	Neil Simpson L CO 3 Leicester
23.01.99	Faisal Mohammed L RSC 2 Cheshunt
25.03.99	Nigel Rafferty L PTS 8 Edgbaston
17.04.99	Ahmet Oner L RSC 1 Dublin
24.10.99	Nigel Rafferty W RSC 4 Wolverhampton
25.03.00	Brian Kilbride W RSC 1 Liverpool
09.04.00	Mark Krence L PTS 6 Alfreton
11.06.00	Glenn Williams L PTS 4 Salford
08.07.00	Tony Dowling L PTS 4 Widnes
23.09.00	John McDermott L RSC 1 Bethnal Green
03.02.01	Scott Baker W RSC 4 Brighton
18.02.01	Hughie Robertson W RSC 2 Southwark
25.02.01	Colin Kenna L RSC 3 Streatham
05.05.01	Danny Percival W CO 1 Edmonton
31.07.01	Neil Hosking L RSC 2 Bethnal Green
07.09.01	Jason Brewster L PTS 6 West Bromwich
22.09.01	Dennis Bakhtov L CO 1 Bethnal Green
22.11.01	Petr Horacek L PTS 4 Paddington
26.01.02	Fola Okesola L RSC 1 Dagenham

Career: 35 contests, won 6, drew 2, lost 27.

Gordon Minors

Holywell. *Born* Enfield, 20 March, 1967
Heavyweight. Ht. 6'2"
Manager Self

14.10.98	Shane MacLaren W RSC 1 Blackpool
29.10.98	Paul Fiske W RSC 3 Newcastle
12.12.98	Willie Clyde W RSC 1 Chester
21.01.99	Karl Andrews W RSC 1 Piccadilly
04.02.99	Keith Long L PTS 6 Lewisham
22.05.99	Danny Watts W CO 1 Belfast
30.09.00	Luke Simpkin DREW 4 Peterborough
23.11.00	Jacklord Jacobs L RSC 4 Bayswater *(Vacant British Masters Heavyweight Title)*
30.06.01	Tomasz Bonin L RSC 4 Tarnow, Poland
24.11.01	John McDermott L RSC 3 Bethnal Green

Career: 10 contests, won 5, drew 1, lost 4.

Lee Minter

Crawley. *Born* Crawley, 21 August, 1976
Welterweight. Ht. 5'8"
Manager A. Gower

20.10.01	Danny Moir L RSC 1 Portsmouth
18.03.02	Andrew Close W PTS 4 Crawley

Career: 2 contests, won 1, lost 1.

Ross Minter

Crawley. *Born* Crawley, 10 November, 1978
Welterweight. Ht. 5'7¾"
Manager F. Warren/F. Maloney

26.03.01	Brian Coleman W PTS 4 Wembley
05.05.01	Trevor Smith W RTD 3 Edmonton
28.07.01	Lee Williamson W PTS 4 Wembley
24.11.01	Karl Taylor W PTS 4 Bethnal Green
15.12.01	Ernie Smith W RSC 2 Wembley
02.03.01	Paul Denton W PTS 6 Bethnal Green
25.05.02	Howard Clarke L RSC 2 Portsmouth

Career: 7 contests, won 6, lost 1.

Ross Minter   Les Clark

(Arvill) Arv Mittoo

Birmingham. *Born* Birmingham, 8 July, 1971
Welterweight. Ht. 5'8"
Manager Self

31.01.96	Alan Bosworth L PTS 6 Stoke
13.02.96	Tommy Janes L PTS 6 Cardiff
21.02.96	Danny Lutaaya L PTS 6 Piccadilly
20.05.96	Terry Whittaker L CO 5 Cleethorpes
29.06.96	Craig Stanley L PTS 4 Erith
23.09.96	Thomas Bradley DREW 6 Cleethorpes
03.10.96	John T. Kelly L PTS 6 Sunderland
01.11.96	David Kirk L PTS 6 Mansfield
14.11.96	Thomas Bradley L RSC 4 Sheffield
22.05.97	Craig Stanley W RSC 3 Southwark
02.09.97	Trevor Tacy L PTS 6 Manchester
22.09.97	Steve Conway L PTS 6 Cleethorpes
09.10.97	Steve Conway L PTS 6 Leeds
23.10.97	Marco Fattore W PTS 6 Mayfair
11.11.97	Kevin McCarthy L PTS 6 Bethnal Green
03.12.97	Marc Smith W PTS 6 Stoke
31.01.98	Harry Andrews L PTS 4 Edmonton
06.03.98	Gavin McGill W PTS 6 Hull
18.03.98	Marc Smith W PTS 6 Stoke
26.03.98	Danny Lutaaya DREW 6 Piccadilly
11.04.98	Charlie Rumbol L PTS 4 Southwark
21.04.98	Adam Spelling W PTS 4 Edmonton
02.10.98	Sammy Smith L PTS 4 Cheshunt
16.10.98	Mark Haslam L PTS 6 Salford
25.11.98	Brian Coleman L PTS 6 Clydach
27.01.99	Ernie Smith DREW 6 Stoke
26.02.99	Mark Payne L PTS 4 Coventry
17.03.99	Marc Smith L PTS 6 Stoke
20.05.99	John Humphrey L PTS 6 Barking
28.05.99	Jamie McKeever L PTS 6 Liverpool
04.06.99	Oscar Hall L PTS 6 Hull
02.07.99	Wahid Fats L PTS 6 Manchester
21.07.99	Brian Gentry L RSC 4 Bloomsbury
20.10.99	Steve Saville L PTS 8 Stoke
31.10.99	Ross McCord L PTS 6 Raynes Park
15.11.99	Lee Sharp L PTS 6 Glasgow
22.11.99	Mohamed Helel L PTS 6 Piccadilly
29.11.99	Peter Swinney L PTS 4 Wembley

11.12.99	Thomas McDonagh L RSC 2 Liverpool
12.02.00	Mally McIver L PTS 4 Sheffield
10.03.00	Jason Hall W RSC 3 Bethnal Green
08.04.00	Junior Witter L PTS 4 Bethnal Green
17.04.00	Gavin Pearson L PTS 6 Glasgow
13.05.00	Chris Steele W RSC 4 Barnsley
21.05.00	Gavin Down L PTS 6 Derby
06.06.00	Casey Brooke W PTS 6 Brierley Hill
15.07.00	Steve Conway L PTS 6 Norwich
30.09.00	Mark Florian L PTS 4 Peterborough
07.10.00	Jesse James Daniel L PTS 4 Doncaster
16.11.00	Lance Crosby L RSC 3 Hull
28.01.01	Stuart Elwell L PTS 6 Wolverhampton
19.02.01	Lee Sharp L PTS 6 Glasgow
26.02.01	Gavin Wake L PTS 4 Nottingham
24.03.01	Richard Holden L PTS 6 Newark
01.04.01	Babatunde Ajayi L PTS 6 Southwark
20.04.01	Manzo Smith L PTS 4 Millwall
08.05.01	Robert Burton L PTS 4 Barnsley
04.06.01	Gary Porter L PTS 6 Glasgow
16.06.01	Gavin Down L PTS 6 Derby
14.07.01	Lee Byrne L PTS 4 Wembley
13.09.01	Lee Meager L PTS 6 Sheffield
23.09.01	Anthony Christopher DREW 6 Shaw
28.10.01	Peter Swinney L PTS 4 Southwark
16.11.01	Terry Ham L PTS 6 Preston
10.12.01	Lee Armstrong L PTS 6 Bradford
23.12.01	John Marshall L RSC 1 Salford
15.04.02	Chris Duggan L PTS 6 Shrewsbury
28.04.02	Peter McDonagh L PTS 6 Southwark
10.05.02	Oscar Hall L PTS 4 Bethnal Green
15.06.02	Chris Saunders L PTS 6 Norwich
23.06.02	Mark Stupple L PTS 6 Southwark

Career: 71 contests, won 9, drew 4, lost 58.

Colin Moffett

Belfast. *Born* Belfast, 15 April, 1975
Flyweight. Ht. 5'6"
Manager B. Hearn

05.11.96	Shane Mallon W RSC 2 Belfast
28.01.97	Anthony Hanna W PTS 4 Belfast
29.04.97	Gary Hickman W PTS 4 Belfast
02.06.97	Jason Thomas L RSC 3 Belfast
20.12.97	Graham McGrath DREW 4 Belfast
18.09.98	Anthony Hanna DREW 4 Belfast
28.11.98	Shaun Norman W PTS 4 Belfast
31.07.99	Waj Khan W CO 1 Carlisle
16.10.99	Delroy Spencer L PTS 4 Bethnal Green
05.06.00	Keith Knox L RSC 3 Glasgow
02.12.00	Dale Robinson L PTS 4 Bethnal Green
15.09.01	Chris Emanuele L RSC 4 Nottingham
27.04.02	Levi Pattison L RSC 2 Huddersfield

Career: 13 contests, won 5, drew 2, lost 6.

Danny Moir

Gateshead. *Born* Gateshead, 21 January, 1972
L. Middleweight. Ht. 5'11"
Manager T. Conroy

04.10.01	Richard Inquieti W PTS 6 Sunderland
20.10.01	Lee Minter W RSC 1 Portsmouth
06.12.01	Gary Jones W PTS 6 Sunderland
08.02.02	Colin McCash W RSC 3 Preston
08.03.02	Martyn Bailey L PTS 6 Ellesmere Port
25.03.02	Gavin Pearson L PTS 6 Sunderland

Career: 6 contests, won 4, lost 2.

(Elton) Tony Montana (Gashi)

Sheffield. *Born* Yugoslavia, 5 August, 1982
L. Welterweight. Ht. 5'8"
Manager B. Ingle

24.11.00	Dave Gibson W PTS 6 Hull
03.12.00	Gary Greenwood DREW 6 Shaw
31.01.01	Pete Buckley W PTS 6 Piccadilly
13.02.01	Barrie Kelley L PTS 6 Brierley Hill
06.03.01	Chris Price W PTS 6 Yarm
18.03.01	Ray Wood DREW 6 Shaw
26.03.01	Francis Barrett L PTS 4 Wembley
24.05.01	Ajose Olusegun L RSC 1 Kensington
07.09.01	Mark Hawthorne L CO 3 Bethnal Green
16.11.01	Young Muttley L PTS 6 West Bromwich
30.11.01	Brian Gifford W PTS 6 Hull
17.12.01	Andrei Ivanov DREW 6 Cleethorpes
31.01.02	James Paisley W PTS 6 Piccadilly
11.02.02	Ernie Smith W PTS 6 Shrewsbury
13.04.02	Nicky Leech L PTS 6 Wolverhampton
11.05.02	Robbie Sivyer L PTS 5 Chesterfield
31.05.02	John Marshall L PTS 6 Hull

Career: 17 contests, won 6, drew 3, lost 8.

Alex Moon

Liverpool. *Born* Fazackerley, 17 November, 1971
Commonwealth S. Featherweight Champion. Former Undefeated WBU Inter-Continental Featherweight Champion. Ht. 5'7½"
Manager T. Gilmour

08.09.95	Marty Chestnut W RSC 3 Liverpool
24.11.95	G. G. Goddard L RTD 2 Chester
03.02.96	Chris Price W RSC 2 Liverpool
06.09.96	Jason Squire W PTS 4 Liverpool
26.10.96	Kelton McKenzie W RSC 3 Liverpool
03.12.96	Keith Jones W RTD 5 Liverpool
01.03.97	David Jeffrey W RSC 2 Liverpool
21.05.97	Miguel Matthews DREW 6 Liverpool
26.09.97	Bamana Dibateza W PTS 6 Liverpool
28.11.97	Elvis Parsley DREW 6 Bethnal Green
12.03.98	Deva Reymond W PTS 8 Liverpool
08.04.98	Stefy Bull W RSC 3 Liverpool
21.07.98	Georghe Parashiv W PTS 8 Widnes
24.10.98	Khayelethu Booi W PTS 12 Liverpool *(Vacant WBU Inter-Continental Featherweight Title)*
13.02.99	Jonjo Irwin L PTS 12 Newcastle *(British Featherweight Title Challenge)*
15.05.99	Jason Thomas W PTS 8 Blackpool
29.02.00	Craig Spacie L PTS 6 Widnes
25.03.00	Keith Jones W PTS 6 Liverpool
19.02.01	Anthony Hanna W PTS 6 Glasgow
20.03.01	Charles Shepherd W PTS 12 Glasgow *(Vacant Commonwealth S. Featherweight Title)*
24.04.01	Karim Nashar W PTS 12 Liverpool *(Commonwealth S. Featherweight Title Defence)*
06.10.01	Affif Djelti L RSC 6 Manchester *(IBO S.Featherweight Title Challenge)*
23.02.02	Pete Buckley W PTS 4 Nottingham
13.04.02	Mick O'Malley W RSC 8 Liverpool *(Commonwealth S. Featherweight Title Defence)*

Career: 24 contests, won 18, drew 2, lost 4.

Jamie Moore

Salford. *Born* Salford, 4 November, 1978
L. Middleweight. Ht. 5'8"
Manager S. Wood

09.10.99	Clive Johnson W RSC 3 Manchester
13.11.99	Peter Nightingale W PTS 4 Hull

19.12.99	Paul King W PTS 6 Salford
29.02.00	David Baptiste W RSC 3 Manchester
20.03.00	Harry Butler W RSC 2 Mansfield
14.04.00	Jimmy Steel W PTS 6 Manchester
27.05.00	Koba Kulu W RTD 3 Southwark
07.10.00	Leigh Wicks W PTS 4 Doncaster
12.11.00	Prince Kasi Kaihau W RSC 2 Manchester
25.11.00	Wayne Shepherd W RSC 3 Manchester
17.03.01	Richie Murray W RSC 1 Manchester
27.05.01	Paul Denton W RSC 3 Manchester
07.07.01	Scott Dixon L CO 5 Manchester *(Vacant WBO Inter-Continental L.Middleweight Title)*
26.01.02	Harry Butler W RSC 3 Dagenham
09.03.02	Andrzej Butowicz W RSC 5 Manchester

Career: 15 contests, won 14, lost 1.

(Jason) J.J. Moore

Mansfield. *Born* Nottingham, 28 February, 1972
S. Featherweight. Ht. 5'6"
Manager J. Ashton

25.02.01	Craig Spacie L PTS 4 Derby
06.03.01	Craig Spacie L PTS 8 Newark
24.03.01	Wayne Wheeler W RSC 4 Newark
19.12.01	Baz Carey W PTS 4 Coventry
18.01.02	Baz Carey DREW 4 Coventry

Career: 5 contests, won 2, drew 1, lost 2.

J.J. Moore   Les Clark

Tony Moran

Liverpool. *Born* Liverpool, 4 July, 1973
Cruiserweight. Ht. 6'6"
Manager T. Gilmour

26.04.01	Shaun Bowes L PTS 6 Gateshead
13.11.01	Paul Bonson L PTS 6 Leeds
19.03.02	Graham Nolan W PTS 6 Slough
10.05.02	Eamonn Glennon W RTD 1 Preston
03.06.02	Dave Clarke W PTS 6 Glasgow

Career: 5 contests, won 3, lost 2.

Leighton Morgan

Treharris. *Born* Caerphilly, 27 February, 1978
Heavyweight. Ht. 6'2"
Manager T. Woodward

16.06.01 Rasmus Ojemaye W RSC 3 Wembley
18.03.02 Dave McKenna W DIS 3 Glasgow
Career: 2 contests, won 2.

Leighton Morgan   Les Clark

Terry Morrill

Hull. *Born* Hull, 2 February, 1965
Cruiserweight. Former Central Area L.
Middleweight Champion. Ht. 5'10¼"
Manager Self

10.12.88 Chris Richards W PTS 6 Crystal Palace
08.02.89 Newton Barnett W PTS 6 Kensington
28.03.89 Skip Jackson L RSC 5 Glasgow
27.06.89 Mark Howell W PTS 6 Kensington
10.10.89 Spencer Alton W PTS 6 Hull
15.11.89 Davey Hughes DREW 4 Lewisham
08.12.89 Tony Baker W PTS 6 Doncaster
22.02.90 Mark Holden W RSC 7 Hull
            *(Central Area L. Middleweight Title
            Challenge)*
10.04.90 Ernie Noble W RSC 7 Doncaster
20.05.90 Jason Rowe L CO 6 Sheffield
            *(Central Area L. Middleweight Title
            Defence)*
31.10.90 Shaun Cummins L RSC 1 Crystal
            Palace
14.03.91 Delroy Waul DREW 8 Middleton
28.05.91 Eamonn Loughran L CO 1 Cardiff
16.10.92 Shamus Casey W PTS 6 Hull
16.09.93 Des Robinson W PTS 8 Hull
12.11.93 Shamus Casey W PTS 8 Hull
09.05.96 Lee Simpkin W RSC 5 Hull
06.11.96 Roy Chipperfield W RSC 1 Hull
28.11.96 Jeff Finlayson W PTS 6 Hull
27.02.97 Prince Kasi Kaihau W PTS 6 Hull
21.11.97 Mark Dawson W PTS 6 Hull
28.03.98 Howard Eastman L RTD 4 Hull
09.06.98 Glenn Williams L PTS 4 Hull
30.09.99 Sven Hamer L PTS 6 Kensington

23.10.99 Danilo Haeussler L PTS 8 Telford
13.11.99 Jamie Warters L PTS 8 Hull
12.02.00 Brian Magee L RTD 4 Sheffield
25.07.00 Konstantin Schvets L PTS 6 Southwark
05.05.01 Peter Haymer L PTS 4 Edmonton
21.07.01 Ruben Groenewald L RSC 4 Sheffield
01.11.01 Tony Booth L RSC 7 Hull
Career: 31 contests, won 15, drew 2, lost 14.

Sam Mottram

Alfreton. *Born* Mansfield, 16 August, 1982
Welterweight. Ht. 5'11"
Manager M. Shinfield

26.04.01 Chris Steele W PTS 6 Gateshead
10.05.01 Chris Steele W PTS 6 Sunderland
03.06.01 Tony Smith W PTS 6 Hanley
03.11.01 Gary Porter L PTS 4 Glasgow
19.11.01 Scott Millar L PTS 6 Glasgow
10.12.01 Tony Smith W PTS 6 Nottingham
Career: 6 contests, won 4, lost 2.

Lee Mountford

Leeds. *Born* Leeds, 1 September, 1972
Cruiserweight. Ht. 6'2"
Manager T. O'Neill

19.04.02 Gary Thompson DREW 4 Darlington
24.06.02 Eamonn Glennon L PTS 6 Bradford
Career: 2 contests, drew 1, lost 1.

Tony Mulholland

Liverpool. *Born* Liverpool, 24 November, 1972
S. Featherweight. Ht. 5'6¾"
Manager Self

16.08.96 Graham McGrath W RSC 3 Liverpool
22.11.96 Keith Jones W PTS 4 Liverpool
04.04.97 Keith Jones W PTS 4 Liverpool
11.09.97 Chris Williams W PTS 4 Widnes
18.04.98 Pete Buckley W PTS 4 Manchester
06.06.98 Pete Buckley W PTS 6 Liverpool
19.12.98 Chris Williams DREW 4 Liverpool
04.09.99 Dean Murdoch W PTS 4 Bethnal Green
06.11.99 Dean Murdoch W RSC 6 Widnes
11.12.99 Gary Flear W PTS 4 Liverpool
29.02.00 Pete Buckley W PTS 4 Widnes
25.03.00 Steve Hanley W PTS 6 Liverpool
08.07.00 Lee Williamson W PTS 6 Widnes
10.02.01 Anthony Hanna W PTS 4 Widnes
10.12.01 Gary Flear W PTS 4 Liverpool
09.03.02 Jimmy Beech W PTS 6 Manchester
13.04.02 Andrew Ferrans W PTS 4 Liverpool
28.05.02 Dariusz Snarski W PTS 6 Liverpool
Career: 18 contests, won 17, drew 1.

Patrick Mullings

Harrow. *Born* Harlesden, 19 October, 1970
Former Undefeated British
S. Bantamweight Champion. Former
Commonwealth Featherweight Champion.
Former IBO S. Bantamweight Champion.
Former Undefeated WBC International &
IBO Inter-Continental
S. Bantamweight Champion. Ht. 5'4½"
Manager F. Maloney

13.12.94 Graham McGrath W PTS 4 Ilford
23.01.95 Des Gargano W PTS 4 Bethnal Green
30.03.95 Graham McGrath W RSC 3 Bethnal
            Green

04.06.95 Des Gargano W PTS 6 Bethnal Green
21.09.95 Pete Buckley W PTS 6 Battersea
15.12.95 Pete Buckley W PTS 4 Bethnal Green
05.02.96 Pete Buckley W PTS 8 Bexleyheath
21.03.96 Danny Ruegg W RSC 3 Southwark
14.05.96 Miguel Matthews W PTS 6 Dagenham
11.12.96 Phil Lashley W RSC 3 Southwark
18.02.97 Spencer Oliver L RSC 10 Cheshunt
            *(Vacant Southern Area
            S. Bantamweight Title)*
20.05.97 Ricky Beard W RTD 3 Edmonton
12.07.97 Francky Leroy W RSC 1 Earls Court
            *(Vacant WBC International
            S. Bantamweight Title)*
06.12.97 Hiviva Hdrian W RSC 1 Wembley
            *(WBC International S. Bantamweight
            Title Defence)*
10.01.98 Euloge Sita Makinza W RTD 5 Bethnal
            Green
28.03.98 Martin Krastev W RSC 3 Hull
            (Vacant IBO S. Bantamweight Title)
02.05.98 Rakhim Mingaleev W PTS 8
            Kensington
08.08.98 Simon Ramoni L PTS 12 Scarborough
            (IBO S. Bantamweight Title Defence)
30.11.98 Marty Chestnut W RSC 2 Peterborough
06.02.99 Brian Carr W PTS 12 Halifax
            (Vacant British S. Bantamweight Title)
24.04.99 Drew Docherty L PTS 12 Peterborough
            *(British S. Bantamweight Title
            Defence)*
10.07.99 Maxim Pougatchev W RSC 4
            Southwark
01.10.99 Ravil Muhamadiarov W PTS 6 Bethnal
            Green
06.11.99 Michael Alldis L PTS 12 Bethnal
            Green
            (Vacant British S. Bantamweight Title)
29.11.99 Eric Odumasi W PTS 12 Wembley
            *(Vacant Commonwealth Featherweight
            Title)*
24.01.00 Scott Harrison L PTS 12 Glasgow
            *(Commonwealth Featherweight Title
            Defence)*
14.04.00 Vladimir Borov W RSC 12 Manchester
            *(Vacant IBO Inter-Continental
            S. Bantamweight Title)*
27.05.00 Simon Ramoni L RSC 8 Southwark
            (IBO S. Bantamweight Title Challenge)
07.04.01 Alexander Tiranov W RSC 3 Wembley
14.07.01 Michael Alldis W PTS 12 Wembley
            *(British S.Bantamweight Title
            Challenge)*

Career: 30 contests, won 24, lost 6.

Gerard Murphy

Uddingston. *Born* Glasgow, 5 October, 1977
L. Middleweight. Ht. 5'10"
Manager F. Warren/A. Morrison

13.06.97 Ivan Walker W PTS 6 Paisley
05.07.97 Paul Salmon W PTS 4 Glasgow
12.09.97 Scott Dixon L PTS 8 Glasgow
28.11.97 Stuart Rimmer W PTS 6 Hull
24.04.98 Dean Bramhald W RSC 2 Glasgow
27.11.98 Les Frost W PTS 6 Hull
07.12.98 Ray Newby W PTS 6 Nottingham
09.04.99 Ivan Walker W RSC 3 Glasgow
21.05.99 Prince Kasi Kaihau W PTS 6 Glasgow
26.11.99 David Kirk W RTD 3 Hull
18.03.00 Paul King W RSC 1 Glasgow
24.06.00 Steve Brumant W PTS 4 Glasgow

17.12.00 Prince Kasi Kaihau W PTS 6 Glasgow
17.11.01 Jason Collins W PTS 4 Glasgow
Career: 14 contests, won 13, lost 1.

Lawrence Murphy

Uddingston. *Born* Bellshill, 9 February, 1976
Middleweight. Ht. 6'1"
Manager A. Morrison

15.05.98 Mark Owens W RSC 2 Edinburgh
17.09.98 Lee Bird W RSC 3 Glasgow
13.11.98 Ian Toby W PTS 6 Glasgow
18.02.99 Mike Duffield W RSC 2 Glasgow
26.06.99 Harry Butler W RSC 1 Glasgow
17.12.00 Michael Alexander W PTS 6 Glasgow
07.09.01 Chris Nembhard DREW 6 Glasgow
17.11.01 Leigh Wicks W PTS 4 Glasgow
16.12.01 Kreshnik Qato W PTS 6 Glasgow
11.03.02 Rob Stevenson W RSC 1 Glasgow
Career: 10 contests, won 9, drew 1.

Oneal Murray

Brixton. *Born* Jamaica, 8 March, 1973
Cruiserweight. Ht. 6'0"
Manager M. Hill

29.03.01 Oddy Papantoniou L PTS 4 Hammersmith
04.10.01 Michael Pinnock W PTS 6 Finsbury
15.10.01 Joe Brame W RSC 2 Southampton
15.12.01 Steven Spartacus L RSC 4 Chigwell
27.01.02 Adam Cale W PTS 6 Streatham
Career: 5 contests, won 3, lost 2.

Oneal Murray　　　　　Les Clark

Richie Murray

Liverpool. *Born* Liverpool, 1 April, 1970
Welterweight. Ht. 5'11"
Manager J. Ingle

13.12.99 Ernie Smith W RSC 5 Cleethorpes
16.05.00 Thomas McDonagh L PTS 4 Warrington

13.11.00 Mickey Yikealo W RSC 3 Bethnal Green
11.12.00 Thomas McDonagh L PTS 6 Widnes
17.03.01 Jamie Moore L RSC 1 Manchester
08.04.02 James Lee W PTS 6 Southampton
28.05.02 Piotr Bartnicki L RSC 2 Liverpool
Career: 7 contests, won 3, lost 4.

Steve Murray　　　　　Les Clark

Steve Murray

Harlow. *Born* Harlow, 5 October, 1975
WBO Inter-Continental Lightweight Champion. Former Undefeated IBF Inter-Continental Lightweight Champion. Ht. 5'6"
Manager F. Warren

10.10.98 Keith Jones W RSC 4 Bethnal Green
14.11.98 Dave Travers W RSC 2 Cheshunt
23.01.99 Marc Smith W RSC 1 Cheshunt
30.01.99 Dewi Roberts W RSC 1 Bethnal Green
03.04.99 Woody Greenaway W CO 2 Kensington
01.05.99 Keith Jones W RSC 6 Crystal Palace
26.06.99 Brian Coleman W PTS 6 Millwall
07.08.99 Pete Buckley W PTS 6 Dagenham
15.11.99 Karl Taylor W RSC 1 Bethnal Green
29.01.00 Keith Jones W PTS 4 Manchester
19.02.00 Juan Carlos Zummaraga W RSC 1 Dagenham
(*Vacant IBF Inter-Continental Lightweight Title*)
29.05.00 Wahid Fats W RSC 3 Manchester
24.06.00 Nono Junior W RSC 4 Glasgow
12.08.00 Alan Temple W RSC 2 Wembley
(*IBF Inter-Continental Lightweight Title Defence. Elim. British Lightweight Title*)
23.09.00 David Kirk W PTS 4 Bethnal Green
24.02.01 Serguei Starkov W PTS 8 Bethnal Green

05.05.01 Bobby Vanzie L RSC 7 Edmonton
(*British Lightweight Title Challenge*)
22.09.01 Darren Melville W PTS 8 Bethnal Green
24.11.01 Keith Jones W RSC 4 Bethnal Green
15.12.01 Jason Hall W RSC 4 Wembley
(*Elim. British Lightweight Title*)
02.03.02 Viktor Baranov W RSC 5 Bethnal Green
(*Vacant WBO Inter-Continental Lightweight Title*)
04.05.02 Rosalin Nasibulin W CO 5 Bethnal Green
Career: 22 contests, won 21, lost 1.

Lee Murtagh

Leeds. *Born* Leeds, 30 September, 1973
British Masters Middleweight Champion. Ht. 5'9¼"
Manager J. O'Neill/K. Walker

12.06.95 Dave Curtis W PTS 6 Bradford
25.09.95 Roy Gbasai W PTS 6 Bradford
30.10.95 Cam Raeside L PTS 6 Bradford
11.12.95 Donovan Davey W PTS 6 Bradford
13.01.96 Peter Varnavas W PTS 6 Halifax
05.02.96 Shamus Casey W PTS 6 Bradford
20.05.96 Shaun O'Neill W PTS 6 Bradford
24.06.96 Michael Alexander W PTS 6 Bradford
28.10.96 Jimmy Vincent L RSC 2 Bradford
14.04.97 Lee Simpkin W PTS 6 Bradford
09.10.97 Brian Dunn W PTS 6 Leeds
05.03.98 Wayne Shepherd W PTS 6 Leeds
08.08.98 Alan Gilbert W PTS 4 Scarborough
13.03.99 Keith Palmer DREW 6 Manchester
27.09.99 Jawaid Khaliq L RSC 5 Leeds
(*Vacant WBF European L. Middleweight Title*)
27.02.00 Gareth Lovell W PTS 6 Leeds
24.09.00 Jon Foster W PTS 6 Shaw
03.12.00 Michael Alexander W PTS 6 Shaw
17.05.01 Ojay Abrahams L RSC 2 Leeds
(*Vacant British Masters L. Middleweight Title*)
03.03.02 Howard Clarke NC 2 Shaw
19.04.02 Neil Bonner W PTS 6 Darlington
21.06.02 Wayne Shepherd W PTS 10 Leeds
(*Vacant British Masters Middleweight Title*)
Career: 22 contests, won 16, drew 1, lost 4, no contest 1.

(Lee) Young Muttley (Woodley)

West Bromwich. *Born* West Bromwich, 17 May, 1976
L. Welterweight. Ht. 5'8½"
Manager M. Shinfield

03.09.99 Dave Hinds W RSC 4 West Bromwich
24.10.99 David Kehoe W RTD 1 Wolverhampton
22.01.00 Wahid Fats L PTS 4 Birmingham
18.02.00 Stuart Rimmer W RSC 1 West Bromwich
27.11.00 Peter Dunn W RSC 3 Birmingham
07.09.01 Jon Honney W RSC 1 West Bromwich
16.11.01 Tony Montana W PTS 6 West Bromwich
26.11.01 Lee Byrne W RSC 1 Manchester
23.02.02 Brian Coleman W PTS 4 Nottingham
23.03.02 Adam Zadworny W RSC 3 Southwark
Career: 10 contests, won 9, lost 1.

Ronnie Nailen

Glasgow. *Born* Belfast, 2 April, 1981
Welterweight. Ht. 5'10"
Manager R. Bannan/K. Morrison

24.05.01 David White W PTS 6 Glasgow
20.10.01 Keith Jones W PTS 4 Glasgow
08.06.02 Brian Coleman W PTS 4 Renfrew
Career: 3 contests, won 3.

Dominic Negus

Havering. *Born* Bethnal Green, 28 July, 1970
Heavyweight. Former Undefeated WBU Inter-Continental S. Cruiserweight Champion. Former Southern Area Cruiserweight Champion. Ht. 6'2"
Manager F. Maloney

03.09.96 Gareth Thomas W RSC 2 Bethnal Green
28.09.96 Patrick Lawrence W RSC 2 Barking
11.01.97 Naveed Anwar W RTD 2 Bethnal Green
04.03.97 Nigel Rafferty W PTS 4 Southwark
20.05.97 Nigel Rafferty W PTS 4 Edmonton
17.06.97 Chris Henry W RSC 10 Cheshunt
(Southern Area Cruiserweight Title Challenge)
02.09.97 Trevor Small DREW 8 Southwark
11.11.97 Constantin Ochrej W CO 6 Bethnal Green
21.04.98 Bruce Scott L RSC 9 Edmonton
(Southern Area Cruiserweight Title Defence)
22.10.98 Kevin Mitchell L RTD 5 Barking
18.02.99 Kevin Mitchell W PTS 10 Barking
(Vacant Southern Area Cruiserweight Title)
13.09.99 Chris Woollas W PTS 10 Bethnal Green
(Elim. British Cruiserweight Title)
08.09.00 Tony Booth L PTS 6 Bristol
06.10.00 Garry Delaney L PTS 10 Maidstone
(Southern Area Cruiserweight Title Defence)
26.05.01 Paul Fiske W CO 1 Bethnal Green
29.09.01 Eamonn Glennon W PTS 6 Southwark
08.12.01 Eddie Knight W CO 2 Dagenham
(Vacant WBU Inter-Continental S.Cruiserweight Title)
26.01.02 Paul Bonson W PTS 4 Bethnal Green
Career: 18 contests, won 13, drew 1, lost 4.

Johnny Nelson

Sheffield. *Born* Sheffield, 4 January, 1967
WBO Cruiserweight Champion. Former Undefeated British & European Cruiserweight Champion. Former Undefeated WBU Heavyweight Champion. Former WBF Heavyweight Champion. Former WBF Cruiserweight Champion. Former Undefeated Central Area Cruiserweight Champion. Ht. 6'2"
Manager B. Ingle/F. Warren

18.03.86 Peter Brown L PTS 6 Hull
15.05.86 Tommy Taylor L PTS 6 Dudley
03.10.86 Magne Havnaa L PTS 4 Copenhagen, Denmark
20.11.86 Chris Little W PTS 6 Bredbury
19.01.87 Gypsy Carman W PTS 6 Mayfair
02.03.87 Doug Young W PTS 6 Huddersfield
10.03.87 Sean Daly W RSC 1 Manchester
28.04.87 Brian Schumacher L PTS 8 Halifax
03.06.87 Byron Pullen W RSC 3 Southwark
14.12.87 Jon McBean W RSC 6 Edgbaston
01.02.88 Dennis Bailey L PTS 8 Northampton
24.02.88 Cordwell Hylton W RSC 1 Sheffield
25.04.88 Kenny Jones W CO 1 Liverpool
04.05.88 Crawford Ashley W PTS 8 Solihull
06.06.88 Lennie Howard W CO 2 Mayfair
31.08.88 Andrew Gerrard W PTS 8 Stoke
26.10.88 Danny Lawford W RSC 2 Sheffield

(Vacant Central Area Cruiserweight Title)
04.04.89 Steve Mormino W RSC 2 Sheffield
21.05.89 Andy Straughn W CO 8 Finsbury Park
(British Cruiserweight Title Challenge)
02.10.89 Ian Bulloch W CO 2 Hanley
(British Cruiserweight Title Defence)
27.01.90 Carlos de Leon DREW 12 Sheffield
(WBC Cruiserweight Title Challenge)
14.02.90 Dino Homsey W RSC 7 Brentwood
28.03.90 Lou Gent W CO 4 Bethnal Green
(British Cruiserweight Title Defence)
27.06.90 Arthur Weathers W RSC 2 Kensington
05.09.90 Andre Smith W PTS 8 Brighton
14.12.90 Markus Bott W RSC 12 Karlsruhe, Germany
(Vacant European Cruiserweight Title)
12.03.91 Yves Monsieur W RTD 8 Mansfield

Johnny Nelson　　　　　　　　　　　Les Clark

(European Cruiserweight Title Defence)
16.05.92 James Warring L PTS 12 Fredericksburg, USA
(IBF Cruiserweight Title Challenge)
15.08.92 Norbert Ekassi L RSC 3 Ajaccio, France
29.10.92 Corrie Sanders L PTS 10 Morula, South Africa
30.04.93 Dave Russell W RSC 11 Melbourne, Australia
(WBF Cruiserweight Title Challenge)
11.08.93 Tom Collins W RSC 1 Mansfield
(WBF Cruiserweight Title Defence)
01.10.93 Francis Wanyama L DIS 10 Waregem, Belgium
(WBF Cruiserweight Title Defence)
20.11.93 Jimmy Thunder W PTS 12 Auckland, New Zealand
(WBF Heavyweight Title Challenge)
05.04.94 Henry Akinwande L PTS 10 Bethnal Green
05.11.94 Nikolai Kulpin W PTS 12 Bangkok, Thailand
(WBF Heavyweight Title Defence)
22.08.95 Adilson Rodrigues L PTS 12 Sao Paulo, Brazil
(WBF Heavyweight Title Defence)
03.12.95 Adilson Rodrigues L PTS 12 Sao Paulo, Brazil
(WBF Heavyweight Title Challenge)
20.01.96 Tony Booth W RSC 2 Mansfield
14.12.96 Dennis Andries W RSC 7 Sheffield
(Vacant British Cruiserweight Title)
22.02.97 Patrice Aouissi W RSC 7 Berck sur Mer, France
(Vacant European Cruiserweight Title)
19.07.97 Michael Murray W PTS 4 Wembley
11.10.97 Dirk Wallyn W RSC 1 Sheffield
(European Cruiserweight Title Defence)
18.07.98 Peter Oboh W RTD 6 Sheffield
27.03.99 Carl Thompson W RSC 5 Derby
(WBO Cruiserweight Title Challenge)
15.05.99 Bruce Scott W PTS 12 Sheffield
(WBO Cruiserweight Title Defence)
07.08.99 Willard Lewis W RTD 4 Dagenham
(WBO Cruiserweight Title Defence)
18.09.99 Sione Asipeli W PTS 12 Las Vegas, USA
(WBO Cruiserweight Title Defence)
06.11.99 Christophe Girard W CO 4 Widnes
(WBO Cruiserweight Title Defence)
08.04.00 Pietro Aurino W RTD 7 Bethnal Green
(WBO Cruiserweight Title Defence)
07.10.00 Adam Watt W RSC 5 Doncaster
(WBO Cruiserweight Title Defence)
27.01.01 George Arias W PTS 12 Bethnal Green
(WBO Cruiserweight Title Defence)
21.07.01 Marcelo Dominguez W PTS 12 Sheffield
(WBO Cruiserweight Title Defence)
24.11.01 Alex Vasiliev W PTS 12 Bethnal Green
(Vacant WBU Heavyweight Title)
06.04.02 Ezra Sellers W CO 8 Copenhagen, Denmark
(WBO Cruiserweight Title Defence)
Career: 55 contests, won 42, drew 1, lost 12.

Chris Nembhard

Leytonstone. *Born* Jamaica, 26 December, 1976
Middleweight. Ht. 6'1"
Manager T. Bowers

29.09.00 Gary Ojuederie W RSC 1 Bethnal Green
02.11.00 Koba Kulu W PTS 6 Kensington
10.11.00 William Webster W RSC 1 Mayfair
15.02.01 Keith Ellwood W RSC 2 Glasgow
23.02.01 David Baptiste W PTS 8 Barking
09.03.01 Rob Stevenson W RSC 2 Millwall
20.04.01 Delroy Mellis L RSC 8 Millwall
(Southern Area L. Middleweight Title Challenge)
31.07.01 Brian Magee L RSC 6 Bethnal Green
07.09.01 Lawrence Murphy DREW 6 Glasgow
24.11.01 Gary Lockett L RSC 2 Bethnal Green
Career: 10 contests, won 6, drew 1, lost 3.

Jason Nesbitt

Birmingham. *Born* Birmingham, 15 December, 1973
S. Featherweight. Ht. 5'9"
Manager N. Nobbs

06.11.00 Stephen Chinnock L PTS 6 Wolverhampton
09.12.00 Lee Meager L RSC 2 Southwark
29.01.01 Henry Castle L CO 6 Peterborough
27.03.01 Billy Smith W PTS 6 Brierley Hill
21.05.01 Sid Razak L PTS 6 Birmingham
04.06.01 Andrew Ferrans L RSC 2 Glasgow
07.07.01 Colin Toohey L PTS 4 Manchester
15.09.01 Colin Toohey L PTS 4 Manchester
22.09.01 John Mackay L PTS 4 Canning Town
01.11.01 Chris Hooper L RSC 6 Hull
16.03.02 Lee Meager L PTS 6 Bethnal Green
27.03.02 Greg Edwards W RSC 5 Mayfair
20.04.02 Henry Castle L PTS 4 Cardiff
04.05.02 Danny Hunt L PTS 4 Bethnal Green
15.06.02 Jesse James Daniel L PTS 4 Leeds
Career: 15 contests, won 2, lost 13.

Dean Nicholas

South Shields. *Born* South Shields, 9 May, 1973
Welterweight. Ht. 5'9"
Manager T. Callighan

22.09.95 David Thompson W PTS 6 Hull
02.11.95 Paul Scott W PTS 6 Houghton le Spring
20.11.95 Shaun Gledhill W RSC 4 Glasgow
14.02.96 Shaun O'Neill W PTS 6 Sunderland
22.04.96 John Smith W PTS 6 Glasgow
09.05.96 John Docherty L PTS 6 Glasgow
23.09.96 Mark Breslin L PTS 8 Glasgow
01.12.96 C. J. Jackson DREW 6 Shaw
27.02.97 Keith Scott L PTS 6 Sunderland
09.10.97 Donovan Davey W PTS 6 Hull
27.10.97 Ray Newby L RSC 4 Nottingham
30.11.97 Lee Molyneux W PTS 6 Shaw
03.02.98 Leon Cessiron L RSC 4 Pont Audemer, France
07.04.98 Jose Etinoff L CO 1 Epernay, France
29.10.98 Richard Inquieti W RSC 1 Newcastle
25.01.99 Glenn McClarnon L CO 1 Glasgow
29.05.99 Peter Dunn W PTS 6 South Shields
29.06.99 Paul Knights L RSC 2 Bethnal Green
17.04.00 James Docherty L RSC 6 Glasgow
23.10.00 James Hare L RSC 1 Glasgow
24.11.00 Oscar Hall L PTS 6 Darlington
05.02.01 Danny Parkinson L PTS 6 Bradford
23.02.01 Richard Inquieti W PTS 6 Irvine
19.03.01 Darren Spencer L RSC 4 Glasgow

22.09.01 Oscar Hall L DIS 9 Newcastle
(Vacant Northern Area Welterweight Title)
Career: 25 contests, won 10, drew 1, lost 14.

Dean Nicholas   Les Clark

Lee Nicholson

Doncaster. *Born* Mexborough, 10 November, 1976
Heavyweight. Ht. 5'11"
Manager J. Rushton

24.09.01 Jason Brewster L PTS 6 Cleethorpes
17.02.02 Jason Brewster L PTS 6 Wolverhampton
11.05.02 Fola Okesola L RSC 1 Dagenham
Career: 3 contests, lost 3.

Mark Nilsen

Sale. *Born* Manchester, 26 July, 1978
Middleweight. Ht. 6'0"
Manager S. Wood/T. Gilmour

17.02.02 Kenroy Lambert W PTS 6 Salford
Career: 1 contest, won 1.

Graham Nolan

Maidenhead. *Born* Maidenhead, 25 February, 1978
Cruiserweight. Ht. 6'0"
Manager J. Evans

19.03.02 Tony Moran L PTS 6 Slough
Career: 1 contest, lost 1.

Danny Norton

Stourbridge. *Born* Wordsley, 8 November, 1969
S. Middleweight. Ht. 6'0"
Manager D. Bradley

07.10.01 Mark Phillips W PTS 6 Wolverhampton
19.04.02 Andy Vickers W CO 2 Darlington
Career: 2 contests, won 2.

Tony Oakey

Portsmouth. *Born* Portsmouth, 2 January, 1976
WBU L. Heavyweight Champion. Former Undefeated Commonwealth & Southern Area L. Heavyweight Champion. Ht. 5'8"
Manager F. Maloney

12.09.98	Smokey Enison W RSC 2 Bethnal Green	

Tony Oakey   Les Clark

21.11.98	Zak Chelli W RSC 1 Southwark	
16.01.99	Jimmy Steel W PTS 4 Bethnal Green	
06.03.99	Mark Dawson W PTS 4 Southwark	
10.07.99	Jimmy Steel W PTS 4 Southwark	
01.10.99	Michael Pinnock W PTS 4 Bethnal Green	
21.02.00	Darren Ashton W PTS 4 Southwark	
13.03.00	Martin Jolley W PTS 6 Bethnal Green	
21.10.00	Darren Ashton W PTS 4 Wembley	
27.01.01	Nathan King W PTS 6 Bethnal Green	
26.03.01	Butch Lesley W PTS 10 Wembley *(Southern Area L. Heavyweight Title Challenge)*	
08.05.01	Hastings Rasani W RSC 10 Barnsley *(Vacant Commonwealth L. Heavyweight Title)*	
09.09.01	Konstantin Ochrej W RSC 4 Southwark	
20.10.01	Chris Davies W PTS 12 Portsmouth *(Commonwealth L.Heavyweight Title Defence)*	
02.03.02	Konstantin Shvets W PTS 12 Bethnal Green *(Vacant WBU L. Heavyweight Title)*	
25.05.02	Neil Simpson W PTS 12 Portsmouth *(WBU L. Heavyweight Title Defence)*	

Career: 16 contests, won 16.

Stephen Oates

Fulham. *Born* Leeds, 11 July, 1975
Bantamweight. Ht. 5'5½"
Manager A. Bowers

29.11.97	Gary Hickman W PTS 4 Norwich	
17.01.98	Chris Emanuele W RSC 4 Bristol	
07.02.98	Stevie Quinn W PTS 4 Cheshunt	
07.03.98	Marty Chestnut W PTS 6 Reading	
16.05.98	Harry Woods W PTS 4 Bethnal Green	
14.07.98	John Matthews L PTS 4 Reading	
10.10.98	Graham McGrath W PTS 4 Bethnal Green	
14.11.98	Chris Jickells W PTS 6 Cheshunt	
13.02.99	Delroy Pryce L PTS 6 Newcastle	
03.04.99	Ross Cassidy W RSC 1 Kensington	
26.06.99	Harry Woods W PTS 6 Millwall	
04.09.99	Danny Ruegg W PTS 6 Bethnal Green	
15.11.99	Jason Thomas W PTS 6 Bethnal Green	
19.02.00	Jason Thomas W PTS 6 Dagenham	
21.10.00	Daniel Ring W RSC 1 Wembley	
16.12.00	Chris Jickells W PTS 4 Sheffield	
17.03.01	Chris Emanuele W PTS 8 Manchester	
09.06.01	Nathan Sting L PTS 8 Bethnal Green	
10.11.01	Kevin Gerowski W PTS 6 Wembley	
23.02.02	Nicky Booth L RSC 7 Nottingham *(British & Commonwealth Bantamweight Title Challenges)*	

Career: 20 contests, won 16, lost 4.

Jon O'Brien

Dublin. *Born* Dublin, 9 May, 1978
S. Middleweight. Ht. 6'0"
Manager Self

18.05.98	Michael Pinnock W PTS 6 Cleethorpes	
19.09.98	Sean Pritchard W PTS 6 Dublin	
19.03.99	Sean Pritchard L PTS 8 Weston super Mare	
19.06.99	Pedro Carragher DREW 4 Dublin	
16.11.01	Simeon Cover W PTS 6 Dublin	

Career: 5 contests, won 3, drew 1, lost 1.

Valery Odin

London. *Born* Guadeloupe, 23 December, 1974
L. Heavyweight. Ht. 6'2½"
Manager T. Bowers

15.06.01	Tom Cannon W PTS 4 Millwall	
22.09.01	Mark Brookes W PTS 4 Canning Town	
09.10.01	Wayne Ellcock L PTS 4 Cardiff	
10.11.01	Tony Dodson L RSC 4 Wembley	
13.12.01	Calvin Stonestreet W RSC 2 Leicester Square	
10.02.02	Radcliffe Green W PTS 6 Southwark	
20.04.02	Toks Owoh W PTS 8 Wembley	
21.05.01	Mark Smallwood L RSC 4 Custom House	

Career: 8 contests, won 5, lost 3.

Valery Odin   Les Clark

Sunkanmi Ogunbiyi

London. *Born* Nigeria, 5 May, 1977
Flyweight. Ht. 5'5"
Manager J. Oyebola

24.05.01	Sergei Tasimov W PTS 4 Kensington
16.06.01	Delroy Spencer W PTS 4 Wembley
13.12.01	Naji Hassan L PTS 6 Leicester Square
13.03.02	Marty Kayes W PTS 4 Mayfair
13.06.02	Lee Georgiou W CO 1 Leicester Square

Career: 5 contests, won 4, lost 1.

Rasmus Ojemaye

London. *Born* Nigeria, 28 May, 1969
Cruiserweight. Ht. 5'10"
Manager J. Oyebola

24.05.01	Collice Mutizwa W CO 2 Kensington
16.06.01	Leighton Morgan L RSC 3 Wembley
09.05.02	Varuzhan Davtyan L RSC 3 Leicester Square

Career: 3 contests, won 1, lost 2.

Fola Okesola

Balham. *Born* Greenwich, 16 May, 1975
Heavyweight. Ht. 6'2½"
Manager B. Hearn

26.01.02	Slick Miller W RSC 1 Dagenham
23.03.02	Piotr Jurczyk W RSC 6 Southwark
13.04.02	Luke Simpkin L PTS 4 Liverpool
11.05.02	Lee Nicholson W RSC 1 Dagenham

Career: 4 contests, won 3, lost 1.

Ajose Olusegun

London. *Born* Nigeria, 6 December, 1979
L. Welterweight. Ht. 5'9"
Manager J. Oyebola

24.05.01	Tony Montana W RSC 1 Kensington
21.06.01	Woody Greenaway W RSC 1 Earls Court
04.10.01	Stuart Rimmer W RTD 2 Finsbury
13.03.02	Gary Flear W PTS 4 Mayfair
13.06.02	Keith Jones W PTS 6 Leicester Square

Career: 5 contests, won 5.

Leo O'Reilly

Bexleyheath. *Born* Gravesend, 4 October, 1979
L. Welterweight. Ht. 5'6"
Manager M. Roe

16.09.00	Dave Hinds W RSC 2 Bethnal Green
30.09.00	Stuart Rimmer W RSC 2 Peterborough
14.10.00	Marco Fattore W PTS 4 Wembley
18.11.00	Dave Travers W RSC 3 Dagenham
09.12.00	Pete Buckley W PTS 4 Southwark
05.02.01	Woody Greenaway W CO 1 Hull
13.03.01	Barrie Kelley W RSC 5 Plymouth
12.05.01	David White W PTS 4 Plymouth
13.09.01	Ernie Smith W PTS 6 Sheffield
16.03.02	Lance Crosby W PTS 8 Bethnal Green
10.05.02	Paul Denton W PTS 6 Bethnal Green

Career: 11 contests, won 11.

(Muhammed) Huggy Osman

Bradford. *Born* Bradford, 7 December, 1971
Cruiserweight. Ht. 6'3"
Manager Self

18.10.99	Geoff Hunter W PTS 6 Bradford
14.11.99	Lennox Williams W PTS 6 Bradford
01.12.99	Steve Loftus W RSC 3 Stoke
06.03.00	Paul Fiske W PTS 6 Bradford
08.07.00	Dave Faulkner DREW 6 Rotherham
04.12.00	Brian Gascoigne W PTS 6 Bradford
15.10.01	Paul Richardson W PTS 6 Bradford
16.11.01	Paul Richardson L PTS 6 Preston

Career: 8 contests, won 6, drew 1, lost 1.

Hussain Osman   Les Clark

Hussain Osman

Paddington. *Born* Syria, 25 July, 1973
Former IBO Inter-Continental & Southern
Area S. Middleweight Champion. Former
Undefeated Southern Area Middleweight
Champion. Ht. 5'9½"
Manager I. Akay

09.05.99	Wayne Asker W PTS 4 Bracknell
20.05.99	Karim Bouali W PTS 4 Barking
15.07.99	Neil Linford W RSC 5 Peterborough
05.10.99	Ojay Abrahams W PTS 4 Bloomsbury
05.02.00	Joey Ainscough W PTS 4 Bethnal Green
01.04.00	George Foreman W PTS 4 Bethnal Green
22.05.00	Steve Timms W RSC 2 Coventry
25.09.00	James Lowther L PTS 8 Barnsley
03.03.01	Gary Lockett L CO 2 Wembley
26.05.01	Lee Molloy W RSC 1 Bethnal Green
04.06.01	Richard Williams L PTS 10 Hartlepool
28.10.01	Gary Logan W PTS 10 Southwark
	(Southern Area Middleweight Title Challenge)
26.01.02	Matthew Barney W RTD 9 Dagenham
	(Vacant IBO Inter-Continental S.Middleweight Title. Southern Area S.Middleweight Title Challenge)
08.04.02	Matthew Barney L PTS 12 Southampton
	(IBO Inter-Continental & Southern Area S. Middleweight Title Defences)
21.05.02	Darren Rhodes W PTS 10 Custom House

Career: 15 contests, won 11, lost 4.

Paul Owen

Sheffield. *Born* Sheffield, 3 October, 1975
S. Middleweight. Ht. 5'10½"
Manager Self

05.05.00	Shane Thomas DREW 6 Pentre Halkyn
08.07.00	Chris Crook W RSC 1 Rotherham
05.10.00	Andy Vickers L PTS 6 Sunderland
24.11.00	Reece McAllister L PTS 6 Darlington
07.12.00	Ian Toby L RTD 5 Sunderland
05.02.01	Steve Timms L RSC 1 Bradford
10.05.01	Gary Dixon W RSC 3 Sunderland
21.06.01	Reece McAllister DREW 6 Sheffield
13.09.01	Reece McAllister W RSC 1 Sheffield
08.02.02	Lee Woodruff W RSC 2 Preston

Career: 10 contests, won 4, drew 2, lost 4.

(Tokunbo) Toks Owoh (Owomoyela)

Belsize Park. *Born* Newham, 21 July, 1972
S. Middleweight. Ht. 5'10½"
Manager F. Warren

24.10.95	Marvin O'Brien W RSC 2 Southwark
08.11.95	Dave Fulton W RSC 1 Bethnal Green
29.11.95	Nicky Wadman W PTS 6 Southwark
19.01.96	Ernie Loveridge W PTS 4 Bracknell
27.03.97	James Branch W RSC 1 Norwich
02.08.97	Peter Vosper W RSC 1 Barnsley
29.11.97	Sven Hamer W PTS 8 Norwich
27.03.98	Darren Ashton W RSC 2 Telford
25.04.98	Omar Sheika L RSC 4 Cardiff
26.09.98	Tony Booth W PTS 6 Norwich
30.01.99	Israel Khumalo W RSC 2 Bethnal Green
03.04.99	Paul Wesley W CO 5 Kensington
26.06.99	Peter Mason W RSC 1 Millwall
23.10.99	Eddie Haley W RSC 3 Telford
29.02.00	Konstantin Okhrej W RTD 4 Widnes
19.06.00	Tony Booth W RSC 3 Burton
23.09.00	Glencoffe Johnson L RSC 6 Bethnal Green
	(Vacant IBF Inter-Continental S.Middleweight Title)
18.01.02	Mondli Mbonambi W PTS 8 Coventry
20.04.02	Valery Odin L PTS 8 Wembley
21.05.02	Erik Teymour L PTS 6 Custom House

Career: 20 contests, won 16, lost 4.

James Paisley

Larne. *Born* Ballymena, 4 January 1980
L. Welterweight. Ht. 5'8"
Manager A. Wilton

09.09.01	Babatunde Ajayi L PTS 4 Southwark
28.10.01	Carl Walton W PTS 4 Southwark
15.12.01	David Barnes L RTD 2 Wembley
31.01.02	Tony Montana L PTS 6 Piccadilly
09.02.02	Michael Jennings L RSC 3 Manchester
11.03.02	Nigel Wright L PTS 4 Glasgow
23.06.02	Jason Gonzalez W PTS 6 Southwark

Career: 7 contests, won 2, lost 5.

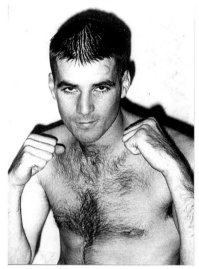

James Paisley   Les Clark

Danny Parkinson

Bradford. *Born* Bradford, 6 August, 1980
Welterweight. Ht. 5'11"
Manager Self

12.06.00	Ram Singh W RSC 3 Bradford
04.12.00	Ram Singh W PTS 6 Bradford
05.02.01	Dean Nicholas W PTS 6 Bradford
19.03.01	Lee Sharp L PTS 6 Glasgow
15.10.01	Richard Inquieti W RSC 1 Bradford
04.03.02	Matt Scriven W PTS 6 Bradford

Career: 6 contests, won 5, lost 1.

Levi Pattison

Leeds. *Born* Kings Lynn, 10 September, 1975
Flyweight. Ht. 5'5½"
Manager M. Marsden

17.07.99	Graham McGrath W PTS 4 Doncaster
15.01.00	Sean Green L PTS 4 Doncaster
25.06.00	Paddy Folan W PTS 6 Wakefield
27.11.00	Chris Edwards L PTS 4 Birmingham
08.05.01	Delroy Spencer W PTS 4 Barnsley
17.05.01	Gary Ford W RSC 5 Leeds
08.10.01	Chris Edwards W PTS 4 Barnsley
24.11.01	Andy Greenaway W PTS 6 Wakefield
28.01.02	Delroy Spencer W RSC 5 Barnsley
27.04.02	Colin Moffett W RSC 2 Huddersfield

Career: 10 contests, won 8, lost 2.

Mark Paxford

Wigan. *Born* Leigh, 18 February, 1979
Welterweight. Ht. 5'9¼"
Manager R. Jones

22.09.00	Colin McCash DREW 6 Wrexham
03.12.00	Paddy Martin W RSC 3 Shaw
04.02.01	Matt Scriven W PTS 6 Queensferry
10.12.01	Pedro Thompson W PTS 6 Bradford
08.02.02	Richard Inquieti W PTS 6 Preston
09.05.02	Gavin Pearson L PTS 6 Sunderland

Career: 6 contests, won 4, drew 1, lost 1.

Gareth Payne

Coventry. *Born* Coventry, 14 April, 1973
British Masters Bantamweight Champion.
Ht. 5'3"
Manager J. Griffin/J. Harding

12.07.99	Lennie Hodgkins W PTS 4 Coventry
22.10.99	Danny Mulligan W RSC 2 Coventry
14.12.99	Paul Quarmby W PTS 4 Coventry
22.01.00	Sean Grant W RSC 1 Birmingham
22.05.00	Nicky Booth L PTS 4 Coventry
28.10.00	Chris Emanuele W CO 1 Coventry
02.01.01	Danny Lawson W RSC 1 Coventry
19.12.01	Delroy Spencer W PTS 4 Coventry
18.01.02	Delroy Spencer L PTS 4 Coventry
25.02.02	Jamie Yelland L RSC 3 Slough
26.04.02	Chris Emanuele W RSC 3 Coventry *(British Masters Bantamweight Title Challenge)*
18.05.02	Jim Betts L PTS 6 Millwall

Career: 12 contests, won 8, lost 4.

Mark Payne

Coventry. *Born* Coventry, 29 March, 1976
S. Bantamweight. Ht. 5'6"
Manager J. Trickett

11.05.98	Dave Travers W RTD 3 Leicester
24.09.98	David Jeffrey W RSC 2 Edgbaston
30.11.98	Danny Lawson W RSC 1 Leicester
11.12.98	Stevie Quinn W RSC 2 Cheshunt
26.02.99	Arv Mittoo W PTS 4 Coventry
12.07.99	John Barnes W PTS 4 Coventry
05.10.99	Isaac Sebaduka W PTS 6 Bloomsbury
14.12.99	Harry Woods W PTS 4 Coventry
10.03.00	Vlado Varhegyi W PTS 6 Bethnal Green
08.09.00	Vladimir Borov W PTS 6 Hammersmith
28.10.00	Rakhim Mingaleev W PTS 6 Coventry
02.01.01	Keith Jones W PTS 6 Coventry
19.05.01	Dazzo Williams L PTS 8 Wembley
22.09.01	Rakhim Mingaleev W PTS 6 Newcastle
19.12.01	Stevie Quinn W RTD 2 Coventry
18.05.02	Michael Hunter L PTS 8 Millwall

Career: 16 contests, won 14, lost 2.

Tommy Peacock

Liverpool. *Born* Liverpool, 24 October, 1969
L. Welterweight. Ht. 5'9"
Manager S. Foster/S. Wood

22.11.96	Wayne Jones W RSC 4 Liverpool
04.04.97	Craig Kelley W PTS 6 Liverpool
13.08.97	John Bailey W PTS 6 Chester, USA
23.09.97	Lee Raheem W PTS 6 Ledyard, USA
17.11.97	Mark Haslam W DIS 5 Manchester
02.02.98	Anthony Campbell DREW 6 Manchester
27.04.98	David Kirk W PTS 6 Manchester
06.06.98	Marc Smith W RSC 4 Liverpool
21.06.98	Dean Bramhald W PTS 6 Liverpool
19.12.98	Darren Underwood W RSC 3 Liverpool
27.02.99	Richard Hatton L RSC 2 Oldham *(Vacant Central Area L. Welterweight Title)*
26.06.99	Mark Ramsey DREW 4 Millwall
06.11.99	Mohamed Helel W PTS 4 Widnes
01.02.00	Souleymane M'Baye L RTD 4 Paris, France
02.03.00	Karim Bouali L PTS 4 Birkenhead
26.05.00	Kevin McIntyre L RSC 5 Glasgow
23.01.01	Kevin Bennett L RSC 5 Crawley
21.07.01	Gavin Down L RSC 1 Sheffield
15.09.01	Nigel Wright L RSC 1 Manchester

Career: 19 contests, won 10, drew 2, lost 7.

Brodie Pearmaine

Lewes. *Born* London, 3 April, 1967
Heavyweight. Ht. 6'0"
Manager R. Davies

24.02.00	Paul Fiske L PTS 6 Sunderland
11.02.02	Mark Gladwell W RSC 3 Southampton
08.04.02	Joe Brame W RSC 1 Southampton
23.06.02	Tommy Eastwood L PTS 4 Southwark

Career: 4 contests, won 2, lost 2.

Brodie Pearmaine   Les Clark

Dave Pearson

Middlesbrough. *Born* Middlesbrough, 1 April, 1974
Middleweight. Ht. 6'2¾"
Manager M. Shinfield

| 15.04.02 | Ian Thomas L CO 3 Shrewsbury |

Career: 1 contest, lost 1.

Gavin Pearson

Bradford. *Born* Bradford, 10 March, 1977
Welterweight. Ht. 5'10"
Manager Self

26.11.98	Bobby Lyndon W PTS 6 Bradford
07.12.98	Dale Lowe L PTS 6 Cleethorpes
21.02.99	Les Frost W PTS 6 Bradford
12.03.99	Piotr Banicki DREW 4 Bethnal Green
03.04.99	Piotr Banicki DREW 4 Carlisle
06.05.99	Paul Swindles W PTS 6 Sunderland
29.05.99	Craig Smith L RSC 1 South Shields
12.09.99	Mike Watson W PTS 6 Nottingham
14.11.99	Chris Steele W PTS 6 Bradford
26.11.99	Peter Dunn DREW 6 Wakefield
09.12.99	John Marsden W PTS 6 Sunderland
06.03.00	John Marsden W PTS 6 Bradford
20.03.00	Joe Miller L PTS 6 Glasgow
17.04.00	Arv Mittoo W PTS 6 Glasgow
15.05.00	John Marsden W CO 5 Bradford
25.06.00	Robbie Sivyer L PTS 6 Wakefield
04.12.00	Dave Hinds W PTS 6 Bradford
05.02.01	Robert Burton L RSC 3 Bradford
17.05.01	Peter Dunn W PTS 6 Leeds
08.10.01	Robert Burton L RSC 2 Barnsley
18.03.02	Richard Inquieti W PTS 6 Glasgow
25.03.02	Danny Moir W PTS 6 Sunderland
29.04.02	Richard Inquieti W PTS 6 Bradford
09.05.02	Mark Paxford W PTS 6 Sunderland

Career: 24 contests, won 15, drew 3, lost 6.

Jon Penn

Pontefract. *Born* Sheffield, 21 January, 1973
Cruiserweight. Ht. 5'8½"
Manager Self

09.10.97	Ian Toby W PTS 6 Hull
11.11.97	Clint Johnson L RSC 2 Leeds
15.12.97	Mike Duffield W RSC 2 Cleethorpes
26.02.98	Ian Toby DREW 6 Sunderland
05.04.98	Jimmy Steel W RSC 5 Shaw
21.05.98	Eddie Haley W RSC 2 Bradford
20.09.98	Jason Barker W PTS 6 Sheffield
28.11.98	Danny Ryan W RSC 4 Belfast
06.03.99	Howard Eastman L RSC 3 Southwark
	(Vacant IBO Inter-Continental S. Middleweight Title)
26.06.99	Mario Veit L RSC 3 Millwall
10.12.99	Milko Stoikov W CO 1 Warsaw, Poland
12.02.00	Jimmy Steel W PTS 6 Sheffield
21.10.00	Paul Bonson W PTS 6 Sheffield
26.03.01	Michael Bowen L RSC 5 Wembley
23.06.01	Neil Linford L RSC 3 Peterborough
13.09.01	Scott Dann W RSC 5 Sheffield
20.10.01	Matthew Barney L RSC 4 Portsmouth
10.12.01	Tony Dodson L RSC 2 Liverpool
	(Vacant Central Area S. Middleweight Title)
26.04.02	Mark Smallwood L PTS 6 Coventry
10.05.02	Spencer Wilding L RTD 1 Preston

Career: 20 contests, won 10, drew 1, lost 9.

Matthew Pepper

Scunthorpe. *Born* Scunthorpe, 23 April, 1979
L. Heavyweight. Ht. 6'0"
Manager T. Petersen

03.12.98	Martin Thompson L CO 4 Hull
30.04.99	Steve Timms L RSC 3 Scunthorpe
26.11.99	Jim Milner W RSC 5 Hull
15.01.00	Damon Hague L CO 1 Doncaster
09.04.00	Damon Hague L RSC 3 Alfreton

11.05.00	Ivan Botton L RSC 4 Newark
09.06.00	Andrew Facey L RSC 1 Hull
30.08.00	Mike Duffield L RSC 4 Scunthorpe
24.03.01	Mark Brookes L RSC 1 Sheffield
30.11.01	Jamie Wilson L RSC 3 Hull

Career: 10 contests, won 1, lost 9.

Mark Phillips

St Clare's. *Born* Carmarthen, 28 April, 1975
S. Middleweight. Ht. 6'0"
Manager C. Sanigar

26.10.00	Shayne Webb W PTS 6 Clydach
12.12.00	Tommy Matthews W PTS 6 Clydach
13.03.01	William Webster W RTD 1 Plymouth
07.10.01	Danny Norton L PTS 6 Wolverhampton
12.12.01	Simon Andrews W PTS 6 Clydach
25.04.02	Mark Ellwood L PTS 6 Hull
10.05.02	Scott Dann L PTS 6 Bethnal Green
23.06.02	Gareth Hogg L PTS 4 Southwark

Career: 8 contests, won 4, lost 4.

Paul Philpott

Southampton. *Born* Southampton, 31 May, 1973
L. Welterweight. Ht. 5'6"
Manager J. Bishop

27.05.00	Mally McIver L PTS 4 Southwark
22.10.00	Chill John L PTS 6 Streatham
15.10.01	Shaune Danskin W RSC 5 Southampton

Career: 3 contests, won 1, lost 2.

Paul Philpott　　　　Les Clark

Esham Pickering

Newark. *Born* Newark, 7 August, 1976
S. Bantamweight. Former Undefeated
British Masters Bantamweight Champion.
Ht. 5'5"
Manager B. Ingle/F. Warren

23.09.96	Brendan Bryce W RSC 5 Cleethorpes
24.10.96	Kevin Sheil W PTS 6 Lincoln

22.11.96	Amjid Mahmood W RSC 2 Hull
09.12.96	Des Gargano W RTD 2 Chesterfield
16.12.96	Graham McGrath W PTS 6 Cleethorpes
20.03.97	Robert Braddock W RSC 6 Newark
12.04.97	Graham McGrath W PTS 4 Sheffield
26.04.97	Mike Deveney W PTS 4 Swadlincote
16.05.97	Chris Price W PTS 6 Hull
26.06.97	Graham McGrath W PTS 6 Salford
01.11.97	Mike Deveney W RSC 8 Glasgow
	(Elim. British Featherweight Title)
09.05.98	Jonjo Irwin L PTS 12 Sheffield
	(Vacant British Featherweight Title)
11.09.98	Louis Veitch W PTS 6 Newark
15.08.99	Chris Lyons W RSC 2 Derby
23.10.99	Ian Turner W PTS 6 Telford
20.11.99	Marc Smith W PTS 6 Grantham
19.02.00	Kevin Gerowski W PTS 10 Newark
	(Vacant British Masters Bantamweight Title. Elim. British Bantamweight Title)
13.08.00	Lee Williamson W PTS 6 Nottingham
16.12.00	Mauricio Martinez L RSC 1 Sheffield
	(WBO Bantamweight Title Challenge)
15.09.01	Carl Allen W PTS 6 Derby
08.12.01	Carl Allen W PTS 8 Chesterfield
20.04.02	Carl Allen W PTS 6 Derby

Career: 22 contests, won 20, lost 2.

Wayne Pinder　　　　Les Clark

Wayne Pinder

Manchester. *Born* Manchester, 15 April, 1978
Middleweight. Ht. 6'0"
Manager S. Wood/T. Gilmour

27.04.98	C. J. Jackson W PTS 6 Manchester
01.06.98	Carlton Williams W PTS 6 Manchester
26.10.98	Mark Owens DREW 6 Manchester
28.02.99	Lee Bird W RSC 5 Shaw
13.03.99	Paul O'Rourke W RSC 3 Manchester
02.05.99	Carl Smith W RSC 5 Shaw
02.07.99	Donovan Davey W PTS 6 Manchester
19.09.99	Paul King W PTS 6 Shaw
11.06.00	Colin Vidler W PTS 6 Salford
01.07.00	Gary Beardsley W PTS 4 Manchester
09.09.00	Ian Toby W PTS 4 Manchester

12.11.00 James Donoghue W PTS 6 Manchester
17.03.01 Leigh Wicks W PTS 4 Manchester
27.05.01 Dean Ashton W PTS 6 Manchester
07.07.01 Ian Toby W RTD 5 Manchester
26.11.01 Howard Clarke W PTS 6 Manchester
09.03.02 Jimmy Steel W PTS 4 Manchester
Career: 17 contests, won 16, drew 1.

Michael Pinnock

Birmingham. *Born* Birmingham, 6 June, 1965
Cruiserweight. Ht. 6'0"
Manager Self

19.05.95 David Flowers L PTS 6 Leeds
13.06.95 Mark Snipe L PTS 6 Basildon
20.06.95 Darren Sweeney L PTS 8 Birmingham
06.09.95 Steve Loftus L PTS 6 Stoke
21.09.95 Luan Morena L PTS 4 Battersea
24.10.95 Graham Townsend L PTS 4 Southwark
17.11.95 Graham Townsend L PTS 4 Bethnal Green
03.12.95 Neville Smith L RSC 5 Southwark
23.01.96 Butch Lesley L PTS 4 Bethnal Green
05.03.96 Panayiotis Panayiotiou L PTS 4 Bethnal Green
16.03.96 Mark Hickey L PTS 6 Barnstaple
25.03.96 Lee Simpkin W PTS 6 Birmingham
03.04.96 Jason Hart L PTS 6 Bethnal Green
24.04.96 Gordon Behan L PTS 6 Solihull
03.05.96 David Larkin DREW 6 Sheffield
14.05.96 Mervyn Penniston L RSC 2 Dagenham
19.07.96 Chris Davies L PTS 6 Ystrad
29.07.96 Stuart Fleet L RSC 3 Skegness
04.10.96 Paul Bonson L PTS 6 Wakefield
28.10.96 Zak Goldman DREW 6 Leicester
14.11.96 Paul Bonson DREW 6 Sheffield
21.11.96 Darren Sweeney W RSC 5 Solihull
26.11.96 Mark Smallwood L PTS 6 Wolverhampton
03.02.97 Neil Simpson L PTS 6 Leicester
09.06.97 Mark Hobson L PTS 6 Bradford
05.07.97 Paschal Collins L PTS 6 Glasgow
02.09.97 Mike Gormley L PTS 6 Manchester
18.09.97 Martin Jolley DREW 6 Alfreton
04.10.97 Zoltan Sarossy L PTS 6 Muswell Hill
27.10.97 Johnny Hooks DREW 6 Nottingham
11.11.97 Graham Townsend L PTS 8 Bethnal Green
25.11.97 Barry Thorogood L PTS 8 Wolverhampton
15.12.97 Greg Scott-Briggs L PTS 6 Nottingham
02.02.98 Glenn Williams L CO 2 Manchester
30.04.98 Bobby Banghar L PTS 6 Purfleet
18.05.98 Jon O'Brien L PTS 6 Cleethorpes
22.10.98 Paul Carr L PTS 6 Barking
29.10.98 Paul Carr DREW 6 Bayswater
05.12.98 Dave Stenner W RSC 3 Bristol
03.04.99 Robert Zlotkowski L PTS 4 Carlisle
15.05.99 Damon Hague L PTS 4 Sheffield
05.06.99 Leif Keiski L PTS 6 Cardiff
02.07.99 Mike Gormley L RSC 6 Manchester
01.10.99 Tony Oakey L PTS 4 Bethnal Green
16.10.99 Brian Magee L RSC 3 Belfast
17.04.00 Gordon Behan L PTS 6 Birmingham
15.05.00 Tony Booth L PTS 6 Cleethorpes
25.05.00 Neil Linford L PTS 4 Peterborough
08.09.00 Steven Spartacus L PTS 4 Hammersmith
10.11.00 Tony Griffiths L PTS 4 Mayfair
01.12.00 Allan Foster L PTS 4 Peterborough
29.01.01 Ivan Botton W PTS 4 Peterborough
20.03.01 Joe Gillon L PTS 6 Glasgow
28.03.01 Darren Ashton DREW 6 Piccadilly

09.06.01 Nathan King L PTS 4 Bethnal Green
21.06.01 Paul Bonson L PTS 6 Sheffield
27.07.01 Mark Brookes L PTS 4 Sheffield
15.09.01 Tony Dowling L PTS 6 Derby
04.10.01 Oneal Murray L PTS 6 Finsbury
21.10.01 Peter Merrall DREW 6 Pentre Halkyn
28.10.01 Radcliffe Green L PTS 4 Southwark
24.11.01 Steven Spartacus L PTS 4 Bethnal Green
09.12.01 Andrew Facey L PTS 6 Shaw
16.12.01 Sam Price L PTS 4 Southwark
16.03.02 Carl Froch L RSC 4 Bethnal Green
Career: 65 contests, won 4, drew 8, lost 53.

Dean Pithie

Coventry. *Born* Coventry, 18 January 1974
Former Undefeated WBC International S. Featherweight Champion. Former WBO Inter-Continental S. Featherweight Champion. Ht. 5'5"
Manager Self

17.02.95 Kid McAuley W RSC 3 Cumbernauld
13.04.95 Kid McAuley W RSC 1 Bloomsbury
01.07.95 Pete Buckley W PTS 4 Kensington
22.07.95 G. G. Goddard W PTS 4 Millwall
21.10.95 Anthony Campbell W PTS 4 Bethnal Green
10.11.95 Kelton McKenzie DREW 6 Derby
26.04.96 Kelton McKenzie W PTS 6 Cardiff
25.06.96 Lewis Reynolds W RSC 2 Mansfield
14.09.96 Miguel Matthews W PTS 4 Sheffield
14.12.96 Marty Chestnut W RSC 3 Sheffield
18.01.97 Harry Escott W RSC 4 Swadlincote
25.02.97 Pete Buckley W PTS 4 Sheffield
26.04.97 David Morris W PTS 8 Swadlincote
11.10.97 Stefy Bull W RSC 11 Sheffield
(Vacant WBO Inter-Continental S. Featherweight Title)
27.03.98 Paul Griffin W RSC 9 Telford
(WBO Inter-Continental S. Featherweight Title Defence)
06.06.98 Gary Thornhill L CO 8 Liverpool
(WBO Inter-Continental S. Featherweight Title Defence)
02.10.98 Keith Jones W PTS 8 Cheshunt
11.12.98 Kelton McKenzie W RSC 7 Cheshunt
(Elim. British S. Featherweight Title)
26.02.99 Andrew Matabola L RSC 8 Coventry
(Vacant WBC International S. Featherweight Title)
12.07.99 Andrew Matebola W RSC 2 Coventry
(WBC International S. Featherweight Title Challenge)
22.10.99 Frank Kiwanuka W RSC 2 Coventry
(WBC International S. Featherweight Title Defence)
14.12.99 Mzonke Fana W PTS 12 Coventry
(WBC International S. Featherweight Title Defence)
29.02.00 Michael Gomez L PTS 12 Widnes
(British S. Featherweight Title Challenge)
22.05.00 Wiseman Jim DREW 12 Coventry
(Vacant WBF Inter-Continental S. Featherweight Title)
28.10.00 Affif Djelti L CO 6 Coventry
(IBO S.Featherweight Title Challenge)
10.04.01 Keith Jones W PTS 8 Wembley
14.07.01 Jason White W PTS 4 Liverpool
17.11.01 Woody Greenaway W PTS 6 Coventry
09.02.02 Isaac Sebaduka W PTS 8 Coventry
26.04.02 Nigel Senior W PTS 6 Coventry
Career: 30 contests, won 24, drew 2, lost 4.

Gary Porter

Glasgow. *Born* Glasgow, 12 September, 1978
Welterweight. Ht. 5'9"
Manager B. Watt

04.06.01 Arv Mittoo W PTS 6 Glasgow
17.09.01 Carl Walton W PTS 6 Glasgow
03.11.01 Sam Mottram W PTS 4 Glasgow
22.04.02 Matt Scriven W PTS 6 Glasgow
03.06.02 Richard Inquieti W PTS 6 Glasgow
Career: 5 contests, won 5.

Marcus Portman

West Bromwich. *Born* West Bromwich, 26 September, 1980
Welterweight. Ht. 6'0"
Manager Self

18.02.00 Ray Wood W PTS 6 West Bromwich
28.03.00 Billy Smith W PTS 6 Wolverhampton
10.09.00 Alan Kershaw W RSC 2 Walsall
15.02.01 Willie Limond L PTS 6 Glasgow
01.04.01 Tony Smith W PTS 6 Wolverhampton
20.04.01 Darren Melville L RSC 3 Millwall
07.09.01 Tony Smith W PTS 6 West Bromwich
15.09.01 Matthew Hatton L RSC 3 Manchester
12.12.01 Ross McCord DREW 4 Clydach
18.01.02 Andy Egan W PTS 4 Coventry
25.02.02 Sammy Smith W PTS 6 Slough
27.04.02 Gavin Wake W PTS 4 Huddersfield
Career: 12 contests, won 8, drew 1, lost 3.

Marcus Portman Les Clark

Duje Postenjak

Glasgow. *Born* Croatia, 13 September, 1975
L. Middleweight. Ht. 5'9¼"
Manager A. Morrison

16.12.01 Tomas da Silva W PTS 6 Glasgow
Career: 1 contest, won 1.

Mark Potter

Walthamstow. *Born* Rush Green, 27
February, 1975
Southern Area Heavyweight Champion.
Ht. 6'1"
Manager Self

19.07.97	J. A. Bugner W PTS 6 Wembley
02.09.97	Rob Albon W RSC 1 Southwark
06.12.97	Johnny Davison W CO 1 Wembley
27.02.98	Lennox Williams W CO 1 Brighton
21.04.98	Geoff Hunter W RSC 1 Edmonton
23.05.98	Shane Woollas W PTS 4 Bethnal Green
12.09.98	Abdelrani Berbachi W RTD 4 Bethnal Green
22.09.98	Antoine Palatis L PTS 8 Pont Audemir, France
21.11.98	Ladislav Husarik W RSC 6 Southwark
08.05.99	Piotr Jurczyk W RSC 1 Bethnal Green
10.07.99	Stanislav Tomcatchov W RSC 3 Southwark
13.09.99	Derek McCafferty W PTS 6 Bethnal Green
29.11.99	Keith Long L PTS 8 Wembley
13.03.00	Danny Watts W RSC 6 Bethnal Green *(Vacant Southern Area Heavyweight Title)*
27.05.00	Mal Rice W CO 1 Southwark
23.09.00	Luke Simpkin W PTS 6 Bethnal Green
21.10.00	Danny Williams L RSC 6 Wembley *(Commonwealth & WBO Inter-Continental Heavyweight Title Challenges. Vacant British Heavyweight Title)*
05.05.01	Michael Murray W PTS 8 Edmonton
28.07.01	Alex Vasiliev L RSC 7 Wembley *(Vacant WBU Inter-Continental Heavyweight Title)*
08.12.01	Gary Williams W RSC 3 Dagenham
26.01.02	Derek McCafferty W PTS 6 Bethnal Green
28.04.02	Neil Kirkwood W RSC 1 Southwark

Career: 22 contests, won 18, lost 4.

Mark Potter   Les Clark

Dean Powell

Peckham. *Born* Salisbury, 4 June, 1970
Middleweight. Ht. 5'9"
Manager B. Lawrence

17.12.96	Matthew Tait L PTS 6 Bethnal Green
11.02.97	Matthew Tait L RSC 4 Bethnal Green
26.09.98	Brian Knudsen L PTS 4 York
12.12.98	Jeff Mills W RSC 3 Southwark
16.01.99	Neil Linford L RSC 1 Bethnal Green
22.11.01	Darren Covill W PTS 4 Mayfair

Career: 6 contests, won 2, lost 4.

Martin Power

Camden Town. *Born* London, 14 February, 1980
Bantamweight. Ht. 5'6"
Manager F. Maloney

09.06.01	Sean Grant W PTS 4 Bethnal Green
28.07.01	Andrew Greenaway W RSC 3 Wembley
22.09.01	Stevie Quinn W RSC 2 Bethnal Green
24.11.01	Anthony Hanna W PTS 4 Bethnal Green
19.01.02	Gareth Wiltshaw W PTS 4 Bethnal Green

Career: 5 contests, won 5.

Martin Power   Les Clark

Sam Price

Reading. *Born* Hillingdon, 6 July, 1981
L. Heavyweight. Ht. 6'0½"
Manager E. Maloney/F. Maloney

16.12.01	Michael Pinnock W PTS 4 Southwark
10.02.02	Calvin Stonestreet W PTS 4 Southwark
19.03.02	Jimmy Steel W PTS 4 Slough

Career: 3 contests, won 3.

Bradley Pryce (Price)

Newbridge. *Born* Newport, 15 March, 1981
IBF Inter-Continental L. Welterweight

Champion. Former Undefeated WBO Inter-
Continental Lightweight Champion.
Ht. 5'11"
Manager E. Calzaghe/F. Warren

17.07.99	Dave Hinds W PTS 4 Doncaster
23.10.99	David Jeffrey W RSC 3 Telford
06.11.99	Eddie Nevins W RSC 2 Widnes
29.01.00	Pete Buckley W PTS 4 Manchester
29.02.00	Carl Allen W PTS 4 Widnes
16.05.00	Carl Allen W RSC 3 Warrington
15.07.00	Gary Flear W RSC 1 Millwall
07.10.00	Gary Reid W RSC 5 Doncaster
27.01.01	Joel Viney W RSC 3 Bethnal Green
17.03.01	Brian Coleman W PTS 4 Manchester
28.04.01	Jason Hall W PTS 12 Cardiff *(Vacant WBO Inter-Continental Lightweight Title)*
21.07.01	Stuart Patterson W RSC 5 Sheffield
09.10.01	Lucky Sambo W PTS 12 Cardiff *(WBO Inter-Continental Lightweight Title Defence)*
12.02.02	Gavin Down W RSC 9 Bethnal Green *(Vacant IBF Inter-Continental L.Welterweight Title)*
20.04.02	Dafydd Carlin W RSC 8 Cardiff
08.06.02	Pete Buckley W RSC 1 Renfrew

Career: 16 contests, won 16.

Kreshnik Qato

Wembley. *Born* Albania, 13 August, 1978
Middleweight. Ht. 5'9½"
Manager F. Warren

28.09.01	Erik Teymour L PTS 6 Millwall
16.12.01	Lawrence Murphy L PTS 6 Glasgow
08.04.02	Ty Browne W PTS 4 Southampton
10.05.02	Paul Jones L PTS 6 Millwall

Career: 4 contests, won 1, lost 3.

Mickey Quinn (McAllister)

Belfast. *Born* Belfast, 7 January, 1979
Middleweight. Ht. 5'10¼"
Manager

01.06.02	Harry Butler W PTS 4 Manchester

Career: 1 contest, won 1.

Stevie Quinn

Newtownards. *Born* Newtonards, 14 November, 1969
S. Bantamweight. Ht. 5'7"
Manager O. McMahon

07.02.98	Stephen Oates L PTS 4 Cheshunt
28.04.98	Tommy Waite L RSC 3 Belfast
11.12.98	Mark Payne L RSC 2 Cheshunt
17.04.99	Chris Edwards W RSC 4 Dublin
22.05.99	Ross Cassidy W PTS 4 Belfast
16.10.99	Anthony Hanna L PTS 4 Belfast
19.02.00	Barry Hawthorne W RSC 5 Prestwick
12.06.00	Mickey Coveney L PTS 4 Belfast
20.10.00	Sean Grant W RSC 2 Belfast
11.11.00	Paul Weir W PTS 4 Belfast
27.01.01	Hussein Hussein L RTD 2 Bethnal Green
01.04.01	Richmond Asante W PTS 4 Southwark
28.04.01	Noel Wilders L RTD 6 Cardiff
22.09.01	Martin Power L RSC 2 Bethnal Green
19.12.01	Mark Payne L RTD 2 Coventry
26.01.02	Michael Hunter L CO 2 Dagenham

Career: 16 contests, won 6, lost 10.

Mark Ramsey

Birmingham. *Born* Birmingham, 24 January, 1968
Welterweight. Ht. 5'7½"
Manager Self

15.11.89	Mick O'Donnell W RSC 1 Lewisham
08.12.89	Dave Pierre L RSC 2 Doncaster
22.02.90	Karl Taylor W RSC 4 Hull
10.04.90	George Jones W RSC 6 Doncaster
20.05.90	Steve Pollard W PTS 6 Sheffield
18.10.90	Neil Haddock L RSC 5 Birmingham
30.05.91	Colin Sinnott W PTS 6 Birmingham
05.12.91	Carl Hook W RSC 5 Oakengates
27.01.93	Andrew Jervis W PTS 6 Stoke
12.02.93	Reymond Deva W PTS 6 Aubervilliers, France
04.03.93	Dave Pierre L PTS 8 Peterborough
01.05.93	Vyacheslav Ianowski L PTS 8 Berlin, Germany
02.07.93	Andreas Panayi DREW 6 Liverpool
05.08.93	Jean Chiarelli W RSC 4 Ascona, Italy
01.10.93	Freddy Demeulenaere W RSC 3 Waregem, Belgium
26.03.94	James Osunsedo W RSC 4 Dortmund, Germany
07.05.94	Andrei Sinepupov L PTS 12 Dnepropetrousk, Ukraine *(Vacant WBO Penta-Continental Lightweight Title)*
30.11.94	Mark Elliot W RSC 10 Wolverhampton *(Elim. British L. Welterweight Title)*
20.05.95	Ahmed Katejev L RTD 5 Hamburg, Germany *(WBC International Welterweight Title Challenge)*
15.09.95	Paul Dyer L PTS 6 Mansfield
23.10.95	Stefan Scriggins L PTS 8 Leicester
12.02.96	Alan McDowall L PTS 8 Glasgow
16.03.96	Alan McDowall L PTS 6 Glasgow
28.06.96	Poli Diaz W RSC 4 Madrid, Spain
12.11.96	Paul Samuels L RSC 4 Dudley
24.02.97	Bobby Vanzie DREW 8 Glasgow
25.03.97	Joshua Clottey L PTS 8 Lewisham
30.04.97	Anthony Campbell L PTS 6 Acton
20.05.97	Peter Richardson L PTS 8 Edmonton
09.08.97	George Scott L PTS 10 San Gennaro Vesuviano, Italy
27.10.97	Steve McLevy L PTS 6 Glasgow
13.12.97	Jawaid Khaliq L PTS 4 Sheffield
07.02.98	Junior Witter DREW 6 Cheshunt
24.02.98	Bruno Wartelle L PTS 10 Porto, Portugal
28.03.98	Justin Juuko L PTS 8 Hull
30.05.98	Richard Hatton L PTS 6 Bristol
18.09.98	Glenn McClarnon L PTS 4 Belfast
23.11.98	Benny Jones W PTS 6 Piccadilly
05.12.98	Jason Williams L PTS 6 Bristol
22.01.99	Neil Sinclair L CO 3 Dublin
12.03.99	Glenn McClarnon L PTS 6 Bethnal Green
23.04.99	Dave Hinds W PTS 6 Clydach
15.05.99	Corey Johnson L PTS 8 Sheffield
07.06.99	Scott Dixon L PTS 8 Glasgow
26.06.99	Tommy Peacock DREW 4 Millwall
17.07.99	Richard Hatton L PTS 6 Doncaster
16.10.99	Bernard McComiskey L PTS 6 Belfast
21.02.00	Charlie Kane L PTS 6 Glasgow
11.03.00	Darren Bruce DREW 6 Kensington
17.04.00	Spencer McCracken L PTS 8 Birmingham
04.09.00	Michael Jennings L PTS 6 Manchester
16.09.00	Zoltan Sarossy W PTS 8 Bethnal Green
28.09.00	Ossie Duran L RSC 2 Kensington
03.11.00	Jason Williams W CO 6 Ebbw Vale
10.11.00	Kevin McIntyre L RSC 4 Glasgow
23.01.01	James Hare L PTS 6 Crawley
17.02.01	Colin Lynes L PTS 6 Bethnal Green
13.03.01	Pavel Melnikov L PTS 8 Plymouth
20.04.01	John Humphrey L PTS 10 Millwall *(Vacant British Masters Welterweight Title)*
19.05.01	David Walker L PTS 4 Wembley
16.06.01	John Tiftik W PTS 6 Dagenham
14.07.01	Darren Bruce W PTS 6 Wembley
03.11.01	Kevin Bennett L PTS 6 Glasgow
08.12.01	Stephan Carr L RSC 3 Dagenham
12.02.02	Ivan Kirpa L CO 5 Bethnal Green
15.03.02	Darren Melville L PTS 6 Millwall

Career: 66 contests, won 19, drew 6, lost 41.

(Shahid) Sid Razak

Birmingham. *Born* Birmingham, 9 March, 1973
Featherweight. Ht. 5'7"
Manager D. Poston

13.02.01	Neil Read W PTS 6 Brierley Hill
27.03.01	Tommy Thomas W RSC 2 Brierley Hill
21.05.01	Jason Nesbitt W PTS 6 Birmingham
08.10.01	Gareth Wiltshaw L PTS 6 Birmingham

Career: 4 contests, won 3, lost 1.

Neil Read   Les Clark

Neil Read

Bilston. *Born* Wolverhampton, 9 February, 1972
Bantamweight. Ht. 5'4"
Manager P. Bowen

08.02.00	Gary Groves W PTS 6 Wolverhampton
10.09.00	Stephen Chinnock L RSC 5 Walsall
30.11.00	Paddy Folan L PTS 6 Blackpool
13.02.01	Sid Razak L PTS 6 Brierley Hill
08.03.01	John-Paul Ryan W PTS 6 Stoke
26.08.01	Lee Holmes L PTS 6 Warrington
06.12.01	Chris Edwards L PTS 8 Stoke
28.01.02	Jamil Hussain L CO 2 Barnsley
13.04.02	Stephen Chinnock L CO 3 Wolverhampton *(Midlands Area Featherweight Title Challenge)*
29.06.02	Jamie Yelland L PTS 6 Brentwood

Career: 10 contests, won 2, lost 8.

Gavin Rees

Newbridge. *Born* Newport, 10 May, 1980
S. Featherweight. WBO Inter-Continental Featherweight Champion. Ht. 5'7"
Manager F. Warren/E. Calzaghe

05.09.98	John Farrell W PTS 4 Telford
05.12.98	Ernie Smith W PTS 4 Bristol
27.03.99	Graham McGrath W RSC 2 Derby
05.06.99	Wayne Jones W RSC 2 Cardiff
11.12.99	Dave Hinds W RSC 2 Liverpool
19.02.00	Pete Buckley W PTS 4 Dagenham
29.05.00	Willie Valentine W RSC 3 Manchester
23.09.00	Pete Buckley W PTS 4 Bethnal Green
13.11.00	Steve Hanley W RSC 1 Bethnal Green
15.01.01	Chris Jickells W RSC 2 Manchester
28.04.01	Vladimir Borov W RSC 4 Cardiff *(Vacant WBO Inter-Continental Featherweight Title)*
21.07.01	Nigel Senior W RSC 2 Sheffield
09.10.01	Nikolai Eremeev W PTS 12 Cardiff *(WBO Inter-Continental Featherweight Title Defence)*
12.02.02	Rakhim Mingaleev W PTS 6 Bethnal Green
20.04.02	Gary Flear W RTD 4 Cardiff

Career: 15 contests, won 15.

Gary Reid

Telford. *Born* Jamaica, 20 November, 1972
Lightweight. Ht. 5'5½"
Manager S. Wood/T. Gilmour

09.12.98	Carl Tilley W CO 1 Stoke
11.02.99	Ted Bami L RSC 2 Dudley
23.03.99	Lee Williamson W PTS 6 Wolverhampton
07.10.99	Stuart Rimmer W RSC 2 Mere
19.12.99	Nono Junior L PTS 6 Salford
14.04.00	Lee Molyneux W PTS 6 Manchester
18.05.00	Sammy Smith W RSC 1 Bethnal Green
23.07.00	Kevin Bennett L RSC 4 Hartlepool
21.09.00	Karim Bouali L PTS 4 Bloomsbury
07.10.00	Bradley Pryce L RSC 5 Doncaster
07.09.01	Willie Limond L PTS 8 Glasgow
22.09.01	Francis Barrett L PTS 4 Bethnal Green
17.02.02	Richie Caparelli W PTS 6 Salford
02.03.02	Paul Halpin L RSC 3 Bethnal Green
26.04.02	Martin Watson L PTS 6 Glasgow
28.05.02	Gareth Jordan DREW 6 Liverpool

Career: 16 contests, won 6, drew 1, lost 9.

Pele Reid

Birmingham. *Born* Birmingham, 11 January, 1973
Former Undefeated WBO Inter-Continental Heavyweight Champion. Ht. 6'3"
Manager Self

24.11.95	Gary Williams W RSC 1 Manchester

20.01.96 Joey Paladino W RSC 1 Mansfield
26.01.96 Vance Idiens W RSC 1 Brighton
11.05.96 Keith Fletcher W CO 1 Bethnal Green
25.06.96 Andy Lambert W CO 1 Mansfield
12.10.96 Eduardo Carranza W CO 2 Milan, Italy
02.11.96 Ricky Sullivan W RSC 2 Garmisch,
          Germany
25.02.97 Michael Murray W RSC 1 Sheffield
28.06.97 Ricardo Kennedy W RSC 1 Norwich
          *(Vacant WBO Inter-Continental
          Heavyweight Title)*
11.10.97 Eli Dixon W CO 9 Sheffield
          *(WBO Inter-Continental Heavyweight
          Title Defence)*
15.11.97 Albert Call W RSC 2 Bristol
06.06.98 Wayne Llewelyn W CO 1 Liverpool
          (Elim. British Heavyweight Title)
19.09.98 Biko Botowamungo W RTD 3
          Oberhausen, Germany
30.01.99 Julius Francis L RSC 3 Bethnal Green
          *(British & Commonwealth
          Heavyweight Title Challenges)*
26.06.99 Orlin Norris L RSC 1 Millwall
22.01.00 Jacklord Jacobs L RSC 2 Birmingham
04.10.01 Mal Rice W PTS 4 Finsbury
13.12.01 Derek McCafferty W RSC 3 Leicester
          Square
27.01.02 Luke Simpkin DREW 4 Streatham
09.05.02 Michael Sprott L RSC 7 Leicester
          Square
          *(Vacant WBF European Heavyweight
          Title)*
Career: 20 contests, won 15, drew 1, lost 4.

Robin Reid

Runcorn. Liverpool, 19 February, 1971
WBF S. Middleweight Champion. Former
WBC S. Middleweight Champion. Ht. 5'9"
Manager Self

27.02.93 Mark Dawson W RSC 1 Dagenham
06.03.93 Julian Eavis W RSC 2 Glasgow
10.04.93 Andrew Furlong W PTS 6 Swansea
10.09.93 Juan Garcia W PTS 6 San Antonio,
          USA
09.10.93 Ernie Loveridge W PTS 4 Manchester
18.12.93 Danny Juma DREW 6 Manchester
09.04.94 Kesem Clayton W RSC 1 Mansfield
04.06.94 Andrew Furlong W RSC 2 Cardiff
17.08.94 Andrew Jervis W RSC 1 Sheffield
19.11.94 Chris Richards W RSC 3 Cardiff
04.02.95 Bruno Westenberghs W RSC 1 Cardiff
04.03.95 Marvin O'Brien W RSC 6 Livingston
06.05.95 Steve Goodwin W CO 1 Shepton
          Mallet
10.06.95 Martin Jolley W CO 1 Manchester
22.07.95 John Duckworth W PTS 8 Millwall
15.09.95 Trevor Ambrose W CO 5 Mansfield
10.11.95 Danny Juma W PTS 8 Derby
26.01.96 Stinger Mason W RSC 2 Brighton
16.03.96 Andrew Flute W RSC 7 Glasgow
26.04.96 Hunter Clay W RSC 1 Cardiff
08.06.96 Mark Dawson W RSC 5 Newcastle
31.08.96 Don Pendleton W RTD 4 Dublin
12.10.96 Vincenzo Nardiello W CO 7 Milan, Italy
          (WBC S. Middleweight Title Challenge)
08.02.97 Giovanni Pretorius W RSC 7 Millwall
          (WBC S. Middleweight Title Defence)
03.05.97 Henry Wharton W PTS 12 Manchester
          (WBC S. Middleweight Title Defence)
11.09.97 Hassine Cherifi W PTS 12 Widnes
          (WBC S. Middleweight Title Defence)
19.12.97 Thulani Malinga L PTS 12 Millwall
          (WBC S. Middleweight Title Defence)

18.04.98 Graham Townsend W RSC 6
          Manchester
13.02.99 Joe Calzaghe L PTS 12 Newcastle
          *(WBO S. Middleweight Title
          Challenge)*
24.06.00 Silvio Branco L PTS 12 Glasgow
          *(WBU S. Middleweight Title
          Challenge)*
08.12.00 Mike Gormley W RSC 1 Crystal
          Palace
          (Vacant WBF S. Middleweight Title)
19.05.01 Roman Babaev W RSC 3 Wembley
          (WBF S. Middleweight Title Defence)
14.07.01 Soon Botes W RSC 4 Liverpool
          (WBF S.Middleweight TitleDefence)
20.10.01 Jorge Sclarandi W CO 3 Glasgow
          (WBF S. Middleweight Title Defence)
19.12.01 Julio Cesar Chavez W PTS 12
          Coventry
          (WBF S. Middleweight Title Defence)
Career: 35 contests, won 31, drew 1, lost 3.

Robin Reid   Harry Goodwin

Darren Rhodes

Leeds. *Born* Leeds, 16 September, 1975
Middleweight. Ht. 5'11"
Manager Self

18.07.98 Andy Kemp W RSC 1 Sheffield
10.10.98 Perry Ayres W CO 2 Bethnal Green
27.02.99 Gareth Lovell W PTS 4 Oldham
01.05.99 Carlton Williams W RSC 4 Crystal
          Palace
29.05.99 Sean Pritchard DREW 4 Halifax
09.10.99 Leigh Wicks W PTS 4 Manchester
11.12.99 Leigh Wicks W PTS 4 Liverpool
25.03.00 Leigh Wicks W PTS 4 Liverpool
29.05.00 Dean Ashton W RSC 3 Manchester
08.07.00 Jason Collins DREW 4 Widnes
04.09.00 Jason Collins L PTS 4 Manchester
11.12.00 Paul Wesley W PTS 4 Widnes
17.03.01 Andrew Facey W PTS 4 Manchester
07.07.01 Wayne Elcock L PTS 4 Manchester
24.11.01 Simeon Cover W RSC 5 Wakefield
02.03.02 Andrew Facey L RSC 6 Wakefield
          *(Vacant Central Area Middleweight
          Title)*
21.05.02 Hussain Osman L PTS 10 Custom
          House
15.06.02 Harry Butler W PTS 4 Leeds
Career: 18 contests, won 12, drew 2, lost 4.

Ryan Rhodes

Sheffield. *Born* Sheffield, 20 November,
1976
Former Undefeated WBO Inter-Continental
Middleweight Champion. Former
Undefeated British & IBF Inter-Continental
L. Middleweight Champion. Ht. 5'8½"
Manager B. Ingle/F. Warren

04.02.95 Lee Crocker W RSC 2 Cardiff
04.03.95 Shamus Casey W CO 1 Livingston
06.05.95 Chris Richards W PTS 6 Shepton
          Mallet
15.09.95 John Rice W RSC 2 Mansfield
10.11.95 Mark Dawson W PTS 6 Derby
20.01.96 John Duckworth W RSC 2 Mansfield
26.01.96 Martin Jolley W CO 3 Brighton
11.05.96 Martin Jolley W RSC 2 Bethnal Green
25.06.96 Roy Chipperfield W RSC 1 Mansfield
14.09.96 Del Bryan W PTS 6 Sheffield
14.12.96 Paul Jones W RSC 8 Sheffield
          (Vacant British L. Middleweight Title)
25.02.97 Peter Waudby W CO 1 Sheffield
          (British L. Middleweight Title Defence)
14.03.97 Del Bryan W RSC 7 Reading
          (British L. Middleweight Title Defence)
12.04.97 Lindon Scarlett W RSC 1 Sheffield
          *(Vacant IBF Inter-Continental
          L. Middleweight Title)*
02.08.97 Ed Griffin W RSC 2 Barnsley
          *(IBF Inter-Continental L. Middleweight
          Title Defence. Vacant WBO
          L. Middleweight Title)*
11.10.97 Yuri Epifantsev W RSC 2 Sheffield
          (Final Elim. WBO Middleweight Title)
13.12.97 Otis Grant L PTS 12 Sheffield
          (Vacant WBO Middleweight Title)
18.07.98 Lorant Szabo W RSC 8 Sheffield
          *(WBO Inter-Continental Middleweight
          Title Challenge)*
28.11.98 Fidel Avendano W RSC 1 Sheffield
          *(WBO Inter-Continental Middleweight
          Title Defence)*
27.03.99 Peter Mason W RSC 1 Derby
17.07.99 Jason Matthews L CO 2 Doncaster
          (Vacant WBO Middleweight Title)
15.01.00 Eddie Haley W RSC 5 Doncaster
16.05.00 Ojay Abrahams W PTS 6 Warrington
21.10.00 Michael Alexander W PTS 6 Wembley
16.12.00 Howard Clarke W PTS 6 Sheffield
21.07.01 Youri Tsarenko W PTS 6 Sheffield
27.10.01 Jason Collins W PTS 4 Manchester
16.03.02 Lee Blundell L RSC 3 Bethnal Green
          *(Vacant WBF Inter-Continental
          Middleweight Title)*
Career: 28 contests, won 25, lost 3.

Mal Rice

Flint. *Born* Mancot, 19 July, 1975
Heavyweight. Ht. 6'2"
Manager J. Davies

26.11.97 Gary Cavey W CO 2 Stoke
29.01.98 Lennox Williams W PTS 6 Pentre
          Halkyn
30.03.98 Bruno Foster L PTS 6 Bradford
30.04.98 Lennox Williams W PTS 6 Pentre
          Halkyn
21.06.98 Shane Woollas L PTS 6 Liverpool
18.02.00 Gary Williams L PTS 6 Pentre Halkyn
13.03.00 Patrick Halberg W RSC 2 Bethnal
          Green
05.05.00 Gary Williams L PTS 4 Pentre Halkyn

27.05.00	Mark Potter L CO 1 Southwark
26.03.01	John McDermott L RSC 2 Wembley
28.07.01	Matt Legg L PTS 4 Wembley
13.09.01	Petr Horacek W RSC 1 Sheffield
04.10.01	Pele Reid L PTS 4 Finsbury
16.12.01	Greg Wedlake L RSC 3 Bristol
18.05.02	Danny Watts L RTD 3 Millwall

Career: 15 contests, won 5, lost 10.

Mark Richards

Wednesbury. *Born* Wednesbury, 30 March, 1972
Middleweight. Ht. 5'9"
Manager Self

01.10.96	Craig Hartwell W PTS 6 Birmingham
12.11.96	Marc Smith W PTS 6 Dudley
22.03.97	Mark Haslam DREW 4 Wythenshawe
19.04.97	Mark McGowan L PTS 6 Plymouth
04.06.98	David Kirk W PTS 6 Dudley
03.10.98	Paul Swindles W CO 1 West Bromwich
11.12.98	Joel Ani W DIS 3 Cheshunt
16.02.99	Dave Fallon W PTS 6 Brentford
15.09.01	Jason Williams L PTS 6 Swansea
27.10.01	Thomas McDonagh DREW 4 Manchester
16.11.01	Harry Butler W PTS 6 West Bromwich
13.04.02	Michael Jones L RSC 1 Liverpool

Career: 12 contests, won 7, drew 2, lost 3.

Paul Richardson

Blackpool. *Born* Oxford, 17 October, 1972
Heavyweight. Ht. 5'10¹/₂"
Manager L. Veitch

09.06.00	Jason Brewster W PTS 6 Blackpool
30.11.00	Dave Faulkner W PTS 6 Blackpool
22.01.01	Paul Fiske W PTS 6 Glasgow
08.03.01	Dave Faulkner W RSC 2 Blackpool
01.04.01	Jason Brewster W RSC 4 Wolverhampton
15.10.01	Huggy Osman L PTS 6 Bradford
16.11.01	Huggy Osman W PTS 6 Preston

Career: 7 contests, won 6, lost 1.

Wayne Rigby

Manchester. *Born* Manchester, 19 July, 1973
WBF L. Welterweight Champion. Former Undefeated IBO Inter-Continental Lightweight Champion. Former British Lightweight Champion. Former Undefeated Central Area Lightweight Champion.
Ht. 5'6"
Manager Self

27.02.92	Lee Fox L PTS 6 Liverpool
08.06.92	Leo Turner W PTS 6 Bradford
02.07.92	Leo Turner W CO 5 Middleton
05.10.92	Colin Innes W PTS 6 Manchester
01.12.92	John T. Kelly L PTS 6 Hartlepool
02.06.94	Kid McAuley W PTS 6 Middleton
13.06.94	Chris Clarkson W PTS 6 Liverpool
22.09.94	Mark Hargreaves W PTS 6 Bury
06.03.95	Kelton McKenzie L PTS 8 Leicester
18.05.95	John T. Kelly W PTS 6 Middleton
05.06.95	Hugh Collins W RSC 4 Glasgow
17.01.96	Kid McAuley W PTS 6 Solihull
24.03.96	Steve Tuckett W PTS 6 Shaw
27.09.96	Jimmy Phelan W PTS 10 Hull
	(Central Area Lightweight Title Challenge)

07.03.97	Alan Bosworth W RSC 5 Northampton
10.01.98	Tanveer Ahmed W PTS 12 Bethnal Green
	(Vacant British Lightweight Title)
11.04.98	Matt Brown W RTD 8 Southwark
	(British Lightweight Title Defence)
17.10.98	Bobby Vanzie L RSC 10 Manchester
	(British Lightweight Title Defence)
31.07.99	Mark McGowan W RSC 4 Carlisle
11.09.99	Alan Temple L PTS 8 Sheffield
04.12.99	Mark Haslam W CO 3 Peterborough
27.05.00	Dariusz Snarski W RSC 8 Mayfair
	(Vacant IBO Inter-Continental Lightweight Title)
01.07.00	Michael Ayers L RSC 10 Manchester
	(IBO Lightweight Title Challenge)
03.03.01	Michael Ayers L PTS 12 Wembley
	(IBO Lightweight Title Challenge)
14.07.01	Keith Jones W CO 3 Wembley
26.11.01	Antonio Ramirez W PTS 12 Manchester
	(Vacant WBF L.Welterweight Title)
09.03.02	Sedat Puskulla W CO 1 Manchester
	(Vacant WBF L. Welterweight Title)
18.05.02	Colin Dunne L RTD 10 Millwall
	(WBU Lightweight Title Challenge. Vacant WBF Lightweight Title)

Career: 28 contests, won 20, lost 8.

Stuart Rimmer

St Helens. *Born* St Helens, 22 April, 1971
L. Welterweight. Ht. 5'6"
Manager Self

13.02.90	Dave Croft W PTS 6 Wolverhampton
07.03.90	Mark Antony L RSC 1 Doncaster

Wayne Rigby   Les Clark

23.04.90 Dave Croft W CO 2 Birmingham
01.05.90 Neil Foran L RSC 2 Oldham
04.06.90 Frankie Foster L PTS 6 Glasgow
27.06.90 Bernard McComiskey L PTS 6 Kensington
12.09.90 Steve Griffith W RSC 2 Bethnal Green
27.09.90 Andrew Morgan W PTS 6 Birmingham
09.10.90 Jim Lawler W CO 2 Wolverhampton
29.10.90 Tony Feliciello L RSC 5 Birmingham
27.11.90 Alan Peacock L RSC 4 Glasgow
12.02.91 Andrew Morgan L PTS 8 Wolverhampton
24.04.91 Steve Winstanley L PTS 6 Preston
04.06.91 Michael Ayers L CO 1 Bethnal Green
10.09.91 Shaun Cooper L RSC 2 Wolverhampton
27.03.96 Wayne Pardoe L RSC 3 Stoke
02.10.96 Vic Broomhead W CO 5 Stoke
29.11.96 Rocky Ferrari W RSC 5 Glasgow
04.12.96 David Kirk L PTS 6 Stoke
23.10.97 Bobby Vanzie L RTD 8 Mayfair
(Vacant Central Area Lightweight Title)
28.11.97 Gerard Murphy L PTS 6 Hull
06.05.98 Brian Coleman W PTS 6 Blackpool
05.06.98 Terry Roberts L PTS 4 Southend
21.07.98 Jamie McKeever L PTS 4 Widnes
01.12.98 Andy Green L RTD 5 Yarm
15.05.99 Gary Ryder L RSC 1 Blackpool
07.10.99 Gary Reid L RSC 2 Mere
18.02.00 Young Muttley L RSC 1 West Bromwich
27.05.00 David Walker L RSC 2 Southwark
30.09.00 Leo O'Reilly L RSC 2 Peterborough
04.10.01 Ajose Olusegun L RTD 2 Finsbury
06.12.01 Drea Dread W PTS 6 Stoke
15.03.02 Oscar Hall L RSC 4 Spennymoor
Career: 33 contests, won 9, lost 24.

Daniel Ring

Peterborough. *Born* Peterborough, 1 November, 1978
Bantamweight. Ht. 5'8"
Manager Self

26.11.98 Paddy Folan DREW 6 Bradford
15.12.98 Waj Khan L PTS 6 Sheffield
17.03.99 Frankie DeMilo L RSC 2 Kensington
17.05.99 Chris Emanuele DREW 6 Cleethorpes
15.08.99 Ross Cassidy L PTS 6 Derby
03.12.99 Chris Edwards W PTS 4 Peterborough
05.03.00 David Jeffrey L PTS 6 Peterborough
22.07.00 Jamie Yelland L PTS 4 Watford
21.10.00 Stephen Oates L RSC 1 Wembley
01.12.00 Danny Lawson W PTS 4 Peterborough
02.02.01 Gary Evans W RSC 4 Portsmouth
11.06.01 Jim Betts L PTS 6 Nottingham
07.07.01 Anthony Hughes L RSC 1 Manchester
Career: 13 contests, won 3, drew 2, lost 8.

Steve Roberts

West Ham. *Born* Newham, 3 December, 1972
WBF L. Middleweight Champion. Former Undefeated WBF S. Middleweight Champion. Former Undefeated Southern Area L. Middleweight Champion. Ht. 5'11"
Manager B. Hearn

16.03.95 Julian Eavis W PTS 6 Basildon
23.05.95 Andy Peach W RSC 3 Potters Bar
13.06.95 Robbie Dunn W RSC 3 Basildon
20.09.95 Jason Hart W RSC 5 Potters Bar

30.09.95 Dick Hanns-Kat W CO 1 Basildon
25.11.95 Ernie Loveridge W PTS 4 Dagenham
23.01.96 Andrew Jervis W PTS 6 Bethnal Green
20.04.96 Peter Vosper W PTS 6 Brentwood
04.05.96 George Richards W PTS 6 Dagenham
27.09.96 Rob Stevenson W PTS 6 Stevenage
27.11.96 Lindon Scarlett W PTS 6 Bethnal Green
08.03.97 Adan Lugo W CO 4 Brentwood
08.04.97 Gilbert Jackson W PTS 10 Bethnal Green
(Vacant Southern Area L. Middleweight Title)
30.08.97 Peter Mitchell W PTS 6 Cheshunt
08.10.97 Darren Covill W PTS 6 Poplar
05.06.98 Danny Quacoe W RTD 4 Southend
20.12.99 Mike Whittaker W PTS 6 Bethnal Green
05.02.00 Danny Thornton W PTS 6 Bethnal Green
01.04.00 Chris Crook W RSC 3 Bethnal Green
16.06.00 Mike Algoet W PTS 12 Bloomsbury

(Vacant WBF S. Middleweight Title)
19.08.00 Scott Dixon W RSC 9 Brentwood
(Vacant WBF L.Middleweight Title)
02.12.00 Mohammed Hissani W RSC 7 Bethnal Green
(WBF L. Middleweight Title Defence)
03.03.01 Sergio Acuna W RSC 1 Wembley
(WBF L. Middleweight Title Defence)
07.04.01 Keith Mullings W RSC 2 Wembley
(WBF L. Middleweight Title Defence)
26.05.01 William Gare W RSC 9 Bethnal Green
(WBF L. Middleweight Title Defence)
15.09.01 Andrzej Butowicz W RTD 7 Nottingham
(WBF L. Middleweight Title)
10.11.01 Ron Weaver W PTS 12 Wembley
(WBF L. Middleweight Title Defence)
28.01.02 Troy Lowry W RSC 4 Barnsley
(WBF L. Middleweight Title Defence)
23.03.02 Kirino Garcia W PTS 12 Southwark
(WBF L. Middleweight Title Defence)
Career: 29 contests, won 29.

Steve Roberts   Les Clark

Dale Robinson

Huddersfield. *Born* Huddersfield, 9 April, 1980
Central Area Flyweight Champion. Ht. 5'4"
Manager T. Gilmour/C. Aston

25.09.00	John Barnes W PTS 4 Barnsley	
28.10.00	Delroy Spencer W RSC 4 Coventry	
02.12.00	Colin Moffett W PTS 4 Bethnal Green	
26.02.01	Christophe Rodrigues W PTS 6 Nottingham	
07.04.01	Andrei Kostin W PTS 6 Wembley	
08.05.01	Terry Gaskin W RTD 3 Barnsley	
	(Central Area Flyweight Title Challenge)	
27.04.02	Jason Thomas W RSC 4 Huddersfield	
18.05.02	Sergei Tasimov W RSC 3 Millwall	
15.06.02	Kakhar Sabitov W PTS 6 Leeds	

Career: 9 contests, won 9.

Steve Robinson

Cardiff. *Born* Cardiff, 13 December, 1968
Former European & WBO Inter-Continental Featherweight Champion.
Former WBO Featherweight Champion.
Former Undefeated WBA Penta-Continental & Welsh Featherweight Champion. Ht. 5'8"
Manager B. Hearn

01.03.89	Alan Roberts W PTS 6 Cardiff
13.03.89	Terry Smith W RTD 4 Piccadilly
06.04.89	Nicky Lucas L PTS 8 Cardiff
04.05.89	John Devine W PTS 6 Mayfair
19.08.89	Marcel Herbert L PTS 6 Cardiff
13.11.89	Shane Silvester W RSC 2 Brierley Hill
10.07.90	Mark Bates L PTS 6 Canvey Island
12.09.90	Tim Driscoll L PTS 8 Bethnal Green
26.09.90	Russell Davison W PTS 8 Manchester
03.10.90	Drew Docherty L PTS 8 Solihull
22.10.90	Alan McKay L PTS 8 Mayfair
19.11.90	Neil Haddock W RSC 9 Cardiff
19.12.90	Brian Roche DREW 6 Preston
24.04.91	Russell Davison W RTD 6 Preston
28.05.91	Colin Lynch W RSC 6 Cardiff
18.07.91	Peter Harris W PTS 10 Cardiff
	(Welsh Featherweight Title Challenge)
31.01.92	Henry Armstrong L PTS 6 Manchester
11.05.92	Neil Haddock L PTS 10 Llanelli
	(Vacant Welsh S. Featherweight Title)
07.10.92	Edward Lloyd W RTD 8 Barry
30.10.92	Stephane Haccoun W PTS 8 Istres, France
01.12.92	Dennis Oakes W RTD 2 Liverpool
19.01.93	Paul Harvey W PTS 12 Cardiff
	(Vacant WBA Penta-Continental Featherweight Title)
13.02.93	Medhi Labdouni L PTS 8 Paris, France
17.04.93	John Davison W PTS 12 Washington
	(Vacant WBO Featherweight Title)
10.07.93	Sean Murphy W CO 9 Cardiff
	(WBO Featherweight Title Defence)
23.10.93	Colin McMillan W PTS 12 Cardiff
	(WBO Featherweight Title Defence)
12.03.94	Paul Hodkinson W CO 12 Cardiff
	(WBO Featherweight Title Defence)
04.06.94	Freddy Cruz W PTS 12 Cardiff
	(WBO Featherweight Title Defence)
01.10.94	Duke McKenzie W CO 9 Cardiff
	(WBO Featherweight Title Defence)
04.02.95	Domingo Damigella W PTS 12 Cardiff
	(WBO Featherweight Title Defence)
07.07.95	Pedro Ferradas W RSC 9 Cardiff
	(WBO Featherweight Title Defence)

30.09.95	Prince Naseem Hamed L RSC 8 Cardiff
	(WBO Featherweight Title Defence)
18.09.96	Kelton McKenzie W PTS 8 Tylorstown
03.02.97	Billy Hardy L PTS 12 Sunderland
	(European Featherweight Title Challenge)
08.03.97	Tomas Serrano W CO 1 Brentwood
	(Vacant WBO Inter-Continental Featherweight Title)
08.05.97	Julio Cesar Sanchez W CO 7 Mansfield
	(WBO Inter-Continental Featherweight Title Defence)
27.09.97	Andrew Matabola W CO 5 Belfast
	(WBO Inter-Continental Featherweight Title Defence)
18.11.97	Aldrich Johnson W RSC 7 Mansfield
	(WBO Inter-Continental Featherweight Title Defence)
25.04.98	Jean Dibateza W PTS 8 Cardiff
03.10.98	Welcome Ncita DREW 12 East London, South Africa
	(WBO Inter-Continental Featherweight Title Defence)
23.02.99	Santiago Rojas W PTS 8 Cardiff
30.04.99	Manuel Calvo W PTS 12 Leganes, Spain
	(Vacant European Featherweight Title)
12.07.99	Martin Krastev W RSC 1 Coventry
02.10.99	Claude Chinon W RSC 10 Cardiff
	(European Featherweight Title Defence)
04.12.99	Jonjo Irwin W PTS 12 Manchester
	(European Featherweight Title Defence)
11.03.00	Juan Carlos Ramirez L RSC 11 Kensington
	(WBO Inter-Continental Featherweight Title Defence)
23.06.00	Istvan Kovacs L PTS 12 Budapest, Hungary
	(European Featherweight Title Defence. WBC International Featherweight Title Challenge)
03.11.00	Cassius Baloyi L PTS 12 Ebbw Vale
	(WBU Featherweight Title Challenge)
25.05.01	Manuel Calvo L PTS 12 Leganes, Spain
	(Vacant European Featherweight Title)
17.11.01	Scott Harrison L RSC 3 Glasgow
	(British & Commonwealth Featherweight Title Challenges)
27.04.02	Steve Conway L PTS 8 Huddersfield

Career: 51 contests, won 32, drew 2, lost 17.

George Robshaw

Leeds. *Born* Hull, 14 March, 1976
S. Middleweight. Ht. 6'0"
Manager F. Maloney

07.10.00	William Webster W PTS 4 Doncaster
16.12.01	Dean Ashton W RTD 2 Southwark

Career: 2 contests, won 2.

Reggie Robshaw

Leeds. *Born* Wakefield, 10 June, 1977
L. Middleweight. Ht. 5'10"
Manager Self

01.04.01	Jason McElligott W PTS 4 Southwark
24.03.02	Pedro Thompson W PTS 6 Streatham

Career: 2 contests, won 2.

Derek Roche

Leeds. *Born* Bedford, 19 July 1972
Welterweight. Former British Welterweight Champion. Former Undefeated Central Area Welterweight Champion. Ht. 5'9"
Manager T. Gilmour

26.09.94	Michael Alexander W RSC 6 Bradford
05.12.94	Shamus Casey W PTS 6 Bradford
30.01.95	Carl Smith W RSC 3 Bradford
23.02.95	Charlie Paine W CO 1 Hull
25.03.95	Rob Stevenson W PTS 6 Rothwell
12.06.95	Paul King W PTS 6 Bradford
25.09.95	Hughie Davey W PTS 6 Bradford
11.11.95	Rick North W RSC 2 Halifax
11.12.95	Kevin McKenzie W RSC 3 Bradford
13.01.96	Shamus Casey W PTS 6 Halifax
07.03.96	Wayne Shepherd W RSC 3 Bradford
23.09.96	Trevor Meikle W PTS 10 Bradford
	(Central Area Welterweight Title Challenge)
23.10.96	Paul Miles W RSC 2 Halifax
09.12.96	Gary Beardsley W RSC 2 Bradford
17.02.97	Michael Alexander W DIS 4 Bradford
09.06.97	Chris Saunders W RSC 4 Bradford
	(Central Area Welterweight Title Defence. Elim. British Welterweight Title)
13.11.97	Hughie Davey W RSC 3 Bradford
23.02.98	Darren McInulty W PTS 6 Glasgow
06.11.98	Del Bryan W RSC 10 Mayfair
	(Vacant IBO Inter-Continental L. Middleweight Title)
10.04.99	Charlie Kane W RSC 7 Manchester
	(Vacant British Welterweight Title)
31.07.99	Georgie Smith W PTS 12 Carlisle
	(British Welterweight Title Defence)
22.10.99	Scott Dixon W PTS 12 Coventry
	(British Welterweight Title Defence)
27.03.00	Harry Dhami L PTS 12 Barnsley
	(British Welterweight Title Defence)
25.09.00	Brian Coleman W PTS 6 Barnsley
11.11.00	Adrian Stone L RSC 2 Belfast
	(IBO L.Middleweight Title Challenge)
08.05.01	Paul Denton W PTS 6 Barnsley
07.07.01	Zoltan Szili W RSC 4 Amsterdam, Holland
08.10.01	Adam Zadworny W RSC 4 Barnsley
26.01.02	Jan Bergman L PTS 12 Bethnal Green
	(WBU Welterweight Title Challenge)
15.06.02	Neil Sinclair L CO 1 Leeds
	(British Welterweight Title Challenge)

Career: 30 contests, won 26, lost 4.

Jim Rock

Dublin. *Born* Dublin, 12 March, 1972
L. Middleweight. All-Ireland S. Middleweight & L. Middleweight Champion. Former Undefeated WAA Inter-Continental S. Middleweight Champion. WBF European L. Middleweight Champion. Ht. 5'11"
Manager M. O'Callaghan

25.11.95	Craig Lynch W PTS 4 Dublin
09.03.96	Peter Mitchell W PTS 6 Millstreet
03.09.96	Rob Stevenson W PTS 6 Belfast
05.11.96	Danny Quacoe W RSC 4 Belfast
28.01.97	Roy Chipperfield W RTD 2 Belfast
12.04.97	George Richards W PTS 6 Sheffield
13.09.97	Robert Njie W CO 3 Millwall
18.04.98	Ensley Bingham L RSC 7 Manchester
19.09.98	Michael Monaghan W PTS 12 Dublin
	(Vacant WAA Inter-Continental S. Middleweight Title)

14.12.98 Perry Ayres W RTD 3 Cleethorpes
22.01.99 Jimmy Vincent W PTS 10 Dublin
20.02.99 Pedro Carragher W RSC 3 Thornaby
*(Vacant WBF European
L. Middleweight Title)*
17.04.99 Michael Alexander W RSC 1 Dublin
*(Vacant All-Ireland S. Middleweight
Title)*
19.06.99 Kevin Thompson W PTS 4 Dublin
15.04.00 Allan Gray W PTS 10 Bethnal Green
*(Vacant All-Ireland L. Middleweight
Title)*
12.06.00 Alan Gilbert W PTS 6 Belfast
20.10.00 Brooke Welby W RSC 3 Belfast
11.11.00 David Baptiste W PTS 4 Belfast
08.12.00 Tommy Attardo W PTS 8 Worcester,
Mass, USA
24.03.01 Hollister Elliott W CO 6 Worcester,
Mass, USA
20.04.01 Jason Collins W PTS 6 Dublin
01.12.01 Ian Cooper L PTS 6 Bethnal Green
24.04.02 Harry Butler W PTS 6 Dublin
Career: 23 contests, won 21, lost 2.

Brendan Rollinson

Hull. *Born* Hull, 8 January, 1974
L. Middleweight. Ht. 6'0"
Manager D. Smith

25.05.00 Pedro Thompson W RSC 2 Hull
25.07.00 Colin Vidler L PTS 4 Southwark
16.11.00 Matthew Ashmole W PTS 6 Hull
23.06.01 Nick Lyon W RSC 4 Peterborough
25.04.02 Darren Covill W PTS 4 Hull
Career: 5 contests, won 4, lost 1.

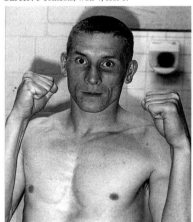

Brendan Rollinson   Les Clark

James Rooney

Hartlepool. *Born* Hartlepool, 30 April, 1978
S. Featherweight. Ht. 5'10"
Manager M. Marsden

26.02.00 Marc Smith W PTS 4 Carlisle
27.03.00 Pete Buckley W PTS 4 Barnsley
13.05.00 Sebastian Hart W PTS 6 Barnsley
23.07.00 Duncan Armstrong W RSC 3
Hartlepool
01.10.00 Nigel Senior W PTS 6 Hartlepool
02.12.00 Gary Flear W PTS 4 Bethnal Green
11.02.01 Dave Hinds W PTS 6 Hartlepool
20.03.01 Lee Williamson W PTS 4 Glasgow

06.05.01 Lee Williamson W PTS 6 Hartlepool
04.06.01 Steve Hanley W PTS 4 Hartlepool
08.10.01 Dave Cotterill W RSC 4 Barnsley
01.12.01 Dariusz Snarski W PTS 6 Bethnal Green
09.03.02 Jamie McKeever L PTS 6 Manchester
05.05.02 Jimmy Beech L RSC 5 Hartlepool
Career: 14 contests, won 12, lost 2.

(James) Jimbo Rooney

Belfast. *Born* Belfast, 18 July, 1978
Flyweight. Ht. 5'3¹/₂"
Manager B. Hearn

18.02.02 Terry Gaskin W RSC 3 Glasgow
11.05.02 Darren Cleary L PTS 4 Dagenham
Career: 2 contests, won 1, lost 1.

Jason Rowland

West Ham. *Born* London, 6 August, 1970
Former Undefeated WBU L. Welterweight
Champion. Former Undefeated British
L. Welterweight Champion. Ht. 5'9¾"
Manager F. Warren

19.09.89 Terry Smith W RSC 1 Millwall
15.11.89 Mike Morrison W PTS 6 Reading
14.02.90 Eamonn Payne W PTS 6 Millwall
17.04.90 Dave Jenkins W CO 1 Millwall
22.05.90 Mike Morrison W PTS 6 St Albans
12.02.91 Vaughan Carnegie W PTS 6 Basildon
07.03.91 Vaughan Carnegie W CO 2 Basildon
11.12.91 Brian Cullen W RSC 4 Basildon
30.04.92 Steve Pollard W RSC 2 Kensington
17.12.92 Jimmy Vincent W PTS 6 Wembley
10.02.93 Seth Jones W RSC 2 Lewisham
18.03.93 John Smith W PTS 6 Lewisham
04.03.94 Dewi Roberts W RSC 1 Bethnal Green
26.04.94 Ray Hood W CO 1 Bethnal Green
12.09.94 Steve Burton W RSC 1 Mayfair
11.10.94 Phil Found W RSC 4 Bethnal Green
09.11.94 Floyd Churchill W RSC 2 Millwall
09.12.94 Richard Swallow W RSC 2 Bethnal
Green
03.03.95 Nigel Bradley W RSC 3 Bethnal Green
29.11.95 Bernard Paul L CO 1 Bethnal Green
*(Southern Area L. Welterweight Title
Challenge. Elim. British
L. Welterweight Title)*
27.03.97 Kevin McKillan W PTS 8 Norwich
13.09.97 Brian Coleman W PTS 8 Millwall
16.05.98 Mark Winters W PTS 12 Bethnal Green
*(British L. Welterweight Title
Challenge)*
01.05.99 Alan Temple W PTS 6 Crystal Palace
15.11.99 Jonathan Thaxton W RSC 5 Bethnal
Green
(British L. Welterweight Title Defence)
21.10.00 Victor Baranov W PTS 12 Wembley
(Vacant WBU L.Welterweight Title)
07.07.01 Richard Hatton L CO 4 Manchester
(WBU L.Welterweight Title Challenge)
Career: 27 contests, won 25, lost 2.

Jason Rushton

Doncaster. *Born* Doncaster, 15 February,
1983
Welterweight. Ht. 5'10"
Manager J. Rushton/F. Warren

27.10.01 Ram Singh W PTS 6 Manchester
09.02.02 Brian Gifford W RSC 1 Manchester
01.06.02 Tony Smith W PTS 4 Manchester
Career: 3 contests, won 3.

Jason Rushton   Les Clark

Roy Rutherford

Coventry. *Born* Coventry, 4 August, 1973
Featherweight. Ht. 5'6"
Manager Self

24.02.98 David Kirk W PTS 6 Edgbaston
26.03.98 Vic Broomhead W PTS 6 Solihull
23.04.98 Dave Hinds W RSC 5 Edgbaston
21.05.98 Carl Allen W PTS 6 Solihull
24.09.98 Dean Murdoch W RSC 3 Edgbaston
14.12.98 Keith Jones W PTS 6 Birmingham
08.03.99 Marc Smith W PTS 6 Birmingham
19.06.99 Marc Smith W RTD 2 Dublin
22.10.99 Woody Greenaway W PTS 4 Coventry
14.12.99 Keith Jones W PTS 4 Coventry
22.01.00 Chris Williams W PTS 8 Birmingham
22.05.00 Alexander Tiranov W PTS 6 Coventry
28.10.00 Richard Evatt L PTS 10 Coventry
07.04.01 Nikolai Eremeev DREW 4 Wembley
26.05.01 Marc Callaghan W RSC 3 Bethnal
Green
10.12.01 Frederic Bonifai W RSC 4 Liverpool
Career: 16 contests, won 14, drew 1, lost 1.

John-Paul Ryan

Northampton. *Born* Enfield, 1 April, 1971
Featherweight. Ht. 5'5"
Manager J. Cox

07.12.00 Paddy Folan W PTS 6 Stoke
08.03.01 Neil Read L PTS 6 Stoke
28.05.02 Paddy Folan W PTS 6 Leeds
25.06.02 Sean Hughes L PTS 6 Rugby
Career: 4 contests, won 2, lost 2.

Gary Ryder

Liverpool. *Born* Fazackerley, 17 December,
1971
L. Welterweight. Ht. 5'7"
Manager T. Gilmour

03.02.96 Andy Davidson W RSC 1 Liverpool
05.03.99 Trevor Tacy W PTS 4 Liverpool
15.05.99 Stuart Rimmer W RSC 1 Blackpool
09.03.00 Benny Jones W PTS 4 Liverpool
19.02.01 Mohamed Helel W RSC 1 Glasgow
04.06.01 Kevin Bennett W RSC 6 Hartlepool
25.09.01 Glenn McClarnon W PTS 8 Liverpool
09.03.02 David Smales W RSC 1 Manchester
Career: 8 contests, won 8.

Paul Samuels

Newport. *Born* Newport, 23 March, 1973
Former Undefeated IBF Inter-Continental
& Welsh L. Middleweight Champion.
Ht. 6'0"
Manager Self

11.11.95	Wayne Windle W RSC 2 Halifax
13.02.96	Jon Harrison W CO 1 Cardiff
05.03.96	Tom Welsh W RSC 3 Bethnal Green
13.03.96	Brian Coleman W PTS 6 Wembley
15.05.96	Gary Hiscox W RSC 3 Cardiff
12.11.96	Mark Ramsey W RSC 4 Dudley
21.06.97	Howard Clarke W PTS 8 Cariff
15.11.97	Justin Simmons W CO 1 Bristol
24.01.98	Prince Kasi Kaihau W CO 3 Cardiff
25.04.98	Del Bryan W PTS 8 Cardiff
05.09.98	Spencer McCracken W PTS 8 Telford
05.12.98	Craig Winter W CO 2 Bristol
	(Vacant Welsh L. Middleweight Title)
27.03.99	Pedro Carragher W RSC 2 Derby
05.06.99	Eric Holland W RSC 9 Cardiff
	(Vacant IBF Inter-Continental
	L. Middleweight Title)
23.10.99	Ojay Abrahams W PTS 8 Telford
19.02.00	Wayne Alexander L RSC 3 Dagenham
	(Vacant British L. Middleweight Title)
23.01.01	Rob Dellapenna DREW 4 Crawley
27.01.02	Howard Clarke W PTS 6 Streatham
29.06.02	Richard Williams T DRAW 3
	Brentwood
	(IBO L. Middleweight Title Challenge)

Career: 19 contests, won 16, drew 2, lost 1.

Inderpaul Sandhu

Eastwood. *Born* Derby, 16 December, 1989
Lightweight. Ht. 5'11"
Manager M. Shinfield

26.02.01	Duncan Armstrong W PTS 4
	Nottingham
11.06.01	Joel Viney W PTS 4 Nottingham
15.09.01	Nigel Senior W PTS 4 Nottingham

Career: 3 contests, won 3.

Chris Saunders

Barnsley. *Born* Barnsley, 15 August, 1969
Former British Welterweight Champion.
Ht. 5'8"
Manager D. Ingle

22.02.90	Malcolm Melvin W PTS 4 Hull
10.04.90	Mike Morrison W PTS 6 Doncaster
20.05.90	Justin Graham W RSC 3 Sheffield
29.11.90	Ross Hale L PTS 6 Bayswater
05.03.91	Rocky Ferrari L PTS 4 Glasgow
19.03.91	Richard Woolgar W RSC 3 Leicester
26.03.91	Felix Kelly L PTS 6 Bethnal Green
17.04.91	Billy Schwer L RSC 1 Kensington
16.05.91	Richard Burton L PTS 6 Liverpool
06.06.91	Mark Tibbs W RSC 6 Barking
30.06.91	Billy Schwer L RSC 3 Southwark
01.08.91	James Jiora W PTS 6 Dewsbury
03.10.91	Gary Flear L PTS 6 Burton
24.10.91	Ron Shinkwin W PTS 6 Dunstable
21.11.91	J. P. Matthews L RSC 4 Burton

30.01.92	John O. Johnson L PTS 6 Southampton
11.02.92	Eddie King W RSC 4 Wolverhampton
27.02.92	Richard Burton L PTS 10 Liverpool
	(Vacant Central Area L. Welterweight
	Title)
09.09.92	John O. Johnson DREW 6 Stoke
01.10.92	Mark McCreath L RSC 4 Telford
01.12.92	Shea Neary L PTS 6 Liverpool
22.02.93	Cham Joof L PTS 4 Eltham
16.03.93	Mark Elliot L PTS 6 Wolverhampton
26.04.93	Dean Hollington W RSC 5 Lewisham
23.10.93	Michael Smyth L PTS 6 Cardiff
02.12.93	Rob Stewart L PTS 4 Sheffield
03.03.94	Kevin Lueshing W RSC 4 Ebbw Vale
04.06.94	Jose Varela W CO 2 Dortmund,
	Germany
26.08.94	Julian Eavis W PTS 6 Barnsley
26.09.94	Julian Eavis W PTS 6 Cleethorpes
26.10.94	Lindon Scarlett W PTS 8 Leeds
17.12.94	Roberto Welin W RSC 7 Cagliari, Italy
15.09.95	Del Bryan W PTS 12 Mansfield
	(British Welterweight Title Challenge)
13.02.96	Kevin Lueshing L RSC 3 Bethnal
	Green
	(British Welterweight Title Defence)
25.06.96	Michael Carruth L RSC 10 Mansfield
09.06.97	Derek Roche L RSC 4 Bradford
	(Central Area Welterweight Title
	Challenge. Elim. British Welterweight
	Title)
27.02.98	Scott Dixon L PTS 10 Glasgow
	(Elim. British Welterweight Title)
17.04.99	Michael Carruth L RSC 5 Dublin
08.12.01	David Kirk W CO 2 Chesterfield
15.06.02	Arv Mittoo W PTS 6 Norwich

Career: 40 contests, won 18, drew 1, lost 21.

Mark Sawyers   Les Clark

Mark Sawyers

Bristol. *Born* Bristol, 19 May, 1967
L. Middleweight. Ht. 5'8"
Manager Self

| 11.02.97 | Peter McCormack W RSC 2 |
| | Wolverhampton |

07.03.97	Alex Mason L PTS 6 Weston super
	Mare
28.06.97	Spencer Fearon L PTS 4 Norwich
18.11.97	Kevin Lang W RSC 1 Mansfield
28.11.97	Matthew Tait L PTS 6 Bethnal Green
08.12.97	Chris Pollock DREW 6 Birmingham
19.12.97	Mehrdud Takaloo L PTS 4 Millwall
13.02.98	Chris Pollock L PTS 8 Weston super
	Mare
23.09.01	Gary Dixon DREW 6 Shaw
15.10.01	James Lee W PTS 6 Southampton
27.10.01	David Barnes L RSC 2 Manchester

Career: 11 contests, won 3, drew 2, lost 6.

Billy Schwer

Luton. *Born* Luton, 12 April, 1969
Former IBO L. Welterweight Champion.
Former Undefeated European Lightweight
Champion. Former Commonwealth
Lightweight Champion. Former Undefeated
British Lightweight Champion. Ht. 5'8½"
Manager Self

04.10.90	Pierre Conan W RSC 1 Bethnal Green
31.10.90	Mark Antony W RSC 2 Wembley
12.12.90	Sean Casey W RSC 1 Kensington
16.01.91	Dave Jenkins W PTS 6 Kensington
07.02.91	John Smith W RSC 2 Watford
06.03.91	Chubby Martin W RSC 3 Wembley
04.04.91	Andy Robins W RSC 2 Watford
17.04.91	Chris Saunders W RSC 1 Kensington
02.05.91	Karl Taylor W RSC 2 Northampton
30.06.91	Chris Saunders W RSC 3 Southwark
11.09.91	Tony Foster W PTS 8 Hammersmith
26.09.91	Felix Kelly W RSC 2 Dunstable
24.10.91	Patrick Kamy W CO 1 Dunstable
20.11.91	Marcel Herbert W PTS 8 Kensington
12.02.92	Tomas Quinones W CO 8 Wembley
25.03.92	Bobby Brewer W RSC 4 Kensington
03.09.92	Wayne Windle W CO 1 Dunstable
28.10.92	Carl Crook W RTD 9 Kensington
	(British & Commonwealth Lightweight
	Title Challenges)
17.12.92	Mauricio Aceves W RSC 3 Wembley
24.02.93	Paul Burke L RSC 7 Wembley
	(British & Commonwealth Lightweight
	Title Defences)
15.06.93	Farid Benredjeb W PTS 8 Hemel
	Hempstead
10.11.93	Paul Burke W PTS 12 Watford
	(British & Commonwealth Lightweight
	Title Challenges)
16.02.94	Sean Murphy W RSC 3 Stevenage
	(British & Commonwealth Lightweight
	Title Defences)
04.03.94	John Roby W RSC 2 Bethnal Green
22.03.94	Edgar Castro W CO 5 Bethnal Green
11.05.94	Howard Grant W RSC 9 Stevenage
	(Commonwealth Lightweight Title
	Defence)
09.11.94	Manuel Hernandez W CO 6 Millwall
28.01.95	Rafael Ruelas L RSC 8 Las Vegas,
	USA
	(IBF Lightweight Title Challenge)
12.05.95	Stephen Chungu W RSC 11 Bethnal
	Green
	(Commonwealth Lightweight Title
	Defence)
23.06.95	Bruno Rabanales W DIS 6 Bethnal
	Green
28.10.95	Ditau Molefyane W CO 8 Kensington
	(Commonwealth Lightweight Title
	Defence)

25.11.95 David Tetteh L RSC 12 Dagenham
(Commonwealth Lightweight Title Defence)
15.03.96 Edward Lloyd W RTD 5 Dunstable
16.05.96 Gareth Jordan W RSC 3 Dunstable
24.10.96 Alan Temple W PTS 8 Wembley
20.11.96 Jean-Michel Moulun W RTD 7 Wembley
25.10.97 Oscar Garcia Cano W RSC 10 Zaragoza, Spain
(European Lightweight Title Challenge)
14.03.98 Jean Gomis W PTS 10 Bethnal Green
12.09.98 Manuel Carlos Fernandes W RTD 7 Bethnal Green
(European Lightweight Title Defence)
16.01.99 Zoltan Kalocsai W RSC 7 Bethnal Green
(European Lightweight Title Defence)
08.05.99 Sandro Casamonica W RTD 8 Bethnal Green
(European Lightweight Title Defence)
29.11.99 Steve Johnston L PTS 12 Wembley
(WBC Lightweight Title Challenge)
14.10.00 Colin Dunne L PTS 12 Wembley
(WBU Lightweight Title Challenge)
07.04.01 Newton Villareal W PTS 12 Wembley
(IBO L. Welterweight Title Challenge)
14.07.01 Pablo Sarmiento L RSC 11 Wembley
(IBO L.Welterweight Title Defence)
Career: 45 contests, won 39, lost 6.

Martin Scotland

West Bromwich. *Born* Birmingham, 8 October, 1975
Middleweight. Ht. 5'10½"
Manager J. Griffin

24.02.00 Pedro Thompson L RSC 4 Edgbaston
20.05.00 Paddy Martin W RSC 5 Leicester
09.03.02 James Davenport L RSC 1 Manchester
13.05.02 Ernie Smith L RTD 2 Birmingham
Career: 4 contests, won 1, lost 3.

Bruce Scott

Hackney. *Born* Jamaica, 16 August, 1969
British, Commonwealth & WBU Inter-Continental Cruiserweight Champion.
Former Undefeated Southern Area Cruiserweight Champion. Ht. 5'9½"
Manager F. Warren

25.04.91 Mark Bowen L PTS 6 Mayfair
16.09.91 Randy B. Powell W RSC 5 Mayfair
21.11.91 Steve Osborne W PTS 6 Burton
27.04.92 John Kaighin W CO 4 Mayfair
07.09.92 Lee Prudden W PTS 6 Bethnal Green
03.12.92 Mark Pain W RSC 5 Lewisham
15.02.93 Paul McCarthy W PTS 6 Mayfair
22.04.93 Sean O'Phoenix W RSC 3 Mayfair
14.06.93 John Oxenham W RSC 1 Bayswater
04.10.93 Simon McDougall W PTS 6 Mayfair
16.12.93 Bobby Mack W Newport
05.04.94 Steve Osborne W RSC 5 Bethnal Green
17.10.94 Bobbi Joe Edwards W PTS 8 Mayfair
09.12.94 John Keeton W CO 2 Bethnal Green
19.04.95 Nigel Rafferty W RSC 2 Bethnal Green
19.05.95 Cordwell Hylton W RSC 1 Southwark
11.11.95 Tony Booth W RSC 3 Halifax
05.03.96 Nick Manners W RSC 5 Bethnal Green
13.07.96 Tony Booth W PTS 8 Bethnal Green
30.11.96 Nicky Piper L RSC 7 Tylorstown

(Commonwealth L. Heavyweight Title Challenge)
15.05.97 Grant Briggs W RSC 2 Reading
04.10.97 Tony Booth L PTS 8 Muswell Hill
21.04.98 Dominic Negus W RSC 9 Edmonton
(Southern Area Cruiserweight Title Challenge)
28.11.98 Darren Corbett W RSC 10 Belfast
(Commonwealth Cruiserweight Title Challenge. Vacant British Cruiserweight Title)
15.05.99 Johnny Nelson L PTS 12 Sheffield
(WBO Cruiserweight Title Challenge)
17.07.99 Juan Carlos Gomez L RSC 6 Dusseldorf, Germany
(WBC Cruiserweight Title Challenge)
08.04.00 Chris Woollas W RSC 2 Bethnal Green
24.06.00 Adam Watt L RSC 4 Glasgow
(Vacant Commonwealth Cruiserweight Title)
16.12.00 John Keeton W CO 6 Sheffield
(Vacant British Cruiserweight Title)
10.03.01 Garry Delaney W RTD 3 Bethnal Green
(British Cruiserweight Title Defence. Vacant Commonwealth Cruiserweight Title)
28.07.01 Rene Janvier W PTS 12 Wembley
(Vacant WBU Inter-Continental Cruiserweight Title)
Career: 31 contests, won 25, lost 6.

Dean Scott

Nottingham. *Born* Kettering, 28 January, 1981
L. Welterweight. Ht. 5'8"
Manager M. Shinfield

11.05.02 Daniel Thorpe L RSC 1 Chesterfield
Career: 1 contest, lost 1.

Matt Scriven

Nottingham. *Born* Nottingham, 1 September, 1973
Welterweight. Ht. 5'10"
Manager M. Shinfield

26.11.97 Shamus Casey W PTS 6 Stoke
08.12.97 Shane Thomas W PTS 6 Bradford
20.03.98 C. J. Jackson L PTS 6 Ilkeston
15.05.98 Lee Bird W RSC 5 Nottingham
08.10.98 Stevie McCready L RTD 3 Sunderland
01.04.99 Adrian Houldey W PTS 6 Birmingham
25.04.99 Danny Thornton L RSC 4 Leeds
27.06.99 Shane Junior L RSC 2 Alfreton
11.09.99 David Arundel L RTD 1 Sheffield
20.03.00 James Docherty L PTS 8 Glasgow
27.03.00 Matt Mowatt L PTS 4 Barnsley
09.04.00 David Matthews W PTS 6 Alfreton
06.06.00 Jackie Townsley L RSC 3 Motherwell
04.11.00 Brett James L RTD 1 Bethnal Green
04.02.01 Mark Paxford L PTS 6 Queensferry
26.02.01 Pedro Thompson W RTD 1 Nottingham
12.03.01 Ernie Smith W PTS 6 Birmingham
20.03.01 James Docherty L RSC 1 Glasgow
21.05.01 Christian Brady L RSC 5 Birmingham
(Vacant Midlands Area Welterweight Title)
21.10.01 Neil Bonner NC 1 Glasgow
04.03.02 Danny Parkinson L PTS 6 Bradford
22.04.02 Gary Porter L PTS 6 Glasgow
28.05.02 Peter Dunn W PTS 8 Leeds
Career: 22 contests, won 8, lost 13, no contest 1.

Matt Scriven   Les Clark

Isaac Sebaduka

Brixton. *Born* Uganda, 1 January, 1976
S. Featherweight. Ht. 5'5¾"
Manager Self

12.07.97 Danny Adams DREW 4 Earls Court
27.10.97 Gary Flear L PTS 6 Nottingham
23.07.98 Chris Williams W RSC 5 Barking
05.10.99 Mark Payne L PTS 6 Bloomsbury
06.11.99 Keith Jones L PTS 4 Bethnal Green
13.03.00 David Jeffrey W RSC 1 Bethnal Green
17.04.00 Richard Evatt W RSC 2 Birmingham
01.07.00 Nikolai Melandovics L RSC 1 Southwark
(Vacant WBF European Featherweight Title)
15.06.01 Darren Melville L PTS 6 Millwall
14.07.01 Charles Shepherd W RSC 5 Wembley
04.10.01 Nono Junior L RSC 4 Finsbury
09.02.02 Dean Pithie L PTS 8 Coventry
Career: 12 contests, won 4, drew 1, lost 7.

Isaac Sebaduka   Les Clark

Surinder Sekhon

Barnsley. *Born* Birmingham, 4 October, 1979
L. Middleweight. Ht. 5'9"
Manager T. Schofield

05.05.02 Franny Jones L PTS 6 Hartlepool
Career: 1 contest, lost 1.

Nigel Senior

Nottingham. *Born* Wallsend, 19 November, 1962
British Masters Lightweight Champion. Ht. 5'5"
Manager J. Gill

03.10.85 Mark Needham W RSC 4 Nottingham
14.10.85 Anthony Brown L PTS 6 Leicester
21.10.85 Peter Bowen DREW 6 Nottingham
11.11.85 Sugar Gibiliru L RSC 5 Liverpool
24.03.86 Joe Donohoe L PTS 6 Mayfair
07.04.86 Billy Joe Dee W PTS 6 Nottingham
15.04.86 Ricky Andrews W PTS 6 Merton
23.04.86 Nigel Haddock L PTS 6 Stoke
19.05.86 Nigel Haddock DREW 6 Nottingham
09.06.86 Nigel Crook W PTS 6 Manchester
23.08.86 Tony Graham DREW 6 Manchester
04.09.86 Gary King W PTS 6 Merton
23.09.86 Carl Cleasby W PTS 6 Batley
20.10.86 Gary Maxwell L PTS 6 Nottingham
29.10.86 Nigel Haddock L PTS 6 Ebbw Vale
11.11.86 Darren Connellan L PTS 6 Batley
28.11.86 Ian Honeywood W RSC 5 Peterborough
16.12.86 Paul Timmons L PTS 6 Alfreton
27.01.87 Russell Davison DREW 8 Manchester
09.02.87 Joe Duffy W CO 3 Glasgow
16.02.87 Dean Bramhall W PTS 8 Glasgow
14.03.87 Floyd Havard L RSC 5 Southwark
13.04.87 John Bennie L PTS 6 Glasgow
01.05.87 Gary de Roux L PTS 8 Peterborough
04.06.87 John Feeney L PTS 8 Sunderland
28.09.87 George Jones L PTS 8 Birmingham
09.11.87 Rocky Lawlor L RSC 5 Birmingham
27.01.88 Ronnie Green L PTS 8 Stoke
24.02.88 John Bennie L PTS 6 Glasgow
08.03.88 Billy Joe Dee W PTS 6 Batley
23.03.88 Glyn Rhodes L PTS 8 Sheffield
30.03.88 Paul Gadney L PTS 6 Bethnal Green
17.04.88 Dave Kettlewell W PTS 6 Peterborough
25.04.88 Dean Bramhall L PTS 8 Nottingham
10.09.88 Herve Jacob L PTS 8 Grande-Synthe, France
07.10.88 Daniel Londas L PTS 8 Bordeaux, France
25.01.89 Henry Armstrong L PTS 8 Stoke
14.02.89 John Davison L RSC 8 Sunderland
20.03.89 Wayne Weekes L PTS 6 Nottingham
24.04.89 Ian Honeywood L PTS 4 Nottingham
10.05.89 Nigel Wenton L RSC 2 Kensington
19.04.90 Les Walsh L PTS 8 Oldham
30.04.90 Kruga Hydes W PTS 6 Nottingham
21.05.90 Peter Konyegwachie L RSC 7 Mayfair
07.09.90 Jimmy Owens L PTS 6 Liverpool
18.10.90 Frankie Foster L CO 2 Hartlepool
(Vacant Northern Area S. Featherweight Title)
03.12.90 Mark Antony L PTS 8 Cleethorpes
10.12.90 Noel Carroll W PTS 6 Nottingham
06.03.91 Richard Joyce L PTS 8 Croydon
01.12.99 Chris Jickells L RSC 2 Stoke
24.02.00 Willie Limond L RSC 6 Glasgow
26.03.00 Steve Brook L PTS 6 Nottingham
17.04.00 Steve Brook L PTS 6 Bradford
11.05.00 John Barnes L PTS 6 Sunderland
20.05.00 Gary Wilson L PTS 6 Rotherham
06.06.00 Barry Hawthorne L PTS 6 Motherwell
10.09.00 Steve Gethin DREW 6 Walsall
22.09.00 Jason Edwards W PTS 6 Wrexham
01.10.00 James Rooney L PTS 6 Hartlepool
09.10.00 Ricky Eccleston L PTS 4 Liverpool
26.10.00 Nigel Leake W PTS 6 Stoke
04.11.00 Marc Callaghan L RSC 4 Bethnal Green
07.12.00 Alex Stewart W PTS 8 Stoke
22.01.01 Craig Docherty L RSC 4 Glasgow
08.03.01 Jason White L PTS 8 Stoke
24.03.01 Carl Greaves L CO 6 Newark
(Vacant Midlands Area S. Featherweight Title)
18.06.01 Dave Cotterill L PTS 6 Bradford
21.07.01 Gavin Rees L RSC 2 Sheffield
15.09.01 Inderpaul Sandhu L PTS 4 Nottingham
24.09.01 Haroon Din L PTS 6 Cleethorpes
07.10.01 Pete Buckley W PTS 6 Wolverhampton
01.11.01 Anthony Hanna W PTS 6 Hull
17.11.01 Gary Greenwood L PTS 6 Coventry
01.12.01 Marc Callaghan W CO 1 Bethnal Green
09.12.01 Pete Buckley L PTS 6 Shaw
17.12.01 Haroon Din L PTS 6 Cleethorpes
25.02.02 Brian Gentry W RSC 8 Slough
(British Masters Lightweight Title Challenge)
26.04.02 Dean Pithie L PTS 6 Coventry
28.05.02 Colin Toohey L PTS 4 Liverpool
Career: 79 contests, won 20, drew 5, lost 54.

Nigel Senior   Les Clark

Charles Shepherd

Carlisle. *Born* Burnley, 28 June, 1970
Former IBO S. Featherweight Champion. Former Undefeated British, Commonwealth & IBO Inter-Continental S. Featherweight Champion. Ht. 5'4"
Manager J. Doughty/T. Gilmour

28.10.91 Chris Aston W PTS 6 Leicester
31.01.92 Alan McDowall L RSC 3 Glasgow
18.05.92 Mark Legg W PTS 6 Marton
25.09.92 George Naylor W RSC 4 Liverpool
22.10.92 Didier Hughes L PTS 4 Bethnal Green
13.02.93 Nigel Wenton W PTS 8 Manchester
23.05.93 Cham Joof W PTS 4 Brockley
21.10.93 Karl Taylor W RTD 5 Bayswater
09.02.94 Justin Juuko L RSC 5 Bethnal Green
21.04.94 Tony Foster L PTS 10 Hull
(Vacant Central Area Lightweight Title)
29.09.94 Frankie Foster W RSC 3 Tynemouth
08.03.95 Bamana Dibateza W PTS 8 Solihull
26.04.95 Kelton McKenzie W RSC 7 Solihull
23.05.95 Michael Ayers L RSC 3 Potters Bar
(British Lightweight Title Challenge)
14.11.95 John Stovin W RSC 4 Bury
22.04.96 Marc Smith W RSC 2 Crystal Palace
29.06.96 P. J. Gallagher L PTS 12 Erith
(British S. Featherweight Title Challenge)
28.10.96 Harry Escott W PTS 8 Glasgow
22.09.97 Dave McHale W RSC 10 Glasgow
(Vacant British S. Featherweight Title)
08.11.97 Matt Brown W PTS 12 Southwark
(British S. Featherweight Title Defence)
02.05.98 Peter Judson W PTS 12 Kensington
(British S. Featherweight Title Defence)
22.01.99 Trust Ndlovu W CO 6 Carlisle
(Vacant Commonwealth S. Featherweight Title)
03.04.99 Smith Odoom W PTS 12 Carlisle
(Commonwealth S. Featherweight Title Defence)
31.07.99 Tom Johnson W PTS 12 Carlisle
(Vacant IBO S. Featherweight Title)
26.02.00 Affif Djelti L RSC 6 Carlisle
(IBO S. Featherweight Title Defence)
05.06.00 Rakhim Mingaleev W PTS 12 Glasgow
(Vacant IBO Inter-Continental S. Featherweight Title)
18.09.00 James Armah L RTD 9 Glasgow
(Vacant Commonwealth S. Featherweight Title)
11.11.00 Tontcho Tontchev L PTS 12 Belfast
(WBA International S. Featherweight Title Challenge)
20.03.01 Alex Moon L PTS 12 Glasgow
(Vacant Commonwealth S. Featherweight Title)
14.07.01 Isaac Sebaduka L RSC 5 Wembley
Career: 30 contests, won 19, lost 11.

Wayne Shepherd

Carlisle. *Born* Whiston, 3 June, 1959
L. Middleweight. Ht. 5'6"
Manager Self

07.10.91 Benji Joseph W PTS 6 Bradford
28.10.91 Noel Henry W PTS 6 Leicester
16.12.91 Dave Maj DREW 6 Manchester
03.02.92 Dave Maj L PTS 6 Manchester
30.03.92 Hughie Davey L PTS 6 Bradford
18.05.92 Dave Whittle W PTS 6 Marton
14.10.92 Richard Swallow L PTS 8 Stoke
31.10.92 George Scott L RSC 6 Earls Court
13.02.93 Delroy Waul L RSC 5 Manchester
31.03.93 Derek Grainger L RSC 4 Barking
11.06.93 Hughie Davey L PTS 6 Gateshead
06.09.93 Shea Neary L RTD 2 Liverpool
26.01.94 James McGee W PTS 6 Stoke

28.02.94	Craig Winter L PTS 6 Manchester
02.03.95	Denny Johnson L PTS 6 Cramlington
06.04.95	Shaun Stokes L PTS 6 Sheffield
22.05.95	Peter Varnavas W PTS 6 Morecambe
01.06.95	Tommy Quinn L PTS 6 Musselburgh
29.07.95	Shaun O'Neill L PTS 4 Whitley Bay
07.10.95	Neil Sinclair L PTS 6 Belfast
30.10.95	John Stronach L PTS 6 Bradford
11.12.95	Shamus Casey L PTS 6 Morecambe
07.03.96	Derek Roche L RSC 3 Bradford
22.04.96	Gilbert Eastman L PTS 4 Crystal Palace
25.06.96	Geoff McCreesh L PTS 4 Stevenage
26.09.96	John Docherty L PTS 6 Glasgow
10.11.96	John Docherty L PTS 6 Glasgow
22.12.96	Chris Barnett L PTS 6 Salford
16.03.97	C. J. Jackson L PTS 6 Shaw
14.10.97	Joe Townsley L PTS 8 Kilmarnock
22.11.97	G. L. Booth L PTS 4 Manchester
05.03.98	Lee Murtagh L PTS 6 Leeds
20.03.98	Wayne Burchell L PTS 6 Leeds
28.04.98	Danny Ryan L DIS 4 Belfast
14.06.98	Matt Mowatt DREW 6 Shaw
20.09.98	Matt Mowatt W PTS 6 Sheffield
12.10.98	Danny Thornton L PTS 6 Bradford
03.12.98	Lee Molloy L PTS 4 Mayfair
22.01.99	Lee Bird W PTS 6 Carlisle
16.02.99	Paul O'Rourke L PTS 6 Leeds
07.08.99	Alan Gilbert DREW 8 Dagenham (Vacant British Masters L. Middleweight Title)
28.10.99	Matt Mowatt W PTS 6 Burnley
15.11.99	James Docherty L PTS 8 Glasgow
14.12.99	Joe Townsley L PTS 6 Coventry
26.02.00	Martin Thompson W PTS 4 Carlisle
05.03.00	Jason Collins L PTS 6 Shaw
21.05.00	Andy Vickers L PTS 6 Shaw
23.10.00	Jackie Townsley L PTS 4 Glasgow
25.11.00	Jamie Moore L RSC 3 Manchester
22.01.01	Joe Townsley L PTS 6 Glasgow
20.03.01	Scott Dixon L PTS 6 Glasgow
28.03.01	Andrew Buchanan L RSC 2 Piccadilly
23.09.01	Richard Inquieti W PTS 6 Shaw
21.10.01	Martyn Bailey L PTS 6 Pentre Halkyn
03.11.01	Ciaran Duffy L PTS 6 Glasgow
10.12.01	Andrei Ivanov W PTS 6 Nottingham
09.02.02	Brendan Halford L PTS 6 Coventry
21.02.02	Ryan Kerr L PTS 6 Sunderland
03.03.02	Conroy McIntosh DREW 6 Shaw
02.06.02	Dean Walker L PTS 6 Shaw
21.06.02	Lee Murtagh L PTS 10 Leeds (Vacant British Masters Middleweight Title)

Career: 61 contests, won 11, drew 4, lost 46.

Gifford Shillingford

Sheffield. *Born* Sheffield, 2 April, 1965
Heavyweight. Ht. 6'2"
Manager B. Ingle

26.09.88	Steve Garber L RSC 4 Bradford
25.01.89	Michael Howells W CO 1 Stoke
21.06.02	Steve Tuck W RSC 1 Leeds

Career: 3 contests, won 2, lost 1.

Charles Shodiya

Hackney. *Born* London, 30 June, 1975
Middleweight. Ht. 6'1¼"
Manager F. Warren

02.03.02	Wayne Elcock L RSC 1 Bethnal Green

Career: 1 contest, lost 1.

Luke Simpkin

Swadlincote. *Born* Derby, 5 May, 1979
Heavyweight. Ht. 6'2"
Manager N. Nobbs

24.09.98	Simon Taylor W CO 3 Edgbaston
16.10.98	Chris P. Bacon L PTS 6 Salford
10.12.98	Jason Flisher W RSC 5 Barking
04.02.99	Danny Watts L CO 3 Lewisham
28.05.99	Tommy Bannister W RSC 4 Liverpool
07.08.99	Owen Beck L PTS 4 Dagenham
11.09.99	Scott Lansdowne L PTS 4 Sheffield
11.03.00	Albert Sosnowski L PTS 4 Kensington
27.03.00	Mark Hobson L PTS 4 Barnsley
29.04.00	Johan Thorbjoernsson L PTS 4 Wembley
23.09.00	Mark Potter L PTS 6 Bethnal Green
30.09.00	Gordon Minors DREW 4 Peterborough
18.11.00	Keith Long L RSC 3 Dagenham
03.02.01	Paul Buttery W RSC 1 Manchester
01.04.01	Wayne Llewelyn L PTS 6 Southwark
24.04.01	Darren Chubbs L PTS 4 Liverpool
06.05.01	Billy Bessey L PTS 6 Hartlepool
09.06.01	John McDermott L PTS 6 Bethnal Green
13.09.01	Mark Krence L PTS 4 Sheffield
10.12.01	Mark Hobson L RTD 3 Liverpool
27,.01.02	Pele Reid DREW 4 Streatham
15.03.02	Mike Holden L PTS 6 Millwall
13.04.02	Fola Okesola W PTS 4 Liverpool
10.05.02	Julius Francis DREW 6 Millwall

Career: 24 contests, won 5, drew 3, lost 16.

Luke Simpkin   Les Clark

Neil Simpson

Coventry. *Born* London, 5 July, 1970
Former Undefeated British &
Commonwealth L. Heavyweight
Champion. Former Midlands Area
L. Heavyweight Champion. Ht. 6'2"
Manager J. Griffin/J. Harding

04.10.94	Kenny Nevers W PTS 4 Mayfair
20.10.94	Johnny Hooks W RSC 2 Walsall
05.12.94	Chris Woollas L PTS 6 Cleethorpes
15.12.94	Paul Murray W PTS 6 Walsall
06.03.95	Greg Scott-Briggs W RTD 5 Leicester
17.03.95	Thomas Hansvold L PTS 4 Copenhagen, Denmark
26.04.95	Craig Joseph L PTS 6 Solihull
11.05.95	Andy McVeigh L CO 2 Dudley
24.06.95	Dave Owens W RSC 1 Cleethorpes
25.09.95	Tony Booth L PTS 8 Cleethorpes
11.10.95	Darren Ashton W RSC 3 Solihull
29.11.95	Greg Scott-Briggs W DIS 7 Solihull (Vacant Midlands Area L. Heavyweight Title)
19.02.96	Stephen Wilson L PTS 6 Glasgow
27.03.96	Tony Booth W PTS 6 Whitwick
26.04.96	Dean Francis L RSC 3 Cardiff
02.10.96	Chris Davies W PTS 4 Cardiff
28.10.96	Nigel Rafferty W PTS 8 Leicester
03.12.96	Danny Peters L PTS 6 Liverpool
03.02.97	Michael Pinnock W PTS 6 Leicester
25.04.97	Stuart Fleet L PTS 10 Cleethorpes (Midlands Area L. Heavyweight Title Defence)
20.10.97	Slick Miller W RTD 1 Leicester
15.12.97	Chris Woollas L PTS 6 Cleethorpes
11.05.98	Greg Scott-Briggs W PTS 6 Leicester
30.11.98	Slick Miller W CO 3 Leicester
26.02.99	Adam Cale W RSC 3 Coventry
12.07.99	Tony Booth W PTS 10 Coventry (Elim. British L. Heavyweight Title)
14.12.99	Darren Corbett L PTS 12 Coventry (Vacant IBO Inter-Continental L. Heavyweight Title)
22.05.00	Mark Baker W PTS 12 Coventry (Vacant British & Commonwealth L. Heavyweight Titles)
18.11.00	Mark Delaney W RSC 1 Dagenham (British L. Heavyweight Title Defence)
02.01.01	Hastings Rasani W CO 4 Coventry (Vacant Commonwealth L. Heavyweight Title)
06.04.01	Yawe Davis L RSC 3 Grosseto, Italy (Vacant European L. Heavyweight Title)
25.05.02	Tony Oakey L PTS 12 Portsmouth (WBU L. Heavyweight Title Challenge)

Career: 32 contests, won 19, lost 13.

Neil Sinclair

Belfast. *Born* Belfast, 23 February, 1974
British Welterweight Champion. Ht. 5'10½"
Manager J. Breen

14.04.95	Marty Duke W RSC 2 Belfast
27.05.95	Andrew Jervis L RSC 3 Belfast
17.07.95	Andy Peach W RSC 1 Mayfair
26.08.95	George Wilson W PTS 4 Belfast
07.10.95	Wayne Shepherd W PTS 6 Belfast
02.12.95	Brian Coleman W RTD 1 Belfast
13.04.96	Hughie Davey W PTS 6 Liverpool
28.05.96	Prince Kasi Kaihau W RSC 2 Belfast
03.09.96	Dennis Berry L PTS 6 Belfast
27.09.97	Trevor Meikle W RSC 5 Belfast
20.12.97	Chris Pollock W RTD 3 Belfast
21.02.98	Leigh Wicks W RSC 1 Belfast
19.09.98	Paul Denton W RSC 1 Dublin
07.12.98	Michael Smyth W CO 1 Acton
22.01.99	Mark Ramsey W CO 3 Dublin
05.06.99	David Kirk W PTS 8 Cardiff
16.10.99	Paul Dyer W RSC 8 Belfast
18.03.00	Dennis Berry W RSC 2 Glasgow
16.05.00	Paul Dyer W RSC 6 Warrington
24.06.00	Chris Henry W RSC 1 Glasgow
12.08.00	Adrian Chase W RSC 2 Wembley

16.12.00	Daniel Santos L CO 2 Sheffield	
	(WBO Welterweight Title Challenge)	
28.04.01	Zoltan Szilii W CO 2 Cardiff	
22.09.01	Viktor Fesetchko W PTS 6 Bethnal Green	
19.11.01	Harry Dhami W RSC 5 Glasgow	
	(British Welterweight Title Challenge)	
20.04.02	Leonti Voronchuk W RSC 4 Cardiff	
15.06.02	Derek Roche W CO 1 Leeds	
	(British Welterweight Title Defence)	

Career: 27 contests, won 24, lost 3.

(Raminderbir) Ram Singh

Wisbech. *Born* Crewe, 13 August, 1969
Welterweight. Ht. 5'11"
Manager Self

06.06.94	Wahid Fats L RSC 3 Manchester
26.09.94	Robert Howard W PTS 6 Morecambe
17.11.94	Terry Whittaker L PTS 6 Sheffield
24.11.94	Paul Scott L PTS 6 Newcastle
05.12.94	Liam Dineen L PTS 6 Houghton le Spring
12.01.95	Steve Tuckett L RSC 6 Leeds
21.02.95	Glen Hopkins L RSC 1 Sunderland
03.04.95	Dave Madden L PTS 6 Northampton
27.04.95	Paul Hamilton W RSC 2 Hull
14.06.95	Terry Whittaker L PTS 6 Batley
28.09.95	John T. Kelly L PTS 6 Sunderland
05.10.95	Garry Burrell L PTS 8 Glasgow
29.01.96	Marco Fattore DREW 6 Piccadilly
21.02.96	Dave Fallon L PTS 6 Piccadilly
19.03.96	Andy Green L PTS 6 Leeds
01.04.96	Hurricane Hughes W PTS 6 Bradford
22.04.96	John T. Kelly L PTS 6 Manchester
09.05.96	Liam Dineen L PTS 6 Sunderland
30.05.96	Steve Conway L PTS 6 Lincoln
13.06.96	Thomas Bradley L RSC 1 Sheffield
24.02.97	Phil Molyneux L PTS 6 Manchester
11.11.97	Franny Hogg L PTS 6 Leeds
04.12.97	Pete Stanway W PTS 6 Hull
03.02.98	John T. Kelly L PTS 6 Yarm
13.02.98	Lee McBride W RSC 5 Barrhead
23.02.98	Jason McElligott L PTS 6 Windsor
20.03.98	Cam Raeside L RSC 4 Ilkeston
21.05.98	Jason Brattley L PTS 6 Bradford
23.07.98	Colin Lynes L CO 1 Barking
12.10.98	Gavin McGill L PTS 6 Nottingham
19.10.98	James Docherty L PTS 6 Glasgow
03.12.98	Peter Lennon W PTS 6 Hull
11.12.98	Jan Cree DREW 4 Prestwick
12.01.99	Glenn McClarnon L RSC 1 Bethnal Green
27.03.99	Gavin McGill L PTS 4 Derby
21.05.99	Mark Halstead DREW 6 Glasgow
02.07.99	Eddie Nevins L CO 1 Manchester
12.06.00	Danny Parkinson L RSC 3 Bradford
15.07.00	Dave Gibson L PTS 6 Norwich
13.08.00	David Kirk L PTS 6 Nottingham
30.08.00	Gavin Down L PTS 6 Scunthorpe
09.09.00	Lee Byrne L RSC 2 Manchester
26.10.00	Peter Dunn L PTS 6 Stoke
04.11.00	Oscar Hall L PTS 6 Derby
19.11.00	Richard Holden L PTS 6 Chesterfield
04.12.00	Danny Parkinson L PTS 6 Bradford
11.12.00	Oscar Hall L CO 4 Cleethorpes
25.02.01	Steve Conway L RSC 2 Derby
08.06.01	Brian Gifford W PTS 6 Hull
23.06.01	Brian Gifford DREW 4 Peterborough
21.07.01	Matthew Hatton L RSC 2 Sheffield
15.09.01	Darrell Grafton L DIS 5 Nottingham
24.09.01	Daniel Thorpe L RSC 4 Cleethorpes
27.10.01	Jason Rushton L PTS 6 Manchester
17.11.01	Matthew Macklin L RSC 1 Glasgow

Career: 55 contests, won 7, drew 4, lost 44.

Robbie Sivyer

Chesterfield. *Born* Chesterfield, 22
September, 1973
Welterweight. Ht. 5'9"
Manager Self

26.04.93	Garry Burrell L PTS 6 Glasgow
07.06.93	Simon Hamblett W PTS 6 Walsall
29.06.93	Mark Allen L PTS 6 Edgbaston
22.09.93	John Stovin L PTS 6 Chesterfield
13.11.93	Wayne Jones L PTS 6 Cullompton
04.03.94	Wayne Jones L PTS 6 Weston super Mare
05.06.95	Trevor Royal W CO 5 Birmingham
02.10.95	T. J. Smith L RSC 4 Birmingham
04.12.95	Robert Grubb W PTS 6 Birmingham
16.03.96	Norman Dhalie W CO 4 Barnstaple
13.06.96	Kid McAuley W PTS 6 Sheffield
01.10.96	Simon Frailing W PTS 6 Birmingham
09.12.96	Chris Price DREW 6 Chesterfield
26.06.97	Roger Sampson L PTS 6 Sheffield
25.06.00	Gavin Pearson W PTS 6 Wakefield
17.11.01	Darren McInulty L RSC 1 Coventry
17.04.02	Richie Caparelli W RSC 6 Stoke
11.05.02	Tony Montana W PTS 6 Chesterfield

Career: 18 contests, won 9, drew 1, lost 8.

David Smales

Birstall. *Born* Staincliffe, 21 May, 1977
Welterweight. Ht. 5'10"
Manager Self

05.06.98	Peter Lennon W CO 6 Hull
15.06.98	Lee Bird W RSC 1 Bradford
25.10.98	Mark Harrison L RSC 4 Shaw
26.11.98	Lee Williamson L PTS 6 Bradford
20.02.99	Paul Swindles L PTS 6 Bradford
14.06.99	Shaun O'Neill L PTS 6 Bradford
18.10.99	Craig Goodman W PTS 6 Glasgow
06.11.99	Piotr Bartnicki L PTS 6 Bethnal Green
01.12.99	Craig Goodman W PTS 6 Stoke
03.03.00	Scott Millar DREW 6 Irvine
28.03.00	Richard Inquieti L PTS 6 Hartlepool
15.05.00	Richard Holden DREW 6 Cleethorpes
22.09.00	Martyn Bailey L RSC 3 Wrexham
07.12.00	Jamie Logan W PTS 6 Stoke
08.04.01	Chris Steele W PTS 6 Wrexham
01.03.02	Scott Millar W PTS 6 Irvine
09.03.02	Gary Ryder L RSC 1 Manchester

Career: 17 contests, won 7, drew 2, lost 8.

Mark Smallwood

Atherstone. *Born* Nuneaton, 30 January,
1975
Cruiserweight. Ht. 6'2"
Manager J. Weaver

22.02.93	John Dempsey W CO 1 Bedworth
17.03.93	Sean Smith W RSC 1 Stoke
10.05.93	Tim Robinson W RSC 4 Cleethorpes
17.06.93	Phil Ball W RSC 1 Bedworth
24.11.93	Darren Littlewood W PTS 8 Solihull
24.02.94	Jerry Mortimer W PTS 6 Walsall
18.04.94	Gil Lewis W RSC 5 Walsall
23.05.94	Dean Ashton W RTD 3 Walsall
11.10.94	Greg Scott-Briggs W PTS 8 Wolverhampton
29.10.94	Greg Scott-Briggs W PTS 6 Cannock
29.11.94	Paul Murray W PTS 8 Wolverhampton
18.01.95	Marvin O'Brien W PTS 6 Solihull
26.11.96	Michael Pinnock W PTS 6 Wolverhampton
16.01.97	Chris Woollas W PTS 8 Solihull

09.05.98	Sven Hamer W PTS 8 Sheffield	
30.11.98	Clinton Woods L RSC 7 Manchester	
15.06.99	Kid Dongo L RSC 6 Tenerife, Spain	
	(Vacant WBA Continental Euro-African L. Heavyweight Title)	
22.03.02	Paul Bonson W PTS 6 Coventry	
26.04.02	Jon Penn W PTS 6 Coventry	
21.05.02	Valery Odin W RSC 4 Custom House	

Career: 20 contests, won 18, lost 2.

Donovan Smillie

Bradford. *Born* Bradford, 9 August, 1975
S. Middleweight. Ht. 5'10½"
Manager J. Ingle

10.04.99	Sean Pritchard W RSC 1 Manchester
02.05.99	Mark Dawson W PTS 6 Shaw
04.12.99	Mark Dawson W PTS 4 Manchester
14.04.00	Dennis Doyley W PTS 4 Manchester
25.11.00	Ojay Abrahams L RSC 2 Manchester
30.11.01	Rob Stevenson W PTS 6 Hull
17.12.01	Mark Chesters W PTS 6 Cleethorpes
17.02.02	William Webster W PTS 6 Salford
20.04.02	Mike Duffield L PTS 4 Derby
15.06.02	Wayne Asker DREW 6 Norwich

Career: 10 contests, won 7, drew 1, lost 2.

Andrew Smith

Bedworth. *Born* Nuneaton, 15 February,
1975
Lightweight. Ht. 5'5"
Manager Self

20.05.94	Marc Smith DREW 6 Neath
16.09.94	Dennis Holbaek Pedersen L RSC 6 Aalborg, Denmark
07.12.94	Jon Pegg DREW 6 Stoke
07.02.95	Jon Pegg W PTS 6 Wolverhampton
22.02.95	Brian Robb L PTS 6 Telford
09.03.95	Robert Grubb DREW 6 Walsall
28.03.95	Robert Grubb W PTS 6 Wolverhampton
03.04.95	Niel Leggett L PTS 6 Northampton
21.04.95	Brian Robb DREW 6 Dudley
13.10.95	Scott Dixon L PTS 4 Glasgow
21.11.95	Chris Lyons W PTS 6 Edgbaston
17.04.02	Peter Allen L PTS 6 Stoke

Career: 12 contests, won 3, drew 4, lost 5.

Danny Smith

Lowestoft. *Born* Great Yarmouth, 6
October, 1979
Middleweight. Ht. 6'0"
Manager S. Pollard

15.07.00	Gary Jones W RSC 1 Norwich
04.11.00	Rob Stevenson DREW 6 Derby
28.03.01	Simeon Cover W PTS 6 Piccadilly
08.06.01	Rob Stevenson W PTS 6 Hull
13.04.02	Freddie Yemofio W PTS 6 Norwich
15.06.02	William Webster W PTS 6 Norwich

Career: 6 contests, won 5, drew 1.

Ernie Smith

Stourport. *Born* Kidderminster, 10 June,
1978
Welterweight. Ht. 5'8"
Manager Self

24.11.98	Woody Greenaway L PTS 6 Wolverhampton
05.12.98	Gavin Rees L PTS 4 Bristol

147

27.01.99	Arv Mittoo DREW 6 Stoke
11.02.99	Tony Smith W PTS 6 Dudley
22.02.99	Liam Maltby W PTS 4 Peterborough
08.03.99	Wayne Jones W PTS 6 Birmingham
18.03.99	Carl Greaves L PTS 6 Doncaster
25.03.99	Brian Coleman L PTS 6 Edgbaston
27.05.99	Brian Coleman L PTS 6 Edgbaston
14.06.99	Dave Gibson W PTS 6 Birmingham
22.06.99	Koba Gogoladze L RSC 1 Ipswich
03.10.99	Gavin Down L RSC 1 Chesterfield
30.11.99	Brian Coleman L PTS 8 Wolverhampton
13.12.99	Richie Murray L RSC 5 Cleethorpes
24.02.00	Brian Coleman L PTS 6 Edgbaston
02.03.00	Oscar Hall L PTS 6 Birkenhead
10.03.00	John Tiftik L PTS 4 Chigwell
18.03.00	Biagio Falcone L PTS 4 Glasgow
07.04.00	Barry Connell L PTS 6 Glasgow
14.04.00	Jose Luis Castro L PTS 6 Madrid, Spain
06.05.00	Matthew Barr L PTS 4 Southwark
15.05.00	Harry Butler L PTS 6 Birmingham
26.05.00	Biagio Falcone L PTS 4 Glasgow
06.06.00	Chris Henry L PTS 8 Brierley Hill
08.07.00	Mehrdud Takaloo L RSC 4 Widnes
13.08.00	Jawaid Khaliq L RSC 4 Nottingham *(Vacant Midlands Area Welterweight Title)*
24.09.00	Shaun Horsfall L PTS 6 Shaw
09.10.00	Dave Gibson W PTS 6 Birmingham
22.10.00	Matthew Barr L PTS 4 Streatham
06.11.00	Stuart Elwell L PTS 6 Wolverhampton
25.11.00	Michael Jennings L PTS 4 Manchester
03.12.00	Shaun Horsfall L PTS 6 Shaw
17.12.00	Kevin McIntyre L PTS 6 Glasgow
20.01.01	David Walker L RTD 1 Bethnal Green
12.03.01	Matt Scriven L PTS 6 Birmingham
24.03.01	Bobby Banghar L PTS 4 Chigwell
12.05.01	Jon Harrison L PTS 4 Plymouth
21.05.01	Brian Coleman W PTS 6 Birmingham
03.06.01	Babatunde Ajayi L PTS 4 Southwark
16.06.01	Bobby Banghar L PTS 4 Dagenham
26.07.01	Andy Abrol L PTS 6 Blackpool
13.09.01	Leo O'Reilly L PTS 6 Sheffield
29.09.01	Brett James L PTS 6 Southwark
01.11.01	Lance Crosby L PTS 6 Hull
17.11.01	Nigel Wright L PTS 4 Glasgow
15.12.01	Ross Minter L RSC 2 Wembley
11.02.02	Tony Montana L PTS 6 Shrewsbury
13.05.02	Martin Scotland W RTD 2 Birmingham
15.06.02	Gavin Wake L PTS 4 Leeds

Career: 49 contests, won 8, drew 1, lost 40.

(Stephen) Manzo Smith

Canning Town. *Born* Enfield, 10 April, 1979
Welterweight. Ht. 5'11"
Manager A. Bowers

18.05.00	Billy Smith W PTS 4 Bethnal Green
30.05.00	Woody Greenaway W PTS 4 Kensington
29.09.00	Jon Honney W PTS 4 Bethnal Green
09.03.01	Dave Travers W PTS 4 Millwall
20.04.01	Arv Mittoo W PTS 4 Millwall
23.11.01	Gary Harrison L PTS 4 Bethnal Green
16.12.01	Kevin McIntyre L PTS 6 Glasgow

Career: 7 contests, won 5, lost 2.

Sammy Smith

Bracknell. *Born* Chichester, 12 May, 1978
Welterweight. Ht. 5'6"
Manager J. Evans

26.03.98	Shaba Edwards W PTS 6 Acton
28.04.98	Les Frost W CO 2 Brentford
02.10.98	Arv Mittoo W PTS 4 Cheshunt
27.10.98	Rudy Valentino W PTS 6 Brentford
07.12.98	Ross McCord L RSC 5 Acton
25.02.99	Trevor Smith W RSC 2 Kentish Town
08.03.99	Brian Coleman W PTS 8 Birmingham
09.05.99	David Kirk W PTS 6 Bracknell
09.04.00	Gavin Down L PTS 6 Alfreton
18.05.00	Gary Reid L RSC 1 Bethnal Green
11.02.02	David Keir W PTS 6 Southampton
25.02.02	Marcus Portman L PTS 6 Slough

Career: 12 contests, won 8, lost 4.

Stephen Smith

Kentish Town. *Born* Hammersmith, 18
July, 1973
IBC L. Welterweight Champion. Former
Undefeated IBF Inter-Continental
Lightweight Champion. Former Undefeated
German International S. Featherweight
Champion. Ht. 5'8"
Manager Self

17.09.94	Marty Chestnut W RSC 5 Leverkusen, Germany
08.10.94	Jason Lepre W RSC 1 Halle, Germany
11.02.95	Fred Reeve W CO 1 Frankfurt, Germany
25.03.95	Pascal Ragaut W PTS 6 Dusseldorf, Germany
27.05.95	Vladimir Komarov W RSC 5 Dortmund, Germany
09.09.95	Juan Leiva W RSC 6 Bielfield, Germany
14.10.95	Abdul Mannon W RSC 3 Munich, Germany
17.02.96	Kid McAuley W RSC 4 Dortmund, Germany
20.04.96	Senturk Ozdemir W PTS 10 Dusseldorf, Germany *(German International S. Featherweight Title Challenge)*
25.05.96	Chris Jickells W RSC 3 Leipzig, Germany
22.06.96	Brian Robb W RSC 4 Dortmund, Germany
31.08.96	Angel Vasilev W PTS 8 Palma de Mallorca
23.11.96	Manny Santiago W PTS 8 Munich, Germany
15.02.97	Ullises Chong W RSC 2 Vienna, Austria
13.04.97	Peter Feher W CO 1 Cologne, Germany
01.06.97	Emmanuel Burton W DIS 3 Riesa, Germany
05.10.97	Bruno Rabanales W RSC 7 Gera, Germany
08.11.97	Rudy Valentino W PTS 8 Southwark
11.04.98	Ervine Blake W RTD 4 Southwark
30.05.98	Ferenc Szakallas W RSC 3 Riesa, Germany
21.11.98	Anthony Maynard W PTS 10 Southwark
06.03.99	Gary Flear W RTD 7 Southwark *(Vacant IBF Inter-Continental Lightweight Title)*
08.05.99	Ivo Golakov W RSC 3 Bethnal Green *(IBF Inter-Continental Lightweight Title Defence)*
13.09.99	David Kehoe W DIS 2 Bethnal Green

21.02.00	Bobby Vanzie L RSC 9 Southwark *(British & Commonwealth Lightweight Title Challenges)*
27.05.00	Michael Davies W PTS 10 Southwark
13.07.00	Assen Vassilev W RSC 1 Bethnal Green
18.11.00	Leonti Voronchuk W PTS 6 Dagenham
10.04.01	Zoltan Kalocsai W PTS 12 Wembley *(Vacant IBC L. Welterweight Title)*
22.09.01	Melikhaya August W CO 4 Newcastle *(IBC L. Welterweight Title Defence)*
28.11.01	Victor Hugo Paz W PTS 12 Bethnal Green *(IBC L. Welterweight Title Defence)*
20.04.02	Rocky Martinez W PTS 12 Wembley *(IBC L. Welterweight Title Defence)*

Career: 32 contests, won 31, lost 1.

Tony Smith   Les Clark

Tony Smith

Sheffield. *Born* Sheffield, 15 August, 1967
L. Middleweight. Ht. 5'8"
Manager Self

12.03.97	Richard Inquieti L RSC 2 Stoke
25.04.97	Dean Bramhald L PTS 6 Cleethorpes
03.05.97	Anas Oweida L RSC 1 Manchester
09.06.97	Christian Brady L RSC 4 Birmingham
10.07.97	Mark Allen L PTS 6 Doncaster
08.10.97	Marc Smith L PTS 6 Stoke
20.11.97	Marc Smith W PTS 6 Solihull
04.12.97	Dean Bramhald L PTS 6 Doncaster
15.01.98	Marc Smith L PTS 6 Solihull
13.05.98	Chris Price W PTS 6 Scunthorpe
21.05.98	Marc Smith L PTS 6 Solihull
21.09.98	Dave Gibson L RSC 6 Cleethorpes
09.12.98	Sean O'Sullivan L PTS 6 Stoke
11.02.99	Ernie Smith L PTS 6 Dudley
18.03.99	Rene Grayel DREW 6 Doncaster
15.09.99	Michael Jennings L RSC 1 Blackpool
04.10.99	Barry Hughes L RSC 5 Glasgow
30.11.99	Craig Clayton L PTS 6 Wolverhampton
08.12.99	Craig Clayton L PTS 6 Stoke
21.05.00	Shaun Horsfall L RSC 4 Shaw

03.02.01	Danny Wray L RSC 1 Brighton
12.03.01	Casey Brooke W PTS 6 Birmingham
01.04.01	Marcus Portman L PTS 6 Wolverhampton
03.06.01	Sam Mottram L PTS 6 Hanley
07.09.01	Marcus Portman L PTS 6 West Bromwich
15.09.01	Ross McCord L PTS 6 Swansea
10.10.01	Jamie Logan L PTS 6 Stoke
10.12.01	Sam Mottram L PTS 6 Nottingham
09.02.02	Andy Egan L PTS 4 Coventry
01.06.02	Jason Rushton L PTS 4 Manchester

Career: 30 contests, won 3, drew 1, lost 26.

Trevor Smith

Birmingham. *Born* Birmingham, 24 October, 1965
L. Welterweight. Ht. 5'8"
Manager Self

04.02.95	Steve Burton W RSC 6 Cardiff
04.03.95	Mark Winters L PTS 6 Livingston
05.05.95	Shaun Stokes DREW 6 Doncaster
02.09.95	Martin Holgate L RSC 2 Wembley
09.10.97	Chris Price W PTS 6 Leeds
11.11.97	Richard Inquieti W RSC 3 Edgbaston
08.12.97	Dave Gibson W PTS 6 Leicester
27.01.98	Benny Jones W PTS 4 Piccadilly
11.03.98	Terry Roberts L PTS 6 Bethnal Green
26.03.98	John Paul Temple W RSC 5 Piccadilly
09.05.98	Oscar Hall L PTS 4 Sheffield
26.05.98	Jason Cook W RSC 1 Mayfair
17.09.98	Tanveer Ahmed L PTS 6 Glasgow
17.10.98	Chris Barnett L RSC 4 Manchester
10.12.98	Colin Lynes L RSC 1 Barking
25.02.99	Sammy Smith L RSC 2 Kentish Town
08.05.99	Kevin McCarthy L RSC 1 Bethnal Green
25.05.00	Lance Crosby L PTS 6 Hull
09.09.00	Dave Gibson W PTS 6 Newark
23.09.00	Francis Barrett L RSC 1 Bethnal Green
28.10.00	Jawaid Khaliq L RSC 1 Coventry
29.01.01	Liam Maltby L PTS 6 Peterborough
17.02.01	Costas Katsantonis L RSC 3 Bethnal Green
03.04.01	Willie Limond L PTS 4 Bethnal Green
05.05.01	Ross Minter L RTD 3 Edmonton
07.07.01	David Barnes L RSC 2 Manchester

Career: 26 contests, won 8, drew 1, lost 17.

Michael Smyth

Barry. *Born* Caerphilly, 22 February, 1970
Former Undefeated Welsh Welterweight Champion. Ht. 5'9¾"
Manager Self

02.05.91	Carl Brasier W RSC 2 Kensington
28.05.91	Rick North W RSC 1 Cardiff
18.07.91	Mike Morrison W RSC 2 Cardiff
03.09.91	Julian Eavis W PTS 6 Cardiff
20.11.91	Mike Russell W RSC 3 Cardiff
17.12.91	Julian Eavis W PTS 6 Cardiff
19.05.92	Ojay Abrahams W PTS 6 Cardiff
07.10.92	David Lake W CO 2 Barry
14.11.92	Des Robinson W PTS 6 Cardiff
10.07.93	Ernie Loveridge W RSC 6 Cardiff
23.10.93	Chris Saunders W PTS 6 Cardiff
12.03.94	Gordon Blair W RSC 4 Cardiff
21.07.94	Maurice Forbes W RSC 3 Battersea
24.09.94	Mike DeMoss W RSC 1 Wembley
25.10.94	Scott Doyle W CO 1 Southwark
25.01.95	Rick North W DIS 4 Cardiff
17.06.95	Kevin Lueshing L RSC 3 Cardiff
	(Final Elim. British Welterweight Title)

20.09.95	Howard Clarke DREW 6 Ystrad
25.10.95	Nigel Bradley W RSC 4 Cardiff
16.12.95	Geoff McCreesh W DIS 4 Cardiff
25.05.96	Maxim Nesterenko L RSC 5 St Petersburg, Russia
	(Vacant WBC International Welterweight Title)
19.07.96	Alexei Perevozchikov W RSC 5 Ystrad
02.10.96	Andrew Murray L PTS 12 Cardiff
	(Commonwealth Welterweight Title Challenge)
26.02.97	Paul King W CO 1 Cardiff
30.08.97	Peter Richardson W RSC 5 Cheshunt
	(Elim. British Welterweight Title)
14.07.98	Geoff McCreesh L PTS 6 Chesterfield
	(British Welterweight Title Challenge)
07.12.98	Neil Sinclair L CO 1 Acton
24.09.99	Jason Williams W RSC 3 Merthyr
	(Vacant Welsh Welterweight Title)
05.02.00	Darren Bruce L CO 5 Bethnal Green
	(IBO Inter-Continental Welterweight Title Challenge)
27.04.01	Kevin McIntyre L PTS 6 Glasgow
08.10.01	Christian Brady W RSC 3 Birmingham
19.03.02	Ted Bami L CO 4 Slough

Career: 32 contests, won 23, drew 1, lost 8.

Mark Snipe

Brighton. *Born* Brighton, 9 March, 1972
L. Heavyweight. Ht. 6'1"
Manager Self

13.06.95	Michael Pinnock W PTS 6 Basildon
27.10.95	Stinger Mason DREW 6 Brighton
26.01.96	Robert Harper W PTS 6 Brighton
13.04.96	Lee Whitehead W PTS 4 Wythenshawe
04.04.97	Darren Ashton L RSC 2 Brighton
11.07.97	Peter Vosper W PTS 6 Brighton
27.02.98	Danny Southam W RSC 2 Brighton
30.03.98	Kid Dongo L PTS 6 Tenerife, Spain
25.10.98	Mark Hobson L RSC 3 Shaw
31.07.01	Allan Foster L PTS 6 Bethnal Green
15.12.01	Andrew Lowe L PTS 4 Chigwell
09.05.02	Peter Haymer L PTS 4 Leicester Square

Career: 12 contests, won 5, drew 1, lost 6.

Mark Snipe   Les Clark

Craig Spacie

Chesterfield. *Born* Chesterfield, 13 March, 1976
S. Featherweight. Ht. 5'5½"
Manager M. Shinfield

18.09.97	Robert Braddock W RSC 6 Alfreton
03.12.97	Dave Travers W RSC 3 Stoke
16.05.98	Michael Gomez L RSC 3 Bethnal Green
14.10.98	Chris Williams W PTS 6 Stoke
02.12.98	David Morris DREW 6 Stoke
17.03.99	Carl Allen L PTS 8 Stoke
03.10.99	Dean Murdoch W RSC 5 Chesterfield
28.11.99	Andy Green W PTS 6 Chesterfield
18.01.00	Marco Fattore W RTD 1 Mansfield
29.02.00	Alex Moon W PTS 6 Widnes
20.03.00	Chris Williams L PTS 6 Mansfield
11.05.00	Pete Buckley W PTS 4 Newark
25.02.01	J.J.Moore W PTS 4 Derby
06.03.01	J.J.Moore W PTS 6 Yarm
17.04.02	Mark Bowen L PTS 8 Stoke
11.05.02	Dave Hinds W PTS 6 Chesterfield

Career: 16 contests, won 11, drew 1, lost 4.

Steven Spartacus (Smith)

Ipswich. *Born* Bury St Edmunds, 3 November, 1976
L. Heavyweight. Ht. 5'10½"
Manager T. Sims

08.09.00	Michael Pinnock W PTS 4 Hammersmith
30.09.00	Martin Jolley W PTS 6 Chigwell
24.03.01	Calvin Stonestreet W PTS 4 Chigwell
16.06.01	Kevin Burton W RSC 1 Dagenham
07.09.01	Rob Stevenson W RSC 4 Bethnal Green
27.10.01	Darren Ashton W PTS 4 Manchester
24.11.01	Michael Pinnock W PTS 4 Bethnal Green
15.12.01	Oneal Murray W RSC 4 Chigwell
19.01.02	Darren Ashton W PTS 4 Bethnal Green

Career: 9 contests, won 9.

John Spence

Cotgrave, *Born* Sheffield, 9 October, 1979
Lightweight. Ht. 5'10"
Manager J. Gill

10.12.01	Mick McPhilbin L RSC 6 Nottingham

Career: 1 contest, lost 1.

Darren Spencer

Liverpool. *Born* Liverpool, 1 September, 1975
Welterweight. Ht. 5'8"
Manager T. Gilmour

20.11.00	Richard Inquieti W RSC 1 Glasgow
03.02.01	Brian Coleman W PTS 6 Manchester
22.02.01	Peter Dunn L PTS 6 Sunderland
19.03.01	Dean Nicholas W RSC 4 Glasgow
25.09.01	Peter Dunn W PTS 4 Liverpool
22.10.01	Gavin Wake L RSC 3 Glasgow

Career: 6 contest, won 4, lost 2.

Delroy Spencer

Walsall. *Born* Walsall, 25 July, 1968
British Masters Flyweight Champion. Ht. 5'4"
Manager T. Marshall

30.10.98	Gwyn Evans L PTS 4 Peterborough
21.11.98	Jamie Evans W PTS 4 Southwark
30.01.99	Ian Napa L PTS 6 Bethnal Green
26.02.99	Chris Edwards W PTS 6 West Bromwich
30.04.99	Nicky Booth L PTS 6 Scunthorpe
06.06.99	Nicky Booth L PTS 4 Nottingham
19.06.99	Willie Valentine L PTS 4 Dublin
16.10.99	Colin Moffett W PTS 4 Bethnal Green
31.10.99	Shane Mallon W PTS 6 Raynes Park
29.11.99	Lee Georgiou L PTS 4 Wembley
19.02.00	Steffen Norskov L PTS 4 Aalborg, Denmark
08.04.00	Ian Napa L PTS 8 Bethnal Green
15.04.00	Lee Georgiou L PTS 4 Bethnal Green
04.07.00	Ankar Miah W RSC 3 Tooting
13.07.00	Darren Hayde W PTS 4 Bethnal Green
30.09.00	Paul Weir L PTS 8 Chigwell
28.10.00	Dale Robinson L RSC 4 Coventry
02.12.00	Keith Knox W PTS 6 Bethnal Green
08.05.01	Levi Pattison L PTS 4 Barnsley
22.05.01	Mimoun Chent L DIS 5 Telde, Gran Canaria
16.06.01	Sunkanmi Ogunbiyi L PTS 4 Wembley
22.11.01	Darren Taylor W PTS 8 Paddington *(Vacant British Masters Flyweight Title)*
09.12.01	Shinny Bayaar L PTS 4 Shaw
19.12.01	Gareth Payne L PTS 4 Coventry
18.01.02	Gareth Payne W PTS 4 Coventry
28.01.02	Levi Pattison L RSC 5 Barnsley

Career: 26 contests, won 9, lost 17.

Michael Sprott

Reading. *Born* Reading, 16 January, 1975
WBF European Heavyweight Champion.
Ht. 6'0¾"
Manager D. Powell

20.11.96	Geoff Hunter W RSC 1 Wembley
19.02.97	Johnny Davison W CO 2 Acton
17.03.97	Slick Miller W CO 1 Mayfair
16.04.97	Tim Redman W CO 2 Bethnal Green
20.05.97	Waldeck Fransas W PTS 6 Edmonton
02.09.97	Gary Williams W PTS 6 Southwark
08.11.97	Darren Fearn W PTS 6 Southwark
06.12.97	Nick Howard W RSC 1 Wembley
10.01.98	Johnny Davison W RSC 2 Bethnal Green
14.02.98	Ray Kane W RTD 1 Southwark
14.03.98	Michael Murray W PTS 6 Bethnal Green
12.09.98	Harry Senior L RSC 6 Bethnal Green *(Vacant Southern Area Heavyweight Title)*
16.01.99	Gary Williams W PTS 6 Bethnal Green
10.07.99	Chris Woollas W RTD 4 Southwark
18.01.00	Tony Booth W PTS 6 Mansfield
14.10.00	Wayne Llewelyn L RSC 3 Wembley
17.02.01	Timo Hoffmann W PTS 8 Bethnal Green
24.03.01	Timo Hoffmann L PTS 8 Magdeburg, Germany
03.11.01	Corrie Sanders L RSC 1 Brakpan, South Africa
20.12.01	Jermell Lamar Barnes W PTS 8 Rotterdam, Holland
12.02.02	Danny Williams L RTD 8 Bethnal Green *(British & Commonwealth Heavyweight Title Challenges)*
09.05.02	Pele Reid W RSC 7 Leicester Square *(Vacant WBF European Heavyweight Title)*

Career: 22 contests, won 17, lost 5.

David Starie

Bury St Edmunds. *Born* Bury St Edmunds, 11 June, 1974
British & Commonwealth S. Middleweight Champion. Former Undefeated IBO Inter-Continental S. Middleweight Champion.
Ht. 6'0"
Manager Self

24.09.94	Paul Murray W RSC 2 Wembley
25.10.94	Dave Owens W PTS 6 Southwark
07.02.95	Marvin O'Brien W PTS 6 Ipswich
30.03.95	Mark Dawson W RSC 1 Bethnal Green
17.05.95	Marvin O'Brien W RSC 5 Ipswich
14.09.95	John Duckworth W PTS 6 Battersea
20.10.95	Hunter Clay W PTS 8 Ipswich
15.12.95	Carlos Christie W CO 4 Bethnal Green
21.03.96	Paul Murray W RSC 1 Southwark
14.05.96	Phil Ball W RSC 1 Dagenham
09.07.96	John Duckworth W RSC 1 Bethnal Green
03.09.96	Pascal Mercier W RSC 3 Bethnal Green
26.11.96	Ray Webb W RSC 6 Bethnal Green
08.04.97	Sammy Storey W RSC 7 Bethnal Green *(Vacant British S. Middleweight Title)*
19.07.97	Dean Francis L RSC 6 Wembley *(British S. Middleweight Title Defence)*
14.02.98	Enzo Giordano W RSC 4 Southwark
28.03.98	Clinton Woods W PTS 12 Hull *(Commonwealth S. Middleweight Title Challenge)*
02.07.98	Danny Juma W RSC 1 Ipswich
21.11.98	Ali Forbes W CO 11 Southwark *(Commonwealth S. Middleweight Title Defence. Vacant British S. Middleweight Title)*
19.01.99	Willie Quinn W RSC 3 Ipswich *(British & Commonwealth S. Middleweight Title Defences)*
24.04.99	Zaourbek Hetagourov W RSC 1 Peterborough
22.06.99	Mark Baker W PTS 12 Ipswich *(British & Commonwealth S. Middleweight Title Defences)*
19.10.99	Teimouraz Kikelidze W PTS 12 Bethnal Green *(Vacant IBO Inter-Continental S. Middleweight Title)*
29.01.00	Joe Calzaghe L PTS 12 Manchester *(WBO S. Middleweight Title Challenge)*
18.11.00	Guy Waters W RSC 6 Dagenham *(Commonwealth S. Middleweight Title Defence)*
09.12.00	Alex Mason W CO 3 Southwark *(British S. Middleweight Title Defence)*
24.03.01	Andrew Flute W RTD 3 Sheffield
25.07.01	Bruno Godoy W RSC 3 Brakpan, South Africa

David Starie   Les Clark

29.09.01	Neil Linford W RSC 6 Southwark
	(British & Commonwealth
	S.Middleweight Title Defences)
08.12.01	Paul Wesley W CO 1 Dagenham
02.03.02	Marc Bargero W CO 1 Brakpan, South
	Africa
	(Commonwealth S. Middleweight Title
	Defence)
08.06.02	Ron Martinez W RSC 1 Memphis,
	Tennessee, USA

Career: 32 contests, won 30, lost 2.

Jimmy Steel

Stoke. *Born* Stoke, 22 June, 1970
L. Heavyweight. Ht. 5'7"
Manager Self

25.04.96	Andy Gray W PTS 6 Mayfair
13.10.96	Johnny Whiteside L RSC 2 Shaw
11.01.97	Enzo Giordano L PTS 4 Bethnal Green
04.04.97	Michael Thomas L PTS 6 Brighton
19.09.97	Jason Ratcliff L PTS 6 Southend
11.11.97	Enzo Giordano L RSC 1 Bethnal Green
21.12.97	Mike Gormley L PTS 6 Salford
06.02.98	Pedro Carragher L PTS 6 Wakefield
17.02.98	Gary Savage W PTS 6 Leeds
17.03.98	Jason Barker L PTS 6 Sheffield
05.04.98	Jon Penn L RSC 5 Shaw
01.06.98	Jeff Finlayson DREW 6 Manchester
09.06.98	Zoltan Sarossy L RSC 1 Hull
17.09.98	Earl Ling DREW 6 Brighton
14.10.98	Jeff Finlayson DREW 6 Blackpool
13.11.98	Tony Griffiths L PTS 4 Brighton
27.11.98	Damon Hague DREW 6 Nottingham
16.01.99	Tony Oakey L PTS 4 Bethnal Green
26.02.99	Ganny Dovidovas L PTS 6 Bethnal
	Green
06.05.99	Dave Johnson L PTS 6 Sunderland
28.05.99	Robert Zlotkowski L PTS 6 Liverpool
10.07.99	Tony Oakey L PTS 4 Southwark
07.10.99	Mike White L PTS 6 Mere
30.10.99	Mike White L PTS 4 Peterlee
14.12.99	Jim Twite L PTS 4 Coventry
12.02.00	Jon Penn L PTS 6 Sheffield
29.02.00	Mike Gormley L RSC 3 Manchester
14.04.00	Jamie Moore L PTS 6 Manchester
13.05.00	Andy Manning L PTS 4 Barnsley
27.05.00	Dean Doyle L PTS 4 Mayfair
19.08.00	Tony Dodson L RSC 3 Brentwood
11.12.00	Mark Brookes L PTS 6 Sheffield
03.12.01	Clint Johnson DREW 6 Leeds
16.12.01	Scott Baker L PTS 4 Southwark
18.02.02	Jason McKay L PTS 4 Glasgow
25.02.02	Tony Strong DREW 4 Slough
09.03.02	Wayne Pinder L PTS 4 Manchester
19.03.02	Sam Price L PTS 4 Slough
20.04.02	Damon Hague L PTS 6 Derby

Career: 39 contests, won 2, drew 6, lost 31.

Chris Steele

Dodworth. *Born* Barnsley, 28 March, 1980
L. Middleweight. Ht. 6'0"
Manager Self

14.11.99	Gavin Pearson L PTS 6 Bradford
02.03.00	Elias Boswell W RSC 4 Blackpool
13.05.00	Arv Mittoo L RSC 3 Barnsley
05.12.00	Colin McCash L RSC 4 Nottingham
08.03.01	Andy Abrol L RSC 6 Blackpool
08.04.01	David Smales L PTS 6 Wrexham
26.04.01	Sam Mottram L PTS 6 Gateshead
10.05.01	Sam Mottram L PTS 6 Sunderland
11.06.01	Darrell Grafton L RSC 1 Nottingham

07.02.02	Andrei Ivanov L PTS 6 Stoke
17.02.02	James Davenport L PTS 6 Salford
22.04.02	Scott Millar L PTS 6 Glasgow
11.05.02	Nicky Leech L PTS 6 Newark

Career: 13 contests, won 1, lost 12.

Blue Stevens

Reading. *Born* Reading, 14 December, 1976
Cruiserweight. Ht. 6'2"
Manager E. Maloney/F. Maloney

08.11.97	L. A. Williams W PTS 6 Southwark
14.03.98	Kevin Mitchell DREW 4 Bethnal
	Green
16.12.01	Tony Booth W PTS 4 Southwark
10.02.02	Darren Ashton W PTS 4 Southwark
19.03.02	Adam Cale W RSC 4 Slough

Career: 5 contests, won 4, drew 1.

Rob Stevenson

Hull. *Born* Hull, 16 March, 1971
S. Middleweight. Ht. 5'9"
Manager Self

28.11.91	Matt Mowatt L PTS 6 Hull
26.03.92	Steve Scott W PTS 6 Hull
04.04.92	Chris Mulcahy L PTS 8 Cleethorpes
29.04.92	Alan Williams W PTS 6 Liverpool
01.06.92	Chris Mulcahy L PTS 6 Manchester
13.10.92	Dean Hiscox L PTS 6 Wolverhampton
26.11.92	Steve Scott L PTS 6 Hull
18.02.93	Warren Stephens W PTS 6 Hull
25.02.93	Ron Hopley DREW 6 Bradford
29.04.93	Billy McDougall DREW 6 Hull
01.07.93	Ron Hopley W PTS 6 York
02.12.93	Ian Noble W PTS 6 Hartlepool
13.12.93	Prince Kasi Kaihau L RSC 5 Doncaster
24.02.94	David Sumner W PTS 6 Hull
24.02.95	Billy Collins L PTS 6 Irvine
25.03.95	Derek Roche L PTS 6 Rothwell
01.07.95	Paul Carr L PTS 6 Kensington
22.09.95	Brian Dunn L PTS 6 Hull
03.11.95	David Bain L PTS 6 Dudley
25.11.95	Jim Webb L PTS 6 Dublin
04.12.95	David Radford L CO 2 Manchester
26.02.96	Shamus Casey W PTS 6 Hull
09.05.96	Carlton Williams L PTS 6 Hull
03.09.96	Jim Rock L PTS 6 Belfast
27.09.96	Steve Roberts L PTS 6 Stevenage
27.02.97	Roy Chipperfield W RSC 5 Hull
20.03.97	Phil Epton L PTS 6 Doncaster
01.05.97	Lee Simpkin W PTS 6 Hull
20.05.97	Ahmet Dottuev L CO 1 Edmonton
04.12.97	Gary Savage L PTS 6 Hull
17.01.98	Darren Dorrington L RSC 3 Bristol
06.03.98	Warren Bowers W PTS 6 Hull
28.03.98	Jason Hart L PTS 6 Crystal Palace
26.09.98	Spencer Fearon L CO 2 Norwich
12.12.99	Butch Lesley L PTS 6 Chigwell
21.02.00	Brian Magee L RSC 5 Southwark
04.11.00	Danny Smith DREW 6 Derby
24.11.00	Lee Bird W PTS 6 Hull
11.12.00	Carl Wall L PTS 4 Widnes
20.01.01	John Tiftik L PTS 6 Bethnal Green
03.02.01	Liam Lathbury L PTS 6 Brighton
25.02.01	Damon Hague L PTS 8 Derby
09.03.01	Chris Nembhard L RSC 2 Millwall
19.05.01	Andrew Lowe L PTS 4 Wembley
08.06.01	Danny Smith L PTS 6 Hull
18.08.01	Simeon Cover L PTS 6 Dewsbury
07.09.01	Steven Spartacus L RSC 4 Bethnal
	Green
01.11.01	Simeon Cover W PTS 6 Hull

30.11.01	Donovan Smillie L PTS 6 Hull
08.12.01	Damon Hague L RSC 7 Chesterfield
11.03.02	Lawrence Murphy L RSC 1 Glasgow

Career: 51 contests, won 12, drew 3, lost 36.

Dave Stewart

Ayr. *Born* Irvine, 5 September, 1975
Lightweight. Ht. 6'0¼"
Manager A. Sims

15.02.01	Danny Connelly W PTS 6 Glasgow
27.04.01	Woody Greenaway W PTS 6 Glasgow
07.09.01	John Marshall W PTS 6 Glasgow
15.06.02	Dave Hinds W PTS 6 Tottenham

Career: 4 contests, won 4.

Adrian Stone

Bristol. *Born* Bristol, 19 July, 1971
Former Undefeated IBO L. Middleweight
Champion. Former Undefeated IBO Inter-
Continental Welterweight Champion. Ht. 5'7"
Manager Self

06.02.93	Sean Daughtry W PTS 6 New York
	City, USA
16.04.93	James Crosby T. DRAW 2 Hamilton,
	USA
08.05.93	Rey Robinson W PTS 4 East Mahanoy,
	USA
28.05.93	Nate Reynolds W RSC 4 Hamilton,
	USA
10.07.93	George Mitchell W RSC 2 Bushill, USA
10.11.93	Ernest Stroman W PTS 4 Atlantic City,
	USA
23.01.94	Sylvie Furlong W CO 1 Boston, USA
20.02.94	Robert West W CO 2 Biloxi, USA
21.04.94	Victor Perez W PTS 8 Ledyard, USA
22.07.94	John Jester W CO 3 Robinsonville,
	USA
18.08.94	Wayne Richards W CO 5 Melville, USA
19.10.94	Curtis Peoples W RSC 7 Catskill, USA
14.12.94	Israel Figueroa W RSC 2 Boston, USA
17.02.95	Ross Thompson W DIS 7 Atlantic City,
	USA
07.04.95	James Hughes L RSC 10 Salem, USA
	(USBA Welterweight Title Challenge)
21.07.95	John Duplessis W RSC 5 New Orleans,
	USA
10.11.95	Roger Turner W RSC 9 Atlantic City,
	USA
03.02.96	Darryl Lattimore W RSC 1 Liverpool
01.04.96	Mroslav Gregoriev W CO 1 Den
	Bosch, Holland
14.05.96	Skipper Kelp L PTS 10 Ledyard, USA
18.10.96	Gilberto Flores T. DRAW 5 New York
	City, USA
15.11.96	Otilio Villareal W PTS 10 Somerset,
	USA
12.12.96	Johar Lashlin W CO 2 Vancouver,
	Canada
	(Vacant IBO Inter-Continental
	Welterweight Title)
27.03.97	John-John Pacquing W RSC 6
	Edmonton, Canada
29.07.97	Greg Johnson W RSC 4 New York
	City, USA
12.12.97	Bobby Butters W RSC 2 Mason City,
	USA
25.04.98	Desi Ford W CO 4 Biloxi, USA
18.08.98	Vernon Forrest L RSC 11 Tunica, USA
	(Vacant NABF Welterweight Title)
18.02.99	Darren Covill W RSC 2 Barking
28.08.99	Benji Singleton W RSC 3 Hamilton,
	USA

14.01.00 Michael Corleone W RSC 3 Long Island, USA
15.04.00 Michael Carruth W RTD 5 Bethnal Green
(Vacant IBO L. Middleweight Title)
15.07.00 Geoff McCreesh W RSC 6 Millwall
(IBO L.Middleweight Title Defence)
11.11.00 Derek Roche W RSC 2 Belfast
(IBO L. Middleweight Title Defence)
13.03.01 Joe Townsley W PTS 12 Plymouth
(IBO L. Middleweight Title Defence)
21.07.01 Shane Mosley L RSC 3 Las Vegas, USA
(WBC Welterweight Title Challenge)
Career: 36 contests, won 30, drew 2, lost 4.

Calvin Stonestreet
Tunbridge Wells. *Born* Pembury, 8 June, 1974
L. Heavyweight. Ht. 5'11½"
Manager M. O'Callaghan

23.01.01 Paul Bonson L PTS 4 Crawley
24.03.01 Steven Spartacus L PTS 4 Chigwell
26.04.01 Oddy Papantoniou W PTS 6 Kensington
16.06.01 John Killian L PTS 4 Wembley
04.07.01 Earl Ling W PTS 4 Bloomsbury
13.12.01 Valery Odin L RSC 2 Leicester Square
10.02.02 Sam Price L PTS 4 Southwark
24.03.02 Alex Gething DREW 4 Streatham
20.04.02 Gabrill Thorli W PTS 4 Wembley
Career: 9 contests, won 3, drew 1, lost 5.

Simon Stowell
Bristol. *Born* Bristol, 12 May, 1971
S. Bantamweight. Ht. 5'7"
Manager C. Sanigar

08.09.00 Danny Lawson W RSC 1 Bristol
06.10.00 Jamie Yelland DREW 4 Maidstone
13.03.01 Danny Lawson W RSC 2 Plymouth
30.09.01 Ian Turner L PTS 4 Bristol
Career: 4 contests, won 2, drew 1, lost 1.

Simon Stowell   Les Clark

Tony Strong
Slough. *Born* London, 22 April, 1970
S. Middleweight. Ht. 5'8"
Manager B. Baker

20.09.01 Darren Ashton L PTS 4 Blackfriars
22.11.01 Adam Cale W CO 1 Mayfair
25.02.02 Jimmy Steel DREW 4 Slough
Career: 3 contests, won 1, drew 1, lost 1.

Darren Stubbs
Oldham. *Born* Manchester, 16 October, 1971
L. Heavyweight. Ht. 5'10"
Manager J. Doughty

02.06.02 Adam Cale W RSC 6 Shaw
21.06.02 Dean Cockburn L RSC 1 Leeds
Career: 2 contests, won 1, lost 1.

Mark Stupple
Bermondsey. *Born* Bermondsey, 23 September, 1970
L. Middleweight. Ht. 5'8"
Manager E. Maloney

28.04.02 Pedro Thompson L RSC 4 Southwark
23.06.02 Arv Mittoo W PTS 6 Southwark
Career: 2 contests, won 1, lost 1.

Michelle Sutcliffe   Les Clark

Michelle Sutcliffe
Leeds. *Born* Leeds, 3 February, 1967
IFBA Flyweight Champion. Former Undefeated WBF & WIBF International Flyweight Champion. Ht. 5'4"
Manager Self

11.02.96 Regina Halmich L RSC 2 Germany
24.05.98 Para Draine L RSC 5 New Jersey, USA
28.06.98 Diane Berry W PTS 5 Warrington
12.02.99 Sengul Ozokcu L PTS 6 Denmark
27.09.99 Veerle Braspenningx W RSC 7 Leeds
(Vacant WIBF International Flyweight Title)
27.02.00 Francesca Lupo W PTS 10 Leeds
(Vacant WBF Flyweight Title)
15.05.00 Jan Wild W PTS 6 Cleethorpes
07.10.00 Regina Halmich L PTS 10 Berlin, Germany
(WIBF L.Flyweight Title Challenge)
19.11.00 Kim Messer L PTS 10 Seoul, South Korea

(IFBA L. Flyweight Title Challenge)
17.05.01 Marietta Ivanova W RSC 5 Leeds
(WBF Flyweight Title Defence. Vacant IFBA Flyweight Title)
29.09.01 Daisy Lang L RSC 7 Hamburg, Germany
(WIBF S. Flyweight Title Challenge)
Career: 11 contests, won 5, lost 6.

Lee Swaby
Lincoln. *Born* Lincoln, 14 May, 1976
Former Undefeated British Masters Cruiserweight Champion. Ht. 6'2"
Manager Self

29.04.97 Naveed Anwar W PTS 6 Manchester
19.06.97 Liam Richardson W RSC 4 Scunthorpe
30.10.97 Phil Ball W RSC 3 Newark
17.11.97 L. A. Williams W PTS 6 Manchester
02.02.98 Tim Redman L PTS 6 Manchester
27.02.98 John Wilson W CO 3 Glasgow
07.03.98 Phill Day L PTS 4 Reading
08.05.98 Chris P. Bacon L RSC 3 Manchester
17.07.98 Chris P. Bacon L PTS 6 Mere
19.09.98 Cathal O'Grady L RSC 1 Dublin
20.12.98 Mark Levy L RTD 5 Salford
23.06.99 Lee Archer W PTS 6 West Bromwich
04.09.99 Garry Delaney L PTS 8 Bethnal Green
03.10.99 Brian Gascoigne DREW 6 Chesterfield
11.12.99 Owen Beck L PTS 4 Liverpool
05.03.00 Kelly Oliver L PTS 10 Peterborough
(Vacant British Masters Cruiserweight Title)
15.04.00 Mark Levy W PTS 4 Bethnal Green
12.05.00 Enzo Maccarinelli W CO 3 Swansea
26.05.00 Steffen Nielsen L PTS 4 Holbaek, Denmark
09.09.00 Tony Dowling W RSC 9 Newark
(Vacant British Masters Cruiserweight Title)
05.02.01 Robert Norton L PTS 8 Hull
24.03.01 Crawford Ashley L PTS 8 Sheffield
30.04.01 Eamonn Glennon W PTS 6 Glasgow
02.06.01 Denzil Browne DREW 8 Wakefield
31.07.01 Stephane Allouane W PTS 4 Bethnal Green
13.09.01 Kevin Barrett W PTS 4 Sheffield
15.12.01 Chris Woollas W RSC 4 Sheffield
27.04.02 Mark Hobson L PTS 10 Huddersfield
(Final Elim. British Cruiserweight Title)
Career: 28 contests, won 13, drew 2, lost 13.

Louis Swales
Hull. *Born* Guisborough, 27 July, 1979
S. Middleweight. Ht. 6'0½"
Manager F. Maloney

16.12.00 Jason Collins DREW 4 Sheffield
10.02.01 Andrew Facey L RSC 3 Widnes
23.09.01 Lee Woodruff L RSC 4 Shaw
Career: 3 contests, drew 1, lost 2.

Peter Swinney
Poplar. *Born* Stepney, 2 November, 1974
Welterweight. Ht. 5'5¾"
Manager F. Maloney

19.10.99 Dennis Griffin W PTS 4 Bethnal Green
29.11.99 Arv Mittoo W PTS 4 Wembley
28.10.01 Arv Mittoo W PTS 4 Southwark
Career: 3 contests, won 3.

T

Mehrdud Takaloo (Takalobigashi)
Margate. *Born* Iran, 23 September, 1975
WBU L. Middleweight Champion. Former
Undefeated IBF Inter-Continental L.
Middleweight Champion. Ht. 5'9"
Manager F. Warren

19.07.97	Harry Butler W RSC 1 Wembley
13.09.97	Michael Alexander W PTS 4 Millwall
15.11.97	Koba Kulu W RSC 3 Bristol
19.12.97	Mark Sawyers W PTS 4 Millwall
07.02.98	Jawaid Khaliq L RSC 4 Cheshunt
16.05.98	Anas Oweida W RSC 1 Bethnal Green
10.10.98	Michael Jones L PTS 6 Bethnal Green
30.01.99	Darren McInulty W RSC 5 Bethnal Green
03.04.99	Gareth Lovell W RSC 6 Kensington
26.06.99	Leigh Wicks W CO 3 Millwall
04.09.99	Carlton Williams W RSC 4 Bethnal Green
23.10.99	Prince Kasi Kaihau W RSC 3 Telford
29.01.00	Paul King W RSC 2 Manchester
08.04.00	Biagio Falcone W RTD 4 Bethnal Green
08.07.00	Ernie Smith W RSC 4 Widnes
12.08.00	Howard Clarke W PTS 12 Wembley *(Vacant IBF Inter-Continental L.Middleweight Title)*
13.11.00	Jason Collins W RSC 2 Bethnal Green
24.02.01	James Lowther W PTS 12 Bethnal Green *(IBF Inter-Continental L.Middleweight Title Defence)*
07.07.01	Anthony Farnell W RSC 1 Manchester *(Vacant WBU L.Middleweight Title)*
22.09.01	Scott Dixon W CO 1 Bethnal Green *(WBU L. Middleweight Title Defence)*
04.05.02	Gary Logan W RSC 10 Bethnal Green *(WBU L. Middleweight Title Defence)*

Career: 21 contests, won 19, lost 2.

Darren Taylor
Bracknell. *Born* Bracknell, 7 December, 1978
Flyweight. Ht. 5'3"
Manager J. Evans

23.11.00	Tommy Thomas W RSC 1 Bayswater
03.06.01	Chris Edwards DREW 6 Hanley
15.10.01	Marty Kayes W PTS 4 Southampton
22.11.01	Delroy Spencer L PTS 8 Paddington *(Vacant British Masters Flyweight Title)*

Career: 4 contests, won 2, drew 1, lost 1.

Mehrdud Takaloo   Les Clark

Karl Taylor   Les Clark

Karl Taylor
Birmingham. *Born* Birmingham, 5 January, 1966
Welterweight. Former Undefeated
Midlands Area Lightweight Champion.
Ht. 5'5"
Manager Self

18.03.87	Steve Brown W PTS 6 Stoke
06.04.87	Paul Taylor L PTS 6 Southampton

12.06.87 Mark Begley W RSC 1 Leamington
18.11.87 Colin Lynch W RSC 4 Solihull
29.02.88 Peter Bradley L PTS 8 Birmingham
04.10.89 Mark Antony W CO 2 Stafford
30.10.89 Tony Feliciello L PTS 8 Birmingham
06.12.89 John Davison L PTS 8 Leicester
23.12.89 Regilio Tuur L RTD 1 Hoogvliet,
Holland
22.02.90 Mark Ramsey L RSC 4 Hull
29.10.90 Steve Walker DREW 6 Birmingham
10.12.90 Elvis Parsley L PTS 6 Birmingham
16.01.91 Wayne Windle W PTS 8 Stoke
02.05.91 Billy Schwer L RSC 2 Northampton
25.07.91 Peter Till L RSC 4 Dudley
(Midlands Area Lightweight Title
Challenge)
24.02.92 Charlie Kane L PTS 8 Glasgow
28.04.92 Richard Woolgar W PTS 6
Wolverhampton
29.05.92 Alan McDowall L PTS 6 Glasgow
25.07.92 Michael Armstrong L RSC 3
Manchester
02.11.92 Hugh Forde L PTS 6 Wolverhampton
23.11.92 Dave McHale L PTS 8 Glasgow
22.12.92 Patrick Gallagher L RSC 3 Mayfair
13.02.93 Craig Dermody L RSC 5 Manchester
31.03.93 Craig Dermody W PTS 6 Barking
07.06.93 Mark Geraghty W PTS 8 Glasgow
13.08.93 Giorgio Campanella L CO 6 Arezzo,
Italy
05.10.93 Paul Harvey W PTS 6 Mayfair
21.10.93 Charles Shepherd L RTD 5 Bayswater
21.12.93 Patrick Gallagher L PTS 6 Mayfair
09.02.94 Alan Levene W RSC 2 Brentwood
01.03.94 Shaun Cogan L PTS 6 Dudley
15.03.94 Patrick Gallagher L PTS 6 Mayfair
18.04.94 Peter Till W PTS 10 Walsall
(Midlands Area Lightweight Title
Challenge)
24.05.94 Michael Ayers DREW 8 Sunderland
12.11.94 P. J. Gallagher L PTS 6 Dublin
29.11.94 Dingaan Thobela W PTS 8 Cannock
31.03.95 Michael Ayers L RSC 8 Crystal Palace
(British Lightweight Title Challenge)
06.05.95 Cham Joof W PTS 8 Shepton Mallet
23.06.95 Poli Diaz L PTS 8 Madrid, Spain
02.09.95 Paul Ryan L RSC 3 Wembley
04.11.95 Carl Wright L PTS 6 Liverpool
15.12.95 Peter Richardson L PTS 8 Bethnal
Green
23.01.96 Paul Knights DREW 6 Bethnal Green
05.03.96 Andy Holligan L PTS 6 Barrow
20.03.96 Mervyn Bennett W PTS 8 Cardiff
21.05.96 Malcolm Melvin L PTS 10 Edgbaston
(Midlands Area L. Welterweight Title
Challenge)
07.10.96 Joshua Clottey L RSC 2 Lewisham
20.12.96 Anatoly Alexandrov L RSC 7 Bilbao,
Spain
28.01.97 Eamonn Magee L PTS 6 Belfast
28.02.97 Mark Breslin L RSC 6 Kilmarnock
30.08.97 Gilbert Eastman L PTS 4 Cheshunt
25.10.97 Tontcho Tontchev L PTS 4
Queensferry
22.11.97 Bobby Vanzie L PTS 6 Manchester
18.04.98 Richard Hatton L RSC 1 Manchester
18.07.98 James Hare L PTS 4 Sheffield
26.09.98 Oktay Urkal L PTS 8 Norwich
28.11.98 Junior Witter L PTS 4 Sheffield
06.03.99 George Scott L RSC 4 Southwark
15.05.99 Jon Thaxton L PTS 6 Sheffield
10.07.99 Eamonn Magee L RTD 3 Southwark
06.11.99 Alan Sebire W PTS 6 Widnes
15.11.99 Steve Murray L RSC 1 Bethnal Green

19.08.00 Iain Eldridge L PTS 4 Brentwood
04.09.00 Tomas Jansson L PTS 6 Manchester
16.09.00 Colin Lynes L PTS 6 Bethnal Green
09.12.00 David Walker L PTS 6 Southwark
10.02.01 Matthew Hatton L PTS 4 Widnes
10.03.01 Francis Barrett L RSC 3 Bethnal Green
10.04.01 Costas Katsantonis L PTS 4 Wembley
16.06.01 Brett James DREW 4 Wembley
15.09.01 David Barnes L PTS 4 Manchester
28.10.01 Babatunde Ajayi L PTS 4 Southwark
24.11.01 Ross Minter L PTS 4 Bethnal Green
15.12.01 Alexandra Vetoux L PTS 4 Wembley
12.02.02 Brett James DREW 4 Bethnal Green
11.03.02 Kevin McIntyre L PTS 4 Glasgow
04.05.02 Matthew Hatton L RSC 3 Bethnal
Green
25.06.02 Rimell Taylor DREW 6 Rugby
Career: 78 contests, won 15, drew 6, lost 57.

Rimell Taylor

Hinckley. *Born* Nuneaton, 28 February,
1981
Welterweight. Ht. 5'11"
Manager J. Weaver

25.06.02 Karl Taylor DREW 6 Rugby
Career: 1 contest, drew 1.

Alan Temple   Les Clark

Alan Temple

Hartlepool. *Born* Hartlepool, 21 October,
1972
Lightweight. Ht. 5'8"
Manager Self

29.09.94 Stevie Bolt W CO 2 Bethnal Green
22.11.94 Phil Found W PTS 6 Bristol
07.02.95 Brian Coleman W PTS 6 Ipswich
27.04.95 Everald Williams L PTS 6 Bethnal
Green
29.09.95 Kevin McKillan W PTS 6 Hartlepool
23.11.95 Rudy Valentino L RSC 3 Marton
02.03.96 Tony Foster W PTS 6 Newcastle
08.06.96 Micky Hall W RSC 2 Newcastle
20.09.96 Scott Dixon L PTS 4 Glasgow

24.10.96 Billy Schwer L PTS 8 Wembley
04.12.96 Harry Escott W PTS 8 Hartlepool
12.02.97 Tanveer Ahmed L RSC 8 Glasgow
(Elim. British Lightweight Title)
13.02.98 Bobby Vanzie L CO 3 Seaham
(Elim. British Lightweight Title)
21.03.98 Michael Ayers L RSC 2 Bethnal Green
31.10.98 Alan Bosworth W PTS 6 Basingstoke
20.02.99 Ivan Walker W PTS 4 Thornaby
05.03.99 David Burke L PTS 8 Liverpool
01.05.99 Jason Rowland L PTS 6 Crystal Palace
22.05.99 Eamonn Magee L CO 3 Belfast
26.06.99 Steve McLevy W RSC 6 Glasgow
11.09.99 Wayne Rigby W PTS 8 Sheffield
02.11.99 Souleymane M'Baye L RTD 7 Ciudad
Real, Spain
12.08.00 Steve Murray L RSC 2 Wembley
(IBF Inter-Continental Lightweight
Title Challenge. Elim. British
Lightweight Title)
26.03.01 Jonathan Thaxton L PTS 4 Wembley
04.06.01 Gary Hibbert W PTS 6 Hartlepool
21.07.01 Junior Witter L CO 5 Sheffield
10.11.01 Colin Dunne L PTS 6 Wembley
09.03.02 Gary Hibbert L RSC 1 Manchester
Career: 28 contests, won 12, lost 16.

(Eranos) Erik Teymour
(Teymurazov)

Canning Town. *Born* Moscow, Russia, 1
March, 1979
S. Middleweight. Ht. 5'8½"
Manager A. Bowers

14.07.01 Dean Ashton W RSC 2 Liverpool
31.07.01 Leigh Wicks W RSC 1 Bethnal Green
28.09.01 Kreshnik Qato W PTS 6 Millwall
23.11.01 Harry Butler W RSC 2 Bethnal Green
16.12.01 Howard Clarke W PTS 6 Southwark
15.03.02 Darren Littlewood W RSC 1 Millwall
26.04.02 Sam Soliman L PTS 8 Glasgow
21.05.02 Toks Owoh W PTS 6 Custom House
Career: 8 contests, won 7, lost 1.

Jonathan Thaxton

Norwich. *Born* Norwich, 10 September,
1974
Lightweight. Former Southern Area, IBF &
WBO Inter-Continental L. Welterweight
Champion. Ht. 5'6"
Manager B. Ingle/F. Warren

09.12.92 Scott Smith W PTS 6 Stoke
03.03.93 Dean Hiscox W PTS 6 Solihull
17.03.93 John O. Johnson W PTS 6 Stoke
23.06.93 Brian Coleman W PTS 8 Gorleston
22.09.93 John Smith W PTS 6 Wembley
07.12.93 Dean Hollington W RSC 3 Bethnal
Green
10.03.94 B. F. Williams W RSC 4 Watford
(Vacant Southern Area L. Welterweight
Title)
18.11.94 Keith Marner L PTS 10 Bracknell
(Southern Area L. Welterweight Title
Defence)
26.05.95 David Thompson W RSC 6 Norwich
23.06.95 Delroy Leslie W PTS 6 Bethnal Green
12.08.95 Rene Prins L PTS 8 Zaandam, Holland
08.12.95 Colin Dunne L RSC 5 Bethnal Green
(Vacant Southern Area Lightweight
Title)
20.01.96 John O. Johnson W RSC 4 Mansfield

13.02.96 Paul Ryan W RSC 1 Bethnal Green
25.06.96 Mark Elliot W CO 5 Mansfield
(Vacant IBF Inter-Continental
L. Welterweight Title)
14.09.96 Bernard Paul W PTS 12 Sheffield
(Vacant WBO Inter-Continental
L. Welterweight Title)
27.03.97 Paul Burke W RSC 9 Norwich
(IBF & WBO Inter-Continental
L. Welterweight Title Defences)
28.06.97 Gagik Chachatrian W RSC 2 Norwich
(IBF & WBO Inter-Continental
L. Welterweight Title Defences)
29.11.97 Rimvidas Billius W PTS 12 Norwich
(IBF & WBO Inter-Continental
L. Welterweight Title Defences)
26.09.98 Emanuel Burton L RSC 7 Norwich

(IBF & WBO Inter-Continental
L. Welterweight Title Defences)
15.05.99 Karl Taylor W PTS 6 Sheffield
07.08.99 Brian Coleman W PTS 6 Dagenham
15.11.99 Jason Rowland L RSC 5 Bethnal Green
(British L. Welterweight Title Challenge)
15.07.00 Kimoun Kouassi W RSC 3 Norwich
21.10.00 Richard Hatton L PTS 12 Wembley
(Vacant British L.Welterweight Title)
26.03.01 Alan Temple W PTS 4 Wembley
28.07.01 David Kirk W PTS 4 Wembley
09.02.02 Eamonn Magee L RSC 6 Manchester
(Commonwealth L.Welterweight Title
Challenge)
13.04.02 Chill John W RSC 2 Norwich
15.06.02 Marc Waelkens W RSC 7 Norwich
Career: 30 contests, won 23, lost 7.

Matthew Thirlwall
Bermondsey. *Born* Middlesbrough, 28 November, 1980
Middleweight. Ht. 5'9½"
Manager R. McCracken

16.03.02 William Webster W RSC 1 Bethnal Green
10.05.02 Leigh Wicks W PTS 4 Bethnal Green
Career: 2 contests, won 2.

Ian Thomas
Stoke. *Born* Stoke, 18 March, 1970
Middleweight. Ht. 5'11¼"
Manager P. Dykes

15.04.02 Dave Pearson W CO 3 Shrewsbury
09.05.02 Gary Firby DREW 6 Sunderland
Career: 2 contests, won 1, drew 1.

Jason Thomas   Les Clark

Jason Thomas
Merthyr Tydfill. *Born* Pontypridd, 7 October, 1976
Bantamweight. Ht. 5'6"
Manager Self

28.11.95 Henry Jones W PTS 4 Cardiff
08.12.95 John Sillo L PTS 6 Liverpool
13.01.96 Paul Griffin L RSC 2 Manchester
02.10.96 Henry Jones L PTS 4 Cardiff
23.10.96 Noel Wilders L PTS 6 Halifax
27.11.96 Jason Booth L PTS 4 Swansea
02.06.97 Colin Moffett W RSC 3 Belfast
02.08.97 Peter Culshaw L PTS 8 Barnsley
14.10.97 Graham McGrath W PTS 6 Wolverhampton
25.10.97 Keith Knox W PTS 8 Queensferry
04.12.97 Sean Green DREW 4 Doncaster
13.02.98 Nick Tooley W PTS 6 Weston super Mare
18.04.98 Hector Orozco DREW 4 Manchester
14.05.98 John Matthews L PTS 6 Acton
03.10.98 Michael Alldis L PTS 6 Crawley
06.02.99 Noel Wilders L PTS 10 Halifax
(Elim. British Bantamweight Title)

Jonathan Thaxton   Les Clark

15.05.99 Alex Moon L PTS 8 Blackpool
24.09.99 Frankie DeMilo W RSC 2 Merthyr
15.11.99 Stephen Oates L PTS 6 Bethnal Green
19.02.00 Stephen Oates L PTS 6 Dagenham
29.03.00 Frankie DeMilo L RSC 8 Piccadilly
(*Vacant British Masters
S. Bantamweight Title*)
06.10.00 Takalani Ndlovu L RSC 2 Maidstone
05.12.00 Kevin Gerowski L PTS 8 Nottingham
24.05.01 Stewart Sanderson DREW 6 Glasgow
08.06.01 Karim Quibir L CO 4 Orense, Spain
17.11.01 Chris Emanuele L RSC 1 Coventry
23.02.02 Jason Booth L PTS 6 Nottingham
27.04.02 Dale Robinson L RSC 4 Huddersfield
Career: 28 contests, won 6, drew 3, lost 19.

Jeff Thomas

St Annes. *Born* Holland, 30 October, 1981
Lightweight. Ht. 5'10"
Manager L. Veitch

09.12.01 Peter Allen W PTS 6 Blackpool
Career: 1 contest, won 1.

Robin Thomas

Liverpool. *Born* Liverpool, 14 January, 1979
Welterweight. Ht. 5'10½"
Manager D. Isaaman

25.06.02 Tony Conroy L RSC 1 Rugby
Career: 1 contest, lost 1.

(Adrian) Carl Thompson

Manchester. *Born* Manchester, 26 May, 1964
Former IBO Cruiserweight Champion.
Former WBO Cruiserweight Champion.
Former Undefeated European, British &
WBC International Cruiserweight
Champion. Ht. 6'0"
Manager Self

06.06.88 Darren McKenna W RSC 2 Manchester
11.10.88 Paul Sheldon W PTS 6
Wolverhampton
13.02.89 Steve Osborne W PTS 6 Manchester
07.03.89 Sean O'Phoenix W RSC 4 Manchester
04.04.89 Keith Halliwell W RSC 1 Manchester
04.05.89 Tenko Ernie W CO 4 Mayfair
12.06.89 Steve Osborne W PTS 8 Manchester
11.07.89 Peter Brown W RSC 5 Batley
31.10.89 Crawford Ashley L RSC 6 Manchester
(*Vacant Central Area L. Heavyweight
Title*)
21.04.90 Francis Wanyama L PTS 6 St
Amandsberg, Belgium
07.03.91 Terry Dixon W PTS 8 Basildon
01.04.91 Yawe Davis L RSC 2 Monaco, Monte
Carlo
04.09.91 Nicky Piper W RSC 3 Bethnal Green
04.06.92 Steve Lewsam W RSC 8 Cleethorpes
(*Vacant British Cruiserweight Title*)
17.02.93 Arthur Weathers W CO 2 Bethnal
Green
(*Vacant WBC International
Cruiserweight Title*)
31.03.93 Steve Harvey W CO 1 Bethnal Green
25.07.93 Willie Jake W CO 3 Oldham
02.02.94 Massimiliano Duran W CO 8 Ferrara,
Italy
(*European Cruiserweight Title
Challenge*)

14.06.94 Akim Tafer W RSC 6 Epernay, France
(*European Cruiserweight Title
Defence*)
10.09.94 Dionisio Lazario W RSC 1
Birmingham
13.10.94 Tim Knight W RSC 5 Paris, France
10.06.95 Ralf Rocchigiani L RSC 11
Manchester
(*Vacant WBO Cruiserweight Title*)
13.04.96 Albert Call W RTD 4 Wythenshawe
09.11.96 Jason Nicholson W PTS 8 Manchester
26.04.97 Keith McMurray W RSC 4 Zurich,
Switzerland
04.10.97 Ralf Rocchigiani W PTS 12 Hannover,
Germany

(*WBO Cruiserweight Title Challenge*)
18.04.98 Chris Eubank W PTS 12 Manchester
(*WBO Cruiserweight Title Defence*)
18.07.98 Chris Eubank W RSC 9 Sheffield
(*WBO Cruiserweight Title Defence*)
27.03.99 Johnny Nelson L RSC 5 Derby
(*WBO Cruiserweight Title Defence*)
03.12.99 Terry Dunstan W CO 12 Peterborough
(*Vacant British Cruiserweight Title*)
13.05.00 Alain Simon W RSC 6 Barnsley
(*Vacant European Cruiserweight
Title*)
25.09.00 Alexei Illiin W RSC 2 Barnsley
(*European Cruiserweight Title
Defence*)

Carl Thompson

Harry Goodwin

03.02.01 Uriah Grant W RSC 5 Manchester
          (IBO Cruiserweight Title Challenge)
26.11.01 Ezra Sellers L RSC 4 Manchester
          (IBO Cruiserweight Title Defence)
Career: 34 contests, won 28, lost 6.

Gary Thompson

Lancaster. *Born* Darwen, 22 June, 1981
Cruiserweight. Ht. 5'9"
Manager B. Myers

22.09.01 Michael Thompson L RSC 3 Newcastle
16.11.01 Adam Cale W PTS 6 Preston
10.12.01 Rob Galloway W PTS 6 Bradford
23.12.01 Lee Whitehead L PTS 4 Salford
08.02.02 Shane White DREW 6 Preston
17.02.02 Lee Whitehead DREW 6 Salford
19.04.02 Lee Mountford DREW 4 Darlington
11.05.02 Tony Dowling L RSC 3 Newark
Career: 8 contests, won 2, drew 3, lost 3.

Michael Thompson

Spennymoor. *Born* Bishop Auckland, 2
March, 1971
Cruiserweight. Ht. 6'3"
Manager Self

13.11.99 Anthony Wright W PTS 4 Hull
20.03.00 Mark Williams W PTS 4 Mansfield
22.09.01 Gary Thompson W RSC 3 Newcastle
15.03.02 Paul Bonson W PTS 6 Spennymoor
19.04.02 Paul Bonson W PTS 6 Darlington
Career: 5 contests, won 5.

Mike Thompson

Northampton. *Born* Andover, 28 May, 1970
S. Middleweight. Ht. 6'1½"
Manager Self

17.02.97 Darren Rees L PTS 6 Bradford
15.04.97 Alex Mason L RSC 2 Edgbaston
26.07.01 Gary Dixon L PTS 6 Blackpool
16.03.02 Simon Andrews W PTS 4 Northampton
Career: 4 contests, won 1, lost 3.

(Patrick) Pedro Thompson

Birmingham. *Born* Birmingham, 27 July,
1962
L. Middleweight. Ht. 5'9½"
Manager Self

03.10.98 Joe Skeldon W RSC 5 West
          Bromwich
25.11.98 Ross McCord L RSC 2 Clydach
22.04.99 Craig Clayton W PTS 6 Dudley
15.05.99 Reagan Denton L PTS 4 Sheffield
20.09.99 Sergei Dziniruk L RTD 2
          Peterborough
02.12.99 Julian Kacanolli W PTS 6
          Peterborough
12.12.99 Darren Boys L PTS 6 Chigwell
24.02.00 Martin Scotland W RSC 4 Edgbaston
23.03.00 Ojay Abrahams DREW 6 Bloomsbury
25.05.00 Brendan Rollinson L RSC 2 Hull
02.10.00 Keith Ellwood L RSC 3 Glasgow
28.11.00 Simon Sherrington L RSC 5 Brierley
          Hill
04.02.01 Martyn Bailey L PTS 6 Queensferry
26.02.01 Matt Scriven L RTD 1 Nottingham
17.09.01 Ryan Kerr L RSC 1 Glasgow
03.12.01 Ciaran Duffy L PTS 6 Leeds
10.12.01 Mark Paxford L PTS 6 Bradford

04.03.02 Lee Williamson L PTS 6 Bradford
24.03.02 Reggie Robshaw L PTS 6 Streatham
28.04.02 Mark Stupple W RSC 4 Southwark
10.05.02 David Walker L RSC 3 Bethnal Green
25.06.02 Sam Gorman L PTS 6 Rugby
Career: 22 contests, won 5, drew 1, lost 16.

Gary Thornhill

Liverpool. *Born* Liverpool, 11 February,
1968
Former Undefeated British Featherweight
Champion. Former Undefeated WBO
Inter-Continental & Central Area
S. Featherweight Champion. Ht. 5'6½"
Manager K. Morrison

27.02.93 Brian Hickey W CO 4 Ellesmere Port
02.07.93 Dougie Fox W CO 1 Liverpool
30.10.93 Miguel Matthews W PTS 6 Chester
01.12.93 Wayne Windle W PTS 6 Stoke
25.02.94 Edward Lloyd DREW 6 Chester
06.05.94 Derek Amory W RSC 1 Liverpool
25.03.95 Craig Kelley W PTS 6 Chester
20.04.95 Michael Hermon W RSC 6 Liverpool
30.06.95 Chip O'Neill W RTD 3 Liverpool
04.11.95 Kid McAuley W PTS 6 Liverpool
08.12.95 Des Gargano W RTD 2 Liverpool
          *(Vacant Central Area S. Featherweight
          Title)*
13.04.96 Dominic McGuigan W RSC 3
          Liverpool
25.06.96 Chris Jickells W PTS 6 Stevenage
11.12.96 Justin Juuko L RSC 8 Southwark
          *(Commonwealth S. Featherweight Title
          Challenge)*
13.12.97 Pete Buckley W PTS 6 Sheffield
06.06.98 Dean Pithie W CO 8 Liverpool
          *(WBO Inter-Continental
          S. Featherweight Title Challenge)*
19.12.98 Steve Conway W RSC 9 Liverpool
          *(WBO Inter-Continental
          S. Featherweight Title Defence)*
07.08.99 Chris Jickells W RSC 4 Dagenham
04.09.99 Michael Gomez L RSC 2 Bethnal
          Green
          (Vacant British S. Featherweight Title)
06.11.99 Marc Smith W PTS 6 Widnes
11.12.99 Pete Buckley W PTS 6 Liverpool
29.02.00 Benny Jones W PTS 6 Widnes
16.05.00 Richie Wenton W RTD 8 Warrington
          (Vacant British Featherweight Title)
09.06.01 Pete Buckley W PTS 4 Bethnal Green
15.09.01 Scott Harrison L RSC 5 Manchester
          *(British & Commonwealth
          Featherweight Title Challenges)*
Career: 25 contests, won 21, drew 1, lost 3.

Danny Thornton

Leeds. *Born* Leeds, 20 July, 1978
Middleweight. Ht. 5'10"
Manager Self

06.10.97 Pedro Carragher L PTS 6 Bradford
13.11.97 Shaun O'Neill DREW 6 Bradford
08.12.97 Shaun O'Neill DREW 6 Bradford
09.02.98 Roy Chipperfield W PTS 4 Bradford
17.03.98 P. J. Maxwell L PTS 6 Sheffield
30.03.98 Mark Owens W PTS 6 Bradford
15.05.98 Danny Bell W PTS 6 Nottingham
15.06.98 Jimmy Hawk W PTS 6 Bradford
12.10.98 Wayne Shepherd W PTS 6 Bradford

21.02.99 Shaun O'Neill W RSC 5 Bradford
25.04.99 Matt Scriven W RSC 4 Leeds
14.06.99 Martin Thompson W PTS 6 Bradford
18.10.99 Paul Henry W PTS 4 Bradford
14.11.99 Dean Ashton W PTS 4 Bradford
06.12.99 Lee Blundell L PTS 6 Bradford
05.02.00 Steve Roberts L PTS 6 Bethnal Green
25.03.00 Lee Molloy W RSC 2 Liverpool
06.06.00 Joe Townsley L RSC 7 Motherwell
          *(IBO Inter-Continental
          L. Middleweight Title Challenge)*
30.11.00 Lee Blundell L RSC 8 Blackpool
          *(Vacant Central Area L. Middleweight
          Title)*
20.03.01 Ian Toby W PTS 8 Leeds
13.11.01 Matt Galer L RSC 4 Leeds
Career: 21 contests, won 12, drew 2, lost 7.

Daniel Thorpe

Sheffield. *Born* Sheffield, 24 September,
1977
L. Welterweight. Ht. 5'7½"
Manager J. Ingle

07.09.01 Brian Gifford DREW 4 Bethnal Green
24.09.01 Ram Singh W RSC 4 Cleethorpes
17.11.01 Mally McIver L PTS 6 Dewsbury
10.12.01 Jason Gonzalez W RSC 2 Birmingham
17.12.01 Joel Viney L RSC 2 Cleethorpes
11.02.02 Gareth Wiltshaw L PTS 6 Shrewsbury
04.03.02 Dave Travers W PTS 6 Birmingham
13.04.02 Jackson Williams L PTS 6 Norwich
11.05.02 Dean Scott W RSC 1 Chesterfield
21.05.02 Chris McDonagh L PTS 6 Custom
          House
08.06.02 Gary Young L RSC 1 Renfrew
Career: 11 contests, won 4, drew 1, lost 6.

John Tiftik

St Pancras. *Born* London, 3 June, 1975
L. Middleweight. Ht. 5'7½"
Manager A. Simms

07.12.98 Mark Weller W CO 4 Acton
10.03.00 Ernie Smith W PTS 4 Chigwell
27.05.00 Colin Vidler W PTS 4 Southwark
07.07.00 Casey Brooke W RSC 2 Chigwell
30.09.00 Lee Bird W PTS 6 Chigwell
02.12.00 Brian Coleman W PTS 4 Chigwell
20.01.01 Rob Stevenson W PTS 4 Bethnal
          Green
16.06.01 Mark Ramsey L PTS 6 Dagenham
13.09.01 Francie Doherty L PTS 4 Sheffield
27.03.02 Darren Covill L RSC 2 Mayfair
Career: 10 contests, won 7, lost 3.

Ian Toby

North Shields. *Born* North Shields, 18 May,
1972
S. Middleweight. Ht. 5'10½"
Manager T. Conroy

22.09.97 Mike Duffield W PTS 6 Cleethorpes
09.10.97 Jon Penn L PTS 6 Hull
21.10.97 Mike Duffield L PTS 6 Yarm
11.11.97 Gary Savage W PTS 6 Leeds
29.11.97 Paul Bowen L RSC 4 Norwich
09.02.98 Darren Rees W PTS 6 Bradford
26.02.98 Jon Penn DREW 6 Sunderland
23.04.98 Mike Whittaker W PTS 6 Newcastle
12.05.98 Wayne Burchell L PTS 6 Leeds

14.06.98	Mike Whittaker L PTS 6 Shaw
29.10.98	Eddie Haley L PTS 10 Newcastle
	(Vacant Northern Area Middleweight
	Title)
13.11.98	Lawrence Murphy L PTS 6 Glasgow
13.02.99	Eddie Haley L RSC 6 Newcastle
	(Northern Area Middleweight Title
	Challenge)
09.04.99	Biagio Falcone L RSC 3 Glasgow
10.06.99	Tony Rowbotham L PTS 4 Hartlepool
26.06.99	Biagio Falcone L PTS 4 Glasgow
15.08.99	Damon Hague L PTS 6 Derby
02.11.99	Javier Martinez W DIS 3 Ciudad Real, Spain
03.12.99	Steven Bendall L PTS 6 Peterborough
29.01.00	Anthony Farnell L RSC 3 Manchester
05.03.00	Lee Blundell L RTD 3 Shaw
11.05.00	Dean Ashton W PTS 6 Sunderland
20.05.00	Matt Mowatt W PTS 6 Rotherham
05.06.00	Albert Rybacki L PTS 4 Glasgow
09.09.00	Wayne Pinder L PTS 4 Manchester
01.10.00	Ian Cooper L RSC 4 Hartlepool
07.12.00	Paul Owen W RTD 5 Sunderland
11.02.01	Andy Vickers L PTS 6 Hartlepool
22.02.01	Matt Mowatt W PTS 6 Glasgow
20.03.01	Danny Thornton L PTS 8 Leeds
30.04.01	Biagio Falcone L RSC 2 Glasgow
07.07.01	Wayne Pinder L RTD 5 Manchester

Career: 32 contests, won 9, drew 1, lost 22.

Colin Toohey

Liverpool. *Born* Liverpool, 19 October, 1975
Lightweight. Ht. 5'7½"
Manager S. Vaughan

07.07.01	Jason Nesbitt W PTS 4 Manchester
15.09.01	Jason Nesbitt W PTS 4 Manchester
28.05.02	Nigel Senior W PTS 4 Liverpool

Career: 3 contests, won 3.

Joe Townsley

Motherwell. *Born* Bellshill, 13 January, 1972
Former Undefeated IBO Inter-Continental
L. Middleweight Champion. Ht. 5'9¼"
Manager T. Gilmour

20.03.95	Hughie Davey L PTS 6 Glasgow
05.04.95	Brian Dunn W RSC 3 Irvine
18.11.95	Kevin Toomey W RSC 6 Glasgow
14.02.96	Shamus Casey W PTS 6 Sunderland
18.03.96	Robbie Bell W PTS 6 Glasgow
03.06.96	Shamus Casey W PTS 6 Glasgow
26.09.96	Prince Kasi Kaihau W PTS 8 Glasgow
10.11.96	Michael Alexander W PTS 8 Glasgow
14.03.97	Michael Alexander W PTS 6 Irvine
02.06.97	Hughie Davey W PTS 8 Glasgow
14.10.97	Wayne Shepherd W PTS 8 Kilmarnock
24.11.97	Tony Walton W PTS 6 Glasgow
23.03.98	Pedro Carragher W PTS 6 Glasgow
21.09.98	Pedro Carragher W PTS 6 Glasgow
11.12.98	Gary Savage W RSC 6 Prestwick
25.01.99	Jim Webb W PTS 12 Glasgow
	(Vacant IBO Inter-Continental
	L. Middleweight Title)
20.09.99	Jon Foster W PTS 6 Glasgow
14.12.99	Wayne Shepherd W PTS 6 Coventry
19.02.00	Oscar Checa W RTD 4 Prestwick
	(IBO Inter-Continental
	L. Middleweight Title Defence)

06.06.00	Danny Thornton W RSC 7 Motherwell
	(IBO Inter-Continental
	L. Middleweight Title Defence)
22.01.01	Wayne Shepherd W PTS 6 Glasgow
13.03.01	Adrian Stone L PTS 12 Plymouth
	(IBO L. Middleweight Title Challenge)
17.11.01	Wayne Alexander L RSC 2 Glasgow
	(British L. Middleweight Title
	Challenge)
08.06.02	Neil Bonner W PTS 6 Renfrew

Career: 24 contests, won 21, lost 3.

Dave Travers

Rowley Regis. *Born* Smethwick, 21 September, 1971
L. Welterweight. Ht. 5'6"
Manager Self

14.10.97	Ian Turner DREW 6 Wolverhampton
20.11.97	Chris Lyons L PTS 6 Solihull
03.12.97	Craig Spacie L RSC 3 Stoke
10.02.98	Kid McAuley W PTS 6 Wolverhampton
18.03.98	Benny Jones L PTS 6 Stoke
11.05.98	Mark Payne L RTD 3 Leicester
11.09.98	Chris Emanuele W RSC 2 Newark
13.10.98	Chris Jickells L PTS 6 Wolverhampton
30.10.98	Liam Maltby L PTS 4 Peterborough
14.11.98	Steve Murray L RSC 2 Cheshunt
27.01.99	John Bermingham W PTS 6 Stoke
09.02.99	Chris Lyons L PTS 6 Wolverhampton
18.02.99	Gary Steadman L PTS 6 Barking
17.03.99	Nigel Leake L PTS 6 Stoke
17.05.99	Jim Betts L RTD 4 Cleethorpes
15.08.99	Gavin McGill L PTS 6 Derby
03.09.99	Jimmy Gould L PTS 6 West Bromwich
20.09.99	Liam Maltby L PTS 6 Peterborough
28.03.00	Duncan Armstrong L PTS 6 Wolverhampton
07.04.00	Kevin McIntyre L RSC 4 Glasgow
20.05.00	Haroon Din L PTS 6 Leicester
06.06.00	Lee Williamson L PTS 6 Brierley Hill
04.07.00	Jaz Malik L PTS 6 Tooting
13.07.00	Danny Hunt L PTS 4 Bethnal Green
12.08.00	Barry Hughes L PTS 4 Wembley
24.09.00	Lee Armstrong L PTS 6 Shaw
02.11.00	Jason McElligott L PTS 4 Kensington
18.11.00	Leo O'Reilly L RSC 3 Dagenham
03.02.01	Chill John L PTS 4 Brighton
13.02.01	Gary Greenwood L PTS 6 Brierley Hill
09.03.01	Manzo Smith L PTS 4 Millwall
27.03.01	Abdul Mannon W PTS 6 Brierley Hill
04.03.02	Daniel Thorpe L PTS 6 Birmingham

Career: 33 contests, won 4, drew 1, lost 28.

Choi Tseveenpurev

Oldham. *Born* Mongolia, 6 October, 1971
British Masters Featherweight Champion.
Ht. 5'5¾"
Manager J. Doughty

21.05.00	David Jeffrey W RSC 2 Shaw
24.09.00	Billy Smith W RTD 2 Shaw
03.12.00	Chris Williams W PTS 4 Shaw
27.04.01	Willie Limond L PTS 8 Glasgow
23.09.01	Steve Hanley W PTS 6 Shaw
06.10.01	Livinson Ruiz W PTS 4 Manchester
09.12.01	Kevin Gerowski W RSC 5 Shaw
	(Vacant British Masters Featherweight
	Title)
22.03.02	Chris Emanuele W PTS 4 Coventry
02.06.02	John Mackay W RSC 5 Shaw

Career: 9 contests, won 8, lost 1.

Steve Tuck

Halifax. *Born* Halifax, 20 June, 1971
Heavyweight. Ht. 6'1½"
Manager K. Walker/T. O'Neill

21.06.02	Gifford Shillingford L RSC 1 Leeds

Career: 1 contest, lost 1.

Ian Turner

Tredegar. *Born* Abergavenny, 6 November, 1975
Bantamweight. Former Undefeated Welsh
Bantamweight Champion. Ht. 5'8"
Manager D. Gardiner

29.05.96	Henry Jones W PTS 6 Ebbw Vale
19.07.96	Marty Chestnut W PTS 6 Ystrad
02.10.96	Kevin Sheil W PTS 6 Cardiff
14.10.97	Dave Travers DREW 6 Wolverhampton
02.12.97	Henry Jones W RSC 8 Swansea
	(Vacant Welsh Bantamweight Title)
03.04.98	Matthew Harris W PTS 8 Ebbw Vale
25.10.98	Ady Lewis DREW 8 Shaw
23.02.99	David Morris L PTS 10 Cardiff
	(Vacant Welsh Featherweight Title)
23.10.99	Esham Pickering L PTS 6 Telford
03.12.99	Frankie DeMilo L PTS 6 Peterborough
12.05.00	David Jeffrey W PTS 6 Swansea
26.05.00	Brian Carr L PTS 6 Glasgow
03.11.00	Frankie DeMilo L PTS 10 Ebbw Vale
	(British Masters S. Bantamweight Title
	Challenge)
08.06.01	German Guartos L PTS 6 Orense, Spain
30.09.01	Simon Stowell W PTS 4 Bristol
01.12.01	John Armour L PTS 8 Bethnal Green
18.03.02	Jim Betts L RTD 4 Crawley

Career: 17 contests, won 7, drew 2, lost 8.

Leo Turner

Bradford. *Born* Bradford, 17 September, 1970
L. Welterweight. Ht. 5'9"
Manager J. Celebanski

08.06.92	Wayne Rigby L PTS 6 Bradford
02.07.92	Wayne Rigby L CO 5 Middleton
12.10.92	Micky Hall L RSC 5 Bradford
14.12.92	Fred Reeve W RSC 2 Bradford
25.01.93	Alan Graham L PTS 6 Bradford
08.11.93	Tim Hill L RTD 4 Bradford
07.02.94	Paul Goode W RSC 3 Bradford
03.03.94	Colin Innes DREW 6 Newcastle
21.04.94	Colin Innes L PTS 6 Gateshead
09.05.94	Ian Richardson DREW 6 Bradford
13.06.94	Colin Innes W PTS 6 Bradford
20.10.94	Carl Roberts W RSC 3 Middleton
24.11.94	Ian Richardson W RSC 6 Newcastle
30.01.95	Trevor George L PTS 6 Bradford
25.06.00	Alan Kershaw L RSC 1 Wakefield
26.10.00	Dave Cotterill W PTS 6 Stoke
13.11.00	Geir Inge Jorgensen L CO 3 Bethnal Green
09.04.01	Duncan Armstrong W PTS 6 Bradford
04.03.02	Pete Buckley W PTS 6 Bradford
15.03.02	Andy McLean L RSC 4 Spennymoor
22.04.02	Tony McPake L RTD 4 Glasgow

Career: 21 contests, won 8, drew 2, lost 11.

Willie Valentine

Dublin. *Born* Dublin, 1 October, 1970
Featherweight. Ht. 5'3"
Manager D. Ingle

19.09.98 Sean Grant W PTS 4 Dublin
22.01.99 Graham McGrath W PTS 4 Dublin
19.03.99 Danny Lawson W RSC 1 Weston super Mare
17.04.99 Kevin Gerowski W PTS 6 Dublin
19.06.99 Delroy Spencer W PTS 4 Dublin
29.05.00 Gavin Rees L RSC 3 Manchester
12.05.01 Harry Woods L PTS 4 Plymouth
16.11.01 John Mackay L RSC 4 Dublin
Career: 8 contests, won 5, lost 3.

Bobby Vanzie

Bradford. *Born* Bradford, 11 January, 1974
British Lightweight Champion. Former
Commonwealth Lightweight Champion.
Former Undefeated Central Area
Lightweight Champion. Ht. 5'5"
Manager J. Doughty/T. Gilmour

22.05.95 Alan Peacock W RSC 1 Morecambe
29.10.95 Steve Tuckett W RSC 2 Shaw
14.11.95 John Smith W PTS 6 Bury
07.03.96 John Smith W PTS 6 Bradford
02.06.96 Anthony Campbell W PTS 6 Shaw
28.10.96 Richard Swallow W PTS 6 Bradford
24.02.97 Mark Ramsey DREW 8 Glasgow
08.06.97 C. J. Jackson W RSC 3 Shaw
23.10.97 Stuart Rimmer W RTD 8 Mayfair
(Vacant Central Area Lightweight Title)
22.11.97 Karl Taylor W PTS 6 Manchester
13.02.98 Alan Temple W CO 3 Seaham
(Elim. British Lightweight Title)
01.06.98 Gary Flear W PTS 6 Manchester
17.10.98 Wayne Rigby W RSC 10 Manchester
(British Lightweight Title Challenge)
01.04.99 Anthony Campbell W PTS 12 Birmingham
(British Lightweight Title Defence)
28.05.99 Athanus Nzau W RSC 10 Liverpool
(Vacant Commonwealth Lightweight Title)
13.09.99 Brian Coleman W PTS 6 Bethnal Green
04.12.99 Vincent Howard W PTS 12 Manchester
(Commonwealth Lightweight Title Defence)
21.02.00 Stephen Smith W RSC 9 Southwark
(British & Commonwealth Lightweight Title Defences)
17.04.00 Paul Kaoma W RSC 2 Birmingham
(Commonwealth Lightweight Title Defence)
09.09.00 Joseph Charles W RSC 6 Manchester
(Commonwealth Lightweight Title Defence)
09.10.00 Laatekwei Hammond W RSC 8 Liverpool
(Commonwealth Lightweight Title Defence)
03.02.01 James Armah L PTS 12 Manchester
(Commonwealth Lightweight Title Defence)
05.05.01 Steve Murray W RSC 7 Edmonton
(British Lightweight Title Defence)
08.10.01 Anthony Maynard W RSC 1 Barnsley
(British Lightweight Title Defence)
01.06.02 Viktor Baranov W PTS 8 Manchester
Career: 25 contests, won 23, drew 1, lost 1.

Andy Vickers

Darlington. *Born* Darlington, 18 June, 1976
Middleweight. Ht. 5'10¾"
Manager T. O'Neill

25.04.99 Matt Mowatt W PTS 6 Leeds
11.10.99 Peter McCormack W PTS 6 Birmingham
30.10.99 Rob Galloway W PTS 6 Peterlee
09.12.99 Martin Thompson W PTS 6 Sheffield
24.02.00 Chris Crook L PTS 6 Sunderland
28.03.00 Steve Timms L RSC 4 Hartlepool
21.05.00 Wayne Shepherd W PTS 6 Shaw
05.10.00 Paul Owen W PTS 6 Sunderland
24.11.00 Keith Palmer W RSC 3 Darlington
11.02.01 Ian Toby W PTS 6 Hartlepool
17.05.01 Reece McAllister L RSC 1 Leeds
03.12.01 Dean Ashton W PTS 6 Leeds
19.04.02 Danny Norton L CO 2 Darlington
Career: 13 contests, won 9, lost 4.

Bobby Vanzie　　　　　Les Clark

159

Jimmy Vincent

Birmingham. *Born* Barnet, 5 June, 1969
British Masters L. Middleweight
Champion. Ht. 5'8"
Manager Self

19.10.87	Roy Williams W PTS 6 Birmingham
11.11.87	Mick Greenwood W PTS 6 Stafford
19.11.87	Darryl Pettit W RSC 6 Ilkeston
24.11.87	Roy Williams W PTS 6 Wolverhampton
14.02.88	Niel Leggett L PTS 6 Peterborough
29.02.88	Billy Cawley W CO 1 Birmingham
13.04.88	Dave Croft W PTS 6 Wolverhampton
16.05.88	Barry North W PTS 6 Wolverhampton
14.06.88	Dean Dickinson W PTS 6 Birmingham
20.09.88	Henry Armstrong L PTS 6 Stoke
10.10.88	Henry Armstrong L PTS 6 Manchester
17.10.88	Dean Dickinson W PTS 6 Birmingham
14.11.88	Peter Gabbitus L PTS 6 Stratford upon Avon
22.11.88	Barry North W RSC 4 Wolverhampton
12.12.88	Tony Feliciello L PTS 8 Birmingham
09.09.92	Mark Dawson L PTS 6 Stoke
23.09.92	Mark Epton W RSC 6 Leeds
17.12.92	Jason Rowland L PTS 6 Wembley
06.03.93	Mark Tibbs W PTS 6 Glasgow
27.08.96	Geoff McCreesh L RSC 1 Windsor
26.09.96	David Bain W RSC 3 Walsall
28.10.96	Lee Murtagh W RSC 2 Bradford
18.01.97	Tommy Quinn W RSC 1 Swadlincote
25.02.97	Kevin Adamson W PTS 6 Sheffield
25.03.97	Gary Jacobs L RSC 1 Lewisham
25.10.97	Ahmed Dottuev L PTS 6 Queensferry
29.01.98	Craig Winter L PTS 6 Pentre Halkyn
28.03.98	Zoltan Sarossy DREW 6 Hull
18.09.98	Danny Ryan L PTS 12 Belfast *(Vacant IBO Inter-Continental S. Middleweight Title)*
24.10.98	Darren Dorrington DREW 6 Bristol
25.11.98	Cornelius Carr L PTS 6 Streatham
05.12.98	Wayne Alexander L RSC 3 Bristol
22.01.99	Jim Rock L PTS 10 Dublin
29.04.99	Anthony McFadden L PTS 6 Bethnal Green
11.12.00	Harry Butler W PTS 6 Birmingham
31.10.01	Jason Williams W PTS 10 Birmingham *(Vacant British Masters L.Middleweight Title)*
10.12.01	Ojay Abrahams W PTS 10 Birmingham *(British Masters L.Middleweight Title Defence)*
26.04.02	Darren McInulty W CO 6 Coventry *(British Masters L. Middleweight Title Defence)*

Career: 38 contests, won 20, drew 2, lost 16.

Joel Viney

Blackpool. *Born* Manchester, 25
September, 1973
Lightweight. Ht. 5'7¾"
Manager L. Veitch

02.03.00	Duncan Armstrong W PTS 6 Blackpool
09.06.00	Gareth Wiltshaw W PTS 6 Blackpool
30.11.00	Dave Cotterill L RSC 1 Blackpool
27.01.01	Bradley Pryce L RSC 3 Bethnal Green
10.03.01	Kevin Lear L RSC 2 Bethnal Green
04.06.01	Barry Hawthorne L PTS 8 Glasgow
11.06.01	Inderpaul Sandhu L PTS 4 Nottingham
26.07.01	Mark Winters L RSC 4 Blackpool
15.10.01	Tasawar Khan L PTS 6 Bradford
29.11.01	Michael Hunter L PTS 6 Hartlepool
09.12.01	Paddy Folan W PTS 6 Blackpool
17.12.01	Daniel Thorpe W RSC 2 Cleethorpes
21.01.02	Andrew Ferrans L PTS 8 Glasgow
17.02.02	John Marshall L RSC 6 Salford
18.03.02	Craig Docherty L CO 1 Glasgow
05.05.02	Andy McLean L PTS 6 Hartlepool
28.05.02	Tony McPake L RSC 1 Liverpool
29.06.02	Matthew Burke L PTS 4 Brentwood

Career: 18 contests, won 4, lost 14.

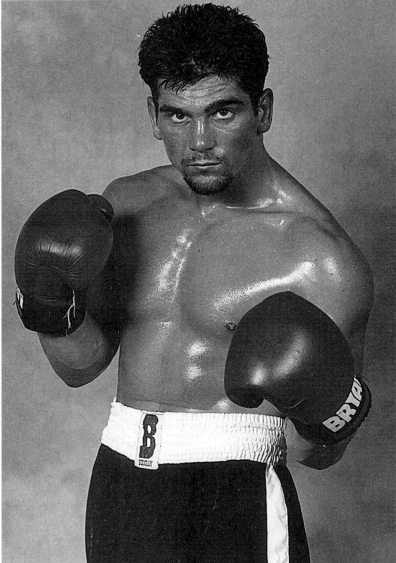

Jimmy Vincent   Chris Bevan

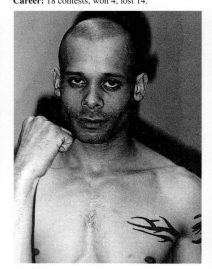

Joel Viney   Les Clark

Tommy Waite

Belfast. *Born* Belfast, 11 March, 1972
All-Ireland Bantamweight Champion.
Former British & Commonwealth
Bantamweight Champion. Ht. 5'4"
Manager B. Hearn

28.05.96	Graham McGrath W PTS 4 Belfast	
03.09.96	Danny Ruegg W RSC 4 Belfast	
05.11.96	Graham McGrath W PTS 4 Belfast	
28.01.97	Rowan Williams W PTS 4 Belfast	
29.04.97	Henry Jones W PTS 4 Belfast	
02.06.97	Louis Veitch W RSC 5 Belfast	
27.09.97	Sean Green L RSC 3 Belfast	
20.12.97	Vince Feeney W PTS 10 Belfast	
	(Vacant All-Ireland Bantamweight Title)	
28.04.98	Stevie Quinn W RSC 3 Belfast	
29.06.99	Anthony Hanna W PTS 4 Bethnal Green	
27.11.99	Kevin Gerowski L PTS 6 Liverpool	
17.04.00	Chris Emanuele W PTS 6 Bradford	
09.09.00	Ady Lewis W RSC 4 Manchester	
	(British & Commonwealth Bantamweight Title Challenges)	
09.10.00	Nicky Booth L PTS 12 Liverpool	
	(British & Commonwealth Bantamweight Title Defences)	
15.09.01	Ady Lewis L PTS 6 Nottingham	

Career: 15 contests, won 11, lost 4.

Gavin Wake   Les Clark

Gavin Wake

Leeds. *Born* Leeds, 25 June, 1979
Welterweight. Ht. 5'11"
Manager M. Marsden

26.02.01	Arv Mittoo W PTS 4 Nottingham	

09.04.01	Richard Inquieti W PTS 6 Bradford	
08.05.01	Brian Coleman W PTS 4 Barnsley	
21.06.01	Lee Williamson W PTS 6 Sheffield	
22.10.01	Darren Spencer W RSC 3 Glasgow	
24.11.01	Richard Inquieti W PTS 6 Wakefield	
27.04.02	Marcus Portman L PTS 4 Huddersfield	
15.06.02	Ernie Smith W PTS 4 Leeds	

Career: 8 contests, won 7, lost 1.

David Walker

Sidcup. *Born* Bromley, 17 June, 1976
Southern Area Welterweight Champion.
Ht. 5'10"
Manager Self

29.04.00	Dave Fallon W RSC 1 Wembley	
27.05.00	Stuart Rimmer W RSC 2 Southwark	
15.07.00	Billy Smith W RTD 2 Millwall	
16.09.00	Keith Jones W PTS 6 Bethnal Green	
14.10.00	Jason Vlasman W RSC 1 Wembley	
18.11.00	Gary Flear W PTS 4 Dagenham	
09.12.00	Karl Taylor W PTS 6 Southwark	
20.01.01	Ernie Smith W RTD 1 Bethnal Green	
17.02.01	Paul Denton W PTS 4 Bethnal Green	
19.05.01	Mark Ramsey W PTS 4 Wembley	
14.07.01	David White W PTS 4 Liverpool	
13.09.01	David Kirk DREW 8 Sheffield	
16.03.02	Paul Dyer W RSC 6 Bethnal Green	
	(Vacant Southern Area Welterweight Title)	
10.05.02	Pedro Thompson W RSC 3 Bethnal Green	

Career: 14 contests, won 13, drew 1.

David Walker   Les Clark

Dean Walker

Sheffield. *Born* Sheffield, 25 April, 1979
L. Middleweight. Ht. 5'11"
Manager D. Hobson

21.10.00	Colin McCash DREW 6 Sheffield	
11.12.00	James Lee L PTS 6 Sheffield	
27.07.01	Chris Duggan W RSC 4 Sheffield	
15.12.01	William Webster W PTS 6 Sheffield	
03.03.02	Shaun Horsfall W PTS 6 Shaw	
02.06.02	Wayne Shepherd W PTS 6 Shaw	

Career: 6 contests, won 4, drew 1, lost 1.

Dean Walker   Les Clark

Carl Walton

Birmingham. *Born* Redditch, 7 June, 1975
Welterweight. Ht. 5'7"
Manager N. Nobbs

17.09.01	Gary Porter L PTS 6 Glasgow	
28.10.01	James Paisley L PTS 4 Southwark	
10.12.01	Chris Duggan L PTS 6 Birmingham	

Career: 3 contests, lost 3.

Martin Watson

Coatbridge. *Born* Bellshill, 12 May, 1981
Lightweight. Ht. 5'8"
Manager R. Bannon/K. Morrison

24.05.01	Shaune Danskin W RSC 3 Glasgow	
20.10.01	Jon Honney W RSC 3 Glasgow	
16.12.01	Richie Caparelli W PTS 6 Glasgow	
11.03.02	Pete Buckley W PTS 4 Glasgow	
26.04.02	Gary Reid W PTS 6 Glasgow	
08.06.02	Scott Miller W RSC 2 Renfrew	

Career: 6 contests, won 6.

Danny Watts

Peckham. *Born* London, 5 April, 1973
Heavyweight. Ht. 6'7"
Manager F. King

02.09.97	Johnny Davison W CO 2 Southwark	
10.01.98	Steve Cranston W RSC 4 Bethnal Green	
11.04.98	Gavin McGhin W PTS 4 Southwark	
12.09.98	Ladislav Husarik W PTS 4 Bethnal Green	
04.02.99	Luke Simpkin W CO 3 Lewisham	
06.03.99	Piotr Jurczyk W PTS 4 Southwark	
22.05.99	Gordon Minors L CO 1 Belfast	
18.12.99	Adey Cook W RSC 1 Southwark	
13.03.00	Mark Potter L RSC 6 Bethnal Green	
	(Vacant Southern Area Heavyweight Title)	
23.03.02	Valery Semishkur W RSC 1 Southwark	
18.05.02	Mal Rice W RTD 3 Millwall	

Career: 11 contests, won 9, lost 2.

Danny Watts   Les Clark

William Webster

Birmingham. *Born* Birmingham, 14 March, 1970
S. Middleweight. Ht. 6'0"
Manager Self

05.06.99	Brian Knudsen L RSC 4 Cardiff
15.08.99	Edwin Cleary L PTS 6 Derby
03.09.99	Steve Timms L RSC 4 West Bromwich
12.11.99	Biagio Falcone L PTS 6 Glasgow
20.11.99	Gary Beardsley L PTS 6 Grantham
02.12.99	Wayne Elcock L PTS 6 Peterborough
13.12.99	Biagio Falcone L RSC 1 Glasgow
21.02.00	Scott Millar L PTS 6 Glasgow
29.02.00	Thomas McDonagh L RTD 2 Widnes
28.03.00	Peter McCormack L PTS 6 Wolverhampton
13.04.00	Steve Ryan L PTS 4 Holborn
15.05.00	Mike Duffield W PTS 6 Birmingham
29.05.00	Michael Jennings L PTS 6 Manchester
19.06.00	Damon Hague L PTS 4 Burton
01.07.00	Alan Page L PTS 4 Manchester
25.09.00	Reagan Denton L PTS 4 Barnsley
07.10.00	George Robshaw L PTS 4 Doncaster
10.11.00	Chris Nembhard L RSC 1 Mayfair
28.01.01	Peter Nightingale L PTS 6 Wolverhampton
17.02.01	Matthew Tait L PTS 4 Bethnal Green
25.02.01	Gary Beardsley L PTS 6 Derby
13.03.01	Mark Phillips L RTD 1 Plymouth
16.06.01	Andrew Lowe L RSC 2 Dagenham
15.12.01	Dean Walker L PTS 6 Sheffield
23.12.01	James Davenport L RSC 5 Salford
17.02.02	Donovan Smillie L PTS 6 Salford
03.03.02	Gary Dixon L PTS 6 Shaw
16.03.02	Matthew Thirlwall L RSC 1 Bethnal Green
15.04.02	Roddy Doran L PTS 8 Shrewsbury
15.06.02	Danny Smith L PTS 6 Norwich

Career: 31 contests, won 1, lost 29.

Greg Wedlake

Minehead. *Born* Bristol, 19 January, 1970
Heavyweight. Ht. 6'2³/₄"
Manager C. Sanigar

19.10.96	Lennox Williams W PTS 4 Bristol
09.12.96	Johnny Davison W PTS 6 Bristol
21.01.97	Johnny Davison W RSC 2 Bristol
05.06.97	David Jules W RSC 3 Bristol
15.09.97	Nick Howard W PTS 6 Bristol
16.12.01	Mal Rice W RSC 3 Bristol

Career: 6 contests, won 6.

Greg Wedlake   Les Clark

Paul Wesley

Birmingham. *Born* Birmingham, 2 May, 1962
S. Middleweight. Ht. 5'9"
Manager Self

20.02.87	B. K. Bennett L PTS 6 Maidenhead
18.03.87	Darryl Ritchie DREW 4 Stoke
08.04.87	Dean Murray W PTS 6 Evesham
29.04.87	John Wright W PTS 4 Loughborough
12.06.87	Leon Thomas W RSC 2 Leamington
16.11.87	Steve McCarthy L CO 8 Southampton
25.01.88	Paul Murray W PTS 8 Birmingham
29.02.88	Paul Murray DREW 8 Birmingham
15.03.88	Johnny Williamson W CO 2 Bournemouth
09.04.88	Joe McKenzie W RSC 6 Bristol
10.05.88	Tony Meszaros W PTS 8 Edgbaston
21.03.89	Carlton Warren L CO 2 Wandsworth
10.05.89	Rod Douglas L CO 1 Kensington
24.10.89	Nigel Rafferty L PTS 6 Wolverhampton
22.11.89	Nigel Rafferty L PTS 8 Stafford
28.11.89	Nigel Rafferty L PTS 6 Wolverhampton
05.12.89	Ian Strudwick L PTS 6 Catford
24.01.90	Rocky Feliciello W PTS 6 Solihull
19.02.90	Nigel Rafferty L PTS 8 Birmingham
22.03.90	John Ashton L PTS 10 Wolverhampton
	(Midlands Area Middleweight Title Challenge)
17.04.90	Winston May DREW 8 Millwall
09.05.90	Alan Richards W PTS 8 Solihull
04.06.90	Julian Eavis W PTS 8 Birmingham
18.09.90	Shaun Cummins L RSC 1 Wolverhampton

17.10.90	Julian Eavis W PTS 6 Stoke
23.01.91	Wally Swift Jnr L PTS 10 Solihull
	(Midlands Area L. Middleweight Title Challenge)
20.03.91	Horace Fleary L RSC 5 Solihull
16.05.91	Delroy Waul L RSC 7 Liverpool
04.07.91	Neville Brown W RSC 1 Alfreton
31.07.91	Francesco dell'Aquila L PTS 8 Casella, Italy
03.10.91	Neville Brown L PTS 8 Burton
29.10.91	Tony Collins DREW 8 Kensington
03.03.92	Antonio Fernandez L PTS 10 Cradley Heath
	(Vacant Midlands Area Middleweight Title)
10.04.92	Jean-Charles Meuret L PTS 8 Geneva, Switzerland
03.06.92	Sumbu Kalambay L PTS 10 Salice Terme, Italy
29.10.92	Ian Strudwick W RSC 1 Bayswater
14.11.92	Paul Busby L PTS 8 Cardiff
24.11.92	Paul Jones W RSC 2 Doncaster
16.03.93	Chris Pyatt L PTS 10 Mayfair
04.06.93	Jacques le Blanc L PTS 10 Moncton, Canada
28.07.93	Antonio Fernandez L RSC 3 Brixton
	(Midlands Area Middleweight Title Challenge)
09.10.93	Warren Stowe W PTS 10 Manchester
	(Elim. British L. Middleweight Title)
09.02.94	Steve Collins L PTS 8 Brentwood
10.02.95	Robert McCracken L PTS 12 Birmingham
	(British L. Middleweight Title Challenge)
24.02.95	Scott Doyle W PTS 8 Weston super Mare
18.03.95	Crisanto Espana L PTS 6 Millstreet
21.04.95	Gilbert Jackson L RSC 6 Dudley
	(Elim. British L. Middleweight Title)
31.01.96	Howard Eastman L RSC 1 Birmingham
21.03.96	Gary Logan L PTS 6 Southwark
13.04.96	Harry Simon L RTD 4 Wythenshawe
26.09.96	Nigel Rafferty DREW 6 Walsall
19.10.96	Glenn Catley L RSC 7 Bristol
25.03.97	Chris Johnson L CO 2 Lewisham
07.02.98	Paul Carr L PTS 6 Cheshunt
07.03.98	Omar Sheika L RTD 4 Reading
23.09.98	Lester Jacobs L CO 4 Bloomsbury
13.02.99	Geoff McCreesh L PTS 8 Newcastle
03.04.99	Toks Owoh L CO 5 Kensington
23.03.00	Lester Jacobs L PTS 6 Bloomsbury
13.04.00	Sam Soliman L PTS 6 Holborn
19.08.00	Adrian Dodson L PTS 4 Brentwood
18.11.00	Paul Bowen L PTS 4 Dagenham
11.12.00	Darren Rhodes L PTS 4 Widnes
08.03.01	Lee Blundell L RSC 3 Blackpool
25.09.01	Tony Dodson L PTS 6 Liverpool
17.11.01	Dean Cockburn L PTS 4 Glasgow
24.11.01	Andrew Lowe L PTS 4 Bethnal Green
08.12.01	David Starie L CO 1 Dagenham

Career: 68 contests, won 16, drew 5, lost 47.

Wayne Wheeler

Plymouth. *Born* Plymouth, 24 February, 1970
Lightweight. Ht. 5'8"
Manager N. Christian

24.03.01	J.J. Moore L RSC 4 Newark
12.05.01	Byron Pryce L RSC 2 Plymouth
16.12.01	Danny Gwilym W RSC 2 Bristol
17.02.02	Dean Hickman DREW 6 Wolverhampton

16.03.02 David Kehoe DREW 6 Northampton
13.04.02 Dean Hickman L PTS 6 Wolverhampton
11.05.02 Carl Greaves L RSC 1 Newark
Career: 7 contests, won 1, drew 2, lost 4.

David White
Cardiff. *Born* Cardiff, 18 April, 1975
Welterweight. Ht. 5'9"
Manager D. Gardiner

23.09.00 Matthew Hatton L PTS 4 Bethnal Green
25.11.00 Matthew Hatton L PTS 4 Manchester
28.01.01 Jimmy Gould L PTS 6 Wolverhampton
05.02.01 Lance Crosby DREW 4 Hull
24.02.01 Francis Barrett L PTS 4 Bethnal Green
28.04.01 Ahmet Kaddour L PTS 4 Cardiff
12.05.01 Leo O'Reilly L PTS 4 Plymouth
24.05.01 Ronnie Nailen L PTS 6 Glasgow
14.07.01 David Walker L PTS 4 Liverpool
18.08.01 Oscar Hall L PTS 6 Dewsbury
Career: 10 contests, drew 1, lost 9.

Jason White
Cardiff. *Born* Cardiff, 18 November, 1978
S. Featherweight. Ht. 5'6"
Manager D. Gardiner

27.11.00 Stephen Chinnock L PTS 4 Birmingham
16.12.00 Scott Miller L PTS 4 Sheffield
08.03.01 Nigel Senior W PTS 8 Stoke
12.05.01 Lee Meager L PTS 4 Plymouth
14.07.01 Dean Pithie L PTS 4 Liverpool
18.08.01 Jesse James Daniel L PTS 6 Dewsbury
Career: 6 contests, won 1, lost 5.

Shane White
Wells. *Born* Bristol, 27 January, 1972
L. Heavyweight. Ht. 5'9"
Manager T. Woodward

08.02.02 Gary Thompson DREW 6 Preston
18.03.02 Billy McClung W RTD 4 Glasgow
Career: 2 contests, won 1, drew 1.

Lee Whitehead
Manchester. *Born* Barton, 16 July, 1965
Cruiserweight. Ht. 5'10¾"
Manager Self

09.10.95 Roy Chipperfield W RSC 2 Manchester
04.12.95 Phil Ball W PTS 6 Manchester
13.01.96 Elwen Brooks W PTS 6 Manchester
26.02.96 Kevin Burton W PTS 6 Manchester
13.04.96 Mark Snipe L PTS 4 Wythenshawe
02.06.96 Andy Fletcher W RSC 2 Shaw
22.08.96 Peter Mason W PTS 6 Salford
19.09.96 Brian Galloway W PTS 4 Manchester
22.12.96 Martin Jolley DREW 6 Salford
18.01.97 Mark Dawson W PTS 6 Manchester
26.06.97 Martin Jolley W PTS 6 Salford
19.09.97 Carl Nicholson L PTS 6 Salford
22.11.97 Kevin Burton DREW 4 Manchester
21.12.97 Mark Dawson L RSC 4 Salford
23.02.98 Peter Federenko L PTS 6 Salford
27.05.01 Darren Ashton L RSC 2 Manchester
23.12.01 Gary Thompson W PTS 4 Salford
17.02.02 Gary Thompson DREW 6 Salford
25.04.02 Earl Ling L PTS 6 Hull
Career: 19 contests, won 10, drew 3, lost 6.

Leigh Wicks
Brighton. *Born* Worthing, 29 July, 1965
S. Middleweight. Ht. 5'6¼"
Manager Self

29.04.87 Fidel Castro W PTS 6 Hastings
26.09.87 Jason Rowe W PTS 6 Hastings
18.11.87 Lou Ayres W PTS 6 Holborn
26.01.88 Theo Marius L PTS 8 Hove
15.02.88 Shamus Casey W PTS 6 Copthorne
26.04.88 Franki Moro DREW 8 Hove
04.05.88 Tony Britton W PTS 8 Wembley
18.05.88 Mark Howell W RSC 8 Portsmouth
25.05.88 Newton Barnett DREW 8 Hastings
22.11.88 Roy Callaghan L PTS 8 Basildon
16.03.89 Tony Britland W PTS 8 Southwark
12.10.89 Tony Gibbs W CO 2 Southwark
08.02.90 Ernie Noble W PTS 8 Southwark
26.04.90 Julian Eavis DREW 8 Mayfair
06.11.90 Gordon Blair W PTS 8 Mayfair
10.01.91 Barry Messam W PTS 6 Wandsworth
14.02.91 Kevin Thompson W PTS 8 Southampton
21.10.91 Tony Britland W RSC 3 Mayfair
20.02.92 Mick Duncan L PTS 8 Glasgow
30.04.92 Darren Morris DREW 6 Mayfair
19.10.92 Bozon Haule W PTS 8 Mayfair
20.01.93 Robert McCracken L PTS 8 Wolverhampton
17.02.93 Kevin Lueshing L PTS 6 Bethnal Green
22.04.93 Warren Stowe L PTS 6 Bury
27.10.95 Danny Quacoe W RSC 4 Brighton
18.11.95 Gary Jacobs L RTD 3 Glasgow
26.01.96 Wayne Appleton L PTS 6 Brighton
05.03.96 Kevin Thompson L PTS 6 Bethnal Green
24.03.97 Ross Hale L PTS 6 Bristol
08.04.97 Ahmet Dottuev L RSC 1 Bethnal Green
29.05.97 Nicky Thurbin L PTS 8 Mayfair
11.07.97 Darren Covill L RSC 2 Brighton
27.11.97 Lester Jacobs L PTS 6 Bloomsbury
06.12.97 Rhoshi Wells L PTS 4 Wembley
21.02.98 Neil Sinclair L PTS 6 Belfast
24.03.98 Ojay Abrahams L PTS 6 Bethnal Green
05.06.98 Darren Bruce L PTS 6 Southend
25.11.98 Darren Covill W PTS 4 Streatham
22.02.99 Neil Linford L PTS 6 Peterborough
26.06.99 Mehrdud Takaloo L CO 3 Millwall
09.10.99 Darren Rhodes L PTS 4 Manchester
27.11.99 Geoff McCreesh L PTS 6 Lubeck, Germany
11.12.99 Darren Rhodes L PTS 4 Liverpool
21.02.00 Sergei Dzinziruk L RSC 2 Southwark
25.03.00 Darren Rhodes L PTS 4 Liverpool
08.04.00 Spencer Fearon L PTS 4 Bethnal Green
02.06.00 Allan Foster L PTS 4 Ashford
24.06.00 Scott Dixon L PTS 4 Glasgow
01.07.00 Karim Hussine L PTS 6 Southwark
30.09.00 Bobby Banghar L PTS 4 Peterborough
07.10.00 Jamie Moore L PTS 4 Doncaster
11.11.00 Brian Knudsen L RSC 5 Belfast
17.03.01 Wayne Pinder L PTS 4 Manchester
29.03.01 Lester Jacobs L PTS 4 Hammersmith
05.05.01 Ty Browne L PTS 6 Brighton
08.06.01 Jason Collins L PTS 4 Hull
21.07.01 Damon Hague L PTS 4 Sheffield
31.07.01 Erik Teymour L RSC 1 Bethnal Green
30.09.01 Liam Lathbury L PTS 4 Bristol
09.10.01 Ruben Groenewald L PTS 6 Cardiff
28.10.01 Allan Gray L PTS 4 Southwark
17.11.01 Lawrence Murphy L PTS 4 Glasgow
08.12.01 Wayne Asker L PTS 4 Dagenham
16.12.01 Allan Gray L PTS 4 Southwark
31.01.02 Freddie Yemofio W PTS 6 Piccadilly
09.02.02 P.J. Maxwell L PTS 4 Manchester
13.04.02 Andrew Facey L PTS 6 Norwich
10.05.02 Matthew Thirlwall L PTS 4 Bethnal Green
Career: 68 contests, won 17, drew 4, lost 47.

Jan Wild (Cooper)
Stockton. *Born* Stockton, 6 June, 1964
Bantamweight. Ht. 5'4½"
Manager T. Miller

01.12.99 Audrey Guthrie W PTS 4 Yarm
15.05.00 Michelle Sutcliffe L PTS 6 Cleethorpes
01.07.00 Cathy Brown L PTS 6 Southwark
(*Vacant WBF Pan-European Flyweight Title*)
Career: 3 contests, won 1, lost 2.

Noel Wilders
Castleford. *Born* Castleford, 4 January, 1975
Former Undefeated IBO, British & Central Area Bantamweight Champion. Ht. 5'5"
Manager T. Callighan

16.03.96 Neil Parry W RTD 4 Sheffield
04.06.96 Graham McGrath W PTS 6 York
04.10.96 Tiger Singh W PTS 6 Wakefield
23.10.96 Jason Thomas W PTS 6 Halifax
12.03.97 John Matthews W PTS 6 Stoke
20.04.97 Shaun Anderson W PTS 6 Leeds
13.11.97 Anthony Hanna W PTS 6 Bradford
06.02.98 Marcus Duncan W RSC 6 Wakefield
(*Vacant Central Area Bantamweight Title*)
21.05.98 Matthew Harris W PTS 6 Bradford
18.07.98 Sean Grant W RSC 4 Sheffield
23.10.98 Fondil Madani W DIS 7 Wakefield
28.11.98 Ross Cassidy W PTS 8 Sheffield
06.02.99 Jason Thomas W PTS 10 Halifax
(*Elim. British Bantamweight Title*)
24.04.99 Anthony Hanna W PTS 6 Peterborough
22.06.99 Ady Lewis W RSC 6 Ipswich
(*Final Elim. British Bantamweight Title*)
30.10.99 Francis Ampofo W PTS 12 Peterlee
(*Vacant British Bantamweight Title*)
18.01.00 Steve Williams W RTD 11 Mansfield
(*British Bantamweight Title Defence*)
20.03.00 Kamel Guerfi W PTS 12 Mansfield
(*Vacant IBO Bantamweight Title*)
15.07.00 Paul Lloyd W PTS 12 Millwall
(*IBO Bantamweight Title Defence*)
28.04.01 Stevie Quinn W RTD 6 Dublin
21.07.01 Chris Emanuele W PTS 6 Sheffield
15.06.02 Sean Grant W RSC 3 Leeds
Career: 22 contests, won 22.

Spencer Wilding
Rhyl. *Born* St Asaph, 26 July, 1972
Cruiserweight. Ht. 6'7"
Manager M. Goodall

08.03.02 Adam Cale W PTS 6 Ellesmere Port
10.05.02 Jon Penn W RTD 1 Preston
Career: 2 contests, won 2.

Danny Williams
Brixton. *Born* London, 13 July, 1973
British & Commonwealth Heavyweight Champion. Former Undefeated WBO Inter-Continental Heavyweight Champion. Ht. 6'3"
Manager F. Warren

21.10.95	Vance Idiens W CO 2 Bethnal Green
09.12.95	Joey Paladino W RSC 1 Bethnal Green
13.02.96	Slick Miller W RSC 1 Bethnal Green
09.03.96	James Wilder W PTS 4 Millstreet
13.07.96	John Pierre W PTS 4 Bethnal Green
31.08.96	Andy Lambert W RSC 2 Dublin
09.11.96	Michael Murray W CO 1 Manchester
08.02.97	Shane Woollas W RSC 2 Millwall
03.05.97	Albert Call W RSC 4 Manchester
19.07.97	R. F. McKenzie W RSC 2 Wembley
15.11.97	Bruce Douglas W RSC 2 Bristol
19.12.97	Derek Amos W RSC 4 New York City, USA
21.02.98	Shane Woollas W RSC 2 Belfast
16.05.98	Antonio Diaz W CO 3 Bethnal Green
10.10.98	Antoine Palatis W PTS 12 Bethnal Green
	(Vacant WBO Inter-Continental Heavyweight Title)
03.04.99	Julius Francis L PTS 12 Kensington
	(British & Commonwealth Heavyweight Title Challenges)
02.10.99	Ferenc Deak W RTD 1 Namur, Belgium
18.12.99	Harry Senior W PTS 12 Southwark
	(Vacant Commonwealth Heavyweight Title)
19.02.00	Anton Nel W CO 5 Dagenham
06.05.00	Michael Murray W RSC 6 Frankfurt, Germany
24.06.00	Craig Bowen-Price W CO 1 Glasgow
23.09.00	Quinn Navarre W RSC 6 Bethnal Green
21.10.00	Mark Potter W RSC 6 Wembley
	(Commonwealth & WBO Inter-Continental Heavyweight Title Defences. Vacant British Heavyweight Title)
09.06.01	Kali Meehan W RSC 1 Bethnal Green
	(Commonwealth Heavyweight Title Defence)
28.07.01	Julius Francis W CO 4 Wembley
	(British & Commonwealth Heavyweight Title Defences)
15.12.01	Shawn Robinson W RSC 2 Mashantucket Connecticut, USA
12.02.02	Michael Sprott W RTD 7 Bethnal Green
	(British & Commonwealth Heavyweight Title Defences)

Career: 27 contests, won 26, lost 1.

(Wayne) Darren Williams

Swansea. *Born* Swansea, 17 July, 1975
Welterweight. Ht. 5'8"
Manager Self

21.06.97	John Smith W PTS 4 Cardiff
26.09.97	Harry Butler W PTS 6 Port Talbot
02.12.97	Steve Tuckett L PTS 6 Swansea
24.01.98	Paul Salmon W PTS 4 Cardiff
23.04.98	Danny Quacoe W PTS 8 Neath
05.09.98	Anthony Farnell L RTD 4 Telford
12.12.00	Gareth Jones DREW 6 Clydach
20.04.01	Richard Inquieti W PTS 6 Dublin
15.09.01	Jon Harrison W PTS 6 Swansea
12.12.01	James Lee W PTS 4 Clydach
24.04.02	Adrian Kirkbride W RSC 2 Dublin

Career: 11 contests, won 8, drew 1, lost 2.

(Darren) Dazzo Williams

Hereford. *Born* Lambeth, 19 March, 1974
S. Bantamweight. Ht. 5'8"
Manager D. Gardiner

24.02.01	Mickey Coveney W CO 1 Bethnal Green
19.05.01	Mark Payne W PTS 8 Wembley
14.07.01	Dimitri Gorodetsky W RSC 3 Liverpool
19.12.01	Mark Alexander W PTS 6 Coventry
18.01.02	Zolani Msolo W RSC 2 Coventry
20.04.02	John Mackay L PTS 6 Wembley

Career: 6 contests, won 5, lost 1.

Danny Williams — Les Clark

Dazzo Williams — Les Clark

Gary Williams

Nottingham. *Born* Nottingham, 25
September, 1965
Heavyweight, Ht. 5'11½"
Manager Self

27.04.92	Damien Caesar L RSC 4 Mayfair
07.09.92	J. A. Bugner L PTS 4 Bethnal Green
06.10.92	Scott Welch L PTS 4 Antwerp, Belgium
01.12.92	Kenny Sandison W PTS 6 Liverpool
27.01.93	Kenny Sandison DREW 6 Stoke
13.02.93	Kevin McBride L PTS 4 Manchester
01.03.93	Ashley Naylor DREW 6 Bradford
29.03.93	Kevin Cullinane W RSC 2 Liverpool
26.04.93	Ashley Naylor W PTS 6 Bradford
10.08.93	Peter Smith L RSC 4 Marula, South Africa
08.12.93	Graham Arnold L PTS 6 Hull
02.02.94	Vincenzo Cantatore L CO 2 Ferrara, Italy
17.03.94	Neil Kirkwood L RSC 1 Lincoln
10.09.94	Clayton Brown L PTS 4 Birmingham
04.10.94	Mike Holden L RSC 4 Mayfair
13.12.94	Damien Caesar L RSC 2 Ilford
18.03.95	Darren Corbett DREW 4 Millstreet
06.05.95	Clayton Brown L PTS 4 Shepton Mallet
10.06.95	Joey Paladino L PTS 6 Manchester
15.09.95	Adrian Kneeshaw W RSC 6 Mansfield
11.10.95	Shane Woollas L PTS 6 Solihull
03.11.95	Tony Henry W PTS 6 Dudley
24.11.95	Pele Reid L RSC 1 Manchester
12.01.96	John Pettersson DREW 4 Copenhagen, Denmark
31.01.96	Robert Norton L RSC 2 Birmingham
21.03.96	Mika Kihlstrom L PTS 4 Southwark
02.04.96	Doug Liggion L PTS 4 Southwark
22.04.96	Shane Woollas L PTS 10 Cleethorpes *(Vacant Midlands Area Heavyweight Title)*
27.05.96	Jukka Jarvinen L PTS 6 Helsinki, Finland
09.07.96	Sugar Raj Kumar Sangwan L PTS 4 Bethnal Green
08.10.96	Owen Bartley L PTS 4 Battersea
26.11.96	Israel Ajose L CO 2 Bethnal Green
18.01.97	Craig Bowen-Price L CO 1 Manchester
28.04.97	Jarrod Corrigan W RSC 4 Hull
02.09.97	Michael Sprott L PTS 6 Southwark
06.10.97	Johnny Davison W PTS 8 Piccadilly
15.12.97	Shane Woollas L RSC 8 Cleethorpes *(Midlands Area Heavyweight Title Challenge)*
15.12.98	Scott Lansdowne L PTS 6 Sheffield
16.01.99	Michael Sprott L PTS 6 Bethnal Green
04.02.99	Rimas Priczmantas L PTS 4 Lewisham
22.02.99	Derek McCafferty L CO 1 Peterborough
27.04.99	Tommy Bannister L PTS 4 Bethnal Green
28.05.99	Albert Sosnowski L RSC 4 Liverpool
26.06.99	Patrick Halberg L PTS 4 Millwall
17.07.99	Roman Bugaj L RSC 4 Gdansk, Poland
07.10.99	Paul Fiske W PTS 6 Sunderland
27.11.99	Tommy Bannister W PTS 4 Liverpool
09.12.99	Paul Fiske W PTS 6 Sunderland
29.01.00	Petr Horacek L PTS 4 Manchester
18.02.00	Mal Rice W PTS 6 Pentre Halkyn
05.05.00	Mal Rice W PTS 4 Pentre Halkyn
20.05.00	Scott Lansdowne L RSC 1 Leicester *(Vacant WBF European S. Cruiserweight Title)*
21.10.00	John McDermott L PTS 4 Wembley
13.11.00	Danny Percival L PTS 4 Bethnal Green
04.06.01	Billy Bessey L PTS 4 Hartlepool

22.09.01	John McDermott L RSC 4 Bethnal Green
08.12.01	Mark Potter L RSC 3 Dagenham
11.05.02	Mark Krence L PTS 6 Chesterfield

Career: 58 contests, won 12, drew 4, lost 42.

Jackson Williams

Norwich. *Born* Norwich, 19 June, 1981
Lightweight. Ht. 5'6½"
Manager J. Ingle

13.04.02	Daniel Thorpe W PTS 6 Norwich
15.06.02	Jason Gonzalez W PTS 6 Norwich

Career: 2 contests, won 2.

(Leon) Jason Williams

Swansea. *Born* Swansea, 11 July, 1974
Welterweight. Ht. 5'11"
Manager C. Sanigar

19.04.97	Jon Harrison L PTS 6 Plymouth
21.06.97	Dewi Roberts W RSC 1 Cardiff
26.09.97	Darren Covill W PTS 6 Port Talbot
15.11.97	Peter Federenko W PTS 4 Bristol
24.01.98	Danny Quacoe W PTS 4 Cardiff
23.02.98	Adrian Chase W PTS 6 Windsor
30.03.98	Rob Pitters W RSC 3 Tenerife
30.05.98	Prince Kasi Kaihau W CO 2 Bristol
14.07.98	Jon Harrison W RTD 2 Reading
05.12.98	Mark Ramsey W PTS 6 Bristol
23.04.99	Harry Butler W RSC 7 Clydach
05.06.99	Paul Miles W RSC 2 Cardiff
02.07.99	Delroy Mellis W PTS 6 Bristol
24.09.99	Michael Smyth L RSC 3 Merthyr *(Vacant Welsh Welterweight Title)*
07.04.00	David Baptiste W PTS 6 Bristol
08.09.00	Karim Bouali L RSC 5 Bristol
03.11.00	Mark Ramsey L CO 6 Ebbw Vale
15.09.01	Mark Richards W PTS 6 Swansea
31.10.01	Jimmy Vincent L PTS 10 Birmingham *(Vacant British Masters L.Middleweight Title)*
16.03.02	Charden Ansoula L RSC 5 Northampton

Career: 20 contests, won 14, lost 6.

Mark Williams

Birmingham. *Born* Birmingham, 16
September, 1969
Cruiserweight. Ht. 6'1"
Manager Self

18.09.98	Mark Levy L PTS 6 Manchester
26.09.98	Faisal Mohammed L RSC 2 Norwich
10.12.98	Anthony Wright W PTS 6 Barking
19.01.99	Cliff Elden W PTS 6 Ipswich
24.03.99	Kenny Gayle DREW 6 Bayswater
29.04.99	Frode Stenasham W RSC 4 Bethnal Green
23.06.99	Jason Brewster DREW 6 West Bromwich
11.12.99	Enzo Maccarinelli L RSC 1 Merthyr
20.03.00	Michael Thompson L PTS 4 Mansfield
04.07.00	Kenny Gayle L PTS 4 Tooting
29.09.00	Paul Maskell W RSC 2 Bethnal Green
20.01.01	Faisal Mohammed L RSC 3 Bethnal Green
24.03.01	Mark Krence L PTS 4 Sheffield
21.06.01	Ali Forbes L PTS 4 Earls Court
07.09.01	Chris Davies L RSC 4 Bethnal Green

Career: 15 contests, won 3, drew 2, lost 10.

Richard Williams

Stockwell. *Born* London, 9 May, 1971
IBO L. Middleweight Champion. Former
Undefeated Commonwealth L.
Middleweight Champion. Ht. 5'9½"
Manager B. Hearn

08.03.97	Marty Duke W RSC 3 Brentwood
30.06.97	Danny Quacoe W PTS 4 Bethnal Green
02.09.97	Michael Alexander L PTS 4 Southwark
16.10.99	Pedro Carragher W RSC 2 Bethnal Green
06.11.99	Lee Bird W RSC 4 Bethnal Green
20.12.99	Harry Butler W RSC 1 Bethnal Green
17.04.00	Kevin Thompson W CO 1 Birmingham
16.06.00	Piotr Bartnicki W RSC 3 Bloomsbury
08.09.00	Dean Ashton W RSC 1 Hammersmith
04.11.00	Howard Clarke W CO 4 Bethnal Green
02.12.00	Aziz Daari W RSC 2 Bethnal Green
23.01.01	Tony Badea W RSC 3 Crawley *(Commonwealth L. Middleweight Title Challenge)*
04.06.01	Hussain Osman W PTS 10 Hartlepool
25.09.01	Andrew Murray W RSC 3 Liverpool *(Commonwealth L. Middleweight Title Defence)*
20.10.01	Viktor Fesetchko W RSC 6 Portsmouth
01.12.01	Shannan Taylor W RSC 4 Bethnal Green *(Commonwealth L. Middleweight Title Defence. Vacant IBO L. Middleweight Title)*
29.06.02	Paul Samuels T DRAW 3 Brentwood *(IBO L. Middleweight Title Defence)*

Career: 17 contests, won 15, drew 1, lost 1.

Steve Williams

Mansfield. *Born* Worksop, 11 October,
1968
Former Undefeated Midlands Area
Bantamweight Champion. Ht. 5'7"
Manager T. Gilmour

06.03.95	Shaun Hall DREW 6 Bradford
06.04.95	Andy Roberts W PTS 6 Sheffield
20.10.95	Terry Gaskin W PTS 6 Mansfield
22.11.95	Neil Parry W PTS 6 Sheffield
22.03.96	Darren Noble W PTS 6 Mansfield
12.09.96	Andy Roberts W PTS 6 Doncaster
01.11.96	Tiger Singh W PTS 6 Mansfield
20.02.97	Neil Parry W PTS 8 Mansfield
08.05.97	Mark Reynolds W RTD 6 Mansfield *(Elim. British Flyweight Title)*
19.03.98	Sean Green W PTS 6 Doncaster
14.10.98	Ross Cassidy W PTS 6 Stoke
18.03.99	Ross Cassidy W PTS 6 Doncaster
27.06.99	Shaun Norman W PTS 10 Alfreton *(Vacant Midlands Area Bantamweight Title)*
18.01.00	Noel Wilders L RTD 11 Mansfield *(British Bantamweight Title Challenge)*
11.05.02	Tasawar Khan W PTS 6 Newark

Career: 15 contests, won 12, drew 1, lost 2.

Lee Williamson

Worcester. *Born* Worcester, 3 February,
1974
Welterweight. Ht. 5'9"
Manager Self

26.10.98	Trevor Tacy L PTS 6 Manchester
26.11.98	David Smales W PTS 6 Bradford
16.01.99	Graham Earl L RSC 4 Bethnal Green

23.03.99   Gary Reid L PTS 6 Wolverhampton
22.04.99   Brian Gifford W PTS 6 Dudley
15.05.99   James Hare L RSC 2 Sheffield
11.10.99   Carl Allen W PTS 6 Birmingham
28.10.99   Mark Hargreaves L PTS 6 Burnley
30.11.99   Marc Smith W PTS 6 Wolverhampton
11.12.99   Brian Carr DREW 6 Liverpool
24.01.00   Craig Docherty L PTS 6 Glasgow
08.02.00   Carl Allen L PTS 8 Wolverhampton
19.02.00   Kevin Lear L PTS 4 Dagenham
04.03.00   Liam Maltby L PTS 6 Peterborough
28.03.00   Carl Allen L PTS 8 Wolverhampton
06.06.00   Dave Travers L PTS 6 Brierley Hill
24.06.00   Kevin McIntyre L PTS 4 Glasgow
08.07.00   Tony Mulholland L PTS 8 Widnes
13.08.00   Esham Pickering L PTS 6 Nottingham
29.09.00   Darren Melville L RSC 4 Bethnal Green
21.10.00   Graham Earl L RSC 3 Wembley
24.11.00   Pete Buckley W PTS 6 Hull
09.12.00   Terry Butwell L PTS 4 Southwark
27.01.01   Danny Hunt W RSC 2 Bethnal Green
10.02.01   Geir Inge Jorgensen L RSC 3 Widnes
20.03.01   James Rooney L PTS 4 Glasgow
26.03.01   Liam Maltby L PTS 6 Peterborough
03.04.01   Danny Hunt L PTS 4 Bethnal Green
06.05.01   James Rooney L PTS 6 Hartlepool

21.06.01   Gavin Wake L PTS 6 Sheffield
14.07.01   Brett James L PTS 6 Wembley
28.07.01   Ross Minter L PTS 4 Wembley
15.09.01   Gavin Down L PTS 6 Derby
10.12.01   David Keir DREW 4 Liverpool
04.03.02   Pedro Thompson W PTS 6 Bradford
13.04.02   David Keir L PTS 4 Liverpool
13.05.02   Chris Duggan W RSC 3 Birmingham
01.06.02   Michael Jennings L PTS 4 Manchester
23.06.02   Brett James L PTS 6 Southwark

Career: 39 contests, won 9, drew 2, lost 28.

Jamie Wilson

Hull. *Born* North Ferriby, 28 May, 1978
L. Heavyweight. Ht. 6'4"
Manager M. Toomey

30.11.01   Matthew Pepper W RSC 3 Hull
31.05.02   Mike Duffield L PTS 6 Hull

Career: 2 contests, won 1, lost 1.

Gareth Wiltshaw

Stoke. *Born* Stoke, 22 August, 1980
S. Featherweight. Ht. 5'7"
Manager W. Swift

17.04.00   John Meade W PTS 6 Bradford
09.06.00   Joel Viney L PTS 6 Blackpool
08.07.00   Kevin England DREW 6 Rotherham
20.11.00   Al Garrett L PTS 6 Glasgow
30.11.00   Mickey Coveney L PTS 4
           Peterborough
18.02.01   Richmond Asante L PTS 4 Southwark
08.04.01   Jason Edwards L PTS 6 Wrexham
20.05.01   Stephen Chinnock L PTS 6
           Wolverhampton
03.06.01   Mickey Coveney L PTS 4 Southwark
08.10.01   Sid Razak W PTS 6 Birmingham
27.10.01   Steve Foster L PTS 4 Manchester
19.01.02   Martin Power L PTS 4 Bethnal Green
11.02.02   Daniel Thorpe W PTS 6 Shrewsbury
02.03.02   Jesse James Daniel L RSC 3 Wakefield
20.04.02   Haroon Din L PTS 6 Derby
04.05.02   Steve Foster L PTS 4 Bethnal Green
13.06.02   Ryan Barrett L PTS 4 Leicester Square

Career: 17 contests, won 3, drew 1, lost 13.

Juliette Winter

Derby. *Born* Whitehaven, 21 February, 1973
Bantamweight. Ht. 5'6"
Manager C. Mitchell

16.06.01   Sara Hall L RTD 4 Derby
20.09.01   Claire Cooper L RSC 4 Blackfriars

Career: 2 contests, lost 2.

Mark Winters

Antrim. *Born* Antrim, 29 December, 1971
Lightweight. Former British
L. Welterweight Champion. Ht. 5'8"
Manager Self

04.03.95   Trevor Smith W PTS 6 Livingston
10.06.95   Mark McGowan W PTS 6 Manchester
09.09.95   Anthony Campbell W PTS 4 Cork
25.11.95   John O. Johnson W RSC 2 Dublin
13.01.96   Rick North W PTS 4 Manchester
09.03.96   Danny Quacoe W RSC 2 Millstreet
08.06.96   Brian Coleman W PTS 4 Newcastle
31.08.96   John Smith W PTS 4 Dublin
30.11.96   Paul Dyer W PTS 6 Tylorstown
14.03.97   Paul Denton W PTS 8 Reading
03.05.97   Jimmy Phelan W PTS 4 Manchester
11.10.97   Carl Wright W PTS 12 Sheffield
           (Vacant British L. Welterweight Title)
21.02.98   Bernard Paul W PTS 12 Belfast
           (British L. Welterweight Title Defence)
16.05.98   Jason Rowland L PTS 12 Bethnal
           Green
           (British L. Welterweight Title Defence)
05.09.98   Junior Witter L PTS 8 Telford
23.10.99   James Hare DREW 6 Telford
11.12.99   Richard Hatton L RSC 4 Liverpool
           *(WBO Inter-Continental
           L. Welterweight Title Challenge)*
04.02.01   David Kirk W PTS 6 Queensferry
20.04.01   David Kirk W PTS 6 Dublin
26.07.01   Joel Viney W RSC 4 Blackpool
15.12.01   Graham Earl L PTS 10 Wembley
           (Elim. British Lightweight Title)

Career: 21 contests, won 16, drew 1, lost 4.

Junior Witter

Bradford. *Born* Bradford, 10 March, 1974
WBU Inter-Continental L. Welterweight
Champion. Former Undefeated WBF L.
Welterweight Champion. Ht. 5'7"
Manager B. Ingle

Richard Williams   Les Clark

18.01.97	Cam Raeside DREW 6 Swadlincote
04.03.97	John Green W PTS 6 Yarm
20.03.97	Lee Molyneux W RSC 6 Salford
25.04.97	Trevor Meikle W PTS 6 Mere
15.05.97	Andreas Panayi W RSC 5 Reading
02.08.97	Brian Coleman W PTS 4 Barnsley
04.10.97	Michael Alexander W PTS 4 Hannover, Germany
07.02.98	Mark Ramsey DREW 6 Cheshunt
05.03.98	Brian Coleman W PTS 6 Leeds
18.04.98	Jan Bergman W PTS 6 Manchester
05.09.98	Mark Winters W PTS 6 Telford
28.11.98	Karl Taylor W PTS 4 Sheffield
13.02.99	Malcolm Melvin W RSC 2 Newcastle *(Vacant WBF L. Welterweight Title)*
17.07.99	Isaac Cruz W PTS 8 Doncaster
06.11.99	Harry Butler W PTS 6 Widnes
21.03.00	Mrhai Iourgh W RSC 1 Telde, Gran Canaria
08.04.00	Arv Mittoo W PTS 4 Bethnal Green
24.06.00	Zab Judah L PTS 12 Glasgow *(IBF L. Welterweight Title Challenge)*
20.10.00	Steve Conway W RTD 4 Belfast
25.11.00	Chris Henry W RSC 3 Manchester
10.03.01	David Kirk W RSC 2 Bethnal Green
22.05.01	Fabrice Faradji W RSC 1 Telde, Gran Canaria
21.07.01	Alan Temple W CO 5 Sheffield
27.10.01	Colin Mayisela W RSC 2 Manchester *(Vacant WBU Inter-Continental L.Welterweight Title)*
16.03.02	Alan Bosworth W RSC 3 Northampton *(Vacant British L.Welterweight Title)*

Career: 25 contests, won 22, drew 2, lost 1.

Junior Witter   Les Clark

Ray Wood (Shearwood)

Liverpool. *Born* Liverpool, 3 May, 1971
L. Welterweight. Ht. 5'6½"
Manager S. Foster/S. Wood

13.11.98	Kevin McIntyre L RSC 4 Glasgow
05.03.99	Brian Gifford W CO 2 Liverpool
15.05.99	Peter Dunn DREW 4 Blackpool

18.02.00	Marcus Portman L PTS 6 West Bromwich
09.03.00	Gary Greenwood L PTS 4 Liverpool
20.10.00	Alan Kershaw L PTS 6 Manchester
12.11.00	Dave Gibson W PTS 6 Manchester
18.03.01	Tony Montana DREW 6 Shaw
19.03.02	Chris McDonagh L PTS 4 Slough

Career: 9 contests, won 2, drew 2, lost 5.

Lee Woodruff

Lancaster. *Born* Lancaster, 27 February, 1980
S. Middleweight. Ht. 5'11"
Manager B. Myers

18.03.01	Tommy Matthews W RSC 2 Shaw
26.04.01	Paul Buchanan L PTS 6 Gateshead
26.07.01	Paul Martin W RSC 1 Blackpool
23.09.01	Louis Swales W RSC 4 Shaw
08.02.02	Paul Owen L RSC 2 Preston

Career: 5 contests, won 3, lost 2.

Clinton Woods

Sheffield. *Born* Sheffield, 1 May, 1972
WBC International L. Heavyweight
Champion. Former Undefeated British,
European & Commonwealth L.
Heavyweight Champion. Former
Commonwealth S. Middleweight
Champion. Former Undefeated Central
Area S. Middleweight Champion. Ht. 6'2"
Manager Self

17.11.94	Dave Proctor W PTS 6 Sheffield
12.12.94	Earl Ling W RSC 5 Cleethorpes
23.02.95	Paul Clarkson W RSC 1 Hull
06.04.95	Japhet Hans W RSC 3 Sheffield
16.05.95	Kevin Burton W PTS 6 Cleethorpes
14.06.95	Kevin Burton W RSC 6 Batley
21.09.95	Paul Murray W PTS 6 Sheffield
20.10.95	Phil Ball W RSC 4 Mansfield
22.11.95	Andy Ewen W RSC 3 Sheffield
05.02.96	Chris Walker W RSC 6 Bradford
16.03.96	John Duckworth W PTS 8 Sheffield
13.06.96	Ernie Loveridge W PTS 6 Sheffield
14.11.96	Craig Joseph W PTS 10 Sheffield *(Vacant Central Area S. Middleweight Title)*
20.02.97	Rocky Shelly W RSC 2 Mansfield
10.04.97	Darren Littlewood W RSC 6 Sheffield *(Central Area S. Middleweight Title Defence)*
26.06.97	Darren Ashton W PTS 6 Sheffield
25.10.97	Danny Juma W PTS 8 Queensferry
26.11.97	Jeff Finlayson W PTS 8 Sheffield
06.12.97	Mark Baker W PTS 12 Wembley *(Vacant Commonwealth S.Middleweight Title)*
28.03.98	David Starie L PTS 12 Hull *(Commonwealth S. Middleweight Title Defence)*
18.06.98	Peter Mason W RTD 4 Sheffield
30.11.98	Mark Smallwood W RSC 7 Manchester
13.03.99	Crawford Ashley W RSC 8 Manchester *(British, Commonwealth & European L. Heavyweight Title Challenges)*
10.07.99	Sam Leuii W RSC 6 Southwark *(Commonwealth L. Heavyweight Title Defence)*
11.09.99	Lenox Lewis W RSC 10 Sheffield *(Commonwealth L. Heavyweight Title Defence)*
10.12.99	Terry Ford W RTD 4 Warsaw, Poland

12.02.00	Kid Dongo W PTS 12 Sheffield *(European L. Heavyweight Title Defence)*
29.04.00	Ole Klemetsen W RSC 9 Wembley *(European L. Heavyweight Title Defence)*
15.07.00	Greg Scott-Briggs W RSC 3 Millwall
24.03.01	Ali Forbes W RTD 10 Sheffield *(Vacant WBC International L. Heavyweight Title)*
27.07.01	Paul Bonson W PTS 6 Sheffield
13.09.01	Yawe Davis W PTS 12 Sheffield *(Final Elim.WBC L.Heavyweight Title)*
16.03.02	Clint Johnson W RSC 3 Bethnal Green

Career: 33 contests, won 32, lost 1.

Martyn Woodward

Cardiff. *Born* Cardiff, 25 September, 1978
Middleweight. Ht. 6'3"
Manager T. Russell

15.09.01	Alan Jones L CO 3 Swansea

Career: 1 contest, lost 1.

Chris Woollas

Epworth. *Born* Scunthorpe, 22 November, 1973
Heavyweight. Midlands Area Cruiserweight Champion. Ht. 5'11"
Manager Self

17.08.94	Darren Littlewood W RSC 4 Sheffield
05.10.94	Robert Norton DREW 6 Wolverhampton
05.12.94	Neil Simpson W PTS 6 Cleethorpes
10.02.95	Monty Wright L RSC 4 Birmingham
30.06.95	Kenny Nevers L RSC 2 Doncaster
25.09.95	Cliff Elden DREW 6 Cleethorpes
08.11.95	Stevie Pettit W PTS 6 Walsall
17.11.95	Markku Salminen L PTS 6 Helsinki, Finland
11.12.95	Cliff Elden DREW 6 Cleethorpes
15.02.96	Pele Lawrence W RSC 6 Sheffield
29.02.96	John Pierre DREW 6 Scunthorpe
16.03.96	David Jules W PTS 6 Sheffield
22.04.96	Jacklord Jacobs DREW 4 Crystal Palace
30.05.96	Martin Langtry L RSC 6 Lincoln *(Midlands Area Cruiserweight Title Challenge)*
03.09.96	Darren Corbett L RSC 7 Belfast
02.10.96	Rocky Shelly W RSC 6 Stoke
09.10.96	Nigel Rafferty W PTS 6 Stoke
28.10.96	Colin Brown L PTS 8 Glasgow
10.11.96	Michael Gale DREW 6 Glasgow
25.11.96	Albert Call L PTS 6 Cleethorpes
17.12.96	Darren Corbett L RSC 1 Doncaster
16.01.97	Mark Smallwood L PTS 8 Solihull
31.01.97	Tim Redman L PTS 6 Pentre Halkyn
14.03.97	Kelly Oliver L PTS 6 Reading
24.03.97	Mikael Lindblad L RSC 7 Helsinki, Finland
19.06.97	Ian Henry W PTS 6 Scunthorpe
02.08.97	Kelly Oliver L RSC 3 Barnsley
15.12.97	Neil Simpson W PTS 6 Cleethorpes
26.01.98	Colin Brown W PTS 6 Glasgow
26.03.98	Cliff Elden L PTS 4 Scunthorpe
06.05.98	Simon McDougall W PTS 6 Blackpool
21.07.98	Matthew Ellis L RSC 5 Widnes
11.09.98	Lennox Williams W PTS 6 Cleethorpes
12.03.99	Albert Sosnowski L PTS 4 Bethnal Green
27.05.99	Nigel Rafferty W PTS 10 Edgbaston

(Midlands Area Cruiserweight Title Challenge)

10.07.99	Michael Sprott L RTD 4 Southwark
13.09.99	Dominic Negus L PTS 10 Bethnal Green

(Elim. British Cruiserweight Title)

09.10.99	Chris P. Bacon L PTS 4 Manchester
30.10.99	Terry Dunstan L RSC 1 Southwark
08.04.00	Bruce Scott L RSC 2 Bethnal Green
13.07.00	Firat Aslan L RSC 2 Bethnal Green
08.09.00	Petr Horacek L PTS 4 Hammersmith
21.10.00	Danny Percival L PTS 4 Wembley
18.11.00	Matthew Ellis L PTS 4 Dagenham
11.12.00	Enzo Maccarinelli L PTS 4 Widnes
15.12.01	Lee Swaby L RSC 4 Sheffield

Career: 46 contests, won 13, drew 6, lost 27.

Shane Woollas

Epworth. *Born* Scunthorpe, 28 July, 1972
Midlands Area Heavyweight Champion.
Ht. 6'2"
Manager Self

26.08.94	Neil Kirkwood L RSC 6 Barnsley
28.07.95	Rob Albon W RTD 4 Epworth
11.10.95	Gary Williams W PTS 6 Solihull
08.11.95	David Jules W PTS 6 Scunthorpe
26.01.96	Nigel Williams W RSC 2 Doncaster
31.01.96	David Jules L PTS 6 Stoke
22.04.96	Gary Williams W PTS 10 Cleethorpes

(Vacant Midlands Area Heavyweight Title)

29.07.96	David Jules L PTS 6 Skegness
31.08.96	Willi Fischer L CO 2 Palma de Mallorca
08.10.96	Mika Kihlstrom L PTS 4 Battersea
06.11.96	Kevin McBride L RSC 2 Hull
08.02.97	Danny Williams L RSC 2 Millwall
19.06.97	Lennox Williams W PTS 6 Scunthorpe
15.12.97	Gary Williams W RSC 8 Cleethorpes

(Midlands Area Heavyweight Title Defence)

11.01.98	Fred Westgeest L PTS 6 Riesa, Germany
21.02.98	Danny Williams L RSC 2 Belfast
23.05.98	Mark Potter L PTS 4 Bethnal Green
21.06.98	Mal Rice W PTS 6 Liverpool
02.07.98	Georgi Kandelaki L RSC 4 Ipswich
11.09.98	Bruno Foster W PTS 6 Cleethorpes
26.09.98	Luan Krasniqi L RSC 3 York
30.11.98	Craig Bowen-Price L RSC 2 Manchester
30.04.99	Brian Gascoigne DREW 6 Scunthorpe
30.10.99	Gavin McGhin L CO 4 Peterlee
12.02.00	Patrick Halberg L PTS 6 Sheffield
05.02.01	Crawford Ashley L RSC 4 Hull
10.04.01	Petr Horacek DREW 4 Wembley
16.06.01	Eric Butterbean Esch L RSC 1 Wembley
27.07.01	Mark Krence L PTS 4 Sheffield

Career: 29 contests, won 9, drew 2, lost 18.

Danny Wray

Shoreham. *Born* Camberwell, 5 July, 1980
Middleweight. Ht. 5'9¼"
Manager R. Davies

03.02.01	Tony Smith W RSC 1 Brighton
05.05.01	Freddie Yemofio W PTS 6 Brighton
09.12.01	Gary Dixon L RSC 4 Shaw

Career: 3 contests, won 2, lost 1.

Carl Wright

Rugby. *Born* Rugby, 26 April, 1978
Cruiserweight. Ht. 6'1¼"
Manager J. Weaver

25.06.02	Dave Clarke W PTS 6 Rugby

Career: 1 contest, won 1.

Nigel Wright

Hartlepool. *Born* Bishop Auckland, 22 June, 1979
L. Welterweight. Ht. 5'9"
Manager G. Robinson

10.02.01	Keith Jones W PTS 4 Widnes
15.09.01	Tommy Peacock W RSC 1 Manchester
17.11.01	Ernie Smith W PTS 4 Glasgow
19.01.02	Woody Greenaway W CO 2 Bethnal Green
11.03.02	James Paisley W PTS 4 Glasgow

Career: 5 contests, won 5.

Nigel Wright   Les Clark

Jamie Yelland

Watford. *Born* London, 5 March, 1975
Bantamweight. Ht. 5'5"
Manager J. Evans

11.03.00	Chris Emanuele W PTS 4 Kensington
22.07.00	Daniel Ring W PTS 4 Watford
06.10.00	Simon Stowell DREW 4 Maidstone
31.10.00	John Barnes W PTS 6 Hammersmith
07.04.01	John Barnes W PTS 4 Wembley
31.07.01	Paddy Folan W RSC 5 Bethnal Green
28.11.01	John Mackay L RSC 6 Bethnal Green
25.02.02	Gareth Payne W RSC 3 Slough
29.06.02	Neil Read W PTS 6 Brentwood

Career: 9 contests, won 7, drew 1, lost 1.

Freddie Yemofio

Hayes. *Born* London, 15 July, 1969
S. Middleweight. Ht. 5'10"
Manager D. Currivan

31.08.93	Lee Sara L PTS 6 Croydon
30.09.93	Martin Rosamond L PTS 6 Hayes
20.05.94	Lee Blundell L RSC 6 Acton

30.09.94	Jason Hart L PTS 6 Bethnal Green
26.05.95	Robert Harper W PTS 6 Norwich
28.04.98	Matthew Tait L PTS 6 Brentford
14.05.98	Matt Galer L RSC 4 Acton
07.12.98	Matthew Barney L PTS 4 Acton
12.08.00	Spencer Fearon L RSC 5 Wembley
02.11.00	Elvis Michailenko L PTS 6 Kensington
09.12.00	Liam Lathbury L PTS 4 Southwark
29.01.01	Francie Doherty L RSC 4 Peterborough
05.05.01	Danny Wray L PTS 6 Brighton
12.05.01	Simon Andrews L PTS 4 Plymouth
31.01.02	Leigh Wicks L PTS 6 Piccadilly
11.02.02	Roddy Doran L PTS 8 Shrewsbury
27.03.02	Kenroy Lambert L PTS 6 Mayfair
13.04.02	Danny Smith L PTS 6 Norwich

Career: 18 contests, won 1, lost 17.

Steve Yorath

Cardiff. *Born* Cardiff, 8 August, 1965
Cruiserweight. Ht. 6'2"
Manager Self

21.11.85	Dai Davies L RSC 5 Blaenavon
13.03.86	John Ashton L CO 3 Alfreton
08.05.90	Rob Albon L PTS 6 Brentford
06.07.90	Phil Soundy L CO 3 Brentwood
17.09.90	Chris Coughlan W PTS 6 Cardiff
24.09.90	John Williams L PTS 6 Mayfair
03.10.90	Phil Soundy L PTS 6 Basildon
19.10.90	Neils H. Madsen L PTS 6 Skive, Denmark
15.04.91	Tony Colclough W PTS 6 Wolverhampton
24.04.91	Phil Soundy W PTS 6 Basildon
28.05.91	R. F. McKenzie W PTS 6 Cardiff
27.06.91	Denzil Browne L PTS 6 Leeds
21.01.92	Graham Arnold W PTS 6 Norwich
31.03.92	Graham Arnold L PTS 6 Norwich
18.05.92	Marco van Spaendonck L PTS 4 Valkenswaard, Holland
23.09.92	Denzil Browne L PTS 8 Leeds
25.11.92	Terry Dunstan L PTS 8 Mayfair
24.02.93	Derek Angol L RSC 5 Wembley
03.04.93	Biko Botowamungu L RSC 5 Vienna, Austria
10.07.93	Chris Okoh L PTS 6 Cardiff
31.08.93	Devon Rhooms L PTS 6 Croydon
04.10.93	Terry Dixon L RSC 4 Mayfair
09.04.94	Dermot Gascoyne L CO 3 Mansfield
27.08.94	Kent Davis W PTS 6 Cardiff
08.09.94	Sean Heron L PTS 6 Glasgow
18.11.94	John Wilson L PTS 6 Glasgow
27.11.94	Owen Bartley DREW 6 Southwark
25.01.95	Kent Davis L PTS 6 Cardiff
05.05.01	Auckland Aumatangi L PTS 6 Perth, Australia
18.06.01	Abel Laulau L PTS 6 Sidney, Australia
24.10.01	Colin Wilson L PTS 6 Southport, Australia
08.02.02	Phil Gregory L PTS 10 Southport, Australia

(Queensland State Heavyweight Title Challenge)

Career: 32 contests, won 6, drew 1, lost 25.

Gary Young

Edinburgh. *Born* Edinburgh, 23 May, 1983
L. Welterweight. Ht. 5'7"
Manager F. Maloney

11.03.02	Paul McIlwaine W CO 2 Glasgow
08.06.02	Daniel Thorpe W RSC 1 Renfrew

Career: 2 contests, won 2.

British Area Title Bouts During 2001-2002

Central Area

Titleholders at 30 June 2002

Fly: Dale Robinson. **Bantam:** *vacant.* **S. Bantam:** *vacant.* **Feather:** *vacant.* **S. Feather:** *vacant.* **Light:** Gary Hibbert. **L. Welter:** *vacant.* **Welter:** Robert Burton. **L. Middle:** *vacant.* **Middle:** Andrew Facey. **S. Middle:** Tony Dodson. **L. Heavy:** *vacant.* **Cruiser:** Denzil Browne. **Heavy:** Neil Kirkwood.

10 December 2001	Tony Dodson W RSC 2 Jon Penn, Liverpool (Vacant S. Middleweight Title)
28 January 2002	Robert Burton W RSC 8 Peter Dunn, Barnsley (Vacant Welterweight Title)
2 March 2002	Andrew Facey W RSC 6 Darren Rhodes, Wakefield (Vacant Middleweight Title)

Between 1 July 2001 and 30 June 2002, Lee Armstrong (S. Feather) vacated, while Lee Blundell (L. Middle) forfeited his title on losing to Anthony Farnell at the weight.

Midlands Area

Titleholders at 30 June 2002

Fly: Anthony Hanna. **Bantam:** *vacant.* **S. Bantam:** Carl Allen. **Feather:** Stephen Chinnock. **S. Feather:** *vacant.* **Light:** Anthony Maynard. **L. Welter:** Gavin Down. **Welter:** Christian Brady. **L. Middle:** *vacant.* **Middle:** Gordon Behan. **S. Middle:** Damon Hague. **L. Heavy:** Darren Ashton. **Cruiser:** Chris Woollas. **Heavy:** Shane Woollas.

15 September 2001	Damon Hague W RTD 2 Dean Ashton, Derby (Vacant S. Middleweight Title)
7 October 2001	Stephen Chinnock W PTS 10 Kevin Gerowski, Wolverhampton (Vacant Featherweight Title)
13 April 2002	Stephen Chinnock W CO 3 Neil Read, Wolverhampton (Featherweight Title Defence)

Between 1 July 2001 and 30 June 2002, Steve Williams (Bantam) and Carl Greaves (S. Feather) forfeited their titles due to a licence expiry and a negative MRI scan, respectively.

Northern Area

Titleholders at 30 June 2002

Fly: *vacant.* **Bantam:** *vacant.* **S. Bantam:** Michael Hunter. **Feather:** *vacant.* **S. Feather:** *vacant.* **Light:** *vacant.* **L. Welter:** *vacant.* **Welter:** Oscar Hall. **L. Middle:** *vacant.* **Middle:** Eddie Haley. **S. Middle:** Ian Cooper. **L. Heavy:** *vacant.* **Cruiser:** *vacant.* **Heavy:** *vacant.*

9 September 2001	Michael Hunter W RSC 8 John Barnes, Hartlepool (Vacant S. Bantamweight Title)
22 September 2001	Oscar Hall W DIS 9 Dean Nicholas, Newcastle (Vacant Welterweight Title)

Robert Burton (left) takes the attack to Peter Dunn on his way to the Central Area welterweight title Les Clark

Northern Ireland Area

Titleholders at 30 June 2002 - None

Scottish Area

Titleholders at 30 June 2002

Fly: *vacant.* **Bantam:** *vacant.* **S. Bantam:** Shaun Anderson. **Feather:** Brian Carr. **S. Feather:** *vacant.* **Light:** *vacant.* **L. Welter:** *vacant.* **Welter:** Kevin McIntyre. **L. Middle:** *vacant.* **Middle:** John Docherty. **S. Middle:** Jason Barker. **L. Heavy:** *vacant.* **Cruiser:** *vacant.* **Heavy:** *vacant.*

26 April 2002	Kevin McIntyre W PTS 10 Craig Lynch, Glasgow (Vacant Welterweight Title)

Southern Area

Titleholders at 30 June 2002

Fly: Ian Napa. **Bantam:** *vacant.* **S. Bantam:** *vacant.* **Feather:** *vacant.* **S. Feather:** *vacant.* **Light:** Graham Earl. **L. Welter:** Costas Katsantonis. **Welter:** David Walker. **L. Middle:** John Humphrey. **Middle:** Allan Gray. **S. Middle:** Matthew Barney. **L. Heavy:** *vacant.* **Cruiser:** Garry Delaney. **Heavy:** Mark Potter.

22 September 2001	Graham Earl W CO 1 Liam Maltby, Bethnal Green (Lightweight Title Defence)
28 October 2001	Gary Logan L PTS 10 Hussain Osman, Southwark (Middleweight Title Defence)
1 December 2001	Paul Dyer L PTS 10 Paul Knights, Bethnal Green (Welterweight Title Defence)
23 November 2001	Costas Katsantonis W RSC 1 Iain Eldridge, Bethnal Green (Vacant L. Welterweight Title)
26 January 2002	Matthew Barney L RTD 9 Hussain Osman, Dagenham (S. Middleweight Title Defence)
16 March 2002	John Humphrey W PTS 10 Ojay Abrahams, Bethnal Green (Vacant L. Middleweight Title)
16 March 2002	David Walker W RSC 6 Paul Dyer, Bethnal Green (Vacant Welterweight Title)
18 April 2002	Hussain Osman L PTS 12 Matthew Barney, Southampton (S. Middleweight Title Defence)
28 April 2002	Allan Gray W PTS 10 Alan Gilbert, Southwark (Vacant Middleweight Title)
10 May 2002	Costas Katsantonis W PTS 10 Gary Harrison, Millwall (L. Welterweight Title Defence)

Between 1 July 2001 and 30 June 2002, Daniel James (L. Welter), Paul Knights (Welter), Delroy Mellis (L. Middle) and Hussain Osman (Middle) relinquished their titles.

Welsh Area

Titleholders at 30 June 2002

Fly: *vacant.* **Bantam:** *vacant.* **S. Bantam:** *vacant.* **Feather:** *vacant.* **S. Feather:** *vacant.* **Light:** *vacant.* **L. Welter:** Jason Cook. **Welter:** *vacant.* **L. Middle:** *vacant.* **Middle:** *vacant.* **S. Middle:** *vacant.* **L. Heavy:** *vacant.* **Cruiser:** Darron Griffiths. **Heavy:** *vacant.*

Between 1 July 2001 and 30 June 2002, Chris Williams (S. Feather) and Paul Samuels vacated and Michael Smyth (Welter) retired.

Western Area

Titleholders at 30 June 2002

Fly: *vacant.* **Bantam:** *vacant.* **S. Bantam:** Frankie DeMilo. **Feather:** *vacant.* **S. Feather:** *vacant.* **Light:** *vacant.* **L. Welter:** *vacant.* **Welter:** *vacant.* **L. Middle:** *vacant.* **Middle:** *vacant.* **S. Middle:** Darren Dorrington. **L. Heavy:** *vacant.* **Cruiser:** *vacant.* **Heavy:** *vacant.*

30 September 2001	Darren Dorrington W RSC 4 Simon Andrews, Bristol (S. Middleweight Title Defence)

John Humphrey (right) won the vacant Southern Area light-middleweight title when defeating Ojay Abrahams   Les Clark

British Title Bouts During 2001-2002

All of last season's title bouts are shown in date order within their weight divisions and give the contestants' respective weights, along with the scorecard if going to a decision. Every contest is summarised briefly and all referees are named.

Flyweight
Jason Booth failed to defend during the period.

Bantamweight
15 September 2001   Nicky Booth 8.6 (England) W RSC 7 Jim Betts 8.6 (England), Harvey Hadden Leisure Centre, Nottingham. Despite keeping the pressure on from the opening bell, Betts, cut on the left eye in the third, eventually found that it was just too much to sustain and gradually wilted as the champion kept hitting back. Eventually, the referee, John Keane, recognised that the challenger had little left and stopped it after 43 seconds of the seventh round. Booth's Commonwealth title was also on the line.

23 February 2002   Nicky Booth 8.6 (England) W RSC 7 Stephen Oates 8.5¼ (England), Harvey Hadden Leisure Centre, Nottingham. In what turned out to be one of the most exciting fights of the season, with both men firing back when hurt, the trained eye could see that this one was never going the distance. Unfortunately, for Oates, every time he seemed to be getting on top, Booth would just come back, which eventually proved just too much for him. Dropped in the fifth and down again in the seventh, John Coyle had seen enough, stopping the fight with 1.42 on the clock. Once again, Booth's Commonwealth title was up for grabs.

S. Bantamweight
14 July 2001   Michael Alldis 8.9¾ (England) L PTS 12 Patrick Mullings 8.10 (England), The Conference Centre, Wembley. Although this one could have gone either way, the referee, Larry O'Connell, made it 115-114 in favour of the challenger, a decision which was never going to please everybody. However, Alldis had gone low on a number of occasions and, although coming on stronger in the closing stages, those punches obviously counted against him. In what should have a new start for Mullings, he forfeited the title in November 2001 after failing an after-the-fight drugs test.

18 March 2002   Michael Alldis 8.9½ (England) W PTS 12 Brian Carr 8.9¾ (Scotland), The Leisure Centre, Crawley. Billed for the vacant title, Alldis put the Mullings fight behind him as he landed Mickey Vann's 117-113 points verdict and with it the Lonsdale Belt, along with Carr's Commonwealth crown. The Scottish southpaw started well enough but, as the fight progressed, Alldis came on stronger and well deserved the decision. Carr finished with a couple of cuts, more to do with some of the rough stuff, but nobody was complaining.

Featherweight
15 September 2001   Scott Harrison 8.13¾ (Scotland) W RSC 5 Gary Thornhill 8.13½ (England), The MEN Arena, Manchester. In making a successful defence of both the British and Commonwealth titles, Harrison again proved what a good fighter he has become. After Thornhill had made a good start, the champion began to overhaul his opponent with a perfect blend of box-fighting before putting the Liverpudlian down with a left hook to the body in the fifth. Although up at four, the referee, Mark Green, felt he was in no condition to defend himself and brought the contest to an end at 0.31 of the round.

17 November 2001   Scott Harrison 9.0 (Scotland) W RSC 3 Steve Robinson 8.12¼ (Wales), Bellahouston Leisure Centre, Glasgow. Using plenty of variety, Harrison took the fight to the former world champion and eventually overwhelmed his opponent with the sheer volume of quality punches. Getting right on top in the third round, the Scot saw his chance and gave Robinson no opportunity to survive, pouring in punches with both hands until Richie Davies called a halt to the action on the 2.51 mark. Harrison's Commonwealth title was also at stake.

Michael Gomez, the former undefeated British super-featherweight champion   Harry Goodwin

S. Featherweight
27 October 2001   Michael Gomez 9.3³/₄ (England) W RSC 2 Craig Docherty 9.3³/₄ (Scotland), The MEN Arena, Manchester. Although cut in the first round, Docherty continued to stand toe-to-toe with Gomez, but ultimately lacked the know how to expose the champion and was unable to hit back and dazed when the referee, Terry O'Connor, jumped in to rescue him at 1.46 of the second round. Gomez relinquished the title in April 2002 to concentrate on a version of the world title.

Lightweight
8 October 2001   Bobby Vanzie 9.8³/₄ (England) W RSC 1 Anthony Maynard 9.8³/₄ (England), The Metrodome, Barnsley. In one of the quickest title defences ever, Vanzie caught Maynard cold and was punching his rival at will on the ropes when Ian John-Lewis came to the challenger's rescue with just 70 seconds on the clock.

L. Welterweight
16 March 2002   Junior Witter 10.0 (England) W RSC 3 Alan Bosworth 9.13¹/₂ (England), The Derngate Centre, Northampton. Billed for the vacant title after Richard Hatton had relinquished the championship belt on winning the WBU championship on 26 March 2001, the local man, Bosworth, did his best but was no match for the rising star, Witter. Durability was not enough as Witter switched easily to deliver blows with precision from varying angles, a left-right putting Bosworth down for a count of three prior to the referee, Marcus McDonnell, calling a halt to proceedings in the third round.

Welterweight
19 November 2001   Harry Dhami 10.6¹/₄ (England) L RSC 5 Neil Sinclair 10.6¹/₂ (Ireland), Bellahouston Leisure Centre, Glasgow. Taking the fight to the champion nearly proved his undoing when dropped for a six count in the first, but Sinclair weathered the storm and came right back, going for the finish as soon as an opportunity presented itself. Despite being cut in the third, the southpaw Irishman was proving irresistible and a thunderous right hander to Dhami's jaw laid him prostate and encouraged the referee, Paul Thomas, to call an immediate halt at 2.44 of the fifth round.

15 June 2002   Neil Sinclair 10.7 (Ireland) W CO 1 Derek Roche 10.6¹/₄ (England), The Town Hall, Leeds. After outboxing his challenger for over two minutes of the opening round, Sinclair landed a cracking left hook to the body, a punch that sent Roche to his knees and unable to get up. Despite trying his best, the punch had knocked all the stuffing out of the local man and, with just 2.20 on the clock, he was counted out by the referee, Paul Thomas, who thus found himself involved in the fastest win in the history of the division.

L. Middleweight
17 November 2001   Wayne Alexander 10.13¹/₄ (England) W RSC 2 Joe Townsley 10.13³/₄ (Scotland), Bellahouston Leisure Centre, Glasgow. Having tripped over in the first and taken a count for the mishap, an angry Alexander twice dropped Townsley, who was also cut under the right eye, before the bell came to his rescue. From then on it was apparent that the Scot had little or no chance and a left hander put him down on one knee where he was counted out by Paul Thomas at 0.29 of the second round.

Middleweight
Howard Eastman failed to defend during the period.

S. Middleweight
29 September 2001   David Starie 12.0 (England) W RSC 6 Neil Linford 11.13¹/₂ (England), Elephant & Castle Leisure Centre, Southwark, London. Having been comfortably outboxed and cut on the left eye in the fourth round, the challenger was beginning to run out of ideas and was continuously punished until John Coyle had seen enough, calling a halt to proceedings at 2.25 of the sixth. In challenging for both the British and Commonwealth title belts, Linford had proved his bravery, but his ability at this level had been exposed by an extremely capable champion.

L. Heavyweight
Neil Simpson relinquished the title in April 2002 to concentrate on a crack at one version or another of the world title.

Cruiserweight
Bruce Scott failed to defend during the period.

Heavyweight
28 July 2001   Danny Williams 17.8 (England) W CO 4 Julius Francis 17.8 (England), The Conference Centre, Wembley. Although both men weighed the same, Williams was much lighter on his feet and outboxed the former champion for three rounds without ever looking to end matters summarily. However, all that changed in the fourth when a tremendous left uppercut put Francis on the floor, clutching his eye and in some pain, to be counted out by Mickey Vann at the 2.15 mark. With his victory, the champion not only retained his British and Commonwealth titles but gained revenge for his only pro defeat.

12 February 2002   Danny Williams (England) 18.5¹/₄ (England) W RTD 7 Michael Sprott 17.4³/₄ (England), York Hall, Bethnal Green, London. Although putting his challenger down heavily at the end of the fourth, Williams was content to get a few more rounds in before pulling the inevitable trigger and doing what was obvious to most of the bystanders. That moment came in the seventh when the champion pinned Sprott on the ropes and punched away incessantly until the towel was thrown in and Richie Davies called it off after 26 seconds of the round. Incidentally, Williams' Commonwealth title was also on the line.

Lord Lonsdale Challenge Belts: Outright Winners

Outright Winners of the National Sporting Club's Challenge Belt, 1909-1935 (21)

Under pressure from other promoters with bigger venues, and in an effort to sustain their monopoly – having controlled championship fights in Britain up until that point in time – the National Sporting Club launched the belt in 1909. They did so on the proviso that there should be eight weight divisions – fly, bantam, feather, light, welter, middle, light-heavy, and heavy – and that to win a belt outright a champion must score three title-match victories at the same weight, but not necessarily consecutively. Worth a substantial amount of money, and carrying a £1 a week pension from the age of 50, the President of the NSC, Lord Lonsdale, donated the first of 22 belts struck. Known as the Lonsdale Belt, despite the inscription reading: 'The National Sporting Club's Challenge Belt', the first man to put a notch on a belt was Freddie Welsh, who outpointed Johnny Summers for the lightweight title on 8 November 1909, while Jim Driscoll became the first man to win one outright. The record time for winning the belt is held by Jim Higgins (279 days).

FLYWEIGHT	Jimmy Wilde; Jackie Brown
BANTAMWEIGHT	Digger Stanley; Joe Fox; Jim Higgins; Johnny Brown; Dick Corbett; Johnny King
FEATHERWEIGHT	Jim Driscoll; Tancy Lee; Johnny Cuthbert; Nel Tarleton
LIGHTWEIGHT	Freddie Welsh
WELTERWEIGHT	Johnny Basham; Jack Hood
MIDDLEWEIGHT	Pat O'Keefe; Len Harvey; Jock McAvoy
L. HEAVYWEIGHT	Dick Smith
HEAVYWEIGHT	Bombardier Billy Wells; Jack Petersen

Note: Both Dick Corbett and Johnny King – with one notch apiece on the 'special' British Empire Lonsdale Belt that was struck in 1933 and later presented to the winner of the Tommy Farr v Joe Louis fight – were allowed to keep their Lonsdale Belts with just two notches secured; Freddie Welsh, also with two notches, was awarded a belt due to his inability to defend because of the First World War; the first bantam belt came back into circulation and was awarded to Johnny Brown; Al Foreman, with just one notch on the second lightweight belt, took it back to Canada with him without the consent of the BBBoC; while the second light-heavy belt was awarded to Jack Smith of Worcester for winning a novices heavyweight competition. Having emigrated to New Zealand, Smith later presented the visiting Her Majesty The Queen with the belt and it now hangs in the BBBoC's offices.

Outright Winners of the BBBoC Lord Lonsdale Challenge Belt, 1936-2002 (108)

Re-introduced by the British Boxing Board of Control as the Lord Lonsdale Challenge Belt, but of less intrinsic value – Benny Lynch's eight-round win over Pat Palmer (16 September 1936 at Shawfield Park, Glasgow) got the new version underway – Eric Boon became the first man to win one outright, in 1939, following victories over Dave Crowley (2) and Arthur Danahar. Since those early days, six further weight divisions have been added and, following on from Henry Cooper's feat of winning three Lonsdale Belts outright, on 10 June 1981 the BBBoC's rules and regulations were amended to read that no boxer shall receive more than one belt as his own property, in any one weight division. From 1 September 1999, any boxer putting a notch on a Lonsdale Belt for the first time will require three more notches at the same weight before he can call the belt his own. However, men who already have a notch on the Lonsdale Belt prior to 1 September 1999 can contest it under the former ruling of three winning championship contests at the same weight. Incidentally, the fastest of the modern belt winners is Ryan Rhodes (90 days), while Chris and Kevin Finnegan are the only brothers to have each won a belt outright.

FLYWEIGHT	Jackie Paterson; Terry Allen; Walter McGowan; John McCluskey; Hugh Russell; Charlie Magri; Pat Clinton; Robbie Regan; Francis Ampofo; Ady Lewis
BANTAMWEIGHT	Johnny King; Peter Keenan (2); Freddie Gilroy; Alan Rudkin; Johnny Owen; Billy Hardy; Drew Docherty; Nicky Booth
S. BANTAMWEIGHT	Richie Wenton; Michael Brodie; Michael Alldis
FEATHERWEIGHT	Nel Tarleton; Ronnie Clayton (2); Charlie Hill; Howard Winstone (2); Evan Armstrong; Pat Cowdell; Robert Dickie; Paul Hodkinson; Colin McMillan; Sean Murphy; Jonjo Irwin

S. FEATHERWEIGHT	Jimmy Anderson; John Doherty; Floyd Havard; Charles Shepherd; Michael Gomez
LIGHTWEIGHT	Eric Boon; Billy Thompson; Joe Lucy; Dave Charnley; Maurice Cullen; Ken Buchanan; Jim Watt; George Feeney; Tony Willis; Carl Crook; Billy Schwer; Michael Ayers; Bobby Vanzie
L. WELTERWEIGHT	Joey Singleton; Colin Power; Clinton McKenzie; Lloyd Christie; Andy Holligan; Ross Hale
WELTERWEIGHT	Ernie Roderick; Wally Thom; Brian Curvis (2); Ralph Charles; Colin Jones; Lloyd Honeyghan; Kirkland Laing; Del Bryan; Geoff McCreesh; Derek Roche
L. MIDDLEWEIGHT	Maurice Hope; Jimmy Batten; Pat Thomas; Prince Rodney; Andy Till; Robert McCracken; Ryan Rhodes; Ensley Bingham
MIDDLEWEIGHT	Pat McAteer; Terry Downes; Johnny Pritchett; Bunny Sterling; Alan Minter; Kevin Finnegan; Roy Gumbs; Tony Sibson; Herol Graham; Neville Brown; Howard Eastman
S. MIDDLEWEIGHT	Sammy Storey; David Starie
L. HEAVYWEIGHT	Randy Turpin; Chic Calderwood; Chris Finnegan; Bunny Johnson; Tom Collins; Dennis Andries; Tony Wilson; Crawford Ashley
CRUISERWEIGHT	Johnny Nelson; Terry Dunstan; Bruce Scott
HEAVYWEIGHT	Henry Cooper (3); Horace Notice; Lennox Lewis; Julius Francis

Note: Walter McGowan and Charlie Magri, with one notch apiece, kept their belts under the three years/no available challengers' ruling, while Johnny King, with two notches, was awarded the belt on the grounds that the Second World War stopped him from making further defences. Incidentally, King and Nel Tarleton are the only men to have won both the NSC and BBBoC belts outright.

Nicky Booth (left) won the bantamweight Lonsdale Belt outright when stopping Stephen Oates in Nottingham last February

Les Clark

British Champions Since Gloves, 1878-2002

The listings below show the tenure of all British champions at each weight since gloves (two ounces or more) were introduced to British rings under Queensberry Rules. Although Charley Davis (147 lbs) had beaten Ted Napper (140 lbs) with gloves in 1873, we start with Denny Harrington, who defeated George Rooke for both the English and world middleweight titles in London on 12 March 1878. We also make a point of ignoring competition winners, apart from Anthony Diamond who beat Dido Plumb for the middles title over 12 rounds, basically because full championship conditions or finish fights of three-minute rounds were not applied. Another point worth bearing in mind, is that prior to the 1880s there were only five weights – heavy, middle, light, feather and bantam. Anything above 154 lbs, the middleweight limit, was classified a heavyweight contest, whereas lightweight, feather and bantamweight poundages were much looser. Therefore, to put things into current perspective, in many cases we have had to ascertain the actual poundage of fighters concerned and relate them to the modern weight classes. Another point worth remembering is that men born outside Britain who won international titles in this country, are not recorded for fear of added confusion and, although many of the champions or claimants listed before 1909 were no more than English titleholders, having fought for the 'championship of England', for our purposes they carry the 'British' label.

Prior to 1909, the year that the Lord Lonsdale Challenge Belt was introduced and weight classes subsequently standardised, poundages within divisions could vary quite substantially, thus enabling men fighting at different weights to claim the same 'title' at the same time. A brief history of the weight fluctuations between 1891 and 1909, shows:

Bantamweight   With the coming of gloves, the division did not really take off until Nunc Wallace established himself at 112 lbs on beating (small) Bill Goode after nine rounds in London on 12 March 1889. Later, with Wallace fighting above the weight, Billy Plimmer was generally recognised as the country's leading eight stoner, following victories over Charles Mansford and Jem Stevens, and became accepted as world champion when George Dixon, the number one in America's eyes, gradually increased his weight. In 1895, Pedlar Palmer took the British title at 112 lbs, but by 1900 he had developed into a 114 pounder. Between 1902 and 1904, Joe Bowker defended regularly at 116 lbs and in 1909 the NSC standardised the weight at 118 lbs, even though the USA continued for a short while to accept only 116 lbs.

Featherweight   Between 1886 and 1895, one of the most prestigious championship belts in this country was fought for at 126 lbs and, although George Dixon was recognised in the USA as world featherweight champion – gradually moving from 114 to 122 lbs – no major international contests took place in Britain during the above period at his weight. It was only in 1895, when Fred Johnson took the British title at 120 lbs, losing it to Ben Jordan two years later, that we came into line with the USA. Ben Jordan became an outstanding champion who, between 1898 and 1899, was seen by the NSC as world champion at 120 lbs. However, first Harry Greenfield, then Jabez White and Will Curley, continued to claim the 126 lbs version of the British title and it was only in 1900, when Jack Roberts beat Curley, that the weight limit was finally standardised at nine stone.

Lightweight   Outstanding champions often carried their weights as they grew in size. A perfect example of this was Dick Burge, the British lightweight champion from 1891-1901, who gradually increased from 134 to 144 lbs, while still maintaining his right to the title. It was not until 1902 that Jabez White brought the division into line with the USA. Later, both White, and then Goldswain, carried their weight up to 140 lbs and it was left to Johnny Summers to set the current limit of 135 lbs.

Welterweight   The presence of Dick Burge fighting from 134 to 144 lbs plus up until 1900, explains quite adequately why the welterweight division, although very popular in the USA, did not take off in this country until 1902. The championship was contested between 142 and 146 lbs in those days and was not really supported by the NSC, but by 1909 with their backing it finally became established at 147 lbs.

On 8 September 1970, Bunny Sterling became the first immigrant to win a British title under the ten-year residential ruling, while earlier, on 28 June 1948, Dick Turpin won the British middleweight title and, in doing so, became the first coloured fighter to win the title, thus breaking down the so-called 'colour bar'.

Note that the Lonsdale Belt notches (title bout wins) relate to NSC, 1909-1935, and BBBoC, 1936-2002.

Champions in **bold** are accorded national recognition.

*Undefeated champions (Does not include men who forfeited titles).

Title Holder	Lonsdale Belt Notches	Tenure	Title Holder	Lonsdale Belt Notches	Tenure	Title Holder	Lonsdale Belt Notches	Tenure
Flyweight (112 lbs)			**Percy Jones**	1	1914	**Joe Symonds**	1	1915-1916
Sid Smith		1911	Joe Symonds		1914	**Jimmy Wilde***	3	1916-1923
Sid Smith	1	1911-1913	**Tancy Lee**	1	1914-1915	**Elky Clark***	2	1924-1927
Bill Ladbury		1913-1914	Jimmy Wilde		1914-1915	**Johnny Hill***	1	1927-1929

Title Holder	Lonsdale Belt Notches	Tenure
Jackie Brown		1929-1930
Bert Kirby	1	1930-1931
Jackie Brown	3	1931-1935
Benny Lynch*	2	1935-1938
Jackie Paterson	4	1939-1948
Rinty Monaghan*	1	1948-1950
Terry Allen	1	1951-1952
Teddy Gardner*	1	1952
Terry Allen*	2	1952-1954
Dai Dower*	1	1955-1957
Frankie Jones	2	1957-1960
Johnny Caldwell*	1	1960-1961
Jackie Brown	1	1962-1963
Walter McGowan*	1	1963-1966
John McCluskey*	3	1967-1977
Charlie Magri*	1	1977-1981
Kelvin Smart	1	1982-1984
Hugh Russell*	3	1984-1985
Duke McKenzie*	2	1985-1986
Dave Boy McAuley*	1	1986-1988
Pat Clinton*	3	1988-1991
Robbie Regan	1	1991
Francis Ampofo	1	1991
Robbie Regan*	2	1991-1992
Francis Ampofo	3	1992-1996
Mickey Cantwell*	1	1996-1997
Ady Lewis*	3	1997-1998
Damaen Kelly	1	1999
Keith Knox	1	1999
Jason Booth	2	1999-

Jason Booth, the current British and Commonwealth flyweight champion

Les Clark

Bantamweight (118 lbs)

Title Holder	Lonsdale Belt Notches	Tenure
Nunc Wallace*		1889-1891
Billy Plimmer*		1891-1895
Tom Gardner		1892
Willie Smith		1892-1896
Nunc Wallace		1893-1895
George Corfield		1893-1896
Pedlar Palmer*		1895-1900
Billy Plimmer		1896-1898
Harry Ware		1899-1900
Harry Ware		1900-1902
Andrew Tokell		1901-1902
Jim Williams		1902
Andrew Tokell		1902
Harry Ware		1902
Joe Bowker		1902-1910
Owen Moran		1905-1907
Digger Stanley		1906-1910
Digger Stanley	2	1910-1913
Bill Beynon	1	1913
Digger Stanley	1	1913-1914
Curley Walker*	1	1914-1915
Joe Fox*	3	1915-1917
Tommy Noble	1	1918-1919
Walter Ross*	1	1919-1920
Jim Higgins	3	1920-1922
Tommy Harrison		1922-1923
Bugler Harry Lake	1	1923
Johnny Brown	3	1923-1928
Alf Pattenden	2	1928-1929
Johnny Brown		1928
Teddy Baldock		1928-1929
Teddy Baldock*	1	1929-1931
Dick Corbett	1	1931-1932
Johnny King	1	1932-1934
Dick Corbett*	1	1934
Johnny King	1+2	1935-1947
Jackie Paterson	2	1947-1949
Stan Rowan*	1	1949
Danny O'Sullivan	1	1949-1951
Peter Keenan	3	1951-1953
John Kelly	1	1953-1954
Peter Keenan	3	1954-1959
Freddie Gilroy*	4	1959-1963
Johnny Caldwell	1	1964-1965
Alan Rudkin	1	1965-1966
Walter McGowan	1	1966-1968
Alan Rudkin*	4	1968-1972
Johnny Clark*	1	1973-1974
Dave Needham	1	1974-1975
Paddy Maguire	1	1975-1977
Johnny Owen*	4	1977-1980
John Feeney	1	1981-1983
Hugh Russell	1	1983
Davy Larmour	1	1983
John Feeney	1	1983-1985
Ray Gilbody	2	1985-1987
Billy Hardy*	5	1987-1991
Joe Kelly	1	1992
Drew Docherty	4	1992-1997
Paul Lloyd	2	1997-1999
Noel Wilders*	2	1999-2000
Ady Lewis	1	2000
Tommy Waite	1	2000
Nicky Booth	4	2000-

S. Bantamweight (122 lbs)

Title Holder	Lonsdale Belt Notches	Tenure
Richie Wenton*	3	1994-1996
Michael Brodie*	3	1997-1999
Patrick Mullings	1	1999
Drew Docherty*	1	1999
Michael Alldis	3	1999-2001
Patrick Mullings	1	2001
Michael Alldis	1	2002-

Featherweight (126 lbs)

Title Holder	Lonsdale Belt Notches	Tenure
Bill Baxter		1884-1891
Harry Overton		1890-1891
Billy Reader		1891-1892
Fred Johnson		1891-1895
Harry Spurden		1892-1895
Jack Fitzpatrick		1895-1897
Fred Johnson		1895-1897
Harry Greenfield		1896-1899
Ben Jordan*		1897-1900
Jabez White		1899-1900
Will Curley		1900-1901
Jack Roberts		1901-1902
Will Curley		1902-1903
Ben Jordan*		1902-1905
Joe Bowker		1905
Johnny Summers		1906
Joe Bowker		1905-1906
Jim Driscoll		1906-1907
Spike Robson		1906-1907
Jim Driscoll*	3	1907-1913
Spike Robson		1907-1910
Ted Kid Lewis*	1	1913-1914
Llew Edwards*	1	1915-1917
Charlie Hardcastle	1	1917
Tancy Lee*	3	1917-1919
Mike Honeyman	2	1920-1921
Joe Fox*	1	1921-1922
George McKenzie	2	1924-1925
Johnny Curley	2	1925-1927
Johnny Cuthbert	1	1927-1928
Harry Corbett	1	1928-1929
Johnny Cuthbert	1	1929-1931
Nel Tarleton	1	1931-1932
Seaman Tommy Watson	2	1932-1934
Nel Tarleton	2	1934-1936
Johnny McGrory	1	1936-1938
Jim Spider Kelly	1	1938-1939
Johnny Cusick	1	1939-1940
Nel Tarleton*	3	1940-1947
Ronnie Clayton	6	1947-1954
Sammy McCarthy	1	1954-1955
Billy Spider Kelly	1	1955-1956
Charlie Hill	3	1956-1959
Bobby Neill	1	1959-1960
Terry Spinks	2	1960-1961
Howard Winstone*	7	1961-1969
Jimmy Revie	2	1969-1971
Evan Armstrong	2	1971-1972
Tommy Glencross	1	1972-1973
Evan Armstrong*	2	1973-1975
Vernon Sollas	1	1975-1977
Alan Richardson	2	1977-1978
Dave Needham	2	1978-1979
Pat Cowdell*	3	1979-1982
Steve Sims*	1	1982-1983
Barry McGuigan*	2	1983-1986

Title Holder	Lonsdale Belt Notches	Tenure
Robert Dickie	3	1986-1988
Peter Harris	1	1988
Paul Hodkinson*	3	1988-1990
Sean Murphy	2	1990-1991
Gary de Roux	1	1991
Colin McMillan*	3	1991-1992
John Davison*	1	1992-1993
Sean Murphy	1	1993
Duke McKenzie*	1	1993-1994
Billy Hardy*	1	1994
Michael Deveney	1	1995
Jonjo Irwin	2	1995-1996
Colin McMillan	1	1996-1997
Paul Ingle*	3	1997-1998
Jonjo Irwin*	2	1998-1999
Gary Thornhill	1	2000
Scott Harrison	3	2001-

S. Featherweight (130 lbs)

Title Holder	Lonsdale Belt Notches	Tenure
Jimmy Anderson*	3	1968-1970
John Doherty	1	1986
Pat Cowdell	1	1986
Najib Daho	1	1986-1987
Pat Cowdell	1	1987-1988
Floyd Havard	1	1988-1989
John Doherty	1	1989-1990
Joey Jacobs	1	1990
Hugh Forde	1	1990
Kevin Pritchard	1	1990-1991
Robert Dickie	1	1991
Sugar Gibiliru	1	1991
John Doherty	1	1991-1992
Michael Armstrong	1	1992
Neil Haddock	2	1992-1994
Floyd Havard*	3	1994-1995
P. J. Gallagher	2	1996-1997
Charles Shepherd	3	1997-1999
Michael Gomez*	5	1999-2002

Lightweight (135 lbs)

Title Holder	Lonsdale Belt Notches	Tenure
Dick Burge		1891-1897
Harry Nickless		1891-1894
Tom Causer		1894-1897
Tom Causer		1897
Dick Burge*		1897-1901
Jabez White		1902-1906
Jack Goldswain		1906-1908
Johnny Summers		1908-1909
Freddie Welsh	1	1909-1911
Matt Wells	1	1911-1912
Freddie Welsh*	1	1912-1919
Bob Marriott*	1	1919-1920
Ernie Rice	1	1921-1922
Seaman Nobby Hall		1922-1923
Harry Mason		1923-1924
Ernie Izzard	2	1924-1925
Harry Mason		1924-1925
Harry Mason*	1	1925-1928
Sam Steward		1928-1929
Fred Webster		1929-1930
Al Foreman*	1	1930-1932
Johnny Cuthbert		1932-1934
Harry Mizler		1934
Jackie Kid Berg		1934-1936
Jimmy Walsh	1	1936-1938
Dave Crowley	1	1938
Eric Boon	3	1938-1944

Title Holder	Lonsdale Belt Notches	Tenure
Ronnie James*	1	1944-1947
Billy Thompson	3	1947-1951
Tommy McGovern	1	1951-1952
Frank Johnson	1	1952-1953
Joe Lucy	1	1953-1955
Frank Johnson	1	1955-1956
Joe Lucy	2	1956-1957
Dave Charnley*	3	1957-1965
Maurice Cullen	4	1965-1968
Ken Buchanan*	2	1968-1971
Willie Reilly*	1	1972
Jim Watt	1	1972-1973
Ken Buchanan*	1	1973-1974
Jim Watt*	2	1975-1977
Charlie Nash*	1	1978-1979
Ray Cattouse	2	1980-1982
George Feeney*	3	1982-1985
Tony Willis	3	1985-1987
Alex Dickson	1	1987-1988
Steve Boyle	2	1988-1990
Carl Crook	5	1990-1992
Billy Schwer	1	1992-1993
Paul Burke	1	1993
Billy Schwer*	2	1993-1995
Michael Ayers*	5	1995-1997
Wayne Rigby	2	1998
Bobby Vanzie	5	1998-

L. Welterweight (140 lbs)

Title Holder	Lonsdale Belt Notches	Tenure
Des Rea	1	1968-1969
Vic Andreetti*	2	1969-1970
Des Morrison	1	1973-1974
Pat McCormack	1	1974
Joey Singleton	3	1974-1976
Dave Boy Green*	1	1976-1977
Colin Power*	2	1977-1978
Clinton McKenzie	1	1978-1979
Colin Power	1	1979
Clinton McKenzie	5	1979-1984
Terry Marsh*	1	1984-1986
Tony Laing*	1	1986
Tony McKenzie	2	1986-1987
Lloyd Christie	3	1987-1989
Clinton McKenzie*	1	1989
Pat Barrett*	2	1989-1990
Tony Ekubia	1	1990-1991
Andy Holligan	3	1991-1994
Ross Hale	4	1994-1995
Paul Ryan	1	1995-1996
Andy Holligan*	1	1996-1997
Mark Winters	2	1997-1998
Jason Rowland*	2	1998-2000
Richard Hatton*	1	2000-2001
Junior Witter	1	2002-

Welterweight (147 lbs)

Title Holder	Lonsdale Belt Notches	Tenure
Charlie Allum		1903-1904
Charlie Knock		1904-1906
Curly Watson		1906-1910
Young Joseph		1908-1910
Young Joseph	1	1910-1911
Arthur Evernden		1911-1912
Johnny Summers		1912
Johnny Summers	2	1912-1914
Tom McCormick		1914
Matt Wells		1914
Johnny Basham	3	1914-1920

Title Holder	Lonsdale Belt Notches	Tenure
Matt Wells		1914-1919
Ted Kid Lewis		1920-1924
Tommy Milligan*		1924-1925
Hamilton Johnny Brown		1925
Harry Mason		1925-1926
Jack Hood*	3	1926-1934
Harry Mason		1934
Pat Butler*		1934-1936
Dave McCleave		1936
Jake Kilrain	1	1936-1939
Ernie Roderick	5	1939-1948
Henry Hall	1	1948-1949
Eddie Thomas	2	1949-1951
Wally Thom	1	1951-1952
Cliff Curvis*	1	1952-1953
Wally Thom	2	1953-1956
Peter Waterman*	2	1956-1958
Tommy Molloy	2	1958-1960
Wally Swift	1	1960
Brian Curvis*	7	1960-1966
Johnny Cooke	2	1967-1968
Ralph Charles*	3	1968-1972
Bobby Arthur	1	1972-1973
John H. Stracey*	1	1973-1975
Pat Thomas	2	1975-1976
Henry Rhiney	2	1976-1979
Kirkland Laing	1	1979-1980
Colin Jones*	3	1980-1982
Lloyd Honeyghan*	2	1983-1985
Kostas Petrou	1	1985
Sylvester Mittee	1	1985
Lloyd Honeyghan*	1	1985-1986
Kirkland Laing	4	1987-1991
Del Bryan	2	1991-1992
Gary Jacobs*	2	1992-1993
Del Bryan	4	1993-1995
Chris Saunders	1	1995-1996
Kevin Lueshing	1	1996-1997
Geoff McCreesh*	4	1997-1999
Derek Roche	3	1999-2000
Harry Dhami	3	2000-2001
Neil Sinclair	2	2001-

L. Middleweight (154 lbs)

Title Holder	Lonsdale Belt Notches	Tenure
Larry Paul	2	1973-1974
Maurice Hope*	3	1974-1977
Jimmy Batten	3	1977-1979
Pat Thomas	3	1979-1981
Herol Graham*	2	1981-1983
Prince Rodney*	1	1983-1984
Jimmy Cable	2	1984-1985
Prince Rodney	2	1985-1986
Chris Pyatt*	1	1986
Lloyd Hibbert*	1	1987
Gary Cooper	1	1988
Gary Stretch	2	1988-1990
Wally Swift Jnr	2	1991-1992
Andy Till	3	1992-1994
Robert McCracken*	3	1994-1995
Ensley Bingham*	2	1996
Ryan Rhodes*	3	1996-1997
Ensley Bingham	3	1997-1999
Wayne Alexander	2	2000-

Middleweight (160 lbs)

Title Holder	Lonsdale Belt Notches	Tenure
Denny Harrington		1876-1880
William Sheriff*		1880-1883

Title Holder	Lonsdale Belt Notches	Tenure
Bill Goode		1887-1890
Toff Wall*		1890
Ted Pritchard		1890-1895
Ted White		1893-1895
Ted White*		1895-1896
Anthony Diamond*		1898
Dick Burge*		1898-1900
Jack Palmer		1902-1903
Charlie Allum		1905-1906
Pat O'Keefe		1906
Tom Thomas	1	1906-1910
Jim Sullivan*	1	1910-1912
Jack Harrison*	1	1912-1913
Pat O'Keefe	2	1914-1916
Bandsman Jack Blake	1	1916-1918
Pat O'Keefe*	1	1918-1919
Ted Kid Lewis		1920-1921
Tom Gummer	1	1920-1921
Gus Platts		1921
Johnny Basham		1921
Ted Kid Lewis	2	1921-1923
Johnny Basham		1921
Roland Todd		1923-1925
Roland Todd		1925-1927
Tommy Milligan	1	1926-1928
Frank Moody		1927-1928
Alex Ireland		1928-1929
Len Harvey	5	1929-1933
Jock McAvoy	3+2	1933-1944
Ernie Roderick	1	1945-1946
Vince Hawkins	1	1946-1948
Dick Turpin	2	1948-1950
Albert Finch	1	1950
Randy Turpin*	1	1950-1954
Johnny Sullivan	1	1954-1955
Pat McAteer*	3	1955-1958
Terry Downes	1	1958-1959
John Cowboy McCormack	1	1959
Terry Downes	2	1959-1962
George Aldridge	1	1962-1963
Mick Leahy	1	1963-1964
Wally Swift	1	1964-1965
Johnny Pritchett*	4	1965-1969
Les McAteer	1	1969-1970
Mark Rowe	1	1970
Bunny Sterling	4	1970-1974
Kevin Finnegan*	1	1974
Bunny Sterling*	1	1975
Alan Minter	3	1975-1977
Kevin Finnegan	1	1977
Alan Minter*	1	1977-1978
Tony Sibson	1	1979
Kevin Finnegan*	1	1979-1980
Roy Gumbs	3	1981-1983
Mark Kaylor	1	1983-1984
Tony Sibson*	1	1984
Herol Graham*	1	1985-1986
Brian Anderson	1	1986-1987
Tony Sibson*	1	1987-1988
Herol Graham	4	1988-1992
Frank Grant	2	1992-1993
Neville Brown	6	1993-1998
Glenn Catley*	1	1998
Howard Eastman	3	1998-

S. Middleweight (168 lbs)

Title Holder	Lonsdale Belt Notches	Tenure
Sammy Storey	2	1989-1990
James Cook*	1	1990-1991
Fidel Castro	2	1991-1992
Henry Wharton*	1	1992-1993
James Cook	1	1993-1994
Cornelius Carr*	1	1994
Ali Forbes	1	1995
Sammy Storey*	1	1995
Joe Calzaghe*	2	1995-1997
David Starie	1	1997
Dean Francis*	2	1997-1998
David Starie	5	1998-

L. Heavyweight (175lbs)

Title Holder	Lonsdale Belt Notches	Tenure
Dennis Haugh		1913-1914
Dick Smith	2	1914-1916
Harry Reeve*	1	1916-1917
Dick Smith*	1	1918-1919
Boy McCormick*	1	1919-1921
Jack Bloomfield*	1	1922-1924
Tom Berry	1	1925-1927
Gipsy Daniels*	1	1927
Frank Moody	1	1927-1929
Harry Crossley	1	1929-1932
Jack Petersen	1	1932
Len Harvey*	1	1933-1934
Eddie Phillips		1935-1937
Jock McAvoy	1	1937-1938
Len Harvey	2	1938-1942
Freddie Mills*	1	1942-1950
Don Cockell	2	1950-1952
Randy Turpin*	1	1952
Dennis Powell	1	1953
Alex Buxton	2	1953-1955
Randy Turpin*	1	1955
Ron Barton*	1	1956
Randy Turpin*	2	1956-1958
Chic Calderwood	3	1960-1963
Chic Calderwood*	1	1964-1966
Young John McCormack	2	1967-1969
Eddie Avoth	2	1969-1971
Chris Finnegan	2	1971-1973
John Conteh*	2	1973-1974
Johnny Frankham	1	1975
Chris Finnegan*	1	1975-1976
Tim Wood	1	1976-1977
Bunny Johnson*	3	1977-1981
Tom Collins	3	1982-1984
Dennis Andries*	5	1984-1986
Tom Collins*	1	1987
Tony Wilson	3	1987-1989
Tom Collins*	1	1989-1990
Steve McCarthy	1	1990-1991
Crawford Ashley*	3	1991-1992
Maurice Core*	2	1992-1994
Crawford Ashley	3	1994-1999
Clinton Woods*	1	1999-2000
Neil Simpson*	2	2000-2002

Cruiserweight (190 lbs)

Title Holder	Lonsdale Belt Notches	Tenure
Sam Reeson*	1	1985-1986
Andy Straughn	1	1986-1987
Roy Smith	1	1987
Tee Jay	1	1987-1988
Glenn McCrory*	2	1988
Andy Straughn	1	1988-1989
Johnny Nelson*	3	1989-1991
Derek Angol*	2	1991-1992
Carl Thompson*	1	1992-1994
Dennis Andries	1	1995
Terry Dunstan*	3	1995-1996
Johnny Nelson*	1	1996-1998
Bruce Scott	1	1998-1999
Carl Thompson*	1	1999-2000
Bruce Scott	2	2000-

Heavyweight (190 lbs +)

Title Holder	Lonsdale Belt Notches	Tenure
Tom Allen*		1878-1882
Charlie Mitchell*		1882-1894
Jem Smith		1889-1891
Ted Pritchard		1891-1895
Jem Smith		1895-1896
George Chrisp		1901
Jack Scales		1901-1902
Jack Palmer		1903-1906
Gunner Moir		1906-1909
Iron Hague		1909-1910
P.O. Curran		1910-1911
Iron Hague		1910-1911
Bombardier Billy Wells	3	1911-1919
Joe Beckett		1919
Frank Goddard	1	1919
Joe Beckett*	1	1919-1923
Frank Goddard		1923-1926
Phil Scott*		1926-1931
Reggie Meen		1931-1932
Jack Petersen	3	1932-1933
Len Harvey		1933-1934
Jack Petersen		1934-1936
Ben Foord		1936-1937
Tommy Farr*	1	1937-1938
Len Harvey*	1	1938-1942
Jack London	1	1944-1945
Bruce Woodcock	2	1945-1950
Jack Gardner	1	1950-1952
Johnny Williams	1	1952-1953
Don Cockell*	1	1953-1956
Joe Erskine	2	1956-1958
Brian London	1	1958-1959
Henry Cooper*	9	1959-1969
Jack Bodell	1	1969-1970
Henry Cooper	1	1970-1971
Joe Bugner	1	1971
Jack Bodell	1	1971-1972
Danny McAlinden	1	1972-1975
Bunny Johnson	1	1975
Richard Dunn	2	1975-1976
Joe Bugner*	1	1976-1977
John L. Gardner*	2	1978-1980
Gordon Ferris	1	1981
Neville Meade	1	1981-1983
David Pearce*	1	1983-1985
Hughroy Currie	1	1985-1986
Horace Notice*	4	1986-1988
Gary Mason	2	1989-1991
Lennox Lewis*	3	1991-1993
Herbie Hide*	1	1993-1994
James Oyebola	1	1994-1995
Scott Welch*	1	1995-1996
Julius Francis	4	1997-2000
Mike Holden*	1	2000
Danny Williams	3	2000-

Retired or Inactive Post-War British Champions: Career Summary

Includes all British champions, along with British boxers who have won major international titles since 1945, who had retired by July 2001 or have been inactive since that date. The section does not include champions still active (for their records see under Active British-Based Boxers), while undefeated champions are those who relinquished their titles, not forfeited them.

George Aldridge British Middleweight Champion, 1962-1963. *Born* 01.02.36. *From* Market Harborough. *Pro Career* 1956-1963 (52 contests, won 36, drew 2, lost 14).

Terry Allen British Flyweight Champion, 1951-1952. Undefeated British Flyweight Champion, 1952-1954. European and World Flyweight Champion, 1950. *Born* 18.06.24. *From* Islington. Birthname - Edward Govier. *Deceased* 1987. *Pro Career* 1942-1954 (74 contests, won 60, drew 1, lost 13).

Brian Anderson British Middleweight Champion, 1986-1987. *Born* 09.07.61. *From* Sheffield. *Pro Career* 1980-1987 (39 contests, won 27, drew 3, lost 9).

Jimmy Anderson Undefeated British S. Featherweight Champion, 1968-1970. *Born* 01.10.42. *From* Waltham Cross. *Pro Career* 1964-1971 (37 contests, won 27, drew 1, lost 9).

Vic Andreetti Undefeated British L. Welterweight Champion, 1969-1970. *Born* 29.01.42. *From* Hoxton. *Pro Career* 1961-1969 (67 contests, won 51, drew 3, lost 13).

Dennis Andries Undefeated British L. Heavyweight Champion, 1984-86. World L. Heavyweight Champion (WBC version), 1986-1987, 1989, and 1990-1991. British Cruiserweight Champion, 1995. *Born* Guyana 05.11.53. *From* Hackney. *Pro Career* 1978-1996 (65 contests, won 49, drew 2, lost 14).

Derek Angol Undefeated British Cruiserweight Champion, 1991-1992. Undefeated Commonwealth Cruiserweight Champion, 1989-1993. *Born* 28.11.64. *From* Camberwell. *Pro Career* 1986-1996 (31 contests, won 28, lost 3).

Evan Armstrong British Featherweight Champion, 1971-1972. Undefeated British Featherweight Champion, 1973-1975. Commonwealth Featherweight Champion, 1974. *Born* 15.02.43. *From* Ayr. *Pro Career* 1963-1974 (54 contests, won 39, drew 1, lost 14).

Michael Armstrong British S. Featherweight Champion, 1992. *Born* 18.12.68. *From* Moston. Birthname - Morris. *Pro Career* 1987-1994 (26 contests, won 18, drew 1, lost 7).

Bobby Arthur British Welterweight Champion, 1972-1973. *Born* 25.07.47. *From* Coventry. *Pro Career* 1967-1976 (41 contests, won 26, lost 15).

Eddie Avoth British L. Heavyweight Champion, 1969-1971. Commonwealth L. Heavyweight Champion, 1970-1971. *Born* 02.05.45. *From* Cardiff. *Pro Career* 1963-1972 (53 contests, won 44, lost 9).

Pat Barrett Undefeated British L. Welterweight Champion, 1989-1990. European L. Welterweight Champion, 1989-1992. *Born* 22.07.67. *From* Manchester. *Pro Career* 1987-1994 (42 contests, won 37, drew 1, lost 4).

Ron Barton Undefeated British L. Heavyweight Champion, 1956. *Born* 25.02.33. *From* West Ham. *Pro Career* 1954-1961 (31 contests, won 26, lost 5).

Jimmy Batten British L. Middleweight Champion, 1977-1979. *Born* 07.11.55. *From* Millwall. *Pro Career* 1974-1983 (49 contests, won 40, lost 9).

Nigel Benn Commonwealth Middleweight Champion, 1988-1989. World Middleweight Champion (WBO version), 1990. World S. Middleweight Champion (WBC version), 1992-1996. *Born* 22.01.64. *From* Ilford. *Pro Career* 1987-1996 (48 contests, won 42, drew 1, lost 5).

Ensley Bingham Undefeated British L. Middleweight Champion, 1996. British L. Middleweight Champion, 1997-1999. *Born* 27.05.63. *From* Manchester. *Pro Career* 1986-1999 (28 contests, won 20, lost 8).

Jack Bodell British Heavyweight Champion, 1969-1970 and 1971-1972. Commonwealth Heavyweight Champion, 1971-1972. European Heavyweight Champion, 1971. *Born* 11.08.40. *From* Swadlincote. *Pro Career* 1962-1972 (71 contests, won 58, lost 13).

Steve Boyle British Lightweight Champion, 1988-1990. *Born* 28.11.62. *From* Glasgow. *Pro Career* 1983-1993 (33 contests, won 25, drew 2, lost 6).

Cornelius Boza-Edwards Undefeated European S. Featherweight Champion, 1982. World S. Featherweight Champion, 1981 (WBC version). *Born* Uganda, 27.05.56. *From* London. *Pro Career* 1976-1987 (53 contests, won 45, drew 1, lost 7).

Jim Brady British Empire Bantamweight Championship Claimant, 1941-1945. *From* Dundee. *Deceased* 1980. *Pro Career* 1932-1947 (169 contests, won 104, drew 15, lost 50).

Jackie Brown British and British Empire Flyweight Champion, 1962-1963. *Born* 02.03.35. *From* Edinburgh. *Pro Career* 1958-1966 (44 contests, won 32, drew 1, lost 10, no contest 1).

Neville Brown British Middleweight Champion, 1993-1998. *Born* 26.02.66. *From* Burton. *Pro Career* 1989-2000 (40 contests, won 32, lost 8).

Frank Bruno Undefeated European Heavyweight Champion, 1985-1986. World Heavyweight Champion (WBC version), 1995-96. *From* Wandsworth. *Pro Career* 1982-1996 (45 contests, won 40, lost 5).

Del Bryan British Welterweight Champion, 1991-1992 and 1993-1995. *Born* 16.04.1967. *From* Birmingham. *Pro Career* 1986-1998 (52 contests, won 32, drew 1, lost 19).

Ken Buchanan Undefeated British Lightweight Champion, 1968-1971, and 1973-1974. Undefeated European Lightweight Champion, 1974-1975. World Lightweight Champion, 1970-1971. World Lightweight Champion, (WBA version), 1971-1972. *Born* 28.06.45. *From* Edinburgh. *Pro Career* 1965-1982 (69 contests, won 61, lost 8).

Joe Bugner British, Commonwealth and European Heavyweight Champion, 1971. Undefeated European Heavyweight Champion, 1972-1975. European Heavyweight Champion, 1976-1977. Undefeated British and Commonwealth Heavyweight Champion, 1976-1977. *Born* Hungary, 13.03.50. *From* Bedford. *Pro Career* 1967-1999 (83 contests, won 69, drew 1, lost 13).

Paul Burke British and Commonwealth Lightweight Champion, 1993. Commonwealth L. Welterweight Champion, 1997 and 1998-1999. *Born* 25.07.66. *From* Preston. *Pro Career* 1987-1999 (43 contests, won 28, drew 2, lost 13).

Alex Buxton British L. Heavyweight Champion, 1953-1955. *Born* 10.05.25. *From* Watford. *Pro Career* 1942-1963 (125 contests, won 78, drew 4, lost 43).

Jimmy Cable British L. Middleweight Champion, 1984-1985. European L. Middleweight Champion, 1984. *Born* 07.09.57. *From* Crawley. *Pro Career* 1980-1988 (41 contests, won 30, drew 2, lost 9).

Chic Calderwood British and British Empire L. Heavyweight Champion, 1960-1963. Undefeated British L. Heavyweight Champion, 1964-1966. *Born* 09.01.37. *From* Craigneuk. Birthname - Charles Calderwood. *Deceased* 1966. *Pro Career* 1957-1966 (55 contests, won 44, drew 1, lost 9, no contest 1).

Johnny Caldwell Undefeated British Flyweight Champion, 1960-1961. British and British Empire Bantamweight Champion, 1964-1965. World Bantamweight Champion (EBU version), 1961-1962. *Born* 07.05.38. *From* Belfast. *Pro Career* 1958-1965 (35 contests, won 29, drew 1, lost 5).

Cornelius Carr Undefeated British S. Middleweight Champion, 1994. *Born* 09.04.69. *From* Middlesbrough. *Pro Career* 1987-2001 (38 contests, won 34, lost 4).

Fidel Castro British S. Middleweight Champion, 1991-1992. *Born* 17.04.63. *From* Nottingham. Birthname - Smith. *Pro Career* 1987-1995 (30 contests, won 22, lost 8).

Ray Cattouse British Lightweight Champion, 1980-1982. *Born* 24.07.52. *From* Balham. *Pro Career* 1975-1983 (31 contests, won 26, drew 3, lost 2).

Ralph Charles Undefeated British and British Empire/Commonwealth Welterweight Champion, 1968-1972. European Welterweight Champion, 1970-1971. *Born* 05.02.43. *From* West Ham. *Pro Career* 1963-1972 (43 contests, won 39, lost 4).

Dave Charnley Undefeated British Lightweight Champion, 1957-1965. British Empire Lightweight Champion, 1959-1962. European Lightweight Champion, 1960-1963. *Born* 10.10.35. *From* Dartford. *Pro Career* 1954-1964 (61 contests, won 48, drew 1, lost 12).

Lloyd Christie British L. Welterweight Champion, 1987-1989. *Born* 28.02.62. *From* Wolverhampton. *Pro Career* 1981-1989 (46 contests, won 24, drew 1, lost 21).

Johnny Clark Undefeated British and European Bantamweight Champion, 1973-1974. *Born* 10.09.47. *From* Walworth. *Pro Career* 1966-1974 (43 contests, won 39, drew 1, lost 3).

Ronnie Clayton British Featherweight Champion, 1947-1954. British Empire Featherweight Championship Claimant, 1947-1951. European Featherweight Champion, 1947-1948. *Born* 09.02.23. *From* Blackpool. *Deceased* 1999. *Pro Career* 1941-1954 (113 contests, won 79, drew 8, lost 26).

Pat Clinton Undefeated British Flyweight Champion, 1988-1991. Undefeated European Flyweight Champion, 1990-1991. World Flyweight Champion (WBO version), 1992-1993. *Born* 04.04.64. *From* Croy. *Pro Career* 1985-1991 (23 contests, won 20, lost 3).

Ray Close Undefeated European S. Middleweight Champion, 1993. *Born* 20.01.69. *From* Belfast. *Pro Career* 1988-1997 (29 contests, won 25, drew 1, lost 3).

Don Cockell British L. Heavyweight Champion, 1950-1952. Undefeated European L. Heavyweight Champion, 1951-1952. Undefeated British Heavyweight Champion, 1953-1956. British Empire Heavyweight Championship Claimant, 1953-1954. Undefeated British Empire Heavyweight Champion, 1954-1956. *Born* 22.09.28. *From* Battersea. *Deceased* 1983. *Pro Career* 1946-1956 (80 contests, won 65, drew 1, lost 14).

Steve Collins Undefeated World Middleweight Champion (WBO version), 1994-1995. Undefeated World S. Middleweight Champion (WBO version), 1995-1997. *Born* 21.07.64. *From* Dublin. *Pro Career* 1986-1997 (39 contests, won 36, lost 3).

Tom Collins British L. Heavyweight Champion, 1982-1984. Undefeated British L. Heavyweight Champion, 1987 and 1989-1990. European L. Heavyweight Champion, 1987-1988 and 1990-1991. *Born* Curacao, 01.07.55. *From* Leeds. *Pro Career* 1977-1993 (50 contests, won 26, drew 2, lost 22).

John Conteh Undefeated British, Commonwealth and European L. Heavyweight Champion, 1973-1974. World L. Heavyweight Champion (WBC version), 1974-1977. *Born* 27.05.51. *From* Liverpool. *Pro Career* 1971-1980 (39 contests, won 34, drew 1, lost 4).

James Cook Undefeated British S. Middleweight Champion, 1990-1991. British S. Middleweight Champion, 1993-1994. European S. Middleweight Champion, 1991-1992. *Born* Jamaica, 17.05.59. *From* Peckham. *Pro Career* 1982-1994 (35 contests, won 25, lost 10).

Johnny Cooke British and British Empire Welterweight Champion, 1967-1968. *Born* 17.12.34. *From* Bootle. *Pro Career* 1960-1971 (93 contests, won 52, drew 7, lost 34).

Gary Cooper British L. Middleweight Champion, 1988. *Born* 31.05.57. *From* Lymington. *Pro Career* 1978-1989 (27 contests, won 16, drew 2, lost 9).

Henry Cooper Undefeated British Heavyweight Champion, 1959-1969. British Heavyweight Champion, 1970-1971. British Empire/Commonwealth Heavyweight Champion, 1959-1971. Undefeated European Heavyweight Champion, 1964 and 1968-1969. European Heavyweight Champion, 1970-1971. *Born* 03.05.34. *From* Bellingham. *Pro Career* 1954-1971 (55 contests, won 40, drew 1, lost 14).

Maurice Core Undefeated British L. Heavyweight Champion, 1992-1994. *Born* 22.06.65. *From* Manchester. Birthname - Maurice Coore. *Pro Career* 1990-1996 (18 contests, won 15, drew 1, lost 2).

Pat Cowdell Undefeated British Featherweight Champion, 1979-1982. Undefeated European Featherweight Champion, 1982-1983. British S. Featherweight Champion, 1986 and 1987-1988. European S. Featherweight Champion, 1984-1985. *Born* 18.08.53. *From* Warley. *Pro Career* 1977-1988 (42 contests, won 36, lost 6).

Carl Crook British and Commonwealth Lightweight Champion, 1990-1992. *Born* 10.11.63. *From* Chorley. *Pro Career* 1985-1993 (31 contests, won 26, drew 1, lost 4).

Maurice Cullen British Lightweight Champion, 1965-1968. *Born* 30.12.37. *From* Shotton. *Deceased* 2001. *Pro Career* 1959-1970 (55 contests, won 45, drew 2, lost 8).

Hughroy Currie British Heavyweight Champion, 1985-1986. *Born* Jamaica, 09.02.59. *From* Catford. *Pro Career* 1981-1989 (29 contests, won 17, drew 1, lost 11).

Brian Curvis Undefeated British and British Empire Welterweight Champion, 1960-1966. *Born* 14.08.37. *From* Swansea. Birthname - Brian Nancurvis. *Pro Career* 1959-1966 (41 contests, won 37, lost 4).

Cliff Curvis Undefeated British Welterweight Champion, 1952-1953. British Empire Welterweight Championship Claimant, 1952. *Born* 02.11.27. *From* Swansea. Birthname - Cliff Nancurvis. *Pro Career* 1944-1953 (55 contests, won 42, drew 1, lost 12).

Najib Daho British S. Featherweight Champion, 1986-1987. Commonwealth Lightweight Champion, 1989-1990. *Born* Morocco, 13.01.59. *From* Manchester. *Deceased* 1993. *Pro Career* 1977-1991 (60 contests, won 34, drew 1, lost 25).

John Davison Undefeated British Featherweight Champion, 1992-1993. *Born* 30.09.58. *From* Newcastle. *Pro Career* 1988-1993 (20 contests, won 15, lost 5).

Gary DeRoux British Featherweight Champion, 1991. *Born* 04.11.62. *From* Peterborough. *Pro Career* 1986-1993 (22 contests, won 13, drew 1, lost 8).

Mike Deveney British Featherweight Champion, 1995. *Born* 14.12.65. *From* Paisley. *Pro Career* 1991-1998 (42 contests, won 22, drew 1, lost 19).

Robert Dickie British Featherweight Champion, 1986-1988. British S. Featherweight Champion, 1991. *Born* 23.06.64. *From* Swansea. *Pro Career* 1983-1993 (28 contests, won 22, drew 2, lost 4).

Alex Dickson British Lightweight Champion, 1987-1988. *Born* 01.10.62. *From* Larkhall. *Pro Career* 1985-1989 (22 contests, won 18, drew 1, lost 3).

Drew Docherty Undefeated British S. Bantamweight Champion, 1999. British Bantamweight Champion, 1992-1997. *Born* 29.11.65. *From* Condorrat. *Pro Career* 1989-2000 (24 contests, won 16, drew 1, lost 7).

John Doherty British S. Featherweight Champion, 1986, 1989-1990, and 1991-1992. *Born* 17.07.62. *From* Bradford. *Pro Career* 1982-1992 (39 contests, won 28, drew 3, lost 8).

Pat Doherty Commonwealth Lightweight Champion, 1989. *Born* 12.04.62. *From* Croydon. *Pro Career* 1981-1989 (32 contests, won 18, drew 3, lost 11).

Dai Dower Undefeated British Flyweight Champion, 1955-1957. Undefeated British Empire Flyweight Champion, 1954-1957. European Flyweight Champion, 1955. *Born* 26.06.33. *From* Abercynon. *Pro Career* 1953-1958 (37 contests, won 34, lost 3).

Terry Downes British Middleweight Champion, 1958-1959 and 1959-1962. World Middleweight Champion (NY/EBU version), 1961-1962. *Born* 09.05.36. *From* Paddington. *Pro Career* 1957-1964 (44 contests, won 35, lost 9).

Richard Dunn British and Commonwealth Heavyweight Champion, 1975-1976. European Heavyweight Champion, 1976. *Born* 19.01.45. *From* Bradford. *Pro Career* 1969-1977 (45 contests, won 33, lost 12).

Terry Dunstan Undefeated British Cruiserweight Champion, 1995-1996. Undefeated European Cruiserweight Champion, 1998. *Born* 21.10.68. *From* Vauxhall. *Pro Career* 1992-1999 (21 contests, won 19, lost 2).

Tony Ekubia British L. Welterweight Champion, 1990-1991. Commonwealth L. Welterweight Champion, 1989-1991. *Born* Nigeria, 06.03.60. *From* Manchester. *Pro Career* 1986-1993 (25 contests, won 21, lost 4).

Joe Erskine British Heavyweight Champion, 1956-1958. British Empire Heavyweight Champion, 1957-1958. *Born* 26.01.34. *From* Cardiff. *Deceased* 1990. *Pro Career* 1954-1964 (54 contests, won 45, drew 1, lost 8).

Chris Eubank Undefeated WBO Middleweight Champion, 1990-1991. WBO S. Middleweight Title, 1991-1995. *Born* 08.08.1966. *From* Brighton. *Pro Career* 1985-1998 (52 contests, won 45, drew 2, lost 5).

George Feeney Undefeated British Lightweight Champion, 1982-1985. *Born* 09.02.57. *From* West Hartlepool. *Pro Career* 1977-1984 (29 contests, won 19, lost 10).

John Feeney British Bantamweight Champion, 1981-1983 and 1983-1985. *Born* 15.05.58. *From* West Hartlepool. *Pro Career* 1977-1987 (48 contests, won 35, lost 13).

Gordon Ferris British Heavyweight Champion, 1981. *Born* 21.11.52. *From* Enniskillen. *Pro Career* 1977-1982 (26 contests, won 20, lost 6).

Darren Fifield Commonwealth Flyweight Champion, 1993-1994. *Born* 09.10.69. *From* Henley. *Pro Career* 1992-1996 (13 contests, won 7, drew 2, lost 4).

Albert Finch British Middleweight Champion, 1950. *Born* 16.05.26. *From* Croydon. *Pro Career* 1945-1958 (103 contests, won 72, drew 9, lost 21, no contest 1).

Chris Finnegan British L. Heavyweight Champion, 1971-1973. Undefeated British L. Heavyweight Champion, 1975-1976. Commonwealth L. Heavyweight Champion, 1971-1973. European L. Heavyweight Champion, 1972. *Born* 05.06.44. *From* Iver. *Pro Career* 1968-1975 (37 contests, won 29, drew 1, lost 7).

Kevin Finnegan British Middleweight Champion, 1977. Undefeated British Middleweight Champion, 1974 and 1979-1980. European Middleweight Champion, 1974-1975 and 1980. *Born* 18.04.48. *From* Iver. *Pro Career* 1970-1980 (47 contests, won 35, drew 1, lost 11).

Hugh Forde British S. Featherweight Champion, 1990. Commonwealth S. Featherweight Champion, 1991. *Born* 07.05.64. *From* Birmingham. *Pro Career* 1986-1995 (31 contests, won 24, lost 7).

Steve Foster Commonwealth L. Middleweight Champion, 1996-1997. *Born* 28.12.60. *From* Salford. *Pro Career* 1981-1999 (39 contests, won 20, drew 2, lost 17).

Johnny Frankham British L. Heavyweight Champion, 1975. *Born* 06.06.48. *From* Reading. *Pro Career* 1970-1976 (40 contests, won 28, drew 1, lost 11).

P.J. Gallagher British S. Featherweight Champion, 1996-1997. *Born* 14.02.73. *From* Wood Green. *Pro Career* 1993-2000 (20 contests, won 19, lost 1).

Jack Gardner British Heavyweight Champion, 1950-1952. British Empire

Heavyweight Championship Claimant, 1950-1952. European Heavyweight Champion, 1951. *Born* 06.11.26. *From* Market Harborough. *Deceased* 1978. *Pro Career* 1948-1956 (34 contests, won 28, lost 6).

John L. Gardner Undefeated British Heavyweight Champion, 1978-1980. Undefeated Commonwealth Heavyweight Champion, 1978-1981. Undefeated European Heavyweight Champion, 1980-1981. *Born* 19.03.53. *From* Hackney. *Pro Career* 1973-1983 (39 contests, won 35, lost 4).

Teddy Gardner Undefeated British and European Flyweight Champion, 1952. British Empire Flyweight Championship Claimant, 1952. *Born* 27.01.22. *From* West Hartlepool. *Deceased* 1977. *Pro Career* 1938-1952 (66 contests, won 55, drew 3, lost 8).

Sugar Gibiliru British S. Featherweight Champion, 1991. *Born* 13.07.66. *From* Liverpool. *Pro Career* 1984-1995 (55 contests, won 16, drew 7, lost 32).

Ray Gilbody British Bantamweight Champion, 1985-1987. *Born* 21.03.60. *From* Warrington. *Pro Career* 1983-1987 (16 contests, won 11, drew 1, lost 4).

Freddie Gilroy Undefeated British and British Empire Bantamweight Champion, 1959-1963. European Bantamweight Champion, 1959-1960. *Born* 07.03.36. *From* Belfast. *Pro Career* 1957-1962 (31 contests, won 28, lost 3).

Tommy Glencross British Featherweight Champion, 1972-1973. *Born* 31.07.47. *From* Glasgow. *Pro Career* 1967-1978 (48 contests, won 31, drew 1, lost 16).

Herol Graham Undefeated British L. Middleweight Champion, 1981-1983. Undefeated Commonwealth L. Middleweight Champion, 1981-1984. Undefeated European L. Middleweight Champion, 1983-1984. Undefeated British Middleweight Champion, 1985-1986. British Middleweight Champion, 1988-1992. European Middleweight Champion, 1986-1987. *Born* 13.09.59. *From* Sheffield. *Pro Career* 1978-1998 (54 contests, won 48, lost 6).

Frank Grant British Middleweight Champion, 1992-1993. *Born* 22.05.65. *From* Bradford. *Pro Career* 1986-1993 (26 contests, won 22, lost 4).

Dave Boy Green Undefeated British and European L. Welterweight Champion, 1976-1977. European Welterweight Champion, 1979. *Born* 02.06.53. *From* Chatteris. *Pro Career* 1974-1981 (41 contests, won 37, lost 4).

Roy Gumbs British Middleweight Champion, 1981-1983. Commonwealth Middleweight Champion, 1983. *Born* St Kitts, 05.09.54. *From* Tottenham. *Pro Career* 1976-1985 (40 contests, won 26, drew 3, lost 11).

Neil Haddock British S. Featherweight Champion, 1992-1994. *Born* 22.06.64. *From* Llanelli. *Pro Career* 1987-1994 (26 contests, won 14, drew 1, lost 11).

Ross Hale British and Commonwealth L. Welterweight Champion, 1994-1995. *Born* 28.02.1967. *From* Bristol. *Pro Career* 1989-1998 (33 contests, won 29, lost 4).

Henry Hall British Welterweight Champion, 1948-1949. *Born* 06.09.22. *From* Sheffield. *Deceased* 1979. *Pro Career* 1945-1952 (66 contests, won 43, drew 3, lost 20).

Billy Hardy Undefeated British Bantamweight Champion, 1987-1991. Undefeated British Featherweight Champion, 1994. Undefeated Commonwealth Featherweight Champion, 1992-1996. European Featherweight Champion, 1995-1998. *Born* 05.09.1964. *From* Sunderland. *Pro Career* 1983-1998 (48 contests, won 37, drew 2, lost 9).

Paul Harvey Commonwealth S. Featherweight Champion, 1991-1992. *Born* 10.11.64. *From* Ilford. *Pro Career* 1989-1994 (22 contests, won 16, drew 1, lost 5).

Floyd Havard British S. Featherweight Champion, 1988-1989. Undefeated British S. Featherweight Champion, 1994-1995. *Born* 16.10.65. *From* Swansea. *Pro Career* 1985-1996 (36 contests, won 34, lost 2).

Vince Hawkins British Middleweight Champion, 1946-1948. *Born* 15.04.23. *From* Eastleigh. *Pro Career* 1940-1950 (86 contests, won 75, drew 1, lost 10).

Lloyd Hibbert Undefeated British L. Middleweight Champion, 1987. Commonwealth L. Middleweight Champion, 1987. *Born* 29.06.59. *From* Birmingham. *Pro Career* 1979-1987 (23 contests, won 19, lost 4).

Herbie Hide Undefeated British Heavyweight Champion, 1993-1994. WBO Heavyweight Champion, 1997-1999. *Born* 27.08.1971. *From* Norwich. *Pro Career* 1989-1999 (33 contests, won 31, lost 2).

Charlie Hill British Featherweight Champion, 1956-1959. *Born* 20.06.30. *From* Cambuslang. *Pro Career* 1953-1959 (36 contests, won 31, lost 5).

Paul Hodkinson Undefeated British Featherweight Champion, 1988-1990. Undefeated European Featherweight Champion, 1989-1991. World Featherweight Champion, 1991-1993 (WBC version). *Born* 14.09.65. *From* Liverpool. *Pro Career* 1986-1994 (26 contests, won 22, drew 1, lost 3).

Andy Holligan British and Commonwealth L. Welterweight Champion,

1991-1994 and 1996-1997. *Born* 06.06.67. *From* Liverpool. *Pro Career* 1987-1998 (30 contests, won 27, lost 3).

Lloyd Honeyghan Undefeated British Welterweight Champion, 1983-1985 and 1985-1986. Undefeated Commonwealth & European Champion, 1985-1986. World Welterweight Champion, 1986. World Welterweight Champion (WBC version), 1986-1987 and 1988-1989. World Welterweight Champion (IBF version), 1986-1987. Commonwealth L. Middleweight Champion, 1993-1994. *From* Bermondsey. *Pro Career* 1980-1995 (48 contests, won 43, lost 5).

Maurice Hope Undefeated British L. Middleweight Champion, 1974-1977. Undefeated Commonwealth L. Middleweight Champion, 1976-1979. Undefeated European L. Middleweight Champion, 1976-1978. World L. Middleweight Champion (WBC version), 1979-1981. *Born* Antigua, 06.12.51. *From* Hackney. *Pro Career* 1973-1982 (35 contests, won 30, drew 1, lost 4).

Mickey Hughes Commonwealth L. Middleweight Champion, 1992-1993. *Born* 13.06.62. *From* St Pancras. *Pro Career* 1985-1993 (31 contests, won 24, lost 7).

Mo Hussein Commonwealth Lightweight Champion, 1987-1989. *Born* 17.11.62. *From* West Ham. *Pro Career* 1982-1989 (27 contests, won 23, lost 4).

Paul Ingle World Featherweight Champion (IBF version), 1999-2000. Undefeated British Featherweight Champion, 1997-1998. Undefeated Commonwealth and European Champion, 1997-1999. *Born* 22.06.72. *From* Scarborough. *Pro Career* (25 contests, won 23, lost 2).

Jonjo Irwin British Featherweight Champion, 1995-1996. Undefeated British Featherweight Champion, 1998-1999. Commonwealth Featherweight Champion, 1996-1997. *Born* 31.05.69. *From* Doncaster. *Pro Career* 1992-1999 (24 contests, won 19, lost 5).

Gary Jacobs Undefeated British Welterweight Champion, 1992-1993. Commonwealth Welterweight Champion, 1988-1989. European Welterweight Champion, 1993-1994. *Born* 10.12.65. *From* Glasgow. *Pro Career* 1985-1997 (53 contests, won 45, lost 8).

Joey Jacobs British S. Featherweight Champion, 1990. *Born* 01.10.60. *From* Manchester. *Pro Career* 1986-1991 (15 contests, won 10, lost 5).

Ronnie James Undefeated British Lightweight Champion, 1944-1947. *Born* 08.10.17. *From* Swansea. *Deceased* 1977. *Pro Career* 1933-1947 (119 contests, won 98, drew 5, lost 16).

Tee Jay British Cruiserweight Champion, 1987-1988. *Born* Ghana, 21.01.62. Birthname - Taju Akay. *From* Notting Hill. *Pro Career* 1985-1991 (19 contests, won 14, drew 1, lost 4).

Bunny Johnson British and Commonwealth Heavyweight Champion, 1975. Undefeated British L. Heavyweight Champion, 1977-1981. *Born* Jamaica, 10.05.47. *From* Birmingham. Birthname - Fitzroy Johnson. *Pro Career* 1968-1981 (73 contests, won 55, drew 1, lost 17).

Frank Johnson British Lightweight Champion, 1952-1953 and 1955-1956. British Empire Lightweight Championship Claimant, 1953. *Born* 27.11.28. *From* Manchester. Birthname - Frank Williamson. *Deceased* 1970. *Pro Career* 1946-1957 (58 contests, won 47, lost 11).

Barry Jones Undefeated WBO S. Featherweight Champion, 1997-1998. *Born* 03.05.74. *From* Cardiff. *Pro Career* 1992-2000 (20 contests, won 18, drew 1, lost 1).

Colin Jones Undefeated British Welterweight Champion, 1980-1982. Undefeated Commonwealth Welterweight Champion, 1981-1984. Undefeated European Welterweight Champion, 1982-1983. *Born* 21.03.59. *From* Gorseinon. *Pro Career* 1977-1985 (30 contests, won 26, drew 1, lost 3).

Frankie Jones British Flyweight Champion, 1957-1960. British Empire Flyweight Champion, 1957. *Born* 12.02.33. *From* Plean. *Deceased* 1991. *Pro Career* 1955-1960 (25 contests, won 17, lost 8).

Peter Kane Undefeated World Flyweight Champion, 1938-1939. European Bantamweight Champion, 1947-1948. *Born* 28.04.18. *From* Golborne. Birthname - Peter Cain. *Deceased* 1991. *Pro Career* 1934-1948 (102 contests, won 92, drew 2, lost 7, no contest 1).

Mark Kaylor British and Commonwealth Middleweight Champion, 1983-1984. *Born* 11.05.61. *From* West Ham. *Pro Career* 1980-1991 (48 contests, won 40, drew 1, lost 7).

Peter Keenan British Bantamweight Champion, 1951-1953 and 1954-1959. British Empire Bantamweight Champion, 1955-1959. European Bantamweight Champion, 1951-1952 and 1953. *Born* 08.08.28. *From* Glasgow. *Deceased* 2000. *Pro Career* 1948-1959 (66 contests, won 54, drew 1, lost 11).

Billy Spider Kelly British Featherweight Champion, 1955-1956. British Empire Featherweight Championship Claimant, 1954. British Empire Featherweight Champion, 1954-1955. *Born* 21.04.32. *From* Londonderry. *Pro Career* 1950-1962 (83 contests, won 56, drew 4, lost 23).

Joe Kelly British Bantamweight Champion, 1992. *Born* 18.05.64. *From* Glasgow. *Pro Career* 1985-1992 (27 contests, won 18, drew 2, lost 7).

John Kelly British and European Bantamweight Champion, 1953-1954. *Born* 17.01.32. *From* Belfast. *Pro Career* 1951-1957 (28 contests, won 24, lost 4).

Johnny King British Bantamweight Champion, 1932-1934 and 1935-1947. British Empire Bantamweight Championship Claimant, 1932-1934. *Born* 08.01.12. *From* Manchester. *Deceased* 1963. *Pro Career* 1926-1947 (222 contests, won 158, drew 15, lost 48, no contest 1).

Keith Knox British and Commonwealth Flyweight Champion, 1999. *Born* 20.06.67. *From* Bonnyrigg. *Pro Career* 1994-2001 (23 contests, won 13, drew 2, lost 8).

Kirkland Laing British Welterweight Champion, 1987-1991. European Welterweight Champion, 1990. *Born* 20.06.54, Jamaica. *From* Nottingham. *Pro Career* 1975-1994 (56 contests, won 43, drew 1, lost 12).

Tony Laing Undefeated British L. Welterweight Champion, 1986. Commonwealth L. Welterweight Champion, 1987-1988. *Born* 22.09.57. *From* Nottingham. *Pro Career* 1977-1988 (18 contests, won 13, drew 1, lost 4).

Davy Larmour British Bantamweight Champion, 1983. *Born* 02.04.52. *From* Belfast. *Pro Career* 1977-1983 (18 contests, won 11, lost 7).

Mick Leahy British Middleweight Champion, 1963-1964. *Born* Cork, 12.03.35. *From* Coventry. *Pro Career* 1956-1965 (72 contests, won 46, drew 7, lost 19).

Stewart Lithgo Commonwealth Cruiserweight Champion, 1984. *Born* 02.06.57. *From* West Hartlepool. *Pro Career* 1977-1987 (30 contests, won 16, drew 2, lost 12).

Paul Lloyd British Bantamweight Champion, 1997-1999. Undefeated Commonwealth Bantamweight Champion, 1996-2000. Undefeated European Bantamweight Champion, 1998-1999. *Born* 07.12.68. *From* Ellesmere Port. *Pro Career* 1992-2000 (27 contests, won 20, lost 7).

Brian London British and British Empire Heavyweight Champion, 1958-1959. *Born* 19.06.34. *From* Blackpool. Birthname - Brian Harper. *Pro Career* 1955-1970 (58 contests, won 37, drew 1, lost 20).

Jack London British Heavyweight Champion, 1944-1945. British Empire Heavyweight Championship Claimant, 1944-1945. *Born* 23.06.13. *From* West Hartlepool. Birthname - Jack Harper. *Deceased* 1964. *Pro Career* 1931-1949 (141 contests, won 95, drew 5, lost 39, no contests 2).

Eamonn Loughran Undefeated Commonwealth Welterweight Champion, 1992-1993. WBO Welterweight Champion, 1993-1996. *Born* 05.06.70. *Fron* Ballymena. *Pro Career* 1987-1996 (30 contests, won 26, drew 1, lost 2, no contest 1).

Joe Lucy British Lightweight Champion, 1953-1955 and 1956-1957. *Born* 09.02.30. *From* Mile End. *Deceased* 1991. *Pro Career* 1950-1957 (37 contests, won 27, lost 10).

Kevin Lueshing British Welterweight Champion, 1996-1997. *Born* 17.04.1968. *From* Beckenham. *Pro Career* 1991-1999 (25 contests, won 21, lost 4).

Danny McAlinden British and Commonwealth Heavyweight Champion, 1972-1975. *Born* Newry, 01.06.47. *From* Coventry. *Pro Career* 1969-1981 (45 contests, won 31, drew 2, lost 12).

Les McAteer British and British Empire Middleweight Champion, 1969-1970. *Born* 19.08.45. *From* Birkenhead. *Pro Career* 1965-1979 (39 contests, won 27, drew 2, lost 10).

Pat McAteer Undefeated British Middleweight Champion, 1955-1958. British Empire Middleweight Champion, 1955-1958. *Born* 17.03.32. *From* Birkenhead. *Pro Career* 1952-1958 (57 contests, won 49, drew 2, lost 6).

Dave McAuley Undefeated British Flyweight Champion, 1986-1988. World Flyweight Champion (IBF version), 1989-1992. *Born* 15.06.61. *From* Larne. *Pro Career* 1983-1992 (23 contests, won 18, drew 2, lost 3).

Sammy McCarthy British Featherweight Champion, 1954-1955. *Born* 05.11.31. *From* Stepney. *Pro Career* 1951-1957 (53 contests, won 44, drew 1, lost 8).

Steve McCarthy British L. Heavyweight Champion, 1990-1991. *Born* 30.07.62. *From* Southampton. *Pro Career* 1987-1994 (17 contests, won 12, drew 1, lost 4).

John McCluskey Undefeated British Flyweight Champion, 1967-1977. Commonwealth Flyweight Champion, 1970-1971. *Born* 23.01.44. *From* Hamilton. *Pro Career* 1965-1975 (38 contests, won 23, lost 15).

John Cowboy McCormack British Middleweight Champion, 1959. European Middleweight Champion, 1961-1962. *Born* 09.01.35. *From* Maryhill. *Pro Career* 1957-1966 (45 contests, won 38, lost 7).

Young John McCormack British L. Heavyweight Champion, 1967-1969. *Born* Dublin, 11.12.44. *From* Brixton. *Pro Career* 1963-1970 (42 contests, won 33, drew 1, lost 8).

Pat McCormack British L. Welterweight Champion, 1974. *Born* Dublin, 28.04.46. *From* Brixton. *Pro Career* 1968-1975 (49 contests, won 30, drew 1, lost 18).

Robert McCracken Undefeated British L. Middleweight Champion, 1994-1995. Commonwealth Middleweight Champion, 1995-1997. *Born* 31.05.68. *From* Birmingham. *Pro Career* 1991-2001 (35 contests, won 33, lost 2).

Geoff McCreesh Undefeated British Welterweight Champion, 1997-1999. *Born* 12.06.70. *From* Bracknell. *Pro Career* 1994-2001 (30 contests, won 23, lost 7).

Glenn McCrory Undefeated British Cruiserweight Champion, 1988. Undefeated Commonwealth Cruiserweight Champion, 1987-1989. World Cruiserweight Champion (IBF version), 1989-1990. *Born* 23.09.64. *From* Annfield Plain. *Pro Career* 1984-1993 (39 contests, won 30, drew 1, lost 8).

Jim McDonnell Undefeated European Featherweight Champion, 1985-1987. *Born* 12.09.60. *From* Camden Town. *Pro Career* 1983-1998 (30 contests, won 26, lost 4).

Tommy McGovern British Lightweight Champion, 1951-1952. *Born* 05.02.24. *From* Bermondsey. *Deceased* 1989. *Pro Career* 1947-1953 (66 contests, won 45, drew 4, lost 17).

Walter McGowan Undefeated British Flyweight Champion, 1963-1966. Undefeated British Empire Flyweight Champion, 1963-1969. World Flyweight Champion (WBC version), 1966. British and British Empire Bantamweight Champion, 1966-1968. *Born* 13.10.42. *From* Hamilton. *Pro Career* 1961-1969 (40 contests, won 32, drew 1, lost 7).

Barry McGuigan Undefeated British Featherweight Champion, 1983-1986. Undefeated European Featherweight Champion, 1983-1985. World Featherweight Champion (WBA version), 1985-1986. *Born* 28.02.61. *From* Clones. *Pro Career* 1981-1989 (35 contests, won 32, lost 3).

Clinton McKenzie British L. Welterweight Champion, 1978-1979 and 1979-1984. Undefeated British L. Welterweight Champion, 1989. European L. Welterweight Champion, 1981-1982. *Born* 15.09.55. *From* Croydon. *Pro Career* 1976-1989 (50 contests, won 36, lost 14).

Duke McKenzie Undefeated British Flyweight Champion, 1985-1986. Undefeated European Flyweight Champion, 1986-1988. World Flyweight Champion (IBF version), 1988-1989. World Bantamweight Champion (WBO version), 1991-1992. World S. Bantamweight Champion (WBO version), 1992-1993. Undefeated British Featherweight Champion, 1993-1994. *Born* 05.05.63. *From* Croydon. *Pro Career* 1982-1998 (46 contests, won 39, lost 7).

Tony McKenzie British L. Welterweight Champion, 1986-1987. *Born* 04.03.63. *From* Leicester. *Pro Career* 1983-1993 (34 contests, won 26, drew 1, lost 7).

Ian McLeod Undefeated Commonwealth S. Featherweight Champion, 2000. *Born* 11.06.69. *From* Kilmarnock. *Pro Career* 1992-2000 (14 contests, won 11, drew 1, lost 2).

Colin McMillan Undefeated British Featherweight Champion, 1991-1992. British Featherweight Champion, 1996-1997. Undefeated Commonwealth Featherweight Champion, 1992. World Featherweight Champion (WBO version), 1992. *Born* 12.02.66. *From* Barking. *Pro Career* 1988-1997 (35 contests, won 31, lost 4).

Noel Magee Commonwealth L. Heavyweight Champion, 1995. *Born* 16.12.65. *From* Belfast. *Pro Career* 1985-1997 (37 contests, won 27, drew 2, lost 8).

Charlie Magri Undefeated British Flyweight Champion, 1977-1981. Undefeated European Flyweight Champion, 1979-1983 and 1984-1985. European Flyweight Champion, 1985-1986. World Flyweight Champion (WBC version), 1983. *Born* Tunisia, 20.07.56. *From* Stepney. *Pro Career* 1977-1986 (35 contests, won 30, lost 5).

Paddy Maguire British Bantamweight Champion, 1975-1977. *Born* 26.09.48. *From* Belfast. *Pro Career* 1969-1977 (35 contests, won 26, drew 1, lost 8).

Terry Marsh Undefeated British L. Welterweight Champion, 1984-1986. European L. Welterweight Champion, 1985-1986. Undefeated World L. Welterweight Champion (IBF version), 1987. *Born* 07.02.58. *From* Basildon. *Pro Career* 1981-1987 (27 contests, won 26, drew 1).

Gary Mason British Heavyweight Champion, 1989-1991. *Born* Jamaica, 15.12.62. *From* Wandsworth. *Pro Career* 1984-1991 (36 contests, won 35, lost 1).

Jason Matthews Undefeated Commonwealth Middleweight Champion, 1999. WBO Middleweight Champion, 1999. *Born* 20.07.70. *From* Hackney. *Pro Career* 1995-1999 (23 contests, won 21, lost 2).

Neville Meade British Heavyweight Champion, 1981-1983. *Born* Jamaica, 12.09.48. *From* Swansea. *Pro Career* 1974-1983 (34 contests, won 20, drew 1, lost 13).

Freddie Mills Undefeated British L. Heavyweight Champion, 1942-1950. British Empire L. Heavyweight Championship Claimant, 1942-1950. Undefeated European L. Heavyweight Champion, 1947-1950. World L. Heavyweight Champion (GB version), 1942-1946. World L. Heavyweight Champion, 1948-1950. *Born* 26.06.19. *From* Bournemouth. *Deceased* 1965. *Pro Career* 1936-1950 (101 contests, won 77, drew 6, lost 18).

Alan Minter British Middleweight Champion, 1975-1977. Undefeated British Middleweight Champion, 1977-1978. European Middleweight Champion, 1977. Undefeated European Middleweight Champion, 1978-1979. World Middleweight Champion, 1980. *Born* 17.08.51. *From* Crawley. *Pro Career* 1972-1981 (49 contests, won 39, lost 9, no contest 1).

Sylvester Mittee British Welterweight Champion, 1985. Commonwealth Welterweight Champion, 1984-1985. *Born* St Lucia, 29.10.56. *From* Bethnal Green. *Pro Career* 1977-1988 (33 contests, won 28, lost 5).

Tommy Molloy British Welterweight Champion, 1958-1960. *Born* 02.02.34. *From* Birkenhead. *Pro Career* 1955-1963 (43 contests, won 34, drew 2, lost 6, no contest 1).

Rinty Monaghan Undefeated British and World Flyweight Champion, 1948-1950. British Empire Flyweight Championship Claimant, 1948-1950. Undefeated European Flyweight Champion, 1949-1950. World Flyweight Champion (NBA version), 1947-1948. *Born* 21.08.20. *From* Belfast. Birthname - John Monaghan. *Deceased* 1984. *Pro Career* 1934-1949 (66 contests, won 51, drew 6, lost 9).

Des Morrison British L. Welterweight Champion, 1973-1974. *Born* Jamaica, 01.02.50. *From* Bedford. *Pro Career* 1970-1982 (50 contests, won 36, drew 2, lost 12).

Sean Murphy British Featherweight Champion, 1990-1991 and 1993. *Born* 01.12.64. *From* St Albans. *Pro Career* 1986-1994 (27 contests, won 22, lost 5).

Charlie Nash Undefeated British Lightweight Champion, 1978-1979. Undefeated European Lightweight Champion, 1979-1980. European Lightweight Champion, 1980-1981. *Born* 10.05.51. *From* Derry. *Pro Career* 1975-1983 (30 contests, won 25, lost 5).

Dave Needham British Bantamweight Champion, 1974-1975. British Featherweight Champion, 1978-1979. *Born* 15.08.51. *From* Nottingham. *Pro Career* 1971-1980 (39 contests, won 30, drew 1, lost 8).

Bobby Neill British Featherweight Champion, 1959-1960. *Born* 10.10.33. *From* Edinburgh. *Pro Career* 1955-1960 (35 contests, won 28, lost 7).

Horace Notice Undefeated British and Commonwealth Heavyweight Champion, 1986-1988. *Born* 07.08.57. *From* Birmingham. *Pro Career* 1983-1988 (16 contests, won 16).

John O'Brien British Empire Featherweight Champion, 1967. *Born* 20.02.37. *From* Glasgow. *Deceased* 1979. *Pro Career* 1956-1971 (47 contests, won 30, lost 17).

Chris Okoh Commonwealth Cruiserweight Champion, 1995-1997. *Born* 18.04.69. *From* Croydon. *Pro Career* 1993-1999 (16 contests, won 14, lost 2).

Spencer Oliver European S. Bantamweight Champion, 1997-1998. *Born* 27.03.75. *From* Barnet. *Pro Career* 1995-1998 (15 contests, won 14, lost 1).

Danny O'Sullivan British Bantamweight Champion, 1949-1951. *Born* 06.01.23. *From* Finsbury Park. *Deceased* 1990. *Pro Career* 1947-1951 (43 contests, won 33, drew 1, lost 9).

Johnny Owen Undefeated British Bantamweight Champion, 1977-1980. Undefeated Commonwealth Bantamweight Champion, 1978-1980. Undefeated European Bantamweight Champion, 1980. *Born* 07.01.56. *From* Merthyr. *Deceased* 1980. *Pro Career* 1976-1980 (28 contests, won 25, drew 1, lost 2).

James Oyebola British Heavyweight Champion, 1994-1995. *Born* Nigeria 10.06.61. *From* Paddington. *Pro Career* 1987-1996 (23 contests, won 18, drew 1, lost 4).

Jackie Paterson British Flyweight Champion, 1939-1948. British Empire Flyweight Championship Claimant, 1940-1948. World Flyweight Champion, 1943-1947. World Flyweight Champion (GB/NY version), 1947-1948. British Bantamweight Champion, 1947-1949. British Empire Bantamweight Championship Claimant, 1945-1949. European Bantamweight Champion, 1946. *Born* 05.09.20. *From* Springfield. *Deceased* 1966. *Pro Career* 1938-1950 (92 contests, won 64, drew 3, lost 25).

Bernard Paul Commonwealth L. Welterweight Champion, 1997-1999. *Born* 22.20.65. *From* Tottenham. *Pro Career* 1991-2000 (35 contests, won 21, drew 4, lost 10).

Larry Paul British L. Middleweight Champion, 1973-1974. *Born* 19.04.52. *From* Wolverhampton. *Pro Career* 1973-1978 (40 contests, won 30, drew 1, lost 9).

David Pearce Undefeated British Heavyweight Champion, 1983-1985.

Born 08.05.59. *From* Newport. *Deceased* 2000. *Pro Career* 1978-1984 (21 contests, won 17, drew 1, lost 3).

Kostas Petrou British Welterweight Champion, 1985. *Born* 17.04.59. *From* Birmingham. *Pro Career* 1981-1988 (37 contests, won 30, lost 7).

Tiger Al Phillips European Featherweight Champion, 1947. British Empire Featherweight Championship Claimant, 1947. *Born* 25.01.20. *From* Aldgate. *Deceased* 1999. *Pro Career* 1938-1951 (89 contests, won 72, drew 3, lost 14).

Nicky Piper Undefeated Commonwealth L. Heavyweight Champion, 1995-1997. *Born* 05.05.66. *From* Cardiff. *Pro Career* 1989-1997 (33 contests, won 26, drew 2, lost 5).

Dennis Powell British L. Heavyweight Champion, 1953. *Born* 12.12.24. *From* Four Crosses. *Deceased* 1993. *Pro Career* 1947-1954 (68 contests, won 42, drew 4, lost 22).

Colin Power Undefeated British L. Welterweight Champion, 1977-1978. British L. Welterweight Champion, 1979. European L. Welterweight Champion, 1978. *Born* 02.02.56. *From* Paddington. *Pro Career* 1975-1983 (34 contests, won 28, drew 1, lost 5).

Kevin Pritchard British S. Featherweight Champion, 1990-1991. *Born* 26.09.61. *From* Liverpool. *Pro Career* 1981-1991 (48 contests, won 23, drew 3, lost 22).

Johnny Pritchett Undefeated British Middleweight Champion, 1965-1969. Undefeated British Empire Middleweight Champion, 1967-1969. *Born* 15.02.43. *From* Bingham. *Pro Career* 1963-1969 (34 contests, won 32, drew 1, lost 1).

Chris Pyatt Undefeated British L. Middleweight Champion, 1986. European L. Middleweight Champion, 1986-1987. Undefeated Commonwealth L. Middleweight Champion, 1991-1992. Commonwealth L. Middleweight Champion, 1995-1996. World Middleweight Champion (WBO version), 1993-1994. *Born* 03.07.63. *From* Leicester. *Pro Career* 1983-1997 (51 contests, won 46, lost 5).

Des Rea British L. Welterweight Champion, 1968-1969. *Born* 09.01.44. *From* Belfast. *Pro Career* 1964-1974 (69 contests, won 28, drew 5, lost 36).

Mark Reefer Undefeated Commonwealth S. Featherweight Champion, 1989-1990. *Born* 16.03.64. Birthname - Mark Thompson. *From* Dagenham. *Pro Career* 1983-1992 (32 contests, won 23, drew 1, lost 8).

Sam Reeson Undefeated British Cruiserweight Champion, 1985-1986. Undefeated European Cruiserweight Champion, 1987-1988. *Born* 05.01.63. *From* Battersea. *Pro Career* 1983-1989 (26 contests, won 24, lost 2).

Robbie Regan Undefeated World Bantamweight Champion (WBO version), 1996-1997. British Flyweight Champion, 1991. Undefeated British Flyweight Champion, 1991-1992. Undefeated European Flyweight Champion, 1992-1993 and 1994-1995. *Born* 30.08.68. *From* Cefn Forest. *Pro Career* 1989-1996 (22 contests, won 17, drew 3, lost 2).

Willie Reilly Undefeated British Lightweight Champion, 1972. *Born* 25.03.47. *From* Glasgow. *Pro Career* 1968-1972 (23 contests, won 13, drew 3, lost 7).

Jimmy Revie British Featherweight Champion, 1969-1971. *Born* 08.07.47. *From* Stockwell. *Pro Career* 1966-1976 (48 contests, won 38, drew 1, lost 9).

Henry Rhiney British Welterweight Champion, 1976-1979. European Welterweight Champion, 1978-1979. *Born* Jamaica, 28.11.51. *From* Luton. *Pro Career* 1973-1980 (57 contests, won 32, drew 6, lost 19).

Alan Richardson British Featherweight Champion, 1977-1978. *Born* 04.11.48. *From* Fitzwilliam. *Pro Career* 1971-1978 (27 contests, won 17, drew 1, lost 9).

Dick Richardson European Heavyweight Champion, 1960-1962. *Born* 01.06.34. *From* Newport. *Deceased* 1999. *Pro Career* 1954-1963 (47 contests, won 31, drew 2, lost 14).

Ernie Roderick British Welterweight Champion, 1939-1948. European Welterweight Champion, 1946-1947. British Middleweight Champion, 1945-1946. *Born* 25.01.14. *From* Liverpool. *Deceased* 1986. *Pro Career* 1931-1950 (142 contests, won 114, drew 4, lost 24).

Prince Rodney Undefeated British L. Middleweight Champion, 1983-1984. British L. Middleweight Champion, 1985-1986. *Born* 31.10.58. *From* Huddersfield. *Pro Career* 1977-1990 (41 contests, won 31, drew 1, lost 9).

Stan Rowan Undefeated British Bantamweight Champion, 1949. British Empire Bantamweight Championship Claimant, 1949. *Born* 06.09.24. *From* Liverpool. *Deceased* 1997. *Pro Career* 1942-1953 (67 contests, won 46, drew 5, lost 16).

Mark Rowe British and Commonwealth Middleweight Champion, 1970. *Born* 12.07.47. *Born* 12.07.47. *From* Camberwell. *Pro Career* 1966-1973 (47 contests, won 38, drew 1, lost 8).

Alan Rudkin British Bantamweight Champion, 1965-1966. Undefeated British Bantamweight Champion, 1968-1972. British Empire Bantamweight

Champion, 1965-1966 and 1968-1969. European Bantamweight Champion, 1971. Undefeated Commonwealth Bantamweight Champion, 1970-1972. *Born* 18.11.41. *From* Liverpool. *Pro Career* 1962-1972 (50 contests, won 42, lost 8).

Hugh Russell Undefeated British Flyweight Champion, 1984-1985. British Bantamweight Champion, 1983. *Born* 15.12.59. *From* Belfast. *Pro Career* 1981-1985 (19 contests, won 17, lost 2).

Paul Ryan British and Commonwealth L. Welterweight Champion, 1995-1996. *Born* 02.02.65. *From* Hackney. *Pro Career* 1991-1997 (28 contests, won 25, lost 3).

Tony Sibson British Middleweight Champion, 1979. Undefeated British Middleweight Champion, 1984 and 1987-1988. Undefeated Commonwealth Middleweight Champion, 1980-1983 and 1984-1988. Undefeated European Middleweight Champion, 1980-1982. European Middleweight Champion, 1984-1985. *Born* 09.04.58. *From* Leicester. *Pro Career* 1976-1988 (63 contests, won 55, drew 1, lost 7).

Steve Sims Undefeated British Featherweight Champion, 1982-1983. *Born* 10.10.58. *From* Newport. *Pro Career* 1977-1987 (29 contests, won 14, drew 1, lost 14).

Joey Singleton British L. Welterweight Champion, 1974-1976. *Born* 06.06.51. *From* Kirkby. *Pro Career* 1973-1982 (40 contests, won 27, drew 2, lost 11).

Kelvin Smart British Flyweight Champion, 1982-1984. *Born* 18.12.60. *From* Caerphilly. *Pro Career* 1979-1987 (29 contests, won 17, drew 2, lost 10).

Roy Smith British Cruiserweight Champion, 1987. *Born* 31.08.61. *From* Nottingham. *Pro Career* 1985-1991 (26 contests, won 18, lost 8).

Vernon Sollas British Featherweight Champion, 1975-1977. *Born* 14.08.54. *From* Edinburgh. *Pro Career* 1973-1977 (33 contests, won 25, drew 1, lost 7).

Terry Spinks British Featherweight Champion, 1960-1961. *Born* 28.02.38. *From* Canning Town. *Pro Career* 1957-1962 (49 contests, won 41, drew 1, lost 7).

Bunny Sterling British Middleweight Champion, 1970-1974. Undefeated British Middleweight Champion, 1975. Commonwealth Middleweight Champion, 1970-1972. European Middleweight Champion, 1976. *Born* Jamaica, 04.04.48. *From* Finsbury Park. *Pro Career* 1966-1977 (57 contests, won 35, drew 4, lost 18).

John H. Stracey Undefeated British Welterweight Champion, 1973-1975. Undefeated European Welterweight Champion, 1974-1975. World Welterweight Champion (WBC version), 1975-1976. *Born* 22.09.50. *From* Bethnal Green. *Pro Career* 1969-1978 (51 contests, won 45, drew 1, lost 5).

Andy Straughn British Cruiserweight Champion, 1986-1987 and 1988-1989. *Born* Barbados, 25.12.59. *From* Hitchin. *Pro Career* 1982-1990 (27 contests, won 18, drew 2, lost 7).

Gary Stretch British L. Middleweight Champion, 1988-1990. *Born* 04.11.65. *From* St Helens. *Pro Career* 1985-1993 (25 contests, won 23, lost 2).

Johnny Sullivan British Empire Middleweight Championship Claimant, 1954. British and British Empire Middleweight Champion, 1954-1955. *Born* 19.12.32. *From* Preston. Birthname - John Hallmark. *Pro Career* 1948-1960 (97 contests, won 68, drew 3, lost 26).

Wally Swift British Welterweight Champion, 1960. British Middleweight Champion, 1964-1965. *Born* 10.08.36. *From* Nottingham. *Pro Career* 1957-1969 (88 contests, won 68, drew 3, lost 17).

Wally Swift Jnr British L. Middleweight Champion, 1991-1992. *Born* 17.02.66. *From* Birmingham. *Pro Career* 1985-1994 (38 contests, won 26, drew 1, lost 11).

Nel Tarleton British Featherweight Champion, 1931-1932 and 1934-1936. Undefeated British Featherweight Champion, 1940-1947. Undefeated British Empire Featherweight Championship Claimant, 1940-1947. *Born* 14.01.06. *From* Liverpool. *Deceased* 1956. *Pro Career* 1926-1945 (144 contests, won 116, drew 8, lost 20).

Wally Thom British Welterweight Champion, 1951-1952 and 1953-1956. British Empire Welterweight Championship Claimant, 1951-1952. European Welterweight Champion, 1954-1955. *Born* 14.06.26. *From* Birkenhead. *Deceased* 1980. *Pro Career* 1949-1956 (54 contests, won 42, drew 1, lost 11).

Eddie Thomas British Welterweight Champion, 1949-1951. European Welterweight Champion, 1951. British Empire Welterweight Championship Claimant, 1951. *Born* 27.07.26. *From* Merthyr. *Deceased* 1997. *Pro Career* 1946-1954 (48 contests, won 40, drew 2, lost 6).

Pat Thomas British Welterweight Champion, 1975-1976. British L. Middleweight Champion, 1979-1981. *Born* St Kitts, 05.05.50. *From* Cardiff. *Pro Career* 1970-1984 (57 contests, won 35, drew 3, lost 18, no contest 1).

Billy Thompson British Lightweight Champion, 1947-1951. European

Lightweight Champion, 1948-1949. *Born* 20.12.25. *From* Hickleton Main. *Pro Career* 1945-1953 (63 contests, won 46, drew 4, lost 13).

Andy Till British L. Middleweight Champion, 1992-1994. *Born* 22.08.63. *From* Northolt. *Pro Career* 1986-1995 (24 contests, won 19, lost 5).

Dick Turpin British Middleweight Champion, 1948-1950. British Empire Middleweight Championship Claimant, 1948-1949. *Born* 26.11.20. *From* Leamington Spa. *Deceased* 1990. *Pro Career* 1937-1950 (103 contests, won 76, drew 6, lost 20, no contest 1).

Randy Turpin Undefeated British Middleweight Champion, 1950-1954. British Empire Middleweight Championship Claimant, 1952-1954. European Middleweight Champion, 1951-1954. World Middleweight Champion, 1951. World Middleweight Champion (EBU version), 1953. Undefeated British L. Heavyweight Champion, 1952, 1955, and 1956-1958. British Empire L. Heavyweight Championship Claimant, 1952-1954. Undefeated British Empire L. Heavyweight Champion, 1954-1955. *Born* 07.06.28. *From* Leamington Spa. *Deceased* 1966. *Pro Career* 1946-1958 (73 contests, won 64, drew 1, lost 8).

Keith Wallace Undefeated Commonwealth Flyweight Champion, 1983-1984. *Born* 29.03.61. *From* Liverpool. *Deceased* 2000. *Pro Career* 1982-1990 (25 contests, won 20, lost 5).

Peter Waterman Undefeated British Welterweight Champion, 1956-1958. Undefeated European Welterweight Champion, 1958. *Born* 08.12.34. *From* Clapham. *Deceased* 1986. *Pro Career* 1952-1958 (46 contests, won 41, drew 2, lost 3).

Michael Watson Undefeated Commonwealth Middleweight Champion, 1989-1991. *Born* 15.03.65. *From* Islington. *Pro Career* 1984-1991 (30 contests, won 25, drew 1, lost 4).

Jim Watt British Lightweight Champion, 1972-1973. Undefeated British Lightweight Champion, 1975-1977. Undefeated European Lightweight Champion, 1977-1979. World Lightweight Champion (WBC version), 1979-1981. *Born* 18.07.48. *From* Glasgow. *Pro Career* 1968-1981 (46 contests, won 38, lost 8).

Paul Weir Undefeated WBO M. Flyweight Champion, 1993-1994. WBO L. Flyweight Champion, 1994-1995. *Born* 16.09.67. *From* Irvine. *Pro Career* 1992-2000 (20 contests, won 14, lost 6).

Scott Welch Undefeated British Heavyweight Champion, 1995-1996. Commonwealth Heavyweight Champion, 1995-1997. *Born* 21.04.1968. *From* Shoreham. *Pro Career* 1992-1999 (26 contests, won 22, lost 4).

Richie Wenton Undefeated British S. Bantamweight Champion, 1994-1996. *Born* 28.10.67. *From* Liverpool. *Pro Career* 1988-2001 (30 contests, won 24, lost 6).

Henry Wharton Undefeated British S. Middleweight Champion, 1992-1993. Undefeated Commonwealth Champion, 1991-1997. Undefeated European S. Middleweight Champion, 1995-1996. *Born* 23.11.1967. *From* York. *Pro Career* 1989-1998 (31 contests, won 27, drew 1, lost 3).

Derek Williams Commonwealth Heavyweight Champion, 1988-1992. European Heavyweight Champion, 1989-1992. *Born* 11.03.65. *From* Peckham. *Pro Career* 1984-1999 (35 contests, won 22, lost 13).

Johnny Williams British Heavyweight Champion, 1952-1953. British Empire Heavyweight Championship Claimant, 1952-1953. *Born* 25.12.26. *From* Rugby. *Pro Career* 1946-1956 (75 contests, won 60, drew 4, lost 11).

Tony Willis British Lightweight Champion, 1985-1987. *Born* 17.06.60. *From* Liverpool. *Pro Career* 1981-1989 (29 contests, won 25, lost 4).

Nick Wilshire Commonwealth L. Middleweight Champion, 1985-1987. *Born* 03.11.61. *From* Bristol. *Pro Career* 1981-1987 (40 contests, won 36, lost 4).

Tony Wilson British L. Heavyweight Champion, 1987-1989. *Born* 25.04.64. *From* Wolverhampton. *Pro Career* 1985-1993 (29 contests, won 20, drew 1, lost 8).

Howard Winstone Undefeated British Featherweight Champion, 1961-1969. European Featherweight Champion, 1963-1967. World Featherweight Champion (WBC version), 1968. *Born* 15.04.39. *From* Merthyr. *Deceased* 2000. *Pro Career* 1959-1968 (67 contests, won 61, lost 6).

Tim Wood British L. Heavyweight Champion, 1976-1977. *Born* 10.08.51. *From* Leicester. *Pro Career* 1972-1979 (31 contests, won 19, drew 1, lost 11).

Bruce Woodcock British Heavyweight Champion, 1945-1950. British Empire Heavyweight Championship Claimant, 1945-1950. European Heavyweight Champion, 1946-1949. *Born* 18.01.21. *From* Doncaster. *Deceased* 1997. *Pro Career* 1942-1950 (39 contests, won 35, lost 4).

Richie Woodhall WBC S. Middleweight Champion, 1998-1999. Commonwealth Middleweight Champion, 1992-1995. Undefeated European Middleweight Champion, 1995-1996. *Born* 17.04.68. *From* Telford. *Pro Career* 1990-2000 (29 contests, won 26, lost 3).

Commonwealth Title Bouts During 2001-2002

All of last season's title bouts are shown in date order within their weight divisions and give the contestants' respective weights, along with the scorecard if going to a decision. Every contest involving a British fighter is summarised briefly and all British officials are named.

Flyweight

Jason Booth (England) failed to defend during the period.

Bantamweight

15 September 2001   Nicky Booth 8.6 (England) W RSC 7 Jim Betts 8.6 (England), Harvey Hadden Leisure Centre, Nottingham, England. Referee: John Keane. For a summary, see under British Title Bouts During 2001-2002.

23 February 2002   Nicky Booth 8.6 (England) W RSC 7 Stephen Oates 8.5¼ (England), Harvey Hadden Leisure Centre, Nottingham, England. Referee: John Coyle. For a summary, see under British Title Bouts During 2001-2002.

S. Bantamweight

3 November 2001   Brian Carr 8.9½ (Scotland) W PTS 12 Mishek Kondwani 8.9 (Zimbabwe), Bellahouston Leisure Centre, Glasgow, Scotland. Billed for the vacant title after Nedal Hussein (Australia) handed in his belt on winning the WBU championship on 29 June 2001, Carr had to call on all his experience and durability to win his first major championship, Larry O'Connell's 115-114 verdict in his favour giving a fair indication of how close it was. Carr, who has never been floored, made an early start, but it was Kondwani who was much stronger at the finish and who would surely have won it had the old 15-round distance still been in place.

18 March 2002   Brian Carr 8.9¾ (Scotland) L PTS 12 Michael Alldis   8.9½ (England), The Leisure Centre, Crawley, England. Referee: Mickey Vann 113-117. For a summary, see under British Title Bouts During 2001-2002.

11 May 2002   Michael Alldis 8.10 (England) W CO 8 Vuyani Phulo 8.9 (South Africa), Goresbrook Leisure Centre, Dagenham, England. Although most of the better boxing came from the champion, Phulo, despite being cut on the right eye, was no push over and offered good resistance right up until the eighth round when he was dropped by a left to the ribs. Quickly under pressure, he went down on one knee and was counted out by Richie Davies in the act of rising, with just a minute of the round gone.

Featherweight

15 September 2001   Scott Harrison 8.13¾ (Scotland) W RSC 5 Gary Thornhill 8.13½ (England), The MEN Arena, Manchester, England. Referee: Mark Green. For a summary, see under British Title Bouts During 2001-2002.

17 November 2001   Scott Harrison 9.0 (Scotland) W RSC 3 Steve Robinson 8.12¼ (Wales), Bellahouston Leisure Centre, Glasgow, Scotland. Referee: Richie Davies. For a summary, see under British Title Bouts During 2001-2002.

11 March 2002   Scott Harrison 8.13¼ W RSC 3 Tony Wehbee 9.0 (Australia), Kelvin Hall, Glasgow, Scotland. Taking complete control early in round two, Harrison began to work both the head and body of the Australian and the end was soon in sight, especially when Wehbee emerged from one exchange with damage both under and over the left eye. Forty eight seconds into round three, the referee, Ian John-Lewis, had seen enough and with the Scot taking his rival systematically apart he called a halt to proceedings.

S. Featherweight

13 April 2002   Alex Moon 9.4 (England) W RSC 8 Mick O'Malley 9.4 (Australia), Everton Park Sports Centre, Liverpool, England. Having been disappointed by the Affif Djelti result, Moon took some time to get going in this one, possibly lacking in confidence, but once he got into gear there was only going to be one winner. By the seventh the champion had begun to outpunch O'Malley, who was now cut on the left eye, as well as outbox him, and in the eighth it was just a matter of time, the referee, Dave Parris, coming to the challenger's rescue at 1.33 on the clock just as the towel came fluttering in.

Lightweight

James Armah (Ghana) failed to defend during the period.

L. Welterweight

27 October 2001   Eamonn Magee 9.13½ (Ireland) W PTS 12 Matthews Zulu 9.11 (South Africa), The MEN Arena, Manchester, England. Somewhat surprisingly, despite the comfortable scoreline of 119-111, Magee found the tough South African a difficult customer and, although doing enough to well deserve Marcus McDonnell's verdict, was unable to stop his man. Concentrating on the head rather than mixing up his shots to maximum effect, at the final bell the champion would have been disappointed with his display.

9 February 2002   Eamonn Magee 10.0 (Ireland) W RSC 6 Jonathan Thaxton 9.12½ (England), Manchester, England. In a battle of southpaws, this was a far different Magee to the one who outpointed Zulu, as the challenger found to his cost. Down in the third, Thaxton was soon fighting an uphill battle and in the sixth, by now carrying damage to the left eye, he was being pounded around the ring when John Coyle rescued him at the 1.10 mark. Magee vacated the title in the week prior to his fight with Richard Hatton on 1 June 2002 for the WBU championship.

Welterweight

17 August 2001   Julian Holland 10.6¾ (Australia) W RSC 7 Shannan Taylor 10.7 (Australia), Sydney, Australia. This one was billed for the vacant title after Jawaid Khaliq (England) relinquished his belt on winning the IBO championship on 11 June 2001.

27 April 2002   Julian Holland 10.5½ (Australia) L RSC 6 James Hare 10.7 (England), The Sports Centre, Huddersfield, England. This was the night that young James Hare came of age, systematically destroying the tough Aussie with a mixture of boxing and quality punches. Cut on the left eye in the third, Holland continued to look dangerous right up until the fifth round when the challenger's better boxing really took effect. The end came at 1.20 of the next round when, having got to his feet after being put down from a cracking right hand to the jaw for six, Holland was swamped with punches from all angles before being rescued by Paul Thomas just as the towel was being thrown in from the champion's corner.

L. Middleweight

25 September 2001   Richard Williams 10.13½ (England) W RSC 3 Andrew Murray 10.13 (Guyana), Everton Park Sports Centre, Liverpool, England. Not the fighter he once was, the challenger soon became easy pickings for Williams, who, despite being cut on the left eye in the first round, really came to life in the third after a fairly quiet start. After being put down and getting to his feet at seven, Murray was quickly nailed by a big left hook, which effectively finished him off and left him reeling around the ring following another count, this time for eight. At this juncture, the referee, Dave Parris, had seen enough and brought matters to a halt at 2.21 on the clock.

1 December 2001   Richard Williams 10.13¾ (England) W RSC 4 Shannan Taylor 10.13¾ (Australia), York Hall, Bethnal Green, London, England. Having been outboxed for the opening couple of rounds, Williams went up a gear in the fourth and was punching lustily without return until the referee, Terry O'Connor, jumped in to rescue the Aussie at the 2.17 mark. Also billed for the vacant IBO title, with John Coyle being one of the judges, Williams automatically relinquished the Commonwealth crown on his victory.

23 March 2002   Joshua Onyango 11.0 (Kenya) W DIS 6 Oswald Maneno 11.0 (Tanzania), Nairobi, Kenya.

28 May 2002   Joshua Onyango 10.13 (Kenya) L RSC 6 Michael Jones 11.0 (England), Everton Park Sports Centre, Liverpool, England. Having boxed in a cloud for the opening six rounds against the inexperienced champion, Jones came out for round six as a man on a mission, punching his rival all around the ring without reply and forcing the referee, Mark Green, to halt matters after just 20 seconds had elapsed. With blood coming from his left eye, following a crack of heads early on, it may have unnerved Jones, but once he had the bit between the teeth there was no stopping him.

Middleweight

Howard Eastman (England) failed to defend during the period.

S. Middleweight

29 September 2001   David Starie 12.0 (England) W RSC 6 Neil Linford 11.13½ (England), Elephant & Castle Leisure Centre, Southwark, London, England. Referee: John Coyle. For a summary, see under British Title Bouts During 2001-2002.

2 March 2002   David Starie 11.13½ (England) W CO 1 Marc Bargero 11.13½ (Australia), Brakpan, South Africa. Unfortunately, despite being the Australian champion, Bargero never presented Starie with any kind of problem whatsoever, apart from spoiling tactics, and was flattened by a four-punch combination after just 1.42 of the opening round.

L. Heavyweight

20 October 2001   Tony Oakey 12.6½ (England) W PTS 12 Chris Davies 12.5½ (Wales), The Mountbatten Centre, Portsmouth, England. This was a good, sporting match-up between two capable fighters, Oakey getting home 116-114 on Dave Parris' scorecard mainly due to his workrate and durability. Davies was always in the contest, despite being outworked at times, and had he mixed up his quality power punches with more work the result could have different. Oakey, meanwhile, relinquished the title after winning the WBU championship on 2 March 2002.

Cruiserweight

Bruce Scott (England) failed to defend during period.

Heavyweight

28 July 2001   Danny Williams 17.8 (England) W CO 4 Julius Francis 17.8 (England), The Conference Centre, Wembley, England. Referee: Mickey Vann. For a summary, see under British Title Bouts During 2001-2002.

12 February 2002   Danny Williams 18.5¼ (England) W RTD 7 Michael Sprott 17.4¾ (England), York Hall, Bethnal Green, London, England. Referee: Richie Davies. For a summary, see under British Title Bouts During 2001-2002.

Commonwealth Champions, 1887-2002

Since the 1997 edition, Harold Alderman's magnificent research into Imperial British Empire title fights has introduced many more claimants/champions than were shown previously. Prior to 12 October 1954, the date that the British Commonwealth and Empire Boxing Championships Committee was formed, there was no official body as such and the Australian and British promoters virtually ran the show, with other members of the British Empire mainly out in the cold. We have also listed Canadian representatives, despite championship boxing in that country being contested over ten or 12 rounds at most, but they are not accorded the same kind of recognition that their British and Australian counterparts are. On 8 September 1970, Bunny Sterling became the first immigrant to win a British title under the ten-year residential ruling and from that date on champions are recorded by domicile rather than by birthplace. Reconstituted as the British Commonwealth Boxing Championships Committee on 22 November 1972, and with a current membership that includes Australia, Bahama, Ghana, Guyana, Jamaica, Kenya, New Zealand, Nigeria, South Africa, Tanzania, Trinidad and Tobago, Zambia, and Zimbabwe, in 1989 the 'British' tag was dropped.

COMMONWEALTH COUNTRY CODE

A = Australia; BAH = Bahamas; BAR = Barbados; BER = Bermuda; C = Canada; E = England; F = Fiji; GH = Ghana; GU = Guyana; I = Ireland; J = Jamaica; K = Kenya; N = Nigeria; NZ = New Zealand; NI = Northern Ireland; PNG = Papua New Guinea; SA = South Africa; SAM = Samoa; S = Scotland; T = Tonga; TR = Trinidad; U = Uganda; W = Wales; ZA = Zambia; ZI = Zimbabwe.

Champions in **bold** denote those recognised by the British Commonwealth and Empire Boxing Championships Committee (1954 to date) and, prior to that, those with the best claims

*Undefeated champions (Does not include men who forfeited titles)

Title Holder	Birthplace/ Domicile	Tenure	Title Holder	Birthplace/ Domicile	Tenure	Title Holder	Birthplace/ Domicile	Tenure
Flyweight (112 lbs)			**Bantamweight (118 lbs)**			Johnny Owen*	W	1978-1980
Elky Clark*	S	1924-1927	**Digger Stanley**	E	1904-1905	Paul Ferreri	A	1981-1986
Harry Hill	E	1929	Owen Moran	E	1905	Ray Minus*	BAH	1986-1991
Frenchy Belanger	C	1929	**Ted Green**	A	1905-1911	John Armour*	E	1992-1996
Vic White	A	1929-1930	**Charlie Simpson***	A	1911-1912	Paul Lloyd*	E	1996-2000
Teddy Green	A	1930-1931	**Jim Higgins**	S	1920-1922	Ady Lewis	E	2000
Jackie Paterson	S	1940-1948	**Tommy Harrison**	E	1922-1923	Tommy Waite	NI	2000
Rinty Monaghan*	NI	1948-1950	**Bugler Harry Lake**	E	1923	Nicky Booth	E	2000-
Teddy Gardner	E	1952	**Johnny Brown**	E	1923-1928			
Jake Tuli	SA	1952-1954	Billy McAllister	A	1928-1930	**S. Bantamweight (122 lbs)**		
Dai Dower*	W	1954-1957	**Teddy Baldock***	E	1928-1930	**Neil Swain**	W	1995
Frankie Jones	S	1957	Johnny Peters	E	1930	**Neil Swain**	W	1996-1997
Dennis Adams*	SA	1957-1962	**Dick Corbett**	E	1930-1932	**Michael Brodie**	E	1997-1999
Jackie Brown	S	1962-1963	**Johnny King**	E	1932-1934	**Nedal Hussein***	A	2000-2001
Walter McGowan*	S	1963-1969	**Dick Corbett**	E	1934	**Brian Carr**	S	2001-2002
John McCluskey	S	1970-1971	Frankie Martin	C	1935-1937	**Michael Alldis**	E	2002-
Henry Nissen	A	1971-1974	Baby Yack	C	1937			
Big Jim West*	A	1974-1975	Johnny Gaudes	C	1937-1939	**Featherweight (126 lbs)**		
Patrick Mambwe	ZA	1976-1979	Lefty Gwynn	C	1939	**Jim Driscoll***	W	1908-1913
Ray Amoo	N	1980	Baby Yack	C	1939-1940	**Llew Edwards**	W	1915-1916
Steve Muchoki	K	1980-1983	**Jim Brady**	S	1941-1945	**Charlie Simpson***	A	1916
Keith Wallace*	E	1983-1984	**Jackie Paterson**	S	1945-1949	Tommy Noble	E	1919-1921
Richard Clarke	J	1986-1987	**Stan Rowan**	E	1949	**Bert Spargo**	A	1921-1922
Nana Yaw Konadu*	GH	1987-1989	**Vic Toweel**	SA	1949-1952	**Bert McCarthy**	A	1922
Alfred Kotey*	GH	1989-1993	**Jimmy Carruthers***	A	1952-1954	**Bert Spargo**	A	1922-1923
Francis Ampofo*	E	1993	**Peter Keenan**	S	1955-1959	**Billy Grime**	A	1923
Daren Fifield	E	1993-1994	**Freddie Gilroy***	NI	1959-1963	**Ernie Baxter**	A	1923
Francis Ampofo	E	1994-1995	**Johnny Caldwell**	NI	1964-1965	Leo Kid Roy	C	1923
Danny Ward	SA	1995-1996	**Alan Rudkin**	E	1965-1966	**Bert Ristuccia**	A	1923-1924
Peter Culshaw	E	1996-1997	**Walter McGowan**	S	1966-1968	Barney Wilshur	C	1923
Ady Lewis*	E	1997-1998	**Alan Rudkin**	E	1968-1969	Benny Gould	C	1923-1924
Alfonso Zvenyika	ZI	1998	**Lionel Rose***	A	1969	**Billy Grime**	A	1924
Damaen Kelly	NI	1998-1999	**Alan Rudkin***	E	1970-1972	Leo Kid Roy	C	1924-1932
Keith Knox	S	1999	**Paul Ferreri**	A	1972-1977	**Johnny McGrory**	S	1936-1938
Jason Booth	E	1999-	**Sulley Shittu**	GH	1977-1978	**Jim Spider Kelly**	NI	1938-1939

Title Holder	Birthplace/ Domicile	Tenure
Johnny Cusick	E	1939-1940
Nel Tarleton	E	1940-1947
Tiger Al Phillips	E	1947
Ronnie Clayton	E	1947-1951
Roy Ankrah	GH	1951-1954
Billy Spider Kelly	NI	1954-1955
Hogan Kid Bassey*	N	1955-1957
Percy Lewis	TR	1957-1960
Floyd Robertson	GH	1960-1967
John O'Brien	S	1967
Johnny Famechon*	A	1967-1969
Toro George	NZ	1970-1972
Bobby Dunne	A	1972-1974
Evan Armstrong	S	1974
David Kotey*	GH	1974-1975
Eddie Ndukwu	N	1977-1980
Pat Ford*	GU	1980-1981
Azumah Nelson*	GH	1981-1985
Tyrone Downes	BAR	1986-1988
Thunder Aryeh	GH	1988-1989
Oblitey Commey	GH	1989-1990
Modest Napunyi	K	1990-1991
Barrington Francis*	C	1991
Colin McMillan*	E	1992
Billy Hardy*	E	1992-1996
Jonjo Irwin	E	1996-1997
Paul Ingle*	E	1997-1999
Patrick Mullings	E	1999-2000
Scott Harrison	S	2000-

S. Featherweight (130 lbs)

Title Holder	Birthplace/ Domicile	Tenure
Billy Moeller	A	1975-1977
Johnny Aba*	PNG	1977-1982
Langton Tinago	ZI	1983-1984
John Sichula	ZA	1984
Lester Ellis*	A	1984-1985
John Sichula	ZA	1985-1986
Sam Akromah	GH	1986-1987
John Sichula	ZA	1987-1989
Mark Reefer*	E	1989-1990
Thunder Aryeh	GH	1990-1991
Hugh Forde	E	1991
Paul Harvey	E	1991-1992
Tony Pep	C	1992-1995
Justin Juuko*	U	1995-1998
Charles Shepherd*	E	1999
Mick O'Malley	A	1999-2000
Ian McLeod*	S	2000
James Armah*	GH	2000-2001
Alex Moon	E	2001-

Lightweight (135 lbs)

Title Holder	Birthplace/ Domicile	Tenure
Jim Burge	A	1890
George Dawson*	A	1890
Harry Nickless	E	1892-1894
Arthur Valentine	E	1894-1895
Dick Burge*	E	1894-1895
Jim Murphy*	NZ	1894-1897
Eddie Connolly*	C	1896-1897
Jack Goldswain	E	1906-1908
Jack McGowan	A	1909
Hughie Mehegan	A	1909-1910

Title Holder	Birthplace/ Domicile	Tenure
Johnny Summers*	E	1910
Hughie Mehegan	A	1911
Freddie Welsh*	W	1912-1914
Ernie Izzard	E	1928
Tommy Fairhall	A	1928-1930
Al Foreman	E	1930-1933
Jimmy Kelso	A	1933
Al Foreman*	E	1933-1934
Laurie Stevens*	SA	1936-1937
Dave Crowley	E	1938
Eric Boon	E	1938-1944
Ronnie James*	W	1944-1947
Arthur King	C	1948-1951
Frank Johnson	E	1953
Pat Ford	A	1953-1954
Ivor Germain	BAR	1954
Pat Ford	A	1954-1955
Johnny van Rensburg	SA	1955-1956
Willie Toweel	SA	1956-1959
Dave Charnley	E	1959-1962
Bunny Grant	J	1962-1967

Title Holder	Birthplace/ Domicile	Tenure
Manny Santos*	NZ	1967
Love Allotey	GH	1967-1968
Percy Hayles	J	1968-1975
Jonathan Dele	N	1975-1977
Lennox Blackmore	GU	1977-1978
Hogan Jimoh	N	1978-1980
Langton Tinago	ZI	1980-1981
Barry Michael	A	1981-1982
Claude Noel	T	1982-1984
Graeme Brooke	A	1984-1985
Barry Michael*	A	1985-1986
Langton Tinago	ZI	1986-1987
Mo Hussein	E	1987-1989
Pat Doherty	E	1989
Najib Daho	E	1989-1990
Carl Crook	E	1990-1992
Billy Schwer	E	1992-1993
Paul Burke	E	1993
Billy Schwer	E	1993-1995
David Tetteh	GH	1995-1997
Billy Irwin	C	1997

Eamonn Magee (left) on his way to victory over Jonathan Thaxton and a successful defence of the Commonwealth light-welterweight title last February

Les Clark

Title Holder	Birthplace/ Domicile	Tenure
David Tetteh	GH	1997-1999
Bobby Vanzie	E	1999-2001
James Armah	GH	2001-

L. Welterweight (140 lbs)

Title Holder	Birthplace/ Domicile	Tenure
Joe Tetteh	GH	1972-1973
Hector Thompson	A	1973-1977
Baby Cassius Austin	A	1977-1978
Jeff Malcolm	A	1978-1979
Obisia Nwankpa	N	1979-1983
Billy Famous	N	1983-1986
Tony Laing	E	1987-1988
Lester Ellis	A	1988-1989
Steve Larrimore	BAH	1989
Tony Ekubia	E	1989-1991
Andy Holligan	E	1991-1994
Ross Hale	E	1994-1995
Paul Ryan	E	1995-1996
Andy Holligan	E	1996-1997
Bernard Paul	E	1997-1999
Eamonn Magee	NI	1999-
Paul Burke	E	1997
Felix Bwalya*	ZA	1997
Paul Burke	E	1998-1999
Eamonn Magee*	NI	1999-2002

Welterweight (147 lbs)

Title Holder	Birthplace/ Domicile	Tenure
Tom Williams	A	1892-1895
Dick Burge	E	1895-1897
Eddie Connelly*	C	1903-1905
Joe White*	C	1907-1909
Johnny Summers	E	1912-1914
Tom McCormick	I	1914
Matt Wells	E	1914-1919
Fred Kay	A	1915
Tommy Uren	A	1915-1916
Fritz Holland	A	1916
Tommy Uren	A	1916-1919
Fred Kay	A	1919-1920
Johnny Basham	W	1919-1920
Bermondsey Billy Wells	E	1922
Ted Kid Lewis	E	1920-1924
Tommy Milligan*	S	1924-1925
Jack Carroll	A	1928
Charlie Purdie	A	1928-1929
Wally Hancock	A	1929-1930
Tommy Fairhall*	A	1930
Jack Carroll	A	1934-1938
Eddie Thomas	W	1951
Wally Thom	E	1951-1952
Cliff Curvis	W	1952
Gerald Dreyer	SA	1952-1954
Barry Brown	NZ	1954
George Barnes	A	1954-1956
Darby Brown	A	1956
George Barnes	A	1956-1958
Johnny van Rensburg	SA	1958
George Barnes	A	1958-1960
Brian Curvis*	W	1960-1966
Johnny Cooke	E	1967-1968
Ralph Charles*	E	1968-1972
Clyde Gray	C	1973-1979

Title Holder	Birthplace/ Domicile	Tenure
Chris Clarke	C	1979
Clyde Gray*	C	1979-1980
Colin Jones*	W	1981-1984
Sylvester Mittee	E	1984-1985
Lloyd Honeyghan*	E	1985-1986
Brian Janssen	A	1987
Wilf Gentzen	A	1987-1988
Gary Jacobs	S	1988-1989
Donovan Boucher	C	1989-1992
Eamonn Loughran*	NI	1992-1993
Andrew Murray*	GU	1993-1997
Kofi Jantuah*	GH	1997-2000
Scott Dixon*	S	2000
Jawaid Khaliq*	E	2000-2001
Julian Holland	A	2001-2002
James Hare	E	2002-

L. Middleweight (154 lbs)

Title Holder	Birthplace/ Domicile	Tenure
Charkey Ramon*	A	1972-1975
Maurice Hope*	E	1976-1979
Kenny Bristol	GU	1979-1981
Herol Graham*	E	1981-1984
Ken Salisbury	A	1984-1985
Nick Wilshire	E	1985-1987
Lloyd Hibbert	E	1987
Troy Waters*	A	1987-1991
Chris Pyatt*	E	1991-1992
Mickey Hughes	E	1992-1993
Lloyd Honeyghan	E	1993-1994
Leo Young	A	1994-1995
Kevin Kelly	A	1995
Chris Pyatt	E	1995-1996
Steve Foster	E	1996-1997
Kevin Kelly	A	1997-1999
Tony Badea	C	1999-2001
Richard Williams*	E	2001
Joshua Onyango	K	2002
Michael Jones	E	2002-

Middleweight (160 lbs)

Title Holder	Birthplace/ Domicile	Tenure
Chesterfield Goode	E	1887-1890
Toff Wall	E	1890-1891
Jim Hall	A	1892-1893
Bill Heffernan	NZ	1894-1896
Bill Doherty	A	1896-1897
Billy Edwards	A	1897-1898
Dido Plumb*	E	1898-1901
Tom Duggan	A	1901-1903
Jack Palmer*	E	1902-1904
Jewey Cooke	E	1903-1904
Tom Dingey	C	1904-1905
Jack Lalor	SA	1905
Ted Nelson	A	1905
Tom Dingey	C	1905
Sam Langford*	C	1907-1911
Ed Williams	A	1908-1910
Arthur Cripps	A	1910
Dave Smith	A	1910-1911
Jerry Jerome	A	1913
Arthur Evernden	E	1913-1914
Mick King	A	1914-1915
Les Darcy*	A	1915-1917

Title Holder	Birthplace/ Domicile	Tenure
Ted Kid Lewis	E	1922-1923
Roland Todd	E	1923-1926
Len Johnson	E	1926-1928
Tommy Milligan	S	1926-1928
Alex Ireland	S	1928-1929
Len Harvey	E	1929-1933
Del Fontaine	C	1931
Ted Moore	E	1931
Jock McAvoy	E	1933-1939
Ron Richards*	A	1940
Ron Richards*	A	1941-1942
Bos Murphy	NZ	1948
Dick Turpin	E	1948-1949
Dave Sands*	A	1949-1952
Randy Turpin	E	1952-1954
Al Bourke	A	1952-1954
Johnny Sullivan	E	1954-1955
Pat McAteer	E	1955-1958
Dick Tiger	N	1958-1960
Wilf Greaves	C	1960
Dick Tiger*	N	1960-1962
Gomeo Brennan	BAH	1963-1964
Tuna Scanlon*	NZ	1964
Gomeo Brennan	BAH	1964-1966
Blair Richardson*	C	1966-1967
Milo Calhoun	J	1967
Johnny Pritchett*	E	1967-1969
Les McAteer	E	1969-1970
Mark Rowe	E	1970
Bunny Sterling	E	1970-1972
Tony Mundine*	A	1972-1975
Monty Betham	NZ	1975-1978
Al Korovou	A	1978
Ayub Kalule	U	1978-1980
Tony Sibson*	E	1980-1983
Roy Gumbs	E	1983
Mark Kaylor	E	1983-1984
Tony Sibson*	E	1984-1988
Nigel Benn	E	1988-1989
Michael Watson*	E	1989-1991
Richie Woodhall	E	1992-1995
Robert McCracken	E	1995-1997
Johnson Tshuma	SA	1997-1998
Paul Jones	E	1998-1999
Jason Matthews*	E	1999
Alain Bonnamie*	C	1999-2000
Sam Soliman	A	2000
Howard Eastman	GU	2000-

S. Middleweight (168 lbs)

Title Holder	Birthplace/ Domicile	Tenure
Rod Carr	A	1989-1990
Lou Cafaro	A	1990-1991
Henry Wharton*	E	1991-1997
Clinton Woods	E	1997-1998
David Starie	E	1998-

L. Heavyweight (175 lbs)

Title Holder	Birthplace/ Domicile	Tenure
Dave Smith*	A	1911-1915
Jack Bloomfield*	E	1923-1924
Tom Berry	E	1927
Gipsy Daniels*	W	1927

189

Title Holder	Birthplace/ Domicile	Tenure
Len Harvey	E	1939-1942
Freddie Mills*	E	1942-1950
Randy Turpin*	E	1952-1955
Gordon Wallace	C	1956-1957
Yvon Durelle*	C	1957-1959
Chic Calderwood	S	1960-1963
Bob Dunlop*	A	1968-1970
Eddie Avoth	W	1970-1971
Chris Finnegan	E	1971-1973
John Conteh*	E	1973-1974
Steve Aczel	A	1975

Title Holder	Birthplace/ Domicile	Tenure
Tony Mundine	A	1975-1978
Gary Summerhays	C	1978-1979
Lottie Mwale	ZA	1979-1985
Leslie Stewart*	TR	1985-1987
Willie Featherstone	C	1987-1989
Guy Waters*	A	1989-1993
Brent Kosolofski	C	1993-1994
Garry Delaney	E	1994-1995
Noel Magee	I	1995
Nicky Piper*	W	1995-1997
Crawford Ashley	E	1998-1999

Title Holder	Birthplace/ Domicile	Tenure
Clinton Woods*	E	1999-2000
Neil Simpson	E	2001
Tony Oakey*	E	2001-2002

Cruiserweight (190 lbs)

Title Holder	Birthplace/ Domicile	Tenure
Stewart Lithgo	E	1984
Chisanda Mutti	ZA	1984-1987
Glenn McCrory*	E	1987-1989
Apollo Sweet	A	1989
Derek Angol*	E	1989-1993
Francis Wanyama	U	1994-1995
Chris Okoh	E	1995-1997
Darren Corbett	NI	1997-1998
Bruce Scott	E	1998-1999
Adam Watt*	A	2000-2001
Bruce Scott	E	2001-

Heavyweight (190 lbs +)

Title Holder	Birthplace/ Domicile	Tenure
Peter Jackson*	A	1889-1901
Dan Creedon	NZ	1896-1903
Billy McColl	A	1902-1905
Tim Murphy	A	1905-1906
Bill Squires	A	1906-1909
Bill Lang	A	1909-1910
Tommy Burns*	C	1910-1911
P.O. Curran	I	1911
Dan Flynn	I	1911
Bombardier Billy Wells	E	1911-1919
Bill Lang	A	1911-1913
Dave Smith	A	1913-1917
Joe Beckett*	E	1919-1923
Phil Scott	E	1926-1931
Larry Gains	C	1931-1934
Len Harvey	E	1934
Jack Petersen	W	1934-1936
Ben Foord	SA	1936-1937
Tommy Farr	W	1937
Len Harvey*	E	1939-1942
Jack London	E	1944-1945
Bruce Woodcock	E	1945-1950
Jack Gardner	E	1950-1952
Johnny Williams	W	1952-1953
Don Cockell	E	1953-1956
Joe Bygraves	J	1956-1957
Joe Erskine	W	1957-1958
Brian London	E	1958-1959
Henry Cooper	E	1959-1971
Joe Bugner	E	1971
Jack Bodell	E	1971-1972
Danny McAlinden	NI	1972-1975
Bunny Johnson	E	1975
Richard Dunn	E	1975-1976
Joe Bugner*	E	1976-1977
John L. Gardner*	E	1978-1981
Trevor Berbick	C	1981-1986
Horace Notice*	E	1986-1988
Derek Williams	E	1988-1992
Lennox Lewis*	E	1992-1993
Henry Akinwande	E	1993-1995
Scott Welch	E	1995-1997
Julius Francis*	E	1997-1999
Danny Williams	E	1999-

Bruce Scott, the Commonwealth cruiserweight champion Les Clark

European Title Bouts During 2001-2002

All of last season's title bouts are shown in date order within their weight division and give the boxers' respective weights, along with the scorecard if going to a decision. There is also a short summary of any bout that involved a British contestant, and British officials are listed where applicable.

Flyweight

16 November 2001   Alexander Mahmutov 7.13¾ (Russia) W RSC 5 Steffen Norskov 8.0 (Denmark), Roskilde, Denmark. Judge: Dave Parris.

5 March 2002   Alexander Mahmutov 7.13¼ (Russia) W PTS 12 Mimoun Chent 7.13¼ (France), Madrid, Spain. Scorecards: 118-110, 117-113, 120-110. Immediately following the fight, Mahmutov relinquished the title in order to protect his WBC number one ranking.

1 June 2002   Mimoun Chent 7.13¾ (France) W TD 8 Jason Booth 7.13¾ (England), Le Havre, France. With the Frenchman accidentally cut on both eyes and deemed unable to continue, and with the scorecards reading 80-73, 78-75 and 78-76 in his favour, he was announced as the winner. It was supposed to be third time lucky for Booth, but he found the champion difficult to tag and was gradually being outboxed prior to the disappointing finish.

Bantamweight

21 September 2001   Alex Yagupov 8.5 (Russia) L RTD 5 Spend Abazi 8.5½ (Denmark), Vejle, Denmark. Referee: Terry O'Connor. Judge: Paul Thomas.

8 February 2002   Spend Abazi 8.6 (Denmark) W RSC 2 Jose Antonio Fuente 8.5¾ (Spain), Copenhagen, Denmark. Judge: Dave Parris.

15 March 2002   Spend Abazi 8.5 (Denmark) W PTS 12 Dimitri Kirilov 8.5¼ (Russia), Viborg, Denmark. Scorecards: Terry O'Connor 117-111, Paul Thomas 115-114, 116-112.

S. Bantamweight

15 September 2001   Salim Medjkoune 8.9½ (France) w rsc 4 Sandor Koczac 8.8½ (Hungary), Agadir, Morocco. Judge: Richie Davies.

18 January 2002   Salim Medjkoune 8.9 (France) T DRAW 4 Mustapha Hame 8.9¼ (France), Clermont Ferrand, France. Medjkoune vacated in June 2002 to concentrate on a crack at Osamu Sato's WBA crown.

Featherweight

15 June 2002   Cyril Thomas 8.13¼ (France) T DRAW 2 Alessandro di Mecco 8.13¼ (Italy), Gubbio, Italy. Referee: Mickey Vann. Billed for the vacant title after Manuel Calvo (Spain) relinquished his belt in January 2002 to concentrate on his forthcoming fight against Prince Naseem Hamed.

S. Featherweight

15 September 2001   Boris Sinitsin 9.2½ (Russia) W PTS

12 Pedro Oscar Miranda 9.2¼ (Spain), Telde, Gran Canaria, Spain. Scorecards: 115-113, 117-112, 115-112. Billed for the vacant title after the previous champion, Tontcho Tontchev (Bulgaria), vacated in June 2001 to pursue a world title shot.

11 November 2001   Boris Sinitsin 9.2 (Russia) W RSC 7 James Fenu 9.2 (Switzerland), Telde, Gran Canaria, Spain.

2 February 2002   Boris Sinitsin 9.1¾ (Russia) L PTS 12 Pedro Oscar Miranda 9.1¼ (Spain), Telde, Gran Canaria, Spain. Scorecards: 114-115, 112-116, 115-115. Referee: Larry O'Connell.

Lightweight

11 August 2001   Stefano Zoff 9.7½ (Italy) w rsc 7 Dariusz Snarski 9.6½ (Poland), Trieste, Italy. Referee: Paul Thomas.

20 October 2001   Stefano Zoff 9.8 (Italy) W RSC 8 Bruno Wartelle 9.8¼ (France), Trieste, Italy. Referee: John Keane. Zoff relinquished in February 2002 in order to challenge Paul Spadafora for the IBF title.

L. Welterweight

17 November 2001   Gianluca Branco 11.0 (Italy) W RSC 6 George Scott 10.9¾ (Sweden), Civitavecchia, Italy. Judge: Terry O'Connor.

9 March 2002   Gianluca Branco 10.0 (Italy) W RTD 10 Allan Vester 10.0 (Denmark), Montegatini, Italy.

Welterweight

29 September 2001   Alessandro Duran 10.6½ (Italy) W DIS 5 Douglas Bellini 10.7 (Belgium), Bondeno, Italy.

18 January 2002   Alessandro Duran 10.6½ (Italy) L PTS 12 Christian Bladt 10.6¾ (Denmark), Thisted, Denmark. Scorecards: 116-112, 113-116, 114-115. Referee: John Coyle.

20 April 2002   Christian Bladt 10.5¾ (Denmark) L PTS 12 Michel Trabant 10.6½ (Germany), Gdansk, Poland. Referee: Richie Davies. Scorecards: 112-117, 112-117, 111-117.

L. Middleweight

19 January 2002   Wayne Alexander 10.13¼ (England) W RSC 3 Paolo Pizzamiglio 10.11½ (Italy), York Hall, Bethnal Green, London, England. Billed for the vacant title after Mamadou Thiam relinquished his belt in December 2001 to concentrate on a prospective WBA title clash against Fernando Vargas, Alexander was a comprehensive winner when pounding Pizzamiglio to defeat. Having smashed his rival to the floor, on arising the Italian, now bleeding under the left eye, was belted along the ropes to be rescued by the referee with just one second of the third round remaining.

Middleweight

1 December 2001   Christian Sanavia 11.4$\frac{1}{2}$ (Italy) W PTS 12 Morrade Hakkar 11.5$\frac{3}{4}$ (France), Padua, Italy. Scorecards: 115-113, 115-113, 113-115. Referee: Larry O'Connell. Billed for the vacant title after Howard Eastman had vacated in November 2001 due to him already being booked to fight William Joppy for what was effectively the WBA interim crown

11 May 2002   Christian Sanavia 11.5$\frac{1}{2}$ (Italy) L RTD 7 Morrade Hakkar 11.5$\frac{1}{4}$ (France), Segrate, Italy. Judge: Mickey Vann.

S. Middleweight

6 October 2001   Danilo Haeussler 11.13 (Germany) W PTS 12 Vincenzo Imparato 12.0 (Italy), Cologne, Germany. Scorecards: 120-108, 117-111, 118-109. Referee: John Coyle.

9 March 2002   Danilo Haeussler 11.12$\frac{3}{4}$ (Germany) W PTS 12 Glenn Catley 11.12$\frac{3}{4}$ (England), Frankfurt, Germany. Scorecards: 114-111, 114-111, 113-113. This was close and had it not been for Catley having two points deducted for dangerous use of the head many felt he would have won. The German finished up looking like a loser, but somehow convinced the judges that he had done enough to win despite being on the floor in the eighth from a body punch. In the post-fight interview, Catley felt that but for protecting a cut right eye, which was damaged in the tenth round, he would have found the aggression required to land the title.

27 April 2002   Danilo Haeussler 11.13$\frac{1}{4}$ (Germany) W RTD 4 Mustapha Iliir 11.11$\frac{1}{2}$ (Yugoslavia), Riesa, Germany. Judge: John Keane.

L. Heavyweight

26 January 2002   Yawe Davis 12.6$\frac{1}{2}$ (Italy) W PTS 12 Kamel Amrane 12.5$\frac{1}{2}$ (France), Aulla, Italy. Judge: Mickey Vann. Scorecards: 115-114, 116-113, 115-113.

Cruiserweight

1 December 2001   Alexander Gurov 13.7 (Ukraine) W CO 4 Rudiger May 13.7 (Germany), Dortmund, Germany. Referee: Mickey Vann. Gurov relinquished in March 2002 to pursue a world title opportunity.

Heavyweight

5 January 2002   Luan Krasniki 15.12$\frac{1}{2}$ (Germany) W PTS 12 Rene Monse 15.12$\frac{1}{2}$ (Germany). Scorecards: 115-113, 115-113, 114-114. Billed for the vacant crown after Vitali Klitschko (Ukraine) relinquished his belt in September 2001 to concentrate on getting a crack at the world title.

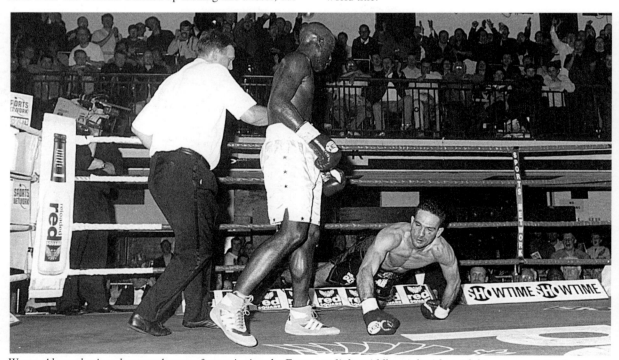

Wayne Alexander is only seconds away from winning the European light-middleweight title, with his opponent, Paolo Pizzamiglio, struggling on the canvas

Les Clark

European Champions, 1909-2002

Prior to 1946, the championship was contested under the auspices of the International Boxing Union, re-named that year as the European Boxing Union (EBU). The IBU had come into being when Victor Breyer, a Paris-based journalist and boxing referee who later edited the Annuaire du Ring (first edition in 1910), warmed to the idea of an organisation that controlled boxing right across Europe, regarding rules and championship fights between the champions of the respective countries. He first came to London at the end of 1909 to discuss the subject with the NSC, but went away disappointed. However, at a meeting between officials from Switzerland and France in March 1912, the IBU was initially formed and, by June of that year, had published their first ratings. By April 1914, Belgium had also joined the organisation, although it would not be until the war was over that the IBU really took off. Many of the early champions shown on the listings were the result of promoters, especially the NSC, billing their own championship fights. Although the (French dominated) IBU recognised certain champions, prior to being re-formed in May 1920, they did not find their administrative 'feet' fully until other countries such as Italy (1922), Holland (1923), and Spain (1924), produced challengers for titles. Later in the 1920s, Germany (1926), Denmark (1928), Portugal (1929) and Romania (1929) also joined the fold. Unfortunately, for Britain, its representatives (Although the BBBoC, as we know it today, was formed in 1929, an earlier attempt to form a Board of Control had been initiated in April 1918 by the NSC and it was that body who were involved here) failed to reach agreement on the three judges' ruling, following several meetings with the IBU early in 1920 and, apart from Elky Clark (fly), Ernie Rice and Alf Howard (light), and Jack Hood (welter), who conformed to that stipulation, fighters from these shores would not be officially recognised as champions until the EBU was formed in 1946. This led to British fighters claiming the title after beating IBU titleholders, or their successors, under championship conditions in this country. The only men who did not come into this category were Kid Nicholson (bantam), and Ted Kid Lewis and Tommy Milligan (welter), who defeated men not recognised by the IBU. For the record, the first men recognised and authorised, respectively, as being champions of their weight classes by the IBU were: Sid Smith and Michel Montreuil (fly), Charles Ledoux (bantam), Jim Driscoll and Louis de Ponthieu (feather), Freddie Welsh and Georges Papin (light), Georges Carpentier and Albert Badoud (welter), Georges Carpentier and Ercole Balzac (middle), Georges Carpentier and Battling Siki (light-heavy and heavy).

EUROPEAN COUNTRY CODE
AU = Austria; BEL = Belgium; BUL = Bulgaria; CRO = Croatia; CZ = Czechoslovakia; DEN = Denmark; E = England; FIN = Finland; FR = France; GER = Germany; GRE = Greece; HOL = Holland; HUN = Hungary; ITA = Italy; KAZ = Kazakhstan; LUX = Luxembourg; NI = Northern Ireland; NOR = Norway; POR = Portugal; ROM = Romania; RUS = Russia; S = Scotland; SP = Spain; SWE = Sweden; SWI = Switzerland; TU = Turkey; UK = Ukraine; W = Wales; YUG = Yugoslavia.

Champions in **bold** denote those recognised by the IBU/EBU

*Undefeated champions (Does not include men who may have forfeited titles)

Title Holder	Birthplace/Domicile	Tenure	Title Holder	Birthplace/Domicile	Tenure	Title Holder	Birthplace/Domicile	Tenure
Flyweight (112 lbs)			Louis Skena*	FR	1953-1954	**Bantamweight (118 lbs)**		
Sid Smith	E	1913	**Nazzareno Giannelli**	ITA	1954-1955	Joe Bowker	E	1910
Bill Ladbury	E	1913-1914	**Dai Dower**	W	1955	Digger Stanley	E	1910-1912
Percy Jones	W	1914	**Young Martin**	SP	1955-1959	**Charles Ledoux**	FR	1912-1921
Joe Symonds	E	1914	**Risto Luukkonen**	FIN	1959-1961	Bill Beynon	W	1913
Tancy Lee	S	1914-1916	**Salvatore Burruni***	ITA	1961-1965	Tommy Harrison	E	1921-1922
Jimmy Wilde	W	1914-1915	**Rene Libeer**	FR	1965-1966	**Charles Ledoux**	FR	1922-1923
Jimmy Wilde*	W	1916-1923	**Fernando Atzori**	ITA	1967-1972	Bugler Harry Lake	E	1923
Michel Montreuil	BEL	1923-1925	**Fritz Chervet**	SWI	1972-1973	Johnny Brown	E	1923-1928
Elky Clark*	S	1925-1927	**Fernando Atzori**	ITA	1973	**Henry Scillie***	BEL	1925-1928
Victor Ferrand	SP	1927	**Fritz Chervet***	SWI	1973-1974	Kid Nicholson	E	1928
Emile Pladner	FR	1928-1929	**Franco Udella**	ITA	1974-1979	Teddy Baldock	E	1928-1931
Johnny Hill	S	1928-1929	**Charlie Magri***	E	1979-1983	**Domenico Bernasconi**	ITA	1929
Eugene Huat	FR	1929	**Antoine Montero**	FR	1983-1984	**Carlos Flix**	SP	1929-1931
Emile Degand	BEL	1929-1930	**Charlie Magri***	E	1984-1985	**Lucien Popescu**	ROM	1931-1932
Kid Oliva	FR	1930	**Franco Cherchi**	ITA	1985	**Domenico Bernasconi**	ITA	1932
Lucien Popescu	ROM	1930-1931	**Charlie Magri**	E	1985-1986	**Nicholas Biquet**	BEL	1932-1935
Jackie Brown	E	1931-1935	**Duke McKenzie***	E	1986-1988	**Maurice Dubois**	SWI	1935-1936
Praxile Gyde	FR	1932-1935	**Eyup Can***	TU	1989-1990	**Joseph Decico**	FR	1936
Benny Lynch	S	1935-1938	**Pat Clinton***	S	1990-1991	**Aurel Toma**	ROM	1936-1937
Kid David*	BEL	1935-1936	**Salvatore Fanni**	ITA	1991-1992	**Nicholas Biquet**	BEL	1937-1938
Ernst Weiss	AU	1936	**Robbie Regan***	W	1992-1993	**Aurel Toma**	ROM	1938-1939
Valentin Angelmann*	FR	1936-1938	**Luigi Camputaro**	ITA	1993-1994	**Ernst Weiss**	AU	1939
Enrico Urbinati*	ITA	1938-1943	**Robbie Regan***	W	1994-1995	**Gino Cattaneo**	ITA	1939-1941
Raoul Degryse	BEL	1946-1947	**Luigi Camputaro***	ITA	1995-1996	**Gino Bondavilli***	ITA	1941-1943
Maurice Sandeyron	FR	1947-1949	**Jesper Jensen***	DEN	1996-1997	**Jackie Paterson**	S	1946
Rinty Monaghan*	NI	1949-1950	**David Guerault***	FR	1997-1999	**Theo Medina**	FR	1946-1947
Terry Allen	E	1950	**Alexander Mahmutov**	RUS	1999-2000	**Peter Kane**	E	1947-1948
Jean Sneyers*	BEL	1950-1951	**Damaen Kelly***	NI	2000	**Guido Ferracin**	ITA	1948-1949
Teddy Gardner*	E	1952	**Alexander Mahmutov**	RUS	2000-2002	**Luis Romero**	SP	1949-1951
			Mimoun Chent	FR	2002-			

Title Holder	Birthplace/ Domicile	Tenure
Peter Keenan	S	1951-1952
Jean Sneyers*	BEL	1952-1953
Peter Keenan	S	1953
John Kelly	NI	1953-1954
Robert Cohen*	FR	1954-1955
Mario D'Agata	ITA	1955-1958
Piero Rollo	ITA	1958-1959
Freddie Gilroy	NI	1959-1960
Pierre Cossemyns	BEL	1961-1962
Piero Rollo	ITA	1962
Alphonse Halimi	FR	1962
Piero Rollo	ITA	1962-1963
Mimoun Ben Ali	SP	1963
Risto Luukkonen	FIN	1963-1964
Mimoun Ben Ali	SP	1965
Tommaso Galli	ITA	1965-1966
Mimoun Ben Ali	SP	1966-1968
Salvatore Burruni*	ITA	1968-1969
Franco Zurlo	ITA	1969-1971
Alan Rudkin	E	1971
Agustin Senin*	SP	1971-1973
Johnny Clark*	E	1973-1974
Bob Allotey	SP	1974-1975
Daniel Trioulaire	FR	1975-1976
Salvatore Fabrizio	ITA	1976-1977
Franco Zurlo	ITA	1977-1978
Juan Francisco Rodriguez	SP	1978-1980
Johnny Owen*	W	1980
Valerio Nati	ITA	1980-1982
Giuseppe Fossati	ITA	1982-1983
Walter Giorgetti	ITA	1983-1984
Ciro de Leva*	ITA	1984-1986
Antoine Montero	FR	1986-1987
Louis Gomis*	FR	1987-1988
Fabrice Benichou	FR	1988
Vincenzo Belcastro*	ITA	1988-1990
Thierry Jacob*	FR	1990-1992
Johnny Bredahl*	DEN	1992
Vincenzo Belcastro	ITA	1993-1994
Prince Naseem Hamed*	E	1994-1995
John Armour*	E	1995-1996
Johnny Bredahl	DEN	1996-1998
Paul Lloyd*	E	1998-1999
Johnny Bredahl*	DEN	1999-2000
Luigi Castiglione	ITA	2000-2001
Fabien Guillerme	FR	2001
Alex Yagupov	RUS	2001
Spend Abazi	SWE	2001-

S. Bantamweight (122 lbs)

Title Holder	Birthplace/ Domicile	Tenure
Vincenzo Belcastro	ITA	1995-1996
Salim Medjkoune	FR	1996
Martin Krastev	BUL	1996-1997
Spencer Oliver	E	1997-1998
Sergei Devakov	UK	1998-1999
Michael Brodie*	E	1999-2000
Vladislav Antonov	RUS	2000-2001
Salim Medjkoune*	FR	2001-2002

Featherweight (126 lbs)

Title Holder	Birthplace/ Domicile	Tenure
Young Joey Smith	E	1911
Jean Poesy	FR	1911-1912
Jim Driscoll*	W	1912-1913
Ted Kid Lewis*	E	1913-1914
Louis de Ponthieu*	FR	1919-1920
Arthur Wyns	BEL	1920-1922
Billy Matthews	E	1922
Eugene Criqui*	FR	1922-1923
Edouard Mascart	FR	1923-1924
Charles Ledoux	FR	1924
Henri Hebrans	BEL	1924-1925
Antonio Ruiz	SP	1925-1928
Luigi Quadrini	ITA	1928-1929
Knud Larsen	DEN	1929
Jose Girones	SP	1929-1934
Maurice Holtzer*	FR	1935-1938
Phil Dolhem	BEL	1938-1939
Lucien Popescu	ROM	1939-1941
Ernst Weiss	AU	1941
Gino Bondavilli	ITA	1941-1945
Ermanno Bonetti*	ITA	1945-1946
Tiger Al Phillips	E	1947
Ronnie Clayton	E	1947-1948
Ray Famechon	FR	1948-1953
Jean Sneyers	BEL	1953-1954
Ray Famechon	FR	1954-1955
Fred Galiana*	SP	1955-1956
Cherif Hamia	FR	1957-1958
Sergio Caprari	ITA	1958-1959
Gracieux Lamperti	FR	1959-1962
Alberto Serti	ITA	1962-1963
Howard Winstone	W	1963-1967
Jose Legra*	SP	1967-1968
Manuel Calvo	SP	1968-1969
Tommaso Galli	ITA	1969-1970
Jose Legra*	SP	1970-1972
Gitano Jiminez	SP	1973-1975
Elio Cotena	ITA	1975-1976
Nino Jimenez	SP	1976-1977
Manuel Masso	SP	1977
Roberto Castanon*	SP	1977-1981
Salvatore Melluzzo	ITA	1981-1982
Pat Cowdell*	E	1982-1983
Loris Stecca*	ITA	1983
Barry McGuigan*	NI	1983-1985
Jim McDonnell*	E	1985-1987
Valerio Nati*	ITA	1987
Jean-Marc Renard*	BEL	1988-1989
Paul Hodkinson*	E	1989-1991
Fabrice Benichou	FR	1991-1992
Maurizio Stecca	ITA	1992-1993
Herve Jacob	FR	1993
Maurizio Stecca	ITA	1993
Stephane Haccoun	FR	1993-1994
Stefano Zoff	ITA	1994
Medhi Labdouni	FR	1994-1995
Billy Hardy	E	1995-1998
Paul Ingle*	E	1998-1999
Steve Robinson	W	1999-2000
Istvan Kovacs*	HUN	2000-2001
Manuel Calvo	SP	2001-2002

S. Featherweight (130 lbs)

Title Holder	Birthplace/ Domicile	Tenure
Tommaso Galli	ITA	1971-1972
Domenico Chiloiro	ITA	1972
Lothar Abend	GER	1972-1974
Sven-Erik Paulsen*	NOR	1974-1976
Roland Cazeaux	FR	1976
Natale Vezzoli	ITA	1976-1979
Carlos Hernandez	SP	1979
Rodolfo Sanchez	SP	1979
Carlos Hernandez	SP	1979-1982
Cornelius Boza-Edwards*	E	1982
Roberto Castanon	SP	1982-1983
Alfredo Raininger	ITA	1983-1984
Jean-Marc Renard	BEL	1984
Pat Cowdell	E	1984-1985
Jean-Marc Renard*	BEL	1986-1987
Salvatore Curcetti	ITA	1987-1988
Piero Morello	ITA	1988
Lars Lund Jensen	DEN	1988
Racheed Lawal	DEN	1988-1989
Daniel Londas*	FR	1989-1991
Jimmy Bredahl*	DEN	1992
Regilio Tuur	HOL	1992-1993
Jacobin Yoma	FR	1993-1995
Anatoly Alexandrov*	KAZ	1995-1996
Julian Lorcy*	FR	1996
Djamel Lifa	FR	1997-1998
Anatoly Alexandrov*	RUS	1998
Dennis Holbaek Pedersen	DEN	1999-2000
Boris Sinitsin	RUS	2000
Dennis Holbaek Pedersen*	DEN	2000
Tontcho Tontchev*	BUL	2001
Boris Sinitsin	RUS	2001-2002
Pedro Oscar Miranda	SP	2002-

Lightweight (135 lbs)

Title Holder	Birthplace/ Domicile	Tenure
Freddie Welsh	W	1909-1911
Matt Wells	E	1911-1912
Freddie Welsh*	W	1912-1914
Georges Papin	FR	1920-1921
Ernie Rice	E	1921-1922
Seaman Nobby Hall	E	1922-1923
Harry Mason	E	1923-1926
Fred Bretonnel	FR	1924
Lucien Vinez	FR	1924-1927
Luis Rayo*	SP	1927-1928
Aime Raphael	FR	1928-1929
Francois Sybille	BEL	1929-1930
Alf Howard	E	1930
Harry Corbett	E	1930-1931
Francois Sybille	BEL	1930-1931
Bep van Klaveren	HOL	1931-1932
Cleto Locatelli	ITA	1932
Francois Sybille	BEL	1932-1933
Cleto Locatelli*	ITA	1933
Francois Sybille	BEL	1934
Carlo Orlandi*	ITA	1934-1935
Enrico Venturi*	ITA	1935-1936
Vittorio Tamagnini	ITA	1936-1937
Maurice Arnault	FR	1937
Gustave Humery	FR	1937-1938
Aldo Spoldi*	ITA	1938-1939
Karl Blaho	AU	1940-1941
Bruno Bisterzo	ITA	1941
Ascenzo Botta	ITA	1941
Bruno Bisterzo	ITA	1941-1942
Ascenzo Botta	ITA	1942
Roberto Proietti	ITA	1942-1943
Bruno Bisterzo	ITA	1943-1946
Roberto Proietti*	ITA	1946
Emile Dicristo	FR	1946-1947
Kid Dussart	BEL	1947
Roberto Proietti	ITA	1947-1948
Billy Thompson	E	1948-1949
Kid Dussart	BEL	1949
Roberto Proietti*	ITA	1949-1950
Pierre Montane	FR	1951
Elis Ask	FIN	1951-1952
Jorgen Johansen	DEN	1952-1954
Duilio Loi*	ITA	1954-1959
Mario Vecchiatto	ITA	1959-1960
Dave Charnley	E	1960-1963
Conny Rudhof*	GER	1963-1964
Willi Quatuor*	GER	1964-1965
Franco Brondi	ITA	1965
Maurice Tavant	FR	1965-1966
Borge Krogh	DEN	1966-1967
Pedro Carrasco*	SP	1967-1969
Miguel Velazquez	SP	1970-1971
Antonio Puddu	ITA	1971-1974
Ken Buchanan*	S	1974-1975
Fernand Roelandts	BEL	1976

Title Holder	Birthplace/ Domicile	Tenure
Perico Fernandez*	SP	1976-1977
Jim Watt*	S	1977-1979
Charlie Nash*	NI	1979-1980
Francisco Leon	SP	1980
Charlie Nash	NI	1980-1981
Joey Gibilisco	ITA	1981-1983
Lucio Cusma	ITA	1983-1984
Rene Weller	GER	1984-1986
Gert Bo Jacobsen	DEN	1986-1988
Rene Weller*	GER	1988
Policarpo Diaz*	SP	1988-1990
Antonio Renzo	ITA	1991-1992
Jean-Baptiste Mendy*	FR	1992-1994
Racheed Lawal	DEN	1994
Jean-Baptiste Mendy*	FR	1994-1995
Angel Mona	FR	1995-1997
Manuel Carlos Fernandes	FR	1997
Oscar Garcia Cano	SP	1997
Billy Schwer*	E	1997-1999
Oscar Garcia Cano	SP	1999-2000
Lucien Lorcy*	FR	2000-2001
Stefano Zoff*	ITA	2001-2002

L. Welterweight (140 lbs)

Title Holder	Birthplace/ Domicile	Tenure
Olli Maki	FIN	1964-1965
Juan Sombrita-Albornoz	SP	1965
Willi Quatuor*	GER	1965-1966
Conny Rudhof	GER	1967
Johann Orsolics	AU	1967-1968
Bruno Arcari*	ITA	1968-1970
Rene Roque	FR	1970-1971
Pedro Carrasco*	SP	1971-1972
Roger Zami	FR	1972
Cemal Kamaci	TU	1972-1973
Toni Ortiz	SP	1973-1974
Perico Fernandez*	SP	1974
Jose Ramon Gomez-Fouz	SP	1975
Cemal Kamaci*	TU	1975-1976
Dave Boy Green*	E	1976-1977
Primo Bandini	ITA	1977
Jean-Baptiste Piedvache	FR	1977-1978
Colin Power	E	1978
Fernando Sanchez	SP	1978-1979
Jose Luis Heredia	SP	1979
Jo Kimpuani	FR	1979-1980
Giuseppe Martinese	ITA	1980
Antonio Guinaldo	SP	1980-1981
Clinton McKenzie	E	1981-1982
Robert Gambini	FR	1982-1983
Patrizio Oliva*	ITA	1983-1985
Terry Marsh	E	1985-1986
Tusikoleta Nkalankete	FR	1987-1989
Efren Calamati	ITA	1989-1990
Pat Barrett	E	1990-1992
Valery Kayumba	ITA	1992-1993
Christian Merle	FR	1993-1994
Valery Kayumba	FR	1994
Khalid Rahilou*	FR	1994-1996
Soren Sondergaard*	DEN	1996-1998
Thomas Damgaard*	DEN	1998-2000
Oktay Urkal*	GER	2000-2001
Gianluca Branco	ITA	2001-

Welterweight (147 lbs)

Title Holder	Birthplace/ Domicile	Tenure
Young Joseph	E	1910-1911
Georges Carpentier*	FR	1911-1912
Albert Badoud*	SWI	1915-1921
Johnny Basham	W	1919-1920
Ted Kid Lewis	E	1920-1924
Piet Hobin	BEL	1921-1925
Billy Mack	E	1923
Tommy Milligan	S	1924-1925

Title Holder	Birthplace/ Domicile	Tenure
Mario Bosisio*	ITA	1925-1928
Leo Darton	BEL	1928
Alf Genon	BEL	1928-1929
Gustave Roth	BEL	1929-1932
Adrien Aneet	BEL	1932-1933
Jack Hood*	E	1933
Gustav Eder	GER	1934-1936
Felix Wouters	BEL	1936-1938
Saverio Turiello	ITA	1938-1939
Marcel Cerdan*	FR	1939-1942
Ernie Roderick	E	1946-1947
Robert Villemain*	FR	1947-1948
Livio Minelli	ITA	1949-1950
Michele Palermo	ITA	1950-1951
Eddie Thomas	W	1951
Charles Humez*	FR	1951-1952
Gilbert Lavoine	FR	1953-1954
Wally Thom	E	1954-1955
Idrissa Dione	FR	1955-1956
Emilio Marconi	ITA	1956-1958
Peter Waterman*	E	1958
Emilio Marconi	ITA	1958-1959
Duilio Loi*	ITA	1959-1963
Fortunato Manca*	ITA	1964-1965
Jean Josselin	FR	1966-1967
Carmelo Bossi	ITA	1967-1968
Fighting Mack	HOL	1968-1969
Silvano Bertini	ITA	1969
Jean Josselin	FR	1969
Johann Orsolics	AU	1969-1970
Ralph Charles	E	1970-1971
Roger Menetrey	FR	1971-1974
John H. Stracey*	E	1974-1975
Marco Scano	ITA	1976-1977
Jorgen Hansen	DEN	1977
Jorg Eipel	GER	1977
Alain Marion	FR	1977-1978
Jorgen Hansen	DEN	1978
Josef Pachler	AU	1978
Henry Rhiney	E	1978-1979
Dave Boy Green	E	1979
Jorgen Hansen	DEN	1979-1981
Hans-Henrik Palm	DEN	1982
Colin Jones*	W	1982-1983
Gilles Elbilia	FR	1983-1984
Gianfranco Rosi	ITA	1984-1985
Lloyd Honeyghan*	E	1985-1986
Jose Varela	GER	1986-1987
Alfonso Redondo	SP	1987
Mauro Martelli*	SWI	1987-1988
Nino la Rocca	ITA	1989
Antoine Fernandez	FR	1989-1990
Kirkland Laing	E	1990
Patrizio Oliva*	ITA	1990-1992
Ludovic Proto	FR	1992-1993
Gary Jacobs*	S	1993-1994
Jose Luis Navarro	SP	1994-1995
Valery Kayumba	FR	1995
Patrick Charpentier*	FR	1995-1996
Andrei Pestriaev*	RUS	1997
Michele Piccirillo*	ITA	1997-1998
Maxim Nesterenko	RUS	1998-1999
Alessandro Duran	ITA	1999
Andrei Pestriaev	RUS	1999-2000
Alessandro Duran	ITA	2000
Thomas Damgaard	DEN	2000-2001
Alessandro Duran	ITA	2001-2002
Christian Bladt	DEN	2002
Michel Trabant	GER	2002-

L. Middleweight (154 lbs)

Title Holder	Birthplace/ Domicile	Tenure
Bruno Visintin	ITA	1964-1966

Title Holder	Birthplace/ Domicile	Tenure
Bo Hogberg	SWE	1966
Yolande Leveque	FR	1966
Sandro Mazzinghi*	ITA	1966-1968
Remo Golfarini	ITA	1968-1969
Gerhard Piaskowy	GER	1969-1970
Jose Hernandez	SP	1970-1972
Juan Carlos Duran	ITA	1972-1973
Jacques Kechichian	FR	1973-1974
Jose Duran	SP	1974-1975
Eckhard Dagge	GER	1975-1976
Vito Antuofermo	ITA	1976
Maurice Hope*	E	1976-1978
Gilbert Cohen	FR	1978-1979
Marijan Benes	YUG	1979-1981
Louis Acaries	FR	1981
Luigi Minchillo*	ITA	1981-1983
Herol Graham*	E	1983-1984
Jimmy Cable	E	1984
Georg Steinherr	GER	1984-1985
Said Skouma*	FR	1985-1986
Chris Pyatt	E	1986-1987
Gianfranco Rosi*	ITA	1987
Rene Jacquot*	FR	1988-1989
Edip Secovic	AU	1989
Giuseppe Leto	ITA	1989
Gilbert Dele*	FR	1989-1990
Said Skouma	FR	1991
Mourad Louati	HOL	1991
Jean-Claude Fontana	FR	1991-1992
Laurent Boudouani	FR	1992-1993
Bernard Razzano	FR	1993-1994
Javier Castillejos	SP	1994-1995
Laurent Boudouani*	FR	1995-1996
Faouzi Hattab	FR	1996
Davide Ciarlante*	ITA	1996-1997
Javier Castillejo*	SP	1998
Mamadou Thiam*	FR	1998-2000
Roman Karmazin*	RUS	2000
Mamadou Thiam*	FR	2001
Wayne Alexander	E	2002-

Middleweight (160 lbs)

Title Holder	Birthplace/ Domicile	Tenure
Georges Carpentier*	FR	1912-1918
Ercole Balzac	FR	1920-1921
Gus Platts	E	1921
Willem Westbroek	HOL	1921
Johnny Basham	W	1921
Ted Kid Lewis	E	1921-1923
Roland Todd	E	1923-1924
Ted Kid Lewis	E	1924-1925
Bruno Frattini	ITA	1924-1925
Tommy Milligan	S	1925-1928
Rene Devos	BEL	1926-1927
Barthelemy Molina	FR	1928
Alex Ireland	S	1928-1929
Mario Bosisio	ITA	1928
Leone Jacovacci	ITA	1928-1929
Len Johnson	E	1928-1929
Marcel Thil	FR	1929-1930
Mario Bosisio	ITA	1930-1931
Poldi Steinbach	AU	1931
Hein Domgoergen	GER	1931-1932
Ignacio Ara	SP	1932-1933
Gustave Roth	BEL	1933-1934
Marcel Thil*	FR	1934-1938
Edouard Tenet	FR	1938
Bep van Klaveren	HOL	1938
Anton Christoforidis	GRE	1938-1939
Edouard Tenet	FR	1939
Josef Besselmann*	GER	1942-1943
Marcel Cerdan	FR	1947-1948
Cyrille Delannoit	BEL	1948

195

Title Holder	Birthplace/ Domicile	Tenure
Marcel Cerdan*	FR	1948
Cyrille Delannoit	BEL	1948-1949
Tiberio Mitri*	ITA	1949-1950
Randy Turpin	E	1951-1954
Tiberio Mitri	ITA	1954
Charles Humez	FR	1954-1958
Gustav Scholz*	GER	1958-1961
John Cowboy McCormack	S	1961-1962
Chris Christensen	DEN	1962
Laszlo Papp*	HUN	1962-1965
Nino Benvenuti*	ITA	1965-1967
Juan Carlos Duran	ITA	1967-1969
Tom Bogs	DEN	1969-1970
Juan Carlos Duran	ITA	1970-1971
Jean-Claude Bouttier	FR	1971-1972
Tom Bogs*	DEN	1973
Elio Calcabrini	ITA	1973-1974
Jean-Claude Bouttier	FR	1974
Kevin Finnegan	E	1974-1975
Gratien Tonna*	FR	1975
Bunny Sterling	E	1976
Angelo Jacopucci	ITA	1976
Germano Valsecchi	ITA	1976-1977
Alan Minter	E	1977
Gratien Tonna	FR	1977-1978
Alan Minter*	E	1978-1979
Kevin Finnegan	E	1980
Matteo Salvemini	ITA	1980
Tony Sibson*	E	1980-1982
Louis Acaries	FR	1982-1984
Tony Sibson	E	1984-1985
Ayub Kalule	DEN	1985-1986
Herol Graham	E	1986-1987
Sumbu Kalambay*	ITA	1987
Pierre Joly	FR	1987-1988
Christophe Tiozzo*	FR	1988-1989
Francesco dell' Aquila	ITA	1989-1990
Sumbu Kalambay*	ITA	1990-1993
Agostino Cardamone*	ITA	1993-1994
Richie Woodhall*	E	1995-1996
Alexandre Zaitsev	RUS	1996
Hassine Cherifi*	FR	1996-1998
Agostino Cardamone*	ITA	1998
Erland Betare*	FR	1999-2000
Howard Eastman*	E	2001
Christian Sanavia	ITA	2001-2002
Morrade Hakkar	FR	2002-

S. Middleweight (168 lbs)

Title Holder	Birthplace/ Domicile	Tenure
Mauro Galvano*	ITA	1990-1991
James Cook	E	1991-1992
Franck Nicotra*	FR	1992
Vincenzo Nardiello	ITA	1992-1993
Ray Close*	NI	1993
Vinzenzo Nardiello	ITA	1993-1994
Frederic Seillier*	FR	1994-1995
Henry Wharton*	E	1995-1996
Frederic Seillier*	FR	1996
Andrei Shkalikov*	RUS	1997
Dean Francis*	E	1997-1998
Bruno Girard*	FR	1999
Andrei Shkalikov	RUS	2000-2001
Danilo Haeussler	GER	2001-

L. Heavyweight (175 lbs)

Title Holder	Birthplace/ Domicile	Tenure
Georges Carpentier	FR	1913-1922
Battling Siki	FR	1922-1923
Emile Morelle	FR	1923
Raymond Bonnel	FR	1923-1924
Louis Clement	SWI	1924-1926
Herman van T'Hof	HOL	1926
Fernand Delarge	BEL	1926-1927
Max Schmeling*	GER	1927-1928
Michele Bonaglia*	ITA	1929-1930
Ernst Pistulla*	GER	1931-1932
Adolf Heuser	GER	1932
John Andersson	SWE	1933
Martinez de Alfara	SP	1934
Marcel Thil	FR	1934-1935
Merlo Preciso	ITA	1935
Hein Lazek	AU	1935-1936
Gustave Roth	BEL	1936-1938
Adolf Heuser*	GER	1938-1939
Luigi Musina*	ITA	1942-1943
Freddie Mills*	E	1947-1950
Albert Yvel	FR	1950-1951
Don Cockell*	E	1951-1952
Conny Rux*	GER	1952
Jacques Hairabedian	FR	1953-1954
Gerhard Hecht	GER	1954-1955
Willi Hoepner	GER	1955
Gerhard Hecht	GER	1955-1957
Artemio Calzavara	ITA	1957-1958
Willi Hoepner	GER	1958
Erich Schoeppner	GER	1958-1962
Giulio Rinaldi	ITA	1962-1964
Gustav Scholz*	GER	1964-1965
Giulio Rinaldi	ITA	1965-1966
Piero del Papa	ITA	1966-1967
Lothar Stengel	GER	1967-1968
Tom Bogs*	DEN	1968-1969
Yvan Prebeg	YUG	1969-1970
Piero del Papa	ITA	1970-1971
Conny Velensek	GER	1971-1972
Chris Finnegan	E	1972
Rudiger Schmidtke	GER	1972-1973
John Conteh*	E	1973-1974
Domenico Adinolfi	ITA	1974-1976
Mate Parlov*	YUG	1976-1977
Aldo Traversaro	ITA	1977-1979
Rudi Koopmans	HOL	1979-1984
Richard Caramonolis	FR	1984
Alex Blanchard	HOL	1984-1987
Tom Collins	E	1987-1988
Pedro van Raamsdonk	HOL	1988
Jan Lefeber	HOL	1988-1989
Eric Nicoletta	FR	1989-1990
Tom Collins	E	1990-1991
Graciano Rocchigiani*	GER	1991-1992
Eddie Smulders	HOL	1993-1994
Fabrice Tiozzo*	FR	1994-1995
Eddy Smulders	HOL	1995-1996
Crawford Ashley	E	1997
Ole Klemetsen*	NOR	1997-1998
Crawford Ashley	E	1998-1999
Clinton Woods*	E	1999-2000
Yawe Davis	ITA	2001-

Cruiserweight (190 lbs)

Title Holder	Birthplace/ Domicile	Tenure
Sam Reeson*	E	1987-1988
Angelo Rottoli	ITA	1989
Anaclet Wamba*	FR	1989-1990
Johnny Nelson*	E	1990-1992
Akim Tafer*	FR	1992-1993
Massimiliano Duran	ITA	1993-1994
Carl Thompson	E	1994
Alexander Gurov	UK	1995
Patrice Aouissi	FR	1995
Alexander Gurov*	UK	1995-1996
Akim Tafer*	FR	1996-1997
Johnny Nelson	E	1997-1998
Terry Dunstan*	E	1998
Alexei Iliin	RUS	1999
Torsten May*	GER	1999-2000
Carl Thompson*	E	2000-2001
Alexander Gurov*	UK	2001-2002

Heavyweight (190 lbs +)

Title Holder	Birthplace/ Domicile	Tenure
Georges Carpentier	FR	1913-1922
Battling Siki	FR	1922-1923
Erminio Spalla	ITA	1923-1926
Paolino Uzcudun	SP	1926-1928
Harry Persson	SWE	1926
Pierre Charles	BEL	1929-1931
Hein Muller	GER	1931-1932
Pierre Charles	BEL	1932-1933
Paolino Uzcudun	SP	1933
Primo Carnera	ITA	1933-1935
Pierre Charles	BEL	1935-1937
Arno Kolbin	GER	1937-1938
Hein Lazek	AU	1938-1939
Adolf Heuser	GER	1939
Max Schmeling*	GER	1939-1941
Olle Tandberg	SWE	1943
Karel Sys*	BEL	1943-1946
Bruce Woodcock	E	1946-1949
Joe Weidin	AU	1950-1951
Jack Gardner	E	1951
Hein Ten Hoff	GER	1951-1952
Karel Sys	BEL	1952
Heinz Neuhaus	GER	1952-1955
Franco Cavicchi	ITA	1955-1956
Ingemar Johansson*	SWE	1956-1959
Dick Richardson	W	1960-1962
Ingemar Johansson*	SWE	1962-1963
Henry Cooper*	E	1964
Karl Mildenberger	GER	1964-1968
Henry Cooper*	E	1968-1969
Peter Weiland	GER	1969-1970
Jose Urtain	SP	1970
Henry Cooper	E	1970-1971
Joe Bugner	E	1971
Jack Bodell	E	1971
Jose Urtain	SP	1971-1972
Jurgen Blin	GER	1972
Joe Bugner*	E	1972-1975
Richard Dunn	E	1976
Joe Bugner	E	1976-1977
Jean-Pierre Coopman	BEL	1977
Lucien Rodriguez	FR	1977
Alfredo Evangelista	SP	1977-1979
Lorenzo Zanon*	SP	1979-1980
John L. Gardner*	E	1980-1981
Lucien Rodriguez	FR	1981-1984
Steffen Tangstad	NOR	1984-1985
Anders Eklund	SWE	1985
Frank Bruno*	E	1985-1986
Steffen Tangstad	NOR	1986
Alfredo Evangelista	SP	1987
Anders Eklund	SWE	1987
Francesco Damiani	ITA	1987-1989
Derek Williams	E	1989-1990
Jean Chanet	FR	1990
Lennox Lewis*	E	1990-1992
Henry Akinwande*	E	1993-1995
Zeljko Mavrovic*	CRO	1995-1998
Vitali Klitschko*	UK	1998-1999
Vladimir Klitschko*	UK	1999-2000
Vitali Klitschko*	UK	2000-2001
Luan Krasniki	GER	2002-

A-Z of Current World Champions

by Eric Armit

Shows the record since 1 July 2001, plus career summary and pen portrait, of all men holding IBF, WBA, WBC and WBO titles as at 30 June 2002. The author has also produced the same data for those who first won titles between 1 July 2001 and 30 June 2002, but were no longer champions at the end of the period in question. Incidentally, the place name given is the respective boxer's domicile and may not necessarily be his birthplace, while all nicknames are shown where applicable in brackets. Not included are British fighters, Lennox Lewis (WBC and IBF heavyweight champion), Joe Calzaghe (WBO super-middleweight champion) and Johnny Nelson (WBO cruiserweight champion). Their full records can be found among the Active British-Based Boxers: Career Records' section.

Jose Antonio (Jaguar) Aguirre

Cardenas, Mexico. *Born* 5 July, 1975
WBC M. Flyweight Champion

Major Amateur Honours: His amateur record shows 15 wins in 18 fights and he was the Mexican Golden Gloves Champion in 1995
Turned Pro: February 1995
Significant Results: Cruz Zamora L PTS 10, Paulino Villalobos W PTS 10, Gustavo Andrade W CO 1, Rafael Orozco W CO 2, Wandee Singwangcha W PTS 12, Jose Luis Zepeda W CO 5, Manny Melchor W PTS 12
Type/Style: A switch hitter and a good technician with a strong body attack, he also has a solid chin
Points of Interest: 5'4" tall. Is the first world champion from Tabasco State and originally studied to be a Doctor. Won the WBC title in February 2000 and, due to a serious shoulder injury and a car crash, has made only four defences. Unbeaten in his last 15 fights

11.11.01	Yasuo Tokimitsu W RSC 3 Okayama *(WBC Mini-Flyweight Title Defence)*

Career: 29 contests, won 27, lost 1, drew 1.

Rosendo (Buffalo) Alvarez

Managua, Nicaragua. *Born* 6 May, 1970
WBA L. Flyweight Champion. Former WBA M. Flyweight Champion

Major Amateur Honours: Competed in the 1991 Pan American Games and claims 66 wins in 78 fights
Turned Pro: December 1992
Significant Results: Jose Bonilla W PTS 12 and W CO 11, Chana Porpaoin W PTS 12, Kermin Guardia W CO 3, Eric Chavez W PTS 12, Songkram Porpaoin W RSC 11, Ricardo Lopez T DRAW 7 and L PTS 12, Beibis Mendoza L DIS 7 and W PTS 12
Type/Style: A fine boxer who is both skilful and fast and a good in-fighter, he also has a fair punch
Points of Interest: 5'5" tall. Has 20 wins inside the distance under his belt and beaten both of the Porpaoin twins. Made five defences of his WBA mini-flyweight title before losing it when he failed to make the weight for his second fight with Ricardo Lopez. Lost for the vacant title to Beibis Mendoza in August 2000 but outpointed him in March 2001 to become champion again. Has had problems with drink and drugs

| 12.12.01 | David Torres W RSC 3 Managua |
| 19.01.02 | Pichitnoi Chor Siriwat W RSC 12 Miami *(WBA L.Flyweight Title Defence)* |

Career: 34 contests, won 31, drew 1, lost 2.

Tim (Cincinnati Kid) Austin

Cincinnati, USA. *Born* 14 April, 1971
IBF Bantamweight Champion

Major Amateur Honours: Was the 1986 US Junior champion, the National Golden Gloves champion in 1990 and 1991 and the Unites States Champion in 1991. Won a bronze medal in the 1992 Olympics and won and lost against Istvan Kovacs. Claims 113 wins in 122 fights
Turned Pro: April 1993
Significant Results: Javier Diaz T Draw 1, Mbulelo Botile W RSC 8, Paul Lloyd W RSC 2, Adrian Kaspari W RSC 1, Sergio Aguila W CO 1, Bernardo Mendoza W RSC 11, Arthur Johnson W PTS 12, Jesus Perez W RSC 6, Steve Dotse W RSC 6
Type/Style: Is a southpaw with a long reach and a knockout punch in each hand

Points of Interest: 5'6" tall. Was inactive for 17 months with a broken jaw before winning the IBF title from Mbulelo Botile in July 1997 and has made only eight defences in five years. Has 21 wins inside the distance, with 11 coming in the first round

15.12.01	Ratanchai Voraphin W PTS 12 Mashantucket *(IBF Bantamweight Title Defence)*

Career: 25 contests, won 24, drew 1.

Tim Austin   Les Clark

Raul (Pepe) Balbi

Buenos Aires, Argentina. *Born* 7 October 1973
Former WBA Lightweight Champion

Major Amateur Honours: Competed in the 1991 Pan American Games and the 1993 World Championships
Turned Pro: November 1993
Significant Results: Faustino Barrios W PTS 10, Manuel Billalba L PTS 10

197

and W PTS 10, Alberto Roda L PTS 10, Artur Grigorian L RSC 11, Carlos Vilchez W CO 2, Santos Rebolledo W PTS 12, Alberto Sicurella W RSC 10

Type/Style: Is a strong, aggressive fighter, who is a heavy-handed hooker, although not always dedicated. Has a good chin

Points of Interest: Beat 14 of his first 16 opponents by kayo or stoppage and now has 33 quick wins. Challenged Artur Grigorian for the WBO title unsuccessfully in 1997 and almost retired later in the year

17.07.01	Vince Howard W RSC 3 Caseros
08.10.01	Julien Lorcy W PTS 12 Paris
	(WBA Lightweight Title Challenge)
05.01.02	Leonard Dorin L PTS 12 San Antonio
	(WBA Lightweight Title Defence)
31.05.02	Leonard Dorin L PTS 12 Bucharest
	(WBA Lightweight Title Challenge)
Career: 55 contests, won 48, drew 1, lost 6.	

Marco Antonio (Baby Faced Assassin) Barrera

Mexico City, Mexico. *Born* 17 January, 1974
Former Undefeated WBC Featherweight Champion. Former Undefeated WBO S. Bantamweight Champion. Former Undefeated Mexican S. Flyweight Champion

Major Amateur Honours: None known, but claims only four losses in 60 fights
Turned Pro: November 1989
Significant Results: Carlos Salazar W PTS 10, Frankie Toledo W RSC 2, Kennedy McKinney W CO 12, Jesse Benavides W CO 3, Junior Jones L DIS 5 and L PTS 12, Richie Wenton W RTD 3, Paul Lloyd W RTD 1, Erik Morales L PTS 12, Jesus Salud W RTD 6, Prince Naseem Hamed W PTS 12
Type/Style: A compact box-fighter with a hard punch in both hands, but is a bit mechanical
Points of Interest: 5'7" tall. Attended the University of Mexico. A natural southpaw who fights right handed, despite losing a hotly disputed decision to Erik Morales in a match for both the WBC and WBO super-bantamweight titles, the WBO reinstated him as champion. Took part in 18 WBO super-bantamweight title fights before relinquishing the title to move up to featherweight. Won the WBC title

when beating Morales but refused to accept it. Took part in 20 WBO super-bantamweight title fights and has 39 wins inside the distance

08.09.01	Enrique Sanchez W RTD 6 Reno
22.06.02	Erik Morales W PTS 12 Las Vegas
	(WBC Featherweight Title Challenge)
Career: 59 contests, won 55, lost 3, no contest 1.	

Johnny Bredahl

Copenhagen, Denmark. *Born* 27 August 1968
WBA Bantamweight Champion. Former Undefeated WBO S. Flyweight Champion. Former Undefeated European Bantamweight Champion

Major Amateur Honours: Bronze medal in the 1986 European Youth Championships and 1987 Senior Championships. A Scandinavian and Danish champion, he competed in the 1988 Olympics
Turned Pro: December 1988
Significant Results: Jose Quirino W PTS 12, Rafael Caban W PTS 12, Wayne McCullough L RSC 8, Efrain Pintor W RSC 2, Alexander Yagupov W PTS 12 (twice), Paul Lloyd W RSC 1, Paulie Ayala L PTS 12
Type/Style: A stylish, upright boxer with an excellent jab and sharp punch. Has good stamina
Points of Interest: 5'8" tall. Failed in bids to win WBC and WBA titles before finding success against Eidy Moya. Unbeaten in eight European title fights, he has 26 wins by stoppage or knockout. Now trained by Freddie Roach

13.10.01	Evangelio Perez W PTS 6 Copenhagen
19.04.02	Eidy Moya W CO 9 Copenhagen
	(WBA Bantamweight Title Challenge)
Career: 54 contests, won 52, lost 2.	

Cruz (Costenito) Carbajal

Veracruz, Mexico. *Born* 3 May, 1974
WBO Bantamweight Champion. Former Undefeated Mexican Bantamweight Champion

Major Amateur Honours: Five times State Champion, he claims only one loss in 39 fights

Turned Pro: May 1992
Significant Results: Jose Luis Bueno W CO 2, Lehlohonolo Ledwaba L PTS 12, Samson Toyota L CO 5, Genaro Garcia W RSC 8, Hugo Dianzo L PTS 10, Johnny Bredahl L PTS 8, Fernando Montiel L RSC 4, Alejandro Estrada W RSC 6
Type/Style: Is a strong and aggressive, hard puncher, but is limited and has a poor defence
Points of Interest: Started boxing at 12 after being inspired by the achievements of Salvador Sanchez. Worked as a butcher and at one stage had a spell of eight losses in ten fights, but now claims 17 wins inside the distance. Almost had the WBO title taken off him due to a dispute over the sanction fee

17.08.01	Hugo Dianzo W PTS 12 Juarez
	(Mexican Bantamweight Title Defence)
16.03.02	Mauricio Martinez W RSC 9 Vera Cruz
	(WBO Bantamweight Title Challenge)
Career: 32 contests, won 21, drew 1, lost 11.	

Julio Pablo Chacon

Las Heras, Argentina. *Born* 22 May, 1975
WBO Featherweight Champion

Major Amateur Honours: Won a bronze medal in the 1996 Olympic Games, a gold medal in the 1995 Pan-American Games and competed in the 1994 World Cup and 1993 Pan-American Games. Claims 53 wins in 62 fights
Turned Pro: October 1996
Significant Results: Ever Beleno W DIS 3, Mauricio Julio W CO 4, Wilson Palacio W RSC 8, Freddie Norwood L PTS 12, Claudio Martinet L PTS 10 and W CO 5, Istvan Kovacs W RSC 6
Type/Style: Is a good stylish boxer with speed and accuracy
Points of Interest: 5'4" tall. Won his first 33 fights, has 31 wins inside the distance and is trained by Amilcar Brusa who looked after Carlos Monzon. Lost to Freddie Norwood in a challenge for the WBA title in May 2000. Beat Istvan Kovacs for the WBO title in June 2001 and has made two defences. His father was also a boxer

11.08.01	Eduardo Barrios W RSC 5 Mendoza
	(WBO Featherweight Title Defence)
17.11.01	Andre Nicola W RTD 3 Buenos Aires
19.01.02	Victor Polo W PTS 12 London
	(WBO Featherweight Title Defence)

Career: 45 contests, won 43, lost 2.

Julio Pablo Chacon   Les Clark

Yo-Sam Choi

South Korea. *Born* 1 March, 1972
WBC L. Flyweight Champion. Former South Korean L. Flyweight Champion

Major Amateur Honours: None known.
Turned Pro: July 1993
Significant Results: San-Gik Yang L PTS 12, Kenzo Ando W PTS 10, Jun Arlos W PTS 12, Saman Sorjaturong W PTS 12 and W CO 7
Type/Style: Is a short, slick, busy two-handed puncher with a rough, tough approach. Is also a good body puncher
Points of Interest: Managed by a lady and sponsored by a Korean Corporation, he has 13 wins by knockout or stoppage. Has only fought outside Korea once. Won the title from Saman Sorjaturong in October 1999 and has made only two defences due to the economic situation in South Korea

23.02.02	Shingo Yamaguchi W RSC 10 Chiba
	(WBC L. Flyweight Title Defence)

Career: 25 contests, won 24, lost 1.

DeMarcus (Chop Chop) Corley

Washington, USA. *Born* 3 June, 1974
WBO L. Welterweight Champion

Major Amateur Honours: National Golden Gloves champion 1995
Turned Pro: May 1996
Significant Results: Dillon Carew T DRAW 3, Daniel Lujan L PTS 10, Ener Julio W PTS 12, Felix Flores W RSC 1
Type/Style: Is a flashy, quick-punching southpaw
Points of Interest: Started boxing at the age of ten, but gave up for a while and worked as a lifeguard. Only received the chance to win the WBO title when the champion, and former victim, Ener Julio, was shown to have cataracts in both eyes five days before a title defence in June 2001, leaving Corley to step in as a late substitute to stop Felix Flores and win the title. Colourful and a designer of his own ring outfits, he has been known to wear red tights and yellow boots into the ring. Suffered two gun shot wounds a few years back when being robbed. Has 16 wins inside the distance, with just the one title defence

19.01.02	Ener Julio W PTS 12 Miami
	(WBO L. Welterweight Title Defence)

Career: 29 contests, won 27, drew 1, lost 1.

Oscar de la Hoya

Montebello, USA. *Born* 4 February, 1973
WBC L. Middleweight Champion. Former WBC Welterweight Champion. Former Undefeated WBC L.Welterweight, IBF and WBO Lightweight and WBO S. Featherweight Champion

Major Amateur Honours: Was the gold medal winner in the 1992 Olympics, the United States champion in 1990 and 1991 and the National Golden Gloves champion in 1989
Turned Pro: November 1992
Significant Results: Genaro Hernandez W RSC 6, Jesse Leija W RSC 2, Julio Cesar Chavez W RSC 4 and W RTD 8, Miguel Gonzalez W PTS 12, Pernell Whitaker W PTS 12, Hector Camacho W PTS 12, Ike Quartey W PTS 12, Oba Carr W RSC 11, Felix Trinidad L PTS 12, Derrell Coley W RSC 7, Shane Mosley L PTS 12

Type/Style: Is a smooth, classy boxer, who is a fast and accurate puncher
Points of Interest: 5'11" tall. Having beaten 14 world or former world champions, he has 28 wins inside the distance and has won six versions of world titles in five divisions. Boxing since the age of six, Oscar lost the WBC title to Felix Trinidad but defeated Derrell Coley in an eliminator and was declared WBC champion again when Trinidad moved up, only to lose the title to Shane Mosley in June 2000

INACTIVE DURING 2001-02
Career: 36 contests, won 34, lost 2.

Nelson Dieppa

Vieques, Puerto Rico. *Born* 25 February, 1971
WBO L. Flyweight Champion

Major Amateur Honours: Won a bronze medal in the 1991 World Championships and a bronze medal in the 1991 Pan-American Games. Also competed in the 1992 Olympic Games
Turned Pro: February 1993
Significant Results: Pablo Tiznado W CO 6, Carlos Murillo L PTS 10, Ramon Hurtado W CO 3, Will Grigsby L PTS 12, Julio Coronel W PTS 10, Andy Tabanas W RSC 11
Type/Style: Is a clever, slick boxer and solid right-hand puncher
Points of Interest: Trained by Felix Trinidad (senior) and has 11 wins inside the distance. His first crack at the title saw the winner, Will Grigsby, fail a drugs test before being stripped. Won the vacant title by beating Andy Tabanas in April 2001 and has made only one defence

29.09.01	Fahlan Sakkririn W PTS 12 New York
	(WBO L. Flyweight Title Defence)

Career: 22 contests, won 19, drew 1, lost 2.

Leonardo (Leo The Lion) Dorin

Montreal, Canada. *Born* Costana, Romania 10 April, 1970
WBA Lightweight Champion

Major Amateur Honours: Won a bronze medal in the 1992 Olympics; a bronze medal in the 1993 European Championships, a gold medal in the 1995 World Championships and was

European Champion in 1995, prior to picking up a bronze in the 1996 Olympics. Competed in the 1997 World Championships and claims only 15 losses in 254 fights
Turned Pro: May 1998
Significant Results: Gustavo Cuello W PTS 10, Gary St Clair W PTS 10
Type/Style: Is a rough, tough, strong and aggressive pressure fighter, but not a big puncher
Points of Interest: 5'4" tall with a 64" reach, his real name is Leonard Doroftei. Has only seven wins inside the distance and is based in Canada

21.07.01	Martin O'Malley W RSC 9 Atlantic City
29.09.01	Emanuel Burton W PTS 10 San Francisco
05.01.02	Raul Balbi W PTS 12 San Antonio *(WBA Lightweight Title Challenge)*
31.05.02	Raul Balbi W PTS 12 Bucharest *(WBA Lightweight Title Defence)*

Career: 21 contests, won 21.

Leonardo Dorin

Steve (Flat Tax) Forbes

Portland, USA. *Born* 26 February, 1977
IBF S. Featherweight Champion

Major Amateur Honours: A five-time Washington and Oregon champion, he competed in the 1994 National Golden Gloves finals. Claims 57 wins in 67 fights
Turned Pro: December 1996
Significant Results: Alejandro Gonzalez L PTS 12, Ernest Zepeda W PTS 10, Moises Pedroza W PTS 10, David Santos W PTS 10, John Brown W RSC 8
Type/Style: Stylish and a quick counter puncher with excellent jab, he also has a solid punch

Points of Interest: Trained by Floyd Mayweather (senior), he started boxing at the age of ten. With only five wins inside the distance, there has been just one title defence since winning the crown by beating John Brown in December 2000

29.09.01	John Brown W PTS 12 Miami *(IBF S. Featherweight Title Defence)*

Career: 21 contests, won 20, lost 1.

Vernon Forrest

Vernon (The Viper) Forrest

Augusta, USA. *Born* 21 February, 1971
WBC Welterweight Champion.
Former Undefeated IBF Welterweight Champion

Major Amateur Honours: A silver medallist in the 1991 World Championships and a competitor in the 1992 Olympics, he won a gold medal in the 1992 World Championships
Turned Pro: November 1992
Significant Results: Adrian Stone W RSC 11, Steve Martinez W RSC 1, Santiago Samaniego W CO 7, Vince Phillips W PTS 12, Raul Frank NC 3 and W PTS 12

Type/Style: Tall and quick, he has a long reach and a strong jab
Points of Interest: 6'0" tall. Attending college under a boxing scholarship, he lost to Kostya Tszyu in the 1991 World Championships, but beat Shane Mosley and Steve Johnston in the Olympic trials. With 25 stoppages or knockouts, his first fight for the vacant IBF title was declared a no contest when Raul Frank was cut. Won the vacant IBF title by outpointing Frank in a return in May 2001, but relinquished the title to challenge Shane Mosley

26.01.02	Shane Mosley W PTS 12 New York *(WBC Welterweight Title Challenge)*

Career: 34 contests, won 33, no contest 1.

Acelino (Popo) Freitas

Salvador de Bahia, Brazil. *Born* 21 September, 1975
WBO and WBA S.Featherweight Champion. Former Brazilian Lightweight Champion

Major Amateur Honours: Won a silver medal in the 1995 Pan-American Games. Claims 72 wins in 74 fights and won 14 Brazilian titles
Turned Pro: July 1995
Significant Results: Anatoly Alexandrov W CO 1, Claudio Martinet W CO 3, Barry Jones W RSC 8, Javier Jauregui W RSC 1, Lemuel Nelson W RSC 2, Carlos Rios W RSC 9, Orlando Soto W RSC 4
Type/Style: Strong and aggressive, he has fast hands, is a quick starter, and packs a crushing punch in his right hand, but gets careless
Points of Interest: 5'7" tall. Brother Luiz Carlos is also a pro and a double Brazilian champion. Won his first 29 fights inside the distance, 22 within the first three rounds, and has 12 first-round finishes. Although it was felt that he was having weight problems it didn't stop him from adding the WBA version of the title to his WBO crown, when beating Joel Casamayor

29.09.01	Alfred Kotey W PTS 10 Miami
12.01.02	Joel Casamayor W PTS 12 Las Vegas *(WBO S. Featherweight Title Defence. WBA S. Featherweight Title Challenge)*

Career: 31 contests, won 31.

Derrick (Smoke) Gainer

Pensacola, USA. *Born* 22 August, 1972
WBA Featherweight Champion

Major Amateur Honours: None, but
had around 30 bouts
Turned Pro: July 1990
Significant Results: Harold Warren W
PTS 12 (twice), Kevin Kelley L CO 8,
Donovan Carey W RSC 6, Diego
Corrales L RSC 3
Type/Style: Has an upright southpaw
style and is a good boxer, although his
chin is not too sound
Points of Interest: 5'9" tall with a 72"
reach. Was managed by Roy Jones,
but broke with him a few months
back. Initially a flyweight when he
turned pro, he lost in a challenge for
the IBF title to Diego Corrales. His
fight with Freddie Norwood went
ahead for the vacant WBA title,
despite the latter being stripped for
failing to make the weight. Has 24
wins inside the distance

INACTIVE DURING 2001-02
Career: 43 contest, won 38, lost 5.

Artur (Atuiz) Grigorian

Tashkent, Uzbekistan. *Born* 20
October,1967
WBO Lightweight Champion

Major Amateur Honours: A gold
medal winner in the 1990 Goodwill
Games, he won a silver medal in the
1991 World Championships and
competed in the 1992 Olympics and
the 1993 World Championships. Also
won a gold medal in the Chemical Cup
in 1994 and claims 361 wins in 384
fights
Turned Pro: April 1994
Significant Results: Antonio Rivera
W CO 12, David Armstrong W PTS
12, Marco Rudolph W RSC 6, Oscar
Garcia Cano W PTS 12, Michael
Clark CO 5, Wilson Galli W RSC 10,
Sandro Casamonica W RSC 9,
Antonio Pitalua W PTS 12, Aldo Rios
W PTS 12
Type/Style: Is a stylish box-fighting
southpaw
Points of Interest: 5'9" tall with a 69"
reach. A former WBO Interim
champion who was awarded the full
title without fighting for it, he has 22
wins inside the distance. The WBO
champion since 1996, with 15 title

defences to his credit, he once beat
Shane Mosley as an amateur

INACTIVE DURING 2001-02
Career: 34 contest, won 34.

Kermin Guardia

Turbo, Colombia. *Born* 17 January,
1970
WBO M. Flyweight Champion.
Former Undefeated Colombian M.
Flyweight Champion

Major Amateur Honours: None known
Turned Pro: June 1991
Significant Results: Marcelino Bolivar
W PTS 12, Ricardo Lopez L PTS 12,
Rosendo Alvarez L CO 3, Eric Jamili
W RSC 5 and W PTS 12, Luis Lazarte
W PTS 12
Type/Style: Southpaw. Is an intelligent,
stylish little boxer with an excellent
jab and hard punch, especially with the
right hook
Points of Interest: Won his first 21
contests, but lost in challenges for the
WBC and WBA titles before winning
the WBO title in May 1998. Has made
only three defences of the WBO title in
three years and was inactive last year.
Has 20 wins inside the distance

INACTIVE DURING 2001-02
Career: 36 contests, won 33, lost 2, no
decision 1.

Bernard (The Executioner) Hopkins

Philadelphia, USA. *Born* 15 January,
1965
WBC, WBA and IBF Middleweight
Champion

Major Amateur Honours: None, but
claims 95 wins in 99 fights
Turned Pro: October 1988
Significant Results: Roy Jones L PTS
12, Lupe Aquino W PTS 12, Segundo
Mercado DREW 12 and W PTS 12,
Robert Allen NC 4 and W RSC 7,
Antwun Echols W PTS 12 and W RSC
10, Syd Vanderpool W PTS 12, Keith
Holmes W PTS 12
Type/Style: Is a strong if mechanical
boxer and a powerful puncher with fast
hands
Points of Interest: 6'0" tall with a 71"
reach. The nephew of former pro, Art
McCloud, after spending five years in
jail he lost his first paid fight. Entering

the ring wearing an executioners mask
and a cape, Bernard has 30 wins inside
the distance. Having lost to Roy Jones
in his first attempt to win the IBF title
and drawn with Segundo Mercado for
the vacant title before beating Mercado
in a return in April 1995, he has now
made 13 title defences of his IBF title
and added the WBC title by
outpointing Keith Holmes in April
2001. Now holds the WBC, IBF and
WBA titles, having defeated Felix
Trinidad for the latter

29.09.01	Felix Trinidad W RSC 12 New York *(IBF and WBC Middleweight Title Defences. WBA Title Challenge)*
02.02.02	Carl Daniels W RTD 10 Reading *(IBF, WBC and WBA Title Defences)*

Career: 45 contests, won 41, drew 1, lost 2,
no contests 1.

Bernard Hopkins

Keitaro Hoshino

Kanagawa, Japan. *Born* 14 August,
1969
WBA M. Flyweight Champion.
Former Undefeated Japanese M.
Flyweight Champion

Major Amateur Honours: None, but
claims 30 wins and seven losses
Turned Pro: November 1988
Significant Results: Ernesto Rubillar
W PTS 10 (twice), Satoshi Yoshida W
PTS 10, Makoto Suzuki W RSC 9,
Jomo Gamboa W PTS 12, Chano
Porpaoin L PTS 12
Type/Style: Is a typical two-fisted,
aggressive battler, but is not a hard
puncher

Points of Interest: Lost his first paid contest and suffered three defeats in four fights in 1993. Inactive throughout 1999, he was the oldest Japanese fighter to win a world title at his first attempt. Managed by the former WBA flyweight champion, Susumu Hanagata, Keitaro has made five defences of his Japanese title and has only six quick wins. First won the WBA title in December 2000 by decisioning Joma Gamboa, but lost it to Chano Porpaoin in April 2001, before beating Gamboa again, this time for the vacant crown

26.09.01	Prabpram Klongphaon W RSC 10 Yokohama
29.01.02	Joma Gamboa W PTS 12 Yokohama *(Vacant WBA M.Flyweight Title)*
Career: 29 contests, won 22, lost 7.	

Vassily (Tiger) Jirov

Yezkazjan, Kazakhstan. *Born* 4 April, 1974
IBF Cruiserweight Champion

Major Amateur Honours: Won a gold medal in the 1996 Olympic Games, where he was also voted the outstanding boxer of the tournament. A bronze medal winner in the 1993 and 1995 World Championships, a gold medallist in the 1992 European Junior Championships, and a bronze medallist in the 1994 Asian Games, he also competed in the 1994 World Cup
Turned Pro: January 1997
Significant Results: Arthur Williams W RSC 7, Dale Brown W CO 10, Saul Montana W RSC 9
Type/Style: Carrying a high guard, he is a busy southpaw with a solid chin and is also a powerful body puncher
Points of Interest: 6'1" tall. Starting boxing at the age of 14, and also known as Valeryvich Zhirov, he has only fought once in his home country as a professional. With 27 wins inside the distance, Vassily has made six defences of the IBF title he won in 1999 when beating Arthur Williams

20.07.01	Adolpho Washington W PTS 10 Canton
08.09.01	Julian Letterlough W RSC 8 Reno *(IBF Cruiserweight Title Defence)*
01.02.02	Jorge Castro W PTS 12 Phoenix *(IBF Cruiserweight Title Defence)*
Career: 31 contests, won 31.	

Roy Jones

Pensacola, USA. *Born* 16 January, 1969
WBC, WBA and IBF L. Heavyweight Champion. Former Undefeated IBF Middleweight and S. Middleweight Champion

Major Amateur Honours: Was a silver medallist in the 1988 Olympics and the National Golden Gloves champion in 1986 and 1987
Turned Pro: May 1989
Significant Results: Bernard Hopkins W PTS 12, James Toney W PTS 12, Mike McCallum W PTS 12, Montell Griffin L DIS 9 and W RSC 1, Virgil Hill W CO 4, Louis del Valle W PTS 12, Reggie Johnson W PTS 12, David Telesco W PTS 12, Richard Hall W RSC 11, Eric Harding W RTD 10, Derrick Harding W RTD 10
Type/Style: A brilliant boxer with fast, skilful, lightning reflexes, he also has a kayo punch in either hand
Points of Interest: 5'11" tall. Originally trained and managed by his father, Roy Snr, he also plays basketball to a high standard and has appeared in films. With 37 wins inside the distance, Roy

was only a welterweight when he won the Golden Gloves and has now made four defences of his IBF/WBC light-heavyweight title. Lost his WBC light-heavyweight title to Montell Griffin in March 1997, but won it back just four months later and is unbeaten since then

28.07.01	Julio Gonzalez W PTS 12 Los Angeles *(WBC,WBA and IBF L. Heavyweight Title Defences)*
02.02.02	Glen Kelly W CO 7 Miami *(WBC, WBA and IBF L. Heavyweight Title Defences*
Career: 47 contests, won 46, lost 1.	

Willie Jorrin

Sacramento, USA. *Born* 21 November, 1969
WBC S. Bantamweight Champion

Major Amateur Honours: The USA Junior Champion in 1984 and an amateur international, he competed in the 1992 Olympic trials. Claims a 158 – 18 record
Turned Pro: February 1993
Significant Results: Antonio Ramirez W PTS 10, George Parra W RSC 7, Aristead Clayton W PTS 12, Marcos

Roy Jones

Badillo W PTS 10, Michael Brodie W PTS 12, Oscar Larios W PTS 12

Type/Style: Is a nimble, clever, busy little fighter with fast hands and a quick in-and-out style. Not a big puncher though and stamina questionable

Points of Interest: 5'5" tall. Originally trained by his father but now trained by Freddie Roach. Willie has eight brothers and two sisters. His record shows 12 wins inside the distance. Won the vacant WBC title with a disputed verdict over Michael Brodie in September 2000 and has made only two defences due to injuries

05.02.02	Osamu Sato DREW 12 Tokyo
	(WBC S. Bantamweight Title Defence)
Career: 29 contests, won 28, drew 1.	

Vladimir (The Steel Hammer) Klitschko

Kiev, Ukraine. *Born* 25 March, 1976
WBO Heavyweight Champion.
Former Undefeated European Heavyweight Champion

Major Amateur Honours: His list of honours include a gold medal in the 1993 European Junior Championships, a silver medal in the 1994 World Junior Championships, a silver medal in the 1994 World Military Championships, a gold medal in the 1995 World Military Championships, a silver medal in the 1996 European Championships and a gold medal in the 1996 Olympics
Turned Pro: November 1996
Significant Results: Ross Puritty L RSC 11, Axel Schulz W RSC 8, Paea Wolfgramm W CO 1, David Bostice W RSC 2, Chris Byrd W PTS 12, Derrick Jefferson W RSC 2
Type/Style: Despite having a mechanical jab and cross approach, his reach and punching power is hard to combat. However, there is some question over his stamina
Points of Interest: 6'7" tall. Originally wanting to be a doctor, his father is a general in the Ukrainian army, Vladimir started boxing at the age of 14, losing his first amateur fight. Has 36 wins inside the distance, of which 26 have come in the first three rounds. He made only one defence of his European title after winning it when beating Axel Schulz in September

1999. Won WBO title by outpointing Chris Byrd in October 2000 and has made four defences. His brother, Vitali, was also the WBO heavyweight champion

04.08.01	Charles Shufford W RSC 6 Las Vegas
	(WBO Heavyweight Title Challenge)
16.03.02	Frans Botha W RSC 8 Stuttgart
	(WBO Heavyweight Title Defence)
29.06.02	Ray Mercer W RSC 6 Atlantic City
	(WBO Heavyweight Title Defence)
Career: 40 contests, won 39, lost 1.	

Roberto (Mako) Leyva

Puerto Penasco, Mexico. *Born* 27 October, 1979
IBF M. Flyweight Champion

Major Amateur Honours: None known
Turned Pro: February 1998
Significant Results: Victor Burgos W RSC 8, Daniel Reyes W PTS 12,

James Page W RSC 7, Larry Marks W PTS 12

Type/Style: An aggressive pressure fighter, he is a southpaw with a hard left-hand punch

Points of Interest: Dad was a fisherman but died when Roberto was very young. Won his first 14 fights inside the distance and now has 18 wins by stoppage or kayo. In his first contest outside of Mexico, he won the IBF title by outpointing Daniel Reyes in April 2001 and has since made only one defence. Nickname means 'The Shark'

29.09.01	Miguel Barrera T DRAW 3 Ensenada
	(IBF M. Flyweight Title Defence)
04.01.02	Frankie Soto W RSC 5 Ensenada
09.03.02	Manny Melchor W PTS 10 Aguscalientes
Career: 22 contests, won 21, drew 1.	

Ricardo Lopez

203

Ricardo (Finito) Lopez

Cuernavaca, Mexico. *Born* 25 July, 1967
IBF L. Flyweight Champion. Former Undefeated WBC, WBA and WBO M. Flyweight Champion

Major Amateur Honours: Mexican Golden Gloves champion in 1984. Lost only one of 41 fights
Turned Pro: January 1985
Significant Results: Saman Sorjaturong W RSC 2, Rocky Lim W CO 2, Ala Villamor W CO 8, Alex Sanchez W RSC 5, Rosendo Alvarez T DRAW 7 and W PTS 12, Will Grigsby W PTS 12, Ratanapol Sowvoraphin W RSC 3
Type/Style: Is a dazzling craftsman and a fast, accurate puncher
Points of Interest: 5'5" tall. Has fought in 26 world title fights, winning 25 and fighting a technical draw with Rosendo Alvarez in the other. Beat Alex Sanchez for the WBO title, but was stripped of it seven months later without defending. Won the WBA title with a victory over Alvarez in November 1998, even though both fighters were over the weight limit. He then won the IBF light-flyweight title when decisioning Will Grigsby in October 1999 and has made only two defences. Is considered to be one of the modern greats

29.09.01	Zolani Petelo W CO 8 New York *(IBF L. Flyweight Title Defence)*	
Career: 51 contests, won 50, drew 1.		

Julien (Bobo) Lorcy

Bezons, France. *Born* 12 April, 1972
Former WBA Lightweight Champion. Former Undefeated European Lightweight and S. Featherweight Champion

Major Amateur Honours: French champion 1991. Competed in the 1990 European Junior Championships, the 1991 World Championships and the 1992 Olympic Games
Turned Pro: October 1992
Significant Results: Jose Sanabria W PTS 8, Boris Sinitsin W RSC 7, Arnulfo Castillo DREW 12 (twice), Anatoly Alexandrov L PTS 12, Jean-Baptiste Mendy W RSC 6, Stefano Zoff L PTS 12, Oscar Cano Garcia W PTS 12
Type/Style: Is a short, aggressive fighter with a typical high guard.

Defence and attitude have let him down at times, but he is a smart boxer
Points of Interest: Unbeaten in his first 40 fights, he failed in three attempts at the WBO super-featherweight title, drawing twice and losing once. Has 36 wins inside the distance. First beat Jean-Baptiste Mendy for the WBA title in April 1999, but lost it in an upset to Stefano Zoff just four months later. Regained the title by beating Takanore Hatakeyama but lost it to Raul Balbi in his first defence

01.07.01	Takanori Hatakeyama W PTS 12 Tokyo *(WBA Lightweight Title Challenge)*	
08.10.01	Raul Balbi L PTS 12 Paris *(WBA Lightweight Title Defence)*	
06.04.02	Ahmed Merichiche W CO 4 Abbeville	
Career: 53 contests, won 50, lost 3.		

Eric Lucas

Montreal, Canada. *Born* 29 May, 1971
WBC S. Middleweight Champion. Former Undefeated Canadian S. Middleweight and L. Heavyweight Champion

Major Amateur Honours: : None known, but claims 65 wins in 84 fights
Turned Pro: December 1991
Significant Results: : Bryant Brannon L PTS 12, Fabrice Tiozzo L PTS 12, Roy Jones L RSF 11, Antwun Echols DREW 8, Segundo Mercado W RSC 5, Alex Hilton W PTS 10, Glenn Catley L RSF 12 and W CO 7
Type/Style: Well schooled, tough, rangy stand-up boxer with a hard right hand punch
Points of Interest: 6'0" tall with a 74" reach. Lost to Fabrice Tiozzo for the WBA light-heavyweight title, to Roy Jones for the IBF super-middleweight title and Glenn Catley for the WBC super-middleweight title before finally beating Catley in a return for the WBC crown. Plays golf and hockey

10.07.01	Glenn Catley W CO 7 Montreal *(Vacant WBC S. Middleweight Title)*	
30.11.01	Dingaan Thobela W RSC 8 Montreal *(WBC S. Middleweight Title Defence)*	
01.03.02	Vinny Pazienza W PTS 12 Ledyard *(WBC S. Middleweight Title Defence)*	
Career: 42 contests, won 35, drew 3, lost 2.		

Felix Machado

Bolivar, Venezuela. *Born* 22 August, 1972
IBF S. Flyweight Champion. Former Undefeated Venezuelan Bantamweight Champion

Major Amateur Honours: Won a silver medal in the 1989 World Junior Championships
Turned Pro: April 1993
Significant Results: Edicson Torres W PTS 10, Fernando Blanco W PTS 12, Adonis Cruz L DIS 8, Daorung Chuwatana L PTS 12, Julio Gamboa DREW 12 and W PTS 12, William de Souza W RSC 3
Type/Style: A tall, methodical southpaw who has a good chin but is not a big puncher
Points of Interest: Lost to Daorung Chuwatana in a challenge for the WBA bantamweight title in 1997 and drew with Julio Gamboa for the vacant IBF super-flyweight title in May 2000 and then beat him in July 2000 to win the title. Has 11 wins by stoppage or kayo since losing his first pro fight and has made three title defences

30.03.02	Martin Castillo W TD 6 Reading *(IBF S. Flyweight Title Defence)*	

Antonio Margarito

Tijuana, Mexico. *Born* 18 March, 1978
WBO Welterweight Champion

Major Amateur Honours: None known
Turned Pro: January 1994
Significant Results: Larry Dixon L PTS 10, Rodney Jones L PTS 10, Alfred Ankamah W CO 4, Danny Perez W PTS 8, David Kamau W CO 2, Frankie Randall W RSC 4
Type/Style: A tall, strong, aggressive banger but a bit one paced, he has a good jab and a strong chin
Points of Interest: 6'0" tall. Turned pro at the age of 15 and suffered three early defeats, but is unbeaten in his last 18 bouts. His fight with Daniel Santos for the WBO title was stopped and declared a no contest due to Antonio suffering a bad cut. Of 30 contests, 18 have come inside the distance

21.07.01	Daniel Santos NC 1 Bayamon *(WBO Welterweight Title Challenge)*	
16.03.02	Antonio Diaz W RSC 10 Las Vegas *(Vacant WBO Welterweight Title)*	
Career: 30 contests, won 26, lost 3, no contest 1.		

Ricardo (El Matador) Mayorga

Costa Rica. *Born* Granada, Nicaragua
3 October, 1973
WBA Welterweight Champion.
Former Undefeated Nicaraguan Light-
Welterweight Champion

Major Amateur Honours: None known
Turned Pro: August 1993
Significant Results: Roger Flores L
PTS 10, Henry Castillo L PTS 10 and
W RSC 7, Diosbelys Hurtado T
DRAW 2, Elio Ortiz W CO 10
Type/Style: A bit wild and unconventional
but strong and a very hard puncher
Points of Interest: Has 21 wins by
kayo or stoppage, having lost his first
professional fight on a stoppage.
Undefeated in his last 17 bouts, his
first fight with Lewis was stopped and
declared a no contest due to Andrew
Lewis getting cut. Born in Nicaragua
but now a Costa Rican citizen

28.07.01	Andrew Lewis NC 2 Los Angeles *(WBA Welterweight Title Challenge)*
30.03.02	Andrew Lewis W RSC 5 Reading *(WBA Welterweight Title Challenge)*
Career:	28 contests, won 23, drew 1, lost 3, no contests 1.

Floyd (Little Stone) Mayweather

Grand Rapids, USA. *Born* 24
February, 1977
WBC Lightweight Champion. Former
Undefeated WBC S. Featherweight
Champion

Major Amateur Honours: The national
Golden Gloves champion in 1993,
1994 and 1996, his first national title
was at 106lbs. Was the United States
champion in 1995 and won a bronze
medal in the 1996 Olympics. Winning
84 of 90 fights, he also competed in
the 1995 World Championships
Turned Pro: October 1996
Significant Results: Genaro Hernandez
W RTD 8, Angel Manfredy W RSC 2,
Carlos Rios W PTS 12, Justin Juuko
W RSC 9, Carlos Gerena W RTD 7,
Gregorio Vargas W PTS 12, Diego
Corrales W RSC 10, Carlos Hernandez
W PTS 12
Type/Style: Talented and flashy with
fast hands, he has great reflexes and a
hard punch
Points of Interest: 5'8" tall. His father,
Floyd Snr, was a good professional

and his uncle, Roger, was the WBA
super-featherweight and WBC light-
welterweight champion. Made eight
title defences at super-feather before
moving up to lightweight, his record
shows 20 wins inside the distance

10.11.01	Jesus Chavez W RTD 9 San Francisco *(WBC S. Featherweight Title Defence)*
20.04.02	Jose Luis Castillo W PTS 12 Las Vegas *(WBC Lightweight Title Challenge)*
Career:	28 contests, won 28.

Manuel (Mantecas) Medina

Tijuana, Mexico. *Born* 30 March,1971
Former IBF Featherweight Champion.
Former WBC Featherweight
Champion. Former Undefeated NABF
Featherweight Champion

Major Amateur Honours: None, had
only four fights
Turned Pro: October 1985
Significant Results: Troy Dorsey W
PTS 12, Tom Johnson W TD 9, Tom
Johnson L PTS 12 (twice), Alejandro
Gonzalez W PTS 12, Luisito Espinosa
L PTS 12, Prince Naseem Hamed L
RSC 11, Paul Ingle L PTS 12, Frankie
Toledo W PTS 10
Type/Style: Awkward and busy with a
good jab and limitless stamina, he can
give any fighter problems, but lacks
punching power
Points of Interest: 5'9" tall with a 71"
reach. Turned pro at the age of 14 and
lied about his age. A three-time IBF
champion, having first won the title in
1991, he was WBC champion for only
three months. Has taken part in 17
world title fights

16.11.01	Frankie Toledo W RSC 6 Las Vegas *(IBF Featherweight Title Challenge)*
27.04.02	Johnny Tapia L PTS 12 New York *(IBF Featherweight Title Defence)*
Career:	72 contests, won 60, lost 12.

Dariusz Michalczewski

Hamburg, Germany. *Born* Gdansk,
Poland, 5 May, 1968
WBO L. Heavyweight Champion.
Former Undefeated WBA and IBF L.
Heavyweight Champion. Former
Undefeated WBO Cruiserweight
Champion

Major Amateur Honours: Won a bronze
medal in the 1986 European Junior
Championships, a silver medal in the
1989 European Championships, and a
gold medal in the 1991 European
Championships
Turned Pro: September 1991
Significant Results: Leonzer Barber W
PTS 12, Nestor Giovannini W CO 10,
Graciano Rocchigiani W DIS 7 and W
RTD 9, Virgil Hill W PTS 12, Nicky
Piper W RTD 7, Mark Prince W RSC
8, Drake Thadzi W RSC 9, Montell
Griffin W RSC 4, Graciano
Rocchigiani W RTD 9
Type/Style: Is a hard-punching and
aggressive pressure fighter, who is
strong with a solid jab but lacks a
sound defence
Points of Interest: Won championships
for both Poland and Germany as an
amateur and had 36 wins inside the
distance. Won WBA and IBF titles by
beating Virgil Hill in June 1997, but
relinquished both in the same month
that he won them. Has made 21
defences of his WBO title

15.12.01	Richard Hall W RSC 11 Berlin *(WBO L. Heavyweight Title Defence)*
20.04.02	Joey De Grandis W CO 2 Gdansk *(WBO L. Heavyweight Title Defence)*
Career:	46 contests, won 46.

Byron (The Hammer from Bama) Mitchell

Jasper, USA. *Born* 31 October, 1973
WBA S. Middleweight Champion

Major Amateur Honours: Won a bronze
medal in the 1994 United States
Championships, a bronze medal in the
1995 PAL Championships and
competed in the 1996 Olympic trials.
Also won amateur international honours
Turned Pro: June 1996
Significant Results: Adam Garland W
RSC 1, Frank Liles W RSC 11, Bruno
Girard DREW 12 and L PTS 12,
Manuel Sciaca W PTS 12
Type/Style: Is a stiff, upright boxer
with only moderate skills, but is a hard
puncher, particularly with the left hook
Points of Interest: 6'0" tall. Having
studied sports medicine, he first won
the WBA title by beating Frank Liles
in June 1999, but lost it to Bruno
Girard in April 2000 before regaining

it following his win over Manuel Siaca in March 2001. Has 17 wins inside the distance

29.09.01	Manuel Siaca W RSC 12 Las Vegas
	(WBA S. Middleweight Title Defence)
Career: 26 contests, won 24, drew 1, lost 1.	

Fernando (Cochulito) Montiel

Los Mochis, Mexico. *Born* 1 March, 1979
WBO S. Flyweight Champion. Former Undefeated WBO Flyweight Champion

Major Amateur Honours: Claims 33 wins in 36 fights and was a local Golden Gloves champion
Turned Pro: December 1996
Significant Results: Paulino Villalobos DREW 10 and W PTS 10, Sergio Millan W PTS 10, Cruz Carbajal W RSC 4, Isidro Garcia W RSC 7, Zoltan Lunka W RSC 7, Juan Domingo Cordoba W CO 1
Type/Style: Is a clever and stylish boxer with a good uppercut
Points of Interest: 5'4" tall. The youngest of a fighting family, his father and four brothers were all boxers. Won his first 11 bouts inside the distance and has 18 wins by knockout or stoppage. Jointly trained by his father Manuel and a Japanese trainer based in Mexico. Won the WBO flyweight title by stopping Isidro Garcia in December 2000 and made three defences before moving up to win the super-flyweight title

08.09.01	Jose Lopez W PTS 12 Reno
	(WBO Flyweight Title Defence)
22.06.02	Pedro Alcazar W RSC 6 Las Vegas
	(WBO S. Flyweight Title Challenge)
Career: 25 contests, won 24, drew 1.	

Eric (Little Hands of Stone) Morel

Madison, USA. *Born* Puerto Rico, 1 October, 1975
WBA Flyweight Champion

Major Amateur Honours: His honours included a silver medal in the 1992 World Junior Championships for Puerto Rico, a silver medal in the 1993 National Golden Gloves, a gold medal in the 1994 National Golden Gloves, and a silver medal in the 1994 and 1996 United States Championships. In

between, he was the USA Junior champion in 1993. Competed in the 1995 Pan-American Games and the 1996 Olympic Games
Turned Pro: October 1996
Significant Results: Rodolfo Blanco W PTS 12, Ysaias Zamudio W RSC 7, Miguel Granados W PTS 12, Sornpichai Kratingdaeng W PTS 12, Gilberto Keb-Baas W PTS 12, Jose de Jesus W RTD 8
Type/Style: Has a string bean, slick upright southpaw style, with a sharp jab
Points of Interest: 5'3" tall. Started boxing as an amateur in 1983 in Puerto Rico and works part time at the Holiday Inn. With 17 wins inside the distance under his belt, he moved down from super-flyweight to win the WBA flyweight title by outpointing Sornpichai Kratingdaeng in August 2000 and has made three defences

| 11.01.02 | Alex Baba W PTS 10 Caguas |
| **Career:** 31 contests, won 31. | |

Jean-Marc Mormeck

Pointe-A-Pitre, Guadeloupe. *Born* 3 June, 1972
WBA Cruiserweight Champion. Former Undefeated French L. Heavyweight Champion

Major Amateur Honours: None, but claims 13 wins in 15 fights
Turned Pro: March 1995
Significant Results: Lee Manuel Osie L PTS 4, Alain Simon W PTS 10, Pascual Warusfel W PTS 10, Valery Vikhor W RSC 3
Type/Style: A strong, stocky, aggressive pressure fighter with a hard clubbing right hand, he is not a devastating puncher though
Points of Interest: Worked as Security Guard at McDonalds and only took up boxing after being injured at football when 15. Although he has had three operations on his right hand, he has still managed 18 wins by stoppage or kayo

04.08.01	Vince Durham W RSC 1 Marseilles
08.10.01	Frank Edmundsen W PTS 8 Paris
23.02.02	Virgil Hill W RTD 8 Marseilles
	(WBA Cruiserweight Title Challenge)
Career: 29 contests, won 27, lost 2.	

Eidy (El Terrible) Moya

Barcelona, Venezuela. *Born* 3, September, 1974
Former WBA Bantamweight Champion

Major Amateur Honours: Was selected for the 1992 Olympic team but was prevented from going by a dispute with the Federation
Turned Pro: July 1994
Significant Results: Dong-Young Kim W CO 1, Felix Machado L PTS 10, Edicson Torres W PTS 12, Diego Andrade W PTS 12, Saohin Sorthanikul W PTS 12
Type/Style: Although a two handed, aggressive fighter his defence is not too good and he is not a puncher
Points of Interest: A stablemate of multi world champion, Leo Gamez, he won the Interim WBA title when beating Saohin Srithai Condo in December 2000. Was farmed out to a gym in South Korea to get experience

14.10.01	Adan Vargas W CO 11 McAllen
	(Vacant WBA Bantamweight Title)
19.04.02	Johnny Bredahl L CO 9 Copenhagen
	(WBA Bantamweight Title Defence)
Career: 17 contests, won 15, lost 2.	

Alexander (Explosivo) Munoz

Miranda, Venezuela. *Born* 8 February, 1979
WBA S. Flyweight Champion

Major Amateur Honours: An outstanding amateur who claims 129 wins in 158 fights, he competed in the World Junior Championships in 1997 and won a silver medal in the Americas championships the same year
Turned Pro: March 1998
Significant Results: Ramon Games W RSC 10, Sornpichai Kratchingdaeng W RSC 5
Type/Style: Has an all out aggressive style with a punch to match and is deadly with the left hook
Points of Interest: Holds the record for the most consecutive inside-the-distance wins by a Venezuelan fighter, having won all of his 22 fights by kayo or stoppage, and had Shoji Kobayashi on the floor five times. Turned pro as a bantamweight

07.07.01	Pedro Medrano W CO 1 Turmero
12.11.01	John Ortiz W CO 3 Turmero
21.12.01	Hernan Berrio W CO 3 Turmero
09.03.02	Celes Kobayashi W RSC 8 Tokyo
	(WBA S.Flyweight Title Challenge)

Career: 22 contests, won 22.

Yutaka Niida

Kanagawa, Japan. *Born* 2 October, 1978
Former Undefeated WBA and Japanese M. Flyweight Champion

Major Amateur Honours: None known
Turned Pro: November 1996
Significant Results: Makoto Suzuki W RSC 9, Daisuke Iida DREW 10
Type/Style: Is aggressive with good speed and a big right-hand punch, but has a suspect chin
Points of Interest: Managed by Mitsunori Seki, who failed in five attempts to win versions of the world featherweight title, he climbed off the floor twice in the first round for his draw with Daisuke Iida. Surprisingly retired immediately after his victory over Chana Porpaoin

25.08.01	Chana Porpaoin W PTS 12 Yokohama
	(WBA M.Flyweight Title Challenge)

Career: 17 contests, won 14, drew 3.

Yober Ortega

La Guaira, Venezuela. *Born* 21 August, 1965
Former WBA S.Bantamweight Champion. Former Undefeated Venezuelan S.Bantamweight Champion

Major Amateur Honours: None known
Turned Pro: September 1990
Significant Results: Antonio Cermeno L PTS 12 (twice), Valdislav Antonov W PTS 12, Kozo Ishii W RSC 11
Type/Style: A southpaw, he is a sturdy fighter with a hard right hook and a good chin
Points of Interest: Already a grand-dad when he won the WBA title. Lost to Antonio Cermeno for both the WBA title and the WBA Interim title before winning the latter by stopping Kozo Ishii in November 2000 and then gaining full recognition following his victory over Jose Rojas. Has 22 wins inside the distance

17.11.01	Jose Rojas W CO 4 Las Vegas
	(Vacant WBA S. Bantamweight Title)
21.02.02	Yoddamrong Sithyodthong L PTS 12 Nakhon
	(WBA S. Bantamweight Title Defence)

Career: 37 contests, won 32, drew 1, lost 4.

Sven Ottke

Berlin, Germany. *Born* 3 June, 1967
IBF S. Middleweight Champion.
Former Undefeated German L. Heavyweight Champion

Major Amateur Honours: A quarter-finalist in the 1988 Olympic Games, he won a bronze medal in the 1989 World Championships, gold medals in the 1991 and 1996 European Championships, a bronze medal in the 1993 European Championships, and a silver medal in the 1994 World Cup. Competed in the 1992 and 1996 Olympics
Turned Pro: March 1997
Significant Results: Charles Brewer W PTS 12, Giovanni Nardiello W CO 3, Thomas Tate W TD 11, Glencoffe Johnson W PTS 12, Lloyd Bryan W PTS 12, Silvio Branco W PTS 12
Type/Style: Good tactically, he is a clever southpaw with an awkward style, although a slow starter and not a hard puncher
Points of Interest: 5'11" tall. Did not turn professional until he was 29, due to a long spell as a world-class amateur. Has only stopped or knocked out five opponents. Having beaten Chris Byrd, Jason Matthews, Juan Carlos Gomez and Michael Moorer while an amateur, Sven has now defended his IBF title 14 times since winning it from Charles Brewer in October 1998

01.09.01	James Butler W PTS 12 Magdeburg
	(IBF S. Middleweight Title Defence)
01.12.01	Tony Mundine W CO 10 Dortmund
	(IBF S. Middleweight Title Defence)
16.03.02	Rick Thornberry W PTS 12 Magdeburg
	(IBF S. Middleweight Title Defence)
01.06.02	Thomas Tate W PTS 12 Nuremburg
	(IBF S. Middleweight Title Defence)

Career: 27 contests, won 27.

Irene (Mambaco) Pacheco

San Juan de Uraba, Colombia. *Born* 26 March, 1971
IBF Flyweight Champion

Major Amateur Honours: None known
Turned Pro: November 1993
Significant Results: Luis Cox W RSC 9, Ferid Ben Jeddu W RSC 4, Pedro Pena W CO 11, Masibulele Makepula W PTS 12
Type/Style: A clever boxer who is mainly southpaw but can switch, he is also a good body puncher
Points of Interest: 5'6" tall. Never fighting for any other major title before becoming IBF champion, he has stopped or knocked out 14 of his last 15 opponents and has only been taken the distance six times. Fighting outside Colombia just three times, Irene has made four title defences since winning the vacant IBF title by beating Luis Cox in April 1999. Has suffered from a brittle right hand and has made only one defence in the past 19 months

09.11.01	Mike Trejo W RSC 4 San Antonio
	(IBF Flyweight Title Defence)

Career: 27 contests, won 27.

Manny Pacquiao

Bukidnon, Philippines. *Born* 12 December, 1976
IBF S. Bantamweight Champion.
Former WBC Flyweight Champion

Major Amateur Honours: None, but started at 13 and won 60 of 64 fights
Turned Pro: January 1995
Significant Results: Chockchai Chokwiwat W CO 5, Melvin Magramo W PTS 10, Chatchai Sasakul W CO 8, Gabriel Mira W CO 4, Medgoen 3K-Battery L CO 3, Reynante Jamili W RSC 2, Arnulfo Barotillo W CO 4, Lehlohonolo Ledwaba W RSC 6
Type/Style: A stocky, aggressive and hard-punching southpaw, his defence is not too hot
Points of Interest: Turned pro at the age of 18. Having won the WBC flyweight title by knocking out Chatchai Sasakul in December 1998, and making one defence before losing it to Medgoen Singsurat in September 1999, he promptly moved straight up to super-bantamweight. Won the IBF title in June 2001 with an upset stoppage victory over Lehlohonolo Ledwaba when he came in as a substitute at two weeks notice. Brother

207

Bobby was also a professional. With 25 wins inside the distance, he is trained by Freddie Roach

10.11.01	Agapito Sanchez T Draw 6 San Francisco *(IBF S. Bantamweight Title Defence. WBO S. Bantamweight Title Challenge)*
08.06.02	Jorge Julio W RSC 2 Memphis *(IBF S. Bantamweight Title Defence)*

Career: 37 contests, won 34, drew 1, lost 2.

Michele Piccirillo

Bari, Italy. *Born* 29 January, 1970
IBF Welterweight Champion. Former Undefeated Italian L. Welterweight Champion. Former Undefeated European Welterweight Champion

Major Amateur Honours: The Italian champion in 1987, 1988, 1989 and 1990, he won a silver medal in the 1990 European Junior Championships, a bronze medal in the 1991 European Championships and competed in the 1991 World Championships and 1992 Olympics
Turned Pro: December 1992
Significant Results: Soren Sondergaard L PTS 12, Geoff McCreesh W RSC 9, Alessandro Duran W PTS 12 and W RSC 5, Juan Martin Coggi W PTS 12, Frankie Randall W PTS 12
Type/Style: Is a neat, precise, thinking boxer with a dangerous right cross
Points of Interest: 5'10" tall. Beat Shane Mosley and Terron Millett but lost to Vernon Forrest as an amateur. Has 23 wins inside the distance. Unbeaten in his last 21 fights

29.09.01	Rafael Pineda W PTS 12 New York
13.04.02	Cory Spinks W PTS 12 Campione d'Italia *(Vacant IBF Welterweight Title)*

Career: 39 contests, won 37, lost 1, no contest 1.

Adonis (Caballo) Rivas

Leon, Nicaragua. *Born* 7 December,1972
WBO Flyweight Champion. Former WBO S.Flyweight Champion

Major Amateur Honours: Won gold and silver medals in the Central American Championships and competed in the 1991 and 1993 Pan-American Games
Turned Pro: October 1995
Significant Results: Sergio Gonzalez L

RSC 4, Antonio Gonzalez DREW 8 and W PTS 10, Diego Morales W PTS 12, Joel Luna Zarate W PTS 12, Pedro Alcazar L PTS 12
Type/Style: : A methodical, aggressive type, he is also a strong infighter with good stamina
Points of Interest: The seventh of ten children, he used to sell Tortillas on the streets. Won the WBO super-flyweight title by beating Diego Morales in November 1999 and made three defences before losing it to Pedro Alcazar in June 2001. Was the Interim flyweight champion until Fernando Montiel won the super-flyweight title in June and that gave Rivas full recognition. Has ten wins by stoppage or knockout

15.12.01	Javier Medina W RTD 5 Managua
04.05.02	Jair Jimenez W PTS 12 Managua *(Vacant WBO Interim Flyweight Title)*

Career: 22 contests, won 18, drew 1, lost 2, no contest 1.

John (The Quite Man) Ruiz

Chelsea, USA. *Born* 4 January, 1972
WBA Heavyweight Champion

Major Amateur Honours: Competed in the World Championships in 1991 and won a gold medal in the 1991 Olympic Festival, before losing in the 1992 Olympic trials
Turned Pro: August 1992
Significant Results: Sergei Kobozev L PTS 10, Julius Francis W CO 4, Danell Nicholson L PTS 12, Boris Powell W PTS 10, David Tua L RSC 1, Tony Tucker W RSC 11, Jerry Ballard W RSC 4, Evander Holyfield L PTS 12 and W PTS 12
Type/Style: Strong with an upright style, he has a solid jab
Points of Interest: 6'2" tall. Named after John Kennedy, he became the first boxer of Puerto Rican origins to win the heavyweight title when he outpointed Holyfield in March 2001. Voted Puerto Rican Fighter of the Year in 2002, although plagued by hand problems, John has 27 wins inside the distance

15.12.01	Evander Holyfield DREW 12 Mashantucket *(WBA Heavyweight Title Defence)*

Career: 42 contests, won 37, drew 1, lost 4.

Veeraphol (Death Mask) Sahaprom

Nakhon Ratchaseema, Thailand. *Born* 16 November, 1968
WBC Bantamweight Champion. Former WBA Bantamweight Champion

Major Amateur Honours: None
Turned Pro: December 1994
Significant Results: Daourang Chuwatana W PTS 12, Nana Yaw Konadu L RSC 2, Rolando Pascua W PTS 10, Joichiro Tatsuyoshi W CO 6, Adan Vargas W PTS 12, Toshiaki Nishioka W PTS 12, Oscar Arciniega W RSC 5
Type/Style: Is a flat-footed, classy stalker with a high, tight guard, who is a big right-hand puncher
Points of Interest: 5'4" tall. Came out of kick boxing into professional boxing, winning the WBC International title in his first fight and the WBA title in his fourth. His real name is Veeraphol Sumranklang, but he now fights as Veeraphol Sahaprom. Holding the WBA title for only four months, he has made nine defences of his WBC title. Getting his nickname from his stony expression when fighting, he has won 26 bouts inside the distance. It is thought that his fight with Julio Coronel was the first world title fight held on a bridge

12.07.01	Den Bermudez W CO 4 Nontaburi
01.09.01	Toshiaki Nishioka DREW 12 Yokohama *(WBC Bantamweight Title Defence)*
19.10.01	Ronny Rogas W RSC 7 Bangkok
11.01.02	Sergio Perez W PTS 12 Thanyaburi *(WBC Bantamweight Title Defence)*
30.03.02	Noel Sungahid W CO 3 Ratanathbet
01.05.02	Julio Coronel W PTS 12 Nonthaburi *(WBC Bantamweight Title Defence)*

Career: 40 contests, won 38, drew 1, lost 1.

Agapito (Cyclone) Sanchez

La Victoria, Dominican Republic. *Born* 14 February, 1970
WBO S. Bantamweight Champion. Former Undefeated Dominican S. Flyweight Champion

Major Amateur Honours: : None known but claims 68 wins in 76 fights
Turned Pro: November 1989
Significant Results: Max Gomez W PTS 12, Marco Antonio Barrera L PTS 12, Javier Marquez L PTS 12, Cesar Soto L RSC 2, Freddie Norwood L

PTS 12, Javier Jauregui W PTS 10, Gustavo Espadas L PTS 10, Oscar Larios W RSC 5, Gerard Martinez W RSC 11, Juan Carlos Ramirez W PTS 10, Jorge Monsalvo W RSC 7
Type/Style: Stocky, muscular and tough, with a good jab, but body punches have a habit of straying low
Points of Interest: Followed an elder brother into boxing. Failed in a previous shot at the WBO title when being outpointed by Marco Antonio Barrera in 1995, before halting Jorge Monsalvo for the vacant title in June 2001. Has 20 wins inside the distance

10.11.01	Manny Pacquiao T DRAW 6 San Francisco *(IBF S. Bantamweight Title Challenge. WBO S. Bantamweight Title Defence)*
Career: 42 contests, won 33, drew 2, lost 7.	

Daniel Santos

San Juan, Puerto Rico. *Born* 10 October, 1975
WBO L. Middleweight Champion. Former Undefeated WBO Welterweight Champion

Major Amateur Honours: Won a bronze medal in the 1992 World Junior Championships, a silver medal in the 1995 Pan-American Games and a bronze medal in the 1996 Olympic Games. Competed in the 1993 and 1995 World Championships and in the 1994 Goodwill Games
Turned Pro: September 1996
Significant Results: Luis Verdugo T DRAW 1, William Ruiz W RSC 3, Ray Lovato W RSC 2, Kofi Jantuah L RSC 5, Ahmed Katajev L PTS 12 and W CO 5, Giovanni Parisi W RSC 4, Neil Sinclair W CO 2
Type/Style: A fast, clever and flashy southpaw, who is a heavy left-handed puncher, he has a questionable chin and is suspect on stamina
Points of Interest: 6'0" tall. Having lost to David Reid in the Pan-American Games, he was unbeaten in his first 21 pro fights prior to losing a disputed decision to Ahmed Katajev in his first challenge for the WBO welterweight title, before the WBO ordered a rematch, which he won in May 2000. With 20 wins inside the distance, he has now made three defences of his welterweight title

21.07.01	Antonio Margarito NC 1 Bayamon *(WBO Welterweight Title Defence)*
16.03.02	Luis Campas W RSC 11 Las Vegas *(Vacant WBO L.Middleweight Title)*
Career: 29 contests, won 25, drew 1, lost 2, no contest 1.	

Osamu Sato

Hyogo, Japan. *Born* 16 December, 1976
WBA S. Bantamweight Champion. Former Undefeated OPBF S. Bantamweight Champion

Major Amateur Honours: None known, but is said to have won 15 out of 21 fights
Turned Pro: September 1995
Significant Results: Gentile Ichihashi L CO 2, Nikolai Eremeev W PTS 10, Max Baro W RSC 5, Yongin Chi W PTS 12
Type/Style: A busy, aggressive combination puncher who mixes to the body and head effectively, although his defence is not too sound
Points of Interest: Had to climb off the floor twice against Willie Jorrin and was also floored by Yongin Chin. Unbeaten in his last 24 fights, he has 15 wins by stoppage or knockout

17.09.01	Wichit Chuwatana W RSC 11 Tokyo *(OPBF S. Bantamweight Title Defence)*
05.02.02	Willie Jorrin DREW 12 Tokyo *(WBC S. Bantamweight Title Challenge)*
18.05.02	Yoddamrong Sithyodthong W CO 8 Saitama *(WBA S. Bantamweight Title Challenge)*
Career: 29 contests, won 26, drew 2, lost 1.	

Harry (Exterminator) Simon

Walvis Bay, Namibia. *Born* 21 October, 1972
WBO Middleweight Champion. Former Undefeated WBO L. Middleweight Champion

Major Amateur Honours: Competed in the 1992 Olympic Games but lost in the first series. An African champion and three times South African champion, he claims just two losses in 273 fights
Turned Pro: January 1994
Significant Results: Del Bryan W RSC 6, Ronald Wright W PTS 12, Kevin Lueshing W RSC 3, Rodney Jones W PTS 12, Wayne Alexander W RSC 5
Type/Style: Strong and powerful, and a charismatic boxer with a sound defence, he has a good chin and plenty of stamina
Points of Interest: Real name Harry Saayman. Having started boxing in 1980 before working in a diamond mine, Harry is the first ever world boxing champion from Namibia. Trained by Brian Mitchell, the former WBA champion, he has 17 wins inside the distance, but made only four WBO title defences in three years. Won the WBO middleweight title by beating Hacine Cherifi, only to have the bout later declared as being for the Interim title

21.07.01	Hacine Cherifi W PTS 12 Bayamon *(Vacant Interim WBO Middleweight Title)*
06.04.02	Armand Krajnc W PTS 12 Copenhagen *(WBO Middleweight Title Challenge)*
Career: 23 contests, won 23.	

Harry Simon   Les Clark

Yoddamrong Sithyodthong

Banrai Uthai, Thailand. *Born* 16 March, 1977
Former WBA S. Bantamweight Champion

Major Amateur Honours: None

Turned Pro: January 1996
Significant Results: Singsaen Porpaoin W PTS 10, Allan Moore W RSC 9, Jesse Maca DREW 12, Ratanchai Sorvorapin W PTS 10
Type/Style: Is a stylish, quick boxer and a good body puncher, but defence is not too good
Points of Interest: Real name is Damrong Kongsuk, but he has adopted the name of his gym. Has 12 wins inside the distance

09.08.01	Dodong Sales W PTS 10 Nontaburi
11.09.02	Alex Escaner W PTS 10 Nontaburi
21.02.02	Yober Ortega W PTS 12 Nakhon *(WBA S. Bantamweight Title Challenge)*
18.05.02	Osamu Sato L CO 8 Saitama *(WBA S. Bantamweight Title Defence)*

Career: 29 contests, won 27, drew 1, lost 1.

Paul (The New Pittsburgh Kid) Spadafora

Pittsburgh, USA. *Born* 5 September, 1975
IBF Lightweight Champion

Major Amateur Honours: Claiming 65 wins in 70 fights, he was twice a State champion and competed in two United States Championships, but failed to win a medal
Turned Pro: October 1995
Significant Results: Troy Fletcher W PTS 8, Sam Girard W PTS 10, Israel Cardona W PTS 12, Renato Cornett W RSC 11, Victoriano Sosa W PTS 12, Billy Irwin W PTS 12, Joel Perez W PS 12
Type/Style: A clever southpaw, he has fast hands, an excellent jab and good footwork, but is not a puncher
Points of Interest: 5'9" tall. A distant cousin to former world light-heavyweight champion, Joey Maxim, his grandfather and brother both being boxers, Paul has had a stormy life with his father dying of a drug overdose and him being shot in the leg by a policeman. Is a natural right hander who fights left handed only because he copied his brother. Having stopped or knocked out 15 opponents, Paul has made six defences since winning the vacant IBF title with the win over Israel Cardona in August 1999

14.08.01	Chuck Tschorniawsky W PTS 10 Chester
09.03.02	Angel Manfredy W PTS 12 Pittsburg *(IBF Lightweight Title Defence)*

Career: 35 contests, won 35.

Johnny (Tap Tap) Tapia

Albuquerque, USA. *Born* 13 February, 1967
IBF Featherweight Champion. Former Undefeated WBO Bantamweight Champion. Former WBA Bantamweight Champion. Former Undefeated WBO and IBF S. Flyweight Champion

Major Amateur Honours: National Golden Gloves Champion in 1983 and 1985
Turned Pro: March 1988
Significant Results: Henry Martinez W RSC 11, Arthur Johnson W PTS 12,

Johnny Tapia   Les Clark

Ricardo Vargas T DRAW 8, Danny Romero W PTS 12, Nana Yaw Konadu W PTS 12, Paulie Ayala L PTS 12, Jorge Julio W PTS 12, Paulie Ayala L PTS 12, Cesar Soto W CO 3
Type/Style: Cool and composed, he is a slick boxer and a hard puncher
Points of Interest: 5'5" tall. Having to overcome numerous battles with drugs and alcohol, he went out of the sport for two years after 1985 National Golden Gloves win. Made 13 title defences at super-flyweight, but lost the WBA bantamweight title in his first defence. With 28 wins by kayo or stoppage, he has taken part in 19 world title fights

19.01.02	Eduardo Alvarez W CO 1 London
27.04.02	Manuela Medina W PTS 12 New York
	(IBF Featherweight Title Challenge)
Career: 56 contests, won 51, drew 2, lost 3.	

Masamori Tokuyama

North Korea. *Born* Tokyo, Japan, 17 September, 1974
WBC S. Flyweight Champion

Major Amateur Honours: None, his record being just 12 wins in 17 fights
Turned Pro: September 1994
Significant Results: Manny Melchor L PTS 10, Nolito Cabato DREW 10 and L TD 7, Hiroki Ioka W RSC 5, Pone Saengmorakot W PTS 12, Injoo Cho W PTS 12 and W CO 5, Akihiko Nago W PTS 12
Type/Style: Tall and upright with a sharp jab and fast hands, he has no punch however
Points of Interest: 5'8" tall. With a real name of Chang-Soo Hong, and the first North Korean to win a world title, his title defence against In-Joo Cho was the first time that a North Korean and a South Korean have fought each other for a world title in Korea. Has seven wins inside the distance and has defended his title four times. His father was a karate teacher

24.09.01	Gerry Penalosa W PTS 12 Yokohama
	(WBC S. Flyweight Title Defence)
23.03.02	Kazuhiro Ryuko W RSC 9 Yokohama
	(WBC S. Flyweight Title Defence)
Career: 29 contests, won 26, drew 1, lost 2.	

Kostya Tszyu

Australia. *Born* Serov, Russia, 19 September, 1969
WBC, WBA and IBF L.Welterweight Champion.

Major Amateur Honours: Was the European Junior champion in 1986, won a World Junior Championship silver medal in 1987, the European Games' gold medal in 1989 and 1991, a bronze medal in the 1989 World Championships and was the gold medal winner in the 1991 World Championships
Turned Pro: March 1992
Significant Results: Jake Rodriguez W RSC 6, Roger Mayweather W PTS 12, Hugo Pineda W RSC 11, Jan Bergman W CO 6, Vince Phillips L RSC 10, Rafael Ruelas W RSC 8, Diosbelys Hurtado W RSC 5, Miguel Gonzalez W RSC 10, Julio Cesar Chavez W RSC 6, Sharmba Mitchell W RTD 7, Oktay Urkal W PTS 12
Type/Style: An aggressive two-fisted fighter, he is a dangerous puncher with both hands
Points of Interest: 5'7" tall. Born in Russia but now based in Australia, Kostya (real christian name is Konstantin) has 23 wins inside the distance and made six defences of the IBF title before being stopped by Vince Phillips in May 1997. Won the vacant WBC title by halting Miguel Gonzalez in August 1999, the WBA title by beating Sharmba Mitchell in February 2001 and became a triple champion with his win over Zab Judah. Wears his hair in a ponytail

03.11.01	Zab Judah W RSC 2 Las Vegas
	(WBC and WBA L. Welterweight Title Defences. IBF L.Welterweight Title Challenge)
18.05.02	Ben Tackie W PTS 12 Las Vegas
	(WBC, WBA and IBF L. Welterweight Title Defences)
Career: 31 contests, won 29, drew 1, lost 1.	

Fernando (Ferocious) Vargas

Oxnard, USA. *Born* 7 December, 1977
WBA L. Middleweight Champion. Former IBF L. Middleweight Champion

Major Amateur Honours: Won a gold medal in the 1994 US Championships,

competed in the 1994 World Junior Championships and won a bronze medal in the 1995 Pan-American Games, before competing in the 1996 Olympic Games
Turned Pro: March 1997
Significant Results: Romallis Ellis W RSC 1, Anthony Stephens W CO 5, Yori Boy Campas W RTD 7, Raul Marquez W RSC 5, Ronnie Wright W PTS 12, Ike Quartey W PTS 12, Ross Thompson W RSC 4, Felix Trinidad L RSC 12
Type/Style: Is very focused and mentally strong with fast hands and a hard punch. Also has good stamina
Points of Interest: 5'10" tall. Started boxing in 1990 and won his first 16 fights inside the distance. Won the IBF title in December 1998 by beating Yori Boy Campas and made six defences before losing it to Felix Trinidad in December 2000. Has stopped or knocked out 20 opponents

22.09.01	Jose Flores W CO 7 Las Vegas
	(Vacant WBA L. Middleweight Title)
Career: 23 contests, won 22, lost 1.	

Fernando Vargas

Pongsaklek Wonjongkam

Nakhornatchaseema, Thailand. *Born* 11 August, 1977
WBC Flyweight Champion

Major Amateur Honours: None
Turned Pro: December 1994
Significant Results: Randy Mangubat W CO 3, Mzukisi Sikali W RSC 1, Juanito Rubillar W PTS 10, Malcolm Tunacao W RSC 1
Type/Style: A tough, aggressive pressure fighter, he is a southpaw with a wicked right hook
Points of Interest: 5'1" tall. His last loss was in December 1995 and he is unbeaten in his last 38 bouts. Has also boxed under the names of Nakornthong Parkview and Sithkanongsak. With 25 wins by stoppage or kayo, he won the WBC title by halting Malcolm Tunacao in March 2001 and has made four defences

15.07.01	Hayato Asai W RSC 5 Nagoya *(WBC Flyweight Title Defence)*
26.10.01	Alex Baba W TD 8 Hat Yai *(WBC Flyweight Title Defence)*
06.12.01	Luis Lazarte W RSC 2 Pattaya *(WBC Flyweight Title Defence)*
19.04.02	Daisuke Naito W CO 1 Khonkaen *(WBC Flyweight Title Defence)*

Career: 45 contests, won 43, lost 2.

Ronald (Winkie) Wright

St Petersburg, USA. *Born* 26 November, 1971
IBF L. Middleweight Champion. Former WBO L. Middleweight Champion

Major Amateur Honours: Won a gold medal at the Olympic Festival after being a 1990 quarter-finalist in the 1989 Golden Gloves. Was an amateur international at the age of 18
Turned Pro: October 1990
Significant Results: Julio Cesar Vasquez L PTS 12, Tony Marshall W PTS 12, Bronco McKart W PTS 12 (twice), Ensley Bingham W PTS 12, Steve Foster W RSC 6, Adrian Dodson W RSC 6, Harry Simon L PTS 12, Fernando Vargas L PTS 12, Keith Mulling W PTS 12
Type/Style: Is a slick and clever southpaw
Points of Interest: 5'10" tall. Floored six times by Julio Cesar Vasquez in an unsuccessful challenge for the WBA title in 1994, he beat Bronco McKart for the WBO title May 1996, but lost it to Harry Simon in August 1998. Lost to Fernando Vargas in a challenge for the IBF title in December 1999, before coming back to land the same title when defeating Robert Frazier. Has 25 wins by stoppage or knockout

12.10.01	Robert Frazier W PTS 12 Indio *(Vacant IBF L.Middleweight Title)*
02.02.02	Jason Papillion W RSC 5 Miami *(IBF L. Middleweight Title Defence)*

Career: 46 contests, won 43, lost 3.

Ronald Wright   Les Clark

World Title Bouts During 2001-2002

by Bob Yalen

All of last season's title bouts for the IBF, WBA, WBC and WBO are shown in date order within their weight division and give the boxers' respective weights, along with the scorecard if going to a decision. There is also a short summary of every bout that involved a British contestant, and British officials, where applicable, are listed. Yet again there were no WORLD TITLE FIGHTS as such – even if you allow for Kostya Tszyu (L. Welter), Bernard Hopkins (Middle) and Roy Jones (L. Heavy), who hold three of the four major titles – just a proliferation of champions recognised by the above four commissions and spread over 17 weight divisions. Below the premier league, come other commissions such as the WBU, IBO, IBC and WBF, etc, etc, which would devalue the world championships even further if one recognised their champions as being the best in the world. Right now, the WBA have decided to continue recognising their champions who move on to claim other commissions' titles as super champions – despite vacating the title and creating a new champion, who, for our purposes, will be classified as an interim champion – which if taken up in general could eventually lead to the best man at his weight being recognised universally as a world champion if the fights can be made.

M. Flyweight

IBF
29 September 2001   Roberto Levya 7.6½ (Mexico) T DRAW 3 Miguel Barrera 7.6½ (Columbia), Ensenada, Mexico.

WBA
25 August 2001   Chana Porpaoin 7.7 (Thailand) L PTS 12 Yutaka Niida 7.5½ (Japan), Yokohama, Japan. Scorecards: 113-116, 113-116, 115-116. On winning the title, Niida promptly retired.

29 January 2002   Keitaro Hoshino 7.7 (Japan) W PTS 12 Joma Gamboa 7.6¾ (Philippines), Yokohama, Japan. Scorecards: 118-110, 118-112, 117-112.

WBC
11 November 2001   Jose Antonio Aguirre 7.7 (Mexico) W RSC 3 Yasuo Tokimitsu 7.6½ (Japan), Okayama, Japan.

WBO
Kermin Guardia (Colombia) made no defences during 2001-2002. On 29 June 2002, in Palma de Mallorca, Spain, Jorge Mata (Spain) stopped Reynaldo Frutos (Panama) in the ninth round to win the interim title.

L. Flyweight

IBF
29 September 2001   Ricardo Lopez 7.9 (Mexico) W CO 8 Zolani Petelo 7.9¾ (South Africa), NYC, New York, USA.

WBA
19 January 2002   Rosendo Alvarez 7.10 (Nicaragua) W RSC 12 Pichitnoi Chor Siriwat 7.10 (Thailand), Miami, Florida, USA.

WBC
23 February 2002   Yo-Sam Choi 7.10 (South Korea) W RSC 10 Shingo Yamaguchi 7.8 (Japan), Chiba, Japan. Earlier, on 20 Ocober 2001, Jorge Arce (Mexico) outpointed Juanito Rubillar (Philippines) over 12 rounds in Tijuana, Mexico to claim the interim title.

WBO
29 September 2001   Nelson Dieppa 7.10 (Puerto Rico) W PTS 12 Fahlan Sakkririn 7.9 (Thailand), NYC, New York, USA. Scorecards: 119-109, 118-110, 118-110.

Flyweight

IBF
9 November 2001   Irene Pacheco 7.13 1/2 (Colombia) W RSC 4 Mike Trejo 7.13½ (USA), San Antonio, Texas, USA.

WBA
Eric Morel (USA) made no defences during 2001-2002.

WBC
15 July 2001   Pongsaklek Wonjongkam 8.0 (Thailand) W RSC 5 Hayato Asai 8.0 (Japan), Nagoya, Japan.

26 October 2001   Pongsaklek Wonjongkam 8.0 (Thailand) W TD 8 Alex Baba 8.0 (Ghana), Hat Yai, Thailand. Referee: Richie Davies. Scorecards: 79-73, 79-73, 79-71.

6 December 2001   Pongsaklek Wonjongkam 8.0 (Thailand) W RSC 2 Luis Lazarte 110½ (Argentina), Pattya, Thailand.

19 April 2002   Pongsaklek Wonjongkam 8.0 (Thailand) W CO 1 Daisuke Naito 8.0 (Japan), Khonkaen, Thailand.

WBO
8 September 2001   Fernando Montiel 8.0 (Mexico) W PTS 12 Jose Lopez 7.13½ (Puerto Rico), Reno, Nevada, USA. Scorecards: 116-110, 116-111, 118-110. On 4 May 2002, Adonis Rivas (Nicaragua) outpointed Jair Jimenez (Colombia) over 12 rounds in Managua, Nicaragua to win the interim title. Rivas was named as champion after Montiel moved up a division to win the WBO super-flyweight crown on 22 June 2002.

S. Flyweight

IBF
30 March 2002   Felix Machado 8.2½ (Venezuela) W TD 6 Martin Castillo 8.3 (Mexico), Reading, Pennsylvania, USA. Scorecards: 58-56, 58-56, 58-56.

WBA
1 September 2001   Celes Kobayashi 8.3 (Japan) W PTS 12 Jesus Rojas 8.2½ (Venezuela), Yokohama, Japan. Scorecards: 116-114, 115-113, 113-116.

9 March 2002   Celes Kobayashi 8.3 (Japan) L RSC 8 Alexander Munoz 8.3 (Venezuela), Tokyo, Japan.

WBC

24 September 2001   Masamori Tokuyama 8.3 W PTS 12 Gerry Penalosa 8.3 (Philippines), Yokohama, Japan. Referee: Larry O'Connell. Scorecards: John Keane 116-113, 115-113, 115-113.

23 March 2002   Masamori Tokuyama 8.3 (Japan) W RSC 9 Kazuhiro Ryuko 8.3 (Japan), Yokohama, Japan.

WBO

5 October 2001   Pedro Alcazar 8.3 (Panama) W PTS 12 Jorge Otero 8.3 (Colombia), Panama City, Panama. Scorecards: 116-112, 116-113, 118-110.

22 June 2002   Pedro Alcazar 8.3 (Panama) L RSC 6 Fernando Montiel 8.3 (Mexico), Las Vegas, Nevada, USA.

Bantamweight
IBF

15 December 2001   Tim Austin 8.6 (USA) W PTS 12 Ratanchai Voraphin 8.6 (Thailand), Mashantuckett, Connecticut, USA. Scorecards: 115-112, 118-109, 117-110.

WBA

14 October 2001   Eidy Moya 8.5 (Venezuela) W CO 11 Adan Vargas 8.6 (Mexico), McAllen, Texas, USA. Billed for the vacant title after Paulie Ayala (USA) forfeited in July 2001 for agreeing to meet Clarence Adams for the IBO championship, which he won on 4 August.

19 April 2002   Eidy Moya 8.6 (Venezuela) L CO 9 Johnny Bredahl 8.5½ (Denmark), Copenhagen, Denmark.

WBC

1 September 2001   Veeraphol Sahaprom 8.6 (Thailand) DREW 12 Toshiaki Nishioka 8.6 (Japan), Yokohama, Japan. Scorecards: 113-115, 116-113, 114-114.

11 January 2002   Veeraphol Sahaprom 8.6 (Thailand) W PTS 12 Sergio Perez 8.5 (Mexico), Thanyaburi, Thailand. Scorecards: 120-108, 118-110, 118-111.

1 May 2002   Veeraphol Sahaprom (Thailand) W PTS 12 Julio Coronel (Colombia), Nonthaburi, Thailand. Scorecards: 117-110, 117-109, 118-109.

WBO

16 March 2002   Mauricio Martinez 8.5½ (Panama) L RSC 9 Cruz Carbajal 8.5¼ (Mexico), Vera Cruz, Mexico..

S. Bantamweight
IBF

10 November 2001   Manny Pacquiao 8.8¼ (Philippines) T DRAW 6 Agapito Sanchez 8.8½ (Dominican Republic), San Francisco, California, USA. Scorecards: 58-54, 55-57, 56-56.

8 June 2002   Manny Pacquiao 8.8½ (Philippines) W RSC 2 Jorge Julio 8.10 (Colombia), Memphis, Tennessee, USA.

WBA

17 November 2001   Yober Ortega 8.8½ (Venezuela) W CO 4 Jose Rojas 8.10 (Venezuela), Las Vegas, Nevada, USA. Billed for the vacant title after Clarence Adams (USA) had been stripped in July for agreeing to take on Paulie Ayala to decide the vacant IBO title on 4 August.

21 February 2002   Yober Ortega 8.10 (Venezuela) L PTS 12 Yoddamrong Sithyodthong 8.10 (Thailand), Nakhon, Thailand. Scorecards: 112-117, 111-118, 112-116.

18 May 2002   Yoddamrong Sithyodthong 8.10 (Thailand) L CO 8 Osamu Sato 8.9¼ (Japan), Saitama, Japan.

WBC

5 February 2002   Willie Jorrin 8.10 (USA) DREW 12 Osamu Sato 8.10 (Japan), Tokyo, Japan. Referee: Terry O'Connor. Scorecards: 114-114, 113-113, 112-114. With Jorrin indisposed, Oscar Larrios (Mexico) stopped Israel Vazquez (Mexico) in the 12th rounds of a contest to decide the interim title in Sacramento, California, USA on 16 May 2002.

WBO

10 November 2001   Agapito Sanchez 8.8½ (Dominican Republic) T DRAW 6 Manny Pacquiao 8.8¼ (Philippines), San Francisco, California, USA. Scorecards: 54-58, 57-55, 56-56.

Featherweight
IBF

16 November 2001   Frankie Toledo 9.0 (USA) L RSC 6 Manuel Medina 9.0 (Mexico), Las Vegas, Nevada, USA.

27 April 2002   Manuel Medina 9.0 (Mexico) L PTS 12 Johnny Tapia 8.13 3/4 (USA), NYC, New York, USA. 113-115, 113-115, 114-114.

WBA

Derrick Gainer (USA) made no defences during 2001-2002.

WBC

28 July 2001   Erik Morales 9.0 (Mexico) W PTS 12 In-Jin Chi 8.13½ (South Korea), Los Angeles, California, USA. Scorecards: 116-111, 117-110, 116-112.

22 June 2002   Erik Morales 9.0 (Mexico) L PTS 12 Marco Antonio Barrera 9.0 (Mexico), Las Vegas, Nevada, USA. Scorecards: 112-116, 113-115, 113-115. Barrera relinquished title on winning.

WBO

11 August 2001   Julio Pablo Chacon 9.0 (Argentina) W RSC 5 Eduardo Barrios 9.0 (Colombia), Mendoza, Argentina.

19 January 2002   Julio Pablo Chacon 8.13½ (Argentina) W PTS 12 Victor Polo 8.13 (Colombia), York Hall, Bethnal Green, London, England. Scorecards: Dave Parris 115-112, Roy Francis 114-113, Paul Thomas 113-114. Following Chacon pulling out at short notice when due to defend against Scott Harrison (Scotland), the WBO gave its blessing to the replacement match between Harrison and Victor Santiago (Puerto Rico) in Renfrew, Scotland on 8 June 2002 going ahead for their interim title. For the record, Santiago was stopped in the sixth round.

S. Featherweight
IBF

29 September 2001   Steve Forbes 9.4 (USA) W PTS 12

John Brown 9.4 (USA), Miami, Florida, USA. Scorecards: 117-111, 115-113, 115-113.

WBA

29 September 2001 Joel Casamayor 9.4 (Cuba) W RSC 8 Joe Morales 9.3^1/$_2$ (USA), Miami, Florida, USA.

12 January 2002 Joel Casamayor 9.3^1/$_2$ (Cuba) L PTS 12 Acelino Freitas 9.3^1/$_2$ (Brazil), Las Vegas, Nevada, USA. Scorecards: 112-114, 112-114, 112-114. With Freitas considered by the WBA to be their super champion, Yodsanan Nanthachkai (Thailand) outpointed Lakva Sim (Mongolia) over 12 rounds in Nakornratchasima, Thailand on 13 April, to claim the secondary title.

WBC

10 November 2001 Floyd Mayweather 9.3^1/$_2$ (USA) W RTD 9 Jesus Chavez 9.3^1/$_2$ (Mexico), San Francisco, California, USA. Mayweather relinquished the title on winning the WBC lightweight championship on 20 April.

WBO

12 January 2002 Acelino Freitas 9.3^1/$_2$ (Brazil) W PTS 12 Joel Casamayor 9.3^1/$_2$ (Cuba), Las Vegas, Nevada, USA. Scorecards: 114-112, 114-112, 114-112.

Lightweight

IBF

9 March 2002 Paul Spadafora 9.9 (USA) W PTS 12 Angel Manfredy 9.8^1/$_2$ (USA), Pittsburgh, Pennsylvania, USA. Scorecards: 115-113, 115-113, 115-113.

WBA

1 July 2001 Takanori Hatakeyama 9.9 (Japan) L PTS 12 Julien Lorcy 9.8^1/$_4$ (France), Tokyo, Japan. Scorecards: 110-118, 111-117, 112-117.

8 October 2001 Julien Lorcy 9.8^1/$_2$ (France) L PTS 12 Raul Balbi 9.8^1/$_2$ (Argentina), Paris, France. Scorecards: 112-115, 110-117, 114-114.

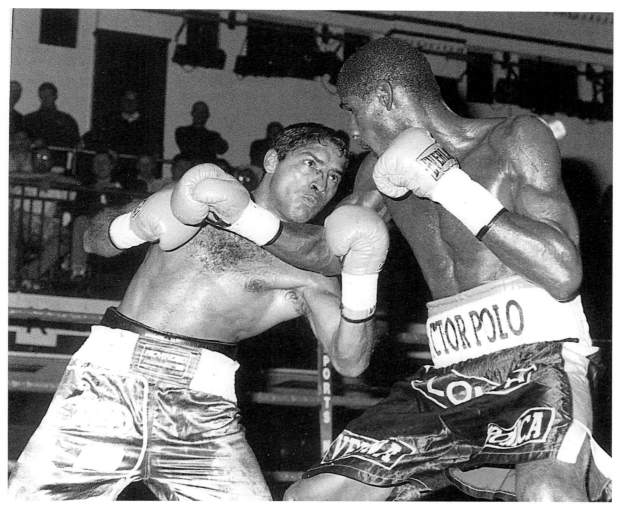

Julio Pablo Chacon (left) successfully defended his WBO featherweight title against Victor Polo in London last January

Les Clark

5 January 2002   Raul Balbi 9.8³/₄ (Argentina) L PTS 12 Leonardo Dorin 9.8 (Romania), San Antonio, Texas, USA. Scorecards: 115-112, 113-114, 112-115.

31 May 2002   Leonardo Dorin 9.8³/₄ (Romania) W PTS 12 Raul Balbi 9.8 (Argentina), Bucharest, Romania. Referee: John Coyle. Scorecards: 118-111, 118-110, 117-112.

WBC

20 April 2002   Jose Luis Castillo 9.8¹/₂ (Mexico) L PTS 12 Floyd Mayweather 9.8 (USA), Las Vegas, Nevada, USA. Scorecards: John Keane 111-115, 111-115, 111-116.

WBO

5 January 2002   Artur Grigorian 9.9 (Uzbekistan) W RSC 8 Ray Martinez 9.9 (USA), Magdeburg, Germany. Referee: Paul Thomas.

L. Welterweight

IBF

3 November 2001   Zab Judah 9.13¹/₂ (USA) L RSC 2 Kostya Tszyu 10.0 (Russia), Las Vegas, Nevada, USA. Judge: John Keane.

18 May 2002   Kostya Tszyu 10.0 (Russia) W PTS 12 Ben Tackie 9.13¹/₂ (Ghana), Las Vegas, Nevada, USA. Scorecards: 120-108, 120-108, 119-109.

WBA

3 November 2001   Kostya Tszyu 10.0 (Russia) W RSC 2 Zab Judah 9.13¹/₂ (USA), Las Vegas, Nevada, USA. Judge: John Keane. As in other divisions, with Tszyu considered to be a super champion by the WBA, Randall Bailey (USA) won the vacant secondary title when stopping Demitrio Ceballos (Panama) in the third round in Reading, Pennsylvania, USA on 2 February 2002. Later, on 11 May 2002, in San Juan, Puerto Rico, Bailey lost the so-called title to Diobelys Hurtado (Cuba) when he was knocked out in the seventh round.

18 May 2002   Kostya Tszyu 10.0 (Russia) W PTS 12 Ben Tackie 9.13¹/₂ (Ghana), Las Vegas, Nevada, USA. Scorecards: 120-108, 120-108, 119-109.

WBC

3 November 2001   Kostya Tszyu 10.0 (Russia) W RSC 2 Zab Judah 9.13¹/₂ (USA), Las Vegas, Nevada, USA. Judge: John Keane.

18 May 2002   Kostya Tszyu 10.0 (Russia) W PTS 12 Ben Tackie 9.13¹/₂ (Ghana), Las Vegas, Nevada, USA. Scorecards: 120-108, 120-108, 119-109.

WBO

19 January 2002   DeMarcus Corley 10.0 (USA) W PTS 12 Ener Julio 10.0 (Colombia), Miami, Florida, USA. Scorecards: 119-105, 118-107, 117-107.

Welterweight

IBF

13 April 2002   Michele Piccirillo 10.7 (Italy) W PTS 12 Cory Spinks 10.6¹/₂ (USA), Campione d'Italia, Italy. Scorecards: 116-111, 115-112, 115-112. Billed for the vacant title after Vernon Forrest was stripped of the championship in December 2001 when challenging Shane Mosley for the WBC crown.

WBA

28 July 2001   Andrew Lewis 10.7 (Guyana) NC 2 Ricardo Mayorga 10.6³/₄ (Costa Rica), Los Angeles, California, USA.

30 March 2002   Andrew Lewis 10.7 (Guyana) L RSC 5 Ricardo Mayorga 10.5¹/₂ (Costa Rica), Reading, Pennsylvania, USA.

WBC

21 July 2001   Shane Mosley 10.7 (USA) W RSC 3 Adrian Stone 10.7 (England), Las Vegas, Nevada, USA. Judge: Mark Green. Up until the finishing blows, the fight had been fairly even, with Stone occasionally forcing the issue. However, once Mosley had found the target with several heavy blows zeroing in, a left-right to the jaw felled the challenger and the fight was stopped at 2.01 of the third, the referee dispensing with the count.

26 January 2002   Shane Mosley 10.6 (USA) L PTS 12 Vernon Forrest 10.7 (USA), NYC, New York, USA. Scorecards: 108-118, 108-117, 110-115.

WBO

21 July 2001   Daniel Santos 10.7 (Puerto Rico) NC 1 Antonio Margarito 10.6 (Mexico), Bayamon, Puerto Rico. Santos relinquished in November 2001 in order to step up and challenge for the WBO light-middleweight crown once held by Harry Simon.

16 March 2002   Antonio Margarito 10.6¹/₂ (Mexico) W RSC 10 Antonio Diaz 10.7 (USA), Las Vegas, Nevada, USA.

L. Middleweight

IBF

12 October 2001   Ronald Wright 10.13³/₄ (USA) W PTS 12 Robert Frazier 10.13 (USA), Indio, California, USA. Scorecards: 120-107, 119-108, 119-108. After Felix Trinidad relinquished the title in May 2001, this one was for the vacant championship.

2 February 2002   Ronald Wright 10.13¹/₄ (USA) W RSC 5 Jason Papillion 10.9¹/₂ (USA), Miami, Florida, USA.

WBA

22 September 2001   Fernando Vargas 10.13¹/₂ (USA) W CO 7 Jose Flores 10.13¹/₂ (Mexico), Las Vegas, Nevada, USA. Billed for the title vacated by Felix Trinidad in May 2001.

WBC

Oscar de la Hoya (USA) made no defences during 2001-2002.

WBO

16 March 2002   Daniel Santos 11.0 (Puerto Rico) W RSC 11 Luis Campas 10.13³/₄ (Mexico), Las Vegas, Nevada, USA. With Harry Simon winning the WBO middleweight title on 21 July 2001, it was expected that he would give up the light-middleweight belt immediately, but, when his win over Hassine Cherifi was later declared to have been for the interim title, it wasn't until November that the championship was officially vacated.

Middleweight

IBF

29 September 2001   Bernard Hopkins 11.3 (USA) W RSC 12 Felix Trinidad 11.4$^{1}/_{2}$ (Puerto Rico), NYC, New York, USA.

2 February 2002   Bernard Hopkins 10.4$^{3}/_{4}$ (USA) W RTD 10 Carl Daniels 11.6 (USA), Reading, Pennsylvania, USA.

WBA

29 September 2001   Felix Trinidad 11.4$^{1}/_{2}$ (Puerto Rico) L RSC 12 Bernard Hopkins 11.3 (USA), NYC, New York, USA. With the WBA recognising Hopkins as a super champion, William Joppy (USA) took over the secondary title when outpointing Britain's Howard Eastman over 12 rounds in Las Vegas, Nevada, USA on 17 November 2001.

2 February 2002   Bernard Hopkins 10.4$^{3}/_{4}$ (USA) W RTD 10 Carl Daniels 11.6 (USA), Reading, Pennsylvania, USA.

WBC

29 September 2001   Bernard Hopkins 11.3 (USA) W RSC 12 Felix Trinidad 11.4$^{1}/_{2}$ (Puerto Rico), NYC, New York, USA.

2 February 2002   Bernard Hopkins 10.4$^{3}/_{4}$ (USA) W RTD 10 Carl Daniels 11.6 (USA), Reading, Pennsylvania, USA.

WBO

3 November 2001   Armand Krajnc 11.6 (Slovenia) W PTS 12 Paolo Roberto 11.6 (Sweden), Lubeck, Germany. Scorecards: 117-111, 118-110, 118-111. Earlier, on 21 July 2001 , in Bayamon, Puerto Rico, Harry Simon (Namibia) outscored Hassine Cherifi (France) over 12 rounds in a fight billed to decide the vacant title. However, with Krajnc refusing to vacate, the WBA were forced to accept that Simon v Cherifi was merely an interim title fight.

6 April 2002   Armand Krajnc 11.5$^{1}/_{2}$ (Slovenia) L PTS 12 Harry Simon 11.4$^{3}/_{4}$ (Namibia), Copenhagen, Denmark. Scorecards: 112-116, 112-116, 113-116.

S. Middleweight

IBF

1 September 2001   Sven Ottke 11.13 (Germany) W PTS 12 James Butler 11.13$^{1}/_{2}$ (USA), Magdeburg, Germany. Scorecards: 118-109, 118-109, 119-108.

1 December 2001   Sven Ottke 11.13 (Germany) W CO 10 Anthony Mundine 11.10$^{1}/_{2}$ (Australia), Dortmund, Germany.

16 March 2002   Sven Ottke 12.0 (Germany) W PTS 12 Rick Thornberry 12.0 (Australia), Magdeburg, Germany. Scorecards: 120-108, 120-108, 120-108.

1 June 2002   Sven Ottke 11.13$^{1}/_{4}$ (Germany) W PTS 12 Thomas Tate 11.13 (USA), Nuremburg, Germany. Scorecards: 119-108, 118-109, 116-111.

WBA

29 September 2001   Byron Mitchell 12.0 (USA) W PTS 12 Manuel Siaca 11.13$^{1}/_{4}$ (Puerto Rico), NYC, New York, USA. Scorecards: 114-112, 114-112, 112-115.

WBC

10 July 2001   Eric Lucas 11.13$^{3}/_{4}$ (Canada) W RSC 7 Glenn Catley 11.13$^{1}/_{4}$ (England), Montreal, Canada. Billed for the vacant title after Dave Hilton (Canada) was jailed for sex crimes in April 2001, Lucas exacted revenge for a previous loss to Catley when he knocked him out at 1.15 of the seventh round. Earlier, the Englishman boxed well, but in the sixth he was floored for a couple of counts before the finishing blow, a right to the jaw, did the damage. Although Catley was out to the world, the referee dispensed with the count to allow immediate aid to the stricken fighter.

30 November 2001   Eric Lucas 11.13$^{3}/_{4}$ (Canada) W RSC 8 Dingaan Thobela 12.0 (South Africa), Montreal, Canada.

1 March 2002   Eric Lucas 11.13 (Canada) W PTS 12 Vinny Pazienza 12.0 (USA), Ledyard, Connecticut, USA. 119-110, 116-110, 117-112.

WBO

13 October 2001   Joe Calzaghe 11.13$^{1}/_{2}$ (Wales) W RSC 4 Will McIntyre 11.13$^{1}/_{2}$ (USA), Copenhagen, Denmark. Judge: Dave Parris. Unfortunately, the American was not an opponent who was going to test Calzaghe, but one who really didn't have a place in the same ring as the champion. Picking his punches throughout, Calzaghe was never in danger of losing to a man who didn't have the tools and when the referee finally called off in 45 seconds in to the fourth with McIntyre the finish was welcomed by all present.

20 April 2002   Joe Calzaghe 11.13$^{3}/_{4}$ (Wales) W PTS 12 Charles Brewer 11.13$^{3}/_{4}$ (USA), The International Arena, Cardiff, Wales. Scorecards: Roy Francis 117-112, 119-109, 118-111. This was a fight where Calzaghe was forced to show his true mettle as Brewer continuously stalked him, always looking to land dangerous punches. In this, his tenth title defence, despite the Welshman being unable to put the challenger on the floor, he was a good winner and again looked the pick of all of the super-middleweights around.

L. Heavyweight

IBF

28 July 2001   Roy Jones 12.5 (USA) W PTS 12 Julio Gonzalez 12.6$^{1}/_{4}$ (USA), Los Angeles, California, USA. Scorecards: 119-106, 118-107, 119-106.

2 February 2002   Roy Jones 12.4 (USA) W CO 7 Glen Kelly 12.6$^{1}/_{2}$ (Australia), Miami, Florida, USA.

WBA

28 July 2001   Roy Jones 12.5 (USA) W PTS 12 Julio Gonzalez 12.6$^{1}/_{4}$ (USA), Los Angeles, California, USA. Scorecards: 119-106, 118-107, 119-106. With the WBA now recognising Roy Jones as their super champion, Bruno Girard (France) and Lou del Valle (USA), met to decide who should be the secondary champion. However, with the fight ending in a split draw in Marseilles, France on 4 August 2001, the so-called title remained vacant. John Coyle refereed. Later, on 22 December 2001, in Orleans, France, Girard finally landed the title when stopping Robert Koon (USA) in the 11th round.

2 February 2002 Roy Jones 12.4 (USA) W CO 7 Glen Kelly 12.6$^{1}/_{2}$ (Australia), Miami, Florida, USA. On 23 May 2002, in Levallois, France, Girard defended the secondary title when outpointing Thomas Hansvoll (Norway) over 12 rounds.

WBC

28 July 2001 Roy Jones 12.5 (USA) W PTS 12 Julio Gonzalez 12.6$^{1}/_{4}$ (USA), Los Angeles, California, USA. Scorecards: 119-106, 118-107, 119-106.

2 February 2002 Roy Jones 12.4 (USA) W CO 7 Glen Kelly 12.6$^{1}/_{2}$ (Australia), Miami, Florida, USA.

WBO

15 December 2001 Dariusz Michalczewski 12.6$^{1}/_{2}$ (Poland) W RSC 11 Richard Hall 12.5$^{1}/_{2}$ (Jamaica), Berlin, Germany.

20 April 2002 Dariusz Michalczewski 12.7 (Poland) W CO 2 Joey DeGrandis 12.7 (USA), Gdansk, Poland.

Cruiserweight

IBF

8 September 2001 Vassily Jirov 13.8 (Kazakhstan) W RSC 8 Julian Letterlough 13.4$^{1}/_{2}$ (USA), Reno, Nevada, USA.

1 February 2002 Vassily Jirov 13.7 (Kazakhstan) W PTS 12 Jorge Castro 13.5 (Argentina), Phoenix, Arizona, USA. Scorecards: 119-110, 119-110, 119-110.

WBA

23 February 2002 Virgil Hill 13.7$^{3}/_{4}$ (USA) L RTD 8 Jean-Marc Mormeck 13.3 (France), Marseilles, France.

WBC

3 November 2001 Juan Carlos Gomez 13.8 (Cuba) W RSC 6 Pietro Aurino 13.8 (Italy), Lubeck, Germany. Referee: Mark Green. Gomez relinquished in early March 2002 in order to campaign in the heavyweight division.

WBO

21 July 2001 Johnny Nelson 13.7$^{3}/_{4}$ (England) W PTS 12 Marcelo Dominguez 13.5$^{1}/_{2}$ (Argentina), Ponds Forge Leisure Centre, Sheffield, England. Scorecards: Paul Thomas 117-110, 117-110, 119-108. Nelson was far too good for the hard man from Buenos Aires, who was a former WBC champion, but was unable to win the fight early. Ultimately, after deciding that he wasn't going to easily knock his challenger over, the champion stuck to his boxing to land the points. Although Dominguez occasionally looked as though he was ready to go, he proved his toughness by his powers of recovery.

6 April 2002 Johnny Nelson 13.7$^{1}/_{2}$ (England) W CO 8 Ezra Sellers 13.7 (USA), Copenhagen, Denmark. With Nelson unable to get going over the first six or seven rounds, having been floored when losing his balance in the fourth round and being hurt in the seventh, he finally put it together in the eighth with a right hander that landed on the dangerous challenger's eye and sent him down for the full count. While there were those who thought that the IBO champion could beat the count, with his eye swelling ominously and obviously still dazed he was counted out in the act of rising.

Heavyweight

IBF

17 November 2001 Hasim Rahman 16.12 (USA) L CO 4 Lennox Lewis 17.8$^{1}/_{2}$ (England), Las Vegas, Nevada, USA. Having blasted his man to defeat in South Africa to win the title, Rahman was expected to do more of the same, but with Lewis well prepared this time he was unable to exact any kind of superiority and was completely outboxed while the fight lasted. The master of cutting down the distance and getting his punches off, Lewis was content to outbox Hassim (or Has-Been as Lewis contually referred to him as) and when the opportunity presented itself he took it. Having landed a solid right hand in the third that had a marked effect on the champion, it was merely a matter of time before Lewis caught up with Rahman and sure enough, early in the fourth, after the left had done its job another long right landed flush on the jaw and Rahman crashed to the floor to be counted out at 1.29 of the round.

8 June 2002 Lennox Lewis 17.11$^{1}/_{4}$ (England) W CO 8 Mike Tyson 16.10$^{1}/_{2}$ (USA), Memphis, Tennessee, USA. This was the one everybody had been waiting for; the defining fight in Lewis' career and the one that would tell us whether Tyson was a spent force. Once the fight was underway, it was clear that all the questions were going to be answered as Tyson, unable to respond to Lewis' left jab and with his right eye cut in the third, was beginning to be gradually taken apart. Pushed over in the fourth, the former 'great' was becoming desperate as he was, by now, being completely outboxed with no idea of how to deal with it. Nearly taken out in the seventh, with the bell coming to his rescue, a left uppercut smashed all remaining resistance out of him in the eighth and he took a count of eight before a tremendous right hand from Lewis landed right on the jaw smashing him to the canvas where he was counted out at the 2.25 mark.

WBA

15 December 2001 John Ruiz 16.8 (USA) DREW 12 Evander Holyfield 15.9 (USA), Mashantucket, Connecticut, USA. Scorecards: 115-113, 112-116, 114-114.

WBC

17 November 2001 Hasim Rahman 16.12 (USA) L CO 4 Lennox Lewis 17.8$^{1}/_{2}$ (England), Las Vegas, Nevada, USA.

8 June 2002 Lenox Lewis 17.11$^{1}/_{4}$ (England) W CO 8 Mike Tyson 16.10$^{1}/_{2}$ (USA), Memphis, Tennessee, USA.

WBO

4 August 2001 Vladimir Klitschko 17.3 (Ukraine) W RSC 6 Charles Shufford 16.10 (USA), Las Vegas, Nevada, USA.

16 March 2002 Vladimir Klitschko 17.4 (Ukraine) W RSC 8 Frans Botha 17.3 (South Africa), Stuttgart, Germany.

29 June 2002 Vladimir Klitschko 17.5 (Ukraine) W RSC 6 Ray Mercer 16.4 (USA), Atlantic City, New Jersey, USA.

World Champions Since Gloves, 1889-2002

Since I began to carry out extensive research into world championship boxing from the very beginnings of gloved action, I discovered much that needed to be amended regarding the historical listings as we know them, especially prior to the 1920s. Although yet to finalise my researches, despite making considerable changes, the listings are the most comprehensive ever published. Bearing all that in mind, and using a wide range of American newspapers, the aim has been to discover just who had claims, valid or otherwise. Studying the records of all the recognised champions, supplied by Professor Luckett Davis and his team, fights against all opposition have been analysed to produce the ultimate data. Because there were no boxing commissions as such in America prior to the 1920s, the yardstick used to determine valid claims were victories over the leading fighters of the day and recognition given within the newspapers. Only where that criteria has been met have I adjusted previous information.

Championship Status Code:

AU = Austria; AUST = Australia; CALIF = California; CAN = Canada; CLE = Cleveland Boxing Commission; EBU = European Boxing Union; FL = Florida; FR = France; GB = Great Britain; GEO = Georgia; H = Hawaii; IBF = International Boxing Federation; IBU = International Boxing Union; ILL = Illinois; LOUIS = Louisiana; MARY = Maryland; MASS = Massachusetts; MICH = Michigan; NBA = National Boxing Association; NC = North Carolina; NY = New York; PEN = Pennsylvania; SA = South Africa; TBC = Territorial Boxing Commission; USA = United States; WBA = World Boxing Association; WBC = World Boxing Council; WBO = World Boxing Organisation.

Champions in **bold** are accorded universal recognition.

*Undefeated champions (Only relates to universally recognised champions prior to 1962 and thereafter WBA/WBC/IBF/WBO champions. Does not include men who forfeited titles).

Title Holder	Birthplace	Tenure	Status
M. Flyweight (105 lbs)			
Kyung-Yung Lee*	S Korea	1987	IBF
Hiroki Ioka	Japan	1987-1988	WBC
Silvio Gamez*	Venezuela	1988-1989	WBA
Samuth Sithnaruepol	Thailand	1988-1989	IBF
Napa Kiatwanchai	Thailand	1988-1989	WBC
Bong-Jun Kim	S Korea	1989-1991	WBA
Nico Thomas	Indonesia	1989	IBF
Rafael Torres	Dom Republic	1989-1992	WBO
Eric Chavez	Philippines	1989-1990	IBF
Jum-Hwan Choi	S Korea	1989-1990	WBC
Hideyuki Ohashi	Japan	1990	WBC
Fahlan Lukmingkwan	Thailand	1990-1992	IBF
Ricardo Lopez*	Mexico	1990-1997	WBC
Hi-Yon Choi	S Korea	1991-1992	WBA
Manny Melchor	Philippines	1992	IBF
Hideyuki Ohashi	Japan	1992-1993	WBA
Ratanapol Sowvoraphin	Thailand	1992-1996	IBF
Chana Porpaoin	Thailand	1993-1995	WBA
Paul Weir*	Scotland	1993-1994	WBO
Alex Sanchez	Puerto Rico	1993-1997	WBO
Rosendo Alvarez	Nicaragua	1995-1998	WBA
Ratanapol Sowvoraphin	Thailand	1996-1997	IBF
Ricardo Lopez*	Mexico	1997-1998	WBC/WBO
Zolani Petelo*	S Africa	1997-2000	IBF
Ricardo Lopez*	Mexico	1998	WBC
Eric Jamili	Philippines	1998	WBO
Kermin Guardia	Colombia	1998-	WBO
Ricardo Lopez*	Mexico	1998-1999	WBA/WBC
Wandee Chor Chareon	Thailand	1999-2000	WBC
Noel Arambulet	Venezuela	1999-2000	WBA
Jose Antonio Aguirre	Mexico	2000-	WBC
Jomo Gamboa	Philippines	2000	WBA
Keitaro Hoshino	Japan	2000-2001	WBA
Chana Porpaoin	Thailand	2001	WBA
Roberto Levya	Mexico	2001-	IBF
Yutaka Niida*	Japan	2001	WBA
Keitaro Hoshino	Japan	2002-	WBA
L. Flyweight (108 lbs)			
Franco Udella	Italy	1975	WBC
Jaime Rios	Panama	1975-1976	WBA
Luis Estaba	Venezuela	1975-1978	WBC
Juan Guzman	Dom Republic	1976	WBA
Yoko Gushiken	Japan	1976-1981	WBA
Freddie Castillo	Mexico	1978	WBC
Sor Vorasingh	Thailand	1978	WBC
Sun-Jun Kim	S Korea	1978-1980	WBC
Shigeo Nakajima	Japan	1980	WBC
Hilario Zapata	Panama	1980-1982	WBC
Pedro Flores	Mexico	1981	WBA
Hwan-Jin Kim	S Korea	1981	WBA
Katsuo Tokashiki	Japan	1981-1983	WBA
Amado Ursua	Mexico	1982	WBC
Tadashi Tomori	Japan	1982	WBC
Hilario Zapata	Panama	1982-1983	WBC
Jung-Koo Chang*	S Korea	1983-1988	WBC
Lupe Madera	Mexico	1983-1984	WBA
Dodie Penalosa	Philippines	1983-1986	IBF
Francisco Quiroz	Dom Republic	1984-1985	WBA
Joey Olivo	USA	1985	WBA
Myung-Woo Yuh	S Korea	1985-1991	WBA
Jum-Hwan Choi	S Korea	1986-1988	IBF
Tacy Macalos	Philippines	1988-1989	IBF
German Torres	Mexico	1988-1989	WBC
Yul-Woo Lee	S Korea	1989	WBC
Muangchai Kitikasem	Thailand	1989-1990	IBF
Jose de Jesus	Puerto Rico	1989-1992	WBO
Humberto Gonzalez	Mexico	1989-1990	WBC
Michael Carbajal*	USA	1990-1993	IBF
Rolando Pascua	Philippines	1990-1991	WBC
Melchor Cob Castro	Mexico	1991	WBC
Humberto Gonzalez	Mexico	1991-1993	WBC
Hiroki Ioka	Japan	1991-1992	WBA
Josue Camacho	Puerto Rico	1992-1994	WBO
Myung-Woo Yuh*	S Korea	1992-1993	WBA
Michael Carbajal	USA	1993-1994	IBF/WBC
Silvio Gamez	Venezuela	1993-1995	WBA
Humberto Gonzalez	Mexico	1994-1995	WBC/IBF
Michael Carbajal*	USA	1994	WBO
Paul Weir	Scotland	1994-1995	WBO
Hi-Yong Choi	S Korea	1995-1996	WBA
Saman Sorjaturong*	Thailand	1995	WBC/IBF
Jacob Matlala*	South Africa	1995-1997	WBO
Saman Sorjaturong	Thailand	1995-1999	WBC
Carlos Murillo	Panama	1996	WBA

Title Holder	Birthplace	Tenure	Status	Title Holder	Birthplace	Tenure	Status
Michael Carbajal	USA	1996-1997	IBF	Betulio Gonzalez	Venezuela	1971-1972	WBC
Keiji Yamaguchi	Japan	1996	WBA	Venice Borkorsor*	Thailand	1972-1973	WBC
Pichitnoi Chor Siriwat	Thailand	1996-2000	WBA	Chartchai Chionoi	Thailand	1973-1974	WBA
Mauricio Pastrana	Colombia	1997-1998	IBF	Betulio Gonzalez	Venezuela	1973-1974	WBC
Jesus Chong	Mexico	1997	WBO	Shoji Oguma	Japan	1974-1975	WBC
Melchor Cob Castro	Mexico	1997-1998	WBO	Susumu Hanagata	Japan	1974-1975	WBA
Mauricio Pastrana	Colombia	1997-1998	IBF	Miguel Canto	Mexico	1975-1979	WBC
Juan Domingo Cordoba	Argentina	1998	WBO	Erbito Salavarria	Philippines	1975-1976	WBA
Jorge Arce	Mexico	1998-1999	WBO	Alfonso Lopez	Panama	1976	WBA
Will Grigsby	USA	1998-1999	IBF	Guty Espadas	Mexico	1976-1978	WBA
Michael Carbajal*	USA	1999-2000	WBO	Betulio Gonzalez	Venezuela	1978-1979	WBA
Ricardo Lopez	Mexico	1999-	IBF	Chan-Hee Park	S Korea	1979-1980	WBC
Yo-Sam Choi	S Korea	1999-	WBC	Luis Ibarra	Panama	1979-1980	WBA
Masibuleke Makepula*	S Africa	2000	WBO	Tae-Shik Kim	S Korea	1980	WBA
Will Grigsby	USA	2000	WBO	Shoji Oguma	Japan	1980-1981	WBC
Beibis Mendoza	Colombia	2000-2001	WBA	Peter Mathebula	S Africa	1980-1981	WBA
Rosendo Alvarez	Nicaragua	2001-	WBA	Santos Laciar	Argentina	1981	WBA
Nelson Dieppa	Puerto Rico	2001-	WBO	Antonio Avelar	Mexico	1981-1982	WBC
				Luis Ibarra	Panama	1981	WBA
				Juan Herrera	Mexico	1981-1982	WBA
Flyweight (112 lbs)				Prudencio Cardona	Colombia	1982	WBC
Johnny Coulon	Canada	1910	USA	Santos Laciar*	Argentina	1982-1985	WBA
Sid Smith	England	1911-1913	GB	Freddie Castillo	Mexico	1982	WBC
Sid Smith	England	1913	GB/IBU	Eleonicio Mercedes	Dom Republic	1982-1983	WBC
Bill Ladbury	England	1913-1914	GB/IBU	Charlie Magri	Tunisia	1983	WBC
Percy Jones	Wales	1914	GB/IBU	Frank Cedeno	Philippines	1983-1984	WBC
Tancy Lee	Scotland	1915	GB/IBU	Soon-Chun Kwon	S Korea	1983-1985	IBF
Joe Symonds	England	1915-1916	GB/IBU	Koji Kobayashi	Japan	1984	WBC
Jimmy Wilde	Wales	1916	GB/IBU	Gabriel Bernal	Mexico	1984	WBC
Jimmy Wilde	Wales	1916-1923		Sot Chitalada	Thailand	1984-1988	WBC
Pancho Villa*	Philippines	1923-1925		Hilario Zapata	Panama	1985-1987	WBA
Fidel la Barba	USA	1925-1927	NBA/CALIF	Chong-Kwan Chung	S Korea	1985-1986	IBF
Fidel la Barba*	USA	1927		Bi-Won Chung	S Korea	1986	IBF
Johnny McCoy	USA	1927-1928	CALIF	Hi-Sup Shin	S Korea	1986-1987	IBF
Izzy Schwartz	USA	1927-1929	NY	Fidel Bassa	Colombia	1987-1989	WBA
Frenchy Belanger	Canada	1927-1928	NBA	Dodie Penalosa	Philippines	1987	IBF
Newsboy Brown	Russia	1928	CALIF	Chang-Ho Choi	S Korea	1987-1988	IBF
Frankie Genaro	USA	1928-1929	NBA	Rolando Bohol	Philippines	1988	IBF
Emile Pladner	France	1929	NBA/IBU	Yong-Kang Kim	S Korea	1988-1989	WBC
Frankie Genaro	USA	1929-1931	NBA/IBU	Duke McKenzie	England	1988-1989	IBF
Midget Wolgast	USA	1930-1935	NY	Elvis Alvarez*	Colombia	1989	WBO
Young Perez	Tunisia	1931-1932	NBA/IBU	Sot Chitalada	Thailand	1989-1991	WBC
Jackie Brown	England	1932-1935	NBA/IBU	Dave McAuley	Ireland	1989-1992	IBF
Jackie Brown	England	1935	GB/NBA	Jesus Rojas	Venezuela	1989-1900	WBA
Benny Lynch	Scotland	1935-1937	GB/NBA	Yukihito Tamakuma	Japan	1990-1991	WBA
Small Montana	Philippines	1935-1937	NY/CALIF	Isidro Perez	Mexico	1990-1992	WBO
Valentin Angelmann	France	1936-1938	IBU	Yul-Woo Lee	S Korea	1990	WBA
Peter Kane*	England	1938-1939	NBA/NY/GB/IBU	Muangchai Kitikasem	Thailand	1991-1992	WBC
Little Dado	Philippines	1938-1939	CALIF	Elvis Alvarez	Colombia	1991	WBA
Little Dado	Philippines	1939-1943	NBA/CALIF	Yong-Kang Kim	S Korea	1991-1992	WBA
Jackie Paterson	Scotland	1943-1947		Pat Clinton	Scotland	1992-1993	WBO
Jackie Paterson	Scotland	1947-1948	GB/NY	Rodolfo Blanco	Colombia	1992	IBF
Rinty Monaghan	Ireland	1947-1948	NBA	Yuri Arbachakov	Russia	1992-1997	WBC
Rinty Monaghan*	Ireland	1948-1950		Aquiles Guzman	Venezuela	1992	WBA
Terry Allen	England	1950		Pichit Sitbangprachan*	Thailand	1992-1994	IBF
Dado Marino	Hawaii	1950-1952		David Griman	Venezuela	1992-1994	WBA
Yoshio Shirai	Japan	1952-1954		Jacob Matlala	S Africa	1993-1995	WBO
Pascual Perez	Argentina	1954-1960		Saen Sorploenchit	Thailand	1994-1996	WBA
Pone Kingpetch	Thailand	1960-1962		Alberto Jimenez	Mexico	1995-1996	WBO
Fighting Harada	Japan	1962-1963		Francisco Tejedor	Colombia	1995	IBF
Pone Kingpetch	Thailand	1963		Danny Romero*	USA	1995-1996	IBF
Hiroyuki Ebihara	Japan	1963-1964		Mark Johnson*	USA	1996-1998	IBF
Pone Kingpetch	Thailand	1964-1965		Jose Bonilla	Venezuela	1996-1998	WBA
Salvatore Burruni	Italy	1965		Carlos Salazar	Argentina	1996-1998	WBO
Salvatore Burruni	Italy	1965-1966	WBC	Chatchai Sasakul	Thailand	1997-1998	WBC
Horacio Accavallo*	Argentina	1966-1968	WBA	Hugo Soto	Argentina	1998-1999	WBA
Walter McGowan	Scotland	1966	WBC	Ruben Sanchez	Mexico	1998-1999	WBO
Chartchai Chionoi	Thailand	1966-1969	WBC	Manny Pacquiao	Philippines	1998-1999	WBC
Efren Torres	Mexico	1969-1970	WBC	Silvio Gamez	Venezuela	1999	WBA
Hiroyuki Ebihara	Japan	1969	WBA	Irene Pacheco	Colombia	1999-	IBF
Bernabe Villacampo	Philippines	1969-1970	WBA	Jose Antonio Lopez	Spain	1999	WBO
Chartchai Chionoi	Thailand	1970	WBC	Sornpichai Pisanurachan	Thailand	1999-2000	WBA
Berkrerk Chartvanchai	Thailand	1970	WBA	Medgoen Singsurat	Thailand	1999-2000	WBC
Masao Ohba*	Japan	1970-1973	WBA	Isidro Garcia	Mexico	1999-2000	WBO
Erbito Salavarria	Philippines	1970-1971	WBC				

Title Holder	Birthplace	Tenure	Status
Malcolm Tunacao	Philippines	2000-2001	WBC
Eric Morel	USA	2000-	WBA
Fernando Montiel*	Mexico	2000-2002	WBO
Pongsaklek Wonjongkam	Thailand	2001-	WBC
Adonis Rivas	Nicaragua	2002-	WBO

S. Flyweight (115 lbs)

Title Holder	Birthplace	Tenure	Status
Rafael Orono	Venezuela	1980-1981	WBC
Chul-Ho Kim	S Korea	1981-1982	WBC
Gustavo Ballas	Argentina	1981	WBA
Rafael Pedroza	Panama	1981-1982	WBA
Jiro Watanabe	Japan	1982-1984	WBA
Rafael Orono	Venezuela	1982-1983	WBC
Payao Poontarat	Thailand	1983-1984	WBC
Joo-Do Chun	S Korea	1983-1985	IBF
Jiro Watanabe	Japan	1984-1986	WBC
Kaosai Galaxy*	Thailand	1984-1992	WBA
Elly Pical	Indonesia	1985-1986	IBF
Cesar Polanco	Dom Republic	1986	IBF
Gilberto Roman	Mexico	1986-1987	WBC
Elly Pical	Indonesia	1986-1987	IBF
Santos Laciar	Argentina	1987	WBC
Tae-Il Chang	S Korea	1987	IBF
Jesus Rojas	Colombia	1987-1988	WBC
Elly Pical	Indonesia	1987-1989	IBF
Gilberto Roman	Mexico	1988-1989	WBC
Jose Ruiz	Puerto Rico	1989-1992	WBO
Juan Polo Perez	Colombia	1989-1990	IBF
Nana Yaw Konadu	Ghana	1989-1990	WBC
Sung-Il Moon	S Korea	1990-1993	WBC
Robert Quiroga	USA	1990-1993	IBF
Jose Quirino	Mexico	1992	WBO
Katsuya Onizuka	Japan	1992-1994	WBA
Johnny Bredahl	Denmark	1992-1994	WBO
Julio Cesar Borboa	Mexico	1993-1994	IBF
Jose Luis Bueno	Mexico	1993-1994	WBC
Hiroshi Kawashima	Japan	1994-1997	WBC
Harold Grey	Colombia	1994-1995	IBF
Hyung-Chul Lee	S Korea	1994-1995	WBA
Johnny Tapia*	USA	1994-1997	WBO
Alimi Goitia	Venezuela	1995-1996	WBA
Carlos Salazar	Argentina	1995-1996	IBF
Harold Grey	Colombia	1996	IBF
Yokthai Sith-Oar	Thailand	1996-1997	WBA
Danny Romero	USA	1996-1997	IBF
Gerry Penalosa	Philippines	1997-1998	WBC
Johnny Tapia*	USA	1997-1998	IBF/WBO
Satoshi Iida	Japan	1997-1998	WBA
In-Joo Cho	S Korea	1998-2000	WBC
Victor Godoi	Argentina	1998-1999	WBO
Jesus Rojas	Venezuela	1998-1999	WBA
Mark Johnson	USA	1999-2000	IBF
Diego Morales	Mexico	1999	WBO
Hideki Todaka	Japan	1999-2000	WBA
Adonis Rivas	Nicaragua	1999-2001	WBO
Felix Machado	Venezuela	2000-	IBF
Masamori Tokuyama	Japan	2000-	WBC
Silvio Gamez	Venezuela	2000-2001	WBA
Celes Kobayashi	Japan	2001-2002	WBA
Pedro Alcazar	Panama	2001-2002	WBO
Alexander Munoz	Venezuela	2002-	WBA
Fernando Montiel	Mexico	2002-	WBO

Bantamweight (118 lbs)

Title Holder	Birthplace	Tenure	Status
Tommy Kelly	USA	1889	
George Dixon	Canada	1889-1890	
Chappie Moran	England	1889-1890	
Tommy Kelly	USA	1890-1892	
Billy Plimmer	England	1892-1895	
Pedlar Palmer	England	1895-1899	
Terry McGovern	USA	1899	USA
Pedlar Palmer	England	1899-1900	GB
Terry McGovern*	USA	1899-1900	
Clarence Forbes	USA	1900	

Title Holder	Birthplace	Tenure	Status
Johnny Reagan	USA	1900-1902	
Harry Ware	England	1900-1902	GB
Harry Harris	USA	1901	
Harry Forbes	USA	1901-1902	
Kid McFadden	USA	1901	
Dan Dougherty	USA	1901	
Andrew Tokell	England	1902	GB
Harry Ware	England	1902	GB
Harry Forbes	USA	1902-1903	USA
Joe Bowker	England	1902-1904	GB
Frankie Neil	USA	1903-1904	USA
Joe Bowker*	England	1904-1905	
Frankie Neil	USA	1905	USA
Digger Stanley	England	1905-1907	
Owen Moran	England	1905-1907	
Jimmy Walsh	USA	1905-1908	USA
Owen Moran	England	1907	GB
Monte Attell	USA	1908-1910	
Jimmy Walsh	USA	1908-1911	
Digger Stanley	England	1909-1912	GB
Frankie Conley	Italy	1910-1911	
Johnny Coulon	Canada	1910-1911	
Monte Attell	USA	1910-1911	
Johnny Coulon	Canada	1911-1913	USA
Charles Ledoux	France	1912-1913	GB/IBU
Eddie Campi	USA	1913-1914	
Johnny Coulon	Canada	1913-1914	
Kid Williams	Denmark	1913-1914	
Kid Williams	Denmark	1914-1915	
Kid Williams	Denmark	1915-1917	
Johnny Ertle	USA	1915-1918	
Pete Herman	USA	1917-1919	
Pal Moore	USA	1918-1919	
Pete Herman	USA	1919-1920	
Joe Lynch	USA	1920-1921	
Pete Herman	USA	1921	
Johnny Buff	USA	1921-1922	
Joe Lynch	USA	1922-1923	
Joe Lynch	USA	1923-1924	NBA
Joe Burman	England	1923	NY
Abe Goldstein	USA	1923-1924	NY
Joe Lynch	USA	1924	
Abe Goldstein	USA	1924	
Eddie Martin	USA	1924-1925	
Charley Rosenberg	USA	1925-1926	
Charley Rosenberg	USA	1926-1927	NY
Bud Taylor*	USA	1926-1928	NBA
Bushy Graham*	Italy	1928-1929	NY
Al Brown	Panama	1929-1931	
Al Brown	Panama	1931	NY/IBU
Pete Sanstol	Norway	1931	CAN
Al Brown	Panama	1931-1933	
Al Brown	Panama	1933-1934	NY/NBA/IBU
Speedy Dado	Philippines	1933	CALIF
Baby Casanova	Mexico	1933-1934	CALIF
Sixto Escobar	Puerto Rico	1934	CAN
Sixto Escobar	Puerto Rico	1934-1935	NBA
Al Brown	Panama	1934-1935	NY/IBU
Lou Salica	USA	1935	CALIF
Baltazar Sangchilli	Spain	1935-1938	IBU
Lou Salica	USA	1935	NBA/NY
Sixto Escobar	Puerto Rico	1935-1937	NBA/NY
Harry Jeffra	USA	1937-1938	NY/NBA
Sixto Escobar	Puerto Rico	1938	NY/NBA
Al Brown	Panama	1938	IBU
Sixto Escobar	Puerto Rico	1938-1939	
George Pace	USA	1939-1940	NBA
Lou Salica	USA	1939	CALIF
Tony Olivera	USA	1939-1940	CALIF
Little Dado	Philippines	1940-1941	CALIF
Lou Salica	USA	1940-1942	NY/NBA
Lou Salica	USA	1941	
Kenny Lindsay	Canada	1941	CAN
Lou Salica	USA	1941-1942	

Title Holder	Birthplace	Tenure	Status
Lou Salica	USA	1942	NY
David Kui Kong Young	Hawaii	1942-1943	H
Manuel Ortiz	USA	1942-1943	NBA
Manuel Ortiz	USA	1943-1945	NY/NBA
Kui Kong Young	Hawaii	1943	TBC
Rush Dalma	Philippines	1943-1945	TBC
Manuel Ortiz	USA	1945-1947	
Harold Dade	USA	1947	
Manuel Ortiz	USA	1947-1950	
Vic Toweel	S Africa	1950-1952	
Jimmy Carruthers*	Australia	1952-1954	
Robert Cohen	Algeria	1954	
Robert Cohen	Algeria	1954-1956	NY/EBU
Raton Macias	Mexico	1955-1957	NBA
Mario D'Agata	Italy	1956-1957	NY/EBU
Alphonse Halimi	Algeria	1957	NY/EBU
Alphonse Halimi	Algeria	1957-1959	
Joe Becerra*	Mexico	1959-1960	
Alphonse Halimi	Algeria	1960-1961	EBU
Eder Jofre	Brazil	1960-1962	NBA
Johnny Caldwell	Ireland	1961-1962	EBU
Eder Jofre	Brazil	1962-1965	
Fighting Harada	Japan	1965-1968	
Lionel Rose	Australia	1968-1969	
Ruben Olivares	Mexico	1969-1970	
Chuchu Castillo	Mexico	1970-1971	
Ruben Olivares	Mexico	1971-1972	
Rafael Herrera	Mexico	1972	
Enrique Pinder	Panama	1972	
Enrique Pinder	Panama	1972-1973	WBC
Romeo Anaya	Mexico	1973	WBA
Rafael Herrera	Mexico	1973-1974	WBC
Arnold Taylor	S Africa	1973-1974	WBA
Soo-Hwan Hong	S Korea	1974-1975	WBA
Rodolfo Martinez	Mexico	1974-1976	WBC
Alfonso Zamora	Mexico	1975-1977	WBA
Carlos Zarate	Mexico	1976-1979	WBC
Jorge Lujan	Panama	1977-1980	WBA
Lupe Pintor*	Mexico	1979-1983	WBC
Julian Solis	Puerto Rico	1980	WBA
Jeff Chandler	USA	1980-1984	WBA
Albert Davila	USA	1983-1985	WBC
Richard Sandoval	USA	1984-1986	WBA
Satoshi Shingaki	Japan	1984-1985	IBF
Jeff Fenech*	Australia	1985-1987	IBF
Daniel Zaragoza	Mexico	1985	WBC
Miguel Lora	Colombia	1985-1988	WBC
Gaby Canizales	USA	1986	WBA
Bernardo Pinango*	Venezuela	1986-1987	WBA
Takuya Muguruma	Japan	1987	WBA
Kelvin Seabrooks	USA	1987-1988	IBF
Chang-Yung Park	S Korea	1987	WBA
Wilfredo Vasquez	Puerto Rico	1987-1988	WBA
Kaokor Galaxy	Thailand	1988	WBA
Orlando Canizales*	USA	1988-1994	IBF
Sung-Il Moon	S Korea	1988-1989	WBA
Raul Perez	Mexico	1988-1991	WBC
Israel Contrerras*	Venezuela	1989-1991	WBO
Kaokor Galaxy	Thailand	1989	WBA
Luisito Espinosa	Philippines	1989-1991	WBA
Greg Richardson	USA	1991	WBC
Gaby Canizales	USA	1991	WBO
Duke McKenzie	England	1991-1992	WBO
Joichiro Tatsuyushi*	Japan	1991-1992	WBC
Israel Contrerras	Venezuela	1991-1992	WBA
Eddie Cook	USA	1992	WBA
Victor Rabanales	Mexico	1992-1993	WBC
Rafael del Valle	Puerto Rico	1992-1994	WBO
Jorge Elicier Julio	Colombia	1992-1993	WBA
Il-Jung Byun	S Korea	1993	WBC
Junior Jones	USA	1993-1994	WBA
Yasuei Yakushiji	Japan	1993-1995	WBC
John Michael Johnson	USA	1994	WBA
Daorung Chuwatana	Thailand	1994-1995	WBA

Title Holder	Birthplace	Tenure	Status
Alfred Kotey	Ghana	1994-1995	WBO
Harold Mestre	Colombia	1995	IBF
Mbulelo Botile	S Africa	1995-1997	IBF
Wayne McCullough	Ireland	1995-1997	WBC
Veeraphol Sahaprom	Thailand	1995-1996	WBA
Daniel Jimenez	Puerto Rico	1995-1996	WBO
Nana Yaw Konadu	Ghana	1996	WBA
Robbie Regan*	Wales	1996-1998	WBO
Daorung Chuwatana	Thailand	1996-1997	WBA
Sirimongkol Singmanassak	Thailand	1997	WBC
Nana Yaw Konadu	Ghana	1997-1998	WBA
Tim Austin	USA	1997-	IBF
Joichiro Tatsuyoshi	Japan	1997-1998	WBC
Jorge Elicier Julio	Colombia	1998-2000	WBO
Johnny Tapia	USA	1998-1999	WBA
Veeraphol Sahaprom	Thailand	1998-	WBC
Paulie Ayala	USA	1999-2001	WBA
Johnny Tapia*	USA	2000	WBO
Mauricio Martinez	Panama	2000-2002	WBO
Eidy Moya	Venezuela	2001-2002	WBA
Cruz Carbajal	Mexico	2002-	WBO
Johnny Bredahl	Denmark	2002-	WBA

S. Bantamweight (122 lbs)

Title Holder	Birthplace	Tenure	Status
Rigoberto Riasco	Panama	1976	WBC
Royal Kobayashi	Japan	1976	WBC
Dong-Kyun Yum	S Korea	1976-1977	WBC
Wilfredo Gomez*	Puerto Rico	1977-1983	WBC
Soo-Hwan Hong	S Korea	1977-1978	WBA
Ricardo Cardona	Colombia	1978-1980	WBA
Leo Randolph	USA	1980	WBA
Sergio Palma	Argentina	1980-1982	WBA
Leonardo Cruz	Dom Republic	1982-1984	WBA
Jaime Garza	USA	1983-1984	WBC
Bobby Berna	Philippines	1983-1984	IBF
Loris Stecca	Italy	1984	WBA
Seung-In Suh	S Korea	1984-1985	IBF
Victor Callejas	Puerto Rico	1984-1986	WBA
Juan Meza	Mexico	1984-1985	WBC
Ji-Won Kim*	S Korea	1985-1986	IBF
Lupe Pintor	Mexico	1985-1986	WBC
Samart Payakarun	Thailand	1986-1987	WBC
Louie Espinosa	USA	1987	WBA
Seung-Hoon Lee*	S Korea	1987-1988	IBF
Jeff Fenech*	Australia	1987-1988	WBC
Julio Gervacio	Dom Republic	1987-1988	WBA
Bernardo Pinango	Venezuela	1988	WBA
Daniel Zaragoza	Mexico	1988-1990	WBC
Jose Sanabria	Venezuela	1988-1989	IBF
Juan J. Estrada	Mexico	1988-1989	WBA
Fabrice Benichou	Spain	1989-1990	IBF
Kenny Mitchell	USA	1989	WBO
Valerio Nati	Italy	1989-1990	WBO
Jesus Salud	USA	1989-1990	WBA
Welcome Ncita	S Africa	1990-1992	IBF
Paul Banke	USA	1990	WBC
Orlando Fernandez	Puerto Rico	1990-1991	WBO
Luis Mendoza	Colombia	1990-1991	WBA
Pedro Decima	Argentina	1990-1991	WBC
Kiyoshi Hatanaka	Japan	1991	WBC
Jesse Benavides	USA	1991-1992	WBO
Daniel Zaragoza	Mexico	1991-1992	WBC
Raul Perez	Mexico	1991-1992	WBA
Thierry Jacob	France	1992	WBC
Wilfredo Vasquez	Puerto Rico	1992-1995	WBA
Tracy Harris Patterson	USA	1992-1994	WBC
Duke McKenzie	England	1992-1993	WBO
Kennedy McKinney	USA	1992-1994	IBF
Daniel Jimenez	Puerto Rico	1993-1995	WBO
Vuyani Bungu	S Africa	1994-1999	IBF
Hector Acero-Sanchez	Dom Republic	1994-1995	WBC
Marco Antonio Barrera	Mexico	1995-1996	WBO
Antonio Cermeno *	Venezuela	1995-1997	WBA
Daniel Zaragoza	Mexico	1995-1997	WBC

Title Holder	Birthplace	Tenure	Status
Junior Jones	USA	1996-1997	WBO
Erik Morales*	USA	1997-2000	WBC
Kennedy McKinney*	USA	1997-1998	WBO
Enrique Sanchez	Mexico	1998	WBA
Marco Antonio Barrera	Mexico	1998-2000	WBO
Nestor Garza	Mexico	1998-2000	WBA
Lehlohonola Ledwaba	S Africa	1999-2001	IBF
Erik Morales	USA	2000	WBC/WBO
Erik Morales*	USA	2000	WBC
Marco Antonio Barrera*	Mexico	2000-2001	WBO
Clarence Adams	USA	2000-2001	WBA
Willie Jorrin	USA	2000-	WBC
Manny Pacquiao	Philippines	2001-	IBF
Agapito Sanchez	Dom Republic	2001-	WBO
Yober Ortega	Venezuela	2001-2002	WBA
Yoddamrong Sithyodthong	Thailand	2002	WBA
Osamu Sato	Japan	2002-	WBA

Featherweight (126 lbs)

Title Holder	Birthplace	Tenure	Status
Ike Weir	Ireland	1889-1890	
Billy Murphy	New Zealand	1890-1893	
George Dixon	Canada	1890-1893	
Young Griffo	Australia	1890-1893	
Johnny Griffin	USA	1891-1893	
Solly Smith	USA	1893	
George Dixon	Canada	1893-1896	
Solly Smith	USA	1896-1898	
Frank Erne	USA	1896-1897	
George Dixon	Canada	1896-1900	
Harry Greenfield	England	1897-1899	
Ben Jordan	England	1897-1899	
Will Curley	England	1897-1899	
Dave Sullivan	Ireland	1898	
Ben Jordan	England	1899-1905	GB
Eddie Santry	USA	1899-1900	
Terry McGovern	USA	1900	
Terry McGovern	USA	1900-1901	USA
Young Corbett II	USA	1901-1903	USA
Eddie Hanlon	USA	1903	
Young Corbett II	USA	1903-1904	
Abe Attell	USA	1903-1904	
Abe Attell	USA	1904-1911	USA
Joe Bowker	England	1905-1907	GB
Jim Driscoll	Wales	1907-1912	GB
Abe Attell	USA	1911-1912	
Joe Coster	USA	1911	
Joe Rivers	Mexico	1911	
Johnny Kilbane	USA	1911-1912	
Jim Driscoll*	Wales	1912-1913	GB/IBU
Johnny Kilbane	USA	1912-1922	USA
Johnny Kilbane	USA	1922-1923	NBA
Johnny Dundee	Italy	1922-1923	NY
Eugene Criqui	France	1923	
Johnny Dundee*	Italy	1923-1924	
Kid Kaplan	Russia	1925	NY
Kid Kaplan*	Russia	1925-1926	
Honeyboy Finnegan	USA	1926-1927	MASS
Benny Bass	Russia	1927-1928	NBA
Tony Canzoneri	USA	1927-1928	NY
Tony Canzoneri	USA	1928	
Andre Routis	France	1928-1929	
Bat Battalino	USA	1929-1932	
Bat Battalino	USA	1932	NBA
Tommy Paul	USA	1932-1933	NBA
Kid Chocolate*	Cuba	1932-1934	NY
Baby Arizmendi	Mexico	1932-1933	CALIF
Freddie Miller	USA	1933-1936	NBA
Baby Arizmendi	Mexico	1934-1935	NY
Baby Arizmendi	Mexico	1935-1936	NY/MEX
Baby Arizmendi	Mexico	1936	MEX
Petey Sarron	USA	1936-1937	NBA
Henry Armstrong	USA	1936-1937	CALIF/MEX
Mike Belloise	USA	1936	NY
Maurice Holtzer	France	1937-1938	IBU

Title Holder	Birthplace	Tenure	Status
Henry Armstrong*	USA	1937-1938	NBA/NY
Leo Rodak	USA	1938	MARY
Joey Archibald	USA	1938-1939	NY
Leo Rodak	USA	1938-1939	NBA
Joey Archibald	USA	1939-1940	
Joey Archibald	USA	1940	NY
Petey Scalzo	USA	1940-1941	NBA
Jimmy Perrin	USA	1940	LOUIS
Harry Jeffra	USA	1940-1941	NY/MARY
Joey Archibald	USA	1941	NY/MARY
Richie Lemos	USA	1941	NBA
Chalky Wright	Mexico	1941-1942	NY/MARY
Jackie Wilson	USA	1941-1943	NBA
Willie Pep	USA	1942-1946	NY
Jackie Callura	Canada	1943	NBA
Phil Terranova	USA	1943-1944	NBA
Sal Bartolo	USA	1944-1946	NBA
Willie Pep	USA	1946-1948	
Sandy Saddler	USA	1948-1949	
Willie Pep	USA	1949-1950	
Sandy Saddler*	USA	1950-1957	
Hogan Kid Bassey	Nigeria	1957-1959	
Davey Moore	USA	1959-1963	
Sugar Ramos	Cuba	1963-1964	
Vicente Saldivar*	Mexico	1964-1967	
Raul Rojas	USA	1967	CALIF
Howard Winstone	Wales	1968	WBC
Raul Rojas	USA	1968	WBA
Johnny Famechon	France	1968-1969	AUST
Jose Legra	Cuba	1968-1969	WBC
Shozo Saijyo	Japan	1968-1971	WBA
Johnny Famechon	France	1969-1970	WBC
Vicente Saldivar	Mexico	1970	WBC
Kuniaki Shibata	Japan	1970-1972	WBC
Antonio Gomez	Venezuela	1971-1972	WBA
Clemente Sanchez	Mexico	1972	WBC
Ernesto Marcel*	Panama	1972-1974	WBA
Jose Legra	Cuba	1972-1973	WBC
Eder Jofre	Brazil	1973-1974	WBC
Ruben Olivares	Mexico	1974	WBA
Bobby Chacon	USA	1974-1975	WBC
Alexis Arguello*	Nicaragua	1974-1977	WBA
Ruben Olivares	Mexico	1975	WBC
David Kotey	Ghana	1975-1976	WBC
Danny Lopez	USA	1976-1980	WBC
Rafael Ortega	Panama	1977	WBA
Cecilio Lastra	Spain	1977-1978	WBA
Eusebio Pedroza	Panama	1978-1985	WBA
Salvador Sanchez*	Mexico	1980-1982	WBC
Juan Laporte	Puerto Rico	1982-1984	WBC
Min-Keun Oh	S Korea	1984-1985	IBF
Wilfredo Gomez	Puerto Rico	1984	WBC
Azumah Nelson*	Ghana	1984-1988	WBC
Barry McGuigan	Ireland	1985-1986	WBA
Ki-Yung Chung	S Korea	1985-1986	IBF
Steve Cruz	USA	1986-1987	WBA
Antonio Rivera	Puerto Rico	1986-1988	IBF
Antonio Esparragoza	Venezuela	1987-1991	WBA
Calvin Grove	USA	1988	IBF
Jeff Fenech*	Australia	1988-1989	WBC
Jorge Paez*	Mexico	1988-1990	IBF
Maurizio Stecca	Italy	1989	WBO
Louie Espinosa	USA	1989-1990	WBO
Jorge Paez*	Mexico	1990-1991	IBF/WBO
Marcos Villasana	Mexico	1990-1991	WBC
Kyun-Yung Park	S Korea	1991-1993	WBA
Troy Dorsey	USA	1991	IBF
Maurizio Stecca	Italy	1991-1992	WBO
Manuel Medina	Mexico	1991-1993	IBF
Paul Hodkinson	England	1991-1993	WBC
Colin McMillan	England	1992	WBO
Ruben Palacio	Colombia	1992-1993	WBO
Tom Johnson	USA	1993-1997	IBF
Steve Robinson	Wales	1993-1995	WBO

Title Holder	Birthplace	Tenure	Status
Gregorio Vargas	Mexico	1993	WBC
Kevin Kelley	USA	1993-1995	WBC
Eloy Rojas	Venezuela	1993-1996	WBA
Alejandro Gonzalez	Mexico	1995	WBC
Manuel Medina	Mexico	1995	WBC
Prince Naseem Hamed*	England	1995-1997	WBO
Luisito Espinosa	Philippines	1995-1999	WBC
Wilfredo Vasquez	Puerto Rico	1996-1998	WBA
Prince Naseem Hamed *	England	1997	WBO/IBF
Prince Naseem Hamed*	England	1997-1999	WBO
Hector Lizarraga	Mexico	1997-1998	IBF
Freddie Norwood	USA	1998	WBA
Manuel Medina	Mexico	1998-1999	IBF
Antonio Cermeno	Venezuela	1998-1999	WBA
Cesar Soto	Mexico	1999	WBC
Freddie Norwood	USA	1999-2000	WBA
Prince Naseem Hamed	England	1999-2000	WBC/WBO
Paul Ingle	England	1999-2000	IBF
Prince Naseem Hamed*	England	2000	WBO
Gustavo Espadas	Mexico	2000-2001	WBC
Derrick Gainer	USA	2000-	WBA
Mbulelo Botile	S Africa	2000-2001	IBF
Istvan Kovacs	Hungary	2001	WBO
Erik Morales	USA	2001-2002	WBC
Frankie Toledo	USA	2001	IBF
Julio Pablo Chacon	Argentina	2001-	WBO
Manuel Medina	Mexico	2001-2002	IBF
Johnny Tapia	USA	2002-	IBF
Marco Antonio Barrera*	Mexico	2002	WBC

S. Featherweight (130 lbs)

Title Holder	Birthplace	Tenure	Status
Johnny Dundee	Italy	1921-1923	NY
Jack Bernstein	USA	1923	NY
Jack Bernstein	USA	1923	NBA/NY
Johnny Dundee	Italy	1923-1924	NBA/NY
Kid Sullivan	USA	1924-1925	NBA/NY
Mike Ballerino	USA	1925	NBA/NY
Tod Morgan	USA	1925-1929	NBA/NY
Benny Bass	Russia	1929-1930	NBA/NY
Benny Bass	Russia	1930-1931	NBA
Kid Chocolate	Cuba	1931-1933	NBA
Frankie Klick	USA	1933-1934	NBA
Sandy Saddler	USA	1949-1950	NBA
Sandy Saddler	USA	1950-1951	CLE
Harold Gomes	USA	1959-1960	NBA
Flash Elorde	Philippines	1960-1962	NBA
Flash Elorde	Philippines	1962-1967	WBA
Raul Rojas	USA	1967	CALIF
Yoshiaki Numata	Japan	1967	WBA
Hiroshi Kobayashi	Japan	1967-1971	WBA
Rene Barrientos	Philippines	1969-1970	WBC
Yoshiaki Numata	Japan	1970-1971	WBC
Alfredo Marcano	Venezuela	1971-1972	WBA
Ricardo Arredondo	Mexico	1971-1974	WBC
Ben Villaflor	Philippines	1972-1973	WBA
Kuniaki Shibata	Japan	1973	WBA
Ben Villaflor	Philippines	1973-1976	WBA
Kuniaki Shibata	Japan	1974-1975	WBC
Alfredo Escalera	Puerto Rico	1975-1978	WBC
Sam Serrano	Puerto Rico	1976-1980	WBA
Alexis Arguello*	Nicaragua	1978-1980	WBC
Yasutsune Uehara	Japan	1980-1981	WBA
Rafael Limon	Mexico	1980-1981	WBC
Cornelius Boza-Edwards	Uganda	1981	WBC
Sam Serrano	Puerto Rico	1981-1983	WBA
Rolando Navarrete	Philippines	1981-1982	WBC
Rafael Limon	Mexico	1982	WBC
Bobby Chacon	USA	1982-1983	WBC
Roger Mayweather	USA	1983-1984	WBA
Hector Camacho*	Puerto Rico	1983-1984	WBC
Rocky Lockridge	USA	1984-1985	WBA
Hwan-Kil Yuh	S Korea	1984-1985	IBF
Julio Cesar Chavez*	Mexico	1984-1987	WBC
Lester Ellis	England	1985	IBF

Title Holder	Birthplace	Tenure	Status
Wilfredo Gomez	Puerto Rico	1985-1986	WBA
Barry Michael	England	1985-1987	IBF
Alfredo Layne	Panama	1986	WBA
Brian Mitchell*	S Africa	1986-1991	WBA
Rocky Lockridge	USA	1987-1988	IBF
Azumah Nelson	Ghana	1988-1994	WBC
Tony Lopez	USA	1988-1989	IBF
Juan Molina*	Puerto Rico	1989	WBO
Juan Molina	Puerto Rico	1989-1990	IBF
Kamel Bou Ali	Tunisia	1989-1992	WBO
Tony Lopez	USA	1990-1991	IBF
Joey Gamache*	USA	1991	WBA
Brian Mitchell*	S Africa	1991-1992	IBF
Genaro Hernandez	USA	1991-1995	WBA
Juan Molina*	Puerto Rico	1992-1995	IBF
Daniel Londas	France	1992	WBO
Jimmy Bredahl	Denmark	1992-1994	WBO
Oscar de la Hoya*	USA	1994	WBO
James Leija	USA	1994	WBC
Gabriel Ruelas	USA	1994-1995	WBC
Regilio Tuur*	Surinam	1994-1997	WBO
Eddie Hopson	USA	1995	IBF
Tracy Harris Patterson	USA	1995	IBF
Yong-Soo Choi	S Korea	1995-1998	WBA
Arturo Gatti*	Canada	1995-1997	IBF
Azumah Nelson	Ghana	1996-1997	WBC
Genaro Hernandez	USA	1997-1998	WBC
Barry Jones*	Wales	1997-1998	WBO
Roberto Garcia	USA	1998-1999	IBF
Anatoly Alexandrov	Kazakhstan	1998-1999	WBO
Takenori Hatakeyama	Japan	1998-1999	WBA
Floyd Mayweather*	USA	1998-2002	WBC
Lakva Sim	Mongolia	1999	WBA
Acelino Freitas*	Brazil	1999-2002	WBO
Diego Corrales*	USA	1999-2000	IBF
Jong-Kwon Baek	S Korea	1999-2000	WBA
Joel Casamayor	Cuba	2000-2002	WBA
Steve Forbes	USA	2000-	IBF
Acelino Freitas	Brazil	2002-	WBO/WBA

Lightweight (135 lbs)

Title Holder	Birthplace	Tenure	Status
Jack McAuliffe	Ireland	1889-1894	USA
Jem Carney	England	1889-1891	
Jimmy Carroll	England	1889-1891	
Dick Burge	England	1891-1896	GB
George Lavigne	USA	1894-1896	USA
George Lavigne	USA	1896	
George Lavigne	USA	1896-1897	
Eddie Connolly	Canada	1896-1897	
George Lavigne	USA	1897-1899	
Frank Erne	Switzerland	1899-1902	
Joe Gans	USA	1902	
Joe Gans	USA	1902-1906	
Jabez White	England	1902-1905	GB
Jimmy Britt	USA	1902-1905	
Battling Nelson	Denmark	1905-1907	
Joe Gans	USA	1906-1908	
Battling Nelson	Denmark	1908-1910	
Ad Wolgast	USA	1910-1912	
Willie Ritchie	USA	1912	
Freddie Welsh	Wales	1912-1914	GB
Willie Ritchie	USA	1912-1914	USA
Freddie Welsh	Wales	1914-1917	
Benny Leonard*	USA	1917-1925	
Jimmy Goodrich	USA	1925	NY
Rocky Kansas	USA	1925-1926	
Sammy Mandell	USA	1926-1930	
Al Singer	USA	1930	
Tony Canzoneri	USA	1930-1933	
Barney Ross*	USA	1933-1935	
Tony Canzoneri	USA	1935-1936	
Lou Ambers	USA	1936-1938	
Henry Armstrong	USA	1938-1939	
Lou Ambers	USA	1939-1940	

Title Holder	Birthplace	Tenure	Status
Sammy Angott	USA	1940-1941	NBA
Lew Jenkins	USA	1940-1941	NY
Sammy Angott*	USA	1941-1942	
Beau Jack	USA	1942-1943	NY
Slugger White	USA	1943	MARY
Bob Montgomery	USA	1943	NY
Sammy Angott	USA	1943-1944	NBA
Beau Jack	USA	1943-1944	NY
Bob Montgomery	USA	1944-1947	NY
Juan Zurita	Mexico	1944-1945	NBA
Ike Williams	USA	1945-1947	NBA
Ike Williams	USA	1947-1951	
Jimmy Carter	USA	1951-1952	
Lauro Salas	Mexico	1952	
Jimmy Carter	USA	1952-1954	
Paddy de Marco	USA	1954	
Jimmy Carter	USA	1954-1955	
Wallace Bud Smith	USA	1955-1956	
Joe Brown	USA	1956-1962	
Carlos Ortiz	Puerto Rico	1962-1963	
Carlos Ortiz*	Puerto Rico	1963-1964	WBA/WBC
Kenny Lane	USA	1963-1964	MICH
Carlos Ortiz	Puerto Rico	1964-1965	
Ismael Laguna	Panama	1965	
Carlos Ortiz	Puerto Rico	1965-1966	
Carlos Ortiz*	Puerto Rico	1966-1967	WBA
Carlos Ortiz	Puerto Rico	1967-1968	
Carlos Teo Cruz	Dom Republic	1968-1969	
Mando Ramos	USA	1969-1970	
Ismael Laguna	Panama	1970	
Ismael Laguna	Panama	1970	WBA
Ken Buchanan*	Scotland	1970-1971	WBA
Ken Buchanan	Scotland	1971	
Ken Buchanan	Scotland	1971-1972	WBA
Pedro Carrasco	Spain	1971-1972	WBC
Mando Ramos	USA	1972	WBC
Roberto Duran*	Panama	1972-1978	WBA
Chango Carmona	Mexico	1972	WBC
Rodolfo Gonzalez	Mexico	1972-1974	WBC
Guts Ishimatsu	Japan	1974-1976	WBC
Esteban de Jesus	Puerto Rico	1976-1978	WBC
Roberto Duran*	Panama	1978-1979	
Jim Watt	Scotland	1979-1981	WBC
Ernesto Espana	Venezuela	1979-1980	WBA
Hilmer Kenty	USA	1980-1981	WBA
Sean O'Grady	USA	1981	WBA
Alexis Arguello*	Nicaragua	1981-1983	WBC
Claude Noel	Trinidad	1981	WBA
Arturo Frias	USA	1981-1982	WBA
Ray Mancini	USA	1982-1984	WBA
Edwin Rosario	Puerto Rico	1983-1984	WBC
Charlie Choo Choo Brown	USA	1984	IBF
Harry Arroyo	USA	1984-1985	IBF
Livingstone Bramble	USA	1984-1986	WBA
Jose Luis Ramirez	Mexico	1984-1985	WBC
Jimmy Paul	USA	1985-1986	IBF
Hector Camacho*	Puerto Rico	1985-1987	WBC
Edwin Rosario	Puerto Rico	1986-1987	WBA
Greg Haugen	USA	1986-1987	IBF
Vinny Pazienza	USA	1987-1988	IBF
Jose Luis Ramirez	Mexico	1987-1988	WBC
Julio Cesar Chavez*	Mexico	1987-1988	WBA
Greg Haugen	USA	1988-1989	IBF
Julio Cesar Chavez*	Mexico	1988-1989	WBA/WBC
Mauricio Aceves	Mexico	1989-1990	WBO
Pernell Whitaker*	USA	1989	IBF
Edwin Rosario	Puerto Rico	1989-1990	WBA
Pernell Whitaker*	USA	1989-1990	IBF/WBC
Juan Nazario	Puerto Rico	1990	WBA
Pernell Whitaker*	USA	1990-1992	IBF/WBC/WBA
Dingaan Thobela*	S Africa	1990-1992	WBO
Joey Gamache	USA	1992	WBA
Miguel Gonzalez*	Mexico	1992-1996	WBC
Giovanni Parisi*	Italy	1992-1994	WBO

Title Holder	Birthplace	Tenure	Status
Tony Lopez	USA	1992-1993	WBA
Fred Pendleton	USA	1993-1994	IBF
Dingaan Thobela	S Africa	1993	WBA
Orzubek Nazarov	Kyrghyzstan	1993-1998	WBA
Rafael Ruelas	USA	1994-1995	IBF
Oscar de la Hoya*	USA	1994-1995	WBO
Oscar de la Hoya*	USA	1995	WBO/IBF
Oscar de la Hoya*	USA	1995-1996	WBO
Phillip Holiday	S Africa	1995-1997	IBF
Jean-Baptiste Mendy	France	1996-1997	WBC
Artur Grigorian	Uzbekistan	1996-	WBO
Steve Johnston	USA	1997-1998	WBC
Shane Mosley*	USA	1997-1999	IBF
Jean-Baptiste Mendy	France	1998-1999	WBA
Cesar Bazan	Mexico	1998-1999	WBC
Steve Johnston	USA	1999-2000	WBC
Julien Lorcy	France	1999	WBA
Stefano Zoff	Italy	1999	WBA
Paul Spadafora	USA	1999-	IBF
Gilberto Serrano	Venezuela	1999-2000	WBA
Takanori Hatakeyama	Japan	2000-2001	WBA
Jose Luis Castillo	Mexico	2000-2002	WBC
Julien Lorcy	France	2001	WBA
Raul Balbi	Argentina	2001-2002	WBA
Leonardo Dorin	Romania	2002-	WBA
Floyd Mayweather	USA	2002-	WBC

L. Welterweight (140 lbs)

Title Holder	Birthplace	Tenure	Status
Pinkey Mitchell	USA	1922-1926	NBA
Mushy Callahan	USA	1926-1927	NBA
Mushy Callahan	USA	1927-1930	NBA/NY
Mushy Callahan	USA	1930	NBA
Jackie Kid Berg	England	1930-1931	NBA
Tony Canzoneri	USA	1931-1932	NBA
Johnny Jadick	USA	1932	NBA
Johnny Jadick	USA	1932-1933	PEN
Battling Shaw	Mexico	1933	LOUIS
Tony Canzoneri	USA	1933	LOUIS
Barney Ross*	USA	1933-1935	ILL
Maxie Berger	Canada	1939	CAN
Harry Weekly	USA	1941-1942	LOUIS
Tippy Larkin	USA	1946-1947	NY/NBA
Carlos Ortiz	Puerto Rico	1959-1960	NBA
Duilio Loi	Italy	1960-1962	NBA
Duilio Loi	Italy	1962	WBA
Eddie Perkins	USA	1962	WBA
Duilio Loi*	Italy	1962-1963	WBA
Roberto Cruz	Philippines	1963	WBA
Eddie Perkins	USA	1963-1965	WBA
Carlos Hernandez	Venezuela	1965-1966	WBA
Sandro Lopopolo	Italy	1966-1967	WBA
Paul Fujii	Hawaii	1967-1968	WBA
Nicolino Loche	Argentina	1968-1972	WBA
Pedro Adigue	Philippines	1968-1970	WBC
Bruno Arcari*	Italy	1970-1974	WBC
Alfonso Frazer	Panama	1972	WBA
Antonio Cervantes	Colombia	1972-1976	WBA
Perico Fernandez	Spain	1974-1975	WBC
Saensak Muangsurin	Thailand	1975-1976	WBC
Wilfred Benitez	USA	1976	WBA
Miguel Velasquez	Spain	1976	WBC
Saensak Muangsurin	Thailand	1976-1978	WBC
Antonio Cervantes	Colombia	1977-1980	WBA
Wilfred Benitez*	USA	1977-1978	NY
Sang-Hyun Kim	S Korea	1978-1980	WBC
Saoul Mamby	USA	1980-1982	WBC
Aaron Pryor*	USA	1980-1984	WBA
Leroy Haley	USA	1982-1983	WBC
Bruce Curry	USA	1983-1984	WBC
Johnny Bumphus	USA	1984	WBA
Bill Costello	USA	1984-1985	WBC
Gene Hatcher	USA	1984-1985	WBA
Aaron Pryor	USA	1984-1985	IBF
Ubaldo Sacco	Argentina	1985-1986	WBA

225

Title Holder	Birthplace	Tenure	Status
Lonnie Smith	USA	1985-1986	WBC
Patrizio Oliva	Italy	1986-1987	WBA
Gary Hinton	USA	1986	IBF
Rene Arredondo	Mexico	1986	WBC
Tsuyoshi Hamada	Japan	1986-1987	WBC
Joe Manley	USA	1986-1987	IBF
Terry Marsh*	England	1987	IBF
Juan M. Coggi	Argentina	1987-1990	WBA
Rene Arredondo	Mexico	1987	WBC
Roger Mayweather	USA	1987-1989	WBC
James McGirt	USA	1988	IBF
Meldrick Taylor	USA	1988-1990	IBF
Hector Camacho	Puerto Rico	1989-1991	WBO
Julio Cesar Chavez*	Mexico	1989-1990	WBC
Julio Cesar Chavez*	Mexico	1990-1991	IBF/WBC
Loreto Garza	USA	1990-1991	WBA
Greg Haugen	USA	1991	WBO
Hector Camacho	Puerto Rico	1991-1992	WBO
Edwin Rosario	Puerto Rico	1991-1992	WBA
Julio Cesar Chavez	Mexico	1991-1994	WBC
Rafael Pineda	Colombia	1991-1992	IBF
Akinobu Hiranaka	Japan	1992	WBA
Carlos Gonzalez	Mexico	1992-1993	WBO
Pernell Whitaker*	USA	1992-1993	IBF
Morris East	Philippines	1992-1993	WBA
Juan M. Coggi	Argentina	1993-1994	WBA
Charles Murray	USA	1993-1994	IBF
Zack Padilla*	USA	1993-1994	WBO
Frankie Randall	USA	1994	WBC
Jake Rodriguez	USA	1994-1995	IBF
Julio Cesar Chavez	Mexico	1994-1996	WBC
Frankie Randall	USA	1994-1996	WBA
Konstantin Tszyu	Russia	1995-1997	IBF
Sammy Fuentes	Puerto Rico	1995-1996	WBO
Juan M. Coggi	Argentina	1996	WBA
Giovanni Parisi	Italy	1996-1998	WBO
Oscar de la Hoya*	USA	1996-1997	WBC
Frankie Randall	USA	1996-1997	WBA
Khalid Rahilou	France	1997-1998	WBA
Vince Phillips	USA	1997-1999	IBF
Carlos Gonzalez	Mexico	1998-1999	WBO
Sharmba Mitchell	USA	1998-2001	WBA
Terron Millett	USA	1999	IBF
Randall Bailey	USA	1999-2000	WBO
Kostya Tszyu*	Russia	1999-2000	WBC
Zab Judah	USA	2000-2001	IBF
Ener Julio	Colombia	2000-2001	WBO
Kostya Tszyu*	Russia	2001	WBA/WBC
DeMarcus Corley	USA	2001-	WBO
Kostya Tszyu	Russia	2001-	WBA/WBC/IBF

Welterweight (147 lbs)

Title Holder	Birthplace	Tenure	Status
Paddy Duffy	USA	1889-1890	
Tommy Ryan	USA	1891-1894	
Mysterious Billy Smith	USA	1892-1894	
Tommy Ryan	USA	1894-1897	USA
Tommy Ryan	USA	1897-1899	
Dick Burge	GB	1897	
George Green	USA	1897	
Tom Causer	GB	1897	
Joe Walcott	Barbados	1897	
George Lavigne	USA	1897-1899	
Dick Burge	GB	1897-1898	
Mysterious Billy Smith	USA	1898-1900	
Bobby Dobbs	USA	1898-1902	
Rube Ferns	USA	1900	
Matty Matthews	USA	1900	
Eddie Connolly	Canada	1900	
Matty Matthews	USA	1900-1901	
Rube Ferns	USA	1901	
Joe Walcott	Barbados	1901-1906	
Eddie Connolly	Canada	1902-1903	GB
Matty Matthews	USA	1902-1903	
Rube Ferns	USA	1903	

Title Holder	Birthplace	Tenure	Status
Martin Duffy	USA	1903-1904	
Honey Mellody	USA	1904	
Jack Clancy	USA	1904-1905	GB
Dixie Kid	USA	1904-1905	
Buddy Ryan	USA	1904-1905	
Sam Langford	Canada	1904-1905	
George Petersen	USA	1905	
Jimmy Gardner	USA	1905	
Mike Twin Sullivan	USA	1905-1906	
Joe Gans	USA	1906	
Joe Walcott	Barbados	1906	USA
Honey Mellody	USA	1906	USA
Honey Mellody	USA	1906-1907	
Joe Thomas	USA	1906-1907	
Mike Twin Sullivan	USA	1907-1911	
Jimmy Gardner	USA	1907-1908	
Frank Mantell	USA	1907-1908	
Harry Lewis	USA	1908-1910	
Jack Blackburn	USA	1908	
Jimmy Gardner	USA	1908-1909	
Willie Lewis	USA	1909-1910	
Harry Lewis	USA	1910-1911	GB/FR
Jimmy Clabby	USA	1910-1911	
Dixie Kid	USA	1911-1912	GB/FR
Ray Bronson	USA	1911-1914	
Marcel Thomas	France	1912-1913	FR
Wildcat Ferns	USA	1912-1913	
Spike Kelly	USA	1913-1914	
Mike Glover	USA	1913-1915	
Mike Gibbons	USA	1913-1914	
Waldemar Holberg	Denmark	1914	
Tom McCormick	Ireland	1914	
Matt Wells	England	1914-1915	AUSTR
Kid Graves	USA	1914-1917	
Jack Britton	USA	1915	
Ted Kid Lewis	England	1915-1916	
Jack Britton	USA	1916-1917	
Ted Kid Lewis	England	1917	
Ted Kid Lewis	England	1917-1919	
Jack Britton	USA	1919-1922	
Mickey Walker	USA	1922-1923	
Mickey Walker	USA	1923-1924	NBA
Dave Shade	USA	1923	NY
Jimmy Jones	USA	1923	NY/MASS
Mickey Walker	USA	1924-1926	
Pete Latzo	USA	1926-1927	
Joe Dundee	Italy	1927-1928	
Joe Dundee	Italy	1928-1929	NY
Jackie Fields	USA	1929	NBA
Jackie Fields	USA	1929-1930	
Young Jack Thompson	USA	1930	
Tommy Freeman	USA	1930-1931	
Young Jack Thompson	USA	1930	
Lou Brouillard	Canada	1931-1932	
Jackie Fields	USA	1932-1933	
Young Corbett III	Italy	1933	
Jimmy McLarnin	Ireland	1933-1934	
Barney Ross	USA	1934	
Jimmy McLarnin	Ireland	1934-1935	
Barney Ross	USA	1935-1938	
Barney Ross	USA	1938	NY/NBA
Felix Wouters	Belgium	1938	IBU
Henry Armstrong	USA	1938-1940	
Fritzie Zivic	USA	1940	
Fritzie Zivic	USA	1940-1941	NY/NBA
Izzy Jannazzo	USA	1940-1942	MARY
Red Cochrane	USA	1941-1942	NY/NBA
Red Cochrane	USA	1942-1946	
Marty Servo	USA	1946	
Sugar Ray Robinson*	USA	1946-1951	
Johnny Bratton	USA	1951	NBA
Kid Gavilan	Cuba	1951-1952	NBA/NY
Kid Gavilan	Cuba	1952-1954	
Johnny Saxton	USA	1954-1955	

Title Holder	Birthplace	Tenure	Status
Tony de Marco	USA	1955	
Carmen Basilio	USA	1955-1956	
Johnny Saxton	USA	1956	
Carmen Basilio*	USA	1956-1957	
Virgil Akins	USA	1957-1958	MASS
Virgil Akins	USA	1958	
Don Jordan	Dom Republic	1958-1960	
Benny Kid Paret	Cuba	1960-1961	
Emile Griffith	Virgin Islands	1961	
Benny Kid Paret	Cuba	1961-1962	
Emile Griffith	Virgin Islands	1962-1963	
Luis Rodriguez	Cuba	1963	
Emile Griffith*	Virgin Islands	1963-1966	
Willie Ludick	S Africa	1966-1968	SA
Curtis Cokes*	USA	1966	WBA
Curtis Cokes*	USA	1966-1967	WBA/WBC
Charley Shipes	USA	1966-1967	CALIF
Curtis Cokes	USA	1968-1969	
Jose Napoles	Cuba	1969-1970	
Billy Backus	USA	1970-1971	
Jose Napoles	Cuba	1971-1972	
Jose Napoles*	Cuba	1972-1974	WBA/WBC
Hedgemon Lewis	USA	1972-1974	NY
Jose Napoles	Cuba	1974-1975	
Jose Napoles	Cuba	1975	WBC
Angel Espada	Puerto Rico	1975-1976	WBA
John H. Stracey	England	1975-1976	WBC
Carlos Palomino	Mexico	1976-1979	WBC
Pipino Cuevas	Mexico	1976-1980	WBA
Wilfred Benitez	USA	1979	WBC
Sugar Ray Leonard	USA	1979-1980	WBC
Roberto Duran	Panama	1980	WBC
Thomas Hearns	USA	1980-1981	WBA
Sugar Ray Leonard	USA	1980-1981	WBC
Sugar Ray Leonard*	USA	1981-1982	
Don Curry*	USA	1983-1984	WBA
Milton McCrory	USA	1983-1985	WBC
Don Curry*	USA	1984-1985	WBA/IBF
Don Curry	USA	1985-1986	
Lloyd Honeyghan	Jamaica	1986	
Lloyd Honeyghan	Jamaica	1986-1987	WBC/IBF
Mark Breland	USA	1987	WBA
Marlon Starling	USA	1987-1988	WBA
Jorge Vaca	Mexico	1987-1988	WBC
Lloyd Honeyghan	Jamaica	1988-1989	WBC
Simon Brown*	Jamaica	1988-1991	IBF
Tomas Molinares	Colombia	1988-1989	WBA
Mark Breland	USA	1989-1990	WBA
Marlon Starling	USA	1989-1990	WBC
Genaro Leon*	Mexico	1989	WBO
Manning Galloway	USA	1989-1993	WBO
Aaron Davis	USA	1990-1991	WBA
Maurice Blocker	USA	1990-1991	WBC
Meldrick Taylor	USA	1991-1992	WBA
Simon Brown*	Jamaica	1991	WBC/IBF
Simon Brown	Jamaica	1991	WBC
Maurice Blocker	USA	1991-1993	IBF
James McGirt	USA	1991-1993	WBC
Crisanto Espana	Venezuela	1992-1994	WBA
Gert Bo Jacobsen*	Denmark	1993	WBO
Pernell Whitaker	USA	1993-1997	WBC
Felix Trinidad*	Puerto Rico	1993-2000	IBF
Eamonn Loughran	Ireland	1993-1996	WBO
Ike Quartey	Ghana	1994-1998	WBA
Jose Luis Lopez	Mexico	1996-1997	WBO
Michael Loewe*	Romania	1997-1998	WBO
Oscar de la Hoya	USA	1997-1999	WBC
Ahmed Kotiev	Russia	1998-2000	WBO
James Page	USA	1998-2000	WBA
Oscar de la Hoya	USA	2000	WBC
Daniel Santos*	Puerto Rico	2000-2002	WBO
Shane Mosley	USA	2000-2002	WBC
Andrew Lewis	Guyana	2001-2002	WBA
Vernon Forrest	USA	2001	IBF

Title Holder	Birthplace	Tenure	Status
Vernon Forrest	USA	2002-	WBC
Antonio Margarito	Mexico	2002-	WBO
Ricardo Mayorga	Nicaragua	2002-	WBA
Michele Piccirillo	Italy	2002-	IBF

L. Middleweight (154 lbs)

Title Holder	Birthplace	Tenure	Status
Emile Griffith*	USA	1962-1963	AU
Denny Moyer	USA	1962-1963	WBA
Ralph Dupas	USA	1963	WBA
Sandro Mazzinghi	Italy	1963-1965	WBA
Nino Benvenuti	Italy	1965-1966	WBA
Ki-Soo Kim	S Korea	1966-1968	WBA
Sandro Mazzinghi	Italy	1968-1969	WBA
Freddie Little	USA	1969-1970	WBA
Carmelo Bossi	Italy	1970-1971	WBA
Koichi Wajima	Japan	1971-1974	WBA
Oscar Albarado	USA	1974-1975	WBA
Koichi Wajima	Japan	1975	WBA
Miguel de Oliveira	Brazil	1975	WBC
Jae-Do Yuh	S Korea	1975-1976	WBA
Elisha Obed	Bahamas	1975-1976	WBC
Koichi Wajima	Japan	1976	WBA
Jose Duran	Spain	1976	WBA
Eckhard Dagge	Germany	1976-1977	WBC
Miguel Castellini	Argentina	1976-1977	WBA
Eddie Gazo	Nicaragua	1977-1978	WBA
Rocky Mattioli	Italy	1977-1979	WBC
Masashi Kudo	Japan	1978-1979	WBA
Maurice Hope	Antigua	1979-1981	WBC
Ayub Kalule	Uganda	1979-1981	WBA
Wilfred Benitez	USA	1981-1982	WBC
Sugar Ray Leonard*	USA	1981	WBA
Tadashi Mihara	Japan	1981-1982	WBA
Davey Moore	USA	1982-1983	WBA
Thomas Hearns*	USA	1982-1986	WBC
Roberto Duran*	Panama	1983-1984	WBA
Mark Medal	USA	1984	IBF
Mike McCallum*	Jamaica	1984-1987	WBA
Carlos Santos	Puerto Rico	1984-1986	IBF
Buster Drayton	USA	1986-1987	IBF
Duane Thomas	USA	1986-1987	WBC
Matthew Hilton	Canada	1987-1988	IBF
Lupe Aquino	Mexico	1987	WBC
Gianfranco Rosi	Italy	1987-1988	WBC
Julian Jackson*	Virgin Islands	1987-1990	WBA
Don Curry	USA	1988-1989	WBC
Robert Hines	USA	1988-1989	IBF
John David Jackson*	USA	1988-1993	WBO
Darrin van Horn	USA	1989	IBF
Rene Jacqot	France	1989	WBC
John Mugabi	Uganda	1989-1990	WBC
Gianfranco Rosi	Italy	1989-1994	IBF
Terry Norris	USA	1990-1993	WBC
Gilbert Dele	France	1991	WBA
Vinny Pazienza*	USA	1991-1992	WBA
Julio Cesar Vasquez	Argentina	1992-1995	WBA
Verno Phillips	USA	1993-1995	WBO
Simon Brown	USA	1993-1994	WBC
Terry Norris	USA	1994	WBC
Vince Pettway	USA	1994-1995	IBF
Luis Santana	Dom Republic	1994-1995	WBC
Pernell Whitaker*	USA	1995	WBA
Gianfranco Rosi	Italy	1995	WBO
Carl Daniels	USA	1995	WBA
Verno Phillips	USA	1995	WBO
Paul Vaden	USA	1995	IBF
Terry Norris*	USA	1995	WBC
Paul Jones	England	1995-1996	WBO
Terry Norris	USA	1995-1997	IBF/WBC
Julio Cesar Vasquez	Argentina	1995-1996	WBA
Bronco McKart	USA	1996	WBO
Ronald Wright	USA	1996-1998	WBO
Laurent Boudouani	France	1996-1999	WBA
Terry Norris	USA	1997	WBC

Title Holder	Birthplace	Tenure	Status
Raul Marquez	USA	1997	IBF
Luis Campas	Mexico	1997-1998	IBF
Keith Mullings	USA	1997-1999	WBC
Harry Simon*	Namibia	1998-2001	WBO
Fernando Vargas	USA	1998-2000	IBF
Javier Castillejo	Spain	1999-2001	WBC
David Reid	USA	1999-2000	WBA
Felix Trinidad*	Puerto Rico	2000	WBA
Felix Trinidad*	Puerto Rico	2000-2001	IBF/WBA
Oscar de la Hoya	USA	2001-	WBC
Fernando Vargas	USA	2001-	WBA
Ronald Wright	USA	2001-	IBF
Daniel Santos	Puerto Rico	2002-	WBO

Middleweight (160 lbs)

Title Holder	Birthplace	Tenure	Status
Nonpareil Jack Dempsey	Ireland	1889-1891	USA
Bob Fitzsimmons	England	1891-1893	USA
Jim Hall	Australia	1892-1893	GB
Bob Fitzsimmons	England	1893-1894	
Bob Fitzsimmons	England	1894-1899	
Frank Craig	USA	1894-1895	GB
Dan Creedon	New Zealand	1895-1897	GB
Tommy Ryan	USA	1895-1896	
Kid McCoy	USA	1896-1898	
Tommy Ryan	USA	1898-1905	
Charley McKeever	USA	1900-1902	
George Gardner	USA	1901-1902	
Jack O'Brien	USA	1901-1905	
George Green	USA	1901-1902	
Jack Palmer	England	1902-1903	GB
Hugo Kelly	USA	1905-1908	
Jack Twin Sullivan	USA	1905-1908	
Sam Langford	Canada	1907-1911	
Billy Papke	USA	1908	
Stanley Ketchel	USA	1908	
Billy Papke	USA	1908	
Stanley Ketchel	USA	1908-1910	
Billy Papke	USA	1910-1913	
Stanley Ketchel*	USA	1910	
Hugo Kelly	USA	1910-1912	
Cyclone Johnny Thompson	USA	1911-1912	
Harry Lewis	USA	1911	
Leo Houck	USA	1911-1912	
Georges Carpentier	France	1911-1912	
Jack Dillon	USA	1912	
Frank Mantell	USA	1912-1913	
Frank Klaus	USA	1912-1913	
Georges Carpentier	France	1912	IBU
Jack Dillon	USA	1912-1915	
Eddie McGoorty	USA	1912-1913	
Frank Klaus	USA	1913	IBU
Jimmy Clabby	USA	1913-1914	
George Chip	USA	1913-1914	
Joe Borrell	USA	1913-1914	
Jeff Smith	USA	1913-1914	
Eddie McGoorty	USA	1914	AUSTR
Jeff Smith	USA	1914	AUSTR
Al McCoy	USA	1914-1917	
Jimmy Clabby	USA	1914-1915	
Mick King	Australia	1914	AUSTR
Jeff Smith	USA	1914-1915	AUSTR
Young Ahearn	England	1915-1916	
Les Darcy*	Australia	1915-1917	AUSTR
Mike Gibbons	USA	1916-1917	
Mike O'Dowd	USA	1917-1920	
Johnny Wilson	USA	1920-1921	
Johnny Wilson	USA	1921-1922	NBA/NY
Bryan Downey	USA	1921-1922	OHIO
Johnny Wilson	USA	1922-1923	NBA
Dave Rosenberg	USA	1922	NY
Jock Malone	USA	1922-1923	OHIO
Mike O'Dowd	USA	1922-1923	NY
Johnny Wilson	USA	1923	
Harry Greb	USA	1923-1926	

Title Holder	Birthplace	Tenure	Status
Tiger Flowers	USA	1926	
Mickey Walker	USA	1926-1931	
Gorilla Jones	USA	1932	NBA
Marcel Thil	France	1932-1933	NBA/IBU
Marcel Thil	France	1933-1937	IBU
Ben Jeby	USA	1933	NY
Lou Brouillard	Canada	1933	NY
Lou Brouillard	Canada	1933	NY/NBA
Vearl Whitehead	USA	1933	CALIF
Teddy Yarosz	USA	1933-1934	PEN
Vince Dundee	USA	1933-1934	NY/NBA
Teddy Yarosz	USA	1934-1935	NY/NBA
Babe Risko	USA	1935-1936	NY/NBA
Freddie Steele	USA	1936-1938	NY/NBA
Fred Apostoli	USA	1937-1938	IBU
Edouard Tenet	France	1938	IBU
Young Corbett III	Italy	1938	CALIF
Freddie Steele	USA	1938	NBA
Al Hostak	USA	1938	NBA
Solly Krieger	USA	1938-1939	NBA
Fred Apostoli	USA	1938-1939	NY
Al Hostak	USA	1939-1940	NBA
Ceferino Garcia	Philippines	1939-1940	NY
Ken Overlin	USA	1940-1941	NY
Tony Zale	USA	1940-1941	NBA
Billy Soose	USA	1941	NY
Tony Zale	USA	1941-1947	
Rocky Graziano	USA	1947-1948	
Tony Zale	USA	1948	
Marcel Cerdan	Algeria	1948-1949	
Jake la Motta	USA	1949-1950	
Jake la Motta	USA	1950-1951	NY/NBA
Sugar Ray Robinson	USA	1950-1951	PEN
Sugar Ray Robinson	USA	1951	
Randy Turpin	England	1951	
Sugar Ray Robinson*	USA	1951-1952	
Randy Turpin	England	1953	GB/EBU
Carl Bobo Olson	Hawaii	1953-1955	
Sugar Ray Robinson	USA	1955-1957	
Gene Fullmer	USA	1957	
Sugar Ray Robinson	USA	1957	
Carmen Basilio	USA	1957-1958	
Sugar Ray Robinson	USA	1958-1959	
Sugar Ray Robinson	USA	1959-1960	NY/EBU
Gene Fullmer	USA	1959-1962	NBA
Paul Pender	USA	1960-1961	NY/EBU
Terry Downes	England	1961-1962	NY/EBU
Paul Pender	USA	1962	NY/EBU
Dick Tiger	Nigeria	1962-1963	NBA
Dick Tiger	Nigeria	1963	
Joey Giardello	USA	1963-1965	
Dick Tiger	Nigeria	1965-1966	
Emile Griffith	Virgin Islands	1966-1967	
Nino Benvenuti	Italy	1967	
Emile Griffith	Virgin Islands	1967-1968	
Nino Benvenuti	Italy	1968-1970	
Carlos Monzon	Argentina	1970-1974	
Carlos Monzon*	Argentina	1974-1976	WBA
Rodrigo Valdez	Colombia	1974-1976	WBC
Carlos Monzon*	Argentina	1976-1977	
Rodrigo Valdez	Colombia	1977-1978	
Hugo Corro	Argentina	1978-1979	
Vito Antuofermo	Italy	1979-1980	
Alan Minter	England	1980	
Marvin Hagler	USA	1980-1987	
Marvin Hagler	USA	1987	WBC/IBF
Sugar Ray Leonard	USA	1987	WBC
Frank Tate	USA	1987-1988	IBF
Sumbu Kalambay	Zaire	1987-1989	WBA
Thomas Hearns	USA	1987-1988	WBC
Iran Barkley	USA	1988-1989	WBC
Michael Nunn	USA	1988-1991	IBF
Roberto Duran	Panama	1989-1990	WBC
Doug de Witt	USA	1989-1990	WBO

Title Holder	Birthplace	Tenure	Status	Title Holder	Birthplace	Tenure	Status
Mike McCallum	Jamaica	1989-1991	WBA	McClellan*	USA	1991-1993	WBO
Nigel Benn	England	1990	WBO	Reggie Johnson	USA	1992-1993	WBA
Chris Eubank*	England	1990-1991	WBO	Gerald McClellan*	USA	1993-1995	WBC
Julian Jackson	Virgin Islands	1990-1993	WBC	Chris Pyatt	England	1993-1994	WBO
James Toney*	USA	1991-1993	IBF	Roy Jones*	USA	1993-1994	IBF
Gerald							

Marvin Hagler, the former world middleweight champion

Pete Goldfield

Title Holder	Birthplace	Tenure	Status		Title Holder	Birthplace	Tenure	Status
John David Jackson	USA	1993-1994	WBA		**Battling Siki**	Senegal	1922-1923	
Steve Collins*	Ireland	1994-1995	WBO		**Mike McTigue**	Ireland	1923-1925	
Jorge Castro	Argentina	1994	WBA		**Paul Berlenbach**	USA	1925-1926	
Julian Jackson	Virgin Islands	1995	WBC		**Jack Delaney***	Canada	1926-1927	
Bernard Hopkins*	USA	1995-2001	IBF		Jimmy Slattery	USA	1927	NBA
Lonnie Bradley*	USA	1995-1998	WBO		Tommy Loughran	USA	1927	NY
Quincy Taylor	USA	1995-1996	WBC		**Tommy Loughran***	USA	1927-1929	
Shinji Takehara	Japan	1995-1996	WBA		Jimmy Slattery	USA	1930	NY
Keith Holmes	USA	1996-1998	WBC		**Maxie Rosenbloom**	USA	1930-1931	
William Joppy	USA	1996-1997	WBA		Maxie Rosenbloom	USA	1931-1933	NY
Julio Cesar Green	Dom Republic	1997-1998	WBA		George Nichols	USA	1932	NBA
William Joppy	USA	1998-2001	WBA		Bob Godwin	USA	1933	NBA
Hassine Cherifi	France	1998-1999	WBC		**Maxie Rosenbloom**	USA	1933-1934	
Otis Grant*	Canada	1998	WBO		Maxie Rosenbloom	USA	1934	NY
Bert Schenk	Germany	1999	WBO		Joe Knight	USA	1934-1935	FL/NC/GEO
Keith Holmes	USA	1999-2001	WBC		Bob Olin	USA	1934-1935	NY
Jason Matthews	England	1999	WBO		Al McCoy	Canada	1935	CAN
Armand Krajnc	Slovenia	1999-2002	WBO		Bob Olin	USA	1935	NY/NBA
Bernard Hopkins*	USA	2001	WBC/IBF		John Henry Lewis	USA	1935-1938	NY/NBA
Felix Trinidad	Puerto Rico	2001	WBA		Gustav Roth	Belgium	1936-1938	IBU
Bernard Hopkins	USA	2001-	WBC/WBA/IBF		Ad Heuser	Germany	1938	IBU
Harry Simon	Namibia	2002-	WBO		**John Henry Lewis**	USA	1938	
					John Henry Lewis	USA	1938-1939	NBA

S. Middleweight (168 lbs)

Title Holder	Birthplace	Tenure	Status		Title Holder	Birthplace	Tenure	Status
Murray Sutherland	Scotland	1984	IBF		Melio Bettina	USA	1939	NY
Chong-Pal Park*	S Korea	1984-1987	IBF		Len Harvey	England	1939-1942	GB
Chong-Pal Park	S Korea	1987-1988	WBA		Billy Conn	USA	1939-1940	NY/NBA
Graciano Rocchigiani*	Germany	1988-1989	IBF		Anton Christoforidis	Greece	1941	NBA
Fully Obelmejias	Venezuela	1988-1989	WBA		Gus Lesnevich	USA	1941	NBA
Sugar Ray Leonard*	USA	1988-1990	WBC		Gus Lesnevich	USA	1941-1946	NY/NBA
Thomas Hearns*	USA	1988-1991	WBO		Freddie Mills	England	1942-1946	GB
In-Chul Baek	S Korea	1989-1990	WBA		**Gus Lesnevich**	USA	1946-1948	
Lindell Holmes	USA	1990-1991	IBF		**Freddie Mills**	England	1948-1950	
Christophe Tiozzo	France	1990-1991	WBA		**Joey Maxim**	USA	1950-1952	
Mauro Galvano	Italy	1990-1992	WBC		**Archie Moore**	USA	1952-1960	
Victor Cordoba	Panama	1991-1992	WBA		Archie Moore	USA	1960-1962	NY/EBU
Darrin van Horn	USA	1991-1992	IBF		Harold Johnson	USA	1961-1962	NBA
Chris Eubank	England	1991-1995	WBO		**Harold Johnson**	USA	1962-1963	
Iran Barkley	USA	1992-1993	IBF		**Willie Pastrano**	USA	1963	
Michael Nunn	USA	1992-1994	WBA		Willie Pastrano*	USA	1963-1964	WBA/WBC
Nigel Benn	England	1992-1996	WBC		Eddie Cotton	USA	1963-1964	MICH
James Toney	USA	1993-1994	IBF		**Willie Pastrano**	USA	1964-1965	
Steve Little	USA	1994	WBA		**Jose Torres**	Puerto Rico	1965-1966	
Frank Liles	USA	1994-1999	WBA		**Dick Tiger**	Nigeria	1966-1968	
Roy Jones*	USA	1994-1997	IBF		**Bob Foster**	USA	1968-1970	
Steve Collins*	Ireland	1995-1997	WBO		Bob Foster*	USA	1970-1972	WBC
Thulani Malinga	S Africa	1996	WBC		Vicente Rondon	Venezuela	1971-1972	WBA
Vincenzo Nardiello	Italy	1996	WBC		**Bob Foster***	USA	1972-1974	
Robin Reid	England	1996-1997	WBC		John Conteh	England	1974-1977	WBC
Charles Brewer	USA	1997-1998	IBF		Victor Galindez	Argentina	1974-1978	WBA
Joe Calzaghe	Wales	1997-	WBO		Miguel Cuello	Argentina	1977-1978	WBC
Thulani Malinga	S Africa	1997-1998	WBC		Mate Parlov	Yugoslavia	1978	WBC
Richie Woodhall	England	1998-1999	WBC		Mike Rossman	USA	1978-1979	WBA
Sven Ottke	Germany	1998-	IBF		Marvin Johnson	USA	1978-1979	WBC
Byron Mitchell	USA	1999-2000	WBA		Victor Galindez	Argentina	1979	WBA
Markus Beyer	Germany	1999-2000	WBC		Matt Saad Muhammad	USA	1979-1981	WBC
Bruno Girard	France	2000-2001	WBA		Marvin Johnson	USA	1979-1980	WBA
Glenn Catley	England	2000	WBC		Mustafa Muhammad	USA	1980-1981	WBA
Dingaan Thobela	S Africa	2000	WBC		Michael Spinks*	USA	1981-1983	WBA
Dave Hilton	Canada	2000-2001	WBC		Dwight Muhammad Qawi	USA	1981-1983	WBC
Byron Mitchell	USA	2001-	WBA		**Michael Spinks***	USA	1983-1985	
Eric Lucas	Canada	2001-	WBC		J. B. Williamson	USA	1985-1986	WBC
					Slobodan Kacar	Yugoslavia	1985-1986	IBF

L. Heavyweight (175 lbs)

Title Holder	Birthplace	Tenure	Status		Title Holder	Birthplace	Tenure	Status
Jack Root	Austria	1903			Marvin Johnson	USA	1986-1987	WBA
George Gardner	Ireland	1903			Dennis Andries	Guyana	1986-1987	WBC
George Gardner	Ireland	1903	USA		Bobby Czyz	USA	1986-1987	IBF
Bob Fitzsimmons	England	1903-1905	USA		Thomas Hearns*	USA	1987	WBC
Jack O'Brien	USA	1905-1911			Leslie Stewart	Trinidad	1987	WBA
Sam Langford	Canada	1911-1913			Virgil Hill	USA	1987-1991	WBA
Georges Carpentier	France	1913-1920	IBU		Charles Williams	USA	1987-1993	IBF
Jack Dillon	USA	1914-1916	USA		Don Lalonde	Canada	1987-1988	WBC
Battling Levinsky	USA	1916-1920	USA		Sugar Ray Leonard*	USA	1988	WBC
Georges Carpentier	France	1920-1922			Michael Moorer*	USA	1988-1991	WBO
					Dennis Andries	Guyana	1989	WBC
					Jeff Harding	Australia	1989-1990	WBC

Title Holder	Birthplace	Tenure	Status
Dennis Andries	Guyana	1990-1991	WBC
Leonzer Barber	USA	1991-1994	WBO
Thomas Hearns	USA	1991-1992	WBA
Jeff Harding	Australia	1991-1994	WBC
Iran Barkley*	USA	1992	WBA
Virgil Hill*	USA	1992-1996	WBA
Henry Maske	Germany	1993-1996	IBF
Mike McCallum	Jamaica	1994-1995	WBC
Dariusz Michalczewski*	Poland	1994-1997	WBO
Fabrice Tiozzo	France	1995-1997	WBC
Virgil Hill	USA	1996-1997	IBF/WBA
Roy Jones	USA	1997	WBC
Montell Griffin	USA	1997	WBC
Dariusz Michalczewski*	Poland	1997	WBO/IBF/WBA
Dariusz Michalczewski	Poland	1997-	WBO
William Guthrie	USA	1997-1998	IBF
Roy Jones*	USA	1997-1998	WBC
Lou del Valle	USA	1997-1998	WBA
Reggie Johnson	USA	1998-1999	IBF
Roy Jones*	USA	1998-1999	WBC/WBA
Roy Jones	USA	1999-	WBC/WBA/IBF

Cruiserweight (190 lbs)

Title Holder	Birthplace	Tenure	Status
Marvin Camel	USA	1979-1980	WBC
Carlos de Leon	Puerto Rico	1980-1982	WBC
Ossie Ocasio	Puerto Rico	1982-1984	WBA
S. T. Gordon	USA	1982-1983	WBC
Marvin Camel	USA	1983-1984	IBF
Carlos de Leon	Puerto Rico	1983-1985	WBC
Lee Roy Murphy	USA	1984-1986	IBF
Piet Crous	S Africa	1984-1985	WBA
Alfonso Ratliff	USA	1985	WBC
Dwight Muhammad Qawi	USA	1985-1986	WBA
Bernard Benton	USA	1985-1986	WBC
Carlos de Leon	Puerto Rico	1986-1988	WBC
Evander Holyfield*	USA	1986-1987	WBA
Rickey Parkey*	USA	1986-1987	IBF
Evander Holyfield*	USA	1987-1988	WBA/IBF
Evander Holyfield*	USA	1988	
Taoufik Belbouli*	France	1989	WBA
Carlos de Leon	Puerto Rico	1989-1990	WBC
Glenn McCrory	England	1989-1990	IBF
Robert Daniels	USA	1989-1991	WBA
Boone Pultz	USA	1989-1990	WBO
Jeff Lampkin*	USA	1990-1991	IBF
Magne Havnaa*	Norway	1990-1992	WBO
Masimilliano Duran	Italy	1990-1991	WBC
Bobby Czyz	USA	1991-1993	WBA
Anaclet Wamba	Congo	1991-1995	WBC
James Warring	USA	1991-1992	IBF
Tyrone Booze	USA	1992-1993	WBO
Al Cole*	USA	1992-1996	IBF
Marcus Bott	Germany	1993	WBO
Nestor Giovannini	Argentina	1993-1994	WBO
Orlin Norris	USA	1993-1995	WBA
Dariusz Michalczewski*	Poland	1994-1995	WBO
Ralf Rocchigiani	Germany	1995-1997	WBO
Nate Miller	USA	1995-1997	WBA
Marcelo Dominguez	Argentina	1995-1998	WBC
Adolpho Washington	USA	1996-1997	IBF
Uriah Grant	USA	1997	IBF
Carl Thompson	England	1997-1999	WBO
Imamu Mayfield	USA	1997-1998	IBF
Fabrice Tiozzo	France	1997-2000	WBA
Juan Carlos Gomez*	Cuba	1998-2002	WBC
Arthur Williams	USA	1998-1999	IBF
Johnny Nelson	England	1999-	WBO
Vassily Jirov	Kazakhstan	1999-	IBF
Virgil Hill	USA	2000-2002	WBA
Jean-Marc Mormeck	Guadeloupe	2002-	WBA

Heavyweight (190 lbs+)

Title Holder	Birthplace	Tenure	Status
John L. Sullivan	USA	1889-1892	USA
Peter Jackson	Australia	1889-1892	

Title Holder	Birthplace	Tenure	Status
Frank Slavin	Australia	1890-1892	GB/AUST
Peter Jackson	Australia	1892-1893	GB/AUST
James J. Corbett	USA	1892-1894	USA
James J. Corbett	USA	1894-1895	
James J. Corbett	USA	1895-1897	
Peter Maher	Ireland	1895-1896	
Bob Fitzsimmons	England	1896-1897	
Bob Fitzsimmons	England	1897-1899	
James J. Jeffries	USA	1899-1902	
James J. Jeffries	USA	1902-1905	
Denver Ed Martin	USA	1902-1903	
Jack Johnson	USA	1902-1908	
Bob Fitzsimmons	England	1905	
Marvin Hart	USA	1905-1906	
Jack O'Brien	USA	1905-1906	
Tommy Burns	Canada	1906-1908	
Jack Johnson	USA	1908-1909	
Jack Johnson	USA	1909-1915	
Sam Langford	USA	1909-1911	
Sam McVey	USA	1911-1912	
Sam Langford	USA	1912-1914	
Luther McCarty	USA	1913	
Arthur Pelkey	Canada	1913-1914	
Gunboat Smith	USA	1914	
Harry Wills	USA	1914	
Georges Carpentier	France	1914	
Sam Langford	USA	1914-1915	
Jess Willard	USA	1915-1919	
Joe Jeannette	USA	1915	
Sam McVey	USA	1915	
Harry Wills	USA	1915-1916	
Sam Langford	USA	1916-1917	
Bill Tate	USA	1917	
Sam Langford	USA	1917-1918	
Harry Wills	USA	1918-1926	
Jack Dempsey	USA	1919-1926	
Gene Tunney*	USA	1926-1928	
Max Schmeling	Germany	1930-1932	
Jack Sharkey	USA	1932-1933	
Primo Carnera	Italy	1933-1934	
Max Baer	USA	1934-1935	
James J. Braddock	USA	1935	
James J. Braddock	USA	1935-1936	NY/NBA
George Godfrey	USA	1935-1936	IBU
James J. Braddock	USA	1936-1937	
Joe Louis*	USA	1937-1949	
Ezzard Charles	USA	1949-1950	NBA
Lee Savold	USA	1950-1951	GB/EBU
Ezzard Charles	USA	1950-1951	NY/NBA
Joe Louis	USA	1951	GB/EBU
Jersey Joe Walcott	USA	1951	NY/NBA
Jersey Joe Walcott	USA	1951-1952	
Rocky Marciano*	USA	1952-1956	
Floyd Patterson	USA	1956-1959	
Ingemar Johansson	Sweden	1959-1960	
Floyd Patterson	USA	1960-1962	
Sonny Liston	USA	1962-1964	
Muhammad Ali	USA	1964	
Muhammad Ali*	USA	1964-1967	WBC
Ernie Terrell	USA	1965-1967	WBA
Muhammad Ali	USA	1967	
Muhammad Ali	USA	1967-1968	WBC
Joe Frazier*	USA	1968-1970	NY/MASS
Jimmy Ellis	USA	1968-1970	WBA
Joe Frazier	USA	1970-1973	
George Foreman	USA	1973-1974	
Muhammad Ali	USA	1974-1978	
Leon Spinks	USA	1978	
Leon Spinks	USA	1978	WBA
Larry Holmes*	USA	1978-1983	WBC
Muhammad Ali*	USA	1978-1979	WBA
John Tate	USA	1979-1980	WBA
Mike Weaver	USA	1980-1982	WBA
Michael Dokes	USA	1982-1983	WBA

Gerrie Coetzee	S Africa	1983-1984	WBA	Herbie Hide	England	1994-1995	WBO
Larry Holmes	USA	1983-1985	IBF	Michael Moorer	USA	1994	WBA/IBF
Tim Witherspoon	USA	1984	WBC	Oliver McCall	USA	1994-1995	WBC
Pinklon Thomas	USA	1984-1986	WBC	George Foreman	USA	1994-1995	WBA/IBF
Greg Page	USA	1984-1985	WBA	Riddick Bowe*	USA	1995-1996	WBO
Tony Tubbs	USA	1985-1986	WBA	George Foreman*	USA	1995	IBF
Michael Spinks	USA	1985-1987	IBF	Bruce Seldon	USA	1995-1996	WBA
Tim Witherspoon	USA	1986	WBA	Frank Bruno	England	1995-1996	WBC
Trevor Berbick	Jamaica	1986	WBC	Frans Botha	S Africa	1995-1996	IBF
Mike Tyson*	USA	1986-1987	WBC	Mike Tyson	USA	1996	WBC
James Smith	USA	1986-1987	WBA	Michael Moorer	USA	1996-1997	IBF
Mike Tyson*	USA	1987	WBA/WBC	Henry Akinwande*	England	1996-1997	WBO
Tony Tucker	USA	1987	IBF	Mike Tyson	USA	1996	WBA
Mike Tyson	USA	1987-1989		Evander Holyfield*	USA	1996-1997	WBA
Mike Tyson	USA	1989-1990	IBF/WBA/WBC	Lennox Lewis*	England	1997-1999	WBC
Francesco Damiani	Italy	1989-1991	WBO	Herbie Hide	England	1997-1999	WBO
James Douglas	USA	1990	IBF/WBA/WBC	Evander Holyfield	USA	1997-1999	IBF/WBA
Evander Holyfield	USA	1990-1992	IBF/WBA/WBC	Vitali Klitschko	Ukraine	1999-2000	WBO
Ray Mercer	USA	1991-1992	WBO	Lennox Lewis*	England	1999-2000	IBF/WBA/WBC
Michael Moorer*	USA	1992-1993	WBO	Chris Byrd	USA	2000	WBO
Riddick Bowe	USA	1992	IBF/WBA/WBC	Lennox Lewis	England	2000-2001	IBF/WBC
Riddick Bowe	USA	1992-1993	IBF/WBA	Evander Holyfield	USA	2000-2001	WBA
Lennox Lewis	England	1992-1994	WBC	Vladimir Klitschko	Ukraine	2000-	WBO
Tommy Morrison	USA	1993	WBO	John Ruiz	USA	2001-	WBA
Michael Bentt	England	1993-1994	WBO	Hasim Rahman	USA	2001	WBA/IBF
Evander Holyfield	USA	1993-1994	WBA/IBF	Lennox Lewis	England	2001-	WBA/IBF

Jersey Joe Walcott (right), at the age of 37, finally won the world heavyweight title at the fifth attempt when knocking out Ezzard Charles in Pittsburgh, USA on 18 July 1951

The Championship History of the Paperweight and Flyweight Classes

by Barry J. Hugman and Harold Alderman

This section has attempted to list in diary format all the leading fights and fighters at weights below 112lbs from the beginning of gloves (1877) through to 2001. When gloved boxing took over from bare-fist fighting, the lowest recognised weight class was bantam, which, like the other weight classes (feather, light, middle and heavy), had no regular ceiling but would have certainly included all weights at 112lbs and below. Later, in Britain, the smallest men would come to be known as paperweights and for our purposes I have taken all weights below 106lbs, in Britain and America, to fall into that category, with those above 106lbs (108lbs in 1897) still seen as bantamweight until 1909 when the National Sporting Club introduced the flyweight class for all men below 112lbs.

Note: Prior to 1923, all fighters listed below without a (country) should be assumed to be British, while any venues shown by town alone belong to Britain. However, from that date onwards, when the flyweight class finally achieved world-wide recognition, all fighters are listed with their country of birth/domicile and likewise for venues. Due to a lack of space, results from the mini and light-flyweight divisions of recent times are not listed.

1877

11 December Punch Dowsett drew 41 Tommy Hawkins, Victoria Skating Rink, Cambridge Heath Road, Hoxton, London. Billed for the English 108lbs title and a £50 silver cup, using two-ounce gloves, when time ran out and the venue had to close at midnight, the referee, Mr Bob Watson, ordered that the bout had to continue the following night. However, on being overruled, a draw was declared.

1878

27 July Tommy Hawkins drew 31 Joe Fowler, St Helen's Grounds, Rotherhithe, London. Billed for the English 110lbs title, to a finish, wearing two-ounce gloves, £15 a side, Hawkins weighed 7st 11lbs to Fowler's 7st 12lbs. The fight was stopped and declared a draw by the referee, Bob Watson, when it was too dark to see.

16 August Tommy Hawkins drew 51 Joe Fowler, Brennan's Yard Assembly Rooms, Bull Lane, Stepney, London. Billed for the English 110lbs title, £25 a side, two-ounce gloves, and the original Joe Hoiles' championship belt (won in 1854). Called a draw when it was getting dark, with Hawkins weighing 7st 11lbs and Fowler 7st 12lbs, the bout is the longest recorded to have taken place in Europe. It is said that the above two contests, which were sporting, but hard fought and skilful, established 'gloved' boxing. Unfortunately, on 27 November 1878, while boxing an exhibition with Punch Dowsett, Fowler dislocated his right arm, the injury ultimately ending his career. Still carrying on in exhibitions, he died in the USA in 1892.

1879

31 July Tommy Hawkins w co 17 Charlie Hipkiss. Billed for the English 108lbs title, this was a finish fight about 50 miles from London before a limited attendance of 45. Using six-ounce gloves and fighting for a £50 purse, Hawkins weighed 7st 9½lbs to Hipkiss' 7st 8lbs.

2 December George Young w co 5 Sam Fitch, 'The Mitre', St Thomas' Street, The Borough, London. Billed for the English 110lbs title and for a £20 cup, the fight would be better remembered for the incident that involved Fitch being bitten by a dog.

1884

23 January Steve Corbett w rtd 20 Jack Hullett, a private show in London. Billed for a finish at 108lbs, with both men scaling 107lbs, Corbett claimed the English title on his victory.

1887

10 January Harry Barnes w pts 10 Steve Corbett, Lambeth School of Arms, Paradise Street, London. No weights or billing reported, but Barnes strengthened his 104lbs English title claim on the result.

30 May (Edwin) Nunc Wallace w co 5 Sam Tongue. Fought in a quiet suburb of Birmingham, and billed for 12 rounds, the winner advertised himself as the English 112lbs champion on the result.

5 October George Camp w co 23 Con Donovan, a private show in London. Billed for the English 108lbs title, and to a finish, Camp weighed 7st 10lbs to Donovan's 7st 8lbs.

16 December George Camp w rtd 15 Jack Sharpe, a private show in London. Although no weights or title billing were reported, later gossip gave Camp as winning the English 112lbs title by this victory.

24 December Hughie Boyle w co 8 Tommy Kelly (USA), NYC, New York, USA. Reported in the *Ring Record Book* to be a contest that decided the American 105lbs title, following extensive research of the New York papers of the day I have yet to find a report of the fight, let alone the fact that it might have involved a claim at the weight in skin-tight gloves.

1888

17 January Bill Lawless w co 18 Jack Tyson, a private show in the west end of London. Although there was no title billing as such, later 'gossip' gave it as an English 108lbs title fight, with Lawless weighing 7st 8lbs to Tyson's 7st 10lbs. Strangely, there is no record of Lawless claiming the championship.

1 February Con Donovan w rtd 63 Tommy Monk, The Baths, Newmarket. Weighing 111lbs to his opponent's 112, this was a finish fight using small gloves and Donovan claimed the English 112lbs title on the result.

25 February Hughie Boyle w rsc 9 Jack Dinan (USA), Staten Island, New York, USA. Contested under MoQ Rules in kid gloves, Boyle (105lbs) claimed the 108lbs title following his win over Dinan (108lbs).

16 March George Camp w co 8 Young Joe Farrell. Stipulated for 12 rounds, and held in private in the City of London, although there was no title billing attached later boxing gossip gave it as a successful defence of Camp's English 112lbs title.

10 May George Dixon (Canada) drew 9 Tommy Kelly (USA), Boston, USA. According to the Boston Post, this was just a seven rounder which was allowed to run to nine because of the interest and was not stopped by the police as intimated in some reports. However, the *Ring Record Book* tells us that, following a ninth-round kayo win for Dixon (105) over Kelly (104¾), his manager, Tom O'Rourke, claimed the American 105lbs title for his charge, although there is no evidence that Dixon ever defended before moving up in weight. On 19 April 1889, the *Philadelphia Item* reported that Tommy Russell had defeated Kelly for the American 105lbs title, but no clarification of that result has come to light as yet. Another defeat for Kelly, on points over 10 rounds, that cannot be substantiated supposedly came on 5 June 1889 in New York City against Chappie Moran.

18 August Jack Dinan (USA) w co 8 Frank Donovan (USA), Winchester, New York, USA. For the American 107lbs championship and a $300 purse, to a finish, Dinan weighed 7st 8½lbs to Donovan's 7st 8lbs.

26 November Goody Jacobs w pts12 Fred Sullivan, Lambeth School of Arms, Paradise Street, London. Billed for the English 106lbs title, it was initially intended to be a finish bout.

3 December Billy Holmes w pts 10 Patsy Sheehan, Pelican Club, Gerrard Street, Soho London. Although being contested at catchweights, following his win over Sheehan (99lbs), Holmes (102lbs) claimed the English 102lbs title.

13 December Tom DeGroat nc 37 Harry Gower, east end of London. Articled to be a finish fight, with three-ounce gloves at catchweights, it was later reported to have been for the English 100lbs title, DeGroat weighing 98lbs to Gower's 100¼lbs. Stopped by police after two hours and 26 minutes, the referee ruled that the fight should be restarted on 27 December. However, although both parties turned up on the day, Gower, refusing to use new gloves and weigh in again, left, whereupon the referee awarded DeGroat the stake money.

1889

12 January Frank Donovan (USA) w co 21 Joe Glassey (USA), Elizabethport, New Jersey, USA. Donovan (105lbs) laid claim to the American 105lbs title following his win over Glassey (102lbs).

5 March Jem Stevens (Bethnal Green) w rtd 6 Ted Hooker (St Luke's), 'The King's Arms', Abbey Street, Bethnal Green, London. Billed for the English 112lbs title.

5 March Nunc Wallace w co 9 Little Bill Goode, a private show in London. Billed for the English 112lbs title, with both men inside 110lbs, the winner had a claim at that weight also and, to add even more confusion, the match had been articled for a finish at 114lbs. Therefore, it was hardly surprising there was a strong feeling that the scales were faulty.

17 April Tom DeGroat w co 20 Patsy Sheehan, a private show in London. To a finish for the English and world 98lb titles, DeGroat scaled 98lbs to Sheehan's 96lbs.

2 May Billy Murray (USA) w co 39 Johnny Lyman (USA), NYC, New York, USA. Contested on the Long Island Sound for the American 110lbs title, to a finish in skin-tight gloves, according to the *Sporting Life* Murray scaled 109¼lbs to Lyman's 105½.

21 May Chappie Moran w rtd 14 Frank Donovan (USA), Staten Island, NYC, USA. With Moran weighing 105lbs to Donovan's 104½lbs, it was billed as being for the world 105lbs title. Fought in skin-tight gloves, it had no real standing in Britain as Moran was not recognised as the English champion at the weight.

28 May Tommy Kelly (USA) w rsc 17 Harry Walton (USA), Cribb AC, Troy, NY, USA. Billed for the American 110lbs title, using two-ounce gloves, both men were inside the stipulated weight.

18 July Tim Buckley w rtd 19 Sid Phillips, a private show on the Surrey side of London. Billed for the English 102 to 104lbs title to a finish, £50 a side. After winning an 112lbs Frank Hindes' championship competition, Buckley announced on 18 December 1889 that he could no longer make the weight

27 August Jimmy Kennard (USA) w rsc 14 Billy Murray (USA), Troy, New York, USA. According to records produced by Tracy Callis this contest was made at 110lbs and billed for the American title.

2 October Alf Gunning drew 24 Jim Pope, 'The Queen's Head', St John Street, West Smithfield, London. Billed for the English 94lbs title, the report in the *Sportsman* states that it lasted 96 minutes (24 three-minute rounds with a one minute interval between) and was refereed by Tom Longer. It was slated to be a fight to the finish.

14 October Tom Gardner w pts 12 Charlie Mansford, Astley's Ampitheatre, Westminster Bridge Road, London. Made at 112lbs, although there was no title billing Gardner staked a claim to the English championship following his victory.

8 November Jimmy Kennard (USA) w rsc 7 Harry Walton (USA), Buffalo, New York, USA. Made at 110lbs, this was a defence of Kennard's claim at the weight.

25 November Jack Dinan (USA) w co 7 Frank Donovan (USA), NYC, New York, USA. Thought to have been a contest that involved the American 107lbs title, this is the last contest I can trace for Dinnan

26 November Bill Bolton w co 16 Jack Tyson, Kennington Social Club, London. With both men inside 100lbs, this fight was looked upon as being for the English title at the weight.

18 December Con Donovan w co 11 Jack Hullett, Hop and Malt Exchange, Borough High Street, London. Set for a finish, with no weights given, later gossip stated this to be a defence of Donovan's English 112lbs title claim with both men inside eight stone.

23 December Alf Gunning w co 11 Enos Gamble, The Chelsea School of Arms, College Street, London. Billed as a fight to the finish, but with no weights given, Gunning was thought to have successfully defended his 94lbs English title claim.

1890

22 January Charlie Mansford w co 11 Harry Saphir, Kennington Social Club, London. Billed for the English 108lbs title to a finish.

31 January Tommy Kelly (USA) w co 10 Chappie Moran, Easton, Pennsylvania, USA. Billed for the world 105lbs title, Kelly was said to have weighed 108¾lbs although his weight was announced as being 106¾lbs to Moran's 104½. Despite Moran continuing to claim the title by default in America, Kelly was still seen to be the champion, but by 26 June 1890 he was defending at 107lbs.

27 February Alf Gower w co 14 Fred Sulllivan, Ormonde Club, Walworth Road, London. Billed for the English 107lbs title, 3.0 pm weigh-in, £50 a side, and a finish, it was the first ever title billing at an odd weight in a British ring. Gower weighed 7st 8½lbs to Sullivan's 7st 9lbs.

11 March Jimmy Kennard (USA) w rsc 2 Johnny Lyman (USA), Buffalo, New York, USA. Billed for the American 110lbs title.

13 March Alf Gunning w co 4 Bill Bolton, Ormonde Club, Walworth Road, London. Although there was no billing as such, with both men scaling 101lbs it was referred to as a title match at the weight in later years. Regardless, Gunning quickly outgrew the weight class.

20 March Bill Moore w rtd 24 Mike Small, a private show in London's west end. Although there was nothing attached, Moore later stated that he won the English 110lbs title in this one.

2 April Billy Plimmer w co 5 Tim Buckley, The South London Gym, Mountford Place, Kennington, London. Billed for the 107lbs English title, £100 purse, and scheduled for 20 rounds, Plimmer weighed 7st 7lbs to Buckley's 7st 8½lbs.

9 April Charlie Mansford w co 13 Harry Saphir, Godwin Club, Kingsland Road, Shoreditch, London. Billed for the English 108lbs title with a finish in mind.

10 April Bill Moore w dis 12 Alf Gunning, The Hop and Malt Exchange, Borough High Street, London. Again, this was a fight that carried no title billing, but was said later to have involved the English 110lbs title.

1 May Mike Small w rtd 12 Jack Hicks, Con Donovan's private show in the west end of London. There were no weights or billing reported, but later gossip shows that the English 102lbs title was involved.

22 May Mike Small w rtd 5 Bill Rose, Con Donovan's private show in the west end of London. No weights or billing stated, and most likely a catchweight match, but Small, inside 102lbs, claimed the English title at the weight.

3 June Alf Gower w co 4 Arthur Westley, Godwin Club, Kingsland Road, Shoreditch, London. Billed for the English 107lbs title, for finish, both men scaled 7st 8lbs. Gower, who had just taken over the 'Essex Arms' in Mile End, stated that he would be unable to defend for some while due to business commitments.

26 June Bill Moore w co 4 A. Gates, a private show in London's west end. Billed for the English 110lbs title, £20 a side, Gates scaled 7st 11lbs to Moore's 7st 12lbs.

26 June Tommy Kelly (USA) w co 3 Benny Murphy, NYC, New York, USA. Although billed for the 105lbs title it had more to do with the 107lbs championship, with Kelly weighing 106½lbs to Murphy's 105½.

2 July Alf Winters w rtd 5 J. O'Grady, Bob Kirby's Lambeth School of Arms, Paradise Street, London. Billed for the English 98lbs title, and £25 a side.

16 July Charley Roberts w co 8 Charlie Mansford, Greyhound

Hotel, Newmarket. Despite reports not giving weights or billing, with both men inside eight stone it was eventually recognised to be a defence of Roberts' English 112lbs title claim.

17 July Joe Portley drew 20 Jim Read, Hop and Malt Exchange, Borough High Street, London. Billed for the English 102lbs title.

24 July Ponk Andrews w rtd 8 Alf Bates. Made at 7st 10lbs, using small gloves, and for £25 a side, Andrews claimed the English 108lbs title following his win. Held in Shoreditch, London, it was a private show.

7 August Mike Small w pts 20 Wag Lansdowne, Queens Head, St John's Street, West Smithfield, London. Thought to involve the English 102lbs title despite a lack of weights and billing

11 August Billy Plimmer w co 13 Arthur Westley, Ormonde Club, Walworth Road, London. Billed for the English 107lbs title and scheduled for 20 rounds, and a £70 purse, Plimmer weighed 7st 7lbs to Westley's 7st 8lbs.

25 August Alf Sparrow w co 15 Alf Winters, Lambeth School of Arms, Paradise Street, London. Billed for the English 101lbs title, and to a finish, the *Sportsman* stated that neither Sparrow or Winters were up to championship standard.

16 September Tommy Kelly (USA) w co 11 Tommy Russell (USA), Hoboken, New Jersey, USA. Although described as a ten-round spar prior to the meet by the *New York World* it was held in private and appears to be more than just a spar, especially when Kelly posted $1,000 with the *Police Gazette* the following day and announced that he was prepared to fight anybody in the world at 105 to 107lbs.

30 September Alf Gunning w rtd 16 Young Hyland, The Ancient Concert Rooms, Great Brunswick Street, Dublin. Stipulated for 20 rounds, but no title billing or weights announced, Gunning's English 94lbs title claim was thought to have been at stake.

4 December Patsy Sheehan w pts 13 Bill Mortimer, a private show in the east end of London. Although there was no title billing or weights published, this is thought to have involved Sheehan's English title claim at 104lbs. Incidentally, an extra round was thrown in for good measure.

16 December Jimmy Kennard (USA) w co 13 Billy Murray (USA), NYC, New York, USA. Articled as a finish fight with skin-tight gloves to decide the American 110lbs title, the *New York World* reported that Kennard would have to face either Tommy Kelly or Martin Flaherty, who beat him at 110lbs, early in 1891 according to unsupported reports, if he wanted to stamp his authority on the weight class.

22 December Jem Stevens w 5 Tom DeGroat, London. The *Mirror of Life* stated that Stevens won the English 100lbs title in this bout, but I have yet to trace.

1891

19 January Tommy Kelly (USA) w pts 10 Frank Donovan (USA), Hoboken, New Jersey, USA. The *New York World* stated that on the day of the fight Kelly was already down to the required 107lbs, with five-ounce gloves to be in use. Although there were reports of him trying to make a match with Eddie Avery a few weeks later, that appears to be the last time we hear of Kelly defending his claim at the weight.

30 January Jem Stevens w rtd 12 Herbert Tarrant, Bob Habbijams' West End School of Arms, Newman Street, off Oxford Street, London. Billed for the English 107lbs title, £50 a side and a £50 purse.

11 February Harry Munro w pts 20 Mike Lanigan, in the east end of London on a Harry Holdsworth private show. Billed for the world and English 90lb titles, the winner was presented with a championship belt.

12 February Joe McGrath drew 15 Alf Gunning, Ancient Concert Rooms, Great Brunswick Street, Dublin. Billed for the English 98lbs title over 12 rounds, the referee, Frank Slavin, ordered the bout to continue for another couple of rounds. However, having asked the men to box a further six sessions, when police interference threatened in the 15th Slavin called a halt and declared a draw.

16 February Harry Munro w co 8 Young Russell, in the east end of London on a private show. Billed for the world and English 90lb titles, to a finish, with two-ounce gloves, and carrying a £5

purse, Russell, who was three inches taller, should not be confused with Jack Russell of Stepney

5 March Jackie McGee drew 15 Ben Slope, The Falstaff Music Hall, Old Street, London. Billed for the English 94lbs title, the winner would receive a silver cup.

18 March George Beach w 7 Mike Small, Albany Club, Holloway Road, London. Billed for the English 102lbs title.

19 March Martin Flaherty (USA) w rtd 26 Link Pope (USA), Streator, USA. According to the *Chicago Tribune*, this was billed for the American 110lbs title with Flaherty recognised as champion. Due to meet Tommy Kelly in Hoboken, New Jersey on 4 September 1891 to decide the American 110lbs title, Flaherty failed to show, and he fights at a higher weight from hereon.

11 May Mike Small w co 6 Bill Mortimer, The Godwin Club, Kingsland Road, Shoreditch, London. Stipulated for a finish, but with no title billing, later reports showed it to have been for the English 102lbs championship. Incidentally, Small scaled 101¾lbs to Mortimer's 100lbs.

30 May Billy Plimmer w rtd 15 Jem Stevens, NSC, King Street, Covent Garden, London. Stipulated for 20 rounds and billed for the English 112lbs title.

8 June Chappie Moran w pts 20 Sid Phillips, NSC, Covent Garden, London. Billed for the world 107lbs title, both men were said to be inside. Moran was a publicity seeker, making claim after claim, and, surprisingly, he was often thought of more than men who were superior. He originally made his name in America, winning the national amateur championship.

15 June Alf Gunning drew 25 Ted Gamble, Ormonde Club, Walworth Road, London. Billed for the English 107lbs title, Gunning claimed the championship on the grounds that he was on top when the bout was stopped well after midnight.

18 June Harry Munro w rtd 9 Bill Stanley, in an east end of London private show. Billed for the world and English 90lb titles, to a finish, with two-ounce gloves.

23 June Harry Munro w co 10 Jim Collins, in an east end of London private show. Billed for the world and English 90lb titles, to a finish, using two-ounce gloves.

3 July Harry Munro w rtd 15 Mick Mahoney, in a west end of London private show. Billed for the world and English 90lb titles, to a finish, with two-ounce gloves.

17 August Mike Small w pts 12 George Murray, 'The Wheatsheaf', Holborn, London. No billing as such, but thought to have involved the English 102lbs title.

17 September Jim Knowles w co 20 Mike Small, Albany Club, Holloway, London. Billed for the English 104lbs title, with a 6.0pm weigh-in and booked for a finish, Knowles scaled 103½lbs to Small's 102.

25 September Bill Mortimer co 8 Joe Gates, Godwin Club, Kingsland Road, Shoreditch, London. Billed for the English title, the winner was challenged by William Cook. For the record, Mortimer weighed 98¾lbs to Gates' 99¾lbs.

13 October Harry Munro w rtd 12 Mick Mahoney, in a west end of London private show. Using two-ounce gloves and to a finish, no title billing was given, but in later gossip it was stated to have involved the world and English 90lb titles.

14 October Bill Moore drew 12 Mike Small, Public Baths, Newmarket. Although there were no weights given, no title billing, and a catchweight contest, it was thought that Moore's 110lbs English title claim was at risk in this one, especially as Small had boxed at 7st 4lbs a month earlier.

19 October Bill Moore w pts 20 Charlie Tilley, a private show in the west end of London. Although not reported as a title bout at 112lbs, it definitely had a bearing on the English championship at the weight.

23 November William Cook w rtd 9 Fred Dove, Pelican Club, Gerrard Street, Soho, London. Billed for the English 110lbs title, £10 a side, four-ounce gloves, 5.0pm weigh-in, one assumes both men made the weight.

30 November George Beach w co 4 Jim Knowles, Albany Club, Holloway, London. Billed for the English 104lbs title over 20 rounds, Beach came in at 102lbs to Knowles' 104, the latter having first weighed in at 105lbs.

5 December Joe Portley w co 3 Bill Moore, Pelican Club, Gerrard

Street, Soho, London. Articled for 110 to 112lbs over 20 rounds, using four-ounce gloves, there was no title billing as such but later gossip gave it as being for the English 110 (with both inside the weight) and 112lbs championships.

1892

4 January Harry Munro w co 9 Bill Haines, in a west end of London private show. Billed to a finish, with two-ounce gloves, despite no weights being given or stipulated it was thought to involve Munro's English (world) 90lbs title claim.

1 February Joe Bennett w rtd 15 Mike Lanigan, a private show in a large ballroom off Regent Street, London. Billed for the English 92lbs title over 20 rounds, and made at 90lbs (ringside weigh-in), give or take two pounds, the fight was contested in a 14 foot ring.

15 February Alf Sparrow w rtd 10 Tom Read, The Hop and Malt Exchange, Borough High Street, London. Although no title billing was given, it was made for 15 rounds and would have extended Sparrow's claim to the English 112lbs title.

26 February Joe Portley w co 11 Charlie Mansford, Kennington Social Club, London. Billed for the English 112lbs title, 1.0pm weigh in, both men made the weight.

7 March Jim Knowles w pts 20 Fred Precious, NSC, Covent Garden, London. Billed for the English 107lbs title, Precious weighing 7st 8lbs to Knowles' 7st 8½lbs, following the result the former asked for a return at the 7st 8lbs limit.

2 April Chappie Moran drew 10 Eddie Avery (USA), Grand Army Hall, Williamsburg, USA. Billed for the world 108lbs title, no weights were announced. With the championship undecided Avery continued with his claim to the title, but it evaporated after he was kayoed in the third round by Dolly Lyons in Brooklyn on 13 May 1892. Scheduled for six rounds, and a catchweight affair, Avery had accepted the challenge of lasting the full distance.

9 May Billy Plimmer w co 10 Tommy Kelly (USA), Coney Island, NYC, USA. Billed for the world 108lbs title, to a finish, using four-ounce gloves which looked more like the two-ounce variety, Kelly was ½lb overweight, while Plimmer came in spot on 7st 10lbs.

19 September Joe Bennett w co 11 Walter Croot, Kennington Social Club, London. Billed for the English 92lbs title over 20 rounds.

24 October Bill Mortimer w co 15 Bill Bolton, NSC, King Street, Covent Garden, London. Billed for the English 102lbs title and a championship belt.

14 December Fred Locke w pts 20 Hiram Cutler, Kennington Social Club, London. In one of the greatest bouts seen, the referee, Watson, was unusual in that he was the only man in British boxing to officiate from inside the ring. Locke claimed the English 106lbs title following his victory at the weight.

19 December Nunc Wallace w co 24 Joe Portley, School of Arms, Newman Street, London. Promoted by Bob Habbijams and articled for a finish, £100 a side and a £100 purse, using four-ounce gloves, it was billed for the English title 112lbs title.

27 December Billy Plimmer w rtd 8 Joe McGrath, Coney Island AC, NYC, USA. Billed for the world 110lbs title, and a $1,500 purse, both men were on the limit.

1893

30 January Alf Sparrow w co 3 Bill Bradford, NSC, Covent Garden, London. Although there was no title billing as such, Sparrow (7st 12lbs) based his claim to the English 110lbs title on this win over Bradford (7st 10lbs).

31 January Alf Buckingham w disq 19 Bill Bolton, Con Donovan's private show, London. Billed for the English 104lbs title over 20 rounds.

13 February Alf Greer w rtd 9 Jim Knowles, NSC, Covent Garden, London. Despite being over the limit, and with no title billing on the table, Greer (7st 13lbs) still claimed the English 110lbs title following his win over the 7st 11lbs Knowles.

6 March Walter Croot w co 11 Bill Bolton, NSC, King Street, Covent Garden, London. Billed for the English 102lbs title, Croot (102) claimed it after Bolton came to the ring at 105lbs. However, Croot had no real right to it as Bolton had lost his title to Bill Mortimer four months previously.

13 March George Beach w rsc 20 Bill Mortimer, NSC, King Street, Covent Garden, London. Billed for the undisputed English 102lbs title, both men weighed 100½lbs (ringside weigh-in).

22 April George Corfield w co 13 Joe Morton, Norfolk Road Drill Hall, Sheffield. Although there was no title billing, Corfield was now claiming the English 112lbs title. On 6 November 1893, Chappie Moran (Coventry, late Birmingham) forfeited to Corfield whom he had been contracted to box in Sheffield on 4 December at £50 a side.

1 May Pedlar Palmer w co 17 Walter Croot, NSC, King Street. Covent Garden, London. Billed for the English 102lbs title, Palmer scaled 101lbs to Croot's 100lbs.

9 October Mike Small w disq 3 Harry Brown, Exchange Hall, Wolverhampton. Billed for the vacant English 102lbs title over 20 rounds, with both men weighing 101¼lbs, the title had become vacant after Palmer, due to meet Brown, realised he could not make the weight and relinquished.

17 October Jimmy Gorman (Paterson, New Jersey, USA) w co 8 Jack Levy, Olympic Club, New Orleans, USA. Billed for the world 102lbs title, with Levy labelled the holder, the latter had earlier said that he would meet Joe Bennett (Deptford), among others, in defence of his English 100lbs title. This was somewhat surprising, as Levy was hardly recognised on this side of the Atlantic.

20 October Bill Moore w rsc 5 Jim Knowles, Chesterfield Goode's Gym, Gerrard Street, Soho, London. Although no billing or weights were reported, following the fight Moore claimed the English 110lbs title and challenged the world.

31 October Jack Maloney w co 9 Harry Munro, Kennington Social Club, London. Billed for the English 96lbs title over 20 rounds, having been made at 94lbs give or take two pounds.

27 November Alf Gower w rsc 3 Fred Locke, NSC, Covent Garden, London. Billed for the English 110lbs title, with Locke (7st 12lbs) reported to be the holder, Gower (7st 10lbs), who was making his comeback after four years out of the ring, was advertised as the 7st 10lbs champion.

5 December Jimmy Barry (Chicago, USA) w co 17 Jack Levy, Roby, Indiana, USA. Billed for the world 100lbs title, with skin-tight gloves the order of the day.

9 December James Kaveney (USA) w co 1 Charley Kelly (USA), Boston, USA. Made at 110lbs, Kelly was inside while Kaveney scaled 110¾lbs. Despite a lack of billing and the fact that he was over the weight, Kaveney claimed the American 110lbs title.

1894

6 February Jimmy Barry (USA) w co 1 Joe McGrath, Colombian AC, Chicago, USA. No weights or title billing were reported, but McGrath was believed to be inside 100lbs.

12 February Charley Kelly (USA) w rsc 1 James Kaveney (USA), Boston, USA. Billed for the American 110lbs title, on his victory Kelly took over Kaveney's claim at the weight.

25 February Jack Pearson w pts 20 Mike Small, NSC, King Street, Covent Garden, London. Billed for the English 102lbs title, and wearing four-ounce gloves, Pearson weighed 102lbs to Small's 101. Surprisingly, Pearson virtually retired after this bout, before coming back in 1897 weighing 116lbs.

9 March Jack Maloney w co 12 Joe Bennett, St Andrew's Hall, Newman Street, off Oxford Street, London. Billed for the English and world 94lb titles over 20 rounds, with a ringside weigh-in.

21 May George Corfield w pts 20 Bill Moore, Norfolk Road Drill Hall, Sheffield. Billed for the English 110lbs title, £50 a side, both men were inside the stipulated 7st 12lbs.

23 May Charley Gledhill w co 2 Jack Murphy, private show in London's west end. Billed for 20 rounds of boxing, and with both men inside 98lbs Gledhill claimed the title at the weight.

2 June Jimmy Barry (USA) w rtd 11 Jimmy Gorman (USA), Olympic Club, New Orleans, USA. Billed for the world 102lbs title, with Gorman labelled the holder, Barry took over as American champion but had moved on by 15 September, on beating Casper Leon for the 105lbs championship.

5 June Bill Mortimer w rsc 13 Alf Buckingham, Ormonde Club, Epsom, Surrey. Although there were no weights reported, the match was made with 20 rounds in prospect and was seen to be an integral part of Mortimer's English 106lbs title claim.

14 June Johnny Connors (USA) w disq 5 Jack Levy, Olympic Club, New Orleans, USA. Having beaten Levy (99lbs), Connors (99½lbs) claimed the title and challenged Jimmy Barry.

25 June Pedlar Palmer w rsc 5 Bill Mortimer, NSC, Covent Garden, London. Billed for the English 106lbs title over 20 rounds, Palmer scaled 105lbs to Mortimer's 103½lbs.

3 July Jimmy Barry (USA) w 4 Harry Brooks (USA), Bradford Falls, USA. Following this win inside 100lbs (the exact poundage has yet to be confirmed), Barry moved up to 105lbs.

30 July Jack Pearson w pts 20 James Carlin, Norfolk Road Drill Hall, Sheffield. Billed for the English 100lbs title.

30 July Chappie Moran w pts 20 Tom Fitzpatrick, Norfolk Road Drill Hall, Sheffield. Billed for the English 107lbs title, both men were on the limit. Moran died on 3 April 1896, after complaining of groin and abdomen pains following a sparring session.

22 August Harry Munro w co 5 Tom Watson, 'The Red Cross', Hare Street, Bethnal Green, London. Billed for 20 rounds with no weights given, it was another fight thought to involve Munro's 90lbs English (world) title claim. As Watson had wanted two-minute rounds it was possibly at catchweights.

29 August Will Curley w co 4 Fred Sullivan, Percy Cottage, Percy Street, Newcastle. Contested in four-ounce gloves for a £25 purse, despite there being no title billing Curley claimed the English 112lbs title.

10 September George Corfield w rtd 12 Alf Gower, Norfolk Road Drill Hall, Sheffield. Billed for the English 110lbs title, £50 a side and a percentage of the gate, and using four-ounce gloves, at the 12 noon weigh in Corfield scaled 7st 11¾lbs to Gower's 7st 10lbs.

15 September Jimmy Barry (USA) w co 25 Casper Leon (Chicago, USA), Lamont, USA. In a finish fight billed for the 105 lbs world title, Barry weighed 104½lbs to Leon's 104¾.

8 October Ernie Brady w disq 13 Charley Gledhill, Percy Cottage, Percy Street, Newcastle. Billed for the English 96lbs title over 15 rounds, Brady was 4½lbs overweight, and although Gledhill was able to claim the title by forfeit he was quite prepared to offer Brady a return at the weight.

15 October Pedlar Palmer w pts 20 Ernie Stanton, NSC, Covent Garden, London. Billed for the 108lbs English title, Palmer scaled 7st 9½lbs to Stanton's 7st 8½lbs. Following the fight, Palmer challenged the world, up to £500 a side.

3 December Mike Small w rsc 18 Ernest Pickard, NSC, King Street, Covent Garden, London. Billed for the English 102lbs title.

1895

11 February Ernie Brady w co 12 Charley Gledhill, Percy Cottage, Percy Street, Newcastle. Billed for the English 100lbs title over 20 rounds.

12 February Albert Gould w disq 1 Jim Williams, Cambridge Gardens, Kilburn, London. Billed for the English 104lbs title over 20 rounds, Williams was disqualified after his second entered the ring when he was floored.

18 March Jack Maloney w pts 20 Ernie Brady, Newcastle. Billed for the English 94lbs to 95lbs title, the fight report stated it to have been made at 96lbs, give or take a pound.

30 March Jimmy Barry (USA) drew 14 Casper Leon (USA), Chicago, USA. Made at 110lbs, with both men inside, Leon, having got up at seven and on the verge of being knocked out, was rescued by a police intervention which resulted in a drawn decision as the matter had been taken out of the referee's hands. At this point in time, Barry was claiming both the 105lbs and 110lbs American (world) titles.

22 April Jack Madden (USA) w pts 25 Johnny Connors (USA), NYC, New York, USA. Billed for the American 105lbs title.

13 May Jack Maloney w pts 20 Ernie Brady, Newcastle. Billed for the English 96lbs title, it was made at 94lbs, give or take two pounds.

28 May Billy Plimmer w co 7 George Corfield, NSC, Covent Garden, London. Billed for the world and English titles at 110lbs, Plimmer (7st 12lbs) would quickly outgrow the weight class and by November was struggling to make 8st. Scheduled for 20 rounds, £200 a side and a £300 purse, and the use of four-ounce gloves, Corfield scaled 7st 10lbs.

3 June Jack Maloney w pts 20 Charley Gledhill, Peoples Palace,

Newcastle. Billed for the 96lbs English title and made at 94lbs, give or take two pounds, following his victory Maloney gave up his claim at 92lbs to 96lbs in order to box at a higher weight.

18 July Jack Wheal w pts 13 Tom Leary, Grimsby. Billed for the English 104lbs title, an extra round was boxed in order to decide the winner. On 24 July, a letter from Ike Booth (Ashton under Lyne) stated that he failed to see how the above fight could have carried title billing when 20 rounds was the recognised distance, with four-ounce gloves.

31 July Joe Elms (USA) w co 2 Jack Levy, Boston Union AC, Boston, USA. Made at 105lbs and booked for 20 rounds, Elms claimed the title regardless of a lack of billing.

9 September George Corfield w co 18 Nunc Wallace, Norfolk Road Drill Hall, Sheffield. Although there was no title billing attached, Corfield claimed the English 112lbs championship on his victory.

21 October Jimmy Barry (USA) w co 4 Jack Madden (USA), Long Island, NYC, USA. Billed for the world 105lbs title, Barry emphasised his superiority over his fellow Americans in this one before moving up a weight class.

23 October Albert Cocksedge drew 20 Young Tiddler, Mafeking Gym, Leicester. Billed for the English 90lbs title.

16 November Joe Nicholls w co 4 Tom Watson, Excelsior Baths, Mansford Street, Bethnal Green, London. Advertised for the English 94lbs title over ten rounds, although not reported as such.

25 November Pedlar Palmer w dis 10 Billy Plimmer, NSC, King Street, Covent Garden, London. Billed for the world 112lbs title, £500 a side, and a £500 purse, both men were dead on the weight, and Palmer never made the mark again, moving up in class.

9 December Harry Ware w pts 20 Dave Job, NSC, King Street, Covent Garden, London. Following his win over Job (103½lbs), despite there being no title billing Ware (102½lbs) claimed the English 104lbs title.

1896

4 January Ike Cohen w rsc 9 Joe Gates, Gymnastic Club, Stalybridge. Billed for the English 104lbs title over 20 rounds, Gates was a late substitute for Jack Pearson, who discovered he could no longer make the weight shortly before the contest was due to take place.

28 January Ted Beach w disq 12 Jack Maloney, Kennington Social Club, London. Billed for the English and world 98lb titles, Maloney came in just under 98lbs, while Beach scaled 96¾lbs. Stipulated for 20 rounds, and a 2.0pm weigh-in.

9 February Bob Bailey w pts 20 Ike Cohen, Norfolk Road Drill Hall, Sheffield. Billed for the English 104lbs title, Bailey scaled 104lbs to Cohen's 102½lbs.

18 February Charlie Taylor w co 15 Ernie Brady, Percy Cottage, Percy Street, Newcastle. Billed for the English 102lbs title, with both men inside the weight.

18 February Bill Bearwish w rtd 6 Sam Goodchild, Con Donovan's private show at the City School of Arms, London. Made with a finish in mind, with both men inside 102lbs, Bearwish's English title claim at the weight had to be at stake.

2 March Mike Small w co 5 Joe Gates, NSC, King Street, Covent Garden, London. Billed for the 102lbs English title over 20 rounds, £25 a side and a £50 purse, after Jack Pearson had earlier renounced his claim.

30 March Harry McDermott w pts 20 Jack Maloney, Albert Hall, Jarrow. Billed for the English 100lbs title, for a £25 purse and £25 a side, McDermott scaled 98½lbs to Maloney's 99½lbs.

4 May Bill Mortimer w rsc 4 Bill Bolton, NSC, King Street, Covent Garden, London. Billed for the English 106lbs title, Bolton came in at 107lbs to Mortimer's 105lbs. The bout went ahead at catchweights, with Mortimer, having waived the forfeit money, rightfully able to claim the title.

8 June Ernie Brady w disq 7 Jack Maloney, Standard Theatre, Gateshead. Made at 104lbs, Brady claimed the English title at the weight following his victory.

14 June Casper Leon (USA) w rsc 9 Johnny Connors (USA), Niagara Falls, New York, USA. Billed for the vacant American 105lbs title.

16 June Dave Sullivan (USA) w co 9 Joe Elms (USA), Boston,

USA. Although made at 112lbs, Sullivan, who scaled less than 110lbs, claimed the American title at the lesser weight but made no defences as such.

9 August Mike Small w co 7 Bob Bailey, Excelsior School of Arms, Sheffield. Billed for the English 104lbs title over 20 rounds, both men scaled 104lbs after the fight had been put back to allow Small an extra week to make the weight.

7 September Billy Plimmer w pts 20 George Corfield, Norfolk Road Drill Hall, Sheffield. Billed for the English 112lbs title.

25 September Harry Brodigan w pts 20 Charlie Taylor, Gymnastic Club, Stalybridge. Brodigan laid claim to the English 100lbs title following this win.

19 October Harry McDermott w disq 15 Ted Beach, Standard Theatre, Gateshead. Billed for the English 100lbs title and due to be contested over 20 rounds.

23 November Harry Ware w co 10 Johnny Thomas, NSC, Covent Garden, London. Billed for the English 108lbs title and scheduled for 20 rounds, Ware was 4lbs overweight so the bout went on at catchweights. Despite losing, Thomas (7st 8lbs) claimed the title by forfeit.

30 November Walter Croot w co 11 Mike Small, NSC, King Street, Covent Garden, London. Billed for the English 102lbs title, Croot scaled 102lbs to Small's 101.

14 December Harry McDermott w co 4 Charlie Taylor, Ginnett's Circus, Newcastle. Despite there being no title billing as such, on winning McDermott challenged the world at 102lbs.

1897

8 February Ted Beach w pts 20 Harry Brodigan, Standard Theatre, Gateshead. Billed for the English 98lbs title, with £50 a side and a £60 purse, both men weighed 97lbs.

1 March Jimmy Barry (USA) w pts 20 Jack Ward (USA), NYC, USA. Although not billed as a title fight, with both men inside 110lbs Barry extended his title claim at the weight in this one.

29 March Harry McDermott w co 10 Mike Small, Standard Theatre, Gateshead. Billed for the English 102lbs title over 20 rounds, it was one of the greatest fights seen, Small being blinded by his own blood almost from the opening bell.

12 April Curly Wood w pts 20 Billy Ray, NSC, King Street, Covent Garden, London. Made at 91lbs, give or take a pound, and for a purse of £50, with £20 a side, both men came in at 91½lbs, Wood claiming the English 92lbs title on the result.

20 April Joe Williams w co 4 Billy Dunn, New City Boxing Club, Sheffield. Although made at catchweights, Williams claimed the English 94lbs title after coming in under 94lbs.

31 May Harry McDermott w disq 8 Harry Brodigan, Standard Theatre, Gateshead. Billed for the English 102lbs title over 20 rounds, £25 a side and a £50 purse, both men scaled 102lbs.

8 June Ernie Brady w disq 7 Jack Maloney, Standard Theatre, Gateshead. Made at 102lbs for the English title, and scheduled for 20 rounds, Brady scaled 101½lbs to Maloney's 102.

2 July Joe Williams w co 16 Michael Kerwin, The Olympic Club, Birmingham. Billed for the English 92lbs title over 20 rounds for a purse of £50, with £50 a side, Kerwin's head hit the ring post as he fell and he died two days later. Bizarrely, he was wearing the trunks and shoes of the late Chappie Moran, whose widow had given them to him on the condition that he only wore them in sparring and not in a contest.

11 October Ernie Brady w co 11 Jack Maloney, NSC, King Street, Covent Garden, London. Given billing for the English 100lbs title, with both men weighing in at 100lbs, the articles actually recorded the bout as being 100lbs, give or take two pounds, which meant that Brady's title claim at the higher weight was at risk. The fight itself was scheduled for 20 rounds.

2 November Jack Walker w rsc 3 Johnny Thomas, NSC, Covent Garden, London. Billed for the vacant English 110lbs title, £50 a side and a £50 purse, both men were stated to be inside the stipulated 7st 12lbs. Incidentally, Walker, despite being billed out of Paddington, was born in Lowestoft.

18 November Joe Williams w co 4 Curly Wood, Glengall Road Gym, Bermondsey, London. Billed for the world 94lbs title over 20 rounds. Articles had earlier called for 90lbs, give or take two

pounds, but was amended to read 92lbs, give or take two pounds, as both men had outgrown the lighter weight class.

22 November Harry McDermott w co 17 Ernie Brady, Standard Theatre, Gateshead. Billed for the English 102lbs title, and scheduled for 20 rounds, £25 a side and a £60 purse, McDermott weighed 101lbs and Brady 102lbs.

6 December Jimmy Barry (USA) w co 20 Walter Croot, NSC, King Street, Covent Garden, London. Billed for the world 108lbs title, with both men inside, Croot was ahead after 19 rounds but instead of boxing his man off he elected to punch it out and was kayoed with just 35 seconds of the bout remaining. Carried from the ring unconscious, he died the following day at 8.30am.

With Pedlar Palmer defending the premier bantam title at 116lbs and with Jimmy Barry coming to the fore at 108lbs among the even lighter men, all weights below 108lbs realistically belong to the paperweight class at this moment in time).

22 December Bill Pincombe w rtd 13 Rocky Knight, The School of Arms, Bristol. Billed for the English title, both men were inside 96lbs at the 1.0pm weigh-in.

1898

22 January Billy Ray w co 8 Curly Wood, Beresford Street Drill Hall, Woolwich, London. Stipulated for 12 rounds, there was no title billing or weights given, but was thought to have involved Wood's 92lbs English title claim.

31 January Mike Small w co 3 Ernie Brady, Standard Theatre, Gateshead. Billed for the English 104lbs title, both men scaled 102lbs.

8 February Alf Rosser w pts 20 Tom Snow, Glengall Road Gym, Bermondsey, London. Billed for the English 98lbs title, £5 a side, the size of the stake shows it should not be taken that seriously.

19 February Steve Flanagan (Philadelphia, USA) drew 20 Danny Dougherty (Philadelphia, USA), Toronto, Canada. With Jimmy Barry now fighting at a higher weight, Flanagan had claimed the American 105lbs title. The *Toronto Daily Mail* reported that the fight was billed for the world title and that both men were inside 105lbs at the ringside weigh-in.

3 March Casper Leon (USA) w pts 15 George Monroe (USA), New Haven Athletic Club, USA. Billed for the American 112lbs title.

14 March Ted Beach w pts 20 Joe Williams, NSC, King Street, Covent Garden, London. Billed for the English 96lbs title, £50 a side and a £100 purse, Williams was the English champion at 94lbs.

16 March Jim Lee drew 20 Ernie Brady, Ancient Concert Rooms, Great Brunswick Street, Dublin. Billed for the English 106lbs title, the fight failed to produce a winner.

28 March Harry McDermott w co 7 Jack Guyon, Standard Theatre, Gateshead. Billed for the English 102lbs title over 20 rounds, £25 a side and a £50 purse, Guyon weighed 101½lbs to McDermott's 102.

3 April Jack Walker w rsc 6 Ike Cohen, The Gymnastic and Athletic Club, Oxford Street, Manchester. Billed for the English 108lbs title, both men weighed 108lbs.

4 April Charlie Exall w disq 7 Harry Brodigan, Standard Theatre, Gateshead. Billed for the English 104lbs title, Exall weighed 100lbs to Brodigan's 102½.

26 May Harry Brodigan w co 6 Jack Hare, Excelsior School of Arms, Sheffield. Billed for the English 104lbs title, both men scaling 104lbs, with 20 x two minute-rounds in place, there was not much recognition forthcoming. Having struggled to make the weight, Lee never defended his claim, while Small had earlier announced that the contest would bring the curtain down on his career.

30 May Jimmy Barry (USA) drew 20 Casper Leon (USA), Lennox AC, NYC, USA. Billed for the world 110lbs title, with Barry reported to be the holder, both men were inside the stipulated weight.

27 June Bob Bailey w rsc 4 Jack Hare, Excelsior School of Arms, Sheffield. Made at 106lbs, despite a lack of billing it was always thought to have involved the English title, but the fact that it was contested over two-minute rounds virtually disqualified it as such.

25 July Harry Brodigan w disq 8 Billy Quinn, Excelsior School of Arms, Sheffield. Billed for the English 104lbs title, Brodigan scaled 104lbs to Quinn's 102.

13 September Jim Lee w co 4 Mike Small, Ancient Concert Rooms, Great Brunswick Street, Dublin. Billed for the English 104lbs title, both men weighed in spot on.

30 September Casper Leon (USA) drew 25 Steve Flanagan (USA), Lennox AC, NYC, USA. Billed for the world 105lbs title, with both men inside, the *New York Evening Telegram* reported that it settled nothing.

4 October Dave Job w disq 7 Ernie Brady, NSC, King Street, Covent Garden, London. Although both men saw it involving the English 104lbs title, the NSC did not, having stipulated it to be for 20 x two-minute rounds. Using the recently introduced six-ounce gloves, Job scaled 102lbs to Brady's 104.

15 November Tom Snow w co 16 Frank Morecombe, New Adelphi Club, The Strand, London. Stipulated for 20 rounds, Morecombe (97½lbs) was walking it until apparently dropping down to be counted out. Although there was no title billing, Snow (96½lbs) based his 98lbs English title claim on his win.

28 November Mike Riley w pts 20 Charlie Exall, NSC, King Street, Covent Garden, London. Billed for the English 104lbs title in some quarters, despite being contested over two-minute rounds, Riley weighed 104lbs and Exall 102.

19 December Alf Rosser w rsc 17 Jim Exall, New Adelphi Club, The Strand, London. Made at 98lbs over 20 rounds, Rosser's English title claim at the weight was at stake.

19 December Fred Delaney w pts 20 Jack Walker, NSC, King Street, Covent Garden, London. Despite a lack of billing, with Delaney weighing 112lbs to Walker's 110 it had some bearing on English 112lb title claims at the time.

29 December Jimmy Barry (USA) drew 20 Casper Leon (USA), City AC, Davenport, Iowa, USA. Billed for the world 110lbs title, this was Barry's penultimate fight before announcing his retirement in September 1899. Leon, who looked a good winner, claimed the title on the result.

Jimmy Barry (USA), a boxing great at weights between 100 and 110lbs

1899

16 January Herbert Rix w disq 7 Jack Maloney, NSC, King Street, Covent Garden, London. Stipulated for 20 two-minute rounds, although there was no title billing, Rix staked his claim to the English 98lbs title on this win. Two-minute rounds were introduced for the first time at the NSC, in the wake of Walter Croot and Tom Turner both losing their lives in fights at the club.

Another new ruling that came into being for this fight was that any boxer who was disqualified would not be paid unless the foul was accidental. Maloney took the NSC to court, but lost on the grounds that he had signed a contract to accept the referee's decision, regardless.

24 January Joe Williams w co 3 Harry Brodigan, Gymnastic Club, Stalybridge. Billed for the English 102lbs title, £50 a side and a £50 purse, Williams weighed 101lbs and Brodigan 102lbs.

20 February Dave Job w disq 14 Jack Guyon, NSC, King Street, Covent Garden, London. Another fight given English title credence outside the domain of the NSC, this time at 104lbs and despite it being contested over 20 x two-minute rounds, Job weighed 102lbs to Guyon's 104.

6 March Jack Walker w rsc 6 Dave Morbin, NSC, Covent Garden, London. Although billed for the 110lbs English title and scheduled for 20 rounds, Morbin was unable to make the weight and was forced to pay forfeit, the fight going on at catchweights.

1 April Casper Leon (USA) drew 20 Danny Dougherty (USA), NYC, USA. With Jimmy Barry inactive, Leon was now claiming the 110lbs title and although the *Brooklyn Standard Union* gave both men to be inside that weight (it was also reported that the two men were inside 108lbs), no title billing was mentioned.

3 April Harry McDermott w co 14 Charlie Exall, Standard Theatre, Gateshead. Billed for the English 102lbs title, while McDermott weighed 102lbs, Exall came in at 105lbs.

29 May Charlie Exall w rsc 19 Mike Riley, Standard Theatre, Gateshead. Billed for the English 102lbs title over 20 rounds, £50 a side and a £50 purse, and using four-ounce gloves, Exall weighed 101lbs to Riley's 101¾lbs.

3 June Patsy Donovan (USA) w pts 20 Casper Leon (USA), NYC, USA. According to the *St Louis Post-Dispatch*, Donovan defeated Leon for the vacant 110lbs title in this one. Not even reported in the *New York Herald*, Donovan's claim seems to go nowhere.

9 June Clarence Forbes (USA) w pts 12 Casper Leon (USA), St Louis, USA. Billed for the American 112lbs title, both men made the weight.

16 September Casper Leon (USA) drew 20 Danny Dougherty (USA), NYC, USA. Still claiming the 110lbs title, despite his loss to Patsy Donovan, this was another billed title fight for Leon at that weight.

4 October Steve Flanagan (USA) drew 20 Casper Leon (USA), St Louis, USA. Billed for the American 112lbs title. Due to box Jack Walker (England) for the world 112lbs title at the Seaside Athletic Club, New York, it was announced that Flanagan had weakened himself when making 105lbs for his contest against Danny Dougherty on 12 March 1900 and was unable to go through with the fight.

23 October Bill Pincombe w pts 20 Joe O'Neill, The City Gym, Bradford. Billed for the English 92lbs title, £100 a side and a £20 purse.

27 October Steve Flanagan (USA) w pts 25 Casper Leon (USA), St Louis, USA. Made at 110lbs, by his victory Flanagan was generally accepted as the champion of the weight class in America.

30 October Joe Williams w co 7 Billy Johnson, New City Boxing Club, Sheffield. Following his win over Johnson (94lbs) in a 20 rounder at catchweights, Williams (96lbs) was acknowledged as the champion at the weight.

30 October Frank Morecombe w pts 20 Dido Vardy, Standard Theatre, Gateshead. Given English title billing at 98lbs, Morecombe weighed 97¾lbs to Vardy's 97½lbs.

1 November Tom Snow w co 11 Frank Exall, New Adelphi Club, The Strand, London. Billed for the English 96lbs title over 20 rounds, after the fight Snow challenged the world.

23 November Harry Ashley drew 20 Alf Rosser, Bob Habbijam's West End School of Arms, Newman Street, off Oxford Street, London. Originally advertised as being for the English 102lbs title, neither man could make the weight and the fight went ahead at catchweights with Ashley (104) called the ex-champion. His opponent, Rosser, weighed 105lbs.

24 November Matt Precious w pts 20 Jim Lee, Gymnastic Club, Stalybridge. Billed for the English 106lbs title, £100 a side and a £60 purse.

11 December Dido Vardy w pts 20 Frank Morecombe, Standard

Theatre, Gateshead. Articled for English 98lbs title, the fight eventually took place at catchweights after Vardy was unable to get below 101½lbs. Morecombe scaled 100½.

21 December Jack Walker w rsc 8 Fred Herring, New Adelphi Theatre, The Strand, London. Billed for the English 110lbs title, £20 a side and a £20 purse, Herring (7st 11lbs), who had won the ABA bantamweight title in 1898, was well beaten by Walker (7st 9¾lbs) in a bout scheduled for 20 rounds.

1900

29 January Matt Precious w rtd 9 Mike Riley, NSC, King Street, Covent Garden, London. Billed for the English 106lbs title, Riley was unable to answer the bell for the tenth round, collapsing and dying the following day.

8 February Tom Snow w pts 20 Ginger Owen, New Adelphi Club, The Strand, London. Billed for the English 96lbs title, and a purse of £75, Snow again challenged the world afterwards and was taken up by Joe Williams (Rotherham). Six months later, Williams asked what had become of Snow, but heard no more.

12 February Dave Job w co 12 Ted Beach, NSC, King Street, Covent Garden, London. Billed for both the world and English 102lb titles, both men were inside the weight.

12 March Danny Dougherty (USA) w co 10 Steve Flanagan (USA), NYC, USA. Following his victory in a match made at 105lbs, Dougherty claimed the American title at the weight.

25 May Danny Dougherty (USA) w pts 20 Tommy Feltz (USA), NYC, USA. Although Feltz weighed 105lbs to Dougherty's 110lbs, the latter laid claim to the 110lbs title on winning.

27 June Joe Williams w co 13 Frank Exall, Ginnett's Circus, Newcastle. Billed as being for the English 98lbs title over 20 rounds, with Williams shown as the holder, both men were inside 7st. Despite some confusion as to whether it was Frank Exall, and not Jim Exall, his brother, who fought Williams, it can be confirmed that it was Frank, and that it was for £50 a side and a £50 purse. There was, in fact, a third Exall, the more famous Charlie, who moved to Newcastle to marry a local girl.

4 August Danny Dougherty (USA) w pts 25 Tommy Feltz (USA), Brooklyn, NYC, USA. Despite being billed as a world bantamweight title fight at 108lbs, the fact that Dougherty was claiming the 110lbs version meant that he was also risking that claim in this one.

30 September George Capstick w co 10 Dummy Forrest, The Gym, West Hartlepool. Billed for the English 98lbs title over 20 rounds, £25 a side and a £30 purse, both men made the weight. Incidentally, Forrest was a deaf mute, hence the nickname.

1901

1 January Ike Cohen w co 1 Alf Hazlegrove, Gymnastic Club, Stalybridge. Having claimed the English 100lbs title on beating Hazlegrove, Cohen was unable to take advantage due to weight-making problems and just seven weeks later he was boxing at 112lbs. Incidentally, the match was made for 20 rounds of boxing, £25 a side and a £30 purse.

6 February Jim Fay w pts 15 Ernie Brady, Mafeking Gym, Leicester. Billed for the English 106lbs title, £25 a side and purse, the fact that it was contested over two-minute rounds ruled it out as a championship fight in the eyes of the purists.

18 February Ike Cohen w dis 4 Ernie Brady, Wonderland, Whitechapel Road, London. Articled for 15 three-minute rounds, and billed for the English 112lbs title, the bout went on at catchweights after Brady weighed in over the weight. Cohen then claimed the championship by forfeit.

4 March Kid Veitch w pts 20 Charlie Exall, Standard Theatre, Gateshead. Billed for the English 106lbs title, £25 a side and a £50 purse.

18 March Tippler Grey w co 4 Mike Small, Gymnastic Club, Stalybridge. Billed for the English 100lbs title, a £25 purse, £25 a side, and stipulated for 20 rounds, this was Gray's 27th win in 30 bouts.

18 March Frank Morecombe w pts 15 Harry McLeavy, Theatre Royal, West Hartlepool. Billed for the English 100lbs title, £25 side and a £25 purse, both men were well inside the weight.

21 May Harry Slough w rtd 15 Jim Fay, Mafeking Gym,

Leicester. Billed for the English 106lbs title, but over two-minute rounds, at the end of 15 rounds the judges could not agree on a decision and ordered an extra round to be fought. However, Fay, who paid forfeit on being well over the weight, refused and the verdict was awarded to Slough.

17 June Charlie Exall w co 8 Kid Veitch, Ginnett's Circus, Newcastle. Billed for the English 106lbs title over 20 rounds, £25 a side and a £50 purse, Exall scaled 7st 6½lbs.

17 June Digger Stanley w pts 20 Owen Moran, Assembly Rooms, Stanley Street, Birmingham. Although both the *Mirror of Life* and the *Sporting Life* gave this one as being at 106lbs, later record books suspiciously show it to have been made at 100lbs. Contested over two-minute rounds, which left a lot to be desired, on 25 June Stanley is challenging all England at 105lbs.

22 July Harry McDermott w pts 20 Charlie Exall, Standard Theatre, Gateshead. Billed for the English 106lbs title, £50 a side and a £127 purse.

26 August Jim Kenrick w co 14 Kid Veitch, Standard Theatre, Gateshead. Made at 108lbs, with both men inside the weight at the 1.0pm weigh-in, Kenrick claimed the English title at the weight despite a lack of billing.

14 September Harry Slough w pts 15 Jack Orton, Mafeking Gym, Leicester. Billed for the English 102lbs title, £25 a side plus purse, it was contested over two-minute rounds.

9 October Owen Moran w pts 15 Harry Slough, Mafeking Gym, Leicester. Billed for the English 102lbs title, £25 a side plus purse, and over two-minute rounds.

24 October Jack Player w co 9 Albert Mortimer, New Adelphi Club, The Strand, London. Scheduled for 20 rounds, with both men inside 107lbs, Player became another claimant to the English 108lbs title.

28 October James Freeman w co 1 Dido Vardy, Standard Theatre, Gateshead. Scheduled for 20 rounds, Vardy (103½) was counted out after just 90 seconds and, while not billed as a championship contest, Freeman (101½) staked his claim to the English 104lbs title.

28 October Harry Slough w co 3 Herbert Gill, The Circus, Lynn Street, West Hartlepool. Scheduled for 12 rounds, it was the final of an English Championship Belt competition.

29 October Harry Slough w co 4 Ernie Brady, Mafeking Gym, Leicester. Billed for the English 106lbs title, Slough created a record when taking part in two English championship fights in successive days.

4 November Charlie Exall w co 6 Matt Precious, Ginnett's Circus, Newcastle. Billed for the English 106lbs title held by Precious (7st 6lbs), £100 a side and £120 purse, the latter had earlier said that he could not get down much below 7st 8lbs Incidentally, Exall also came in at 7st 6lbs. Following the bout, Harry McDermott objected to it carrying title billing as, in his eyes, Precious had forfeited the title when he refused to go through with their planned-for championship fight of an earlier date.

11 December Harry Slough drew 15 Terry Kid McCormac, Mafeking Gym, Leicester. Billed as an English 106lbs title bout, but again over two-minute rounds, £25 a side and a £15 purse, it should not be considered as such. Prior to the bout, McCormac had challenged the world, but was later proved to have been a novice. Also, the *Leicester Sporting News* gave the result as a retirement win for Slough, but failed to name the round. Slough relinquished his claim to the title in September 1905 when unable to make the weight.

26 December Albert Cocksedge w co 3 Young Tiddler, Mafeking Gym, Leicester. There is some doubt over the credence of this billed 98lbs English title bout as Leicester promotions were normally held over two-minute rounds.

27 December Tommy Feltz (USA) w rsc 1 Kid Henning (USA), Savannah, USA. Billed for the American 112lbs title and scheduled for 25 rounds, the *Toronto Daily Mail* reported it as a world title bout. However, this was the last time Feltz boxed at the weight and three fights later he had moved up to 115lbs, when challenging Harry Forbes for the American title at that weight.

1902

23 January Digger Stanley drew 12 Frank Morecombe,

Wonderland, Whitechapel Road, London. Although there was no title billing and contested over two-minute rounds, £10 a side and a purse, both men were inside 106lbs, with Stanley weighing 104lbs to Morecombe's 105lbs. Later in the year (1 October), Stanley challenged Owen Moran (Birmingham) at the weight, 20 rounds, up to £100 a side, but, gaining weight quickly took his claim up a class.

10 February Charlie Exall w pts 20 Jack Walker, Ginnett's Circus, Newcastle. Billed for the English 108lbs title with the use of four-ounce gloves, Exall, who stated that he weighed 105lbs to Walker's 111lbs, claimed the title by forfeit, even though it was known that Walker could never have made the weight and had released his title claim prior to the fight. Following the fight, Exall stated that he now held both the English 106lb and 108lbs titles.

12 May Owen Moran w pts 10 Jim Kenrick, NSC, King Street, Covent Garden, London. Made at 108lbs and contested under the new ruling at the club of all bouts being scheduled for ten rounds or under, Moran, who scaled 108lbs to Kenrick's 105lbs, laid claim to the title.

25 June Johnny Hughes w pts 20 Tibby Watson (Australia), New Adelphi Club, The Strand, London. Billed for the world and Imperial British Empire 108lb titles, both men were inside the weight.

27 September Charlie Exall w disq 8 Harry McDermott, Ginnett's Circus, Newcastle. With only two-minute rounds stipulated and no title billing, McDermott appeared well on top when he was badly cut by a head butt and left the ring feeling that Exall would be disqualified. Unfortunately, for him, the referee did not and was left with no other option than to disqualify McDermott, thus leaving Exall's English 106lbs title claim intact.

22 October Jack Walker w pts 15 Jim Kenrick, Bob Habbijams' West End School of Arms, Newman Street, off Oxford Street, London. Billed for the English 110lbs title, £25 a side and a £50 purse, both men being inside the 7st 12lbs limit at the 1.0pm weigh-in, Kenrick was down twice in the 15th.

25 October Harry McDermott w co 8 Tibby Watson (Australia), Ginnett's Circus, Newcastle. Reported in some places as being for the world 108lbs title, there was no mention of weights.

15 November Harry McDermott w pts 15 Jim Kenrick, Ginnett's Circus, Newcastle. Billed for the English 106lbs title, although he made the weight Kenrick announced that he had such a struggle to make 7st 8lbs that he would be fighting in a higher weight class in future.

29 December Owen Moran w co 2 Jack Morris, Adelphi Theatre, Liverpool. Although not billed as a title bout, with both men inside 7st 12lbs Moran's win gained him a good claim to the English 110lbs championship in the eyes of his supporters.

1903

17 January Charlie Exall drew 15 Jim Kenrick, Ginnett's Circus, Newcastle. Billed for the English 108lbs title, Exall scaled 106lbs to Kenrick's 108.

20 January Willie Schumacher (USA) w co 10 Johnny Watson (USA), Glen Falls, New York, USA. Billed for the world 105lbs title, a record produced by Luckett Davis brings to light that Schumacher, a brilliant amateur, was taking part in only his third pro fight.

14 February Barney Sloane w rtd 7 Eddie Sullivan, Ginnett's Circus, Newcastle. Billed for the English 94lbs title, following this Sloane challenged all.

19 February Frank Morecombe w pts 15 Patsy Haley, Coronation Gym, Liverpool. Made at the 7st 8lbs limit, 4pm weigh-in, and £25 a side and £50 purse, although there was no title billing on the night, later reports stated that the English 106lbs title was involved.

21 February Jim Kenrick w pts 20 Charlie Exall, Ginnett's Circus, Newcastle. Billed for the English 108lbs title, Kenrick came in at 110lbs, thus allowing Exall (106lbs) to hold on to his claim. Despite this, in the 1 April issue of the *Sporting Life* Kenrick was still claiming to be the champion of the weight class.

2 March Digger Stanley w pts 12 Jack Walker, Wonderland, Whitechapel Road, London. Billed for the world and English 110lb titles, Walker weighing 7st 11lbs to Stanley's 7st 12lbs, the former maintained that as it had been contested over 12 three-minute rounds and not a recognised championship distance, the titles were invalidated.

26 March Jimmy Walsh (Boston, USA) w pts 10 Willie Schumacher (USA), Boston, USA. Billed for the American 105lbs title, as reported in the *Boston Post*, Walsh quickly moved up in weight leaving Schumacher as the obvious candidate to reclaim the title.

2 April Digger Stanley w pts 10 Jack Guyon, Wonderland, Whitechapel Road, London. Although it was not billed as involving the English 110lbs title, Stanley was advertised as the 7st 12lbs champion and Guyon as the 7st 10lbs titleholder.

3 April Jack Walker w rsc 10 James Freeman, The New Adelphi Club, The Strand, London. Billed for the English 110lbs bantamweight title, Walker weighed in at 7st 11lbs to 7st 8lbs for Freeman, who must not be confused with Newcastle's Jim Freeman.

13 April Matt Precious w pts 15 Ernie Godwin, The Horse Repository, Hill Street, Birmingham. Although billed as an English 7st 7lbs title fight, Godwin insisted that it was the 110lbs world championship that was on offer at £100 a side.

25 May Owen Moran w pts 15 Jack Walker, NSC, King Street, Covent Garden, London. Articled for the English 112lbs title, Moran weighing 112lbs to Walker's 111½, this was the start of Moran's claim at the weight.

24 October Harry McDermott w rtd 6 Jack Player, Ginnett's Circus, Newcastle. Scheduled for 20 rounds, with both men inside 108lbs, McDermott based his claim to the English 108lbs title on this win despite a lack of billing.

14 November Harry McDermott w co 5 Jack Fitzpatrick, Ginnett's Circus, Newcastle. Made at 108lbs, but with no title billing, it did not stop McDermott furthering his English title claim at the weight.

19 November Willie Schumacher (USA) w pts 15 Kid Murphy (USA), New York, USA. A record produced by Luckett Davis shows Schumacher winning this one to land the vacant American 105lbs title. However, although the writer has yet to trace it there is every chance that it was held in private as contests of this duration were outlawed in New York at the time.

14 December Digger Stanley w pts 15 Jack Walker, NSC, King Street, Covent Garden, London. Billed for the English 112lbs title and £150.

17 December Jim Exall w pts 15 Frank Morecombe, International Athletic Club, Marylebone, London. Billed for the English 102lbs title and Championship Belt, both men weighed 100½lbs.

19 December Charlie Exall w co 5 Ernie Godwin, Ginnett's Circus, Newcastle. Billed for the English 108lbs title, while Exall made 107lbs Godwin came in well over the weight at 110lbs.

26 December Harry McDermott w co 3 Johnny Hughes, Ginnett's Circus, Newcastle. Billed for the world 108lbs title claimed by Hughes, unfortunately, the Londoner was two pounds over the weight, but that did not stop the brilliant McDermott (107lbs) claiming the title by forfeit.

1904

25 January Jim Kenrick w pts 15 Fred Herring, NSC, King Street, Covent Garden, London. Made at 110lbs, despite a lack of billing Kenrick's English title claim at the weight was on the line in this one.

1 February Frank Morecombe w pts 15 Jim Exall, International Athletic Club, Marylebone, London. Although no weights or title billing was given at the time, in later years Morecombe stated that he won the English 102lbs title in this one.

6 February Harry McDermott w co 7 Jack Guyon, Ginnett's Circus, Newcastle. Billed for the world 108lbs title using four-ounce gloves, both men made the weight.

13 February Charlie Exall w pts 15 Tibby Watson (Australia), Ginnett's Circus, Newcastle. There was no title billing as such, but with both men inside 108lbs, Exall's claim at the weight would have been at stake.

20 February Harry Slough w co 6 Harry Brodigan, The Circus, Lynn Street, West Hartlepool. Billed for the 112lbs English championship, Slough scaled 110½lbs to Brodigan's 112.

7 March Dave Job w rsc 2 James Freeman, NSC, King Street, Covent Garden, London. Although no billing as such, with both men inside 7st 8lbs, £50 a side and a £50 purse, this fight was reckoned to involve the 106lbs English championship.

12 March Barney Sloane w co 3 Ben Gray, Ginnett's Circus, Newcastle. Although no weights were announced, Sloane was reported as the English 94lbs champion. The title then lapsed until Jimmy Wilde came good.

31 March Kid Murphy (USA) w pts 25 Benny Franklin (USA), Belair AC, Baltimore, USA. Billed for the American 105lbs title, and reported as a 25 round draw in the *Boston Post*, prior to the contest the *Baltimore Sun* reported that Murphy had been claiming the American 105lbs title for the past three years, despite his record showing no evidence to support this statement. On 10 May, also in Baltimore, Murphy outpointed Franklin over 15 rounds of a contest that some latter day historians thought might have involved the 105lbs title, although there was nothing in print to substantiate that. The only clue that something might have been at stake here were challenges to the winner coming in from Willie Schumacher, Jimmy Walsh, Willie Gibbs and Billy Taylor, the so-called English champion. However, on 25 May, in Baltimore, Murphy undoubtedly took over Schumacher's claim to the title when the latter, unable to make the weight for their proposed title fight, forfeited any rights he may have had to it. Two days earlier, the *Baltimore Sun* reported that Murphy was already down to weight while Schumacher still had to take off a couple of pounds, which ultimately he was unable to do.

18 April Digger Stanley w pts 20 Jimmy Walsh (USA), NSC, King Street, Covent Garden, London. Billed for the world 112lbs title with both men inside the weight.

30 May Jim Kenrick w rsc 12 Dave Job, NSC, King Street, Covent Garden, London. Despite the fact that there was no championship billing attached, in later years Kenrick claimed that it was a scheduled 15-round defence of his English 108lbs title, with both men inside the weight.

6 June Digger Stanley drew 20 Jimmy Walsh (USA), NSC, King Street, Covent Garden, London. Again billed for the world 112lbs title with both men inside the weight.

25 June Harry Slough w co 14 Charlie Exall, The Circus, Lynn Street, West Hartlepool. Billed for the English 108lbs title, with no weights announced some reports stated that it had been for the 110lbs title. Confirmation of that came in the shape of a return fight between the pair, booked for 25 July 1904, at 108lbs, that was later cancelled.

30 June Jack Wise w pts 15 Frank Morecombe, Alma Grounds, Barking Road, Canning Town, London. The final of Joe Smith's 106lbs World Championship Belt competition saw just 20 of the 62 entries make the weight. As the Australian, Tibby Watson, was one of them the world championship label was correct, Watson not being eligible to fight for the English title.

11 July Digger Stanley w co 6 Harry McDermott, Ginnet's Circus, Newcastle. Billed for both the world and English 108lb titles over 15 rounds, the light-punching Stanley (107lbs), having been put down five times in the fifth, kayoed McDermott (also 107lbs) with a right to the jaw which was regarded with some suspicion in the light of the latter's past record with regard to 'throwing' fights.

1 August Boyo Driscoll w dis 10 Owen Moran, Queens Hall, Cardiff. Despite being billed for the English 112lbs title, the winner, real name being Patrick, received no recognition as such due to the fight being contested over two-minute rounds. This was supported by the 3 September issue of the *Mirror of Life*, which reported Moran as still being champion.

16 September Frank Morecombe w pts 15 Ernie Godwin, Cosmopolitan Club, Marylebone Road, London. Both were safely inside the 106lbs limit at the 2pm weigh-in and while there was no English title billing given, later 'gossip' showed it to have involved the championship.

17 October Digger Stanley w co 19 Harry McDermott, Ginnett's Circus, Newcastle. Billed for the world and 108lb English titles, and scheduled for 20 rounds, Stanley weighed 108lbs to McDermott's 107lbs. This was to be Stanley's last fight at the weight and a month later he had challenged the world at 114lbs.

27 October Frank Morecombe drew 15 Albert Cocksedge,

Cosmopolitan Club, Marylebone Road, London. Although stated to have been at catchweights, with both men almost certainly inside 7st 8lbs Morecombe's 106lbs English title claim had to be at stake.

17 November Albert Cocksedge w pts 15 Frank Morecombe, Cosmoplitan Club, Marylebone Road, London. Although there was no English title billing, the fact that it was made at 7st 8lbs would have seen Morecombe's 106lbs claim passing to Cocksedge.

26 November Harry McDermott w rtd 2 Jack Christian, Ginnett's Circus, Newcastle. Billed for the English 112lbs title, McDermott scaled 109lbs to Christian's 111.

1905

6 January Tibby Watson (Australia) w rsc 7 Jack Daly, Corn Exchange, Ashford, Kent. Although given world title billing at 108lbs, in reality it had to be at catchweights with the heavier Daly later claiming that he was in excess of the advertised weight.

16 January Young Bill Smith drew 12 Smokey Bishop, Lecture Hall, Deptford, London. Billed for the English 106lbs title, there was much dispute as to the validity of said billing with many feeling that the championship of Kent and south London might have been more apt. For the record, Smith weighed 7st 7¹/₂lbs to Bishop's 7st 6lbs.

30 January Tibby Watson (Australia) w co 13 Con Canning, Olympic Club, Sheffield. Despite being given world title billing at 104lbs, there was no recognition forthcoming as the match had been made over 20 x two-minute rounds.

20 February Harry McDermott w rsc 9 Charlie Exall, Ginnett's Circus, Newcastle. Scheduled for 15 rounds and billed for the English 108lbs title, both men were inside the weight.

27 February Jim Kenrick w pts 15 Boyo Driscoll, NSC, King Street, Covent Garden, London. Billed for the English 112lbs title and a championship belt.

27 March Mark Verrall w pts 10 Frank Morecombe, NSC, King Street, Covent Garden, London. Not given title billing and not over the championship distance, Verrall (104lbs) claimed the English 104lbs title following the win. Morecombe scaled 103¹/₂lbs.

10 April Jim Kenrick w pts 15 Ike Bradley, NSC, King Street, Covent Garden, London. Billed for the English 112lbs title, the *Mirror of Life* gave Kenrick as 111lbs to Bradley's 109, while the *Sporting Life* had him as 109lbs and 107, respectively. On 4 May, at the former Adelphi Theatre in Liverpool, the two men drew over 20 two-minute rounds, which had no credence as a title fight and was not articled as such. Another two-minute rounder at the Adelphi Theatre, on 25 May, saw Kenrick beat Johnny Hughes on an 11th-round disqualification.

18 May Frank Morecombe drew 15 Ernie Godwin, Gymnastic Club, Liverpool. Although there was no title billing for this one, it was later reported to have been for the English 102lbs championship, £75 a side and a £75 purse.

27 July Jim Kenrick w pts 15 Ike Bradley, The Gymastic Club (Late Adelphi Theatre), Liverpool. At 112lbs, with four-ounce gloves, despite a lack of billing it has to be seen as a defence for Kenrick.

25 September Harry Slough w co 3 Harry McDermott, Ginnett's Circus, Newcastle. Billed for the English and world 108lbs titles, both men weighing 107lbs, Slough, who had great difficulty making the weight, relinquished the titles immediately after giving his greatest display.

12 October Jim Kenrick w co 8 Charlie Exall, Gymnastic Club, Liverpool. Billed for the 108lbs title, with no weights given the *Sporting Life* reported the title involved to be at 112lbs and over 15 rounds, not 20.

30 October Ike Bradley w disq 4 Harry Slough, Ginnett's Circus, Newcastle. Billed for the English 112lbs title, Slough was disqualified after his seconds entered the ring when he had been floored and looked unlikely to beat the count.

27 November Jim Kenrick w pts 15 Jack Guyon, NSC, Covent Garden, London. Made at 110lbs, Kenrick weighing 110lbs to Guyon's 109, despite a lack of title billing both Kenrick's and Guyon's English title claims at the weight would have been at risk.

1906

4 January Mark Verrall w pts 15 Ernie Godwin, Gymnastic Club, Liverpool. Although scheduled for two-minute rounds, Verrall claimed the English 106lbs title nonetheless, challenging all England five days later.

20 January Digger Stanley w pts 20 Ike Bradley, The Gymnastic Club, Liverpool. Billed for the world 112lbs title.

2 February Mark Verrall w dis 3 Jim Kenrick, NSC, King Street, Covent Garden, London. Billed for the English 108lbs title with Kenrick called the champion.

21 May Digger Stanley w rsc 18 Harry Slough, Ginnett's Circus, Newcastle. Billed for the English 112lbs title, £25 a side and a £60 purse.

2 June Charlie Exall w co 4 Jack Daly, Ginnett's Circus, Newcastle. Billed for the English 108lbs title and scheduled for 20 rounds, Exall was such an overwhelming favourite that there were no bets laid.

28 July Ginger Osborne w co 12 Harry Slough, The Circus, Lynn Street, West Hartlepool. Billed for the English 110lbs title, both men came in spot on the weight.

2 October Albert Cocksedge w pts 20 Charlie Dew, NSC, King Street, Covent Garden, London. Having outscored Dew (102½lbs), despite there being no title billing attached, Cocksedge (103lbs) laid claim to the English 104lbs championship.

29 October Sam Keller w co 9 Mark Verrall, NSC, King Street, Covent Garden, London. Scheduled for 15 rounds and billed for the English 108lbs title, Keller came in at 108lbs to Verrall's 107. Strangely, when challenged to a return, Keller claimed that the bout had been articled at 109lbs.

8 November Ike Dorsett (Canada, late London) w pts Joe Daly (USA), Buenos Aires, Argentine. Reported in the *Sporting Life*, although there was no information about the boxers' weights or the duration of the contest, the article stated that it was billed for the world 7st 8lbs championship. Incidentally, Dorsett was better known as Young Bill Smith.

10 December Albert Cocksedge w pts 15 Charlie Dew, NSC, King Street, Covent Garden, London. Billed for the English 104lbs title, winner to defend against Charlie Exall, both men scaled 102lbs.

1907

18 January Joe Percival w pts 15 Joe Donnelly, Ginnett's Circus, Newcastle. Following his win at about 100lbs, Percival claimed the title at the weight. However, Donnelly had looked a good winner after the judges had disagreed on the verdict, Percival winning on the casting vote of the referee, Tom Murphy.

15 February Bert Chatterton w co 6 Albert Cocksedge, Harry Cullis Gym, Monument Road, Birmingham. Billed for the English 104lbs title over 20 rounds and a £25 purse, it was only the 12th bout of Chatterton's career.

1 March Kid Murphy (USA) w pts 10 Johnny Coulon (Canada), Milwaukee, Wisconsin, USA. Billed for the world 105lbs title, both men made the weight.

14 March Tom Sayers w co 7 Bill Shaw, Tower's School of Physical Culture, Upton Park, London. Billed for the English 98lbs title over 15 rounds, with a silver championship belt at stake.

23 March Joe Percival w pts 10 Tom Brown, Ginnett's Circus, Newcastle. Although no weights or billing was given, it seems certain that Percival was defending his 100lbs English title claim in this one.

27 April Tom Brown w pts 15 Joe Percival, The Circus, Lynn Street, West Hartlepool. Made at 100lbs, Percival's English title claim at the weight passed to Brown.

12 June Albert Cocksedge w co 4 Bert Chatterton, Harry Cullis Gym, Monument Road, Birmingham. Although there was no title billing and only over 12 rounds, following his win Cocksedge once again assumed control of the 104lbs weight class. However, in fact, Cocksedge was unable to make the weight again and moved on.

3 July Kid Murphy (USA) drew 15 Young Britt (Baltimore, USA), Belair AC, Baltimore, USA. Billed for the world 105lbs title.

27 July Tommy Brown w rtd 5 Jim Forester, The Circus, Lynn Street, West Hartlepool. Stipulated for 15 rounds of boxing and billed for the English 100lbs title. Brown's 11th-round kayo win over Frank Exall (Bermondsey) at the same venue on 7 September 1907 was stated to be at catchweights with no title billing. The fact that Exall had been boxing between 7st 8lbs and 8st during the past three years made it highly unlikely that Brown's title claim was involved.

5 October Tommy Brown w rtd 11 Jim Freeman, The Circus, Lynn Street, West Hartlepool. Billed for the English 100lbs title and over 15 rounds, this was not the Jim (James) Freeman who won the ABA title in 1900.

14 October Ike Bradley w co 19 Jim Southway, The National Club, Merthyr. Billed for the English 112lbs title, both men scaled 110lbs.

22 October Albert Cocksedge w pts 15 Charlie Exall, Ginnett's Circus, Newcastle. With Cocksedge still claiming the English 106lbs title, although fought at catchweights and contested over two-minute rounds, it was thought that both men were inside 7st 8lbs.

2 November Tommy Brown w pts 15 Frank Morecombe, The Circus, Lynn Street, West Hartlepool. Billed for the English 100lbs title.

21 December Tommy Brown w pts 15 Frank Morecombe, The Circus, Lynn Street, West Hartlepool. Billed for the English 100lbs title, Brown appears to be fighting above the weight from heron.

1908

8 January Johnny Coulon (Canada) w pts 10 Kid Murphy (USA), Peoria, Ill, USA. Billed for the world 105lbs title.

29 January Johnny Coulon (Canada) w pts 10 Kid Murphy (USA), Peoria, Ill, USA. Billed for the world 105lbs title, some reports claimed that the American 105lbs title fights should be ignored as being seen as legitimate championship matches, as ten rounds was not an acceptable distance to judge 'endurance'.

10 February Albert Cocksedge w pts 15 Harry McDermott, Ginnett's Circus, Newcastle. Billed for the English 108lbs title, although not reported as such both men agreed that they had made 108lbs for the contest.

17 February Charlie Dew w pts 15 Joe Percival, Ginnett's Circus, Newcastle. Billed for the English 104lbs title, while Percival (102) made the weight comfortably Dew (104) struggled.

20 February Johnny Coulon (Canada) w co 9 Cooney Kelly (Peoria, Ill, USA), Peoria, Ill, USA. Billed for the world 105lbs title over ten rounds.

13 March Johnny Coulon (Canada) w pts 10 Young Terry McGovern (USA), Peoria, Ill, USA. Billed for the world 105lbs title, Coulon weighed 103½lbs to McGovern's 104.

15 June Albert Cocksedge w pts 20 Harry Badger, New City Boxing Club, Sheffield. Made at catchweights, £20 a side and a £20 purse, despite a lack of billing it was thought to involve Cocksedge's 106lbs English title claim.

26 June Tibby Watson (Australia) w rtd 9 Frank Morecombe, Cosmopolitan Gym, Plymouth. Although there were no weights given, both were thought to be inside 108lbs, thus putting Watson's claim at risk.

7 September Curly Osborne drew 20 Joe Percival, Royal Engineers Drill Hall, Leeds. Billed for the English 104lbs title, Percival had earlier, on 23 March, been accorded a 15-round points win over the Londoner in Leeds, a result that was refuted by Osborne, who claimed never to have been in the town prior to 7 September.

19 October Curly Osborne w pts 20 Joe Percival, Royal Engineers Drill Hall, Leeds. Billed for the English 104lbs title, both men scaled 104lbs.

21 December Sam Keller w pts 20 Ralph Marshall, Scottish National AC, Charles Street, Bridgeton, Glasgow. Billed for the English 110lbs title, £100 a side and a £50 purse, with both men on the 7st 12lbs limit, the fact that it was contested over two-minute rounds disqualifies it from having any real credence.

26 December James Easton w pts 20 Mango Pitt, Scottish National AC, Charles Street, Bridgeton, Glasgow. Although billed for the English 98lbs title, with Easton scaling 96½lbs to Pitt's

97lbs, again, the fact that it was contested over two-minute rounds meant that the fight itself carried little or no credence whatsoever.

28 December Curly Osborne w co 4 Harry Kid Furness, Scottish National Athletic Club, Glasgow. Billed for the English 104lbs title.

1909

1 February Curly Osborne w pts 20 Joe Percival, Royal Engineers Drill Hall, Leeds. Although made at catchweights, with both men inside 7st 8lbs Osborne laid claim to the English 106lbs title.

8 February Sid Smith w pts 15 Albert Cocksedge, NSC, King Street, Covent Garden, London. Reported as being for the English 108lbs title, Smith scaled 105lbs to Cocksedge's 107. Surprisingly, Cocksedge was still advertising himself as the 108lb champion of England in the 13 February issue of the *Mirror of Life*.

At a meeting on 11 February 1909 at the NSC, it was stated that flyweight (112lbs) would be recognised as the lowest championship weight that a British (formerly English) title would be contested at. Regardless of that announcement, all the English weight classes at every two pounds below 112lbs merely carried on until Jimmy Wilde's total domination of virtually all weights up to 112lbs took effect.

11 February Johnny Coulon (Canada) w rtd 5 Kid Murphy (USA), NYC, USA. Billed for the world 105lbs title, with both men inside, this would be Coulon's last defence at the weight prior to him moving up to 108lbs. Incidentally, this one was a no-decision contest.

25 March Curly Osborne w co 15 Joe Percival, Birkenhead. Scheduled for 20 rounds, although no weights or billing were given it was later stated that Osborne had won the English 106lbs title with this victory. On 17 August, Osborne was outpointed over 20 rounds at the Central Hall, Manchester by Salford's Billy Marchant, but the latter, both taller and heavier, would not have been placed to land Osborne's title claim.

11 May Curly Osborne drew 20 Joe Percival, Scottish National AC, Charles Street, Bridgeton, Glasgow. Billed for the English 104lbs title. On 15 May, when Sid Smith challenged all England between 104lbs and 108lbs, it was obvious that men such as himself were not happy giving away a lot of weight to opponents who scaled close to the 112lbs mark. The problem had come about following the meeting at the NSC on 11 February, when it was decided that, in order to stop the profusion of fights at every two pounds, especially among the lower weights, there would not be an official championship weight below 112lbs. Unfortunately, this meant that men of Smith's weight were being unfairly treated and because there was a proliferation of small men at the time it was argued on their behalf that there should be at least two paperweight classes below the new flyweight division.

28 May Johnny Coulon (Canada) w co 10 Tibby Watson (Australia), Dayton, Ohio, USA. Billed for the world 108lbs title, the original plan was to make the fight at 105lbs, but neither man could make that poundage anymore and Coulon moved his claim up following his win.

3 June Paddy Carroll w pts 20 Joe Percival, Drill Hall, Birkenhead. Although there was no billing as such, Carroll later claimed that he won the English 108lbs paperweight title in this one.

25 June Curly Osborne w pts 15 James Easton, Theatre Royal, Belfast. Billed as an English title bout at 104lbs, on the same day in the *Sporting Life* Osborne was reported as a claimant to the title.

15 July Paddy Carroll w rtd 13 Curly Osborne, Drill Hall, Birkenhead. Billed as a fight that involved a claim to the English 104lbs title over 20 rounds, Osborne struggled to make the weight and, with Carroll also unable to get down to 104lbs again, the title lapsed.

4 September Young Joey Smith w pts 20 Joe Shears, Forrester's Music Hall, Cambridge Heath Road, Mile End, London. Originally billed for the English 100lbs title, and Mr Harman's Championship Belt, Smith (106lbs) came in 6lbs overweight and the fight went on at catchweights. Shears, weighing just 98lbs, could have claimed the title by forfeit if the contest had more standing, it being contested over two-minute rounds, but, amazingly, it was Smith who was presented with the belt and who then claimed the English title at 106lbs on the substance of this result.

6 September Sam Keller drew 20 Albert Cocksedge, Scottish National AC, Glasgow. Billed for the 112lbs British title, but no weights given. On 9 December, the American promoter, Jim Coffroth, claimed that, under the new weight scales published by the NSC, the Canadian-born Johnny Coulon should be recognised as the undisputed flyweight champion of the world.

29 September Young Joey Smith w pts 20 Eddie Morgan, Millfield Hotel, Pontypridd. Billed for the English and world 106lbs titles, but contested over two-minute rounds (therefore having no validity as such), Smith scaled 106lbs to Morgan's 98½lbs.

4 October Joe Percival w pts 20 Curly Osborne, Newcastle. Contested at catchweights, but with Percival thought to be inside 106lbs Osborne's title claim is certainly on the slide from hereon and, on 11 November, Paddy Carroll (Liverpool) outpointed him over 20 rounds at the International AC, Liverpool.

13 November Joe Shears drew 15 Llew Probert, Welsh NSC, Merthyr. Billed for the 102lbs English title and carrying a £40 purse, it was probably a misprint with both Shears (98lbs) and Probert (99lbs) being inside 100lbs.

6 December Joe Sheers w pts 20 James Easton, Scottish National AC, Charles Street, Bridgeton, Glasgow. Again billed for the English 98lbs title, but again contested over two-minute rounds.

20 December Harry McDermott w rtd 11 Curly Osborne, St James' Hall, Newcastle. Billed for the English 108lbs paperweight title, both men came in on the weight.

20 December Young Joey Smith w rtd 9 Kid Sullivan, Millfield Hotel, Pontypridd. Billed for the world 106lbs title over 25 rounds (20 was also reported), £50 a side and 60% of the gate, Smith backed up his claim.

1910

15 January Johnny Coulon (Canada) w pts 10 George Kitson (USA), New Orleans, Louisiana, USA. Although not billed for the 112lbs title, following the result Coulon claimed the world crown at the weight.

24 January James Easton drew 20 Young George Dando, Scottish National AC, Charles Street, Bridgeton, Glasgow. Billed for the English 98lbs title, Easton scaled 97lbs to Dando's 96lbs. The fight was presumably contested over two-minute rounds.

29 January Young Joey Smith drew 20 Young Johnny Cohen, Wonderland, Whitechapel Road, London. Billed for both the British and world 106lbs titles, the fact that it was contested over two-minute rounds disqualified it as a genuine championship bout. On 11 February, at the Brighton Dome, Smith knocked out Harry Ray in the tenth of a 20 rounder at catchweights. Almost certainly articled for two-minute rounds, it was yet another fight for Smith that would not be taken seriously and, on 1 May 1910, he relinquished his claim due to increasing weight problems.

29 January Johnny Coulon (Canada) w co 9 Earl Denning (USA), New Orleans, Louisiana, USA. Billed for the American and world 112lbs flyweight title.

31 January Harry McDermott w pts 20 Joe Percival, Newcastle. Billed for the English 110lbs title, no weights were announced.

19 February Johnny Coulon (Canada) w pts 10 Jim Kenrick, New Orleans, Louisiana, USA. Billed for the world 112lbs title, this was the last time that Coulon boxed at the weight.

2 April Louis Ruddick w pts 15 Teddy Murphy (USA), Central Academy, Manchester. Despite not being billed as such, it was reported to carry the world 98lbs title, with both men on the weight. However, Murphy was a substitute for Ginger James. Incidentally, Ruddick twice defeated James at catchweights, with the latter weighing under 98lbs, while Ruddick scaled 104lbs and 109lbs, respectively.

14 April Albert Cocksedge w pts 20 Harry McDermott, Newcastle. Billed for the English 110lbs title, no weights were published.

27 June Bill Kyne w pts 20 Albert Cocksedge, Newcastle. Billed as an English 110lbs title defence for Cocksedge, no weights were published.

18 July Bill Kyne w co 2 Curly Osborne, St James' Hall, Newcastle. Scheduled for 20 rounds and billed for the English 110lbs title, again there were no weights made available.
22 August Bill Kyne w co 6 Joe Wilson, St James' Hall, Newcastle. Billed for the English 110lbs title, £25 a side plus purse, the winner was challenged by Harry McDermott for £100 a side. Following on from this there were a number of contests for Kyne which carried no title billing as such and the 110lbs weight class disappeared.
17 October Young Joe Fox w pts 20 Joe Percival, Leeds. Thought to involve Percival's English 106lbs title claim, but no billing or weights were reported, as in his next two fights. All three were stipulated for 20 rounds.
21 November Joe Percival w dis 4 Young Joe Fox, Leeds. Thought to have involved the English 106lbs title.
7 December Joe Percival w co 2 Jack Madden, Leeds. Yet another fight for Percival thought to involve the English 106lbs title.

Jim Kenrick was one of Britain's leading 112 pounders at the turn of the last century

1911

30 January Sid Smith w pts 15 George Peters, Manor Place Baths, Walworth, London. Made at 112lbs, but not a billed title fight, it did not stop Smith from claiming to be the British champion, especially as he had defeated the Scot, Alex Lafferty, on points over 20 rounds in a catchweight bout at the Victoria AC, Glasgow on 5 December. With Smith inside the articled weight of 112lbs, Lafferty failed to make the weigh-in, being well over the required limit.
8 May Joe Percival w pts 20 Louis Ruddick, Carlton Hill Barracks, Leeds. Billed for the English 106lbs title, £25 a side and a £60 purse, both men scaled 7st 8lbs.
25 September Sid Smith w pts 20 Stoker Bill Hoskyne, The Ring, Blackfriars, London. Billed for the 112lbs title, it was disqualified from being recognised as such by the boxing public at large due to two-minute rounds being contested.
16 October Bill Ladbury w co 7 Albert Cocksedge, Belgrave Rink, Leicester. Billed for the British 112lbs title, Ladbury received limited recognition.
16 October Jim Berry w dis 12 Joe Percival, Newcastle. Again thought to involve Percival's English 106lbs title claim and

scheduled for 20 rounds, there was no billing or weights given in the *Mirror of Life* report.
19 October Sid Smith w pts 20 Louis Ruddock, The Stadium, Liverpool. Although there was no billing as such, the fight was thought to have involved Smith's British title claim at 112lbs.
4 December Sid Smith w pts 20 Joe Wilson, NSC, King Street, Covent Garden, London. By winning the Lonsdale Belt, Smith could justifiably claim to be the leading man at 112lbs in the world despite a lack of further billing. However, following a derisory purse offer for a defence against Johnny Hughes, Smith returned the belt to the Club and went in search of better financial opportunities.
18 December Louis Ruddick w dis 4 Jim Berry, Newcastle. Scheduled for 20 rounds, despite a lack of weights and billing Ruddick was thought to have taken over Berry's claim at the weight, but quickly moved on. That was it as far as the 106lbs weight class was concerned until Tal Jones outpointed Harry Aarons over 15 rounds at the NSC on 21 June 1921. Although not billed as such, later gossip stated that Jones won the British title in this fight, but no more is heard of championship fights at weights below 112lbs from then on.

1912

20 July Jimmy Wilde w rtd 4 Kid Morris, Cardiff. Billed for the British 94lbs title over 20 rounds.
19 September Sid Smith w pts 20 Curley Walker, The Ring, Blackfriars, London. Contested under full championship conditions, it was billed for the 112lbs world title outside the jurisdiction of the NSC.
4 November Billy Padden drew 15 Kid Morris, Scottish National AC, Charles Street, Bridgeton, Glasgow. Although there was no title billing accorded, later articles on Padden show this to have been an English title bout at 104lbs. Padden weighed 104lbs to Morris' 100.
2 December Billy Padden w pts 15 Kid Morris, Scottish National AC, Charles Street, Bridgeton, Glasgow. As in their previous bout, later reports give this as being for the English 104lbs title, but following Padden's 18th-round defeat at the hands of Jimmy Wilde at 112lbs his claim disintegrated.

1913

1 January Jimmy Wilde w rtd 18 Billy Padden, Victoria AC, Glasgow. Billed for the English 98lbs title over 20 rounds (2.0pm weigh-in), *Boxing* stated that Wilde retained his title, while the *Mirror of Life* reported that Padden had been the champion until defeated by Wilde.
18 January Jimmy Wilde w rtd 7 Tommy Hughes, The Hippodrome, Tonypandy. Later stated to have involved the English 100lbs title, Wilde (94lbs), with bigger fish to fry, never bothered to pursue his claim. Hughes weighed 100lbs.
30 March Jimmy Wilde w co 6 Eugene Husson (France), NSC, King Street, Covent Garden, London. With Wilde weighing 94lbs to the Frenchman's 87½, this was a 20 rounder billed for the world 'gnatweight' title over 20 rounds.
11 April Sid Smith w pts 20 Eugene Criqui (France), Paris, France – GB/France. Billed for the 112lbs world title.
2 June Bill Ladbury w rsc 11 Sid Smith, The Ring, Blackfriars, London – GB. Billed for the world 112lbs title.
22 September Jimmy Wilde w pts 20 Young George Dando, Westgate Street Skating Rink, Cardiff. Billed for the Welsh and English 108lbs paperweight titles, Wilde scaled 96lbs to Dando's 92.
6 December Jimmy Wilde w disq 18 Young George Dando, Merthyr. Again billed for the Welsh and English 108lbs paperweight titles, Wilde weighed in at 96lbs while Dando made 107lbs.
16 December Jimmy Wilde w rtd 9 Harry Brooks, Free Trade Hall, Manchester. Although there was no title billing, with Wilde weighing 96lbs to Brooks' 106lbs his 108lbs 'paperweight' title claim was obviously at risk in this one.

1914

3 January Jimmy Wilde w pts 20 Kid Nutter), The Pavilion,

Tonypandy. Although there was no title billing accredited, Wilde (6st 10lbs) later stated that his British and world 94lb titles had been at stake in this one, with Nutter scaling 88lbs.

26 January Percy Jones w pts 20 Bill Ladbury, NSC, King Street, Covent Garden, London – GB/IBU. Billed for the world 112lbs title.

2 February Jimmy Wilde w pts 15 Kid Nutter, Drill Hall, Birkenhead. Again, although no title billing, with both men inside the weight limit, Wilde's 94lbs championship claim at the weight was automatically at stake. Nutter (90lbs) was killed in action in France.

26 March Percy Jones w pts 20 Eugene Criqui (France), The Stadium, Liverpool – GB/IBU. Defeated on an 18th round stoppage by Joe Symonds at the Old Cosmo Rink, Plymouth on 15 May 1914 in a billed 112lbs title bout, Jones should have forfeited his GB/IBU version of the title on the scales when weighing-in two and a half pounds overweight. However, after the NSC refused to recognise the winner and matched Jones against Jimmy Berry at the Club, the Welshman successfully weighed-in only for Berry not to turn up. Berry later stated that he had informed the officials earlier that he was unable to make 112lb. Finally, on 19 October 1914, Jones forfeited any right he had to his version of the title when he failed to make the weight for a defence against Tancy Lee at the NSC. The fight went ahead at catchweights with Lee winning on a 14th-round stoppage and effectively being recognised by the Club as the new champion.

16 November Jimmy Wilde w pts 15 Joe Symonds, The Ring, Blackfriars, London. With the NSC not recognising Symonds' claim he was matched by the promoters at the Blackfriars' Ring against the sensational Jimmy Wilde for their version of the 112lbs title.

3 December Jimmy Wilde w co 9 Sid Smith, The Stadium, Liverpool. Wilde successfully defended his claim to the 112lbs title in this fight before going to the NSC to meet Tancy Lee in a bout where the winner would be generally recognised on this side of the Atlantic as world champion.

1915

25 January Tancy Lee w rsc 17 Jimmy Wilde, NSC, King Street, Covent Garden, London – GB/IBU. Billed for the British 112lbs, it also took on board Wilde's world title claim at the weight.

18 October Joe Symonds w rsc 16 Tancy Lee, NSC, King Street, Covent Garden, London – GB/IBU. While being billed for the British 112lbs title, Lee's world title claim at the weight automatically passed to Symonds.

1916

14 February Jimmy Wilde w rsc 12 Joe Symonds, NSC, King Street, Covent Garden, London – GB/IBU. Wilde took over the British 112lbs title and, at the same time, regained his world title claim at the weight.

24 April Jimmy Wilde w rtd 11 Johnny Rosner (USA), The Stadium, Liverpool – GB/IBU. Billed for the world 112lbs title.

26 June Jimmy Wilde w rsc 11 Tancy Lee, NSC, King Street, Covent Garden, London – GB/IBU. Billed for the British 112lbs championship, it automatically involved Wilde's world title claim at the weight.

31 July Jimmy Wilde w co 10 Johnny Hughes, Kensal Rise Athletic Ground, London – GB/IBU. Yet another British 112lbs championship contest in which Wilde's world title claim was at risk.

18 December Jimmy Wilde w co 11 Young Zulu Kid (USA), Holborn Stadium, London. Billed for the world 112lbs title, Wilde was recognised in most quarters as the champion following his victory.

1917

12 March Jimmy Wilde w rtd 4 George Clark, NSC, King Street, Covent Garden, London. Billed for the British 112lbs championship and recognised by the press as involving Wilde's world title claim at the weight.

18 October Tal Jones w dis 3 Billy Padden, The Stadium, Liverpool. Following his win, Jones (100lbs) gained a sound claim to the English title at the weight.

22 October Dick Heasman w pts 15 Tommy Davis, NSC, King Street, Covent Garden, London. Although not billed for a title, reports stated that Heasman (100lbs), by his win over Davis (99lbs), countered Tal Jones claim to the English 100lbs championship.

22 November Tal Jones w pts 20 Billy Padden, The Stadium, Liverpool. Although there was no title billing as such, with Jones scaling 100lbs it was looked upon as a defence of his English title claim at the weight.

1918

4 February Dick Heasman w pts 15 Tal Jones, NSC, King Street, Covent Garden, London. Although the NSC did not officially recognise any weight below 112lbs and, therefore, gave this fight no title billing, with the match made at 100lbs Heasman proved himself the best man at the weight, bar Jimmy Wilde.

29 April Jimmy Wilde w rtd 2 Dick Heasman, NSC, King Street, Covent Garden, London. Despite the NSC failing to recognise any weight below 112lbs in championship terms, with Wilde scaling 100½lbs to Heasman's 102 the press saw this being a world title match at the weight and had Wilde lost there was the possibility that he would have forfeited his 112lb honours. With Wilde now recognised on the other side of the Atlantic as the world champion, Johnny Rosner had earlier claimed the American title on knocking out the Young Zulu Kid inside seven rounds on 28 September 1917 in New York City, USA, but Wilde had already defeated both men and there was little recognition forthcoming for Rosner. However, with the little Welshman fighting mainly in the bantamweight ranks there was a renewed interest in the States to find a worthy challenger for the title, especially after Young Montreal took over Rosner's American title claim on outpointing the latter over 12 rounds in Providence, Rhode Island, USA on 10 April 1919, but he too decided to campaign among the bantams.

The incomparable Jimmy Wilde

With Wilde's total domination at all weights up to and including 112lbs, and with the NSC and other leading authorities failing to recognise even smaller men, the paperweight class faded into obscurity despite persisting in Wales up until around 1929.

1920

12 March Jimmy Wilde nd-w pts 12 Frankie Mason (USA), Toledo, Ohio, USA. Billed as a world flyweight title fight despite the Articles of Agreement calling for both men to be inside 108lbs. Earlier, on 3 March 1920 in Philadelphia, USA Wilde won a six-round newspaper decision over Patsy Wallace (USA), with both men inside 112lbs. Two further no-decision bouts during his tour saw Wilde risking his title over short distances, Battling Murray (USA) being counted out in the eighth round on 21 April 1920 in Camden, New Jersey and being then knocked out in the second on 13th May 1920 in Philadelphia. The final contest for Wilde (105lbs) during his 1919-1920 tour of North America saw him outpoint America's Patsy Wallace (112lbs) over 10 rounds in Toronto, Canada on 24 May 1920. Billed as a title fight, there was little or no risk for Wilde with the contest being contracted at 116lbs in order to protect his title. Following Wilde's defeat at the hands of world bantam champion, Pete Herman, in a catchweight bout at the NSC on 13 January 1921, in order to find an American titleholder at the weight Johnny Buff (112) outpointed Frankie Mason (108) over 15 rounds in New Orleans on 11 February 1921, despite the match being made at 116lbs. Then, fighting over 15 rounds in New York City, Buff went on to kayo Abe Goldstein inside two rounds on 31 March 1921, both men weighing 110lbs, before he, in turn, was knocked out by the Filipino, Pancho Villa, on 14 September 1922. Although Villa (109½) lost the American title to Frankie Genaro (110½) over the same distance in New York City on 1 March 1923, when the promoter, Tex Rickard, lulled Wilde out of semi-retirement for a title defence it was not Genaro who was selected to meet the world champion but Villa, on the grounds that he was bigger box office.

1923

18 June Pancho Villa (Philippines) w co 7 Jimmy Wilde (Wales), NYC, New York, USA.
13 October Pancho Villa (Philippines) w pts 15 Benny Schwartz (USA). Baltimore, Maryland, USA.

1924

30 May Pancho Villa (Philippines) w pts 15 Frankie Ash (England), NYC, New York, USA.

1925

1 May Pancho Villa (Philippines) w pts 15 Clever Sencio (Philippines), Manila, Philippines.Villa died from a poisoned tooth infection on 14 July 1925 and the title became vacant. As the reigning American champion, Frankie Genaro claimed the title on the strength of his 1923 victory over Villa, but before outright acceptance was forthcoming he was asked to defend his American title against Fidel LaBarba.
22 August Fidel LaBarba (USA) w pts 10 Frankie Genaro (USA), Los Angeles, California, USA – NBA/CALIFORNIA. Although the fight was billed for the vacant world championship as well as the American title, it went unrecognised as such in Europe.

1926

8 July Fidel LaBarba (USA) w pts 10 Georgie Rivers (USA), Los Angeles, California, USA – NBA/CALIFORNIA. Following this American title fight, LaBarba was matched against the European champion, Elky Clark, in order to once again unify the title.

1927

21 January Fidel LaBarba (USA) w pts 12 Elky Clark (Scotland), NYC, New York, USA. LaBarba relinquished the title on announcing his retirement in August 1927 and the NBA, then California and New York, and later Britain and the IBU, all instigated their own tournaments to find a successor. On 22 October 1927 in Bridgeport, Connecticut, Pinky Silverberg (USA) beat Ruby Bradley (USA) on a seventh-round disqualification, which was reported by Ring Magazine as Silverberg becoming champion of the world in the eyes of 24 States and four countries. However, the *Boston Post* clarified the situation when it stated that the fight was supposed to have been sanctioned by the NBA as a title bout, but at their convention four days earlier the NBA stated that a series of eliminators involving men such as Frenchy Belanger, Newsboy Brown and Frankie Genaro were being set up to find an opponent for England's Ernie Jarvis to decide the championship of the world. Regardless of this, one can be sure that this was an eliminator and, following a poor performance, Silverberg dropped out of the reckoning.
28 October Johnny McCoy (USA) w pts 10 Tommy Hughes (USA), Los Angeles, California, USA – CALIFORNIA.
16 December Izzy Schwartz (USA) w pts 15 Newsboy Brown (USA), NYC, New York, USA – NY.
19 December Frenchy Belanger (Canada) w pts 12 Ernie Jarvis (England), Toronto, Canada – NBA. Earlier, on 28 November 1927 in Toronto, Belanger had outpointed Frankie Genaro over ten rounds of an NBA final eliminator (reported in some quarters as being for the NBA title).

1928

3 January Newsboy Brown (USA) w pts 10 Johnny McCoy (USA). Los Angeles, California, USA – CALIFORNIA.
6 February Frankie Genaro (USA) w pts 10 Frenchy Belanger (C). Toronto, Canada – NBA.
9 April Izzy Schwartz (USA) w pts 15 Routier Parra (Chile), NYC, New York, USA – NY. On 9 May 1928, in Fort Wayne, Indiana, Schwartz gained a ten-round press victory over Happy Atherton, the Indianapolis flyweight, and although there was no mention of weights and it was outside the jurisdiction of the NYSAC the local paper reported that while Atherton was not expected to wrest the title from Schwartz a good showing would do much to gain him a bout where the crown would be very much at stake. Despite the newspaper expectancy, this one was almost certainly an over-the-weight contest.
24 April Newsboy Brown (USA) w co 6 Speedy Dado (Philippines), Los Angeles, California, USA – CALIFORNIA.
20 July Izzy Schwartz (USA) w disq 4 Frisco Grande (Philippines), Rockaway, New York, USA – NY.
23 July Frankie Genaro (USA) drew 10 Steve Rocco (Canada), Toronto, Canada – NBA.
3 August Izzy Schwartz (USA) w co 4 Little Jeff Smith (USA), Rockaway, New York, USA – NY. Following the passing of the Altman Bill, which permitted 15-round fights to a decision in New Jersey, Schwartz knocked out Frisco Grande (Philippines) inside eight rounds at Long Branch on 31 August 1928. While the *New York Times* reported it to be a title fight (Schwartz held the New York version of the title), it was contested outside the jurisdiction of the NYSAC. However, with both men inside 112lbs, had Schwartz lost he would have undoubtedly been stripped of his title.
29 August Johnny Hill (Scotland) w pts 15 Newsboy Brown (USA). Clapton Stadium, London, England. Billed by the promoters as a world title fight, while Brown certainly lost his Californian recognition on the result and Hill was recognised in Scotland as being the world champion, support for the winner was not totally forthcoming in Britain, even though he was the European champion. Support for Hill further diminished on 7 February 1929 when he was knocked out in Paris by the Frenchman, Emile Pladner, despite the match being made at 115lbs.
15 October Frankie Genaro (USA) w pts 10 Frenchy Belanger (Canada), Toronto, Canada – NBA.
14 December Frankie Genaro (USA) w disq 2 Steve Rocco (Canada), Detroit, Michigan, USA – NBA.

1929

2 March Emile Pladner (France) w co 1 Frankie Genaro (USA), Paris, France – NBA. Having won the NBA title, Pladner was proclaimed the IBU world flyweight champion on 20 March 1929. Incidentally, with the finish timed at 58 seconds, this was the shortest world title fight on record at that moment in time.

12 March Izzy Schwartz (USA) w pts 12 Frenchy Belanger (Canada), Toronto, Canada – NY. Contested on NBA territory, the NYSAC gave Schwartz permission to defend their title against Belanger as long as the winner promised to meet their number one contender, Emile Pladner, within a designated period. On 22 August 1929 in Newark, New Jersey, Schwartz was outpointed over 15 rounds by Willie LaMorte (USA). Although being a member of the NBA, who recognised Frankie Genaro as champion, the New Jersey Boxing Commission permitted the promoter to advertise the contest as a championship fight while insisting that both men make the limit, before announcing immediately prior to the battle that no title was at stake. Following the fight, the NYSAC withdrew its support of Schwartz and, in refusing to recognise LaMorte, set up an elimination tournament at Madison Square Gardens to find a new champion. A four-legged affair on 4 November 1929, saw Black Bill, Eugene Huat, Ruby Bradley and Midget Wolgast outscore Willie Davies, Schwartz, Ernie Peters and Johnny McCoy, respectively, before the Cuban, Bill, eliminated Huat, also on points over 10 rounds, to book himself a place in the final against Wolgast, who drew a bye after Bradley pulled out.

21 March Johnny Hill (Scotland) w pts 15 Ernie Jarvis (England), Albert Hall, Kensington, London, England. Advertised as a British and European title fight, Hill's version of the world championship was also at stake.

18 April Frankie Genaro (USA) w disq 5 Emile Pladner (France), Paris, France – NBA/IBU.

29 June Johnny Hill (Scotland) w disq10 Ernie Jarvis (England), Cartyne Greyhound Track, Glasgow, Scotland. Billed for the British title, Hill's version of the world championship was yet again automatically at stake. Due to meet Frankie Genaro for the NBA title, Hill's claim dissolved on 27 September 1929, the day of his untimely death.

17 October Frankie Genaro (USA) w pts 15 Ernie Jarvis (England), Albert Hall, Kensington, London, England – NBA/IBU. On 21 November 1929 in Paterson, New Jersey, Willie LaMorte (USA) stopped the Filipino, Frisco Grande, inside seven rounds of a billed title fight. However, it was not recognised as such by the NYSAC, or in New Jersey, who, as a member of the NBA, still viewed Frankie Genaro as champion. Naturally, LaMorte, a New Yorker by birth, continued to claim the championship with good cause until being defeated by Midget Wolgast in a challenge on the New York title. Also, at the end of 1929, Pablo Dano, a Filipino who had beaten LaMorte and drawn with Izzy Schwartz, laid claim to the title to further confuse the issue. Despite being a good fighter, Dana 's claim fell on deaf ears and he received no official backing.

1930

18 January Frankie Genaro (USA) w rtd 12 Yvon Trevidic (France), Paris, France –NBA/IBU.

21 March Midget Wolgast (USA) w pts 15 Black Bill (Cuba), NYC, New York, USA – NY. Five days later, concurring with the NYSAC ruling, Wolgast was acclaimed as world champion by the Pennsylvanian Boxing Commission, an authority who had failed to recognise any fighter as a champion following the demise of Pancho Villa.

16 May Midget Wolgast (USA) w co 6 Willie LaMorte (USA), NYC, New York, USA – NY.

10 June Frankie Genaro (USA) w pts 10 Frenchy Belanger (Canada), Toronto, Canada – NBA/IBU.

26 December Frankie Genaro (USA) drew 15 Midget Wolgast (USA), NYC, New York, USA.

1931

25 March Frankie Genaro (USA) drew 15 Victor Ferrand (Spain), Madrid, Spain – NBA/IBU. At the finish, Ferrand was four points ahead on the referee's scorecard, but, under IBU rules, the challenger had to have a lead of at least five points for the title to change hands.

13 July Midget Wolgast (USA) w pts 15 Ruby Bradley (USA), NYC, New York, USA – NY. Despite not defending the New York version of the championship again, and competing mainly in

the bantamweight ranks from hereon, Wolgast continued to be recognised as their champion right up to his defeat at the hands of Small Montana in September 1935.

30 July Frankie Genaro (USA) w co 6 Jackie Harmon (USA), Waterbury, Connecticut, USA – NBA/IBU.

3 October Frankie Genaro (USA) w pts 15 Valentin Angelmann (France), Paris, France – NBA/IBU.

27 October Young Perez (France) w co 2 Frankie Genaro (USA), Paris, France – NBA/IBU.

1932

31 October Jackie Brown (England) w rsc 13 Young Perez (France), Belle Vue, Manchester, England – NBA/IBU.

1933

12 June Jackie Brown (England) w pts 15 Valentin Angelmann (France), Olympia, London, England – NBA/IBU.

11 September Jackie Brown (England) w pts 15 Valentin Angelmann (France), Belle Vue, Manchester, England – NBA/IBU.

11 December Jackie Brown (England) w pts 15 Ginger Foran (England), Belle Vue, Manchester – NBA/IBU.

1934

18 June Jackie Brown (England) drew 15 Valentin Angelmann (France), Belle Vue, Manchester, England – NBA/IBU. Brown forfeited IBU recognition at their annual conference on 6 June 1935, for failing to meet Angelmann in a return match. The fact that Brown had already signed for a defence against Benny Lynch was given no due consideration.

1935

9 March Benny Lynch (Scotland) w rtd 2 Jackie Brown (England), Belle Vue, Manchester, England – GB/NBA. Immediately following his victory, the IBU, who had not recognised Brown v Lynch as a title fight, gave Lynch until 25 September to sign for a contest against Valentin Angelmann. When he failed to do so they announced that the Frenchman would box the current European champion, Kid David, for their version of the title.

16 September Small Montana (Philippines) w pts10 Midget Wolgast (USA), Oakland, California, USA – NY/CALIFORNIA.

16 December Small Montana (Philippines) w pts10 Tuffy Pierpont (USA), Oakland, California, USA – NY/CALIFORNIA.

1936

6 January Valentin Angelmann (France) w rtd 5 Kid David (Belgium), Paris, France – IBU.

16 September Benny Lynch (England) w co 8 Pat Palmer (England) Shawfield Park, Glasgow, Scotland – GB/NBA.

12 December Valentin Angelmann (France) w pts 15 Ernst Weiss (Austria), Paris, France – IBU. During an international boxing convention held in Rome during the third week of April 1938, the IBU agreed to refuse to recognise all individually made world champions, including Angelmann, in an effort to stand by one universally recognised titleholder.

1937

19 January Benny Lynch (Scotland) w pts 15 Small Montana (Philippines), The Arena, Wembley, England – GB/NBA/NY.

13 October Benny Lynch (Scotland) w co13 Peter Kane (England), Shawfield Park, Glasgow, Scotland – GB/NBA/NY. From hereon, Lynch's career lurched from one catastrophe to another. Contracted to defend the world title in a return against Kane at the Liverpool Stadium on 24 March 1938, he failed to make the weight and, although the contest went ahead, resulting in a 12-round draw, he was fortunate not to forfeit the championship. Following that debacle, he did finally forfeit the title on the scales when weighing in six and a half pounds overweight for a championship match against the American, Jackie Jurich, at Shawfield Park, Glasgow on 29 June 1938. That fight also went ahead, with Jurich being counted out in the 11th round, but the little Scot's career was effectively over and Kane was matched against Jurich for the vacant title, while the claims of the Filipino eight stoners, Little Dado and Small Montana, were strongly supported in California.

1938

22 September Peter Kane (England) w pts 15 Jackie Jurich (USA), Anfield Football Ground, Liverpool, England – GB/NY/IBU/NBA. Having won the title, Kane also found that he was having a struggle to make the weight and in May 1939 he announced that he was relinquishing the title in order to campaign as a bantamweight.

30 November Little Dado (Philippines) w pts 10 Small Montana (Philippines), Oakland, California, USA – CALIFORNIA. Although Dado was recognised in California as world champion, it did not stop a promotion going ahead in the same town, matching the loser, Montana, with Jackie Jurich on 3 March 1939 for the vacant American title, the latter winning via a seventh-round kayo. Then, on 1 September 1939, the newly formed World Championship Committee agreed to recognise the winner of Dado v Enrico Urbinati (European champion) as world champion, but, unfortunately, due to the war, that fight fell through. Meanwhile, in defence of his American title, Jurich outpointed Montana after ten rounds on 4 October 1939, before suffering a tenth-round kayo defeat at the hands of Little Pancho in Los Angeles on 11 December 1939. Both men were inside 112lbs and, three days later, Little Dado was proclaimed NBA flyweight champion. Prior to that, around the end of October, Little Pancho had asked the NBA to consider him as their champion, but ultimately lost out to his compatriot.

1940

17 June Little Dado (Philippines) drew 10 Little Pancho (Philippines), San Francisco, California, USA – CALIFORNIA. With Dado still recognised by the NBA, this contest was authorised by the Californian Boxing Commission for their version of the title.

Peter Kane, pictured beating Baltazar Sangchilli in 1939, won the world flyweight title in 1938 on Benny Lynch being stripped

1941

21 February Little Dado (Philippines) w pts 10 Jackie Jurich (USA), Honolulu, Hawaii – NBA. Inactive for almost all of 1942, Dado came back towards the end of that year as a fully-fledged bantam, but reigned on as champion until 14 October 1943, the day the NBA formally decided he could no longer make the weight.

1943

19 June Jackie Paterson (Scotland) w co 1 Peter Kane (England), Hampden Park, Glasgow, Scotland – GB/NY. With Kane still able to make eight stone, and despite having earlier relinquished the title, the Englishman was allowed to 'defend' his old title against Paterson in a fight seen by Britain and the NYSAC as being for the championship. Paterson was eventually recognised by the NBA when they stripped Little Dado in October 1943.

1946

10 July Jackie Paterson (Scotland) w pts 15 Joe Curran (England), Hampden Park, Glasgow, Scotland. Paterson forfeited NBA recognition in July 1947, having thrice pulled out of title defences against Dado Marino, and a match between the latter and Rinty Monaghan was announced to decide the championship. Initially, Paterson had also been stripped by the BBBoC but, following an injunction in the High Court, he was later reinstated.

1947

20 October Rinty Monaghan (Northern Ireland) w pts 15 Dado Marino (Hawaii), Harringay Arena, London, England – NBA.

1948

23 March Rinty Monaghan (Northern Ireland) w co 7 Jackie Paterson (Scotland), King's Hall, Belfast, Northern Ireland.

1949

5 April Rinty Monaghan (Northern Ireland) w pts 15 Maurice Sandeyron (France), King's Hall, Belfast, Northern Ireland.
30 September Rinty Monaghan (Northern Ireland) drew 15 Terry Allen (England), King's Hall, Belfast, Northern Ireland. Monaghan retired as undefeated champion in April 1950 and the two leading contenders, Terry Allen and the French champion, Honore Pratesi, were matched for the vacant title.

1950

25 April Terry Allen (England) w pts 15 Honore Pratesi (France), Harringay Arena, London, England.
1 August Dado Marino (Hawaii) w pts 15 Terry Allen (England), Honolulu, Hawaii.

1951

1 November Dado Marino (Hawaii) w pts 15 Terry Allen (England), Honolulu, Hawaii.

1952

19 May Yoshio Shirai (Japan) w pts 15 Dado Marino (Hawaii), Tokyo, Japan.
15 November Yoshio Shirai (Japan) w pts 15 Dado Marino (Hawaii), Tokyo, Japan.

1953

18 May Yoshio Shirai (Japan) w pts 15 Tanny Campo (Philippines), Tokyo, Japan.
27 October Yoshio Shirai (Japan) w pts 15 Terry Allen (England), Tokyo, Japan.

1954

23 May Yoshio Shirai (Japan) w pts 15 Leo Espinosa (Philippines), Tokyo, Japan.
26 November Pascual Perez (Argentina) w pts 15 Yoshio Shirai (Japan), Tokyo, Japan.

1955

30 May Pascual Perez (Argentina) w co 5 Yoshio Shirai (Japan),

Tokyo, Japan. On a number of occasions, Perez risked his championship in non-title fights when allowing his opponent to make less than eight stone without contractual conditions in place. One such fight was on 22 October 1955, when he outpointed the Filipino, Danny Kid (111¼), over ten rounds in Buenos Aires, Argentina.

1956

11 January Pascual Perez (Argentina) w pts 15 Leo Espinosa (Philippines), Buenos Aires, Argentina. Yet another fight where Perez appeared to risk his title was a ten-round points win over fellow Argentinian, Marcelo Quiroga (111½), in Buenos Aires, Argentina on 31 March 1956.

30 June Pascual Perez (Argentina) w rtd 11 Oscar Suarez (Cuba), Montevideo, Uruguay. Two more 10-round non-title fights that saw Perez and his fellow Argentinians weighing in publicly at less than 112lbs came against Ricardo Valdez (w rsc 5 in Buenos Aires on 3 August 1956) and Hector Almaraz (w co 3 in Rosario on 25 August 1956).

1957

30 March Pascual Perez (Argentina) w co 1 Dai Dower (Wales), Buenos Aires, Argentina. Both Urbieta Sosa (w co 3 in Buenos Aires on 2 August 1957) and Pablo Sosa (w co 3 in Buenos Aires on 16 August 1957) weighed in at less that 112lbs for non-title contests against Perez, but from then on there appears to be no record of it happening again.

7 December Pascual Perez (Argentina) w co 3 Young Martin (Spain) Buenos Aires, Argentina.

1958

19 April Pascual Perez (Argentina) w pts 15 Ramon Arias (Venezuela), Caracas, Venezuela.

15 December Pascual Perez (Argentina) w pts 15 Dommy Ursua (Philippines), Manila, Philippines.

1959

10 August Pascual Perez (Argentina) w pts 15 Kenji Yonekura (Japan), Tokyo, Japan.

5 November Pascual Perez (Argentina) w co 13 Sadao Yaoita (Japan), Osaka, Japan.

1960

16 April Pone Kingpetch (Thailand) w pts 15 Pascual Perez (Argentina), Bangkok, Thailand.

22 September Pone Kingpetch (Thailand) w rsc 8 Pascual Perez (Argentina), Los Angeles, California, USA.

1961

27 June Pone Kingpetch (Thailand) w pts 15 Mitsunori Seki (Japan), Tokyo, Japan.

1962

30 May Pone Kingpetch (Thailand) w pts 15 Kyo Noguchi (Japan), Tokyo, Japan.

10 October Fighting Harada (Japan) w co 11 Pone Kingpetch (Thailand), Tokyo, Japan.

1963

12 January Pone Kingpetch (Thailand) w pts 15 Fighting Harada (Japan), Tokyo, Japan.

18 September Hiroyuki Ebihara (Japan) w co 1 Pone Kingpetch (Thailand), Tokyo, Japan.

1964

23 January Pone Kingpetch (Thailand) w pts 15 Hiroyuki Ebihara (Japan), Bangkok, Thailand.

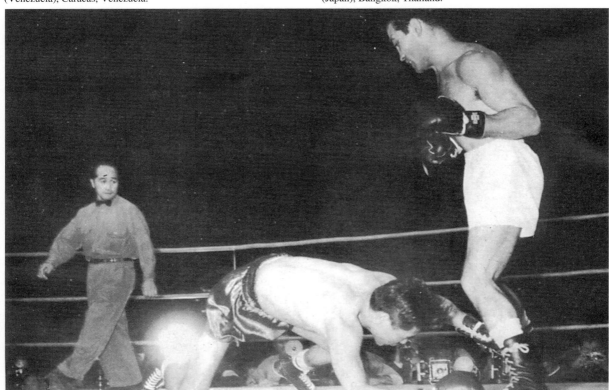

Pascual Perez (Argentina) won the flyweight title in 1954, beating Yoshio Shirai in Japan. Perez is seen here knocking Shirai out in their return contest on 30 May 1955

1965

23 April Salvatore Burruni (Italy) w pts 15 Pone Kingpetch (Thailand), Rome, Italy. Burruni forfeited WBA recognition in November1965 after failing to defend against the number one challenger, Hiroyuki Ebihara, within the given deadline. Following the announcement, the latter was matched for the vacant WBA title against Horacio Accavallo, who had outpointed Burruni three months earlier, but he had to be replaced by Katsuyoshi Takayama when injured in training.

2 December Salvatore Burruni (Italy) w co 13 Rocky Gattellari (Australia), Sydney, Australia – WBC.

1966

1 March Horacio Accavallo (Argentina) w pts 15 Katsuyoshi Takayama (Japan), Tokyo, Japan – WBA.

14 June Walter McGowan (Scotland) w pts 15 Salvatore Burruni (Italy), The Arena, Wembley, England – WBC.

15 July Horacio Accavallo (Argentina) w pts 15 Hiroyuki Ebihara (Japan), Buenos Aires, Argentina – WBA.

10 December Horacio Accavallo (Argentina) w pts 15 Efren Torres (Mexico), Buenos Aires, Argentina – WBA.

30 December Chartchai Chionoi (Thailand) w rsc 9 Walter McGowan (Scotland), Bangkok, Thailand – WBC.

1967

26 July Chartchai Chionoi (Thailand) w co 3 Puntip Keosuriya (Thailand), Bangkok, Thailand – WBC.

13 August Horacio Accavallo (Argentina) w pts 15 Hiroyuki Ebihara (Japan), Buenos Aires, Argentina – WBA. Accavallo retired as undefeated WBA champion in October 1968.

19 September Chartchai Chionoi (Thailand) w rsc 7 Walter McGowan (Scotland), The Arena, Wembley, England – WBC.

1968

28 January Chartchai Chionoi (Thailand) w rsc 13 Efren Torres (Mexico), Mexico City, Mexico – WBC.

10 November Chartchai Chionoi (Thailand) w pts 15 Bernabe Villacampo (Philippines), Bangkok, Thailand – WBC.

1969

23 February Efren Torres (Mexico) w rsc 8 Chartchai Chionoi (Thailand), Mexico City, Mexico – WBC.

30 March Hiroyuki Ebihara (Japan) w pts 15 Jose Severino (Brazil), Sapporo, Japan – WBA.

19 October Bernabe Villacampo (Philippines) w pts 15 Hiroyuki Ebihara (Japan), Tokyo, Japan – WBA.

28 November Efren Torres (Mexico) w pts 15 Susumu Hanagata (Japan), Guadalajara, Mexico – WBC.

1970

20 March Chartchai Chionoi (Thailand) w pts 15 Efren Torres (Mexico), Bangkok, Thailand – WBC.

6 April Berkrerk Chartvanchai (Thailand) w pts 15 Bernabe Villacampo (Philippines), Bangkok, Thailand – WBA.

21 October Masao Ohba (Japan) w rsc 13 Berkrerk Chartvanchai (Thailand), Tokyo, Japan – WBA.

7 December Erbito Salavarria (Philippines) w rsc 2 Chartchai Chionoi (Thailand), Bangkok, Thailand – WBC.

1971

1 April Masao Ohba (Japan) w pts 15 Betulio Gonzalez (Venezuela), Tokyo, Japan – WBA.

30 April Erbito Salavarria (Philippines) w pts 15 Susumu Hanagata (Japan), Manila, Philippines – WBC.

23 October Masao Ohba (Japan) w pts 15 Fernando Cabanela (Philippines), Tokyo, Japan – WBA.

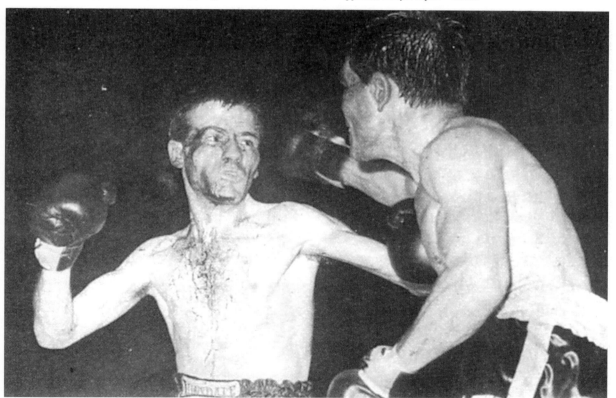

Scotland's Walter McGowan (left) joined a long line of British flyweights who ruled the 112lbs division, when beating the Italian, Salvatore Burruni, in 1966

20 November Erbito Salavarria (Philippines) drew 15 Betulio Gonzalez (Venezuela), Caracas, Venezuela – WBC. Salavarria forfeited WBC recognition immediately after the fight for allegedly using an illegal stimulant and Gonzalez was proclaimed champion.

1972
4 March Masao Ohba (Japan) w pts 15 Susumu Hanagata (Japan), Tokyo, Japan – WBA.
3 June Betulio Gonzalez (Venezuela) w co 4 Socrates Batoto (Philippines), Caracas, Venezuela – WBC.
20 June Masao Ohba (Japan) w co 5 Orlando Amores (Panama), Tokyo, Japan – WBA.
29 September Venice Borkorsor (Thailand) w rtd 10 Betulio Gonzales (Venezuela), Bangkok, Thailand – WBC.

1973
2 January Masao Ohba (Japan) w rsc 12 Chartchai Chionoi (Thailand), Tokyo, Japan – WBA. Ohba left his WBA version of the title vacant in January 1973 when he died in a road accident.
9 February Venice Borkorsor (Thailand) w pts 15 Erbito Salavarria (Philippines), Bangkok, Thailand – WBC. Borkorsor relinquished his WBC version of the title in August 1973 to campaign as a bantamweight.
17 May Chartchai Chionoi (Thailand) w rsc 4 Fritz Chervet (Switzerland), Bangkok, Thailand – WBA.
4 August Betulio Gonzalez (Venezuela) w pts 15 Miguel Canto (Mexico), Caracas, Venezuela – WBC.
27 October Chartchai Chionoi (Thailand) w pts 15 Susumu Hanagata (Japan), Bangkok, Thailand – WBA.
17 November Betulio Gonzalez (Venezuela) w rsc 11 Alberto Morales (Mexico), Caracas, Venezuela – WBC.

1974
27 April Chartchai Chionoi (Thailand) w pts 15 Fritz Chervet (Switzerland), Zurich, Switzerland – WBA.
20 July Betulio Gonzalez (Venezuela) w rsc 10 Franco Udella (Italy), Sabbiadoro, Italy – WBC.
1 October Shoji Oguma (Japan) w pts 15 Betulio Gonzalez (Venezuela), Tokyo, Japan – WBC.
18 October Susumu Hanagata (Japan) w rsc 6 Chartchai Chionoi (Thailand), Yokohama, Japan – WBA. Chionoi forfeited his WBA version of the title before the fight when he weighed in at 115¼lbs. However, the contest went ahead and, following the decision, Hanagata was proclaimed champion.

1975
8 January Miguel Canto (Mexico) w pts 15 Shoji Oguma (Japan), Sendai, Japan – WBC.
1 April Erbito Salavarria (Philippines) w pts 15 Susumu Hanagata (Japan), Toyama City, Japan – WBA.

108lbs to 112lbs (On 4 April 1975, the light-flyweight division was introduced at weights up to 108lbs).

24 May Miguel Canto (Mexico) w pts 15 Betulio Gonzalez (Venezuela), Monterrey, Mexico – WBC.
23 August Miguel Canto (Mexico) w rsc 11 Jiro Takada (Japan), Merida, Mexico – WBC.
7 October Erbito Salavarria (Philippines) w pts 15 Susumu Hanagata (Japan), Yokohama, Japan – WBA.
13 December Miguel Canto (Mexico) w pts 15 Ignacio Espinal (Dominican Republic), Merida, Mexico – WBC.

1976
27 February Alfonso Lopez (Panama) w rsc 15 Erbito Salavarria (Philippines), Manila, Philippines – WBA.
21 April Alfonso Lopez (Panama) w pts 15 Shoji Oguma (Japan), Tokyo, Japan – WBA.
15 May Miguel Canto (Mexico) w pts 15 Susumu Hanagata (Japan), Merida, Mexico – WBC.
2 October Guty Espadas (Mexico) w rsc 13 Alfonso Lopez (Panama), Los Angeles, California, USA – WBA.
3 October Miguel Canto (Mexico) w pts 15 Betulio Gonzalez (Venezuela), Caracas, Venezuela – WBC.

19 November Miguel Canto (Mexico) w pts 15 Orlando Javierta (Philippines), Los Angeles, California, USA – WBC.

1977
1 January Guty Espadas (Mexico) w rtd 7 Jiro Takada (Japan), Tokyo, Japan – WBA.
24 April Miguel Canto (Mexico) w pts 15 Reyes Arnal (Venezuela), Caracas, Venezuela – WBC.
30 April Guty Espadas (Mexico) w rsc 13 Alfonso Lopez (Panama), Merida, Mexico – WBA.
15 June Miguel Canto (Mexico) w pts 15 Kimio Furesawa (Japan), Tokyo, Japan – WBC.
17 September Miguel Canto (Mexico) w pts 15 Martin Vargas (Chile), Merida, Mexico – WBC.
19 November Guty Espadas (Mexico) w co 8 Alex Santana (Nicaragua), Los Angeles, California, USA – WBA.
30 November Miguel Canto (Mexico) w pts 15 Martin Vargas (Chile), Santiago, Chile – WBC.

1978
2 January Guty Espadas (Mexico) w rsc 7 Kimio Furesawa (Japan), Tokyo, Japan – WBA.
4 January Miguel Canto (Mexico) w pts 15 Shoji Oguma (Japan), Tokyo, Japan – WBC.
18 April Miguel Canto (Mexico) w pts 15 Shoji Oguma (Japan), Tokyo, Japan – WBC.
13 August Betulio Gonzalez (Venezuela) w pts 15 Guty Espadas (Mexico), Maracay, Venezuela – WBA.
4 November Betulio Gonzalez (Venezuela) w rsc 12 Martin Vargas (Chile), Maracay, Venezuela – WBA.
20 November Miguel Canto (Mexico) w pts 15 Tacomron Vibonchai (Thailand), Houston, Texas, USA – WBC.

1979
29 January Betulio Gonzalez (Venezuela) drew 15 Shoji Oguma (Japan), Hamamatsu, Japan – WBA.
10 February Miguel Canto (Mexico) w pts 15 Antonio Avelar (Mexico), Merida, Mexico – WBC.
18 March Chan-He Park (South Korea) w pts 15 Miguel Canto (Mexico), Pusan, South Korea – WBC.
19 May Chan-He Park (South Korea) w pts 15 Tsutomo Igarashi (Japan), Seoul, South Korea – WBC.
6 July Betulio Gonzalez (Venezuela) w co 12 Shoji Oguma (Japan), Utsunomiya, Japan – WBA.
9 September Chan-He Park (South Korea) drew 15 Miguel Canto (Mexico), Seoul, South Korea – WBC.
16 November Luis Ibarra (Panama) w pts 15 Betulio Gonzalez (Venezuela), Maracay, Venezuela – WBA.
16 December Chan-He Park (South Korea) w co 2 Guty Espadas (Mexico), Pusan, South Korea – WBC.

1980
9 February Chan-He Park (South Korea) w pts 15 Arnel Arrozal (Philippines), Seoul, South Korea – WBC.
16 February Tae-Shik Kim (South Korea) w co 2 Luis Ibarra (Panama) Seoul, South Korea – WBA.
13 April Chan-He Park (South Korea) w pts 15 Alberto Morales (Mexico), Taegu, South Korea – WBC.
18 May Shoji Oguma (Japan) w co 9 Chan-He Park (South Korea), Seoul, South Korea – WBC.
29 June Tae-Shik Kim (South Korea) w pts 15 Arnel Arrozal (Philippines), Seoul, South Korea – WBA.
28 July Shoji Oguma (Japan) w pts 15 Sung-Jun Kim (South Korea), Tokyo, Japan – WBC.
18 October Shoji Oguma (Japan) w pts 15 Chan-He Park (South Korea), Sendai, Japan – WBC.
13 December Peter Mathebula (South Africa) w pts 15 Tae-Shik Kim (South Korea), Los Angeles, California, USA – WBA.

1981
3 February Shoji Oguma (Japan) w pts 15 Chan-He Park (South Korea), Tokyo, Japan – WBC.

28 March Santos Laciar (Argentina) w rsc 7 Peter Mathebula (South Africa), Soweto, South Africa - WBA.
12 May Antonio Avelar (Mexico) w co 7 Shoji Oguma (Japan), Mito City, Japan – WBC.
6 June Luis Ibarra (Panama) w pts 15 Santos Laciar (Argentina), Buenos Aires, Argentina - WBA.
30 August Antonio Avelar (Mexico) w co 2 Tae-Shik Kim (South Korea), Seoul, South Korea – WBC.
26 September Juan Herrera (Mexico) w co 11 Luis Ibarra (Panama), Merida, Mexico – WBA.
26 December Juan Herrera (Mexico) w rsc 7 Betulio Gonzalez (Venezuela), Merida, Mexico – WBA.

1982
20 March Prudencio Cardona (Colombia) w co 1 Antonio Avelar (Mexico), Tampico, Mexico – WBC.
1 May Santos Laciar (Argentina) w rsc 13 Juan Herrera (Mexico), Merida, Mexico – WBA.
24 July Freddie Castillo (Mexico) w pts 15 Prudencio Cardona (Colombia), Merida, Mexico – WBC.
14 August Santos Laciar (Argentina) w pts 15 Betulio Gonzalez (Venezuela), Maracaibo, Venezuela – WBA.
5 November Santos Laciar (Argentina) w rsc 13 Steve Muchoki (Kenya), Copenhagen, Denmark – WBA.
6 November Eleoncio Mercedes (Dominican Republic) w pts 15 Freddie Castillo (Mexico), Los Angeles, California, USA – WBC.

1983
4 March Santos Laciar (Argentina) w co 9 Ramon Neri (Dominican Republic), Cordoba, Argentina – WBA.
15 March Charlie Magri (England) w rsc 7 Eleoncio Mercedes (Dominican Republic), The Arena, Wembley, England – WBC.
5 May Santos Laciar (Argentina) w rsc 2 Suichi Hozumi (Japan), Shizuoka, Japan – WBA.
17 July Santos Laciar (Argentina) w co 1 Hi-Sup Shin (South Korea), Cheju, South Korea – WBA.
27 September Frank Cedeno (Philippines) w rsc 6 Charlie Magri (England), The Arena, Wembley, England – WBC.
24 December Soon-Chun Kwon (South Korea) w co 5 Rene Busayong (Philippines), Seoul, South Korea – IBF.

1984
18 January Koji Kobayashi (Japan) w rsc 2 Frank Cedeno (Philippines), Tokyo, Japan – WBC.
28 January Santos Laciar (Argentina) w pts 15 Juan Herrera (Mexico), Marsala, Sicily, Italy – WBA.
25 February Soon-Chun Kwon (South Korea) w td 12 Roger Castillo (Philippines), Seoul, South Korea – IBF. Ahead on the judges' scorecards at the time, Kwon retained his title by decision after he was accidentally cut and pulled out of the fight by the doctor.
9 April Gabriel Bernal (Mexico) w co 2 Koji Kobayashi (Japan), Tokyo, Japan – WBC.
19 May Soon-Chun Kwon (South Korea) w pts 15 Ian Clyde (Canada), Daejon, South Korea – IBF.
1 June Gabriel Bernal (Mexico) w rsc 11 Antoine Montero (France), Nimes, France – WBC.
7 September Soon-Chun Kwon (South Korea) w rsc 12 Joaquin Caraballo (Philippines), Chungju, South Korea – IBF.
15 September Santos Laciar (Argentina) w co 10 Prudencio Cardona (Colombia), Cordoba, Argentina – WBA.
8 October Sot Chitalada (Thailand) w pts 12 Gabriel Bernal (Mexico), Bangkok, Thailand – WBC.
8 December Santos Laciar (Argentina) w pts 15 Hilario Zapata (Panama), Buenos Aires, Argentina – WBA.

1985
25 January Soon-Chun Kwon (South Korea) drew 15 Chong-Kwan Chung (South Korea), Daejon, South Korea – IBF.
20 February Sot Chitalada (Thailand) w rtd 4 Charlie Magri (England), Alexandra Pavilion, London, England – WBC.
14 April Soon-Chun Kwon (South Korea) w co 3 Shinobu Kawashima (Japan), Pohang, South Korea – IBF.

6 May Santos Laciar (Argentina) w pts 15 Antoine Montero (France), Grenoble, France – WBA. Laciar relinquished his WBA version of the title in July 1985 due to increasing weight problems.
22 June Sot Chitalada (Thailand) drew 12 Gabriel Bernal (Mexico), Bangkok, Thailand – WBC.
17 July Soon-Chun Kwon (South Korea) drew 15 Chong-Kwan Chung (South Korea), Masan, South Korea – IBF.
5 October Hilario Zapata (Panama) w pts 15 Alonzo Gonzales (USA), Panama City, Panama – WBA.
20 December Chong-Kwan Chung (South Korea) w rsc 4 Soon-Chun Kwon (South Korea), Taegu, South Korea – IBF.

1986
31 January Hilario Zapata (Panama) w pts 15 Javier Lucas (Mexico), Panama City, Panama – WBA.
22 February Sot Chitalada (Thailand) w pts 12 Freddie Castillo (Mexico), Kuwait City, Kuwait – WBC.
7 April Hilario Zapata (Panama) w pts 15 Suichi Hozumi (Japan), Nirasaki, Japan –WBA.
27 April Bi-Won Chung (South Korea) w pts 15 Chong-Kwan Chung (South Korea), Pusan, South Korea – IBF.
5 July Hilario Zapata (Panama) w pts 15 Dodie Penalosa (Philippines), Manila, Philippines – WBA.
2 August Hi-Sup Shin (South Korea) w rsc 15 Bi-Won Chung (South Korea), Inchon, South Korea – IBF.
13 September Hilario Zapata (Panama) w pts 15 Alberto Castro (Colombia), Panama City, Panama – WBA.
22 November Hi-Sup Shin (South Korea) w rsc 13 Henry Brent (USA), Chunchon, South Korea – IBF.
6 December Hilario Zapata (Panama) w pts 15 Claudemir Dias (Brazil), Salvador, Brazil – WBA.
10 December Sot Chitalada (Thailand) w pts 12 Gabriel Bernal (Mexico), Bangkok, Thailand – WBC.

1987
13 February Fidel Bassa (Colombia) w pts 15 Hilario Zapata (Panama), Barranquilla, Colombia – WBA.
22 February Dodie Penalosa (Philippines) w co 5 Hi-Sup Shin (South Korea), Inchon, South Korea – IBF.
25 April Fidel Bassa (Colombia) w co 13 Dave McAuley (Ireland), King's Hall, Belfast, Northern Ireland – WBA.
15 August Fidel Bassa (Colombia) drew 15 Hilario Zapata (Panama), Panama City, Panama – WBA.
5 September Chang-Ho Choi (South Korea) w co 11 Dodie Penalosa (Philippines), Manila, Philippines – IBF.
5 September Sot Chitalada (Thailand) w co 4 Rae-Ki Ahn (South Korea), Bangkok, Thailand – WBC.
18 December Fidel Bassa (Colombia) w pts 12 Felix Marty (Dominican Republic), Cartagena, Colombia – WBA.

1988
16 January Rolando Bohol (Philippines) w pts 15 Chang-Ho Choi (South Korea), Manila, Philippines – IBF.
31 January Sot Chitalada (Thailand) w rsc 7 Hideaki Kamishiro (Japan), Osaka, Japan – WBC.
26 March Fidel Bassa (Colombia) w pts 12 Dave McAuley (Ireland), King's Hall, Belfast, Northern Ireland – WBA.
6 May Rolando Bohol (Philippines) w pts 15 Cho-Woon Park (South Korea), Manila, Philippines – IBF.
23 July Yong-Kang Kim (South Korea) w pts 12 Sot Chitalada (Thailand), Pohang, South Korea – WBC.
2 October Fidel Bassa (Colombia) w pts 12 Raymond Medel (USA) San Antonio, Texas, USA – WBA.
5 October Duke McKenzie (England) w co 11 Rolando Bohol (Philippines), Grand Hall, Wembley, England – IBF.
13 November Yong-Kang Kim (South Korea) w pts 12 Emil Romano (Philippines), Chungju, South Korea – WBC.

1989
3 March Elvis Alvarez (Colombia) w pts 12 Miguel Mercedes (Dominican Republic), Medellin, Colombia – WBO. Alvarez relinquished his WBO version of the title in October 1989 in order to try for a crack at one of the other organisation's crowns.

5 March Yong-Kang Kim (South Korea) w pts 12 Yukhito Tamakuma (Japan), Aomori, Japan – WBC.

8 March Duke McKenzie (England) w rsc 4 Tony de Luca (USA), Albert Hall, London, England – IBF.

15 April Fidel Bassa (Colombia) w rsc 6 Julio Gudino (Panama), Barranquilla, Colombia – WBA.

3 June Sot Chitalada (Thailand) w pts 12 Yong-Kang Kim (South Korea), Trang, Thailand – WBC.

7 June Dave McAuley (Ireland) w pts 12 Duke McKenzie (England), The Arena, Wembley, England – IBF.

30 September Jesus Rojas (Venezuela) w pts 12 Fidel Bassa (Colombia), Barranquilla, Colombia – WBA.

8 November Dave McAuley (Ireland) w pts 12 Dodie Penalosa (Philippines), Grand Hall, Wembley, England – IBF.

1990

30 January Sot Chitalada (Thailand) w pts 12 Ric Siodoro (Philippines), Bangkok, Thailand – WBC.

10 March Yul-Woo Lee (South Korea) w pts 12 Jesus Rojas (Venezuela), Taejon, South Korea – WBA.

17 March Dave McAuley (Ireland) w pts 12 Louis Curtis (USA), King's Hall, Belfast, Northern Ireland – IBF.

1 May Sot Chitalada (Thailand) w pts 12 Carlos Salazar (Argentina), Bangkok, Thailand – WBC.

28 July Yuhhito Tamakuma (Japan) w rsc 10 Yul-Woo Lee (South Korea), Mito, Japan – WBA.

18 August Isidro Perez (Mexico) w rsc 12 Angel Rosario (Puerto Rico), Ponce – WBO.

9 September Sot Chitalada (Thailand) w co 1 Richard Clark (Jamaica), Kingston, Jamaica – WBC.

15 September Dave McAuley (Ireland) w pts 12 Rodolfo Blanco (Colombia) King's Hall, Belfast, Northern Ireland – IBF.

3 November Isidro Perez (Mexico) w pts 12 Alli Galvez (Chile), Acapulco, Mexico – WBO.

24 November Sot Chitalada (Thailand) w pts 12 Jung-Koo Chang (South Korea), Seoul, South Korea – WBC.

6 December Yukihito Tamakuma (Japan) drew 12 Jesus Rojas (Venezuela), Aomori, Japan – WBA.

1991

15 February Muangchai Kitikasem (Thailand) w rsc 6 Sot Chitalada (Thailand), Ayuthaya, Thailand – WBC.

14 March Elvis Alvarez (Colombia) w pts 12 Yukihito Tamakuma (Japan), Tokyo, Japan – WBA.

11 May Dave McAuley (Ireland) w pts 12 Pedro Feliciano (Puerto Rico), Maysfield Leisure Centre, Belfast, Northern Ireland – IBF.

18 May Muangchai Kitikasem (Thailand) w rsc 12 Jung-Koo Chang (South Korea), Seoul, South Korea – WBC.

1 June Yong-Kang Kim (South Korea) w pts 12 Elvis Alvarez (Colombia), Seoul, South Korea – WBA.

10 August Isidro Perez (Mexico) w pts 12 Alli Galvez (Chile), Santiago, Chile – WBO.

7 September Dave McAuley (Ireland) w co 10 Jacob Matlala (South Africa), Maysfield Leisure Centre, Belfast, Northern Ireland – IBF.

5 October Yong-Kang Kim (South Korea) w pts 12 Silvio Gamez (Venezuela), Inchon, South Korea – WBA.

25 October Muangchai Kitikasem (Thailand) w pts 12 Alberto Jimenez (Mexico), Bangkok, Thailand – WBC.

1992

28 February Muangchai Kitikasem (Thailand) w rsc 9 Sot Chitalada (Thailand) Samut Prakan, Thailand – WBC.

18 March Pat Clinton (Scotland) w pts 12 Isidro Perez (Mexico), Kelvin Hall, Glasgow, Scotland – WBO.

24 March Yong-Kang Kim (South Korea) w co 6 Jon Penalosa (Philippines), Inchon, South Korea – WBA.

11 June Rodolfo Blanco (Colombia) w pts 12 Dave McAuley (Ireland), Bilbao, Spain – IBF.

23 June Yuri Arbachakov (Armenia) w co 8 Muangchai Kitikasem (Thailand), Tokyo, Japan – WBC.

19 September Pat Clinton (Scotland) w pts 12 Danny Porter (England), Scottish Exhibition Centre, Glasgow, Scotland – WBO.

26 September Aquiles Guzman (Venezuela) w pts 12 Yong-Kang Kim (South Korea), Pohang, South Korea – WBA.

20 October Yuri Arbachakov (Armenia) w pts 12 Yun-Un Chin (South Korea), Tokyo, Japan – WBC.

29 November Pichit Sitbangprachan (Thailand) w co 3 Rodolfo Blanco (Colombia), Bangkok, Thailand – IBF.

15 December David Griman (Venezuela) w pts 12 Aquiles Guzman (Venezuela), Caracas, Venezuela – WBA.

1993

6 March Pichit Sitbangprachan (Thailand) w rsc 4 Antonio Perez (Mexico), Uttaridit, Thailand – IBF.

20 March Yuri Arbachakov (Armenia) w rsc 9 Muangchai Kitikasem (Thailand), Lopburi, Thailand – WBC.

15 May Jacob Matlala (South Africa) w rsc 8 Pat Clinton (Scotland), Scottish Exhibition Centre, Glasgow, Scotland – WBO.

21 June David Griman (Venezuela) w rsc 8 Hiroki Ioka (Japan), Osaka, Japan – WBA.

11 July Pichit Sitbangprachan (Thailand) w rsc 1 Kyung-Yun Lee (South Korea), Bangkok, Thailand – IBF.

16 July Yuri Arbachakov (Armenia) w pts 12 Ysaias Zamudio (USA), Kobe City, Japan – WBC.

3 October Pichit Sitbangprachan (Thailand) w rsc 9 Miguel Martinez (Mexico), Chaiyaphum, Thailand – IBF.

4 October David Griman (Venezuela) w pts 12 Alvaro Mercado (Colombia), Puerta la Cruz, Venezuela – WBA.

4 December Jacob Matlala (South Africa) w rtd 7 Luigi Camputaro (Italy), Sun City, South Africa – WBO.

13 December Yuri Arbachakov (Armenia) w pts 12 Nam-Hoon Cha (South Korea), Kyoto – WBC.

1994

23 January Pichit Sitbangprachan (Thailand) w pts 12 Arthur Johnson (USA), Surat Thani, Thailand – IBF.

13 February Saen Sorploenchit (Thailand) w pts 12 David Griman (Venezuela), Chachoengsao, Thailand – WBA.

10 April Saen Sorploenchit (Thailand) w pts 12 Jesus Rojas (Venezuela), Samut Prakan, Thailand – WBA.

8 May Pichit Sitbangprachan (Thailand) w pts 12 Jose Luis Zepeda (Mexico), Rajburi, Thailand – IBF. Sitbanprachan relinquished his IBF version of the title in October 1994 due to extended inactivity.

11 June Jacob Matlala (South Africa) w rtd 9 Francis Ampofo (England), York Hall, Bethnal Green, London, England – WBO.

12 June Saen Sorploenchit (Thailand) w pts 12 Aquiles Guzman (Venezuela), Bangkok, Thailand – WBA.

1 August Yuri Arbachakov (Armenia) w co 8 Hugo Soto (Argentina), Tokyo, Japan – WBC.

25 September Saen Sorploenchit (Thailand) w pts 12 Yong-Kang Kim (South Korea), Kanchanaburi, Thailand – WBA.

15 October Jacob Matlala (South Africa) w pts 12 Domingo Lucas (Philippines), Sun City, South Africa – WBO.

25 December Saen Sorploenchit (Thailand) w rsc 11 Danny Nunez (Dominican Republic), Rayong, Thailand – WBA.

1995

30 January Yuri Arbachakov (Armenia) w pts 12 Oscar Arciniega (Mexico), Sapporo, Japan – WBC.

11 February Alberto Jiminez (Mexico) w rsc 8 Jacob Matlala (South Africa), Hammanskraal, South Africa – WBO.

18 February Francisco Tejedor (Colombia) w rtd 7 Jose Luis Zepeda (Mexico), Cartagena, Colombia – IBF.

22 April Danny Romero (USA) w pts 12 Francisco Tejedor (Colombia), Las Vegas, Nevada, USA – IBF.

7 May Saen Sorploenchit (Thailand) w pts 12 Evangelio Perez (Panama), Songkhla, Thailand – WBA.

17 June Alberto Jiminez (Mexico) w rtd 9 Robbie Regan (Wales), National Ice Rink, Cardiff, Wales – WBO.

29 July Danny Romero (USA) w co 6 Miguel Martinez (Mexico), San Antonio, Texas, USA – IBF. With Romero injured following a non-title loss to Willy Salazar, Robbie Regan (Wales) stopped Ferid Ben Jeddou (Tunisia) in the the second round on 16 December 1995 at Cardiff, Wales in a so-called interim title fight.

A month later, Romero relinquished the crown, while Regan moved up to bantam to challenge Daniel Jimenez for the WBO title.

25 September Yuri Arbachakov (Armenia) w pts 12 Chatchai Sasakul (Thailand), Tokyo, Japan – WBC.

9 October Alberto Jimenez (Mexico) w rsc 2 Zolile Mbitye (South Africa), Tijuana, Mexico – WBO.

17 October Saen Sorploenchit (Thailand) w rsc 10 Hiroki Ioka (Japan), Osaka, Japan – WBA.

1996

14 January Saen Sorploenchit (Thailand) w pts 12 Yong-Soon Chang (South Korea), Nontaburi, Thailand – WBA.

05 February Yuri Arbachakov (Armenia) w pts 12 Raul Juarez (Mexico), Osaka, Japan – WBC.

23 March Alberto Jimenez (Mexico) w rsc 5 Mike Martinez (Mexico), Las Vegas, Nevada, USA – WBO.

23 March Saen Sorploenchit (Thailand) w pts 12 Silvio Gamez (Venezuela), Tathum Thani, Thailand – WBA.

04 May Mark Johnson (USA) w co 1 Francisco Tejedor (Colombia), Anaheim, California, USA – IBF.

1 June Alberto Jimenez (Mexico) w pts 12 Jose Lopez (Puerto Rico), Lake Tahoe, Nevada, USA – WBO.

5 August Mark Johnson (USA) w rsc 8 Raul Juarez (Mexico), Los Angeles, California, USA – IBF.

26 August Yuri Arbachakov (Armenia) w rsc 9 Takato Toguchi (Japan), Tokyo, Japan – WBC. With Arbachakov sidelined due to a broken wrist, Chatchai Sasakul (Thailand) outpointed Ysaias Zamudio (USA) on points over 12 rounds in Bangkok, Thailand on 9 May 1997 to win the interim title. On 1 August 1997, with Arbachakov still not available, Sasakul forced Juan Domingo Cordoba (Argentine) to retire inside seven rounds in Bangkok.

6 September Alberto Jimenez (Mexico) drew 12 Carlos Salazar (Argentina), Buenos Aires, Argentina – WBO.

8 September Saen Sorploenchit (Thailand) w pts 12 Alexander Mahmoutov (Russia), Nakhon Phanom, Thailand – WBA.

23 November Jose Bonilla (Venezuela) w pts 12 Saen Sorploenchit (Thailand), Bangkok, Thailand – WBA.

13 December Carlos Salazar (Argentine) w rsc 10 Alberto Jimenez (Mexico), Buenos Aires, Argentina – WBO.

1997

10 February Mark Johnson (USA) w pts 12 Alejandro Montiel (Mexico), Los Angeles, California, USA – IBF.

25 February Jose Bonilla (Venezuela) w rsc 7 Hiroki Ioka (Japan), Osaka, Japan – WBA.

8 March Carlos Salazar (Argentina) drew 12 Antonio Ruiz (Mexico), Mexicali, Mexico – WBO.

23 May Carlos Salazar (Argentina) w pts 12 Antonio Ruiz (Mexico), Saenz Pena, Argentina – WBO.

1 June Mark Johnson (USA) w co 2 Cecilio Espino (Mexico), Uncasville, Connecticut, USA – IBF.

19 July Carlos Salazar (Argentina) w pts 12 Salvatore Fanni (Italy), Porto Rotonde, Sardinia, Italy – WBO.

23 August Jose Bonilla (Venezuela) w pts 12 Evangelio Perez (Panama), Cumana, Venezuela – WBA.

16 September Mark Johnson (USA) w pts 12 Angel Almena (Puerto Rico), Nashville, Tennessee, USA – IBF.

10 October Carlos Salazar (Argentina) w pts 12 Everardo Morales (Mexico), Resistencia, Argentina – WBO.

12 November Chatchai Sasakul (Thailand) w pts 12 Yuri Arbachakov (Armenia), Sapporo, Japan – WBC.

22 November Jose Bonilla (Venezuela) w rsc 6 Keiji Yamaguchi (Japan), Osaka, Japan – WBA.

1998

22 February Mark Johnson (USA) w co 1 Arthur Johnson (USA), Washington DC, USA – IBF.

27 February Chatchai Sasakul (Thailand) w pts 12 Yong-Jin Kim (South Korea), Bangkok, Thailand – WBC.

21 March Carlos Salazar (Argentina) w pts 12 Jose Lopez (Puerto Rico), Rocque Saenz Pena, Chaco, Argentina – WBO.

1 May Chatchai Sasakul (Thailand) w co 5 Yong-Soon Chang (South Korea), Bangkok, Thailand – WBC.

29 May Hugo Soto (Argentina) w pts 12 Jose Bonilla (Venezuela), Las Vegas, Nevada – USA. With Soto unavailable, Mauricio Pastrana (Colombia) outpointed Jose Bonilla (Venezuela) over 12 rounds in Caracas, Argentine on 3 October 1998 to win the interim title.

26 July Mark Johnson (USA) w pts 12 Luis Rolon (Puerto Rico), Verona, New York, USA – IBF.

14 August Ruben Sanchez (Mexico) w td 8 Carlos Salazar (Argentina), Mexicali, Mexico – WBO.

4 September Mark Johnson (USA) w rtd 7 Jose Laureano (Puerto Rico), Atlantic City, New Jersey, USA – IBF. Johnson vacated the title in October 1998 to fight at a higher poundage.

4 December Manny Pacquiao (Philippines) w rsc 8 Chatchai Sasakul (Thailand), Bangkok, Thailand – WBC.

18 December Ruben Sanchez (Mexico) w pts 12 Salvatore Fanni (Italy), Cagliari, Italy – WBO.

1999

13 March Silvio Gamez (Venezuela) w rsc 3 Hugo Soto (Argentina), NYC, New York, USA – WBA.

10 April Irene Pacheco (Colombia) w rsc 9 Luis Cox (Peru), Barranquilla, Colombia – IBF.

23 April Jose Antonio Lopez (Spain) w rsc 3 Ruben Sanchez (Argentina), Zaragoza, Spain – WBO.

24 April Manny Pacquiao (Philippines) w co 4 Gabriel Mira (Mexico), Manila, Philippines – WBC.

4 June Jose Antonio Lopez Bueno (Spain) w rsc 7 Igor Gerasimov (Russia), Malaga, Spain – WBO. Bueno forfeited WBO version of the title in December 1999 following a motor cycle accident.

3 September Sornpichai Pisanurachan (Thailand) w co 8 Silvio Gamez (Venezuela), Mukdaham, Thailand – WBA.

17 September Medgoen Singsurat (Thailand) w co 3 Manny Pacquiao (Philippines), Nakhon, Thailand – WBC. Pacquiao (113lbs) lost his title on the scales and Singsurat was declared the new champion on his victory.

16 October Irene Pacheco (Colombia) w rsc 4 Ferid Ben Jeddou (Tunisia), Barranquilla, Colombia – IBF.

18 December Isidro Garcia (Mexico) w pts 12 Jose Lopez (Puerto Rico), Indio, California, USA – WBO.

2000

14 January Irene Pacheco (Colombia) w co 11 Pedro Pena (USA), El Paso, Texas, USA – IBF.

25 February Medgoen Singsurat (Thailand) w pts 12 Masaki Kawabata (Japan), Samut Sakorn, Thailand – WBC.

8 April Sornpichai Pisanurachan (Thailand) w rsc 5 Gilberto Gonzalez (Venezuela), Bangkok, Thailand – WBA.

19 May Malcolm Tunacao (Philippines) w rsc 7 Medgoen Singsurat (Thailand), Udon Thani, Thailand – WBC.

5 August Eric Morel (USA) w pts 12 Sornpichai Pisanurachan (Thailand), Madison, Wisconsin, USA – WBA.

12 August Isidro Garcia (Mexico) w rsc 6 Jose Rafael Sosa (Argentina), Cordoba, Argentina – WBO.

20 August Malcolm Tunacao (Philippines) drew 12 Celes Kobayashi (Japan), Tokyo, Japan – WBC.

7 October Eric Morel (USA) w pts 12 Alberto Ontiveros (Mexico), Las Vegas, Nevada, USA – WBA.

10 November Irene Pacheco (Colombia) w pts 12 Masibulele Makepula (South Africa), Las Vegas, Nevada, USA – IBF.

15 December Fernando Montiel (Mexico) w rsc 7 Isidro Garcia (Mexico), Ciudud Obregon, Mexico – WBO.

15 December Eric Morel (USA) w pts 12 Gilberto Keb-Baas (Mexico), Madison, Wisconsin, USA – WBA.

2001

2 March Pongsaklek Wonjongkam (Thailand) w rsc 1 Malcolm Tunacao (Philippines), Pichit Province, Thailand – WBC.

24 March Fernando Montiel (Mexico) w rsc 7 Zoltan Lunka (Romania), Munich, Germany - WBO.

25 May Fernando Montiel (Mexico) w co 1 Juan Domingo Cordoba (Argentina), Acapulco, Mexico – WBO.

8 June Eric Morel (USA) w rtd 8 Jose de Jesus (Venezuela), Baraboo, Wisconsin, USA – WBA.

Highlights from the 2001-2002 Amateur Season

by Chris Kempson

The season proved to be a successful one both at domestic and international level on the junior and senior fronts, leading to the extremely competitive European Senior Championships in Perm, Russia (12-21 July) and the eagerly awaited Commonwealth Games in Manchester (25 July-3 August). So travel through these pages and see who made the headlines in 2001-2002.

JULY

England's Anthony Quigley set the standard, a gold standard in fact with a fine 63.5kgs success at the annual international Junior Olympic tournament held in Marquette, Michigan from 4-6 July. England also secured nine silvers and a bronze in an event for 15 and 16-year-olds from the United States, Canada and Mexico.

Liverpool, staged the European Cadet (Under-17) Championships in the splendid surroundings of the St George's Hall from 16-23 July. England scooped four medals. Sunderland's Tony Jeffries (71kgs) landed gold, while Brian Rose (Blackpool and Fylde) 60 kgs, east Londoner Grant Skehill (St George's, Stepney) 63.5kgs and Liam Anthony (67kgs) from Chadd's ABC in the

Midland Counties each won a bronze medal, in an event where traditionally boxers from Eastern Europe do well. Ireland's Eric Donovan also achieved a bronze in the 57kgs division.

AUGUST

The National Training and Coaching Centre in Limerick was the setting for the Four Nations Junior Tournament (18-19 August). England came out on top with six golds, Wales netted three, Scotland two and the Irish host nation the other.

Ireland visited Poland and squeezed home with a 5-4 victory over the host nation in Tarnow on 25 August.

SEPTEMBER

Scottish light-welterweight Kevin Anderson from Denbeath was the only medal winner from Britain or Ireland at the European Junior Championships in Sarajevo, Croatia from 20-30 September. He landed bronze, beating two opponents before losing to the eventual gold medallist.

On 25 September the new and very enterprising Peacock ABC based in Canning Town in east-London

Andy Morris (left) seen on his way to the ABA lightweight title, when outpointing Femi Fehintola

Les Clark

pulled off a first for London by introducing the Kid Gloves scheme to the Raines Foundation School in Bethnal Green.

OCTOBER

In the aftermath of the 11 September terrorist attacks in the United States, both England and Ireland withdrew from the World Cadet Championships in Baku, Azerbaijan from 11-22 October.

Both England and Scotland performed very well in the Tammer multi-nations tournament in Tampere, Finland from 18-21 October.

Stephen Matthews (Salisbury, Liverpool) received a silver in the light-welterweight division for England, who also landed four bronze medals via Darran Langley (Hollington) at light-fly, Mark Moran (Golden Gloves, Liverpool) at bantam, Steven Bell (Nichols Police) at feather and Karmand's Gavin Smith at light-welter. Not to be denied, the Fauldhouse southpaw, Colin McNeil, won gold for Scotland at welterweight, while up at light-heavyweight Lee Ramsay (Kingdom) picked up a silver for the Scots.

The inaugural All-Ireland Under-21 Championships took place from 26-28 October in the refurbished National Stadium in Dublin.

On 27 October in Hirtshals, (Denmark), England thumped the host nation 5-1 in an international encounter.

On 31 October, for the first time in 90 years, Irish women boxed in open competition in the National Stadium in Dublin on a Central Council tournament.

NOVEMBER

Ireland went to France and lost twice there. First at Laon on 16 November by 7 bouts to 2 and on 18 November, by 6 bouts to 3 at Pont-Audemer, whilst earlier, on 3 November, Young Ireland lost 5-4 to their French counterparts in Abbeville.

On 17 November, the experiment of staging amateur and professional shows in the same venue on the same day (Bellahouston Sports Centre) saw Scotland beaten 7-4 by an Australian squad. A week earlier, on 9 November, at the Pettycur Leisure Centre in Kinghorn, the Scots had held the Aussies to a 6-6 draw.

Young England beat Young Ireland 5-3 in an Under-19 match in Weymouth on 17 November, while two days later, on 19 November on the senior front, England edged out the United States 4-3 at the annual HABAD charity dinner show at the Park Lane Hilton. Broad Street's world silver medallist, heavyweight David Haye, being the host nation's hero when clinching the match for England.

Scotland's outstanding and talented welterweight, Colin McNeil, continued his fine international form with a silver medal at the prestigious Feliks Stamm multi-nations tournament in Warsaw from 12-18 November. Repton and England's Tony Cesay netted bronze, retiring at the end of the third round against McNeil in their all-southpaw semi-final.

England's juniors were very successful at the Under-19 multi-nations tournament in Salonika, Greece from 20-26 November. David Pendleton (Durham Academy) won gold

at light-heavy, light-fly Dean Swanson (Tower Hill) and flyweight Nick McDonald (Vauxhall) scooped silver, while there were bronze medals for Karmand light-welter, James Fletcher, and Cheshunt super-heavy, Colin Goldhawk.

England's two-man team arrived back from the Copenhagen Box-Cup (21-26 November) with a medal apiece. Paul Smith (Rotunda) claimed a silver at light-middleweight, while Stowe featherweight, Billy Corcoran, got bronze, losing to the eventual gold medallist in his semi-final. Scotland's light-welterweight, Kevin Anderson, continued his excellent form when securing a bronze medal.

The Irish Intermediate Championships took place in Dublin and straddled the period 23, 24 and 30 November and 1 and 7 December.

DECEMBER

The NACYP Class 'A' finals took place at the Britannia Adelphi Hotel in Liverpool on 4 December, the Class 'B' concluded on 14 December at the Seaham Leisure Centre in County Durham, while the Class 'C' finals were staged at London's Royal Lancaster Hotel on 10 December.

The National ABA Novice finals were boxed off at the Knottingley Sports Centre on 15 December.

Two international matches took place this month. France trounced the Irish once more, the scoreline reading 7-1 in favour of the French at Pessac on 14 December, while the Welsh were beaten 4-1 by Norway in Tonsberg on 15 December.

JANUARY

The New Year saw some excellent domestic performances in both the 48th Bocskai Cup in Debrecen, Hungary from 21-26 January and in the Norway Box Cup in Oslo's Jordalhallen from 24-26 January. In Hungary, Repton's young light-welterweight, Darren Barker, boxed three times for gold, while Plains Farm's David Dolan, competing in the 95kgs division, won a bronze. The event was held using AIBA's new weight categories which came in on 1 January only to be quickly rescinded, but it was too late to revert to the old 12 divisions.

In Norway, Welsh bantamweight, Darren Edwards (Cwmavon Hornets), struck gold by beating Mark Moran (Golden Gloves, Liverpool) in the final. It was the first-ever mixed (male and female) ABA team at a multi-nations tournament. Courtney Fry, now with the Salisbury Club in Liverpool, won silver in the 81kgs division, while West Wythenshawe lightweight, Andrew Morris, secured a bronze. For the women, Mickila Jones (Arrow) got silver in the 57 kgs division and there was bronze for Nicola Adams of east Leeds at bantamweight.

England had a successful inaugural trip to New Delhi, India, taking part in the junior multi-nations tournament held there. Wombwell's light-welter, Thomas Coward, and Finchley light-middle, Joe Smyth, both brought home gold. Welterweight Kaylem Lowe (St George's Stepney) won silver and there was a bronze each for Nathan Brough (Salisbury, Liverpool) at featherweight, Brian Rose

(Blackpool and Fylde) at lightweight, and light-middle, Lee Siner (Salisbury, Liverpool). On 25 January, at the Ringside Club in Dublin, Young Ireland avenged an earlier defeat when beating the French youngsters 5-3.

FEBRUARY

Young England scored a good victory over Young France by 5 bouts to 2 at the Royal Lancaster Hotel in London on 4 February.

The National Stadium in Dublin hosted the Irish Senior Championships on 8, 9, 15, 16 and 22 February.

MARCH

Ireland swept to a fine victory 8-4 over Canada in Dublin on 1 March, but in a second team match in Maam Cross, Galway two nights later on 3 March, the Canadians got their 'revenge' by 7 bouts to 5.

The Metrodome in Barnsley was the setting for the 55th National Schoolboy Finals on 9 and 10 March.

The Afan Lido in Port Talbot hosted the Welsh ABA Finals on 15 March.

The Time Capsule, Monklands, Coatbridge was the venue for the Scottish Senior Finals on 16 March.

England's heavyweight star, David Haye, won the gold medal at the 20th Italian multi-nations in Rome, 19-22 March, with West Ham flyweight, Matthew Marsh, notching up a bronze, as did three of Scotland's four-man squad. The bronze medallists were: Colin McNeil (welter), Jamie Coyle (light-middle) and Steve McGuire (middle).

On the international stage, Ireland failed once again to conquer France, going down 5-3 in Dublin on 15 March. Two days later in Dundalk, the French jinx struck yet again, France repeating their win, on this occasion by 4-2.

Ireland then ventured to the United States and won two matches against 'native American champions', first by 7-1 on 19 March and then by 5-2 on 25 March.

APRIL

The ABA Senior Finals were again held at the Metrodome in Barnsley (5 April) and with two walkovers there were only 11 bouts. The North West Counties bagged five titles and James Dolan (Plains Farm) picked up his third consecutive cruiserweight crown without having to box, following the double disqualification in the Southern semi-final a few days earlier. London won three titles with, arguably, Rosehill's Lenny Daws at light-welterweight being seen as the revelation of the season.

England picked up a silver medal via super-heavyweight, Ian Lewison (Miguels), and a bronze from light-welterweight, Lee Beavis (Dale Youth), in the Gee Bee multi-nations in Helsinki (4-8 April).

Nathan Brough of Salisbury, Liverpool won a bronze medal at featherweight for England in the Under-19 multi-nations event held in Bydgoszcz, Poland from 15-21 April.

The second annual Four Nations Senior Championships were held on 18 and 19 April at Ireland's national Events Centre, Gleneagle Hotel in Killarney and the host nation captured six golds, four silver and a bronze by way of their medal haul. England were second with 5-2-4, followed by Wales with 1-2-4 and Scotland with 0-4-3.

In Trondheim, Norway on 27 April, England beat Box-Team Trondheim 4-1, while on this double bill Young Scotland defeated Young Norway 5-2. Also on the international front, Ireland hosted Denmark, winning 5-3 at the National Stadium in Dublin (12 April) and 3-2 at the Waterford Forum (4 April).

The inaugural Schoolboy Four Nations Tournament took place in Port Talbot, Wales on 26 and 27 April. The Irish youngsters carried all before them, winning 11 gold, six silver and five bronze medals. England came second with seven golds, five silver and seven bronze, with Wales third 2-5-11 and Scotland in fourth place on 2-5-8.

MAY

The English team for the Commonwealth Games in Manchester was announced during the first few days in May and was greeted with jubilation by some, heartache by others, as well as some measure of surprise and disbelief. Only three of the team were current ABA champions at their selection weight, while half of the Manchester team did not enter the ABAs this year. Only time will tell about the merits, or not, of those chosen to box in Manchester.

The ABA Youth Finals were boxed off at the Sports Centre in Knottingley on 11 May, with Liverpool's Tower Hill Club winning three titles.

Tuning up for the Commonwealth Games, Scotland headed for Canada and won the first and drew the second of their international matches there. On 10 May in Regina, the Scots triumphed 5-4, while in Moose Jaw on 13 May, the scores were tied at 5-5.

England landed two bronze medals from the Arena Cup in Pula, Croatia from 22-25 May. Lightweight, Savdhul Zaman (Middlesbrough), and Hollington flyweight, Stewart Langley, bagging the spoils.

The 23rd Acropolis Cup tournament was held in Athens, Greece from 29 May-3 June, where both England and Ireland performed very well. For the Irish, bronze medals were claimed by Liam Cunningham (flyweight), Noel Monteith (lightweight) and David Conlon (welterweight). England's medal winners were David Mulholland, the reigning ABA featherweight champion from Salisbury, Liverpool, who struck silver, Rosehill's current ABA light-welterweight titleholder, Lenny Daws (bronze), and light-heavyweight, Courtney Fry, from Salisbury, Liverpool (bronze).

JUNE

Young England beat their Irish counterparts 7-5 at Dublin's National Stadium on 7 June, while the Irish senior squad ventured to Poland, losing 6-2 in Ostroviec on 13 July.

The Four Nations Juniors Tournament was held at the Marriott Hotel in Glasgow on 25 and 26 June. England proved to be the most successful with five golds, three silvers and two bronze. Runners-up were Ireland 4-4-2, Wales were in third place on 2-1-6, with the host nation in fourth slot on 0-3-8.

The year was rounded off in fine style with two English boxers securing silver medals in the Balaton Cup Under-19 multi-nations event in Hungary from 26 June-1 July. The lightweight, Michael Grant (Haringey Police and Community), seemed very unlucky to lose in the final against Dudas of the host nation, while Wombwell light-welterweight, Thomas Coward, did well to lift silver in his first appearance at this level.

With our fast emerging and very promising junior talent, coupled with our well established senior stars, the future of amateur boxing in these islands is as bright as it has been for many years. This can only be for the good of our sport.

Matthew Grainger landed the ABA super-heavyweight title for the second year running

Les Clark

ABA National Championships, 2001-2002

Eastern Counties/Home Counties v Combined Services

Essex Division The Toot, Tilbury – 8 February
L. Fly: no entries. **Fly:** no entries. **Bantam:** final: B. Nguyen (Harlow) wo. **Feather:** no entries. **Light:** no entries. **L. Welter:** *final:* N. Wicks (Chelmsford) w pts O. Pinnock (Southend). **Welter:** no entries. **L. Middle:** no entries. **Middle:** *final:* J. Cullinane (Southend) wo. **L. Heavy:** *semi-finals:* H. Mahdavian (Stanford le Hope) wo, F. Flanagan (Brook) w pts R. O'Rourke (Chelmsford); *final:* F. Flanagan w pts H. Mahdavian. **Cruiser:** no entries. **Heavy:** no entries. **S. Heavy:** no entries.

Mid-Anglia Division (No Entries)

Norfolk Division Ocean Rooms, Gorleston – 30 January
L. Fly: no entries. **Fly:** no entries. **Bantam:** no entries. **Feather:** *final:* C. Weston (Norwich Lads) wo. **Light:** no entries. **L. Welter:** *final:* J. Williams (Norwich City) wo. **Welter:** no entries. **L. Middle:** *final:* M.Cooper (Aylesham) wo. **Middle:** no entries. **L. Heavy:** *final:* M. Redhead (Kingfisher) wo. **Cruiser:** no entries. **Heavy:** no entries. **S. Heavy:** no entries.

Suffolk Division Pontins, Pakefield – 8 February
L. Fly: no entries. **Fly:** no entries. **Bantam:** no entries. **Feather:** no entries. **Light:** no entries. **L. Welter:** *final:* K. Jackson (Haverhill) wo. **Welter:** *final:* P. Devlin (Lowestoft) w rsc 2 L. Rudd (New Astley). **L. Middle:** no entries. **Middle:** *final:* A. Burnett (Triple A) wo. **L. Heavy:** *final:* P. Davis (Lowestoft) wo. **Cruiser:** no entries. **Heavy:** no entries. **S. Heavy:** no entries.

Eastern Counties Semi-Finals & Finals St Andrew's Hall, Norwich – 22 February
L. Fly: no entries. **Fly:** no entries. **Bantam:** *final:* B. Nguyen (Harlow) wo. **Feather:** *final:* C. Weston (Norwich Lads) wo. **Light:** no entries. **L. Welter:** N. Wicks (Chelmsford) withdrew; *final:* K. Jackson (Haverhill) w pts J. Williams (Norwich City). **Welter:** *final:* P. Devlin (Lowestoft) wo. **L. Middle:** *final:* M. Cooper (Aylesham) wo. **Middle:** *final:* J. Cullinane (Southend) w pts A. Burnett (Triple A). **L. Heavy:** F. Flanagan (Brook) withdrew; *final:* M. Redhead (Kingfisher) w pts P. Davis (Lowestoft). **Cruiser:** no entries. **Heavy:** no entries. **S. Heavy:** no entries.

Home Counties Football Ground, Thame – 2 March
L. Fly: no entries. **Fly:** *final:* C. Jury (Reading) w pts D. Culling (Stevenage). **Bantam:** *final:* L. Lewis (Wolvercote) wo. **Feather:** no entries. **Light:** *final:* G. Crouch (Thame) w pts J. Cleary (Lewsey Centre). **L. Welter:** *semi-finals:* N. Ward (Reading) wo, A. Lever (Bedford) w pts P. Steadman (Wolvercote); *final:* N. Ward w rsc 3 A. Lever. **Welter:** *semi-finals:* C. Pratt (Bracknell) wo, P. Malcolm (Luton Shamrock) J. Grant (Berinsfield); *final:* C. Pratt w pts P. Malcolm. **L. Middle:** *semi-finals:* E. Matthews (Callowland) wo, A. Dennis (Stevenage) w pts C. Wood (Wolvercote); *final:* E. Matthews w pts A. Dennis. **Middle:** no entries. **L. Heavy:** *semi-finals:* E. Ikeagwu (Luton Shamrock) wo, J. Hearn (Marlow) w pts C. Ifekoya (Haileybury); *final:* J. Hearn w pts E. Ikeagwu. **Cruiser:** no entries. **Heavy:** *final:* P. Reading (Hitchin) w rsc 3 R. James-Bowen (Milton Keynes Royals). **S. Heavy:** *final:* P. Joyce (Wolvercote) wo.

Home Counties v Eastern Counties Ocean Rooms, Gorleston – 9 March
L. Fly: no entries. **Fly:** C. Jury (Reading) wo. **Bantam:** L. Lewis w pts B. Nguyen (Harlow). **Feather:** C. Weston (Norwich Lads) wo. **Light:** G. Crouch (Thame) wo. **L. Welter:** N. Ward (Reading) w pts K. Jackson (Haverhill). **Welter:** C. Pratt (Bracknell) w pts P. Devlin (Lowestoft). **L. Middle:** M. Cooper (Aylesham) w pts E. Matthews (Callowland). **Middle:** J. Cullinane (Southend) wo. **L. Heavy:** M. Redhead (Kingfisher) w pts J. Hearn (Marlow). **Cruiser:** no entries. **Heavy:** P. Reading (Hitchin) wo. **S. Heavy:** P. Joyce (Wolvercote) wo.

Combined Services Royal Navy Barracks, Portsmouth – 24 January
L. Fly: no entries. **Fly:** *final:* D. Barriball (Army) wo. **Bantam:** *final:* P. Murray (Army) wo. **Feather:** *final:* D. Webb (Army) wo. **Light:** *final:* N. Robinson (Army) w pts K. Davie (RN). **L. Welter:** *final:* J. Cusick (RN) w rsc 4 N. Burchett (Army). **Welter:** *final:* S. Briggs (Army) w pts K. Green (RN). **L. Middle:** *final:* A. Morrison (Army) w pts R. Maxwell (RN). **Middle:** *final:* D. Frost (Army) w pts D. Tang (RN). **L. Heavy:** *final:* L. Spare (Army) wo. **Cruiser:** *semi-finals:* N. Okoth (Army) wo, T. Hindley (RN) w pts I. Aldridge (RAF); *final:* N. Okoth w rsc 2 T. Hindley. **Heavy:** *final:* M. O'Connell (RN) wo. **S. Heavy:** *final:* N. Hosking (RAF) wo.

Eastern Counties/Home Counties v Combined Services The Fire Service Sports Club, Aveley – 15 March
L. Fly: no entries. **Fly:** D. Barriball (Army) w pts C. Jury (Reading). **Bantam:** L. Lewis (Wolvercote) w pts P. Murray (Army). **Feather:** C. Weston (Norwich Lads) w pts D. Webb (Army). **Light:** N. Robinson (Army) w pts G. Crouch (Thame). **L. Welter:** N. Ward (Reading) w pts S. Patterson (Army) – replaced J. Cusick (RN). **Welter:** S. Briggs (Army) w pts C. Pratt (Bracknell). **L. Middle:** M. Cooper (Aylesham) w pts A. Morrison (Army). **Middle:** D. Frost (Army) w pts J. Cullinane (Southend). **L. Heavy:** M. Redhead (Kingfisher) w pts L. Spare (Army). **Cruiser:** N. Okoth (Army) wo. **Heavy:** M. O'Connell (RN) w pts P. Reading (Hitchin). **S. Heavy:** N. Hosking (RAF) w pts P. Joyce (Wolvercote).

Midland Counties v North-East Counties

Midland Counties Northern Zone The Social Club, Newdigate – 16 February & The Jungle Club, Leicester – 21 February
L. Fly: no entries. **Fly:** *final:* J. Mulhern (Standard Triumph) wo. **Bantam:** *final:* F. Holmes (Kingsthorpe) wo. **Feather:** *final:* D. Walton (Willenhall) wo. **Light:** *semi-finals:* C. Johnson (Chesterfield) w pts M. Teague (Grimsby SoB), R. Munro (Old Robin Hood) w rsc 1 M. Vasey (Eastwood); *final:* C. Johnson. **L. Welter:** *semi-finals:* C. Smith (Desborough) w rsc 2 A. Hill (South Normanton SoB), T. Feecham (Coventry Colliery) w rtd 3 P. McKervey (Bulkington); *final:* C. Smith w pts T. Feecham. **Welter:** *semi-finals:* D. McClelland (Chesterfield) wo, J. Flynn (Standard Triumph) w rsc 1 C. Hartley (Retford); *final:* J. Flynn w pts D. McClelland. **L. Middle:** *semi-finals:* J. Elliott (South Normanton SoB) wo, M. Concepcion (Belgrave) w

pts N. Lyon (Boston); *final:* M. Concepcion w pts J. Elliott. **Middle:** *final:* R. Samms (Phoenix) w rsc 3 L. Hepburn (Phoenix). **L. Heavy:** *final:* D. Grainger (Chesterfield) wo. **Cruiser:** *final:* A. Williams (Bulkington) wo. **Heavy:** *final:* S. Wilson (Standard Triumph) w rsc 3 D. England (Wellingborough). **S. Heavy:** *final:* J. Callum (Coventry Colliery) w pts P. Butlin (Melton Mowbray).

Midland Counties Southern Zone   Garrington's Social Club – 17 & 24 February
L. Fly: no entries. **Fly:** no entries. **Bantam:** *semi-finals:* A. Odud (Birmingham City Police) wo, S. Walton (Donnington Ex-Serviceman's) w pts C. Male (Pleck); *final:* A. Odud w pts S. Walton. **Feather:** *semi-finals:* M. Gethin (Wednesbury) wo, R. Wyatt (Lye) w pts N. Marston (Shrewsbury Severnside); *final:* M. Gethin w rsc 2 R. Wyatt. **Light:** *semi-finals:* W. Neath (Small Heath) wo, T. Davies (Donnington Ex-Serviceman's) w pts D. Harrison (Wednesfield); *final:* T. Davies w pts W. Neath. **L. Welter:** *final:* T. Walker (Tamworth) w rsc 3 G. Coombs (Birmingham Irish). **Welter:** *semi-finals:* J. Scanlon (Birmingham City Police) w co 1 S. Jolley (Aston), W. Johnston (Queensberry Police) w pts D. English (Burton); *final:* J. Scanlon w pts W. Johnston. **L. Middle:** *semi-finals:* G. Harris (Ironworks) wo, T. Adams (Birmingham Irish) w rsc 1 M. Greening (Droitwich); *final:* T. Adams w pts G. Harris. **Middle:** *semi-finals:* H. Jamil (Birmingham City Police) w pts M. Curley (Hobbs Moat), K. Smith (Heath Town) w pts J. Finnegan (Burton); *final:* H. Jamil w dis 4 K. Smith. **L. Heavy:** *final:* M. Shafquat (Birmingham City Police) w pts M. Hough (Pleck). **Cruiser:** no entries. **Heavy:** *final:* S. Wood (Premier) w pts P. Scope (Burton). **S. Heavy:** no entries.

Midland Counties Finals   Tile Hill ABC, Coventry – 2 March
L. Fly: no entries. **Fly:** J. Mulhern (Standard Triumph) wo. **Bantam:** F. Holmes (Kingsthorpe) w pts A. Odud (Birmingham City Police). **Feather:** D. Walton (Willenhall) w pts M. Gethin (Wednesbury). **Light:** T. Davies (Donnington Ex-Serviceman's) w dis 3 R. Munro (Old Robin Hood). **L. Welter:** C. Smith (Desborough) w pts T. Walker (Tamworth). **Welter:** J. Flynn (Standard Triumph) w pts J. Scanlon (Birmingham City Police). **L. Middle:** M. Concepcion (Belgrave) w pts T. Adams (Birmingham Irish). **Middle:** R. Samms (Phoenix) w pts H. Jamil (Birmingham City Police). **L. Heavy:** D. Grainger (Chesterfield) w pts M. Shafquat (Birmingham City Police). **Cruiser:** A. Williams (Bulkington) wo. **Heavy:** S. Wilson (Standard Triumph) w pts S. Wood (Premier). **S. Heavy:** J. Callum (Coventry Colliery) wo.

Tyne, Tees & Wear Division   The Country Club, Marton – 13 & 21 February
L. Fly: no entries. **Fly:** *final:* J. Watson (Grainger Park) wo. **Bantam:** *final:* R. Boyle (Birtley Police) wo. **Feather:** *final:* I. Ward (Darlington) w pts G. Gibson (Aycliffe). **Light:** *final:* S. Zaman (Middlesbrough) w pts J. Sayers (Newcastle East End). **L. Welter:** *semi-finals:* A. Turnbull (Ormesby) w rsc 1 P. Robinson (Hartlepool Boys), A. Marksby (Darlington) w pts A. Palmer (Newbiggin); *final:* A. Turnbull w pts A. Marksby. **Welter:** *semi-finals:* G. Harmison (Newbiggin) wo, M. McLean (Birtley Police) w pts M. Marshall (Plains Farm); *final:* G. Harmison w pts M. McLean. **L. Middle:** *semi-finals:* F. Jones (Darlington) w pts I. Greenwell (Sunderland), D. Grey (Plains Farm) w pts A. Mooney (Booker); *final:* F. Jones w co 2 D. Grey. **Middle:** *quarter-finals:* G. Barr (Birtley Police) wo, C. McIntyre (Newbiggin) wo, M. Denton (Hartlepool Headland) wo, S. McCrone (Spennymoor) w pts S. Ward (Sunderland); *semi-finals:* G. Barr w pts C. McIntyre, M. Denton w pts S. McCrone; *final:* G. Barr w co 1 M. Denton. **L.**

Heavy: *final:* T. Marsden (Birtley Police) wo. **Cruiser:** *final:* J. Dolan (Plains Farm) wo. **Heavy:** *final:* D. Dolan (Plains Farm) wo. **S. Heavy:** *final:* B. Robinson (Plains Farm) w pts K. Maloney (Ormesby).

Yorkshire & Humberside Division   Mill Lane WMC, South Kirby – 14 February & Woodseats WMC, Sheffield – 20 February
L. Fly: no entries. **Fly:** *final:* E. Heagney (Cleckheaton) wo. **Bantam:** *final:* R. Nelson (Karmand) w pts S. Doherty (Bradford Police Boys). **Feather:** *final:* J. Dyer (Burmantofts) wo. **Light:** *semi-finals:* L. McGonnell (Doncaster Plant) wo, F. Fehintola (Karmand) w rsc 3 L. Smedley (Eastfield); *final:* F. Fehintola w pts L. McGonnell. **L. Welter:** *final:* T. Fletcher (Karmand) wo. **Welter:** *final:* C. Sebine (Burmantofts) w pts D. Hill (St Paul's). **L. Middle:** *final:* S. Sekhon (Hoyle Mill) wo. **Middle:** *final:* D. Teasdale (Unity) wo. **L. Heavy:** *final:* A. Khan (Unity) wo. **Cruiser:** no entries. **Heavy:** *final:* N. McGarry (Doncaster Plant) wo. **S. Heavy:** *final:* C. Baker (Unity) wo.

North-East Counties Finals   The High Pit Club, Cramlington – 2 March
L. Fly: no entries. **Fly:** E. Heagney (Cleckheaton) w pts J. Watson (Grainger Park). **Bantam:** R. Nelson (Karmand) w pts R. Boyle (Birtley Police). **Feather:** I. Ward (Darlington) w co 3 J. Dyer (Burmantofts). **Light:** F. Fehintola (Karmand) w pts S. Zaman (Middlesbrough). **L. Welter:** T. Fletcher (Karmand) w pts A. Turnbull (Ormesby). **Welter:** C. Sebine (Burmantofts) w pts G. Harmison (Newbiggin). **L. Middle:** F. Jones (Darlington) w pts S. Sekhon (Hoyle Mill). **Middle:** G. Barr (Birtley Police) w pts D. Teasdale (Unity). **L. Heavy:** T. Marsden (Birtley Police) w pts A. Khan (Unity). **Cruiser:** J. Dolan (Plains Farm) wo. **Heavy:** D. Dolan (Plains Farm) w rsc 4 N. McGarry (Doncaster Plant). **S. Heavy:** C. Baker (Unity) w pts B. Robinson (Plains Farm).

Midland Counties v North-East Counties   Triumph Social Club, Coventry - 16 March
L. Fly: no entries. **Fly:** E. Heagney (Cleckheaton) w pts J. Mulhern (Standard Triumph). **Bantam:** F. Holmes (Kingsthorpe) w pts R. Nelson (Karmand). **Feather:** I. Ward (Darlington) w rsc 2 D. Walton (Willenhall). **Light:** F. Fehintola (Karmand) w pts T. Davies (Donnington Ex-Servicemen's). **L. Welter:** T. Fletcher (Karmand) w rsc 1 C. Smith (Desborough). **Welter:** J. Flynn (Standard Triumph) w pts C. Sebine (Burmantofts). **L. Middle:** M. Concepcion (Belgrave) w co 2 F. Jones (Darlington). **Middle:** R. Samms (Phoenix) w rsc 3 Gary Barr (Birtley Police). **L. Heavy:** T. Marsden (Birtley Police) w co 2 D. Grainger (Chesterfield). **Cruiser:** J. Dolan (Plains Farm) w rsc 4 A. Williams (Bulkington). **Heavy:** D. Dolan (Plains Farm) w pts S. Wilson (Standard Triumph). **S. Heavy:** C. Baker (Unity) w dis 3 J. Callum (Coventry Colliery).

North-West Counties v London

East Lancs & Cheshire Division   Wythenshawe Forum, Manchester – 15 February
L. Fly: no entries. **Fly:** no entries. **Bantam:** *semi-finals:* N. Naghizadeh (Sale West), J. Kays (Nichols Police) w rsc 2 D. Wolfenden (Moss Side); *final:* J. Kays w pts N. Naghizadeh. **Feather:** no entries. **Light:** *semi-finals:* A. Morris (West Wythenshawe) wo, J. Burrows (Bredbury & Stockport) w pts D. Boone (Centurians); *final:* A.Morris w co 1 D. Boone. **L. Welter:**

final: L. Graves (Chorley) w pts C. White (Lancaster Lads). **Welter:** *semi-finals:* O. Choudhry (Hamer) wo, B. Alston (Sale West) w pts C. McGrory (Droylesden); *final:* O. Choudhry w pts B. Alston. **L. Middle:** no entries. **Middle:** no entries. **L. Heavy:** no entries. **Cruiser:** *final:* T. Green (Bredbury & Stockport) wo. **Heavy:** *final:* C. Campbell (Nichols Police) wo. **S. Heavy:** *final:* G. Wilson (Bury) wo.

West Lancs & Cheshire Division Everton Park Sports Centre, Liverpool – 8 & 15 February

L. Fly: *final:* C. Lyon (Wigan) wo. **Fly:** *final:* S. Ungi (Golden Gloves) wo. **Bantam:** *final:* D. Matthews (Salisbury) wo. **Feather:** *final:* D. Mulholland (Salisbury) wo. **Light:** *semi-finals:* S. Mullin (Golden Gloves) w pts A. Corish (Marsh Lane), M. Murray (St Helens Town) w pts L. Jennings (Tower Hill); *final:* M. Murray w pts S. Mullin. **L. Welter:** *semi-finals:* A. Davis (Tower Hill) w pts C. McGowan (Tuebrook), D. Angus (Salisbury) w pts P. Grice (Wigan); *final:* D. Angus wo A. Davis. **Welter:** *semi-finals:* S. Farmer (Marsh Lane) w pts S. Harkin (Kirkdale), P. Jones (Stockbridge) w pts M. Murphy (Wigan); *final:* P. Jones w pts S. Farmer. **L. Middle:** *semi-finals:* D. Price (Wigan) wo, P. Smith (Rotunda) w pts L. Andrews (Salisbury); *final:* P. Smith w pts D. Price. **Middle:** *final:* N. Perkins (Kirkdale) w pts S. Birch (St Helens Town). **L. Heavy:** *final:* P. Keir (Rotunda) w pts J. Ainscough (Kirkdale). **Cruiser:** *final:* M. Whitty (Rotunda) w dis 2 M. Carroll (Golden Gloves). **Heavy:** *final:* M. Stafford (Kirkby) wo. **S. Heavy:** *final:* D. Price (Salisbury) w pts D. Alcock (Phoenix).

North-West Counties Finals Olympia, Liverpool – 25 February

L. Fly: C. Lyon (Wigan) wo. **Fly:** S. Ungi (Golden Gloves) wo. **Bantam:** D. Matthews (Salisbury) w co 2 J. Kays (Nichols Police). **Feather:** D. Mulholland (Salisbury) wo. **Light:** A. Morris (West Wythenshawe) w pts M. Murray (St Helens Town). **L. Welter:** L. Graves (Chorley) w pts D. Angus (Salisbury). **Welter:** P. Jones (Stockbridge) w pts O. Choudhry (Hamer). **L. Middle:** P. Smith (Rotunda) wo. **Middle:** N. Perkins (Kirkdale) wo. **L. Heavy:** P. Keir (Rotunda) wo. **Cruiser:** M. Whitty (Rotunda) w rsc 3 T. Green (Bredbury & Stockport). **Heavy:** M. Stafford (Kirkby) w rtd 2 C. Campbell (Nichols Police). **S. Heavy:** D. Price (Salisbury) w rsc 3 G. Wilson (Bury).

London North-East Division York Hall, Bethnal Green – 6 February

L. Fly: no entries. **Fly:** no entries. **Bantam:** *final:* L. Otte (West Ham) w pts M. Gadaffi (Repton). **Feather:** *final:* W. Dodd (Dagenham) wo. **Light:** *final:* R. Sictorness (Repton) wo. **L. Welter:** no entries. **Welter:** *semi-finals:* T. Cesay (Repton) w pts J. B. Mbou (Dagenham), M. Lomax (Broad Street) w pts J. Benn (Peacock); *final:* M. Lomax w pts T. Cesay. **L. Middle:** *final:* D. Cadman (Repton) w dis 4 P. Masterson (Peacock). **Middle:** *semi-finals:* D. Robinson (Repton) wo, E. Monteith (Peacock) w pts F. Davies (Broad Street); *final:* D. Robinson w pts E. Monteith. **L. Heavy:** *final:* A. Boyd (Peacock) w rsc 3 D. Verdi (Repton). **Cruiser:** *final:* M. Lee (Repton) wo. **Heavy:** *final:* J. Zikic (Repton) wo. **S. Heavy:** *semi-finals:* J. Young (Repton) wo, T. Foy (Dagenham) w pts R. McCallum (Broad Street); *final:* J. Young w rsc 2 T. Foy.

London North-West Division The Irish Centre, Camden Town – 7 February

L. Fly: no entries. **Fly:** no entries. **Bantam:** no entries. **Feather:** *final:* W. Corcoran (Stowe) wo. **Light:** *semi-finals:* K. Elias (Dale)

wo, M. Grant (Haringey Police) w pts W. Gure (Hayes); *final:* M. Grant w rsc 3 K. Elias. **L. Welter:** *semi-finals:* A. Theophane (All Stars) w pts Jamal Morrison (All Stars), L. Beavis (Dale) w pts T. Neunie (Haringey Police); *final:* L. Beavis w pts A. Theophane. **Welter:** *semi-finals:* S. Johnson (Trojan Police) wo, Jamie Morrison (All Stars) w pts John Barrett (Trojan Police); *final:* S. Johnson w pts Jamie Morrison. **L. Middle:** *final:* V. Antanavicius (All Stars) wo. **Middle:** *semi-finals:* G. Synetos (Haringey Police) wo, C. Campbell (Trojan Police) w pts R. Aguilar (St Pancras); *final:* C. Campbell w pts G. Synetos. **L. Heavy:** *quarter-finals:* Jimmy Barrett (Trojan Police) wo, A. Coward (St Pancras) wo, D. Mohseni (All Stars) wo, T. Simao (All Stars) w pts J. O'Connor (Trojan Police); *semi-finals:* Jimmy Barrett w pts A. Coward, D. Mohseni w pts T. Simao; *final:* Jimmy Barrett w pts D. Mohseni. **Cruiser:** *semi-finals:* A. Aliy (Haringey Police) wo, C. Barrett (Trojan Police) w pts S. Goodwin (St Pancras); *final:* C. Barrett w pts A. Aliy. **Heavy:** *final:* A. Al-Sady (All Stars) wo. **S. Heavy:** *final:* P. Danquah (All Stars) wo.

London South-East Division National Sports Centre, Crystal Palace – 31 January

L. Fly: *final:* D. Langley (Hollington) w pts S. McDonald (Fitzroy Lodge). **Fly:** *final:* S. Langley (Hollington) wo. **Bantam:** *final:* S. Gregory (Samuel Montague) wo. **Feather:** *final:* S. Mullins (Fisher) wo. **Light:** *final:* A. Ideh (Lynn) wo. **L. Welter:** *semi-finals:* D. Byrnes (Fisher) w pts K. Erdene (Fitzroy Lodge), G. Woolcombe (Marvels Lane) w pts D. Gregory (Fitzroy Lodge); *final:* D. Byrnes w pts G. Woolcombe. **Welter:** *semi-finals:* E. Mbwakongo (Fisher) w pts P. McDonagh (Fisher), M. Reigate (Fitzroy Lodge) w pts A. Small (Fitzroy Lodge); *final:* E. Mbwakongo w rsc 3 M. Reigate. **L. Middle:** *semi-finals:* S. Webb (Bromley & Downham) w pts A. Wanogho (Lynn), W. Aird (Fisher) w pts J. Hudson (Fitzroy Lodge); *final:* S. Webb w pts W. Aird. **Middle:** *semi-finals:* Mark Thirlwall (Fisher) w pts S. Tobin (Fitzroy Lodge), D. Woodhouse (Fitzroy Lodge) w pts C. Imaga (Miguel's); *final:* Mark Thirlwall w rtd 2 D. Woodhouse. **L. Heavy:** *final:* A. Thomas (Lynn) w pts D. Barnaby (Fitzroy Lodge). **Cruiser:** no entries. **Heavy:** *final:* S. McDonald (Lynn) wo. **S. Heavy:** *final:* I. Lewison (Miguel's) wo.

London South-West Division Earlsfield ABC, Wandsworth – 8 February

L. Fly: no entries. **Fly:** no entries. **Bantam:** no entries. **Feather:** no entries. **Light:** no entries. **L. Welter:** *final:* Lenny Daws (Rosehill) w pts A. Freeman (Kingston). **Welter:** *final:* Luke Daws (Rosehill) wo. **L. Middle:** *final:* E. Plekalkiewkz (Earlsfield) w pts S. Barr (Kingston). **Middle:** no entries. **L. Heavy:** *final:* D. Nairn (Battersea) w rsc 3 S. Hutchinson (Balham). **Cruiser:** *final:* R. McIntosh (Battersea) wo. **Heavy:** no entries. **S. Heavy:** *final:* no entries.

London Semi-Finals & Finals York Hall, Bethnal Green – 14 & 21 February

L. Fly: *final:* D. Langley (Hollington) wo. **Fly:** *final:* S. Langley (Hollington) wo. **Bantam:** *final:* L. Otte (West Ham) w pts S. Gregory (Samuel Montague). **Feather:** *semi-finals:* S. Mullins (Fisher) wo, W. Corcoran (Stowe) w pts W. Dodd (Dagenham); *final:* W. Corcoran w rsc 2 S. Mullins. **Light:** *semi-finals:* R. Sictorness (Repton) wo, M. Grant (Haringey Police) w pts A. Ideh (Lynn); *final:* M. Grant w rsc 4 R. Sictorness. **L. Welter:** *semi-finals:* Lenny Daws (Rosehill) wo, L. Beavis (Dale) w pts D. Byrnes (Fisher); *final:* Lenny Daws w pts L. Beavis. **Welter:** *semi-finals:* Luke Daws (Rosehill) w pts E. Mbwakongo (Fisher), M. Lomax (Broad Street) w pts S. Johnson (Trojan Police); *final:* M. Lomax w rsc 3 Luke Daws. **L. Middle:** *semi-finals:* S. Webb

(Bromley & Downham) w pts E. Plekalkiewkz (Earlsfield), D. Cadman (Repton) w pts V. Antanavicius (All Stars); *final:* S. Webb w dis 4 D. Cadman. **Middle:** *semi-finals:* D. Robinson (Repton) wo, Mark Thirlwall (Fisher) w pts C. Campbell (Trojan Police); *final:* Mark Thirlwall w pts D. Robinson. **L. Heavy:** *semi-finals:* A. Boyd (Peacock) wo D. Nairn (Battersea), A. Thomas (Lynn) w pts J. Barrett (Trojan); *final:* A. Thomas w pts A. Boyd. **Cruiser:** *semi-finals:* C. Barrett (Trojan Police) wo, M. Lee (Repton) w co 1 R. McIntosh (Battersea); *final:* C. Barrett w rsc 1 M. Lee. **Heavy:** *semi-finals:* A. Al-Sady (All Stars) wo, J. Zikic (Repton) w pts S. McDonald (Lynn); *final:* J. Zikic w pts A. Al-Sady. **S. Heavy:** *semi-finals:* P. Danquah (All Stars) wo, J. Young (Repton) w pts I. Lewison (Miguel's); *final:* J. Young w co 1 P. Danquah.

North-West Counties v London   Olympia, Liverpool – 15 March
L. Fly: D. Langley (Hollington) w pts C. Lyon (Wigan). **Fly:** S. Langley (Hollington) w pts S. Ungi (Golden Gloves). **Bantam:** D. Matthews (Salisbury) w rtd 1 S. Gregory (Samuel Montague) – replaced L. Otte (West Ham). **Feather:** D. Mulholland (Salisbury) w pts W. Corcoran (Stowe). **Light:** A. Morris (West Wythenshawe) w pts M. Grant (Haringey Police). **L. Welter:** Lenny Daws (Rosehill) w pts L. Graves (Chorley). **Welter:** M. Lomax (Broad Street) w pts P. Jones (Stockbridge). **L. Middle:** P. Smith (Rotunda) w pts S. Webb (Bromley & Downham). **Middle:** N. Perkins (Kirkdale) w pts Mark Thirlwall (Fisher). **L. Heavy:** P. Keir (Rotunda) w pts A. Thomas (Lynn). **Cruiser:** M. Whitty (Rotunda) w rsc 3 C. Barrett (Trojan Police). **Heavy:** M. Stafford (Kirkby) w pts J. Zikic (Repton). **S. Heavy:** D. Price (Salisbury) w pts J. Young (Repton).

Southern Counties v Western Counties

Southern Counties   The Rifle Range, Bisley – 16 February & The Planets, Woking – 22 February
L. Fly: *final:* B. Brazil (Aldershot & Farnham) wo. **Fly:** no entries. **Bantam:** *final:* J. Convey (St Mary's) wo. **Feather:** *semi-finals:* J. Mitchell (Basingstoke) wo, A. Gardner (St Mary's) w pts A. Graham (Whitehawk); *final:* A. Gardner w pts J. Mitchell. **Light:** *final:* L. Cook (Foley) wo, W. Dunkley (Swanley) w pts S. Calvert (Leigh Park); *final:* W. Dunkley w pts L. Cook. **L. Welter:** *quarter-finals:* A. Martin (Foley) wo, A. Balmer (Southwick) wo, J. Xavier (St Mary's) wo, F. Jones (Woking) w pts J. Berry (Sandwich); *semi-finals:* A. Martin w pts A. Balmer, J. Xavier w rsc 3 F. Jones; *final:* J. Xavier w pts A. Martin. **Welter:** *quarter-finals:* S. James (Broadstairs) wo, A. Daffy (Medway Golden Gloves) wo, J. Morris (Newport) wo, I. Hudson (Faversham) w pts D. Larter (Southwick); *semi-finals:* J. Morris w pts I. Hudson, S. James w pts A. Daffy; *final:* J. Morris w pts S. James. **L. Middle:** *semi-finals:* J. Hull (Camberley) w pts David Taylor (Foley), K. Said (Lawrence) w pts Daniel Taylor (Foley); *final:* K. Said w pts J. Hull. **Middle:** *quarter-finals:* M. Thornton (Horsham) wo, D. Wakefield (Dorking) wo, J. Cole (Newport) wo, A. Ewence (Woking) w pts E. Kahlow (West Hill); *semi-finals:* A. Ewence w pts J. Cole, M. Thornton w co 1 D. Wakefield; *final:* A. Ewence w pts M. Thornton. **L. Heavy:** *semi-finals:* J. St John (Woking) w rsc 2 T. Maxwell (Shepway), R. Walls (Owlsmore) w pts G. Kelly (Fareham); *final:* R. Walls w pts J. St John. **Cruiser:** *final:* D. Candasarmy (Woking) w rsc 4 S. Reid (Southwick). **Heavy:** no entries. **S. Heavy:** *final:* M. Grainger (Woking) wo.

Western Counties Southern Division   Badger Hill Public House, Frome – 8 February & Broad Plain Leisure Centre, Bristol – 9 February
L. Fly: no entries. **Fly:** no entries. **Bantam:** *final:* L. Haskins (Empire) wo. **Feather:** no entries. **Light:** *final:* J. Nicholas (National Smelting) w pts R. Scutt (Sydenham). **L. Welter:** *final:* A. Woodward (Watchet) w pts J. Hicks (Yeovil/Reckleford). **Welter:** *semi-finals:* A. Berkely (Empire) wo, Justin Turley (Penhill RBL) w pts A. Cummings (National Smelting); *final:* J. Turley w pts A. Berkely. **L. Middle:** *final:* S. Mullins (Penhill RBL) wo. **Middle:** *semi-finals:* D. Guthrie (Yeovil/Reckleford) wo, M. Banton (Viking) w rtd 2 S. Baines (Gloucester); *final:* D. Guthrie w rsc 3 M. Banton. **L. Heavy:** no entries. **Cruiser:** *final:* M. Jennings (Amalgamated) wo. **Heavy:** no entries. **S. Heavy:** *final:* B. Harding (Penhill RBL) wo.

Western Counties Northern Division   Acorn Youth Centre, Torquay – 2 February & The University, Exeter – 16 February
L. Fly: no entries. **Fly:** no entries. **Bantam:** *final:* N. Ahmed (Bournemouth) wo. **Feather:** *final:* J. Saygi (Paignton) w rsc 2 P. Wiffen (Weymouth). **Light:** *final:* M. Marshall (Paignton) wo. **L. Welter:** *quarter-finals:* M. Stuckey (Torbay) wo, J. Vanemmemis (Bideford) wo, A. Coles (Camborne), A. Wyatt (Paignton) w pts A. Kennedy (Devonport); *semi-finals:* M. Stuckey w pts J. Vanemmemis, A. Wyatt w rsc 3 A. Coles; *final:* A. Wyatt w pts M. Stuckey. **Welter:** *final:* B. Partrick (Devonport) wo. **L. Middle:** *final:* C. Drake (Mayflower) wo. **Middle:** *final:* P. Brown (Phoenix) wo. **L. Heavy:** no entries. **Cruiser:** no entries. **Heavy:** *final:* S. Luscombe (Mayflower) wo. **S. Heavy:** *final:* N. Kendall (Apollo) w rsc 4 M. Elkins (Barnstaple).

Western Counties Finals   Butlins Holiday Camp, Minehead – 2 March
L. Fly: no entries. **Fly:** no entries. **Bantam:** L. Haskins (Empire) w pts N. Ahmed (Bournemouth). **Feather:** J. Saygi (Paignton) wo. **Light:** M. Marshall (Paignton) w pts J. Nicholas (National Smelting). **L. Welter:** A. Woodward (Watchet) w pts M. Stuckey (Torbay) – replaced A. Wyatt (Paignton). **Welter:** J. Turley (Penhill RBL) w rsc 3 B. Partrick (Devonport). **L. Middle:** C. Drake (Mayflower) w pts S. Mullins (Penhill RBL). **Middle:** D. Guthrie (Yeovil/Reckleford) w pts P. Brown (Phoenix). **L. Heavy:** no entries. **Cruiser:** M. Jennings (Amalgamated) wo. **Heavy:** S. Luscombe (Mayflower) wo. **S. Heavy:** B. Harding (Penhill RBL) w rsc 2 N. Kendall (Apollo).

Southern Counties v Western Counties The Planets, Woking – 8 March
L. Fly: B. Brazil (Aldershot & Farnham) wo. **Fly:** no entries. **Bantam:** J. Convey (St Mary's) w dis 2 L. Haskins (Empire). **Feather:** A. Gardner (St Mary's) w pts J. Saygi (Paignton). **Light:** W. Dunkley (Swanley) w pts M. Marshall (Paignton). **L. Welter:** J. Xavier (St Mary's) w pts A. Woodward (Watchet). **Welter:** J. Turley (Penhill RBL) w pts J. Morris (Newport). **L. Middle:** K. Said (Lawrence) w pts C. Drake (Mayflower). **Middle:** D. Guthrie (Yeovil/Reckleford) w pts A. Ewence (Woking). **L. Heavy:** R. Walls (Owlsmore) wo. **Cruiser:** D. Candasarmy (Woking) w co 4 M. Jennings (Amalgamated). **Heavy:** S. Luscombe (Mayflower) wo. **S. Heavy:** M. Grainger (Woking) w pts B. Harding (Penhill RBL).

English ABA Semi-Finals & Finals

The Sports Academy, Eston – 22 March, York Hall, Bethnal Green – 30 March & The Metrodome, Barnsley – 5 April

L. Fly: *final:* D. Langley (Hollington) w pts B. Brazil (Aldershot & Farnham). **Fly:** *semi-finals:* S. Langley (Hollington) wo, D. Barriball (Army) w pts E. Heagney (Cleckheaton); *final:* D. Barriball w pts S. Langley. **Bantam:** *semi-finals:* D. Matthews (Salisbury) w pts J. Convery (St Mary's), F. Holmes (Kingsthorpe) w pts L. Lewis (Wolvercote); *final:* D. Matthews w pts F. Holmes. **Feather:** *semi-finals:* I. Ward (Darlington) w rsc 1 C. Weston (Norwich Lads), D. Mulholland (Salisbury) w pts A. Gardner (St Mary's); *final:* D. Mulholland w pts I. Ward. **Light:** *semi-finals:* F. Fehintola (Karmand) w pts N. Robinson (Army), A. Morris (West Wythenshawe) w pts W. Dunkley (Swanley); *final:* A. Morris w pts F. Fehintola. **L. Welter:** *semi-finals:* Lenny Daws (Rosehill) w rsc 3 J. Xavier (St Mary's), T. Fletcher (Karmand) w pts N. Ward (Reading); *final:* Lenny Daws w pts T. Fletcher. **Welter:** *semi-finals:* M. Lomax (Broad Street) w pts J. Turley (Penhill RBL), S. Briggs (Army) w pts J. Flynn (Standard Triumph); *final:* M. Lomax w pts S. Briggs. **L. Middle:** *semi-finals:* M. Concepcion (Belgrave) w rsc 2 M. Cooper (Aylesham), P. Smith (Rotunda) w pts K. Said (Lawrence); *final:* P. Smith w pts M. Concepcion. **Middle:** *semi-finals:* D. Frost (Army) w pts R. Samms (Phoenix), N. Perkins (Kirkdale) w rsc 4 D. Guthrie (Yeovil/Reckleford); *final:* N. Perkins w pts D. Frost. **L. Heavy:** *semi-finals:* T. Marsden (Birtley Police) w pts M. Redhead (Kingfisher), R. Walls (Owlsmere) w pts P. Keir (Rotunda); *final:* T. Marsden w rsc 3 R. Walls. **Cruiser:** *semi-finals:* J. Dolan (Plains Farm) w pts N. Okoth (Army), M. Witty (Rotunda) and D. Candasarmy (Woking) both disqualified in 4th; *final:* J. Dolan wo. **Heavy:** *semi-finals:* D. Dolan (Plains Farm) w pts M. O'Connell (RN), M. Stafford (Kirkby) w pts S. Luscombe (Mayflower); *final:* D. Dolan w pts M. Stafford. **S. Heavy:** *semi-finals:* M. Grainger (Woking) w pts D. Price (Salisbury), N. Hosking (RAF) w pts C. Baker (Unity); *final:* M. Grainger w pts N. Hosking.

Rotunda's Paul Smith (right) landed the ABA light-middleweight title following a points win over the highly touted Martin Concepcion

Les Clark

Irish Championships, 2001-2002

Senior Tournament

The National Stadium, Dublin - 8, 9, 15, 16 & 22 February
L. Fly: *quarter-finals:* S. McKimm (Abbey, Down) wo, J. P. Kinsella (Ballybrack, Dublin) wo, P. Baker (Immaculata, Belfast) wo, Paul Hyland (Golden Cobra, Dublin) w rsc 3 J. Moore (St Francis', Limerick); *semi-finals:* J. P. Kinsella w pts P. Baker, Paul Hyland w pts S. McKimm; *final:* J. P. Kinsella w pts Paul Hyland. **Fly:** *semi-finals:* L. Cunningham (Saints, Belfast) wo, D. Campbell (St Saviour's, Dublin) w pts T. Lee (Oughterard, Galway); *final:* L. Cunningham w pts D. Campbell. **Bantam:** *quarter-finals:* D. McKenna (Holy Family, Belfast) wo, M. Lindsay (Immaculata, Belfast) wo, Patrick Hyland (Golden Cobra, Dublin) wo, D. Lawlor (St Michael's, Athy) w rsc 3 S. McAnee (Ring, Derry); *semi-finals:* M. Lindsay w pts D. Lawlor, D. McKenna w pts Patrick Hyland; *final:* M. Lindsay w pts D. McKenna. **Feather:** *quarter-finals:* S. Ormond (Quarryvale, Dublin) wo, J. P. Campbell (South Meath) wo, R. Kane (Shamrock, Tyrone) wo, G. Brown (Crumlin, Dublin) w rsc 3 N. Hazlett (St Bridgid's, Derry); *semi-finals:* S. Ormond w pts J. P. Campbell, G. Brown w co 1 R. Kane; *final:* S. Ormond w pts G. Brown. **Light:** *quarter-finals:* N. Monteith (Dockers, Belfast) wo, K. Hogg (Larne, Antrim) w pts S. Mallon (Cluan Mhuire, Newry), E. McAneaney (Dealgan, Dundalk) w pts T. Carlyle (Sacred Heart, Dublin), A. Murray (Cavan/Clonoe) w pts E. Hyland (Golden Cobra, Dublin); *semi-finals:* A. Murray w pts E. McAneaney, N. Monteith w pts K. Hogg; *final:* A. Murray w pts N. Monteith. **L. Welter:** *quarter-finals:* M. Kelly (Dealgan, Dundalk) wo, R. Sheahan (St Michael's, Athy) w rsc 2 M. J. Sweeney (Sligo), S. Barrett (Rylane, Cork) w pts R. Cardwell (Monkstown, Belfast), P. McCloskey (St Canice's, Derry) w pts A. Carlyle (Sacred Heart, Dublin); *semi-finals:* R. Sheahan w pts M. Kelly, P. McCloskey w pts S. Barrett; *final:* P. McCloskey w pts R. Sheahan. **Welter:** *prelims:* J. Moore (Arklow) wo, P. Walsh (St Coleman's, Cork) wo, T. Blaney (Westside, Cork) wo, P. Jennings (Quarryvale, Dublin) wo, F. Turner (St Ibar's, Wexford) wo, H. Joyce (St Michael's, Athy) w pts M. Donovan (Ennis), J. Harkin (Dunfanaghy, Donegal) w rsc 4 A. Tierney (St Anthony's, Tuam), D. Conlon (Crumlin, Dublin) w pts G. McClure (Abbey, Antrim),; *quarter-finals:* J. Moore w rsc 3 H. Joyce, P. Walsh w rsc 2 J. Harkin, T. Blaney w pts P. Jennings, D. Conlon w pts F. Turner; *semi-finals:* J. Moore w rsc 2 P. Walsh, D. Conlon w pts T. Blaney; *final:* J. Moore w rsc 3 D. Conlon. **L. Middle:** *quarter-finals:* J. Duddy (Ring, Derry) wo, D. Sutherland (St Saviour's, Dublin) w rsc 2 E. O'Kane (St Canice's, Derry), A. Gibson (Larne) w pts A. Whiston (Crumlin, Dublin), K. Byrne (Darndale, Dublin) w rsc 2 I. Lapko (Drimnagh, Dublin); *semi-finals:* J. Duddy w pts D. Sutherland, A. Gibson w rsc 3 K. Byrne; *final:* J. Duddy w pts A. Gibson. **Middle:** *prelims:* K. Egan (Neilstown, Dublin) wo, L. Senior (Crumlin, Dublin) wo, K. Whelan (Saviou's/Crystal, Waterford) wo, T. Moran (St Anne's, Westport) wo, C. Carmichael (Holy Trinity, Belfast) wo, F. O'Brien (Drimnagh, Dublin) wo, T. Fitzgerald (Glen, Cork) wo, M. Lee (Oughterard, Galway) w pts J. Waldron (Midfield, Mayo); *quarter-finals:* K. Egan w pts L. Senior, K. Whelan w pts T. Moran, C. Carmichael w pts F. O'Brien, M. Lee w rsc 4 T.

Fitzgerald; *semi-finals:* K. Egan w pts K. Whelan, M. Lee w pts C. Carmichael; *final:* K. Egan w pts M. Lee. **L. Heavy:** *quarter-finals:* S. O'Grady (St Saviour's, Dublin) wo, I. Timms (Quarryvale, Dublin) w rsc 2 S. O'Hagan (Bishop Kelly, Tyrone), M. McDonough (Brosna, Offaly) w pts P. Smith (Keady, Antrim), B. Ferry (Dunfanaghy, Donegal) w pts J. Kelly (Sean McDermott, Leitrim); *semi-finals:* I. Timms w pts S. O'Grady, M. McDonough w pts B. Ferry; *final:* I. Timms w dis 4 M. McDonough. **Heavy:** *final:* A. Reynolds (St Joseph's, Sligo) w rsc 2 P. Sharkey (Crumlin, Dublin). **S. Heavy:** *quarter-finals:* E. Falvey (St Coleman's, Cork) wo, J. Upton (Crumlin, Dublin) wo, T. Crampton (St Broughan's, Offaly) w rsc 3 G. Dargan (CIE, Dublin), C. McMonagle (Holy Trinity, Belfast) w rsc 3 D. Sweeney (Sligo); *semi-finals:* E. Falvey w pts T. Crampton, C. McMonagle w rsc 4 J. Upton; *final:* E. Falvey w pts C. McMonagle.

Intermediate Finals

The National Stadium, Dublin – 7 December
L. Fly: S. McGinn (Abbey, Down) w rsc 4 M. Regan (Claremorris, Mayo). **Fly:** T. Lee (Oughterard, Galway) w rtd 2 T. McDonald (Cabra, Dublin). **Bantam:** P. Hyland (Golden Cobra, Dublin) w pts R. Simpson (Savior's/Crystal, Waterford). **Feather:** D. Moore (St Joseph's, Derry) w pts B. Gillespie (Twin Towns, Donegal). **Light:** P. Simpson (St Saviour's/Crystal, Waterford) w pts G. Dunne (Neilstown, Dublin). **L. Welter:** J. Wasson (Eastside, Belfast) w pts D. Cassidy (Dromore, Tyrone). **Welter:** T. Blaney (Westside, Cork) w rsc 3 M. O'Donovan (Ennis, Clare). **L. Middle:** E. O'Kane (St Canice's, Derry) w pts M. Woods (Mount Tallant, Dublin). **Middle:** T. Moran (St Anne's, Laois) w pts P. Murray (St Matthew's, Dublin). **L. Heavy:** M. McDonagh (Brosna, Westmeath) w rsc 1 P. Cowan (Cluain Mhuire, Newry). **Heavy:** C. Barrett (Olympic, Galway) w pts S. McClafferty (Dunfanaghy, Donegal). **S. Heavy:** G. Riggs (St Saviour's, Dublin) w pts D. Nevin (Dunboyne, Neath).

Junior Finals

The National Stadium, Dublin – 24 May
L. Fly: Paul Hyland (Golden Cobra, Dublin) w pts C. Ahern (Baldoyle, Dublin). **Fly:** D. Murphy (St. Saviour's, Dublin) w pts B. Gillen (Draperstown, Derry). **Bantam:** E. Tuohy (Moate, Westmeath) w pts T. Ward (Ballina, Mayo). **Feather:** P. Roche (Nielstown, Dublin) w pts D. Byrne (Crumlin, Dublin). **Light:** P. Brolly (Errigal, Derry) w pts D. Towman (Sacred Heart, Newry). **L. Welter:** R. Sheehan (St. Michael's, Athy) w rtd 4 J. McDonagh (Brosna, Westmeath). **Welter:** C. McAuley (Dungloe, Donegal) w pts J. Sweeney (Sligo). **L. Middle:** A. Lee (St. Francis, Limerick) w pts P. Moffett (Abbey, Down). **Middle:** M. Keenan (Sunnyside, Cork) w pts B. Fitzpatrick (West Finglas, Dublin). **L. Heavy:** D. O'Neill (Paulstown, Kilkenny) w rsc 2 P. Coyle (Geesala, Mayo). **Heavy:** J. Walsh (Claremorris, Mayo) w pts D. Goughran (Bay City, Dublin). **S. Heavy:** no entries.

Scottish and Welsh Senior Championships, 2001-2002

Scotland ABA

The Time Capsule, Coatbridge – 9 February & 16 March, The Tree Tops Hotel, Aberdeen – 22 February & Pettycur Leisure Centre, Kinghorn – 1 March

L. Fly: *final:* U. Hussain (Kinross) w pts I. McCabe (Lesmahagow). **Fly:** *final:* L. Munro (Dennistoun) w rsc 3 S. Bartlett (Inverness). **Bantam:** *semi-finals:* K. Townsley (Blantyre) wo, J. Ancliff (Granite City) w pts G. Izzat (Clovenstone); *final:* K. Townsley w pts J. Ancliff. **Feather:** *quarter-finals:* J. Simpson (Port Victoria) w rsc 4 R. Park (Blantyre), S. Young (Lothian) w pts F. Rafiq (Dennistoun), J. Gilhaney (Blantyre) w pts M. Murray (Inverness), S. Flynn (Clovenstone) w pts R. Nichol (Phoenix); *semi-finals:* S. Flynn w pts J. Gilhaney, J. Simpson w pts S. Young; *final:* J. Simpson w pts S. Flynn. **Light:** *prelims:* M. Hastie (Forgewood) wo, G. Clark (Gilmerton) wo, L. Spence (Inverness) wo, J. Bothwell (Dennistoun) wo, T. Graham (Auchengeich) w pts S. Green (Glenrothes), S. Carroll (Granite City) w pts P. Best (O'Neils), G. McMillan (Blantyre) w pts J. Devine (Barn), P. King (Newarthill) w pts G. McArthur (Clydebank); *quarter-finals:* G. Clark w pts L. Spence, M. Hastie w rsc 2 J. Bothwell, T. Graham w pts S. Carroll, G. McMillan w pts P. King; *semi-finals:* M. Hastie w rsc 2 G. Clark; G. McMillan w pts T. Graham; *final:* M. Hastie w pts G. McMillan. **L. Welter:** *quarter-finals:* K. Anderson (Denbeath) wo, L. McAllister (Granite City) wo, C. Black (Barn) w pts J. McKeown (Barrhead), B. Morrison (Forgewood) w rsc 2 M. Tierney (Glenrothes); *semi-finals:* K. Anderson w pts L. McAllister, B. Morrison w pts C. Black; *final:* B. Morrison w pts K. Anderson. **Welter:** *quarter-finals:* M. Cittadini (Dennistoun) wo, J. Murphy (Barn) w pts M. Reid (Insch), B. Lee (Arbroath) w rsc 1 N. Murray (Gorbals), D. Hendry (Port Victoria) w pts C. Dickson (Noble Art); *semi-finals:* B. Lee w pts D. Hendry, J. Murphy w rsc 3 M. Cittadini; *final:* J. Murphy w pts B. Lee. **L. Middle:** *prelims:* C. Thompson (Glenrothes) wo, J. Coyle (Bannockburn) wo, V. Baldassara (Clydebank) wo, C. McEwan (Clovestone) wo, S. McCarroll (Clydebank) wo, R. Morrison (Bannockburn) wo, W. Blackwood (Garnock Valley) wo, B. Peacock (Barrhead) w pts S. Rao (Dennistoun); *quarter-finals:* J. Coyle w rsc 3 V. Baldassara, C. McEwan w rsc 2 S. McCarroll, R. Morrison w pts W. Blackwood, C. Thompson w rsc 1 B. Peacock; *semi-finals:* R. Morrison w pts C. Thompson, C. McEwan w pts J. Coyle; *final:* C. McEwan w rsc 3 R. Morrison. **Middle:** *quarter-finals:* S. McGuire (Glenrothes) wo, A. Will (Insch) wo, I. Donnelly (Broadwood), W. Moore (Perth Railways) w pts A. Garbett (Granite City); *semi-finals:* W. Moore w pts I. Donnelly, S. McGuire w rtd 4 A. Will; *final:* S. McGuire w pts W. Moore. **L. Heavy:** *quarter-finals:* M. Ross (Larkhall) wo, W. Clark (Glenrothes) wo, G. King (Inverness) wo, L. Ramsay (Kingdom) w pts M. Loughlin (Leith Victoria); *semi-finals:* L. Ramsay w rsc 2 M. Ross, W. Clark w rsc 4 G. King; *final:* L. Ramsay w pts W. Clark. **Cruiser:** *semi-finals:* S. Simmons (Leith Victoria) w pts W. Graham (Newarthill), S. Henvey (Wellmeadow) w pts A. Tait (Lothian); *final:* S. Henvey w pts S. Simmons. **Heavy:** *semi-finals:* G. Wilson (Springhill) wo, A. Young (Inverness) w pts A. Robb (Lochside); *final:* A. Young w rsc 2 G. Wilson. **S. Heavy:** *quarter-finals:* R. McPhee (Garnock Valley) wo, J. Perry (Larkhall) wo, J. McKechnie (Wellmeadow) w pts A. Boyle (Bannockburn), I. Millarvie (Glasgow Phoenix) w rsc 2 P. Malone (Arbroath); *semi-finals:* J. Perry w pts R. McPhee, I. Millarvie wo J. McKechnie; *final:* I. Millarvie w pts R. McPhee.

Wales ABA

Afan Lido Sports Centre, Port Talbot – 9 February & 15 March, Fairwater Sports & Social Club, Cwmbran – 22 February & The Dockers Club, Swansea – 27 February

L. Fly: *final:* Y. Essa (Peacocks) wo. **Fly:** *semi-finals:* M. Edmonds (St Joseph's East) wo, K. Foley (St Joseph's South) w pts J. Mwasingallah (Splott Adventure); *final:* M. Edmonds wo K. Foley. **Bantam:** *semi-finals:* D. Davies (Merthyr) wo, D. Edwards (Cwmavon Hornets) w pts H. Janes (Highfields); *final:* D. Edwards w pts D. Davies. **Feather:** *semi-finals:* P. Ashton (St Joseph's South) wo, J. Alger-Crees (Prince of Wales) w pts D. Rees (Swansea Premier); *final:* P. Ashton w pts J. Alger-Crees. **Light:** *quarter-finals:* A. Evans (Carmarthen) wo, M. Roberts (Wrexham) wo, I. Ghaney (Grange Catholic) wo, J. Arthur (Coed Eva) w pts J. Evans (Army); *semi-finals:* J. Arthur w rsc 4 A. Evans, M. Roberts w pts I. Ghaney; *final:* J. Arthur w pts M. Roberts. **L. Welter:** *quarter-finals:* C. Hope (Merthyr) wo, C. Hall (Penyrheol) w co 2 P. Hayhurst (Carmarthen), N. Burchett (Army) w dis 3 K. Bryan (Splott Adventure), V. Bryan (Splott Adventure) w rsc 3 M. Burnett (Ferndale); *semi-finals:* C. Hall w pts C. Hope, V. Bryan w pts N. Burchett; *final:* C. Hall w pts V. Bryan. **Welter:** *quarter-finals:* L. Owen (Blaen-y-maes) wo, W. Lukins (Splott Adventure) w rsc 3 A. Knox (Sports Connection), S. Phillips (Cwmavon Hornets) w pts H. Evans (Carmarthen), A. Doherty (Pontypool & Panteg) w co 1 A. Hay (Pembroke); *semi-finals:* A. Doherty w rsc 3 W. Lukins, L. Owen w pts S. Phillips; *final:* A. Doherty w co 2 L. Owen. **L. Middle:** *prelims:* J. Hull (Highfields) wo, K. McIver (Barry West End) wo, M. Morgan (Merthyr) wo, A. Davies (Carmarthen) wo, R. Allen (Palace) wo, A. Evans (Merthyr) wo, R. Davies (Davies Hornets) wo, L. Jones (Kyber Colts) w pts K. Thomas (Prince of Wales); *quarter-finals:* J. Hull w co 1 K. McIver, M. Morgan w pts A. Davies, R. Allen w pts A. Evans, L. Jones w rsc 2 R. Davies; *semi-finals:* M. Morgan w co 4 J. Hull, L. Jones w pts R. Allen; *final:* L. Jones w pts M. Morgan. **Middle:** *quarter-finals:* P. Astley (Kyber Colts) wo, J. Jones (Army) wo, M. Allen (Palace) w dis 3 D. Radham (Pembroke), F. Borg (Prince of Wales) w pts S. Goody (Victoria Park); *semi-finals:* J. Jones w pts P. Astley, M. Allen w pts F. Borg; *final:* M. Allen w pts J. Jones. **L. Heavy:** *quarter-finals:* J. Walters (Prince of Wales) wo, D. Evans (Pontypool & Panteg) wo, E. Davies (Aberaman) wo, J. Whitfield (Army) w pts M. Lloyd (Penyrheol); *semi-finals:* J. Walters w rsc 4 D. Evans, J. Whitfield w pts E. Davies; *final:* J. Whitfield w rsc 2 J. Walters. **Heavy:** *semi-finals:* D. Mais (Splott Adventure) wo, L. Milsjen (Coed Eva) w pts D. Morgan (Penyrheol); *final:* L. Milsjen w pts D. Mais. **S. Heavy:** *quarter-finals:* K. Evans (Carmarthen) wo, S. Gammer (Pembroke) wo, L. Ali (Splott Adventure) wo, D. Morgan (Portmead & Blaenymaes) w pts A. Thomas (Merthyr); *semi-finals:* S. Gammer wo L. Ali, K. Evans w rsc 1 D. Morgan; *final:* K. Evans w pts S. Gammer.

Four Nations Tournament, 2002

National Events Centre, Gleneagle Hotel, Killarney 18 & 19 April

L. Fly: *semi-finals:* J. P. Kinsella (I) w rsc 4 Y. Essa (W), D. Langley (E) w pts G. Jones (S) – replaced U. Hussain; *final:* D. Langley w pts J. P. Kinsella. *3rd place:* G. Jones w pts Y. Essa. **Fly:** *semi-finals:* D. Campbell (I) – replaced L. Cunningham - w pts M. Edmonds (W), D. Barriball (E) w pts L. Muro (S); *final:* D. Campbell w pts D. Barriball. *3rd place:* M. Edmonds w pts L. Munro. **Bantam:** *semi-finals:* S. Flynn (S) – replaced K. Townsley - wo D. Matthews (E), D. McKenna (I) – M. Lindsay - w pts D. Edwards (W), *final:* D. McKenna w pts S. Flynn. *3rd place:* D. Edwards wo. **Feather:** *semi-finals:* S. Ormond (I) w pts J. Simpson (S), D. Mulholland (E) w pts P. Ashton (W); *final:* D. Mulholland w co 1 S. Ormond. *3rd place:* J. Simpson w pts P. Ashton. **Light:** *semi-finals:* A. Murray (I) w pts M. Hastie (S), F. Fehintola (E) – replaced A. Morris - w pts J Arthur (W); *final:* A. Murray w pts F. Fehintola. *3rd place:* M. Hastie w pts J. Arthur. **L. Welter:** *semi-finals:* N. Burchett (W) – replaced C. Hall - w pts L. McAllister (S) – replaced B. Morrison, Lenny Daws (E) w pts R. Sheahan (I) – replaced P. McCloskey; *final:* Lenny Daws w rsc 3 N. Burchett. *3rd place:* R. Sheahan w pts L. McAllister. **Welter:** *semi-finals:* A. Doherty (W) w pts M. Lomax (E), J. Moore (I) w rsc 3 J. Murphy (S); *final:* J. Moore w pts A. Doherty. *3rd place:* M. Lomax w pts J. Murphy. **L. Middle:** *semi-finals:* C. McEwan (S) w rsc 2 L. Jones (W), J. Duddy (I) w pts P. Smith (E); *final:* J. Duddy w pts C. McEwan. *3rd place:* P. Smith wo L. Jones. **Middle:** *semi-finals:* K. Egan (I) w rsc 3 S. McGuire (S), N. Perkins (E) w rsc 3 M. Allen (W); *final:* N. Perkins w rsc 3 K. Egan. *3rd place:* S. McGuire wo M. Allen. **L. Heavy:** *semi-finals:* T. Marsden (E) w rsc 2 J. Whitfield (W), L. Ramsay (S) w rsc 2 I. Timms (I); *final:* T. Marsden w pts L. Ramsay. *3rd place:* J. Whitfield wo I. Timms. **Heavy:** *semi-finals:* A. Young (S) w rtd 2 L. Milsjen (W), A. Reynolds (I) w pts M. Stafford (E) – replaced D. Dolan; *final:* A. Reynolds w rsc 1 A. Young. *3rd place:* M. Stafford wo L. Milsjen. **S. Heavy:** *semi-finals:* K. Evans (W) w pts D. Price (E) – replaced M. Grainger, C. McMonagle (I) – replaced E. Falvey - wo I. Millarvie (S); *final:* K. Evans w pts C. McMonagle. *3rd place:* D. Price wo.

Code: E = England, I = Ireland, S = Scotland, W = Wales

David (left) and James Dolan of Plains Farm ABC each made it a hat trick of successive ABA title wins in 2002   Les Clark

British and Irish International Matches, 2001-2002

Does not include multi-nation tournaments, despite them being recognised as international appearances, merely because space will not allow. We apologise if any international matches have been missed, but we have covered all we have been made aware of.

Ireland (5) v Poland (4)   Tarnow, Poland – 25 August
(Irish names first): **L. Fly:** J. P. Kinsella l pts M. Jaworek, P. Baker w pts R. Roczniak. **Fly:** D. Campbell l pts A. Rzany. **Bantam:** M. Lindsay w pts T. Mazur. **Feather:** J. P. Campbell l pts K. Szot. **Light:** E. McEneaney w pts A. Nycz, T. Carlyle l pts S. Klasa. **L. Welter:** H. Joyce w pts K. Chudecki. **L. Middle:** D. Sutherland w pts A. Zwarycz.

England (5) v Denmark (1)   Hirtshals, Denmark – 27 October
(English names first): **Light:** A. Morris l pts M. Kristjansen. **L. Welter:** D. Happe w pts S. Manuel. **Welter:** M. Lomax w pts M. Ali. **L. Heavy:** C. Fry w pts A. H. Nielsen. **Heavy:** P. Souter w pts K. S. Nielsen, D. Dolan w pts J. Andersen.

Young Ireland (4) v Young France (5)   Abbeville, France – 3 November
(Irish names first): **L. Fly:** A. Hopkins l pts P. Fresnois. **Fly:** B. Gillen l pts G. Fresnois, D. Murphy l pts J. Outin. **Bantam:** Patrick Hyland l pts A. Vastine, E. Tuohy w pts H. Ziouti. **Feather:** P. Roche w pts K. Abessalem, E. Donovan w pts K. Maachou. **Welter:** C. McAuley w pts T. Bastard. **L. Heavy:** W. McLaughlin l pts S. Rachid.

Scotland (6) v Australia (6)   Pettycur Leisure Centre, Kinghorn – 9 November
(Scottish names first): **L. Fly:** D. Birrell l pts J. Goodwin, U. Hussain w pts S. Percy. **Bantam:** G. Izzatt l pts M. Garlett. **Feather:** J. Simpson w pts R. Fletcher, D. Burns l pts B. Wilson. **Light:** S. Green l pts T. Johns. **L. Welter:** R. Brown l pts T. Kidd, K. Anderson w pts J. Fletcher. **Welter:** J. Lovell w pts B. Gervaise. **L. Middle:** M. Reid l co 3 M. Kramer. **Middle:** W. Moore w rsc 2 S. McConville, S. McGuire w rsc 3 D. Baff.

Ireland (2) v France (7)   Laon, France – 16 November
(Irish names first): **Fly:** D. Campbell l pts J. Thomas, H. Cunningham l pts G. Fresnois. **Light:** P. Simpson l pts G. Salingue, E. Hyland l pts B. Dangnoko. **L. Welter:** M. Kelly l pts X. Noel, T. Carlyle l pts S. Bouzaine. **L. Middle:** D. Sutherland w pts D. Bertu, A. Lee w rsc 3 T. Karl. **L. Heavy:** B. Ferry l pts J. Dovi. Note: Lee represented Ireland at junior level.

Scotland (4) v Australia (7)   The Bellahouston Leisure Centre, Glasgow – 17 November
(Scottish names first): **L. Fly:** I. McCabe l pts S. Percy. **Bantam:** P. Pollock l rsc 1 M. Garlett. **Feather:** D. Burns l pts B. Wilson, J. Simpson w pts R. Fletcher. **Light:** J. McKeown l pts T. Johns. **L. Welter:** J. Carlin l pts T. Kidd, B. Morrison w pts J. Fletcher. **Welter:** C. O'Neil w pts B. Gervaise. **Middle:** G. Bullock l co 3 M. Kramer, P. Kearney l pts S. McConville, B. Peacock w pts D. Baff.

Young England (5) v Young Ireland (3)   The Pavilion Ocean Rooms, Weymouth – 17 November
(English names first): **L. Fly:** J. Watson l pts Paul Hyland, S. McDonald w rsc 3 J. Moore. **Bantam:** E. Heagney l pts Patrick

Hyland. **Feather:** N. Brough w pts S. Ormond. **Light:** A. Morris w pts M. Hogan. **L. Welter:** A. Woodward l pts R. Sheahan. **Welter:** R. Ashworth w pts D. Barrett. **Middle:** J. Boyd w pts B. Fitzpatrick.

Ireland (3) v France (6)   Pont-Audemer, France – 18 November
(Irish names first): **Fly:** D. Campbell l pts G. Fresnois, H. Cunningham l pts J. Thomas. **Bantam:** T. Lee l pts A. Vastine. **Light:** P. Simpson l rtd 2 G. Salingue, A. Magee l pts A. Kebir. **L. Welter:** M. Kelly w pts S. Bouzaine. **L. Middle:** D. Sutherland w pts J. M. Ismael. **Middle:** D. O'Hagan w pts E. Adolf. **L. Heavy:** B. Ferry l pts M. Benzeghiba. Note: Lee, Magee and O'Hagan represented Ireland at junior level.

England (4) v USA (3)   The Park Lane Hilton, Mayfair, London – 19 November
(English names first): **Bantam:** M. Moran l pts J. Litzau. **Feather:** S. Bell w pts D. Rodela. **L. Welter:** G. Smith w pts L. Gonzalez. **L. Middle:** S. Birch l pts S. Powell. **Middle:** D. Frost l pts A. Ward. **L. Heavy:** T. Marsden w pts J. Pastorella. **Heavy:** D. Haye w pts C. Ellis.

Ireland (1) v France (7)   Pessac, France – 14 December
(Irish names first): **Fly:** M. Lindsay l pts J. Thomas. **Light:** A. Murray l rsc 3 Z. Yahudi, D. Carron l rsc 3 G. Salingue. **L. Welter:** T. Hamill l pts S. Bouzaine. **Welter:** P. McCloskey l pts X. Noel. **L. Middle:** J. Duddy w pts I. Lahmar. **Middle:** C. Carmichael l rsc 3 C. Karl. **S. Heavy:** C. Barrett l pts M. Aouiche.

Wales (1) v Norway (4)   Tonsberg, Norway – 15 December
(Welsh names first): **Light:** K. Hope l pts A. Pursharif. **Welter:** A. Doherty w pts M. Hansen. **L. Middle:** R. Davies l pts K. Tverberg. **Middle:** M. Allen l pts B. Norve. **L. Heavy:** J. Walters l rsc 2 M. Macura.

Young Ireland (5) v Young France (3)   Ringside Club, Dublin – 25 January
(Irish names first): **L. Fly:** G. Casey l pts S. Takoucht, A. Hopkins w pts Alexis Vastine. **Fly:** D. Murphy w pts J. Outin. **Bantam:** E. Tuohy w pts Adriani Vastine. **Feather:** E. Donovan l pts K. Maachou. **Light:** W. McLoughlin w pts K. Abessalem. **L. Welter:** M. Gallagher l pts S. Rachidi. **L. Middle:** A. Lee w pts K. Piquet.

Young England (5) v Young France (2)   Royal Lancaster Hotel, Lancaster Gate, London – 4 February
(English names first): **L. Fly:** J. Fowl l pts S. Takought. **Fly:** D. Broadhurst w pts J. Outin. **Bantam:** K. Mitchell l pts A. Vastine. **Light:** S. Jennings w pts K. Abdessalem. **L. Welter:** A. Quigley w pts S. Rachidi. **Welter:** R. Ashworth w pts L. Aitchaouche. **L. Middle:** T. Jeffries w pts K. Piquet.

Ireland (8) v Canada (4)   National Stadium, Dublin – 1 March
(Irish names first): **L. Fly:** J. P. Kinsella w rsc 2 J. Kalimuthu. **Fly:** L. Cunningham w pts S. Gauthier. **Bantam:** D. Lawlor l pts A. Kooner.

Feather: S. Ormond l pts B. Gaudet. **Light:** D. Kennedy l pts A. Decarie. **L. Welter:** P. McCloskey w pts R. Romero. **Welter:** J. Moore w rsc 3 R. Savage. **L. Middle:** D. Sutherland l pts J. Pascal. **Middle:** K. Egan w pts M. Walchuk. **L. Heavy:** S. O'Grady w pts J. Hurst. **Heavy:** A. Reynolds w pts J. Douglas. **S. Heavy:** E. Falvey w pts M. Mychajliv.

Ireland (5) v Canada (7)   Maam Cross, Galway – 3 March
(Irish names first): **L. Fly:** Paul Hyland w pts J. Kalimuthu. **Fly:** T. Lee w pts S. Gauthier. **Bantam:** Patrick Hyland l pts A. Kooner. **Feather:** G. Brown w pts B. Gaudet. **Light:** S. Mallon l pts A. Decarie. **L. Welter:** R. Sheehan w pts R. Romero. **Welter:** D. Conlon l pts R. Savage. **L. Middle:** H. Coyle l pts J. Pascal. **Middle:** T. Moran l pts M. Walchuk. **L. Heavy:** J. Kelly l pts J. Hurst. **Heavy:** A. Reynolds w pts J. Douglas. **S. Heavy:** T. Crampton l pts M. Mychajliv.

Ireland (3) v France (5)   National Stadium, Dublin – 15 March
(Irish names first): **Fly:** D. Lawlor l pts J. Thomas. **Bantam:** Patrick Hyland l pts A. Hallab. **Feather:** S. Ormond w pts B. Dangnoko. **Light:** A. Murray w pts A. Janfouah. **L. Welter:** A. Carlyle l rsc 3 W. Blain. **Welter:** D. Conlon w pts X. Noel. **L. Middle:** H. Joyce l pts D. Bertu. **L. Heavy:** I. Timms w pts M. Diambang.

Ireland (2) v France (4)   Fairways Hotel, Dundalk – 17 March
(Irish names first): **Feather:** J. P. Campbell l pts B. Dangnoko. **Light:** N. Monteith w rsc 3 A. Janfouah. **L. Welter:** M. Kelly w pts W. Blain. **Welter:** T. Blaney l rsc 2 X. Noel. **L. Middle:** E. O'Kane l pts D. Bertu. **S. Heavy:** T. Crampton l pts M. Aouiche.

Ireland (5) v Denmark (3)   National Stadium, Dublin – 12 April
(Irish names first): **Feather:** P. Roche w pts W. Mirza. **Light:** E. Hyland l rsc 4 M. Kristjansen. **L. Welter:** D. Murphy w rsc 3 J. Hansen. **Welter:** C. McAuley w pts O. Carlsen. **L. Middle:** A. Lee w rsc 3 T. Claxton. **L. Heavy:** S. O'Grady l rsc 3 A. Nielsen. **Heavy:** P. Sharkey l rsc 3 J. Andersen, S. Curran w rsc 3 M. Steengaard. Note: Roche, Murphy, McAuley, Lee and Curran represented Ireland at junior level.

Ireland (3) v Denmark (2)   The Forum, Waterford – 14 April
(Irish names first): **Light:** P. Simpson l pts M. Kristjansen. **L. Welter:** A. Foley w pts J. Hansen. **L. Middle:** J. Roche w pts O. Carlsen, P. Whelan w rsc 3 T. Claxton. **Heavy:** C. Barrett l pts J. Andersen. Note: Foley, Roche and Whelan represented Ireland at junior level.

Scotland (5) v Canada (4)   Regina, Canada   10 May
(Scottish names first): **Bantam:** K. Townsley l rsc 3 A. Kooner. **Feather:** J. Simpson l pts B. Gaudet. **L. Welter:** K. Anderson w pts R. Romero. **Welter:** C. McNeil w pts R. Savage. **L. Middle:** C. McEwan w pts J. Pascal. **Middle:** S. McGuire l pts M. Walchuk. **L. Heavy:** L. Ramsay w pts J. Hurst. **Heavy:** A. Young l rsc 3 J. Douglas. **S. Heavy:** I. Millarvie w pts D. Cadieux.

Scotland (5) v Canada (5)   Moose Jaw, Canada – 13 May
(Scottish names first): **Bantam:** K. Townsley l rsc 2 A. Kooner. **Feather:** J. Simpson l pts B. Gaudet. **Light:** M. Hastie w pts A. Decarie. **L. Welter:** K. Anderson w pts R. Romero. **Welter:** C. McNeil w rsc 3 R. Savage. **L. Middle:** C. McEwan l pts J. Pascal. **Middle:** S. McGuire l pts M. Walchuk. **L. Heavy:** L. Ramsay w pts J.

Hurst. **Heavy:** A. Young l pts J. Douglas. **S. Heavy:** I. Millarvie w pts D. Cadieux.

Young Ireland (5) v Young England (7)   National Stadium, Dublin – 7 June
(Irish names first): **L. Fly:** M. Brady l pts M. Gallet, P. Keyes l pts S. Leonard. **Fly:** D. Murphy w pts F. Gavin, G. Casey l pts E. Corcoran. **Bantam:** A. Hopkins w pts W. Bloomfield. **Feather:** E. Donovan w pts J. O'Donnell. **Light:** D. Toman w pts S. Kennedy. **L. Welter:** J. J. McDonagh l pts B. Rose. **Welter:** G. Hogan l pts N. Gittus. **L. Middle:** C. Tohill l rsc 2 J. Smythe. **Middle:** P. Lee w pts R. Collins. **L. Heavy:** M. Healy l pts D. Price.

Ireland (2) v Poland (6)   Ostroviec, Poland – 13 June
(Irish names first): **L. Fly:** J. P. Kinsella l pts T. Zajaczkowski. **Fly:** D. Campbell w pts Z. Kolacz. **Light:** A. Murray l pts A. Nycz. **L. Welter:** M. Kelly w pts A. Bojanowski. **Welter:** D. Conlon l rsc 2 M. Cendrowski. **Middle:** K. Egan l pts P. Wilczewski. **Heavy:** T. Sheahan l rsc 3 A. Kuziemski. **S. Heavy:** J. Upton l rsc 2 G. Kielsa.

Ireland (1) v Poland (5)   Sosnaviec, Poland – 15 June
(Irish names first): **Fly:** D. Campbell l pts Z. Kolacz. **Light:** A. Murray l pts R. Szikora. **L. Welter:** M. Kelly w pts S. Malinowski. **Welter:** D. Conlon l pts C. Naroznik. **Heavy:** T. Sheahan l rsc 2 A. Kuziemski. **S. Heavy:** J. Upton l rtd 1 G. Kielsa.

David Dolan, a regular England international at heavyweight   Les Clark

ABA Champions, 1881-2002

L. Flyweight

1971 M. Abrams
1972 M. Abrams
1973 M. Abrams
1974 C. Magri
1975 M. Lawless
1976 P. Fletcher
1977 P. Fletcher
1978 J. Dawson
1979 J. Dawson
1980 T. Barker
1981 J. Lyon
1982 J. Lyon
1983 J. Lyon
1984 J. Lyon
1985 M. Epton
1986 M. Epton
1987 M. Epton
1988 M. Cantwell
1989 M. Cantwell
1990 N. Tooley
1991 P. Culshaw
1992 D. Fifield
1993 M. Hughes
1994 G. Jones
1995 D. Fox
1996 R. Mercer
1997 I. Napa
1998 J. Evans
1999 G. Jones
2000 J. Mulherne
2001 C. Lyon
2002 D. Langley

Flyweight

1920 H. Groves
1921 W. Cuthbertson
1922 E. Warwick
1923 L. Tarrant
1924 E. Warwick
1925 E. Warwick
1926 J. Hill
1927 J. Roland
1928 C. Taylor
1929 T. Pardoe
1930 T. Pardoe
1931 T. Pardoe
1932 T. Pardoe
1933 T. Pardoe
1934 P. Palmer
1935 G. Fayaud
1936 G. Fayaud
1937 P. O'Donaghue
1938 A. Russell
1939 D. McKay
1944 J. Clinton
1945 J. Bryce
1946 R. Gallacher
1947 J. Clinton
1948 H. Carpenter
1949 H. Riley
1950 A. Jones
1951 G. John
1952 D. Dower
1953 R. Currie

1954 R. Currie
1955 D. Lloyd
1956 T. Spinks
1957 R. Davies
1958 J. Brown
1959 M. Gushlow
1960 D. Lee
1961 W. McGowan
1962 M. Pye
1963 M. Laud
1964 J. McCluskey
1965 J. McCluskey
1966 P. Maguire
1967 S. Curtis
1968 J. McGonigle
1969 D. Needham
1970 D. Needham
1971 P. Wakefield
1972 M. O'Sullivan
1973 R. Hilton
1974 M. O'Sullivan
1975 C. Magri
1976 C. Magri
1977 C. Magri
1978 G. Nickels
1979 R. Gilbody
1980 K. Wallace
1981 K. Wallace
1982 J. Kelly
1983 S. Nolan
1984 P. Clinton
1985 P. Clinton
1986 J. Lyon
1987 J. Lyon
1988 J. Lyon
1989 J. Lyon
1990 J. Armour
1991 P. Ingle
1992 K. Knox
1993 P. Ingle
1994 D. Costello
1995 D. Costello
1996 D. Costello
1997 M. Hunter
1998 J. Hegney
1999 D. Robinson
2000 D. Robinson
2001 M. Marsh
2002 D. Barriball

Bantamweight

1884 A. Woodward
1885 A. Woodward
1886 T. Isley
1887 T. Isley
1888 H. Oakman
1889 H. Brown
1890 J. Rowe
1891 E. Moore
1892 F. Godbold
1893 E. Watson
1894 P. Jones
1895 P. Jones
1896 P. Jones
1897 C. Lamb

1898 F. Herring
1899 A. Avent
1900 J. Freeman
1901 W. Morgan
1902 A. Miner
1903 H. Perry
1904 H. Perry
1905 W. Webb
1906 T. Ringer
1907 E. Adams
1908 H. Thomas
1909 J. Condon
1910 W. Webb
1911 W. Allen
1912 W. Allen
1913 A. Wye
1914 W. Allen
1919 W. Allen
1920 G. McKenzie
1921 L. Tarrant
1922 W. Boulding
1923 A. Smith
1924 L. Tarrant
1925 A. Goom
1926 F. Webster
1927 E. Warwick
1928 J. Garland
1929 F. Bennett
1930 H. Mizler
1931 F. Bennett
1932 J. Treadaway
1933 G. Johnston
1934 A. Barnes
1935 L. Case
1936 A. Barnes
1937 A. Barnes
1938 J. Pottinger
1939 R. Watson
1944 R. Bissell
1945 P. Brander
1946 C. Squire
1947 D. O'Sullivan
1948 T. Profitt
1949 T. Miller
1950 T. Lawrence
1951 T. Nicholls
1952 T. Nicholls
1953 J. Smillie
1954 J. Smillie
1955 G. Dormer
1956 O. Reilly
1957 J. Morrissey
1958 H. Winstone
1959 D. Weller
1960 F. Taylor
1961 P. Benneyworth
1962 P. Benneyworth
1963 B. Packer
1964 B. Packer
1965 R. Mallon
1966 J. Clark
1967 M. Carter
1968 M. Carter
1969 M. Piner
1970 A. Oxley
1971 G. Turpin

1972 G. Turpin
1973 P. Cowdell
1974 S. Ogilvie
1975 S. Ogilvie
1976 J. Bambrick
1977 J. Turner
1978 J. Turner
1979 R. Ashton
1980 R. Gilbody
1981 P. Jones
1982 R. Gilbody
1983 J. Hyland
1984 J. Hyland
1985 S. Murphy
1986 S. Murphy
1987 J. Sillitoe
1988 K. Howlett
1989 K. Howlett
1990 P. Lloyd
1991 D. Hardie
1992 P. Mullings
1993 R. Evatt
1994 S. Oliver
1995 N. Wilders
1996 L. Eedle
1997 S. Oates
1998 L. Pattison
1999 M. Hunter
2000 S. Foster
2001 S. Foster
2002 D. Matthews

Featherweight

1881 T. Hill
1882 T. Hill
1883 T. Hill
1884 E. Hutchings
1885 J. Pennell
1886 T. McNeil
1887 J. Pennell
1888 J. Taylor
1889 G. Belsey
1890 G. Belsey
1891 F. Curtis
1892 F. Curtis
1893 T. Davidson
1894 R. Gunn
1895 R. Gunn
1896 R. Gunn
1897 N. Smith
1898 P. Lunn
1899 J. Scholes
1900 R. Lee
1901 C. Clarke
1902 C. Clarke
1903 J. Godfrey
1904 C. Morris
1905 H. Holmes
1906 A. Miner
1907 C. Morris
1908 T. Ringer
1909 A. Lambert
1910 C. Houghton
1911 H. Bowers
1912 G. Baker

1913 G. Baker
1914 G. Baker
1919 G. Baker
1920 J. Fleming
1921 G. Baker
1922 E. Swash
1923 E. Swash
1924 A. Beavis
1925 A. Beavis
1926 R. Minshull
1927 F. Webster
1928 F. Meachem
1929 F. Meachem
1930 J. Duffield
1931 B. Caplan
1932 H. Mizler
1933 J. Walters
1934 J. Treadaway
1935 E. Ryan
1936 J. Treadaway
1937 A. Harper
1938 C. Gallie
1939 C. Gallie
1944 D. Sullivan
1945 J. Carter
1946 P. Brander
1947 S. Evans
1948 P. Brander
1949 H. Gilliland
1950 P. Brander
1951 J. Travers
1952 P. Lewis
1953 P. Lewis
1954 D. Charnley
1955 T. Nicholls
1956 T. Nicholls
1957 M. Collins
1958 M. Collins
1959 G. Judge
1960 P. Lundgren
1961 P. Cheevers
1962 B. Wilson
1963 A. Riley
1964 R. Smith
1965 K. Buchanan
1966 N. Baxter
1967 K. Cooper
1968 J. Cheshire
1969 A. Richardson
1970 D. Polak
1971 T. Wright
1972 K. Laing
1973 J. Lynch
1974 G. Gilbody
1975 R. Beaumont
1976 P. Cowdell
1977 P. Cowdell
1978 M. O'Brien
1979 P. Hanlon
1980 M. Hanif
1981 P. Hanlon
1982 H. Henry
1983 P. Bradley
1984 K. Taylor
1985 F. Havard
1986 P. Hodkinson

1987 P. English	1935 F. Frost	1953 D. Hughes	1970 D. Davies	1987 A. Holligan
1988 D. Anderson	1936 F. Simpson	1954 G. Martin	1971 M. Kingwell	1988 A. Hall
1989 P. Richardson	1937 A. Danahar	1955 F. McQuillan	1972 T. Waller	1989 A. Hall
1990 B. Carr	1938 T. McGrath	1956 D. Stone	1973 N. Cole	1990 J. Pender
1991 J. Irwin	1939 H. Groves	1957 D. Stone	1974 P. Kelly	1991 J. Matthews
1992 A. Temple	1944 W. Thompson	1958 R. Kane	1975 J. Zeraschi	1992 D. McCarrick
1993 J. Cook	1945 J. Williamson	1959 R. Kane	1976 C. McKenzie	1993 P. Richardson
1994 D. Pithie	1946 E. Thomas	1960 R. Day	1977 J. Douglas	1994 A. Temple
1995 D. Burrows	1947 C. Morrissey	1961 B. Brazier	1978 D. Williams	1995 A. Vaughan
1996 T. Mulholland	1948 R. Cooper	1962 B. Brazier	1979 E. Copeland	1996 C. Wall
1997 S. Bell	1949 A. Smith	1963 R. McTaggart	1980 A. Willis	1997 R. Hatton
1998 D. Williams	1950 R. Latham	1964 R. Taylor	1981 A. Willis	1998 N. Wright
1999 S. Miller	1951 R. Hinson	1965 R. McTaggart	1982 A. Adams	1999 D. Happe
2000 H. Castle	1952 F. Reardon	1966 W. Hiatt	1983 D. Dent	2000 N. Wright
2001 S. Bell	1953 D. Hinson	1967 B. Hudspeth	1984 D. Griffiths	2001 G. Smith
2002 D. Mulholland	1954 G. Whelan	1968 E. Cole	1985 I. Mustafa	2002 L. Daws

Lightweight

1881 F. Hobday
1882 A. Bettinson
1883 A. Diamond
1884 A. Diamond
1885 A. Diamond
1886 G. Roberts
1887 J. Hair
1888 A. Newton
1889 W. Neale
1890 A. Newton
1891 E. Dettmer
1892 E. Dettmer
1893 W. Campbell
1894 W. Campbell
1895 A. Randall
1896 A. Vanderhout
1897 A. Vanderhout
1898 H. Marks
1899 H. Brewer
1900 G. Humphries
1901 A. Warner
1902 A. Warner
1903 H. Fergus
1904 M. Wells
1905 M. Wells
1906 M. Wells
1907 M. Wells
1908 H. Holmes
1909 F. Grace
1910 T. Tees
1911 A. Spenceley
1912 R. Marriott
1913 R. Grace
1914 R. Marriott
1919 F. Grace
1920 F. Grace
1921 G. Shorter
1922 G. Renouf
1923 G. Shorter
1924 W. White
1925 E. Viney
1926 T. Slater
1927 W. Hunt
1928 F. Webster
1929 W. Hunt
1930 J. Waples
1931 D. McCleave
1932 F. Meachem
1933 H. Mizler
1934 J. Rolland

1955 S. Coffey
1956 R. McTaggart
1957 J. Kidd
1958 R. McTaggart
1959 P. Warwick
1960 R. McTaggart
1961 P. Warwick
1962 B. Whelan
1963 B. O'Sullivan
1964 J. Dunne
1965 A. White
1966 J. Head
1967 T. Waller
1968 J. Watt
1969 H. Hayes
1970 N. Cole
1971 J. Singleton
1972 N. Cole
1973 T. Dunn
1974 J. Lynch
1975 P. Cowdell
1976 S. Mittee
1977 G. Gilbody
1978 T. Marsh
1979 G. Gilbody
1980 G. Gilbody
1981 G. Gilbody
1982 J. McDonnell
1983 K. Willis
1984 A. Dickson
1985 E. McAuley
1986 J. Jacobs
1987 M. Ayers
1988 C. Kane
1989 M. Ramsey
1990 P. Gallagher
1991 P. Ramsey
1992 D. Amory
1993 B. Welsh
1994 A. Green
1995 R. Rutherford
1996 K. Wing
1997 M. Hawthorne
1998 A. McLean
1999 S. Burke
2000 A. McLean
2001 S. Burke
2002 A. Morris

L. Welterweight

1951 W. Connor
1952 P. Waterman

Lenny Daws (Rosehill ABC), one of two fighting brothers, seen here after landing the ABA light-welter title

Les Clark

Welterweight

1920 F. Whitbread
1921 A. Ireland
1922 E. White
1923 P. Green
1924 P. O'Hanrahan
1925 P. O'Hanrahan
1926 B. Marshall
1927 H. Dunn
1928 H. Bone
1929 T. Wigmore
1930 F. Brooman
1931 J. Barry
1932 D. McCleave
1933 P. Peters
1934 D. McCleave
1935 D. Lynch
1936 W. Pack
1937 D. Lynch
1938 C. Webster
1939 R. Thomas
1944 H. Hall
1945 R. Turpin
1946 J. Ryan
1947 J. Ryan
1948 M. Shacklady
1949 A. Buxton
1950 T. Ratcliffe
1951 J. Maloney
1952 J. Maloney
1953 L. Morgan
1954 N. Gargano
1955 N. Gargano
1956 N. Gargano
1957 R. Warnes
1958 B. Nancurvis
1959 J. McGrail
1960 C. Humphries
1961 A. Lewis
1962 J. Pritchett
1963 J. Pritchett
1964 M. Varley
1965 P. Henderson
1966 P. Cragg
1967 D. Cranswick
1968 A. Tottoh
1969 T. Henderson
1970 T. Waller
1971 D. Davies
1972 T. Francis
1973 T. Waller
1974 T. Waller
1975 W. Bennett
1976 C. Jones
1977 C. Jones
1978 E. Byrne
1979 J. Frost
1980 T. Marsh
1981 T. Marsh
1982 C. Pyatt
1983 R. McKenley
1984 M. Hughes
1985 E. McDonald
1986 D. Dyer
1987 M. Elliot
1988 M. McCreath
1989 M. Elliot
1990 A. Carew
1991 J. Calzaghe
1992 M. Santini
1993 C. Bessey
1994 K. Short
1995 M. Hall
1996 J. Khaliq
1997 F. Barrett
1998 D. Walker
1999 A. Cesay
2000 F. Doherty
2001 M. Macklin
2002 M. Lomax

L. Middleweight

1951 A. Lay
1952 B. Foster
1953 B. Wells
1954 B. Wells
1955 B. Foster
1956 J. McCormack
1957 J. Cunningham
1958 S. Pearson
1959 S. Pearson
1960 W. Fisher
1961 J. Gamble
1962 J. Lloyd
1963 A. Wyper
1964 W. Robinson
1965 P. Dwyer
1966 T. Imrie
1967 A. Edwards
1968 E. Blake
1969 T. Imrie
1970 D. Simmonds
1971 A. Edwards
1972 L. Paul
1973 R. Maxwell
1974 R. Maxwell
1975 A. Harrison
1976 W. Lauder
1977 C. Malarkey
1978 E. Henderson
1979 D. Brewster
1980 J. Price
1981 E. Christie
1982 D. Milligan
1983 R. Douglas
1984 R. Douglas
1985 R. Douglas
1986 T. Velinor
1987 N. Brown
1988 W. Ellis
1989 N. Brown
1990 T. Taylor
1991 T. Taylor
1992 J. Calzaghe
1993 D. Starie
1994 W. Alexander
1995 C. Bessey
1996 S. Dann
1997 C. Bessey
1998 C. Bessey
1999 C. Bessey
2000 C. Bessey
2001 M. Thirwall
2002 P. Smith

Middleweight

1881 T. Bellhouse
1882 A. H. Curnick
1883 A. J. Curnick
1884 W. Brown
1885 M. Salmon
1886 W. King
1887 R. Hair
1888 R. Hair
1889 G. Sykes
1890 J. Hoare
1891 J. Steers
1892 J. Steers
1893 J. Steers
1894 W. Sykes
1895 G. Townsend
1896 W. Ross
1897 W. Dees
1898 G. Townsend
1899 R. Warnes
1900 E. Mann
1901 R. Warnes
1902 E. Mann
1903 R. Warnes
1904 E. Mann
1905 J. Douglas
1906 A. Murdock
1907 R. Warnes
1908 W. Child
1909 W. Child
1910 R. Warnes
1911 W. Child
1912 E. Chandler
1913 W. Bradley
1914 H. Brown
1919 H. Mallin
1920 H. Mallin
1921 H. Mallin
1922 H. Mallin
1923 H. Mallin
1924 J. Elliot
1925 J. Elliot
1926 F. P. Crawley
1927 F. P. Crawley
1928 F. Mallin
1929 F. Mallin
1930 F. Mallin
1931 F. Mallin
1932 F. Mallin
1933 A. Shawyer
1934 J. Magill
1935 J. Magill
1936 A. Harrington
1937 M. Dennis
1938 H. Tiller
1939 H. Davies
1944 J. Hockley
1945 R. Parker
1946 R. Turpin
1947 R. Agland
1948 J. Wright
1949 S. Lewis
1950 P. Longo
1951 E. Ludlam
1952 T. Gooding
1953 R. Barton
1954 K. Phillips
1955 F. Hope
1956 R. Redrup
1957 P. Burke
1958 P. Hill
1959 F. Elderfield
1960 R. Addison
1961 J. Caiger
1962 A. Matthews
1963 A. Matthews
1964 W. Stack
1965 W. Robinson
1966 C. Finnegan
1967 A. Ball
1968 P. McCann
1969 D. Wallington
1970 J. Conteh
1971 A. Minter
1972 F. Lucas
1973 F. Lucas
1974 D. Odwell
1975 D. Odwell
1976 E. Burke
1977 R. Davies
1978 H. Graham
1979 N. Wilshire
1980 M. Kaylor
1981 B. Schumacher
1982 J. Price
1983 T. Forbes
1984 B. Schumacher
1985 D. Cronin
1986 N. Benn
1987 R. Douglas
1988 M. Edwards
1989 S. Johnson
1990 S. Wilson
1991 M. Edwards
1992 L. Woolcock
1993 J. Calzaghe
1994 D. Starie
1995 J. Matthews
1996 J. Pearce
1997 I. Cooper
1998 J. Pearce
1999 C. Froch
2000 S. Swales
2001 C. Froch
2002 N. Perkins

L. Heavyweight

1920 H. Franks
1921 L. Collett
1922 H. Mitchell
1923 H. Mitchell
1924 H. Mitchell
1925 H. Mitchell
1926 D. McCorkindale
1927 A. Jackson
1928 A. Jackson
1929 J. Goyder
1930 J. Murphy
1931 J. Petersen
1932 J. Goyder
1933 G. Brennan
1934 G. Brennan
1935 R. Hearns
1936 J. Magill
1937 J. Wilby
1938 A. S. Brown
1939 B. Woodcock
1944 E. Shackleton
1945 A. Watson
1946 J. Taylor
1947 A. Watson
1948 D. Scott
1949 *Declared no contest*
1950 P. Messervy
1951 G. Walker
1952 H. Cooper
1953 H. Cooper
1954 A. Madigan
1955 D. Rent
1956 D. Mooney
1957 T. Green
1958 J. Leeming
1959 J. Ould
1960 J. Ould
1961 J. Bodell
1962 J. Hendrickson
1963 P. Murphy
1964 J. Fisher
1965 E. Whistler
1966 R. Tighe
1967 M. Smith
1968 R. Brittle
1969 J. Frankham
1970 J. Rafferty
1971 J. Conteh
1972 W. Knight
1973 W. Knight
1974 W. Knight
1975 M. Heath
1976 G. Evans
1977 C. Lawson
1978 V. Smith
1979 A. Straughn
1980 A. Straughn
1981 A. Straughn
1982 G. Crawford
1983 A. Wilson
1984 A. Wilson
1985 J. Beckles
1986 J. Moran
1987 J. Beckles
1988 H. Lawson
1989 N. Piper
1990 J. McCluskey
1991 A. Todd
1992 K. Oliver
1993 K. Oliver
1994 K. Oliver
1995 K. Oliver
1996 C. Fry
1997 P. Rogers
1998 C. Fry
1999 J. Ainscough
2000 P. Haymer
2001 C. Fry
2002 T. Marsden

Cruiserweight

1998 T. Oakey
1999 M. Krence
2000 J. Dolan
2001 J. Dolan
2002 J. Dolan

Heavyweight

1881 R. Frost-Smith
1882 H. Dearsley

1883 H. Dearsley	1910 F. Storbeck	1945 D. Scott	1972 T. Wood	1999 S. St John
1884 H. Dearsley	1911 W. Hazell	1946 P. Floyd	1973 G. McEwan	2000 D. Dolan
1885 W. West	1912 R. Smith	1947 G. Scriven	1974 N. Meade	2001 D. Dolan
1886 A. Diamond	1913 R. Smith	1948 J. Gardner	1975 G. McEwan	2002 D. Dolan
1887 E. White	1914 E. Chandler	1949 A. Worrall	1976 J. Rafferty	
1888 W. King	1919 H. Brown	1950 P. Toch	1977 G. Adair	**S. Heavyweight**
1889 A. Bowman	1920 R. Rawson	1951 A. Halsey	1978 J. Awome	1982 A. Elliott
1890 J. Steers	1921 R. Rawson	1952 E. Hearn	1979 A. Palmer	1983 K. Ferdinand
1891 V. Barker	1922 T. Evans	1953 J. Erskine	1980 F. Bruno	1984 R. Wells
1892 J. Steers	1923 E. Eagan	1954 B. Harper	1981 A. Elliott	1985 G. Williamson
1893 J. Steers	1924 A. Clifton	1955 D. Rowe	1982 H. Hylton	1986 J. Oyebola
1894 H. King	1925 D. Lister	1956 D. Rent	1983 H. Notice	1987 J. Oyebola
1895 W. E. Johnstone	1926 T. Petersen	1957 D. Thomas	1984 D. Young	1988 K. McCormack
1896 W. E. Johnstone	1927 C. Capper	1958 D. Thomas	1985 H. Hylton	1989 P. Passley
1897 G. Townsend	1928 J. L. Driscoll	1959 D. Thomas	1986 E. Cardouza	1990 K. McCormack
1898 G. Townsend	1929 P. Floyd	1960 L. Hobbs	1987 J. Moran	1991 K. McCormack
1899 F. Parks	1930 V. Stuart	1961 W. Walker	1988 H. Akinwande	1992 M. Hopper
1900 W. Dees	1931 M. Flanagan	1962 R. Dryden	1989 H. Akinwande	1993 M. McKenzie
1901 F. Parks	1932 V. Stuart	1963 R. Sanders	1990 K. Inglis	1994 D. Watts
1902 F. Parks	1933 C. O'Grady	1964 C. Woodhouse	1991 P. Lawson	1995 R. Allen
1903 F. Dickson	1934 P. Floyd	1965 W. Wells	1992 S. Welch	1996 D. Watts
1904 A. Horner	1935 P. Floyd	1966 A. Brogan	1993 P. Lawson	1997 A. Harrison
1905 F. Parks	1936 V. Stuart	1967 P. Boddington	1994 S. Burford	1998 A. Harrison
1906 F. Parks	1937 V. Stuart	1968 W. Wells	1995 M. Ellis	1999 W. Bessey
1907 H. Brewer	1938 G. Preston	1969 A. Burton	1996 T. Oakey	2000 J. McDermott
1908 S. Evans	1939 A. Porter	1970 J. Gilmour	1997 B. Stevens	2001 M. Grainger
1909 C. Brown	1944 M. Hart	1971 L. Stevens	1998 N. Hosking	2002 M. Grainger

Matthew Grainger wins the ABA super-heavyweight title for the second year running, his opponent, Neil Hosking, having re-joined the 'Simon Pures' after just one pro contest

Les Clark

International Amateur Champions, 1904-2002

Shows all Olympic, World, European & Commonwealth champions since 1904. British silver and bronze medal winners are shown throughout, where applicable.

Country Code

ALG = Algeria; ARG = Argentina; ARM = Armenia; AUS = Australia; AUT = Austria; AZE = Azerbaijan; BE = Belarus; BEL = Belgium; BUL = Bulgaria; CAN = Canada; CEY = Ceylon (now Sri Lanka); CI = Channel Islands; CUB = Cuba; DEN = Denmark; DOM = Dominican Republic; ENG = England; ESP = Spain; EST = Estonia; FIJ = Fiji Islands; FIN = Finland; FRA = France; GBR = United Kingdom; GDR = German Democratic Republic; GEO = Georgia; GER = Germany (but West Germany only from 1968-1990); GHA = Ghana; GUY = Guyana; HOL = Netherlands; HUN = Hungary; IND = India; IRL = Ireland; ITA = Italy; JAM = Jamaica; JPN = Japan; KAZ = Kazakhstan; KEN = Kenya; LIT = Lithuania; MAS = Malaysia; MEX = Mexico; MRI = Mauritius; NKO = North Korea; NIG = Nigeria; NIR = Northern Ireland; NOR = Norway; NZL = New Zealand; PAK = Pakistan; POL = Poland; PUR = Puerto Rico; ROM = Romania; RUS = Russia; SAF = South Africa; SCO = Scotland; SKO = South Korea; SR = Southern Rhodesia; STV = St Vincent; SWE = Sweden; TCH = Czechoslovakia; THA = Thailand; TUR = Turkey; UGA = Uganda; UKR = Ukraine; URS = USSR; USA = United States of America; UZB = Uzbekistan; VEN = Venezuela; WAL = Wales; YUG = Yugoslavia; ZAM = Zambia.

Olympic Champions, 1904-2000

St Louis, USA - 1904
Fly: G. Finnegan (USA). **Bantam:** O. Kirk (USA). **Feather:** O. Kirk (USA). **Light:** H. Spangler (USA). **Welter:** A. Young (USA). **Middle:** C. May (USA). **Heavy:** S. Berger (USA).

London, England - 1908
Bantam: H. Thomas (GBR). **Feather:** R. Gunn (GBR). **Light:** F. Grace (GBR). **Middle:** J.W.H.T. Douglas (GBR). **Heavy:** A. Oldman (GBR).
Silver medals: J. Condon (GBR), C. Morris (GBR), F. Spiller (GBR), S. Evans (GBR).
Bronze medals: W. Webb (GBR), H. Rodding (GBR), T. Ringer (GBR), H. Johnson (GBR), R. Warnes (GBR), W. Philo (GBR), F. Parks (GBR).

Antwerp, Belgium - 1920
Fly: F. Genaro (USA). **Bantam:** C. Walker (SAF). **Feather:** R. Fritsch (FRA). **Light:** S. Mossberg (USA). **Welter:** T. Schneider (CAN). **Middle:** H. Mallin (GBR). **L. Heavy:** E. Eagan (USA). **Heavy:** R. Rawson (GBR).
Silver medal: A. Ireland (GBR).
Bronze medals: W. Cuthbertson (GBR), G. McKenzie (GBR), H. Franks (GBR).

Paris, France - 1924
Fly: F. la Barba (USA). **Bantam:** W. Smith (SAF). **Feather:** J. Fields (USA). **Light:** H. Nielson (DEN). **Welter:** J. Delarge (BEL). **Middle:** H. Mallin (GBR). **L. Heavy:** H. Mitchell (GBR). **Heavy:** O. von Porat (NOR).
Silver medals: J. McKenzie (GBR), J. Elliot (GBR).

Amsterdam, Holland - 1928
Fly: A. Kocsis (HUN). **Bantam:** V. Tamagnini (ITA). **Feather:** B. van Klaveren (HOL). **Light:** C. Orlando (ITA). **Welter:** E. Morgan (NZL). **Middle:** P. Toscani (ITA). **L. Heavy:** V. Avendano (ARG). **Heavy:** A. Rodriguez Jurado (ARG).

Los Angeles, USA - 1932
Fly: I. Enekes (HUN). **Bantam:** H. Gwynne (CAN). **Feather:** C. Robledo (ARG). **Light:** L. Stevens (SAF). **Welter:** E. Flynn (USA). **Middle:** C. Barth (USA). **L. Heavy:** D. Carstens (SAF). **Heavy:** A. Lovell (ARG).

Berlin, West Germany - 1936
Fly: W. Kaiser (GER). **Bantam:** U. Sergo (ITA). **Feather:** O. Casanova (ARG). **Light:** I. Harangi (HUN). **Welter:** S. Suvio (FIN). **Middle:** J. Despeaux (FRA). **L. Heavy:** R. Michelot (FRA). **Heavy:** H. Runge (GER).

London, England - 1948
Fly: P. Perez (ARG). **Bantam:** T. Csik (HUN). **Feather:** E. Formenti (ITA). **Light:** G. Dreyer (SAF). **Welter:** J. Torma (TCH). **Middle:** L. Papp (HUN). **L. Heavy:** G. Hunter (SAF). **Heavy:** R. Iglesas (ARG).
Silver medals: J. Wright (GBR), D. Scott (GBR).

Helsinki, Finland - 1952
Fly: N. Brooks (USA). **Bantam:** P. Hamalainen (FIN). **Feather:** J. Zachara (TCH). **Light:** A. Bolognesi (ITA). **L. Welter:** C. Adkins (USA). **Welter:** Z. Chychla (POL). **L. Middle:** L. Papp (HUN). **Middle:** F. Patterson (USA). **L. Heavy:** N. Lee (USA). **Heavy:** E. Sanders (USA).
Silver medal: J. McNally (IRL).

Melbourne, Australia - 1956
Fly: T. Spinks (GBR). **Bantam:** W. Behrendt (GER). **Feather:** V. Safronov (URS). **Light:** R. McTaggart (GBR). **L. Welter:** V. Jengibarian (URS). **Welter:** N. Linca (ROM). **L. Middle:** L. Papp (HUN). **Middle:** G. Schatkov (URS). **L. Heavy:** J. Boyd (USA). **Heavy:** P. Rademacher (USA).
Silver medals: T. Nicholls (GBR), F. Tiedt (IRL).
Bronze medals: J. Caldwell (IRL), F. Gilroy (IRL), A. Bryne (IRL), N. Gargano (GBR), J. McCormack (GBR).

Rome, Italy - 1960
Fly: G. Torok (HUN). **Bantam:** O. Grigoryev (URS). **Feather:** F. Musso (ITA). **Light:** K. Pazdzior (POL). **L. Welter:** B. Nemecek (TCH). **Welter:** N. Benvenuti (ITA). **L. Middle:** W. McClure (USA). **Middle:** E. Crook (USA). **L. Heavy:** C. Clay (USA). **Heavy:** F. de Piccoli (ITA).
Bronze medals: R. McTaggart (GBR), J. Lloyd (GBR), W. Fisher (GBR).

Tokyo, Japan - 1964
Fly: F. Atzori (ITA). **Bantam:** T. Sakurai (JPN). **Feather:** S. Stepashkin (URS). **Light:** J. Grudzien (POL). **L. Welter:** J. Kulej (POL). **Welter:** M. Kasprzyk (POL). **L. Middle:** B. Lagutin (URS). **Middle:** V. Popenchenko (URS). **L. Heavy:** C. Pinto (ITA). **Heavy:** J. Frazier (USA).
Bronze medal: J. McCourt (IRL).

Mexico City, Mexico - 1968
L. Fly: F. Rodriguez (VEN). **Fly:** R. Delgado (MEX). **Bantam:** V. Sokolov (URS). **Feather:** A. Roldan (MEX). **Light:** R. Harris (USA). **L. Welter:** J. Kulej (POL). **Welter:** M. Wolke (GDR). **L. Middle:** B. Lagutin (URS). **Middle:** C. Finnegan (GBR). **L. Heavy:** D. Poznyak (URS). **Heavy:** G. Foreman (USA).

Munich, West Germany - 1972
L. Fly: G. Gedo (HUN). **Fly:** G. Kostadinov (BUL). **Bantam:** O. Martinez (CUB). **Feather:** B. Kusnetsov (URS). **Light:** J. Szczepanski (POL). **L. Welter:** R. Seales (USA). **Welter:** E. Correa (CUB). **L. Middle:** D. Kottysch (GER). **Middle:** V. Lemeschev (URS). **L. Heavy:** M. Parlov (YUG). **Heavy:** T. Stevenson (CUB).
Bronze medals: R. Evans (GBR), G. Turpin (GBR), A. Minter (GBR).

Montreal, Canada - 1976
L. Fly: J. Hernandez (CUB). **Fly:** L. Randolph (USA). **Bantam:** Y-J. Gu (NKO). **Feather:** A. Herrera (CUB). **Light:** H. Davis (USA). **L. Welter:** R. Leonard (USA). **Welter:** J. Bachfield (GDR). **L. Middle:** J. Rybicki (POL). **Middle:** M. Spinks (USA). **L. Heavy:** L. Spinks (USA). **Heavy:** T. Stevenson (CUB).
Bronze medal: P. Cowdell (GBR).

Moscow, USSR - 1980
L. Fly: S. Sabirov (URS). **Fly:** P. Lessov (BUL). **Bantam:** J. Hernandez (CUB). **Feather:** R. Fink (GDR). **Light:** A. Herrera (CUB). **L. Welter:** P. Oliva (ITA). **Welter:** A. Aldama (CUB). **L. Middle:** A. Martinez (CUB). **Middle:** J. Gomez (CUB). **L. Heavy:** S. Kacar (YUG). **Heavy:** T. Stevenson (CUB).
Bronze medals: H. Russell (IRL), A. Willis (GBR).

Los Angeles, USA - 1984
L. Fly: P. Gonzalez (USA). **Fly:** S. McCrory (USA). **Bantam:** M. Stecca (ITA). **Feather:** M. Taylor (USA). **Light:** P. Whitaker (USA). **L. Welter:** J. Page (USA). **Welter:** M. Breland (USA). **L. Middle:** F. Tate (USA). **Middle:** J-S. Shin (SKO). **L. Heavy:** A. Josipovic (YUG). **Heavy:** H. Tillman (USA). **S. Heavy:** T. Biggs (USA).
Bronze medal: B. Wells (GBR).

Seoul, South Korea - 1988
L. Fly: I. Mustafov (BUL). **Fly:** H-S. Kim (SKO). **Bantam:** K. McKinney (USA). **Feather:** G. Parisi (ITA). **Light:** A. Zuelow (GDR). **L. Welter:** V. Yanovsky (URS). **Welter:** R. Wangila (KEN). **L. Middle:** S-H. Park (SKO). **Middle:** H. Maske (GDR). **L. Heavy:** A. Maynard (USA). **Heavy:** R. Mercer (USA). **S. Heavy:** L. Lewis (CAN).
Bronze medal: R. Woodhall (GBR).

Barcelona, Spain - 1992
L. Fly: R. Marcelo (CUB). **Fly:** C-C. Su (NKO). **Bantam:** J. Casamayor (CUB). **Feather:** A. Tews (GER). **Light:** O. de la Hoya (USA). **L. Welter:** H. Vinent (CUB). **Welter:** M. Carruth (IRL). **L. Middle:** J. Lemus (CUB). **Middle:** A. Hernandez (CUB). **L. Heavy:** T. May (GER). **Heavy:** F. Savon (CUB). **S. Heavy:** R. Balado (CUB).
Silver medal: W. McCullough (IRL).
Bronze medal: R. Reid (GBR).

Atlanta, USA - 1996
L. Fly: D. Petrov (BUL). **Fly:** M. Romero (CUB). **Bantam:** I. Kovaks (HUN). **Feather:** S. Kamsing (THA). **Light:** H. Soltani (ALG). **L. Welter:** H. Vinent (CUB). **Welter:** O. Saitov (RUS). **L. Middle:** D. Reid (USA). **Middle:** A. Hernandez (CUB). **L. Heavy:** V. Jirov (KAZ). **Heavy:** F. Savon (CUB). **S. Heavy:** Vladimir Klitschko (UKR).

Sydney, Australia - 2000
L. Fly: B. Aslom (FRA). **Fly:** W. Ponlid (THA). **Bantam:** G. Rigondeaux Ortiz (CUB). **Feather:** B. Sattarkhanov (KAZ). **Light:** M. Kindelan (CUB). **L. Welter:** M. Abdullaev (UZB). **Welter:** O. Saitov (RUS). **L. Middle:** Y. Ibraimov (KAZ). **Middle:** J. Gutierrez Espinosa (CUB). **L. Heavy:** A. Lebziak (RUS). **Heavy:** F. Savon (CUB). **S. Heavy:** A. Harrison (ENG).

World Champions, 1974-2001

Havana, Cuba - 1974
L. Fly: J. Hernandez (CUB). **Fly:** D. Rodriguez (CUB). **Bantam:** W. Gomez (PUR). **Feather:** H. Davis (CUB). **Light:** V. Solomin (URS). **L. Welter:** A. Kalule (UGA). **Welter:** E. Correa (CUB). **L. Middle:** R. Garbey (CUB). **Middle:** R. Riskiev (URS). **L. Heavy:** M. Parlov (YUG). **Heavy:** T. Stevenson (CUB).

Belgrade, Yugoslavia - 1978
L. Fly: S. Muchoki (KEN). **Fly:** H. Strednicki (POL). **Bantam:** A. Horta (CUB). **Feather:** A. Herrera (CUB). **Light:** D. Andeh (NIG). **L. Welter:** V. Lvov (URS). **Welter:** V. Rachkov (URS). **L. Middle:** V. Savchenko (URS). **Middle:** J. Gomez (CUB). **L. Heavy:** S. Soria (CUB). **Heavy:** T. Stevenson (CUB).

Munich, West Germany - 1982
L. Fly: I. Mustafov (BUL). **Fly:** Y. Alexandrov (URS). **Bantam:** F. Favors (USA). **Feather:** A. Horta (CUB). **Light:** A. Herrera (CUB). **L. Welter:** C. Garcia (CUB). **Welter:** M. Breland (USA). **L. Middle:** A. Koshkin (URS). **Middle:** B. Comas (CUB). **L. Heavy:** P. Romero (CUB). **Heavy:** A. Jagubkin (URS). **S. Heavy:** T. Biggs (USA).
Bronze medal: T. Corr (IRL).

Reno, USA - 1986
L. Fly: J. Odelin (CUB). **Fly:** P. Reyes (CUB). **Bantam:** S-I. Moon (SKO). **Feather:** K. Banks (USA). **Light:** A. Horta (CUB). **L. Welter:** V. Shishov (URS). **Welter:** K. Gould (USA). **L. Middle:** A. Espinosa (CUB). **Middle:** D. Allen (USA). **L. Heavy:** P. Romero (CUB). **Heavy:** F. Savon (CUB). **S. Heavy:** T. Stevenson (CUB).

Moscow, USSR - 1989
L. Fly: E. Griffin (USA). **Fly:** Y. Arbachakov (URS). **Bantam:** E. Carrion (CUB). **Feather:** A. Khamatov (URS). **Light:** J. Gonzalez (CUB). **L. Welter:** I. Ruzinkov (URS). **Welter:** F. Vastag (Rom). **L. Middle:** I. Akopokhian (URS). **Middle:** A. Kurniavka (URS). **L. Heavy:** H. Maske (GDR). **Heavy:** F. Savon (CUB). **S. Heavy:** R. Balado (CUB).
Bronze medal: M. Carruth (IRL).

Sydney, Australia - 1991
L. Fly: E. Griffin (USA). **Fly:** I. Kovacs (HUN). **Bantam:** S. Todorov (BUL). **Feather:** K. Kirkorov (BUL). **Light:** M. Rudolph (GER). **L. Welter:** K. Tsziu (URS). **Welter:** J. Hernandez (CUB). **L. Middle:** J. Lemus (CUB). **Middle:** T. Russo (ITA). **L. Heavy:** T. May (GER). **Heavy:** F. Savon (CUB). **S. Heavy:** R. Balado (CUB).

Tampere, Finland - 1993
L. Fly: N. Munchian (ARM). **Fly:** W. Font (CUB). **Bantam:** A. Christov (BUL). **Feather:** S. Todorov (BUL). **Light:** D. Austin (CUB). **L. Welter:** H. Vinent (CUB). **Welter:** J. Hernandez (CUB). **L. Middle:** F. Vastag

(ROM). **Middle:** A. Hernandez (CUB). **L. Heavy:** R. Garbey (CUB). **Heavy:** F. Savon (CUB). **S. Heavy:** R. Balado (CUB).
Bronze medal: D. Kelly (IRL).

Berlin, Germany - 1995
L. Fly: D. Petrov (BUL). **Fly:** Z. Lunka (GER). **Bantam:** R. Malachbekov (RUS). **Feather:** S. Todorov (BUL). **Light:** L. Doroftel (ROM). **L. Welter:** H. Vinent (CUB). **Welter:** J. Hernandez (CUB). **L. Middle:** F. Vastag (ROM). **Middle:** A. Hernandez (CUB). **L. Heavy:** A. Tarver (USA). **Heavy:** F. Savon (CUB). **S. Heavy:** A. Lezin (RUS).

Budapest, Hungary - 1997
L. Fly: M. Romero (CUB). **Fly:** M. Mantilla (CUB). **Bantam:** R Malakhbekov (RUS). **Feather:** I. Kovacs (HUN). **Light:** A. Maletin (RUS). **L. Welter:** D. Simion (ROM). **Welter:** O. Saitov (RUS). **L. Middle:** A. Duvergel (CUB). **Middle:** Z. Erdei (HUN). **L. Heavy:** A. Lebsiak (RUS). **Heavy:** F. Savon (CUB). **S. Heavy:** G. Kandelaki (GEO).
Bronze medal: S. Kirk (IRL).

Houston, USA - 1999
L. Fly: B. Viloria (USA). **Fly:** B. Jumadilov (KAZ). **Bantam:** R. Crinu (ROM). **Feather:** R. Juarez (USA). **Light:** M. Kindelan (CUB). **L. Welter:** M. Abdullaev (UZB). **Welter:** J. Hernandez (CUB). **L. Middle:** M. Simion (ROM). **Middle:** U. Haydarov (UZB). **L. Heavy:** M. Simms (USA). **Heavy:** M. Bennett (USA). **S. Heavy:** S. Samilsan (TUR).
Bronze medal: K. Evans (WAL).

Belfast, Northern Ireland - 2001
L. Fly: Y. Bartelemi Varela (CUB). **Fly:** J. Thomas (FRA). **Bantam:** G. Rigondeaux Ortiz (CUB). **Feather:** R. Palyani (TUR). **Light:** M. Kindelan Mesa (CUB). **L. Welter:** D. Luna Martinez (CUB). **Welter:** L. Aragon Armenteros (CUB). **L. Middle:** D. Austin Echemendia (CUB). **Middle:** A. Gogolev (RUS). **L. Heavy:** E. Makarenko (RUS). **Heavy:** O. Solis Fonte (CUB). **S. Heavy:** R. Chagaev (UZB).
Silver medal: D. Haye (ENG).
Bronze medals: J. Moore (IRL), C. Froch (ENG).

World Junior Champions, 1979-2000

Yokohama, Japan - 1979
L. Fly: R. Shannon (USA). **Fly:** P. Lessov (BUL). **Bantam:** P-K. Choi (SKO). **Feather:** Y. Gladychev (URS). **Light:** R. Blake (USA). **L. Welter:** I. Akopokhian (URS). **Welter:** M. McCrory (USA). **L. Middle:** A. Mayes (USA). **Middle:** A. Milov (URS). **L. Heavy:** A. Lebedev (URS). **Heavy:** M. Frazier (USA).
Silver medals: N. Wilshire (ENG), D. Cross (ENG).
Bronze medal: I. Scott (SCO).

Santo Domingo, Dominican Republic - 1983
L. Fly: M. Herrera (DOM). **Fly:** J. Gonzalez (CUB). **Bantam:** J. Molina (PUR). **Feather:** A. Miesses (DOM). **Light:** A. Beltre (DOM). **L. Welter:** A. Espinoza (CUB). **Welter:** M. Watkins (USA). **L. Middle:** U. Castillo (CUB). **Middle:** R. Batista (CUB). **L. Heavy:** O. Pought (USA). **Heavy:** A. Williams (USA). **S. Heavy:** L. Lewis (CAN).

Bucharest, Romania - 1985
L. Fly: R-S. Hwang (SKO). **Fly:** T. Marcelica (ROM). **Bantam:** R. Diaz (CUB). **Feather:** D. Maeran (ROM). **Light:** J. Teiche (GDR). **L. Welter:** W. Saeger (GDR). **Welter:** A. Stoianov (BUL). **L. Middle:** M. Franek (TCH). **Middle:** O. Zahalotskih (URS). **L. Heavy:** B. Riddick (USA). **Heavy:** F. Savon (CUB). **S. Heavy:** A. Prianichnikov (URS).

Havana, Cuba - 1987
L. Fly: E. Paisan (CUB). **Fly:** C. Daniels (USA). **Bantam:** A. Moya (CUB). **Feather:** G. Iliyasov (URS). **Light:** J. Hernandez (CUB). **L. Welter:** L. Mihai (ROM). **Welter:** F. Vastag (ROM). **L. Middle:** A. Lobsyak (URS). **Middle:** W. Martinez (CUB). **L. Heavy:** D. Yeliseyev (URS). **Heavy:** R. Balado (CUB). **S. Heavy:** L. Martinez (CUB).
Silver medal: E. Loughran (IRL).
Bronze medal: D. Galvin (IRL).

San Juan, Puerto Rico - 1989
L. Fly: D. Petrov (BUL). **Fly:** N. Monchai (FRA). **Bantam:** J. Casamayor (CUB). **Feather:** C. Febres (PUR). **Light:** A. Acevedo (PUR). **L. Welter:** E. Berger (GDR). **Welter:** A. Hernandez (CUB). **L. Middle:** L. Bedey (CUB). **Middle:** R. Garbey (CUB). **L. Heavy:** R. Alvarez (CUB). **Heavy:** K. Johnson (CAN). **S. Heavy:** A. Burdiantz (URS).
Silver medals: E. Magee (IRL), R. Reid (ENG), S. Wilson (SCO).

Lima, Peru - 1990
L. Fly: D. Alicea (PUR). **Fly:** K. Pielert (GDR). **Bantam:** K. Baravi (URS). **Feather:** A. Vaughan (ENG). **Light:** J. Mendez (CUB). **L. Welter:** H.

Vinent (CUB). **Welter:** A. Hernandez (CUB). **L. Middle:** A. Kakauridze (URS). **Middle:** J. Gomez (CUB). **L. Heavy:** B. Torsten (GDR). **Heavy:** I. Andreev (URS). **S. Heavy:** J. Quesada (CUB).
Bronze medal: P. Ingle (ENG).

Montreal, Canada - 1992
L. Fly: W. Font (CUB). **Fly:** J. Oragon (CUB). **Bantam:** N. Machado (CUB). **Feather:** M. Stewart (CAN). **Light:** D. Austin (CUB). **L. Welter:** O. Saitov (RUS). **Welter:** L. Brors (GER). **L. Middle:** J. Acosta (CUB). **Middle:** I. Arsangaliev (RUS). **L. Heavy:** S. Samilsan (TUR). **Heavy:** G. Kandeliaki (GEO). **S. Heavy:** M. Porchnev (RUS).
Bronze medal: N. Sinclair (IRL).

Istanbul, Turkey - 1994
L. Fly: J. Turunen (FIN). **Fly:** A. Jimenez (CUB). **Bantam:** J. Despaigne (CUB). **Feather:** D. Simion (ROM). **Light:** L. Diogenes (CUB). **L. Welter:** V. Romero (CUB). **Welter:** E. Aslan (TUR). **L. Middle:** G. Ledsvanys (CUB). **Middle:** M. Genc (TUR). **L. Heavy:** P. Aurino (ITA). **Heavy:** M. Lopez (CUB). **S. Heavy:** P. Carrion (CUB).

Havana, Cuba - 1996
L. Fly: L. Hernandez (CUB). **Fly:** L. Cabrera (CUB). **Bantam:** P. Miradal (CUB). **Feather:** E. Rodriguez (CUB). **Light:** R. Vaillan (CUB). **L. Welter:** T. Mergadze (RUS). **Welter:** J. Brahmer (GER). **L. Middle:** L. Mezquia (CUB). **Middle:** V. Pletniov (RUS). **L. Heavy:** O. Simon (CUB). **Heavy:** A. Yatsenko (UKR). **S. Heavy:** S. Fabre (CUB).
Bronze medal: R. Hatton (ENG).

Buenos Aires, Argentina - 1998
L. Fly: S. Tanasie (ROM). **Fly:** S. Yeledov (KAZ). **Bantam:** S. Suleymanov (UKR). **Feather:** I. Perez (ARG). **Light:** A. Solopov (RUS). **L. Welter:** Y. Tomashov (UKR). **Welter:** K. Oustarkhanov (RUS). **L. Middle:** S. Kostenko (UKR). **Middle:** M. Kempe (GER). **L. Heavy:** H. Yohanson Martinez (CUB). **Heavy:** O. Solis Fonte (CUB). **S. Heavy:** B. Ohanyan (ARM).
Silver medal: H. Cunningham (IRL).
Bronze medal: D. Campbell (IRL).

Budapest, Hungary - 2000
L. Fly: Y. Leon Alarcon (CUB). **Fly:** O. Franco Vaszquez (CUB). **Bantam:** V. Tajbert (GER). **Feather:** G. Kate (HUN). **Light:** F. Adzsanalov (AZE). **L. Welter:** G. Galovkin (KAZ). **Welter:** S. Ustunel (TUR). **L. Middle:** D. Chernysh (RUS). **Middle:** F. Sullivan Barrera (CUB). **L. Heavy:** A. Shekmourov (RUS). **Heavy:** D., Medzhydov (UKR). **S. Heavy:** A. Dmitrienko (RUS).
Bronze medal: C. Barrett (IRL).

European Champions, 1924-2002

Paris, France - 1924
Fly: J. McKenzie (GBR). **Bantam:** J. Ces (FRA). **Feather:** R. de Vergnie (BEL). **Light:** N. Nielsen (DEN). **Welter:** J. Delarge (BEL). **Middle:** H. Mallin (GBR). **L. Heavy:** H. Mitchell (GBR). **Heavy:** O. von Porat (NOR).

Stockholm, Sweden - 1925
Fly: E. Pladner (FRA). **Bantam:** A. Rule (GBR). **Feather:** P. Andren (SWE). **Light:** S. Johanssen (SWE). **Welter:** H. Nielsen (DEN). **Middle:** F. Crawley (GBR). **L. Heavy:** T. Petersen (DEN). **Heavy:** B. Persson (SWE). **Silver medals:** J. James (GBR), E. Viney (GBR), D. Lister (GBR).

Berlin, Germany - 1927
Fly: L. Boman (SWE). **Bantam:** K. Dalchow (GER). **Feather:** F. Dubbers (GER). **Light:** H. Domgoergen (GER). **Welter:** R. Caneva (ITA). **Middle:** J. Christensen (NOR). **L. Heavy:** H. Muller (GER). **Heavy:** N. Ramm (SWE).

Amsterdam, Holland - 1928
Fly: A. Kocsis (HUN). **Bantam:** V. Tamagnini (ITA). **Feather:** B. van Klaveren (HOL). **Light:** C. Orlandi (ITA). **Welter:** R. Galataud (FRA). **Middle:** P. Toscani (ITA). **L. Heavy:** E. Pistulla (GER). **Heavy:** N. Ramm (SWE).

Budapest, Hungary - 1930
Fly: I. Enekes (HUN). **Bantam:** J. Szeles (HUN). **Feather:** G. Szabo (HUN). **Light:** M. Bianchini (ITA). **Welter:** J. Besselmann (GER). **Middle:** C. Meroni (ITA). **L. Heavy:** T. Petersen (DEN). **Heavy:** J. Michaelson (DEN).

Los Angeles, USA - 1932
Fly: I. Enekes (HUN). **Bantam:** H. Ziglarski (GER). **Feather:** J. Schleinkofer (GER). **Light:** T. Ahlqvist (SWE). **Welter:** E. Campe (GER). **Middle:** R. Michelot (FRA). **L. Heavy:** G. Rossi (ITA). **Heavy:** L. Rovati (ITA).

Budapest, Hungary - 1934
Fly: P. Palmer (GBR). **Bantam:** I. Enekes (HUN). **Feather:** O. Kaestner GER). **Light:** E. Facchini (ITA). **Welter:** D. McCleave (GBR). **Middle:** S. Szigetti (HUN). **L. Heavy:** P. Zehetmayer (AUT). **Heavy:** G. Baerlund (FIN).
Bronze medal: P. Floyd (GBR).

Milan, Italy - 1937
Fly: I. Enekes (HUN). **Bantam:** U. Sergo (ITA). **Feather:** A. Polus (POL). **Light:** H. Nuremberg (GER). **Welter:** M. Murach (GER). **Middle:** H. Chmielewski (POL). **L. Heavy:** S. Szigetti (HUN). **Heavy:** O. Tandberg (SWE).

Dublin, Eire - 1939
Fly: J. Ingle (IRL). **Bantam:** U. Sergo (ITA). **Feather:** P. Dowdall (IRL). **Light:** H. Nuremberg (GER). **Welter:** A. Kolczyski (POL). **Middle:** A. Raadik (EST). **L. Heavy:** L. Musina (ITA). **Heavy:** O. Tandberg (SWE).
Bronze medal: C. Evenden (IRL).

Dublin, Eire - 1947
Fly: L. Martinez (ESP). **Bantam:** L. Bogacs (HUN). **Feather:** K. Kreuger (SWE). **Light:** J. Vissers (BEL). **Welter:** J. Ryan (ENG). **Middle:** A. Escudie (FRA). **L. Heavy:** H. Quentemeyer (HOL). **Heavy:** G. O'Colmain (IRL).
Silver medals: J. Clinton (SCO), P. Maguire (IRL), W. Thom (ENG), G. Scriven (ENG).
Bronze medals: J. Dwyer (SCO), A. Sanderson (ENG), W. Frith (SCO), E. Cantwell (IRL), K. Wyatt (ENG).

Oslo, Norway - 1949
Fly: J. Kasperczak (POL). **Bantam:** G. Zuddas (ITA). **Feather:** J. Bataille (FRA). **Light:** M. McCullagh (IRL). **Welter:** J. Torma (TCH). **Middle:** L. Papp (HUN). **L. Heavy:** G. di Segni (ITA). **Heavy:** L. Bene (HUN).
Bronze medal: D. Connell (IRL).

Milan, Italy - 1951
Fly: A. Pozzali (ITA). **Bantam:** V. Dall'Osso (ITA). **Feather:** J. Ventaja (FRA). **Light:** B. Visintin (ITA). **L. Welter:** H. Schelling (GER). **Welter:** Z. Chychla (POL). **L. Middle:** L. Papp (HUN). **Middle:** S. Sjolin (SWE). **L. Heavy:** M. Limage (BEL). **Heavy:** G. di Segni (ITA).
Silver medal: J. Kelly (IRL).
Bronze medals: D. Connell (IRL), T. Milligan (IRL), A. Lay (ENG).

Warsaw, Poland - 1953
Fly: H. Kukier (POL). **Bantam:** Z. Stefaniuk (POL). **Feather:** J. Kruza (POL). **Light:** V. Jengibarian (URS). **L. Welter:** L. Drogosz (POL). **Welter:** Z. Chychla (POL). **L. Middle:** B. Wells (ENG). **Middle:** D. Wemhoner (GER). **L. Heavy:** U. Nietchke (GER). **Heavy:** A. Schotzikas (URS).
Silver medal: T. Milligan (IRL).
Bronze medals: J. McNally (IRL), R. Barton (ENG).

Berlin, West Germany - 1955
Fly: E. Basel (GER). **Bantam:** Z. Stefaniuk (POL). **Feather:** T. Nicholls (ENG). **Light:** H. Kurschat (GER). **L. Welter:** L. Drogosz (POL). **Welter:** N. Gargano (ENG). **L. Middle:** Z. Pietrzykowski (POL). **Middle:** G. Schatkov (URS). **L. Heavy:** E. Schoeppner (GER). **Heavy:** A. Schotzikas (URS).

Prague, Czechoslovakia - 1957
Fly: M. Homberg (GER). **Bantam:** O. Grigoryev (URS). **Feather:** D. Venilov (BUL). **Light:** K. Pazdzior (POL). **L. Welter:** V. Jengibarian (URS). **Welter:** M. Graus (GER). **L. Middle:** N. Benvenuti (ITA). **Middle:** Z. Pietrzykowski (POL). **L. Heavy:** G. Negrea (ROM). **Heavy:** A. Abramov (URS).
Bronze medals: R. Davies (WAL), J. Morrissey (SCO), J. Kidd (SCO), F. Teidt (IRL).

Lucerne, Switzerland - 1959
Fly: M. Homberg (GER). **Bantam:** H. Rascher (GER). **Feather:** J. Adamski (POL). **Light:** O. Maki (FIN). **L. Welter:** V. Jengibarian (URS). **Welter:** L. Drogosz (POL). **L. Middle:** N. Benvenuti (ITA). **Middle:** G. Schatkov (URS). **L. Heavy:** Z. Pietrzykowski (POL). **Heavy:** A. Abramov (URS).
Silver medal: D. Thomas (ENG).
Bronze medals: A. McClean (IRL), H. Perry (IRL), C. McCoy (IRL), H. Scott (ENG).

Belgrade, Yugoslavia - 1961
Fly: P. Vacca (ITA). **Bantam:** S. Sivko (URS). **Feather:** F. Taylor (ENG). **Light:** R. McTaggart (SCO). **L. Welter:** A. Tamulis (URS). **Welter:** R. Tamulis (URS). **L. Middle:** B. Lagutin (URS). **Middle:** T. Walasek (POL).

L. Heavy: G. Saraudi (ITA). **Heavy:** A. Abramov (URS).
Bronze medals: P. Warwick (ENG), I. McKenzie (SCO), J. Bodell (ENG).

Moscow, USSR - 1963
Fly: V. Bystrov (URS). **Bantam:** O. Grigoryev (URS). **Feather:** S. Stepashkin (URS). **Light:** J. Kajdi (HUN). **L. Welter:** J. Kulej (POL). **Welter:** R. Tamulis (URS). **L. Middle:** B. Lagutin (URS). **Middle:** V. Popenchenko (URS). **L. Heavy:** Z. Pietrzykowski (POL). **Heavy:** J. Nemec (TCH).
Silver medal: A. Wyper (SCO).

Berlin, East Germany - 1965
Fly: H. Freisdadt (GER). **Bantam:** O. Grigoryev (URS). **Feather:** S. Stepashkin (URS). **Light:** V. Barranikov (URS). **L. Welter:** J. Kulej (POL). **Welter:** R. Tamulis (URS). **L. Middle:** V. Ageyev (URS). **Middle:** V. Popenchenko (URS). **L. Heavy:** D. Poznyak (URS). **Heavy:** A. Isosimov (URS).
Silver medal: B. Robinson (ENG).
Bronze medals: J. McCluskey (SCO), K. Buchanan (SCO), J. McCourt (IRL).

Rome, Italy - 1967
Fly: H. Skrzyczak (POL). **Bantam:** N. Giju (ROM). **Feather:** R. Petek (POL). **Light:** J. Grudzien (POL). **L. Welter:** V. Frolov (URS). **Welter:** B. Nemecek (TCH). **L. Middle:** V. Ageyev (URS). **Middle:** M. Casati (ITA). **L. Heavy:** D. Poznyak (URS). **Heavy:** M. Baruzzi (ITA).
Silver medal: P. Boddington (ENG).

Bucharest, Romania - 1969
L. Fly: G. Gedo (HUN). **Fly:** C. Ciuca (ROM). **Bantam:** A. Dumitrescu (ROM). **Feather:** L. Orban (HUN). **Light:** S. Cutov (ROM). **L. Welter:** V. Frolov (URS). **Welter:** G. Meier (GER). **L. Middle:** V. Tregubov (URS). **Middle:** V. Tarasenkov (URS). **L. Heavy:** D. Poznyak (URS). **Heavy:** I. Alexe (ROM).
Bronze medals: M. Dowling (IRL), M. Piner (ENG), A. Richardson (ENG), T. Imrie (ENG).

Madrid, Spain - 1971
L. Fly: G. Gedo (HUN). **Fly:** J. Rodriguez (ESP). **Bantam:** T. Badar (HUN). **Feather:** R. Tomczyk (POL). **Light:** J. Szczepanski (POL). **L. Welter:** U. Beyer (GER). **Welter:** J. Kajdi (HUN). **L. Middle:** V. Tregubov (URS). **Middle:** J. Juotsiavitchus (URS). **L. Heavy:** M. Parlov (YUG). **Heavy:** V. Tchernishev (URS).
Bronze medals: N. McLaughlin (IRL), M. Dowling (IRL), B. McCarthy (IRL), M. Kingwell (ENG), L. Stevens (ENG).

Belgrade, Yugoslavia - 1973
L. Fly: V. Zasypko (URS). **Fly:** C. Gruescu (ROM). **Bantam:** A. Cosentino (FRA). **Feather:** S. Forster (GDR). **Light:** S. Cutov (ROM). **L. Welter:** M. Benes (YUG). **Welter:** S. Csjef (HUN). **L. Middle:** A. Klimanov (URS). **Middle:** V. Lemechev (URS). **L. Heavy:** M. Parlov (YUG). **Heavy:** V. Ulyanich (URS).
Bronze medal: J. Bambrick (SCO).

Katowice, Poland - 1975
L. Fly: A. Tkachenko (URS). **Fly:** V. Zasypko (URS). **Bantam:** V. Rybakov (URS). **Feather:** T. Badari (HUN). **Light:** S. Cutov (ROM). **L. Welter:** V. Limasov (URS). **Welter:** K. Marjaama (FIN). **L. Middle:** W. Rudnowski (POL). **Middle:** V. Lemechev (URS). **L. Heavy:** A. Klimanov (URS). **Heavy:** A. Biegalski (POL).
Bronze medals: C. Magri (ENG), P. Cowdell (ENG), G. McEwan (ENG).

Halle, East Germany - 1977
L. Fly: H. Srednicki (POL). **Fly:** L. Blazynski (POL). **Bantam:** S. Forster (GDR). **Feather:** R. Nowakowski (GDR). **Light:** A. Rusevski (YUG). **L. Welter:** B. Gajda (POL). **Welter:** V. Limasov (URS). **L. Middle:** V. Saychenko (URS). **Middle:** I. Shaposhnikov (URS). **L. Heavy:** D. Kvachadze (URS). **Heavy:** E. Gorstkov (URS).
Bronze medal: P. Sutcliffe (IRL).

Cologne, West Germany - 1979
L. Fly: S. Sabirov (URS). **Fly:** H. Strednicki (POL). **Bantam:** N. Khrapzov (URS). **Feather:** V. Rybakov (URS). **Light.** V. Demianenko (URS). **L. Welter:** S. Konakbaev (URS). **Welter:** E. Muller (GER). **L. Middle:** M. Perunovic (YUG). **Middle:** T. Uusiverta (FIN). **L. Heavy:** A. Nikolyan (URS). **Heavy:** E. Gorstkov (URS). **S. Heavy:** P. Hussing (GER).
Bronze medal: P. Sutcliffe (IRL).

Tampere, Finland - 1981
L. Fly: I. Mustafov (BUL). **Fly:** P. Lessov (BUL). **Bantam:** V. Miroschnichenko (URS). **Feather:** R. Nowakowski (GDR). **Light:** V. Rybakov (URS). **L. Welter:** V. Shisov (URS). **Welter:** S. Konakvbaev (URS). **L. Middle:** A. Koshkin (URS). **Middle:** J. Torbek (URS). **L.**

Heavy: A Krupin (URS). **Heavy:** A. Jagupkin (URS). **S. Heavy:** F. Damiani (ITA).
Bronze medal: G. Hawkins (IRL).

Varna, Bulgaria - 1983
L. Fly: I. Mustafov (BUL). **Fly:** P. Lessov (BUL). **Bantam:** Y. Alexandrov (URS). **Feather:** S. Nurkazov (URS). **Light:** E. Chuprenski (BUL). **L. Welter:** V. Shishov (URS). **Welter:** P. Galkin (URS). **L. Middle:** V. Laptev (URS). **Middle:** V. Melnik (URS). **L. Heavy:** V. Kokhanovski (URS). **Heavy:** A. Jagubkin (URS). **S. Heavy:** F. Damiani (ITA).
Bronze medal: K. Joyce (IRL).

Budapest, Hungary - 1985
L. Fly: R. Breitbarth (GDR). **Fly:** D. Berg (GDR). **Bantam:** L. Simic (YUG). **Feather:** S. Khachatrian (URS). **Light:** E. Chuprenski (BUL) **L. Welter:** S. Mehnert (GDR). **Welter:** I. Akopokhian (URS). **L. Middle:** M. Timm (GDR). **Middle:** H. Maske (GDR). **L. Heavy:** N. Shanavasov (URS). **Heavy:** A. Jagubkin (URS). **S. Heavy:** F. Somodi (HUN).
Bronze medals: S. Casey (IRL), J. Beckles (ENG).

Turin, Italy - 1987
L. Fly: N. Munchyan (URS). **Fly:** A. Tews (GDR). **Bantam:** A. Hristov (BUL). **Feather:** M. Kazaryan (URS). **Light:** O. Nazarov (URS). **L. Welter:** B. Abadjier (BUL). **Welter:** V. Shishov (URS). **L. Middle:** E. Richter (GDR). **Middle:** H. Maske (GDR). **L. Heavy:** Y. Vaulin (URS). **Heavy:** A. Vanderlijde (HOL). **S. Heavy:** U. Kaden (GDR).
Bronze medal: N. Brown (ENG).

Athens, Greece - 1989
L. Fly: I.Mustafov (BUL). **Fly:** Y. Arbachakov (URS). **Bantam:** S. Todorov (BUL). **Feather:** K. Kirkorov (BUL). **Light:** K. Tsziu (URS). **L. Welter:** I. Ruznikov (URS). **Welter:** S. Mehnert (GDR). **L. Middle:** I. Akopokhian (URS). **Middle:** H. Maske (GDR). **L. Heavy:** S. Lange (GDR). **Heavy:** A. Vanderlijde (HOL). **S. Heavy:** U. Kaden (GDR).
Bronze Medal: D. Anderson (SCO).

Gothenburg, Sweden - 1991
L. Fly: I. Marinov (BUL). **Fly:** I. Kovacs (HUN). **Bantam:** S. Todorov (BUL). **Feather:** P. Griffin (IRL). **Light:** V. Nistor (ROM). **L. Welter:** K. Tsziu (URS). **Welter:** R. Welin (SWE). **L. Middle:** I. Akopokhian (URS). **Middle:** S. Otke (GER). **L. Heavy:** D. Michalczewski (GER). **Heavy:** A. Vanderlijde (HOL). **S. Heavy:** E. Beloussov (URS).
Bronze medals: P. Weir (SCO), A. Vaughan (ENG).

Bursa, Turkey - 1993
L. Fly: D. Petrov (BUL). **Fly:** R. Husseinov (AZE). **Bantam:** R. Malakhbetov (RUS). **Feather:** S. Todorov (BUL). **Light:** J. Bielski (POL). **L. Welter:** N. Suleymanogiu (TUR). **Welter:** V. Karpaclauskas (LIT). **L. Middle:** F. Vastag (ROM). **Middle:** D. Eigenbrodt (GER). **L. Heavy:** I. Kshinin (RUS). **Heavy:** G. Kandelaki (GEO). **S. Heavy:** S. Rusinov (BUL).
Bronze medals: P. Griffin (IRL), D. Williams (ENG), K. McCormack (WAL).

Vejle, Denmark - 1996
L. Fly: D. Petrov (BUL). **Fly:** A. Pakeev (RUS). **Bantam:** I. Kovacs (HUN). **Feather:** R. Paliani (RUS). **Light:** L. Doroftei (ROM). **L. Welter:** O. Urkal (GER). **Welter:** H. Al (DEN). **L. Middle:** F. Vastag (ROM). **Middle:** S. Ottke (GER). **L. Heavy:** P. Aurino (ITA). **Heavy:** L. Krasniqi (GER). **S. Heavy:** A. Lezin (RUS).
Bronze medals: S. Harrison (SCO), D. Burke (ENG), D. Kelly (IRL).

Minsk, Belarus - 1998
L. Fly: S. Kazakov (RUS). **Fly:** V. Sidorenko (UKR). **Bantam:** S. Danilchenko (UKR). **Feather:** R. Paliani (TUR). **Light:** K. Huste (GER). **L. Welter:** D. Simion (ROM). **Welter:** O. Saitov (RUS). **L. Middle:** F. Esther (FRA). **Middle:** Z. Erdei (HUN). **L. Heavy:** A. Lebsiak (RUS). **Heavy:** G. Fragomeni (ITA). **S. Heavy:** A. Lezin (RUS).
Silver Medals: B. Magee (IRL), C. Fry (ENG).
Bronze medal: C. Bessey (ENG).

Tampere, Finland - 2000
L. Fly: Valeri Sidorenko (UKR). **Fly:** Vladimir Sidorenko (UKR). **Bantam:** A. Agagueloglu (TUR). **Feather:** R. Paliani (TUR). **Light:** A. Maletin (RUS). **L. Welter:** A. Leonev (RUS). **Welter:** B. Ueluesoy (TUR). **L. Middle:** A. Catic (GER). **Middle:** Z. Erdei (HUN). **L. Heavy:** A. Lebsiak (RUS). **Heavy:** J. Chanet (FRA). **S. Heavy:** A. Lezin (RUS).

Perm, Russia - 2002
L. Fly: S. Kazakov (RUS). **Fly:** G. Balakshin (RUS). **Bantam:** K. Khatsygov (BE). **Feather:** R. Malakhbekov (RUS). **Light:** A. Maletin (RUS). **L. Welter:** D. Panayotov (BUL). **Welter:** T. Gaidalov (RUS). **L.**

Middle: A. Mishin (RUS). **Middle:** O. Mashkin (UKR). **L. Heavy:** M. Gala (RUS). **Heavy:** E. Makarenko (RUS). **S. Heavy:** A. Povetkin (RUS).

Note: Gold medals were awarded to the Europeans who went the furthest in the Olympic Games of 1924, 1928 & 1932.

European Junior Champions, 1970-2001

Miskolc, Hungary - 1970
L. Fly: Gluck (HUN). **Fly:** Z. Kismeneth (HUN). **Bantam:** A. Levitschev (URS). **Feather:** Andrianov (URS). **Light:** L. Juhasz (HUN). **L. Welter:** K. Nemec (HUN). **Welter:** Davidov (URS). **L. Middle:** A. Lemeschev (URS). **Middle:** N. Anfimov (URS). **L. Heavy:** O. Sasche (GDR). **Heavy:** J. Reder (HUN).
Bronze medals: D. Needham (ENG), R. Barlow (ENG), L. Stevens (ENG).

Bucharest, Romania - 1972
L. Fly: A. Turei (ROM). **Fly:** Condurat (ROM). **Bantam:** V. Solomin (URS). **Feather:** V. Lvov (URS). **Light:** S. Cutov (ROM). **L. Welter:** K. Pierwieniecki (POL). **Welter:** Zorov (URS). **L. Middle:** Babescu (ROM). **Middle:** V. Lemeschev (URS). **L. Heavy:** Mirounik (URS). **Heavy:** Subutin (URS).
Bronze medals: J. Gale (ENG), R. Maxwell (ENG), D. Odwell (ENG).

Kiev, Russia - 1974
L. Fly: A. Tkachenko (URS). **Fly:** V. Rybakov (URS). **Bantam:** C. Andreikovski (BUL). **Feather:** V. Sorokin (URS). **Light:** V. Limasov (URS). **L. Welter:** N. Sigov (URS). **Welter:** M. Bychkov (URS). **L. Middle:** V. Danshin (URS). **Middle:** D. Jende (GDR). **L. Heavy:** K. Dafinoiu (ROM). **Heavy:** K. Mashev (BUL).
Silver medal: C. Magri (ENG).
Bronze medals: G. Gilbody (ENG), K. Laing (ENG).

Izmir, Turkey - 1976
L. Fly: C. Seican (ROM). **Fly:** G. Khratsov (URS). **Bantam:** M. Navros (URS). **Feather:** V. Demoianeko (URS). **Light:** M. Puzovic (YUG). **L. Welter:** V. Zverev (URS). **Welter:** K. Ozoglouz (TUR). **L. Middle:** W. Lauder (SCO). **Middle:** H. Lenhart (GER). **L. Heavy:** I. Yantchauskas (URS). **Heavy:** B. Enjenyan (URS).
Silver medal: J. Decker (ENG).
Bronze medals: I. McLeod (SCO), N. Croombes (ENG).

Dublin, Ireland - 1978
L. Fly: R. Marx (GDR). **Fly:** D. Radu (ROM). **Bantam:** S. Khatchatrian (URS). **Feather:** H. Loukmanov (URS). **Light:** P. Oliva (ITA). **L. Welter:** V. Laptiev (URS). **Welter:** R. Filimanov (URS). **L. Middle:** A. Beliave (URS). **Middle:** G. Zinkovitch (URS). **L. Heavy:** I. Jolta (ROM). **Heavy:** P. Stoimenov (BUL).
Silver medals: M. Holmes (IRL), P. Hanlon (ENG), M. Courtney (ENG).
Bronze medals: T. Thompson (IRL), J. Turner (ENG), M. Bennett (WAL), J. McAllister (SCO), C. Devine (ENG).

Rimini, Italy - 1980
L. Fly: A. Mikoulin (URS). **Fly:** J. Varadi (HUN). **Bantam:** F. Rauschning (GDR). **Feather:** J. Gladychev (URS). **Light:** V. Shishov (URS). **L. Welter:** R. Lomski (BUL). **Welter:** T. Holonics (GDR). **L. Middle:** N. Wilshire (ENG). **Middle:** S. Laptiev (URS). **L. Heavy:** V. Dolgoun (URS). **Heavy:** V. Tioumentsev (URS). **S. Heavy:** S. Kormihtsine (URS).
Bronze medals: N. Potter (ENG), B. McGuigan (IRL), M. Brereton (IRL), D. Cross (ENG).

Schwerin, East Germany - 1982
L. Fly: R. Kabirov (URS). **Fly:** I. Filchev (BUL). **Bantam:** M. Stecca (ITA). **Feather:** B. Blagoev (BUL). **Light:** E. Chakimov (URS). **L. Welter:** S. Mehnert (URS). **Welter:** T. Schmitz (GDR). **L. Middle:** B. Shararov (URS). **Middle:** E. Christie (ENG). **L. Heavy:** Y. Waulin (URS). **Heavy:** A. Popov (URS). **S. Heavy:** V. Aldoshin (URS).
Silver medal: D. Kenny (ENG).
Bronze medal: O. Jones (ENG).

Tampere, Finland - 1984
L. Fly: R. Breitbart (GDR). **Fly:** D. Berg (GDR). **Bantam:** K. Khdrian (URS). **Feather:** O. Nazarov (URS). **Light:** C. Furnikov (BUL). **L. Welter:** W. Schmidt (GDR). **Welter:** K. Doinov (BUL). **L. Middle:** O. Volkov (URS). **Middle:** R. Ryll (GDR). **L. Heavy:** G. Peskov (URS). **Heavy:** R. Draskovic (YUG). **S. Heavy:** L. Kamenov (BUL).
Bronze medals: J. Lowey (IRL), F. Harding (ENG), N. Moore (ENG).

Copenhagen, Denmark - 1986
L. Fly: S. Todorov (BUL). **Fly:** S. Galotian (URS). **Bantam:** D. Drumm (GDR). **Feather:** K. Tsziu (URS). **Light:** G. Akopkhian (URS). **L. Welter:**

F. Vastag (ROM). **Welter:** S. Karavayev (URS). **L. Middle:** E. Elibaev (URS). **Middle:** A. Kurnabka (URS). **L. Heavy:** A. Schultz (GDR). **Heavy:** A. Golota (POL). **S. Heavy:** A. Prianichnikov (URS).

Gdansk, Poland - 1988
L. Fly: I. Kovacs (HUN). **Fly:** M. Beyer (GDR). **Bantam:** M. Aitzanov (URS). **Feather:** M. Rudolph (GDR). **Light:** M. Shaburov (URS). **L. Welter:** G. Campanella (ITA). **Welter:** D. Konsun (URS). **L. Middle:** K. Kiselev (URS). **Middle:** A. Rudenko (URS). **L. Heavy:** O. Velikanov (URS). **Heavy:** A. Ter-Okopian (URS). **S. Heavy:** E. Belusov (URS).
Bronze medals: P. Ramsey (ENG), M. Smyth (WAL).

Usti Nad Labem, Czechoslovakia - 1990
L. Fly: Z. Paliani (URS). **Fly:** K. Pielert (GDR). **Bantam:** K. Baravi (URS). **Feather:** P. Gvasalia (URS). **Light:** J. Hildenbrandt (GDR). **L. Welter:** N. Smanov (URS). **Welter:** A. Preda (ROM). **L. Middle:** A. Kakauridze (URS). **Middle:** J. Schwank (GDR). **L. Heavy:** Iljin (URS). **Heavy:** I. Andrejev (URS). **S. Heavy:** W. Fischer (GDR).
Silver medal: A. Todd (ENG).
Bronze medal: P. Craig (ENG).

Edinburgh, Scotland - 1992
L. Fly: M. Ismailov (URS). **Fly:** F. Brennfuhrer (GER). **Bantam:** S. Kuchler (GER). **Feather:** M. Silantiev (URS). **Light:** S. Shcherbakov (URS). **L. Welter:** O. Saitov (URS). **Welter:** H. Kurlumaz (TUR). **L. Middle:** Z. Erdie (HUN). **Middle:** V. Zhirov (URS). **L. Heavy:** D. Gorbachev (URS). **Heavy:** L. Achkasov (URS). **S. Heavy:** A. Mamedov (URS).
Silver medals: M. Hall (ENG), B. Jones (WAL).
Bronze medals: F. Slane (IRL), G. Stephens (IRL), C. Davies (WAL).

Salonika, Greece - 1993
L. Fly: O. Kiroukhine (UKR). **Fly:** R. Husseinov (AZE). **Bantam:** M. Kulbe (GER). **Feather:** E. Zakharov (RUS). **Light:** O. Sergeev (RUS). **L. Welter:** A. Selihanov (RUS). **Welter:** O. Kudinov (UKR). **L. Middle:** E. Makarenko (RUS). **Middle:** D. Droukovski (RUS). **L. Heavy:** A. Voida (RUS). **Heavy:** Vladimir Klitschko (UKR). **S. Heavy:** A. Moiseev (RUS).
Bronze medal: D. Costello (ENG).

Sifok, Hungary - 1995
L. Fly: D. Gaissine (RUS). **Fly:** A. Kotelnik (UKR). **Bantam:** A. Loutsenko (UKR). **Feather:** S. Harrison (SCO). **Light:** D. Simon (ROM). **L. Welter:** B. Ulusoy (TUR). **Welter:** O. Bouts (UKR). **L. Middle:** O. Bukalo (UKR). **Middle:** V. Plettnev (RUS). **L. Heavy:** A. Derevtsov (RUS). **Heavy:** C. O'Grady (IRL). **S. Heavy:** D. Savvine (RUS).
Silver medal: G. Murphy (SCO).
Bronze medal: N. Linford (ENG).

Birmingham, England - 1997
L. Fly: G. Balakshine (RUS). **Fly:** K. Dzhamoloudinov (RUS). **Bantam:** A. Shaiduline (RUS). **Feather:** D. Marciukaitis (LIT). **Light:** D. Baranov (RUS). **L. Welter:** A. Mishine (RUS). **Welter:** D. Yuldashev (UKR). **L. Middle:** A. Catic (GER). **Middle:** D. Lebedev (RUS). **L. Heavy:** V. Uzelkov (RUS). **Heavy:** S. Koeber (GER). **S. Heavy:** D. Pirozhenko (RUS).
Silver medal: S. Miller (ENG).
Bronze medals: S. Burke (ENG), M. Dean (ENG), P. Pierson (ENG), M. Lee (IRE).

Rijeka, Croatia - 1999
L. Fly: Kibalyuk (UKR). **Fly:** A. Bakhtin (RUS). **Bantam:** V. Simion (ROM). **Feather:** Kiutkhukow (BUL). **Light:** Pontilov (RUS). **L. Welter:** G. Ajetovic (YUG). **Welter:** S. Nouaouria (FRA). **L. Middle:** S. Kazantsev (RUS). **Middle:** D. Tsariouk (RUS). **L. Heavy:** Alexeev (RUS). **Heavy:** Alborov (RUS). **S. Heavy:** Soukhoverkov (RUS).
Bronze medal: S. Birch (ENG).

Sarejevo, Croatia - 2001
L. Fly: A. Taratokin (RUS). **Fly:** E. Abzalimov (RUS). **Bantam:** G. Kovaljov (RUS). **Feather:** M. Hratchev (RUS). **Light:** S. Aydin (TUR). **L. Welter:** D. Mikulin (RUS). **Welter:** O. Bokalo (UKR). **L. Middle:** M. Korobov (RUS). **Middle:** I. Bogdanov (UKR). **L. Heavy:** R. Kahkijev (RUS). **Heavy:** V. Zuyev (BE). **S. Heavy:** I. Timurziejev (RUS).
Bronze medal: K. Anderson (SCO).

Note: The age limit for the championships were reduced from 21 to 19 in 1976.

Commonwealth Champions, 1930-2002

Hamilton, Canada - 1930
Fly: W. Smith (SAF). **Bantam:** H. Mizler (ENG). **Feather:** F. Meacham

(ENG). **Light:** J. Rolland (SCO). **Welter:** L. Hall (SAF). **Middle:** F. Mallin (ENG). **L. Heavy:** J. Goyder (ENG). **Heavy:** V. Stuart (ENG).
Silver medals: T. Pardoe (ENG), T. Holt (SCO).
Bronze medals: A. Lyons (SCO), A. Love (ENG), F. Breeman (ENG).

Wembley, England - 1934
Fly: P. Palmer (ENG). **Bantam:** F. Ryan (ENG). **Feather:** C. Cattarall (SAF). **Light:** L. Cook (AUS). **Welter:** D. McCleave (ENG). **Middle:** A. Shawyer (ENG). **L. Heavy:** G. Brennan (ENG). **Heavy:** P. Floyd (ENG).
Silver medals: A. Barnes (WAL), J. Jones (WAL), F. Taylor (WAL), J. Holton (SCO).
Bronze medals: J. Pottinger (WAL), T. Wells (SCO), H. Moy (ENG), W. Duncan (NIR), J. Magill (NIR), Lord D. Douglas-Hamilton (SCO).

Melbourne, Australia - 1938
Fly: J. Joubert (SAF). **Bantam:** W. Butler (ENG). **Feather:** A. Henricus (CEY). **Light:** H. Groves (ENG). **Welter:** W. Smith (AUS). **Middle:** D. Reardon (WAL). **L. Heavy:** N. Wolmarans (SAF). **Heavy:** T. Osborne (CAN).
Silver medals: J. Watson (SCO), M. Dennis (ENG).
Bronze medals: H. Cameron (SCO), J. Wilby (ENG).

Auckland, New Zealand - 1950
Fly: H. Riley (SCO). **Bantam:** J. van Rensburg (SAF). **Feather:** H. Gilliland (SCO). **Light:** R. Latham (ENG). **Welter:** T. Ratcliffe (ENG). **Middle:** T. van Schalkwyk (SAF). **L. Heavy:** D. Scott (ENG). **Heavy:** F. Creagh (NZL).
Bronze medal: P. Brander (ENG).

Vancouver, Canada - 1954
Fly: R. Currie (SCO). **Bantam:** J. Smillie (SCO). **Feather:** L. Leisching (SAF). **Light:** P. van Staden (SR). **L. Welter:** M. Bergin (CAN). **Welter:** N. Gargano (ENG). **L. Middle:** W. Greaves (CAN). **Middle:** J. van de Kolff (SAF). **L. Heavy:** P. van Vuuren (SAF). **Heavy:** B. Harper (ENG).
Silver medals: M. Collins (WAL), F. McQuillan (SCO).
Bronze medals: D. Charnley (ENG), B. Wells (ENG).

Cardiff, Wales - 1958
Fly: J. Brown (SCO). **Bantam:** H. Winstone (WAL). **Feather:** W. Taylor (AUS). **Light:** R. McTaggart (SCO). **L. Welter:** H. Loubscher (SAF). **Welter:** J. Greyling (SAF). **L. Middle:** G. Webster (SAF). **Middle:** T. Milligan (NIR). **L. Heavy:** A. Madigan (AUS). **Heavy:** D. Bekker (SAF).
Silver medals: T. Bache (ENG), M. Collins (WAL), J. Jordan (NIR), R. Kane (SCO), S. Pearson (ENG), A. Higgins (WAL), D. Thomas (ENG).
Bronze medals: P. Lavery (NIR), D. Braithwaite (WAL), R. Hanna (NIR), A. Owen (SCO), J. McClory (NIR), J. Cooke (ENG), J. Jacobs (ENG), B. Nancurvis (ENG), R. Scott (SCO), W. Brown (WAL), J. Caiger (ENG), W. Bannon (SCO), R. Pleace (WAL).

Perth, Australia - 1962
Fly: R. Mallon (SCO). **Bantam:** J. Dynevor (AUS). **Feather:** J. McDermott (SCO). **L. Light:** E. Blay (GHA). **L. Welter:** C. Quartey (GHA). **Welter:** W. Coe (NZL). **L. Middle:** H. Mann (CAN). **Middle:** M. Calhoun (JAM). **L. Heavy:** A. Madigan (AUS). **Heavy:** G. Oywello (UGA).
Silver medals: R. McTaggart (SCO), J. Pritchett (ENG).
Bronze medals: M. Pye (ENG), P. Benneyworth (ENG), B. Whelan (ENG), B. Brazier (ENG), C. Rice (NIR), T. Menzies (SCO), H. Christie (NIR), A. Turmel (CI).

Kingston, Jamaica - 1966
Fly: S. Shittu (GHA). **Bantam:** E. Ndukwu (NIG). **Feather:** P. Waruinge (KEN). **Light:** A. Andeh (NIG). **L. Welter:** J. McCourt (NIR). **Welter:** E. Blay (GHA). **L. Middle:** M. Rowe (ENG). **Middle:** J. Darkey (GHA). **L. Heavy:** R. Tighe (ENG). **Heavy:** W. Kini (NZL).
Silver medals: P. Maguire (NIR), R. Thurston (ENG), R. Arthur (ENG), T. Imrie (SCO).
Bronze medals: S. Lockhart (NIR), A. Peace (SCO), F. Young (NIR), J. Turpin (ENG), D. McAlinden (NIR).

Edinburgh, Scotland - 1970
L. Fly: J. Odwori (UGA). **Fly:** D. Needham (ENG). **Bantam:** S. Shittu (GHA). **Feather:** P. Waruinge (KEN). **Light:** A. Adeyemi (NIG). **L. Welter:** M. Muruli (UGA). **Welter:** E. Ankudey (GHA). **L. Middle:** T. Imrie (SCO). **Middle:** J. Conteh (ENG). **L. Heavy:** F. Ayinla (NIG). **Heavy:** B. Masanda (UGA).
Silver medals: T. Davies (WAL), J. Gillan (SCO), D. Davies (WAL), J. McKinty (NIR).
Bronze medals: M. Abrams (ENG), A. McHugh (SCO), D. Larmour (NIR), S. Oglivie (SCO), A. Richardson (ENG), T. Joyce (SCO), P. Doherty (NIR), J. Rafferty (SCO), L. Stevens (ENG).

Christchurch, New Zealand - 1974
L. Fly: S. Muchoki (KEN). **Fly:** D. Larmour (NIR). **Bantam:** P. Cowdell

(ENG). **Feather:** E. Ndukwu (NIG). **Light:** A. Kalule (UGA). **L. Welter:** O. Nwankpa (NIG). **Welter:** M. Muruli (UGA). **L. Middle:** L. Mwale (ZAM). **Middle:** F. Lucas (STV). **L. Heavy:** W. Knight (ENG). **Heavy:** N. Meade (ENG).
Silver medals: E. McKenzie (WAL), A. Harrison (SCO).
Bronze medals: J. Bambrick (SCO), J. Douglas (SCO), J. Rodgers (NIR), S. Cooney (SCO), R. Davies (ENG), C. Speare (ENG), G. Ferris (NIR).

Edmonton, Canada - 1978
L. Fly: S. Muchoki (KEN). **Fly:** M. Irungu (KEN). **Bantam:** B. McGuigan (NIR). **Feather:** A. Nelson (GHA). **Light:** G. Hamill (NIR). **L. Welter:** W. Braithwaite (GUY). **Welter:** M. McCallum (JAM). **L. Middle:** K. Perlette (CAN). **Middle:** P. McElwaine (AUS). **L. Heavy:** R. Fortin (CAN). **Heavy:** J. Awome (ENG).
Silver medals: J. Douglas (SCO), K. Beattie (NIR), D. Parkes (ENG), V. Smith (ENG).
Bronze medals: H. Russell (NIR), M. O'Brien (ENG), J. McAllister (SCO), T. Feal (WAL).

Brisbane, Australia - 1982
L. Fly: A. Wachire (KEN). **Fly:** M. Mutua (KEN). **Bantam:** J. Orewa (NIG). **Feather:** P. Konyegwachie (NIG). **Light:** H. Khalili (KEN). **L. Welter:** C. Ossai (NIG). **Welter:** C. Pyatt (ENG). **L. Middle:** S. O'Sullivan (CAN). **Middle:** J. Price (ENG). **L. Heavy:** F. Sani (FIJ). **Heavy:** W. de Wit (CAN).
Silver medals: J. Lyon (ENG), J. Kelly (SCO), R. Webb (NIR), P. Hanlon (ENG), J. McDonnell (ENG), N. Croombes (ENG), H. Hylton (ENG).
Bronze medals: R. Gilbody (ENG), C. McIntosh (ENG), R. Corr (NIR).

Edinburgh, Scotland - 1986
L. Fly: S. Olson (CAN). **Fly:** J. Lyon (ENG). **Bantam:** S. Murphy (ENG). **Feather:** B. Downey (CAN). **Light:** A. Dar (CAN). **L. Welter:** H. Grant (CAN). **Welter:** D. Dyer (ENG). **L. Middle:** D. Sherry (CAN). **Middle:** R. Douglas (ENG). **L. Heavy:** J. Moran (ENG). **Heavy:** J. Peau (NZL). **S. Heavy:** L. Lewis (CAN).
Silver medals: M. Epton (ENG), R. Nash (NIR), P. English (ENG), N. Haddock (WAL), J. McAlister (SCO), H. Lawson (SCO), D. Young (SCO), A. Evans (WAL).
Bronze medals: W. Docherty (SCO), J. Todd (NIR), K. Webber (WAL), G. Brooks (SCO), J. Wallace (SCO), C. Carleton (NIR), J. Jacobs (ENG), B. Lowe (NIR), D. Denny (NIR), G. Thomas (WAL), A. Mullen (SCO), G. Ferrie (SCO), P. Tinney (NIR), B. Pullen (WAL), E. Cardouza (ENG), J. Oyebola (ENG), J. Sillitoe (CI).

Auckland, New Zealand - 1990
L. Fly: J. Juuko (UGA). **Fly:** W. McCullough (NIR). **Bantam:** S. Mohammed (NIG). **Feather:** J. Irwin (ENG). **Light:** G. Nyakana (UGA). **L. Welter:** C. Kane (SCO). **Welter:** D. Defiagbon (NIG). **L. Middle:** R. Woodhall (ENG). **Middle:** C. Johnson (CAN). **L. Heavy:** J. Akhasamba (KEN). **Heavy:** G. Onyango (KEN). **S. Heavy:** M. Kenny (NZL).
Bronze medals: D. Anderson (SCO), M. Edwards (ENG), P. Douglas (NIR).

Victoria, Canada - 1994
L. Fly: H. Ramadhani (KEN). **Fly:** P. Shepherd (SCO). **Bantam:** R. Peden (AUS). **Feather:** C. Patton (CAN). **Light:** M. Strange (CAN). **L. Welter:** P. Richardson (ENG). **Welter:** N. Sinclair (NIR). **L. Middle:** J. Webb (NIR). **Middle:** R. Donaldson (CAN). **L. Heavy:** D. Brown (CAN). **Heavy:** O. Ahmed (KEN). **S. Heavy:** D. Dokiwari (NIG).
Silver medals: S. Oliver (ENG), J. Cook (WAL), M. Renaghan (NIR), M. Winters (NIR), J. Wilson (SCO).
Bronze medals: D. Costello (ENG), J. Townsley (SCO), D. Williams (ENG).

Kuala Lumpar, Malaysia - 1998
L. Fly: S. Biki (MAS). **Fly:** R. Sunee (MRI). **Bantam:** M. Yomba (TAN). **Feather:** A. Arthur (SCO). **Light:** R. Narh (GHA). **L. Welter:** M. Strange (CAN). **Welter:** J. Molitor (CAN). **L. Middle:** C. Bessey (ENG). **Middle:** J. Pearce (ENG). **L. Heavy:** C. Fry (ENG). **Heavy:** M. Simmons (CAN). **S. Heavy:** A. Harrison (ENG).
Silver medal: L. Cunningham (NIR).
Bronze medals: G. Jones (ENG), A. McLean (ENG), C. McNeil (SCO), J. Townsley (SCO), B. Magee (NIR), K. Evans (WAL).

Manchester, England - 2002
L. Fly: M. Ali Qamar (IND). **Fly:** K. Kanyanta (ZAM). **Bantam:** J. Kane (AUS). **Feather:** H. Ali (PAK). **Light:** J. Arthur (WAL). **L. Welter:** D. Barker (ENG). **Welter:** D. Geale (AUS). **L. Middle:** J. Pascal (CAN). **Middle:** P. Miller (AUS). **L. Heavy:** J. Albert (NIG). **Heavy:** J. Douglas (CAN). **S. Heavy:** D. Dolan (ENG).
Silver medals: D. Langley (ENG), P. Smith (ENG), S. Birch (ENG).
Bronze medals: M. Moran (ENG), A. Morris (ENG), C. McEwan (SCO), A. Young (SCO), K. Evans (WAL).

British Junior Championship Finals, 2001-2002

National Association of Clubs for Young People (NACYP)

Britannia Adelphi Hotel, Liverpool – 4 December

Class A: L. Fort (Jim Driscoll's) wo J. McDonnell (Hatfield). 45 kg: P. Edwards (Salisbury) w pts T. Mills (St Mary's). 48 kg: L. Allon (St Paul's) w rtd 3 C. Minter (Dale Youth). 51 kg: J. Trotman (Medway Golden Gloves) w pts J. McElvaney (South Bank). 54 kg: B. Saunders (Spennymoor) w pts R. Ward (Dagenham). 57 kg: W. Bilan (Denbeath) w pts S. Turner (Lawrence). 60 kg: R. Pickard (Repton) w pts C. Mullen (Horsley Hill). 63. 5 kg: E. Brook (St Thomas') w pts M. Lobb (Berinsfield). 67 kg: K. Chiverton (Mansfield) w pts S. O'Donnell (Dale Youth). 71 kg: N. Scott (Trojan Police) w pts J. Lee (Altrincham).

The Leisure Centre, Seaham – 14 December

Class B: 45 kg: M. Grimes (Golden Gloves) w pts M. O'Donnell (Dale Youth). 48 kg: F. Gavin (Small Heath) w pts M. Graydon (Broad Plain). 51 kg: W. Mitchell (Shamrock) w pts P. Quinn (Dagenham). 54 kg: W. Broomfield (New Astley) w pts M. Robinson (Tower Hill). 57 kg: J. Selkirk (Rotunda) w pts R. Owen (Gwent). 60 kg: T. Nevin (Repton) wo J. McQuillan (Keady). 63. 5: J. Phillips (Gwent) w rsc 1 R. Taylor (Handsworth). 67 kg: L. Veness (Newham) w pts C. Johnson (Boston). 71 kg: M. Boylan (Radford) w pts J. Smyth (Finchley). 75 kg: A. Jeffries (Sunderland) w rsc 3 B. Frankham (Westree).

Royal Lancaster Hotel, Lancaster Gate – 10 December

Class C: 48 kg: J. Fowl (Haileybury) w pts I. McCabe (Lesmahagow). 51 kg: D. Broadhurst (Birmingham Irish) w pts M. Edmonds (St Joseph's East). 54 kg: F. Holmes (Kingsthorpe) w pts M. Walsh (Norwich Lads). 57 kg: R. Barrett (Eltham) w pts M. Gethin (Wednesbury). 60 kg: M. Grant (Haringey Police) w pts S. Jennings (Tower Hill). 63. 5 kg: L. Graves (Chorley) w pts J. Xavier (St Mary's). 67 kg: A. Quigley (Tower Hill) w pts K. Lowe (St George's). 71 kg: C. McDonagh (Hanwell) wo L. Siner (Salisbury). 75 kg: M. Hall (Collyhurst) w rsc 1 M. Davies (Gwent). 81 kg: P. Trott (Altrincham) w pts J. Guntert (Abingdon).

Schools

The Metrodome, Barnsley – 9 & 10 March

Class 1: 32 kg: S. Cosgrave (Hartlepool Catholic) w pts W. Buckland (Repton). 34 kg: K. D'eath (Northside) w pts C. Broad (Exeter). 36 kg: M. McGuire (Kettering) w pts J. Chericato (Canterbury). 39 kg: G. Hancock (Horden) w pts E. Corcoran (Trojan Police). 42 kg: W. Saunders (Cheshunt) w pts G. Watson (Hartlepool Catholic). 45 kg: P. Stokes (Trojan Police) w pts T. Costello (Birmingham City). 48 kg: H. Burton (Ardwick Lads) w pts J. Gosling (Southend). 51 kg: R. Smith (Darlington) w pts R. Garvey (Earlsfield). 54 kg: L. Ripley (Eltham) w pts P. Steel (Blaydon). 57 kg: W. Eastwood (Onslow) w pts L. Bullock (Old Robin Hood). 60 kg: P. O'Connor (Northolt) wo.

Class 2: 36 kg: M. Ward (Birtley Police) w pts B. Fowl (Haileybury). 39 kg: J. Saunders (Belhus Park) w pts M. Fagin (Vauxhall Motors). 42 kg: J. Bowman (Northside) w pts L. Turner (Repton). 45 kg: L. Gray (Stevenage) w pts D. Rogers (Hinckley Olympic) – replaced R. Lawson (Northside). 48 kg: S. Alker-Hall (Chorley) wo. 51 kg: A. Sexton (Finchley) w pts E. Welsh (Darlington). 54 kg: C. Riley (Wellington) w pts B. Skeete (Earlsfield). 57 kg: J. Gillingwater (Canvey) w pts K. Kirkham (Blackpool & Fylde). 60 kg: T. Jacobs (Harwich) w pts J. Wale (Mexborough). 63 kg: D. Niven (Thame) w rsc 2 D. Robinson (Kirkdale). 66 kg: G. Groves (Dale Youth) w rsc 2 O. Sykes (Sandygate). 69 kg: L. Jarvis (Leigh Park) wo M. Davies (Ironworks).

Class 3: 39 kg: D. Hylands (Salisbury) w pts J. Radford (Newham). 42 kg: V. Mitchell (West Ham) w pts A. Silk (Northside). 45 kg: P. Edwards (Salisbury) w pts C. Smith (Onslow). 48 kg: A. Crolla (Fox) w pts R. O'Grady (Portsmouth). 51 kg: J. McElvaney (South Bank) w pts J. Bowen (Repton). 54 kg: R. Ward (Dagenham) w pts A. Downs (Wythenshawe East). 57 kg: A. Khan (Bury) w co 1 S. Turner (Lawrence). 60 kg: N. Ripley (Eltham) w pts P. Maddison (Salisbury). 63 kg: M. Pardoe (Droitwich) w pts K. Shinkwin (Bushey). 66 kg: T. Saunders (Cheshunt) w pts J. Brown (Oldham). 72 kg: M. Singh (St Theresa's) w pts J. O'Connor (Northolt). 69 kg: D. Booth (Pool of Life) w pts J. Davis (Slough).

Class 4: 42 kg: J. McDonnell (Hatfield) w pts J. McCully (Danson Youth). 45 kg: L. Mulholland (St Paul's) w pts M. Grimes (Golden Gloves). 48 kg: F. Gavin (Small Heath) w pts T. Mills (St Mary's). 51 kg: G. Reay (Spennymoor) w pts J. Trotman (Medway Golden Gloves). 54 kg: B. Saunders (Spennymoor) w pts D. Clark (Repton). 57 kg: C. Kipling (West Hull) w pts J. O'Donnell (Dale Youth). 60 kg: R. Pickard (Repton) w rsc 3 C. Mullen (Horsley Hill). 63. 5 kg: G. Skehill (St George's) w pts D. Halsall (Preston & Fulwood). 67 kg: T. Crewe (Plains Farm) w pts S. O'Donnell (Dale Youth). 71 kg: T. Hill (Golden Ring) w pts J. Lewis-Dickenson (Birtley Police). 75 kg: V. Collingwood (St Paul's) w pts N. Scott (Trojan Police). 81 kg: J. Degale (Dale Youth) w pts D. Price (Westway Eastfield).

ABA Youth

The Sports Centre, Knottingley – 11 May

Class 5 (born 1985): 45 kg: M. Gallett (Pleck) w rsc 2 S. Joyce (Canvey). 48 kg: S. Leonard (Darlington) w pts P. Jamieson (Transport). 51 kg: M. Robinson (Tower Hill) w pts A. Brennan (Triumph). 54 kg: W. Broomfield (New Astley) w pts L. Cutter (Southampton). 57 kg: J. O'Donnell (Dale Youth) w pts R. Mitchell (New Astley). 60 kg: L. Shinkwin (Bushey) w pts B. Zacharkin (Phoenix). 63. 6 kg: B. Rose (Blackpool) w pts S. Joplin (Westway). 67 kg: N. Gittus (East Durham) w pts L. Veness (Newham). 71 kg: A. Jeffries (Sunderland) w pts A. Hakim (Newham). 75 kg: R. Collins (Premier) w pts B. Frankham (Westree). 81 kg: D. Price (Westway) w pts T. Dallas (Medway). 86 kg: M. Khanekevich (All Stars) w pts D. Garside (Harlepool Catholic). 91 kg: B. Smith (Kings Lynn) wo.

Class 6 (born 1984): 48 kg: A. Bibby (Sandy) w pts R. Todd (Hamer). 51 kg: N. McDonald (Vauxhall Motors) w pts D. Broadhurst (Birmingham Irish). 54 kg: K. Mitchell (West Ham) wo. 57 kg: G. Sykes (Cleckheaton) w pts J. Murray (Northside). 60 kg: S. Jennings (Tower Hill) w co 2 D. Herdman (Stevenage). 63. 6 kg: A. Quigley (Tower Hill) w rsc 3 A. Clegg (White Rose). 67 kg: R. Ashworth (Scarborough) w pts L. Calvert (Finchley). 71 kg: L. Siner (Salisbury) w pts B. McDonagh (Old Robin Hood). 75 kg: M. Hall (Collyhurst & Moston) w rsc 1 G. Paterson (Craghead). 81 kg: J. Boyd (Donnington) w rsc 4 A. Gibbens (Bognor Regis). 86 kg: L. Robinson (Trinity) wo. 91 kg: S. Sexton (Norwich Lads) w rsc 1 M. Grainger (Darnhill & Heywood).

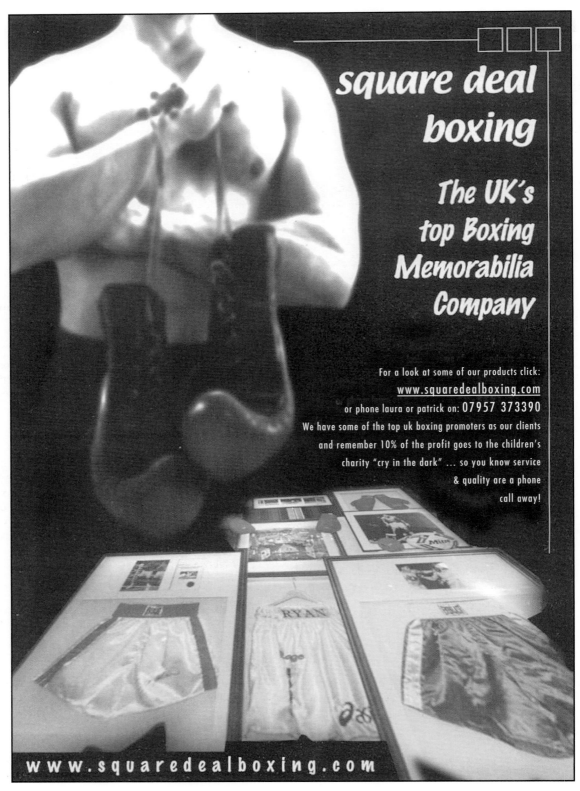

282

The Triple Hitters' Boxing Quiz (Part 7)

Compiled by Ralph Oates

QUESTIONS

1. Over how many rounds did Marvin Hart outpoint Jack Johnson on 28 March 1905?
   A. 12.   B. 13.   C. 20.

2. On 12 December 1907, Stanley Ketchel outpointed Joe Thomas over 20 rounds. In which part of America did this contest take place?
   A. New York.   B. San Francisco.   C. Boston.

3. Which boxer was nick-named 'The Black Panther'?
   A. Sam Langford.   B. Harry Wills.
   C. Peter Jackson.

4. On 13 October 1924, Tommy Loughran and Harry Greb met in a ten-round contest. What was the result?
   A. Points win for Loughran.   B. A draw.
   C. Points win for Greb.

5. On 5 April 1933, Frankie Genaro outpointed Joey Archibald over how many rounds?
   A. Six.   B. Eight.   C. Ten.

6. On 23 December 1944, Kid Gavilan outpointed Miguel Acevedo over ten rounds. In which country did the contest take place?
   A. Cuba.   B. America.   C. Canada

7. On 30 May 1951, Ezzard Charles retained his world heavyweight title against Joey Maxim. By which method?
   A. Six-round knockout.   B. Nine-round stoppage.
   C. 15-round points decision.

8. Who was the referee for the Charles v Maxim contest?
   A. Frank Gilmer.   B. Clarence Rosen.
   C. Mark Conn.

9. On 7 March 1952, Ernie Fossey and Bernard Cottrell met in a six-round contest. What was the result?
   A. A draw.   B. Points win for Fossey.
   C. Points win for Cottrell.

10. Over how many rounds did Henry Cooper outpoint Cliff Purnell on 8 February 1955?

A. Four.   B. Six.   C. Eight.

11. Howard Winstone stopped Colin Salcombe in round six on 4 February 1960. Where did the contest take place?
    A. Cardiff.   B. Birmingham.   C. Manchester.

12. On 22 October 1963, Maurice Cullen lost a ten-round points decision to which opponent?
    A. Eddie Perkins.   B. Sammy McSpadden.
    C. Carlos Ortiz.

13. In which round did Billy Walker knock out Charley Powell on 26 January 1965?
    A. One.   B. Two.   C. Three.

14. Which opponent did John Conteh, the former world, European, British and Commonwealth light-heavyweight champion, not meet in the professional ranks?
    A. Johnny Frankham.   B. Les Stevens.
    C. Billy Aird.

15. On 29 January 1970, Ken Buchanan lost his undefeated professional record in his 34th professional contest in Spain, when outpointed over 15 rounds for the vacant European lightweight title by Miguel Velasquez. In later fights, Velasquez went on to capture a WBC world championship. In which weight division?
    A. Lightweight.   B. Light-Welterweight.
    C. Welterweight.

16. On 2 March 1974, Jim Watt outpointed Kokkie Oliver over ten rounds. In which country did this contest take place?
    A. Nigeria.   B. France.   C. South Africa.

17. How many bouts did tbe former British featherweight champion, Terry Spinks, have during his professional career?
    A. 48.   B. 49.   C. 50.

18. Which opponent did Charlie Magri, the former world, European and British flyweight champion, not

283

meet during his professional career?
A. Mike Stuart.   B. Candy Iglesias.
C. Keith Wallace.

19. In which country did the former British and European middleweight champion, Kevin Finnegan, not box during his professional career?
A. America.   B. South Africa.   C. Mexico.

20. Which championship did Tim Wood win at light-heavyweight during his professional career?
A. British.   B. Commonwealth.   C. European.

21. On 7 May 1977, Clinton McKenzie outpointed Fernand Roelandts over eight rounds. In which country did the contest take place?
A. England.   B. Belgium.   C. France.

22. Which version of the world middleweight championship did Chris Pyatt once hold?
A. WBO.   B. WBA.   C. WBC.

23. On 5 November 1982, Colin Jones won the European welterweight title in Denmark when he stopped the holder, Hans Henrik Palm, in round two. Prior to Jones, who was the previous British holder of this championship?
A. Dave Boy Green.   B. John H. Stracey.
C. Henry Rhiney.

24. On 4 March 1986, in a final eliminator for the WBA heavyweight title, Frank Bruno knocked out Gerrie Coetzee in the opening round. Which version of the world championship did Coetzee formerly hold?
A. IBF.   B. WBA.   C. WBC.

25. On 18 May 1988, Paul Hodkinson won the British featherweight title when he stopped the holder, Peter Harris, in round 12. At that time, how many professional contests had Hodkinson participated in?
A. 11.   B. 12.   C. 13.

26. On 2 November 1988, Brian Mitchell made a successful defence of his WBA super-featherweight crown when he outpointed which challenger over 12 rounds?
A. Jim McDonnell.   B. Jose Rivera.
C. Salvatore Bottiglieri.

27. On 11 August 1992, in Atlantic City, Lennox Lewis stopped Mike Dixon in round four. At this stage of his professional career, Lewis was undefeated in how many contests?

A. 19.   B. 20.   C. 21.

28. On 30 April 1993, Johnny Nelson won the WBF cruiserweight title when he stopped the holder, Dave Russell, in round 11. In which country did this contest take place?
A. Australia.   B. New Zealand.   C. England.

29. On 24 February 1997, Bobby Vanzie met Mark Ramsey in an eight-round contest. What was the result?
A. Points win for Vanzie.   B. A draw.
C. Points win for Ramsey.

30. In his American debut on 19 December 1997, Prince Naseem Hamed retained his WBO featherweight title in New York when he knocked out Kevin Kelley in round four. Which version of the world featherweight championship did Kelley previously hold?
A. WBA.   B. IBF.   C. WBC.

31. On 13 February 1999, Joe Calzaghe retained his WBO super-middleweight title when he outpointed Robin Reid over 12 rounds. At this stage of his career, Calzaghe was undefeated in how many professional contests?
A. 26.   B. 27.   C. 28.

32. Peter Culshaw retained his WBU flyweight crown on 15 May 1999 when he stopped Adrian Ochoa in round nine. Where did this contest take place?
A. Newcastle.   B. Blackpool.   C. Manchester.

33. Which lady boxer was born on 12 August 1968?
A. Jane Couch.   B. Cathy Brown.
C. Audrey Guthrie.

34. Over how many rounds did Nicky Cook outpoint Vlado Varhegyi on 20 August 1999?
A. Four.   B. Six.   C. Eight.

35. On 16 October 1999, Jason Booth won the British and Commonwealth flyweight championship when he stopped the holder, Keith Knox. In which round?
A. Nine.   B. Ten.   C. 11.

36. Which boxer is not from Scotland?
A. Keith Knox.   B. Scott Harrison.
C. Francis Ampofo.

37. In defence of his WBO Inter-Continental light-welterweight crown on 11 December 1999, Ricky Hatton stopped Mark Winters in round four. In

which weight division was Winters formerly a British champion?
A. Lightweight. B. Light-Welterweight.
C. Welterweight.

38. On 20 March 2000, Noel Wilders won the vacant IBO bantamweight title when he outpointed Kamel Guerfi over 12 rounds. At this stage of his career, Wilders was undefeated in how many professional contests?
A. 16. B. 17. C. 18.

39. In which round on 13 May 2000 did Roy Jones stop Richard Hall in defence of his WBC, WBA and IBF light-heavyweight titles?
A. Ten. B. 11. C. 12.

40. On 1 July 2000, Cathy Brown won the vacant WBF European flyweight title when she outpointed Jan Wild over six rounds. In which country did this contest take place?
A. Belgium. B. France. C. England.

41. In which year did manager, trainer and promoter, Graham Moughton, represent Great Britain in the Olympic Games?
A. 1968. B. 1972. C. 1976.

42. On 18 February 2001, Rob Hayes-Scott made his professional debut, stopping Kevin Burton in the opening round. Who was his manager?
A. Tania Follett. B. Dai Gardiner. B. Bruce Baker.

43. On 10 April 2001, Colin Lynes outpointed David Kirk over six rounds. At this stage of his career, Lynes was undefeated in how many professional contests?
A. 11. B. 12. C. 13.

44. Michelle Sutcliffe defended her WBF flyweight crown and won the vacant IFBA flyweight title on 17 May 2001 when she stopped Marietta Ivanova in round five. Where did this contest take place?
A. Manchester. B. Leeds. C. London.

45. How tall is Anthony Farnell?
A. 5'9". B. 5'10". C. 5'11".

46. Over how many rounds did Jane Couch outpoint Viktoria Oleynikov on 16 June 2001?
A. Four. B. Five. C. Six.

47. On 23 June 2001, Kostya Tszyu retained his WBC and WBA light-welterweight titles when he defeated Oktay Urkal. By which method was this achieved?
A. Six-round stoppage. B. Eight-round knockout.
C. 12-round points decision.

48. Robin Reid retained his WBF super-middleweight championship against Julio Cesar Vasquez on 19 December 2001, following a 12-round points decision in his favour. In which weight division was Vasquez a former WBA world title holder?
A. Welterweight. B. Light-Middleweight.
C. Middleweight.

49. Ricky Hatton retained his WBU light-welterweight title on 9 February 2002 when he stopped Mikhail Krivolapov in round nine. Who was the referee for this contest?
A. Mickey Vann. B. Richie Davies.
C. John Coyle.

50. Michael Sprott failed in his bid to win the British and Commonwealth heavyweight titles on 12 February 2002 when stopped in which round by the defending champion, Danny Williams.
A. Five. B. Six. C. Seven.

LONDON
FOR ALL YOUR
BOXING
ESSENTIALS

LONSDALE SPORTS EQUIPMENT LTD.,
47 Beak Street, London W1F 9SE

Tel: 020 7437 1526

Fax: 020 7734 2094

Tel:
Leicester
(0116)
2629287

Mobile:
07989
215287

JOHNNY GRIFFIN
BOXING PROMOTIONS & MANAGEMENT
Licensed by BBBoC
Member of the Professional Boxing Promoters' Association

I am calling for 'Open Shows' involving both amateur and professional boxers appearing side by side. The current dialogue between the BBBoC and both the Amateur Boxing Association of England and Amateur Boxing Scotland is to be welcomed, but it is paramount it continues and is extended to include Wales and Northern Ireland. We need to develop more shows for both codes and it is time that the amateurs and professionals reached some kind of agreement on the joint organisation of the sport. Nothing ventured, nothing gained.

Under these circumstances I am sure a revival of small-hall boxing would be possible right across the country, with both sides benefiting from the stimulation. The small-hall culture must be protected and an academy to maintain certain basic values, which are fundamental to the development and continued enhancement of both amateur and professional boxing throughout the United Kingdom, would not be amiss.

We must examine certain aspects of our sport with a view to bringing about changes for the good of all. In short, this should be the dawn of a new era.

Directory of Ex-Boxers' Associations

by Ron Olver

BOURNEMOUTH Founded 1980. Dai Dower (P); Percy Singer (T); Dave Fry (VC); Doug Mitchell (S); Peter Fay (C), 24 Monkswell Green, Purewell, Christchurch, Dorset BH23 1MN.

CORK Founded 1973. HQ: Glen Boxing Club, Blackpool, Cork. William O'Leary (P & C); John Martin (S); Phil Murray (VC); John Donovan (T).

CORNWALL Founded 1989. HQ: Truro City Football Club. Stan Cullis (P); Jimmy Miller (T); John Sandow (C); Chris Trembath (VC); Bill Matthews (S), 33 Victoria Road, St Austell, Cornwall PL25 4QF.

CROYDON Founded 1982. HQ: Ivy House Club, Campbell Road, West Croydon. Bill Flemington (VC & T); Richard Evans (PRO & S); Barry Penny (C); Gilbert Allnutt (P), 37 Braemar Avenue, Thornton Heath, Croydon CR9 7RJ.

EASTERN AREA Founded 1973. HQ: Norfolk Dumpling, Cattle Market, Hall Road, Norwich. Brian Fitzmaurice (P); Ron Springall (C); Clive Campling (VC), 57 Northfields, Norwich NR4 7ES.

HULL & EAST YORKSHIRE Founded 1996. HQ: The Rising Sun Hotel, Hull. Don Harrison (C); Micky Brooks (S); Geoff Rymer (PRO); Bert Smith (T), 54 St Aidan Road, Bridlington, E. Yorks.

IPSWICH Founded 1970. HQ: Loco Club, Ipswich. Alby Kingham (P); Vic Thurlow (C & T); Michael Thurlow (S), 147 Clapgate Lane, Ipswich IP3 0RF.

IRISH Founded 1973. HQ: National Boxing Stadium, South Circular Road, Dublin. Val Harris (P); Richard O'Reilly (C); Tommy Butler (T); Willie Duggan (S), 175 Kimmage Road West, Dublin 6W.

KENT & SUSSEX Founded 1997. HQ: RAFA Club, Chatham. Mick Smith (P & C); Ray Lambert (PRO); Paul Nihill, MBE (S & T), 5 Acre Close, Rochester, Kent ME1 2RE.

LEEDS Founded 1952. HQ: North Leeds WMC, Burmantofts, Lincoln Green, Leeds 9. Alan Richardson (P); Greg Steene (HP); Kevin Cunningham (C & S); Alan Alster (T); Frank Johnson (PRO), Franwyn, 7 Allenby Drive, Leeds.

LEICESTER Founded 1972. HQ: Belgrave WMC, Checketts Road, Leicester. Mick Greaves (P & C); Mrs Rita Jones (T); Norman Jones (S), 60 Dumbleton Avenue, Leicester LE3 2EG.

LONDON Founded 1971. HQ; St Pancras Social Club, Argyle Square, London. Stephen Powell (P); Micky O'Sullivan (C); Andy Williamson (VC); Ron Olver (PRO); Ray Caulfield (T); Mrs Mary Powell (S), 36 St Peters Street, Islington, London N1 8JT.

MANCHESTER Founded 1968. HQ: LMR Club, Whitworth Street West, Manchester. Tommy Proffitt (P); Jack Edwards (C); Kenny Baker (T); Jimmy Lewis (VC); Eddie Copeland (S), 9 Lakeside, Hadfield, Glossop, Derby SK13 1HW.

MERSEYSIDE (Liverpool) Founded 1973. HQ: Transport Drivers Club, Hockenhall Alley, Liverpool. Johnny Cooke (P); Terry Riley (C); Jim Boyd (VC); Jim Jenkinson (T), 13 Brooklands Avenue, Waterloo, Liverpool L22 3XY.

MIDLANDS EBA Ron Gray (P); Barry DeLacy (C); Lee Potts (T); Jerry Hjelter (S), 67 Abberley Avenue, Stourport on Severn, Worcs DY13 0LY.

NORTHAMPTON DISTRICT Founded 2001. Jeff Tite (P); Sam Monks (C); Joe Grundler (T); Sid Green (S), 8 Friars Close, Delapre, Northampton NN4 8PU.

NORTHAMPTONSHIRE Founded 1981. HQ: Cue Club, Bridge Street, Northampton. Dick Rogers (P); Gil Wilson (C); Peter Cripps (T); Mrs Pam Ward (S), 6 Derwent Close, Kings Heath, Northampton.

NORTHERN FEDERATION Founded 1974. Several member EBAs. Annual Gala. Eddie Monahan (S), 16 Braemar Avenue, Marshside, Southport.

NORTHERN IRELAND Founded 1970. HQ: Ulster Sports Club, Belfast. Derrick Wade (P); Paddy Graham (C); Tucker Adams (VC); Micky Hannah (T); Freddie Gilroy (PRO); Al Gibson (S), 900 Crumlin Road, Belfast.

NORTH STAFFS & SOUTH CHESHIRE Founded 1969. HQ: The Saggar Makers Bottom Knocker, Market Place, Burslem, Stoke on Trent. Tut Whalley (P); Roy Simms (VC); Les Dean (S); John Greatbach (T); Billy Tudor (C & PRO), 133 Springbank Road, Chell Heath, Stoke on Trent, Staffs ST6 6HW.

NORWICH HQ: West End Retreat, Brown Street, Norwich. Les King (P); John Pipe (C); Jack Wakefield (T); Dick Sadd (S), 76 Orchard Street, Norwich.

NOTTINGHAM Founded 1979. HQ: The Earl Howe, Carlton Road, Sneinton, Nottingham. Len Chorley (P); Walter Spencer (C); Terry Bradley (VC); Diane Rooksby (T); John Kinsella (PRO); Graham Rooksby (S), 42 Spinney Road, Keyworth, Notts NG12 5LN.

PLYMOUTH Founded 1982. HQ: Exmouth Road Social Club, Stoke, Plymouth. Tom Pryce-Davies (C); Doug Halliday (VC & S); Arthur Willis (T); Buck Taylor (P & PRO), 15 Greenbank Avenue, St Judes, Plymouth PL4 9BT.

PRESTON Founded 1973. HQ: Barney's Piano Bar, Church Street, Preston. John Allen (C); Tommy Smith (T); Peter Osborne (P & S), 39 Prospect Place, Ashton, Preston PR2 1DL.

ST HELENS Founded 1983. HQ: Royal Naval Association, Volunteer Street, St Helens. Johnny Molloy (P); Ray Britch (C); Tommy McNamara (T); Paul Britch (S), 16 Oxley Street, Sutton, St Helens WA9 3PE

SCOTTISH Founded 1997. HQ: Iron Horse Public House, West Nile Street, Glasgow. Walter McGowan, MBE (P); Andy Grant (C); Charlie Sexton (VC); Frank O'Donnell (LP); Peter Baines (T); Liam McColgan (S), 25 Dalton Avenue, Linnvale, Clydebank G81 2SH.

SHEFFIELD HQ: Darnall Liberal Working Mens Club, Irvine Street, Sheffield 9. Billy Calvert (P); Peter Skinner (C); Harry Carnall (VC); Jim Daly (T); John Redfern (S), 33 Birch Avenue, Chapeltown, Sheffield S35 1RQ.

SQUARE RING Founded 1978. HQ: Snooty Fox Hotel, St Marychurch. George Pook (P); Johnny Mudge (S); Jim Banks (T); Paul King (C), 10 Pine Court Apartments, Middle Warberry Road, Torquay.

SUNDERLAND Founded 1959. HQ: River Wear Social Club,

Sunderland. George Martin (P); Terry Lynn (C); Les Simm (T & S), 21 Orchard Street, Pallion, Sunderland SR4 6QL.

SWANSEA & SOUTH WEST WALES Founded 1983. HQ: Villiers Arms, Neath Road, Hafod, Swansea. Cliff Curvis (P); Gordon Pape (C); Ernie Wallis (T); Len Smith (S), 105 Cockett Road, Swansea SA2 0FG.

TRAMORE Founded 1981. HQ: Robinson Bar, Main Street, Tramore, Co Waterford. T. Flynn (P); C. O'Reilly (C); L. O'Brien (VC); W. Hutchinson (T); Peter Graham (S), 3 Riverstown, Tramore.

TYNESIDE Founded 1970. HQ: Pelaw Social Club, Heworth, Pelaw. Billy Charlton (P); Maxie Walsh (C); Harry Greenwood (VC); Malcolm Dinning (T); Alan Gordon (S), 16 Dove Court, Birtley, Chester le Street, Durham PH3 1HB.

WELSH Founded 1976. HQ: Rhydyfelin Labour Club, Pontypridd. Robbie Regan (P); Ken Shannon (C); Ron Bruzas (T); Don James (S), 28 Woodfield Road, Talbot Green, Pontyclun, Mid-Glamorgan. Patron - Lord Brooks.

The above information is set at the time of going to press and no responsibility can be taken for any changes in officers or addresses of HQs that may happen between then and publication or changes that have not been notified to me.

ABBREVIATIONS

P - President. HP - Honorary President. LP - Life President. AP - Acting President. C - Chairman. VC - Vice Chairman. T - Treasurer. S - Secretary. PRO - Public Relations Officer and/or Press Officer.

Ron Olver (right), Vice-President and P.R.O. of the London Ex-Boxers' Association presents former heavyweight, Joe Crickmar, with the Alf Paolozzi award at LEBA's Annual Awards Luncheon.

Derek Rowe

Obituaries

by Derek O'Dell

It is impossible to list everyone, but I have again done my best to include final tributes for as many of the well-known boxers and other familiar names within the sport who have passed away since the 2002 Yearbook was published. We honour them and will remember them.

ALCAZAR Pedro *From* Panama. *Died* June 2002. WBO super-flyweight champion lost not only his title and unbeaten record but also his life, following his defence against Mexico's Fernando Montiel. Pedro appeared to be well in his dressing room following the fight, but collapsed later in his hotel room. Although there were rumours that he had weight problems, he did not appear to be dehydrated going into the fight and it was felt that a contributory factor in his death could have been a car accident on 1 February in which he received back injuries. In 26 previous contests, Pedro had only lost once, to Edgar Monserrat, and had won the WBO version of the title when outpointing Adonis Rivas on 16 June 2001 before successfully defending against Jorge Otero prior to the contest against Montiel.

ANDREWS Karl *From* Bristol. *Died* 10 January 2002, aged 26. Despite having no amateur experience, he turned pro in 1996 and had six contests, beating Gavin McGhin and Nick Howard and drawing with Tim Redman, but losing inside the distance to Gary Cavey, Bruno Foster and Gordon Minors. A heavyweight, who was managed by Chris Sanigar, he died of injuries received in a street brawl in Tenerife.

Karl Andrews   Les Clark

ARNETT Peter *Died* 20 April 2002, aged 79. A boxing promoter who put on several boxing shows in Hampshire after the last war, he had built up a leisure services business after starting out as a fishmonger. In middle age he returned from the continent with a fish van full of gambling machines, which he distributed in pubs and cafes. Gradually he built up the business of Peter Arnett Leisure and went on to operate bingo halls in the Portsmouth area. He successfully promoted wrestling as well as boxing before the era of televised sport.

AZTECA Kid *From* Mexico. *Died* 18 March 2002, aged 87. Azteca held the Mexican welterweight title from 1932 until 1949 and had an outstanding record. Born Villanueva Paramo, he adopted the name of 'Kid Azteca' in his early professional career, but actually began as 'Kid Chino'. A pro at 14 who had his last fight at 43, he twice beat Ceferino Garcia in 1933 and went on to beat Cocoa Kid, Baby Joe Gans, Izzy Jannazzo, Al Chavez, Saverio Turiello, Al Manfredo, Fritzie Zivic, Nick Moran and Bobby Yaeger, but dropped decisions to Bep van Klaveren, Baby Casanova, Zivic, Sammy Angott and, in his swan-song, to Joe Borell. Azteca died in Mexico from liver and kidney problems.

BAKER Bob *From* Pittsburgh, Pennsylvania, USA. *Died* April 2002, aged 75. A good heavyweight whose brittle hands possibly prevented him from reaching world-title status, Bob went unbeaten in his first 26 contests before losing to Clarence Henry, and ran up a fine record with wins over Walter Hafer, Marty Marshall, Rusty Payne, Abel Cestac, Omelio Agramonte (2), Jimmy Bivins, Cesar Brion, Nino Valdes (2), Joe Baksi, Coley Wallace (2), Jimmy Slade, Rex Layne (3), Julio Mederos, John Holman and George Chavalo, before coming over here to clearly outpoint Dick Richardson in 1957. In a subsequent fight in Britain he lost a return with Richardson and his form began to suffer and in five contests, he won only one. Retired from boxing in the knowledge that he had met the best and had faced Archie Moore when the old Mongoose was cutting a swathe through the ranks. Other men to beat him included Bob Satterfield, Tommy 'Hurricane' Jackson (2) and Eddie Machen, all leading contenders at one time or another.

BARRY Kevin *From* Adelaide. *Died* 18 November 2002, aged 43, from a heart ailment. The Australian southpaw heavyweight, who had 20 fights of which won ten, unsuccessfully challenged Dean Walters for the Australian title in December 1988 but was knocked out in four rounds.

BARTOLO Sal (Salvatore) *From* Boston, Mass, USA. *Died* March 2002, aged 84. Although a former NBA world featherweight champion, Sal Bartolo is one of the underrated performers of the 1940s thanks to being around at the same time as Willie Pep, who beat him for the world title in 1946. They met three times and Pep always came away as the winner but had a close shave in their first encounter in April 1943. With Pep thinking it would be an easy fight, Bartolo proved to be a difficult foe and ran him to a very close decision. Sal twice beat Phil Terranova in NBA title bouts and also defended against Willie Roache and Spider Armstrong before losing to Pep. Not many men beat him in a 97-fight career that started in 1937 and finished on a winning note in 1949. At his peak, only Chalky Wright, Maxie Shapiro, Gus Mell and Pep could get the better of him, while he bested men such as Bobby 'Poison' Ivy, Everette Rightmire, Joey Archibald, Lefty LaChance and Jock Leslie among others.

BEBBINGTON Dennis *From* West Ham. *Died* June 2002, aged 69. Had a fine amateur career in which he fought Peter Toch the one-time ABA heavyweight champion. Dennis won several junior titles and turned pro under Sam Burns, but lost his first bout due to a cut eye, his opponent being Terence Murphy of Hoxton, who went on to become a top challenger in the light-heavyweight division. Dennis' other opponents included Jack Streek of Sidcup, Billy Middleton of British Honduras and Billy Edwards. His fight with Edwards drew nubbins and was one of the best small-hall contests of the 1950s. After beating Middleton, Dennis, who came from a famous fighting family, retired from boxing.

BLOXHAM Stan *Died* January 2002, aged 65, after suffering from cancer. A member of the fine RAF team back in the mid 1950s, Stan never turned pro but was a good test for many of the leading amateurs of the day, having won an ABA youth title in 1952. As a senior he became the North-West London divisional champion in 1953 whilst boxing for the Alexandra club. After retirement, he moved to Worthing.

BONILLA Jose *From* El Tigre, Venezuela. *Died* June 2002, aged 34, from an asthma attack. A former WBA flyweight champion from Venezuela, Bonilla was a hard-punching and tactically clever champion who fought in Japan, Thailand, USA and his native South America, defending his world title three times before losing to Hugo Soto. Also the Latin-American flyweight champion, in 33 pro fights he won 28 and lost five before retiring in 1999, notching victories over good men such as Edicson Torres, Saen Sorploenchit, Hiroki Ioka, and Jose de Jesus Lopez. He proved what a tough nut he was to crack when taking the heavy-punching Rosendo Alvarez into the 11th round when contesting the Latin-American mini-flyweight title in 1994.

BROOKS Mickey *From* Camberwell. *Died* in June 2002, aged 57. After reaching the London ABA welterweight finals in 1966, losing to Peter Cragg the eventual champion, Mickey turned pro and was unbeaten in his first eight contests. He beat men such as Ray Fallone, Lloyd Wallace and Freddie Goodman, but lost to Ivan Drew, Malcolm McKenzie and Jackie Turpin (twice), the last two defeats at the hands of Turpin forcing his retirement from the game.

CAMPBELL Davy *From* Enniskillen. *Died* December 2001, aged 47. Turned pro in 1977, having represented Ireland as an amateur international and been a national champion at light-welter, which he eventually emulated in the paid ranks. However, he never quite fulfilled the promise he had shown in his amateur days and retired in 1983 with a record of 20 contests, having won 11 and lost nine. A favourite sparring partner to Barry McGuigan, who paid his friend a glowing tribute when informed of his death by suicide.

CHABIN Herve *From* France. *Died* following a car crash in January 2002, aged 36. In a 27 fight career, Chabin won 13 and drew one. Despite what, on paper appears to be a spotty record, he was good enough to twice fight for the French bantamweight championship, both Redka Abbas and Louis Mancini staving off strong challenges from him.

CHAMBERLAIN Bill *From* Croydon. *Died* 7 December 2001. Having served with the Chindits in Burma, on his return home he turned pro under the management of Tom Powell, boxing as a welterweight out of the Gun Gym in Croydon. Bill was a powerfully built man who was popular at Beckenham Baths, where he drew with Steve Curtis and knocked out Johnny Jones. Being a long distance lorry driver wasn't really conducive to being available for fights and despite retiring early he never lost his love of the sport, being a founder member of Croydon EBA and becoming involved with the Hillcrest BC.

CHICHESTER Ray *Died* July 2002. The Welsh Area's Chief Inspector since 1984, Ray died suddenly, but left behind a legacy of service to Welsh boxing. He was always ready to support any function connected with boxing.

CONNORS George *From* Islington. *Died* 22 February 2002, aged 69. Boxing as a flyweight who was active in early 1950s, Ron Olver saw him beat Les Daw on the first show that he reported for the trade paper. Connors joined Charlie Woods' booth and the experience instilled him with enough savvy to look after himself against Britain's four-star bantamweights, beating Hughie Byrne, Wilf Briers and Billy Downer, but being unlucky to lose a hair-line decision to Joe Quinn. His services as a sparring partner were much in demand and he was very proud of how he helped Al Phillips, Jake Tuli and the O'Sullivan bothers, but after losing to Malcolm McLeod and then Johnny O'Callaghan he finally quit the sport in 1958.

COOPER George *From* Orpington. *Died* 8 February 2002, aged 68. Turned pro in 1952, having just four fights as a heavyweight in his first two years before coming back in 1957 to beat Dave Sammons, the Board's Dennis Lockton, George Naufahu and Paddy Slavin prior to being beaten by Maxie Earle and Basil Kew and retiring in 1958. Often confused with Henry Cooper's brother, George, who had to box professionally as 'Jim' due to George already being licensed. A regular performer on the boxing booths, along with his friend Billy Dean, who also passed away recently, George was also active in the film industry as an extra.

COSSEMYNS Pierre *From* Brussels, Belgium. *Died* December 2001, aged 71. Having won the Belgian amateur championship in 1951, he immediately turned pro and boxed through to 1963. A crack bantam and twice Belgian champion, he rose up the ratings to become one of the best men at his weight in the world. His first most notable victory was over future world champion, Hogan 'Kid' Bassey, at Leeds in 1952. He popped over to Belfast 18 months later and stopped John Kelly in nine rounds. The first Brit to beat him was Peter Keenan but there was not a lot in it, even though some of Cossemyns' best form had deserted him at that time, having just lost to Billy Peacock in Sydney. On the way home he had dropped off in Singapore to train Lin-Kee Chon. Australia was not a happy hunting ground for the Belgian. He lost to Kevin Jones and Gaetano Annalora there, but got back on the winning side back home by regaining the Belgian title. He lost twice to Terry Spinks and to Freddie Gilroy in 1958 but was too good for George Bowes, Tommy Miller and Cherif Hamia, another notable scalp. Seemed to get a new lease of life in 1961, when winning the vacant European title by stopping Freddie Gilroy and defending against Piero Rollo. Although Rollo beat him in the return, Cossemyns went on for another year (he was 33), to finish his career by beating Jean-Claude Leroy.

CRAWFORD Bruce *From* Thornaby. *Died* 6 October 2001, aged 72. This hard-punching middleweight turned pro in 1949 and quickly established himself as a dangerous contender for the title. He beat that tough New Zealand scrapper, Billy Coloulias, inside the scheduled distance and outpointed Billy Stevens, Tom Meli and Jimmy Bray. All this in his first year of punching for pay. Dick Langley beat him in 1950, but he continued to establish his reputation by stopping the much-heralded Sammy Sullivan. However, his form went to pieces in 1953 and following defeats by Johnny Sullivan, Arthur Howard and Billy Ellaway, Bruce decided to call it a day. He was only 25.

CULLEN Maurice *From* Shotton. *Died* 29 November 2001, aged 63. The younger brother of Terry Cullen, it was only a lack of punching power that prevented Maurice's entry into the ranks of the all-time greats. He was a pure boxer and a really good one at that with an abundance of stamina, due to a slow heartbeat, with skill to match. He held the British lightweight championship between 1965 and 1968, winning it by defeating Dave Coventry before losing it to Ken Buchanan. His first attempt at the

championship failed when Dave Charnley edged him out over 15 rounds at Manchester. Cullen fought two world champions in Carlos Ortiz and Eddie Perkins and each time he gave an excellent account of himself but lost on points.

DEAN Billy *From* Greenwich. *Died* June 2002, aged 74. Dean, a light-heavy, began boxing in 1949, beating Brian Anders in his third pro outing before being stopped by the experienced Reg Spring. He came back to beat Joe Plant of Hackney and the useful Canadian, Gene Fowler, but lost to the British title challenger, George Walker (brother of Billy), and three fights later scored what was one of his best wins to beat Johnny Barton. In a 35 bout career, of which he won 20, other top names he met before bowing out in 1957 were Albert Finch, Arthur Howard and Jimmy Davis.

DENNINGTON Claude *From* Peckham. *Died* 16 December 2001, aged 78. One of the many good lightweights operating in the early post-war years, Claude took on many of the top men around at the same time with Cyril Gallie, Billy Thompson, Peter Fallon, George Daly, Bert Hornby, Tommy McGovern and Elis Ask all appearing on his record. He also had two fights in Australia, losing on points to George Barnes and Alfie Clay and also took Elis Ask to a close decision in Stockholm. Unfortunately, Army service interrupted his career and a controversial defeat by Cliff Curvis in 1948 put him out of the British lightweight title eliminators. His younger brother, Ron, also boxed as a pro.

DUNNE Jimmy *From* Liverpool. *Died* March 2002, aged 60. The ABA lightweight champion in 1964 and an Olympic Games quarter finalist, Jimmy had a fine amateur career before turning pro in 1964. Started his paid career with wins over Paddy Winters and Johnny Wakefield before drawing with Kevin Hylands and stopping Peter Carney. Surprisingly stopped by Lex Hunter, Jimmy decided the paid ranks weren't for him, promptly retiring in February 1965, and it will be for his amateur achievements that he will be remembered. Was the uncle of Colin Dunne, the current lightweight star.

EDSON Jay *Died* 10 December 2001, aged 77. Made his name as one of the better boxing referees and handled just under 50 world-title fights before opting for less strenuous pursuits, becoming an adviser and co-ordinator for Top Rank. As a referee, Edson was involved with contests featuring Mohammad Ali, George Foreman, Marvin Hagler, Roberto Duran and Jesus Chavez and was still a key figure in the fight game when cancer cut him down.

EXLEY Billy *From* Newcastle. *Died* 17 March 2002, aged 81. Born in Glasgow, Billy began boxing in October 1946 and retired in 1950. A good fighter, he consolidated his claim to be one of this country's top welterweight when he twice knocked out the formidable Stan Hawthorne. Johnny Ryan was the only amateur known to have beaten him and Billy always fought in good company, his power punching bringing over a half of his 25 wins to an early conclusion. His record is studded with men of championship standard such as Eddie Thomas, Henry Hall, Jimmy Malloy, Willie Whyte, Claude Ritter, Jeff Tite and the Aussie star, Mickey Tollis.

FRANCIS George *Died* 3 April 2002, aged 73. A clean-living man, dedicated to boxing, George, who had been a reasonable amateur with the St Pancras ABC before graduating as a coach, gave up his work on London's Covent Garden to train Bunny Sterling and it was a matter of great pride to him when Sterling won the British, Commonwealth and European titles. Although Sterling was his first major success, he proceeded to take John Conteh to a world championship soon after, his disciplined training being a prime factor in Conteh's victory over Jorge Ahumada. George, who went on to handle Frank Bruno, Cornelius Boza-Edwards and John Mugabi, was a great family man and after becoming depressed when losing his wife and son to cancer, and his son in law in a car accident, it is believed that he took his own life.

Eddie Futch   Les Clark

FUTCH Eddie *From* the USA. *Died* 10 October 2001, aged 90. Active until recently, the veteran trainer was one of the most respected men in the game. Three of his fighters - Joe Frazier, Ken Norton and Larry Holmes beat Muhammad Ali and it was due to Futch's keen analysis of Ali's style, that they were able to do so. His connections with the game went back to the days of Joe Louis. He saw them all and was loved and respected by them all, being a magnificent trainer and cornerman to some of the greatest fighters of recent years.

GARRY Bobby *From* Levenmouth, Fife. *Died* 27 April 2002, aged 41. A former Scottish international amateur star, Bobby died suddenly at his home. Despite representing Scotland many times he never won a major title before nose injuries eventually forced him to retire. He then became a referee and judge.

GODDEN Barry *From* Wakefield. *Died* 16 September 2001, aged 66. A serving airman, he first came to prominence as a 21-year-old amateur light-heavyweight, reaching the 1956 ABA semi-finals by beating Redvers Sangoe in the ISBA finals. Although outpointed by Johnny Cole, he never bettered that performance, despite being an RAF champion several times and winning various Command titles and representing the RAF in the Britannia Shield.

GOLDBERG Benny *From* Detroit, USA. *Died* September 2001, aged 83. Turning pro in 1938, having lost out to Jackie Wilson in the 1936 Olympic trials, Goldberg proved to be a clever southpaw bantamweight cum feather with victories over many of the top names, going undefeated for six years. At one time ranked by Ring Magazine as the number one contender in both divisions, he numbered Manuel Ortiz, Joey Archibald, Luis Castello, Lou Transperenti and Tony Olivera among his victims. In his New York debut he knocked out Danny Carabella, but was avoided by Willie Pep, Phil Terranova and Sal Bartolo. A tricky boxer who could make even the greats look bad, he got one title shot but was narrowly beaten by an old foe in Manuel Ortiz before calling it a day in 1946. On retiring his record shows him to have had 60 wins from 63 fights, only a no contest against the dangerous KO Morgan and losses to Ortiz and Billy Miller marring his pro career.

GOODALL Manny *Died* June 2002, aged 79. A key figure in northern boxing circles for many years, Goodall turned his hand to promoting in 1977 when he paired John Conteh with Len Hutchins at Liverpool. He was involved, one way or another, with most post-war boxing events in Blackpool, Liverpool and Leeds.

GREEN Harold *From* Brooklyn, New York. *Died* September 2001, aged 78. Green was a very busy middleweight from 1942 through to 1954 when retiring and fought four world champions during his career in Marcel Cerdan, Rocky Graziano, Fritzie Zivic and Joey Giardello. At his peak he beat Graziano in two of their three meetings, outpointed Zivic but lost to Cerdan and split a pair of verdicts with Giardello. Green also beat Morris Reif, Sammy Secret (2) and Pete Mead and fought some top contenders in Paddy Young, Rocky Castellani, Ernie Durando, Pierre Langlois, Herbie Kronovitz, Johnny Greco and Bobby Ruffin. Harold was born in New York and did the bulk of his fighting there but died in Las Vegas from a heart attack.

GUZMAN Hugo Benjamin *Died* July 4 2002, aged 29. Guzman, a super-featherweight from Argentina, went into a coma after being knocked out by Cesar Celso Romaro. It was a second round stoppage and Guzman never recovered after he had left the ring, dying in hospital.

GWYNNE Horace *From* Toronto, Canada. *Died* November 2000, aged 88. Better known as 'Lefty', Gwynne won a gold medal for Canada in the 1932 Olympics, becoming only the second Canadian to do so, beating Vito Melis (Italy), Jose Villeneuve (Philippines) and the European champion, Hans Ziglarski (Germany) in the final before turning pro. A 5'2" bantamweight who hit like a 'sledgehammer', he lost just one contest as an amateur but won all his professional fights, winning the Canadian title in 1938 before retiring the next year. With a good job in a car manufacturing plant, which he later quit for a lucrative position as a recreation supervisor for the city of Toronto, there just wasn't enough money in the game to make it worth his while.

HERMAN Vic *From* Glasgow. *Died* 7 March 2002, aged 73. A flamboyant and game flyweight from the Gorbals district, Vic Herman was around when the division teemed with talent. From 1947 to 1954 he fought them all and came close to winning a British title against Terry Allen in 1951. He also fought the world titleholder, Japan's Yoshio Shirai, in Tokyo. The chance came when Vic was past his prime, but he gave it his all and was fighting back against an in-form champion, going ten rounds before the referee intervened. Most of all he will be remembered for his playing of the bagpipes on the way to the ring. On one occasion he said to the MC: "Make it a long introduction, it's a long walk from the dressing room and I'm knackered". Vic was also a talented artist as well as a musician and had an exhibition of his paintings shown in London many years ago. His fine record shows that he beat Skeets Gallagher, Charlie Squire, Jackie Bryce, Eddie Carson, Norman Tennant (3), Norman Lewis, Tino Cardinale, Theo Nolten, Dante Bini, Henry Carpenter, Jackie Briers, Mickey McKay, Alex Bollaert, and includes the names of Joe Murphy, Louis Skena, Teddy Gardner, Jimmy Pearce, Honore Pratesi, Dickie O'Sullivan, Joe Cairney, Jake Tuli, Chamrern Songkitrat and Maurice Sandeyron before he bowed out of boxing in 1954 following a hat-trick of defeats at the hands of Peter Keenan.

HOLMES Fred *Died* 1 June 2002, aged 18. Holmes, who lost to Derry Matthews in the 2002 ABA finals at

Fred Holmes (right)

Les Clark

293

bantamweight, met a tragic end when he drowned in a lake near Peterborough. First came to notice with the Focus club, reaching the schoolboy finals in 1999, the ABA Youth finals in 2000 and winning an NABC title in 2000. He then moved on to Kingsthorpe ABC to capture another title, this time in the NABC 'C' class before entering the senior championships. Having also won a silver medal in the 2000 junior Olympics, he was obviously a youngster with a bright future.

IREI Yoshihiro *From* Tokyo, Japan. *Died* 9 April 2002, aged 22. A promising youngster who had previously won all eight of his flyweight contests, Irei lost on points over six rounds to Yoshinori Naito on 24 March before losing consciousness in the dressing room and failing to recover.

JONES Benny *From* Stoke. *Died* April 2002, aged 88. Benny was one of the best bantamweights to come out of the Potteries, drawing with Jackie Brown but losing two subsequent fights to the former world champion. He lost only three of his first 40 fights, but such was the depth of talent in those days that it was not until his seventh year as a professional that he got his chance with the big names of the bantamweight division. Having twice beaten Phil Milligan, he was slightly over the hill by 1937 and uncharacteristically lost five consecutive contests to good men, including the aforementioned Jackie Brown, Tut Whalley and Jim Brady. He closed the year with a great performance by drawing with Brown and most critics were of the opinion that the verdict flattered the world champion. Even when past his best, he fought the best men around.

JOSAMU Gilbert *From* Zimbabwe. *Died* October 2001. A former 11 stone champion of Zimbabwe, Gilbert challenged for the Commonwealth title in 1988 but lasted only one round with Australia's Troy Walters. He was also beaten in two appearances in Britain, by Chris Pyatt and Anthony Logan.

LECTOURE Tito *From* Buenos Aires, Argentina. *Died* 1 March 2002, aged 65. From 1956 to 1987 Tito Lectoure was Argentine boxing, having taken over the ruins of the famous Luna Park Arena in Buenos Aires and built up a solid boxing empire. Carlos Monzon, Victor Galindez, Sergio Palma and Nicolina Loche were all part of that empire and with regular shows and top-class competition, world-class fighters sprung up like daises. Unfortunately, Argentinian boxing has slumped since he ceased promoting in 1987.

LOVELL Santiago Alberto *From* Argentina. *Died* in 2002, aged 60. An Argentinian heavyweight active in the 1960s and '70s, he was the son of the 1932 Olympic heavyweight king. Although beaten inside two rounds by Joe Bugner in 1974, Lovell had good wins on his record, Jose Urtain, Roberto Davila and Eduardo Corletti all succumbing to him. While men like Alfredo Evangelista and Oscar Bonavena were also too experienced for him, he always fought in good company and his record is studded with names of rated boxers like Charlie Polite, Bernt August, Miguel Paez and Lorenzo Zanon, etc.

McDOUGALL Simon *From* Blackpool. *Died* June 2002, aged 33. A very tough and durable heavyweight who was active between 1988 and 1998, Simon often had to go into an opponent's back yard and was rarely given an easy fight. He fought some of the best in Europe, seldom with success but always finishing on his feet. In 45 contests, he only won 14, including stoppage victories over Roland Ericsson and Stefan Angehrn and a points win over the up-and-coming Monty Wright. However, among the good men he met were Andrea Magi, Garry Delaney (2), Mark Prince, Bruce Scott, Christophe Girard, Ole Klemetsen, John Keeton, Michael Gale and Rudiger May. He was found dead in his flat.

Simon McDougall   Harry Goodwin

MacLEOD Stix *From* Zimbabwe. *Died* 2002, aged 42. A former all-African bantamweight champion Stix died following a stroke. The talented Zimbabwean looked set for big things until Francis Musankabala knocked him out in his eighth fight. He was good enough though to twice take on Paul Ferreri of Australia for the Commonwealth title, but was beaten inside the distance on both occasions before closing his career in 1983 following another defeat at the hands of Musankabala.

MAGEE Len *From* St Austell. *Died* 19 January 2002. The President of the Cornwall EBA, Len boxed from 1945 to

1952, much of his action coming as a member of Sam McKeown's boxing booth. Was a regular on the fairgrounds, travelling with Peter Fay, Harry Legge, Gordon Goodman, Rinty Monaghan and many others.

MANUEL Sandy *From* Nigeria. *Died* 3 May 2002, aged 69. Sandy came to Britain in 1952, along with Hogan 'Kid' Bassey and was based in Liverpool. Born Emanuel Babarinsa, he adopted his nom de ring to make life easier for promoters and ring announcers. Quickly becoming a travelling fighter, his services were used in continental rings, in Australia and Nigeria as well as here, and he proved to be a clever fighter rather than a puncher, as well as a busy one. In 1953, he squeezed in nine contests from January to March and lost only one of them. In August of that year he travelled to Ireland and stopped both Al Sharpe and Gerry Smythe and in November he lost a ten rounder in Italy to Dulio Loi, which was considered to be a blatant home-town decision. The 'Rochdale Thunderbolt', otherwise known as Johnny Butterworth, also beat him but Sandy finished the year with a knockout win over Ricky McCullough. Among some of the other prominent men who Sandy beat were Mick Leahy, Boswell St Louis, Frank Johnson, Albert Carroll and Freddie Teidt.

MURFITT Maurice *From* Little Downham. *Died* 16 June 2002, aged 70. Although often billed out of Downham Market, Maurice lived in Little Downham all his life. One of seven brothers and the only to take up boxing, from 1951 to 1959 he had 59 recorded fights and won half of them. This moderate record belies that was a fighter of some ability, beating Owen Randall, Clive Campling, Rufus Cobson and Charlie Williams. In 1952, he drew with Ron Dennington and went on to lose to Ron Hinson at Wembley. He also won and lost in two fights with Johnny Pipe and could always be relied on to give a good account of himself. He took up farming after retirement from the ring and had a family of seven children, four girls and three boys.

MURRAY Andrew *From* Georgetown, Guyana. *Died* 26 January 2002, aged 30 following a car crash. The undefeated Commonwealth welterweight champion between 1993 and 1997, Murray defeated Tony Swift and Michael Smyth in two of his three visits to Britain, before being beaten by Richard Williams in an unsuccessful light-middleweight Commonwealth title challenge last September. Had a crack at the WBA world welterweight title in 1995, but was beaten inside four rounds by Ghana's Ike Quartey. A pro since 1990, his record from 35 fights was 27 wins (17 inside the distance), one draw and seven defeats.

OLLA Ted *From* Milwaukee, USA. *Died* 25 June 2001, aged 71, having suffered from Alzheimer's. Began as a pro in 1949, losing his first fight, he became a useful middleweight who will be remembered for his 1955 fight with Sugar Ray Robinson in which Robinson stopped his game opponent in the third round. Following that, he retired from the ring and became a poker dealer in Las Vegas. Prior to turning professional, Ted won the Wisconsin Golden Gloves novice middleweight title in 1948.

OLSON Carl Bobo *From* Hawaii. *Died* 16 January 2002, aged 73, following a long battle with Alzheimers. Having turned pro at the age of 16 in 1944, the former world middleweight champion was unfortunate to be around at the same time as Sugar Ray Robinson, who beat him four times. Olson campaigned for eight years before getting an abortive shot at Sugar Ray's middleweight crown, being knocked out in 1950, but was successful in 1953 when he beat Randolph Turpin for the vacant championship on Robinson's retirement. A move up the scale to challenge for the light-heavyweight title was disastrous, Archie Moore knocking him out in three rounds in 1955, and in December of that year he lost his middleweight title to Robinson. He had just one fight in 1956, which ended in another kayo title defeat at the hands of Robinson. However, on coming back as a light-heavyweight he regained much of his form against Joey Maxim, who he beat on points, but from then on he only had the occasional successes, lasting only one round with Jose Torres and being outpointed by Don Fullmer before quitting boxing in 1966. Men he beat in his prime included Anton Raadik, Tommy Yarosz, Milo Savage, Lloyd Marshall, Chuck Hunter, Walter Cartier, Jimmy Beau, Robert Villemain, Eugene Hairston, Lee Sala, Norman Hayes (2), Paddy Young (2), Kid Gavilan, Rocky Castellani, Piere Langlois, Ralph Tiger Jones, Jimmy Martinez, Joey Giambra and Rory Calhoun.

PARKES Frank *From* Beeston, Nottingham. *Died* August 2002, aged 82. Turned pro in 1937 at the age of 16 and was soon making a name for himself, having had excellent sparring with men like Frank Bonsor and George Marsden. Unfortunately, World War 11 got in the way and Frank spent almost six years in the Navy, being involved at Dunkirk and seeing action elsewhere. On permanently returning to the ring, he had grown into a lightweight and, prior to retiring in 1956, he numbered among his victims men of the calibre of Jack 'Kid' Berg, Phineas John, Joe Connolly, Johnny McManus, Johnny King, Kid Tanner, Bert Jackson, Ben Duffy, Alan Tanner, Ivor Germain, Maurice Mancini, Johnny Mann, Darkie Hughes, Cliff Anderson, Jackie Turpin and Mickey Flanagan. His final fight came when he called it a day after losing his Midlands Area title to the up-and-coming Johnny Mann on 17 April 1956. Known as the 'Fighting Butcher', he was a master boxer of the old school, who was held in the highest respect by all those who knew him and was a founder member and Life President of the Nottingham EBA.

PEHI Sonny *From* New Zealand. *Died* 7 March 2002, aged 67. Made history as the first Maori to win a New Zealand professional title when he knocked out Roy Stevens in 11 rounds in 1958. He successfully defended against Charlie Beaton (1959) before the boxing authority took his title away in 1960 for failing to take a medical when requested. Won 14 out of 17 contests, including a points victory over the American, Chuck Wadsworth, who had recently defeated Kitione Lave.

PERALTA Gregorio *From* San Juan, Argentina. *Died* 2002, aged 66. An 'evergreen' light-heavyweight and heavyweight from South America, Peralta was one of two talented and top-rated fighting brothers. He fought just once for the world title, in 1964, when Willie Pastrano beat him, having outpointed Pastrano five months earlier. Was a long-time holder of the South American heavyweight title and for the five years of his career he was based in Europe, mainly proving too good for whatever European boxers he fought. Some of the big names on his record are Mauro Mina, Wayne Thornton, Roberto Davila, Oscar Bonavena, George Foreman, Jose Menno, Jose Urtain and Ron Lyle, while in his European campaign, he beat Rocky Campbell, Gerhard Zech, Billy Aird, Bill Drover, Horst Benedens and drew with Ron Lyle.

POWELL Tom *Died* 7 March 2002, aged 87. In the days that he was a licensed timekeeper, Tom Powell became the oldest holder of a boxing licence in this country, but years earlier he had started his pro career as a fighter under the management of Albert Teal, his fights spanning just one year. Following a debut points defeat by Harry Barker, Tom proceeded to beat Cyril Rhodes, Harry Hepton, Bill Ringer, Don Harvey and Billy Webb. This run of victories culminated in a third-round kayo win over Gunner Bill Yeo, for which Tom received £1.10s after expenses. Quitting the game because he realised that big money just wasn't there for him, he became part of the promotional team at Croydon's Abacus Hall prior to taking out a time-keeper's licence. He was instrumental in forming Croydon EBA.

PRIEST Al *From* Boston, Mass, USA. *Died* 5 January 2001, aged 80. Al 'Red' Priest who was 13 fights into his career on resuming fighting for pay in 1945, following his discharge from World War 11, fought many of the leading lights of the time, including -world champions, Kid Gavilan and Fritzie Zivic. He wasn't a heavy puncher but he knew all the tricks, beating Pete Mead and Charlie Fusari in 1948 and then offering both men return matches. He again outscored Mead, but the talented Fusari turned the tables. Joe Rindone, Ralph Zanelli, Anton Raadik and Joey De John also beat him but they had to fight hard to do so, while Coley Welch, Ruben Shank and Vinnie Cidone all failed to halt the progress of the Massachusetts middleweight who fought on to 1952 before calling it a day.

PUDGE Joe *From* Cardiff. *Died* 17 November 2001, aged 90. The eldest of a large family of boxing brothers, Joe Pudge, who boxed as 'Joe Douglas', will remain one of those men whose early fighting record is obscure and fragmented. Boxing in the 1930s when so many shows outside of the capital went unreported, only 34 fights are on his account of 'known contests' and only six losses can be

traced. However, two Welsh champions, Ronnie Bishop and Jack Kiley, fell before his fists in the days where area champions were class performers.

REID Chris *From* Brooklyn, New York. *Died* June 2001, aged 38, the 'Big C' being his final opponent. Turning pro in 1984 after losing in the semi-finals of the 1984 USA Olympic trials, Chris, under the management of Mickey Duff and trained by Teddy Atlas, ran up an impressive tally of 19 wins before being stopped by Fulgencio Obelnegias. In 25 contests (two draws and one no contest), his only other defeat was in 1988 against Graciano Rocchigiani in a bid for the German's IBF super-middleweight title. Retired soon after and later became a trainer in New Jersey where he established the Long Branch BC.

Sandy Saddler

SADDLER Sandy *From* Boston, Mass, USA. *Died* 18 September 2001, aged 77. Joe 'Sandy' Saddler who beat Willie Pep three times out of four was an all-time great and one of the hardest punching featherweights ever. After a good start as an amateur he turned professional in 1944 and ran up an impressive record, despite being stopped by Jock Leslie in his second outing, but had nearly 100 fights before his big chance came in 1948. He then stunned the boxing world by knocking out Willie Pep for the world featherweight title. Pep was considered unbeatable but had no answer to Saddler's power in one of the greatest upsets ever. In the return match, Willie turned in one of his most brilliant of victories to beat Sandy, but it was the only fight of their series in which he was returned the winner. Twice appearing in Europe, Saddler was far too good for Ireland's

Jim Keery (1949) and the French ace, Ray Famechon (1954). After regaining the title from Pep, he defended it against Red Top Davis and Flash Elorde before retiring undefeated champion in 1957 due to eye problems. In later years he was victim of a street assault which was the start of deterioration in health, failing eyesight and Alzheimer's Disease forcing him to spend his final years in a nursing home. His record of 162 fights (144 wins, two draws, 16 losses) is littered with names of world champions such as Phil Terranova, Joe Brown, Jimmy Carter, Harold Dade, Paddy DeMarco and Lauro Salas.

SEYS José *From* Belgium. *Died* 7 March 2002, aged 43, from sudden heart failure. Turning pro in 1981, he was a difficult man to box against and scored several stunning victories when the odds were stacked against him; the most typical example being when he pricked the Errol Christie bubble in less than a minute. Seys returned to Britain to take on Herol Graham but was predictably stopped in six rounds. He won 31 out of 55 fights, losing most of the 18 that went against him in the twilight of his career. Along the way he beat Luc Goossens, Jon Marie Emebe, Yves Monsieur, Dave Owens and picked up the Belgian title. A shot at the European title, however, ended in failure when Eric Nicoletta stopped him in Montpelier and soon afterwards Eddie Smulders beat him for the Benelux title. There was nothing of note after that and he retired in 1995.

SHEA Jim *Died* June 2002. A Board of Control steward, and Chief Medical Officer of the Scottish Area Council, Jim passed away after a long illness. He was a long-serving member of the Scottish Council.

SNELLING Fred *Died* 6 November 2001, aged 85. Fred, who was one of the most efficient boxing scribes of his day, first produced published articles for *Everybody's* in the 1940s under the name of 'Oscar Frederick' and in the difficult days of paper rationing produced three booklets that quickly sold out: *Fight Quiz, Battling Bruce* and *White Hope*. In 1972 he hit the jackpot with two best-sellers in *James Bond – A Report* and *A Bedside Book of Boxing*, the last of which ranks alongside A J Liebling's *Sweet Science* as one of the most sought-after boxing books. Fred became production editor of the newly launched *Boxing Monthly* and then took over as editor of *The Southern Ex-Boxer*, a magazine that is still enjoying a wide circulation. He also submitted several articles to *The British Boxing Yearbook* and was still churning out copy right up until his death. He left behind an unsurpassed legacy of books and articles on James Bond, films, literature and boxing.

SNOEK Wim *From* Amsterdam, Holland. *Died* 27 October 2001, aged 74. Boxing from light-heavyweight to heavyweight, Snoek, a good-class European fighter, first aroused British interest when in his second year of fighting he beat Peckham's Dick Langley in Rotterdam. He then came in as a sub to easily beat Albert Finch and Alex Buxton before his winning run against British-based boxers was halted in 1954 by Yolande Pompey, who stopped him in three rounds. Snoek carried on for another couple of years with mixed success before heading for Central and South America, where his form deserted him. On returning to Europe, he lost to Randolph Turpin in London and then travelled to Africa, Germany, Italy and Sweden with varying success. A good journeyman fighter, and twice holder of the Dutch light-heavyweight title, Wim fought challengers for the European championship and gave Ingemar Johansson no end of trouble in a fight at the heavyweight poundage.

SODERMAN Bob *Died* 26 February 2002, aged 80. A dedicated researcher into boxing and baseball history, Bob spent many hours of his life at newspaper libraries to dig out results and facts that had never been published previously. Correspondence from Bob was detailed and always bulky. He did an enormous amount of work in a short space of time, -such was his energy. A founder member of IBRO and an expert on Joe Louis and Jack Dempsey, Bob was the first man to fathom out the early record of Archie Moore after discovering that it included many of his contests as an amateur.

TAYLOR Kenny *From* Norwich. *Died* October 2001, aged 71. A lightweight who did the bulk of his fighting in the Eastern Counties after turning pro in 1950, Taylor was a solid puncher with inside the distance wins over Jimmy McLachlan of Hackney, Dick Levers, Jack Armstrong and Harold Palmer. He outpointed Ernie Fossey and Tony Brazil in 1952 and repeated against Fossey in 1953 before his career fizzled out after Laurie Davies stopped him in four rounds at Great Yarmouth in September 1953. There would be just five more fights in the next four years, the final one coming at Wembley Town Hall in April 1957 when, after decking the up-and-coming Arthur Murphy (Camden Town) three times in the first round, he was forced to retire with a badly cut tongue at the end of the fourth.

TETTEH Joe *From* Ghana. *Died* February 2002, aged 64. Apart from being a boxing craftsman who could look after himself against the best men of his day, he was also the first holder of the Commonwealth light-welterweight championship and, typically, had to fight in his opponent's (Joey Santos) backyard to win. Having turned pro in Ghana in the late '50s before coming to Britain in 1964 following a losing Commonwealth featherweight title fight against Floyd Robertson, he made a reputation as a travelling journeyman, a real pro, and a very well liked man. Lost a heart-breaking decision to Des Morrison for the British ten stone title, but took his defeat in a typical sporting manner. Tetteh never dodged a fight and was often a last minute substitute, being far, far better than his 44-30-5 record suggested. Beat Bobby Fisher, Billy Calvert, Peter Cheevers and Pat McCormack before bowing out in 1974 after being knocked out by the former world lightweight champion, Ken Buchanan.

TREE Jack *Died* February 2002, aged 81. As the long-time European correspondent for *The Ring* magazine (as Sgt Jack Tree of BAOR), Jack was a mine of information on continental boxing. He also reported for *Boxing News*, *Boxing Weekly* and *South African Boxing World*, but will be mainly remembered for his contribution to *The Ring* for which he never received a single dollar in payment. Yet his enthusiasm for the game was such that he continued to file boxing reports right up to his death. We had close dealings when I was writing the old timers' section of *Boxing Monthly* and *Boxing Weekly*. Jack would never let a piece of useful information pass me by and is sadly missed. He leaves behind a widow, Gisela, and a host of friends.

VALDEZ Emiliano *From* Dominican Republic. *Died* March 2002, aged 28. Never recovered from injuries received in a fight against Teddy Reid in February 2000. Represented his country at the 1995 Pan American Games before turning professional and having 14 fights, of which he won ten and drew one. Unfortunate to be matched too ambitiously against Kofi Jantuah, Kassim Ouma, and then Teddy Reid on 23 January 2000, he went into a coma after the Reid fight and although hanging on for two years eventually succumbed to head injuries received in that fight.

VALE Ronnie *From* Leamington. *Died* March 2002, aged 67. A good eight-round scrapper with plenty of punching power, and a pro from 1955 to 1964, Vale fought once for the Midland Area middleweight title but was disqualified against Maxie Smith. Although he beat good men like George Blazeby, Roy Thomas, Dave George, Paddy Delargy and Tommy Hayes, in general he found the next level up, such as Harry Scott, Orlando Paso and Gert van Heerden, too much for him.

WEBBER Kenny *Died* 18 February 2002, aged 49. Turned pro in 1972 after a brilliant amateur career and got off to a good start by beating Bobby Ruffe, Bob Langley and Derek Simpson before dropping an eight-round points decision to Rod Griffiths. He did well to draw with Des Rea in his tenth pro fight and he beat Trevor Francis twice out of three fights they had, but started to flounder after back-to-back defeats by Des Morrison and Peter Morris and was inactive in 1978 and 1979. His comeback was going well until he journeyed to Italy to meet Luigi Minchillo, who knocked him out in five rounds and it was downhill after that. After retiring from boxing in 1981, Kenny suffered bouts of depression, which ultimately led to him taking his own life.

WEIDIN Joe *From* Austria. *Died* 26 June 2002, aged 79. Weidin, real name Weidinger, was a tough old campaigner who was effective at European level but proved to be just short of world class. He is best remembered over here for his defiant stand against Jack Gardner in 1951 when Gardner took over the European heavyweight title that Weidin had won from French-Pole, Stephane Olek. Earlier in his career, Joe fought in America under the tutelage of Jack Dempsey who could see potential class in the big Austrian. The story goes that Joe saw the great Willie Pep at his best and realising that his own skills were so inferior to those of the featherweight champion, decided to pack his bags and return home. A pro from 1946, he retired from boxing in 1952 and while he could number Robert Eugene (2), Nisse Anderssen, Alf Brown (2), Don Mogard, Hein Lazek among his victims, he was defeated by top Americans, Freddie Beshore and Lee Oma.

WESTON Stanley *Died* 23 April 2002, aged 82. Weston was once Nat Fleischer's gardener and, like his employer, a keen boxing buff. He was also a brilliant portrait artist and designed several of *The Ring* magazine covers, which eventually led to a staff position on the magazine. In the early 1950s, Weston was given a free hand in designing Joe Wender's *Boxing and Wrestling* magazine and the readership benefited from Stanley's superb collection of photos. On Fleischer's death, however, he took over *The Ring* and *KO* magazines and although *The Ring* couldn't compete with the pictorial image of *Boxing Illustrated* (formerly *Boxing and Wrestling*), Weston didn't want to see the old journal fade out, thus it was the latter that folded. A knowledgeable boxing historian, Weston's contribution to the game was immense.

WILLIAMS Gus *From* Hartlepool. *Died* in March 2002. A diminutive flyweight who boxed between 1951 and 1956, mainly in the West Hartlepool venue, he never reached more than the six round stage but he always gave good value in the ten recorded fights that I could find for him.

WISEMAN Jim *From* Capetown, South Africa. *Died* 20 July 2002, aged 29. A good class super-featherweight, Jim was found hanged in a gym in his native Capetown. In May 2000, Wiseman had looked a clear winner over Britain's Dean Pithie before having to settle for a draw and more recently, in April 2001, had been knocked out in the 12th and final round when challenging Mzonke Fana for the national title.

WOMACK Ricky *From* Detroit, USA. *Died* 19 January 2002, aged 40. As an amateur he beat Evander Holyfield in half of their eight fights and looked set for a brilliant career, but it never worked out that way. Undefeated in 13 paid outings with a great future ruined by terms in jail, the most recent being 16 years for armed robbery and attempted murder, he threw away his chances and disenchanted his trainers before taking his own life. Mental illness was quoted as the cause of his suicide.

ZAYAS Manuel *From* Philippines. *Died* April 2002, aged 21. Three days after being stopped by Alex Escaner in the ninth of a ten round fight, the young super-bantamweight died from injuries sustained during the fight. Zayas had first lost consciousness whilst being examined by a doctor in his corner after the referee had called a halt.

A Boxing Quiz with a Few Below the Belt (Part 7)
Compiled by Les Clark

QUESTIONS

1. Vitali Klitschko has won the vacant European Heavyweight title on two occasions. Against whom?

2. During 1981 to 1984, Wilfredo Benitez had a total of eight fights. How many were title fights?

3. What's the nickname of Clarence Adams?

4. What title did Patrice Aouissi win in March 1995?

5. Who beat Jose Luis Bueno in a WBC bantamweight title fight in March 1996?

6. What is the nickname for Peter Culshaw?

7. From whom did Darren Corbett take the Commonwealth belt?

8. Who did Istvan Kovacs defeat to win the WBO featherweight belt in January 2001?

9. What was the fighting name of Sidney Walker?

10. How many fights did Cassius Clay have before taking the world title from Sonny Liston?

11. Who did Tyrone Booze beat to win the inaugural WBO cruiserweight title?

12. Against whom was Nino Benvenuti's last win?

13. In what round did Javier Castillejo stop Javier Martinez in defence of his WBC junior-middleweight belt?

14. What title did Tontcho Tontchev win when he defeated Anatoly Alexandrov in January 2001?

15. Which was the last world title that Simon Brown fought for and against whom?

16. Livingston Bramble had only one fight in 1985. Who was his opponent?

17. Which was the last title fight to go beyond 15 rounds?

18. Miguel Angel Gonzalez went eight years and 42 fights before his first loss. Who beat him?

19. On how many occasions has Montell Griffin fought in England?

20. Who was the last fighter to stop the former WBO champion, Herbie Hide?

21. WBA champion, William Joppy, has fought in England on only one occasion. Can you name the opponent and the venue?

22. Who retained his WBO welterweight belt by defeating Giovanni Parisi in June 2000?

23. How many British fighters did Emile Griffith meet?

24. Between winning the title from Alan Minter and losing it to Sugar Ray Leonard, how many successful defences did Marvin Hagler make?

25. Gene Fulmer's last three fights were against the same person. Can you name him?

26. Who beat Mickey Cantwell to retain his IBF strawweight title in June 2000?

27. What was the fighting name of Giuseppe Carrora?

28. Marcelo Dominguez fought for a version of the world cruiserweight title in July 2001. Name the opponent?

29. What is the nickname for Arturo Gatti?

30. Can you name the man who beat Wayne McCullough in the final of the 1992 Olympics?

31. Who brought about the first defeat of Tony 'TNT' Tubbs?

32. Can you give me the full name of Mike Tyson?

33. Who did Ray Mancini lose to in a world title challenge in March 1989?

34. Who did Richard Hatton beat to win the British light-welterweight title?

35. Who did Mauricio Martinez beat in the first defence of his WBO bantamweight title?

36. Name Marcel Cerdan's last opponent?

37. Who was the first Colombian to win a world title?

38. Alfred Kotey has fought on eight occasions in Britain. How many times was he defeated and by whom?

39. In 1979, Larry Holmes defended the WBC heavyweight title three times, stopping each of his opponents. Can you name them?

40. Jesse James Leija had 30 fights, with 28 wins and two draws, before losing to Gabriel Ruelas. Can you name the two men he drew with?

41. Former WBA heavyweight champion, Mike Weaver, lost his first two fights to the same man. Who was he?

42. Who were the boxers that took part in the first world title fight in a communist country?

43. Who holds the record for the longest uninterrupted reign as a featherweight champion?

44. What did Stanley Ketchel, Young Perez and Eleoncio Mercedes have in common?

45. Vito Antuofermo's career total was 50-7-2 and of his seven losses three were to British fighters. Can you name them?

46. Marcel Cerdan had only four losses in his career. Who was the first man to beat him and where was the fight held?

47. What have former world champions, Duane Thomas, Jimmy Paul and Milton McCrory have in common?

48. Which of the following boxers – George Benton, Don Fullmer and Ruben Carter – did former world heavyweight champion, Jimmy Ellis, fight and what were the results?

49. Bob Foster won the world light-heavyweight title from Dick Tiger. How many successful defences did he make?

50. Have either of the Spinks brothers, Michael or Leon, ever fought in Britain?

Leading BBBoC License Holders: Names and Addresses

Licensed Promoters

Jack Bishop
76 Gordon Road
Fareham
Hants
PO16 7SS
0132 928 4708

Paul Boyce
79 Church Street
Briton Ferry
Neath, Wales
0163 981 3723

David Bradley
Aston Hall, Aston Lane
Claverley
Nr Wolverhampton
WV5 7DZ
0174 671 0287

Pat Brogan
112 Crewe Road
Haslington
Crewe, Cheshire
0127 087 4825

Tony Burns
67 Peel Place
Clayhill Avenue
Ilford, Essex IG5 0PT
0208 551 3791

Trevor Callighan
40 Prescott Street
Halifax
West Yorkshire
HX1 2QW
0142 232 2592

Roy Cameron
43 Beaulieu Close
Colindale
London NW9 6SB
0208 205 2949

Capitol Promotions
Capitol Gymnasium
180 Longford Road
Coventry CV6 6DR
0247 636 4237

David Casey
424 Barking Road
London E13 8HJ
0207 377 6333

Annette Conroy
144 High Street East
Sunderland
Tyne and Wear
SR1 2BL
0191 567 6871

Pat Cowdell
129a Moat Road
Oldbury, Warley
West Midlands
0121 552 8082

Denis Cross
6 Partington Street
Newton Heath
Manchester M40 2AQ
0161 205 6651

David Currivan
15 Northolt Avenue
South Ruislip
Middlesex HA4 6SS
0208 841 9933

Michael Dalton
16 Edward Street
Grimsby
South Humberside
0147 231 0288

Ronnie Davies
3 Vallensdean Cottages
Hangleton Lane
Portslade
Sussex
0127 341 6497

Evans-Waterman Promotions
88 Windsor Road
Bray
Berkshire SL6 2DJ
0162 862 3640

Joe Frater
The Cottage
Main Road
Grainthorpe
Louth,
Lincolnshire
0147 234 3194

Dave Garside
33 Lowthian Road
Hartlepool
Cleveland
TS26 8AL
0142 929 1611

Jimmy Gill
45 Blandford Road
Chilwell
Nottingham
NG9 4GY
0115 913 5482

Golden Fists Promotions
119 High Road,
Loughton
Essex IG10 4LT
0208 502 1415

Ron Gray
Ingrams Oak
19 Hatherton Road
Cannock
Staffordshire
0154 350 2279

Johnny Griffin
0116 2262 9287
07989 215287

GSC Promotions
Ian Mcleod
c/o Glasgow Moat House
Congress Road
Glasgow G3 8QT
0141 222 2577

Jess Harding
c/o UK Industrial Pallets
Ltd
Travellers Lane
Industrial Estate
Travellers Lane
Welham Green
Hatfield
Herts AL9 7HF
0170 727 0440

Dennis Hobson
130 Handsworth Road
Sheffield
South Yorkshire
S9 4AE

Harry Holland
12 Kendall Close
Feltham
Middlesex
0208 867 0435

Lloyd Honeyghan
PO Box 17216
London
SE17 1ZU
0795 640 5007

Hull & District Sporting Club
Mick Toomey
25 Purton Grove
Bransholme
Hull HU7 4QD
0148 282 4476

Alma Ingle
26 Newman Road
Wincobank
Sheffield S9 1LP
0114 281 1277

John Ingle
20 Rockmount Road
Wincobank
Sheffield
S9 1NF
0114 261 7934

Lester Jacobs
2 Radnor Road
Peckham
London
SE15 6UR
0207 639 4734

Lion Promotions
Lennox Lewis & Adrian
Ogun, Suite 201
Gainsborough House
81 Oxford Street
London W1D 2EU
0207 903 5074

Malcolm McKillop
14 Springfield Road
Mangotsfield
Bristol
0117 957 3567

Owen McMahon
3 Atlantic Avenue
Belfast
BT15 2HN
0123 274 3535

Eugene Maloney
Maloney's Fight Factory
516 Old Kent Road
London SE1
0207 740 2876

Matchroom
Barry Hearn
10 Western Road
Romford
Essex
RM1 3JT
0170 878 2200

Midland Sporting Club
John Mills
24 Perton Road
Wolverhampton
WV6 8DN
0121 505 2141

Alex Morrison
197 Swanston Street
Laird Business Park
Dalmarnock
Glasgow
G40 4HW
0141 554 7777

Katherine Morrison
197 Swanston Street
Laird Business Park
Dalmarnock
Glasgow
G40 4HW
0141 554 7777

William Murray
49 Garnerville Road
Belfast
BT4 2QQ
0289 076 3282

National SC (Charity)
Cafe Royal
68 Regents Street
London W1R 6EL

North Staffs Sporting Club
J Baddeley
29 Redwood Avenue
Stone
Staffordshire
ST15 0DB
0178 220 2242

Panix Promotions
Panos Eliades
6 Bloomsbury Square
London WC1A 2LP
0207 242 2358

Peacock Promotions
Anthony Bowers
Peacock Gym
Caxton Street North
Canning Town
London E16 1JR
0207 511 3799

Steve Pollard
899 Beverley High Road
Hull HU6 9NJ
0148 280 3455

Prince Promotions
John Sheppard
Prince House
172 Psalter Lane
Sheffield
South Yorkshire
S11 8UR
0114 220 3000

Joe Pyle
36 Manship Road
Mitcham
Surrey CR4 2AZ
0208 395 6907

R & R Events
Ricky Manners
Mabgate Mills
Mill 6, Unit B
Macauley Street
Mabgate
Leeds LS9 7DZ
0113 243 6017

Glyn Rhodes
70 Oldfield Road
Stannington
Sheffield S6
0114 233 1687

Ringside Sporting Promotions
Ensley Bingham &
Martin Matthews
13 Osborne Road
Altrincham
Cheshire
WA15 8EU
0161 929 8088

St Andrew's Sporting Club
Tommy Gilmour
Holiday Inn
Bothwell Street
Glasgow
G2 7EN
0141 248 5461

Kevin Sanders
135 Coneygree Road
Peterborough
Cambridgeshire
PE1 8LQ
0173 355 5916

Chris Sanigar
Bristol Boxing Gym
40 Thomas Street
St Agnes
Bristol
Avon
BS2 9LL
0117 949 6699

Showsport International
Paul Hennessey
9 Warple Road
Quinton
Birmingham
B32 1RL
0121 242 1356

Sports Network
Frank Warren
Centurion House
Bircherley Green
Hertford
Hertfordshire
SG14 1AP
0199 250 5550

Sportsman Promotions
Frank Quinlan
Hollinthorpe Low Farm
Swillington Lane
Leeds
Yorkshire
LS26 8BZ
0113 287 0167

Kevin Spratt
8 Springfield Road
Guisley
Leeds
LS20 8AL
0194 387 6229

Tara Promotions
Jack Doughty
Lane End Cottage
Golden Street
Off Buckstone Road
Shaw
Oldham
OL1 8LY
01706 845753

Louis Veitch
35 Clinton Avenue
Blackpool
FY1 4AE
0125 329 3083

VIP Promotions
Stephen Wood
Edward Street
Cambridge Industrial Area
Salford
Manchester
M7 1RL
0161 834 9496

Keith Walker
Wayside Bungalow
Selby Road
Eggborough
DN14 0LN
0197 766 2616

Geraldine Williams
17 Kings Street
Lostwithiel
Cornwall
PL22 0AQ
0120 887 1194

Philip Williams
18 Queens Avenue
Sandycroft
Deeside
CH5 2PR
0124 453 9344

World Sports Organisation
Unit 5, Ella Mews
Cressy Road
London
NW3 2NH
0207 284 2133

Yorkshire Executive Sporting Club
John Celebanski
87 Crowtree Lane
Allerton
Bradford
B8 0AN
0127 482 4015

Licensed Managers

Sam Adair
Ashfield Cottage
Barnstaple
Devon
EX31 4DB
0123 747 4989

Isola Akay
129 Portnall Road
Paddington
London W9 3BN
0208 960 7724

Kofi Asante
102 Old Hospital Close
St James Drive
Balham
London
SW12 8SS
0208 672 0475

Chris Aston
23 Juniper Grove Mews
Netherton
Huddersfield
West Yorkshire
HD4 7WG
0148 432 9616

Bruce Baker
PO Box 25188
London
SW1V 3WL
0207 592 0102

Robert Bannan
1c Thornton Street
Townhead, Coatbridge
North Lanarkshire
ML5 2NZ
0123 660 6736

John Baxter
53 Battenburg Road
Leicester
LE3 5HB
0116 243 2325

Tony Behan
Flat 6, 29 Roundlea Rd
Northfield
Birmingham
B31 1DA
0771 002 2862

Sam Betts
The Railway Hotel
115 Station Road
Kirkham
Lancashire
PR4 2HD
0177 268 7973

Jack Bishop
76 Gordon Road
Fareham
Hants
PO16 7SS
0132 928 4708

Tony Borg
39 Clarence Street
Newport
Gwent
Wales
0163 378 2824

Peter Bowen
50 Newman Avenue
Lanesfield
Wolverhampton
West Midlands
WV4 6BZ
0190 282 8159

Jackie Bowers
36 Drew Road
Silvertown
London E16
0207 476 5530

Tony Bowers
3 The Green Walk
Chingford
London E4
0208 523 8113

David Bradley
The Dovecote
Aston Hall
Claverley
WV5 7DZ
0174 671 0287

John Branch
44 Hill Way
Holly Lodge Estate
London
NE6 4EP

John Breen
Cedar Lodge
589 Antrim Road
Belfast
BT15
0123 277 0238

Mike Brennan
2 Canon Avenue
Chadwell Heath
Romford
Essex
0208 599 4588

Michael Brooks
490 Hessle Road
Hull
HU6 5AA
0148 227 1163

Steve Butler
107 Cambridge Street
Normanton
West Yorkshire
WF6 1ES
0192 489 1097

Trevor Callighan
40 Prescott Street
Halifax
West Yorkshire
HX1 2QW
0142 232 2592

Enzo Calzaghe
51 Caerbryn
Pentwynmawr
Newbridge
Gwent
South Wales
0149 524 8988

Ernie Cashmore
4 Beech Court
Birmingham
B43 6AB
0121 357 5841

John Celebanski
87 Crowtree Lane
Allerton
Bradford
8 0AN
01274 824015/542903

Nigel Christian
80 Alma Road
Plymouth
Devon
PL3 4HU
0175 225 2753

William Connelly
72 Clincart Road
Mount Florida
Glasgow G42
0141 632 5818

Tommy Conroy
144 High Street East
Sunderland
Tyne and Wear
0191 567 6871

Pat Cowdell
129a Moat Road
Oldbury
Warley
West Midlands
BG8 9EE
0121 552 8082

John Cox
11 Fulford Drive
Links View
Northampton NN2 7NX
0160 471 2107

Dave Currivan
15 Northolt Avenue
South Ruislip
Middlesex
0208 841 9933

David Davies
10 Bryngelli
Carmel
Llanelli
Dyfed SA14 7EL
0126 984 3204

John Davies
Unit 14, Rectors Yard
Rectors Lane
Penre Sandycroft
Deeside
Flintshire CH5 2DH
0124 453 8984

Ronnie Davies
3 Vallensdean Cottages
Hangleton Lane
Portslade
Sussex
0127 341 6497

Peter Defreitas
6 Stroud Close
Chadwell Heath
Romford
Essex RM6 4AD
0183 678 1700

Owen Delargy
37 Leamington Road
Coventry
CV3 6GF
0120 369 0771

Brendan Devine
80 Fallbrook Drive
West Derby
Liverpool
L12 5NA
0151 263 1179

John Donnelly
15 Birkdale Avenue
St Annes on Sea
Lancashire
0125 371 2612

Jack Doughty
Lane End Cottage
Golden Street
Off Buckstones Road
Shaw
Oldham
OL2 8LY
01706 845753

Phil Duckworth
The Hampton Hotel
Longclose Lane
Richmond Hill
Leeds
LS9 8NP

Mickey Duff
c/o Mrs E Allen
16 Herga Court
Harrow on the Hill
Middlesex
HA1 3RS
0208 423 6763

Paul Dykes
51 Port Vale Court
Hamil Road
Burslem
Stoke on Trent
ST6 1DF
0783 177 7310

Gwyn Evans
1 Merchistoun Road
Horndean
Portsmouth
Hants
PO8 9LS
0239 259 4504

Jim Evans
88 Windsor Road
Maidenhead
Berkshire
SL6 2DJ
0162 823 640

Norman Fawcett
4 Wydsail Place
Gosforth
Newcastle upon Tyne
NE3 4QP
0191 213 1294

Stuart Fleet
269 St Nicholas Drive
Grimsby
South Humberside
0147 228 0181

Colin Flute
84 Summerhill Road
Coseley
West Midlands
WV14 8RE
0190 240 2699

Tania Follett
123 Calfridus Way
Bracknell
Berkshire
RG12 3HD
0134 445 5547

Steve Foster
62 Overdale
Swinton
Salford M27 5WE
0161 794 1723

Dai Gardiner
13 Hengoed Hall Drive
Cefn Hengoed
Mid Glamorgan
CF8 7JW
0163 328 4810

Dave Garside
33 Lowthian Road
Hartlepool
Cleveland
TS26 8AL
0142 929 1611

Anthony Gee
56 Bloombury Street
London
WC1B 3QT
0207 746 9100

Jimmy Gill
69 Inham Road
Chilwell
Nottingham
NG9 4GT
0115 913 5482

Tommy Gilmour
St Andrew's Sporting
Club
Holiday Inn
Bothwell Street
Glasgow G2 7EN
0141 248 5461

Mike Goodall
Gibbs Lane
Offenham
Evesham
Worcestershire
0138 644 2118

Alex Gower
22 Norwood Avenue
Rush Green
Romford
Essex RM7 0QH
0170 875 3474

Billy Graham
116 Stockport Road
Mossley
Ashton under Lyme
Manchester
0145 783 5100

Lee Graham
28 Smeaton Court
50 Rockingham Street
London SE1 6PF

Ron Gray
Ingrams Oak
19 Hatherton Road
Cannock
Staffordshire
0154 350 2279

Johnny Griffin
0116 262 9287
07989 215287

Carl Gunns
14 Whiles Lane
Birstall
Leicester LE4 4EE

Christopher Hall
3 Dewhurst Road
Cheshunt
Hertford EN8 9PG

Jess Harding
c/o UK Industrial Pallets
Ltd
Travellers Lane
Industrial Estate
Travellers Lane
Welham Green
Hatfield
Herts AL9 7HF
0170 727 0440

Billy Hardy
23 Pembrey Court
Sothall
Sheffield
Yorkshire
S20 2GY
0114 247 7318

Tony Harris
237 Stapleford Road
Trowell
Nottingham
NG9 3QE

Kevin Hayde
162 Western Avenue
North
Cardiff
Wales
0122 222 7606

Pat Healy
1 Cranley Buildings
Brookes Market
Holborn
London EC1
0207 242 8121

Barry Hearn
Matchroom
10 Western Road
Romford
Essex RM1 3JT
0170 878 2200

Mick Hill
35 Shenstone House
Aldrington Road
Streatham
London SW16
0208 769 2218

Dennis Hobson
73 Darnall Road
Sheffield
S9 5AH
0124 643 1116

Harry Holland
12 Kendall Close
Feltham
Middlesex
0208 737 4886

Gordon Holmes
15 Robert Andrew
Close
Morley St Botolph
Wymondham
Norfolk
NR18 9AA
0195 360 7887

Lloyd Honeyghan
PO Box 17216
London
SE17 1ZU

Geoff Hunter
6 Hawkshead Way
Winsford
Cheshire
CW7 2SZ
0160 686 2162

John Hyland
The Morton Suite
The Moat House Hotel
1 Paradise Street
Liverpool
L1 8JD
0151 708 8331

Brendan Ingle MBE
26 Newman Road
Wincobank
Sheffield S9 1LP
0114 281 1277

Dominic Ingle
26 Newman Road
Sheffield
S9 1LP
0114 281 1277

John Ingle
20 Rockmount Road
Wincobank
Sheffield S9
0114 261 7934

Richard Jones
1 Churchfields
Croft
Warrington
Cheshire
WA3 7JR
0192 576 5167

Thomas Jones
13 Planetree Road
Hale
Cheshire
WA15 9JL
0161 980 2661

Brian Lawrence
50 Willow Vale
London W12
0208 723 0182

Buddy Lee
The Walnuts
Roman Bank
Leverington
Wisbech
Cambridgeshire
PE13 5AR
0194 558 3266

Pat Lynch
Gotherington
68 Kelsey Lane
Balsall Common
Near Coventry
CV7 7GL
0167 633374

Paul McCausland
20 Invernook Drive
Belfast
Northern Ireland
BT4 1RW
0123 220 2355

Robert McCracken
16 Dusard Way
Droitwich
Worcestershire
WR9 8UX
0190 579 8976

Gary McCrory
Croftside
Low Enterprise Park
Greencroft
Stanley
Co Durham DH9 8NN
0120 723 7117

Jim McDonnell
2 Meadway
Hillside Avenue
Woodford Green
Essex IG8 7RF
07860 770006

John McIntyre
941 Aikenhead Road
Glasgow G44 4QE
0141 632 9114

Ian McLeod
14 Stewarton Crescent
Kilmarnock
Scotland
0141 222 2577

Owen McMahon
3 Atlantic Avenue
Belfast BT15
0289 074 3535

Colin McMillan
60 Billet Road
Chadwell Heath
Romford
Essex RM6 5SU
0208 597 4464

Charlie Magri
Victoria Pub
110 Grove Road
London E3 5TH
0795 652 4060

Frank Maloney
Sports Network
Centurion House
Bircherley Green
Hertfordshire
SG14 1AP
0199 250 5550

Eugene Maloney
Maloney's Fight Factory
516 Old Kent Road
London SE1 5BA
0207 740 2876

Dennie Mancini
16 Rosedew Road
Off Fulham Palace Road
London W6 9ET
0207 437 1526

Ricky Manners
Mabgate Mills
Mill 6, Unit B
Macauley Street
Mabgate
Leeds LS9 7DZ
0113 243 6017

Michael Marsden
1 North View
Roydes Lane
Rothwell
Leeds LS26 0BQ
0192 482 6499

Terry Marsh
141 Great Gregorie
Basildon
Essex

Tony Marshall
29 Seagull Bay Drive
Coseley
West Midlands
WV14 8AL
0121 520 3212

Tommy Miller
128 Clapton Mount
King Cross Road
Halifax
West Yorkshire
0142 236 1147

Clifton Mitchell
The Penine Hotel
Derby
Derbyshire DE1
0133 229 5380

Alex Morrison
197 Swanston Street
Laird Business Park
Dalmarnock
Glasgow
G40 4HW
0141 554 7777

Katherine Morrison
197 Swanston Street
Laird Business Park
Dalmarnock
Glasgow G40 4HW
0141 554 7777

James Murray
87 Spean Street
Glasgow G44 4DS
0141 637 7926

Bert Myers
The Lodge
Lower House Lane
Burnley
Lancashire
0128 277 9300

Paul Newman
12 Edgehill Way
Portslade
Brighton BN41 2PU
0127 341 9777

Norman Nobbs
364 Kings Road
Kingstanding
Birmingham B44 0UG
0121 355 5341

Stewart Nubley
94 Richmond Road
Kirkby in Ashfield
Nottinghamshire
NG17 7PW
0162 343 2357

Mark O'Callaghan
1 Keel Gardens
Southborough
Tunbridge Wells
Kent TN4 0JQ
0189 268 9979

Terry O'Neill
48 Kirkfield View
Colton Village
Leeds LS15 9DX
0113 225 6140

James Oyebola
194 Portnall Road
London W9
0208 930 9685

Terry Petersen
21 Lynwood Crescent
Pontefract
West YorkshireWF8 3QT
0197 770 3512

Alan Phillips
Glendowor Lodge
Coventry Road
Wolvey
Hinckley
LeicestershireLE10 3LD

Steve Pollard
899 Beverley High Road
Hull HU6 9NJ
0148 280 9455

David Poston
2 Whitegate Road
Daisy Bank
Bliston
West Midlands
WV14 8UY
0190 249 3040

Dean Powell
41(a) Grosvenor Terrace
Camberwell
London SE5 0NW
0795 690 5741

Michael Quinn
64 Warren Road
Wanstead
London
E11 2NA
0208 989 0082

Howard Rainey
9 Castlebeck Drive
Sheffield S2 1NP
0114 264 4106

Paul Rees
41 Alsop Close
London Colney
Herts AL2 1BW
0172 776 7656

Glyn Rhodes
70 Oldfield Road
Stannington
Sheffield S6
0114 233 1687

Gus Robinson, MBE
Stranton House
Westview Road
Hartlepool
TS24 0BB
0142 923 4221

John Rooney
51 Kirby Estate
Southwark Park Road
London
SE16 2EG
0788 407 7024

Ronnie Rush
4 Marcross Road
Ely
Cardiff
South Glamorgan
CF5 4RP
0122 259 3902

John Rushton
20 Alverley Lane
Balby
Doncaster
DN4 9AS
0130 231 0919

Kevin Sanders
135 Coneygree Road
Peterborough
Cambridgeshire
PE1 8LQ
0173 355 5916

Chris Sanigar
Bristol Boxing Gym
40 Thomas Street
St Agnes
Bristol BS2 9LL
0117 949 6699

Trevor Schofield
234 Doncaster Road
Barnsley
South Yorkshire
S70 1UQ
0122 629 7376

Mike Shinfield
126 Birchwood Lane
Somercotes
Derbyshire
DE55 4NE
0177 360 3124

Tony Sims
205 Collier Row Lane
Romford
Essex
RM5 3JA
0170 874 9940

Darkie Smith
21 Northumberland
House
Gaisford Street
London
NW5 2EA
0207 916 1784

Les Southey
Oakhouse
Park Way
Hillingdon
Middlesex
0189 525 4719

Norrie Sweeney
3 Saucehill Terrace
Paisley
Scotland PA2 6SY
0141 580 0269

Wally Swift
12 Garden Close
Knowle
Solihull
West Midlands B93 92F
0156 477 5140

Glenroy Taylor
73 Aspen Lane
Northolt
Middlesex U35 6XH
0795 645 3787

Jimmy Tibbs
44 Gyllyngdune
Gardens
Seven Kings, Essex
0208 806 8700

Terry Toole
6 Churchwell Close
Chipping Onger
Essex CM5 9BH
0127 736 2372

Mick Toomey
25 Purton Grove
Bransholme
Hull
HU7 4QD
0148 282 4476

Jack Trickett
Acton Court Hotel
187 Buxton Road
Stockport
Cheshire
SK2 7AB
0161 483 6172

Stephen Vaughan
c/o Lee Maloney
72 East Damswood Road
Speke
Liverpool
L24 7RJ
0797 102 4704

Louis Veitch
35 Clinton Avenue
Blackpool FY1 4AE
0125 329 3083

Keith Walker
Walkers Boxing
Promotions
Headland House
Suite 21-35
Spawd Bone Lane
Knottingley
West Yorks
WF11 0HY
0197 763 6905

Frank Warren
Centurion House
Bircherley Green
Hertford
Hertfordshire SG14 1AP
0199 250 5550

Robert Watt
32 Dowanhill Street
Glasgow G11
0141 334 7465

Jack Weaver
301 Coventry Road
Hinckley
Leicestershire LE10 0NE
0145 561 9066

Malcolm Webb
51 Bedwellty Road
Aberbargoed, Bargoed
Mid Glamorgan
Wales CF81 9AX
0144 387 9118

Paul Weir
11 Hopetown Bank
Irvine
Ayrshire KA11 1DX
0794 112 2373

Derek Williams
65 Virginia Road
Surrey CR7 8EN
0208 458 0511

Derek Williams
17 Kings Street
Lostwithiel
Cornwall PL22 0AQ

John Williams
3a Langham Road
Tottenham
London N15 3QX
0794 933 5787

Alan Wilton
The Bridge
42 Derryboy Road
Crossgar
BT30 9LH
0289 754 2195

Barry Winter
9 McNeill Avenue
Linnvale
Clydebank
G81 2TB
0141 952 9942

Stephen Wood
Viking Promotions
Edward Street
Cambridge Industrial
Area
Salford
Manchester M7 1RL
0161 834 9496

Tex Woodward
Spaniorum Farm
Compton Greenfield
Bristol
BS12 3RX
0145 463 2448

Licensed Matchmakers

Neil Bowers
59 Carson Road
Canning Town
London E16 4BD
0207 473 5631

Ernie Fossey
26 Bell Lane
Brookmans Park
Hatfield
Hertfordshire
0170 765 6545

Steve Foster
62 Overdale
Swinton
Salford M27 5WZ
0161 794 1723

Dave Garside
33 Lowthian Road
Hartlepool
Cleveland TS26 8AL
0142 929 1611

John Gaynor
7 Westhorne Fold
Counthill Drive
Brooklands Road
Crumpsall
Manchester M8 4JN
0161 740 6993

Tommy Gilmour
St Andrew's SC
Holiday Inn
Bothwell Street
Glasgow G2 7EN
0141 248 5461

Ron Gray
Ingrams Oak
19 Hatherton Road
Cannock
Staffordshire
0154 350 2279

John Ingle
20 Rockmount Road
Wincobank
Sheffield S9 1LP
0114 261 7934

Terry Johnson
1 Launceston Road
Park Hall
Walsall WS5 3ED
0192 262 6209

Graham Lockwood
106 Burnside Avenue
Skipton
N. Yorkshire
BD23 2DB
0175 679 2726

Dennie Mancini
16 Rosedew Road
Off Fulham Palace Road
Hammersmith
London W6 9ET
0207 437 1526

Tommy Miller
128 Clapton Mount
King Cross Road
Halifax
West Yorkshire
0142 236 1147

Ken Morton
3 St Quintin Mount
'Bradway'
Sheffield S17 4PQ
0114 262 1829

Stewart Nubley
94 Richmond Road
Kirkby in Ashfield
Nottinghamshire
NG17 7PW
0162 343 2357

Dean Powell
41(a) Grosvenor Terrace
Camberwell
London SE5 0NW
0207 701 3843

Richard Poxon
148 Cliffefield Road
Sheffield S8 9BS
0114 225 7856

Len Slater
78 Sutcliffe Avenue
Nunsthorpe, Grimsby
Lincolnshire

Terry Toole
6 Churchwell Close
Chipping Onger
Essex CM5 9BH
0127 736 2372

Ian Watson
2 Jed Moor
Hepburn Village
Tyne & Wear
NE31 1ET

Licensed BBBoC Referees, Timekeepers, Ringwhips and Inspectors

Licensed Referees

Class 'B'
Billy Aird	Southern Area
Dean Bramhald	Midland Area
Mark Curry	Northern Area
Seamus Dunne	Southern Area
Kevin Durrand	Central Area
Andrew East	Central Area
Stephen Gray	Central Area
Christopher Kelly	Central Area
Shaun Messer	Midlands Area
David Morgan	Welsh Area
Roy Snipe	Central Area
Alton Spencer	Midlands Area
Paul Webster	Central Area
Pete Wolstencroft	Central Area
Andrew Wright	Northern Area

Class 'A'
Ivor Bassett	Welsh Area
Terence Cole	Northern Area
Lee Cook	Midlands Area
Kenneth Curtis	Southern Area
Philip Edwards	Central Area
Roddy Evans	Welsh Area
Howard Foster	Central Area
Keith Garner	Central Area
Paul Graham	Scottish Area
Anthony Green	Central Area
Michael Heatherwick	Welsh Area
Jeff Hinds	Southern Area
Al Hutcheon	Scottish Area
David Irving	Northern Ireland
Wynford Jones	Welsh Area
Phil Kane	Central Area
Victor Loughin	Scottish Area
Grant Wallis	Western Area

Class 'A' Star
John Coyle	Midlands Area
Richard Davies	Southern Area
Mark Green	Southern Area
Ian John-Lewis	Southern Area
John Keane	Midlands Area
Marcus McDonnell	Southern Area
Larry O'Connell	Southern Area
Terry O'Connor	Midlands Area
Dave Parris	Southern Area
Paul Thomas	Midlands Area
Mickey Vann	Central Area

Licensed Timekeepers
Roy Bicknell	Midlands Area
Arnold Bryson	Northern Area
Neil Burder	Welsh Area
Richard Clark	Central Area
Anthony Dunkerley	Midlands Area
Robert Edgeworth	Southern Area
Harry Foxall	Midlands Area

Eric Gilmour	Scottish Area
Gary Grennan	Central Area
Brian Heath	Midlands Area
Greg Hue	Southern Area
Jon Lee	Western Area
Peter McCann	Southern Area
Norman Maddox	Midlands Area
Barry Pinder	Central Area
Raymond Rice	Southern Area
Colin Roberts	Central Area
James Russell	Scottish Area
David Walters	Welsh Area
Kevin Walters	Northern Area
Paul Webster	Central Area
Nick White	Southern Area

Licensed Ringwhips
Lester Arthur	Western Area
Albert Brewer	Southern Area
Michael Burke	Scottish Area
Steve Butler	Central Area
John Davis	Southern Area
Ernie Draper	Southern Area
Mike Goodall	Midlands Area
Simon Goodall	Midlands Area
Lee Gostolo	Central Area
Denzil Lewis	Western Area
Stuart Lithgo	Northern Area
Tommy Miller (Jnr)	Central Area
Kenneth Morton	Central Area
Tommy Rice	Southern Area
Sandy Risley	Southern Area
Ed Robinson	Southern Area
Trevor Russell	Welsh Area
James Wallace	Scottish Area

Inspectors
Herold Adams	Southern Area
Alan Alster	Central Area
William Ball	Southern Area
Richard Barber	Southern Area
Michael Barnett	Central Area
Don Bartlett	Midlands Area
Graham Bingham	Midlands Area
Fred Breyer	Southern Area
David Brown	Western Area
Walter Campbell	Northern Ireland
Harry Carroll	Welsh Area
Geoff Collier	Midlands Area
Michael Collier	Southern Area
Constantin Cotzias	Southern Area
Julian Courtney	Welsh Area
Kevin Crawford	Central Area
John Crowe	Midlands Area
Jaswinder Dhaliwal	Midlands Area
Kevin Fulthorpe	Welsh Area
Bob Galloway	Southern Area
Paul Gooding	Northern Area

Eddie Higgins	Scottish Area
Michael Hills	Northern Area
Neil Holland	Midlands Area
Alan Honnibal	Western Area
David Hughes	Welsh Area
Terry Hutcheon	Scottish Area
Francis Keenan	Northern Ireland
James Kirkwood	Scottish Area
Eddie Lillis	Central Area
Fred Little	Western Area
Bob Lonkhurst	Southern Area
Paul McAllister	Northern Ireland
Sam McAughtry	Northern Ireland
Dave McAuley	Northern Ireland
Liam McColgan	Scottish Area
Billy McCrory	Northern Ireland
Gerry McGinley	Scottish Area
Paul McKeown	Northern Ireland
Pat Magee	Northern Ireland
David Ogilvie	Northern Area
Dave Porter	Southern Area
Fred Potter	Northern Area
Les Potts	Midlands Area
Chris Rattenbury	Western Area
Steve Ray	Central Area
Bob Rice	Midlands Area
Geoffrey Rogers	Southern Area
Hugh Russell	Northern Ireland
Charlie Sexton	Scottish Area
Neil Sinclair	Southern Area
Bert Smith	Central Area
Nigel Underwood	Midlands Area
David Venn	Northern Area
Phil Waites	Midlands Area
Ernie Wallis	Welsh Area
Ron Warburton	Central Area
Bob Williams	Southern Area
Geoff Williams	Midlands Area
Trevor Williams	Midlands Area
Barney Wilson	Northern Ireland

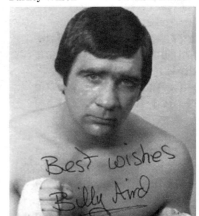

Billy Aird. Once a leading heavyweight contender, now a Class 'B' referee

PROFESSIONAL BOXING PROMOTERS' ASSOCIATION

UNDER BBB OF C RULES

PRESENTS

THE BRITISH MASTERS CHAMPIONS

HEAVY:	JACKLORD JACOBS
CRUISER:	GARRY DELANEY
LIGHT-HEAVY:	VACANT
SUPER-MIDDLE:	RUBEN GROENEWALD
MIDDLE:	LEE MURTAGH
LIGHT-MIDDLE:	JIMMY VINCENT
WELTER:	VACANT
LIGHT-WELTER:	GAVIN DOWN
LIGHT-WEIGHT:	NIGEL SENIOR
SUPER-FEATHER:	VACANT
FEATHER:	CHOI TSEVEENPUREV
SUPER-BANTAM:	FRANKIE DEMILO
BANTAM:	GARETH PAYNE
FLYWEIGHT:	DELROY SPENCER

THE PBPA
P O BOX 25188
LONDON
SW1V 3WL

TEL: 020 7592 0102
FAX: 020 7592 0087
EMAIL: bdbaker@tinyworld.co.uk

CHAIRMAN: Bruce Baker
GENERAL SECRETARY: Greg Steene
DIRECTORS: B. Baker, G. Steene, P. Brogan, J. Gill, J. Evans, R. Cameron, J. Griffin

MEMBERSHIP OPEN TO ALL SMALL HALL PROMOTERS

CHRIS SANIGAR
Boxing Management Training
BRISTOL BOXING GYM, 40 THOMAS STREET
ST AGNES, BRISTOL BS2 9LL
Email address: csanigar@aol.com
TEL: 0117 949 6699 FAX: 0117 904 9373 Mobile: 07831 359978

PEACOCK PROMOTIONS

PROMOTER/MANAGER: TONY BOWERS
AGENT/MATCHMAKER: ROY HILDER
TRAINERS: MARTIN BOWERS/JACKIE BOWERS/ALI FORBES/
JOHN BOSCOE/JOHN HUMPHREY SNR
SECRETARY: ALAN RITCHINGS

WE ARE VERY PROUD TO BOTH PROMOTE AND MANAGE THE FOLLOWING LIST OF PROFESSIONAL BOXERS:

Boxer	Weight	Title	Record
JULIUS FRANCIS (36)	HEAVY	EX BRITISH & COMMONWEALTH CHAMPION	22-10-1
HARRY DA SILVA (31)	CRUISER		16-9-2
ALORYI MOYOYO (28)	CRUISER		8-1-0
GARRY DELANEY (31)	CRUISER	BRITISH MASTERS CHAMPION	30-6-1
ELVIS MICHAILENKO (26)	LIGHT-HEAVY	W.B.F. EUROPEAN CHAMPION	11-0-1
ERIK TEYMOUR (21)	SUPER-MIDDLE		7-1-0
CHRIS NEMBHARD (23)	MIDDLE		6-3-1
SCOTT DIXON (25)	LIGHT-MIDDLE	W.B.O. INTER-CONTINENTAL CHAMPION	25-7-2
THOMAS DA SILVA (24)	LIGHT-MIDDLE		4-3-1
JOHN 'BOY' HUMPHREY (21)	WELTER	SOUTHERN AREA CHAMPION. FORMER UNDEFEATED BRITISH MASTERS CHAMPION	12-2-0
MANZO SMITH (24)	WELTER		5-2-0
CRAIG LYNCH (30)	WELTER		3-5-1
LUKE RUDD (20)	WELTER	PROFESSIONAL DEBUT	
DANIEL JAMES (25)	LIGHT-WELTER		12-2-0
DARREN MELVILLE (26)	LIGHT-WELTER		9-1-1
KARIM BOUALI (27)	LIGHT	W.B.U. INTER-CONTINENTAL CHAMPION	9-3-1
STEPHEN OATES (24)	SUPER-BANTAM		16-4-0
JOHN MACKAY (20)	SUPER-BANTAM		5-3-0
ROCKY DEAN (24)	BANTAM		5-1-0
JOSEPH AGBEKO (21)	BANTAM	W.B.F. WORLD CHAMPION	13-0

READY, WILLING AND ABLE
ANYTIME, ANYPLACE, ANYWHERE

Tony Burns Promotions

67 Peel Place
Clayhall Avenue
Ilford
Essex IG5 0PT

Office: 020 8550 8911
Fax: 020 8550 8915
Mobile: 07979 536925
E-Mail: tburnsltd@aol.com

Licensed by The British Boxing Board of Control Ltd

Tony Sims
Boxing Manager and Trainer

205 Collier Row Lane
Romford
Essex RM5 3JA

Office: 01708 749 940
Fax: 020 8550 8915
Mobile: 07984 977 629

Boxing Trainer & Fitness Conditioner: T. Steward

BOXERS:

Weight	Boxer	Record
Heavyweight	Mark Potter	20-4
Light-Heavyweight	Steve Spartacus	9-0
Light-Heavyweight	Andrew Lowe	7-0
Light-Welterweight	Ben Hudson	1-0-1
Lightweight	Dave Stewart	4-0

Licensed by The British Boxing Board of Control Ltd

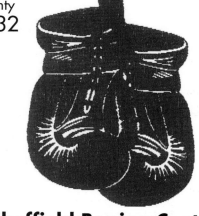

Boxers' Record Index